ENCYCLOPEDIA OF
THE AMERICAN
PRESIDENCY

Other Books

BY MICHAEL A. GENOVESE

The Supreme Court, The Constitution, and Presidential Power (Washington, D.C.: University Press of America, 1980)

Politics and Cinema: An Introduction to Political Films (Lexington, Mass.: Ginn Press, 1986)

The Nixon Presidency: Power and Politics in Turbulent Times (Westport, Conn.: Greenwood Publishing Group, 1990)

The Presidency in an Age of Limits (Westport, Conn.: Greenwood Publishing Group, 1993)

Women as National Leaders (editor) (Newbury, Calif.: Sage Publishing, 1993)

The Presidential Dilemma (New York: HarperCollins, 1995)

The Paradoxes of the American Presidency (with Thomas E. Cronin) (New York: Oxford University Press, 1998)

The Political Film (New York: Simon & Schuster, 1998)

The Watergate Crisis (Westport, Conn.: Greenwood Press, 1999)

The Power of the American Presidency, 1789–2000 (New York: Oxford University Press, 2000)

The Presidency and Domestic Policy: Comparing Leadership Styles, FDR to Clinton (with William W. Lammers) (Washington, D.C.: Congressional Quarterly Press, 2000)

The Presidency and the Law: The Clinton Legacy (with David Gray Adler) (Lawrence: University Press of Kansas, 2002)

Polls and Politics (with Matt Streb) (Albany: State University of New York Press, 2004)

ENCYCLOPEDIA OF THE AMERICAN PRESIDENCY

Michael A. Genovese

Facts On File, Inc.

To Gaby, the most beautiful woman I've ever seen.
How did I get so lucky? And, remember,
"We'll always have Paris."

Encyclopedia of the American Presidency

Copyright © 2004 by Michael A. Genovese

Facts On File, Inc.
132 West 31st Street
New York NY 10001

Library of Congress Cataloging-in-Publication Data

Genovese, Michael A.
Encyclopedia of the American Presidency / Michael A. Genovese.
p. cm.
Includes bibliographical references and index.
ISBN 0-8160-4699-9
1. Presidents—United States—Encyclopedias. 2. Presidents—
United States—Biography. I. Title
JK511.G45 2004
973'.09'9—dc222003049254

Facts On File books are available at special discounts when purchased in bulk
quantities for businesses, associations, institutions, or sales promotions. Please call
our Special Sales Department in New York at (212) 967-8800 or (800) 322-8755.

You can find Facts On File on the World Wide Web at http://www.factsonfile.com.

Text design by Joan M. Toro

Cover design by Cathy Rincon

Printed in the United States of America

VB FOF 10 9 8 7 6 5 4 3 2 1

This book is printed on acid-free paper.

Contents

List of Entries

Contributor List

Adkins, Randall E., University of Nebraska, Omaha
Adler, David Gray, Idaho State University
Alpert, Eugene J., The Washington Center
Anderson, Donald F., University of Michigan, Dearborn

Bailey, Michael E., Berry College
Baker, Nancy, New Mexico State University
Bimes, Terri, Harvard University
Blakesley, Lance, Loyola Marymount University
Blanchard, Colleen, Georgia State University
Bose, Meena, United States Military Academy
Borrelli, Mary Anne, Connecticut College
Brattebo, Douglas M., United States Naval Academy
Brownell, Roy E. II, Washington, D.C.

Carey, Michael, Portland, Oregon
Comiskey, Michael, Penn State, Fayette
Corrigan, Matthew, University of North Florida
Cox-Han, Lori, Austin College
Crockett, David A., Trinity University

Daynes, Byron W., Brigham Young University
Deen, Rebecca E., University of Texas, Arlington
Dewhirst, Robert E., Northwest Missouri State University
Dougherty, Richard J., University of Dallas
Duquette, Gerold J., Central Connecticut State University

Ellis, Richard J., Williamette University

Faletta, Jean-Philippe, University of St. Thomas
Farrar-Myers, Victoria, University of Texas, Austin

Garrison, Jean, University of Wyoming
Gerstmann, Evan, Loyola Marymount University
Glad, Betty, University of South Carolina
Grafton, Carl, Auburn University, Montgomery

Heith, Diane, Saint John's University
Hedgepath, Donna, University of South Carolina
Hoff, Samuel B., Delaware State University
Holmes, F. Owen, California State University, Fullerton

Kan, Paul, Air Command and Staff College, Maxwell
   Air Force Base
Kassop, Nancy, State University of New York, New Paltz
Kelly, Sean Q., Niagara University
Korzi, Michael, Towson State University
Krukones, Michael G., Bellarmine University

Langston, Thomas, Tulane University
Lawrence, Adam B., University of Pittsburgh
Lendler, Marc, Smith College

Matheson, Sean C., Knox College
Matthews, Elizabeth, Rochester Institute of
   Technology
Mullen, Stephanie, Queen's University

Patterson, Bradley H., Bethesda, Maryland
Pederson, William, Louisiana State University
Pfiffner, James P., George Mason University
Pitney, John J., Claremont McKenna University
Ponder, Daniel E., University of Colorado,
   Colorado Springs

Renshon, Stanley A., City University of New York

Savage, Sean J., Saint Mary's College
Schier, Steven E., Carleton College
Shogan, Colleen, George Mason University
Shull, Steven A., University of New Orleans
Smaha, Joseph, Gainesville, Florida
Sorrentino, Frank M., St. Francis College

Spitzer, Robert J., State University of New York, Cortland
Streb, Matt, Loyola Marymount University
Strong, Robert A., Washington and Lee University
Stuckey, Mary E., Georgia State University

Tatalovich, Raymond, Loyola University, Chicago
Tomkin, Shelley Lynne, Trinity College, Washington

Underwood, James E., Union College

Warber, Adam L., Texas A&M University
Wert, Joseph, Indiana University Southeast
Whittington, Keith, Princeton University
Wolf, Thomas P., Indiana University Southeast

Yalof, David, University of Connecticut

Preface

No single volume, encyclopedia or other, could capture the full measure of the U.S. presidency. It is a complex, contradictory, paradoxical institution, at once protean and powerful, while simultaneously weak and constrained.

The strength and power of the presidency emanates less from a constitutional grant of power than from the evolutionary growth of the office as it faced crises, wars, and the emergence of the U.S. as the dominant power in the world.

The weakness and limits on the office stem from the Madisonian system of CHECKS AND BALANCES so important to the separation of powers established by the framers of the Constitution.

This encyclopedia of the American presidency is organized alphabetically for ease of use. It is designed to answer questions about presidents and the presidency. Most entries list bibliographic references for those who wish to further explore their subjects. Entries bear the names of their authors; all entries not so designated were written by the volume's editor. The content of the entries is solely the work of the contributors and does not necessarily reflect the views of the contributors' employers.

My deepest thanks go out to all my friends and colleagues in the Presidency Research Group of the American Political Science Association who consented to write entries for this encyclopedia. Their contribution has been valuable beyond expression and I owe you all a great deal.

Loyola Marymount University in Los Angeles was of great help in completing this project, supplying me with release time and typists. Two typists labored over this manuscript, and I thank them both: Julie Steed and Katherine Puglisi. My research assistant, Chris Zepeda, was absolutely amazing. His organizational work, attention to detail, and his patience with a boss who could be a real problem helped keep the project on track and finally to completion.

Owen Lancer at Facts On File was a patient and understanding editor. Owen's gentle nudging and overall support helped turn this nightmare into a book, and I thank him for being such a gentleman.

Finally, and most important, I wish to thank my wife, Gaby, without whom nothing would be possible, and life would be devoid of meaning.

Introduction

The presidency is the most powerful and important political institution in the United States. It was not always so, nor was it so intended by the framers of the Constitution. The Constitution gives Congress most of the power in the U.S. separation-of-powers system of government. Presidents have very few independent, constitutionally granted powers. So why, then, is the presidency of today so powerful and important?

Over time, crises, both domestic and foreign, wars, and the rise of the United States as the dominant, or hegemonic, power of the world all conspired to create a stronger and more centralized presidency. While the president may not have been granted a great deal of formal or constitutional power, the president is well positioned to exercise informal authority. That is to say that while the president's constitutional power is limited, the office is well positioned to exercise political leadership. The presidency of today reflects the historical growth of the office as well as the responses of previous presidents to wars and crises, and the demands of leadership in the international arena.

An encyclopedia is not the place to tell this tale in detail. There are several very good histories of the American presidency which have done just that. This work is an effort to assist readers in answering questions about the operation of the presidency, the institution, and the people who have occupied the office. This is a reference or research aide, not a narrative text. To fully understand the office and its occupants is a lifetime effort, but if full knowledge may be unattainable, at least we can make some sense of this complex, contradictory, and paradoxical institution. It is our hope that this encyclopedia contributes to that goal.

A

acceptance addresses

The acceptance address constitutes the penultimate moment of a political nominating convention. Conventions, of course, mark the end of intra-party primary campaigning and the beginning of the interparty election campaign. As transitional moments, conventions serve to heal the wounds of the primary battles and refocus attention toward what the party shares and how it differs from the opposing party or parties. In the contemporary context, conventions are often the first campaign event that garners significant attention from many voters.

The rhetoric of the important convention addresses (keynotes, vice presidential and presidential acceptance addresses) is designed to further these partisan goals and to help accomplish a smooth transition from the primary to the general election. Keynote addresses focus attention on the broad political context, set the theme of the convention, and legitimate the political party as a means of collective action. Acceptance addresses continue the convention's theme, reflect the broad context of the party, and shift the focus from the party to the candidates, placing them as the primary agent of political action.

Like all campaign speeches, acceptance addresses have both instrumental and consummatory functions. Instrumentally, campaigns motivate voters, foster dialogue on issues, and legitimate leaders and their policies. They also contribute to the process of community building through ubiquitous participation in shared rituals. The acceptance address is an important part of the conventional ritual.

In the television age, acceptance addresses are the first opportunities candidates have to appear "presidential" before a national audience. The form and style of the address is therefore formal, the content is frequently full of clichés, and the thrust of the speech is toward creating authority for the speaker. Incumbent presidents rely on the rhetoric of affirmation, which legitimates their current administration and justifies the campaign for a second term—Ronald REAGAN's 1984 address that offered a vision of "Morning in America" and Bill CLINTON's 1996 theme of a "bridge to the 21st century" are good recent examples. Challengers tend to use the rhetoric of purification, which affirms the sanctity of the American mission but offers a correction to the present path. In the first paragraph of his 2000 address, for instance, George W. BUSH said, "Together, we will renew America's purpose." In both cases, the candidates define themselves in relation to the opposing candidate and to the opposing political party.

As Karlyn Kohrs Campbell and Kathleen Hall Jamieson note, acceptance addresses assume the form of a jeremiad, or sermon designed to call the faithful back to the true path. Candidates will define American history in terms that are favorable to their campaigns, detail the negative consequences of deviation from the principles that form the basis of those campaigns, and promise a bright future if the deviation is corrected by supporting a particular candidate's bid for the presidency. This view of history generally traces the highlights of national history with specific reference to the party's heroes, who serve as exemplars of the values espoused by that party. Republicans, for instance, often focus on exemplars of freedom (Abraham LINCOLN, Teddy ROOSEVELT, Ronald Reagan), while Democrats tend to prefer examples that illuminate their commitment to equality (Franklin D. Roosevelt, John KENNEDY), although both parties reference iconic presidents from the founding (George WASHINGTON, Thomas JEFFERSON) and trace their political genealogy to these exemplars, gaining legitimacy and authority from the implied continuity from the founding to the candidate.

In placing the candidate rather than the party at the center of the speech, contemporary acceptance addresses reflect and perhaps contribute to the phenomenon of "candidate-centered politics," and perhaps also to the comparative weakness of the political parties as campaign organizations.

Further reading: Benoit, William L. "Acclaiming, Attacking, and Defending in Presidential Nominating Acceptance Addresses, 1960–1996," *Quarterly Journal of Speech* 85 (1999): 247–267; Ritter, Kurt W. "American Political Rhetoric and the Jeremiad Tradition: Presidential Nomination Acceptance Addresses, 1960–1976," *Central States Speech Journal* 31 (1980): 153–172; Trent, Judith S., and Robert V. Friedenberg. *Political Campaign Communication: Principles and Practices,* 4th ed. New York: Praeger, 2000.

—Mary E. Stuckey & Colleen Blanchard

accountability

Presidential accountability suggests that in a democratic or republican form of government, a president must be held accountable, or made to answer for his actions. In some areas—foreign policy and war, for example—the president has perhaps too much power. In other areas, such as DOMESTIC POLICY and ECONOMIC POLICY, the president often seems quite weak. The former means we often get heroic but undemocratic leadership; the latter means we often lead presidential lambs to political slaughter.

There are three types of accountability: (1) *ultimate accountability* (which the United States has via the impeachment process); (2) *periodic accountability* (provided for by general elections); and (3) *daily accountability* (somewhat contained in the separation of powers). James MADISON believed that elections provided the "primary check on government" and that the separation of powers ("ambition will be made to counteract ambition") plus "auxiliary precautions" would take care of the rest.

Of course, there *are* times when presidents abuse power or behave corruptly. But even in the three most recent bouts with presidential abuses, WATERGATE, the IRAN-CONTRA SCANDAL, and the Clinton affair, the president was stopped by the countervailing forces of a free press, an independent Congress, an independent judiciary, and (belatedly) an aroused public.

Presidents can be held accountable, but can they be held responsible? That is, can they muster enough power to govern? One means to improve accountability and also empower leadership is to strengthen the party system in America. Our parties are—at least by European standards—weak, undisciplined, and nonideological. A stronger party system could organize and mobilize citizens and government, diminish the fragmentation of the separation of powers, and mitigate the atomization of our citizenry. If the parties were more disciplined and programmatic, the government's ability to govern, as well as be held accountable, could be greatly changed.

A more responsible party system would also ground presidents in a more consensus-oriented style of leadership and thereby diminish the independent, unconnected brand of leadership so often attempted by recent presidents.

Acheson, Dean (1893–1971) *secretary of state*

Secretary of state and close confidant of President Harry Truman, Acheson served Truman from 1949 to the end of the president's term. Responsible for implementing the MARSHALL PLAN for European recovery, and for helping establish NATO, Acheson was a hard-liner toward the Soviet Union and, although attacked by Senator Joseph MCCARTHY, maintained a tough adversarial position toward the Soviets.

Dean Acheson worked especially closely with President Truman, more closely than almost any secretary of State in the modern era, and was credited with a hand in nearly all the major foreign policy moves of the administration at a time when U.S. power was at its post–World War II peak and when a new postwar international regime was being created. As the COLD WAR dawned, Truman and Acheson had to build a new regime out of the ashes of world war at a time when the Western powers were being challenged by the Soviet Union. Acheson was "present at the creation" of the policy of CONTAINMENT, the development of NATO, the MARSHALL PLAN and TRUMAN DOCTRINE, and the development of international aid programs that have been in effect for more than 50 years. He was a monumental figure at a time of great importance.

Further reading: Acheson, Dean. *Present at the Creation.* New York: Norton, 1969; Brinkley, Douglas. *Dean Acheson: The Cold War Years, 1953–71.* New Haven, Conn.: Yale University Press, 1992; Smith, Gaddis. *Dean Acheson.* New York: Cooper Square Publishers, 1972.

Adams, Abigail Smith (1744–1818) *first lady*

Of the early FIRST LADIES, Abigail Adams is perhaps the most widely known to the general public. Her extraordinary correspondence, with its cogent analysis and well-phrased declarations, is an extraordinary legacy. Yet Adams did not confine her opinions to the written page. Her conversations with her husband and with other decision makers were consistently substantive, so much so that she was sometimes criticized for her attentiveness to politics and political debate.

Although Abigail Adams was not formally educated, she did receive considerable tutoring from her father throughout her childhood. A minister with a formidable library, he provided his daughter with an extensive training in the liberal arts. The intellectual curiosity that his teaching fostered was one of Adams's most notable traits. Years later, she would supplement her children's formal education, teaching herself Latin so that she could introduce them to the classics. Her subsequent marriage to John ADAMS required some negotiation: At their first meeting, John initially described Abigail as a "wit," while reserving judgment about her personality; and Abigail's family felt that she would be marrying beneath herself in accepting John's proposal.

The Adams marriage was marked by frequent and long separations. There were five children: Abigail Amelia ("Nabby," 1765–1813), John Quincy (1767–1848), Susanna (1768–1770), Charles (1770–1800), and Thomas Boylston (1772–1832). Abigail Adams was effectively a single parent for most of their lives. In addition to running the family farm in Braintree, Massachusetts, she gradually assumed responsibility for managing virtually all of John's investments. This practice continued throughout their marriage, with numerous biographers noting that her assumption of these roles left John free to pursue his political career. More precisely, she often generated the income that underwrote his political success. This was particularly evident in the White House years, when she stretched the president's meager salary, in an inflationary period, to meet their extensive social obligations.

In commenting on Abigail Adams's politics, biographers have described Adams as both radical and conservative. Cited in support of the contention that her views were comparatively radical is her support for the American Revolution, as well as her ongoing belief that women were not men's inferiors. As evidence of her conservatism, there is her general lack of support for the French Revolution and her belief that this uprising would lead to violence and abuses of liberty in the United States. There is also her acceptance of a family-centered role for women and her belief that marriage and family were two of society's most foundational institutions. What was unequivocally radical about Adams, however, was her willingness to publicly comment on politics, a practice that led to some controversy during the presidential term. Her outspoken comments were a concern because they were made by a woman, because they were made by the wife of the president, and because they advertised the belief that politics was a partisan enterprise.

Abigail Adams died of typhoid fever in 1818. She was survived by her husband, two of her five children, and numerous grandchildren.

Further reading: Anthony, Carl Sferrazza. *First Ladies.* New York: William Morrow and Company, Inc., 1991; Caroli, Betty Boyd. *First Ladies*, expanded ed. New York: Oxford University Press, 1995. There have been a number of published collections of Abigail Adams's letters, of which more than 2,000 are extant.

—Mary Anne Borelli

Abigail Smith Adams, from an original painting by Gilbert Stuart *(Library of Congress)*

Adams, John (1735–1826) *second U.S. president*
The second president of the United States (1797–1801), Adams was born on October 30, 1735, in Braintree (now Quincy), Massachusetts. He graduated from Harvard College in 1755 and began to practice law, but the call to revolution interested Adams and he became active in the movement to break with Great Britain.

Short (5'6"), stocky, balding, habitually in poor health, this New England Puritan had a reserved, distant, and aloof personality. While greatly ambitious and in need of personal recognition, John Adams was nonetheless uncomfortable in public situations, of a suspicious nature bordering on paranoia, and prone to depression. Following the dignified and statuesque George WASHINGTON, Adams seemed almost a comic figure—pompous, vain, and yearning for a stature that nature denied him.

Biographer Gilbert Chinaid called Adams "honest, stubborn, and somewhat narrow," but a fierce patriot who contributed much to the making of America. Peter Shaw saw in Adams a man of contradictions, at war with himself. His passion for fame led to a pomposity which in the end deflated him. He was, in some respects, his own worst enemy.

His private writings revealed a pettiness and resentment, a vanity and smallness unbecoming a person of his

John Adams, second president of the United States. Painted by John Singleton Copley, 1800 *(Library of Congress)*

stature. He could be rude and grumpy, stubborn and strong willed, cold and narrow-minded, conceited and overly ambitious. In a letter to James MADISON, Thomas JEFFERSON wrote of Adams: "He is vain, irritable, and a bad calculator of the force and probable effect of the motives which govern men." Benjamin Franklin said Adams was "always an honest man, often a wise one, but sometimes, and in some things, absolutely out of his senses." In private, George Washington ridiculed Adams (his vice president) for his "ostentatious imitations and mimicry of Royalty."

Accused of being too sympathetic to monarchy, Adams once proposed the pompous title "His Highness the President of the United States of America and Protector of the Rights of the Same." Besides being a mouthful, this suggestion aroused ridicule among his contemporaries.

As the nation's first vice president, Adams was known to preside over the Senate dressed in a powdered wig, and he often appeared at ceremonial functions with a sword strapped at his waist. Such things made him the object of abuse and derision, earning him the sobriquet "His Rotundity." He even went so far as to predict that eventually the United States would fully embrace the British system.

As was the custom of the times, Adams did not actively campaign for the presidency. Such public-office seeking was frowned upon as unseemly. It was a time when the landed gentry still dominated the public arena, and the democratization of politics had yet to take place.

George Washington was, to say the least, a tough act to follow. Succeeding an icon is an unenviable task. It was, Adams himself noted, "a novelty" in political affairs, this "sight of the sun setting full-orbit, and another rising (though less splendid)."

Adams's inauguration marked the first of what would be many peaceful and orderly transfers of power. As he entered office, the United States was a mere child, eight years old. The U.S. population was less than 5 million, two-thirds of whom lived within 100 miles of the Atlantic coast.

Adams's presidency was not a happy one. Marked by the beginning of a bitter partisan split between the Federalists (Adams, Alexander HAMILTON), and the Jeffersonian faction, this split signified the beginning of party politics in the new nation.

Adams believed himself to be limited in the art and craft of politics because he was "unpracticed in intrigues of power." Nowhere is this statement more evident than in one of his first presidential decisions. Hoping (in vain as it turned out) to establish continuity with the Washingtonian past, Adams asked all of Washington's department heads to remain in his CABINET. This was a grave mistake, as these men proved unloyal to Adams and often looked to Hamilton for guidance. He later described this decision as his greatest mistake, which he believed resulted in the destruction of his presidency.

The cabinet, led by the ambitious and resentful Alexander Hamilton, was often in conflict with the president, who was supposed to control the administration. Adams's political foe, Thomas Jefferson, noted the internal disputes within Adams's cabinet, remarking that the "Hamiltonians who surround him [Adams], are only a little less hostile to him than to me."

From the moment he entered office, Adams was confronted with a serious crisis: a possible war with France. Still smarting from Washington's NEUTRALITY PROCLAMATION, the leaders of France pressured the United States to join them in the ongoing war against Great Britain. France, in an effort to press the issue, refused to recognize U.S. diplomats and threatened to hang any American sailor captured on British ships.

Adams called a special session of Congress and boldly declared he would not permit the United States to be intimidated by these French threats. He called upon Congress to pass legislation to prepare for the nation's defense. Would the dogs of war be unchained?

In early 1798 Adams received word that the French were interested in a deal. Agents of the French government, referred to simply as X, Y, and Z, secretly demanded the payment of bribes before the American envoy could see the foreign minister, Talleyrand. Furious about this demand, Adams at first favored war, but the United States was not prepared for war. Adams went to Congress with a request that American merchant ships be armed, but the Congress resisted. Adams then made the XYZ dispatches public and proclaimed "Millions for defense, but not one cent for tribute."

As preparation for war moved ahead, Adams called George Washington back into the active service of his country. Washington reluctantly agreed. During this war scare, the Federalists who controlled Congress passed the ALIEN AND SEDITION ACTS, granting extraordinary powers to the government. These acts, clear and direct violations of the Bill of Rights, were used by Adams to shut down opposition-controlled newspapers and to threaten political opponents.

In early 1799 Adams, still hoping to avoid a war for which the United States was ill-prepared, launched another diplomatic overture to France. This caused angry dissent in his own FEDERALIST PARTY. When several Federalist senators warned Adams they would not support him in this, the president threatened to resign and turn the presidency over to Thomas Jefferson. Nothing put greater fear in the hearts of Federalists than the thought of "that radical" Jefferson in the presidency. Adams's peace overtures to France proved successful, and war was averted.

Unfortunately this incident left scars. Hamilton vowed to wrestle power away from Adams, and in late 1799 and early 1800, the president discovered that Hamilton had been secretly trying to control the cabinet. Enraged, Adams forced his entire cabinet to resign.

In the aftermath of these internecine battles, and with Hamilton writing scathing broadsides against Adams, the Federalists lost the election of 1800 to their dreaded adversary Thomas Jefferson.

For all his limitation and difficulties, Adams ranks in the above average category of American presidents. While not an adroit politician (Adams refused to actively lead Congress), and in spite of possessing a quirky personality and somewhat limited view of the office, Adams nonetheless helped establish the presidency and its foreign affairs powers. The first president to live in the still unfinished White House (as it is now called), and much influenced by a strong and outspoken wife (Abigail ADAMS was derisively referred to as "Mrs. President"), Adams saw America through threatening and turbulent times. He avoided what certainly would have been a costly and probably unwinnable war and brought the country through the early and potentially explosive era of party formation and conflict.

During Adams's time, the government became firmly established in what Jefferson called "that Indian swamp in the wilderness," Washington, D.C. Jefferson was not alone in his criticism of the nation's capital city. In 1862 novelist Anthony Trollope said, "I . . . found the capital still under the empire of King Mud. . . . Were I to say that it was intended to be typical of the condition of the government, I might be considered cynical."

Adams lived to the age of 90. He died on July 4, 1826, the same day as his rival and later friend, Thomas Jefferson. Adams's last words were "Thomas Jefferson still survives." Jefferson, unbeknownst to Adams, had died earlier that day.

Further reading: Brown, Ralph A. *The Presidency of John Adams.* Lawrence: Regents Press of Kansas, 1975; Ellis, Joseph J. *Passionate Sage: The Character and Legacy of John Adams.* New York: W. W. Norton, 1993; Ferling, John E. *John Adams: A Life.* Knoxville: University of Tennessee Press, 1992; Smith, Page. *John Adams.* 2 vols. Garden City, N.Y.: Doubleday, 1962.

Adams, John Quincy (1767–1848) *sixth U.S. president*

The first son of a president to become president, John Quincy Adams was born on July 11, 1767, in Braintree (now Quincy), Massachusetts. He graduated from Harvard College in 1787.

Often dour and disagreeable, enigmatic, prone to bouts of depression, the 5'7" balding John Quincy Adams was the first president to be photographed and also the first elected without receiving a plurality of either the popular or electoral college votes. He was the son of President John ADAMS. John Quincy Adams was a distinguished diplomat and a mediocre president. "I am a man of reserved, cold, austere, and forbidding manners," Adams said of himself. James BUCHANAN said of Adams, "His disposition is as perverse and mulish as that of his father." William Henry HARRISON said of Adams: "It is said he is a disgusting man to do business with. Coarse, dirty, and clownish in his address and stiff and abstracted in his opinions, which are drawn from books exclusively."

The election of 1824 was one of the most bitter and hostile in history. The results of the general election were inconclusive:

Jackson	99 electoral votes	153,544 popular votes
Adams	84 electoral votes	108,740 popular votes
Crawford	41 electoral votes	46,618 popular votes
Clay	37 electoral votes	47,136 popular votes

John Quincy Adams, sixth president of the United States. Painted by Thomas Sully; engraved by A. B. Durand, ca. 1826 *(Library of Congress)*

Thus, the election was thrown into the House of Representatives. Andrew JACKSON led the race but was 32 electoral votes short of victory. Clay, who came in fourth, was dropped from the race, and he could turn his votes over to Jackson or Adams and, in effect, determine the outcome.

On January 9, 1825, Clay met with Adams. The details of their conversation are not known, but shortly thereafter, Clay's support went to Adams, prompting Jackson to complain of a "corrupt bargain." Clay was later appointed by Adams as secretary of state.

As a result of the questionable nature of his election, Adams took office severely wounded. In his inaugural address he noted he was "less possessed of [public] confidence in advance than any of my predecessors." Undeterred, Adams decided to work to strengthen the presidency, and was the first president to attempt to lead Congress openly. In his first annual message to Congress, he called for expansive internal improvements and a variety of other new programs. Adams's predecessors harbored

doubts about the constitutionality of such spending measures, but Adams rejected this narrow view. In this way, Adams was the first president "to demonstrate the real scope of creative possibilities of the constitutional provision to 'recommend to their [Congress's] consideration such measures as he shall judge necessary and expedient.'"

In Paul C. Nagel's words, "His four years [1825–29] in the White House were a misery for him. . . . For the remaining twenty years of his life, he reflected on his presidency with distaste, convinced that he had been the victim of evildoers. His administration was a hapless failure and best forgotten, save for the personal anguish it cost him."

The Adams years were a time of harsh political strife but also of great economic expansion. By the end of his presidency, King Caucus, the method whereby congressional caucuses selected presidential candidates, was being replaced by political PARTY CONVENTIONS. Adams was not a strong president, but his bold reform proposals did open the door for future presidents to promote their legislative programs more openly.

Further reading: Bemis, Samuel F. *John Quincy Adams and the Union.* New York: Knopf, 1956; Hecht, Marie B. *John Quincy Adams: A Personal History of an Independent Man.* New York: Macmillan, 1972; Nagel, Paul C. *John Quincy Adams.* New York: Knopf, 1998.

Adams, Sherman (1899–1986) *governor*

The former New Hampshire Governor Adams became well known during the EISENHOWER administration as one of Ike's closest aides. Adams was the equivalent of Ike's CHIEF OF STAFF and in 1955 was forced to resign when he was charged with receiving gifts in exchange for influencing government policy.

administrative presidency

One of the fundamental and enduring questions of American government, indeed of any democratic government, is that of the proper relationship between politicians and bureaucrats, and by extension political appointees and careerists in the EXECUTIVE BRANCH. Traditional public administration theory held that there should be a line between politics and administration that was not to be crossed by practitioners on either side of the divide. In other words, elected politicians made policy and career officials implemented that policy.

Over time, many began to abandon the traditional orthodoxy as unfeasible. Many presidents (e.g., NIXON, CARTER, REAGAN) came to Washington expecting their greatest battles to be in the congressional arena but found their most immovable obstacle to be in their own house, the executive branch BUREAUCRACY. Presidents found themselves frustrated in trying to provide consistent, coherent policy direction, largely because they perceived bureaucracy to be indifferent or actively hostile to their wishes. Whether or not this was actually true (and some evidence suggests it was, at least to a certain degree), that was their perception.

The administrative presidency was developed as a partial solution to this problem. The strategy basically holds that presidents can strengthen their capacity for providing direction by taking an active role in the administrative, or management, side of government, the very location traditional public administration had strongly advocated they should stay away from. In contrast to the traditional legislative route, by which policy is advocated, proposed, debated, passed, and signed into law, the administrative presidency advocates using managerial capabilities to their fullest extent, especially in the area of policy implementation.

The most direct mechanism toward this end is for presidents to fully use their APPOINTMENT POWER. The basic goal is to put people devoted to the president's philosophy as deep into the bureaucracy as possible. Obviously this means the president needs to choose ideologically compatible people for cabinet positions but also extend this authority to the subcabinet level. Normally, presidents had taken responsibility for approving cabinet secretaries and perhaps one or two assistants just under the secretary. An administrative presidency strategy calls for the president to appoint as many layers as feasible, thereby virtually "infecting" the bureaucracy with presidential loyalists who will strongly advocate and champion the president's agenda, thereby relieving the president of the responsibility to micromanage departmental action.

The role of the White House staff (WHS) in this process is not so clear. Some scholars see a disciplined, responsive WHS as acting in concert with a politicized bureaucracy, while others feel active White House participation only serves to strengthen the hand of lower level career bureaucrats, the very people least susceptible to presidential control. In essence, the administrative presidency strategy argues for the centralization of policy in the president's branch. That is, policy making is done largely in the White House or the departments, with implementation undertaken by political appointees to the greatest extent possible, rather than leaving it to the bureaucrats who get and keep their jobs via the CIVIL SERVICE system.

While the appointment power is generally seen as the most important component of an administrative presidency strategy, other factors help the president gain and maintain control of the executive branch. Some of these include full use of the budget power, delegation of program authority, the use of central clearance where policy proposals are filtered through the presidency (particularly the OFFICE OF MANAGEMENT AND BUDGET), and cost benefit analysis.

It should be noted that while many agree that the appointment authority is the best bet for presidents in enhancing their power, these others are more of a mixed bag and might even decrease presidential influence in the administrative state. Richard Waterman, for example, argues that in many cases, the administrative presidency strategy can be effective when combined with a more traditional legislative approach. This argument does not negate the effectiveness of the administrative presidency strategy but rather sees presidential influence as enhanced if presidents employ the strategy with a cooperative vein and sensitivity to political realities and the possibilities they engender.

Further reading: Nathan, Richard P. *The Administrative Presidency.* New York: John Wiley and Sons, 1983; Waterman, Richard W. *Presidential Influence and the Administrative State.* Knoxville: University of Tennessee Press, 1989; Aberbach, Joel, Robert D. Putnam, and Bert A. Rockman, *Bureaucrats and Politicians in Western Democracies.* Cambridge, Mass.: Harvard University Press, 1981.

—Daniel E. Ponder

Administrative Procedure Act (APA)

As the scope of governmental responsibility increased during the GREAT DEPRESSION under the auspices of the NEW DEAL, the U.S. government experienced an explosion in the number and types of administrative agencies. This explosion necessitated the promulgation of regulations to guide and restrain the activities of these new agencies. Regulations are basically policy that is set by the agency, under authority delegated by CONGRESS AND THE PRESIDENT. The rapid increase in agencies, accompanied by the unprecedented growth in regulations, led to a concern on the part of the Congress and President Franklin D. ROOSEVELT as to the consistency with which regulations were issued across agencies. Roosevelt instructed his attorney general to convene a Committee on Administrative Proceedings in 1939, and that committee issued a report to Congress in 1941.

The Administrative Procedure Act (APA) extends due process provisions of the Bill of Rights to administrative agencies. The Act became law after Congress had originally passed a much more stringent set of procedures (the Vilalter-Logan Act of 1940), which would have required agencies to implement "court-like" procedures for most policy making promulgated by administrative agencies. This, as one scholar put it, would have formalized most of what agencies had done in the past. Franklin Roosevelt vetoed that legislation. In 1946 Congress passed a much looser and less judicial APA. In doing so, it substantially relaxed requirements on administrative agencies and set informal rules by which agencies could (but do not necessarily have to) provide due process to potential litigants. For example, section 554 relieves agencies of having to hold court-like hearings, except when the enabling legislation explicitly mandates such hearings.

In many instances, the APA limits the scope of what can be adjudicated. Indeed, the APA is not applicable to the president of the United States (though it is to executive agencies under his auspices). Generally, the APA, as noted, requires administrative agencies to adhere to due process; allow for broad decision-making participation; be amenable to solicitation of input from interest groups and concerned parties; and provide a clear linkage between evidence presented and their decision. All 50 states have since adopted some form of the APA, and most have used the federal version as a guide.

Further reading: Carter, Lief H. *Administrative Law and Politics: Cases and Comments.* Boston: Little Brown, 1983.
—Daniel E. Ponder

administrative reforms of the presidency

The history of administrative reforms is also a history of the struggle for dominance between Congress and the presidency. During the 19th century, Congress dominated the relationship with few exceptions, but the 20th century saw a change. The president came into his own and presidential dominance became a reality. As this happened, presidents began to pursue administrative reform. During the 20th century several attempts were made at reform with varying degrees of success.

Goals of reform have been fourfold: to gain more control over the BUREAUCRACY, to gain more control over the budgetary process, to expand the White House staff, and to rearrange cabinet offices by purpose.

The history of administrative reform can be divided into four periods, roughly corresponding to the major attempts at reform. The efforts in the three decades prior to the New Deal are best represented by the TAFT COMMISSION, the period of the New Deal reforms by the BROWNLOW COMMITTEE, the period immediately after World War II by the two HOOVER COMMISSIONS; recent reform attempts, begin with the ASH COUNCIL and go to the present time.

Early Attempts at Reform:
The Taft Commission (1905–1933)

The first major attempts at administrative reform came at the beginning of the 20th century in the administration of Theodore ROOSEVELT. This was the height of the Progressive era, when big government was beginning to come into its own. Advocates of a strong presidency wanted to release

the president from his constraints so he could act as needed. This could be done through administrative reform. Yet Roosevelt's attempt at reform was weak, focusing on micro-level management rather than the macro side. The Keep Commission, created by Roosevelt in 1905, did however set the precedent that all other presidents of the 20th century (and presumably beyond) would follow. The only lasting effects of the Keep Commission, its final recommendations being rather mundane ones having to do with minor administrative matters, involved the use of envelopes with windows and some suggestions for changes in records management.

William Howard Taft had a little more luck with his attempt. The so-called Taft Commission (its official name was the Commission on Economy and Efficiency), formulated in 1909, was more ambitious than its predecessor. Persistent deficits and the expanding role of the federal government necessitated budgetary and administrative reforms. The recommendations of the commission were of two types: Minor administrative details, and reforms that would centralize the executive branch. Some of these were adopted by Congress, the most important of which was the centralization of government publications in the Government Printing Office.

As deficits continued to climb through the early 1900s, more pressure came on Congress to reform the budgeting process. This, as well as the increasing complexity of dealing with annual federal budgets, brought Congress to the passage of BUDGET AND ACCOUNTING ACT OF 1921. This major piece of legislation was the most important reorganization of the executive branch undertaken to date. The act established the BUREAU OF THE BUDGET to assist the president with his new budgetary authority. The act also created the GENERAL ACCOUNTING OFFICE, which was to be the auditing arm of Congress.

New Deal Reform:
The Brownlow Committee (1933–1945)

The Great Depression led to the speeding up of the federal government getting involved in policy areas once reserved for the states. Coming into the White House on the promise to "do something" about the depression, Franklin Delano ROOSEVELT led the way. As more programs were passed by Congress, and more bureaucratic agencies sprang up, Roosevelt found himself increasingly frustrated at dealing with the bureaucracy. If all of the recommendations of the BROWNLOW COMMITTEE were instituted, it would have meant the largest reorganization yet of the executive branch. The committee made recommendations in the following areas: White House staff, personnel management, fiscal management, planning management, administrative reorganization, and ACCOUNTABILITY of the executive branch to Congress. As it was, Roosevelt got only a minor part of what he wanted. Two years after Roosevelt made his recommendations to Congress, he was given reorganization authority for a period of two years, subject to several stipulations. In addition, he was given the authority to hire six assistants—the beginnings of the EXECUTIVE OFFICE OF THE PRESIDENT.

Post–WWII Attempts:
The Two Hoover Commissions (1946–1960)

Another spate of reorganization came about after WWII. This time, it was led by a Republican-controlled Congress, who named former president HOOVER to lead the commission to reorganize the postwar government. The first Hoover Commission delivered its report in 1949 and included 27 recommendations in such areas as centralizing discretionary authority in department heads rather than in bureau chiefs, grouping executive departments more closely by function, and increasing the president's staff. Many of the recommendations were adopted by Congress. A second Hoover Commission was called together in the early part of the EISENHOWER administration by another Republican Congress. The work of this commission was hampered by two things. A Republican Congress created the commission and it was formulated without regard to BIPARTISANSHIP; however, by the time the commission's reports were written, control of Congress had switched. Second, at the same time the commission was working, Eisenhower had a second group (President's Advisory Committee for Government Organization, or PACGO) trying to accomplish similar goals. Thus a lack of cooperation between Eisenhower and the commission that hampered the commission's success.

Recent Reorganization Attempts:
(1960–present)

Since the two Hoover Commissions, administrative reform has become institutionalized in the presidency. Every president since Kennedy, with the exceptions of Gerald FORD and George H. W. BUSH, engaged in large-scale reform attempts. Lyndon JOHNSON commissioned two task forces that ended up making several recommendations regarding the reorganization of departments and the organization of the many GREAT SOCIETY programs. Not much was done with the recommendations of these task forces, mainly because of Johnson's unwillingness, and because of the preoccupation with the Vietnam War. Some of the recommendations from the second task force found their way to Richard NIXON's ASH COUNCIL.

Nixon, believing the bureaucracy too sympathetic to Democratic policies, sought through the Ash Council to gain more presidential control over the executive branch. Out of the recommendations made by the Ash Council, Congress implemented only the suggestions for reconsti-

tuting the BUREAU OF THE BUDGET, giving it more managerial functions and renaming it the OFFICE OF MANAGEMENT and BUDGET.

Carter's presidency saw the largest effort at reorganization ever attempted by a president. The changes approved by Congress included reforming the budgetary process through the use of the zero-based budgeting technique (later ended by REAGAN) and the passage of the Civil Service Reform Act. This act fundamentally changed the CIVIL SERVICE system and also created the Senior Executive Service. Carter also successfully created the EDUCATION DEPARTMENT and ENERGY DEPARTMENT.

Since Carter, administrative reform efforts have been scaled down. The Reagan presidency saw the use of ideological tests in the appointment process and also increased centralization of the review process for administrative regulations. Reagan also sought to devolve many federal government functions to the states. The Clinton administration, battling further budget deficits, instituted the National Performance Review (NPR), which sought to change the way government operated. In addition to cutting thousands of jobs from the federal payroll, NPR also sought to institute private sector businesslike procedures for federal government agencies, making them more quality and customer focused. Currently, as a result of the SEPTEMBER 11, 2001, attack, the Bush administration is attempting reform of the executive branch by creating a DEPARTMENT OF HOMELAND SECURITY, which would centralize much of the intelligence gathering into one federal department.

Further reading: Arnold, Peri. *Making the Managerial Presidency.* Princeton, N.J.: Princeton University Press, 1998; Hart, John. *The Presidential Branch: From Washington to Clinton,* 2d ed. New York: Seven Bridges Press, 1995; Mansfield, Harvey. "Federal Executive Reorganization: Thirty Years of Experience," *Public Administration Review* (July/August 1969); Nathan, Richard. *The Administrative Presidency.* Upper Saddle River, N.J.: Prentice Hall, 1983.

—Joseph Wert

advice and consent

The Constitution's advice-and-consent provision put into practice the system of separation of powers and CHECKS AND BALANCES designed by the framers. In the wake of colonial rule under the king of England, the framers distrusted the use of unchecked EXECUTIVE POWER. Their experience under the Articles of Confederation, however, showed them the benefit that could be derived by having a single head of state in dealing in FOREIGN AFFAIRS. Similarly, the practice of executive appointment and Senate approval of executive and judicial branch officials offered what Alexander HAMILTON called in *Federalist No.* 76 "an efficacious source of stability in the administration" of government.

According to Article II, Section 2, of the U.S. Constitution,

> "[The President] shall have power, by and with the advice and consent of the Senate, to make treaties, provided two thirds of the Senators present concur; and he shall nominate, and by and with the advice and consent of the Senate, shall appoint ambassadors, other public ministers and consuls, judges of the Supreme Court, and all other officers of the United States, whose appointments are not herein otherwise provided for, and which shall be established by law: but the Congress may by law vest the appointment of such inferior officers, as they think proper, in the President alone, in the courts of law, or in the heads of departments."

Although it would appear from the constitutional wording regarding advice and consent that the executive and Congress are on equal footing in terms of nominations, appointments, and treaties, this is far from how events have historically transpired. Many questions have arisen about the proper role, power, and authority each institution has vis-à-vis the other in terms of appointments and treaties. Many of these questions have been litigated, and some have found their way to the Supreme Court to clarify the lines that delineate one institution's power from the permitted checks of the other. Among the more prominent cases in this area are: *MARBURY V. MADISON,* 5. U.S. (1 Cr.) 137 (1803) (Chief Justice MARSHALL calling the nomination process the "sole act of the president" and "completely voluntary"); *MYERS V. UNITED STATES,* 272 U.S. 52 (1926) (the power to remove executive branch officials originally approved of by the Senate "vested in the President alone"); and *Altman & Co. v. United States,* 224 U.S. 583 (1912) (EXECUTIVE AGREEMENTS are valid international accords even though they are not approved by Congress).

In terms of nominations and appointments, President George WASHINGTON began the practice of seeking advice from the Senate regarding his nominations. However, as soon as the Senate seemed to dismiss his choices without any consultation, Washington became a bit weary. Later, President MADISON rebuffed a Senate committee that was created to confer with him prior to making appointments. From these encounters, senatorial courtesy emerged and evolved—the practice of the president consulting the senator from the state from which the nominee hailed. This informal practice has been used frequently by presidents to avoid embarrassing moments.

Divisions over nominations and appointments arise most especially over judicial appointments, especially Supreme Court nominees. Judicial appointments in general have been rife with political battles, as senators often hold up their confirmations in order to win concessions on other legislative matters by the executive. After all, the Constitution requires only that the Senate must approve nominees before they take office; it does not prescribe the method, manner, or timing of the Senate's approval process. Partisan squabbles came to a head in 1987 with the nomination by Ronald REAGAN of Robert H. Bork for the U.S. Supreme Court. The confirmation battle was rife with partisan rancor and eventually led to the rejection of Bork. More recently, congressional inaction on presidential judicial appointments to lower federal courts during the administrations of Bill CLINTON and George W. BUSH has created an additional strain on the burgeoning workload of the federal judiciary.

The Senate's process for approving cabinet officers and other executive branch officials tends to be less confrontational than for Supreme Court appointments. Nevertheless, problems for presidents do sometimes arise. On rare occasions, the Senate may reject an executive branch appointment, as it did in 1989 to John G. Tower, President George H. W. BUSH's nominee for secretary of Defense. Another possibility is for the president or a nominee facing trouble to withdraw the appointment from consideration before a vote is cast, such as with President Bill Clinton's appointments of Zoe Baird and Kimba Wood for attorney general, and President George W. Bush's appointment of Linda Chavez for secretary of Labor. All in all, events like the Bork encounter and Baird/Wood/Chavez withdrawals have led many critics to believe these "advice and consent" processes will continue to be merely a partisan battleground rather than an avenue for reaping the benefits of a system of separation of powers and checks and balances.

Unlike the nominations and appointments process above, where the constitutional language regarding the process focuses solely on the executive, the wording in the Constitution regarding treaties (i.e., "shall have Power, by and with the Advice and Consent of the Senate, to make Treaties,") seems to tie the two branches more closely together in the formulation of these documents. President Washington originally turned to the Senate to assist him with a treaty that was to be negotiated with the Southern Indians, but the Senate rebuffed this overture. And although it is true presidents have continued to seek advice from the Senate, this instance did set precedence for presidents to act before seeking advice. Treaty termination and reinterpretation have been continual sources of controversy between the branches. So, too, has the advent of executive agreements; they have the force of a treaty but do not require advice and consent by the Senate. The use of these instruments by the president has led to much debate both inside and outside legal venues about their circumvention of the Senate. More important, according to some critics, these agreements seem to violate the whole advice-and-consent system established by the Constitution. Further, other manifestations like the *fast track* provision (allowing for only an up or down vote by the Senate on an executive negotiated treaty) have also called into question the original design and meaning of the advice and consent provisions of the Constitution.

Further reading: Fisher, Louis. *Constitutional Conflicts Between Congress and the President,* 3d ed. Lawrence, Kans.: University Press of Kansas, 1991.

—Victoria Farrar-Myers

advisers, presidential

Presidents are boundedly rational individuals, and as such their capacities for gaining and processing information are limited. So that they do not have to do all of the heavy lifting themselves, they surround themselves with advisers, people whose job it is to bring to the president information, distill it, and provide a perspective from which the president can make an informed decision. As basic as this notion sounds, it has not always been this way. Historically, most advice that came to presidents came from cabinet officials. For example, George WASHINGTON's closest advisers came from two warring members of his administration, Secretary of State Thomas JEFFERSON and Secretary of the Treasury Alexander HAMILTON. Presidents had little if anyone in the way of institutionalized staff to even so much as help them sort through information. This was not terribly daunting for the early presidents, because much of what they did was administrative, and they did not face the array of policy issues that face their more modern successors.

In more recent days, the president has had a powerful impact on the congressional agenda. Much of what he proposes gets at least cursory attention in Congress. Thus, much of what the government does emerges from the EXECUTIVE BRANCH, and much of that from the White House. Presidents and their staffs have had to be innovative and at least conversant with technological issues. This is most stark since the evolution of the NEW DEAL, during which demands on the national government began to grow and have never really slowed since. Thus, presidents began to develop an administrative staff for two purposes: first, to help organize the presidency, and second, to provide advice as to how to best go about getting what they want done. The genesis of the growth of the presidential staff came in 1936 when President Franklin D. ROOSEVELT appointed the BROWNLOW COMMITTEE to make recommendations on how presidents could best manage their own offices. In what has become one of the most oft-cited phrases in the presidential literature, the Brownlow Committee famously proclaimed "The President needs help." While only providing for six staffers, even this was initially rejected by Congress as too much expansion and aggrandizement of presidential power. In 1939, however, Congress passed most of what Brownlow suggested, and with that came a presidential staff and, by extension, advisers.

This staff has grown over time, and presidential advisers can be found almost anywhere. On the surface, just looking at the list of White House Staff (WHS) and the EXECUTIVE OFFICE OF THE PRESIDENT (EOP), it is tempting to interpret these advisers as neatly compartmentalized into functional units. While there is some truth to this, mostly for purposes of organizational flowcharts, it masks considerable overlap, coordination, and teamwork (what might be termed "functional interdependence") that occur more or less behind the scenes. This overlap and functional interdependence gives rise to the notion of an advisory system of interconnected strands of information and advice. The increased interlocking of policy areas necessitates overlapping structures. For example, DOMESTIC POLICY often has much to say about ECONOMIC POLICY, and vice versa. Much of what American government does has some implication for foreign policy. This policy overlap leads to overlap in advisory processes.

Advisers can be located within government, outside of government, or straddle both worlds. Over time, task forces and commissions have come to play a significant role in advising presidents. Quite often, people from business, academics, the arts, and government staff them. They provide advisory services, often with a wide variety of information born of their differing perspectives, and address a specific need.

More traditionally, advisers are located either in the White House or in the EOP. Cabinet members continue to play an important advisory function, but over time presidents have come to centralize policy making in the White House. Presidents have what amount to in-house staffs covering domestic policy (usually termed the OFFICE OF POLICY DEVELOPMENT), foreign policy (the NATIONAL SECURITY COUNCIL staff in the EOP), and economic policy (the COUNCIL OF ECONOMIC ADVISERS). More recent presidents, such as Bill CLINTON, have given formal status to the interdependent nature of most policy areas and have constructed advisory apparatuses that mirror this overlap, such as councils that are responsible simultaneously for economic and domestic policy, with a strong foreign policy component. These structures are often large and unwieldy, but the effort to combine these policy areas is made more and more frequently.

While many proposals come from the executive departments, the nature of the advisory staff in the White House shifts depending on timing, presidential interest, the nature of the policy under consideration, and so forth. For example, when a policy proposal is extremely important to the president, advisory staff physically situated in the White House or EOP often take the lead in developing proposals, soliciting advice from outside entities purely for the sake of information. Staff then plays the role of policy director. When policy tends to overlap with several departments and is particularly complicated, the staff tends to act more as a facilitator, brokering agreements among the departments or agencies, and taking an active role in the process. Finally, when proposals fit nearly into the purview of one department or agency, that entity is often charged with formulating the proposal but under the supervision of the staff, this time playing the role of monitor.

While the demarcation is often more detailed, advisers generally provide a combination of political and policy advice. The two, though related, need to be distinguished. Political advice takes account of the political needs of the president, or the promises and commitments he has made to various groups or the public, how best to handle them, what groups can be counted on to rise in protest, with what impact, how Congress and the public are likely to react, and so forth. Policy advice takes a long-term perspective in that it is often technical, unrelated to political interests, or keeps those interests to a minimum. The central task, then, is to combine the two into workable policy proposals that satisfy the political needs of the president (or at minimum do not do them irreparable harm) and adequately address the substantive problem at hand. This is easier said than done in most cases, especially those proposals that are politically charged.

Further reading: Dickinson, Matthew. *Bitter Harvest: FDR, Presidential Power and the Growth of the Presidential Branch.* New York: Cambridge University Press, 1997; Hult, Karen. "Advising the President," in *Researching the Presidency: Vital Questions, New Approaches,* eds. George C. Edwards III, John H. Kessel, and Bert A. Rockman. Pittsburgh, Pa.: University of Pittsburgh Press, 1993, 111–159; Patterson, Bradley H., Jr. *The White House Staff: Inside the West Wing and Beyond.* Washington, D.C.: Brookings, 2000; Ponder, Daniel E. *Good Advice: Information and Policy Making in the White House.* College Station: Texas A&M University Press, 2000; Rudalevige, Andrew. *Managing the President's Program.* Princeton, N.J.: Princeton University Press, 2002; Walcott, Charles E., and Karen M. Hult. *Governing the White House: From Hoover Through LBJ.* Lawrence: University of Kansas, 1995.

—Daniel E. Ponder

African Americans

The relationship between the African-American experience and the EXECUTIVE BRANCH of the U.S. government defies easy summary. In many ways it parallels the history of African Americans. Before the incorporation of African Americans into full participation in the political system, the attention afforded them by individual presidents was episodic, at best. For example, President LINCOLN met with Frederick Douglass, a former slave who was an important abolitionist advocate, on the subject of emancipation. President Theodore ROOSEVELT's meeting with Booker T. Washington was the first time an African American dined with a president in the White House, and Roosevelt was sharply criticized by many of his contemporaries.

The extent to which presidents have incorporated African Americans into their administration also varies considerably across time. The first African-American presidential appointment was in 1869, when President GRANT appointed Ebenezer Don Carlos Bassett as minister to Haiti. Real strides toward racial parity, however, were not made until a century later. President JOHNSON appointed Thurgood Marshall the first African American to the Supreme Court. President NIXON appointed approximately 30 African Americans to positions within the executive branch, albeit in subcabinet appointments. This was three times that of his predecessor. Similarly, President CARTER appointed African Americans to the executive branch at three times the rate of President Nixon. Unlike President Nixon, President Carter's appointments included some high-profile nominations, such as Andrew Young as ambassador to the United Nations, Drew Days as assistant attorney general for civil rights, and Wade McCree as the solicitor general. Carter's successor, President Ronald REAGAN, also made prominent appointments of African Americans, notably General Colin POWELL as Adviser to the NATIONAL SECURITY COUNCIL. In the next administration, President G. H. W. BUSH was successful in his nomination of Clarence Thomas (former head of the Civil Rights Commission under Reagan) to the Supreme Court, replacing Thurgood Marshall. President William Jefferson CLINTON appointed more African Americans than any other administration and, more significantly, these appointments were for positions other African Americans had not previously held. These appointments included four at the cabinet level in both his first and second terms. Additionally, Clinton appointed 29 black men and eight black women to the federal judiciary.

While individual presidents have been involved with and committed to the struggle of African Americans for rights and equality, these presidents have all been white men. Shirley Chisholm was the first African-American woman to mount a major campaign for the presidency. As the first African-American woman to be elected to Congress in 1968, she ran an independent bid for the presidency in 1972. Though others have run for the presidency, perhaps the best known is the Reverend Jesse Jackson, who vied for the Democratic Party's nomination in 1984 and

Andrew Young, shown here being sworn in as U.S. ambassador to the United Nations by Supreme Court Justice Thurgood Marshall, as President Jimmy Carter and First Lady Rosalynn Carter look on. *(Library of Congress)*

1988. In 1996 and 2000, Alan Keyes, a Republican, ran in that party's presidential nomination contests.

African Americans, in the extent to which they have been a consistent voting block, have been an important potential constituency group for presidents. Historically, African Americans have been a part of the Democratic Party's coalition. Sources vary, but the percentage of African-American voters supporting the Democrat running for president generally ranges from 80 to 90 percent.

Further reading: Chisholm, Shirley. *Unbought and Unbossed.* New York: Houghton, 1970; McClain, Paula D., and Joseph Stewart, eds. *Can We All Get Along? Racial and Ethnic Minorities in American Politics,* 2d ed. Boulder, Colo.: Westview Press, 1998; Shull, Steven A. *American Civil Rights Policy from Truman to Clinton: The Role of Presidential Leadership.* New York: M. E. Sharpe, 1999.
—Rebecca E. Deen

Agency for International Development (AID)

This semi-independent government agency is a branch of the U.S. International Development Corporation Agency (IDCA). Its function is to develop economic and technical assistance programs for foreign nations, mostly in the developing world. Created by Congress in 1961 to promote President Kennedy's ALLIANCE FOR PROGRESS program, AID is headed by a director who runs the agency and advises the president on foreign aid issues. In the 1980s significant budget cuts limited the agency's ability to effectively perform its task of assisting developing nations.

agenda

Given that the U.S. Constitution enumerates the legislative power in Article I, it would appear that the U.S. Congress would be the purveyor of the national agenda. Certainly, the framers saw the legislature as the first branch of government. However, Article II of the Constitution, outlining the EXECUTIVE BRANCH, leaves open the possibility for the presidency to have a say in this area. Over time, the president had become the leading figure in setting the federal government's priorities.

Article II, Section 3 calls for the Executive to "from time to time give to the Congress Information on the State of the Union, and recommend to their Consideration such

Measures as he shall judge necessary and expedient." As a result, presidents have used their STATE OF THE UNION ADDRESSES to set forth their vision for the political agenda as well as to create a "laundry list" of items for congressional action. Throughout much of the first part of the nation's history, presidents delivered their annual message in written form to Congress. The message usually was comprised of a mix of reporting of executive branch activities combined with modest proposals for legislative actions. In 1887 Grover CLEVELAND took the ambitious step of devoting his third annual message to a single issue: the tariff. Woodrow Wilson restored the practice, observed by Washington and Adams but abandoned by JEFFERSON and his successors, of delivering the message in person to Congress. Each president since then has followed Wilson's suit. The State of the Union address has become a preeminent political event each year, garnering prime-time live coverage by the major television networks.

Over the years, presidents have acquired other mechanisms by which they can set the political agenda. Perhaps the most significant tool stems from the BUDGET AND ACCOUNTING ACT OF 1921 as well as subsequent related legislation, which require the president to submit an executive budget to Congress. Whereas before this act presidents had little authority in developing the federal government's budget, the president was given an ability to set the nation's priorities and to highlight needed action to supplement the president's budget and the presidency was granted the ability to set the legislative agenda by being responsible for developing the federal government's budget.

Much of the current agenda-setting process has been institutionalized. For example, to provide presidents with the necessary resources to address the institution's new budgetary responsibilities, the Budget and Accounting Act of 1921 also created the BUREAU OF THE BUDGET, housed in the TREASURY DEPARTMENT. The Bureau later became the OFFICE OF MANAGEMENT AND BUDGET, a separate entity within the EXECUTIVE OFFICE OF THE PRESIDENT with increased powers and broader responsibilities, where presidents have at their disposal well-trained staff and advisers who develop and hone the NATIONAL ECONOMIC COUNCIL (created by President Clinton). In addition to these formal structures, presidents retain informal means to pursue their legislative agendas, such as the power to persuade and the ability to appeal to the public for support.

Given the increased authority of the presidency, the public and the media have come to look toward the president to lead and highlight key areas for action. Further, in times of crisis, the energy of the executive has given presidents the advantage (vis-à-vis Congress) to demonstrate their leadership capabilities. The fact that the public expects the president to be the nation's leader, though, creates a double-edged sword for the presidency. On one hand, it allows presidents greater ability to pursue their preferred alternatives or courses of action to address problems. For example, some presidents have successfully pursued ambitious agendas under grand themes, even when certain individual proposals may have not been so widely accepted: Franklin Roosevelt's NEW DEAL, Harry Truman's FAIR DEAL, Lyndon Johnson's GREAT SOCIETY, and, to a lesser degree, John Kennedy's NEW FRONTIER and Richard Nixon's New Federalism. On the other hand, the public perception of presidential LEADERSHIP creates the expectation that the president can and should solve any problem plaguing the nation, even if that problem is beyond the scope of the presidency's powers.

Political scientist Paul C. Light has undertaken perhaps the most comprehensive analysis regarding the development and pursuit of presidential domestic agendas. Light identifies two sets of resources that directly bear on a president's agenda. The first is comprised of internal resources, such as time, information, expertise, and energy. The second takes in external resources: party support in Congress, public approval, electoral margin, and PATRONAGE. These external resources help shape the amount of "presidential capital," meaning the status, authority, and influence that a president may have at any given time. All these factors figure into determining two cycles that affect both the timing of presidential initiatives and the size of the president's agenda. Light calls the first cycle the *cycle of decreasing influence*, reflecting that as time goes on presidents often lose political capital because of declining party support in Congress, lack of time to pursue major proposals, lame-duck status in a second term, etc. The other cycle Light identifies is the *cycle of increasing effectiveness*. Simply stated, the longer that presidents and their administrations remain in office and engage in the policy-making process, the more they learn and the better they become at garnering congressional and public support for their proposals. The point at which these two cycles peak to provide a president with the best opportunity to pursue his most ambitious proposals is at the start of his second term (assuming he is reelected). During this time, the administration has four years of on-the-job training under its belt and is coming off an electoral victory that the president can portray as reaffirming his priorities for the country.

Just what issues presidents decide to pursue, which alternatives are selected, at what time proposals are offered, and how much emphasis such proposals are given all are subject to variations in the policy-making process generally. Given the limited nature of presidential capital, presidents generally do not doggedly pursue issues that will spend too much capital and offer too little in return on the investment. As a result, a president may call for Congress to pursue a certain legislative proposal year after year in his State of the Union address but not follow up his call with any affirmative action.

Political scientist John W. Kingdon offers a model for understanding the agenda-setting and policy-making processes. He identifies three streams flowing through the political system that affect these processes. The first stream involves the process by which conditions in the political system are defined as problems that require governmental attention. The second stream consists of the various policy communities that generate, debate, craft, and accept alternatives. The third stream, the political stream, "is composed of such factors as swings of national mood, administration or legislative turnover, and interest group pressure campaigns" (Kingdon). When the three streams come together, a short window of opportunity opens up allowing for the government to enact legislation.

Further reading: Kernell, Samuel. *Going Public: New Strategies Of Presidential Leadership,* 3d ed. Washington, D.C.: CQ Press, 1997: Kingdon, John W. *Agendas, Alternatives, and Public Policies,* 2d ed. New York: Longman, 1985; Light, Paul C. *The President's Agenda: Domestic Policy Choice From Kennedy to Reagan,* 2d ed. Baltimore, Md.: Johns Hopkins University Press, 1991.

—Victoria Farrar-Myers

Agnew, Spiro T. (1918–1996) *U.S. vice president*
Born to Greek immigrants on November 9, 1918, just outside of Baltimore, Maryland, Agnew was Richard M. Nixon's vice president. After serving in the military in the World War II, he graduated from the University of Baltimore's Law School in 1947. Agnew practiced law first at a Baltimore firm, and then eventually moved to setting up his own practice in Towson, Maryland. In his transition to the suburbs, although his father had been a lifelong Democrat with heavy involvement in local party politics, he switched party affiliation. After a brief stint on the zoning board, he ran for associate circuit judge in 1960. In 1961 the new county executive dropped Agnew from the zoning board. In protest, he ran for county executive in 1962. Taking advantage of a deep split in the ranks of the Democrats, Agnew was able to get elected the first Republican Baltimore County Executive in the 20th century. While in office Agnew exhibited liberal and progressive tendencies. This enabled him, when he ran as the Republican gubernatorial nominee in 1966, to position himself to the left of his Democratic opponent, George Mahoney. However, once in the governor's office, he was much more conservative on racial matters and issues dealing with civil disorder. When NIXON surprised the Republican party establishment and political pundits alike by picking Agnew as his running mate in 1968, he actively campaigned as a get-tough, law- and-order political figure that attacked VIETNAM WAR protesters and college students who questioned "traditional" American

Spiro T. Agnew *(Library of Congress)*

values. Once elected, Nixon was preoccupied with the war in Vietnam throughout his first term. In order to blunt the steady stream of criticism emanating from the media and members of Congress, Nixon decided to use Agnew. It was in this role that Agnew became famous for several slogans such as "nattering nabobs of negativism" in reference to the media, and "radiclibs," for radical liberals. Agnew's appeal was evidence to Nixon that a new conservative coalition could be constructed using blue-collar ethnic voters and white-collar suburbanites. However, after the disappointing results in the 1970 MIDTERM ELECTIONS, Nixon's confidence in Agnew was shaken. The president had decided to use the vice president to stump for congressional candidates, but Agnew's abrasive style resulted in several Republican candidates requesting that he stay out of their district or state. As his 1972 reelection campaign approached, Nixon considered replacing Agnew with Treasury Secretary John Connally. However, Nixon won reelection by a comfortable enough margin that his vice-presidential running mate seemed irrelevant. As the WATERGATE events unfolded, Agnew informed H. R. Haldeman of a problem of his own on April 10, 1973: He himself had been ensnared in a bribery scandal in Maryland. In addition, even while VICE PRESIDENT, Agnew had continued to accept payments in his

White House office. It had seemed that Agnew had been Nixon's insurance against IMPEACHMENT. However, if both Nixon and Agnew were impeached simultaneously, the end result would be a Democrat ascending to the presidency. Nixon's new White House CHIEF OF STAFF, Alexander Haig, eventually convinced Agnew to resign. In return, Agnew received a suspended sentence and a $10,000 fine. Following his RESIGNATION, this controversial vice president quickly faded into obscurity. He died from leukemia on September 17, 1996.

Further reading: Cohen, Richard M. *A Heartbeat Away: The Investigation and Resignation of Vice President Spiro T. Agnew.* New York: Viking Press, 1994; *Washington Post,* September 19, 1996; Witcover, Jules. *White Knight: The Rise of Spiro Agnew.* New York: Random House, 1972.
—Jean-Philippe Faletta

Agriculture Department (USDA)

Established in 1862 during the LINCOLN presidency, the Agriculture Department (USDA) is today the sixth-largest CABINET department, employing approximately 100,000 full-time workers. It is responsible for a variety of federal programs such as subsidies, food stamps, rural development loans, food safety, nutrition, school lunch programs, managing for national parks and forests, as well as overseas food distribution programs.

Elevated to cabinet status in 1889, the Agriculture Department came under fire during the REAGAN years when the president called for the elimination of many food support programs. Political pressure from farmers and Congress forced the administration to retreat, and most of the programs continued unaltered.

agriculture policy

Agriculture is a policy arena strongly influenced by demographic changes, advances in science and technology, and growing awareness of environmental challenges, as well as changes in international trade patterns. Presidents increased their influence over agriculture policy as Congress lost influence in the post–WORLD WAR II period. This change in dominant institutional influence has gone through several fluctuations in the 20th century and promises to continue in the 21st.

The idea of a nation of yeoman self-sufficient farmers, trading their products and eventually joining the cash economy while the plantation system waxed and then waned in the South, has a basis in both fact and myth in the 19th century. Frontiersmen-turned-farmers helped lead the expansion into territory occupied by aboriginal peoples. In any other context this expansion of a people and a new style of economy across a continent, displacing the original inhabitants, would be called IMPERIALISM. Instead presidents, political leaders, and the public saw this MANIFEST DESTINY as inevitable and positive.

Development of the industrial revolution coincided with rising productivity on farms, freeing labor to move to factory jobs. The laissez-faire approach of presidents in the 19th-century era reinforced a generally hands-off national agriculture policy. In the early 20th century the pattern of modernization in farming accelerated due to more mechanization and reached a crescendo by the post-WWII period. The farm-based population shrank. Without significant deliberation, modern agribusiness ever more fully replaced the yeoman farmers. Today agribusiness continues this pattern of accelerated change and concentration in agriculture production especially since the CARTER and REAGAN administrations. Farmers still in the business today increasingly work under contract and purchase inputs such as seed, fertilizer, and pesticides from an ever-smaller number of concentrated agribusinesses. Similar production concentrations are occurring in the meat industry as the cartelization of agriculture continues. End products are increasingly manufactured, that is, processed by agribusiness to fit with modern marketing practices to sell food products. Changes in logistics, the distribution and transportation process, also contribute to the accelerated concentration of agriculture in the hands of agribusiness. Presidents in the 20th century pursued agricultural policies allowing this transformation of U.S. agriculture. Policy processes, without much in the way of public discussion or discourse, have smoothed the way for concentration.

Broadly, changes in agriculture policy in the 20th century featured increasing governmental intervention in some aspects of agriculture while ignoring others. Congress rather than the president had been the dominant force in much of U.S. agricultural policy. Starting with Franklin D. ROOSEVELT, presidents have had an increasing influence, partly due to population shifts that result in decreased power and influence for Congress. Rural districts are much less powerful than they once were.

Presidents' growing influence through their secretaries of agriculture, a cabinet office since 1889, and the Department of Agriculture focused on new knowledge and the application of science through, for example, extension services. Secretary of Agriculture James Wilson, who served from 1897 to 1913 under Presidents MCKINLEY, Theodore ROOSEVELT, TAFT, and WILSON, focused policy extensively on experiment stations. Later, in the Depression era, more direct economic tools were used to influence the direction of agriculture. In the 1930s the primary goal was salvaging farm incomes. Some of the tools utilized were price controls, marketing agreements, loan programs, and various other subsidies. The upsurge in executive influence occurred in the Roosevelt era. Republican presidents, however, did not return to a laissez-faire version of agricultural policy. In part that was due to the declining yet still effective influence of farm district legislators who held powerful committee positions in Congress and protected their constituents' incomes. However, the dramatic drop in farm population as the productivity of farmers radically increased led eventually to the decline in power of agri-district members of Congress, though it took well-known federal court decisions to effect the change.

On the executive side, the Department of Agriculture, and at the state level, universities focused on applying science to agriculture, made impressive progress. As productivity increased, the inevitable surpluses followed. Presidents in the COLD WAR era used foreign aid food programs, such as PL 480, established in the EISENHOWER administration, to reduce surpluses.

Technological advances in the research labs augmented trends in Third World agriculture, culminating in new worldwide production patterns. This in turn effected demand for U.S. agriculture exports. International politics intruded as well. Agriculture suffered in what became a foreign policy battle between president and Congress, rather than one purely over the direction of agriculture policy. Anti-DÉTENTE forces in the Senate opposed to CARTER'S policy with the Soviets embargoed grain sales. Ostensibly the embargo's purpose was to improve Jewish immigration from the Soviet Union. Interestingly, a leader of the anti-détente forces was from a wheat exporting state. The unintended but obvious outcome was a grand opening for agri-producers in other parts of the world who promptly stepped in to fill the void.

Urbanized America today is far different from the earlier times when agriculture was more easily recognized as an important component of the overall economy. Increasingly urban interests and demands have shaped agriculture policy. These include food stamp and nutrition programs, food product labeling, residual pesticides, genetically modified products, and fertilizer usage. The latter three topics overlap with environmental concerns that Republican and Democratic presidents alike cannot ignore. The domain of the Agriculture Department is no longer subject to only farmer or agribusiness influence. Organized interests representing consumers and environmental issues are now part of the president's agriculture policy concerns.

Competing claims to scarce resources further complicate presidents' agriculture policy picture as well. President CLINTON and now BUSH may wish otherwise, but in various regions of the nation, issues such as water impinge on agriculture and executive department decision making. Where irrigation from water diversion programs created an agricultural base, such as in the arid West, there now arise challenges by competing claims for the limited resource. In other regions groundwater supplies from giant aquifers pose similar long-term problems that will eventually face future presidents. In many ways these new problems are more complex and volatile than the price controls, cropland diversion, commodity programs, and export programs that have been the focus of previous executive agricultural decision making. The new issues involve many more constituent groups than older style agri-policy issues.

Another problematic aspect for Presidents REAGAN, George H. W. BUSH, Clinton, and George W. Bush is the globalization of agricultural trade. Indeed this expansion is occurring and it is a two-way street. Open trade and lowered tariffs and quotas create new markets for U.S. agribusiness. At the same time, U.S. markets are also more open than ever to foreign agricultural products. In any supermarket, consumers find fresh and frozen fruits, vegetables, fish and meat, and manufactured food items such as pasta in abundance from all corners of the globe. In the process of global trade, agribusiness interests in the United States may be undercut by price competition. In this case, what is good for the consumer may hurt selected producers. The long-term effect may be fewer food producers in the United States and/or changes in what they produce. Presidents could come under significant political pressure if the current low level of criticism regarding globalization of agriculture should ever increase.

Further reading: Cochrane, Willard, and Mary Ryan. *American Farm Policy, 1948–1973.* Minneapolis: University of Minnesota Press, 1976; Hadwiger, Don, and Ross Talbot. "Food Policy and Farm Programs," *Proceedings of the Academy of Political Science* vol. 34 (1982); Talbot, Ross, and Don Hadwiger. *The Policy Process in American Agriculture.* San Francisco: Chandler Publishing Co., 1968.
—Michael Carey

Air Force One

Presidential air transport began in 1944 when a C-54 called the *Sacred Cow* was put into service for President Franklin D. ROOSEVELT. The *Independence*, a DC-6, transported President Harry S TRUMAN until 1953. President Dwight D. EISENHOWER flew on the *Columbine II* and *Columbine III*. During the 1950s the radio call sign of the presidential aircraft became *Air Force One*, but it was not until the Kennedy administration that the term was widely used as the title of the President's aircraft.

Perhaps the most historically significant presidential aircraft entered into service in 1962. Tail number 26000 carried President KENNEDY to Dallas on November 22, 1963, and returned his body to Washington, D.C., following his assassination. At Love Field, Lyndon B. JOHNSON was sworn into office as the 36th president on board the plane.

Air Force One over Mount Rushmore *(United States Air Force)*

In 1972 President Richard M. NIXON made historic visits aboard 26000 to the People's Republic of China and to the former Soviet Union. Tail number 26000 was retired in May 1998 and is on display at the U.S. Air Force Museum in Ohio.

Tail number 27000 replaced 26000 and was used to fly Presidents Nixon, FORD, and CARTER to Cairo, Egypt, on October 19, 1981, to represent the United States at the funeral of Egyptian president Anwar Sadat. It also flew former president Carter and former vice president MONDALE to Germany to greet the American hostages released from Iran. The president who flew on 27000 the most was Ronald REAGAN. After arriving to Berlin in 1987 on 27000, Reagan famously stated, "Mr. Gorbachev, tear down this wall." Tail number 27000 is now on display at the Reagan Library in Simi Valley, California.

Currently, the presidential fleet consists of two specially designed Boeing 747200B's with tail numbers 28000 and 29000. The planes used as *Air Force One* are state-of-the-art flying machines. Accommodations for the president include an executive suite consisting of a stateroom (with dressing room, lavatory, and shower) and office. A conference and dining room area is also available for the president, staff, family, guests, and news media. *Air Force One* is a fully equipped "flying White House" with 87 separate phone lines, numerous televisions, a provisional medical facility, and two kitchens equipped to serve up to 100 passengers.

Further reading: *Air Force One*. National Geographic documentary, released on July 11, 2001; Chitester, Ken. *Aboard Air Force One: 200,000 Miles With a White Mouse*

Aide. Santa Barbara, Calif.: Fithian Press, 1997; Holder, Bill. *Planes of the Presidents: An Illustrated History of Air Force One.* Atglen, Pa.: Schiffer Publishing, Ltd., 2000; Von Hardesty. *"Air Force One": The Aircraft That Shaped the Modern Presidency.* Chauhassen, Minn.: Creative Publishing, 2003.

—Colleen J. Shogan

Alaska Purchase

The Alaska Purchase, which took place under the administration of Andrew JOHNSON, marked the end of Russian occupation of America and a significant purchase of land (and resources) by the United States. The treaty, negotiated by Secretary of State William H. SEWARD, originally met with some criticism and was derisively referred to as "Seward's folly." Over time the purchase for $7.2 million was considered an excellent deal. The treaty making the Alaska Purchase official was approved by Congress (after some difficulty) and signed on March 30, 1867.

Alien and Sedition Acts

The Alien and Sedition Acts were passed by Congress in the summer of 1798. They were intended to suppress domestic opposition to the John ADAMS administration, while preparing the country for hostilities with France. Continuing conflicts between France and Britain made American neutrality difficult. The Federalists who controlled the government from the Founding until 1801 favored Britain over France, especially after the French Revolution, and there was a series of diplomatic and naval incidents between the United States and France. By contrast, the growing Jeffersonian opposition favored an alliance with France and distrusted Britain. There was little experience at the time with legitimate political parties, and the Federalists regarded criticism of the sitting administration as disloyalty to the American government.

The Alien and Sedition Acts actually consisted of four statutes, three of which dealt with aliens. The Naturalization Act nearly tripled the residency requirement for aliens to become eligible for citizenship in the United States, extending the requirement to 14 years from the five years set in 1795 (which in turn had extended the two-year requirement set in 1790). The Act also required aliens to declare their intent to become citizens five years before their actual admission into citizenship. More immediately, it substantially delayed the voting privileges that accompanied citizenship for a population that was assumed to largely favor the Jeffersonians. The Alien Act and the Alien Enemies Act imposed new restrictions on resident aliens. The Alien Act gave the president sweeping new powers to order, in peacetime, any resident alien that the president

regarded as "dangerous to the peace and safety of the United States" to leave the country, unless licensed by the president to remain under whatever conditions the CHIEF EXECUTIVE might choose. Ships arriving in the United States were required to file a report on all aliens on board. Violators of the presidential orders were subject to fines and imprisonment, but there were no trials or other legal procedures required for the president to declare an alien dangerous. In time of war, the Alien Enemies Act authorized the president to imprison or deport all natives of the hostile nation who had not already become naturalized American citizens. The Alien Act was never enforced.

The Sedition Act was the most controversial of the four laws. The Sedition Act was formally entitled "an act for the punishment of certain crimes against the United States," and it included a number of provisions regarding interference with government officials, conspiracies for insurrections, and the like. More important, the second section of the statute made it a crime to "print, utter or publish" anything "false, scandalous, or malicious" against the government, to bring the government or its institutions into "contempt or disrepute," or to "excite against them . . . the hatred of the good people of the United States." Seditious speech was a crime recognized in the British common law, but there was substantial public resistance to the American federal courts accepting prosecutions based only on the judge-made common law. In writing seditious speech into the federal criminal law, Congress actually moderated the British legal standard. In contrast to British law, the Sedition Act made the truth of the statement a defense against conviction, made the jury the judge of the fact of the libel, and required the prosecution to demonstrate criminal intent. The Sedition Act was aggressively used by the Adams administration against prominent Jeffersonian writers, editors, and even politicians, though juries often refused to convict. In the Virginia and Kentucky resolutions and elsewhere, the Jeffersonians denounced the Sedition Act as unconstitutional for exceeding the powers of the federal government and for violating the First Amendment guarantee of free speech, and they used opposition to the statute to help mobilize their own victorious electoral campaign of 1800. In the process, they developed a broader understanding of the requirements of free speech in a democracy.

The Naturalization Act of 1798 was repealed in April 1802. The Alien Act expired by its own terms in 1800, and the Sedition Act expired in 1801. Neither statute was renewed. The Alien Enemies Act remains on the books in amended form and has been employed at various times in American history. Supreme Court Justice Samuel Chase, who oversaw a number of particularly prominent and politically charged trials in the 1790s, was impeached by the House of Representatives in 1804 but was not removed by the Senate.

Further reading: Elkins, Stanley, and Eric McKitrick. *The Age of Federalism.* New York: Oxford University Press, 1993; Levy, Leonard W. *Emergence of a Free Press.* New York: Oxford University Press, 1985; Miller, John C. *Freedom's Fetters: The Alien and Sedition Acts.* Boston: Little, Brown and Company, 1951.

—Keith E. Whittington

Alliance for Progress

When John F. KENNEDY became president in 1961, U.S. relations with Latin America posed a formidable challenge to the incoming administration. Hostility from Latinos ran high, as many viewed the United States as a "counterrevolutionary bully" who favored right-wing dictatorships at the expense of democratic insurgencies. American citizens saw it differently, as they tended to focus on Fidel Castro and his alleged efforts to export communism. As Kennedy biographer James N. Giglio puts it, "Kennedy's Latin American policy was both an idealistic and a practical response to hemispheric and economic needs and to a perceived Communist threat."

During the election campaign of 1960, Kennedy proposed a partnership with Latin America, an Adianza para el Progresso (Alliance for Progress), in which the United States would engage in a MARSHALL PLAN of sorts for Latin America. He formally proposed it to a meeting of Latin American diplomats at the White House in March of 1961. The Alliance for Progress consisted of three parts: economic assistance, land and tax reform, and a new commitment to leaders and policies who supported democratic ideals, principles, and practices. The plan, which focused particular attention on restructuring the social, political, and economic character of the region, constituted an enormously ambitious plan, never before attempted by an American president, to influence the fundamental nature of Latin America.

The Alliance was modestly successful, providing funds for the construction of infrastructure, schools, hospitals, and low-cost housing. However, it failed to win the popular support enjoyed by the Peace Corps, nor did it achieve the more basic goals of the administration, particularly the restructuring of society in the region. Reasons for its modest success included the fact that, unlike the Marshall Plan, the financing included only loans and loan guarantees rather than grants, the administration's insistence that some of the money be used to buy U.S. goods at U.S. prices, the unanticipated population explosion in the region which made it impossible to meet economic development goals, and particularly bureaucratic and organizational problems such as putting the Alliance under the AGENCY FOR INTERNATIONAL DEVELOPMENT rather than making it an independent agency such as the Peace Corps. This latter problem in particular is blamed for stifling a kind of creativity that could have kept the Alliance from being captured by so-called bureaucratic intransigence and functioning more in line with what Kennedy had intended.

Further reading: Giglio, James N. *The Presidency of John F. Kennedy.* Lawrence: University Press of Kansas, 1991; Schlesinger, Arthur M., Jr. "The Alliance for Progress: A Retrospective." In *Latin America: The Search for a New International Role,* edited by Ronald G. Hellman and H. Jan Rosenbaum. New York: John Wiley, 1975.

—Daniel E. Ponder

ambassadors, receiving and appointing

Article II, Section 2 of the Constitution says that the president "shall nominate, and by and with the Advice and Consent of the Senate, shall appoint Ambassadors, other public Ministers and Consuls." Thus, the president appoints, subject to Senate approval, all U.S. ambassadors to other nations. This gives the president foreign policy authority in that the president selects and instructs those who are sent abroad to represent the United States to other governments. The president's "receiving" power stems from Article II, Section 3, which says that the president "shall receive Ambassadors and other public Ministers." This allows the president to be the chief recipient of information from other nations. This two-way dialogue—appointing and receiving ambassadors—places the president at the center of the foreign policy loop, granting him considerable power and influence. While Alexander HAMILTON underestimated this authority, writing in *Federalist No. 69* that the power to receive ambassadors was "more a matter of dignity than of authority," over time presidents have used this method to enhance their control over foreign policy. Also, the power to receive has been linked over time with the power—not mentioned in the Constitution—to "recognize" other governments.

amnesty

Amnesty and pardon are forms of generic clemency which derive from Article II, Section 2, of the Constitution giving the president "Power to grant Reprieves and Pardons for Offenses against the United States, except in Cases of Impeachment." Legal scholars often draw artificial distinctions between amnesty and pardon, but presidential exercise of this power has tended to undercut such academic delineations. Overall, amnesties pertain to large groups and pardons to single individuals. Regardless of what the form of clemency is termed, the exercise of it typically is unpopular among the public since it short-circuits the normal judicial process. Yet that is precisely why the CHIEF EXECUTIVE was given this power; it sometimes is needed in special circumstances and may serve as a safety valve to dispel national tension. Alexander HAMILTON defended the power in *Federalist No. 74.* Hamilton understood that law is not always an absolute black and white matter. Hamilton's defense of presidential clemency power was based upon his understanding of how George WASHINGTON used this prerogative during the American Revolution. Washington set the precedent for clemency while a military commander during the American Revolution, called for its application to Loyalists after the war was won, and exercised it with classical prudence during his presidency, since it is the only unchecked constitutional power granted to the executive.

The fundamental empirical question is the type of clemency exercised—limited or broad, regardless of what it is called, and if there is a pattern discernible among presidential personalities. Clemency patterns emerge from the historic record of presidents. There is a consistent, if largely unrecognized, presidential behavior common to America's MOUNT RUSHMORE quartet: This most active and flexible group of chief executives granted amnesties and granted more of them than all other presidents combined. In addition to Washington, Abraham LINCOLN's "with malice toward none" policy personifies both the tone and character of this type of president and corresponding clemency records. Lincoln, a "compassionate conservative," granted the second greatest number of amnesties, adhering to a prudent clemency policy. The Mount Rushmore—and other active-flexible—chief executives were willing to risk and withstand the inevitable public criticism clemency triggers. Gerald FORD's controversial pardon of Richard NIXON is a classic example not only of why the Founders favored executive pardons but also why active-flexible presidents, even conservative ones, are willing to act, regardless of public backlash.

Most presidents are too passive to grant clemency, especially amnesty, for amnesty represents the most visible kind of clemency—it requires a proclamation by the chief executive. Warren G. HARDING first favored clemency for World War I opponents, only to reverse his stance in the wake of the criticism heaped upon him for pardoning Eugene V. Debs. Calvin COOLIDGE appointed the first clemency commission, in effect creating a political shield for himself before he would grant amnesty. The southern-born Woodrow WILSON demonstrated an extremist streak that prevented leniency toward those who opposed his presidential foreign policy. Wilson was an extremist at the opposite end of the spectrum from Andrew JOHNSON, who holds the distinction of having issued the most amnesties in American history. Of course, Johnson's real offense was more political—subverting the policy of radical Republicans who wanted to punish southerners for the CIVIL WAR. He misused presidential clemency to secure political support among fellow southerners.

Good presidents may make errors in granting individual pardons, but a survey of the presidential amnesty record suggests that use of this executive prerogative confirms the Founders' wisdom in conferring such an unchecked judicial power on the executive. It allows for contemporary decency and creates the foundation for an admirable political legacy.

Further reading: Moore, Kathleen D. *Pardons: Justice, Mercy, and the Public Interest.* New York: Oxford University Press, 1989; Pederson, William D. "Amnesty and Presidential Behavior." In *The "Barberian" Presidency,* edited by William D. Pederson, 113–128. New York: P. Lang, 1989; Pederson, William D. "Amnesties and Pardons." In *The American Revolution, 1775–1783,* Volume 1, edited by Richard L. Blanco, 32–33. New York: Garland Publishing, 1983; Pederson, William D., and Frank J. Williams. "America's Presidential Triumvirate: Quantitative Measures." In *George Washington, Foundation of Presidential Leadership and Character,* edited by Ethan Fishman, William D. Pederson, and Mark Rozell, 143–161. Westport, Conn.: Praeger, 2001.

—William D. Pederson

Anderson, John B. (1922–   ) *congressman*

In 1980 longtime Republican member of the House John B. Anderson left his party to run for president as an independent. Unhappy with the choices being offered the voters in the 1980 presidential election, and sensing a strategic opening to run as a moderate candidate, Anderson tried to exploit the relative unpopularity of President CARTER and the perception that Governor Ronald REAGAN was too conservative to appeal to most voters.

Anderson tried to position himself as a centrist alternative to President Carter and Republican Reagan, but after attracting some early attention, Anderson slipped, receiving only 6.6 percent of the popular vote.

announcement speeches

During the years between presidential elections, presidential aspirants travel to states holding early PRIMARIES AND CAUCUSES in order to "test the waters" and determine the likely success of their candidacies. Laying the groundwork for a successful presidential campaign requires raising money, constructing an organization, and developing a message that resonates with voters. Aspirants typically spend months or even years doing so without ever making formal their intent to seek the OVAL OFFICE.

Eventually a candidate states his intent through an official announcement speech recognizing the formal kickoff of the campaign. Following the McGovern-Fraser reforms in the DEMOCRATIC PARTY, the length of the campaign grew as candidates announced their decision to seek the White House earlier. For example, in 1968 the Democratic nominee, Hubert HUMPHREY, declared his intent to seek the Democratic nomination in late April prior to the August convention. Less than three years later in January of 1971 the eventual Democratic nominee, George MCGOVERN, announced the formation of his campaign organization—an unprecedented 18 months prior to the July convention! Given that announcement speeches are often the formal introduction of the candidate to many voters across the nation, they tend to focus on the biography of the candidate and his or her policy positions. Thus, these major media events tend to occur in either the birthplace or hometown of the candidate.

The timing of announcement speeches tends to be political. While long-shot candidates often announce early in order to gain as much support as possible, front-runners who enjoy significant name recognition prior to entering the campaign tend to delay formal entrance as long as possible. In fact, until the success of DARK HORSE candidate Jimmy CARTER in 1976, early announcement of candidacy was considered a sign of weakness. It was then that candidates recognized the benefits of early announcement, which include free media coverage that facilitates both grassroots campaigning and additional fund-raising. Today the nature of testing the waters is changing. In the past three nomination cycles as many as seven major Democratic or Republican presidential contenders announced their candidacies only to later withdraw after recognizing that their message was not resonating with either campaign donors or voters.

Further reading: Polsby, Nelson, and Aaron Wildavsky. *Presidential Elections.* New York: Chatham House Publishers, 2000; Wayne, Stephen. *Road to the White House.* Boston: Bedford/St. Martin's, 2000.

—Randall E. Adkins

Antideficiency Act

The Constitution grants all spending power to the Congress. However, the president as CHIEF EXECUTIVE claims some discretionary authority over spending. In an effort to curb overspending by executive departments, Congress in 1905 and again in 1906 passed antideficiency laws aimed at curbing spending. In 1950, Congress rewrote the Antideficiency Act in an effort to curb spending and reclaim some of its budgeting authority.

In the early 1970s, Richard NIXON used a provision of the 1950 act to claim broad authority to impound funds appropriated by Congress. Often courts were called on to intervene in disputes between Nixon and Congress over the IMPOUNDMENT OF FUNDS. Usually the president lost in court. Congress then passed a budget act in 1974 to put a halt to the impoundment of funds by a president. The Budget Enforcement Act of 1990 again attempted to tighten controls over discretionary spending.

Anti-Federalists

Many contemporary critics look at the Anti-Federalists as "men of little faith," but to others they were prophets of the fissures that would drive future political conflicts in American democracy. Although the Anti-Federalists lost the original Constitutional debate, their philosophy and ideals permeate our political culture.

Who were the Anti-Federalists? History describes them as the opponents to the new Constitution, but they also were the proponents of government closer to the people, the need for representatives from the middle-class yeomanry mirroring their constituents in government, and the ability of humans to be virtuous. The Anti-Federalists' greatest fear was that people would become complacent with the new national government, so far removed from their daily lives. Without the citizens' constant participation in government, like those of the localities and states, and within juries, new entities like the national executive and judiciary would become too powerful and magisterial. The Anti-Federalists feared the necessary and proper clause (Article I, Section 8), dubbing it the "elastic clause," through which the new national government would grow.

Although some considered the presidency a well-conceived office, the majority Anti-Federalist view opposed the idea of a strong executive and the powers that came with the office. Some favored a plural executive—the single executive struck too closely with the English monarchical system. Other concerns included the presidential VETO, COMMANDER IN CHIEF, and APPOINTMENT POWERS. Perhaps the harshest criticisms were cast toward the president's general authority to execute the laws faithfully. As William Symmes wrote, "Should a Federal law happen to be as generally expressed as the President's authority; must he not interpret the Act! For in many cases he must execute the laws independent of any judicial decision. . . . Is there no instance in which he may reject the sense of the legislature, and establish his own, and so far, would he not be to all intents and purposes absolute?" Or consider Patrick Henry's more flamboyant rhetoric on a similar issue:

> "If your American chief, be a man of ambition, and abilities, how easy is it for him to render himself absolute . . . I would rather infinitely . . . have a King, Lords, and Commons, than a Government so replete with such insupportable evils. If we make a King, we may prescribe the rules by which he shall rule his people, and interpose such checks as shall prevent him from infringing them: But the President, in the field, at the

head of his army, can prescribe the terms on which he shall reign master, so far that it will puzzle any American ever to get his neck from under the galling yoke."

As a group, the Anti-Federalists were a patchwork of many individuals like Patrick Henry, George CLINTON, Brutus, and Melancton Smith, who never quite congealed as a singular voice in the way that MADISON, HAMILTON, and JAY did with the FEDERALIST PAPERS. Their haphazard style, some contend, cost them the original debate. However, their ideals resonated right away in the passage of the first ten amendments, the Bill of Rights, which Anti-Federalist forces in states like New York won as a concession from the Federalists for ratification. When originally passed, these ten amendments held the national government in check; now, through incorporation (the process through which the Supreme Court has used the Fourteenth Amendment to apply many of these rights to the states), these rights form the foundation of our key individual protections in the United States today.

Further reading: Ketcham, Ralph. *The Anti-Federalist Papers; and, The Constitutional Convention Debates.* New York: New American Library, 1986; Storing, Herbert J. *What The Anti-Federalists Were For.* Chicago: University of Chicago Press, 1981.

—Victoria Farrar-Myers

Anti-Masonic Party

Americans have long been suspicious of secret societies and have feared conspiratorial, behind-the-scenes efforts to gain power. Such fears spawned the creation of America's first third party, the Anti-Masonic Party. After the 1826 disappearance under suspicious circumstances of William Morgan of New York, a fallen member of the Masonic Order (Masons), various communities in the northeast began to form anti-Mason societies. Morgan was about to reveal the "secrets" of the Masonic Order, and it was widely believed that the Masons killed him to keep their secrets safe.

In 1830 anti-Masonic parties formed. In 1832 they became the first political party to hold a political convention. The Anti-Masonic Party was strongly anti-Jackson (Andrew JACKSON was a Mason), and they offered their own ticket: William Wirt of Maryland as president, and Amos Ellmaker of Pennsylvania as vice president. The Anti-Masonic ticket won only Vermont, and Jackson was easily reelected in 1832.

The Anti-Masonic Party, like most third parties, was a single-issue coalition, one united in its fears of the Masons. After 1836 they disbanded and the leading figures of the Party such as William H. SEWARD and Thaddeus Stevens gravitated toward the Whig Party.

Further reading: Vaughn, William Preston. *The Anti-Masonic Party in the United States, 1826–1843.* Lexington: University Press of Kentucky, 1983.

Antitrust Policy

The goal of antitrust policy is to insure fairness in business practices. As the United States became an industrial power in the 1890s, calls for business reform became more pronounced as "trusts" (a form of business monopolies) developed. In 1890, President Benjamin HARRISON signed the Sherman Antitrust Act, prohibiting monopolies and restraint on trade. While underenforced, it was nonetheless the first effort to insure fairness in business practice against the growing trend toward trusts.

President Theodore ROOSEVELT more vigorously enforced the act and became known as a "trustbuster." In 1914 President Wilson signed the CLAYTON ACT, an attempt to control price-fixing and mergers.

As business has become more global, efforts to enforce antitrust policies have proven deficient. Today, megacorporations with international reach dominate the world economy.

Further reading: Adams, Walter, and James W. Brock. *Antitrust Economics on Trial: A Dialogue on the New Laissez-Faire.* Princeton, N.J.: Princeton University Press, 1991; Hawley, Ellis W. *The New Deal and the Problem of Monopoly.* Princeton, N.J.: Princeton University Press, 1966.

ANZUS Treaty

On September 1, 1951, Australia, New Zealand, and the United States signed a mutual defense treaty that went into effect on April 28, 1952. For over three decades it was regarded as the model of such agreements.

The treaty was brief, referred to as flexible, but one could regard that to be a euphemism for vague or ambiguous. It noted its compatibility with the UNITED NATIONS Charter and with existing security agreements. Unlike NATO, for example, it did not have a secretariat, a joint command, or require its member nations to have standing armies in each other's territories. Its conditions have never been explicitly invoked, which its defenders argue demonstrates its effectiveness.

The impetus for ANZUS emerged from the collapse of the British Empire and the onset of the COLD WAR. It gave Australia desired special access to Washington and enabled Washington, if only symbolically, to reward Australia and New Zealand for their contributions to UN efforts in the KOREAN WAR. It was one in a series of the U.S. treaties that came to fruition in the EISENHOWER administration and which were designed to contain international communism.

Over the years, reaction to incidents in Pacific Rim locales reflected the differing national interests of the signatories: Taiwan (1955), Indonesia (1958–64), Indochina (1964), and the Indian Ocean (1979–81) either demonstrated the flexibility of ANZUS or its ineffectiveness, depending on one's point of view.

As early as the mid-1950s, John Foster DULLES suggested that ANZUS was redundant with the creation of SEATO. A far more damaging blow occurred in 1985 when New Zealand's Labour government, headed by David Lange, denied admission for an American naval vessel to enter New Zealand harbors unless it would declare that it had no nuclear weapons. Following standard American policy, the ship declined to do so. This followed several months of diplomatic maneuverings on Labour's antinuclear stance, a position that was enacted into law and maintained by the subsequent National Party government. In reaction, Washington discontinued military exercises and suspended most other activities with New Zealand forces. New Zealand was essentially no longer a member of ANZUS.

After the break, New Zealand adopted a defense policy based on conventional weapons—one that was essentially neutralist and sought closer ties with the island nations of the south Pacific. Antinuclear sentiment continued strong among the New Zealand people. Meanwhile, Australia's commitment to New Zealand through the 1944 ANZAC pact was strained and Australia strengthened its relations with United States.

In September 2001, the United States and Australia issued a joint statement commemorating the 50th anniversary of the treaty, noting it had been "a pillar of strength in the Asia-Pacific region," and reaffirming their commitment to the alliance. Others noted that the acronym was then 16 years out of date and that the treaty had become a United States–Australia alliance.

Further reading: Baker, Richard W. *The ANZUS States and Their Region.* Westport, Conn.: Praeger, 1994; Bercovitch, Jacob. *ANZUS in Crisis: Alliance Management in International Affairs.* New York: St. Martin's Press, 1988; Donnini, Frank P. *ANZUS in Revision: Changing Defense Features of Australia and New Zealand in the Mid-1980s.* Maxwell Air Force Base, Ala.: Air University Press, 1991.

—Thomas P. Wolf

appointment power

Article II, Section 2, of the Constitution grants the president the power—with the advice and consent of the Senate—to appoint officers of the United States. Congress may also delegate to the president the power to appoint "inferior Officers."

Overall, the president appoints more than 1,000 officials, mostly members of his own party, to top posts. Controversies over appointment and removal were quite common. In general the Supreme Court has given presidents wide latitude in both appointing and removing officials.

The appointment power is an important tool for a president in gaining control of his administration and national policy. All presidents want "their people" to staff key government positions so that the partisan and ideological goals of the president can be met. If disloyal or opposition forces sit in key positions, the president will not be able to elicit from them the support and loyalty essential for governing.

Over the years there have been some dramatic and pointed battles over presidential appointments. In the summer of 1991, during the presidency of George H. W. BUSH, the president nominated Clarence Thomas to a seat on the Supreme Court. During Thomas's confirmation hearings in the Senate, law professor Anita Hill came forward and claimed that Thomas had sexually harassed her when she worked for him at the Department of Education. Thomas angrily denied the accusations, and the hearings degenerated into a circus-like atmosphere with accusations and cross accusations flying on all sides. Thomas was eventually confirmed, but the legacy of this incident tarnished him for years.

Further reading: Heclo, Hugh. *A Government of Strangers: Executive Politics in Washington.* Washington, D.C.: Brookings Institution, 1977; Mackenzie, G. Calvin, ed. *The In-and-Outers: Presidential Appointees and Transient Government in Washington.* Baltimore: Johns Hopkins University Press, 1987.

arms control

Presidents are the principal arms control negotiators for the United States, and while the history of arms control can be traced back to the Rush-Bagot agreement of 1817 (an agreement that eliminated naval deployments on the Great Lakes), it is really in the COLD WAR era that arms control has been a prominent and politically persistent AGENDA item.

In the cold war era, presidents have dominated the arms control agenda. They set the agenda, conduct negotiations, agree to terms, and either sign EXECUTIVE AGREEMENTS or submit treaties to the Senate for approval. The first major nuclear arms agreement was the Limited Test Ban Treaty of the KENNEDY administration. Kennedy's successor, Lyndon JOHNSON, concluded the Outer Space Treaty, banning nuclear weapons in space, and the Nuclear Nonproliferation Treaty. Johnson also got the STRATEGIC ARMS LIMITATION TALKS (SALT) started.

Under President NIXON, the United States and the Soviet Union signed the SALT I agreement, as well as the Anti-ballistic Missile (ABM) treaty. Jimmy CARTER, building on work done in the FORD administration, negotiated the SALT II agreement. His successor, Ronald REAGAN, opposed SALT II, but he eventually proposed drastic cuts in the nuclear arsenals, along with the development of a "Star Wars" missile defense system. Reagan and Mikhail Gorbachev concluded an Intermediate Nuclear Force (INF) treaty.

George H. W. BUSH continued to pursue arms control, agreeing to the Conventional Forces in Europe (CFE) treaty. President CLINTON made the peaceful destruction of Soviet nuclear missiles and nuclear nonproliferation the centerpiece of his arms control policy.

George W. BUSH continued down the arms control path with reduction agreements with Russia but also heightened tensions by withdrawing the United States from the ABM treaty and attempting to develop a missile defense system.

Further reading: Krepon, M., and D. Caldwell, eds. *The Politics of Arms Control Treaty Ratification.* New York: St. Martin's Press, 1991; Newhouse, J. *Cold Dawn: The Story of SALT.* New York: Holt, Rinehart and Winston, 1973; Talbott, S. *Deadly Gambits.* New York: Vintage Books, 1984; Talbott, S. *Endgame: The Inside Story of SALT II.* New York: Harper & Row, 1979.

Arms Control and Disarmament Act of 1961

The U.S. ARMS CONTROL AND DISARMAMENT AGENCY was created by this act. It was designed to conduct research and aid in ARMS CONTROL and disarmament efforts. Controversial, this act created the means by which presidents could pursue disarmament and nonproliferation policies.

Arms Control and Disarmament Agency (ACDA)

On September 26, 1961, President KENNEDY signed the ACDA Act, establishing the Arms Control and Disarmament Agency. The ACDA Act called for the director to advise the president and secretary of state on ARMS CONTROL and disarmament issues. The act also directed the agency to assist in negotiations, conduct research, and inform the public on these issues. Later amendments to the act call for the agency to present annual reports to the president on arms control compliance. The president is required to submit this report to Congress.

Over time the ACDA has been actively involved in a number of international negotiations on arms control and disarmament, including the 1963 Limited Test Ban Treaty, the 1968 Nuclear Nonproliferation Treaty, the 1972 Bio-

logical Weapons Convention, and the 1992 Chemical Weapons Convention.

Some presidents prefer to bypass ACDA and negotiate bilaterally, using the secretary of state or another official as chief negotiator. Since the breakup of the Soviet Union and end of the COLD WAR, ACDA's responsibilities have shifted toward nuclear nonproliferation and arms reduction efforts.

arms sales

Prior to the 1970s, the president controlled the sale of arms to other nations as part of the president's foreign policy authority. After VIETNAM and WATERGATE, and as U.S. arms sales grew in volume and controversy, Congress began to demand a greater role.

In 1974 Congress passed the Foreign Assistance Act, which included a provision allowing Congress, by joint resolution, to veto any arms sale. This "LEGISLATIVE VETO" was also part of the Arms Export Control Act of 1976.

The Supreme Court, however, in *INS v. CHADHA* (1983), invalidated the legislative veto. Congress then (1986) created a "joint resolution of disapproval," which was subject to a presidential veto.

In spite of Congress's efforts to develop better oversight of arms sales, it has generally been unable to stop resolute presidents from selling arms abroad.

Arthur, Chester A. (1829–1886) *twenty-first U.S. president*

Chester Alan Arthur was born in Fairfield, Vermont, on October 5, 1829. A graduate of Union College, Arthur became a lawyer and was vice president under James A. GARFIELD.

At 6'2", sporting full side-whiskers and a mustache, Chester A. Arthur cut an imposing figure. Nicknamed "The Gentleman Boss," Arthur was a machine politician whom *The Nation* referred to as "a mess of filth." Woodrow Wilson called him "a non-entity with side whiskers."

The Congress continued to dominate in this age of smaller presidents, but forces were brewing that would soon contribute to an enlarging of the presidency and a shrinking of the Congress. The United States was emerging as an economic force in the world and soon would take a more prominent place on the world stage.

Institutional tugs-of-war aside, the presidency, even in this period of congressional ascendancy, was continuing to be subtly transformed. In 1881 William Graham Sumner noted that "the intention of the constitution-makers has gone for very little in the historical development of the presidency." Sumner felt that "the office has been molded by the tastes and faiths of the people." President Garfield's

Chester Alan Arthur, 21st president of the United States. Photograph by Charles Milton Bell, 1882 *(Library of Congress)*

assassination enflamed public passions against machine politics and the spoils, or PATRONAGE, system. Surprisingly, Arthur, who became president upon Garfield's death, supported and worked for civil service reform, culminating with the passage of the PENDLETON ACT.

Chester A. Arthur's greatest impact as president (1881–85) came in the area of DOMESTIC POLICY. While he had a reputation as a product of the corrupt political machine politics of the time, Arthur made a serious attempt to govern with fairness and integrity, and historians generally agree that he succeeded in overcoming his machine past. He made a series of capable appointments and worked hard for civil service reform.

He campaigned hard for a rather expansive domestic agenda, even calling for the repeal of all internal taxes except for excise duties on tobacco and liquor. He fought unsuccessfully for an ITEM VETO, called for reform of the presidential succession process, and worked for the regulation of interstate commerce.

He succeeded in vetoing the Chinese exclusion bill (which would have excluded laborers for a 20-year period)

and pushed for the development of a modern navy. Arthur was a man of limited talent who loved the ceremonial aspects of the office but sometimes faltered at the substance of the job.

Further reading: Doenecke, Justus D. *The Presidencies of James A. Garfield and Chester A. Arthur.* Lawrence: Regents Press of Kansas, 1981; Reeves, Thomas C. *Gentleman Boss: The Life of Chester Alan Arthur.* New York: Knopf, 1975.

Ash Council

Shortly after Richard NIXON took office in 1969, he created the Advisory Council on Government Organization. Dubbed the "Ash Council" after its chairman, Roy Ash, its purpose was to reorganize the EXECUTIVE BRANCH in a way to make it more manageable from the president's office.

As the first partisan Republican president in nearly 40 years, Nixon believed the BUREAUCRACY was controlled by those who were closely allied with Democrats in Congress and thus were committed to Johnson's Great Society programs and hostile to his own. The task of the Ash Council was to apply methods of business organization to the federal bureaucracy in order to make it a more rational structure and, at the same time, more controllable by the president.

The recommendations of the Ash Council were manifold and far-reaching. It suggested reorganizing the Executive Office by reconstituting the BUREAU OF THE BUDGET, giving it more managerial responsibilities, adding a mid-level management layer of political appointees, and renaming it the OFFICE OF MANAGEMENT AND BUDGET. It was also suggested that a separate Domestic Policy Council be created that would act much like the NATIONAL SECURITY COUNCIL in managing DOMESTIC POLICY.

A second area of recommendations involved reorganizing several cabinet departments into something of a "supercabinet." All current domestic cabinet departments would be absorbed into four new departments—Natural Resources, Economic Affairs, Human Resources, and Community Development.

A third area of recommendations came in reorganizing the environmental organizations. This involved the merging of authority over ENVIRONMENTAL POLICY held by several departments into one ENVIRONMENTAL PROTECTION AGENCY. In the final and related area of recommendations, the council proposed that four new regulatory agencies be developed incorporating the existing regulatory agencies. These new agencies would be the Transportation Regulatory Agency, Federal Power Agency, Securities and Exchange Agency, and the Federal Trade Practices Agency.

In the end, Congress rejected all of the Ash Council's recommendations except the reconstitution of the Bureau of the Budget. Nixon also created the Domestic Policy Council without congressional approval.

Further reading: Arnold, Peri E. *Making the Managerial Presidency: Comprehensive Reorganization Planning, 1905–1996.* Lawrence: University Press of Kansas, 1998; Noll, Roger. *Reforming Regulation: An Evaluation of the Ash Council Proposals.* Washington, D.C.: Brookings Institution, 1971.

—Joseph Wert

Ashcroft, John (1942–) *U.S. attorney general*
John Ashcroft, former Missouri governor and U.S. senator, was nominated to be U.S. attorney general by President George W. BUSH. After a difficult confirmation battle, he was confirmed by the Senate by a vote of 58 to 42, the closest of any confirmed attorney general.

Born in 1942 in Chicago, Ashcroft grew up in Springfield, Missouri, the son and grandson of Assembly of God preachers. He graduated from Yale University and the University of Chicago law school. He taught at Southwest Missouri State University and coauthored two college textbooks with his wife, Janet Ashcroft. During his time on Capital Hill, he also gained attention as a member of the Singing Senators.

Ashcroft began his public life in 1972, when he was appointed state auditor after an unsuccessful run for Congress. From 1974 to 1976 he worked for the state attorney general, John Danforth, along with a young Clarence Thomas. In 1976 Ashcroft was elected to succeed Danforth, serving two terms as attorney general. He was elected governor in 1984 and reelected in 1988, serving until 1992. When Danforth announced his Senate retirement in 1994, Ashcroft easily won the seat. After rejecting a White House run, he ran for reelection to the Senate in 2000 but lost to a Democratic opponent who had been killed a month before the election. It was at that point that he was tapped to join the new Bush administration.

Ashcroft established a conservative record as governor and U.S. senator. In his last year in the Senate, he garnered 100 percent approval ratings from both the Christian Coalition and the American Conservative Union, and a zero percent rating from the National Organization for Women and the League of Conservation Voters. He also had a reputation as a strong proponent of states' rights. This position appeared to change after he joined the Bush administration, particularly in the aftermath of September 11, 2001. Since that time, he has championed a broad expansion of federal law enforcement authority vis-à-vis the states, and executive branch power.

While he received high public approval in the weeks after 9/11, his aggressive antiterrorism measures have been criticized for threatening CIVIL LIBERTIES. Ashcroft's outspoken policy positions have led some to call him the most polarizing member of the Bush cabinet.

Further reading: Ashcroft, John, with Gary Thomas. *Lessons from a Father to His Son.* Nashville, Tenn.: Thomas Nelson Publishers, 1998; Toobin, Jeffrey. "Profiles: Ashcroft's Ascent." *The New Yorker,* 15 April 2002.

—Nancy V. Baker

assassinations

An assassination is the murder of a prominent person. There have been far more attempts to assassinate American presidents than have actually been successful. The most recent assassination attempt as of this writing was in March 1981, when Ronald REAGAN survived being shot by John Hinckley. To date, four presidents have died at the hands of an assassin.

Abraham LINCOLN was assassinated on April 14, 1865, and succumbed to his wounds early in the morning of the 15th. As the president who served during the CIVIL WAR, Lincoln partially expected that he would be the target of disgruntled expatriates determined to take his life. On Good Friday, Lincoln and his wife Mary attended a presentation of the play *Our American Cousin* at Ford's Theater in Washington, D.C. John Wilkes BOOTH, 26, an actor and Southern sympathizer, entered the Presidential Box and shot Lincoln in the back of the head from close range. Lincoln was carried to the Peterson House across the street from the theater, where he died at 7:22 the next morning.

James A. GARFIELD was the next president to die at the hands of an assassin (though many believe that the shooter did not ultimately cause the president's death). Garfield had been president for only a short time when on July 2, 1881, he was about to board the train at the Washington Train Depot, on his way to Elberton, New Jersey, to visit his ailing wife. Charles GUITEAU, a mentally unstable lawyer, who was disgruntled with Garfield because he was not appointed ambassador to France, fired two shots into Garfield. Garfield lingered for 80 days until he finally succumbed on September 19, 1881. Guiteau was later hanged.

Garfield's death is particularly interesting for two reasons. The first is that it indirectly led to the end of the spoils system and prompted Congress to move the bureaucracy into the modern CIVIL SERVICE, where the principle of merit is employed for hiring and promotion, rather than political or partisan considerations. The second is that it is widely reported that Garfield did not die from the wound inflicted by the gunshot. Indeed, the bullet lodged in a rather safe place, several inches from his spine. Rather, it

Leon Czolgosz shoots President McKinley with a concealed revolver at the Pan-American Exposition reception, September 6, 1901. Photograph of a wash drawing by T. Dart Walker *(Library of Congress)*

is likely he died as a result of unsanitary methods doctors used at the time, such as probing the gunshot wound with unwashed hands. In other words, it is unlikely he would have died had the doctors done nothing but close the wound.

William MCKINLEY was shot in Buffalo, New York, while attending the Pan-American Exposition on September 6, 1901. The assassin, an anarchist by the name of Leon CZOLGOSZ, fired twice from a revolver hidden beneath a handkerchief on his right hand. One bullet rebounded off of a button on the president's vest, but the second bullet penetrated the president's stomach. Similar to Garfield's circumstance, it is quite possible that McKinley would have survived had it not been for infection caused at least in part by the medical practices of the day. He died on September 14, 1901. His assassin's connections with "legitimate" anarchists of the day, especially Emma Goldman, were dubious at best, but he appears to have believed that the greatest

good he could contribute was to kill the leader of the "greatest" capitalist nation on earth, the United States. He was executed in the electric chair fewer than two months after McKinley's death.

By far the greatest controversy surrounding any president's death is that of John F. KENNEDY. Kennedy was traveling in Texas, in part to assuage political tensions between key Democratic politicians. On November 22, 1963, he was shot in the head and neck while riding in a motorcade, en route to a speaking engagement at the World Trade Mart in Dallas. He died approximately 30 minutes later; Vice President Lyndon JOHNSON was sworn in on AIR FORCE ONE, immediately prior to departure for Washington, D.C.

Kennedy's assassination has become the stuff of legend. The official version of the tragedy was released by the Warren Commission and pinned sole responsibility for the shooting on Lee Harvey OSWALD, an employee of the Texas School Book Depository, from where he allegedly fired the fatal shots. Oswald was himself gunned down by nightclub owner Jack Ruby as Oswald was about to be transported to a more secure lockup. However, almost from the beginning, questions were raised about whether or not Oswald really had acted alone. For example, photographs and documents linked Oswald to the Soviet Union and to Cuba, thus potentially implicating the communist world in the plot (if one indeed existed). Other conspiracy theories have budded, most owing to ballistics evidence which indicates that Oswald could not have fired all of the shots with a single-loaded gun, as well as autopsy and photographic evidence that shows that the angle from which Kennedy was hit could not have come from the School Book Depository. The most notorious evidence comes from witnesses who saw smoke and the shadow of a man on the so-called Grassy Knoll just to the right of where Kennedy's car was when the fatal bullets struck his head. No one has ever been found, and the legend and folklore have grown dramatically. Movies, television shows, documentaries, and numerous websites have added fuel to the controversy. Possible perpetrators include everyone from the CIA (which reportedly had a stake in keeping the VIETNAM WAR going), to foreign governments (most notably Cuba and the USSR), to the mafia who might have been angry with Kennedy's crackdown on organized crime. While the official record remains "closed," via the findings of the Warren Report, the case appears to be far from solved.

Further reading: Giglio, James N. *The Presidency of John F. Kennedy.* Lawrence: University Press of Kansas, 1991; http://www.netcolony.com/news/presidents/assassinations.html.

—Daniel F. Pondor

Atlantic Alliance

In the aftermath of World War II, fears of possible Soviet expansion into Western Europe spawned efforts to develop a more unified Europe, with links to the United States. President Truman's MARSHALL PLAN was one such effort, and British Foreign Secretary Ernest Bevin's attempt to bring Western Europe into an alliance was another such effort.

After the 1948 Soviet takeover of Czechoslovakia, President TRUMAN pushed for the development of what became known as the Atlantic Alliance. The first tangible step in this process was the Brussels Pact signed by France, Britain, and the Benelux countries. President Truman called on Congress to join this coalition, and on June 11, 1948, the Senate passed the Vandenberg Resolution, 64 to 4, committing the United States to this collective security pact.

In April of 1949 the United States, France, Britain, and the Benelux countries, along with Canada, Denmark, Iceland, Italy, Norway, and Portugal signed the North Atlantic Treaty. This led to the development of NATO and the COLD WAR alliance that shaped Western policy toward the Soviet Union.

Atlantic Charter

A result of the August 1941 Atlantic Conference between Franklin D. ROOSEVELT and British Prime Minister Winston Churchill aboard ship off the coast of Newfoundland, the two leaders issued a statement of general principles. Issued by Roosevelt as a press release in order to avoid submitting the agreement to the isolationist-oriented Congress as a treaty for ratification, the Atlantic Charter, as it soon became known, was an agreement between Roosevelt and Churchill establishing the broad principles to guide the actions of the United States and Great Britain.

Designed to show how close the United States and Great Britain were (and how different the Nazis were to the allies), these principles called for both powers to eschew territorial gain, guarantee freedom of the seas, and promote self-determination for all nations.

In September of 1941, 15 nations, including the Soviet Union, agreed to the principles of the Atlantic Charter.

atomic bomb

The atomic bomb is based on the principle of nuclear fission. Fission refers to the splitting of an atom's nucleus into fragments and the resulting emission of neutrons and energy. The emitted neutrons hit other nuclei causing them to split, producing more energy and more neutrons which in turn generate more fission reactions, and so forth in a chain reaction that can result in a massive explosion. Fission is accomplished with isotopes (versions) of the heavy elements uranium and plutonium. Even more powerful explosions can be produced with the fusion of two light elements such as hydrogen isotopes deuterium and tritium. This is the principle behind the hydrogen bomb.

The first fission chain reaction was produced in a laboratory setting in Chicago on December 2, 1942. The first atomic bomb was exploded at Alamogordo, New Mexico, on July 16, 1945. On August 6 and 9, 1945, the United States dropped two atomic bombs on Hiroshima and Nagasaki, Japan. On August 29, 1949, the Soviet Union detonated its first atomic device. The United States successfully tested its first hydrogen bomb on October 31, 1952, and it was followed on November 22, 1955, by the explosion of the Soviet Union's first hydrogen bomb.

Two major political debates have surrounded the atomic bomb and subsequent nuclear weapons. The first is whether it should have been used against Japan during WORLD WAR II. The second is how it should be developed, deployed, brandished, or limited vis-à-vis the United States's two post–World War II enemies, the Soviet Union and China. Both issue areas, especially the second, encompass a host of issues and topics too numerous even to list in this entry.

Months before the atomic bombing of Japan it was well known by U.S. decision-makers that its Pacific adversary had been defeated militarily by conventional means. The U.S. insistence on unconditional surrender prevented the Japanese government from ending the war. The Japanese were especially concerned that after the surrender the emperor be maintained without harm. Japanese attempts to communicate this message and American attempts to soften its position via diplomatic back channels were badly handled and complicated by splits in the Japanese government. The Japanese government remained divided over details of surrender for almost a week even after suffering the devastation of Hiroshima and Nagasaki and the USSR's entry into the war against it. With the perspective afforded by historians' access to documents and interviews of many of the decision-makers on both sides, it seems clear that a blockade and continued conventional bombing together with more competent diplomatic efforts (especially by the Japanese) would have produced a surrender without the use of atomic bombs.

Further reading: Wainstock, Dennis D. *The Decision to Drop the Atomic Bomb.* Westport, Conn.: Praeger, 1996.

—Carl Grafton

Atomic Energy Commission (AEC)

The U.S. Atomic Energy Commission (AEC) was created by the Atomic Energy Act of 1946 (also known as the McMahon Act). This statute transferred authority over all aspects of atomic energy from the wartime MANHATTAN PROJECT that developed the atomic bombs to the AEC.

Composed of five civilian members appointed by the president with the ADVICE AND CONSENT of the Senate to five-year terms, the AEC was given exclusive administrative authority over nuclear weapons development and civilian applications such as power generation and nuclear medicine. It was also responsible for nuclear safety regulation.

The McMahon Act permitted only the AEC to own fissionable materials and related facilities or to have access to previously classified information, thus precluding participation in nuclear research and development by the private sector. This constraint slowed nuclear reactor development for electrical power generation by preventing the participation of large corporations such as General Electric or Westinghouse. Accordingly, the Atomic Energy Act of 1954 somewhat loosened AEC control.

Soon after passage of the 1954 Act, the AEC and its corporate partners began development and construction of nuclear electrical generation plants. In the peak period 1970–74 orders for 142 such plants were placed. In addition, the AEC had research and development contracts with hundreds of corporations and made research grants to more than 200 universities.

Federal agencies are often created and reorganized as responses to the occurrence of large-scale social, economic, or technological changes. Thus the development of atomic energy resulted in the AEC's creation in 1946, but other large-scale changes brought the AEC's demise. The first was post–WORLD WAR II chemistry that gave birth in the 1960s to the environmental movement. Initially, environmentalists saw nuclear power plants as cleaner than coal-fired plants, but the damaging effects on fish of thermal pollution produced by nuclear plants was a different matter. Making matters worse, the AEC essentially refused responsibility for this problem, thus highlighting the conflict of interest inherent in the agency's twin role of promoting nuclear power on one hand and regulating safety on the other. In 1971 concerns over nuclear plant safety and possible AEC covers of reactor shortcomings produced a torrent of criticism. The 1973 Arab oil boycott dealt the agency a second blow. Many concerned with energy shortages wanted a broad-gauged research effort aimed at developing a variety of energy sources, not just a single increasingly dangerous looking technology; the AEC was not the answer to environmental, energy, or safety concerns.

The AEC was abolished in 1975. It was replaced by the more broadly based Energy Research and Development Administration and the Nuclear Regulatory Commission, which was responsible only for safety regulation.

Further reading: Duffy, Robert J. *Nuclear Politics in America.* Lawrence: University Press of Kansas, 1997; Grafton, Carl. "Response to Change: The Creation and Reorganization of Federal Agencies." In *Political Reform,* edited by R. Miewald and M. Steinman, 25–42. Chicago: Nelson-Hall, 1983.

—Carl Grafton

Attorney General, Office of the

The U.S. Attorney General is the chief law officer of the national government, head of the DEPARTMENT OF JUSTICE, and a key presidential adviser in many administrations. The attorney general is named by the president and confirmed with the ADVICE AND CONSENT of the Senate.

One of the oldest functions of the office is to represent the U.S. government before the Supreme Court, a role largely delegated to the solicitor general in 1870. Another venerable function is providing legal advice to the CHIEF EXECUTIVE, a quasijudicial role that has largely been assigned to the Office of Legal Counsel. The third role is administrative, overseeing the large federal BUREAUCRACY of the Justice Department. The department includes the FEDERAL BUREAU OF INVESTIGATION, the Immigration and Naturalization Service, the Federal Bureau of Prisons, the U.S. Marshals Service, and the Drug Enforcement Agency, as well as the Civil, Criminal, Civil Rights, Tax, Antitrust, and Environment and Natural Resources divisions.

The Office of the Attorney General has undergone dramatic changes since its creation by the Judiciary Act of 1789, the statute that established the federal judiciary. Early attorney generals served only part-time, encouraged to maintain a private law practice that would supplement their income and—it was believed—hone their legal skills. While a member of the CABINET since 1792, the attorney general was not paid on par with other cabinet officers until 1853. The first clerk was not hired until 1819, and the first office space was not provided until 1821. Institutionalization came gradually, first during the long tenure of William Wirt in the Monroe administration, followed by the tenure of the activist Caleb Cushing, who served under PIERCE. In 1870 the attorney general became the head of the new Department of Justice, created in the aftermath of the CIVIL WAR to handle the explosion in federal litigation.

The 20th century brought greater expansion in the scope of the attorney general's duties. The trend has accelerated in the past 20 years, as evidenced in the growth of the Justice Department's budget authority, from $2.35 billion in FY 1981 to more than $24 billion in FY 2002. Its budget request of $30 billion for FY 2003 includes funding for new programs related to combating terrorism.

Further reading: Baker, Nancy V. *Conflicting Loyalties: Law and Politics in the Attorney General's Office.* Lawrence: University Press of Kansas, 1992; Clayton, Cornell W. *The Politics of Justice: The Attorney General and the Making of Legal Policy.* Armonk, N.Y.: M. E. Sharpe, 1992.

—Nancy V. Baker

B

backgrounds of presidents

George Walker Bush is the 43rd president, but only the 42nd man to hold the office since Grover CLEVELAND was both the 22nd and 24th president.

Presidential Geography

James K. POLK was the first president born after the United States became independent from England. As of 2002, 23 of the 42 presidents were born in one of four states or colonies. Eight were from Virginia (WASHINGTON, JEFFERSON, MADISON, MONROE, W. H. HARRISON, TYLER, TAYLOR, and WILSON), seven from Ohio (GRANT, HAYES, GARFIELD, B. HARRISON, MCKINLEY, TAFT, HARDING), four each from Massachusetts (J. ADAMS, J. Q. ADAMS, KENNEDY, G. H. W. Bush), and New York (VAN BUREN, FILLMORE, T. Roosevelt, F. Roosevelt). The states of birth for the remaining presidents were: Two each from Texas (EISENHOWER, L. JOHNSON), North Carolina (POLK, A. JOHNSON) and Vermont (ARTHUR, COOLIDGE) and one each from Arkansas (CLINTON), California (NIXON) Connecticut (G. W. Bush) Georgia (CARTER), Illinois (REAGAN), Iowa (HOOVER), Kentucky (LINCOLN), Missouri (TRUMAN), Nebraska (FORD), New Hampshire (PIERCE), New Jersey (CLEVELAND), Pennsylvania (BUCHANAN), and South Carolina (JACKSON). Thus 20 states have been presidential birthplaces.

Several presidents were elected from states other than that in which they were born. Seventeen or nearly 40 percent no longer were residents of their native states when elected president or became vice president. Three of those came from Tennessee (Jackson, Polk, A. Johnson), two each from Illinois (Lincoln, Grant), New York (Arthur, Cleveland) and Texas (both Bushes), and one each from California (Reagan), Indiana (B. Harrison), Kansas (Eisenhower), Louisiana (Taylor), Massachusetts (Coolidge), Michigan (Ford), New Jersey (Wilson), and Ohio (W. Harrison).

Family

Fourteen of the 42 presidents or 33.3 percent were the first-born child or only child in their families, but birth order is not associated with significant success or lack of it as president. Two presidents, Ford and Clinton, were adopted.

Ten or nearly one-fourth of the presidents came from five families: The two Bushs (father and son), the two Roosevelts (cousins), the two Harrisons (grandfather and grandson), the two Adamses (father and son), and James Madison and Zachary Taylor, who shared grandparents. Moreover, Tyler was Truman's great uncle.

Contrary to the log cabin myth, most presidents were from middle class or higher socioeconomic families. That relationship is even more likely for those presidents ranked as the most successful, including Lincoln. In addition, presidents tend to marry into families that have a social rank above theirs, if only slightly higher.

For several CHIEF EXECUTIVES, their wives were crucial to their political success. Abigail ADAMS was the second president's closest confidant, including advice on policy matters. Dolley MADISON, who served as a hostess for the widowed President JEFFERSON, had a vivacious personality that compensated for her husband's dour public demeanor. Sarah Polk encouraged her husband's political ambition, regularly read and marked key passages in official papers before he read them, and was his chief adviser. Mary Todd LINCOLN, Julia Grant, Helen Taft, and Florence Harding encouraged their husbands to attain high status, although Mrs. Lincoln was a liability when her husband was president. Lucy Hayes and Lucretia Garfield sublimated their careers and political views to avoid impairing their husbands' careers, as did Lou Henry HOOVER, fluent in five languages, holder of a geology degree, and board member of national nonprofit organizations, who had lived for extensive periods abroad and spoken publicly for women's issues. After her husband's polio attack, Eleanor ROOSEVELT became his eyes, ears, and spokeswoman, making numerous appearances before key organizations and keeping his name prominent in the political arena. Although she had reservations about his seeking the presidency, she served as a sounding board for him in the White House years. Throughout their marriage, her husband relied on Bess Truman's advice, although she disclaimed a public role as first lady. Jacqueline KENNEDY, who disliked politics, radiated an aura of fashion that enhanced her husband's image as a youthful, dynamic leader. Lady Bird Johnson's southern manner and business acumen were significant assets to her notably ambitious husband. Rosalynn CARTER and Hillary CLINTON were active partners in their husband's political careers. Nancy Reagan encouraged her husband's political career and offered advice on political issues and personnel.

Religion

It is no simple task to categorize the religious beliefs of presidents. If they are classified according to formal membership or the church they attended regularly: Fourteen were Episcopalian, eight were Presbyterian, seven were Methodists, five were either Baptist or Unitarian/Congregational, three were Disciples of Christ, two each were Dutch Reformed or Quaker, and one was Roman Catholic. Those figures include six that claimed to have no formal faith: Jefferson, Polk, Tyler, Lincoln, A. Johnson, and Hayes. All but Jefferson often attended their wives' church. Hayes illustrates the diversity of religious practice: He was baptized Presbyterian, attended Episcopalian services until his marriage, after which he regularly attended his wife's Methodist church, but claimed no formal church membership. Nonetheless, he was notable for banning liquor from the White House. The totals include multiple members, e.g., Bush, Jr., was reared in an Episcopalian family but became a Methodist after marrying.

A few presidents (Garfield, McKinley, Wilson) were notably devout, and two, J. Q. Adams (Unitarian) and Eisenhower (Presbyterian), did not join a church until becoming president. Yet Eisenhower initiated the custom of opening cabinet meetings with a prayer and launched the White House Prayer Breakfast. Cleveland (Presbyterian), the son of a minister, fathered a child out of wedlock.

Education and Occupation

Thirty-three presidents (more than 75 percent) attended college, most receiving degrees, but one, James Monroe, was at William and Mary for only a few weeks. Six attended Harvard for either undergraduate or graduate studies; five were at Yale in those pursuits (Bush, Jr., received degrees from both). William and Mary was the college of three, as was Princeton. Four of the first six presidents had college degrees, putting them in the rarefied educational elite of their era.

Truman was the last, and the only one since Cleveland, not to have a college degree. Twenty-four were lawyers, although that was not always the primary occupation, as with Jefferson and Wilson. Taft had the most distinguished

legal career, serving as a federal judge, and after his presidency as Chief Justice of the U.S. Supreme Court. Twenty-one had military service, ranging from very limited duty, such as that of Madison, L. Johnson, and Bush, Jr., to life careers, as with Grant and Eisenhower.

Seven presidents, including plantation owners Washington, Jefferson, and Madison, were in agriculture. For W. Harrison, Grant, Truman, and Carter, farming was their livelihood for only part of their careers. Only Washington and Carter were successful in this occupation. Fillmore, Garfield, Wilson, and L. Johnson were educators, and Eisenhower served briefly as a university president. The two Bushes and Truman were businessmen, although this was only a brief occupation for Truman. Harding and Kennedy were in journalism. Tailoring, engineering, and acting were the occupations of A. Johnson, Hoover, and Reagan, respectively.

For many presidents, specifying an occupation is difficult. T. Roosevelt, for example, never had a constant occupation, unless it was author, since he was persistently in public service.

Immediate Pre–White House Experience

Since 14 VICE PRESIDENTs were subsequently president, it might be presumed that that office is the obvious threshold to the presidency. That is a bit misleading. Thirteen presidents were vice presidents immediately before becoming president. Only four, J. Adams, Jefferson, Van Buren, and Bush, Sr., were elected directly from the vice presidency. Eight became president upon the death of their predecessor. Ford assumed the office upon the RESIGNATION of Nixon. The fourteenth, Nixon, became president eight years after leaving the vice presidency. So unless the vice president's ticket mate has ill health or is assassinated, the vice presidency is not the most likely immediate stepping-stone to the top job.

Public service is the common thread for eventual residents of the White House, but nine presidents were in private life when elected. Seven were sitting governors, five were in the CABINET, four were in Congress (three Senators), three in the military, and one in diplomatic service.

Other Previous Public Service

Presidential pre–White House experience falls into several categories: 33 served in Congress, 17 in the House and 16 in the Senate. Eleven served in both chambers. Nineteen had served in state legislatures; that same number served as governors, which includes two that were governors of pre-state territories. Nine had diplomatic appointments. Nine had been cabinet members, most commonly secretary of state (six). Some had been in more than one cabinet post. Of the nine, only Taft (War), Grant (War ad interim), and Hoover did not serve at State. Monroe briefly held the War post simultaneously with that of State. Hoover, Secretary of Commerce during the technological changes of the 1920s, had the most impressive record of all who directed that department. Three future presidents held subcabinet appointments: the Roosevelts, each of whom was assistant secretary of the navy, and Bush, Sr., a previous director of the CIA. Several presidents had held positions, elective and appointive, in local government.

Lack of Prior Public Office

Only six presidents held no elective office before entering the White House. The first five were Taylor, Grant, Arthur, Taft, and Hoover. The last four of those, although briefly for Grant, had served in appointive public office. The last president with no prior service in elective office was Eisenhower, who along with W. Harrison, Taylor, and Grant, was elected primarily because of his military prowess. None of the half-dozen without previous elective experience are ranked among the top presidents; Eisenhower is rated highest among the six.

In conclusion, there are no certain pathways to the presidency. A law degree may be useful, but of the 39th through 43rd presidents only one held that degree. Being born into a presidential family can be an asset. For military service, battlefield experience may be less important than the level of military command: Eisenhower was never in a combat situation while Truman, not identified as military figure, led an artillery unit in WORLD WAR I. Extensive public service is characteristic, but a few persons attained the highest office with little or no previous record in that sector.

Further reading: Baltzell, E. Digby, and Howard G. Schneiderman. "Social Class in the Oval Office." *Society*, September/October 1988; Degregerio, William A. *The Complete Book of U.S. Presidents*. Fort Lee, N.J.: Barricade Books, 2001; Whitney, David C. *The American Presidents*. Pleasantville, N.Y.: Reader's Digest, 1996.

—Thomas P. Wolf

Baker, Howard, Jr. (1925–) *U.S. senator*

Born in Huntsville, Tennessee, Howard Baker attended the University of the South and graduated from Tulane University before receiving his J.D. from the University of Tennessee. He served in the Navy during World War II. In 1950 he began his political career by managing the first of his father's seven successful campaigns for Congress. In 1966 he became the first Republican ever popularly elected to the U.S. Senate from Tennessee. He was reelected to two additional terms in 1972 and 1978. His first marriage was to Joy Dirksen, who died in 1993. She was daughter of the late Senator Everett McKinley Dirksen, who had once

served as minority leader of the Senate. Baker served as Senate Minority Leader from 1977 to 1981.

He came to national attention during the 1973 WATER-GATE investigation hearings. As vice chairman of the panel, Baker was known for his direct and insightful questioning of witnesses, and especially for asking, "What did the President know and when did he know it?" This prominence gave rise to his selection as keynote speaker at the 1976 Republican convention and talk of a possible presidential run in 1980.

Although Baker's run for the presidency in 1980 was ill-fated, his national stature was enhanced. When Ronald REAGAN captured the White House, bringing in with him a Republican-controlled Senate, Baker was elected Senate majority leader, a post he held from 1981 to 1985, after which he retired from the Senate.

During the Iran-contra scandal, with the need to demonstrate better management of the White House and restore confidence in Reagan's presidency, Baker was called upon by President Reagan to succeed Donald Reagan as his CHIEF OF STAFF, a post he held from 1987 to 1988. Baker is credited with improving White House relations with Congress and setting the stage for historic arms agreements with the Soviet Union. Baker's acceptance of the position was widely understood to mean that he would have to forgo a possible run for the presidency in 1988.

When Baker left the Senate he joined the law firm of Baker, Donelson, Bearman and Caldwell in Washington, D.C., and in 1996 he married U.S. Senator Nancy Kassebaum. Upon the election of George W. BUSH as president, he was appointed and confirmed by the Senate to be Ambassador to Japan, a post traditionally held by former congressional leaders.

—Eugene J. Alpert

Baker, James A., III (1930–) *secretary of state, secretary of the treasury, undersecretary of commerce, White House chief of staff*

One of Washington, D.C.'s premier Republican "insiders," Baker served as George H. BUSH's campaign manager in Bush's unsuccessful bid for a Senate seat in 1970. He later served as undersecretary of commerce in the FORD administration and chaired Ford's reelection effort in 1976.

Baker ran George H. Bush's unsuccessful presidential bid in 1976, but he so impressed the REAGAN team that Baker was the surprise appointment as Reagan's CHIEF OF STAFF. Baker was a part of the Reagan "troika" with Baker serving as the chief of staff, Michael Deaver as head of communications, and Ed MEESE as head of policy. These three men worked closely together and ran an efficient White House operation. The troika was held together by the capable hands of Baker, who was in many ways the most important man in the Reagan White House in the first term. After a successful stint as chief of staff, Baker, to the shock of many inside and outside the administration, switched jobs with Treasury Secretary Donald Regan. The White House operation deteriorated, and the Reagan White House became inefficient and insensitive to the nuances of politics and management. Baker left Treasury to head George H. Bush's successful run for the presidency. He was rewarded with the post of secretary of state, a position Baker handled capably. He was secretary during the Gulf War. In 1992 Baker left State to head President Bush's unsuccessful bid for a second term.

Baker was called back into service by the Bushes again to head George W. BUSH's effort to resolve the disputed election of 2000. In that capacity Baker successfully employed a delaying strategy that allowed the U.S. Supreme Court to intervene and select Bush as president.

Baker, Newton Diehl (1871–1937) *secretary of war*
Newton Baker, born in Martinsburg, West Virginia, was Woodrow Wilson's secretary of war (1916–21), following the resignation of Lindley M. Garrison. At 44, Wilson's youngest cabinet member, Baker, an 1892 graduate of Johns Hopkins University where he first met WILSON, earned a law degree from Washington and Lee University in 1894.

After serving as secretary to the postmaster general in the second Cleveland administration, Baker moved to Cleveland, Ohio, where he was city solicitor (1901–09) and mayor (1911–15). It was there that, the diminutive (5'6", 125 lbs.) Baker earned these sobriquets: "Big Little Mayor," "ND" (Never Defeated), "Boy Mayor" (along with two others, Cincinnati's H. T. Hunt and Toledo's Brand Whitlock), and "Three Cent" (for his efforts to keep ice cream cones in city parks and streetcar fares at three cents each). Throughout his career he was associated with the progressive movement, including public utilities reform and municipal beautification in Cleveland. Unlike progressives generally, Baker rejected nonpartisanship, proportional representation, and the long ballot.

Although manifesting pacifist inclinations, he presided over the introduction and administration of conscription, assuring the public that this was essential to the war effort and it would be terminated at war's end. Baker effectively raised both the manpower and the material to wage war on a scale without precedent, while drastically reducing the ratio of men lost to disease as compared to battlefield casualties and strengthening the role of CHIEF OF STAFF, which improved the operation of the War Department. At war's end, he created the University of the American Expeditionary Force in Europe for soldiers awaiting demobilization. This became a model for the Special Services Division in WORLD WAR II.

Further reading: Beaver, Daniel R. *Newton D. Baker and the American War Effort, 1917–1919.* Lincoln: University of Nebraska Press, 1966; Cramer, Clarence H. *Newton D. Baker: A Biography.* New York: Garland Publishing, 1961.
— Thomas P. Wolf

Baker Accords

In the early to mid 1980s much of the Third World, particularly countries in Latin America, was engulfed in a debt crisis. Many countries, such as Mexico, had either defaulted or were near default on various loans and loan guarantees that had been extended by wealthier nations such as the United States. Indeed, in 1982 the United States had provided funds and incentives to bail Mexico out of defaulting. Many of these types of piecemeal solutions were successful, but only for a time. By the mid 1980s Mexico, for example, was ready to default again. The United States under the Reagan administration had adopted a largely passive stance toward debtor nations and their efforts at debt reduction. However, by 1985 the situation had grown so bad that portions of their international economy were in jeopardy.

Secretary of State James A. Baker proposed a three-pronged plan to provide another set of structural incentives and monetary infusion that would theoretically expand opportunities for economic growth in the region. The Baker Accords consisted first of providing monetary support for encouraging investment in southern export industries. Second, the administration proposed supply-side (as opposed to demand-side) strategies for expanding economic growth. Finally, the United States actively encouraged world-lending institutions, such as the World Bank and the International Monetary Fund, to expand lending and credit to the debtor nations.

Though aimed at expanding growth and development in the Third World, these measures were largely unsuccessful. Some analysts attribute this to the fact that the United States did not encourage nor practice large-scale debt reduction, nor engage in other practices commonly used to prop up failing economies. Additionally, the Baker Accords were long on "encouraging" lending activity but did not actively pursue compliance. As a result, many industries did not heed the letter or the spirit of the Accords. As a result of these problems, coupled with the fact that northern markets were unable to absorb southern exports at that time, Third World debt continued to rise without enhancing an ability to pay. Thus, the Baker Accords largely failed, and the debt crisis continued for some time.

Further reading: Lairson, Thomas D., and David Skidmore. *International Political Economy: The Struggle for Power and Wealth,* 2d ed. New York: Harcourt Brace, 1997.
—Daniel E. Ponder

Bank Holiday of 1933

The Depression of 1929 caused a slew of bank failures. When Franklin Roosevelt became president in 1933, he issued an executive order imposing a "bank holiday." Several days later he submitted a proposal to Congress granting emergency assistance to the more solid banks in hopes of extending public confidence in the banking system and ending the crisis.

In June of 1933, Congress passed the Glass-Steagall Banking Act, strengthening the role of the Federal Reserve's power over banks, as well as separating commercial from investment banks.

Bank of the United States

Alexander HAMILTON, President George WASHINGTON's secretary of the treasury, proposed a central bank as part of a master plan for putting the new nation's finances on

BORN TO COMMAND.

OF VETO MEMORY.

HAD I BEEN CONSULTED.

KING ANDREW THE FIRST.

A caricature of Andrew Jackson as a despotic monarch drawn in response to Jackson's order to remove all federal deposits from the Bank of the United States *(Library of Congress)*

sound footing. The First Bank of the United States, created when Hamilton's plans were approved, was successful but unpopular. The national bank demanded that state banks redeem their own paper currency in gold or silver, which clashed with the interest of many states in sometimes inflating their own currency. The national bank, moreover, was associated in the popular imagination, and in reality, with the interests of wealthy creditors in the nation's biggest cities. When the First Bank's charter expired in 1811, Congress declined to keep the bank alive. It took another war, the WAR OF 1812, to bring Congress to the recognition that a national bank might be a practical if unsavory necessity, and the Second Bank of the United States was created in 1816. The Second Bank, with 18 branches, a capital stock of $35 million, and one-fifth government ownership, seemed to its supporters a model of modern management.

After a few skirmishes over Bank administration early in the first term of President Andrew JACKSON's administration, the president of the Bank and his congressional allies publicly challenged President Jackson. Nicholas Biddle, the Bank's president, thought his institution was so helpful to the nation that it must therefore be popular. To trap President Jackson into declaring himself irrevocably for or against the Bank, its congressional supporters passed a bill in Jackson's reelection year to recharter the institution—four years before the Bank's old charter was to expire. Jackson vetoed the bill and sent back to Congress an angry letter of explanation, accusing the Bank and its supporters of having corrupted the nation's politics and damaged its economy.

The campaign of 1832 thus became one of the most significant in U.S. history. Because both sides during the election did all in their power to focus attention on the Bank, Jackson was able to proclaim after his reelection the mandate theory of the presidency. In the election the people had spoken, Jackson declared. They wanted him, as their representative, to kill the "Monster Bank." By forcing the withdrawal of government funds from the institution, the Bank was demolished.

The consequences of the Bank War were ironic. The nation would undergo industrialization without a central bank, until the creation of the FEDERAL RESERVE SYSTEM in 1913. While the nation took a step into the past in the killing of its bank, it simultaneously leaped into the future with the democratization of the presidency.

Further reading: St. Clair Clarke, M., and D. A. Hall, compilers. *Legislative and Documentary History of the Bank of the United States. New York: Augustus M. Kelly Publishers, 1967; Remini, Robert V. Andrew Jackson and the Bank War: A Study in the Growth of Presidential Power. New York: W. W. Norton, 1967.

—Thomas S. Langston

Barbary War

In 1815 the Barbary states, Algeria, Morocco, and Tunis, resumed piracy of U.S. ships in the southern Mediterranean. President JEFFERSON had, 10 years earlier, sent war ships to defeat the piracy, but as the piracy began again President MADISON asked Congress for a declaration of war. It was granted in 1815.

Madison sent two squadrons under the command of Stephen Decatur. The United States quickly defeated the Barbary powers, but when they refused to comply with peace terms, Madison again threatened the use of force and the Barbary powers complied. Madison, unlike Jefferson, sought and was granted a declaration of war, as he felt he was constitutionally obligated to gain congressional consent prior to military involvement.

Barkley, Alben W. (1877–1956) U.S. vice president

Alben W. Barkley was born in Lowes, Kentucky, on November 24, 1877. Barkley, a Democrat, was elected to the U.S. House of Representatives from Kentucky in 1912 and to the Senate in 1926. As an agrarian populist, Barkley was a staunch supporter of Woodrow WILSON's progressive legislation and Franklin D. Roosevelt's NEW DEAL. Favored by Roosevelt to become Senate majority leader in 1937, Barkley was elected to this position by a vote of 38-37 against conservative Democratic Senator Byron "Pat" Harrison of Mississippi.

During the remainder of ROOSEVELT's presidency, Barkley was generally loyal to the president and effective in organizing Senate support for major administration bills. In 1944, however, Barkley openly opposed Roosevelt's veto of a tax cut bill and briefly vacated his Senate leadership position in protest. Barkley later claimed that this public disagreement with Roosevelt was the reason why Roosevelt did not choose the Kentuckian as his running mate in 1944.

Barkley continued to serve as majority and then minority leader of the Senate during the initial period of Harry S Truman's presidency. After Barkley delivered a rousing keynote address at the 1948 Democratic national convention, Truman chose Barkley as his running mate. After Truman won the election and the Democrats regained control of Congress in 1948, Barkley enjoyed a fairly leisurely vice presidency. Barkley briefly ran for the Democratic presidential nomination of 1952, but he withdrew from the race at the party's national convention. Elected again to the Senate from Kentucky in 1954, Barkley died of a heart attack on April 30, 1956.

Further reading: Barkley, Alben W. *That Reminds Me.* Garden City, N.Y.: Doubleday, 1954; Libbey, James K. *Dear Alben.* Lexington: University Press of Kentucky, 1979;

Savage, Sean J. *Truman and the Democratic Party.* Lexington: University Press of Kentucky, 1997.

—Sean J. Savage

Bates, Edward (1793–1869) U.S. attorney general

First a Whig, then a member of the Know-Nothing (American) Party, Bates joined the REPUBLICAN PARTY in the mid 1850s and sought the party's presidential nomination in 1860 only to be defeated by Abraham LINCOLN. As president, Lincoln chose Bates to serve as his attorney general. In 1864 Bates suffered a stroke and resigned in November of that year.

Bay of Pigs

When he became president, John KENNEDY inherited a plan devised in the EISENHOWER administration for an invasion of Cuba by CIA-trained Cuban expatriates (with U.S. support). Cuba was controlled by Fidel Castro, a communist, and was a thorn in the side of the United States.

In April of 1961 the invasion commenced. Almost immediately, it became clear that the plan was doomed from the start. The CENTRAL INTELLIGENCE AGENCY did not fully inform the president of the collateral needs of the plan, hoping that Kennedy, once the invasion began, would approve additional and overt U.S. support for the rebels. But the President did not give the go-ahead for overt U.S. military support, and the invasion failed.

Kennedy was new to the office of president and did not ask deep and probing questions when presented with a plan that to the trained and inquiring mind should have alerted him to the dangers inherent in the project. The failed invasion proved a great embarrassment to the United States and a public relations windfall for Cuba and the Soviet Union.

Bell, John (1797–1869) secretary of war, U.S. senator, U.S. representative

In 1860 Bell was the presidential nominee of the short-lived Constitutional Union Party, a party formed for the purpose of preventing a CIVIL WAR over the issue of slavery. Prior to the presidential bid, Bell served as Speaker of the House, and as U.S. Senator from Tennessee. Amid the secessionist crisis of the 1850s and 1860s, Bell was a moderate and a peacemaker. Although himself a Southerner and a slaveholder, Bell attempted to chart a middle ground at a time when tempers and positions were extreme.

benefits, presidential

The White House has been called the nation's most elaborate example of public housing, and although opulent, most presidents and their families find life within its walls confining and difficult. The White House is both the president's home and office. Family rooms are located on the second floor and are furnished and maintained at government expense. Presidents pay for food and phone charges, but any state or official function is paid for by the government.

The president receives a salary, but the "other" benefits far exceed any financial compensation. The president's security detail—supplied by the SECRET SERVICE—official travel, CAMP DAVID retreat, and all job-related expenses are paid for by the government.

Berlin Crisis

After WORLD WAR II Berlin became a divided city, with the United States and its allies controlling part of the German city (the West), and the Soviet Union controlling the rest (East Berlin), plus the land surrounding the city. In the heat of the COLD WAR, Berlin became a symbol of the divisions of the world between the U.S. and Soviet blocs.

In 1958 Soviet leader Nikita Khrushchev initiated a crisis by threatening the security of the U.S.-controlled sectors. These threats continued until August 4, 1961, when the Kennedy administration got an agreement from NATO to defend Berlin with force if necessary.

The East German government began to restrict travel to and from East Berlin, causing chaos as many East Germans attempted to flee to West Berlin. The communists constructed barriers—the Berlin wall—to restrict migration. On August 12 the communists sealed the border and the city became physically as well as ideologically and politically divided.

President KENNEDY ordered a U.S. battle group to drive through East German checkpoints into West Berlin. Finally, in December, Khrushchev backed away from his BRINKSMANSHIP, and the crisis—and war—were averted.

Further reading: Schlesinger, Arthur M., Jr. *A Thousand Days: John F. Kennedy in the White House.* Boston: Houghton Mifflin, 1965; Walton, Richard J. *Cold War and Counterrevolution: The Foreign Policy of John F. Kennedy.* New York: Viking Press, 1972.

Biddle, Francis Beverly (1886–1968) *jurist*

A graduate of Harvard College (1909) and Harvard Law School (1911), Biddle clerked for Supreme Court Justice Oliver Wendell Holmes (1911–12) before being admitted to the Pennsylvania bar. He then entered private practice, acquiring an expertise in corporate and trial work. Biddle served in the U.S. Army during WORLD WAR I and was a special assistant to the U.S. attorney for the Eastern District of

Pennsylvania (1922–26), but his early career was centered around private practice.

In 1932 Biddle changed his party affiliation from Republican to Democratic. Subsequently appointed chair of the National Labor Relations Board (1934–35), he contributed to the development of labor law and to its administration by the federal government. He was subsequently named a Class C director and deputy chair of the Federal Reserve Bank (1935–39), during which time he also served as chief counsel to the investigators committee for the TENNESSEE VALLEY AUTHORITY (TVA). His analysis defended the TVA against charges of waste and mismanagement and set new cost and performance standards for public utilities.

Biddle reluctantly accepted an appointment to the Third Circuit of the U.S. Circuit Court of Appeals in 1939. He did so with the expectation of being on the bench for a brief stretch of time, ROOSEVELT having promised to name him solicitor general as part of a more general reformation of the CABINET and subcabinet. Named SOLICITOR GENERAL in 1940, he was nominated as attorney general in 1941. During his years at the DEPARTMENT OF JUSTICE, he was involved in transferring immigration and nationalization agents from the Labor Department to Justice, in advising about the JAPANESE-AMERICAN INTERNMENT, in prosecuting the sedition trials of the 1940s, and in antitrust negotiations.

Having left public service shortly after TRUMAN entered the OVAL OFFICE, Biddle returned in 1945, when he was appointed to the international military tribunal for the Nazi war crimes trials in Nuremberg. As much diplomatic as legal in content, the trials and rulings allowed Biddle to exercise the full range of his professional talents. When he returned to the United States, however, his long association with the Roosevelt administration caused Republican senators to oppose any further presidential nominations. Biddle retired from public service and chose not to resume the private practice of law, but he continued to write extensively.

Further reading: Biddle, Francis B. *In Brief Authority.* Garden City, N.Y.: Doubleday, 1962. Francis Biddle's papers are deposited at the Franklin D. Roosevelt Library and at Georgetown University.

—Mary Anne Borrelli

bipartisanship

In order to advance their policy agendas, presidents must often cooperate with lawmakers from the opposing party. DIVIDED GOVERNMENT is one reason for this bipartisanship. The president's party controlled both houses of Congress in just six of the 32 years between the inauguration of Richard NIXON and the departure of Bill CLINTON. During the other 26 years, presidents had no choice but to court the other side of the aisle. Though they often met with frustration, they also scored successes. In 1981, for instance, President REAGAN secured passage of his economic program by winning votes from Southern Democrats in the House.

Bipartisanship is not quite as important when the same party controls Congress and the White House. In 1993 President Clinton managed to win approval of his economic program without a single Republican vote in either chamber. On certain issues, however, enough members of the president's party may break with the administration that it needs votes from the minority party. Occasionally the administration may have to get the bulk of its support from the other side. When President Clinton sought legislation in 1993 to carry out the North American Free Trade Agreement, the Democratic majority in the House voted against it by a margin of 102 to 156. Yet the measure still passed because 132 Republicans backed it, with only 43 against.

In the Senate bipartisanship may be necessary even when the president's party enjoys both unity and majority status. Because Senate filibusters have become more common in recent decades, important legislation often cannot pass without the support of the 60 senators it takes to stop a filibuster. Neither party usually has that many seats.

Bipartisan cooperation may trigger intraparty conflict. During times of divided government, members of the president's party in Congress may worry that the administration is "selling out" to the legislative majority. In 1990, when President George H. W. Bush acceded to Democratic demands for a tax increase, many Republican conservatives fought the measure. In 1996, when President Clinton compromised with congressional Republicans on welfare reform and other initiatives, some Democrats complained that he had put his own reelection ahead of their interests and principles. Conversely, Republican presidential candidate Bob Dole believed that his former colleagues on Capitol Hill had deprived him of campaign issues that he might have used against President Clinton.

An old saying holds that "politics stops at the water's edge," meaning that political leaders prefer bipartisanship on foreign policy and national security. This tendency is most evident in national emergencies such as the 1941 attack on Pearl Harbor or the 2001 attacks on New York and Washington. When President Franklin ROOSEVELT asked for a declaration of war and when President George W. BUSH sought a congressional resolution approving a military response, support was nearly unanimous. In both cases, only a single House member voted in opposition.

The saying notwithstanding, politics often continues at the water's edge. As wars dragged on in Korea and Vietnam, partisan criticism mounted. When President George H. W. BUSH sought congressional approval of the Gulf War, most Democrats voted no. The measure passed because of solid support from Republicans, along with such notable Democratic exceptions as Senators Albert GORE of Tennessee and Joseph LIEBERMAN of Connecticut.

Since the 1970s, congressional Republicans have become more uniformly conservative and Democrats more uniformly liberal. This ideological chasm has posed a challenge to presidents seeking bipartisan cooperation. President Clinton responded with a strategy of "triangulation," placing himself between liberal Democrats and conservative Republicans. He achieved mixed results.

Further reading: Campbell, Colton C., and Nicol Rae, eds. *The Contentious Senate: Partisanship, Ideology, and the Myth of Cool Judgment.* Lanham, Md.: Rowman & Littlefield Publishers, 2001; Drew, Elizabeth. *Whatever It Takes: The Real Struggle for Political Power in America.* New York: Viking, 1997.

—John J. Pitney, Jr.

Blaine, James G. (1830–1893) *secretary of state*
James G. Blaine had a long and distinguished career of public service. After serving three years in the Maine State House of Representatives, Blaine was elected to Congress in 1862. He served in the House for 12 years, the last six as Speaker. In 1876 he switched over to the Senate and served there until 1881. Blaine was a candidate at five Republican national conventions for the party's presidential nomination. In 1884 he headed the party's ticket and lost narrowly to Grover CLEVELAND (48.50 percent to 48.25 percent; 219 electoral votes to 182). He was an acknowledged leader in the REPUBLICAN PARTY for a quarter century. His name evoked strong responses from both devoted followers and opponents, including certain factions within the GOP. Blaine's greatest legacy, however, may stem from his role as secretary of state, a position he held first under James GARFIELD, continued for a short while during Chester Alan ARTHUR's term, and to which he was reappointed under Benjamin HARRISON. His tenures as secretary of state involved a handful of military commitments abroad in such places as Hawaii, Haiti, Argentina, and Chile, as well as diplomatic disputes such as an ongoing clash with England over seal fisheries in the Bering Sea. Blaine's most significant contribution rested in the development of commercial relations with Pan-American nations. His Latin American policies strove to prevent war in the hemisphere, to increase commercial activity, and to have the United States serve more as a mediator among nations rather than a forceful intervener. Blaine was the driving force behind the Pan-American Trade Conference, an effort that he started in 1881 as Garfield's secretary of state and that finally came to fruition in 1889. By that time, Blaine was serving his second term as secretary and was elected president of the Trade Conference. As one scholar has said

about Blaine and his policies, "today the principles which he so earnestly upheld for the relations of the United States to the other States of this hemisphere have been accepted as maxims of American policy."

Further reading: Muzzey, David Saville. *James G. Blaine: A Political Idol of Other Days.* New York: Dodd, Mead & Company, 1934; Stanwood, Edward. *James Gillespie Blaine.* New York: Houghton, Mifflin and Company, 1905.

—Victoria Farrar-Myers

Blair House

Across from the White House, at 1651 Pennsylvania Avenue, sits Blair House. Blair House was built by Army Surgeon General Joseph Lovell. He lived there from 1824 to 1836. Blair House was also the home of newspaper editor Francis Preston Blair. He was an adviser to President Andrew JACKSON, part of his KITCHEN CABINET. Blair's daughter married into the Robert E. Lee family (they lived next door). Abraham LINCOLN used Blair House to offer the command of the Union Army to General Robert E. Lee. Lee rejected the offer and instead commanded the Confederate Army. Portraits of Lovell, Blair, and Lee now hang in Blair House. The government purchased Blair House in 1942 for $175,000. Today, the Blair House complex is primarily used for ceremonial functions and guest quarters for foreign heads of state. Rumor has it that Eleanor ROOSEVELT encouraged the purchase of Blair House for use as a guest house for dignitaries. Late one night, Mrs. Roosevelt found Britain's Prime Minister Winston Churchill wandering the White House looking for President Franklin Roosevelt in order to continue an earlier meeting. She decided that the president might get a better night's sleep with VIP's across the street. President Truman was the only president to reside at Blair House. The Truman family lived in Blair House while the White House was being renovated from 1948 to 1951. While they were residing at Blair House, there was an assassination attempt on President Truman. A White House police officer was shot and killed by Puerto Rican nationalists protecting President Truman on November 1, 1950. As a result, in 1951 Congress authorized Secret Service protection for the president and his family (Public Law 82-79). A plaque by the door to Blair House commemorates the sacrifice made by Officer Leslie Coffelt. The president-elect has awaited his inauguration at Blair House. Some government work also occurred at Blair House. Vice President Al GORE's effort to rethink and rework government service took place in Blair House, and the end result was termed the "Blair House Papers."

—Diane Heith

Boland Amendments

Congress enacted amendments, chiefly sponsored by Representative Edward Boland (Dem.-Mass.), to appropriations bills that expressly banned any agency or entity of the United States from spending funds available to it to support military or paramilitary operations in Nicaragua. These amendments became controversial during the IRAN-CONTRA AFFAIR when Reagan administration officials attempted to divert the profits from arms sales to Iran to the contras—a Nicaraguan military group that was attempting to overthrow the Sandinista government.

After the first Boland Amendment, President REAGAN stated he was deeply committed to the contras and compared them to the American Founding Fathers. The administration proceeded to assist the contras in their effort to overthrow the Nicaraguan government. The controversy involves three dimensions: (1) The National Security Council was not specifically mentioned in the Boland Amendments and is, strictly speaking, not an intelligence agency. (2) The sale of arms to Iran was done through intermediaries, and the claim was made that they could dispense the profits to whomever they desired. (3) The theory of INHERENT POWERS as articulated in *United States. v. Curtiss-Wright* (1936) gives the president independent power to conduct foreign policy, and therefore the Congress had unconstitutionally attempted to limit the president's constitutional prerogatives.

The House and Senate Select Committees concluded that the National Security Council had violated the Boland Amendment. In addition, they concluded that the full purchase price of the arms sold to Iran was available to the CIA and therefore could not be diverted to the contras. Lastly, they concluded that the EXECUTIVE BRANCH's legal opinion was faulty and cursory.

The Boland Amendments were in the tradition of the COOPER-CHURCH AMENDMENT to utilize the appropriations process to cut funds for the implementation of the War in Indochina, and the Clark Amendment, which banned aid to private groups that were assisting military groups in Angola.

—Frank Sorrentino

Bonus Army

In the midst of the GREAT DEPRESSION, veterans groups began agitating for increased benefits. In 1931 Congress passed a bill that would have allowed veterans to borrow up to 50 percent of the value of their WORLD WAR I certificates. President HOOVER vetoed the legislation, but Congress overrode the veto.

In 1932 a group of about 10,000 veterans, referred to as the Bonus Expeditionary Force (BEF) or the Bonus Army, met in Washington, D.C., to demand full value on their certificates. The Senate refused, and most of the protesters disbanded.

Those who remained, about 2,000, were a cause of some concern. President Hoover told General Douglas MacArthur to keep the Bonus Army under control but not to drive them away. MacArthur violated this order, and on July 28, 1932, with tanks and a thousand armed soldiers, he drove the Bonus Army out of their encampment at Anacosta Flats, setting the camp ablaze.

Hoover did not publicly reprimand MacArthur, and the impression was left that MacArthur ordered the assault. Hoover, in fact, took full responsibility for what took place. MacArthur would, decades later, be fired by President TRUMAN for insubordination.

Booth, John Wilkes (1838–1865) *actor, assassin*

Assassin of President Abraham LINCOLN, Booth was a successful actor from a family of actors, and his racist and pro-slavery ideals made him a Confederate sympathizer during the CIVIL WAR. He took particular note of Lincoln's use of PREROGATIVE POWER, seeing in Lincoln's actions evidence that he was a tyrant. Booth initially plotted to kidnap Lincoln and hold him hostage in an attempt to bargain for peace on Confederate terms, but the plot fell apart. Motivated by a desire for revenge for the Southern defeat, Booth reformed the conspiracy around the assassination of several top federal officials, including Vice President Andrew JOHNSON and Secretary of State William SEWARD.

Booth learned that Lincoln would be attending the English comedy *Our American Cousin* at Ford's Theater in Washington, D.C. on April 14, 1865. When Lincoln's lone guard left his post during the play, Booth had free access to the presidential box. He fired one shot into Lincoln's head and, after slashing Major John Rathbone with a knife, leaped to the stage, shouting, "*Sic semper tyrannis*," a Latin phrase meaning "thus always to tyrants." Lincoln died the next morning.

The wider conspiracy failed. Seward, although badly injured by one of the plotters, survived his attack. Johnson's assassin lost his nerve. Booth fled Ford's Theater but was trapped and killed by Union soldiers on April 26. The other conspirators were captured and hanged.

The consequences of Booth's act were profound. Lincoln's death left Andrew Johnson as president, a Democrat who lacked both Lincoln's political skills and partisan support. Unable to manage the difficult process of RECONSTRUCTION, Johnson fought fierce battles with the Republican Congress. Impeached and disgraced, he left a Reconstruction policy that scarred the nation for decades to come.

Further reading: Clarke, James W. *American Assassins: The Darker Side of Politics*, 2d rev. ed. Princeton, N.J.: Princeton University Press, 1990; Hanchett, William. *The Lincoln Murder Conspiracies*. Urbana: University of Illinois Press, 1983.

—David A. Crockett

box scores, presidential

Ever since presidents have been involved in the legislative process, observers of American politics have been interested in how "successful" the president is in that arena. The first sustained systematic record-keeping effort was begun by the *Congressional Quarterly* organization, which tracked presidential success with Congress from 1953 to 1975. These results are generally reported in the *Congressional Quarterly Almanacs*, published annually by CQ Press.

The box scores include specific legislative requests by presidents, contained in presidential messages to Congress and other public statements during the calendar year in which *CQ* tracks legislation. As such, they are a good first cut at the president's AGENDA and agenda activity.

Perhaps more important from a research orientation is what the box scores exclude from analysis, rather than what they include. Excluded are proposals advocated by executive branch officials but not specifically by the president; nominations and suggestions that Congress consider or study particular topics even when legislation is not specifically requested; legislation dealing with the District of Columbia; routine appropriation requests for regular, continuing government operations.

One potential area of concern, which *CQ* editors admit and try to correct for, is the fact that the legislative process in Congress is messy. For example, a piece of legislation could be proposed by the president but changed so radically during the course of congressional committee action, hearings, amending action, and so forth, that the final product does not resemble very much of what the president proposed. *CQ*'s editors recognized this and have made a judgment call on whether or not the final version of the bill originally proposed by the president is a reasonable approximation of his intentions. If so, it is counted as a victory (assuming it passes and is signed); if not, it is considered a failure even if it is passed.

Many of these exclusions are perfectly reasonable, and *CQ* does well to specify what it does and does not include. As such, it is a solid start for researchers, reporters, and citizens interested in tracking the fate of the president's program. Because of its exclusions, and in some cases the way that it counts requests, ultimately the box scores do not tell us much more than the percentage of time that a piece of legislation, requested by a president and conforming the *CQ*'s restrictive criteria, makes it through the legislative process. As such, they are of limited use to researchers and were ultimately discontinued in 1975. In what remains of this article, I detail some of the more glaring problems with the box score methodology.

Because the presidential box score is a tabular checklist of the president's program, it counts all pieces of legislation as equal, regardless of the content and relative import of the proposal. This tends to artificially inflate or deflate (depending on the distribution of wins and losses) each president's success rate.

Scholars are also in general agreement on other drawbacks of using box scores. These include such potential problems as timing, where *CQ* calculates success and failure in a calendar year, whereas many presidential proposals take more than a year to make their way through the legislative process. Another pitfall involves ambiguity in identifying when a measure has failed (e.g., some proposals are killed by Congress via roll call voting; others are denied congressional activity; still others begin the legislative process but die in committee or somewhere else in the maze of the congressional process). Yet another problem arises when one recognizes that much of what constitutes presidential LEADERSHIP or influence in Congress involves presidential requests that are outside the legislative process, such as presidential nominations and the requirement of Senate consent. Finally, the calculation of presidential success in Congress depends on the analysis of legislation proposed by the president. However, a great deal of legislation begins in Congress, with the president playing a decidedly reactive role. Since the legislative process is decidedly interdependent, presidents often care about these congressionally based initiatives and are actively involved in either promoting their passage or working for their defeat. These problems, largely recognized by the editors at *CQ*, prompted them to discontinue calculating box scores in 1975.

Further reading: Presidential box scores can be found in: *Congressional Quarterly Almanac* (editions 1953–75). Washington: Congressional Quarterly; Edwards, George C., III. *At the Margins: Presidential Leadership of Congress.* New Haven: Yale University Press, 1989; Bond, Jon R., and Richard Fleisher. *The President in the Legislative Arena.* Chicago: University of Chicago Press, 1990, pages 55–60.

—Daniel E. Ponder

brain trust

When a *New York Times* reporter coined the term *brain trust* in September 1932, Governor Franklin ROOSEVELT had already been meeting regularly with its members for over a year. Looking toward the coming presidential campaign, Roosevelt's counselor, Samuel Rosenman, foresaw

the need for answers to the stream of questions that a presidential candidate is assaulted with by the press. With Roosevelt's input, Rosenman began recruiting idea men for the coming national campaign.

Raymond Moley, a criminology expert and professor of government at Columbia University, was the nominal head of the group that emerged to advise the candidate. Moley believed that the government must "harmonize" the interests of business and society, but that conglomerates, trusts, and even certain monopolies were the products of the "maturation" of the U.S. economy. Adolf A. Berle, Jr., and Rexford Tugwell, also Columbia University professors, were less sanguine about the growth of big business. These men thought the government needed to provide directive intelligence and, if need be, coercion, to balance the overweening influence of private corporations in the economy. In a speech that Roosevelt delivered to the Commonwealth Club of San Francisco, September 23, 1932, the influence of Berle and Tugwell was plainly evident. "Our task now," Roosevelt stated, "is not discovery or exploitation of natural resources, or necessarily producing more goods. It is the soberer, less dramatic business of administering resources and plants already in hand . . . of adapting existing economic organizations to the service of the people." "The day of the manager," Roosevelt went on to declare, "has come."

Once Roosevelt took office, the brain trusters scattered to government jobs in different departments, though they were all on call to help the president as he wanted their help. The sometimes-utopian sentiments of Roosevelt's intellectuals, especially Tugwell, led to criticism of the Brain Trust in the press and on Capitol Hill. "We have turned our backs on competition," Tugwell proclaimed on behalf of the new administration at one point, "and have chosen control." These were strong words, and although they were no stronger than Roosevelt's own words from his first inaugural address, Tugwell and the other brain trusters served Roosevelt as lightning rods, attracting the strikes that Roosevelt himself might otherwise have had to endure.

The enduring significance of the Brain Trust was that it opened new opportunities for intellectuals in presidential service, and that it illustrates clearly the lack of any single philosophy behind the NEW DEAL. Berle and Tugwell agreed more often than not with each other, but they were frequently at odds with Moley. These three, meanwhile, were joined at times in the informal listing of Brain Trusters by Hugh Johnson, a protégé of the business-minded financier Bernard Baruch. Working outside the Brain Trust, meanwhile, were other men of intelligence and learning, such as Louis Brandeis and Felix Frankfurter, who also deeply influenced Roosevelt, but who rejected the very premise of the brain trusters, that the future of America lay in big business working in concert with big government.

Further reading: Langston, Thomas S. *Ideologues and Presidents: From the New Deal to the Reagan Revolution.* Baltimore: Johns Hopkins University Press, 1992; Moley, Raymond. *After Seven Years.* New York: Harper Brothers, 1939.

—Thomas Langston

Breckinridge, John C. (1821–1875) *U.S. vice president*

Elected as James BUCHANAN's vice president at age 36, John C. Breckinridge is the youngest VICE PRESIDENT in history. Breckinridge, a staunch defender of states' rights, served as vice president as the winds of war approached. Though sympathetic to the Southern cause, he attempted to hold the Union together.

In 1860 the Democrats split into several factions and the Southern faction nominated Breckinridge as its presidential candidate. He lost to LINCOLN and shortly thereafter was appointed senator of Kentucky. In September of 1861, just seven months into his term, he left the Senate and moved to Virginia, where he was made a Confederate general. A federal grand jury in Kentucky issued an indictment against Breckinridge for treason, the Senate expelled him (he had already resigned), and in February of 1865 he was appointed Confederate secretary of war.

At the end of the war, Breckinridge fled the United States for Cuba, then England. When President Andrew JACKSON issued an AMNESTY, Breckinridge returned to Kentucky to practice law.

Bretton Woods

An agreement reached at the International Monetary and Financial Conference of the United States and Associated Nations, which met in Bretton Woods, New Hampshire, in July of 1944. The agreement, signed by 44 nations, was an attempt to promote international development and, importantly, to regulate the international economic system and create an environment amenable to free trade. The agreement also sought to avoid world economic recession such as that which followed the conclusion of WORLD WAR I. After some doubt about its support, Congress approved the Bretton Woods agreement in 1945. The agreement created two key institutions, the International Monetary Fund (IMF) and the International Bank for Reconstruction and Development, known most commonly as the World Bank. The job of the World Bank was to act as a lending institution to aid development and reconstruction efforts throughout the world, particularly in those economies adversely effected by WORLD WAR II. The IMF was charged with promoting economic coordination between nations, especially with regard to their currency valuations and their trading decisions. This was to insure increased growth and productivity in general in the international economy as well as balanced growth among nations. By the 1990s, 180 nations had become members of the World Bank and IMF, although the United States and Western nations still hold considerable power within the organizations.

The world economic system was governed by the Bretton Woods agreement from 1946 to 1971, with the IMF being a key actor in managing international economic and trade decisions. In the effort to stabilize currency and maintain fixed rates of exchange, the U.S. dollar came to be used as the standard by which to judge and assess other currencies. In other words, the United States essentially became the banker to the world. This system worked rather well for other countries and the United States through the 1950s. For instance, Japan and European nations experienced substantial economic recovery in the aftermath of Bretton Woods. The United States reaped several important advantages, economic and political. With the dollar as the official standard currency of the world, U.S. companies were encouraged to invest in foreign nations and to expand their productivity. The attractiveness of the dollar also allowed the United States to engage in a substantial buildup of its military in Europe. But no advantage was as important as the strengthening of the United States's position of leadership in the international world. With the dollar having such a critical impact on the economies and thus nations of the world, the United States solidified its position as an international hegemony and leader of the industrialized nations, and the American presidency likewise was invested with considerable power and prestige.

The system, however, encountered significant problems in the 1960s, and these problems culminated in Nixon's shocking decision in 1971 to no longer back the U.S. dollar with gold and thus suspend the Bretton Woods system. The dollar had been used as the standard currency because of the large reserves of gold held in the United States and the government's willingness to back the dollar with gold. By the 1960s, however, confidence in the dollar, and the United States's ability to back the dollar with gold, waned as the United States experienced a negative balance-of-payments in the international economy. One key outcome of this lack of confidence was foreign countries' and investors' decisions to demand gold in exchange for their dollars, thus causing the U.S. gold reserve to shrink by more than 50 percent between 1949 and 1971. With Nixon's decision in 1971, the dollar would now have a "floating" rate rather than an exchange rate tied to gold and thus other nations' currencies would "float" or fluctuate as well, depending on market conditions. In this post-Bretton Woods system, exchange rates are managed through a combination of national monetary decisions and multilateral agreements with other nations, with the United States continuing to exercise strong, but not dominant, leadership. The IMF continues to exert an important influence on international monetary decisions, even with the floating nature of exchange rates; however, the World Bank today operates largely to aid developing nations.

Further reading: Diner, Daniel C., and Dean J. Patterson. "Chapter 6: Chief Economist," in *Powers of the Presidency*, 2d ed. Washington, D.C.: Congressional Quarterly Press, 1997; Frendreis, John P., and Raymond Tatalovich. *The Modern Presidency and Economic Policy.* Itasca, Ill.: F. E. Peacock Publishers, Inc., 1994; Kegley, Charles W., Jr., and Eugene R. Wittkopf. *American Foreign Policy: Pattern and Process*, 3d ed. New York: St. Martin's Press, 1987; Kirshner, Orin, ed. *The Bretton Woods-GATT System: Retrospect and Prospect After Fifty Years.* London: M. E. Sharpe, 1996.

—Michael J. Korzi

Bricker Amendment

Proposed in September 1951 by Senator John W. Bricker (Rep.-Ohio) and never adopted, the Bricker Amendment would have barred presidents from making EXECUTIVE AGREEMENTS with foreign governments and prohibited any treaty that abridged American constitutional freedoms or governed "any other matters essentially within the domestic jurisdiction of the United States" or of state and local governments. The Amendment was partly a reaction to what Bricker and other conservatives saw as an unconstitutional expansion of presidents' ability to make foreign agreements during WORLD WAR II and the COLD WAR.

It also reflected fears that American social and ECONOMIC POLICY could be dictated by the terms of international agreements such as the draft UN International Covenant on Human Rights, which guaranteed citizens social and economic rights such as the right to housing, education, health care, and membership in a labor union. In *MISSOURI V. HOLLAND*, 252 U.S. 416 (1920), the U.S. Supreme Court had held that the terms of a treaty, which under Article VI of the Constitution becomes part of the "supreme Law of the Land," could authorize Congress to legislate on subjects previously beyond its reach. The Amendment's supporters feared that this doctrine, combined with American ratification of the Covenant, would authorize or even require Congress to legislate a vast expansion of American social welfare programs.

The Senate rejected the amendment in 1954 after the EISENHOWER administration, which opposed the amendment as a crippling restriction on the president's ability to negotiate international agreements, persuaded moderate Republicans to oppose it.

Further reading: Pach, Chester J., and Elmo Richardson. *The Presidency of Dwight D. Eisenhower.* Lawrence: University Press of Kansas, 1991; Tananbaum, Duane. *The Bricker Amendment Controversy: A Test of Eisenhower's Political Leadership.* Ithaca, N.Y.: Cornell University Press, 1988.

—Michael Comiskey

brinksmanship

A term used in foreign policy making, brinksmanship refers to the intentional threat of war as a tactic to get an adversary to comply with your wishes. Brinksmanship is a dangerous and infrequently used tactic. The term is believed to have been coined by Dwight D. EISENHOWER's secretary of state, John Foster DULLES, who in an interview stated that in the COLD WAR era, the United States had to be ready to go to the brink of war in order to secure the peace.

Brownell, Herbert, Jr. (1904–1996) *lawyer, campaign strategist*

A graduate of the University of Nebraska (1924) and of Yale Law School (1927), Brownell specialized in corporate law. His expertise, however, was in campaign strategizing.

Active in HOOVER's 1928 presidential campaign, Brownell subsequently entered political office as a New York State Assemblyman (1933–37). He was identified with progressive legislation that established minimum wage standards, liberalized alimony laws, reorganized New York city government, and provided unemployment relief and family assistance.

Though Brownell claimed to leave the legislature to devote more time to his legal practice, his political activities in subsequent years suggested otherwise. Among the city, state, and national campaigns he managed were the gubernatorial (1938 and 1942) and presidential (1944 and 1948) campaigns of Thomas E. Dewey. From 1944 to 1946 he chaired the Republican National Committee.

In 1952 Brownell managed the EISENHOWER presidential campaign, leading efforts to defeat Robert Taft at the national party convention. An adviser during Eisenhower's presidential transition, he become attorney general.

Brownell entered the Justice Department soon after it had endured a series of scandals, which led him to distance some departmental appointments from partisan politics. His other initiatives related to policing the U.S.-Mexico border, admitting Hungarian refugees in 1956, and enforcing antitrust legislation. He was unable to secure passage of a constitutional amendment providing for presidential DISABILITY and succession. His anticommunist stances drew criticism from both liberals and conservatives. For example, Brownell endorsed wiretapping without court supervision in national security cases, though he was willing to have the findings ruled inadmissible in court. He opposed making membership in the Communist Party illegal but indicted leaders of the American Communist Party under the Smith Act. An adviser to the president on the nomination of Chief Justice Earl Warren, Brownell was a pivotal figure in enforcing the Court's rulings at Little Rock (1957) and in securing passage of the Civil Rights Act of 1957.

Leaving the CABINET in 1957, Brownell returned to private practice and to managing Republican campaigns. He also served as a special ambassador negotiating the Colorado River salinity problem with Mexico (1972–74) and chaired the National Study Commission on Records and Documents of Federal Officials (1975–77).

Further reading: Brownell, Herbert. *Advising Ike: The Memoirs of Attorney General Herbert Brownell.* Lawrence, Kansas: University Press of Kansas, 1993; Herbert Brownell's papers are deposited at the Dwight D. Eisenhower Library.
—Mary Anne Borrelli

Brownlow Committee

The President's Committee on Administrative Management, popularly known as the Brownlow Committee, was appointed by President Franklin D. ROOSEVELT to recommend changes to enable the CHIEF EXECUTIVE to efficiently manage the modern welfare state that emerged from New Deal measures. Within the context of the spread of European fascism and communism, as well as the development of modern social science, the president appointed a three-member committee to develop recommendations that would refute autocratic claims that democratic government was too outdated to meet the changing demands of the 20th century. The committee is credited to Harold Ickes (1874–1952), Franklin Roosevelt, and Charles E. Merriam (1874–1953), the originator of the idea and the father of the behavioral movement in political science. He exemplified the academic specialist in the emerging role of the government consultant.

Merriam assigned the task for developing the idea to his friend, Louis Brownlow (1879–1963), who chaired the Public Administration Committee of the Social Science Research Council. Brownlow had been a prominent journalist before President Woodrow Wilson appointed him as commissioner of the District of Columbia (1915–20). In February 1936 Brownlow drafted "Rough Notes on the Kind of Study Needed," a one-page summary of his thoughts. He met with FDR in early March 1936 and agreed to chair the committee. Merriam also recruited Luther H. Gulick III (1892–1993) to the committee. Gulick had been a student of Columbia University's Progressive historian Charles A. Beard, later succeeding him as the

director of the Training School for Public Service of the New York Bureau of Municipal Research. Gulick established Columbia University's Institute of Public Administration and served as its president for more than 40 years.

The committee had nine months to research and prepare its findings. Its resources included a $50,000 budget and a staff of 26 experts, including some who later became well-known political scientists, e.g., Robert E. Cushman (1889–1969), Merle Fainsod (1907–72), Arthur N. Holcombe (1884–1977), and Arthur W. Macmahon (1890–1980).

The report was timed for issuance after the November 1936 elections. The report's overall theme was to give the president managerial power commensurate with his role of overseeing the largest BUREAUCRACY in the world. Specifically, it proposed enhancing the American presidency in five ways: (1) enlarging the staff; (2) expanding the merit system; (3) improving fiscal management; (4) creating a permanent planning agency; and (5) adding two cabinet posts and placing executive agencies, including regulatory commissions, under the major cabinet departments.

On January 11, 1937, FDR held a news conference about the report, which he then transmitted to Congress. Congressional hearings began in February, unfortunately coinciding with introduction of FDR's Supreme COURT PACKING PLAN. The president had failed to consult with Congress on either matter and had insisted on total secrecy while the Brownlow Committee prepared its findings. On May 31, Brownlow had a heart attack, removing him from the legislative battle. Opponents now termed the Brownlow bill a call for executive dictatorship. It was defeated by a narrow margin in April 1938.

Ultimately, however, FDR triumphed in the administrative war. The Reorganization Act of 1939 and subsequent legislation enacted most of the bold vision for the American presidency that the Brownlow Report had outlined. Unfortunately, most of the original recommendations have been overlooked. For example, what was recommended as a small increase in staff mushroomed into a 600-employee White House Office, and presidential assistants who were to have a "passion for anonymity" are now better known than many cabinet members. Violating the spirit of the Report has led to a milieu of excesses that yielded WATERGATE and the IRAN-CONTRA AFFAIR. Nonetheless, the Report recommendations have been the most important contribution to a strong and responsible presidency since the FEDERALIST PAPERS.

Further reading: Brownlow, Louis. *The Autobiography of Louis Brownlow.* Chicago: University of Chicago Press, 1958; Pederson, William D. "Brownlow Committee." In *A Historical Guide to the U.S. Government,* edited by George T. Kurian. New York: Oxford University Press, 1998; Pederson, William D., and Stephen N. Williams. "The President and the White House Staff." In *Dimensions of the Modern Presidency*, edited by Edward N. Kearney, 139–156. Saint Louis, Mo.: Forum Press, 1982; Polenberg, Richard. *Reorganizing Roosevelt's Government: The Controversy over Executive Organization, 1936–1939*. Cambridge, Mass.: Harvard University Press, 1966; *Report of the President's Committee on Administrative Management*, 1937.

—William D. Pederson

Bryan, William Jennings (1860–1925) *politician*

William Jennings Bryan was the standard bearer of the DEMOCRATIC PARTY in three losing efforts to claim the presidency. Bryan, born in Illinois in 1860, graduated from Union College of Law in 1883 and settled afterward in Lincoln, Nebraska, from where he was elected to the House of Representatives in 1891. As editor in chief of the *Omaha World-Herald* from 1894 to 1896, Bryan maintained a high profile and was chosen as a speaker at the 1896 convention of the Democratic Party.

At that convention, Bryan's fiery rhetoric, in which he proclaimed that rich Americans were attempting to crucify ordinary families on a "cross of gold," rallied the convention delegates to endorse him as their candidate for president. The nation's adherence to a gold standard for its currency, Bryan and his supporters believed, was impoverishing farmers, who had to repay debts in hard currency that they often did not have, following the depression of the early 1890s. The Democratic Party's answer was the "free coinage of silver," which would have the effect of inflating the currency and thus helping debtors. The Populist Party, gratified at his embrace of inflationary economics and other aspects of their program, endorsed Bryan as their candidate for president as well in 1896.

Before Bryan's campaign, a major party presidential candidate almost never gave what we today would consider standard campaign speeches, in which a nominee makes promises and asks for votes. Bryan broke this tradition, reinforcing his reputation as an orator and a candidate unrestrained by old ways of thinking. In rousing speeches across the nation, the 36-year-old Democratic and Populist candidate called for free coinage of silver, government ownership of the railroads, and a graduated income tax. Against a fearful and fantastically well-financed opposition, Bryan won only 47 percent of the popular vote, to Republican William MCKINLEY's 51 percent.

Bryan reprised his role as the Democratic Party nominee for president in 1900, when he campaigned on old themes, as well as the new issue of U.S. IMPERIALISM, following the Spanish-American War of 1898. In 1908 Bryan again ran for the Democrats, this time against Republican William Howard TAFT. Though the economy was prospering in that year, Bryan continued to call for the economic panaceas of his first campaign, and he was soundly defeated. After assisting in Woodrow Wilson's victorious campaign of 1912, Bryan was confirmed as secretary of state. He resigned that post in 1915, over objections to Wilson's drift toward participation in World War I.

In private life afterward, Bryan crusaded for Prohibition and died shortly after appearing as a star witness for the prosecution in the famous "Monkey Trial" of 1925, in which a school teacher was placed on trial for teaching the theory of evolution to his students.

Further reading: Ashby, LeRoy. *William Jennings Bryan: Champion of Democracy*. Boston: Twayne, 1987; Bryan, William Jennings, with Mary Baird Bryan. *The Memoirs of William Jennings Bryan*. Chicago: John C. Winston Company, 1925.

—Thomas S. Langston

Buchanan, James (1791–1868) *fifteenth U.S. president*

Regarded as one of the least effective presidents in U.S. history, James Buchanan was born on April 23, 1791, in Cove, Pennsylvania. He graduated from Dickinson College in 1809.

The presidency of James Buchanan (1857–61) was dominated, even overwhelmed, by the tensions between the North and the South over the issue of slavery. While Buchanan thought slavery was a moral evil, he also recognized a constitutional right of Southern states to allow slavery to exist. He tried to steer a middle course between the pro- and anti-slavery forces. He failed.

The nation's only bachelor president, Buchanan, 6 feet tall and droopy-eyed, proved a weak and ineffective president, who failed to head off Southern secession. Ulysses S. GRANT, in a letter to a friend, referred to Buchanan as "our present granny executive."

Although Buchanan was a strong Unionist, his limited conception of presidential power prevented him from taking steps to stem the breakup. Once secession began, Buchanan sat paralyzed, believing the federal government had no authority to coerce the Southern states to remain a part of the Union. He sat idly by when action was needed.

Buchanan was a strict constitutional constructionist. He believed the president was authorized to take only the action clearly permitted by the Constitution. This limited view of the office limited Buchanan's efforts to end domestic strife and allowed events to accelerate beyond hope. In his final message to Congress, Buchanan said of the presidency: "After all, he is no more than the chief executive officer of the Government. His province is not to make but to execute the laws."

Two days after Buchanan took office, the U.S. Supreme Court announced its decision in *DRED SCOTT V. SANDFORD*.

JAMES BUCHANAN,
DEMOCRATIC CANDIDATE FOR PRESIDENT OF THE UNITED STATES.

Proof for a large woodcut campaign banner for James Buchanan *(Library of Congress)*

Finding slavery to be lawful under the Constitution, it ruled that blacks whose ancestors had arrived in America as slaves did not qualify as U.S. or state citizens and thus did not have a citizen's right to sue in federal courts. Also, an enslaved black who escaped to a free state or territory must be returned as property to his or her owner. It further held that Congress had no right to ban slavery in a territory and that the Missouri Compromise of 1820 was unconstitutional. The Dred Scott case, rather than resolving the slavery question, added fuel to the already hot flames.

To make matters worse, in August of 1857 a severe economic downturn hit the banking industry, leading to the panic of 1857. This plunged the nation into a depression and further heightened the already explosive tensions.

It was the secession threat that most worried Buchanan. While he believed secession was unconstitutional, he also believed the federal government's hands were tied—that it was unconstitutional for the federal government to use force against a secessionist state. Buchanan's unwillingness to be flexible and move beyond this very limited (and given the

times, dangerous) view further emboldened Southern secessionists. In his last message to Congress, delivered on December 3, 1860, Buchanan meekly noted "Apart from the execution of the laws, so far as this may be practical, the Executive has no authority to decide what shall be the relations between the Federal Government and South Carolina. . . ."

On December 20, 1860, South Carolina officially seceded from the Union. Two weeks later, President Buchanan sent a special message to Congress pleading that it was not too late for a compromise. Within weeks, six more Southern states withdrew from the Union. It was either disunion or war.

Buchanan operated in difficult times, but he was weak and ineffective. His vacillation and timidity in the face of impending crisis reflected not only his own shortcomings (as great as they were) but the collapse of presidential LEADERSHIP generally in the pre–CIVIL WAR period.

In his final speech to Congress he said, "I at least meant well for my country." Well meaning or not, Buchanan left his successor a seemingly unsolvable crisis. "If you are as happy, Mr. Lincoln, on entering this house as I am in leaving it and returning home," Buchanan told Abe LINCOLN, "you are the happiest man in this country."

Further reading: Curtis, George T. *Life of James Buchanan, Fifteenth President of the United States*, 2 vols. New York: Harper, 1883; Klein, Philip S. *President James Buchanan: A Biography*. University Park: Pennsylvania State University Press, 1962; Smith, Elbert B. *The Presidency of James Buchanan*. Lawrence: University Press of Kansas, 1975.

Buckley v. Valeo, 424 U.S. 1 (1976)

In the aftermath of the WATERGATE scandal and revelations of corruption in the 1972 presidential race, Congress passed CAMPAIGN FINANCE reform in 1974. The law limited the amounts both individuals and POLITICAL ACTION COMMITTEES (PACs) could donate to political campaigns. Further, it extended public financing to cover the nomination phase and created a FEDERAL ELECTION COMMISSION to enforce the law.

This law was immediately challenged, and in *BUCKLEY V. VALEO*, the Supreme Court upheld the limits on the amount individuals and PACs could contribute and allowed that public financing of primaries was constitutional, but it ruled that limiting how much a candidate could contribute to their own campaign was unconstitutional, arguing that such spending was a form of "speech."

Budget and Accounting Act of 1921

The Budget and Accounting Act of 1921 was a groundbreaking legislative initiative in two respects: It facilitated the evolution of the 20th-century presidency, and it transformed executive branch departments and agencies into more professionalized operations in order to keep pace with the demands for public services that they would face in the years to come.

Of primary significance is the fact that the Budget and Accounting Act granted the president the statutory responsibility to compile, prepare, and publish the Budget of the United States Government on an annual basis and to submit it to Congress. This grant of authority to the president did much to increase presidential power. Prior to the Budget Act, individual bureaus in the EXECUTIVE BRANCH either submitted their budget requests directly to the Congress in a format called *The Book of Estimates* or disseminated them through the Treasury Department, which had no legal right to alter them. While prior to the Budget and Accounting Act a number of presidents had tried to review, change, or comment on the bureau requests, the lack of statutory authority could still undermine their efforts in this regard.

The Budget and Accounting Act reversed this line of authority. After 1921 executive branch agencies would no longer be permitted to submit budget requests to Congress that had not been cleared by the BUREAU OF THE BUDGET (BOB). BOB had also been established by the Budget Act to assist the president in his newly acquired budget preparation mandate. This office bolstered presidential clout in the budgetary process in that it immediately afforded the president professional staff assistance and was headed by a director whose appointment did not require Senate confirmation. Moreover, in 1939, when BOB became part of the newly created EXECUTIVE OFFICE OF THE PRESIDENT (EOP), presidential control over federal budgeting was further enhanced. (The BOB was renamed the OFFICE OF MANAGEMENT AND BUDGET [OMB] in 1970 and later, during the FORD administration in the wake of the WATERGATE scandal, Congress voted to require Senate confirmation for the OMB Director.) From 1921 to 1974, the president's access to staff assistance and information so outpaced that of congressional appropriations committees that Congress usually could do little more than change the president's budget at the margins.

The Budget and Accounting Act also created the GENERAL ACCOUNTING OFFICE (GAO) to aid the Congress in overseeing implementation of statues in the departments and agencies by providing it with a nonpartisan staff office to review programmatic efficiency and economy. The GAO would be headed by a comptroller general to be appointed by the president and confirmed by the Senate for a 15-year term.

The Congress is usually not so inclined to delegate broad authority to the president. Why did it do so in this instance? Scholar Howard Shuman describes how a convergence of economic conditions, events, and public opinion trends precipitated passage of the Budget Act—but it took more than 25 years to come to fruition. The key economic triggers were years of deficits after long periods of surplus and unprecedented mushrooming of government spending. The budget was in deficit from 1894 to 1899 and in 1904–05 and 1908–10 after being in surplus from 1867 to 1893. There were also periods of substantial increase in the size of federal budgets such as that which occurred from 1899 to 1912 due to costs connected with the construction of the Panama Canal, the cost of military pensions, and the Spanish American War.

Economic problems led to the creation of study commissions such as the Cockrell-Dockery Commission, the Keep Commission, and finally in 1910 President TAFT's Commission on Economy and Efficiency. The commissions cited numerous examples of waste and inefficiency in budgeting and government management in general and in military contracting in particular. The progressive movement that blossomed at the time, with its emphasis on reforming government operations through scientific management and on ridding government of political corruption, also created a favorable climate for establishment of an executive budget. A related public budget movement also took root that stressed the importance of increasing rationality, accountability, and accuracy in federal budgeting. However, when economic conditions temporarily improved and the budget moved into surplus in 1911 and 1912, the issue was shelved until after WORLD WAR I when deficits, spending, and inflation ballooned considerably beyond prewar levels.

Shuman reports that conditions were so pronounced that they brought both government reformers and politically powerful members of the business establishment together in their support for the proposals that would culminate in the Budget and Accounting Act of 1921. A first effort was vetoed by President Wilson because it allowed the Congress to remove the comptroller general without formal presidential approval. This was altered in a second legislative attempt which successfully passed Congress because it required the president's signature for removal of the comptroller general. President HARDING signed the Budget and Accounting Act on June 10, 1921. In many respects it was to become the defining blueprint for federal budgeting from 1921 until 1974, when the CONGRESSIONAL BUDGET AND IMPOUNDMENT CONTROL ACT added new layers to the congressional budget process.

Further reading: Fisher, Louis. *Presidential Spending Power.* Princeton, N.J.: Princeton University Press, 1975; Mosher, Frederick, C. *A Tale of Two Agencies, A Comparative Analysis of the General Accounting Office and the Office of Management and Budget.* Baton Rouge: Louisiana State University Press, 1984; Shuman, Howard E. *Politics and the Budget: The Struggle between the President and the Congress.* Englewood Cliffs, N.J.: Prentice Hall, 1992; Tomkin, Shelley L. *Inside OMB: Politics and Process in the President's Budget Office.* Armonk, N.Y.: M. E. Sharpe, 1998.

—Shelley Lynne Tomkin

budgetary process, the presidency and the

The president is responsible for submitting a detailed federal budget proposal to Congress on an annual basis. Encompassing hundreds of pages and sometimes presented in several volumes, the president's budget includes programmatic breakdowns of budget requests and their justifications, revenue receipts and projections, and other information required by various statutes. Since the 1980s presidents have also increasingly tracked the progress of that budget as it is considered by the Congress and negoti-

ated to win support for presidential priorities. Whether Congress sends the president individual appropriations bills or massive omnibus budget packages with multiple appropriations and tax actions, the president must decide whether to sign or veto them in their entirety. (President CLINTON was briefly afforded a limited line-item veto authority in 1996, but the Line-Item Veto Act was overturned by the Supreme Court in 1998 as overstepping the Constitution's grant of executive authority.) The president also apportions the funds to federal agencies and programs.

The president and the White House staff are assisted in all of these responsibilities by the OFFICE OF MANAGEMENT AND BUDGET (OMB), a key unit in the EXECUTIVE OFFICE OF THE PRESIDENT. OMB's 500-person career staff review executive branch budget requests, compile the president's budget proposal, and track that budget once it is submitted to Congress. The president usually provides input to OMB's budget preparation process by articulating broad policy guidelines and priorities and by hearing appeals from departmental agencies at the end of the process before final decisions are reached. OMB's political appointees—about 20 in number—assist the White House in negotiating with the Congress and interest groups on budgetary issues.

In the 20th century, the president's involvement throughout the federal budget process—including budget preparation, congressional passage, and execution—has evolved into a role that is as significant as it is challenging. Since presidential budget decisions potentially impact the economic health of the nation and the public tends to hold incumbent presidents accountable for economic downturns, the president's budget actions can directly drive presidential approval ratings and/or whether a president will win a second term in office. Budgetary issues are also inextricably connected with pursuit of most presidential agendas, whether they endorse cutting taxes or funding a president's favored programs or both. Moreover, preparation of a coordinated presidential budget proposal to Congress on an annual basis for the entire federal government is a congressionally mandated responsibility that a president must attend to in spite of other unanticipated challenges he might face. Just as a president who remains aloof from personal engagement in economic issues does so at his own peril, so too presidents who largely turn budget issues over to surrogates must take extraordinary care as to the skills and capacities of the surrogates they appoint.

The president's budget role is doubly challenging for other reasons as well. Many factors beyond a president's control affect the broader economy as well as how much leverage a president has to tinker with the overall budget. These include unforeseen emergencies or crises (national or global economic downturns or upturns, natural disasters, epidemics, wars) and revenues that are unavailable for the president's priorities due to agreements or laws made in the past through entitlement programs, budgetary ceilings, lock boxes, or budget process guidelines such as the GRAMM-RUDMAN-HOLLINGS ACT or the Budget Enforcement Act. In addition, the president's budget powers are shared with Congress. Today the president must sell his budgetary priorities through often drawn-out and exhausting negotiations with Congresses that since the 1970s have enhanced staffing and procedural capabilities. So too, over the last 50 years DIVIDED GOVERNMENT has been the rule and not the exception.

It is difficult to evaluate presidential performance in the budgetary area precisely because of inexact linkages between budget actions and economic outcomes. Still, a composite view of performance and outcome can be approximated. How knowledgeable was the president with respect to budgetary matters and their interplay with the economy? How knowledgeable were key surrogates such as the budget director? The same question can be applied to political skills generally and those involving relationships with the Congress in particular. Did the president's congressional strategies achieve presidential programmatic objectives to the degree possible within a given political environment or did they result in mere stalemate or failure? If achieved, were the president's desired objectives associated with an improving or a deteriorating economy? Was the AGENDA perceived as being reasonably equitable or not? Thus in the final analysis successful presidential performance in the budgetary realm constitutes both an art form and a science, calling into play many of the skills and personal characteristics that would be required to achieve distinction in other avenues of presidential LEADERSHIP.

History of Presidential Involvement in the Budgetary Process (1921–1993)

Presidential involvement and influence in federal budgeting derives largely from the BUDGET AND ACCOUNTING ACT OF 1921, which authorized the White House to control the departmental agency budget requests to Congress and to compile and submit a coordinated budget proposal to Congress on an annual basis. Previously, executive branch offices sought funds directly from Congress on an individual basis—a reality that often resulted in inefficiency and pork barrel spending deemed out of control by government reformers of the time. The Budget Act also established a BUREAU OF THE BUDGET (BOB) housed in the Treasury Department to provide staff assistance to enable the president to execute this new responsibility. (In 1970 under the NIXON administration, the Budget Bureau's name was changed to the Office of Management and Budget.) Presidential clout in the budgetary arena was further increased during the Roosevelt administration when the size of the EXECUTIVE BRANCH and the reach of federal

programs expanded and when the Bureau of the Budget was transferred from the Treasury Department to the newly created Executive Office of the President (EOP) in 1939. BOB/OMB has served presidents of both parties by applying programmatic budgetary expertise to the task of translating broad presidential policy positions into specific budget requests and by compiling the entire presidential budget to be transmitted to Congress.

Until the late 1970s and early 1980s, the president's budget tended to emerge relatively intact from the congressional appropriations process subject only to relatively minor and intermittent alterations. The president's influence outweighed that of Congress in this shared budgetary power because the White House's command of information and expertise through executive branch agencies and BOB/OMB far surpassed that of the congressional appropriations committees.

Congress reasserted its clout in the budget process through passage of the CONGRESSIONAL BUDGET AND IMPOUNDMENT CONTROL ACT OF 1974. This statute succeeded in placing the Congress on a more equal footing with the president in several respects. It established the Congressional Budget Office (CBO) to provide nonpartisan budgetary and economic analysis to the Congress. House and Senate budget committees were created to oversee new procedures such as the preparation of budget resolutions designed to provide spending ceilings and guidelines for the appropriations and authorization committees. Moreover, presidential discretion to impound funds already appropriated was constrained.

These institutional changes, a growing deficit, and wholly or partially divided government during the 1980s produced a new budgetary dynamic between the president and the Congress. As budget expert Allen Schick aptly described it, the presidential budget was transformed from an authoritative blueprint for government spending to an opening negotiating position in a White House–congressional bargaining process that would often result in stalemates continuing beyond the span of a single fiscal year. Deadlock would only be resolved after high-level White House–congressional budget negotiating sessions, which were conducted at the same time that government operated at the previous year's funding levels.

In this environment, the White House and OMB had to devise new staff units and strategies to allow the president to exert an impact in the congressional budgetary arena. Political skills, knowledge of arcane congressional budget rules, and personal acquaintance with key members of Congress and staff became increasingly significant to the White House and OMB. The number of OMB political appointees multiplied in the decade from the 1970s to the 1980s for these reasons. Neither Presidents Ronald REAGAN nor George Herbert Walker BUSH could be characterized as being deeply engaged or knowledgeable with respect to the details of programmatic budget issues or congressional budget procedures. Both presidents however selected knowledgeable OMB directors with a superlative grasp of the intricacies of the federal budget, evolving congressional budget rules, and the politics of the congressional budget process.

David Stockman, Reagan's first budget director, who had been a member of Congress before joining the Reagan administration, led the charge in preparing and negotiating to congressional passage a budget and economic plan that cut domestic program budgets by an unprecedented $38 billion dollars. This part of the so-called Reagan revolution in concert with a tax cut and a sizable increase in the military budget all reflected President Reagan's ideological agenda. Associated outcomes were a mounting deficit from an administration that campaigned on balancing the budget, a recession in the early 1980s, and White House–congressional deadlock for the remainder of Reagan's two terms. President Reagan was not engaged in the details of budgeting to a degree that would have enabled him to heed the implications of his evolving agenda. In his memoir of the period, Stockman faults himself for not adequately communicating to the president the implications of budget decisions and the likelihood of Congress cutting the domestic budget to the degree required to balance the affects of the tax cut and the military buildup.

Summitry and deadlock continued under President George Herbert Walker Bush. President Bush's inability to keep his campaign pledge not to raise taxes, to stem deficit growth, and most importantly to mount a convincing effort to remedy joblessness and recession in 1992, probably cost him reelection. It is to his credit in general and to the credit of his budget director Richard Darman in particular, along with a small group of congressional Democratic and Republican leaders that the Omnibus Reconciliation Act of 1990 and its accompanying Budget Enforcement Act (BEA) began to lay a constructive and realistic foundation for a turnabout in the deficit and the economy. The BEA had more modest goals than did its predecessor deficit reduction devises—Gramm-Rudman-Hollings I and II. Without seeking to eliminate the deficit through draconian deadlines, the BEA did aim to control discretionary spending through the setting of flexible ceilings and the offsetting of new entitlement commitments through a pay-as-you-go (paygo) system. Notable for the purposes of this discussion was the fact that presidential budget authorities were much enhanced under the terms of the BEA. Scholar Howard Shuman wrote soon after the passage of the law that the president through OMB was given the authority to determine whether spending ceilings were being maintained and whether flexible deficit reduction goals and paygo provisions were being met. Still, at the end of the Bush administration, deficit projections had reached 290 billion dollars and the nation was experiencing a recession.

Clinton and the Budgetary Process

Perhaps more than any president of recent memory, President Bill CLINTON was personally involved and informed concerning the formulation of his presidential budgets and their relationship to his policy goals. He was able to harness the federal budget process to achieve measured progress on his designated objectives to the degree possible within the economic and political environment of the times. By the end of his second term in office, the budgetary actions, decisions, and agenda of the Clinton administration were considered at least partially responsible for an extraordinary improvement in the economy in a way that benefited a range of different economic sectors. Certainly, Clinton was the beneficiary of certain fortuitous economic factors—the high-tech surge of the early and middle nineties and the growth of the global marketplace. Political skill and keen understanding of macroeconomic factors also played a critical role. The Clinton budget and economic policy team exhibited a high level of intellectual sophistication regarding the budget relationship with macroeconomic trends, bond markets, and interest rates. Its tactics and strategies also took into account the often arcane complexities of executive and congressional budgetary processes and melded these with the political gamesmanship that the 1990s brought forth.

Clinton and the Budget—Phase One

Clinton's decision in 1993 to make his first budget and economic plan the top priority for the new administration was a crucial first step. Taking a cue from the Reagan/Stockman strategy, Clinton grasped the importance of moving early and dramatically to get the budget through Congress while retaining some vestige of a HONEYMOON PERIOD. Indeed, a number of the actions taken during his first year in office turned out to be decisive for the following seven years. From the beginning, Clinton showcased his sophisticated economic and budgetary knowledge by chairing an economic summit before taking office and by impressing upon Federal Reserve Chairman Alan Greenspan that he understood how serious deficit reduction efforts could signal the bond markets in a way that could lower interest rates. He established a NATIONAL ECONOMIC COUNCIL (NEC) designed to play an honest broker role in his first budget preparation process. Another wise action was the appointment of former Budget Committee Chairman Leon Panetta to head the OMB. A budget director schooled in the ways of Washington in general and the congressional budget process in particular, Panetta had taken part in writing the congressional rules that Clinton would have to play within and enjoyed good relations on both sides of the aisle.

In fact, all four of his budget directors had excellent congressional budget experience and contacts.

His first budget team was balanced between deficit hawks and advisers from the campaign who lobbied for putting-people-first spending programs. This advisory balance served him well in the long run, since he ended up with a five-year budget plan that balanced deficit reduction strategies with measured investments in Clinton's priority areas, including expansion of the earned income tax credit (EITC) and the creation of Americorps. Despite some concessions, the final reconciliation package preserved more than 70 percent of the Clinton team's recommended budgetary investments.

Clinton's razor-thin victory in passing the 1993 Budget Agreement was to accelerate a crucial turn in the nation's economic fortunes. With both House and Senate Republicans predicting that the law would bring on a recession, the 1993 budget agreement instead constituted a first step toward creating an environment that would spark the longest peacetime economic expansion in U.S. history. Moreover, this change of direction spurred favorable response from the bond markets by signaling new fiscal constraint and investment. Interest rates began to drop and the deficit started to shrink over the next few months. The public, however, did not begin to feel the impact of an improving economy until later, and in November of 1994 the Democrats lost their majorities in both houses of Congress.

Phase Two: Clinton, the Republican Congress, and Budget Balancing

The 1994 election ushered in a second phase in the chronicle of the Clinton administration's budgetary history. At the outset, the period seemed reminiscent of the Reagan era's budgetary wars during a period of divided government. Recovering from the shock of the election, the White House challenged the Republican Congress to produce a congressional budget showing how it intended to balance the budget in seven years. In June of 1995 the White House released its own 10-year plan to balance the budget. Over the next few months, there followed a semantical war over which party's economic projections were more credible. Well beyond the beginning of the new fiscal year, the president and Congress were unable to reach a budgetary agreement. Unlike the budget stalemates of the 1980s when CONTINUING RESOLUTIONS funded the government at the previous year's level until budget deals were reached, in 1995 the Congress attached critical policy changes to the resolutions that Clinton subsequently vetoed. Thus ensued the government shutdown of 1995–96.

Both sides were taking an enormous risk in pursuing such BRINKSMANSHIP, but it was Clinton who was to win one of his most dramatic political victories when the Republican Congress was blamed by the public for the government shutdown. What conditions and presidential actions factored into this victory? First, as budget scholar Allen Schick observes, Clinton used his VETO POWER effectively to keep congressional Republicans off balance by vetoing some bills and threatening to veto others. Second, the White House adroitly communicated positions, which reflected the public's priorities of supporting funding to bolster the quality of public education and to preserve Medicare, social security, and the environment. Third, the public was beginning to feel the effects of the expanding economy and job creation to a degree that it had not a year earlier. Finally, Clinton's ability to project empathy to victims' families after the Oklahoma City bombing refocused the spotlight on Clinton's remarkable public communications skills.

In early 1996 the two sides funded the government, froze the deficit debate, and turned to the campaign trail. It became clear before the end of the 1996 election that the economic projections of both the White House and the Congress had been too pessimistic. The deficit just kept dropping. If there was any message to be taken from the 1996 election, which retained a government divided between a Democratic president and a Republican Congress, it was that the electorate wanted less partisan wrangling and more compromise and economic results for the public. That atmosphere and the steadily improving economy that was making the budget ever more easy to balance led to a budget-balancing agreement signed in the summer of 1997.

The Clinton White House's contribution to this achievement was a willingness to seek consensus and allow the Republicans to score some wins on tax cuts and defense spending in order to achieve policy goals that never would have been approved by a Republican Congress otherwise. Clinton was also able to realize several critical policy goals that had been frustrated due to the deficit. These included $30 billion worth of higher educational tax credits and the creation and funding of the Children's Health Insurance Program for uninsured children whose parental incomes fell below $30,000.

Observers at the time perceived some downsides to the agreement as well. They noted at the time that the budget-balancing plan was markedly unrealistic in one respect—it clearly shortchanged budgetary support for established governmental functions that were not protected by vocal interest groups and constituencies. It also did little to solve the long-term budgetary problems connected with maintaining SOCIAL SECURITY and Medicare solvency that economists had projected into the future. The period from the summer of 1997 until the winter of 1998 showed the degree to which the previous economic projections had been off point. While the hard-fought budget-balancing agreement of 1997 had aimed for a balanced budget in five years by 2002, it was to take just one and a half years to realize a projected budget surplus for 1998.

Phase Three: Surplus Wars

The final phase of the Clinton budgetary presidency was ushered in as the deficit wars were transformed into surplus wars between the Republican Congress and the Clinton White House. Clinton's major objectives during this final period of his budgetary presidency were to prevent the Republican Congress from dissipating the surplus with a massive tax cut and to reach an agreement with the Congress that would extend the solvency of the Social Security system in preparation for baby boomer retirements. Clinton effectively used the latter objective to pursue the former when he beseeched the Congress to save Social Security first and to refrain from using the Social Security trust fund for general fund expenditures. Over the next three years, he successfully reduced the public appetite for large tax cuts. Moreover, as time went on, public opinion polls showed that the Clinton White House was more trusted to handle the Social Security issue than was the Republican Congress.

During the first budget cycle in this period, most congressional Republicans did little to organize their own forces effectively to pass their desired tax cut, since they were counting on a massive public disaffection with the president to swell their ranks in the 1998 midterm election. Not only did the public disaffection never materialize, but in the final weeks before the 1998 election, the White House was able to extract significant concessions from the Republican leadership and to increase funding for White House priorities considerably. Anxious to go home and campaign and becoming concerned about their prospects, most members left negotiations for the final deal to the leadership and the White House. In this the White House was able to score incremental victories for administration priority areas such as increased education funding. During the remainder of Clinton's term in office, the same pattern generally prevailed. In 1999, for example, Clinton won significant concessions from the Congress on funding for teachers, police, and on the environment. On the latter point, Clinton successfully used veto threats to stop 12th-hour legislative riders designed to aid business interests at the expense of environmental protections involving public lands and wildlife. Though congressional Republicans had become better organized and were able to pass a $792 billion tax cut that year, the Republican loss of seats in 1998 made Clinton's September 1999 veto final.

In the last year of Clinton's term, the size of the actual and the projected surplus continued to mushroom beyond the expectations of all the experts. In this environment, elimination of the federal debt by the year 2013 and targeted tax credits for health insurance and retirement

accounts for the middle class and working poor had become stated administration goals.In retrospect, it is also interesting to note that Clinton's 2000 budget included $10 billion in budget proposals to deter and to prepare for terrorist attacks after the embassy bombings in Kenya and Tanzania.

Generally, the administration had maintained marked discipline in its budget preparation and in congressional negotiations during six years of divided government. It was thus able to painstakingly win incremental funding increases for its highest priority areas. Joe Klein concluded in a retrospective on the Clinton presidency in December of 2000 that these programmatic enhancements were significant in their result—a government that had dramatically improved the lives of millions of the poorest, hardest-working Americans. Clinton's bravado performances in public addresses arguing for his budgets, his comfort with one-on-one lobbying of members of Congress of both parties, and his personal powers of persuasion in negotiating sessions also factored into his successes. To some degree the Clinton presidency also wrested control of agenda setting from the Republican Congress. In the end, in order to satisfy their constituents, many Republicans changed their previous stances and supported increased funding for new Democratic policy priorities such as education—a very different atmosphere from that which prevailed in 1995 after the REPUBLICAN PARTY won control of the House and the Senate.

George W. Bush and the Budget Process

Two years into the Bush administration, the president's budget legacy has yet to be determined, but several observations can be made within the framework set earlier in this discussion. During the preparation of his first budget, President Bush assumed a CEO role in that he was personally disengaged from detailed programmatic budget discussions. The first Bush budget was crafted through a disciplined decision-making process that was tightly controlled by a senior council directed by Vice President Richard CHENEY and which included White House CHIEF OF STAFF Andrew Card, Treasury Secretary Paul O'Neill, Budget Director Mitchell Daniels, and economic adviser Lawrence B. Lindsey. Appeals for spending increases from cabinet officials were not welcome and were to be ironed out before ever being brought to the president. This contrasts with the preparation of the first Clinton budget and economic plan, a process marked by considerable cabinet-level involvement and input and long meetings and discussions with the president on large and small details.

Of highest priority during the early months of the Bush administration was selling a $1.6 trillion tax cut to a House of Representatives and Senate closely divided along partisan lines. The president compromised on a $1.35 trillion tax cut phased in over 10 years that passed the Congress in

June of 2001. Explanations for Bush's success with a closely divided Congress include early White House involvement in preparing the tax cut proposal, aggressive engagement with Congress to sell the plan, and some willingness to compromise.

Budget issues that were intertwined with the tax cut did not receive the immediate and close attention from the White House that was afforded the tax cut. In fact the White House budget strategy was characterized by observers as a "tax cuts first, budget cuts later" approach. This strategy produced a status quo budget for the first year with phased-in reductions and freezes in succeeding years in a variety of domestic programs, which had been bolstered during the Clinton years. These areas included child care, school construction, AIDS treatment, and public housing. Though many Clinton-era investment agenda items were unfunded under President Bush's budget plan, others such as the earned income tax cut (EITC) were maintained.

Even though $5 trillion 10-year surpluses were being projected at the time of the passage of the tax cut, budget experts immediately issued cautions. Observers worried that the tax cut/budget planning did not provide adequate cushioning for unforeseen economic downturns or emergencies that could deplete the projected surpluses. Others were concerned that the tax cut/budget plans did not contain the necessary funding for increases in defense spending (which were not included in the original Bush budget), education funding—a key focus of the president's compassionate conservative agenda—and prescription drug Medicare supports, all promised by the Bush administration without having to borrow from the Social Security trust fund.

As with so many other aspects of the political landscape, the September 11th terrorist attack on the World Trade Center changed budgetary/economic realities. Shortly after the disaster, a bipartisan consensus brought forth agreement on funding for the war on terrorism, relief efforts for New York, and an airline bailout. Within a two-month period the United States was clearly enveloped in a broad but shallow recession, and by November of 2001 the cautionary notes of only a few months earlier had come to fruition—Mitch Daniels projected that by 2002 the budget surplus would go into a deficit, not to be balanced again before 2005. Republicans blamed the war expenditures and the uncontrollable aspects of the recession and looked to further tax cuts to prime the economy, while Democrats pointed to the tax cut of only six months earlier as well as to the other two factors.

Further reading: Klein, Joe. "Bill Clinton Looks Back." *The New Yorker,* 16 and 23 October 2000; Schick, Allen, and Felix Lostracco. *The Federal Budget: Politics, Policy, Process.* Washington, D.C.: Brookings Institution, 2000; Shuman, Howard E. *Politics and the Budget: The Struggle between the President and the Congress.* Englewood Cliffs, N.J.: Prentice Hall, 1992; Tomkin, Shelley L. *Inside OMB: Politics and Process in the President's Budget Office.* Armonk, N.Y.: M. E. Sharpe, 1998; Woodward, Bob. *The Agenda: Inside the Clinton White House.* New York: Simon & Schuster, 1994.

—Shelley Lynne Tomkin

Bull Moose Party

Technically called the Progressive Party, the Bull Moose Party was a third-party effort led by former president Theodore ROOSEVELT in 1912. The term *Bull Moose* was coined after Roosevelt said he felt "like a bull moose." Less a legitimate organized alternative to the two major parties than a vehicle for Roosevelt's personal ambition, the party split Republican voters in 1912, allowing Woodrow Wilson to win with just 42 percent of the popular vote.

There were two principal reasons for the rise of the Bull Moose Party. First, younger reform-minded leaders in the REPUBLICAN PARTY, hailing largely from the West and Midwest, and led by Wisconsin Senator Robert La Follette, joined a growing insurgency against the more conservative "Old Guard" Republicans. Second, Roosevelt and his handpicked successor, William Howard TAFT, experienced a severe rupture in their relationship that threatened to tear the party apart. Upon leaving the presidency in 1909, Roosevelt went on a lengthy safari in Africa. He returned to find Taft lacking the energy and vigor Roosevelt thought was necessary in the presidency. He came to believe that Taft was under the control of reactionary forces. Roosevelt then became personally insulted when Taft, acting in accordance with the Sherman Antitrust Act, moved against U.S. Steel for conducting merger activities that Roosevelt had approved of when he was president.

Roosevelt challenged Taft for the Republican nomination, winning most of the primaries he entered, but the party leaders were united behind Taft, and the party machine won the credentials battles at the national convention, giving Taft the nomination. Roosevelt forces bolted to a rump convention, eventually forming the Progressive Party. They made Roosevelt their presidential candidate instead of La Follette and nominated Hiram Johnson as his running mate. The Progressive Party convention was a veritable religious camp meeting, a crusade against an unholy system. Delegates sang "The Battle Hymn of the Republic" and "Onward Christian Soldiers," and Roosevelt said, "We stand at Armageddon, and we battle for the Lord." The party's platform was called a "Covenant with the People," and supported such things as a progressive income tax, an inheritance tax, women's suffrage, direct election of senators, direct primaries, a minimum wage, prohibition of child labor, the initiative, the referendum, recall of elected officials, unemployment insurance, and old-age pensions.

The election was a three-way contest between Taft, Roosevelt, and Wilson. With Roosevelt splitting Republican support, Wilson won the election. With the exception of the birth of the Republican Party itself, the Bull Moose effort was the most successful third-party effort in American history, garnering more than 27 percent of the popular vote and 88 electoral votes. Taft came in third, with only eight electoral votes. The party even won 14 House seats. However, the party was based on the personality of Roosevelt, and when he returned to the GOP in 1916 the party disintegrated, its ideas absorbed by the DEMOCRATIC PARTY.

Further reading: Cooper, John Milton, Jr. *The Warrior and the Priest: Woodrow Wilson and Theodore Roosevelt.* Cambridge, Mass.: Belknap Press of Harvard University Press, 1983; Crunden, Robert M. *Ministers of Reform: The Progressives' Achievement in American Civilization, 1889–1920.* New York: Basic Books, 1982; Rosenstone, Steven J., Roy L. Behr, and Edward H. Lazarus. *Third Parties in America,* 2d rev. ed. Princeton, N.J.: Princeton University Press, 1996.

—David A. Crockett

bully pulpit

The start of the RHETORICAL PRESIDENCY and the president's use of the bully pulpit are credited to Theodore ROOSEVELT. He advanced the president's role as the national leader of public opinion and used his rhetorical skills to increase the power of the presidency through popular support. Roosevelt believed that the president was the steward of the people and that weak presidential LEADERSHIP during the 19th century had left the American system of government open to the harmful influence of special interests. He expanded presidential power to the furthest limits of the Constitution by drawing on broad discretionary powers, the first president to do so during peacetime, as opposed to a more conservative and literal reading of presidential powers within the Constitution. Roosevelt's "Stewardship Doctrine" demanded presidential reliance on popular support of the people and also increased the public's expectation of the man and the office. He often appealed directly to the American public through his active use of the bully pulpit to gain support of his legislative AGENDA in an attempt to place public pressure on Congress. He referred to his speaking tours around the country as "swings around the circle." Roosevelt's use of the presidency as a bully pulpit changed Americans' view of the office and helped to shift power from the legislative to EXECUTIVE BRANCH during the 20th century. Later presidents, though not all, would follow Roosevelt's strategy of relying on the bully pulpit to elevate the power of the office as an attempt to lead democratically as the spokesperson for the American public. Woodrow WILSON contributed to a more dominant view of the presidency through his use of the bully pulpit, and he broke with a 113-year tradition by becoming the first president since John ADAMS to deliver his State of the Union address in person before the Congress in 1913. Through his rhetorical skills, especially during World War I, Wilson established the presidency as a strong position of leadership at both the national and international level. Franklin D. ROOSEVELT relied heavily on the bully pulpit, particularly in his use of radio, to gradually persuade the American public to support his New Deal policies during the 1930s and America's involvement in World War II during the 1940s.

Use of the bully pulpit has become especially important since the start of the television age, where a president's overall success or failure as a leader can be determined by his rhetorical skills and public influence. Since the 1950s, three presidents stand out as successful in their use of the bully pulpit—John F. KENNEDY, Ronald REAGAN, and Bill CLINTON. All were known for their frequent use of inspiring and eloquent speeches about public policy and their visions for the country. Kennedy talked of a "NEW FRONTIER" and motivated many Americans to become active in public service. Reagan saw the bully pulpit as one of the president's most important tools, and relying on his skills as an actor he provided a strong image of moral leadership that restored Americans' faith in government institutions. Clinton's skills as an orator, and his ability to speak in an extemporaneous and empathetic manner, aided his leadership on some, if not all, of his legislative priorities, like affirmative action and education.

Other presidents during the 20th century either abdicated the bully pulpit or used it ineffectively, which diminished presidential power during their terms and curtailed their leadership potential by allowing other political actors to shape the public debate. As it has evolved during the past century, a president's skillful use of the bully pulpit is necessary to promote his philosophy for governing as well as the overall moral and political vision of the administration. It can also determine the effectiveness of presidential governance and whether or not a president can accomplish his policy and broader ideological objectives through rhetorical skills. However, some view this as an institutional dilemma for the modern presidency. Since the current political culture now demands the president to be a popular leader by fulfilling popular functions and serving the nation through mass appeal, this suggests that the presidency has greatly deviated from the original constitutional intentions of the founders. The rhetorical presidency, through the use of the bully pulpit, is viewed by some as a constitutional aberration by removing the buffer between citizens and their representatives that the framers established.

Further reading: Cronin, Thomas E., and Genovese, Michael A. *The Paradoxes of the American Presidency.* New York: Oxford University Press, 1998; Gelderman, Carol. *All the Presidents' Words: The Bully Pulpit and the Creation of the Virtual Presidency.* New York: Walker and Co., 1997; Lammers, William W., and Genovese, Michael A. *The Presidency and Domestic Policy: Comparing Leadership Styles, FDR to Clinton.* Washington, D.C.: CQ Press, 2000; Milkis, Sidney M., and Nelson, Michael. *The American Presidency: Origins And Development.* Washington, D.C.: CQ Press, 1999; Tulis, Jeffrey K. *The Rhetorical Presidency.* Princeton, N.J.: Princeton University Press, 1987.

—Lori Cox-Han

bureaucracy

The federal bureaucracy is comprised of hundreds of government agencies that implement Congressional and presidential directives and act as a major force in shaping presidential decisions and congressional legislation.

The structure of the federal bureaucracy consists of three basic types: cabinet departments, independent executive agencies, and independent regulatory commissions.

CABINET *departments* are 14 in number and are the major components of the federal bureaucracy. Originally there were three departments. By the mid 19th century, there were a total of six cabinet departments: Departments of WAR, STATE, TREASURY, the Post Office, the Navy, and the INTERIOR. All were small and easily subject to the scrutiny of both the CONGRESS and THE PRESIDENT. The industrial revolution helped to establish the Departments of AGRICULTURE and COMMERCE and LABOR.

After the Great Depression and WORLD WAR II, the government became involved in a wider range of international and domestic problems, leading to the consolidation of the armed forces (the Departments of War and Navy) into the Department of Defense (1940). In 1953 several agencies dealing with domestic welfare were combined into the Department of HEALTH, EDUCATION AND WELFARE (HEW).

In the 1960s, concern about urban areas and transportation led to the creation of the Department of HOUSING AND URBAN DEVELOPMENT (1965) and the Department of TRANSPORTATION (1966). Concern over energy led to the development of the Department of ENERGY in 1977. Educational groups successfully demanded that education be given its own cabinet department, the Department of EDUCATION (1980). The former HEW then became known as the Department of HEALTH AND HUMAN SERVICES. In 1989 the Veterans Administration was elevated to cabinet-level status and renamed the Department of Veterans Affairs. The ENVIRONMENTAL PROTECTION AGENCY is presently being considered for cabinet-level status, as environmental concerns have become a higher priority with many Americans. Each department reflects the recognition of a group's status and interests and the role of government to protect those interests.

Departments are organized to respond to interest groups. This leads to a Small Business Administration in the Department of Commerce, for small business people, and a Bureau of Fish and Wildlife in the Department of Interior, for sportsmen. While this broadens the political base of each department, it can create a system that is run from the subunit up rather than the other way around.

The president appoints the cabinet secretary and numerous other officials—undersecretaries, deputy undersecretaries, assistant secretaries, and some bureau chiefs. There is a strict line of hierarchy, under which bureau executives report to the cabinet secretary who reports to the president. This appears to be a tight organizational structure, but the mere size and complexity prevents significant presidential control.

Independent executive agencies and government corporations are agencies that report to the president in the same manner as departments though they are not in cabinet departments. The president appoints the heads of these agencies and may dismiss them without consulting Congress. They were placed independent of a cabinet department primarily for political and symbolic reasons.

The National Aeronautics and Space Administration (NASA) could have been placed in the Department of DEFENSE; however, this would suggest that the space program was intended primarily for military purposes rather than civilian purposes such as satellite communications and space exploration. It also allows for this agency to be more accountable to academic and communication interest groups.

The independent executive agency can also be useful in implementing a new program. President JOHNSON, for example, conducted the War on Poverty (a series of government measures intended to eradicate poverty) from the Office of Economic Opportunity rather than scatter the program throughout the cabinet departments. This gave greater coordination and gave the president better control by making new appointments and avoiding the institutionalized web of power relations that exist between the cabinet departments, interest groups, and congressional committees. Other examples of independent executive agencies are the CENTRAL INTELLIGENCE AGENCY (CIA) and the Selective Service.

GOVERNMENT CORPORATIONS became popular during the NEW DEAL and after WORLD WAR II and were intended to increase professionalism and minimize politics. They were established to accomplish specific tasks such as extending credit to banking facilities. Government corporations were given more freedom of action, especially with fiscal affairs. Their directors are appointed by the president and approved by the Senate. They have been established to insure bank deposits (Federal Deposit Insurance Corporation), to develop a regional utility (TENNESSEE VALLEY AUTHORITY), to operate intercity rail service (National Railroad Passenger Corporation or Amtrak) and more recently to deliver mail (United States Postal Service).

Independent regulatory commissions are unique in that they are administratively independent of all three branches of government and their work combines legislative, executive, and judicial aspects.

Each commission is responsible for establishing the rules and regulations that govern certain aspects of the private sector economy. The rules have the effect of law and therefore are considered quasi-legislative bodies. They also have a quasi-judicial function by conducting hearings and passing judgments in cases arising under their regulations.

The commissioners are appointed by the president with the consent of the Senate; however, they do not report to the president but to Congress. The commission must contain members from both major political parties, and they cannot be removed by the president before the end of their fixed term except for cause.

They were established to provide greater expertise in complex and technical areas. Furthermore, with fixed terms, membership from both parties, and immunity from executive and congressional directives, the goals were that the rules would be more objectively drawn, enforced, and adjudicated.

The goals were not achieved. Powerful interest groups have high stakes in the proceedings of the various commissions. Licenses to operate a television station or to operate a nuclear plant are worth millions of dollars to those groups. Interest groups are, therefore, willing to use significant amounts of their political and financial resources to make sure that the commissioners selected are sympathetic to the industry. Critics have concluded that regulatory agencies in many cases become servants of industry instead of regulating the interest of the larger public.

Further reading: Nathan, Richard P. *The Administrative Presidency.* New York: Wiley, 1983; Rourke, Francis E., ed. *Bureaucratic Power in National Policy Making.* Boston: Little, Brown, 1986; Wilson, James Q. *Bureaucracy: What Government Agencies Do and Why They Do It.* New York: Basic Books, 1989.

—Frank M. Sorrentino

Bureau of the Budget (BOB)

In 1921 the BUDGET AND ACCOUNTING ACT created the Bureau of the Budget (BOB). Responsible for preparing the budget of the United States, the BOB, originally a part of the TREASURY, was moved to the EXECUTIVE OFFICE OF THE PRESIDENT (EOP) in 1939. In 1970 the responsibilities of the BOB were expanded and the office was renamed the OFFICE OF MANAGEMENT AND BUDGET.

Burns, James MacGregor (1918–) *scholar*

James MacGregor Burns is a political scientist and biographer whose works have had significant influence on how political leadership is viewed and analyzed. His mammoth book *Leadership,* published in 1978, helped to establish leadership studies as a recognized interdisciplinary field of research and education. Since retiring from a teaching position at Williams College, Burns has served as a senior scholar at the James MacGregor Burns Academy of Leadership at the University of Maryland, College Park, Maryland.

Burns writes for a broad audience, and his literary accomplishments include the Pulitzer Prize and the National Book Award, for his biographies of Franklin Delano ROOSEVELT, *Roosevelt: The Lion and the Fox* (1956) and *Roosevelt: The Soldier for Freedom.* Burns's service to his intellectual communities includes the past presidency of the American Political Science Association and the International Society of Political Psychology. His service to his community outside of his profession includes a run for Congress as a Democratic nominee in 1958, and attending four Democratic National Conventions as a delegate.

Like the popular historian Arthur M. Schlesinger, Jr., Burns makes no attempt to distinguish his partisan views from his professional analyses. He is a Democrat, proud of the tradition of Franklin Roosevelt, and thoroughly disenchanted with moderates such as Bill CLINTON and Al GORE. A traditional Democratic Party liberal on social issues, Burns believes it to be blatantly obvious that the American nation is in peril from "grotesque" income inequalities and related societal injustices, and he calls for activist government to address these ills. Given the configuration of the political parties and their makeup among the population, it is obvious to Burns that only the DEMOCRATIC PARTY can hope to be relevant to the framing of the necessary solutions.

What is noteworthy about Burns's writings, however, is not their partisanship but their theoretical argument and depth of historical detail. Burns distinguishes between "transactional" or deal-making leadership, and a bolder style of leadership which he terms "transformational." Transforming leadership aims at "sustained and planned social transformation;" it "raises the level of human conduct and ethical aspiration of both leader and led."

Because of the presidency's centrality to the government and his relationship to the people, the presidency is an office of potential transformational leadership. Typically, transformational leaders have emerged in crisis, but it is not necessary, Burns writes, for those that call for transformational leadership to await a crisis. "One of the arts of great leadership," Burns writes, "is the capacity to convert latent crises into visible and dramatic ones." In this way, Franklin Roosevelt became the "Great Educator" as president, and in much the same way Theodore ROOSEVELT and Lyndon JOHNSON focused the nation's attention on problems that a majority of Americans would have preferred to ignore. Great leaders, in fact, might at times create a crisis atmosphere to advance their transformational AGENDA.

In the 21st century, America is in need, Burns has written, of a "transformational president with the necessary transactional skills—a 21st century LBJ." To give the president more power in domestic affairs, but less in foreign and military affairs, where a weak president "often sees his chance for greatness," Burns favors consideration of structural reforms, such as abolishing off-year elections and "institutionalizing the kind of group that helped Kennedy deal with the Cuban missile crisis."

Further reading: Burns, James MacGregor. "Dive in Gents: Boldness Is No Vice." *Washington Post*, 14 May 2000, Outlook section; *Leadership*. New York: Harper & Row, 1978; ———. *Roosevelt: The Lion and the Fox*. New York: Harcourt, Brace, 1956.

—Thomas S. Langston

Burr, Aaron (1756–1836) *politician, U.S. senator, U.S. vice president*
Burr was a politician and man of intrigues from the early period of the American republic whose major public actions had an important impact on the development of the nation and the office of the presidency, particularly the administration of Thomas JEFFERSON. Burr was born in 1756, studied at Princeton University, served in the Revolutionary War, and then after the war commenced his political career in New York City as a lawyer. Burr quickly established a reputation for himself in New York political circles and won election to the U.S. Senate in 1791. Although he would not win reelection in 1797, by this time he was a force in New York State politics, and because of his power and influence he would be placed on the presidential ticket with Jefferson in 1800. It is the election of 1800 where Burr made his first major impact on American politics.

Jefferson's burgeoning political party, the Democratic-Republicans, in order to win New York State (key to winning the presidency), nominated Burr as Jefferson's running mate in the 1800 election. The discipline of the partisan electors was too strong, as Jefferson and Burr both received the same amount of electoral votes, 73 each. Prior to the Twelfth Amendment to the Constitution, electors did not vote separately for president and vice president. Rather, the top vote-getter would be president and the second in line, vice president. With the tie, the choice for president was thrown to the House of Representatives, a lame-duck session controlled by the rival FEDERALIST PARTY. Although Jefferson had been the Democratic-Republicans' clear choice for president, Federalists decided to create havoc and considered promoting Burr to the presidency. Burr did not publicly disavow these plans and thereby earned Jefferson's long-standing distrust and antipathy. In the end it was Jefferson's political rival, the Federalist Alexander HAMILTON, who persuaded the congressional Federalists to support Jefferson for president, leaving the vice presidency for Burr. The ambiguous and potentially destabilizing outcome of this election led directly to the passage of the Twelfth Amendment, which, among other things, created separate Electoral College votes for president and vice president.

Being largely cut out of the administration by Jefferson (a response to Burr's duplicitous behavior in the aftermath of the 1800 election), Burr accepted the overtures of New York Federalists to run for governor of New York in 1804. Burr's political ambition was quite large and Federalists wanted to wrest political power away from the Democratic-Republicans, so a marriage of political convenience was arranged. Alexander Hamilton, a chief rival of Burr's even before he helped to sway congressional Federalists to Jefferson's side in the 1800 election, entered the picture again in opposition to Burr. Hamilton swayed Federalists away from Aaron Burr a second time, now toward the Democratic-Republican candidate for governor, Morgan Lewis. Lewis won the election, but the acrimonious feud between Burr and Hamilton led to the former challenging the latter to a duel. In July 1804, Alexander Hamilton, a major American founder and leading light of the Federalist Party, died after dueling with Burr. Even though he rid himself of his arch rival, Burr's political career was now effectively over; however, he would continue to exert influence over the nation's political course over the next several years.

Although wanted in both New York and New Jersey on charges stemming from the duel, Burr remained vice president and was called into service in that capacity later in 1804 to preside over the impeachment trial of Supreme Court Justice Samuel Chase. The IMPEACHMENT of Chase represented a critical juncture in American constitutionalism. Chase was a Federalist partisan despised by the Democratic-Republicans, who sought to remove him from office for his political views. Democratic-Republicans, including Jefferson, hoped that Burr could be counted on to preside over the trial in such manner as to assure Chase's conviction. To sweeten the deal for Burr, Jefferson offered him several patronage appointments in the Louisiana territory, which Burr accepted. Nevertheless, Burr presided over the trial of Chase with strict observation of the law, thereby making it impossible for the politically motivated prosecution of Chase to succeed. Chase was acquitted and thus did Burr help to preserve the sanctity of an independent judiciary.

Denied the vice presidency for Jefferson's second term, Burr devoted his attention to a still not fully understood conspiracy in the Western states of the United States, one which he had already been planning prior to the impeachment trial. The conspiracy, as far as historians can gather, was most likely an attempt by Burr, with the aid of General James Wilkinson (governor of the Louisiana territory but also in the pay of the Spanish government), among others, to break the Western states away from the Union, forming an independent state under the command of Burr, that would then make war on Spain in order to seize Mexico. (A more generous interpretation, however, suggests that Burr's plan was more likely just an attack on Spanish territories rather than also a secessionist movement.) To this end, Burr traveled through the West in 1805 gathering supporters for his cryptic plans. He also met with representatives of Spain and England at various points to solicit support for his schemes. Burr's movements and meetings caused much suspicion throughout the West and Jefferson soon became aware of Burr's intrigues.

By late 1806, Wilkinson abandoned Burr, writing to Jefferson about conspiracies in the West. Jefferson, compiling anecdotal evidence against Burr for some time, issued a proclamation warning citizens against attacking Spain and authorized federal and state officials to capture the leaders of the conspiracy (although Burr was not mentioned by name). In time, in 1807, Burr was in the possession of federal authorities and brought before Supreme Court Chief Justice John MARSHALL on two charges, treason and a misdemeanor charge of preparing to engage in military action against Mexico. Although Burr was acquitted, since the government was unable to prove the charges according to Marshall's strict standards, his trial was significant for two reasons, both stemming from the bitter confrontation between the Federalist chief justice and the Democratic-Republican president. First, the trial was not Marshall's shining moment and he displayed considerable partisanship (although Jefferson did so as well). This led Jefferson and Republicans to push for reforms of the judiciary making judges more dependent on presidential authority and limiting their terms. Even though these reforms came to naught, they formed an important piece of the Democratic-Republican perspective on popular democracy and the courts, a legacy which survives to the current day. Second, the case established an important precedent for EXECUTIVE PRIVILEGE. Marshall had allowed during the trial that the president should respond to a subpoena by the defense. While Jefferson did send the documents requested, he never formally responded to the subpoena, maintaining that the executive reserved the right to decide which documents would be shared and which withheld. The Burr case would be used by later presidents to defend their right to executive privilege.

Aaron Burr had henceforth no significant role in public affairs. He died in New York in 1836.

Further reading: Abernethy, Thomas Perkins. *The Burr Conspiracy.* New York: Oxford University Press, 1954; Johnstone, Robert M. Jr. *Jefferson and the Presidency: Leadership in the Young Republic.* Ithaca, N.Y.: Cornell University Press, 1978; McDonald, Forrest. *The Presidency of Thomas Jefferson.* Lawrence: University Press of Kansas, 1976.

—Michael J. Korzi

Bush, Barbara (1925–) *first lady*
American first lady (1989–93), the wife of George Herbert Walker Bush, 41st president of the United States and U.S. vice president (1981–89), and the mother of President George Walker Bush (2000–) and Governor of Florida Jeb Bush (1998–), Barbara Pierce was born on June 8, 1925, in Rye, New York, to Marvin Pierce, who later became president of McCall Corporation, and Pauline Robinson Pierce.

Barbara Pierce attended Ashley Hall boarding school in South Carolina and attended but did not graduate from Smith College in Northampton, Massachusetts. She married George Herbert Walker Bush on January 6, 1945. In 1948 the couple moved to Texas, where George Bush went into the oil business and Barbara Bush focused her attention on raising their children: George, Robin, John (Jeb), Neil, Marvin, and Dorothy. Their daughter, Robin, died in 1953 at the age of three from leukemia.

Probably due in no small part to her warm image as "everybody's grandmother," Barbara Bush was one of the most popular FIRST LADIES in recent times. The American people and the media seemed to appreciate her friendly, forthright style. When she entered the White House in 1989, she adopted a more traditional role as first lady and called working for a more literate America the "most important issue we have." As wife of the vice president, she had selected the promotion of literacy as her special cause, and she continued her involvement with many organizations devoted to the cause as first lady, becoming honorary chairman of the Barbara Bush Foundation for Family Literacy. A strong advocate of volunteerism, Mrs. Bush helped many other charitable causes as first lady, including the homeless, the elderly, and school volunteer programs.

Barbara Bush remains active in charitable organizations, serving on the Boards of AmeriCares and the Mayo

First Lady Barbara Bush *(Library of Congress)*

Clinic, and continues her prominent role in the Barbara Bush Foundation. She lives with her husband in Houston, Texas.

Further reading: Bush, Barbara. *Barbara Bush: A Memoir.* New York: Scribner's Sons, 1994; Gould, Lewis. *American First Ladies,* 2d ed. New York: Routledge, 2001; Radcliffe, Donnie. *Simply Barbara Bush.* New York: Warner Books, 1990.

—Stephanie Mullen

Bush, George H. W. (1924–) *forty-first U.S. president*

Born into wealth and power (his father was a U.S. Senator from Connecticut) in 1924, in Milton, Massachusetts, George Bush served one term as president from 1989 to 1993. A decorated hero of WORLD WAR II, Bush, the nation's 41st president, is father of George W. BUSH, the nation's 43rd president.

George Bush had the best résumé in Washington: Congressman, U.S. envoy to China, national chairman of the REPUBLICAN PARTY, director of the CIA, and VICE PRESIDENT for eight years. Critics wondered what he had

accomplished in all these impressive posts: He left few footprints, they said.

Tall at 6'2", thin, to the manor born, educated at Yale, Bush was a man of uncompromising grayness. He was elected in the afterglow of the Reagan revolution, but he was not a Reaganite true believer. Bush was more cautious, more moderate, more pragmatic than REAGAN. Bush was a manager at a time when the nation needed a leader, a status quo president in a time of change, a minimalist in a momentous time. The end of the COLD WAR opened a window of opportunity to exert creative leadership, but Bush was shackled by a vastly depleted resource base (the legacy of Reagan's economic mismanagement) and an intellectual cupboard that was bare (no vision for a post–cold war future). Bush often seemed a passive observer in a dramatically changing world.

Bush was at his best when he had a clear goal to achieve (e.g., the Gulf War), a goal imposed upon him by events, but when it came time for him to choose, to set priorities, to decide on a direction, he floundered. As conservative columnist George Will commented, "When the weight of the (presidency) is put upon a figure as flimsy as George Bush, the presidency buckles. . . ."

George Bush served as a managerial president, not a leader. In a time that cried out for vision, Bush seemed paralyzed. There was no clear aspiration to accomplish any grand goals. Bush's successes include the Persian GULF WAR and a winding down of the cold war, but his failures—his inability to build on the concept of a New World Order or to counter rising deficits, his lack of a domestic AGENDA, and his standoffish attitude as the economy tumbled—opened the door to Bush's opponents in the 1992 election. When it came time for the public to render judgment on President Bush, it chose a relative unknown instead of him.

There seemed to be no central core to Bush, no clear set of beliefs. As Bert A. Rockman noted, "Bush seems to be not well anchored by a strong set of personal values that put him in control of his circumstances. Instead, he seems to be largely buffeted by circumstances, making his choices to be more susceptible to a raw calculus of what he personally has to lose or gain from them."

Bush was a reactive president, not an initiator, a caretaker or maintaining president, not a visionary. He had an aimless style, which failed to provide clear direction to his staff or to the machinery of government. How could someone with so much government experience, with such an impressive résumé, be so devoid of ideas and have so few policy preferences? Although Bush did have the most impressive résumé in politics, it is equally true that he left few footprints along the way. Bush was a manager, not a leader; he executed other people's ideas, not his own. When he was elected, Bush had precious few ideas that he was determined to translate into policy. His was not an idea-driven administration. President Bush wanted to better manage the status quo.

Bush was pulled between his temperament, which sought stability and continuity, and the demands of the times, which called for dramatic change. It was not a good fit between the leader and the times.

The Bush leadership style—cautious, prudent, and managerial—did indeed seem a poor fit for times that begged for vision. The procedural presidency of George Bush turned out to be process-centered, but not idea-driven. The times called for leadership, yet Bush supplied prudence. As events moved rapidly, Bush moved slowly. Bush liked to play the insider game (he has been referred to as the Rolodex president), not the grand strategy game. He often acted late; therefore, the United States was given less input as events unfolded around the world. Soon, the other powers sensed that they no longer needed to defer to the United States: Germany unified, and the United States watched; China repressed dissidents, and the United States issued a mild reproach; Eastern Europe exploded, and the United States watched. Bush's style of leadership was often criticized as being more reactive than proactive; more adrift than imaginative. Bush's was called the Revlon presidency because of his practice of offering only cosmetic solutions to problems. *U.S. News & World Report* called Bush's first year "The Year of Living Timorously." The Bush team was a fairly small, close-knit group of longtime acquaintances, all highly professional. Bush preferred to work with a few key, close advisers—Secretary of State James BAKER, National Security Adviser Brent Scowcroft, Defense Secretary Dick CHENEY, and Joint Chiefs of Staff General Colin POWELL—all of whom were strong in FOREIGN AFFAIRS, but less interested in DOMESTIC POLICY. Their driving theme seemed to be, in Bert Rockman's words, "to do nothing well." Their primary goal was not to accomplish great things, but to protect and better manage the status quo. This would have been acceptable in normal times, but the world was going through revolutionary convulsions. The times, and U.S. interests, demanded a leader. Instead, the United States got a manager.

Bush had few deeply held policy beliefs. In domestic policy he alienated conservatives by reneging on his "no new taxes" pledge, helped undo a Reagan-era excess by resolving the savings and loan crisis, and promoted "a kinder, gentler America" than his predecessor. But domestically his policy was less rather than more.

It was in foreign affairs that President Bush felt most at home. By the late 1980s, the tectonic plates of the international system were shifting dramatically. The Soviet Union was breaking apart, Eastern Europe was achieving independence, democracy was taking root in South America, and new powers in economics (Japan) and politics (a more united Western Europe) were rising. It was a time of extraordinary events that created an opportunity for a visionary leader to shape a new world order.

In his inaugural address, the new president spoke of a new breeze that was blowing around the world, refreshed by freedom. Only the United States, Bush asserted, could provide the leadership necessary to meet the challenges of this new world order. The United States had leadership, but, Bush noted, it had "more will than wallet."

It is true that Bush boldly exerted presidential prerogative by unilaterally ordering the invasion of Panama in 1989. The United States deposed Manuel Noriega and brought him to the United States for trial on drug charges. But where was the far-reaching vision to animate U.S. policy in this new and changing world?

In 1989 the Soviet Union collapsed. Only China, North Korea, and Cuba remained as communist strongholds. The West had won the cold war, and George Bush presided over this seminal event. But what would follow (replace) the cold war?

In August 1990 Iraq invaded Kuwait. George Bush put together a multilateral coalition, and in January 1991 this coalition invaded Iraq and drove the Iraqis back, out of Kuwait. Bush had done a masterful job of coalition building.

President George H. W. Bush and Vice President Dan Quayle *(George Bush Presidential Library)*

After the successful war, Bush's popularity rose to an unprecedented 90 percent. He seemed all but invincible, but as the economy soured, Bush's popularity fell. Domestic problems replaced the jubilation over the war, and as Bush had no response to the nation's domestic and economic problems, the public grew increasingly impatient.

As president when the Soviet Union's power dissolved and the cold war ended, Bush had a distinct advantage over his predecessors. Gone was the overwhelming burden of cold war confrontation, but Bush still faced enormous problems, not the least of which was the economic legacy of the Reagan years. Facing economic insolvency, Bush pursued a more cooperative, bargaining, coalition-building style of international leadership. The United States was in the lead on this, but the style of leadership was more one of bargaining than commanding. With Soviet power in retreat, the pressures on Bush were eased, and U.S. minimalist hegemony in a bargaining atmosphere emerged.

Structurally, the bipolar world had collapsed, and either a loose unipolar world (with the United States at the helm) or a diffuse multipolar world (with strong U.S. influence) would emerge. In this new world, the United States had less power to impose its will, but was in a heightened position to persuade. This shift in the nature of U.S. power called for a shift in the early stages of the Gulf crisis. In the end though, Bush retreated into the foggy certainty of old methods: force and war.

Given the dramatically new circumstances facing George Bush, could we have reasonably expected him to devise a new policy approach and stick with it? Bush's early efforts at developing a new world order reflected a new approach to a new era. However, Bush was afraid he might be wrong, so he abandoned hope for a new model and left it in the ashes of war.

As the Soviet Union collapsed, it became clear that President Bush had an enormous window of opportunity to initiate dramatic change. With high popularity ratings and a weak opposition, he had room to maneuver politically. With the end of the cold war, Bush had more freedom to move in new directions than any of his predecessors since Harry S TRUMAN. He could have set the political agenda for the nation and, perhaps, the world, but Bush was a reactor, not an initiator. To his credit, he reacted well to the Gulf crisis, pursuing a model form of leadership in an age of limits. To his detriment, he could not dream grand dreams, set new standards, or pursue bold changes. This lost opportunity may yet come back to haunt the United States. As Alan Tonelson notes:

> Bush's foreign policy conservatism is exacting considerable and mounting costs on America. It is, after all, a conservatism that is less reasoned than felt—or perhaps, more accurately, learned by rote. Consequently, it is less

a strategy than an impulse. Indeed, Bush's incessant, almost ritualistic invocation of cold war ideals—collective security, stability, international law, and above all, United States world leadership—indicates that his conservatism is becoming an intellectual cage. Mantras seem to be in command, instead of ideas.

The tragedy of Bush's term is the tragedy of missed opportunities. Bush was at the helm when the Soviet empire collapsed, when Eastern Europe achieved independence, when Western Europe united, and when Latin America embraced democracy. It was an opportunity to engage in visionary leadership, a chance to create a new world order, and an opportunity to refashion the way the international system operated. Such opportunities come along rarely, but Bush was the wrong man for the times; a cautious manager when a visionary leader was required. After flirting with transforming leadership (the early days of the Gulf War), Bush quickly retreated into the false security of politics as usual. This was a style of leadership almost totally inappropriate for the times.

Further reading: Duffy, Michael. *Marching in Place: The Status Quo Presidency of George Bush.* New York: Simon & Schuster, 1992; Greene, John Robert. *The Presidency of George Bush.* Lawrence: University Press of Kansas, 2000; Parmet, Herbert S. *George Bush: The Life of a Lone Star Yankee.* New York: Scribner, 1997.

Bush, George W. (1946–) *forty-third U.S. president*
George Walker Bush was born in July 1946, in New Haven, Connecticut, while his father was an undergraduate at Yale University. The younger George Bush grew up in Texas. First in Midland and then in Houston, George W. imbibed the frontier culture of the Texas oil business. Like his father before him, he "prepped" for Yale by attending the Phillips Academy at Andover, Massachusetts. At Andover, Bush, nicknamed "Lip" for his garrulous and sarcastic manner, was a social leader and head cheerleader. At Yale he played baseball and was tapped for Skull and Bones, the college's most exclusive secret society.

With the possibility of being drafted into the Vietnam War ever present for American men of his generation, Bush found a comparatively safe haven in the Texas Air National Guard in 1968. From 1968 to 1973 he flew fighter jets, helped out in the political campaigns of family friends, and lived the life of a carefree bachelor. In 1973 he enrolled in Harvard University for a two-year master's in business administration.

From 1975 to 1986, Bush attempted to emulate his father's success in the independent oil business and to join the true family business, politics. On both fronts, he failed in these early efforts. His oil company, Arbusto, drilled too many dry wells to turn a profit, and when he turned to politics he was soundly defeated in 1978 when he sought to represent Midland in the U.S. House of Representatives. Bush was more successful in his personal life, marrying Laura Welch, a teacher and librarian from Midland, in 1977. The couple became the parents of twin daughters, Barbara and Jenna, four years later.

In the mid to late 1980s, George W. Bush's life changed. What his detractors said about his past in his run for the presidency was largely true. In his 30s, Bush had been a habitual drinker with a sharp tongue and a quick temper. When he reached 40, however, he stopped drinking and began to take a deep, personal interest in RELIGION. (Bush, raised Episcopalian, is a Methodist.)

Out of the oil business by 1986, Bush found greater success in his subsequent ventures. He was an aide in his father's presidential campaign of 1988 and continued to serve his father unofficially during his administration. In December 1991, when President Bush needed to ease out of office his CHIEF OF STAFF, John Sununu, it was the younger George Bush who executed the presidential wish. The younger Bush also at last made his fortune, through part ownership of the Texas Rangers baseball team. From 1989 to 1994 Bush was managing general director of the team. When the team was sold in 1998, Bush had a $15 million payday.

In 1994 Bush won the Texas governorship, against incumbent Ann Richards. Bush's strategy in that election was to start campaigning early and to stick to a simple platform throughout the lengthy campaign: reform of education, juvenile crime, welfare, and "lawsuit abuse." Bush, moreover, scored points by treating his opponent with respect, while she seemed incapable of taking Bush seriously as an opponent. With 53.5 percent of the vote, Bush assumed the governorship in 1995 for a four-year term.

The Texas governorship is constitutionally weak, forcing its occupant to work closely with the legislative branch and its leader, the lieutenant governor, or risk becoming irrelevant in Austin. Bush thrived in the office, establishing a close relationship with Bob Bullock, the Democratic lieutenant governor. In 1998 Bullock crossed party lines to endorse Bush for reelection. With 68 percent of the vote, including 49 percent of the Hispanic vote, Bush became the first Texas governor to win consecutive four-year terms.

Looking towards the 2000 presidential campaign, Bush became the early leader among Republicans. Bush, a moderate conciliator, was appealing to party elders in part because of his famous name, and in part because the value of moderation had been underlined in 1998. In that year, the public rallied behind the beleaguered president and the DEMOCRATIC PARTY, in reaction to the House Republicans' IMPEACHMENT of the president.

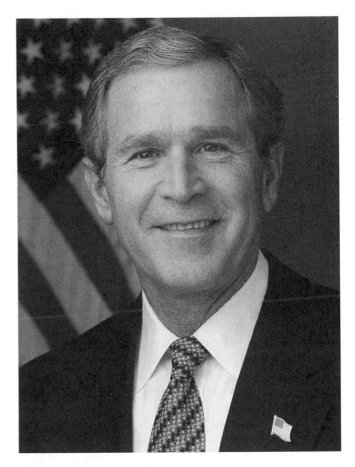

President George W. Bush. *(Photo by Eric Draper, White House)*

As in his initial run for the governorship of Texas, Bush worked with his adviser, Karl Rove, to identify key AGENDA items, and ran a determined campaign against his foremost Republican challenger, Senator John McCain, and the Democratic nominee, Vice President Al GORE. In the general election, Bush won the Electoral College balloting after losing the popular vote, 48.4 percent to 47.9 percent. The outcome in the ELECTORAL COLLEGE hinged, moreover, on Florida's contested tally. Finally, on December 12, 2000, five of the nine members of the Supreme Court called a halt to recounting in Florida, effectively naming Bush the victor. During a truncated transition, president-elect Bush and vice president-elect Dick Cheney appointed a diverse and experienced cabinet and began to reach out to Democrats in Washington.

From January 20, 2001, to September 11, 2001, the George W. Bush presidency was focused on implementing his CAMPAIGN PLEDGES. He launched a "charm offensive" on Capitol Hill and worked effectively with Congress to cut taxes, achieving the clearest victory of this stage of his presidency. Bush also lobbied Congress for other items on his agenda, achieving at least partial success on a faith-based welfare provision, nationally mandated school testing, and a national missile defense. At the same time, Bush worked to solidify his support on the right wing of the REPUBLICAN PARTY. Bush's first substantive act as president was to sign an executive order banning U.S. government funds from use by international groups that supported abortion. On environmental issues, Bush's early steps, which included revoking a regulation that aimed to reduce arsenic in drinking water, caused considerable controversy.

In May 2001 Vermont Senator James Jeffords switched from the Republican to the Democratic Party, giving control of the Senate to his new party. With the return of DIVIDED GOVERNMENT, and an economy headed toward recession, public approval of the president dropped during the summer. After the August congressional recess, the Gallup Poll showed Bush with a new low in public approval. A majority of Americans did not think the president understood "problems of people like you."

The Bush presidency was altered dramatically on SEPTEMBER 11, 2001. Bush responded to the terrorist attacks of that day by issuing an ultimatum to the Taliban government of Afghanistan, which was providing refuge for the terrorist organization responsible for the attacks. "They will hand over the terrorists," Bush said, "or they will share in their fate." In a remarkably successful military operation, Bush backed up his words. U.S. troops, working with anti-Taliban forces from Afghanistan, caused the collapse of Taliban rule in Afghanistan. To coordinate the U.S. effort against terrorism, President Bush, moreover, signed an EXECUTIVE ORDER creating a new OFFICE OF HOMELAND SECURITY. In November 2001 the president established military tribunals to try certain suspected terrorists and unilaterally withdrew the United States from the Anti-Ballistic Missile Treaty, against weak protestations from Russia. Some observers saw a president enlarged by circumstance; others, such as R. W. Apple of *The New York Times*, wondered if Bush were merely "growing into the clothes of the presidency."

In the spring of 2003 the United States, after failing to gain UNITED NATIONS support for an invasion of Iraq, launched an invasion with what the president called a "coalition of the willing." Iraq had long been a thorn in the side of the United States and was suspected of amassing weapons of mass destruction. In a preemptive assault, the United States, Great Britain, and others swept through Iraq and the war ended less than a month after it began.

After a little more than two years of the George W. Bush presidency, the president's future is uncertain. His father led the nation to victory in the Gulf War, enjoyed enormous popularity as a consequence, and was voted out of office in 1992 partially due to voter concern about the U.S. economy. George W. Bush knows this history painfully well and will do all in his power to avoid its repetition.

Further reading: Minutaglio, Bill. *First Son: George W. Bush and the Bush Family Dynasty*. New York: Times Books, 1999; Mitchell, Elizabeth. *W: Revenge of the Bush Dynasty*. New York: Hyperion, 2000.

—Thomas S. Langston

Bush v. Gore, 531 U.S. (2000)

The presidential election of 2000 was one of the most bizarre and contested elections in U.S. history. On election night the results were so close that the winner could not be determined. At the end of the evening, the election hinged on the results of the vote in the state of Florida. At first, the networks awarded the state to Democrat Al GORE, only moments later to withdraw the announcement, followed by giving the state to Republican George W. BUSH, followed later by an announcement that the vote was too close to call.

In dispute were the contested ballots in several areas of the state. With George W. Bush slightly ahead, the Republicans argued that the existing vote, and the award of the state to Bush, should proceed. This was the view of Florida Secretary of State Kathleen Harris as well. Harris was also one of the heads of the Bush campaign team in Florida.

The Democrats protested, calling for a recount. They believed that a true count of all the votes in Florida would give Gore the state, and the presidency.

It took 36 days and several different court decisions before the contest was decided. At first the question of how to proceed went to the courts in Florida, and in general, they sided with the Gore position. When these cases reached the Florida Supreme Court, the Gore team felt confident, as a majority of that court was composed of Democrats. Indeed the Florida Supreme Court did side with the Gore position (count more votes), and the Bush team appealed to the United States Supreme Court for reversal.

The Supreme Court is comprised of a majority of justices who are Republicans, and the Bush team felt that was their best chance for a victory. After sending the case back to the Florida Supreme Court, the case again landed on the desk of the U.S. Supreme Court, and as time was running out, it became clear that the Supreme Court would likely have the last word in determining the winner of the presidential contest.

In *Bush v. Gore* (531 U.S., 2000), the Supreme Court ultimately decided in favor of the Bush position, thereby effectively precluding any further challenges by the Gore team and giving the presidency to George W. Bush. The irony was that to reach its conclusion, the Supreme Court overturned one of its most cherished principles that it had upheld time after time in the past few years: state sovereignty. The Court had consistently sided with states over the federal government in cases where states' rights or state supremacy were concerned, but in *Bush v. Gore,* the Court overturned a decision by the Florida Supreme Court and handed the presidency to George W. Bush.

In a dissenting opinion, Justice Stevens noted the damage done to respect for the law by this case, writing,

> The endorsement of that [Bush's] position by the majority of this Court can only lend credence to the most cynical appraisal of the work of judges throughout the land. It is confidence in the men and women who administer the judicial system that is the true backbone of the rule of law. Time will one day heal the wound to that confidence that will be inflicted by today's decision. One thing, however, is certain. Although we may never know with complete certainty the identity of the winner of this year's presidential election, the identity of the loser is perfectly clear. It is the Nation's confidence in the judge as an impartial guardian of the rule of law.

See also CHAD.

Further reading: Dershowitz, Alan M. *Supreme Injustice: How the High Court Hijacked Election 2000.* New York: Oxford University Press, 2001; Gillman, Howard. *The Votes That Counted: How the Supreme Court Decided the 2000 Presidential Election.* Chicago: University of Chicago Press, 2001; Posner, Richard A. *Breaking the Deadlock: The 2000 Election, The Constitution, and the Courts.* Princeton, N.J.: Princeton University Press, 2001.

business policy

Business policy refers to the relationship between government and business. In terms of the fundamentals of our political economy, because Americans believe so firmly in private property, free enterprise, and competitive markets, the viability of capitalism is a given and presidents try to reassure corporate America by appointing a friendly voice as secretary of the Treasury. President EISENHOWER, who was impressed with entrepreneurs who managed huge corporations, appointed many successful businessmen to his CABINET. President KENNEDY appointed Douglas Dillon, a Republican, as Treasury secretary, and President CLINTON appointed Robert Rubin, a Wall Street brokerage executive.

Yet, in terms of partisan politics, arguably Republicans are more sympathetic to business interests because Democrats get electoral and financial support from organized labor. Both Franklin D. ROOSEVELT and Harry TRU-MAN wanted to nurture organized labor. For FDR, reforming capitalism meant a host of new regulatory agencies, unionization (National Labor Relations Board), and protection for workers through minimum wage/maximum hours laws. Truman vetoed (it was overridden) the Taft-Hartley Act of 1947, which restricted strikes imperiling the national economy and seized private steel mills to prevent a work stoppage during the KOREAN WAR.

The government-business relationships can become testy during inflationary periods, such as President Kennedy's confrontation with Big Steel over its desire to raise prices. Kennedy later made amends by advocating a reduction of corporate and individual income taxes, which were enacted under President Lyndon JOHNSON. Johnson also "jawboned" big business to limit price increases, although what doomed LBJ's voluntary wage-price guidelines was the refusal of certain large unions to accept wage restraint. Though sympathetic to corporate America, President NIXON took the unprecedented peacetime step of imposing wage-price controls to curb inflation. He also signed landmark environmental legislation imposing expensive air and water quality regulations on businesses. However, economists began arguing that onerous governmental regulations were hurting business, disrupting markets, and causing inflation. Their agitation for "DEREGULATION" of industries like trucking and the airlines had its first success under Democrat Jimmy CARTER and continued with Republican Ronald REAGAN. As a determined conservative, Reagan believed that most federal regulations discouraged the spirit of entrepreneurship in America.

Once President George W. BUSH shifted his attention from the War on Terrorism to the lackluster economy, his nearly $700 billion stimulus package explicitly appealed to investors by recommending the end of double taxation on corporate dividends. President Clinton was arguably the most pro-business Democratic president. The 1990s saw the stock market climb to its highest levels, the nation experience its most sustained period of prosperity, and the return (since 1969) of balanced federal budgets. In many respects Clinton acted more like a Republican in his economic stewardship, particularly his embrace of the North American Free Trade Accord despite the opposition of unions and congressional Democrats.

Further reading: Cohen, Jeffrey E. *Politics and Economic Policy in the United States,* 2d ed. Boston: Houghton Mifflin Company, 2000; Lindeen, James W. *Governing America's Economy.* Englewood Cliffs, N.J.: Prentice-Hall, 1994.

—Raymond Tatalovich

C

cabinet

The cabinet is a group of department secretaries, the head administrators of the major government agencies, who also serve the president in an advisory capacity. The cabinet is not mentioned in the Constitution nor is it required by law. It is a creature of custom and is, consequently, a weak institution.

Each president uses it in different ways. The cabinet was first formed by George Washington, and it included the secretaries of STATE, TREASURY, and WAR, and the attorney general.

By 2002 it had grown to 15 members including the vice president, the attorney general, and the secretaries of STATE, TREASURY, DEFENSE, INTERIOR, AGRICULTURE, COMMERCE, LABOR, HEALTH AND HUMAN SERVICES, HOUSING AND URBAN DEVELOPMENT, TRANSPORTATION, ENERGY, EDUCATION, and VETERAN AFFAIRS. In the past, the UNITED NATIONS ambassador has had cabinet status though he or she does not head a major department. Ironically, George Bush, a former UN ambassador, removed it from cabinet status.

Among recent presidents, Franklin ROOSEVELT used it sparingly as an advisory group, while Dwight D. EISENHOWER used it as his principal vehicle for advisement and decision-making. John KENNEDY believed that cabinet meetings were a "waste of time." Lyndon JOHNSON held regular meetings but never discussed the Vietnam War.

Richard NIXON initially indicated he would revive the cabinet; however, he used it very infrequently as a formal advisement bureau, preferring the NATIONAL SECURITY COUNCIL, the committee of the principal government officials that handles national defense, and the Domestic Council as alternatives. Nixon also unsuccessfully proposed the creation of a Super Cabinet to increase coordination and to reduce the cabinet to a more manageable size.

Jimmy CARTER held regular meetings; however, it was not his principal advisement body. Ronald REAGAN held regular cabinet meetings and used it more for advice than

any other recent President. George H. W. BUSH held regular cabinet meetings but preferred to use his staff as the major vehicle for advice and decision-making. Bill CLINTON utilized the cabinet sporadically. George W. BUSH, with his focus on the War on Terrorism, has used the National Security Council as his principal source of advice.

Beginning with Andrew JACKSON, presidents have developed a KITCHEN CABINET, composed of close friends and advisers. Presidents believe these groups and the White House staff are more loyal to the president and his agenda.

The cabinet has not lived up to expectations of many scholars on American government, and there are several reasons for this. Cabinet members must be approved by the Senate. Therefore, a president must negotiate with the Senate leaders and party leaders throughout the country. The results are that many positions are given to individuals whom the president may hardly know or trust. Also, because a president may need to offer a position to a group that he needs the support of for the upcoming election or to help pass legislation that he desires, these individuals tend to be more loyal to their political benefactors than to the president. Bill Clinton appointed Donna Shalala to Health and Human Services despite her reluctance on welfare reform. George Bush appointed Colin POWELL as secretary of State despite his support for the ABM Treaty.

The cabinet's relationship with Congress was an unresolved issue. Congress's authority to investigate and to authorize budgets meant that they needed access to the executive departments. WASHINGTON preferred that all communications occur though him. This proved to be ineffective because of the increasing complexity of the work of the departments. In addition, beginning with Secretary of the Treasury HAMILTON, cabinet officials have found that direct communications with Congress are a more effective means of promoting the president's AGENDA and dealing with Congress's constitutional responsibilities.

The issue of whether the president should have exclusive authority in removing cabinet officials has been contentious. Presidents have argued that their responsibility to make sure that "the laws are faithfully executed" gives them this authority. Congressional advocates claim that they are given the constitutional authority to confirm appointees, which implies they should be involved in any termination decision. In addition, they have the power to investigate, impeach, and create or destroy executive departments. This issue came to a head in the IMPEACHMENT OF ANDREW JOHNSON. Congress had passed the TENURE OF OFFICE ACT (1867), which required that the Senate had to confirm a successor before the president could remove a cabinet secretary. When Johnson removed Secretary of War Edwin Stanton, Congress impeached Johnson. In his trial in the Senate he was not convicted by one vote.

The Supreme Court has visited this issue on several occasions. In *MYERS V. UNITED STATES* (1926), the Court, headed by Chief Justice and former President William Howard Taft, seemed to find that President Wilson had unlimited authority to remove a postmaster.

In *Humphrey's Executor v. United States* (1935), however, the Court held that President Roosevelt did not have the right to remove officials from the Federal Trade Commission, because it is a regulatory agency which is given legislative powers by the Congress.

In 1958 the Supreme Court further clarified the president's REMOVAL POWER. President TRUMAN had appointed Myron Wiener to serve on the War Claims Commission and he was later removed from office by Eisenhower. In *Wiener v. United States* (1958), the Court ruled that if officials are engaged in adjudicative (judicial) functions, presidents may not remove them for political reasons.

In *Morrison v. Olson* (1988), the Court upheld the INDEPENDENT COUNSEL provision of the ETHICS IN GOVERNMENT ACT OF 1978, thereby further limiting the president's right to dismiss the independent counsel. Chief Justice Rehnquist concluded that the president's ability to govern was not damaged by his inability to remove an independent counsel. Some have speculated that the Court may find other positions that may be protected from presidential removal authority.

Former vice president Charles G. DAWES said, "The members of the Cabinet are a president's natural enemy." This is partly true because cabinet members often adopt the views and interests of their departments. They become advocates of the programs and needs of their bureaucracies which may be in competition with other cabinet members for higher budgets and presidential support. A cabinet member is responsible not only to the president but also to his or her department. In addition, he or she is accountable to Congress, which approves the appointment, creates the department along with its legal authority, and approves the budget. Thus, the cabinet member, if he or she is to gain the loyalty of his or her department, must become an effective champion of its interests and needs rather than being exclusively the president's person. Consequently, presidents have been wary of cabinet members' advice. President LINCOLN, who had similar problems with his cabinet, once remarked "Seven nays, one aye; the ayes have it." The cabinet will continue to remain an institution of ambiguous significance and status.

Further reading: Bennett, Anthony J. *The American President's Cabinet from Kennedy to Bush.* New York: St. Martin's Press, 1996; Fenno, Richard E. *The President's Cabinet.* Cambridge, Mass.: Harvard University Press, 1959; Grossman, Mark. *The Encyclopedia of the United States Cabinet.* Santa Barbara, Calif.: ABC-CLIO, 2000; Koenig, Louis W. *The Chief Executive.* Fort Worth, Tex.: Harcourt Brace College Publishers, 1996; Reich, Robert B. *Locked in the Cabinet.* Thorndike, Maine: Thorndike Press, 1997.

—Frank M. Sorrentino

cabinet formation, theories of

According to Richard E. Fenno, CABINET appointments are shaped by five variables: (1) Presidential influence—a president may be closely involved in selecting a nominee or give the position only casual attention. (2) Incentives and drawbacks—potential nominees must weigh the likelihood of lower income and the ability to affect policy, as well as the prestige of the appointment, some cabinet positions being more important than others. (3) The conditions of the time—nominees may sense an obligation to serve when a crisis confronts the nation or be willing to accept an appointment when the national climate shifts, e.g., to one favorable to business, as in the EISENHOWER years. (4) The cabinet norm—this implies that a nominee must have the qualifications to carry out the appointment, as well as working with others in the cabinet. (5) Availability and balance—the former refers to having the obvious qualities expected for the position, e.g., the secretary of agriculture must come from a state with a substantial agricultural economy. The latter pertains to a cabinet having an accepted mix of geography, personal loyalty, party involvement, and appropriate expertise.

In Nelson W. Polsby's view there are five theories or bases on which presidents form their cabinets. The client-oriented approach assumes that cabinet posts should be filled by persons who have substantial standing with the clientele that each department serves and will operate to satisfy that constituency. For example, the secretary of agriculture should have links to the agricultural sector. The specialist alternative fills the cabinet with individuals that have expertise with the department that they are to lead; this appointment will have internalized the norms of performance expected by its department and the professionals associated with that agency. The third option is appointment of Washington careerists, persons who have worked inside the Beltway for several years and will during their careers serve in more than one presidential administration. Joseph Califano and Richard CHENEY are examples. Presidential ambassadors are the fourth category. These are longtime acquaintances of the president with whom he has the greatest confidence since he knows them well and they have demonstrated loyalty to him. Finally, there are the symbolic appointments that represent specific segments of society, such as women, blacks, and Hispanics. These groups are recognized as deserving representation in a presidential cabinet, and their appointments serve to shore up presidential support with those symbolic groups. No cabinet is composed entirely of only one of these forms of cabinet appointments, but the mix from these groups offer clues to a president's preferences and priorities.

Further reading: Cohen, Jeffrey E. *The Politics of the U.S. Cabinet: Representation in the Executive Branch, 1789–1984.* Pittsburgh, Pa.: University of Pittsburgh Press, 1988; Fenno, Richard E. *The President's Cabinet.* Cambridge, Mass.: Harvard University Press, 1959; Polsby, Nelson W. *Consequences of Party Reform.* New York; Oxford University Press, 1983; "Presidential Cabinet Making: Lessons for the Political System," *Political Science Quarterly* (spring 1978).

—Thomas P. Wolf

Calhoun, John C. (1782–1850) *U.S. vice president*
John C. Calhoun was a leading political figure and thinker of the "second generation" of Americans after the Founding. He was born on the South Carolina frontier, where his father was a political leader. A precocious student, Calhoun attended Yale College and studied law in South Carolina and Connecticut. He joined the South Carolina state legislature in 1808 and was first elected to the U.S. House of Representatives in 1810. In Congress, Calhoun was one of the leading "War Hawks," a group of young nationalists in Congress who supported the War of 1812 with Britain. He left Congress to become secretary of war from 1817 to 1825 under President James MONROE and was credited as an efficient administrator.

He first ran for president in 1824 but found little support in a crowded field of candidates and settled for serving as vice president during the John Quincy ADAMS administration. As vice president, Calhoun proved to be an active and able presiding officer of the Senate, where he worked diligently to assist the supporters of Andrew JACKSON. He was again elected VICE PRESIDENT for Jackson's first term of office, from 1829 to 1832. Although initially a strong con-

tender to succeed Jackson to the presidency, Calhoun personally and politically broke from Jackson during the president's first term. Calhoun resigned the vice presidency when he was elected to the U.S. Senate by the South Carolina legislature in December 1832. In leaving the administration, he led a small "States' Rights Party" that associated itself with the opposition Whigs until returning to the DEMOCRATIC PARTY in 1837. In 1843 Calhoun resigned the Senate for another unsuccessful run for the Democratic nomination for the presidency. He agreed to serve as John TYLER's secretary of State, from 1844 to 1845, where he negotiated the admission of Texas into the union. He returned to the Senate in 1845, where he remained until his death in the midst of the debate over the Compromise of 1850 that gave California statehood.

Although an advocate of building national strength in the years surrounding the WAR OF 1812, Calhoun soon became sharply critical of "consolidated" government, the leading theorist of states' rights, and the political voice of the South. The "Tariff of Abominations" of 1828 provoked bitter opposition in South Carolina and elsewhere in the cotton-growing South that was dependent on foreign markets. While serving as Jackson's vice president, Calhoun anonymously developed and published the doctrine of state NULLIFICATION, which held that a state could block enforcement of an unconstitutional federal law. By popular convention in November 1832, South Carolina adopted the theory and threatened to block the collection of tariff duties in state ports, which Calhoun elaborately defended upon leaving the administration in the midst of the crisis. The standoff was resolved with the passage of the Compromise Tariff of 1833. Over the next two decades, Calhoun often returned to his central themes of the federal union as a compact of independent states, as the federal government as a common trust of the states, and the dangers of majority tyranny. He was a strong defender of the presidential veto as a check on legislative abuses, and he also became an aggressive defender of Southern slavery. In two posthumously published works, the *Disquisition on Government* and the *Discourse on the Constitution*, Calhoun elaborated on his constitutional theory of "concurrent majorities" by which political decisions can only be made by the separate consent of multiple political majorities. Extending this logic, he proposed in the *Discourse* the creation of a dual presidency, each with a veto power, separately representing the North and the South in order to preserve the union.

Further reading: Peterson, Merrill D. *The Great Triumvirate: Webster, Clay, and Calhoun.* New York: Oxford University Press, 1987; Wiltse, Charles M. *John C. Calhoun,* 3 vols. Indianapolis: Bobbs-Merrill, 1944–51.

—Keith E. Whittington

campaign finance

Throughout most of American history, campaign financing for federal offices was mostly unregulated and the public knew very little of candidates' campaign finance activity. Congress passed only a handful of laws relating to the fundraising and spending in federal elections. For example, after President Theodore Roosevelt addressed the issue of corporations participating in campaigns in an annual message, Congress passed the Tillman Act in 1907, which banned corporations and national banks from making contributions to federal candidates. Congress also passed a series of laws in 1910 and 1911 imposing a narrow set of disclosure requirements and spending limits for congressional candidates.

After the TEAPOT DOME SCANDAL in 1925, Congress passed the Federal Corrupt Practices Act, which provided the primary campaign finance framework until the reforms of the 1970s. This act closed some loopholes, revised spending limit amounts, and prohibited offering money in exchange for a vote, but its scope was otherwise narrow and the act did not provide enforcement mechanisms. Congress later added the HATCH ACT in 1939, which prohibited federal employees from actively participating in political activity, and amended it the next year to limit fund-raising and expenditures of multistate party committees, to limit the amount individuals could contribute to candidates, and to regulate primary elections. In addition, Congress enacted the TAFT-HARTLEY ACT, which banned political contributions from labor unions.

The largely unregulated framework for federal election campaign financing changed dramatically with the passage of the 1971 Federal Election Campaign Act (FECA), its amendments in 1974, 1976, and 1979, and the Revenue Act of 1971 and its 1974 amendments. The 1971 Revenue Act established public funding of presidential elections via the one-dollar-check-off box on income tax forms (later raised to three dollars). Presidential candidates could be eligible for public funds if they limited their spending (among certain other requirements). The 1971 FECA was a broad piece of legislation addressing many areas related to campaign financing. The act strengthened the existing bans on contributions by corporations and labor unions but also provided the legal basis for such organizations, and others as well, to form POLITICAL ACTION COMMITTEES. The 1971 FECA furthered tightened campaign financing disclosure requirements and extended them to primary elections. Finally, it placed strict limits on media advertising by campaigns and on how much money individual candidates and their immediate families could contribute to their campaigns.

The break-in at the Democratic Party headquarters at the WATERGATE complex in 1972 and the ensuing scandal had many effects on the American political system, one of which was a call for greater reform of the government. As a result, Congress amended FECA in 1974 to provide the most comprehensive set of campaign finance laws adopted. The 1974 amendments to the FECA included the following provisions:

1. limits on direct contributions: from individuals, PACs, and party committees;
2. spending limits for political parties expenditures on behalf of federal candidates (so-called coordinated expenditures);
3. candidate spending limits for House, Senate, and presidential candidates, which replaced the media expenditure ceilings in the 1971 FECA;
4. limits on independent expenditures for expenditures by individuals or interest groups made independently of a candidate's campaign to advocate the election or defeat of a federal candidate;
5. the Federal Election Commission: the FEC was created to implement and enforce the federal campaign finance laws;
6. new disclosure and reporting rules requiring quarterly contributions and spending reports from candidates, with such reports made publicly available; and
7. amending the presidential election public funding system to allow major party presidential nominees to receive public funds up to a preset spending limit, provided they do not accept any additional private money, and to establish a voluntary system of public matching funds in presidential primary campaigns.

The Supreme Court significantly limited the scope of the 1974 FECA Amendments in *BUCKLEY V. VALEO*, 424 U.S. 1 (1976) by striking down certain provisions while letting others stand. For example, on one hand, the Court upheld the limits on direct contributions from individuals, PACs, and political parties, reasoning that such limits were appropriate legislative mechanisms to protect against the reality or appearance of undue influence stemming from large contributions. On the other hand, however, the Court struck down the spending limits for expenditures by House and Senate candidates, the spending limits on independent expenditures, and the contribution limits for candidates and families to their own campaigns. Here, the Court saw the activities that Congress sought to limit as constitutionally protected political speech that could not be involuntarily limited and thus struck down the FECA amendments' restrictions as violating the First Amendment right to free speech. Nevertheless, the Court allowed the spending limits for presidential candidates who accept public funding to stand. Such limits were voluntary and thus different from those that the Court invalidated.

Advocates of campaign finance reform often criticize the Court's reasoning in *Buckley v. Valeo* because it equates money with speech (i.e., limits on campaign expenditures and independent expenditures are unconstitutional limits on free speech). They point to the unequal levels of money that candidates are capable of raising—for example, congressional incumbents who are able to raise more funding than their challengers—and to the unequal resources that individuals and groups control. Thus, so the argument goes, the *Buckley* decision implies an unequal right to free speech—the candidates who can raise more from the wealthiest individuals and groups receive "more speech" than most congressional challengers and the small individual contributor.

As a result of the *Buckley* decision, Congress amended FECA in 1976 to comply with the Court's rulings. In 1979 Congress further modified FECA to address unforeseen problems that arose in implementing the act and its previous amendments. For example, Congress streamlined candidates' reporting requirements, which were seen as too burdensome and costly. More significantly, Congress addressed concerns raised by party organizations that the spending limits imposed on them forced the parties to choose between election-related media advertising on candidates and traditional grassroots party-building activities such as voter registration and get-out-the-vote drives. In the 1979 FECA amendments, Congress exempted parties from spending limits for certain party building activities, thus allowing such organizations to spend unlimited amount of federal (i.e., "hard") money on such pursuits.

Hard money must be raised from regulated sources such as PACs and individuals, and expenditures of hard money must be reported to the Federal Election Commission. Soft money, by contrast, refers to funds that parties collect in unlimited amounts for party-building activities, often from sources such as corporations and labor unions that are otherwise prohibited from participating directly in the campaign finance system. The advent of soft money did not come about from the 1979 FECA amendments, as is often believed to be the case, but instead from two FEC rulings interpreting those amendments. The dramatic increase since 1979 in the amount of soft money flowing into the political parties and the expenditures of soft money has been the subject of great concern for campaign finance reformers and one of the core components of recent reform efforts in Congress.

Such efforts have been led in the Senate by Senators John McCain (Rep.-Ariz.) and Russell Feingold (Dem.-Wis.) and in the House by Representatives Christopher Shays (Rep.-Conn.) and Marty Meehan (Dem.-Mass.). Their attempts to pass reform legislation focusing on banning soft money and regulating certain independent expenditures have met with mixed results. In the 105th and 106th Congresses, reformers passed legislation in the House, only to meet defeat in the Senate. Finally, in the 107th Congress, both chambers of Congress approved campaign finance reform legislation, and President George W. BUSH signed the bill into law. This legislation, among other provisions, bans soft money at the national level, prohibits state parties from spending soft money on federal candidates, increases the individual contribution limit to individual candidates from a fixed $1,000 to $2,000 indexed to inflation, and requires disclosure of expenditures by individuals and groups who spend at least $10,000 in a calendar year on electioneering communications. Congressional opponents, however, have vowed to fight the legislation in the courts, so the bill's long-term effect has yet to be determined.

Overall, FECA has had a number of desirable and undesirable effects. As campaign finance expert Anthony Corrado contends:

> the new campaign finance system [created by FECA and its amendments] represented a major advancement over the patchwork of regulations it replaced. The disclosure and reporting requirements dramatically improved public access to financial information and regulators' ability to enforce the law. The contribution ceilings eliminated the large gifts that had tainted the process in 1972. Public financing quickly gained widespread acceptance among the candidates, and small contributions became the staple of presidential campaign financing.

Without limits on candidate expenditures, however, the cost of congressional campaigns has continued to rise. Moreover, a number of presidential candidates, such as George W. Bush, Ross Perot, and Steve Forbes, have forgone public financing so as to not be limited by spending limitations that accompany accepting public funds. As a result, the ever-increasing focus on fund-raising has led many to believe that candidates for federal office are perhaps even more beholden to moneyed interests than in the unregulated pre-FECA days.

Further reading: Corrado, Anthony, Thomas E. Mann, Daniel R. Ortiz, Trevor Potter, and Frank J. Sorouf, eds. *Campaign Finance Reform: A Sourcebook.* Washington, D.C.: Brookings Institution, 1997; Dwyre, Diana, and Victoria A. Farrar-Myers. *Legislative Labyrinth: Congress and Campaign Finance Reform.* Washington, D.C.: CQ Press, 2001.
—Victoria Farrar-Myers

campaign pledges

Presidential elections have changed enormously over the last few decades. Almost immediately after the presidential election, candidates begin testing the waters to run in the next one. Therefore, presidential candidates need to distinguish themselves from the rest of the pack.

We have come to expect lofty accomplishments from our presidents. We expect them to make bold proposals that will move the country forward, and we demand that they live up to their promises. We want large tax cuts; we want substantial improvement regarding education; we want a reformed health-care system; we want a decrease in crime rates. While we insist on sweeping pledges from our presidential candidates, the president can do little without Congress's support. For example, the president does not have nearly the power of his constitutional counterpart in Britain. If the president is unable to get his campaign pledges enacted because Congress is not on board, his public approval ratings are likely to drop substantially.

In general, the public does not believe that presidential candidates keep their promises. The common perception is that candidates will say anything to get elected; once they win, they will not follow their word. The public and the media constantly criticized President Bill CLINTON for not enacting his campaign pledges. In some ways, these criticisms were justified. Clinton promised universal health care (a position that some credited with his election) and failed to deliver. He argued for a repeal of the ban on gays in the military but was forced to compromise. In some cases, Clinton went counter to his campaign pledges. Instead of lowering the gas tax, for example, he proposed one.

Contrary to the conventional wisdom, however, presidents usually follow their campaign pledges (or at least try to enact them). Using Clinton again as an example, he raised the minimum wage, cut the size of government, reformed welfare, put new police officers on the street, passed an assault weapons ban, and created a national service program, all of which he promised on the campaign trail. Clinton is not alone. A study by Jeff Fishel found that a majority of proposals by KENNEDY, JOHNSON, NIXON, CARTER, and REAGAN were quite comparable to the promises they made during the campaign. Certainly presidents do not follow through on all of their campaign pledges, but it is difficult to argue that they are simply saying something to get elected and then completely ignore their promises.

However, the public does not always look favorably upon candidates' campaign pledges. When Walter MONDALE stated during his 1984 acceptance speech that he would raise taxes to help combat the budget deficits created by the Reagan administration, the public reacted negatively. Campaign pledges can also come back to hurt a candidate as well. The public did not forget that George H. W. Bush raised taxes after emphatically stating "Read my lips, no new taxes" in his 1988 acceptance speech. Many consider Bush's tax increase to be a major factor in his defeat in 1992.

Further reading: Fishel, Jeff. *Presidents and Promises.* Washington, D.C.: CQ Press, 1985; Mendoza, Mark, and Kathleen Hall Jamieson. "The Morning After: Do Politicians Keep Their Promises?" In *Everything You Think You Know About Politics and Why You're Wrong,* edited by Kathleen Hall Jamieson. New York: Basic Books, 2000.
—Matt Streb

campaign strategies

Because of the uniqueness of the ELECTORAL COLLEGE, presidential candidates are not vying to win a plurality of the popular vote but instead a majority of the electoral vote. This forces candidates to focus most of their attention on key "battleground states." A battleground state is one that has a medium to large-sized population and whose polls indicate that the race is close. It is also a state that has the potential to determine the outcome of the election. Florida, Pennsylvania, Michigan, and New Jersey are often battleground states. Some large states, like California, New York, and Texas, have not been considered battleground states in recent elections because they overwhelmingly supported one of the two major candidates.

Campaign strategies differ some depending on the candidates' party affiliations. Republicans usually do well in the Midwest, West, and South. The South has not always been a Republican stronghold. In fact, in was not until the 1964 election that southern states really became associated with the REPUBLICAN PARTY at the presidential level (although Dwight EISENHOWER did campaign in the South in 1952 and 1956 and won some southern states). In that year, Barry GOLDWATER carried the five states of the Deep South largely because of his support of states' rights and opposition to the 1964 CIVIL RIGHTS ACT. Richard NIXON began to perfect the so-called Southern Strategy in 1968 and 1972. Since that time, the South has voted predominantly Republican in presidential elections. In fact, a nonsouthern Democrat has not carried a southern state since Hubert H. HUMPHREY in 1968. In 1984, 1988, and 2000, Republican candidates swept the South, gaining a huge advantage in the Electoral College. In 2000 the South accounted for slightly more than half of the 270 votes needed for victory.

Democrats have traditionally faired best in the Northeast, Mid-Atlantic, and Pacific Coast. Nevertheless, more states have had stronger ties to the Republican Party. In the last nine presidential elections, the Democrats have won only the District of Columbia and Minnesota at least eight times (13 electoral votes). On the other hand, Republican candidates have carried 16 states in at least eight of the past nine elections (128 electoral votes; roughly half of the number of votes needed to win the election). Because the Republicans have the advantage in so many states, it is especially imperative that Democrats do well in the battleground states.

While the Electoral College forces candidates to focus on certain states, they also must have a clear theme with which the American public can identify. In 1992 CLINTON adviser James Carville's constant reminder, "It's the economy, stupid" resonated with voters. Clinton consistently focused on President George H. W. BUSH's failure to stimulate the economy and lack of a future plan to do so. Clinton also employed another successful strategy in 1992. He took similar positions on foreign policy issues as Bush. People considered Bush's strength to be foreign policy, especially after the victory in the Persian Gulf the year before. By taking similar stances as Bush on foreign policy, Clinton was hoping to make it a nonissue in the election, instead keeping all of the attention on the economy (where Clinton had the upper hand).

In 1996 Clinton, under the direction of political consultant Dick Morris, successfully employed a strategy called "triangulation." On most issues, there is a liberal position and a conservative position; according to triangulation, the candidate wants to place himself/herself somewhere in between. Regarding affirmative action, for example, Clinton chose to "mend it, not end it" and he promised to "end welfare as we know it." Triangulation can be quite successful because the majority of the public falls somewhere in the middle on most issues. It can also be dangerous, however, because people may argue that the candidate does not stand for anything—he/she is constantly straddling the fence—a criticism that Clinton often faced.

Another key aspect of campaign strategy is to have a quick response to your opponent's charges. Again, Clinton's 1992 campaign was quite successful at doing so. The Clinton campaign created a "War Room," led by consultants James Carville and George Stephanopoulos. While the War Room was in charge of campaign strategy, it also focused on immediately responding to Bush's attacks against Clinton. The War Room often received advance copies of Bush's ads or speeches and would respond to them almost instantaneously. These quick responses by the Clinton campaign kept Bush's charges from gaining much traction.

Strategies also change slightly depending on whether a candidate is an incumbent or a challenger. To put it simply, an incumbent will run on his record and argue that the country has been better off under his leadership. A challenger must convince the public that they are not better off than four years ago. While some scholars have questioned whether campaigns even matter because evidence has indicated that the performance of the economy often can predict the outcome of the election, clearly campaigns are important. Were they not significant, Al GORE would have easily won the 2000 presidential election.

Further reading: Caesar, James W., and Andrew E. Busch. *The Perfect Tie: The True Story of the 2000 Presidential Election*. Lanham, Md.: Rowman & Littlefield, 2001; *The War Room*. Vidmark Entertainment, 1993; Wayne, Stephen J. *The Road to the White House 2000*. Boston, Mass.: Bedford/St. Martin's, 2001.

—Matthew Streb

Camp David

Located 50 miles northwest of Washington, D.C., and nestled in the Catoctin Mountains of Maryland, Camp David is the president's vacation, work, and retreat house. Built in 1942 and originally named Shangri-La by Franklin ROOSEVELT, it was renamed by President EISENHOWER after his grandson. In 1978 Camp David was the location of negotiations between President Carter, Egyptian President Anwar Sadat, and Israeli Prime Minister Menachem Begin that led to the signing of the historic CAMP DAVID ACCORDS.

Camp David Accords

When Jimmy CARTER was elected president there was a general consensus among Middle East experts that the time had come to move beyond the step-by-step approach to peace negotiations that Henry KISSINGER had pursued after the 1973 war. The Carter administration's early efforts to find an international forum in which to discuss a comprehensive Middle East settlement failed.

Then Egyptian President Anwar Sadat broke the stalemate and changed all the calculations about the prospects for a Middle East peace with his dramatic trip to Jerusalem in November of 1977. When the expectations raised by Sadat's bold initiative began to fade, Carter stepped in and invited both Sadat and Israeli Prime Minister Menachem Begin to join him for private talks at CAMP DAVID. He did so against the advice of many of his foreign policy advisers who held out little hope of substantial progress in face-to-face negotiations between Middle East enemies.

For 13 days in September of 1978 Carter devoted his considerable energies to the negotiation of a peace treaty between Israel and Egypt. The Israelis agreed to return the Sinai desert, captured in the 1967 Six-Day War, to Egypt in exchange for a normalization of relations with the largest of their Arab neighbors. The Camp David Accords also contained general principles to be followed in subsequent negotiations that would tackle the more difficult questions regarding the West Bank, Gaza, the future of Jerusalem, and the fate of the Palestinians scattered across the Middle East.

Both the Egyptians and the Israeli delegations at Camp David agreed that Carter was the indispensable mediator of the agreements that were reached. After early sessions with all three leaders produced very little, Carter carried messages between the delegations, drafted proposed treaty language, and personally persuaded Sadat and Begin to remain at the presidential retreat when each threatened to leave. Carter's foreign policy team, often at odds over other issues, worked well to support the president's personal DIPLOMACY with the Egyptian and Israeli leaders.

A final round of high-level negotiations, including a presidential trip to Cairo and Jerusalem, was necessary to convert the Camp David agreements into an Egyptian-Israeli peace treaty that was signed on the White House lawn on March 26, 1979. In the years that followed, the general outline for the resolution of the remaining Middle East issues that was contained in the Camp David Accords influenced the agreements reached in Oslo and the peace proposals made by President Clinton during his final months in office. Of course, none of these negotiations took place on the optimistic timetable that had been expected in the euphoria following the Camp David Accords. For their efforts Sadat and Begin shared the Nobel Peace Prize in 1978; Carter won his in 2002.

Further reading: Quandt, William. *Peace Process: American Diplomacy and the Arab-Israeli Conflict since 1967*, rev. ed. Los Angeles: University of California Press, 2001; Telhami, Shibley. *Power and Leadership in International Bargaining: The Path to the Camp David Accords*. New York: Columbia University Press, 1990.

—Robert A. Strong

Camp David Negotiations, the

The Middle East Agreements arising out of the Camp David talks in the fall of 1978 were Jimmy CARTER's greatest accomplishment. The Sinai was returned to Egypt, diplomatic relations between Israel and Egypt were established, and a framework for peace was designed to guide subsequent negotiations on Palestinian self-governance and its relationship to Israel.

These accomplishments at CAMP DAVID were in large part due to the skills of several people, aided by the U.S. Secretary of State Cyrus Vance and a harmonious and expert American support team. President Jimmy Carter became the chief diplomat in two simultaneous but in some ways separate U.S. negotiations with Israel and Egypt. The Egyptian president, Anwar Sadat, straining against strong opposition from members of his own negotiating team, made compromises without which no deal could have been reached. Members of the Israeli negotiating team—Defense Minister Ezer Weizman, Attorney General Aharon Barak, and Foreign Minister Moshe Dayan—pushed the negotiations forward by advising the Americans on what issues to play and how to deal with a more truculent Israeli prime minister, Menachem Begin. One

final sticking point, the dissolution of Israeli settlements in the Sinai, was only resolved when General Abrahm Tamir of the Israel delegation called Agricultural Minister General Arik Sharon (later prime minister) and secured his agreement that concession should be made on this matter to avoid what would have been a conference failure.

The near-intractability of the problems confronted at Camp David delayed any final settlement on the Israeli-Egyptian peace treaty for six months and the framework for peace would have little impact on the resolutions of the Palestinian issue for several years. The CAMP DAVID ACCORDS, however, did stop a downward cycle in hostilities that could have had even more negative consequences for the Middle East. Shortly before the talks began, Begin and Sadat had been exchanging hostile remarks. Saudi Arabia was pressuring Sadat to reconcile his differences with Syria's Hafez Assad, a hard-liner in the Middle East conflict. Such reconciliation could have brought Sadat back into the radical Arab bloc, thereby enhancing the likelihood of another round of Middle East wars, a resurgence of Soviet influence in the area, and a possible oil embargo against the United States. At the bottom of the slope, in short, a renewed conflict in the Middle East and Soviet intervention therein was a distinct possibility.

In the fall of 1978 Begin and Sadat received Nobel Peace Prizes for their work at Camp David. Jimmy Carter's contribution to the process was not recognized until the fall of 2002, when he too was awarded the Nobel Peace Prize.

—Betty Glad

Carter, Jimmy (1924–) *thirty-ninth U.S. president*

In the wake of the WATERGATE scandal, the voters were looking for an open, honest man to serve in the White House. Jimmy Carter, the former governor of Georgia, was able to appeal to disaffected voters and narrowly won the presidency in 1976.

As part of the continuing fallout of Watergate, the voters rejected Gerald FORD and chose instead an unknown former Democrat governor of Georgia ("Jimmy who?" people asked), who spoke openly in biblical terms and promised "I'll never lie to you." Jimmy Carter, 5'10", with sandy hair and a toothy smile, came out of nowhere to the White House.

No president in the last 50 years had so little experience in government as Carter. But it was a time when being a Washington politician was a liability. The voters wanted an "outsider," someone who was not tainted by the evils of Washington politics, and so Jimmy Carter was the first of two consecutive D.C. outsiders to occupy the White House.

Carter's relaxed informality, ready smile of prominent teeth, and down-home style convinced people that he was one of them, not a professional politician. Astonished at the public's desire to have a nonpolitician in the nation's most highly politicized job, critics lamented, "If you needed brain surgery you'd go to a professional and experienced brain surgeon; why, when choosing a president, do you want an amateur in the White House?" But such concerns were lost on a public grown cynical from years of Vietnam and Watergate.

President Carter set out to de-pomp and demythologize the IMPERIAL PRESIDENCY. While he was one of the most intelligent men to serve as a president, he never articulated a sense of purpose or overall vision beyond his frequently expressed moralism. "Carterism does not march and it does not sing," said historian Eric Goldman. "It is cautious, muted, grayish, at times even crabbed."

A number of characteristics have been used to describe Jimmy Carter. Aide James Fallows, after departing in 1979, stressed Carter's basic fairness and decency. To Fallows, Carter would be an ideal person to judge one's soul. He also emphasized, however, that Carter seemed to conduct a pas-

President Jimmy Carter, thirty-ninth president of the United States *(Jimmy Carter Library)*

sionless presidency. Others have pointed to Carter's honesty and forthrightness, self-discipline, and tenacious pursuit of personal goals in all activities, including even sporting contests. Less flattering assessments have also been applied, with an emphasis on his naiveté about the nature of government, limited creativity and innovativeness, and tendencies toward self-righteousness and feelings of moral superiority.

Carter's four years as president were difficult and contentious. He had trouble leading his party, did a mediocre job at leading Congress, and failed to inspire the public. During his term, inflation rose and productivity faltered.

"I learned the hard way," Carter wrote in his memoirs, "that there was no party loyalty or discipline when a complicated or controversial issue was at stake—none. Each legislator had to be wooed and won individually. It was every member for himself, and the devil take the hindmost!"

In spite of the many setbacks, there were also some impressive victories. Carter's emphasis on HUMAN RIGHTS had significant long-term effects across the globe. His CAMP DAVID ACCORDS between Israel and Egypt were a stunning success; he normalized U.S. relations with China, won the Panama Canal Treaty, pushed Strategic Arms Limitation Talks (SALT II), pushed for the transition to black rule in Zimbabwe; and, on the home front, he won CIVIL SERVICE reform, appointed the first black women to the CABINET, created both the Energy and Education Departments, and avoided major scandal.

On November 4, 1979, a mob of Iranian youths seized the U.S. embassy in Tehran, taking 63 Americans hostage. Carter saw no way to get the hostages released short of an attack that would have endangered their lives. Negotiations and sanctions failed to move the Iranians.

Carter's inability to resolve this crisis successfully became the dominating event of his presidency. A failed rescue mission in 1980 only made Carter look more helpless. Eventually Carter was able to win the release of all the hostages, but by then it was too late for him. The Iranians released the hostages on the morning Carter left office.

Hendrik Hertzberg, a onetime Carter speechwriter, said of his former boss, "He was and is a moral leader more than a political leader," adding that "[h]e spoke the language of religion and morality far more, and far more effectively, than he spoke the language of politics." Jimmy Carter was a very good man, but not an especially adept politician. He was the first of several "outsiders" to be elected president in an age of cynicism.

Although Carter avoided many of the excesses of other recent presidents, he was unable to generate sufficient support or to exercise decisive leadership. His presidency ended with Gallup poll ratings in the 20 percent range. Consequently, he was defeated in his 1980 bid for reelection. Not since 1932, with Herbert HOOVER in the midst of THE GREAT DEPRESSION, has an incumbent president been so totally defeated. As a sign of Carter's low standing, Ronald REAGAN, in 1984 bid for reelection, was still running against the memory of Jimmy Carter!

Many argue that Carter is the greatest "ex-president" in history. After leaving the White House, Carter devoted himself to a series of humanitarian activities that included working for Habitat for Humanity, building houses for the poor, working as an international peacemaker and conflict negotiator, and writing numerous books on peace, justice, and politics. In 2002 he was honored with the Nobel Peace Prize.

Further reading: Dumbrell, John, ed. *The Carter Presidency: A Re-Evaluation.* Manchester, England: Manchester University Press, 1993; Hargrove, Erwin C. *Jimmy Carter as President: Leadership and the Politics of the Public Good.* Baton Rouge: Louisiana State University Press, 1988; Jones, Charles O. *The Trusteeship Presidency: Jimmy Carter and the United States Congress.* Baton Rouge: Louisiana State University Press, 1988; Kaufman, Burton I. *The Presidency of James Earl Carter, Jr.* Lawrence: University Press of Kansas, 1993.

Carter, Rosalynn (1927–   ) *first lady, social activist*
Wife of President Jimmy CARTER, Rosalynn Carter took an active part in her husband's presidency, occasionally sitting in on cabinet meetings. She was an active campaigner for her husband and enlarged the scope of the first lady's role in politics. The Carters were an especially close couple, both politically and personally, and the president would often bounce ideas off his politically astute wife. She was an influential voice in the president's ear, and the senior staff appreciated her political instincts and policy advice.

Carter Doctrine
In response to the Soviet Union's invasion of Afghanistan, Jimmy CARTER declared in his STATE OF THE UNION ADDRESS on January 23, 1980, that any "attempt by an outside force to gain control of the Persian Gulf region will be regarded as an assault on the vital interests of the United States of America." He added that any such attack "will be repelled by any means necessary, including military force." The Carter Doctrine, as it became known, was intended to serve as a warning to the Soviet Union not to encroach on the Persian Gulf region.

The Carter Doctrine was an attempt to shore up the president's weakened position caused by two international crises. First, on November 4, 1979, radical students overran the U.S. Embassy in Tehran, Iran, and took 63 members of

First Lady Rosalynn Carter *(White House)*

the American staff hostage. Although 14 were later released, the remaining hostages were kept as leverage to demand that the United States cut its ties with the shah and return him to Iran for trial. Second, in late December 1979, the Soviet Union sent some 80,000 troops into Afghanistan, a country bordering Iran. Only six months after the United States and Soviet Union had made a major breakthrough with the signing of the SALT (Strategic Arms Limitation Talks) II treaty and a much-publicized embrace between Carter and Soviet Premier Brezhnev, the Soviet Union sent troops outside its sphere of influence for the first time since World War II.

The Carter administration recognized that the invasion of Afghanistan represented a strategic challenge in the Persian Gulf. The Carter Doctrine was modeled on the TRUMAN DOCTRINE and was designed to link the security of the Persian Gulf region to that of the United States. It was acknowledgment that the security of the United States was interdependent with that of the Persian Gulf. The invasion of Afghanistan raised the fear that it was only the first step in a Soviet plan to cut off access of the Western powers to the oil from that region. The goal of the Carter Doctrine was to serve warning to the Soviet Union that encroachment in regions deemed vital to U.S. interests would lead to engagement with the United States.

While the speech was generally well received, critics argued it was merely an idle threat because it was not backed by significant force. Ronald REAGAN used such claims in his successful bid for the presidency in 1980. In response to the invasion of Afghanistan, in addition to the enunciation of the Carter Doctrine, the president also removed the SALT II treaty from Senate consideration, increased defense spending, imposed a grain embargo against the Soviet Union, called for a boycott of the Olympic Games in Moscow (a boycott in which 62 nations, including the United States, participated), and banned high-technology transfers. Despite these moves, the American public felt he was not "tough enough" in his dealings with the Soviet Union. Carter's weakened foreign policy position, failure to enunciate a clear vision for the country, and severe economic crisis cost him a second term as president.

Further reading: Brzezinski, Zbigniew. *Power and Principle: Memoirs of the National Security Advisor 1977–1981.* New York: Farrar, Straus, Giroux, 1983; Morris, Kenneth E. *Jimmy Carter: American Moralist.* Athens: University of Georgia Press, 1996.

—Elizabeth Matthews

Case Act

The Case Act of 1972 was sponsored by Senator Clifford Case (Rep.-N.J.) and Representative Clement Zablocki (Dem.-Wis.). It required that the EXECUTIVE BRANCH report to Congress all EXECUTIVE AGREEMENTS (a written or verbal pact or understanding reached by the president or another authorized official with a foreign government) within 60 days after they have been finalized. In addition, it requires that the executive branch inform Congress of all executive agreements in effect at the time of the passage of the act. Lastly it provides that the House and Senate Committees with jurisdiction over FOREIGN AFFAIRS be informed of any executive agreements that the president determines needed to be kept secret to ensure national security.

The purpose of the Case Act was to improve congressional monitoring of America's foreign commitments. Congress determined that this information was crucial and indispensable if Congress is to meet its constitutional responsibilities in the formulation of foreign policy. The Case Act was motivated by the fact that executive agreements, unlike treaties, do not require any congressional approval. The Case Act was also motivated by the discovery of many secret agreements made during the period of 1964–72 relating to the Indochina War. The Case Act can be seen as one of the attempts by Congress to restrain presidential domination of foreign policy and war making. The

Case Act was a more modest attempt than the Bricker Amendment in 1953, which had aimed to establish congressional review of executive agreements and to make treaties unenforceable without accompanying legislation.

The Case Act was amended in 1978 to cover all oral international agreements which were used particularly by the DEFENSE DEPARTMENT to bypass the formal written reporting requirements to Congress. In addition, it required a written presidential explanation for a delay beyond 60 days in reporting to Congress and authorized the State Department to coordinate all agreements by other executive agencies.

The Case Act does not prevent the executive branch from engaging in executive agreements; however, it allows Congress the information that they could use to block appropriations to implement them and to conduct hearings that can impact on public opinion.

Further reading: Franck, Thomas M., and Edward Weisband. *Foreign Policy by Congress.* New York: Oxford University Press, 1979; Johnson, Loch K. *The Making of International Agreements.* New York: New York University Press, 1984; Margolis, Lawrence. *Executive Agreements and Presidential Power in Foreign Policy.* New York: Praeger, 1986.

—Frank Sorrentino

Cass, Lewis (1782–1866) *politician*

Born in New Hampshire, Lewis Cass served as a territorial governor, minister to France, secretary of war under Andrew JACKSON, U.S. senator from Michigan, unsuccessful Democratic Party presidential nominee in 1848, and secretary of state under James BUCHANAN. A committed Jeffersonian Democrat, Cass was an avid nationalist and resigned from Buchanan's CABINET when the president refused to resupply forts threatened by secessionists in South Carolina. He died in 1866.

Further reading: Woodford, Frank B. *Lewis Cass: The Last Jeffersonian.* New York: Octagon Books, 1973.

caucuses, presidential nominating

While presidential primary contests attract the most attention in the race for the nomination, another method of delegate section is the caucus. From 1796 to 1824 a congressional caucus selected the presidential nominees for the party. Later, as primaries replaced the congressional caucuses, some states chose to let a party caucus of members select the states' delegates to the presidential nominating convention. Today, roughly 20 percent of the convention delegates come from caucus status.

censure

A censure resolution is a formal reprimand of a person either by the House of Representatives, the Senate, or both chambers acting together. Censure does not remove an official from office, but it brings a formal judgment of disapproval against wrongdoing not thought to rise to the level of an impeachable offense. Censure has been used sparingly, extraordinarily so against persons outside of Congress. The only president to be censured by a full chamber of Congress was President Andrew JACKSON, by the Senate, but censure measures have been introduced (and ultimately rejected) against Presidents John ADAMS, John TYLER, James POLK, Abraham LINCOLN, and former President James BUCHANAN.

Andrew Jackson was censured by the Senate in 1834 for perceived abuse of presidential power. Jackson, who strongly opposed the BANK OF THE UNITED STATES, had vetoed its rechartering in 1832 and worked to hasten its demise, scheduled for 1836, by withdrawing federal funds on deposit in the bank and distributing them to several state banks. Senator Henry CLAY led the campaign for censure against Jackson, claiming that Jackson's presidency was "approaching tyranny" in its destruction of a legitimate governmental institution and unfair dismissal of Secretary of the Treasury William Duane when he refused to transfer the federal deposits to the states. Jackson was furious at the censure, and he called on his attorney general, Benjamin Butler, to prepare a formal protest. Jackson's protest held that the censure unconstitutionally subverted the distribution of powers between the branches and also bypassed the constitutionally prescribed impeachment process. Without a formal IMPEACHMENT, Jackson reasoned, he was not afforded a political trial to defend himself. Though the Senate refused to enter Jackson's protest into its official journal, in 1837 it expunged the censure from its records. Censure reemerged as an issue in 1998 when the DEMOCRATIC PARTY introduced a joint resolution in Congress to censure CLINTON as an alternative to impeachment. Republicans argued that censure had no explicit constitutional warrant, undermined the power of impeachment, upset the balance of powers by encouraging petty congressional harassment of EXECUTIVE POWER, and violated the constitutional injunction against Bills of Attainder. Democrats countered that censure was a more commensurate punishment for Clinton's misdeed than impeachment, reflected the traditional legislative authority to register the mind of the House or Senate, and did not constitute a Bill of Attainder because it did not take away a person's life, liberty, or property. The scholarly community weighed in on the issue, largely favoring the legality of censure, but the point became moot when the House voted to impeach President Clinton.

Further reading: Posner, Richard. *An Affair of State.* Cambridge, Mass.: Harvard University Press, 1999; U.S. Congress. House. *Report of the Judiciary House of Representatives to Accompany H. Res. 611;* Van Tassel, Emily Field, and Paul Finkelman. *Impeachable Offenses.* Washington, D.C.: CQ Press, 1999.

—Michael E. Bailey

Central Intelligence Agency (CIA)

Created as part of the National Security Act of 1947, the Central Intelligence Agency (CIA) possesses five *official functions:* advise the NATIONAL SECURITY COUNCIL (NSC) in matters relating to intelligence activities; make recommendations to the NSC for the coordination of intelligence; correlate, evaluate, and disseminate intelligence information within the government; perform additional functions for the benefit of existing intelligence agencies; and assume other functions related to intelligence as the NSC may direct.

In its initial era of activity from 1947 until the early 1970s, the CIA was engaged in many political and paramilitary assignments abroad. Among the more noteworthy COVERT OPERATIONS during this span were the overthrow of President Jacobo Arbenz of Guatemala in 1954, repeated efforts to overthrow or assassinate Cuban leader Fidel Castro in the 1960s, and the destabilization of Chilean president Salvador Allende's government in 1973.

It was the revelation of CIA participation in Allende's ouster by a military junta which, along with the collapse of anticommunist consensus due to the VIETNAM WAR, CIA association with the WATERGATE break-in and ensuing cover-up, and reports that the CIA had thousands of domestic files on antiwar activists and political dissenters, spawned a major decline in the agency's influence and prestige. A presidential commission was appointed by Gerald FORD in 1975, charged with the task of investigating the entire intelligence structure and suggesting reforms. The resulting changes included a downsizing of CIA covert personnel, increased oversight of intelligence activities by the EXECUTIVE BRANCH, and the establishment of intelligence committees in both chambers of Congress.

Just as the period between 1975 and 1980 represented the nadir of the CIA's use of covert operations, so the election of Ronald REAGAN to the presidency in 1980 represented an opportunity for a fresh approach to American intelligence and security policy. The Reagan administration immediately initiated a program to revitalize the national intelligence system. As a result, the CIA undertook covert operations in more than a dozen nations, including Afghanistan, Angola, Libya, Ethiopia, and Cambodia among others. The most salient CIA activity in the early 1980s was the assistance given to rebels fighting the Marxist Sandinista government in Nicaragua. In addition to delivering arms, uniforms, and equipment to the rebels, known as the contras, the CIA mined Nicaragua's harbors.

In late 1986 it was learned that the contras received money diverted from illegal ARMS SALES to Iran. The ensuing outcry from the IRAN-CONTRA scandal sent the CIA reeling again. In an eerie repetition of the mid-1970s, both a presidential commission and congressional committees were formed to probe the latter affair. Though it was discovered that the CIA played a secondary role to the NSC, the agency did not escape criticism. Another round of reform measure was enacted, including three measures in 1989. These laws led to the establishment of an independent inspector general within the CIA, the prohibition against U.S. FOREIGN AID being used to pressure recipients into violating American law, and a statute imposing criminal penalties on public officials who permit sales of restricted arms to terrorist states. A 1991 law signed by President George H. W. Bush additionally codified and restricted the authority of presidential "findings," outlawed use of covert action to influence domestic policies or groups, and strengthened reporting requirements to the congressional intelligence committees.

The decline of communism in Eastern Europe, which culminated with the fall of the Soviet Union in late 1991, left the CIA searching for a purpose. First, the agency's budget was extensively trimmed. Second, a proposal that intelligence agencies assist with commercial spying on behalf of American business interests was rejected. Third, the agency's critics insisted on faster declassification of documents so that more records were accessible to the public. Fourth, a 1996 law signed by President Bill CLINTON required Senate confirmation of the CIA's general counsel in order to prevent political influence over the position. Still, the CIA had some notable achievements during the 1990s, such as its successful monitoring of North Korea's nuclear weapons development.

As America entered the 21st century, many questioned the continued need for the CIA. Those doubts were largely put to rest after the heinous events of September 11, 2001. The CIA, which had helped to apprehend international terrorist "Carlos the Jackal" in Sudan in 1994, became an integral part of the war on terrorism launched by the United States. The CIA dispatched many personnel to Afghanistan to ferret out Taliban and al Qaeda forces under the control of Osama bin Laden and to assist the U.S. military in defeating them. The very successful operation resulted in the death of only a single agent. Meanwhile, the budget of the CIA was increased and the agency began actively recruiting new personnel. Apparently, the pendulum has swung again in favor of the CIA and its mission.

Further reading: Dulles, Allen. *The Craft of Intelligence.* New York: New American Library, 1965; Hoff, Samuel B. "Toward 2000: The CIA's Role in American Foreign and Security Policy." In *Strategic Challenges to U.S. Foreign Policy in the Post-Cold War,* edited by Marco Rimanelli. Tampa, Fla.: Saint Leo Press, 1998; Miller, Nathan. *Spying for America: The Hidden History of U.S. Intelligence.* New York: Paragon House, 1989; Wise, David, and Thomas Ross. *The Invisible Government.* New York: Vintage Books, 1974; Woodward, Bob. *Veil: The Secret Wars of the CIA, 1981–1987.* New York: Simon & Schuster, 1987.

—Samuel B. Hoff

chad

A piece of waste material from a computer punch card that became a central issue in the 2000 presidential election recount in the state of Florida. The Oxford English Dictionary defines *chad* as a "piece of waste material from punched cards or tape during punching." Due to the closeness of the 2000 presidential election, the voting outcome in the state of Florida would give an electoral college victory to either Al GORE (Dem.) or George W. BUSH (Rep.). After the final tally on election night in Florida, Bush led Gore by 1,784 votes, close enough to trigger an automatic recount. This recount ensured that voting procedures in Florida would be examined closely.

During the 2000 elections, punch card machines were used in many Florida counties. These punch cards became a central issue in the recount because of various reports of undervoting across Florida. Undervoting occurs when a counting machine registers no vote on a punch card ballot for a particular office. In the 2000 presidential election in Florida, there were thousands of undervotes across the state.

Some of these undervotes were caused by partially punched chads or chad buildup in voting machines. Thus a major controversy in the recount was how to count votes on punch card ballots where chads had been partially punched. Since the Florida courts and Florida statutes gave little guidance, elections administrators and canvassing boards in Florida had to decide whether to count votes with chads punched on one corner, two corners, three corners, or "pregnant" (chads were bubbled but not punched out). Depending on the counting standard used, the presidential election could have been decided by how these chads were punched. The word *chad* became a favorite of comedians and international commentators, who joked about the U.S. presidency being decided on by waste paper. The Supreme Court put an end to the counting of undervotes and the examination of chads with their decision in *BUSH V. GORE* that ended the recount in Florida.

Further reading: Toobin, Jeffrey. *Too Close to Call.* New York: Random House, 2001.

—Matthew Corrigan

character

Character and personality have always been important elements in understanding presidential politics. In 1972 James David Barber published his influential book, *The Presidential Character*, arguing that we needed to look at and understand the inner, or psychological, components that effected presidential behavior. Barber looked closely at a president's style (active or passive) and character (positive or negative), combining those features to produce four personality types: Active-Positive, Active-Negative, Passive-Positive, and Passive-Negative.

Initially, Barber's work won a great deal of attention and praise. However, over time Barber's personalistic/psychological approach met with a great deal of criticism from scholarly circles.

Attention refocused on the inner life of presidents during the presidency of Bill Clinton, when character issues relating to the president's alleged flaws took center stage. Could, it was asked, someone be a "bad" person but a good president? Evidently the American public believed so as Clinton's job approval ratings were in the 60 percent range, while ratings of his character hovered in the 30 percent range, creating what many referred to as a "character gap."

Further reading: Barber, James David. *The Presidential Character: Predicting Performance in the White House,* 4th rev. ed. Englewood Cliffs, N.J.: Prentice Hall, 1992; Cronin, Thomas, and Michael Genovese. "President Clinton and Character Questions." *Presidential Studies Quarterly* (Fall 1998): 892–897; George, Alexander. "Assessing Presidential Character." *World Politics* 26 (1974): 234–282; Nelson, Michael. "The Psychological Presidency." In *The Presidency and the Political System,* 3d ed., edited by Michael Nelson, 189–212. Washington, D.C.: CQ Press, 1990.

character issues and presidential politics

Debate on public issues and candidates' stands on them have traditionally been the focus of American presidential campaigns. In recent decades, however, an important change has taken place. Rather than ask candidates where they stand, the public now wants to know who they are. Rather than depend on what a candidate promises, the public wants to know why he wishes to do it. Presidential elections increasingly revolve around issues of character, judgment, and leadership.

These changes are a partial result of the decreasing importance of party labels as a surrogate for policy positions and the corresponding rise of "personal" politics. They also reflect increasing public awareness that the character, judgment, and leadership qualities of leaders are important measures by which to judge candidates and presidents. A central question, therefore, is on what basis these judgments might reasonably be made.

As the term implies, character issues lie at the intersection of psychological and political theory and partisan politics. Candidates are now asked to explain publicly what had in the past been considered private, often because of charges made by their opponents. Direct questions about whether they have committed adultery, had psychological counseling of any type, or even, as in the case of the 1990 election, raised their children in conformity with their religious beliefs have become routine. The line between the public and private lives of our political leaders has blurred dramatically in the past two decades.

At a distance and in a short time, it is generally difficult to obtain the kind of information that would go into making adequate judgments of character and judgment. We get to know both best by paying attention to a myriad of details about a person's behavior in relationships of many kinds (with family, friends, associates, strangers, and even cultural commodities, like money) and having some knowledge of the psychological history and reasons for what we observe.

There are, moreover, strong forces at work to limit what will be revealed during a campaign. Presidential candidates ultimately run to be elected, not intimately known. Aware that character is an issue, campaigns have responded by investing enormous resources in shaping candidates' personas and portraying the result as "character." They attempt to present candidates as they would prefer to be seen, rather than how they are. One ironic result is that the most accurate assessments of character and judgment are being made by those with the least interest in a full public disclosure.

However, as the importance of character has publicly increased, so has media attention and potentially useful information among them: candidate's opponents who may raise character issues in the hope of obtaining political advantage, news organizations (especially those with investigative capabilities), former associates of the candidate, political scientists and psychologists who study candidates and leadership, and the candidate or leader's own response to situations or direct questions.

Not all of this information is of equal value. However, the overall result of these contributions to public information is a substantial increase in the amount of data on which to make character judgments. The only thing that seems to be lacking sometimes is a way to make sense of it.

Some judgments are easy to make. A president who backdates a bill of sale to gain tax preferences, or who lies about his previous political experience or education raises issues of character and suitability. Yet, other areas are not so easy. Does the fact that a 45-year-old presidential candidate admits to having smoked marijuana more than 20 years ago disqualify him for office and, if so, on what grounds? Does a past extramarital affair represent grounds for disqualification? What if, as was the case with Gary Hart, that affair took place in the middle of a presidential campaign? What about having attempted to evade the draft during an unpopular war, or a tendency to drink too much before achieving sobriety at age 40?

What are we to make of a public display of feelings? Why, for example, when Edmund Muskie "choked up" while delivering a speech in 1972 against a man who printed scurrilous things about his wife, were his "strength" and "stability" questioned—yet when President Ronald REAGAN openly cried at the funeral service for soldiers killed in an airplane crash, no one raised a question. Neither did anyone question George W. BUSH's tendency to "wear his emotions on his sleeve."

Posing these questions suggests that obtaining relevant information may not be the only, or even the most difficult, problem. Along with the information there must be some framework of understanding which helps to make sense of it. Theory, of course, is the solution.

The Nature of Character

Character is the foundation of personality but not synonymous with it. If character is the foundation of individual psychology, personality is its superstructure. Many important elements of personality can be traced to their origins in character psychology. However, personality characteristics are rarely a simple reflection of character. The reason for this is that character and personality develop to some degree in response to maturation, learning, and experience.

The term *character* refers to a set of basic psychological building blocks of intrapsychic and interpersonal functioning that, over time, become integrated into a package. I conceptualize character in terms of three basic elements of psychological functioning: the domains of ambition, integrity, and relatedness.

Character is a vertical psychological concept, not solely a horizontal one. That is, the effects of character are evident throughout an individual's psychological functioning. Character is found not only in the deepest recesses of an individual's psyche but also in the everyday world of accessible and observable behavior. It is that fact that makes the psychological assessment of presidents and leaders possible. An individual's choices reflect what he stands for and his capacity to sustain his fidelity to it (the domain of integrity), the level and means by which he pursues his life purposes (the domain of ambition), and how the individual organizes his interpersonal relationships (the domain of relatedness). A president's choices and their context are often manifestly evident, even to untrained observers. What the trained observer can often do, aided by knowledge of the range of ways these elements can manifest themselves, is to place these observed "facts" into a framework of meaning that allows us to draw theoretical implications.

Presidential Performance

A useful theory requires three elements: a theory of *ordinary* character functioning; a theory of presidential performance; and an appreciation of how and under what circumstances the two fit together. Trait theories are helpful in developing linkages between specific personality characteristics (for example, achievement motivation) and other single characteristics relevant to performance, such as ambition. However, it is a long conceptual and causal way from an individual trait—say sociability—to a person's basic stance toward others. Many "charming" people, for example, use their charm for self-interested purposes. Moreover, single traits present only the thinnest slice of presidential psychology and performance.

While there are many ways to conceptualize presidential performance, every president must decide and lead. Making good choices is helped by having developed good judgment—the quality of analysis, reflection, and ultimately insight that informs the making of politically consequential decisions. Effective political leadership involves three tasks: mobilization, orchestration, and consolidation. Mobilization refers to the president's ability to arouse public support, orchestration to the coordination of various institutional and support elements to achieve his purposes, and consolidation to the ability to develop policy structures that translate his ability to mobilize and orchestrate into enduring policy structures.

Character and Presidential Performance

Presidential performance is always shaped by circumstances. A useful initial hypothesis is that character and psychological functioning are important in shaping presidential performance, *including the president's selection of his responses to circumstances*. By examining the range of choices available to the president and those he selects in similar and different circumstances, one can begin to discern the underlying patterns of psychology that shape his behavior. This is, in reality, something of a minimalist hypothesis. The purpose of a psychologically informed analysis is not to prove that character or presidential psychology explains everything. It will rarely do that in any event. Rather, the challenge of such an analytical focus is to specify what psychological aspects of functioning affect which aspects of presidential performance and further clarify the circumstances under which they do so.

Presidential performance is not reducible to character nor are psychological factors necessarily determinative. Character and psychology do shape presidential performance. However, they are mediated through a number of important filters, including the president's beliefs, his political and personal skills, and the political calculus of the circumstances he must confront.

Presidential judgment, for example, is a complex reflection of character, the ways in which problems are framed, information processing, and experience. The three elements of political leadership (arousal, orchestration, and consolidation) require interpersonal and conceptual skills. They as well require determination (a character element) and vision (an intuitive/cognitive element). A psychologically grounded theory of character and presidential performance will have to make use of a variety of psychological and political theories, not just one.

The Psychological Context of Presidential Performance

Context has a psychological component. Every president is evaluated on his success in addressing and resolving one or more *basic public dilemmas*—the fundamental unresolved public questions concerning public psychology facing the president on taking office. It is not a specific question about public policy but rather a more basic question that raises issues of the public's psychological connections to its institutions, leaders, political process, and each other. This unresolved public concern underlies and frames the more specific policy debates.

One such dilemma among modern presidents was the one faced by Franklin D. ROOSEVELT as to whether and how the government would respond to potentially major national economic and social dislocations in 1932. For Lyndon JOHNSON, in 1964, the question was whether and how the government should implement major programs designed to further the civil rights and economic opportunities for disadvantaged and politically marginal groups. For Gerald FORD (after Richard NIXON), and for Jimmy CARTER (after Johnson, Nixon, and Ford), the basic public dilemma was whether a president could accomplish his policy purposes honestly as well as competently. For Ronald REAGAN in 1984 the question revolved around the restoration of public faith in the office of the president after the flawed presidencies of Lyndon Johnson, Richard Nixon, and, as the public perceived it, the well-intentioned but ineffectual presidencies of Gerald Ford and Jimmy Carter. For Bill CLINTON the major public dilemma was that of public trust in public policy and America's increasing diversity—raising issues of national integration amid traditions of group identifications.

When presidents fail to successfully address their basic public dilemmas, they leave old tasks to new presidents. Thus, George W. BUSH must address issues of public trust, the dilemmas of American diversity, and after 9/11, the dilemma of reconciling freedom and security.

Character as a Political Resource

Honesty, integrity, and trustworthiness may well be virtues in themselves, but they are important for the nation's political life. Political leadership involves the mobilization, orchestration, and consolidation of public mindedness for common purposes. A dishonest political leader forfeits the assumption of public trust that underlies social capital. A president whose positions do not reflect his convictions leaves us wondering which, if either, we should credit. And a political leader whose political self-interest can be counted on to supersede his public mindedness raises the question of whether we are being enlisted for his, or our, purposes. One important function of character integrity, therefore, is to provide an anchor for ambition. It also provides the public with a sense of reassurance that they have given their legitimacy to someone honest enough to deserve it. And it serves as the basis for extending to the leader the benefits of trust-time in which to complete his work, the benefit of the doubt in conflicted circumstances, and the capacity to tolerate setbacks. In a divided society, character integrity is a critical element of leadership capital.

Further reading: Barber, James David. *Presidential Character: Predicting Performance in the White House.* Englewood Cliffs, N.J.: Prentice Hall, 1972; Post, Jerrold M., ed. *The Psychological Assessment of Political Leaders: Theories, Methods, and Applications.* Ann Arbor: University of Michigan Press, 2003; Renshon, Stanley A. *The Psychological Assessment of Presidential Candidates.* New York: Routledge, 1998; Schultz, William. *Handbook of Psychobiography.* New York: Oxford University Press, 1995.
—Stanley A. Renshon

Chase, Salmon P. (1808–1873) *chief justice, secretary of the treasury, U.S. senator*

Born on January 13, 1808, in Cornish, New Hampshire, Chase attended Dartmouth College, then studied law under U.S. Attorney General William Wirt. His lifelong ambition was to become president.

Chase was a U.S. senator from Ohio, Lincoln's secretary of the Treasury, governor of Ohio, and in 1864 was nominated to be the sixth chief justice of the Supreme Court. Throughout his career, Chase was passionately antislavery. He was unsuccessful in his bid for the Republican Party presidential nomination in 1860.

In 1868, as chief justice, Chase presided with dignity and fairness over the Senate impeachment trial of President Andrew JOHNSON. Chase died on May 7, 1873, in New York City.

Further reading: Blue, Frederick J. *Salmon P. Chase: A Life in Politics.* Kent, Ohio: Kent State University Press, 1987.

checks and balances

The structure of the U.S. government is predicated on the principle of separation of powers, perhaps best justified by James MADISON in *Federalist No. 51*. Briefly, separation of powers (as opposed to a fusion of powers practiced in many other democracies, most notably Great Britain) is the idea that different institutions will be primarily responsible for executing the major functions of government (i.e., lawmaking, enforcement, and interpretation). There is overlap, to be sure, and it is likely correct that we have a system not of fully separated powers, but, in Richard Neustadt's famous phrase, separated institutions sharing power. This sharing of power is founded on a system of checks and balances that would, presumably, protect the system from falling prey to tyranny. The framers of the Constitution were particularly concerned that their new creation would not become what they were rebelling against, namely, a strong and despotic monarchy. Checks and balances were thus instituted as a partial means of ensuring that no one institution would gain enough power to strip the other institutions of power and thus come to dominate government.

In *Federalist No. 51* Madison not only makes the case for a system of separated powers but also notes that in order for these institutions (Congress, the presidency, and the courts) to work effectively, they must be given the means to counteract attempts for either individual aggrandizement or encroachment upon the legitimate power sources or structures of their competing institutions. In his words, "Ambition must be made to counteract ambition." In other words, each institution would be given a "check" on the other institutions so as to "balance" the set of power bases given to each by the Constitution.

Most of the checks and balances are found in the Constitution, though some are derivative of the Constitution without finding voice within the document itself. In constructing this intricate system, the framers placed checks and balances at many different levels and generally upon the system, as well as endowing institutions with specific checks.

Any understanding of the general nature of checks and balances must begin with FEDERALISM. By splitting legitimate political authority between a centralized, national government and the disparate states, the Constitution endows both with sovereign power that cannot be usurped by another level. This is, of course, somewhat dampened by the fact that Article VI endows the national government with "supreme" power (known as the supremacy clause), but this does not mean that the states are mere extensions of the national government, as is the case with unitary governments. Second, the Constitution separates the elections of the various institutions of government. Thus, as is the case with parliamentary governments, the executive cannot be derivative of the legislature. This gives each an independent power base. Closely related is the fact that each institution serves for differing periods of time, with representatives elected for two years, the president for four, and senators for six. These different time horizons provide a

natural check on one another as the staggered terms alter political perceptions of the public good. Third is bicameralism, meaning a legislature (that is, Congress) with two houses. The main component of bicameralism is the requirement that almost all lawmaking must pass both the House and the Senate in identical form. This avoids a situation wherein one house possesses all legitimate political authority, as is the case in Britain, where the House of Commons is for all intents and purposes the only legislative authority.

Specific checks exist for each institution on the others and are found both within and outside the Constitution. Internal checks for the president on Congress, for example, include the presidential veto. For the courts, the president nominates judges to the federal courts, including the Supreme Court. Congress (in this case, the Senate) confirms or rejects these nominations. Additionally, the president can negotiate treaties, but they are subject to the ADVICE AND CONSENT provisions of the Senate. The House of Representatives can impeach the president, with the Senate sitting as the tribunal charged with deciding whether or not the president is guilty and therefore should be removed from office. Congress also controls the federal budget to a great degree, therefore having a very real check on the activities of the president in the realm of the EXECUTIVE BRANCH, the branch that the president ostensibly presides over. Congressional checks on the courts include IMPEACHMENT, setting the size of the Supreme Court, and jurisdictions of lower courts.

One very important check that is not explicitly found in the Constitution is the ability for courts to declare various acts, including legislation, of both the Congress and the executive branch unconstitutional and therefore null and void. This provision, called judicial review, is at best implied in the Constitution and was given voice by Chief Justice John MARSHALL in 1803 in the landmark MARBURY V. MADISON. Judicial review, at least in theory, sets the parameters by which presidents and Congress can act.

Other "checks" that exist are not strictly derived from the Constitution but might be considered derivative of it. These are the activities that each branch undertakes in its own sphere but that are subject to external checks by another institution with overlapping power. For example, the president is the COMMANDER IN CHIEF but cannot, according to the Constitution, engage in warfare unilaterally. According to the Constitution, the president can ask Congress for a declaration of war, and Congress can then assent or refuse that request. By implication, Congress cannot declare war in the absence of a presidential request. Also, as already mentioned, Congress by and large controls the purse strings, which could also roll back the unilateral authority of the president to engage in war. However, presidents have been able to get around the checks of Congress by relying on the opinions in several court cases (e.g., *U.S. v. Pink*), as well as by using the moniker of commander in chief. Congress technically has the constitutional muscle to take back what it has lost or abdicated but has so far failed to do so. One example of congressional effort to enforce its check on the presidency was the passage of the WAR POWERS RESOLUTION over President Nixon's veto in 1973. However, no president has formally complied with its provisions (though many have done so informally), given that its provisions (especially those dealing with the ability of congress to veto presidential action after 60 days) might very well constitute a giant LEGISLATIVE VETO, which the court ruled unconstitutional in another setting in 1984.

For the most part, however, the system of checks and balances has been remarkably successful. Though American political history sports examples of times when the separation of powers was violated, these checks generally meet the Madisonian ideal that ambition be made to counteract ambition, and thus the democratic objective of government not only governing others, but especially in governing itself, is largely realized in the American political system.

Further reading: James Madison. *Federalist 51, The Federalist Papers;* Robert A. Dahl. *A Preface to Democratic Theory.* Chicago: The University of Chicago Press, 1957.
—Daniel E. Ponder

Cheney, Richard B. (1941–   ) *deputy assistant to the president, White House chief of staff, congressman, secretary of defense, chief executive officer of Halliburton Company, U.S. vice president*

Dick Cheney was born in Lincoln, Nebraska, and was raised in Casper, Wyoming. He earned B.A. and M.A. degrees in political science from the University of Wyoming. Cheney began his career in public service in 1969 during the NIXON administration. He served in several positions at the Cost of Living Council, Office of Economic Opportunity, and on the WHITE HOUSE staff. During the brief FORD administration, he served as deputy assistant and later as CHIEF OF STAFF. Ford wanted the position to have a lower profile compared to that of Nixon's chief of staff, H. R. Haldeman.

After Ford's defeat, Cheney successfully ran and served as a congressman from Wyoming. He served on the Committee on Intelligence and the Committee to investigate the IRAN-CONTRA AFFAIR. He was elected chairman of the House Republican Conference in 1987 and House minority whip in 1988. During the first BUSH administration, after John Tower was rejected by the Senate, Cheney was nominated and unanimously confirmed to be secretary of Defense. He was called upon to develop America's new post–COLD WAR defense strategy, which entailed

Vice President Dick Cheney (left) walks with Secretary of Defense Donald Rumsfeld into the Pentagon, April 8, 2003. *(Department of Defense)*

reduced budgets and personnel, alongside a significant increase in technology. In addition, he was asked to develop a new definition of America's strategic interest in a vastly altered international environment.

As Defense secretary, he was responsible for Operation Just Cause, which successfully captured Panama's dictator, Manuel Noriega. In addition, he supervised Operation Desert Storm, which successfully turned back Iraq's invasion of Kuwait. Cheney contended that the operation, which involved a half million troops, could be waged on the authority of the president as commander in chief. Congress rejected this argument. The GULF WAR, while successful, was criticized for leaving in power Iraq's dictator Saddam Hussein. However, for his role in Desert Storm, President Bush awarded Cheney the Medal of Freedom.

Upon Bush's defeat for reelection, Cheney returned to the private sector and became the chief executive officer of Halliburton Company, an energy company. Later, as VICE PRESIDENT, Cheney was hounded by accusations that he received special privileges and had been improperly compensated for his work for Halliburton.

In 2000 Cheney was asked to head the search for a vice presidential candidate to run with George W. BUSH, the Republican nominee for president. Bush surprisingly selected Cheney. It was believed that he added NATIONAL SECURITY and Washington experience to the ticket.

As vice president, Cheney has been a partner in all of the Bush administration's proposals and policies. He headed a commission to develop a new energy policy and has been deeply involved in developing the policies relating to the War on Terrorism. Critics have argued that his close ties to the energy industry created a conflict of interest and that his heart problems make him a risky choice for vice president. He has, however, enjoyed high professional and public approval and enjoys the confidence of President Bush.

Further reading: Cheney, Richard B., and Lynne V. Cheney. *Kings of the Hill: Power and Personality in the House of Representatives.* New York: Simon & Schuster, 1996; Andrews, Elaine K. *Richard B. Cheney: A Life of Public Service.* Brookfield, Conn.: Millbrook Press, 2001.
—Frank M. Sorrentino

chief executive

Article II, Section 1, of the U.S. Constitution opens with the words "The executive Power shall be vested in a President . . .," thereby making the president the nation's chief executive, or its chief administrator.

This responsibility is often seen in conjunction with the constitutional requirement that the president must faithfully execute the law. Together, the two are seen as a significant grant of authority and power.

While the president is the nation's chief executive, his control over the management of the government is limited in significant ways by Congress. The president shares many powers with Congress and clashes over managerial, policy, and procedural matters are not uncommon.

chief of staff

The WHITE HOUSE chief of staff is a relatively new position and represents the growing power of the presidency and America's role in the world. The White House served primarily as the president's residence, and until WORLD WAR II, Franklin D. ROOSEVELT maintained a small staff at the White House under his secretary, Stephen Early. The president would have meetings with CABINET officials, advisers, and others at the White House. The war transformed the presidency, making the president the central figure in both foreign and domestic policies, and the White House began to house large numbers of staffers to analyze, evaluate, and propose policy. Roosevelt preferred a freewheeling style and did not appoint a chief of staff so that he would have access to a wide range of views and perspectives.

Harry TRUMAN initially wanted to reduce the White House staff to its previous level. However, as a result of the COLD WAR, the president proposed a NATIONAL SECURITY COUNCIL, which would be staffed at the White House. In addition, the role of government had grown so substantially during the 20th century that the president needed advisers to help with proposals and for monitoring the BUREAUCRACY in which he was nominally in charge. He appointed presidential assistant John Stedman to coordinate and supervise all those advisers who did not have direct access to the president.

It was President Dwight EISENHOWER who formalized the chief-of-staff role. Eisenhower drew on his experience in the military where he utilized a chief of staff who coordinated all activities, issues, and personnel. Eisenhower appointed SHERMAN ADAMS, who also served as the presidential gatekeeper. Except for foreign relations, Adams was in charge of PATRONAGE, communications, press relations and Congressional relations. In addition, he served as liaison to the cabinet. Adams was forced to resign when he was accused of accepting favors. It raised the question of significant power being wielded by unelected and virtually unaccountable officeholders.

Both Presidents KENNEDY and JOHNSON preferred informal managerial systems. They contrasted themselves to Eisenhower, and they wanted to avoid having one individual with a dominant voice. They filled their staffs with loyalists who could be counted on to support and protect the president. Critics have argued that this may lead to a groupthink situation in which the president rarely gets critical feedback.

Richard NIXON reinstated the chief-of-staff position by appointing H. R. Haldeman, a former advertising executive with little political experience. Haldeman's control over the staff was considerable for the reclusive Nixon. Critics have suggested that despite Haldeman's managerial ability, his principal asset to Nixon was loyalty. While the White House staff was well managed, there were too few voices that were free to object to questionable political strategies, especially during the WATERGATE affair. President FORD had Donald RUMSFELD and Dick CHENEY serve as chief of staff but without the imperial manner of Haldeman.

President Jimmy CARTER originally wanted to avoid appointing a chief of staff but ultimately yielded when he became overburdened with details. He appointed his former campaign manager Hamilton Jordan to the post.

Ronald REAGAN, during his first term, was innovative. He divided the functions of chief of staff among three aides. Ed MEESE was in charge of policy, Michael Deaver of communication, and James BAKER of administration. This created competition and access while maintaining a sense of orderliness. In his second term Reagan appointed Donald Regan to the post.

President George H. W. BUSH appointed former New Hampshire Governor John Sununu. Bush believed that he would combine managerial orderliness with political judgment. President Bill CLINTON originally appointed Thomas F. McLarty, his childhood friend and a former utility executive, to the post but switched to former congressman Leon Panetta. President George W. BUSH made Andrew Card his first appointment as chief of staff. This reflects the importance that Bush places on the position and his style of management.

The chief of staff serves closest to the president and performs several functions. Their primary duty is to make sure that the president has access to the necessary information and individuals to make adequate decisions and make sure that important issues are given priority. The chief of staff must also serve as the president's disciplinarian, making sure that individuals working for the White House are performing up to the expectations of the president.

In addition, the chief of staff will be asked to coordinate policy that may cut across departments and bruise the egos of top officials. Lastly, the chief of staff must serve the nation and not hesitate to bring negative information about problems, policies, and personnel to the president. The president and the nation are best served by an honest broker.

The role of chief of staff will vary from president to president. It will reflect their personalities, their work habits, and their style of management. The chief-of-staff position, whether formally or informally stated, is an integral part of the modern presidency. The staff around the president has grown in size and importance over the years, and it needs to be coordinated and managed to serve each president's needs.

While the chief of staff does not require Senate approval, it is a position of immeasurable importance because it serves as a gatekeeper for the president of information and individuals. It is a position that requires managerial ability, political judgment, and loyalty. However, no chief of staff can substitute for a president who is not engaged in the intellectual and political issues of his administration. The president is ultimately accountable for the effective functioning of the White House staff.

Further reading: Hess, Stephen. *Organizing the Presidency*. Washington, D.C.: Brookings Institution, 1988; Koenig, Louis W. *The Chief Executive*. San Diego, Calif.: Harcourt Brace Jovanovich, 1986; Nathan, Richard P. *The Administrative Presidency*. New York: Wiley, 1983.

—Frank M. Sorrentino

chief of state

Many countries of the world, especially democracies, have both a symbolic and substantive leader. For example, Britain has the monarchy, which is largely symbolic and ceremonial, while substantive authority rests with the cabinet, particularly the prime minister. In the United States both the symbolic and the substantive roles are fused within the personage of the president and the office of the presidency. The role of chief of state is normally distinguished from the head of government, but given the fact that they coexist in one institution, the two can be separated for analytic purposes. This entry deals primarily with the chief of state, while elsewhere the head of government is treated.

The chief of state and the head of government are not necessarily opposed to one another, but the chief of state is largely symbolic. The reason for this is that part of a country's identity is based on its cultural symbols. The American people and their political culture focus in large part on the president, the presidency, and the trappings of the office, including the WHITE HOUSE, the OVAL OFFICE, the PRESIDENTIAL SEAL, AIR FORCE ONE (the presidential airplane), and the like. When the president is "acting presidential" he is often depicted in one of these settings. It is here that the presidential connection to the people is often made.

For example, when the president hosts a reception for Boy Scouts and Girl Scouts, or when he speaks to the nation in a time of crisis, or travels abroad to attend the funeral of a foreign leader, he is acting as the American chief of state. When Bill CLINTON threw out the first pitch at the World Series, or Ronald REAGAN spoke to the crowds and, thanks to television, the world at the 40th anniversary of the Invasion of Normandy, or George W. BUSH spoke to the country in the wake of the September 11, 2001, terrorist attacks, these presidents were fulfilling our expectations of national leadership and acting as representative of the nation.

To a significant degree, the role of chief of state is tied to the expectation gap, wherein the expectations heaped upon the president and presidency significantly outstrip the capacities to meet those expectations. As a symbolic leader, the president tends to reap the benefits in terms of popularity, approval, and prestige that attend good news (such as a good economy and peace at home and abroad). When the news is not so good, the president often suffers, even if whatever has turned "bad" is beyond his ability to control. In that case, the president might resort to his role as chief of state in order to regain some of his lost prestige. Speeches, trips abroad, highly publicized ceremonies in the White House Rose Garden, and the like can help recoup his losses in the short term but do not seem to have lasting impact in the long term.

Further reading: Rossiter, Clinton. *The American Presidency*. New York: Harcourt, Brace, and World, Inc., 1956.

—Daniel E. Ponder

Church Committee

This was a select congressional committee formed in the Senate in 1975, and chaired by Sen. Frank Church, to investigate allegations of illegal CIA behavior. The Church Committee's 15-month investigation produced a voluminous final report and numerous recommendations and helped to substantially redefine the relationship between Congress and the presidency regarding intelligence. Created by the National Security Act of 1947, until the 1970s the CENTRAL INTELLIGENCE AGENCY experienced virtual carte blanche in its conduct of intelligence operations. Although formally responsible to the Armed Services and Appropriations committees in the House and Senate, congressional OVERSIGHT by these committees was characterized by deference if not active support of the intelligence community. This relationship changed substantially with the 1974 publication of *New York Times* articles by Seymour Hersh alleging that the CIA had engaged in illegal monitoring of American citizens and domestic dissidents, a violation of the charter of the CIA. The stories set off a firestorm of criticism and led the FORD administration to appoint a commission (the Rockefeller Commission) to investigate the accusations. Congress also set up special committees to investigate the allegations, the Church Committee in the Senate and the Nedzi and Pike Committees in the House (the Nedzi committee was short-lived and was replaced by the Pike Committee).

The Church Committee got started in late January of 1975 and conducted a thoroughgoing 15-month investigation into the numerous allegations swirling around the intelligence community. Hersh's article drew in part on an internal CIA report, dubbed the Family Jewels, that also revealed, most notably, plans within the CIA to assassinate foreign leaders and topple foreign governments. The full ambit of the Family Jewels allegations served as the committee's subject matter. In 1976, after extensive public and private hearings, the committee released its sizable final report. The committee made 183 recommendations to the Senate to improve intelligence operations, the most important of these recommendations revolving around improving the ability of Congress to oversee the intelligence community through special standing committees on intelligence. The Pike Committee, incidentally, became embroiled in acrimonious internal bickering, and the full House voted against the release of its final report.

In 1976 the Senate created the Senate Select Committee on Intelligence (the House created a counterpart in 1977) to oversee the intelligence community. Until this time there had never been standing congressional committees charged solely with overseeing intelligence. Empowered with legislative muscle and institutional legitimacy, the Intelligence Committees in the House and Senate have become important players in the intelligence arena since the late 1970s. Further intelligence blunders and cover-ups, such as Iran-contra, have fueled a vigilance on the part of the Congress, particularly the Intelligence Committees, to maintain a watchful eye over the EXECUTIVE BRANCH in its intelligence and COVERT OPERATIONS. Although initially fought by Republicans as an intrusion into the prerogatives of the presidency and executive branch, many Republicans in Congress have since accepted the newly expanded oversight role for Congress in intelligence and have vigorously supported congressional prerogatives in recent years. While congressional assertiveness in intelligence appears to be entrenched, congressional deference may return somewhat as a result of the terrorist attacks on the United States on September 11, 2001.

Further reading: Johnson, Lock K. *A Season of Inquiry.* Chicago: Dorsey Press, 1988; Knott, Stephen F. "The Great Republic Transformation in Oversight." *International Journal of Intelligence and Counter Intelligence* 13 (2000): 49–63; Lowenthal, Mark M. *U.S. Intelligence: Evolution and Anatomy,* 2d ed. Westport, Conn.: Praeger, 1992; Smist, Frank J., Jr. *Congress Oversees the United States Intelligence Community,* 2d ed. Knoxville: University of Tennessee Press, 1994.

—Michael Korzi

Civilian Conservation Corps (CCC)

Many Americans alive in the 1930s could remember the days when most of their countrymen lived and worked on farms and settlers would trek westward into the frontier. When Franklin ROOSEVELT came into office in 1933, he, like many other thoughtful people of the time, looked with nostalgia upon days gone by. Urban life, it was said, was less healthy than rural life, and young men raised without having labored out of doors were commonly thought to have missed an important formative experience. To this nostalgia were added concerns for the quality of national parks and wildlife areas, for the loss of forestland to logging, and for the erosion of soil. Out of this mix came one of the most famous of the New Deal programs of the Franklin Roosevelt administration.

The Civilian Conservation Corps (CCC) was created by statute in the FIRST HUNDRED DAYS of the Roosevelt presidency and did not expire until 1942. Over the course of its existence, almost three million young American men were put to work in the program. CCC laborers worked at soil conservation, reforestation, the control of wildfires, and the restoration of parks and battlefields.

Roosevelt's "Tree Army" was the president's favorite New Deal program, according to First Lady Eleanor ROOSEVELT. The men in the CCC were paid $30 a month and were required to send all but five dollars home to their families. The Army supervised the workers and boasted in annual reports of the program's effectiveness in turning boys into men. When the nation mobilized for WORLD WAR II, most of the CCC's veterans returned once more to Army supervision, this time on a more strictly military mission.

Further reading: Hill, Edwin G. *In the Shadow of the Mountain: The Spirit of the CCC.* Pullman, Wash.: Washington University Press, 1990; Leuchtenburg, William E. *Franklin D. Roosevelt and the New Deal, 1932–1940.* New York: Harper & Row, 1963.

—Thomas Langston

civil liberties

The president and the attorney general can play a key role in the expansion or denial of civil liberties in the United States. Almost from the beginning of the republic, questions of presidential power over civil liberties have caused controversy and concern.

During the presidency of John ADAMS, the Federalists passed the ALIEN AND SEDITION ACTS, limiting freedom of speech and press, and making it a crime to print "any false, scandalous and malicious writings" directed against the government, Congress, or the president. Adams vigorously enforced the law, convicting 10 men. The courts were of no help as they were in the hands of the Federalists. MADISON and JEFFERSON were forced to write anonymous attacks on the policy.

In the WORLD WAR I era, civil liberties were curtailed via the Espionage Act of 1917 and the Alien Act of 1918. President WILSON's attorney general, A. Mitchell Palmer, was especially repressive in his efforts to attack leftist labor organizations (see the PALMER RAIDS).

WORLD WAR II saw efforts to curtail the liberties of Japanese-American citizens when in 1942, President ROOSEVELT, using Executive Order 9066, had U.S. citizens of Japanese descent herded into detention centers. Amazingly, the Supreme Court, in *Hirabayashi v. U.S.* (1943) and *Korematsu v. U.S.* (1944), upheld the legality of these restrictions of freedom.

In the COLD WAR era, the denial of civil liberties became part of the political football of the age as loyalty tests and loyalty programs were enacted.

During the NIXON presidency further assaults on civil liberties took place as the president and top aides sought to expand illegal wiretapping, engaged in burglary and domestic espionage, corrupted elections, and bypassed the FBI in a series of attempts to establish a secret investigative unit under the control of the president. Nixon also attempted to impose prior restraints on the press in the Pentagon Papers case, but the courts intervened on behalf of publication.

In the aftermath of the 9/11 tragedy, President George W. BUSH and John ASHCROFT, his attorney general, limited a number of freedoms in their effort to root out terrorists.

Further reading: Irons, Peter. *Justice at War: The Story of the Japanese American Interment Cases.* New York: Oxford University Press, 1983; Neely, Mark E., Jr. *The Fate of Liberty: Abraham Lincoln and Civil Liberties.* New York: Oxford University Press, 1991; Smith, James Morton. *Freedom's Fetters: The Alien and Sedition Laws and American Civil Liberties.* Ithaca, N.Y.: Cornell University Press, 1956.

civil religion

A term of unusual ambiguity and controversy, CIVIL RELIGION is the religious dimension of social life which relates citizenship and society to the conditions of ultimate existence and meaning. Though the concept dates back to Greek and Roman civil theology, the term *civil religion* was coined by Jean-Jacques Rousseau in *The Social Contract.* Rousseau used the term to signify the body of religious beliefs required of citizens in his ideal regime. Aimed at cementing the social bond and calming political passions erupting from competing religious systems, the tenets of Rousseau's civil religion included belief in the existence of a powerful and beneficent God; life after death; reward for just behavior; punishment of transgressive behavior; and the sanctity of the social contract.

More recently, Robert Bellah's 1967 article "Civil Religion in America" has set in motion a scholarly flurry to better understand and document civil religion. Bellah argued that in the United States civil religion is neither church religion nor state-sponsored religion but rather exists side by side with church religion while drawing from religious and secular sources such as the Declaration of Independence. Its function, roughly, is twofold: to legitimate existing political arrangements (the priestly function) while also holding the nation and her political leaders responsible to a transcendent ethical standard (the prophetic function).

Civil religion in the United States has no formal institutional basis but it is in presidential INAUGURAL ADDRESSES that it finds its most explicit political expression. Common civil religious themes in the inaugural addresses include sacrifice, the sanctity of freedom, American destiny under God, and America as a chosen nation. Though every president has acknowledged God in the inaugural addresses, the addresses of WASHINGTON, LINCOLN, WILSON, Franklin ROOSEVELT, KENNEDY, and REAGAN stand out in the degree to which they place civil religion front and center. Abraham LINCOLN's Second Inaugural Address is perhaps the most cited document of civil religion in American history.

No consensus has been forged on civil religion since Bellah's 1967 article. The scope, locus, function, history, and even existence of civil religion are still hotly debated. While most critics of civil religion agree that politics often entails an element of piety or religious expression, many dispute that this religious dimension constitutes a bona fide religion. Others acknowledge the existence of civil religion but believe that it poses a threat to church religion, secular political discourse, or both.

Further reading: Gehrig, Gail. *American Civil Religion: An Assessment.* Storrs, Conn.: Society for the Scientific Study of Religion, 1981; Richey, Russell E., and Donald G. Jones, eds. *American Civil Religion.* New York: Harper & Row, 1974; Rousseau, Jean-Jacques. *On the Social Contract.* Translated and edited by Judith R. Masters and Roger D. Masters. New York: St. Martin's Press, 1978.

—Michael E. Bailey

Civil Rights Act

The history of civil rights legislation largely parallels the history of race relations and the civil rights movement in general. The first laws regarding civil rights, in 1866 and 1875, were enacted during the RECONSTRUCTION era after the CIVIL WAR. However, it was not until the late 1950s and the 1960s that a confluence of political and social forces created the political will for major civil rights legislation. The effectiveness of the African-American community in organization and mobilization increased substantially in the post-WORLD WAR II era. With the help of organizations like the Southern Christian Leadership Conference (SCLC) and the Student Nonviolent Coordinating Committee (SNCC), and leaders such as Dr. Martin Luther King, Jr., AFRICAN AMERICANS were able to put substantial pressure on the business and political establishments. Through the use of sit-ins and other nonviolent direct actions, civil rights workers were able to create a climate in which it became more politically feasible for CIVIL RIGHTS POLICY to be changed. Violence between demonstrators and groups that opposed them intensified the pressure put on the political establishment. By the spring of 1963, violent reaction to the peaceful demonstrations of Birmingham, Alabama, was so destructive that President KENNEDY threatened to mobilize the National Guard.

Though in the modern civil rights era legislation addressing civil rights was introduced every year from 1945 to 1957, it was not until 1957 that a modest bill was signed into law. It was, however, in 1964, that a substantial, sweeping and far-reaching Civil Rights Act was enacted. The leadership of President John F. Kennedy is credited with the bill's introduction and President Lyndon B. JOHNSON played a key role in pushing the legislation through Congress after Kennedy's assassination. The administration's proposal covered many aspects of civil rights: voting; education; public accommodations; discrimination in federal programs; and the formation of an Equal Employment Opportunities Commission (EEOC).

As passed, the 1964 law enacted many of the president's requests. It prohibited discrimination in voter registration and all public accommodations and facilities engaged in interstate commerce. It facilitated desegregation of public schools by authorizing the Justice Department to file suit against offending school districts as well as authorizing the withholding of funds from schools that refused to desegregate. Finally, it also prohibited discrimination in employment for all businesses with more than 25 employees and created the EEOC to review complaints.

The 1964 law was not a panacea; there were many loopholes. For example, it exempted private clubs from the accommodations requirement. Similarly, small businesses were exempt from employment provisions. Also, the EEOC lacked real enforcement powers. However, its existence, combined with the 1965 Voting Rights Act, signaled an important step in the battle for equal rights and protections for African Americans that had been waged at the grassroots and federal government level since the end of the Civil War.

By the latter part of the 20th century, the very notion of civil rights had evolved. Attempts to carry out the mission of the 1964 law led to affirmative action practices. Controversial from their inception, these practices proved to be divisive, and fights over them were highly partisan. By the 1980s and 1990s, with the administrations of Presidents Ronald REAGAN and George H. W. BUSH, anti-affirmative action forces had mounted an all-out campaign to change the practices, charging that the remedy for past civil rights abuses had itself become a mechanism for injustice and inequity. Many of these advocates argued for a "color-blind" society, where race (and now gender, age, sexual orientation, and other protected classifications) were irrelevant to laws pertaining to education, employment, accommodations, and the other protections offered under the 1964 Act.

The focus of the Civil Rights Act of 1991 was employment. The Act was the subject of a great deal of conflict between the Democratic Congress and President Bush. While he was on record as supporting affirmative action, he was nevertheless opposed to earlier versions of the 1991 law (including a 1990 version he vetoed), on the grounds that they would lead to the use of quotas in hiring practices. The version signed into law on November 21, 1991, had many provisions that spoke directly to hiring practices, discrimination, and sexual harassment. Specifically, in response to a series of Supreme Court cases, employers would bear the burden of proving that any questionable hiring practices constituted business necessities. Also, employers could be held liable for discrimination by one employee

President Lyndon Johnson signs the Civil Rights Act of 1964 as Martin Luther King, Jr., looks on. *(Johnson Library)*

against another. Finally, it allowed women to receive compensatory damages for sexual harassment and discrimination, expanding on the provisions of the 1964 law that only allowed for the payment of court costs.

Further reading: Belknap, Michael R. *Securing the Enactment of Civil Rights Legislation, 1946–1960.* New York: Garland, 1991; Shull, Steven A. *American Civil Rights Policy from Truman to Clinton: The Role of Presidential Leadership.* New York: M. E. Sharpe, 1999.

—Rebecca E. Deen

civil rights policy

Prior to the CIVIL WAR, civil rights policy—to the extent that one could say there was one—focused on the issue of slavery. At first the issue centered around the possible expansion of slavery to newly established states. Later questions of abolition surfaced and took center stage.

After the Civil War, controversies centered around reconstruction policies, leading up to passage of the Thirteenth Amendment, which abolished slavery, and the Civil Rights Act of 1866. This bill was enacted over President Andrew JOHNSON's veto.

The GRANT administration attempted to enforce civil rights policy but met with limited success. Then the "Compromise of 1876" led to a retreat from presidential involvement in civil rights for a quarter of a century.

President Theodore ROOSEVELT caused a stir when he invited prominent African-American leader Booker T. Washington to dinner at the White House. The gesture caused such an outrage that Roosevelt backed away from even that cursory effort.

In the 1930s President Franklin D. ROOSEVELT and his NEW DEAL policies drew African-American voters away from the REPUBLICAN PARTY to the DEMOCRATIC PARTY, and they would remain a key element in the Democratic Party for the next 70 years. From that point, civil rights became more and more important in presidential politics.

Harry S Truman banned discrimination in the military and created a presidential committee on civil rights in 1946. That committee's report, issued in 1947 and entitled *To Secure These Rights,* called for Congress to pass antilynching laws and a variety of other civil rights provisions.

In the 1950s the Supreme Court decision in *Brown v. Board of Education* (1954) called for an end to segregation in our schools. Resistance to desegregation caused a confrontation in Little Rock, Arkansas, and President EISEN-HOWER felt compelled, reluctantly, to send in federal troops to enforce the law.

From that point on the civil rights movement put pressure on the government to act on behalf of minorities in the U.S. Though the Civil Rights Act of 1957 was a watered-down piece of legislation, nonetheless its passage exhibited the growing power of the civil rights movement.

By the 1960s civil rights had become one of the central issues of the times. Martin Luther King, Jr., became an outspoken and effective leader of the nonviolent wing of the movement, and some calling for violence also rose to prominence. The Kennedy administration, supportive but initially reluctant (for political reasons) to back the civil rights movement, finally gave its full support in 1963, and after Kennedy's untimely death, Congress, with a major push from President Lyndon JOHNSON, passed the CIVIL RIGHTS ACT of 1964, the Voting Rights Act of 1965, and the Civil Rights Act of 1968. In 1967 President Johnson appointed the first African American to the Supreme Court: Thurgood Marshall.

By the 1970s a political backlash against civil rights was welling up. Antibusing for schools became a rallying cry, and President NIXON, while promoting the PHILADELPHIA PLAN (an affirmative action policy) also exploited the anti-civil rights sentiments for his own political gain.

The 1980s saw a further retreat away from presidential involvement in the civil rights movement. The REAGAN administration argued in favor of granting tax-exemption status to a school (Bob Jones University) that prohibited interracial dating, and argued to weaken antidiscrimination standards in the workplace.

In the late 1960s and 1970s, the concept of civil rights began to extend beyond the issue of race to include age (Age Discrimination in Employment Act, 1967), and disability (Americans with Disabilities Act, 1991).

Further reading: Amaker, Norman C. *Civil Rights and the Reagan Administration.* Lanham, Md.: University Press of America, 1988; Graham, Hugh Davis. *The Civil Rights Era: Origins and Development of National Policy, 1960–1972.* New York: Oxford University Press, 1990; Sitkoff, Harvard. *A New Deal for Blacks.* New York: Oxford University Press, 1978; Stern, Mark. *Calculating Visions: Kennedy, Johnson, and Civil Rights.* New Brunswick, N.J.: Rutgers University Press, 1992.

civil service

For most of the 19th century, employment in the EXECU-TIVE BRANCH of the national government was based on the principle of the spoils system. Under this system, which essentially began under Andrew JACKSON, nonelected government jobs were given largely as PATRONAGE, that is, on the basis of politics rather than merit. This was to ensure both that political supporters would be rewarded, thereby maintaining future support, and to maximize political compatibility with the elected person. To be sure, the educated were drawn upon, since the pool of qualified candidates was small. Nonetheless, otherwise qualified candidates were often left out of the resource pool because they were of the wrong party affiliation, different from the current governing regime.

After the CIVIL WAR, however, there emerged a growing concern that the work of the national government could not be done, or done as well as it otherwise could, utilizing the talents of individuals whose main qualification was an amity for and with the party in power. Still, while many were in favor of reform, the issue did not carry political clout such that anyone was willing to do the hard work required to pass meaningful action. Consciousness began to rise somewhat during the GRANT administration, when several of his appointees were party to external interests who sought to defraud the government.

The issue of civil service reform got an unexpected boost when a disgruntled office seeker assassinated President James A. GARFIELD in 1881. Many saw this as evidence that the spoils system was inherently corrupt and, at least in this instance, led to murder. This, combined with severe Republican losses in the 1882 MIDTERM ELECTIONS and a growing fear that they would also lose the 1884 presidential election, propelled many Republicans to jump behind a bill originally proposed by Senator George Pendleton of Ohio, which established the modern-day civil service. Under this system, such fundamental tasks as hiring and promotion were done through a merit system (rather than the spoils system). In addition, the PENDLETON ACT insulated civil servants from political pressures by removing them from the possibility of being fired for political reasons. Finally, government employees were guaranteed political neutrality by prohibiting their being coerced into making political contributions or serving on political campaigns.

Members of the civil service, often called "bureaucrats," perform the day-to-day tasks of implementing governmental policy. Civil servants are not elected, as already noted, but work for and in the executive branch departments and agencies. While it has become fashionable for politicians and pundits to engage in BUREAUCRACY (and sometimes bureaucrat) bashing and decry a "leviathan" government that has grown unmanageably large, the fact of the matter is that government employment of nonmilitary personnel has remained largely stable since the mid 1950s, at about 2.5 million workers.

Merit governs hiring and promotion within the civil service. Pay rates come under the General Schedule (GS) system, ranging from GS 1 to GS 15. Levels GS 1–7 are made up mostly of clerical workers, while GS 8–15 are composed of professional and administrative positions.

Civil servants are not, contrary to popular myth, incompetent. Rather, the bulk of them are highly educated, skilled, motivated, and committed to their jobs. Many are prevented from striking outright, but most have some access to collective bargaining. Civil servants have been able to join unions since 1912 but have had a limited right to strike only since 1962, though they gained a firmer foothold to strike in the Civil Service Reform Act (CSRA) of 1978. Firing an employee has never been a problem when inefficient or incompetent workers are involved. It has been harder to accomplish, though, when seeking to discharge an employee deemed adequate; in other words, when the employee is merely meeting minimal expectations.

The CSRA of 1978 marked a watershed in bureaucratic reform. Among other things, it created the OFFICE OF PERSONNEL MANAGEMENT, charged with administering, executing, and enforcing civil service laws and regulations. The bipartisan Merit Standards Personnel Board decides employee appeals of personnel activities. The Federal Labor Relations Authority governs worker organizations and unions. It has made personnel management easier and created a Senior Executive Service (SES), which offers tenure to the uppermost members of the GS. In exchange, members give up their rights to particular assignments. Thus, it is easier for political executives to move SES members to other agencies if they deem it necessary, after a congressionally prescribed four-month waiting period after a new agency head is appointed.

In general, the civil service operates well and far more efficiently than most members of the public or politicians give it credit for. Inefficiencies do exist, to be sure, mostly given the often-cited criticism that the bureaucracy generally lacks the profit incentive that is endemic to the market mechanism. However, many argue that this is necessary for governing and that privatization of services (one remedy often proposed) will not necessarily, or even in most circumstances, outdistance the work of the civil service.

Further reading: Fester, James W., and Donald F. Kettl. *The Politics of the Administrative Process,* 2d ed. Chatham, N.J.: Chatham House, 1996; Mosher, Frederick. *Democracy and the Public Service,* 2d ed. New York: Oxford University Press, 1982; Nigro, Felix A., and Lloyd G. Nigro. *Modern Public Administration,* 6th ed. New York: Harper and Row, 1984.

—Daniel E. Ponder

Civil War

One nation, or two? All free, or half slave? These questions characterized the split between North and South and precipitated the single greatest crisis in the history of the republic.

Before Abraham LINCOLN became president, the succession of Southern states from the union had already begun. Lincoln, determined to maintain the union, led the North to a victory that both preserved the union and freed the slaves.

During the war, Lincoln grabbed power without congressional authorization and acted with near-dictatorial authority, initiating military action, suspending the writ of habeas corpus, putting civilians on trial in military courts, and utterly dominating decision making. Arguing that the emergency created authority, Lincoln did not wait for Congress—he acted. He explained his reasoning in an 1864 letter to his friend Albert Hodges:

> Was it possible to lose the nation and yet preserve the Constitution? By general law, life and limb must be protected, yet often a limb must be amputated to save a life; but a life is never wisely given to save a limb. I felt that measures otherwise unconstitutional might become lawful by becoming indispensable to the preservation of the nation. Right or wrong, I assumed this ground and now avow it.

During the war, Lincoln issued the EMANCIPATION PROCLAMATION, freeing the slaves. With victory, Lincoln proposed a lenient RECONSTRUCTION for the South. However, his assassination on April 14, 1861, ended his hopes for such a plan. The Civil War marks a dramatic increase in the power of the president during an emergency. After the war, the nation returned to a congressionally dominated regime.

Lincoln ranks as possibly the greatest president in U.S. history. His conduct of the war, freeing of the slaves, preservation of the Union, and inspiring rhetoric place him at the top of most scholars' lists as the most highly rated of the U.S. presidents.

Further reading: McPherson, James M. *Abraham Lincoln and the Second American Revolution.* New York: Oxford University Press, 1990; *Battle Cry of Freedom.* New York: Oxford University Press, 1988; Neely, Mark E. *The Fate of Liberty: Abraham Lincoln and Civil Liberties.* New York: Oxford University Press, 1991; Wills, Garry. *Lincoln at Gettysburg: The Words That Remade America.* New York: Simon & Schuster, 1992.

Clark, Ramsey (1927–) U.S. attorney general

A key Justice Department attorney during the administrations of presidents John KENNEDY and Lyndon JOHNSON, Ramsey Clark was U.S. attorney general from 1967 to 1969. During his time in President Johnson's CABINET, Clark was known best for his aggressive support of civil rights and CIVIL LIBERTIES, particularly for protecting free speech for unpopular people and groups and the rights of criminal defendants. His actions included filing the first racial desegregation case against a school district in a northern state. In office, Clark also worked to develop new programs to reform federal prisons, enforce antitrust provisions, aggressively prosecute organized crime, strengthen national drug rehabilitation programs, and upgrade criminal law enforcement training. He was known for his vigorous opposition to the death penalty and strengthening gun control laws. In addition, he was frequently critical of government wiretaps of citizen telephone conversations, although he authorized their use in cases involving national security. Clark joined the Kennedy administration in 1961 as assistant attorney general in charge of the lands division but soon was reassigned to oversee school desegregation efforts in southern states. He became deputy attorney general in 1965 and acting attorney general in October 1966, a position he held until his nomination was approved the following February. A native of Texas, Clark is the son of Tom C. Clark, a member of the U.S. Supreme Court from 1949 to 1967. The senior Clark resigned from the Court to avoid the possibility of a conflict of interest when his son became attorney general.

After leaving government service, Clark taught in law schools and practiced law in New York City. He frequently was attacked, particularly by Republicans and conservatives, as being "soft on crime," and for representing unpopular defendants and for his aggressive criticism of several American military actions overseas.

Further reading: Clark, Ramsey. *Crime in America.* New York: Simon & Schuster, 1970; Harris, Richard. *Justice.* New York: E.P. Dutton, 1970.

—Robert E. Dewhirst

Clay, Henry (1777–1852) *secretary of state, candidate for president, speaker of the House, U.S. senator, U.S. representative*

Perhaps the most influential politician of the first half of the 19th century, Henry Clay, called the "Great Compromiser" because he brokered several significant deals between the North and South over the issue of slavery, several times ran for, but was never elected, president.

An eloquent speaker and brilliant politician, Clay promoted an "American System" of reforms—the building of roads and canals, internal improvements, tariffs—that brought him to loggerheads with President Andrew JACKSON. Clay was elected Speaker of the House on his first day as a representative from Kentucky. He dominated the House and had a profound influence on U.S. politics for 40 years.

Clayton Act

Enacted in 1914, the Clayton Act extended the SHERMAN ANTITRUST ACT's prohibition against price fixing and monopolistic practices and exempted labor unions from antitrust laws. The act also limited the jurisdiction of the courts to issue injunctions against labor unions, but this provision faced opposition by the courts and required subsequent legislation to establish this limitation. The Clayton Act, named after the Senate sponsor Henry Clayton of Alabama, was one of the planks of President WILSON's NEW FREEDOM platform.

Further reading: Adams, Walter, and James W. Brock. *Antitrust Economics on Trial: A Dialogue on the New Laissez-Faire.* Princeton, N.J.: Princeton University Press, 1991; Jones, Eliot. *The Trust Problem in the United States.* New York: Macmillan, 1927.

Cleveland, Grover (1837–1908) *twenty-second and twenty-fourth U.S. president*

Grover Cleveland's place in American history is secured if for no other reason than to provide an answer to several trivia questions. Cleveland is the only president to serve two nonconsecutive terms. He was the only Democrat elected president during a span dating from before the CIVIL WAR (James BUCHANAN elected as a Democrat in 1856) almost to World War I (Woodrow Wilson elected in 1912). Cleveland also represents a more substantial figure in the development of the presidency than these bits of trivia suggest. While in office, Cleveland offered a counterpoint to the Whiggish notion of the presidency that dominated much of American political thought during the latter part of the 19th century. He showed a willingness to use the tools of the presidency, such as the veto and the annual message, to a degree that they had not been used before. Further, his approach to foreign policy during the 12 years that separated his first year in office (1885) and his last (1897) reflected the growing international presence of the United States.

Grover Cleveland was born in Caldwell, New Jersey, on March 18, 1837, and moved with his family to New York State when he was four. He did not attend college due to his father's unexpected death in 1853. Nevertheless, he was admitted to the bar in 1859 after studying law at a Buffalo law firm, a position his uncle helped him obtain. Although drafted to serve in the Civil War, Cleveland paid $150 to a Polish immigrant to serve for him, a practice allowed under the Conscription Act of 1863.

Cleveland's political career started when he was elected ward supervisor in 1862, also serving as assistant district attorney for Erie County from 1836 to 1865. He became county sheriff in 1871, serving in that position for two years. In 1882 he became mayor of Buffalo and developed a reputation as the "veto mayor" for blocking high-priced city contracts. The following year he was elected governor of New York. In that office, he demonstrated many of the traits that he would later exhibit in the White House, vetoing private bills, rebuffing the party bosses at Tammany Hall, generally favoring merit over PATRONAGE for government jobs, and otherwise promoting CIVIL SERVICE reform.

Cleveland entered the 1884 Democratic convention as the party's front-runner and secured the nomination for president on the second ballot. His Republican opponent was James G. Blaine, former secretary of State and longtime party leader. The campaign has been called the dirtiest in American history, as its primary focus centered on the morality of both candidates. Democrats charged Blaine for using his positions of power for personal financial gain. Cleveland was susceptible to attacks for a premarital affair with Maria C. Halpin in the early 1870s. Ms. Halpin gave birth to a son and named Cleveland as the father. Although the child's paternity was never established (Ms. Halpin apparently had several affairs with other married men), Cleveland accepted responsibility for the child and helped arrange for the child's adoption when Ms. Halpin suffered a mental breakdown. As a campaign issue, the affair gave rise to chants like "Ma, Ma where's my Pa? Gone to the White House, Ha, Ha, Ha!" But Cleveland was able to diffuse the issue by directing his supporters to "tell the truth" about the affair. At the end of the day, Cleveland defeated Blaine by 219-182 in the ELECTORAL COLLEGE and garnered a 63,000-vote margin in the popular vote.

As Cleveland entered office, he continued his trait of favoring merit over patronage for doling out federal government jobs. He strictly adhered to the PENDLETON ACT and dutifully poured over the qualifications of applicants for positions outside that act's scope. Nevertheless, Cleveland did favor appointing meritorious Democrats over Republicans and made use of the TENURE OF OFFICE ACT's provision that allowed him to suspend (but not remove) incumbent Republican federal employees in favor of Democratic appointees. As with several of his predecessors, Cleveland had an early showdown with the Senate over the presidency's appointment-and-removal powers—a showdown that Cleveland won both with the Senate and in the realm of public opinion. A few months later, Congress repealed the Tenure of Office Act altogether, an action that Cleveland later referred to an "an expurgation of the last pretense of statutory sanction to an encroachment upon constitutional Executive prerogatives." Although the issue of the REMOVAL POWER would not be settled until the 1920s with the Supreme Court case of MYERS V. UNITED STATES, the repeal of the Tenure of Office Act was an important step in the development of the presidency, representing a clear victory for the independent authority of the institution.

Congress passed several major pieces of legislation during Cleveland's first administration. With the passage of the Interstate Commerce Act of 1887, Congress created the Interstate Commerce Commission, the nation's first regulatory agency, thereby recognizing a need to provide some checks on the nation's emerging industrial economy. Congress also passed the PRESIDENTIAL SUCCESSION ACT of 1886, the first revision of presidential succession laws since 1792; the Dawes Severalty Act of 1887, which granted citizenship and land to Indians who were ready to adopt "the habits of civilized life;" and the HATCH ACT of 1887, establishing agricultural experiment stations at agricultural colleges. As with most legislation during this era, however, the president played only a small role in the passage of these bills, such as lending some measure of public support to congressional efforts and, as constitutionally required, signing the bills into laws.

The more significant impact that Cleveland's first term had on the presidency's institutional development lies in bills and proposals that did not become law. For example, Cleveland wielded his veto pen like no other president before him. His favorite targets were private pension bills for Civil War veterans that Cleveland saw as adding excessive costs for the federal government and promoting fraud and dishonesty among claimants. Cleveland vetoed 228 pension bills. However, one should note this equals just over 10 percent of the total private bills passed by Congress during the president's first term. He also combined constructive criticism with occasional mockery in his veto messages, thereby irritating Congress and angering the Grand Army of the Republic, the Civil War veterans' organization.

As another example of Cleveland's impact on the presidency's institutional development, he devoted his entire third annual message in December 1887 solely to the issue of the tariff. The president's STATE OF THE UNION address traditionally had been a mix of reporting of executive branch activities combined with modest proposals for legislative actions. Never before, however, had the annual message been such an aggressive tool for calling for legislative action in one policy area. Cleveland was concerned about the growing Treasury surplus that was accumulating due to the high protectionist tariffs then in effect. Cleveland laid out his analysis of the cause and effects of the high tariff, and in the end he recommended significantly lower tariff rates on all necessaries and raw materials. He believed that doing so would result both in reducing consumer prices domestically and in opening markets to American products abroad. In the end, however, Congress did not pass any tariff legislation in the wake of Cleveland's speech. Nevertheless, his message reflects a more proactive conception of the CHIEF EXECUTIVE—one that becomes more embroiled in legislative affairs and one that differs considerably from the Whiggish notion of the presidency, best typified by Cleveland's successor in office Benjamin HARRISON. Moreover, many scholars would define this speech as a key economic address that would foreshadow later expansive involvement by executives in the economic realm.

Harrison defeated Cleveland in the 1888 election, even though Cleveland won the popular vote nationwide. Cleveland's long-standing battle with the Tammany Hall machine caused him to lose his home state of New York and, as a result, cost him the election. After leaving office, Cleveland practiced law in New York City. He generally stayed out of the public realm during the first few years of the Harrison presidency but returned with his "Silver Letter" of February 1891. In this letter, Cleveland broke with Western Democrats but gained favor with Eastern Democrats and even some moderate Republican Mugwumps by criticizing

President Grover Cleveland *(Library of Congress)*

the idea of the "dangerous and reckless experiment" posed by "free, unlimited and independent silver." Cleveland continued his public profile throughout 1891 and into 1892 and entered the Democratic convention once again as the front-runner. Despite opposition from Silver Democrats and Tammany Hall, he garnered the party's nomination on the first ballot. The primary issue of the campaign was the Tariff Act of 1890; Cleveland continued his call to reduce tariff rates. Cleveland won the election handily in the ELECTORAL COLLEGE, 277-145, with Populist candidate James Weaver, whose campaign centered on the free coinage of silver, garnering 22 electoral votes from the West.

Cleveland's second administration was marked by the nation's economic problems. As president, Cleveland took an even more proactive approach than his first term to addressing these issues. His efforts cost him the support of his DEMOCRATIC PARTY but once again represented an expanded use of presidential powers and expanded notion of presidential authority.

The nation experienced an economic panic starting in February 1893, followed by a four-year depression. One important cause of these problems was the nation's declining gold reserves, which Cleveland attributed to the Sherman Silver Purchase Act passed during the HARRISON administration. Cleveland took the significant step of calling for a special session of Congress to address the problem. Although Congress repealed the Purchase Act, Cleveland alienated significant portions of his party. The western and southern silver-wing of the party, led by William Jennings BRYAN, who was emerging as a national force, opposed Cleveland's policy. Meanwhile, congressional party leaders resented Cleveland's interventionist approach on a domestic policy issue as well as his tactic of threatening to withhold all patronage appointments unless Congress passed an unconditional repeal of the Purchase Act.

Cleveland also brought a more activist approach to the tariff in his second term. In his first term, even though he dedicated his third annual message to the issue, he did not get involved in the legislative process. In the second term, however, Cleveland cowrote the original legislation that eventually became the Wilson-Gorman Tariff Act of 1894. As conceived, the bill would have resulted in significantly lower tariff rates. After working its way through Congress, though, the legislation resulted in moderate reductions of three base rates but also added charges to other goods, thus earning the nickname of the "Mongrel Tariff." Cleveland charged his fellow Democrats with "party perfidy and party dishonor," but he allowed the bill to become law without his signature.

In 1894 employees of the Pullman Palace Car Company went on strike when George Pullman cut his employees' wages. The strike quickly spread to other railroad companies, spearheaded by the American Railway Union and its leader, Eugene V. Debs. The strike severely constricted rail traffic from Chicago to points west, and violence broke out in Blue Island, Illinois, a town south of Chicago. Spurred on by the course of events and perhaps overly influenced by his attorney general, Richard Olney (who had developed a close relationship with a consortium of railroad managers), President Cleveland ordered federal troops into Chicago. As a result, the strike eventually was broken, and Debs and other union leaders were arrested. Cleveland biographer Richard E. Welch, Jr., perhaps best summarizes the unprecedented nature of the president's actions: "Cleveland was not the first American president to send federal troops to maintain law and order during a railroad strike. . . . Cleveland was, however, the first president to do so at his own initiative and not at the application of a state governor." By undertaking the actions he did, Cleveland relied on neither any legislative approval from Congress nor a request from a state's governor generally responsible for exercising police powers over his state's citizenry. Instead, Cleveland relied on his notion of the presidency's constitutional authority, a position that the Supreme Court subsequently upheld when Debs challenged his arrest.

Cleveland's primary focus during his two terms was on domestic issues: the tariff, civil service reform, the economy, etc. Yet his approach to foreign policy offers lessons about the changing role of the United States in the world in the last past of the 19th century. Cleveland entered office in 1885 calling for "peace, commerce, and honest friendship with all nations; entangling alliances with none." He held true to his premise in the first major foreign policy issue he faced when he withdrew the Frelinghuysen-Zavala treaty, which would have created a canal through Nicaragua (one similar to the Panama Canal), from Senate consideration because of its implications for creating permanent alliances. The president took a similar approach in regard to a treaty with Hawaii, but Cleveland's approach to foreign policy has been characterized as being inconsistent and not having any grand theme. Thus, Cleveland sometimes exhibited a more aggressive approach to FOREIGN AFFAIRS, such as using American warships to counter the German presence in Samoa in 1888–89. The most dramatic international event of Cleveland's tenure, though, involved a boundary dispute between Venezuela and the British colony Guiana. Cleveland viewed his stance in the dispute, developed in conjunction with Secretary of State Richard Olney (who switched to the position from attorney general in 1895), as merely being a reaffirmation of the long-standing MONROE DOCTRINE. Critics, however, suggest that Cleveland unnecessarily brought the nation to the brink of war with Great Britain over a dispute that was not of great national importance. The long-term effect of Cleveland's actions was to spark a sense of "militant nationalism" among the public

and to raise the Monroe Doctrine in the public's eye to be an almost inviolate principle of American foreign policy.

Further reading: Milkis, Sidney M., and Michael Nelson. *The American Presidency: Origins and Development, 1776–1993,* 2d ed. Washington, D.C.: CQ Press, 1994; Nevins, Allan. *Grover Cleveland: A Study in Courage.* New York: Dodd, Mead & Company, 1933; Welch, Richard E., Jr. *The Presidencies of Grover Cleveland.* Lawrence: University Press of Kansas, 1988.

—Victoria Farrar-Myers

Clifford, Clark McAdams (1906–1998) *secretary of defense, assistant to the president*

Clark Clifford, characterized by James Reston as a person who had a career of rescuing presidents, was born in Fort Scott, Kansas, and attended Washington University in St. Louis, the city in which he began his law practice in 1928. Although a father and past draft age, he enlisted in the U.S. Navy in 1943 and was assigned in 1944 as a naval aide to the WHITE HOUSE. After TRUMAN became president, his fellow Missourian soon became a presidential speechwriter, then special COUNSEL TO THE PRESIDENT. Clifford helped shape the MARSHALL PLAN, NATO, the NATIONAL SECURITY ACT, which created the CIA and unified the armed services, and interceded for Truman with George C. MARSHALL when Truman granted diplomatic recognition to the new state of Israel over Marshall's objection. During the 1948 presidential election campaign that stunned the world when Truman won, Clifford was closely involved in developing and implementing campaign strategy.

Although his standard admonition to new or prospective clients was that his services did not involve providing influence with governmental agencies, when he left government service in 1949, he quickly had a stable of impressive corporate clients that would include Trans World Airlines, ABC, General Electric, RCA, and Du Pont.

After leaving the White House, Clifford continued to be a trusted adviser to Democratic presidents. For John KENNEDY he was personal lawyer during Kennedy's Senate years, leader of the presidential transition team, and member, then chair, of the Foreign Intelligence Committee that was created in the aftermath of the BAY OF PIGS fiasco. President CARTER sought Clifford's advice in handling accusations raised against Office of Management and Budget Director Bert Lance during his years as a Georgia banker. Clifford was one of the first persons that Lyndon JOHNSON telephoned when Johnson became president.

In 1967 he was appointed secretary of Defense and soon became convinced that the war in Southeast Asia was not winnable. Initially, this created a rift between him and President Johnson, a friend for more than 20 years.

Unfortunately for his reputation, Clifford's last years were tinged with scandal swirling around his connections with the Bank of Credit and Commercial International. Although he claimed no knowledge of the charges (fraud, bribing bank regulators, and laundering drug money), and his partner was acquitted, it was only a few weeks before his death that the last charges, including a hefty fine, against Clifford were resolved.

No one recalls him ever raising his voice. His flawless speeches, like Churchill's, were carefully rehearsed, and he was invariably meticulously groomed.

Further reading: Clifford, Clark, with Richard Holbrooke. *Counsel to the President.* New York: Random House, 1991; Frantz, Douglas, and David McKean. *Friends in High Places: The Rise and Fall of Clark Clifford.* Boston: Little, Brown, 1995.

—Thomas P. Wolf

Clinton, George (1739–1812) *U.S. vice president, governor*

This powerful multiterm governor of New York was a prominent figure in the politics of the founding era, and a two-term vice president. The confusion over how voters selected presidential versus vice presidential candidates led to the passage of the Twelfth Amendment, allowing a president and vice president to run as a "team." The Virginian JEFFERSON chose New Yorker Clinton as his vice president and they easily won the 1804 election.

However, Clinton was frail and aging, and he proved to be an ineffective vice president, fumbling through his duties as presiding officer of the Senate. In 1808 he hoped to become president, but James MADISON won the nod and accepted Clinton as his vice president. While victorious, this team did not have a happy relationship, as Clinton often and openly disagreed with Madison. In 1811 Clinton cast the tiebreaking vote in the Senate against rechartering the BANK OF THE UNITED STATES. Madison held a contrary view! On April 20, 1812, Clinton became the first VICE PRESIDENT to die in office, leaving the position unfilled for a short time.

Clinton, Hillary Rodham (1947–) *first lady, U.S. senator*

Prominent lawyer, activist for children's rights, former first lady to President Bill CLINTON (1993–2000), U.S. Senator (Dem.-N.Y.), Hillary Rodham Clinton has an extensive résumé. Born in Chicago, Illinois, on October 26, 1947, to parents Hugh and Dorothy Rodham, she excelled at an early age. At Wellesley College, in Massachusetts, she studied political science and psychology. Graduating with high honors in 1969, she was chosen commencement speaker by her fellow graduates, the first student to receive such an honor.

First Lady Hillary Rodham Clinton *(Library of Congress)*

Her experiences at Yale Law School shaped her future, both personally and professionally. As the editor of the *Yale Review of Law and Social Action,* she became interested in the rights and interests of children and their families. After graduation from Yale in 1973, she took a position working for the Children's Defense Fund as a staff attorney and, later, as a member of the board of directors. In 1974 she worked briefly for the House Judiciary Committee in the WATERGATE investigations. The following year, however, she moved to Arkansas, taking a position as assistant professor at the University of Arkansas Law School. In that year, she also married Bill Clinton, whom she had met in her second year at Yale.

Throughout her career, Clinton has worked in family and education policy development and advocacy. In Arkansas, Governor Clinton appointed her to chair the Educational Standards Committee and she also founded the Arkansas Advocates for Children and Families. In 1977 she was appointed by President CARTER to be chair of the Legal Services Corporation. She was named one of the *National Journal*'s 100 Most Influential Lawyers in 1988 and 1991, and in 1987 she chaired the American Bar Association's Committee on Women in the profession.

When President Clinton took office in 1993, Mrs. Clinton expanded the role of the office of the first lady. She was the first to have an office in the prestigious West Wing of the WHITE HOUSE and, when she was called to testify about her dealings in the failed Whitewater land development affair, became the first first lady to be subpoenaed before a federal grand jury. When President Clinton was campaigning for the office in 1992, he quipped that the country would get two for the price of one (in reference to the policy role that his wife would assume); this was not universally well received. In her position as the chair of the President's Task Force on Health Care (the working group charged with developing a proposal to reform the health care system), she drew a substantial amount of criticism from several fronts. Some opposition was political, by those who differed with the administration's policy goals. Other forces opposed her expansion of the role of first lady away from ceremonial duties toward substantive policy. Still others questioned the high-powered role of someone who held neither an elected office nor one that required Senate confirmation. In response to a suit brought against her by the Association of American Physicians and Surgeons, a federal appeals court held that the first lady was a government employee.

Even after the Clintons left the White House following the completion of President Clinton's second term as president, Hillary Rodham Clinton continued to make history. No other first lady had run for elected office, either prior to or after occupying the White House. In 2000 Mrs. Clinton won election to the U.S. Senate representing New York. In the 107th Congress she serves on the following committees: Budget; Environment and Public Works; and Health, Education, Labor and Pensions.

Further reading: Burden, Barry, and Anthony Mughan. "Public Opinion and Hillary Rodham Clinton." *Public Opinion Quarterly* 63 (1999): 237–251; Burrell, Barbara. *Public Opinion, the First Ladyship, and Hillary Rodham Clinton.* New York: Garland Publishers, 1997; Eksterowicz, Anthony, and Kristen Paynter. "The Evolution of the Role and Office of the First Lady: The Movement Toward Integration with the White House Office." *Social Science Journal* 37 (2000): 547–563.

—Rebecca E. Deen

Clinton, William Jefferson (1946–) *forty-second U.S. president*

Bill Clinton is the most paradoxical president to occupy that office. He left office the same way that he entered it —a man of dazzling talents, towering ambitions, substantial personal deficiencies, and, not surprisingly, enormous controversy. He is widely recognized as one of the most knowledgeable, politically insightful, rhetorically fluent, and adroit modern politicians to occupy the OVAL OFFICE. Yet he is also recognized as a president who squandered his political and historical potential because his personal flaws

trumped his enormous talents. Many marveled at his capacity to rescue himself after seeming to throw himself off one or another personal or political precipice. Others wondered why it was necessary for him to do that so often.

A President of Enormous Contradictions
Clinton had trouble throughout his career with these issues. Ironically, the president who promised the "most ethical administration" in history presided over one in which resignations for ethical cause, indictments, convictions, judicial reprimands, appointments of special investigative prosecutors, and continuing questions about ethical and possibly criminal lapses played a defining role.

In his 1992 presidential campaign, among the many issues that he and the public had to face were: his less than candid answers to questions about his draft deferment, marijuana use, marital fidelity, and the use of questionable deductions for an inside land deal (Whitewater) loans on his tax returns. Once in office he faced controversy and criticism for a number of highly questionable contributions to his reelection campaign, the use of the White House to both solicit money and to reward contributors, his Whitewater legal defense fund, the questionable and highly controversial pardons he gave right before leaving office, and, of course, his IMPEACHMENT because of questionable behavior with a 21-year-old intern and his subsequent misrepresentations, under oath, to a federal court and grand jury.

Public Response to President Clinton
Clinton's paradoxical and uneven performance as president was mirrored in large part by the public's response to him. So, while Clinton did not inspire public trust, he managed throughout his term—including during his impeachment—to retain public support. Surveys found that 58 percent of the public approved of Clinton's performance as a president, but 61 percent disapproved of him as a person. At the height of his impeachment hearings 65 percent of those asked said they approved of the way President Clinton was handling the presidency, yet only 35 percent thought him honest and trustworthy, and only 29 percent felt he had high personal moral and ethical standards. Fifty-five percent of the public opposed the House passing impeachment articles and sending them on to the Senate. However, if they did, 44 percent of the public thought he should then resign and save the country (them?) a damaging Senate trial. At the same time, 57 percent thought that if the House passed articles of impeachment, the Senate should not remove him from office.

At the end of his time in office, seven in 10 Americans said they were tired of the problems associated with this administration, and fewer than one-third wished that he could run for a third term. Fifty-four percent said they would be "glad to see him go," and only 39 percent said they would be "sorry to see him go." One could sum up the

William Jefferson Clinton (*Library of Congress*)

evidence from these and similar surveys regarding the public's response to President Clinton as follows: They supported the president, but not his behavior; they wanted him severely reprimanded, but not punished; and they wanted him to remain in office and not be removed after his Senate trial, but were happy to see him leave.

Domestic Politics and Policy

Clinton campaigned for and won office promising to govern as a "New Democrat" but immediately appeared to govern as an old one. After promising to focus like a laser on the economy, almost his first order of business was to insist that gay soldiers be allowed to openly serve in the military. After promising not to raise taxes on the middle class to pay for new government programs, he did so relying on the distinction between tax increases that increased general revenues and thus could be used to pay for new programs and tax increases directly mandated for new programs. And the last straw for the public was the president's declaration of a health-care "crisis" and his proposed massive federalization of the health care system as a solution—one that was roundly defeated by Congress.

In the 1994 MIDTERM ELECTIONS, the public overwhelmingly repudiated his leadership. The GOP gained control of both houses of Congress and made enormous gains in state governorships and legislatures. Thereafter, he survived by temporarily borrowing the policies and premises of his opponents—a process dubbed "triangulation"—and by proposing numerous small-gauge policies. In 1996 he won reelection, the only Democrat to do so since FDR, by promising, again, to govern from the political center.

Domestically, his administration was successful in maintaining a robust economy (which some attribute to GOP control of Congress after 1995), in passing a landmark welfare reform shortly before his reelection campaign after twice vetoing similar efforts, in championing free trade and winning approval of NAFTA (North America Free Trade Agreement) over the objections of union leaders who were strong supporters of his party, and in attempting to reorient the Democrats away from a singular focus on interest-group liberalism toward a more capitalist-friendly stance.

Consistent with the ambiguities and paradoxes of this administration, Clinton promised in his 1996 State of the Union address that "the era of big government was over," even as he was adding new programs and expanding old ones. He promised to make abortion "safe, legal, and rare" but repeatedly vetoed any measure to circumscribe it. He promised to "mend, not end" the controversial policy of racial preferences. He mended the government's racial preferences in procurement policy by opening it up to whites who "could prove they had been victims of chronic discrimination." Individual minority applications had no such burden of proof, it was assumed. And to these obvious rhetorical and policy inconsistencies, one must add Clinton's trenchant, prescient insight regarding America's ethnic diversity: "It is really potentially a great thing for America that we are becoming so multi-ethnic . . . but it's also potentially a powder keg of problems and heart break and division and loss." This was followed by the President's Initiative on Race—"One America"—that was roundly criticized as not being sufficiently politically diverse, encouraging platitudes rather than real issue engagement, and framing the issues as black-white rather than focused on America's increasing ethnic diversity.

Foreign Policy

Although less interested in foreign than in DOMESTIC POLICY, Clinton's contribution to the development of a post-COLD WAR world can be summed up as emphasizing multilateralism, the importance of written agreements and corresponding commitment to the importance of international systems of issue resolution, and a reluctance to use military force. Clinton was a tireless promoter of resolving long-festering international problems—among them the Catholic-Protestant conflict in Northern Ireland and the

Arab-Israeli conflict. He gained agreements in both conflicts, but no lasting peace in either. Some wondered whether his repeated immersion in the latter conflict escalated expectations for further gains among Palestinians, leading them to ultimately reject the final accord the president so desperately tried to achieve.

President Clinton was a reluctant world leader when Serbia began to undertake the ethnic cleansing of ethnic Muslims in the former republic of Yugoslavia. Yet, after a reluctant start, U.S. air power was instrumental in bringing about the Dayton Accords, which ended the fighting but not the conflict. Mr. Clinton was equally reluctant in confronting Saddam Hussein and insisting that expelled UN weapons inspectors be allowed back in to continue their work, and he preferred the minimalist military approach of shooting cruise missiles in response to an Iraqi plot to assassinate former president George H. W. BUSH, or to terrorist bombing of the World Trade Towers in 1993, rather than making full use of American military and diplomatic power. In light of 9/11, reports that Saudi Arabia offered to turn over Osama Bin Laden to the United States but was rebuffed because the president and his advisers felt there wasn't enough legal evidence to make a strong court case, must be judged a missed opportunity and a matter of regret.

A President of Paradoxes: Why?

The dazzling array of personal and political paradoxes that characterize the Clinton presidency are a result of the mismatch between the president's large policy ambitions and a public that had tired of large ineffective solutions to public problems that continued in spite—some would say because—of them. Clinton saw himself as the heir to Roosevelt and Kennedy, doing big and great things with the presidency he had prepared himself for and wanted since early adolescence. And he correctly felt that he had the intelligence, drive, and political skill to accomplish it.

He was faced with a public that had become reticent to support large government policy programs—however well intentioned—that seemed after many decades to not solve problems and perhaps even to exacerbate them. He was then faced with a choice: Either persuade the public that his programs would be different, or try to finesse the public's reluctance by not being clear and forthright about his views and purposes. In welfare reform, race relations, abortion, his economic program, the nation's child-care programs, and vaccine production, and most paradigmatically his massive health care program hidden behind "regional alliances," Mr. Clinton chose to finesse rather than persuade.

President Clinton's Legacy

Even before leaving office, Clinton was much concerned with his public legacy and place in history. Frustrated by

the public and later by the Republican Congress that elected to check him, he was denied the chance to create the grand policy monuments to his own personal and public ambitions that he sought. Yet, our best presidents are not remembered primarily for the number and expansiveness of their programs. Who remembers George WASHINGTON's policy initiatives, or thinks that FDR's greatness lies in the creation of big government?

These, and other modern presidents—Harry TRUMAN, Dwight EISENHOWER, and Ronald REAGAN come to mind—are well regarded historically for one of two primary reasons. Either, like Washington, Truman, and Eisenhower, they exemplified in their conduct an honest, steady, and competent reliability that made them trustworthy anchors during turbulent political times. Or, like ROOSEVELT in response to the depression or Reagan in response to widespread public malaise, they were able through the force and example of their characters to help change the political climate—for Roosevelt from despair to optimism, for Reagan from alienation to confidence.

President Clinton will not be recalled as having accomplished either. He will be recalled most as a president who resided during a prosperous period, and perhaps, if people forget the role the REPUBLICAN PARTY and his reelection needs played, as the president who transformed welfare. In foreign policy the successful risks he took to help start the Irish peace process must be balanced against the decidedly mixed results and legacy of the administration in Haiti, Somalia, Rwanda, Bosnia, Iraq, the Middle East, and his response to the opening salvos in the age of catastrophic terrorism.

The tragedy of his presidency is not to be found in the Monica Lewinsky sex scandal. It is that his promise to be a "New Democrat" correctly reflected what the country desperately needed, policies that were fair across the board, and not only to those who supported the DEMOCRATIC PARTY, smaller targeted policies that solved old problems without creating new ones, and a president who could and would honestly explain his thinking in ways the public could understand and support. Those promises were discarded at the beginning of Clinton's presidency.

Clinton will be remembered as being a supremely astute politician, but a man whose personal psychology both furthered and stained his presidency. He will also be remembered for managing to remain in office through many scandals by combination of guile, determination, and the benefits of public cynicism that, paradoxically, he was instrumental in propagating. And he will, I think, poignantly be remembered as a president whose missed opportunities and personal failings compromised a presidency that might have ranked among the very best. And finally, he will be remembered, fondly by some and angrily by others, as the president whose erratic personal and public performance provided the public fatigue and readiness for change that resulted in the election of George W. BUSH.

Further reading: Drew, Elizabeth. *On the Edge: The Clinton Presidency.* New York: Simon & Schuster, 1994; Klein, Joe. *The Natural: The Misunderstood Presidency of Bill Clinton.* New York: Doubleday, 2002; Mariness, David. *First in His Class: A Biography of Bill Clinton.* New York: Simon & Schuster, 1995; Renshon, Stanley A. *High Hopes: The Clinton Presidency and the Politics of Ambition.* New York: Routledge, 1998.

—Stanley A. Renshon

Clinton v. Jones, 520 U.S. 681 (1997)

This was a Supreme Court decision that held that a sitting president is not temporarily immune from civil suit for private acts committed prior to taking office. The case involved a civil suit brought against President Bill CLINTON by Paula Corbin Jones, an Arkansas state employee, who alleged that while governor of Arkansas, Clinton made unwanted sexual advances toward her. Jones contended that following her rebuff of then-Governor Clinton, she was treated in a hostile fashion by her coworkers and that her duties at work were diminished as a result. She sued Clinton (and a state trooper) for damages for a number of claims including sexual harassment. The federal court trial judge ruled that discovery in the case could proceed but that the trial itself would be delayed until after Clinton's presidency. Jones appealed and won at the federal court of appeals, a decision that Clinton in turn appealed to the Supreme Court.

A decade and a half before *Clinton v. Jones,* the Supreme Court decided in *Nixon v. Fitzgerald* that the president was immune from suit for actions taken in his official capacity. Clinton tried to build on that precedent by arguing that a sitting president should be temporarily immune from suit for private actions that preceded his tenure in office. In support of his position, Clinton argued that subjecting the CHIEF EXECUTIVE to civil suits would distract the president from important state business. This argument would ultimately prove prescient.

Prior to Jones's suit against President Clinton, there had been only three sitting presidents who had ever been defendants in civil suits for actions preceding their term of office. Theodore ROOSEVELT and Harry TRUMAN each had complaints dismissed against them before they became president, and those dismissals were later upheld after they assumed office. John F. KENNEDY had two companion suits brought against him for an incident before his presidency, but he settled the suits following his inauguration. Other presidents had participated in a variety of legal proceedings while in office: Thomas JEFFERSON had provided papers

relevant to Vice President Aaron BURR's trial for treason, James MONROE responded to written interrogatories, U.S. GRANT and Gerald FORD each gave depositions in criminal cases, Jimmy CARTER and Clinton each gave videotaped testimony for use in criminal trials, and Richard NIXON produced tape-recorded conversations pursuant to a subpoena *duces tecum* arising out of the WATERGATE affair.

In *Clinton v. Jones,* the Supreme Court, speaking through Justice John Paul Stevens, concluded unanimously that the president did not enjoy immunity for actions taken prior to his term of office. The Court reasoned that the basis for providing the president (or any other government official) with immunity is so that he can perform his official functions without fear of liability. The Court stated that such a rationale was absent in a suit brought for nonofficial actions. The justices were unimpressed with the argument that the suit would distract the president. The Court closed its opinion by indicating that although no constitutional provision governed such an immunity claim, Congress possessed the authority to pass legislation addressing this legal lacuna.

The Court's interpretation of precedent was virtually unassailable, there being little in the constitutional text, relevant case law, or historical practice to suggest such a civil immunity existed. However, the importance of practical considerations, such as those raised by Clinton's attorneys, soon manifested themselves as the Jones suit progressed and conflated with INDEPENDENT COUNSEL Kenneth Starr's investigation into the Whitewater land transaction, which involved both the president and first lady. The two interrelated scandals would nearly culminate in President Clinton's undoing following his misleading, if not perjurious, deposition in the Jones suit and his similarly misleading testimony before the grand jury impaneled by Starr. The president's mendacious testimony about the nature of his relationship with WHITE HOUSE intern Monica Lewinsky ultimately prompted his 1998 IMPEACHMENT by the House of Representatives and acquittal by the Senate in early 1999.

Clinton's efforts to dismiss the Jones suit and the impeachment trial as legally meritless were frustrated by the terms of both his out-of-court settlement with Jones and his settlement with the independent counsel. Both involved Clinton making large cash settlements, the latter also involving the suspension of Clinton's Arkansas law license for five years.

While it is too early to evaluate the significance of *Clinton v. Jones* on the institution of the presidency, the immediate effect of the decision on the Clinton presidency proved devastating. It consumed his presidency for the better part of a year and poisoned his already uneasy relationship with the Republican Congress, dramatically undercutting the Supreme Court's prophesy in its opinion that "it appears to us highly unlikely [that this case will] . . . occupy any substantial amount of [the President's] time."

Further reading: Miller, Randall K. "Presidential Sanctuaries after the Clinton Sex Scandals." *Harvard Journal of Law & Public Policy* 22 (1999); Posner, Richard A. *An Affair of State.* Cambridge, Mass.: Harvard University Press, 1999.

—Roy E. Brownell II

Clinton v. City of New York, 524 U.S. 417 (1998)

This was a Supreme Court decision that held the Line Item Veto Act to be unconstitutional. In 1996, in response to growing concern over persistent federal budget deficits, Congress passed and President Clinton signed into law a statute providing the president with "enhanced rescission authority." Although this power was popularly termed a "line item veto," such a characterization was an inaccurate portrayal of this delegated power.

The statute granted the president conditional authority to cancel certain spending and revenue provisions within five days of the president's signing a bill into law. (A true "line item veto" would have authorized the president to strike certain provisions from the statute immediately preceding presidential signature.) To invoke this power, the president had to make a determination that the cancellation would lower the federal budget deficit, would not hinder vital governmental functions, and would not adversely affect the national interest. Presidential cancellation of provisions rendered them without "legal force or effect"; the savings brought about by these actions would then be channeled toward deficit reduction. Presidential cancellations were then of course subject to congressional reappropriation through the traditional lawmaking process.

President Clinton made liberal use of this enhanced rescission authority, striking down 82 provisions, almost half of which were later reappropriated by Congress over the president's traditional veto. One of the cancellations involved a favorable provision through which the City of New York received a waiver of funds it owed to the Department of HEALTH AND HUMAN SERVICES. Another cancellation involved the abolition of a tax benefit aiding the Snake River Potato Growers. Both parties and two hospital associations brought suit challenging the constitutionality of the cancellations.

In a 6-3 decision, the Supreme Court struck down the act as an unconstitutional violation of the Presentment Clause, the constitutional provision that lays out the proper lawmaking procedure. The Court reasoned that by rendering the statutory provisions without "legal force or effect" the president had essentially "amended two Acts of Congress by repealing a portion of each." The Court concluded that both enactment and repeal of statutes had to follow the "'single, finely wrought and exhaustively considered, procedure'" provided in the Constitution.

The Court's decision and the alleviation of the budget deficit problem together ensured that the line item veto (manifested as either a constitutional amendment or through other statutory means) disappeared for the time being from the political landscape. More broadly, the Court's strict interpretation of the Presentment Clause in *INS v. Chadha* and in later striking down the Line Item Veto Act, stands in stark contrast to the Court's loose treatment of the nondelegation doctrine, a principle that theoretically limits Congress in its delegations to the EXECUTIVE BRANCH. The Court's permissive treatment of this doctrine has permitted agencies to perform their own derivative lawmaking function through the issuance of regulations. In the wake of *Chadha,* courts have done little to resolve this tension in the jurisprudence of lawmaking.

Further reading: Brownell, Roy E., II. "The Unnecessary Demise of the Line Item Veto Act: The Clinton Administration's Costly Failure to Seek Acknowledgment of 'National Security Rescission.'" *American University Law Review* 47 (1998): 1273; Kelleher, Leslie H. "Separation of Powers and Delegations of Authority to Cancel Statutes in the Line Item Veto Act and Rules Enabling Act." *George Washington Law Review* 68 (2000): 395.

—Roy E. Brownell II

coattails

A presidential candidate is said to have coattails, in the metaphor promulgated by Abraham LINCOLN, when his popularity translates into votes for congressional candidates of his party, helping to increase their margins of victory and even sweeping them into office along with him. Coattail votes matter more when they determine the winner in elections to the House and Senate than when they merely increase congressional candidates' percentage of the vote. Coattails often were quite significant in the 19th and early 20th centuries because straight ticket voting was the norm. The fortunes of the House and Senate candidates of a presidential candidate's party almost always rose or fell with his own. Coattails have diminished markedly since Franklin D. ROOSEVELT's presidency, however. Party identification among voters has waned, and widespread split-ticket voting is the main cause of the modern paucity of presidential coattails.

Coattails are significant for a president because legislators who have ridden his popularity into office may feel obligated to him, which can translate into support for his policy initiatives. New legislators often are elected to modify the existing policies that the presidential candidate has criticized. FDR's NEW DEAL, Lyndon JOHNSON's GREAT SOCIETY, and Ronald Reagan's changes in ECONOMIC POLICY were fueled in large part by a shift in the partisan balance in Congress brought about by each president's coattails. By backing the president's AGENDA, new members of Congress may send a public signal that they stand by him and his policies, thus hoping to solidify their standing with their constituents.

Because few congressional races are truly competitive, a presidential candidate must attract a large number of coattail votes in many distinct constituencies to make a difference in more than a handful of House and Senate races nationwide. This has proved a steadily more difficult task for presidential candidates, however. Close presidential elections almost never produce coattails, and even a landslide victory like Richard NIXON's over George MCGOVERN in 1972 did not shake the DEMOCRATIC PARTY's hold in Congress. Since FDR, in fact, the only nonincumbent presidential candidate with coattails of any significance was Ronald REAGAN in 1980. Emblematic of the reality of shorter coattails, especially for challengers, was Bill CLINTON's victory in 1992: Every Democratic senator and representative elected that year garnered more votes in his or her state or district than Clinton did. The existence of "reverse coattails"—instances in which legislators of the president's party run ahead of him in their own states and districts—has become a staple of modern presidential elections. This trend is particularly pronounced in the Northeast (home to more than half of all House Republicans from districts that voted Democratic at the presidential level in 2000) and the South (home to half of all House Democrats from districts that voted Republican at the presidential level in 2000).

The prospects for longer presidential coattails in future elections do not look bright. With roughly one-third of Americans no longer identifying as members of either major political party and presidential and congressional candidates running campaigns emphasizing their individuality more than any overarching party philosophy, it would seem that only a fortuitous combination of factors could lengthen presidential coattails. Such an improbable confluence might include a national partisan realignment borne of foreign crisis and/or domestic economic calamity, along with the emergence of a presidential candidate possessing a galvanizing personality and agenda. Future presidents, apt to come to office without significant coattails, are likely to have to govern like their recent predecessors, assembling diverse coalitions of legislators across party lines.

Further reading: Cook, Rhodes. "The Election of 2000: Part Retro, Part New Age." *Public Perspective,* November/December 2001; Edwards, George C., III. *The Public Presidency.* New York: St. Martin's Press, 1983; Greenfield, Jeff. "Of Landslides and Coattails." Available on-line. URL: cnn.com. Downloaded April 19, 2000.

—Douglas M. Brattebo

cold war

When did the cold war begin? There is no answer acceptable to everyone. For William Hyland, it began with the Molotov-Ribbentrop Pact of 1939; for Clark CLIFFORD, in September 1946; Dean ACHESON, in February 1946. Perhaps when FDR, returned from Yalta, perceived that Joseph Stalin would not comply with the agreements reached there? Or when Winston Churchill gave his 1946 "Iron Curtain" speech at Westminster College in Fulton, Missouri? Was it initiated when Bernard Baruch first gave the term public utterance in 1947?

Whatever the date, for more than 40 years the United States and the Soviet Union were in a state of military, political, and economic tension and competition that structured the context in which international relations were conducted. A bipolar world was created in which the two superpowers sought to gain allies and prevent the other from extending its influence around the world.

The optimism that greeted the end of WORLD WAR II soon faded, as the UNITED NATIONS, created to resolve international problems, became an arena for contention between the American and Soviet blocs. The Soviets, who suffered by far the greatest loss of life among the victorious European allies, quickly expanded its control over nations along its borders—nations the Red Army freed from the Third Reich and its puppet regimes. Western apprehension about this Soviet tactic was augmented by Stalin's obstinacy in negotiations on a peace treaty for Germany, his installation of a communist government in the Soviet zone there, the near overthrow of the Greek government by communist insurgents, which brought forth the TRUMAN DOCTRINE, and the fall of Czechoslovakia to communist rule.

In the late 1940s, the United States adopted a policy of CONTAINMENT, meaning that military force would not be employed to liberate Soviet satellite nations, but attempts to expand Soviet domination would be resisted, by force if need be.

Conduct of the Presidency

To gain public and congressional support for anticommunist programs, TRUMAN and his successors often overstated Soviet power, although it was no easy task to determine Soviet economic and military capability. Despite the constitutional prerogative of Congress to declare war, the president was authorized to launch a full-scale military response if he determined that the Soviets were attacking the United States.

As with conventional wars, the president was granted extended authority. Charges, at times nearly hysterical, that communists held key positions in the American government accentuated fear of the international communist threat. There were communist agents in the United States and Britain that passed security information, such as that central to the construction of the first Soviet atomic bomb, but this Red Scare challenged the constitutional rights of many citizens who had not supported the USSR. Both public and private institutions implemented loyalty oaths for their employees. Conscription continued into the 1970s.

Alliance and Counter-Alliance

To help Europe rebuild and make Western Europe less susceptible to the communist threat there, the MARSHALL PLAN (1947) was launched. In 1949 the North Atlantic Treaty Organization (NATO) was created to provide a multinational military umbrella for the defense of Western Europe. The Soviet bloc, which could have benefited from the Marshall Plan, declined—at Stalin's order. In response to NATO, the Warsaw Pact was created. To coordinate economic efforts, COMECON, the Council for Mutual Economic Assistance, was established within Eastern Europe, with Moscow directing policy.

During the EISENHOWER administration, Secretary of State John Foster DULLES pursued a policy of forging regional alliances such as SEATO in Southeast Asia. Coupled with this was Eisenhower's assumption that Americans would not accept the costs of maintaining a conventional military force equivalent to that of the Iron Curtain bloc. Instead the United States would rely on a less costly nuclear deterrent.

Military Hostilities

On occasion, the United States intervened militarily, not in direct confrontation with the Soviets, but with their surrogates—in Korea (1950–53), in Vietnam (1960s–1970s), and, oddly, in Grenada (1983). The KOREAN WAR was perceived by the West as an effort of Stalin to expand the communist empire. Americans were bewildered that "brainwashing" by the communists persuaded 325 UN prisoners of war, including 22 Americans, to refuse repatriation at the war's end. The 1949 triumph of communism in China and its INTERVENTION in Korea augmented the perception that liberal democracy was losing around the globe.

Following the example of Korea in halting the spread of communist rule, the United States under Eisenhower provided only military supplies and advisers to the government of South Vietnam. KENNEDY sent combat forces to that nation, a policy expanded by JOHNSON and NIXON. Vietnam proved to be different militarily and politically from Korea. In Vietnam there was no clear military front. Instead, the Vietcong enemy effectively infiltrated the South Vietnam countryside. Further complicating the American task were the facts that Ho Chi Minh, the leader of North Vietnam, was popular in the South, and prominent South Vietnamese governmental leaders were Catholic, although the nation was predominately Buddhist. Ultimately, U.S. forces were withdrawn from South Vietnam rather than continue to lose lives.

The Soviets had a similar experience with Afghanistan, beginning in 1979, where a decade-long effort to support a communist regime demonstrated that Soviet military tactics and technology could not overcome partisans surreptitiously aided by American arms and supplies.

In Nicaragua during the 1980s, American-backed contras sought to overthrow the Soviet-supported Sandinista regime. The circumvention of congressional mandate and unauthorized use of government funds might have brought impeachment and removal from office of a less popular president than REAGAN, or one not so near the end of his term.

Patience When Confronted with Provocation

Throughout the cold war, the West exercised restraint when the Soviet military either threatened to intervene on behalf of communist allies—Czechoslovakia (1948)—or forcefully suppressed protest in its client states: East Berlin (1953), Hungary (1956), Czechoslovakia (1968). In other instances, such as in Poland (1970), indigenous military and law enforcement, operating according to Soviet wishes, crushed protest.

America and its allies refused to respond militarily to dramatic Soviet provocations: the Berlin Blockade (1948–49), the erection of the Berlin Wall (1961), and the CUBAN MISSILE CRISIS (1962). The United States protested and in the last instance demanded the withdrawal of the Soviet weaponry from Cuba. The Blockade illustrates the point-counterpoint nature between the two blocs: It was, at least in part, a response to the movement of France, Britain, and the United States to first establish a common currency for their occupation zones in Germany, followed by creating the German Federal Republic (West Germany) from those territories. Similarly, the Berlin Wall staunched the flow of skilled East German professionals fleeing through West Berlin. The Wall stabilized the communist regime.

Espionage

Not all competition was openly evident. The CENTRAL INTELLIGENCE AGENCY and the Soviet KGB waged their own version of the cold war with Berlin as a crucial focus of intelligence gathering and defection by spies. If a new government was viewed as sympathetic to Soviet overtures, the United States was not above overthrowing that government by subversion or assassination, as occurred in Guatemala (1953) and Chile (1973).

Presidents Gorbachev, Reagan, and Bush at the close of the cold war era, New York Harbor *(Ronald W. Reagan Library)*

Thaws

The cold war was not a period in which tension between the two superpowers remained constant. With the death of Stalin in 1953, relations between the Soviet Union and the United States thawed. In 1955 the first summit involving these two nations was held at Geneva. Cultural exchange, which would ebb and flow, commenced, letting Soviet and American citizens visit each other's homeland. The 1963 Nuclear Test Ban Treaty prohibited testing nuclear bombs in the atmosphere. In the 1960s the doctrine of Mutually Assured Destruction (MAD) was formulated; it recognized that each superpower could destroy the other and therefore neither should build a defense system that would upset this balance. DÉTENTE, initiated by Nixon and Leonid Brezhnev, was the lengthiest and most complicated effort to reduce cold war tension. It accepted Soviet nuclear parity, offered Soviet-American cooperation in several fields, and supported most favored nation status for the Soviets, enabling them to acquire large amounts of American grain.

Other Forms of Competition

Competition extended to technology and economic spheres. While spies facilitated Soviet development of nuclear weapons and jet aircraft, the 1957 launching of Sputnik demonstrated that Soviet technological success was not dependent upon stealing secrets from the West. This first spacecraft set off a competition that the United States would win upon landing astronauts on the moon in 1969.

Each side offered economic aid, frequently supplemented by military equipment, to its allies or potential allies. From the early 1960s Cuba became dependent on Soviet economic assistance. American policy enabled numerous noncommunist but nondemocratic regimes to stay in power or seize it. East and West both sought to demonstrate that their respective systems were superior.

Radio Free Europe offered an open window for Eastern Europe. Despite jamming of the broadcasts by the communist governments, Eastern Europeans learned more and more about life in the West, especially after West Germany's *Ostpolitik* of the early 1970s permitted visits by West Germans to their East German relatives. Except in places such as Cuba, Radio Moscow had no impact comparable to Radio Free Europe.

The Third World
By the 1960s, India, Yugoslavia, and others led a bloc of nations that claimed to be nonaligned, or not favoring either the Western bloc or the Soviet one. Unquestionably, some Third World nations, for example Egypt under Gamal Abdel Nasser, were more sympathetic to the Soviets. Cold war competition extended to nations emerging from colonial domination, particularly in Africa, where Soviet agents actively backed independence movements and the end of apartheid in South Africa.

Cracks in the Soviet Edifice
Perception of communism as a monolith controlled by the Soviet Union, which was pervasive among the American right, became increasingly defective. In the late 1940s Tito's Yugoslavia demonstrated its willingness to defy Stalin. By the 1970s China was opposing Moscow on key issues, a posture that Nixon sought to exploit by resuming contacts with Peking in 1972. Albania supported China and followed its own cold war path. Further fractures of the Soviet empire emerged in Poland, Hungary, Romania, and Czechoslovakia.

The End of the Cold War
Gorbachev, who became head of the Soviet Union in 1985, was aware that communist economic systems were falling behind those of capitalism, notably in Asia. To reverse the Soviet economic decline, he introduced *glasnost* (openness) and *perestroika* (restructuring). Increased exposure by Soviet-bloc citizens to the West from television and personal visits revealed economic benefits and personal freedom there. Heavy costs of countering containment continued. Once the Soviet system began to open up and Gorbachev proceeded to reorganize it, he could not reverse its disintegration without resorting to force. He refused to do that.

With the fall of the Berlin Wall in November 1989, it would have been impossible to put the genie of the Soviet empire back in the bottle. The collapse of the Soviet Union did not occur until 1991, but both sides already conceded that the cold war was no more after the Wall was breached.

Although all adhered to Truman's containment policy, each president brought his own signature to the cold war: Truman's Marshall Plan, NATO, and the Korean conflict

waged under UN auspices; Eisenhower's nuclear BRINKSMANSHIP and multilateral defense treaties; Kennedy's missile crisis response and escalation in Vietnam; Johnson's Vietnam quagmire; Nixon's détente and opening relations with China; FORD's signing of the Helsinki Agreement (1975) that lead to increased rights for persons behind the Iron Curtain; Carter's human rights emphasis; Reagan's rejection of both the concept of Mutually Assured Destruction (MAD) and détente but negotiation of the first arms reduction agreement; the first BUSH's cautious but fruitful DIPLOMACY as the Soviet empire disintegrated.

Further reading: Beschloss, Michael R., and Strobe Talbott. *At the Highest Levels: The Inside Story of the End of the Cold War.* Boston: Little, Brown, 1993; Crockatt, Richard. *The Fifty Years War.* New York: Routledge, 1995; Gaddis, John L. *We Now Know: Rethinking the Cold War.* New York: Oxford University Press, 1997; Hyland, William G. *The Cold War: Fifty Years of Conflict.* New York: Times Books, 1991.
—Thomas P. Wolf

Colfax, Schuyler (1823–1885) *U.S. vice president*
Colfax served in the House of Representatives and, in 1863–69, as Speaker of the House. He was Ulysses S. GRANT's first vice president (1869–73). Known as "smiler" or "the great joiner" for his propensity to join organizations, Colfax was denied his party's nomination for a second term as vice president, a move that later proved prescient, as Colfax became linked to the CREDIT MOBILIER SCANDAL at the end of his vice presidency.

commander in chief
The Constitution grants to the president the narrow authority to direct the nation's military: "The President shall be Commander in Chief of the Army and Navy of the United States, and of the Militia of the several States, when called into the actual service of the United States." In reality, presidents have acquired, with congressional assent, both the power to direct the use of force *and* the responsibility of deciding under what conditions the defense of the nation requires a military response.

The first president set precedents for a strong interpretation of the commander in chief clause. By sending the army to campaign against hostile Indians, backed by the British, who had not abandoned all the forts they had theoretically lost in their war against the colonies, President WASHINGTON established a precedent for presidential direction of the use of military force against external threats. By simultaneously employing a multistate militia force against rebellious frontiersmen in the WHISKEY REBELLION of 1794, Washington established the precedent for presidential use of the nation's soldiery against threats from its own citizens.

Since Washington's time, Congress and the Supreme Court have typically exercised only loose oversight of the commander in chief during actual war, but they have sought to restore constitutional balance in the return to peace. As in all areas of presidential responsibility, some presidents have excelled at the performance of this role, while others have performed less credibly.

The low point of 19th-century presidential command came in President James Madison's time in office. Pressured by Congress into a war for which the nation's military was utterly unprepared, President MADISON struggled to command a military that his own pacific policies had enfeebled.

The U.S.-Mexican War, 1846–48, was a victory for the professional American military and for the vastly energetic commander in chief James K. POLK. In this expedition on foreign soil, President Polk determined the general strategy of the war, gave attention to problems of organization and logistics, chose his commanding generals, and used his CABINET to organize the war effort. This was the first demonstration of the presidency's enormous capacity as an administrative agency.

During the CIVIL WAR, President Abraham LINCOLN directed a true "presidential war." Lincoln took it upon himself to declare a blockade of the South, the equivalent of declaring war, and personally exercised vast PREROGATIVE POWERS during the emergency. The commander in chief clause, Lincoln argued, when joined with the "take care" clause and the president's OATH OF OFFICE, gave to the president a seemingly bottomless reservoir of "war powers." During the war, members of Congress sought to pressure the president by extensive use of the Congress's responsibility for OVERSIGHT of executive affairs, but they seldom questioned the president on the larger issue of "war powers." After the war, the Supreme Court sought to draw boundaries around presidential power by overturning certain acts of the president identical to those which the Court had prudently permitted during the fighting.

Theodore ROOSEVELT made the president's role of commander in chief more steady, by asserting the United States' duty to maintain a global military presence in peacetime. The next expansion of the president's war powers occurred in WORLD WAR I. During the brief American participation in the war, Congress delegated to the president vast powers over the domestic economy and society. This was not just "presidential war," but "total war." The president and his agents decided to an extent never seen in the United States before what Americans might sell and buy, what prices they might sell their goods at, and even what they might say and write about their government.

In WORLD WAR II Presidents Franklin ROOSEVELT and Harry TRUMAN fulfilled their obligations as commander in chief with great political as well as military skill. Roosevelt,

like Polk and Lincoln before him, was a nonveteran, but a highly successful commander in chief. He exercised strict civilian control over the military during the war, deciding—against the urgings of his senior military leadership—to delay the cross-channel invasion that eventually won the war in Europe, and to send U.S. forces instead into Africa. Roosevelt also delicately balanced the competing demands for resources among the services.

After World War II the nation for the first time accepted the need for a large standing military force in peacetime. The United States had maintained a global naval presence for decades, but its combined military strength in peacetime had been puny by comparison to the armed forces of the major European powers. After World War II that changed, and a succession of commanders in chief were now faced with the task of leading a vastly enlarged, and seemingly permanent, military establishment.

The commander in chief role during the COLD WAR proved fraught with political as well as military dangers. Harry Truman left office a hugely unpopular president because of the stalemate in the "police action" in Korea; John KENNEDY's presidency received a serious setback in the BAY OF PIGS assault on Cuba; Lyndon JOHNSON wrestled with the problem of VIETNAM unsuccessfully until his decision not to run for reelection in 1968; and Richard NIXON was so outraged by criticism over his handling of that war that he authorized the creation of a "plumbers" unit to plug government leaks. The plumbers wound up burgling the offices of the Democratic National Committee Chairman in the WATERGATE office complex, which led to Nixon's RESIGNATION from office in 1974. All the other presidents of the COLD WAR similarly faced some of their toughest choices as president in the exercise of this important power.

With the end of the cold war, will American presidents continue to be bedeviled, and their powers expanded, by their role as commander in chief? On the one hand, surveys of voters show that the mass public was indifferent to military and defense issues in the elections of 1992 through 2000. On the other hand, President CLINTON and the two Presidents BUSH made some of their most important decisions as president while exercising the duty of commander in chief, and Congress has thus far not reclaimed any lost constitutional ground. After the events of September 11, 2001, moreover, President George W. BUSH asserted that he as president should be entrusted with considerable discretionary power over the use of force for the duration of the nation's open-ended war against terrorism.

Further reading: Dawson, Joseph G., III, ed. *Commanders in Chief: Presidential Leadership in Modern Wars.* Lawrence: University Press of Kansas, 1993; Halberstam, David. *War in a Time of Peace: Bush, Clinton, and the Generals.* New York: Scribner, 2001.

—Thomas Langston

Commerce Department

A cabinet-level department headed by a secretary appointed by the president with the advice and consent of the Senate, the Commerce Department was established in 1913, when the Department of Commerce and Labor (founded in 1903) was split into two separate departments.

The Commerce Department is expected to promote international trade, commerce, and economic growth. In recent years it has promoted U.S. competitiveness and international free trade and open competition.

commissions, presidential

Presidential commissions have played a significant role in providing guidance, advice, and possible courses of action to presidents in response to national crises. The first "presidential" commission was established by President George WASHINGTON, in an attempt to deal with the WHISKEY REBELLION, a revolt of Western Pennsylvania farmers on a recently imposed federal tax on spirits. Although ineffective in dealing with the rebellion, the precedent was set for forming and utilizing an ad hoc body to advise the president. The modern-day "father" of the presidential commission is considered to be President Theodore ROOSEVELT.

Two major presidential commissions focused on the study and investigation of the circumstances of the assassination of President John F. KENNEDY. On November 29, 1963, one week after President Kennedy's assassination, President Lyndon B. JOHNSON, by Executive Order 11130, established the President's Commission on the Assassination of President John F. Kennedy. This commission, commonly known as the WARREN COMMISSION, was charged with investigating the assassination. The commission's work was completed in 10 months and a final report was issued.

The chair of the commission was Earl Warren, Chief Justice of the United States. Other members included: Richard B. Russell, Democratic senator from Georgia and chairman of the Senate Armed Services Committee; John Sherman Cooper, Republican senator from Kentucky and U.S. Ambassador to India; Hale Boggs, Democratic representative from Louisiana and majority whip in the House of Representatives; Gerald R. FORD, Republican representative from Michigan and chairman of the House Republican Conference; Allen W. Dulles, lawyer and former Director of the CENTRAL INTELLIGENCE AGENCY; John J. McCloy, lawyer, former president of the International Bank for Reconstruction and Development, and former U.S. High Commissioner for Germany.

In 1975 President Gerald R. Ford established the Commission to Investigate the Central Intelligence Agency Activities Within the United States. This commission was referred to as the Rockefeller Commission. Only a portion of this commission's work related to the Kennedy assassination. The major focus of its work related to assassination attempts on Cuban leader Fidel Castro.

Following the precedents of their peers, recent presidents have established a variety of commissions, including one to create a National Agenda for the Eighties (Carter), study U.S. Olympic Sports (Ford), establish a White House Fellows program (NIXON), study America's Strategic Forces, particularly nuclear missiles (REAGAN), study the Assignment of Women in the Armed Forces (George H. W. BUSH), and investigate Seaport Crime and Security (CLINTON).

Further reading: Flitner, David, Jr. *The Politics of Presidential Commissions: A Public Policy Perspective.* Dobbs Ferry, N.Y.: Transnational Publishers, Inc., 1986; Zink, Steven D. *Guide to the Presidential Advisory Commissions, 1973–1984.* Alexandria, Va.: Chadwick-Healey, Inc., 1987; Information on the Warren, Rockefeller and other presidential Commissions is available on-line. URL: http://www.nara.gov/research/jfk/gil_42.html#prescomm. Downloaded September 1, 2001.

—Owen Holmes

compassionate conservative

The term was coined by George W. BUSH during his campaign for the presidency in 2000. It was meant to signify a "kinder, gentler" conservatism: one that cared about people. Bush repeatedly called for a compassionate conservatism during his campaign.

Congress and the president

Although it is common to claim that the framers created a governmental system of "separation of powers," Richard NEUSTADT corrects this misleading description and notes that what they created, instead, was a system of "separated institutions *sharing* powers." Charles O. Jones refines this by going one step further to claim that "these separated institutions often *compete* for shared powers." The sharing, or overlapping, of powers was the key ingredient for James MADISON who, as the architect for the structure of the system, sought balance among the powers and a carefully crafted monitoring by each branch over the other two. In *The Federalist No. 51,* Madison explained that the best way to keep each branch from invading the powers of the others was "by so contriving the interior structure of the government as its several constituents parts may, by their mutual relations, be the means of keeping each other in their proper places. . . ."

Constitutionally, Congress and the president possess separate as well as shared powers. Article I delegates to Congress a long list of specific, exclusive powers in Section 8, such as the power to tax and spend, to declare war, to coin money, to regulate commerce, and to raise and support armies, while the final clause in Article I extends a more general power "to make all laws which shall be necessary and proper for carrying into execution the foregoing powers. . . ." Article II provides the president with some specific, exclusive powers, too, though far fewer than Congress, such as the power to pardon, to receive ambassadors, to make RECESS APPOINTMENTS, and to give a STATE OF THE UNION message to Congress. The president is also authorized, more broadly, "to take care that the laws be faithfully executed," and even the first clause in Article II, "The executive power shall be vested in a president of the United States of America," is often relied upon as a source of general executive authority.

What is clear, however, is that the *most* important duties for both branches are the ones they exercise jointly that require affirmative action from both. Congress's power to legislate requires the president's participation, as the very least, at the final step in the process, either by his signature or his veto (or, in rare cases, his abstention from either, which will permit the bill to become law without his signature). But the president routinely enters the process at its beginning, recommending legislation to Congress, followed by the dispatching of his aides to Capitol Hill to engage in continuous discussions and negotiations throughout the process. Conversely, the president's powers (a) to appoint executive officials and federal judges, and (b) to make treaties with foreign nations that cannot be completed without Senate participation, consisting of (a) its advice and consent to nominations, and (b) its ratification by a two-thirds vote of presidentially negotiated treaties. Even the president's designation as "Commander-in-Chief of the Army and Navy of the United States" technically operates only "when called into the actual service of the United States," meaning, when Congress declares war or authorizes the president to use military force.

This interdependence, or mutual action, between Congress and the president, in order for most of these powers to operate successfully, serves simultaneously as the "check" against abuse that was so embedded in Madison's design. The president's veto of an enrolled bill from Congress negates that proposal in the same way that Senate rejection of an executive or judicial nominee or failure to ratify a treaty ends those efforts. Not only can each branch judge whether the other has overstepped its bounds *constitutionally* to abuse authority or usurp the prerogatives of the other, but each one can also disapprove for *political* reasons.

The political dimension was equally as important as the constitutional one to Madison. Not only would his system of "auxiliary precautions" enable the policing of each branch by the other, but it would also insure that policies enacted into law would have the accumulated support of these two institutions and would be the product of deliberation and joint negotiations.

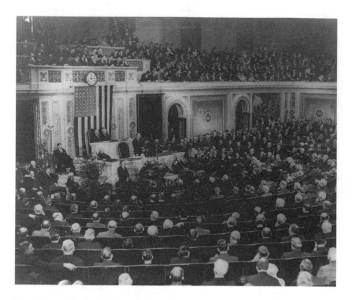

President Herbert Hoover addresses a joint session of Congress, 1932. *(Library of Congress)*

Historically, the relationship between Congress and the president has been a dynamic and changing one. At different times, one may possess more political influence than the other. Jones was not incorrect to characterize their relations as a competition for power. Each is possessive of its own prerogatives, acts to protect against incursion by the other, and, where possible, may venture out to "raid" the other, if the circumstances are ripe.

Madison's genius, once again, informs us in *The Federalist No. 51* that "in republican government, the legislative authority necessarily predominates." The difference in the number and scope of powers delegated by the framers to Congress as compared to those delegated to the president is evidence that they not only considered the legislature to be the dominant branch but also, as such, the branch to fear most as the one more likely to aggrandize power. Although the framers understood well the dangers of excessive EXECUTIVE POWER, as they had experienced under King George III in Great Britain, their concern for potentially abusive executive power was overshadowed by what seemed a more pressing worry for legislative excess. A president was to "execute," or carry out, the laws, much as a clerk simply implementing an order or directive supplied by another. Presidential discretion, or judgment, in the implementation process, or claims to independent action, or expansion of executive authority through creative constitutional interpretation, all seemed distant to the framers.

And yet, history has recorded that certain presidents have set precedents in office that, once exercised, rarely recede but rather become institutionalized and cemented into the job description. Over time, as these precedents accumulated, it was all but inevitable that the power, size, and scope of the presidency would increase, often at the expense of congressional power.

George WASHINGTON, Andrew JACKSON, and Abraham LINCOLN were among the early presidents who asserted strong claims on behalf of their office vis-à-vis Congress. Washington claimed the right to proclaim neutrality; Jackson vetoed legislation for policy reasons; and Lincoln took numerous actions as a wartime president that established the rationale for emergency power. Then congressional power returned to dominate the latter half of the 19th century. Scholars then jumped forward to Theodore ROOSEVELT and Woodrow WILSON as the next two presidents who were responsible for expanding the president's legislative role as the national government itself increased in size and complexity to address the issues of industrialization and urbanization. Roosevelt established the practice of sending to Congress a defined legislative program, and Wilson was also equally engaged in active negotiations with Congress over legislative proposals.

The modern presidency, as we know it today, with its heightened profile as well as heightened public expectations, began with Franklin D. ROOSEVELT and the quantum leap he engineered in the size and responsibility of the national government, as a consequence of the need to address the economic emergency brought on by the Depression and, later, the military emergency created by the attack on Pearl Harbor in December 1941 and the entry of the United States into WORLD WAR II. War again would be the catalyst for increased presidential power when Harry TRUMAN took the action into war against Korea in 1950 without congressional authorization, and when Lyndon JOHNSON and Richard NIXON gradually increased commitment of U.S. troops, against growing public opposition, in Vietnam in the 1960s and early 1970s. A public backlash, born of a combination of its disenchantment with presidential deception during the VIETNAM WAR and the disgrace of a sitting president's (Nixon's) RESIGNATION from office rather that to face assured IMPEACHMENT, contributed to the characterization of the presidency as "imperial" by historian Arthur Schlesinger, Jr., in 1973. Congress recognized that it had allowed the president to encroach on its prerogatives, especially the war power, and that the legislature needed to recapture some of its authority and to restore a lost constitutional balance. The mid 1970s witnessed a series of legislative enactments, such as the WAR POWERS RESOLUTION of 1973, the CONGRESSIONAL BUDGET AND IMPOUNDMENT CONTROL ACT OF 1974, and the NATIONAL EMERGENCIES ACT of 1976, designed to "take back" these powers from the president and to set in place mechanisms that would insure careful congressional monitoring in these policy areas to prevent future usurpations by the president.

The record of these efforts over the last 30 years has not been encouraging to Congress. In the competition for shared powers, it appears that the president has won the largest proportion, contrary to the framers' expectations 200 years ago. History and precedents, rather than constitutionally delegated powers, have merged to produce a powerful executive who leads, rather than follows, Congress.

Further reading: Bond, Jon R., and Richard Fleisher, eds. *Polarized Politics: Congress and the President in a Partisan Era.* Washington, D.C.: CQ Press, 2000; Fisher, Louis. *The Politics of Shared Power: Congress and the Executive.* College Station: Texas A & M University Press, 1998; Hamilton, Alexander, James Madison, and John Jay. *The Federalist Papers.* 1787–1788. Reprint: New York: The New American Library, 1961; Jones, Charles O. *The Presidency in a Separated System.* Washington, D.C.: The Brookings Institution, 1994; Neustadt, Richard E. *Presidential Power: The Politics of Leadership.* New York: John Wiley & Sons, Inc., 1964; Peterson, Mark A. *Legislating Together: The White House and Capitol Hill from Eisenhower to Reagan.* Cambridge, Mass.: Harvard University Press, 1990; Schlesinger, Arthur M. *The Imperial Presidency.* New York: Popular Library, 1974.

—Nancy Kassop

Congressional Budget and Impoundment Control Act of 1974

The Congressional Budget and Impoundment Control Act of 1974 is best understood by examining the economic and political events and conditions that led to its passage in 1974. A budget crisis in the late 1960s and early 1970s contributed to troubling inflation rates and increasing deficits. Growth of the federal budget was deemed increasingly irreversible due to a complex set of circumstances including uncontrollable spending in entitlement programs only changeable through new legislation. The growing budgets and deficits were linked to the economic problems.

Several study commissions leading up to passage of the 1974 Budget Act concluded that Congress lacked the institutional means to inject the requisite restraint into its appropriations process. There were insufficient mechanisms to link spending and taxation, to weigh competing priorities to set annual spending ceilings, or to provide independent nonpartisan budgetary and economic estimates to parallel those the OFFICE OF MANAGEMENT AND BUDGET offered the president. Congressional authority and responsibility was fragmented and divided among appropriations and authorization subcommittees. No one unit or committee within the Congress was charged with centralized responsibility for the budget as a whole.

At the same time controversy was brewing over unprecedented impoundments imposed by President

NIXON. Presidents had long been authorized to withhold spending on appropriated projects under the Antideficiency Act in order to promote efficiency and savings or if unforeseen circumstances rendered funding for an action unnecessary. Previous presidents had exercised restraint in their use of this authority and had aroused little concern. The Nixon impoundments involved much larger sums of money, sometimes canceled entire programs, and undermined congressional intent. Spending was withheld in a variety of programs including but not limited to those dealing with housing and urban development, water pollution control, waste treatment facilities, the Farmers Home Administration, and the Rural Electrification Administration. Nixon in turn shifted the blame to the Congress's inability to tighten its budgetary belt and used tortured interpretations of statutes to defend his actions.

For all of these reasons, there was strong bipartisan support for budgetary reform to address all of these problems by increasing the discipline and ACCOUNTABILITY of both the CONGRESS AND THE PRESIDENT and establishing the institutional and legal means to do so. To these ends the Congressional Budget and Impoundment Control Act created new congressional committees, units, budget process procedures, and legislative schedules to spur the Congress to assume a more responsible role in federal budgeting. The act also mandated procedures that limited the president's discretion in impounding funds. The Congressional Budget Office (CBO) was established to provide nonpartisan budgetary and economic analysis to the Congress. No longer would the Congress be dependent on executive branch budgetary and economic estimates. A new budget process and timeline were superimposed over the existing appropriations and authorizations processes. Budget Committees in both houses were created to oversee new procedures designed to introduce greater discipline and broader scope into congressional budgeting. The Budget Committees were charged with looking at the larger economic picture, including revenue intake, projected deficits, and economic conditions, and determining how they related to the president's budget proposal. Further, the committees were to provide funding ceilings and guidelines for appropriations and authorization committees to work within the form of budget resolutions.

A reconciliation process was created in the Budget Act, which provided a vehicle to obligate authorization and tax writing committee actions to comply with the budget resolution. Both budget resolutions and reconciliation procedures allowed members to vote on total budgets as opposed to individual programs, thus promoting budgetary discipline by providing political cover for those representatives who did not wish to be seen by constituents and special interest groups as cutting certain projects or programs.

David Stockman, President REAGAN's budget director and a former member of Congress, was able to use his knowledge of the small print in the reconciliation provisions in the statute to quickly move massive domestic budget cuts through Congress in 1981.

The Budget Act also included provisions that eliminated opportunities for future presidents to refuse to release appropriated moneys for their intended functions. By virtue of the Congressional Budget and Impoundment Control Act, the president was required to report to the Congress on anticipated recisions (cases where he intended to cancel funding permanently) and deferrals (when the president would temporarily delay expenditures). In the case of deferrals the president could delay funding unless Congress objected. With recisions, both chambers were required to approve the cancellation within a 45-day period. (After the Supreme Court's 1983 decision in INS v. CHADHA, deferrals were handled through appropriations laws.)

The significance of the Congressional Budget and Impoundment Control Act should not be underestimated. It succeeded in placing Congress on a more equal footing with the president in the budgetary arena. It decisively limited presidential spending powers. Moreover, as budget process expert Allen Schick has suggested, the Budget Act was one factor in transforming the president's budget proposal from an authoritative budgetary blueprint into merely the first phase of a complex and newly empowered congressional budget process.

Further reading: Fisher, Louis. *Presidential Spending Power.* Princeton, N.J.: Princeton University Press, 1975; Schick, Allen. *Congress and Money.* Washington, D.C.: Urban Institute, 1980; Shuman, Howard. *Politics and the Budget: The Struggle between the President and the Congress.* Englewood Cliffs, N.J.: Prentice Hall, 1992.

—Shelley Lynne Tomkin

Connally Amendment

Passed in 1946, the Connally Amendment limited jurisdiction of the International Court of Justice (the World Court) on the United States and its citizens. This amendment accepted the jurisdiction of the World Court, but exempted U.S. involvement in "disputes with regard to matters which are essentially within the domestic jurisdiction of the United States of America." Thus, the United States would make final determinations as to World Court jurisdictional boundaries.

In 1986 President REAGAN terminated the United States' acceptance of the World Court's compulsory jurisdiction. This also terminated the Connally Amendment.

Further reading: Damrosch, Lori Fisler, ed. *The International Court of Justice at a Crossroads.* Dobbs Ferry, N.Y.: Transnational Publishing, 1987.

conservation policy   See ENVIRONMENTAL POLICY.

constitution and the presidency, the

The framers invented a presidency of some strength, but little independent power. They put the president in a position to lead (influence, persuade), but not command (order).

What structure or skeleton of power and government did the founders of the U.S. system design? The chief mechanisms they established to control as well as to empower the executive are as follows: (1) Limited Government, a reaction against the arbitrary, expansive powers of the king or state, and a protection of personal liberty; (2) Rule of Law, so that only on the basis of legal or constitutional grounds could the government act; (3) SEPARATION OF POWERS, so that the three branches of government each would have a defined sphere of power; and (4) CHECKS AND BALANCES, so that each branch could limit or control the powers of the other branches of government.

In this structure, what *powers* and *resources* has the president? Limited powers. Constitutionally, the United States faces a paradox: The Constitution both *empowers* and *restrains* government. In fact, the Constitution does not clearly spell out the power of the presidency. Article I is devoted to the Congress, the first and constitutionally the most powerful branch of government. Article II, the executive article, deals with the presidency. The president's power cupboard is—compared to that of the Congress— nearly bare. Section 1 gives the "executive power" to the president but does not reveal whether this is a grant of tangible power or merely a title. Section 2 makes the president commander in chief of the armed forces but reserves the *power* to declare war for the Congress. Section 2 also gives the president absolute power to grant reprieves and pardons, power to make treaties (with the ADVICE AND CONSENT of the Senate), and the power to nominate ambassadors, judges, and other public ministers (with the advice and consent of the Senate). Section 3 calls for the president to inform the Congress on the State of the Union and to recommend measures to Congress, grants the power to receive ambassadors, and imposes upon the president the duty to see that the laws are faithfully executed. These powers are significant, but in and of themselves they do not suggest a very strong or independent institution, and certainly not a national leadership position.

Presidential power, when viewed from a constitutional perspective, is both specific and obscure: Specific in that some elements of presidential power are clearly spelled out (e.g., the veto power, a PARDON POWER); obscure in that the limits and boundaries of presidential power are either ill-defined or open to vast differences in interpretation (e.g., the president's power in FOREIGN AFFAIRS and his

power over the military). In an effort to understand presidential power, the Constitution is a starting point, but it provides few definitive answers. The Constitution, as it relates to the powers of the president, raises more questions than it answers.

As historical circumstances have changed, so too has the meaning or interpretation of the Constitution. The scope and meaning of the executive clause (Article II) of the Constitution has changed to meet the needs of the times and the wishes (demands) of strong presidents. The skeleton-like provisions of Article II have left the words open to definition and redefinition by courts and presidents. This skeleton-like wording leaves it up to an aggressive CHIEF EXECUTIVE and a willing Supreme Court to shape the actual parameters of such powers. In effect, history has rewritten the Constitution. For two centuries, we have been debating just what the words of the Constitution mean, and this debate is by no means over. The words are "flexible" enough to mean different things in different situations. Thus one can see the elasticity of options open for both the Supreme Court and the president. On the whole though, a more "expansive" view of presidential power has taken precedence over a more "restrictive" view. The history of the meaning of presidential power through the Constitution has been one of the expansion of power and the enlargement of the meaning of the words of the Constitution.

The presidential office gets power from a variety of sources, both constitutional and extra-constitutional. While the Constitution must be the starting point for any analysis of presidential power, it is by no means the final word on the subject. The loose construction of the words of the Constitution: "the executive power shall be vested in a president . . . take care that the laws be faithfully executed . . . etc.," has been used to view the powers of the president in expansive or elastic terms.

The Constitution gives us an outline of the powers of the president, but not a picture. For the president is much more than the Constitution leads us to believe. As Haight and Johnson write: ". . . the Presidency is above all an integrated institution, all of whose parts interlock with one another. Any description that discusses these parts individually cannot help being partially misleading." Thus, one cannot simply look at the Constitution and define and describe "presidential power." The presidency is more than the sum of its constitutional parts.

Presidential power exists in two forms: *formal* powers and *informal* powers. To understand presidential power, one must understand how both the formal and informal powers work and interact and how the combination of the two can lead to dominance by a president who, given the proper conditions and abilities, is able to exploit his power sources.

Formal Powers

The formal powers of the president revolve around the constitutional powers to "command." They involve those areas of the Constitution that clearly place powers and responsibilities on the shoulders of the president.

The formal powers of the president are derived essentially from the Constitution. Those powers "derived" from the Constitution extend, however, beyond the strictly legalistic or specifically granted powers that find their source in the literal reading of the words of the constitution. Additionally, presidents have

Enumerated powers (those that the Constitution expressly grants);

Implied powers (those that may be inferred from power expressly granted);

Resulting powers (those that result when several enumerated powers are added together); and

Inherent powers (those powers in the field of external affairs that the Supreme Court has declared do not depend upon constitutional grants but grow out of the existence of the national government).

Informal Powers

This in part leads us to the informal powers of the president, which find their source in the "political" as opposed to the "constitutional." They are the powers that are either not spelled out in the Constitution, acquired through politics, or which are "missing" from the Constitution. Richard NEUSTADT, in his *Presidential Power,* discussed the informal power of the president to "persuade." Neustadt and others feel that the power to persuade is the most important of all the presidential powers.

These informal powers of the president rely upon his ability to engage in the personal part of politics. All presidents have and can use their formal powers, but the informal powers require skill at persuasion, personal manipulation, and mobilization. These skills may be difficult to cultivate but, in the long run, changing the minds of people may be more powerful than ordering someone into compliance. In the informal powers of the president, some can see the breaking point between those presidents characterized as "great" or aggressive and those who rate less favorably in the eyes of historians. The great presidents have been able and willing to exploit the informal powers at the disposal of a president.

Thus, the president has two types of power: *formal*, the ability to command, and *informal*, the ability to persuade. The president's formal powers are limited and (often) shared. The president's informal powers are a function of skill, situation, and the political times. While the formal power of the president remains fairly constant over time, the president's informal powers are quite variable, dependent on the skill of each individual president. This is not to suggest that the president's formal powers are static—over time, presidential power has increased significantly—but the pace of change has been such that it was well over a hundred years before the presidency assumed primacy in the U.S. political system.

The constitutional structure of the government *disperses* or *fragments* power: With no recognized, authoritative vital center, power is fluid and floating, and no one branch can very easily or freely act without the consent (formal or tacit) of another branch. Power was designed to counteract power; ambition to check ambition. This structure was developed by men whose memories of tyranny and the arbitrary exercise of power by the king of England were fresh in their minds. It was a structure designed to force a *consensus* before the government could act. The structure of government created by the framers did not create a leadership institution, but several—three separate, semiautonomous institutions—that shared power. As James Pfiffner notes, "The Framers designed a system of shared powers within a system that is purposefully biased against change." The forces of the status quo were given multiple veto opportunities; the forces of change were forced to go into battle nearly unarmed.

Because there are so many potential veto points, the American system generally alternates between stasis and crisis, paralysis and spasm. On occasion the branches are able to cooperate and work together to promote change, but it is especially difficult for the president and Congress—deliberately disconnected by the framers—to forge a union. The resulting paralysis has many parents, but the separation of powers is clearly the most determinative.

Further reading: Charles C. Thach. *The Creation of the Presidency.* Baltimore: Johns Hopkins University Press, 1922; Cronin, Thomas E., ed. *Inventing the American Presidency.* Lawrence: University Press of Kansas, 1989.

constitutional amendments

While the Constitution has remained largely unchanged in over two hundred years, several amendments do relate to the presidency. The TWELFTH AMENDMENT, adopted in 1804, relates to the election of presidents, clarifying how votes for president and vice president are cast. The TWENTIETH AMENDMENT deals with the date of presidential INAUGURATIONS. The TWENTY-SECOND AMENDMENT (1951) limits the president to two terms. The TWENTY-THIRD AMENDMENT allows citizens residing in the District of Columbia to vote in presidential elections. The Twenty-fourth Amendment eliminates the poll tax. The TWENTY-FIFTH AMENDMENT deals with filling a vacancy in the vice presidency and also covers the temporary transferal of power to the vice president in case of illness of the president. The Twenty-sixth Amendment gives 18-year-olds the right to vote. See Appendix I for these Constitutional amendments.

constitutional convention

The American presidency was a deliberate creation, an invention. In this respect the presidency is unlike the office of the British prime minister, which evolved gradually during the 18th century without ever being codified. No one can definitively say who was the first prime minister, but every schoolboy and girl knows that George WASHINGTON was the first president. Prior to 1787 there was no American presidency; indeed there was no national CHIEF EXECUTIVE of any sort. There was an office with the title of "president" under the old national confederation, but it bears no relationship to the presidency established by Article II of the Constitution. The president between 1775 and 1787 was elected annually by the Continental Congress from among its members and served as little more than the presiding officer of that body.

The delegates selected to attend the 1787 Constitutional Convention agreed that the new constitution should establish a distinct EXECUTIVE BRANCH, but they had very different ideas about what that branch should look like. The delegates faced a host of contentious questions. Should the executive be plural or single? If single, should the executive have to seek the ADVICE AND CONSENT of an executive council, as most state constitutions required the governor to do? What powers should the executive be given? Should the executive have the power to veto legislation? Should the executive be given the power to make appointments, grant pardons, draw up treaties, conduct war? How should the executive be removed, and for what causes? Who should succeed the executive if he were to be removed or die in office? Should there be restrictions on who could become the executive? What should they call the executive?

The starting point for the delegates was the Virginia Plan, which was drafted by the Virginia delegation immediately prior to the start of the convention. The plan was vague on the subject of EXECUTIVE POWER. It did not even indicate whether the executive was to be unitary or plural, probably because the Virginia delegation was almost evenly split on the question. Deciding whether there should be one president or many was the first order of business when the convention took up the plan's resolution that "a National Executive be instituted." The first motion that the delegates considered relating to executive power was from Pennsylvania's James WILSON, who moved that the executive "consist of a single person." Opponents of a single executive feared that it would be "the foetus of monar-

chy," in the words of the Virginia governor Edmund Randolph. At least a quarter of the delegates shared Randolph's preference for a plural executive, but after several days of debate the delegates made the fateful decision (with seven states in favor and three opposed) to vest the executive power in a single person.

That was the easy part; the hard part was agreeing on a system for selecting the president. During the last two months of the convention 10 days were given up in whole or in large part to the issue. Why did the framers have so much difficulty devising a scheme to select the president? The short answer is that there were 13 states and only one president. How the president was selected would determine which states would exercise the greatest power over the nation's most important political office. If the president was elected directly by the people, as Wilson advocated, the most populous states stood to benefit. Pennsylvania had 10 times the number of people as Delaware. The three most populous states had nearly as many white inhabitants as the other 10 states combined, but far more than naked state interests were at stake in this debate. There was a widely shared feeling among the delegates that the people in a nation as vast as the United States would not be in a position to evaluate the merits and demerits of national political leaders. As George Mason put the point: "It would be as unnatural to refer the choice of a proper character for chief Magistrate to the people, as it would, to refer a trial of colors to a blind man." The popular choice, many feared, would be ill-informed and parochial.

The obvious alternative to popular election was selection by the national legislature, as the Virginia Plan proposed at the outset. The New Jersey Plan, offered as the small states' substitute for the Virginia Plan, was identical to the latter in its provisions for presidential selection. Throughout most of the convention this seemed the only realistic option to the great majority of the delegates. Contributing to the delegates' bias toward legislative selection was the fact that at the state level most governors were chosen by the state legislatures. Of the 12 states represented at the convention, only four (Connecticut, Massachusetts, New York, and New Hampshire) had any experience with a popularly elected chief executive. In every southern state the chief executive was selected by the legislature.

Selection by the legislature also was perceived to have serious drawbacks, none more so than the way it threatened to undermine the independence of the executive. If the president relied on the legislature for his appointment, how could he be expected to act as an effective check on the legislative branch? If the legislature was to select the president, most of the delegates agreed, executive independence could only be secured by a relatively long term of office and especially by making the executive ineligible for a second term. Only a president who had no hope of reelection would have the will to defend executive prerogatives against legislature encroachments. Legislative selection raised another problem as well, especially for those more fearful of executive power than they were concerned to safeguard executive independence. An executive selected by the legislature and eligible for reelection might use the powers of his office (particularly the appointive power) to corrupt the legislature by buying legislators' support. These twin concerns over maintaining executive independence from the legislature and avoiding corruption of the legislature were so acute that on July 17, four state delegations voted in favor of allowing the president to serve "during good behavior" rather than have him be made eligible for reelection. Over the next two weeks the delegates considered a range of alternative proposals but without making any headway. They ended up at the end of July where they had begun at the beginning of June: with an executive selected by the legislature, serving a seven-year term, and ineligible for reelection.

And yet doubts continued to linger. Many delegates disliked making the executive ineligible for reelection. If the president was doing a good job why shouldn't he be kept in the job? No rotation in office was required of national legislators, so why should rotation exist for the executive, where there was arguably greater need for continuity, experience, and stability? If the president was made, as James MADISON put it, the "tenant of an unrenewable lease," might it not take away "one powerful motive to a faithful & useful administration"? Was it wise for the nation to tie its hands so that at some critical juncture it might be unable to choose a chief executive deemed to be "essential to the public safety"? More ominously still, would a chief executive who was denied a legitimate means for his political ambitions be tempted to seek violent and unconstitutional means to maintain himself in power? "Shut the Civil road to Glory," Gouverneur MORRIS warned the convention, "and he may be compelled to seek it by the sword."

When the convention returned again to the issue of presidential selection toward the end of August these philosophical doubts mixed potently with state interests to stymie the convention once again. It was all very well to agree that the legislature should select the president, but that formulation left out how the legislature should select the president. If the president were to be selected by joint ballot of the two houses of Congress, the advantage would go to the larger states. If, on the other hand, each house was granted a negative on the vote of the other house, or if the legislature cast votes by state rather than by individuals, then the smaller states would be advantaged. It was this raw clash of state interests that forced the convention to hand the matter over to the Committee on Postponed Matters (the Brearly Committee), out of which emerged the most original part of the founders' handiwork, the ELECTORAL COLLEGE.

It is often said that the framers expected that except in rare circumstances the electoral college would essentially be a nominating device, with the final selection left to the legislature. George Mason's estimate that 19 times in 20 the legislature would make the selection is frequently taken as representative of the thinking of the framers, but a close reading of the convention debates suggests that opinion on this question was sharply divided. Those who agreed with Mason that the electoral college would rarely make the final selection believed that the voting for president would almost invariably be highly fragmented because electors would vote for their own state's favorite son. Mason's view was strongly challenged on the floor by members of the Brearly Committee. Georgia's representative on the committee, Abraham Baldwin, countered that "increasing intercourse among the people of the States" would make national figures better known and thus make it increasingly likely that a candidate would gain a majority in the electoral college. The primary spokesman for the Brearly Committee on the convention floor, Morris, pointed out that the requirement that electors vote for two candidates, only one of whom could be from the elector's own state, made it probable that the election would be settled in the electoral college. Madison, Virginia's representative on the committee, defended the committee's decision to vest the contingency election in the Senate on the grounds that since the small states predominated in the Senate, the large states would have a strong incentive to avoid the contingency election and make sure the selection was made by the electoral college.

The creation of the electoral college was a mixed-motive game. Delegates from large states could support it in the knowledge that they would dominate the electoral college, which they had sound reasons to expect would make the final selection. Small state representatives could support it in the plausible hope that elections would frequently be thrown into the Senate (or, as it was amended on the floor, in the House of Representatives with each state possessing an equal vote). It was a compromise made possible by the uncertainty that inevitably accompanied an institution with which no delegate had any practical experience. For instance, the provision that electors must cast two votes could be seen as helping candidates from the smaller states since, as Hugh Williamson explained, the second vote would be "as probably of a small as a large [state]," but a case could also be made that it would advantage the large states since, as Morris emphasized, it would make it less likely that the selection would be thrown into the legislature. Theories and reasons abounded but in truth no delegate had a clear sense of how this novel creation would actually work, which probably explains why critics and defenders alike did such a poor job of anticipating the problems the electoral college would generate, problems that became apparent to many of the framers in the first presidential election.

Having settled how the president was to be selected, the delegates were in a better position to resolve questions about the powers that should be assigned to the president. The Virginia Plan had specifically granted the executive just one power, the power to veto legislation, and even this power could be exercised only with the consent of a council drawn from the judiciary and could be overridden by an unspecified portion of the legislature. The idea of an executive council of revision quickly ran into strong opposition from those who felt such a council violated the separation of powers by giving judges a role in the legislative process. Instead (on the same day they decided on a single executive) the delegates opted to vest a qualified veto power in the president alone. A few delegates preferred giving the president an absolute veto, including Wilson, Morris, and Alexander HAMILTON, but that proposal failed spectacularly, without a single state in support. The delegates originally opted for a two-thirds legislative override of an executive veto, but in the middle of the August a motion by Williamson to require a three-fourths vote in both the Senate and the House was narrowly carried. On September 12, the day the Committee of Style presented the final draft of the Constitution to the delegates, the convention again changed its mind, narrowly accepting a motion (again from Williamson) to revert to a two-thirds override. Madison objected strenuously that a two-thirds veto would be insufficient to "check legislative injustice and encroachments," but more delegates agreed with Charles Pinckney that a three-quarter veto placed "a dangerous power" in the hands of the president and a small number of legislators.

The British monarch possessed an absolute veto power, but rarely used it. More worrying to delegates fearful of executive power was the power of appointments, which they believed the king had used to corrupt the legislature by offering offices to members of Parliament. The delegates' fear of the executive APPOINTMENT POWER manifested itself in their early decision to follow most state constitutions and vest the appointment of JUDGES in the legislature. The Virginia plan lodged the appointment of judges in the "National Legislature," and on June 13 the convention placed the power in the hands of the Senate alone. On July 21 Madison proposed to give the executive the power to nominate judges "unless disagreed to by 2/3 of the second branch of the Legislature," but the idea was firmly rejected by the convention. The appointment of judges remained in the hands of the Senate until the Committee on Postponed Matters, on September 4, reported out a proposal to have the president "nominate and by and with the consent of the Senate appoint" judges as well as ambassadors and other "public Ministers." The proposal, barely imaginable in the opening days of the convention, sailed through without serious opposition.

The power to negotiate treaties was another power that for most of the convention was securely lodged in the hands of the Senate. Again it was the Committee on Postponed Matters that for the first time placed the treaty-making power in the hands of the president, subject to the consent of two-thirds of the Senate. Having given Congress the power to declare war, made the president commander in chief, and divided treaty-making power between the president and the Senate, the convention clearly signaled that the control of foreign and military policy was to be, as Hamilton put in *Federalist No. 75*, a "joint possession." That today the president seems to have sole ownership of foreign and military policy would have pleased Hamilton but is certainly not a result anticipated by the framers.

The changes made in the closing weeks of the convention, particularly those made by the Committee on Postponed Matters, significantly strengthened the presidency. Had the convention finished its business shortly after the Committee of Detail's report on August 6, it would have produced a considerably weaker presidency. The president would have been selected by the legislature for a single seven-year term, without any power in the treaty-making process and without any role in the appointment of ambassadors or judges. To be sure, the executive would still have had the power to veto legislation subject to a two-thirds legislative override, would have been COMMANDER IN CHIEF of the armed forces, and would have possessed an almost unrestricted PARDON POWER. But a president picked by the legislature, without the ability to seek reelection, and without any role in the selection of Supreme Court and federal justices or in the making of treaties would have occupied a dramatically different office. It would have doubtless altered the course of American history in ways that none of us can fully comprehend. What the framers created during that muggy Philadelphia summer continues to profoundly shape politics in the United States and even the world.

Further reading: Cronin, Thomas E., ed. *Inventing the American Presidency.* Lawrence: University Press of Kansas, 1989; Ellis, Richard J., ed. *Founding the American Presidency.* Lanham, Md.: Rowman & Littlefield, 1999; Farrand, Max. *The Records of the Federal Convention,* 4 vols. New Haven, Conn.: Yale University Press, 1934; Thach, Charles C., Jr. *The Creation of the Presidency, 1775–1789.* Baltimore, Md.: Johns Hopkins Press, 1923.

—Richard J. Ellis

containment

The policy of containment finds its origins in the post-war presidency of Harry TRUMAN and in the publication of George Kennan's article in *Foreign Affairs.* Kennan believed that the Soviets were motivated by two beliefs: the inherent opposition between capitalism and socialism and the infallibility of the communist party leadership. As such, American foreign policy should incorporate the "adroit and vigilant application of counterforce at a series of constantly shifting geographic and political points, corresponding to the shifts and maneuvers of Soviet policy." The means should be "long term, patient but firm and vigilant containment."

Containment became the defining conception of American postwar policy and set the tone for the American and Soviet relationship that would last a generation. The implications of containment were clear: The Soviet Union would test American resolve by applying pressure to certain strategic points. For the Truman administration in 1947, Greece represented such a point. If Greece fell into the communist sphere, it was reasoned, Turkey would be next, and soon the Middle East would be dominated by pro-Soviet governments. Such reasoning represented an early version of the "domino theory," which argued that a socialist triumph in one state would knock over the free governments of neighboring countries.

The year 1950 was another pivotal one for the policy of containment. The Truman administration, spurred into action by the fall of China to communism and by Soviet acquisition of the ATOMIC BOMB, sought more funding to begin a massive and rapid construction of political, economic, and military strength in the Free World. National Security Council Resolution 68 (NSC 68) institutionalized containment as the policy of the United States. Containment equaled INTERVENTION. In fact, containing communism was the primary strategy used to protect America's construction and consolidation of its leadership. To keep communism from spreading outside Eastern Europe and the Soviet Union, the United States would react aggressively to any early warning of communist infiltration of a free nation. Military advice and economic aid would not necessarily be enough to prevent a government from falling. The use of American military force would be applied in dire situations where geopolitical considerations demanded it, such as Korea, Vietnam, and Grenada. In the seventies and eighties, direct involvement by U.S. troops was limited and proxy wars were launched against pro-Soviet governments and insurgencies.

Although the policy of containment ended with the dissolution of Soviet Union in 1991, containment continues to be debated as a policy option for dealing with potentially expansionist powers like Iraq and China.

Further reading: Ambrose, Stephen. *Rise to Globalism,* 8th ed. New York: Penguin Publishers, 1997; Kennan, George. "Long Telegram." In *Foreign Relations of the United States.* Washington, D.C.: U.S. Government Printing Office, 1969; Kennan, George. "The Sources of Soviet Conduct." *Foreign Affairs* (July 1947).

—Paul Rexton Kan

contempt of Congress

Contempt of Congress consists of deliberate interference with Congress's duties and powers. Most often, it consists of disobeying a subpoena to provide a committee with testimony or documents. The Constitution does not explicitly empower Congress to punish contempt by anyone but its own members. In 1821, however, the Supreme Court ruled that Congress does indeed have such authority. According to Justice William Johnson, the idea "that such an assembly should not possess the power to suppress rudeness, or repel insult is a supposition too wild to be suggested" (*Anderson v. Dunn,* 19 U.S. 204, 229 [1821]).

Either house of Congress may cite an individual for contempt. Under the inherent contempt power, the House or Senate may actually try offenders and then jail them in the Capitol. Neither chamber has used this procedure since 1934 because of its potential for consuming time and creating bad publicity. It would seem odd to imprison people in a building whose highest point is the Statue of Freedom.

The major alternative is the statutory criminal contempt power, which dates back to 1857 and appears in Title 2, Sections 192 and 194, of the United States Code. The law applies to anyone who defies a congressional subpoena by refusing to appear, answer pertinent questions, or produce requested materials. The offense is a misdemeanor that may bring up to a $1,000 fine and up to a year in jail. The process starts when a House or Senate committee reports a contempt resolution, which goes to the full chamber for a vote. The president pro tem of the Senate or the Speaker of the House then certifies the report to the appropriate U.S. Attorney, "whose duty it shall be to bring the matter before the grand jury for its action."

Contempt resolutions are a questionable tool for extracting information from the EXECUTIVE BRANCH, since enforcement depends on the executive branch itself. In 1982 the House approved a contempt resolution against Anne Gorsuch (later Anne Burford), administrator of the ENVIRONMENTAL PROTECTION AGENCY. The U.S. Attorney for the District of Columbia, however, declined to take the case to the grand jury. He ran into severe criticism from the chairman of the committee that had originated the resolution, but the House counsel conceded that the language of the statute provided for prosecutorial discretion. Another law (28 U.S.C. § 1365) provides the Senate with a civil contempt mechanism, but it exempts subpoenas to the executive branch.

Of course, Congress is scarcely powerless in its struggles for information. Lawmakers can use many informal bargaining chips, such as power over appropriations, to get what they want. And although contempt resolutions may not result in prosecution, they can be an extremely unpleasant experience for their targets. "Well, one never likes being cited for contempt," said Attorney General Janet Reno in 1998 after a House committee voted to cite her for failing to turn over papers in one of the CLINTON probes. So when committee chairs utter the words "contempt of Congress," the affected officials of the executive branch will pay attention.

Further reading: Fisher, Louis. *Constitutional Conflicts Between Congress and the President,* 4th ed. Lawrence: University Press of Kansas, 1997; Rosenburg, Morton. *Investigative Oversight: An Introduction to the Law, Practice and Procedure of Congressional Inquiry.* New York: Nova Science Publishers, 2003.

—John J. Pitney

continuing resolutions

As the normal calendar of the budget process often breaks down, means must be found to fund the activities of the federal government in light of Congress's inability to establish policy in a timely manner. Continuing resolutions are one such means.

If Congress is unable to pass appropriations bills by the start of the fiscal year they resort to a continuing resolution. In recent years these resolutions have become more important—and controversial—as they are often used not just to fund the activities of the government but to change policy outside of the normal channels.

Continuing resolutions are not bound by the rule of the House of Representatives that prohibits attaching substantive legislation onto an appropriations bill. Therefore, in negotiating the terms of a continuing resolution, members of the House and Senate appropriations committees can use the process to change policy. For example, it was through a continuing resolution that, in the late 1980s, a provision was inserted in a resolution that allowed states to raise the speed limit to 65 miles per hour. Critics also assert that continuing resolutions limit the president's ability and willingness to exercise the veto power.

conventions See PARTY CONVENTIONS.

Coolidge, Calvin (1872–1933) *thirtieth U.S. president*

The thirtieth president, Calvin Coolidge was born in Plymouth Notch, Vermont, in 1872. A graduate of Amherst College, Coolidge practiced law prior to his entry into politics. A state legislator, governor, and vice president, Coolidge became president during the "Roaring Twenties."

Calvin Coolidge, thin and standing 5'9", known as "Silent Cal" due to his quiet, taciturn, even mundane manner, was probably America's first "feel good" president. "Keep Cool With Coolidge" was his motto, and Coolidge kept cool by sleeping more than any other president in U.S.

President Calvin Coolidge *(Library of Congress)*

history. He seemed convinced that the less a president did, the better. H. L. Mencken said: ". . . while he yawned and stretched the United States went slam bang down the hill—and he lived just long enough to see it fetch up with a horrible bump at the bottom." The chronically shy Coolidge was a man of few words. George Creel said he was "distinguishable from the furniture only when he moved."

During the 1924 campaign, a reporter asked him: "Have you any statement on the campaign?" "No," replied Coolidge. "Can you tell us something about the world situation?" asked another. "No." "Any information about Prohibition?" "No." When the reporters started to leave, Coolidge said solemnly: "Now, remember—don't quote me." At a

White House social event, a woman approached Coolidge: "You must talk to me, Mr. President," she said. "I made a bet today that I could get more than two words out of you." "You lose" was the reply. Foreign diplomats said Coolidge "can be silent in five languages."

In a way Coolidge fit the mood of the times. "I think the American public wants a solemn ass as a president. And I think I'll go along with them," he once said. And humorist Will Rogers said, "He did not do nothing, but that's what we wanted done."

Coolidge was straitlaced and a man of unbending grayness, a man newspaper editor William Allen White referred to as "a Puritan in Babylon." Teddy ROOSEVELT's daughter, Alice, said Coolidge "looked like he had been weaned on a pickle."

Coolidge rejected the activist view of the presidency and was deferential to congressional leadership. One of his few strongly held beliefs was that "the business of the American people is business," and Coolidge vowed nonintervention in the affairs of business. This gave the commercial interests in America a free hand to pursue their goals unencumbered by government supervision.

Coolidge was president in the midst of the "Roaring Twenties." In 1921 automobile registration in the United States was at 9.3 million. By 1929 that number soared to 26.7 million. The telephone was revolutionizing communication. Radio was introduced. Moving pictures became a popular pastime. In 1922, 40 million movie tickets were sold per week. By 1929 the number had climbed to 100 million. And in 1920 women won the right to vote. Prohibition was in force, *The Jazz Singer* was released, Sacco and Vanzetti were executed, Babe Ruth went on his home run binge, Al Capone and Mickey Mouse captured the popular imagination, Charles Lindbergh flew the first solo flight across the Atlantic, and an economic boom swept the land. It was a time of individualism and materialistic extravagance. And Silent Cal was president during the Roaring Twenties— it was a paradox that made sense.

Silent Cal let Congress do the talking. Other than proposing tax reductions, Coolidge had virtually no legislative AGENDA. In this way, he more closely resembled 19th- than 20th-century presidents. Having abandoned the role of legislator-in-chief, he chose instead to use the veto pen to limit legislative activity.

During the Coolidge years, the HARDING scandals were exposed, Congress passed the Immigration Act of 1924 (which limited the number of Italians and Jews who could enter the country, raised quotas for northern Europeans, and excluded Japanese ["America must be kept American," Coolidge said]), the Revenue Acts of 1924 and 1926 (tax cuts) were enacted, the Veteran's Bonus Act of 1924 was passed (over Coolidge's veto), the McNary-Haugen Bill of 1927 was passed (over Coolidge's two vetoes), and in *MYERS*

v. UNITED STATES (1926) the Supreme Court gave constitutional sanction to a broad interpretation of the president's REMOVAL POWER. In FOREIGN AFFAIRS, the Pact of Paris (the KELLOGG-BRIAND PACT) of 1928 was approved.

Coolidge's reluctance to regulate business in spite of some early warning signs helped lead to the GREAT DEPRESSION, which hit six months after he left office. Coolidge, committed to a laissez-faire approach, decided to leave business alone. He ignored the mounting economic troubles that would soon plunge the nation into a deep depression.

Coolidge built up a meager record as president. He probably wanted it that way. He shrunk the presidency and left several key problems unaddressed. His failure to supply leadership, to recognize and even anticipate problems, contributed to the Great Depression.

Silent Cal died of a heart attack on January 5, 1933. On hearing the news of Coolidge's death, writer Dorothy Parker cynically asked, "How can they tell?"

Further reading: Fuess, Claude M. *Calvin Coolidge, The Man from Vermont.* Boston: Little, Brown, 1940; McCoy, Donald R. *Calvin Coolidge, The Quiet President.* Lawrence: University Press of Kansas, 1988; Murray, Robert K. *The Politics of Normalcy: Governmental Theory and Practice in the Harding-Coolidge Era.* New York: W. W. Norton, 1973.

Cooper-Church Amendment

The Cooper-Church Amendment was passed by Congress to force the withdrawal of U.S. forces in Cambodia during the VIETNAM WAR.

In 1970 President NIXON had secretly ordered U.S. forces into Cambodia to attack communist sanctuaries. When Nixon announced the operation on April 30, 1970, many college campuses exploded into protest against the perceived expansion of the war. Four students were killed by national guard troops at Kent State University in Ohio, and other students were shot by police officers at Jackson State University in Mississippi. An estimated 100,000 protesters marched on Washington, and Congress received in excess of two million letters protesting Nixon's actions.

Congress responded to the public outcry. Senators John Sherman Cooper (Rep.-Ky.) and Frank Church (Dem.-Idaho) of the Senate Foreign Relations Committee introduced a measure to force the government to recall the troops from Cambodia. Congress was utilizing the power of the purse by cutting off funding for any action in Cambodia after July 1, 1970. Nixon withdrew U.S. troops from Cambodia claiming he had intended to do so anyway, regardless of Cooper-Church.

The Cooper-Church Amendment marked the first time in U.S. history that the Senate threatened to curb the president's use of military force and marked the beginning of a resurgent Congress attempting to reclaim its role in war-making. Cooper-Church was the first of many measures Congress utilized, including the repeal of the GULF OF TONKIN RESOLUTION, the WAR POWERS RESOLUTION, the CASE ACT, and the Hughes Ryan Act, that transformed the executive/legislative relationship with regard to foreign policy.

Further reading: Fisher, Louis. *Presidential War Powers.* Lawrence: University Press of Kansas, 1995; Johnson, Lock K. *America as a World Power: Foreign Policy in a Constitutional Framework.* New York: McGraw-Hill, 1991.
—Frank M. Sorrentino

Corcoran, Thomas (1900–1981) *political adviser*

Thomas (Tommy, "The Cork") Corcoran was a top adviser to FDR during the GREAT DEPRESSION. Corcoran headed the Reconstruction Finance Corporation, but his reach extended far beyond this agency, as Corcoran was instrumental in the development of Roosevelt's NEW DEAL. He lobbied Congress, wrote legislation, and served as one of FDR's key political strategists. With the onset of WORLD WAR II, Corcoran's influence waned. He left government service in 1940 and became a prominent and controversial lawyer and lobbyist.

Corwin, Edward S. (1878–1963) *scholar*

A founding member of the modern discipline of political science, Corwin was known for his major contributions to public law and to the study of the American presidency. His magisterial book, *The President: Office and Powers,* is a sweeping analysis of the presidency's constitutional and historical roots and development.

Corwin received his B.A. in history, Phi Beta Kappa, from the University of Michigan in 1900. He earned his Ph.D. at the University of Pennsylvania in 1905, after which he was one of Princeton University's instructors or "preceptors" recruited by university President Woodrow WILSON. At Princeton, Corwin helped found the Politics Department, becoming its first chair. He was named McCormick Professor of Jurisprudence in 1918 and remained so until his retirement in 1946. He worked for the Franklin D. ROOSEVELT administration as adviser to the Public Works Administration, consultant to the attorney general, and later as editor for the Library of Congress. Among other honors, Corwin served as president of the American Political Science Association in 1931.

Corwin's approach to the study of American politics and the presidency was deeply rooted in history, law, philosophy, and judicial processes. Supreme Court Justice Benjamin Cardozo once said of Corwin, "I find I have frequent occasion to draw upon your learning." Corwin's vast legal knowledge shaped and formed his study of the presidency, and it also led him to the view that the modern, post-Roosevelt presidency had come to unhealthily dominate the national political landscape. Much of the standard wisdom accepted about the presidency today traces directly to his analysis of the office.

Corwin noted at the outset that the office's vaguely articulated parameters opened the door to accelerating EXECUTIVE POWER. The office always struggled between its constitutional subservience to the legislative branch and its drive toward greater autonomy and power. Yet in noting this, Corwin did not focus on rules and laws alone; he readily acknowledged that the office at any given time was substantially the product of the individual holding it, and of the balance between normalcy and crisis in the country. In *The President,* published in four editions (1940, 1941, 1948, and 1957, with a revised fifth edition published in 1984), Corwin examines the organic beginnings of the office, beginning with the nature of executive power and the means by which it arose from the CONSTITUTIONAL CONVENTION and early presidencies. He then explores election, succession, removal, and DISABILITY; presidential administrative responsibilities; CHIEF EXECUTIVE powers and prerogatives, including EMERGENCY POWERS and their consequences; the president's preeminent role as chief organ in foreign policy; commander-in-chief powers, with particular focus on the CIVIL WAR and the world wars; and the president's LEGISLATIVE LEADERSHIP. Presidential power is cyclical, Corwin concluded. Yet its generalized upward march has been fed by two structural erosions: the decline of dual FEDERALISM, and of the separation of powers. Congress in particular has shared much of the responsibility for the latter, having readily yielded to the presidency much power and prerogative. The explosion of administrative rule making has also fed executive fires.

Corwin's themes reverberate throughout the modern literature on the presidency and are too often rediscovered, as though they had not been articulated a half-century earlier. *The President* continues in print, published by New York University Press. Its analysis is as trenchant and insightful today as the day it was penned.

Further reading: Corwin, Edward S. *The President: Office and Powers.* Edited by Randall W. Bland, Theodore T. Hindson, and Jack W. Peltason. New York: New York University Press, 1984; *Presidential Power and the Constitution: Essays.* Edited by Richard Loss. Ithaca: Cornell University Press, 1976; Utter, Glenn H., and Charles Lockhart, eds. *American Political Scientists.* Westport, Conn.: Greenwood Press, 1993.
—Robert J. Spitzer

Council of Economic Advisers (CEA)

Established by the EMPLOYMENT ACT OF 1946, the Council of Economic Advisers (CEA) is composed of three members appointed by the president (one of whom serves as chair), with the ADVICE AND CONSENT of the Senate. The CEA assists the president of providing advice on ECONOMIC POLICY as well as preparing economic forecasts.

Council on Environmental Quality (CEQ)

The Council on Environmental Quality (CEQ) was created in 1970 as an office within the EXECUTIVE OFFICE OF THE PRESIDENT (EOP) to formulate and recommend to the president national policies to improve the quality of the environment. It maintains three types of responsibilities: to develop and analyze ENVIRONMENTAL POLICY; to coordinate environmental programs from other agencies; and to gather and assess environment-related information. Much CEQ activity is focused on preparation and dissemination of studies and reports for the president and Congress. Since 1971 the CEQ has published an annual, detailed report analyzing and summarizing environmental trends. In addition, the CEQ oversees the preparation of environmental impact statements within the federal government.

The CEQ is governed by a three-member board appointed by the president, subject to Senate confirmation. One of the three is designated by the president to serve as chair. The Office of Environmental Quality (OEQ) provides staff support to implement the organization's mission.

The CEQ was created by Congress as part of the National Environmental Policy Act of 1969 (PL 91-190; 83 Stat. 852). Its primary proponent was Senator Henry M. Jackson (Dem.-Wash.), who first promoted the idea in 1967. President Richard NIXON initially opposed the idea but signed the bill creating the office into law. The CEQ presented its first report in August 1970. The CEQ's influence has waxed and waned according to the extent to which presidential administrations maintained an interest in environmental matters. Its influence and size was greatest during Jimmy CARTER's presidency, owing to the administration's keen interest in the environment. The REAGAN presidency slashed CEQ staff from 49 to 15 and cut its budget by half, reflecting its lack of interest in environmental matters. The marginalization of the CEQ continued under George H. W. BUSH. The more environmental-friendly CLINTON administration surprised many when it initially proposed replacing the CEQ with a White House environmental policy adviser. The agency survived, but with little influence over national environmental policy.

Further reading: Relyea, Harold, ed. *The Executive Office of the President.* Westport, Conn.: Greenwood Press, 1997; Rosenbaum, Walter A. *Environmental Politics and Policy,* 4th ed. Washington, D.C.: CQ Press, 1998.

—Robert J. Spitzer

counsel to the president

Every president beginning with Franklin Delano ROOSEVELT has had one or more aides with the title of "counsel" or "special counsel" or "counselor to the president," although the functions associated with that position have varied greatly. Samuel Rosenman was the first person to hold the title of special counsel, when he was brought to the White House by FDR as a speechwriter and adviser on DOMESTIC POLICY during WORLD WAR II. Others with that title and similar functions in later administrations included Clark CLIFFORD and Charles Murphy under TRUMAN, Gerald Morgan under EISENHOWER, Theodore Sorensen under KENNEDY, Harry McPherson under JOHNSON, and John Ehrlichman in 1969–70 under NIXON. It was John Dean, however, who was named as Nixon's counsel in 1970, who brought a central focus on "lawyering" to the position and who set the foundation for the modern office of counsel to the president as a separate unit in the White House Office.

Today, the counsel's office is viewed as the lawyer to the institution of the presidency, but its responsibilities, though emanating from legal ones, extend, also, deep into the policy and political realms. It is perhaps more accurate to describe the counsel as a "monitor" to the president—one who watches over every aspect of the work that goes into and comes out of the OVAL OFFICE, as an early warning system for any potential legal or ethical issues that might arise.

The counsel's office performs many routine tasks throughout the course of an administration, and it prefers to do its work out of the glare of the public spotlight. However, when scandals hit the White House, attention quickly turns to the counsel's office as the locus for information and advice on high-profile, sticky legal issues that affect the office of the presidency. When charges involve claims of personal, rather than official, wrongdoing by a president, the CHIEF EXECUTIVE hires private legal counsel, whose responsibility is to the *person* who occupies the Oval Office, rather than to the office itself.

The size of the counsel's office has varied over the years, rising to a high during the CLINTON years of as many as 40 lawyers to as few as two or three in the early years. Commonly, the number is approximately seven or eight lawyers. It usually consists of the counsel to the president, one or two deputy counsels, and the remaining associate counsels. Some factors that have affected the size of the office include the increased scope and specialization of its work, as well as a more hostile contemporary environment in Washington, where legal and ethical controversies become fodder for political conflicts.

The clearest way to understand just how central the work of the counsel's office is to the functioning of the White House is to acknowledge its relentless pace and immense breadth of responsibilities. The basic functions have come to include: (1) overseeing the process for all presidential nominations and appointments to the executive and judicial branches; (2) advising the president on the exercise of EXECUTIVE PRIVILEGE and other constitutional prerogatives of the office (e.g., war powers and presidential disability and succession); (3) participating in policy-making to ensure adequate oversight over any possible legal controversies; (4) advising on all actions the president takes within the legislative process (e.g., review of proposed legislation, drafting of signing statements and veto messages, monitoring negotiations over treaty issues in the Senate); (5) issuing ethics regulations at the beginning of an administration and insuring that all White House staffers are well-informed about such rules—a job that takes on added importance during election campaigns, where strict separation between government and campaign work must be maintained; (6) acting as the point of contact with the White House for all EXECUTIVE BRANCH departments and agencies, whose general counsels maintain communication with the counsel's office; and (7) coordinating and overseeing all contacts from the White House and executive branch departments agencies to the DEPARTMENT OF JUSTICE.

The Department of Justice is the governmental unit with the closest relationship to the counsel's office, and an understanding of that relationship will clarify the distinct duties associated with each. The attorney general, as the chief administrator of the Department of Justice, is responsible for establishing legal policy for the nation and for administering the nation's justice system. The Office of Legal Counsel in the Department of Justice is a highly specialized unit of approximately seven or eight lawyers whose role is to provide legal opinions to the president and the CABINET on constitutional questions. Those opinions are provided directly to the counsel's office in the White House, and carry with them the expectation that they will be followed. The potential for a clash of opinions between the Office of Legal Counsel in the Department of Justice and the Office of Counsel to the President is a real one, and tensions occasionally arise between them. The source of this tension is attributed to the fact that the counsel's office is part of the White House staff and, as such, is always sensitive to the political impact of any action or position the president is considering. Thus, the counsel's office needs to be able to reconcile both legal and political advice to the president, insuring that its opinions are both legally sound as well as politically astute—two dimensions that are not always so compatible. Former counsels to the president have lamented that trying to provide advice that does not sacrifice one of these dimensions for the other is an enor-

mous challenge. The Office of Legal Counsel in the Department of Justice is under no such constraint: Its opinions are purely legal, and the authority for its existence and functions is statutory, unlike the White House staff units, which exist as personal aides to the president. There is a strong presumption, then, that the counsel's office should heed the opinions of the Office of Legal Counsel, and it ignores them at its own peril.

Further reading: Borrelli, Mary Anne, Karen Hult, and Nancy Kassop. "The White House Counsel's Office." *Presidential Studies Quarterly* 31, no. 4 (December 2001): 561–584; Powell, H. Jefferson. *The Constitution and the Attorneys General.* Durham, N.C.: Carolina Academic Press, 1999.

—Nancy Kassop

court packing plan

The Judicial Reform Bill of 1937, popularly known as the "court packing plan," was a product of Franklin D. ROOSEVELT's frustration with the U.S. Supreme Court, which had declared many aspects of the NEW DEAL unconstitutional. It also reflected Roosevelt's hubris after the legislative success of his first term and the huge margin of his reelection victory (in 1936 he won roughly 60 percent of the popular vote and 98 percent of the ELECTORAL COLLEGE, taking 523 of 531 electoral votes). As a result of these previous successes, Roosevelt believed that the New Deal represented good policy and an overwhelming national mandate, both of which were endangered by the "nine old men" of the Supreme Court. On February 7, 1937, he proposed the Judicial Reform Bill, which sanctioned the appointment of one new justice for each one who failed to retire after reaching the age of 70. This would potentially allow Roosevelt to nominate as many as six new justices. While nothing like it had ever been proposed before, the plan was not entirely without precedent. The number of justices on the Supreme Court is fixed by statute, not by the Constitution, and that number has varied between a low of five in 1789 to a high of 10 between 1863 and 1865.

Roosevelt failed to consult with Congress before advocating judicial reform. He also failed to prepare the public and to justify the proposal in a clear and consistent manner. Once he announced the plan, he appeared to lose all interest in it. He made little effort initially to organize congressional or public support for the bill. His opponents were not so reticent. Roosevelt was quickly accused of attempting to "pack" the Court in what was widely considered to be an illegitimate attempt to exert presidential control over the judiciary.

That spring, the president's position was further weakened when the Court handed down a series of decisions favorable to the New Deal, the most important of which was a ruling affirming the constitutionality of the WAGNER ACT. In addition, Senator Joseph Robinson, a key Roosevelt supporter, died. This complicated the already difficult political situation for Roosevelt. Finally, on the day that the House Judiciary Committee was scheduled to begin hearings on the Judicial Reform Bill, Justice Willis Van Devanter announced his decision to retire from the Court. This combination of events ensured the bill's defeat.

This defeat was a product of the nature of the bill as well as the politics surrounding its short legislative life. Roosevelt attempted to portray the bill as part of a government-wide reorganization to mitigate the charges that he was improperly interfering with another branch of government, but in fact, that is exactly what he proposed doing, and that intention was clear from the outset.

Regardless of the merits of the bill, Roosevelt failed to consult with Congress, and he took his party's support for granted. He also allowed the bill to be interpreted publicly in personal rather than in political or policy-oriented ways, and provided misleading and non-credible justifications for it, focusing on the age and workloads of the justices rather than on the real source of his aggravation with the Court. This made the accusations of dictatorial behavior more plausible.

This defeat was an inauspicious beginning to what would prove to be a difficult second term. It helped to foster an environment in which Roosevelt's motives as well as his actions were considered suspect. The failure of the Judicial Reform Bill also led to worsened relations with Congress that in turn rendered the second term less than productive legislatively.

Further reading: Burns, James MacGregor. *Roosevelt: The Lion and the Fox.* New York: Harper and Brace, 1956; McJimsey, George. *The Presidency of Franklin Delano Roosevelt.* Lawrence: University Press of Kansas, 2000; Ryan, Halford R. *Franklin D. Roosevelt's Rhetorical Presidency.* New York: Greenwood Press, 1988; Savage, Sean J. *Roosevelt: The Party Leader, 1932–1945.* Lexington: Kentucky University Press, 1991.

—Mary E. Stuckey

courts and the president, the

The president and the federal courts exist within a two-way relationship: The president affects the courts by appointing federal judges, and the courts pronounce judgment on presidential actions or on other policies the president may favor. The impact, in both directions, may have momentous and long-term consequences, since federal judges have lifetime appointments, often leading to 30- or even 40-year tenures, long outlasting the president who appointed them, and

court decisions have, at times, profoundly affected a president's political options—the most dramatic being the 1974 U.S. Supreme Court decision in the NIXON tapes case that was the catalyst for his RESIGNATION from office. Even when the ramifications from presidential-judicial relations are not as spectacular as this, the degree of interdependence between these two institutions is significant.

Article II of the Constitution provides the president with the power to "nominate, and by and with the advice and consent of the Senate, shall appoint . . . judges of the Supreme court, and all other officers of the United States. . . ." This authority extends not only to Supreme Court justices, but to judges at all levels of the federal courts, consisting of the 94 district courts and the 13 courts of appeals. In the CONSTITUTIONAL CONVENTION, MADISON proposed giving the appointment of JUDGES solely to the Senate, while James Wilson suggested that the president be given this exclusive power. Eventually, the compromise of nomination by the president and consent by the Senate won the approval of the convention delegates. What was clear at the convention was support for a considerable role for the Senate in the selection process; but the placement of the process among the president's powers in Article II suggests that, in practice, the CHIEF EXECUTIVE was to be the primary player here.

The appointment process for all three levels is similar, with additional attention at the district court level and with a larger role played in the first stage by senators from the president's party of the home state of a nominee. If a prospective nominee is not favored by his senator, the president, respecting the tradition of "senatorial courtesy," will not move the name forward.

The selection process contains many players, although principal responsibility is lodged jointly in the DEPARTMENT OF JUSTICE and the OFFICE OF COUNSEL TO THE PRESIDENT for the generating of names of potential candidates and for the extensive "vetting," or background checks, of each nominee who also must submit personal information to the FBI. The American Bar Association practice of evaluating judicial candidates began in the 1950s, although the administration of George W. BUSH has claimed that it will refuse to consider these ratings. The president is presented with the results of the inquiry efforts of the Justice Department and the White House Counsel, and he makes his decision. The nomination is sent to the Senate, where it is referred to the Judiciary Committee for a public hearing. Any objection at that point by a home state senator usually signals the demise of a nomination, and the committee will decline to proceed with a hearing. When hearings are held, the nominee appears in person to answer questions from senators. The committee then votes on the nomination, and, where approved, the full Senate subsequently acts on the nomination as the final step in the process.

Presidential appointments to the judiciary come under closer scrutiny by the Senate than appointments to the EXECUTIVE BRANCH. The Senate jealously guards its prerogative to screen candidates carefully, recognizing the weighty significance these appointments carry. Lifetime tenure and judicial independence largely insulate federal judges, once confirmed by the Senate, from further ACCOUNTABILITY. Both the president and the Senate are mindful of the political and ideological makeup of each court and of the impact that any new appointment can make on that court's decisions and, ultimately, on the substance of the law.

Senate rejection of Supreme Court nominees is rare, although a total of 27 nominations, or about 20 percent throughout the nation's history, have not succeeded, mostly during the 19th century. Long periods of DIVIDED GOVERNMENT, in more recent decades, have raised the political stakes for both the president and the Senate and have made the confirmation process quite contentious.

Four other types of presidential-judicial relations bear mentioning. One is the president's selection of the solicitor general, the third-ranking official in the Justice Department, who serves as the attorney for the executive branch. This official is nominated by the president and confirmed by the Senate and contributes to setting the agenda of the federal appellate courts. The solicitor general determines which cases the government will appeal (when it loses) from the district courts, and, similarly, which cases from the courts of appeal will be petitioned to the Supreme Court. As a frequent player in the federal court system, the office of solicitor general has earned an enviable and influential reputation, and it has established an exceptionally high success rate (about 80 percent) of Supreme Court granting of certiorari to hear its cases as well as an actual success rate (about 75 percent) of winning those cases for the government. It is nicknamed "the tenth justice" for its closeness to the high court. At the same time, although the office was intended, historically, to be relatively independent, with its only requirement of someone who is "learned in the law," recent solicitors general have functioned much more as political advocates for the president.

The second relationship between the president and the courts concerns the president's authority to recommend legislation to Congress affecting the federal courts. The most famous example of this is Franklin ROOSEVELT's "COURT PACKING PLAN" of 1937, in an effort to break free of the "nine old men" on the Court who had frustrated his attempts to pass urgent NEW DEAL legislation to address the economic emergency. The Court declared unconstitutional 13 laws from 1934 to 1936. Roosevelt's strategy here was to ask Congress to increase the number of justices on the Court, thus permitting him to select additional justices who might offset those hostile to the NEW DEAL. In effect, Roosevelt's plan, had it passed, would have undermined judicial independence by manipulating the size, and, ultimately, the voting alignments, on the Court to promote decisions favorable to the president. Congress refused to pass this legislation, and the Court, on its own, began to uphold New Deal legislation with the 1937 decision of *West Coast Hotel v. Parrish.*

Third, the courts depend on the executive branch to enforce their decisions. Stark reminders of this dependence occurred in 1957, when President EISENHOWER called out federal troops to enforce court-ordered school desegregation in Little Rock, Arkansas, and when President KENNEDY took similar action with federal troops in 1961 to enforce a desegregation order at the University of Mississippi.

The most dramatic examples of a president's responsibility to enforce the law occur when the court's decision directly affects the president and his executive powers. It is rare for the courts to rule against a sitting president, although the exceptions to this rule are the ones most often remembered. President TRUMAN was scolded by the Court in the Steel Seizure case in 1952 when it declared unconstitutional his executive order seizing the steel mills in an effort to avert a labor strike during the KOREAN WAR. He complied with the decision, returning the mills to their owners, and a strike followed. In August 1974 the nation waited for almost two weeks in suspense before learning whether President NIXON would, in fact, comply with the Court order in *UNITED STATES V. NIXON* and turn over the WATERGATE tapes to special prosecutor Leon JAWORSKI. In agreeing to do so, the Court's decision had the cataclysmic effect of moving the president into realizing that he would be unable to survive an impeachment effort, and thus that his only option was to resign from office.

Judicial review of the constitutionality of a president's actions is, perhaps, the most direct effect the courts can have on a sitting president. This oversight was nowhere mentioned in the Constitution, but Chief Justice Marshall's decision in *MARBURY V. MADISON* erased any doubt that that federal courts would exercise this power over legislative and executive actions.

Conflicts between the president and the courts occur when the president's interpretation of his constitutional authority is challenged. Many of Lincoln's actions as a wartime president were questioned, with differing results from the Court at various points in time. His suspension of the writ of habeas corpus was struck down in the *Ex parte Milligan* (1866) case, after the war had ended, while his 1861 blockage of Southern ports was upheld by the Court in *THE PRIZE CASES* in 1863, while war was ongoing.

FOREIGN AFFAIRS, especially, is an area where federal courts are reluctant to enter, preferring to leave questions of policy to the "political" branches. The classic example of the Supreme Court's deference to the president in this policy area is the 1936 case of *UNITED STATES V. CURTISS-*

WRIGHT EXPORT CORPORATION, where the Court waxed expansively on the president as "the sole organ of the federal government in the field of international relations." In fact, the Court's decision went far beyond the facts of the case, which only asked whether the Congress's delegation of power to the president was constitutional. The Court took the opportunity, instead, to articulate an inherent, exclusive EXECUTIVE POWER to act in foreign affairs, giving the president more power than the Constitution ever intended.

Finally, even when court decisions have resulted in rejection of the president's claims, many have limited the narrow construction to the facts before them in the specific case but have articulated a principle which, in fact, validates an expansive view of the law and of executive power. The court rejected Truman's assertion of emergency power in the Steel Seizure case, but at least six justices acknowledged that if Congress had not acted previously to deny emergency seizure power, the outcome might have been different. A similar pattern was apparent in both the *U.S. v. Nixon* case and the 1971 *NEW YORK TIMES V. UNITED STATES* (Pentagon Papers) case. In *Nixon,* the court rejected the president's claim of an absolute, unqualified EXECUTIVE PRIVILEGE over OVAL OFFICE communications, but the decision, for the first time, announced that a qualified executive privilege *was* entitled to constitutional protection. In the Pentagon Papers case, six members of the Court agreed that the government had not met the heavy burden of proof needed to justify an injunction to halt all publication of a top-secret, stolen DEFENSE DEPARTMENT document—but, if the government *could* have proven that national security would be directly, immediately, and irreparably harmed, the Court would have upheld the injunction.

The most controversial decision by the Court affecting a president was its interpretation of constitutional provisions and federal and state statutes that guided the electoral process in the 2000 presidential election. An unprecedented spectacle occurred, where the Supreme Court determined the election outcome by its December 2000 ruling in *BUSH v. GORE,* ending the hand recount of votes in Florida and delivering the necessary 25 electoral votes to George W. BUSH to assure him of an election victory. It would be hard to imagine a closer connection between the president and the courts than this, or one that would arouse greater public skepticism.

Further reading: Abraham, Henry J. *Justices and Presidents: A Political History of Appointments to the Supreme Court,* 2d ed. New York: Oxford University Press, 1985; Caplan, Lincoln. *The Tenth Justice: The Solicitor General and the Rule of Law.* New York: Vintage Books, 1987; Goldman, Sheldon. *Picking Federal Judges: Lower Court Selection from Roosevelt through Reagan.* New Haven, Conn.: Yale University Press, 1997.

—Nancy Kassop

covert operations

The term *covert activities* refers to secret activities engaged in by a government in support of policy objectives. Such activities as propaganda, financial support, arms, paramilitary activities, and efforts to overthrow or destabilize governments and foreign leaders are common forms of covert operations.

Except in wartime, covert activities were sporadically used by the United States up until the onset of the COLD WAR in the late 1940s. In the 1950s, President EISENHOWER used covert operations as a key part of his foreign policy. From that point on, covert actions became frequent and problematic.

Covert operations undermine democratic ACCOUNTABILITY, as their purpose is to be secret. Yet, since their consequences can be significant—for example, political ASSASSINATIONS, or overthrowing democratically elected governments—they raise serious questions for a democracy.

In the KENNEDY administration, a series of covert activities, many directed against Fidel Castro of Cuba, followed by even more covert actions in the NIXON years, led the Senate to hold hearings (the CHURCH COMMITTEE, named after the committee chair, Frank Church of Idaho) and attempted to impose some democratic controls and accountability. But such efforts (e.g., setting up a Senate Committee on Intelligence) have been weak and have done little to control presidents determined to violate the law.

In the REAGAN years, the IRAN-CONTRA scandal began as a series of covert and illegal activities, indicating that a president willing to violate the law can get away with a great deal if willing to use covert operation to cover up his activities.

Further reading: Johnson, Loch K. *America's Secret Power: The CIA in a Democratic Society.* New York: Oxford University Press, 1989; Prados, John. *Presidents' Secret Wars: CIA and Pentagon Covert Operations since World War II.* New York: W. Morrow, 1986.

Cox, Archibald, Jr. (1912–) *lawyer*

Archibald Cox was a Harvard Law School professor who had served as solicitor general under Attorney General Robert F. KENNEDY, but who will be most remembered for the role he played as the first special prosecutor investigating executive branch wrongdoing in the WATERGATE scandal during the Nixon administration.

Cox was appointed under an arrangement in May 1973 connected to the Senate confirmation of Elliott Richardson to be attorney general. Richardson had been nominated by President NIXON to succeed Richard Kleindienst as attorney general, and the new nominee pledged to the Senate as a commitment during his hearings that he would appoint a special prosecutor to investigate possible criminal conduct by presidential aides and even the president himself. Richardson offered to name the person during the hearings so that the Senate could informally determine if it approved or not. Cox had been Richardson's professor at Harvard Law School. He accepted the position, he later wrote, "out of the belief in the importance of trying to demonstrate that our system of law and government is capable of investigating, thoroughly and fairly, any plausible charges of wrongdoing, even at the very highest levels of government . . . I promised that I would pursue the trail, wherever it led, even to the Presidency."

Cox's work as special prosecutor would eventually lead him to subpoena tapes of OVAL OFFICE conversations between the president and his aides. The U.S. Court of Appeals for the District of Columbia sustained the District Court's order to the president, but Nixon refused to comply with it, declined to appeal it, and, additionally, ordered Cox to refrain from demanding the tapes. Instead, Nixon proposed that he would provide summaries, rather than the original tapes, to Cox, a deal that Cox rejected because he knew that if he intended to use evidence from the tapes at a subsequent trial, the court would accept only the original version.

Upon Cox's refusal to accept Nixon's deal, Nixon ordered the firing of Cox on October 20, 1973, setting into motion what has been called the "Saturday Night Massacre." This label refers to the fact that it took three Justice Department officials before Nixon found one who would carry out his directive. In its wake, Attorney General Richardson resigned, rather than carry out the order to fire Cox. Richardson believed that Cox had not committed "extraordinary improprieties," the only condition for which he could be fired, as provided in the JUSTICE DEPARTMENT regulation establishing the office. With Richardson gone, the president turned to the Deputy Attorney General William Ruckelshaus and ordered him to dismiss Cox. Ruckelshaus refused and was about to resign but was fired before he had a chance. Next in line at the Justice Department was the SOLICITOR GENERAL, Robert Bork, who complied with Nixon's order and fired Cox.

Cox will be remembered as a public servant who pursued justice, and who challenged a sitting president to provide evidence that the president knew would be damaging to himself, his aides, and his office.

Further reading: Cox, Archibald. *The Court and the Constitution.* Boston: Houghton Mifflin, 1987; Harriger, Katy J. *The Special Prosecutor in American Politics,* 2d rev. ed. Lawrence: University Press of Kansas, 2000.

—Nancy Kassop

creation of the presidency

The presidency was invented more than 200 years ago as a relatively small, controlled office with limited powers.

Today, the office is larger, more powerful, but still (usually) quite controlled and limited.

At the time of the colonists' break with Great Britain, antimonarchical sentiment was strong. JEFFERSON's *Declaration of Independence* was, in addition to being an eloquent expression of democratic and revolutionary faith, a laundry list of charges leveled against the tyrannical king. And propagandist supreme Tom Paine stigmatized England's King George III as "The Royal Brute of Britain."

Anti-executive feelings were so strong that when the post-revolutionary leadership assembled to form a government, their *Articles of Confederation* contained *no executive!* So weak and ineffective were the Articles that Noah Webster said they were "but a name, and our confederation a cobweb." Over time, however, the absence of an executive proved unworkable, and slowly and quite grudgingly an acceptance of the inevitability of an executive became more commonly accepted.

This would be no strong, independent executive. The new nation was reluctant, but willing, to accept the necessity of an executive, but the fear of tyranny continued to lead them in the direction of a very limited and constrained office.

The ideas on which the framers drew in inventing a presidency are diverse and complex. They took a negative example away from their experiences with the king of England. Their fear of the executive imbedded in the framers a determination *not* to let the new American executive squint toward monarchy.

Several European political theorists opened the framers' imaginations to new possibilities for governing. John Locke's *Second Treatise on Government* (1690) and Montesquieu's *The Spirit of the Laws* (1748) were especially influential.

From their understanding of history the framers drew several lessons. In studying the collapse of Greek (Athenian) democracy, the founders deepened their already profound suspicions of democracy. Thus, they were determined to prevent what some framers referred to as mobocracy. A tyranny of the people was just as frightening as a tyranny of the monarchy. From their examination of the Roman Republic and its collapse from the weight of empire, the founders understood how delicate the balance was between the Senate and the will of the emperor. An emperor armed as tribune of the people, bent on imperial pursuits, led to tyranny just as surely as monarchy and mobocracy.

While less understood, the lessons the framers drew from the Native Americans clearly had an impact on the writing of the Constitution. While the framers looked across the Atlantic and saw hereditary monarchies, they looked down the road and could see a sophisticated, democratic, egalitarian government in action: the Iroquois Confederation. This union of six tribes/nations, organized along lines similar to a separation-of-powers system, was the model for Ben Franklin's 1754 Albany Plan of Union and was much studied by several of the framers.

On July 27, 1787, the drafting committee of the CONSTITUTIONAL CONVENTION met at the Indian Queen Tavern to agree on a draft of the Constitution to submit to the entire convention. The committee's chair, John Rutledge of South Carolina, opened the meeting by reading aloud an English translation of the Iroquois tale of the founding of the Iroquois Confederacy. Rutledge's purpose was to underscore the importance for the new nation of a concept embedded in the tradition of the Iroquois Confederacy: "We" the people, from whence all power derives. While this concept also has European roots, nowhere in the Old World was it being practiced. The neighbors of the Constitution's framers, however, had for decades been living under a Constitution that brought this concept to life, and one which had an impact on the men who met in Philadelphia in that hot summer of 1787.

The experience with colonial governors further added to the framers' storehouse of knowledge. Those states with weak executives, states dominated by the legislature with a defanged governor seemed less well run than states like New York, which had a fairly strong, independent governor. Such examples softened the fears of executive tyranny among the founders. Thus, slowly over time, the anti-executive sentiments began to wane, and there developed a growing recognition that while executive tyranny was still to be feared, an enfeebled executive was also a danger to good government.

Under the Articles, the national government was weak and ineffective. In each state, minor revolts of debtors threatened property and order. The most famous of these was Shays's Rebellion (1787). These mini-revolutions put a fear into the propertied classes. Some longed for the imposed order of a monarchy. "Shall we have a king?" John JAY asked of Washington during the Shays's Rebellion.

As the framers met in Philadelphia, most of those present recognized (some quite reluctantly) the need for an independent executive with *some* power. But what? No useful model existed anywhere in the known world. They would have to invent one.

The American Revolution against Great Britain was in large part a revolution against authority. Historian Bernard Bailyn said the rebellion against Britain made resistance to authority "a doctrine according to godliness." The colonists were for the most part defiant, independent, egalitarian, and individualistic. The symbols and rallying cries were antiauthority in nature, and once it became necessary to establish a new government, it was difficult to reestablish the respect for authority so necessary for an effective government.

Reconstructing authority, especially executive authority, was a slow, painful process. By 1787, when the framers

met in Philadelphia "for the sole and express purpose of revising the Articles of Confederation . . . [in order to] render the federal constitution adequate to the exigencies of government and the preservation of the Union," there was general agreement that a limited executive was necessary to promote good government. But what kind of executive? One person or several? How should he be selected? For how long a term? With what powers?

No decision at the convention was more difficult to reach than the scope and nature of the executive. They went through proposals, counterproposals, decisions, reconsiderations, postponements, reversals, until finally a presidency was invented.

The confusion reflected what political scientist Harvey C. Mansfield, Jr., referred to as the framers' "ambivalence of executive power." There were widespread and divergent views on the creation of an executive office. Initially, most delegates were considered "congressionalists," hoping to create a government with a strong Congress and a plural executive with very limited power. Delegate George Mason proposed a three-person executive, one chosen from each region of the nation. Delegate Roger Sherman described this plural executive as "no more than an institution for carrying the will of the legislature into effect."

There were also advocates for a strong, unitary executive. Alexander HAMILTON initially wanted to institute a version of the British system of government on American soil, along with a monarch. However, there was little support for such a proposal, and Hamilton quickly backed away.

James MADISON, often referred to as the father of the U.S. Constitution, had surprisingly little impact on the invention of the presidency, even going so far as to write in a letter to George WASHINGTON shortly before the convention, "I have scarcely ventured as yet to form my own opinion either of the manner in which [the executive] ought to be constituted or of the authorities with which it ought to be clothed."

Probably the most influential framer on the invention of the presidency was James Wilson of Pennsylvania. At first, Wilson sought the direct popular election of the president, but eventually he lost that battle and instead helped develop what became the ELECTORAL COLLEGE. He also greatly influenced the choice of a single over a plural executive.

In the end, the framers wanted to strike a balance in EXECUTIVE POWER. Making the presidency too strong would jeopardized liberty; making the office too weak would jeopardize good government—but just how to achieve balance remained a thorny issue.

Unlike the Congress and the Judiciary, for which there was ample precedent to guide the framers, the presidency was truly new, invented in Philadelphia, different from any executive office that preceded it. The president would not be a king, he would not be sovereign. He would swear to protect and defend a higher authority: the Constitution.

The framers faced several key questions. First, how many? Should it be a single (unitary) or plural executive? Initial sympathy for a plural executive eventually gave way to a single executive, primarily because that was the best way to assign responsibility (and blame) for the execution of policy. The second question was how to choose the executive. Some proposed popular election, which was rejected because the framers feared the president might become tribune of the people. Others promoted selection by the Congress, but this was rejected on grounds that it might make the president the servant of Congress, and it would undermine the separation of powers. Finally, the framers invented an Electoral College as the best of several unappealing alternatives.

Next, how long? Should the president serve for life? A fixed term? Two years, four years, six years? If for a fixed term, should he be eligible for reelection? After much hemming and hawing they decided on a four-year term with reeligibility as an option, but the president could be removed—impeached—for certain not very clearly delineated offenses.

The toughest question related to how much power the president should be given. In a way, the framers deftly avoided this issue. Since they could not reach a clear consensus on the president's power, they decided to create a bare skeleton of authority. They left many areas vague and ambiguous; they left gaping silences throughout Article II. How could the framers—so afraid of the mob and the monarchy—leave so important an issue so poorly answered? The answer is: George Washington.

Any examination of the invention of the presidency that did not take George Washington into account would be remiss. Each day, as debate after debate took place, the men of Philadelphia could look at the man presiding over the convention, secure in the knowledge that whatever else became of the presidency, George Washington would be its first officeholder. So confident were the framers (and the public as well) of Washington's skills, integrity, and republican sentiments, they felt comfortable leaving the presidency unfinished and incomplete. They would leave it to Washington to fill in the gaps and set the proper precedents.

After the convention, delegate Pierce Butler acknowledged Washington's influence in this excerpt from a letter to Weedon Butler:

> I am free to acknowledge that his powers (the President's) are full great, and greater than I was disposed to make them. Nor, *entre nous*, do I believe they would have been so great had not many of the members cast their eyes towards George Washington as President; and shaped their ideas of the powers to be given to a President by their opinions of his virtue.

Of course, Washington would not always be the president. Thus, while the framers trusted Washington, could they trust all of his successors? Leaving the presidency unfinished opened the door for future problems in the executive. Ben Franklin pointed to this when he noted "The first man, put at the helm, will be a good one. Nobody knows what sort may come afterwards."

Washington, then, is the chief reason why the presidency is so elastic. The office was left half finished with the expectation that Washington would fill in the gaps. In many ways he did, but this also left openings that future presidents were able to exploit on the road to an expanding conception of executive power.

The presidency that emerged from the Philadelphia convention was an office with "very little plainly given, very little clearly withheld . . . the Convention . . . did not define: it deferred." This meant that the presidency would be shaped, defined, and created by those people who occupied the office and the times and demands of different eras. The framers thus invented a very "personal presidency," and much of the history of presidential power stems from the way presidents have understood and attempted to use the office to attain their goals. As Alan Wolfe has written: "The American presidency has been a product of practice, not theory. Concrete struggles between economic and political forces have been responsible for shaping it, not maxims from Montesquieu." The unsettled nature of the presidency was a marked characteristic of this peculiar office and, to some, the genius of the framers. The Constitution that emerged from the Philadelphia convention was less an act of clear design and intent and more a "mosaic of everyone's second choices." The presidency, left unfinished and only partially formed, had yet to be truly invented.

Further reading: Thach, Charles C. *The Creation of the Presidency.* Baltimore: Johns Hopkins University Press, 1922; Cronin, Thomas E., ed. *Inventing the American Presidency.* Lawrence: University Press of Kansas, 1989.

Crédit Mobilier scandal

When the REPUBLICAN PARTY came to power in the 1860s, the federal government took steps to promote the nation's economic development. The railroads became prime beneficiaries of government support. To some unscrupulous railroad operators, however, the lure of legal profits and subsidies was not enough. In the most notorious case of political corruption in the second half of the 1800s, Thomas Durant, chief operating officer of the Union Pacific railroad company, purchased a holding company in 1864, gave it an impressive sounding name, Crédit Mobilier, and assigned to it the job of constructing the Union Pacific (UP) line westward out of Omaha. Durant thereupon systematically overcharged the railroad for the benefit of the holding company, which was paid in cash and UP stock. The scheme made money because the federal government approved the bills of the railroad corporation, and Durant was in league with members of Congress not averse to being bribed. Eventually, Crédit Mobilier owned all of the Union Pacific, and the government and UP shareholders lost out.

When details of this corruption came to light within Congress, the company sought to influence congressional investigators by selling deeply discounted shares of Crédit Mobilier stock to leading members of Congress. Oakes Ames, a Republican representative from Massachusetts, served as the company's agent in making payoffs to other members of Congress. Among those later exposed as having accepted stock under these circumstances were House Speaker (and later Vice President) Schuyler COLFAX and Representative (and later President) James GARFIELD. Vice President Colfax was dropped from the Republican ticket in 1872 as a consequence of his part in the scheme.

Ulysses S. Grant, president at the time, was not personally implicated, but Crédit Mobilier was only one of many scandals surrounding his administration.

Further reading: Schultz, Jeffrey D. *Presidential Scandals.* Washington, D.C.: CQ Press, 2000.

—Thomas Langston

crisis management

A crisis is a situation that occurs suddenly, heightens tensions, carries a high level of threat to a vital interest, provides only limited time for making decisions, and possesses an atmosphere of uncertainty. Crisis management involves both precrisis planning and the handling of the situation during a crisis. The Constitution makes no mention of crises or EMERGENCY POWERS, but during a crisis, the president assumes (and is ceded) added power to confront the crisis situation. Thus, the normal system of CHECKS AND BALANCES recedes, and a form of quasi-presidential government emerges.

After the attack on the United States on September 11, 2001, President George W. BUSH grabbed power, and the Congress and public generally supported extra-constitutional actions by Bush. Standards of democratic accountability suffer during a crisis as presidents assume greater unchecked power.

Further reading: Genovese, Michael A. "Presidential Leadership and Crisis Management." *Presidential Studies Quarterly* 16 (1986): 300–309; ———. Presidents and Crisis: Developing a Crisis Management System in the Executive Branch." *International Journal on World Peace* 4

(1987): 81–101; Janis, Irving L. *Crucial Decisions: Leadership in Policy Making and Crisis Management.* New York: Free Press, 1989; Rossiter, Clinton. *Constitutional Dictatorship: Crisis Government in the Modern Democracies.* New York: Harcourt, Brace & World, 1963.

Cronin, Thomas E. (1940–) *scholar*

One of the preeminent presidency scholars of the modern era, Thomas E. Cronin was instrumental in helping establish the Presidency Research Group of the American Political Science Association in the early 1980s. Through his influence as a scholar he helped revive presidency studies, and by his mentoring of young scholars Cronin brought a number of outstanding young academics into the field.

Cronin received his Ph.D. in political science from Stanford University. He served as a White House Fellow in 1966–67. Among his influential books are *The Presidential Advisory System* (1969), *The Presidency Reappraised* (1974), *The State of the Presidency* (1975), *Inventing the Presidency* (1989), and *The Paradoxes of the American Presidency* (1998).

Cronin was awarded the prestigious Charles E. Merriam Award for Outstanding Contributions to the Art of Government by the American Political Science Association. In 1993 he assumed the presidency of Whitman College in Walla Walla, Washington.

Thomas E. Cronin's impact on the study of the presidency cannot be measured merely by a listing of his influential books, articles, and numerous awards. Cronin was able, with the help of others, to reinvigorate the field of presidency studies, build an institution (the Presidency Research Group) to support the study of the presidency, inspire a range of young scholars to devote themselves to the study of the presidency, and serve as a role model of the gentleman and scholar.

Cuban missile crisis

The Cuban missile crisis of 1962 was significant for U.S. foreign policy and the Kennedy administration for a number of reasons. It was President KENNEDY's most serious foreign policy encounter, and its successful conclusion proved to be a turning point in his presidency after such events as the creation of the Berlin Wall and the failed invasion of the BAY OF PIGS. The crisis also brought the two superpowers of the U.S. and the USSR the closest to war in the nuclear era that they had ever been and eventually led to the signing of the Limited Test Ban Treaty between the two nations in 1963.

President Kennedy had met with Premier Nikita Khrushchev in Vienna in June of 1961. The Soviet leader had presented an ultimatum on Berlin with Kennedy's

Picture from a spy satellite showing a missile launch site in Cuba *(John F. Kennedy Library)*

reaction being that prospects for war were "very real." Khrushchev left the meeting unimpressed with the young leader and proceeded to assist the East Germans in the building of the Berlin Wall a few months later. Kennedy believed that any confrontation with the Soviet Union would occur over Berlin and not Cuba.

While President Kennedy did not want to take a hard line on Berlin with the Soviet Union, since he felt that "a wall is a hell of a lot better than a war," he approved an increase in the military budget of $3.5 billion. Also he authorized a program named Operation Mongoose to destabilize Castro and placed the program under the direction of Attorney General Robert Kennedy.

Relations between the United States and the Soviet Union continued to grow more tense through 1961 and into 1962. By the middle of 1962 intelligence reports indicated that the Russians were transporting medium and intermediate range ballistic missiles, mobile tactical nuclear weapons, and surface to air missile batteries to Cuba. In early September, Robert Kennedy met with Soviet ambassador Anatoly Dobrynin who presented Khrushchev's guarantee that no suface-to-surface missiles or offensive weapons had been placed in Cuba.

On October 14th a U-2 reconnaissance plane gathered photographic evidence of medium-range ballistic missile sites near San Cristobal and one near San Diego de los Banos. Other sources indicated that the missile sites would be operational in two weeks. At this point the president and his closest advisers formed an executive committee (ExComm) of the NATIONAL SECURITY COUNCIL to begin

President John F. Kennedy meeting with his ExComm group during the Cuban missile crisis, October 29, 1962
(John F. Kennedy Library)

to weigh the alternatives. A number of approaches were considered, ranging from a protest note to Khrushchev to a direct nuclear retaliation against the Soviet Union with the middle-range choices being the most popular. These choices included a naval blockade of Cuba, a surgical air strike to remove the bases, and an invasion of the island.

Of these alternatives an air strike against missile bases and an invasion of Cuba were ruled out because they might provoke a war with the Soviet Union, especially if Russian personnel were killed. A quarantine of the island through a naval blockade seemed to be the most rational choice since it exhibited U.S. strength without resorting to violence, and it allowed the Soviet Union to back away from any direct confrontation by having its ships change course.

On October 22 President Kennedy ended the secretive element of the Cuban situation by appearing on television and informing the American public of his decision to establish a quarantine against Cuba. The president also stated that "any nuclear missile launched from Cuba against any nation in the Western hemisphere" would be regarded "as an attack by the Soviet Union on the U.S. requiring a full retaliatory response on the Soviet Union."

The next day the Organization of American States unanimously came out in support of the quarantine along with NATO members. Russian ships stopped at the quarantine line while Kennedy gave orders delaying the boarding of Soviet ships and placed Russian-speaking U.S. personnel on ships at the quarantine line.

On October 24 UN secretary-general U Thant proposed a two-week cooling off period which Khrushchev accepted; Kennedy rejected it, indicating that no other alternatives but the removal of missiles from Cuba were possible. In the UN the next day Ambassador Adlai Stevenson challenged the Soviet Ambassador Valerian Zorin to admit the existence of the missiles, indicating that he would wait for an answer "until hell freezes over."

By October 26 Soviet ships heading toward Cuba were changing course. That evening Khrushchev sent a telegram to Kennedy stating his willingness to remove the missiles if there was a guarantee of no invasion of Cuba by the United States. The president saw this as an agreeable proposal. The following morning, though, Khrushchev sent another telegram that was more severe in nature, which required the United States to dismantle its missiles in Turkey in order for Russia to remove missiles from Cuba. Kennedy and his advisers decided to ignore the second telegram and accepted the first proposal. The president was concerned that by accepting the second Soviet proposal, the Russians could whittle away at U.S. missile sites in future confrontations. Kennedy thus presented Khrushchev with the ultimatum of removing the missiles or weighing the possibility of other measures being taken. Khrushchev accepted the first proposal. At the same time, though, Robert Kennedy reached a private agreement with Anatoly Dobrynin to remove U.S. missiles in Turkey for the missiles in Cuba. The missiles in Turkey were removed by April of 1963.

Thus, the Cuban missile crisis gave every indication of a U.S. victory. The United States acted in a forceful yet diplomatic manner in getting the Soviet Union to remove its missiles from Cuba. The event is important, though, for the fact that President Kennedy showed himself to be an effective foreign policy leader in his design of a decision-making unit (ExComm), which involved people with different points of view. The actions of the Kennedy administration in this situation also made it possible to negotiate a partial test-ban treaty with the Soviet Union in 1963 and to install a "hot line" between the White House and the Kremlin to reduce the chances of future occurrences such as the one in Cuba. On the other hand, the actions taken by the United States in this event gave it a feeling of invulnerability in foreign policy that carried over into U.S. involvement in Vietnam.

Further reading: Allison, Graham. *Essence of Decision: Explaining the Cuban Missile Crisis.* Boston: Little, Brown, 1971; Blight, James G., and David A. Welch. *On the Brink: Americans and Soviets Reexamine the Cuban Missile Crisis.* New York: Hill and Wang, 1989; Nathan, James. *Anatomy of the Cuban Missile Crisis.* Westport, Conn.: Greenwood Press, 2001; Weldes, Jutta. *Constructing National Interests: The U.S. and the Cuban Missile Crisis.* Minneapolis: University of Minnesota Press, 1999.

—Michael G. Krukones

Curtis, Charles (1860–1936) *U.S. vice president, U.S. senator, U.S. representative*
One of Charles Curtis's grandparents was Native American, and Curtis was born on an Indian reservation in 1860. He served in the House of Representatives and Senate. In 1928 he was chosen as Herbert HOOVER's running mate and served one term as vice president. Hoover kept Curtis at a distance and thus he played no significant role in the administration.

Czolgosz, Leon (1873–1901) *assassin*
Leon Czolgosz was an anarchist, the American-born son of immigrants from Czechoslovakia. He had a history of anti-establishment activity, opposing the economic system and those who were in power. He believed that all rulers were enemies of the working people, and his stated reason for assassinating MCKINLEY was that "he was the enemy of the good people—the good working people."

McKinley was only six months into his second term as president when he went to the Pan-American Exposition in Buffalo, New York. While there, he participated in a reception at the Temple of Music on September 6, 1901. Numerous guards, soldiers, and Secret Service agents were in McKinley's vicinity, but his closest guards were not ideally placed to protect the president as he greeted people in a receiving line, and Czolgosz apparently had little thought for his own life. Czolgosz wrapped his gun in a handkerchief—not an unusual sight on the hot day—and shot twice as he approached the president. One bullet lodged in the president's stomach. Czolgosz was tackled immediately, while McKinley expressed concern for his wife, and commented that the assassin was "some poor misguided fellow." McKinley's health wavered, but eight days later he died of a gangrenous infection.

Czolgosz was tried, convicted, and executed within two months. His background prompted a wider effort to investigate and arrest other anarchists, aided by the fact that some anarchist leaders praised McKinley's assassination as a selfless act.

The most immediate consequence of Czolgosz's act was the elevation to the presidency of Theodore ROOSEVELT, one of the architects of the expanded vision of presidential power evident in the 20th century. McKinley's assassination also led to permanent and full-time SECRET SERVICE protection for the president.

Further reading: Clarke, James W. *American Assassins: The Darker Side Of Politics,* 2d rev. ed. Princeton, N.J.: Princeton University Press, 1990; Leech, Margaret. *In the Days of McKinley.* New York: Harper, 1959.

—David A. Crockett

D

Dallas, George Mifflin (1792–1864) *U.S. vice president*

In 1844 the Democrats met in Baltimore and nominated James K. POLK for president. They then unanimously chose Senator Silas Wright of New York as Polk's vice-presidential running mate. Wright, however, refused the nomination (the first and only time such an event has occurred). The convention then turned to George Dallas, an experienced diplomat, senator, and statesman, who accepted his party's nomination.

Dallas sought the presidential nomination in 1848, but a falling out with Polk over patronage issues caused the party to split, and the nomination went instead to a rival candidate. The city of Dallas, Texas, is named in honor of George Dallas, in appreciation for his support for annexation of Texas. He died in Philadelphia on December 31, 1864.

Dames & Moore v. Regan, 453 U.S. 654 (1981)

This case led to a Supreme Court decision that upheld the president's power pursuant to a sole executive agreement to settle the claims of American nationals. The case involved a number of EXECUTIVE ORDERS and regulations promulgated by Presidents Jimmy CARTER and Ronald REAGAN during and following the IRANIAN HOSTAGE CRISIS. Through these orders and regulations, and pursuant to an executive agreement between the two nations, the president nullified attachments and liens on Iranian assets in the United States and directed that the assets be transferred to Iran. The president also suspended claims by U.S. nationals against Iran in American courts and directed that they be presented to an international claims tribunal. The executive agreement was submitted neither to the Senate nor to Congress as a whole for subsequent approval. While the president's nullification of attachments and liens was carried out in accordance with the International Emergency Economic Powers Act (IEEPA), the president's suspension of claims was performed without express legislative sanction.

Dames & Moore was an American company that was owed money for services rendered by its subsidiary in Iran. Following the actions of the president, the company sued to prevent the execution of the executive agreement and the regulations issued thereunder. The company contended that in concluding the agreement and issuing the regulations, the president's actions exceeded his constitutional and statutory powers. The Court read IEEPA broadly, however, and concluded that the statute did in fact authorize the president's nullification of attachments and liens. With respect to the suspension of claims, on the other hand, the Court acknowledged that no statutory authority had been delegated to the president by either IEEPA or the Hostage Act. The Court reasoned that Congress's acquiescence constituted tacit authorization, and thus the president's actions were legally justified.

Although the Court refused to find that the president possesses plenary authority to settle claims, there can be little doubt that *Dames & Moore* extended presidential power in the area of FOREIGN AFFAIRS. Whereas, in *UNITED STATES V. BELMONT* and *UNITED STATES V. PINK,* the president had concluded EXECUTIVE AGREEMENTS and settled claims pursuant to his power of diplomatic recognition, in *Dames & Moore* the Court upheld the president's power to conclude agreements affecting claims outside of his RECOGNITION POWER. Moreover, the president appeared to remove an entire set of cases from the jurisdiction of the federal courts and possibly to effect a taking of property.

On a broader level, the decision stands as the opposite of (and may represent a retreat from) the Court's earlier rulings in *YOUNGSTOWN SHEET AND TUBE V. SAWYER* and *LITTLE V. BARREME.* In those cases, the Court concluded that Congress's failure to authorize presidential actions effectively constituted a prohibition of such activity. In *Dames & Moore*, on the other hand, the Court concluded that congressional silence constituted an implicit authorization. The tension between these two sets of cases reflects the divided nature of the jurisprudence governing unilateral presidential actions.

Further reading: Symposium. "Dames & Moore v. Regan." *UCLA L. Rev.* 29 (1982): 977; Marks, Lee R., and John C. Grabow. "The President's Foreign Economic Powers after *Dames & Moore v. Regan:* Legislation by Acquiescence." *Cornell L. Rev.* 68 (1982).

—Roy E. Brownell II

dark horse

A dark horse is a person who is considered to be a long shot to gain his party's nomination. This aspirant is not initially included among the front-runners for the party's endorsement. As with such terms as party whip, "dark horse" was evidently borrowed from the British. It was apparently first used in Benjamin Disraeli's 1831 novel *The Young Duke*.

James K. POLK of Tennessee, the DEMOCRATIC PARTY's nominee in 1844, is considered to be the first successful dark horse. He trailed former President Martin VAN BUREN and Lewis CASS of Michigan in early balloting at the convention but prevailed on the ninth ballot. Other dark horses that gained their party's nomination include Franklin PIERCE, Rutherford B. HAYES, Warren G. HARDING, and Wendell Willkie. Adlai Stevenson could also fit this category, although there was sizable support for him within the DEMOCRATIC PARTY before he announced his candidacy as the party convention opened in 1952. Given the length of the presidential nominating campaign and the amount of funds needed, by the 1980s it was unlikely that a dark horse could prevail.

Dark horse is part of the traditional terminology used to refer to presidential aspirants in American politics. One breeding ground for dark horses was the "favorite son." This referred to a prominent political figure, whose state delegation to the national convention would put his (or her) name in nomination. This was usually done to offer public honor to the person and to put the state in the convention spotlight, however briefly, and perhaps to enable that state's delegation to bargain with other aspirants for the nomination. With the changes in Democratic Party rules in the early 1970s, favorite son nominations were no longer permitted. The REPUBLICAN PARTY soon discontinued the practice too.

Further reading: Safire, William. *Safire's New Political Dictionary.* New York: Random House, 1993.

—Thomas P. Wolf

Davis, Jefferson (1808–1889) *secretary of war, U.S. senator, U.S. representative, president of the Confederate States of America*

Though best known as the president of the Confederate states during the CIVIL WAR, it should be pointed out that Davis, while serving as senator from Mississippi, was a leading spokesman for Southern interests but was not, until 1860, an advocate of secession.

Once the secessionist movement became a political reality, Davis resigned from the Senate, and on February 9, 1861, a convention of Southern states met in Montgomery, Alabama, and selected him president of the Confederate States of America. His inauguration took place on February 18, 1861, two weeks before Abraham LINCOLN became president.

Davis, an advocate of a limited executive while a member of the legislature, became a very powerful CHIEF EXECUTIVE as he led the Confederate States through the tough times of the Civil War. In early 1865, with the outcome of the war clear, Davis left Richmond, the Southern capitol, but was soon arrested by Northern troops. Though he was indicted for treason and spent two years in a prison, Davis never stood trial. He was released and lived in Canada and Europe before returning to Mississippi. On December 6, 1889, he died in New Orleans.

Dawes, Charles Gates (1865–1951) *U.S. vice president*

Dawes, the nation's 30th vice president, served in that office from 1925 to 1929 under President Calvin COOLIDGE. Born in Ohio on August 27, 1865, and educated at Marietta College and Cincinnati Law School, Dawes practiced law in Lincoln, Nebraska, and was a successful banker before venturing into national politics as a Republican. Prior to the vice presidency, Dawes was controller of the currency, budget director, ambassador to Great Britain, and director of the Reconstruction Finance Corporation. Dawes is known for the "Dawes Plan" that reconstructed German war reparations.

Although he was given no substantial role as vice president, Dawes amazingly told Coolidge he did not wish to attend CABINET meetings! Charles Dawes's impact on the presidency can be seen in his service as the nation's first budget director, and he established the legitimacy of this fledgling office at a time when the budget process was chaotic and unorganized. His career ended abruptly when in 1932, after serving only four months as director of the Reconstruction Finance Corporation, his integrity was called into question due to an RFC loan that aided his faltering Chicago Bank. He died on April 23, 1951, in Evanston, Illinois.

Further reading: Leach, Paul R. *That Man Dawes.* Chicago: The Reilly & Lee Co., 1930; Timmons, Bascom N. *Portrait of an American: Charles G. Dawes.* New York: H. Holt, 1953.

death of a president

Eight presidents have died in office, four by assassination and four from natural causes. All were succeeded by their vice presidents; all lay in state in the East Room of the White House. All but KENNEDY were returned to their home areas for burial. All were grieved for as the symbol of the nation.

The first two presidents to die in office were the only Whigs elected to the presidency. William Henry HARRISON died of pneumonia on April 4, 1841, one month after he delivered the longest inaugural address in presidential his-

tory, during a driving rain. Zachary TAYLOR, like Harrison an older man nominated for office for his record as a war hero, died at the age of 65 on July 9, 1850, having become ill after a Fourth of July feast.

Abraham LINCOLN was assassinated by John Wilkes BOOTH, a Confederate sympathizer, in a plot to kill leading government officials. Lincoln, the only target of this conspiracy actually killed, died from a gunshot wound on April 14, 1865, the day after being struck by Booth's shot as he attended a play at Ford's Theater not far from the White House. As his body was carried back to Illinois on a 20-day journey, more than a million people walked past his coffin at stops along the way.

James GARFIELD was shot in the back by Charles J. GUITEAU, a man who claimed divine instruction, but who also expressed earthly resentment that he had not been awarded with a diplomatic appointment for having passed

Franklin D. Roosevelt's funeral procession on Pennsylvania Avenue, Washington, D.C., April 24, 1945 *(Library of Congress)*

out campaign literature in Garfield's election. Garfield died on September 19, 1881, after doctors probed unsuccessfully for two months for a bullet lodged near his spine.

William MCKINLEY was shot twice with bullets fired by an anarchist, Leon CZOLGOSZ, from a concealed revolver during a public reception at Buffalo, New York. He died on September 14, 1901, and was succeeded to the presidency by his VICE PRESIDENT, Theodore ROOSEVELT.

Warren G. HARDING died in a San Francisco hotel on August 2, 1923, of medical problems probably linked to his high blood pressure. After his death, Mrs. Harding refused to permit an autopsy, and the nation was soon treated to a series of revelations concerning rampant corruption among Harding's CABINET members and the president's intimate association with several women. A popular book was soon published alleging Mrs. Harding's participation in a plot to poison her husband.

The outpouring of grief following Harding's death is sometimes cited as evidence of an irrational, symbol-laden attachment by the American people to their president, since Harding is remembered as one of the worst of all presidents. But when Harding died, the scandals that reduced his legacy to ashes were not yet known, and his administration had achieved many of its objectives.

Franklin ROOSEVELT died in Warm Springs, Georgia, of a cerebral hemorrhage, on April 12, 1945, shortly after attending the postwar conference of allied leaders at Yalta.

John Kennedy, the most recent president to have died in office, was killed in Dallas, Texas, by Lee Harvey OSWALD, on November 22, 1963, and was buried at Arlington National Cemetery. Ninety-five percent of American adults tuned in or listened to the burial ceremonies on television or radio. Following three days of nonstop funeral coverage, a majority of American adults in surveys reported symptoms of personal grieving. Conspiracy theories abound regarding the death of Kennedy, but there has never been credible evidence to discredit the lone gunman hypothesis endorsed by the WARREN COMMISSION that investigated his assassination.

In several of these instances, a president's death left to successors hugely difficult choices and dilemmas and left the fallen leader with a more positive historical legacy than might otherwise have been the case. Could President Lincoln have engineered a more successful RECONSTRUCTION of the South than his ill-remembered successor, President Andrew JOHNSON? Would Franklin Roosevelt have dealt more successfully than Harry TRUMAN with the domestic problems associated with the return to peace? Would, finally, President Kennedy have found a way to pull back from America's commitment to the defense of South Vietnam? We will, of course, never know, as death left these problems to other men.

Further reading: Manchester, William. *Death of a President, November 20–November 25, 1963.* New York: Harper & Row, 1967; Posner, Gerald. *Case Closed: Lee Harvey Oswald and the Assassination of JFK.* New York: Random House, 1993.

—Thomas Langston

debates, presidential

Debates have become a staple of presidential elections, as much as primaries or PARTY CONVENTIONS. However, this was not always the case. In fact, it was not until 1960 that the first presidential debate occurred. Roughly 77 million people watched the four televised debates between John F. KENNEDY and Richard NIXON. Among academicians, the Kennedy-Nixon debates are the most commonly discussed debates because of their perceived impact on the outcome of the election.

The circumstances surrounding the 1960 election made debates an essential part of the campaign. Kennedy was not as well known as Nixon and believed that the debates would provide an opportunity for him to present his message to the American public. Nixon, a successful debater in college, felt he could not back down from Kennedy's challenge even though he was so advised by many in the REPUBLICAN PARTY. The first debate was widely considered to be disastrous for Nixon. He had just undergone knee surgery, bumped his knee right before the debate, and was in considerable pain. He was a profuse sweater and refused to wear makeup. As a result, he looked pale and had beads of sweat on his brow and upper lip throughout the debate. On the other hand, Kennedy was quite tanned, having just spent time in Florida. Kennedy looked at the camera, while Nixon looked at Kennedy. In the eyes of many viewers, Kennedy looked more "presidential" in the first debate. Among those who *watched* the first debate on television, a majority felt that Kennedy had won. However, the majority of people who *listened* to the debate on the radio believed Nixon was victorious. Unfortunately for Nixon, far more people watched the debate than listened to it. While many believed he fared better in the final three debates, Nixon never was able to recover from his initial performance. For the first time, "telegenicity" became a major factor in a presidential campaign.

Presidential debates took a hiatus for the next three elections, mainly because no candidate wanted to repeat Nixon's mistakes. In 1964 Lyndon JOHNSON was the incumbent and well ahead of Barry GOLDWATER in the polls; he would have benefited little from debating. In 1968 and 1972 Nixon had significant leads over Hubert HUMPHREY and George MCGOVERN and refused to debate. It was not until 1976, when an incumbent president was electorally vulnerable, that candidates participated in another presidential debate. It was also the first time that vice presidential candidates debated.

Since 1976 the public has come to expect presidential debates, and the debates have provided some memorable moments. In 1976 Gerald FORD, widely characterized as clumsy and aloof, did nothing to change that perception when he mistakenly asserted that Eastern Europe was not under Soviet rule. Certainly Ford's pardon of Nixon was a larger factor in his close loss, but the major gaffe in the debate did nothing to help his candidacy. Others have hurt their campaigns by poor debate performances as well. In 1988 Michael DUKAKIS failed to overcome the belief that he was cold and emotionless when he responded to a question regarding the death penalty. Asked whether he would support the death penalty if his wife were raped and murdered, Dukakis responded with an unemotional answer that startled many viewers. In 2000 Al GORE, generally thought to be a more capable debater than George W. BUSH, offended many viewers by constantly sighing and rolling his eyes when Bush spoke.

Vice presidential candidates have occasionally turned in poor debate performances as well. Trying to answer charges that he was too inexperienced to be vice president, Dan QUAYLE compared himself to John Kennedy, which prompted Lloyd Bentsen to reply with his infamous, but rehearsed, line, "Senator, I served with Jack Kennedy. I knew Jack Kennedy. Jack Kennedy was a friend of mine. Senator, you are no Jack Kennedy." This exchange has haunted Quayle throughout his career.

Such memorable moments do not always have a negative effect on a candidate, however. In 1980 Ronald REAGAN asked the famous question, "Are you better off than you were four years ago?" Voters overwhelmingly agreed with Reagan that their lives had not been improved by the CARTER administration. Reagan benefited from his performances during the 1984 debates as well. He eased voters' concerns about his age when he appeared sharp and witty. When asked if a man of his age could face the pressures of being president, he quipped, "I will not make age an issue in this campaign. I am not going to exploit, for political purposes, my opponent's youth and inexperience."

Recently, the format of presidential debates has begun to change. The traditional debate format featured candidates standing behind lecterns facing a panel of questioners. While this format is occasionally still used, others have become common as well. In 1992, for the first time, a "town hall" format was used where an audience of undecided voters asked the candidates questions, while a moderator presided over the debate. This format provided advantageous to Bill CLINTON, who was quite relaxed in the town hall setting. On the other hand, George H. W. BUSH was

clearly uncomfortable and, at one point, was even caught on camera glancing at his watch. In 2000 another format was employed for the first time. A single moderator presided over a debate, sitting with the two candidates around a table.

The debate format is more important than most people realize. As the Kennedy-Nixon debates illustrated, it is not always what the candidate says that is most important in the viewers' minds, but how he looks. Image preparation has become as important as issue preparation. For example, advisers instruct candidates when to look at the camera and when to look at the opponent. The importance of image has led to some humorous controversies. In 1988 Michael Dukakis stood on a riser behind his lectern to make him appear taller and more "presidential." In 2000 the Bush and Gore camps sparred over the amount of swivel the candidates' chairs would have.

While image is important, candidates do spend a great deal of time preparing for the debates. Candidates normally hold mock debates where an adviser plays the opponent. Staff members pepper the candidate with almost every question and situation imaginable. They also plan specific strategies, deciding when to attack or ignore an opponent, when to answer a question head-on and when to talk around the answer. Candidates are also given lines that must be constantly repeated. For example, in 2000 George W. BUSH frequently referred to Democrat Al GORE's criticisms of Bush's plan for the federal surplus as "fuzzy math."

With the concern over image and preparation, candidates believe that their performances in the debates will have a significant impact on the outcome of the election. Debates are usually evaluated in a winner/loser scenario. Immediately after the debate, advisers give the media their biased impressions of the debate and explain why their candidate won. News organizations conduct instant polls to determine whom the television audience felt performed better. Usually, however, the effects of the debates are minimal. Some studies have indicated that viewers do learn new information about the candidates' positions on issues. Clearly, some factors, such as Ford's statement that Eastern Europe was not under Soviet domination, have affected the public's perception of candidates. While the debates may influence weaker partisans and independents, they mostly solidify partisan support. Nevertheless, debates remain an essential feature of presidential campaigns.

Further reading: Commission on Presidential Debates. *http://www.debates.org; Debating Our Destiny.* MacNeil/Lehrer Productions, 2000; Wayne, Stephen J. *The Road to the White House 2000.* Boston, Mass.: Bedford/St. Martin's, 2000.

—Matt Streb

Debs, Eugene V. (1855–1926) *socialist leader, labor activist*

Eugene Debs, born in Terre Haute, Indiana, in 1855, was remembered for his leadership in the labor movement, as well as his tireless work for the Socialist Party in the United States. Beginning his working career in the railroad yards in Terre Haute, he established the American Railway Union, the largest union in the United States at the time, becoming its president in 1893. This union survived until 1894, when it became entangled in the well-known Chicago Pullman Palace Car Company strike. As a result of Debs's participation and leadership in this strike, he was imprisoned for six months in 1895 in the Woodstock, Illinois, prison.

An important result of his imprisonment was his initial exposure to socialism and his conversion three years later that led to his initial support of the newly formed Social Democratic Party (SDP). This party subsequently became the Socialist Party of America in 1901 after the SDP merged with a wing of the Socialist Labor Party.

Eugene Debs remained an activist in the socialist movement during his entire life. While he was not a socialist theoretician, he was more a political evangelist who represented the Socialist Party as a presidential candidate five different times during the years of 1900, 1904, 1908, 1912, and 1920. In 1900 he only polled 96,000 votes, but by 1904 he had raised his total popular votes to 400,000. While 1908 showed that Debs had only raised his total vote 20,000 votes above his 1904 total, it may have been his most colorful campaign, since the Socialist Party that year chartered a train labeling it "The Red Special," carrying Debs on a 15,000-mile whistle-stop tour around the United States. In 1912—the same election that had WILSON beating TAFT and Theodore ROOSEVELT—Debs received 901,255 votes, or 6 percent of the popular vote cast. In 1920, his last election, he secured even more popular votes—919,801—but it was only 3.5 percent of the total popular votes cast. This election was his most unusual, since at the time he was an inmate of the Atlanta penitentiary, having been found guilty of violating the 1918 Espionage Act for speaking out against our involvement in WORLD WAR I and attempting to obstruct recruitment. For this he was sentenced to 10 years in prison. His campaign slogan that year was "From the Jail house to the White House." He did not have to serve the full 10 years, however, since President Warren G. HARDING, who had defeated him in the election, commuted his sentence in 1921. Harding did what Woodrow Wilson had refused to do, given that Wilson considered Debs a traitor to the country. Debs's commutation, however, was not without difficulties since he did lose his citizenship, and it was not returned to him until 1976—posthumously. He died in 1926 in Lindlahr Sanitarium, Elmhurst, Illinois.

Further reading: Currie, Harold W. *Eugene V. Debs.* Boston: Twayne Publishers, 1976; Morgan, Howard Wayne. *Eugene V. Debs.* Syracuse, N.Y.: Syracuse University Press, 1962; Salvatore, Nick. *Eugene V. Debs: Citizen and Socialist.* Urbana: University of Illinois Press, 1982.

—Byron W. Daynes

Defense Department

Created in 1941, the mission of the Department of Defense (DOD) is to promote national security by being prepared for war. The DOD is comprised of the military branches: army, navy, air force, and marines. The secretary heads the department and advises the president on military and national security matters.

defense policy

Defense policy refers to decisions and actions that seek to protect U.S. interests. While homeland defense, or the protection of U.S. territory and borders, represents the most basic meaning of defense policy, the term also encompasses international actions that serve to further U.S. security. American defense policy has evolved gradually in the past two hundred years, often proportionally to the expansion of the U.S. role in the world that originated in the late 19th century. During the COLD WAR, the United States institutionalized the development of defense policy by creating a formal executive BUREAUCRACY to assist the president in making defense decisions. In the aftermath of the terrorist attacks of September 11, 2001, the United States is reviewing its defense policy infrastructure and adapting it to the needs of the 21st century.

In the century after its inception, U.S. defense policy concentrated primarily on establishing international legitimacy of the new nation and protecting its borders, which expanded steadily throughout the contiguous United States. In 1803 Thomas JEFFERSON nearly doubled the territory of the United States through the LOUISIANA PURCHASE, which ensured control of the Mississippi River and its trade routes. The WAR OF 1812 narrowly but definitively established the independence of the new nation from Great Britain. The MONROE DOCTRINE of 1823 expanded U.S. defense policy from the country to the hemisphere with its famous declaration that "We should consider any attempt on [the Europeans'] part to extend their system to any portion of this hemisphere as dangerous to our peace and safety." President James K. POLK expanded U.S. borders westward in the MEXICAN WAR of 1846–48 through the annexation of the territory that would become California and New Mexico. Texas and Oregon also became part of the United States in the 1840s. The expansion of the

United States through the continent in this period would come to be known as MANIFEST DESTINY.

By the end of the 19th century, the growing economy in the United States spurred a greater interest in international affairs, in part to find new markets for trade but also for political reasons. As Frederick Jackson Turner wrote, "at the end of a hundred years of life under the Constitution, the frontier has gone, and with its going has closed the first period of American history." Manifest Destiny now would extend beyond the Western Hemisphere, making the United States a world power and increasing its defense commitments. In the SPANISH-AMERICAN WAR the United States gained control of Cuba and Puerto Rico in the Caribbean and also Guam and the Philippines in the Pacific. Yet the United States remained ambivalent over its responsibilities for collective defense vis-à-vis its allies. It did not enter WORLD WAR I until 1917, three years after the global conflict began, and then only because German submarine warfare refused to recognize the rights of neutral countries such as the United States. Although American defense interests had grown, defense was still defined largely in national terms.

The first U.S. effort to incorporate collective security into defense policy failed miserably. After World War I, President Woodrow WILSON launched a grassroots campaign to build support for the TREATY OF VERSAILLES, but the treaty failed to garner a two-thirds vote in the Senate, falling short by seven votes. Consequently, the United States did not participate in the LEAGUE OF NATIONS. For the next decade, U.S. defense policy focused primarily on protecting economic opportunities and limiting military spending. The United States hosted an international conference on naval disarmament in 1921–22, which limited the naval power of the United States, Great Britain, Japan, France, and Italy. As Hitler rose to power in Germany in the 1930s, the United States passed neutrality laws four times to ensure that it would not participate in the burgeoning conflict. After WORLD WAR II began, the United States provided some aid to its allies through "cash and carry" and Lend-Lease programs, but its defense policy remained narrowly focused. Only after Japan attacked Pearl Harbor on December 7, 1941, did fighting World War II become part of American defense policy.

The Allied victory renewed questions about American global responsibilities in defense policy. While defense spending dropped sharply following World War II, U.S. security interests had expanded considerably with the origins of the cold war. The TRUMAN DOCTRINE and MARSHALL PLAN illustrated the U.S. commitment to defending itself and its allies from the encroachment of communism. To assist the president in making defense policy, Congress passed the NATIONAL SECURITY ACT of 1947, which created the NATIONAL SECURITY COUNCIL, the Department of Defense (previously the Department of War), and the CENTRAL INTELLIGENCE AGENCY and formally authorized the positions of the JOINT CHIEFS OF STAFF. The United States institutionalized the development of defense policy to ensure that its wide-ranging interests in the cold war would be pursued fully and systematically.

U.S. defense policy during the COLD WAR can be defined broadly as CONTAINMENT of communism, though important variations emerged in different administrations. John Lewis Gaddis writes that U.S. defense policy in the cold war shifted regularly between "symmetrical" strategies, which aimed to meet any challenge posed by the Soviets regardless of cost, and "asymmetrical" strategies, which focused on selective interests and sought to control costs. The Truman Administration's initial containment policy focused primarily on political and economic interests, although it did emphasize collective security with the creation of the North Atlantic Treaty Organization (NATO). After the KOREAN WAR began, TRUMAN sharply increased defense spending and U.S. interests in the cold war were more broadly defined. Dwight D. EISENHOWER reined in defense spending with his "New Look" policy, while John F. KENNEDY and Lyndon B. JOHNSON pursued a policy of "Flexible Response" that again expanded U.S. interests and costs.

During the Nixon administration, the United States made significant advances in reducing threats to its defense by renewing ties with both China and the Soviet Union. Jimmy CARTER tried to continue DÉTENTE, but his efforts halted over the Soviet invasion of Afghanistan in 1979. Ronald REAGAN initially viewed the Soviet Union suspiciously, calling it an "evil empire" and increasing defense spending so the United States would be prepared to meet any threat posed by the communist superpower. In particular, Reagan initiated the STRATEGIC DEFENSE INITIATIVE (SDI), popularly known as the "Star Wars" plan, which aimed to create a defense shield to protect the United States from attack. While Reagan steadfastly maintained his dedication to SDI, in his second term he also began to pursue ARMS CONTROL negotiations with Soviet leader Mikhail Gorbachev. The two leaders eventually participated in four summit meetings and signed the Intermediate Nuclear Forces Treaty in 1987. The United States also restructured its defense policy apparatus with the Goldwater-Nichols Act of 1986, which gave more power to the chairman of the JOINT CHIEFS OF STAFF as well as to regional military commanders.

The ending of the cold war prompted a reassessment of U.S. defense policy in the 1990s. The "New World Order," as George H. W. BUSH famously called it, permitted nations to work together in ways not possible during the cold war. When Iraq invaded Kuwait in the summer of 1990, the United States and the Soviet Union stood together in opposing the aggression. Bush successfully negotiated a United Nations resolution supporting the use of force against Iraq, and Congress ultimately passed a joint resolution supporting the use of force just days before the Persian GULF WAR began. Thus, the United States developed both internal and allied coalitions that viewed Saddam Hussein's actions as threats to the international order and their own defense interests.

Defense policy took a secondary role in the CLINTON administration because the public and the president were concerned foremost about the economy. Without immediate threats to U.S. security, U.S. defense policy lacked clear direction. Humanitarian interventions in Somalia and Haiti, and NATO intervention in Bosnia and Kosovo, served interests other than American defense and prompted many debates about U.S. defense needs in the post-cold war era. The Clinton Administration tried to replace the containment strategy of the cold war with a strategy of "democratic enlargement," defined as expanding "the world's free community of market democracies." Although the phrase did not serve to replace "containment," it did illustrate how defense policy in the 1990s focused more on promoting common economic interests with other nations than on traditional security concerns.

When George W. BUSH assumed the presidency in 2001, he made some important changes in defense policy, most notably by announcing that the United States would withdraw from the 1972 ABM Treaty so it could pursue national missile defense freely. Bush also declared that the United States would work to contain proliferation of nuclear weapons and other weapons of mass destruction. At the same time, Bush promised to limit U.S. defense commitments, especially in the area of nation-building. The terrorist attacks of September 11, 2001, recast the focus of defense policy to homeland security, an issue that had not commanded public attention since the cold war. Just as defense policy in the 19th century referred to protection of U.S. borders, so, too, does the term today signify foremost protection of U.S. territory. While global concerns in pursuing the continuing campaign against terrorism remain part of American defense policy, the need for homeland defense is sharply etched into the public conscience and will remain so for the foreseeable future.

As presidents develop American defense policy in the coming years, they will have to balance U.S. interests with the concerns of U.S. allies. In particular, questions about U.S. INTERVENTION, especially preemptive action, will require both domestic and international justification. While the definition of defense policy remains the same as it was in the early days of the republic, the audience that witnesses, and participates in, the practice of American defense is much larger.

Further reading: Ambrose, Stephen E., and Douglas G. Brinkley. *Rise to Globalism: American Foreign Policy Since 1938.* New York: Penguin Books, 1997; Gaddis, John Lewis. *Strategies of Containment: A Critical Appraisal of Postwar American National Security Policy.* New York: Oxford University Press, 1952; LaFeber, Walter. *The American Age: United States Foreign Policy at Home and Abroad,* 2d ed. New York: W. W. Norton, 1994.

—Meena Bose

delegation of legislative power

Article I, Section 1, of the Constitution provides that "All legislative powers herein granted shall be vested in a Congress of the United States, which shall consist of a Senate and House of Representatives." May Congress delegate these powers to the other branches or to private parties? In 1825 Chief Justice John MARSHALL wrote: "The difference between the departments undoubtedly is, that the legislature makes, the executive executes, and the judiciary construes the law; but the maker of the law may commit something to the discretion of the other departments, and the precise boundary of this power is a subject of delicate and difficult inquiry, into which a Court will not enter unnecessarily."

This "delicate and difficult inquiry" continues into the 21st century.

Some delegation is inevitable since Congress can scarcely anticipate each circumstance under which officials have to apply its laws. In drafting air-quality legislation, for instance, lawmakers would have a hard time listing every existing pollutant, and it would be impractical for them to pass an additional statute whenever polluters emitted a new chemical compound. For such specifics, Congress must rely on executive officials who have the requisite flexibility and expertise. Delegation can also serve a political purpose. Enacting vague legislation allows lawmakers to shift responsibility for contentious issues of detail.

Although delegation may be a fact of life, it is a troubling one. The bureaucrats who wield so much delegated power may be dedicated public servants, but they do not answer to the voters. Since their decisions usually get little publicity, narrow interests may "capture" them without drawing attention. And while the Constitution does not explicitly deal with the issue, judges have held that there are limits on delegation, referring to the legal maxim, *delegata non potestas non potest delegari* ("delegated power cannot be delegated"). As John Locke explained in *The Second Treatise on Civil Government:* "The legislative cannot transfer the power of making laws to any other hands; for it being a delegated power from the people, they who have it cannot pass it over to others."

This principle of nondelegation is tricky to carry out. In the realm of foreign policy and national security, the courts have interpreted it loosely to allow great power to the president. In *UNITED STATES V. CURTISS-WRIGHT EXPORT CORP.* (1936), the Supreme Court held that Congress must often give the president discretion "which would not be admissible were domestic affairs alone involved." Congress has tried to restrain this discretion, most notably through the WAR POWERS RESOLUTION, but with limited success.

Even in DOMESTIC POLICY, the Court has only twice overturned laws because of unconstitutional delegation. In *PANAMA REFINING CO. V. RYAN* (1935), the Court invalidated legislation authorizing the president to prohibit the interstate shipment of oil production that exceeded state quotas. In a more famous case, *SCHECHTER POULTRY CORP. V. UNITED STATES* (1935), the Court struck down provisions of the NATIONAL INDUSTRIAL RECOVERY ACT allowing the president to establish "codes of fair competition" for business. In a memorable concurring opinion, Justice Cardozo wrote: "The delegated power of legislation which has found expression in this code is not canalized within banks that keep it from overflowing. It is unconfined and vagrant. . . . This is delegation running riot." In these cases, the Court said that when lawmakers want to delegate power, they must write a law that spells out the underlying policy, sets standards for monitoring how the EXECUTIVE BRANCH carries it out, and specifies the findings of fact that the president must make before acting.

As Theodore Lowi points out in *The End of Liberalism,* the *Schechter* precedent still stands, but courts have largely ignored it. Even in the case of *CLINTON V. CITY OF NEW YORK,* which struck down the statutory line-item veto, the Court did not rely on the nondelegation principle but on the Presentment Clause, which requires Congress to present entire bills to the president for signature or veto but does not provide for selective cancellation of their provisions.

Congress has taken certain steps to keep delegation from running riot. The 1946 ADMINISTRATIVE PROCEDURE ACT lays out elaborate procedures that the executive branch must follow in issuing administrative rules. In 1995 the House of Representatives established the Corrections Calendar, an expedited procedure to correct or repeal laws, rules, and regulations that have proved to be obsolete or ineffectual. Critics argue that these laws do not go far enough and that Congress should consider further reforms.

Further reading: Barber, Sotirios A. *The Constitution and the Delegation of Congressional Power.* Chicago: University of Chicago Press, 1975; Kerwin, Cornelius M. *Rulemaking: How Government Agencies Write Law and Make Policy,* 2d ed. Washington, D.C.: CQ Press, 1999; Schoenbrod, David. *Power Without Responsibility: How Congress Abuses the People through Delegation.* New Haven, Conn.: Yale University Press, 1993.

—John J. Pitney, Jr.

Democratic Leadership Council (DLC)

After losing the White House in 1968, 1972, 1980, and 1984, a group of moderate and conservative Democrats, believing their best chance of recapturing the presidency was to offer moderate, not liberal, candidates, formed the Democratic Leadership Council. Founded in 1985 and spearheaded by Al From, the DLC quickly became a force within the DEMOCRATIC PARTY. With its outreach programs and bimonthly magazine, *The New Democrat,* the DLC promoted a "third way" in politics, as an alternative between the old party's left and the increasingly conservative direction of the Republicans.

Bill CLINTON was a DLC proponent, and he turned "third way" politics into what was called "triangulation," where Clinton positioned himself between the left-leaning Democrats in Congress and the hard-right forces of Newt Gingrich in the REPUBLICAN PARTY. This strategy was popular with the voters and helped Clinton win the presidency in 1988 and 1992. The DLC also had influence abroad as countries like Great Britain embraced "third way" politics (Tony Blair and the Labor Party) with great electoral and policy success.

Democratic Party

For the purposes of political participation, electoral processes, and governing, the Democratic Party is one of the two major parties in the United States. It is the oldest existing political party in the world. During the deliberations of the CONSTITUTIONAL CONVENTION in 1787 in Philadelphia, two major, rival factions of delegates developed and emerged from that meeting. The FEDERALISTS favored a strong national government, clear supremacy of the national government over the states, and a flexible interpretation of the Constitution, especially for executive and judicial powers. By contrast, the ANTI-FEDERALISTS favored a more limited national government, strict interpretation of the Constitution, and the adoption of a Bill of Rights to protect states' rights and individual liberties from the national government. The Anti-Federalists then established the Democratic-Republican Party in 1793 with Thomas JEFFERSON and James MADISON as its most prominent founders.

With the election of Thomas Jefferson to the presidency in 1800, the Democratic-Republicans consistently controlled the presidency and Congress for the next 24 years. With its pro–states' rights, strict constructionistic ideology, the Democratic-Republican Party relentlessly and aggressively opposed national bank and high tariff policies advocated by the Federalists.

Renaming the Democratic-Republican Party the Democratic Party, the Democrats decisively won the presidential and congressional elections of 1828. The Democrats soon adopted the use of national conventions for nominating presidential and vice presidential candidates and drafting national platforms for articulating their party's ideology and policy AGENDA. National conventions enabled President Andrew JACKSON and Martin VAN BUREN, Jackson's second vice president and successor, to circumvent congressional caucuses and develop the Democratic Party as a larger, more diverse, mass-based majority party. They justified their aggressive use of an expanded PATRONAGE or "spoils" systems in distributing federal jobs and contracts by asserting an appropriate connection in a democratization between political participation, that is, party service and loyalty.

Following Martin Van Buren's failure to be reelected in 1840, the growing controversy over slavery increasingly divided and weakened the Democratic Party regionally. The newly established REPUBLICAN PARTY won the presidential election of 1860. It also elected most presidents and usually controlled Congress until 1932. During and shortly after the CIVIL WAR, more strident Republicans often denounced northern Democrats as treasonous "Copperheads" who sympathized with the Confederacy and slavery. With most voters outside of the South identifying with the Republican Party, the Democratic electoral base in national politics was mostly limited to Southern whites and Irish Catholics concentrated in northern cities.

The growing rift between the progressive and conservative wings of the Republican Party enabled Democrat Woodrow WILSON to be elected president in 1912 with approximately 42 percent of the popular votes. During his two-term presidency, Wilson and a Democratic-controlled Congress enacted economic reform legislation and identified the Democratic Party with a moralistic, interventionistic foreign policy with the American role in WORLD WAR I and Wilson's failed effort to make the United States an active, leading member of the LEAGUE OF NATIONS.

The Democrats failed to become the majority party among voters, and the Republicans soon won control of the presidency and Congress. This resumption of Republican dominance was evident in the pro–big business, high-tariff, and isolationist policies of the 1920s and early 1930s. The ability of the Democrats to unite and effectively challenge the Republicans was hampered by the religious, regional, and cultural conflicts between urban, Catholic, northern Democrats and rural, Protestant, southern Democrats, especially over the national prohibition of alcohol.

The widespread economic suffering of the GREAT DEPRESSION and the resulting unpopularity of Republican president Herbert HOOVER enabled Democrat Franklin D. ROOSEVELT to easily defeat Hoover and for the Democrats to gain large majorities of Congress. But it was not until Roosevelt's landslide reelection in 1936 that most voters were registered Democrats for the first time since 1856. Roosevelt identified his presidency and the Democratic Party with his NEW DEAL economic policies, such as public works projects to relieve unemployment, new banking and stock market regulations, and new social welfare benefits, such as retirement pensions. New Deal programs, Roosevelt's party leadership, and the shrewd distribution of patronage jobs enabled the Democrats to broaden and diversify their party's coalition to also include labor unions, AFRICAN AMERICANS, Jews, and Catholics in general. Roosevelt and his party's national image became more identified with liberalism and greater federal intervention to solve both social and economic problems.

Harry TRUMAN protected and sought to further the liberal identity of the Democratic Party through his FAIR DEAL policy proposals, which included civil rights legislation, and the continuation of an interventionistic American foreign policy in World War II and then the COLD WAR. His upset victory and the return of Congress to Democratic control in the 1948 elections reaffirmed the endurance of the Democratic Party as the majority party in voter identification and policy making.

Despite the eight-year Republican presidency of Dwight EISENHOWER, the Democrats controlled Congress during six of those eight years and retained majority status in voter identification. Conservative Southern whites were more openly alienated from the national Democratic Party, not only because of its more liberal positions on civil rights but also because of its closer affiliation with labor unions, Northern cities, and liberal activists.

Like Roosevelt and Truman, Democrat John F. KENNEDY faced bipartisan conservative opposition in Congress to his domestic policy proposals, especially on civil rights, education, antipoverty programs, and Medicare. Following Kennedy's assassination in November 1963, President Lyndon B. JOHNSON gained enough support in Congress and public opinion to secure passage of a major income tax cut and the CIVIL RIGHTS ACT of 1964. Johnson's landslide victory and increase in the number of non-Southern liberal Democrats elected to Congress in 1964 enabled Johnson and his allies in Congress to enact more liberal laws and programs, collectively known as the GREAT SOCIETY.

In 1968 the anti-Johnson, anti–VIETNAM WAR presidential campaigns of Democratic Senators Eugene MCCARTHY and Robert F. KENNEDY, the assassination of the latter candidate, riots outside of the 1968 Democratic National Convention in Chicago, and the minor party presidential candidacy of George WALLACE all contributed to the election of Republican Richard M. NIXON as president in 1968.

Except for Jimmy CARTER's one term (1977–81) Democratic presidency, the Republicans usually won presidential elections from 1968 until 1992. During that period, though, the Democrats always controlled the House of Representatives and usually controlled both houses of Congress. Due to the sharp increase in the number of proportions of voters identifying themselves as independents, the Democratic Party lost its status as the majority party in voter identification after 1968. In federal elections voters increasingly preferred to vote Republican for president and Democratic for Congress, especially for U.S. representatives, until 1994. Seniority, constituency service, gerrymandering of congressional districts, and their aggressive defense of Social Security benefits and other middle-class entitlements during the 1970s and 1980s benefited Democratic congressional incumbents.

In a three-way race in 1992, Democrat Bill CLINTON was elected president with approximately 43 percent of the popular vote. Like Kennedy, Clinton had effective media skills and had proven himself to be an effective fundraiser and campaigner, but controversies of his policy behavior regarding a national health plan proposal, the legal acceptance of homosexuals in the military, and a new gun control law all contributed to the election of Republican majorities to Congress in 1994.

In both his rhetoric and policy compromises with Republicans, especially on the Welfare Reform Act of 1996, Clinton repositioned himself as a moderate reformer. With a more populist, centrist image with the voters and a prosperous economy, Clinton was easily reelected in 1996. Despite Clinton's IMPEACHMENT and later acquittal by a Republican-controlled Congress because of legal issues pertaining to a sex scandal, Clinton continued to receive high job-approval ratings in public opinion polls.

In the 2000 presidential campaign, Al GORE, Clinton's vice president, was the Democratic presidential nominee. He closely associated himself with the prosperity of the Clinton era but distanced himself from Clinton's more controversial, unethical personal image. Gore received almost 600,000 more popular votes than George W. BUSH, the Republican presidential nominee, but Gore did not clearly win a majority of Electoral College votes. The growing political and legal controversy of the popular, and, therefore, electoral, vote results of Florida eventually led to the Supreme Court's decision that Bush receive Florida's Electoral College votes, consequently making Bush president.

Analysts and scholars of the popular vote and public opinion polling results of the 2000 presidential election frequently commented on how Americans were almost evenly divided on such social issues as gun control, abortion, and school prayer and how this division was reflected in the virtually equal political strength in voter appeal of the Democratic and Republican parties.

Further reading: Goldman, Ralph M. *Search for Consensus: The Story of the Democratic Party.* Philadelphia: Temple University Press, 1979; Savage, Sean J. *Roosevelt: The Party Leader, 1932–1945.* Lexington: University Press of Kentucky, 1991.

—Sean J. Savage

deregulation

Deregulation is a term that became popularly known during the 1970s for the process and policies by which various federal controls on the economy are reduced or eliminated. Most federal regulatory commissions and agencies, such as the Interstate Commerce Commission (ICC), Federal Trade Commission (FTC), and Federal Reserve Board, were established during the late 19th century and early 20th century in order to protect the public from abusive, monopolistic practices by big business. By the late 1960s, however, more economists began to criticize the development of "regulatory regimes" in which federal regulatory commissions used their powers to protect entrenched business interests rather than the public good.

A bipartisan consensus in Congress in the early 1970s emerged in support of deregulation in certain agencies and within certain industries, such as interstate airline and trucking transportation, for the purposes of reducing inflation, promoting efficiency, growth, and greater competition within certain heavily regulated businesses, and providing consumers with more choices. Presidents Gerald FORD, Jimmy CARTER, and Ronald REAGAN appointed members to certain regulatory agencies who favored deregulation. Carter, though, also wanted to increase federal regulations in some policy areas, such as civil rights, environmental protection, occupational safety, and consumer product safety. Reagan, by contrast, implemented a more comprehensive, aggressive program of deregulation, partially overseen by the OFFICE OF MANAGEMENT AND BUDGET (OMB), that aroused the opposition of liberal interest groups and most Democrats in Congress.

Nonetheless, the Airline Deregulation Act of 1978, which was signed into law by Carter, gradually reduced the economic regulatory powers of the Civil Aeronautics Board (CAB) until it entirely eliminated the CAB on January 1, 1985. This action made the CAB the first major federal regulatory commission created during peacetime to be abolished. The legislative success of this 1978 law motivated Congress to pass and Carter to sign similar legislation, the Motor Carrier Act of 1980. This law reduced the powers of the ICC over interstate truck transportation, especially freight rates. The deregulation of long distance telephone rates and services, however, was primarily achieved through federal court decisions and administrative rulings by the Federal Communications Commission (FCC).

Through an administrative strategy, Republican presidents have sought to weaken or eliminate economic regulations through their influence on their appointees in the EXECUTIVE BRANCH, EXECUTIVE ORDERS, and administrative rulings.

Like Jimmy Carter, another Democratic president, Bill CLINTON wanted to encourage certain specific economic deregulation for the promotion of low-inflation economic growth and more consumer choices. Also like Carter, though, Clinton wanted to strengthen existing rules or increase the number of new regulations in such noneconomic policy areas as civil rights, environmental protection, and occupational safety. Confronting a Republican-controlled Congress during most of his presidency, Clinton employed an administrative strategy in order to strengthen or at least defend existing regulations in the above noneconomic policy areas. The most significant event of deregulation during his presidency was Clinton's elimination of the ICC, the nation's first regulatory commission, in 1996.

Further reading: Nathan, Richard P. *The Administrative Presidency.* New York: Wiley, 1983; Quirk, Paul, and Martha Derthick. *The Politics of Deregulation.* Washington, D.C.: Brookings Institution, 1985.

—Sean J. Savage

détente

A French word that means calm or relaxation, détente in English typically suggests an easing of tensions between two opposing parties. During the COLD WAR, détente referred to the Nixon administration's policy toward the Soviet Union, which included the negotiation of two pathbreaking ARMS CONTROL treaties. Détente continued into the early Carter Administration years but ended abruptly with the Soviet invasion of Afghanistan in December 1979 and then resumed in the second half of the REAGAN Administration. Although détente still has cold war connotations, it also can be used to identify more recent examples of cooperation between nations.

Richard NIXON entered office in 1969 determined to halt U.S. involvement in VIETNAM, a goal that he pursued through fostering ties with the Soviet Union and China. NATIONAL SECURITY ADVISER Henry KISSINGER developed a strategy known as "linkage," which held that improved relations with the two largest Communist nations would serve to put pressure on North Vietnam. Together, Nixon and Kissinger worked to achieve linkage by negotiating the first arms-control treaties with the Soviet Union, thus promoting détente. (During the KENNEDY administration, the United States had signed a treaty banning nuclear testing in the atmosphere, but the Nixon administration's treaties would be the first to place limits on numbers of nuclear weapons.)

Nixon's strategy of détente aimed to protect U.S. interests in the cold war by maintaining a balance of power between the United States and the Soviet Union. Recognizing that the United States did not have unlimited resources, Nixon decided that negotiations in areas of common interest with opponents would best serve U.S. goals. While the United States had enjoyed strategic superiority over the Soviet Union in the 1950s and early 1960s, the Soviets subsequently launched a crash missile-development program that sought to halt U.S. dominance in the field. Nixon wanted to maintain U.S. superiority, but he declared that his administration would focus foremost on sufficiency, or the procurement of enough weapons to protect U.S. interests.

Sufficiency required that the United States work with the Soviet Union to impose limits on the arms race. In 1972 the two superpowers signed two landmark arms-control treaties: the Anti-Ballistic Missile (ABM) Treaty, which limited each side's missile defense sites and missile launchers; and the STRATEGIC ARMS LIMITATION TALKS (SALT), which limited numbers of offensive weapons. The treaties were primarily of symbolic value, as they did not restrict the number of warheads each side could have, but they nevertheless marked an important advancement in U.S.-Soviet relations. They also recognized the concept of Mutually Assured Destruction (MAD), which held that some vulnerability on each side would deter nuclear attack.

Nixon also pursued détente with China in 1972, visiting Peking and signing the Shanghai Communiqué, which moved toward normalizing relations between the two countries. The Communiqué marked a sharp departure from U.S. policy since 1949, when the "loss" of China to Mao Tse-tung's Communist Party prompted the United States to recognize only the Nationalist government of Chiang Kai-shek in Taiwan. At the time, Nixon sharply criticized the TRUMAN administration for not doing more to support the Nationalist forces. As president, however, he determined that pursuing relations with both China and the Soviet Union would prevent them from forming an alliance against the United States. Although détente did not achieve "linkage" with respect to halting Chinese and Soviet aid to North Vietnam, it did serve to recognize common strategic and economic interests between the United States and the two communist nations.

Like Nixon, CARTER wanted to pursue détente with the Soviet Union and China, but his achievements fell short of his ambitions. Carter entered office determined to negotiate a second arms-control treaty with the Soviet Union, but he and Soviet leader Leonid Brezhnev did not sign SALT II until June 1979. Six months later, the Soviet Union invaded Afghanistan, and in response to this aggression, Carter halted grain and high-technology sales to Russia, boycotted the 1980 Olympics in Moscow, and withdrew SALT II from Senate consideration. The United States did extend full recognition to China in 1979, but this accomplishment was soon overshadowed by the widening rift with the Soviet Union, as well as by the American hostages in Iran.

When REAGAN became president, then, détente had virtually disappeared. Reagan campaigned on a platform of increased defense spending that would restore American prestige and point out the weaknesses of the Soviet system. In 1983 Reagan famously referred to the Soviet Union as an "evil empire," and although he used the phrase only

Premier Mikhail Gorbachev and President Ronald W. Reagan sign the Intermediate Nuclear Forces Treaty. *(Collection of the District of Columbia Public Library)*

once in a speech, it came to symbolize U.S. views about the Soviet Union. Reagan's staunch anticommunist beliefs were matched only by his fervent dislike of nuclear weapons, and his desire to free the world from the risk of nuclear attack resulted in four meetings with Soviet leader Mikhail Gorbachev from 1985 to 1988. Thus, détente returned in the second Reagan administration with the signing of the Intermediate Nuclear Forces Treaty in 1987, and the first trip by a U.S. president to Moscow since the Nixon administration.

Now that the cold war is over, détente seems to refer, much like Reagan said of the phrase "evil empire" during the Moscow summit in 1988, to "another time, another era." When the United States announced in 2001 that it would withdraw from the ABM Treaty, critics feared the consequences of permitting antiballistic missile defense development, but the end of détente was not discussed. Détente can be used today to identify the easing of tensions between nations, such as cooperation between India and Pakistan, or Israeli-Palestinian negotiations. By definition, however, it will always be associated with the improvement in U.S.-Soviet relations that began in the Nixon administration.

Further reading: Ambrose, Stephen E., and Douglas G. Brinkley. *Rise to Globalism: American Foreign Policy since 1938.* New York: Penguin Books, 1997; Gaddis, John Lewis.

Strategies of Containment: A Critical Appraisal of Postwar American National Security Policy. New York: Oxford University Press, 1982; Kissinger, Henry. *Diplomacy.* New York: Simon & Schuster, 1994; Oberforfer, Don. *From the Cold War to a New Era: The United States and the Soviet Union, 1983–1991,* updated ed. Baltimore: Johns Hopkins University Press, 1998.

—Meena Bose

diplomacy

Diplomacy refers to discussions between states on political matters. It encompasses routine interactions between foreign service professionals, formal meetings between heads of state, and specific negotiations about issues over which states have different interests. On a daily basis, diplomacy serves to maintain smooth working relationships between states. When states disagree, diplomacy becomes especially important because it seeks to prevent disputes from escalating into military conflict. States turn first to diplomacy to mediate competing interests, making it one of the most significant instruments of policy, as it aims to resolve disputes peacefully and at low cost.

The history of diplomacy dates back to ancient times, but its usage today refers most often to relations in the balance-of-power international system created by the

Peace of Westphalia in 1648. The rise of the modern state made diplomacy an essential component of pursuing national interests by means other than war. According to Henry KISSINGER, the balance-of-power concept held that "each state, in pursuing its own selfish interests, would somehow contribute to the safety and progress of all the others." By pursuing their national interests diplomatically, states developed a secular political system, one that was grounded in the independent right of states to exist, rather than in a broader moral or religious justification. Kissinger describes this concept as *raison d'état*, which held that "the well-being of the state justified whatever means were employed to further it; the national interest supplanted the medieval notion of a universal morality." After the Peace of Westphalia, he writes, "the doctrine of *raison d'état* grew into the guiding principle of European diplomacy."

In the United States *raison d'état* has never served as sufficient justification for international diplomacy. From its inception, the United States has maintained an uneasy relationship with the idea that its foreign policy decisions are based upon political rather than ideological considerations, and in its early years, it sought to limit international engagements as much as possible. While George WASHINGTON made important diplomatic decisions, most notably the NEUTRALITY PROCLAMATION of 1793, which declared that the United States would not take sides in the Anglo-French war, he left office advising the people to steer clear of "permanent" alliances. As he wrote in his FAREWELL ADDRESS, the United States should avoid becoming involved in European politics, as "our detached and distant situation invites and enables us to pursue a different course."

Washington's address reflected the president's constitutional authority to define the limits of U.S. diplomacy. The Constitution left diplomacy largely to the EXECUTIVE BRANCH, making the president responsible for receiving ambassadors from other states, nominating ambassadors and top foreign policy officials, and drafting treaties. The Senate approved appointments by majority vote and ratified treaties by two-thirds vote, but the president was expected to serve as "chief diplomat." To assist the president in these areas, the first Congress established a STATE DEPARTMENT and approved Washington's nomination of Thomas JEFFERSON as secretary of state.

Although the United States engaged in both diplomacy and war to expand its territory in the 19th century, for the most part, it heeded Washington's admonition to avoid entanglement in European diplomatic games. As secretary of state, John Quincy ADAMS famously declared on July 4, 1821, that the United States "goes not abroad in search of monsters to destroy. She is the well-wisher to the freedom and independence of all. She is the champion and vindicator only of her own. . . ." While some members of Congress argued that the United States should recognize newly independent Latin American states, Adams was concerned that

doing so would hinder U.S. relations with Spain. Two years later, though, in a message that became known as the MONROE DOCTRINE, President James MONROE declared that the United States "should consider any attempt on [the Europeans'] part to extend their system to any portion of this hemisphere as dangerous to our peace and safety." Thus, the United States remained ambivalent about its diplomatic commitments.

By the end of the 19th century, however, the growing military and economic strength of the United States spurred international leadership. President William MCKINLEY committed the country to a global role with the SPANISH-AMERICAN WAR of 1898, in which the United States acquired control over Cuba, Puerto Rico, Guam, and the Philippines. From this point onward, only the extent of U.S. international leadership would be debated.

Two presidents in the early 20th century defined the spectrum of choices for the United States in international diplomacy: Theodore ROOSEVELT and Woodrow WILSON. Roosevelt emphasized the need for the United States to maintain a global balance of power, which for him meant "muscular diplomacy in the Western Hemisphere." He expanded the essentially defensive posture of the Monroe Doctrine to a policy that promised more aggressive behavior by the United States in the Western Hemisphere. Known as the Roosevelt Corollary, this policy declared that "Chronic wrongdoing, or an impotence which results in the general loosening of the ties of civilized society, may . . . force the United States, however reluctantly, in flagrant cases of such wrongdoing or impotence, to the exercise of an international police power." Although diplomacy was preferred to use of force, Roosevelt's policy served to justify U.S. INTERVENTION over the next 30 years in Mexico, Nicaragua, Cuba, the Dominican Republic, and Haiti.

Like Roosevelt, Woodrow Wilson believed that the United States possessed the power to support an activist foreign policy, but Wilson's vision derived not from balance-of-power politics but from his belief that the United States had a moral responsibility to promote its values abroad. As he declared before WORLD WAR I, "the world must be made safe for democracy." Thus even the war had a diplomatic purpose for the United States, namely, to spread its democratic values around the world. After the war Wilson traveled to Paris to draft a treaty with European leaders that would prevent the outbreak of another war. Although the United States never ratified the TREATY OF VERSAILLES (it garnered a majority vote in the Senate but fell seven votes short of the required two-thirds), Wilson's personal diplomacy and interest in collective security would serve as a model for future administrations.

Throughout the 20th century, U.S. diplomacy shifted between Rooseveltian realism and Wilsonian idealism, often couching Roosevelt's balance-of-power politics in Wilson's principles. After WORLD WAR II the United States led the effort to create the UNITED NATIONS, in marked contrast to U.S. resistance to joining the LEAGUE OF NATIONS 25 years earlier. The COLD WAR, in many respects, represented a triumph of diplomacy and deterrence, as the United States and the Soviet Union never engaged in a direct military conflict. When the two nations came closest to war during the CUBAN MISSILE CRISIS in October 1962, secret negotiations between U.S. President John F. KENNEDY and Soviet Premier Nikita S. Khrushchev ultimately defused the conflict. While both countries did become involved in protracted military engagements during the cold war—the United States in Korea and Vietnam, the Soviet Union in Afghanistan—diplomacy did serve to maintain relations between the two superpowers and eventually to pursue ARMS CONTROL treaties and other agreements that ultimately contributed to the ending of the cold war.

After the fall of the Berlin Wall in November 1989, diplomacy took on even greater importance as the primary means by which the United States would pursue its interests and promote its values in an uncertain, and no longer bipolar, world. Before the GULF WAR in 1991, President George H. W. BUSH personally spoke with heads of state to build a multilateral coalition to oppose Iraq's invasion of Kuwait. President Bill CLINTON brokered peace accords in Ireland and made every effort to produce an Israeli-Palestinian agreement. When diplomacy did not succeed, as with U.S. efforts to contain Slobodan Milosevic in Bosnia and Kosovo, the United States conducted air strikes to bring warring parties to the negotiating table. Critics argued that the United States pursued diplomacy even when no prospects for agreement existed, but again American interests in using power to promote political ends wrestled with American commitments to spreading democratic principles peacefully.

In the aftermath of the SEPTEMBER 11, 2001, ATTACKS on the United States, diplomacy will be one of the means that American foreign policy employs to capture terrorists and prevent future attacks. Diplomacy alone will not serve to protect U.S. interests, as the recent military conflict in Afghanistan demonstrates. Nevertheless, protecting American power and values requires that presidents practice diplomacy painstakingly, and they follow a long, hallowed tradition in doing so.

Further reading: Jentleson, Bruce W. *American Foreign Policy: The Dynamics of Choice in the 21st Century.* New York: W. W. Norton, 2000; Kissinger, Henry. *Diplomacy.* New York: Simon & Schuster, 1994; LaFeber, Walter. *The American Age: U.S. Foreign Policy at Home and Abroad, 1750 to the Present,* 2d ed. New York: W. W. Norton, 1994; Schulzinger, Robert D. *American Diplomacy in the Twentieth Century,* 4th ed. New York: Oxford University Press, 1998.

—Meena Bose

disability

Although both William Henry HARRISON and Zachary TAYLOR died early in their terms of office, their illnesses were so brief that the issue of presidential disability did not arise. The 1881 assassination of James A. GARFIELD first made presidential disability an active issue. In the 10 weeks (July 2–September 19) after he was shot, his CABINET and the nation were confronted with the prospect that his condition would leave the nation without a president indefinitely. The issue arose again in the final months of Woodrow WILSON's presidency. Suffering a major stroke, Wilson was shielded from the public while many speculated that his second wife was actually carrying out the duties of his office.

Robert H. Ferrell suggests that the disability question should have been broached during the presidency of Grover CLEVELAND, who was operated upon for cancer of the mouth in 1893. Only in 1917 did this become public when one of his surgical team revealed Cleveland's illness, considered to be fatal in that era. Ferrell speculates that in addition to the Wilson and Cleveland presidencies, presidential disability may have occurred in those of Warren G. HARDING, Franklin D. ROOSEVELT, Dwight D. EISENHOWER, John F. KENNEDY, Ronald W. REAGAN, and George H. W. BUSH. Chester Alan ARTHUR, a victim of Bright's disease, might be added to the list.

A central issue is the effect that an illness or disability has upon a president's effectiveness in his duties. Although Ferrell establishes that FDR's health was declining long before the Yalta Conference, Robert Gilbert refers to several at that meeting who noted that FDR was astute in his assessments of the issues before the conferees, and that in the weeks before his death he realized that the Soviet Union was not complying with those agreements.

At one extreme is the Wilson case, where the president was incapacitated; at the other was Calvin COOLIDGE, who after the death of his son was so depressed that Gilbert notes his presidential role changed from an assertive one to one in which he deferred matters to his cabinet.

Without providing guidelines to what constitutes a disability, the TWENTY-FIFTH AMENDMENT designates who shall determine that a disability has occurred and when it may be concluded. Ferrell, along with Edward MacMahon and Leonard Curry, notes that the disability issue is compounded by a history of incompetent presidential physicians or ones that have deliberately kept the public from knowing the actual state of a president's health. They suggest that the presidential physician be confirmed by the Senate to encourage more candor about a president's health.

Further reading: Bayh, Birch. *One Heartbeat Away: Presidential Disability and Succession.* Indianapolis, Ind.: Bobbs-Merrill, 1968; Ferrell, Robert H. *Ill-Advised: Presi-*

dential Health and Public Trust. Columbia: University of Missouri Press, 1992; Gilbert, Robert E. *The Mortal Presidency: Illness and Anguish in the White House.* New York: Basic Books, 1992; MacMahon, Edward B., and Leonard Curry. *Medical Cover-Ups in the White House.* Washington, D.C.: Farragut Pub. Co., 1987.

—Thomas P. Wolf

divided government

Presidents cannot govern alone, especially in a separation-of-power system such as the United States. They need help to lubricate the machinery of government. One such lubricant has historically been the political party. When the White House and Congress are both controlled by the same political party, governing becomes a bit easier, as party links help presidents join what the framers of the Constitution separated: the executive and legislative branches.

In recent decades, voters have been less likely to vote straight party tickets and increasingly have split their votes. That is, they may vote for a Democrat for president and a Republican for Congress. Divided government occurs when one party controls one branch and the other party controls the other branch. For example, in 1996, a Democrat, Bill CLINTON, served as president, but the Republicans controlled the House and Senate. While this often makes for conflictual behavior, it should also be noted that often the business of government gets done in spite of the difficulties presented by divided government.

doctrines, presidential

A presidential doctrine establishes a strategy that is the recognized "approach" or policy of the U.S. government. These doctrines relate primarily to foreign policy. The first famous presidential foreign policy doctrine was the MONROE DOCTRINE.

In recent years, almost every president has been associated with a foreign policy doctrine. Each president attempts to stamp his own philosophy onto the strategic policy of the United States. For example, the CARTER DOCTRINE of 1980 was a statement announcing that an attempt by any outside force to gain control of the Persian Gulf would be regarded as a threat to the vital national interest of the United States. The REAGAN Doctrine involved an announcement that the United States would oppose Communism by supporting opposition to Communist regimes around the world. The BUSH Doctrine, articulated after the 9/11 tragedy, called for the United States to engage in preemptive action to eliminate threats to U.S. national security.

These doctrines are not formally binding. They are a statement of purpose and intent, establishing a guidepost for action and setting policy for the government.

dollar diplomacy

During the TAFT presidency, the United States developed a new approach to Central America and the Caribbean. The United States would use its economic leverage to promote political and fiscal reform. President Taft announced that dollars would be used instead of bullets as an instrument of U.S. policy. This soon became known as "dollar diplomacy."

domestic policy

By domestic, we mean that which occurs within the territorial confines of the United States. Domestic policy refers to those government programs designed to affect the internal nature of the United States.

Constitutionally, the Congress has the most authority to deal with domestic policy, as it possesses legislative and funding power. The president, through his STATE OF THE UNION ADDRESS, his legislation agenda, and through lobbying Congress and exercising his veto authority, has a strong influence over the outcome of domestic policy.

Historically Congress was the dominant branch in establishing domestic policy, but ever since the NEW DEAL in the 1930s, the president has been a significant, if not dominant, player in the domestic policy process.

Democrat presidents tend to be more programmatic in domestic affairs, attempting to use the power of the federal government to advance social policies. Republican presidents have generally been more reliant on the private sector in domestic affairs.

domestic policy adviser

Beginning with Herbert HOOVER, most presidents have had some sort of institutional apparatus charged with overseeing the domestic policy-making apparatus. The position of domestic policy adviser can be traced back at least as far as Clark CLIFFORD under President Harry TRUMAN. With the possible exception of Dwight EISENHOWER, every president since has designated at least one person to serve as an assistant for DOMESTIC POLICY. Lyndon JOHNSON set up a formalized office of domestic policy, which has become a mainstay of the INSTITUTIONAL PRESIDENCY.

The position of assistant to the president for domestic policy has gradually become institutionalized since the Hoover administration. The position (or at least the need for someone to spearhead the coordination of domestic policy initiatives) grew in importance following the BUDGET AND ACCOUNTING ACT OF 1921, which virtually mandated that the president present some sort of legislative agenda to the Congress. However, in the period before 1946, there existed no sustained mechanism for coordinating domestic policy formulation. In the years immediately following the development of the EXECUTIVE OFFICE OF THE PRESIDENT (EOP), the WHITE HOUSE OFFICE (WHO) and the BUREAU OF THE BUDGET (BOB) shared responsibility in the domestic policy realm. These tasks were performed primarily by senior aides in the WHO, who also assisted in developing policy priorities. The manner in which these were accomplished was through speech preparation, messages to Congress, other important policy statements, and drafting legislation to be submitted to Congress. Likewise, it was commonplace for first drafts of speeches in any subject matter to originate in the department that was primarily concerned with the subject matter, to be consolidated later in the White House.

The actual role of assistant to the president for domestic policy went to another level with the work of Clark Clifford, who held the title of Special Council to the President under Truman. Clifford's first assignment was to develop and consolidate the FAIR DEAL legislative program offered by Truman in the 1947 STATE OF THE UNION ADDRESS. Charles Murphy, who performed essentially the same tasks, utilizing to a great extent the newly formed Research Division of the Democratic National Committee, succeeded Clifford in 1950. The duties performed by Clifford were to facilitate the clearance process in a new White House role. His role was to formulate and develop ideas, rather than fully develop proposals, which was done in the departments.

No formal office was designated during the Eisenhower administration. However, under KENNEDY and Johnson, the nucleus of a permanent advisory process began to take shape. When Kennedy became president, he designated Theodore Sorensen to coordinate proposals, though Sorensen was never officially designated as assistant for domestic policy. Lyndon Johnson expanded Sorensen's role to two people, Bill Moyers and Joseph Califano. The role was further institutionalized by the creation of the Domestic Council pursuant to the provisions of the ASH COUNCIL and was put under the directorship of John Ehrlichman. James Cannon held the position during the FORD administration. Jimmy CARTER slightly altered the parameters of the council and renamed it the Domestic Policy Staff, but the role was continued under the strong leadership of Stuart Eizenstat. Further institutionalization of the role is evidenced by the fact that Ehrlichman, Cannon, and Eizenstat were given professional staffs. Under REAGAN, the office changed names again to the OFFICE OF POLICY DEVELOPMENT, and its status in the administration downgraded. George H. W. BUSH utilized Roger Porter in the domestic and economic realms, as well as Chief of Staff John Sununu, but his focus on foreign policy as well as his lack of major domestic initiatives kept the office from being elevated to the status it enjoyed during the Carter years. CLINTON renamed the office the Domestic Policy Council (DPC), and it was headed by Carol Rasco, an adviser on welfare issues since Clinton's days as Arkansas governor. The DPC under Clinton was not fully functional until nine months after his inauguration, and even then performed most of its work in an ad hoc fashion. George W. BUSH has so far not designated an official assistant for domestic policy, with much of the work being done by senior advisers Karl Rove and Karen Hughes, with economic input from Economic Adviser Lawrence Lindsey. This may be reflective of the fact that many of the more recent presidents have tended to explicitly recognize the interdependence of economic and domestic policy, so future administrations may do away with the notion of a simply domestic policy adviser altogether.

Further reading: Burke, John. *The Institutional Presidency: Organizing and Managing the White House from FDR to Clinton,* 2d ed. Baltimore, Md.: Johns Hopkins University Press, 2000; Hart, John. *The Presidential Branch: From Washington to Clinton,* 2d ed. Chatham, N.J.: Chatham House, 1995; Ponder, Daniel E. *Good Advice: Information and Policy Making in the White House.* College Station: Texas A&M University Press, 2000.
—Daniel E. Ponder

Douglas, Stephen A. (1813–1861) *U.S. senator, representative, state supreme court judge*

Stephen Douglas will always be the shadow of his Illinois political opponent, Abraham LINCOLN. Douglas and Lincoln were rivals in the 1858 Senate race that is more remembered for the moving and eloquent debates than for the outcome (Douglas won). Lincoln and Douglas were rivals two years later, this time for the presidency, this time Lincoln victorious.

Born on April 23, 1813, in Brandon, Vermont, Douglas, as a U.S. senator, introduced the Kansas-Nebraska Bill, allowing both states into the Union, canceling the Missouri Compromise (setting a northern boundary on slave states).

A skilled politician, nicknamed the "Little Giant" (he stood a mere five feet, four inches tall), Douglas's career all but ended after his defeat in 1860. After the CIVIL WAR erupted, Douglas toured the North speaking out in support of the Union. He fell ill in May and died on June 31, 1861.

Further reading: Johannsen, Robert W. *Stephen A. Douglas.* New York: Oxford University Press, 1973; Wells, Damon. *Stephen Douglas: The Last Years, 1857–1861.* Austin: University of Texas Press, 1971.

Dred Scott v. Sandford (1857)

Dred Scott, a slave, first attempted to obtain his freedom through a St. Louis circuit court in 1853. Scott's second owner, Dr. John Emerson, an army surgeon, took Scott from Missouri to Illinois and into the Wisconsin territory, where slavery was illegal. On his return to St. Louis, Dred Scott and his family were sold to John F. A. Sandford of New York, due to Emerson's death.

In 1853 Scott filed suit for his freedom in the St. Louis circuit court, arguing that he had entered free territory. He lost in the Missouri State Supreme Court but then filed suit in a federal court against his final owner, John F. S. Sandford. On losing this decision, he appealed to the U.S. Supreme Court.

On March 6, 1857, Chief Justice Roger B. Taney, along with six associate justices, delivered the majority decision against Scott. The Taney opinion concluded that Scott was not a citizen of the U.S. because he was a slave, the same as *personal property*. As a result, Scott had no right to bring this case to court. Taney did not stop with Scott but went further to suggest that the federal government had no right to prohibit slavery in any portion of the United States, regardless of what the Missouri Compromise might have said.

Two important dissents, written by Justices John McLean and Benjamin R. Curtis, defended Scott and were printed for public release as soon as they were written. Taney held back on his written opinion until he had read the dissents. This situation led to a heated exchange of letters in 1857 between Justices Taney and Curtis that resulted in the eventual resignation of Curtis from the Court.

The decision was important for a number of reasons. It was only the second case decided that tested the legitimacy of judicial review, coming 50 years after the first case, MAR-BURY v. MADISON. In addition, Taney's conclusions regarding slavery undermined the prestige of the Court for years. Most critics were particularly concerned that Taney had gone so far as to void the Missouri Compromise—that document that had determined which territories should be free territories. His broadened dicta in this case disturbed the uneasy balance between North and South and heightened citizens' emotions regarding the issue of slavery and probably brought the beginning of the CIVIL WAR ever closer.

Newspapers supporting the Republican cause in 1857, like the Albany, New York, *Evening Journal,* were furious with the decision. As it stated on March 10: "The half million of men and women paralyzed . . . by the atheistic logic of the decision of the case of Dred Scott, . . . will be to all free and uncorrupted souls a complete denial of the bad law and worse conscience, with which the Supreme Court has pronounced its departure from Republicanism and its entrance into slavery." Democratic reaction defended the decision in equally strong terms. The *Richmond, Virginia, Enquirer* stated on March 10 that "a politico-legal question . . . [has] been decided emphatically in favor of the advocates and supporters of the Constitution and the Union, the equality of the States and the rights of the South, in contradistinction to and in repudiation of the dia-

bolical doctrines inculcated by factionists and fanatics; and that too by a tribunal of jurists, as learned, impartial and unprejudiced as perhaps the world has ever seen."

Further reading: Fehrenbacher, Don E. *The Dred Scott Case.* New York: Oxford University Press, 1978; Hopkins, Vincent C. *Dred Scott's Case.* New York: Russell & Russell, 1967; Kutler, Stanley I., ed. *The Dred Scott Decision: Law or Politics.* Boston: Houghton Mifflin, 1967.

—Byron W. Daynes

drug policy

Since the 1970s, presidents have paid a great deal of attention to drug policy, but attention and results are two very difficult things.

Richard NIXON was the first president to declare a "war on drugs." He appointed the first "drug czar" and focused a great deal of concern on the growing problems of drugs and street crime. Since that time, presidents have been compelled to devote time and resources to this thorny problem.

The increased attention has resulted in a mixed record of success. Thus, while drug policy will continue to be politically important, presidents can and will probably have only a limited impact in eliminating the scourge of drugs from society.

Dukakis, Michael (1933–   ) *politician*

Michael Dukakis was the highly regarded governor of Massachusetts in 1975–79 and 1983–91. In 1988 he was the DEMOCRATIC PARTY nominee for president. In the general election, he faced Vice President George BUSH, who, after attacking Dukakis in the campaign, won the presidency with 54 percent of the popular vote.

Dukakis, born in 1933 to Greek immigrant parents, attended Swarthmore College and Harvard Law School, then worked his way up the political ladder from town council to Massachusetts state legislature to the governorship. After his loss in 1988, he taught at several colleges and served as head of the Amtrak board.

Further reading: Nyhan, David. *The Duke: The Inside Story of a Political Phenomenon.* New York: Warner Books, 1988.

Dulles, John Foster (1888–1959) *secretary of state, U.S. ambassador, diplomat, U.S. senator*

Best known as secretary of state (1953–59) during the presidency of Dwight D. EISENHOWER, Dulles was the third in his family to be secretary of state; his grandfather served under Benjamin HARRIS and his uncle served under Woodrow WILSON at the Versailles Peace Conference. He was an undergraduate at Princeton (with a major in philosophy), attended the Hague Peace Conference of 1907 with his grandfather (and acted as a secretary for the Chinese delegation), and then attended George Washington University Law School. Although it appeared he was destined for DIPLOMACY, he became an extremely successful lawyer and was the senior partner of his firm. In 1917 Woodrow Wilson sent him to Central America to negotiate the protection of the Panama Canal and he participated as counsel in the Versailles Peace Conference following WORLD WAR I. In 1945 he served as an adviser at the conference in San Francisco that created the UNITED NATIONS, and in mid 1949 he was appointed to fill a vacated Senate seat, where he immediately expressed support for the North Atlantic Treaty. He ran for the Senate seat in November, campaigning on anticommunism, but lost, and in 1950 he was named as a consultant for the STATE DEPARTMENT. In this post, he served as the chief negotiator for the peace treaty with Japan.

Although already acquaintances, in 1952 Dulles and Eisenhower discovered that their views were compatible, especially on the subject of opposition to communism, collective defense, and the idea of freedom for Soviet satellites when they met at the Supreme Headquarters of the Allied Powers in Europe (SHAPE). Dulles was less inclined to compromise than Eisenhower and more inclined to accept military options. On January 21, 1952, Dulles became Eisenhower's secretary of state and the two worked closely together. His commitment to anticommunism and his power as secretary of state seemed to embolden him with a moral self-righteousness. He believed communism was morally wrong and inherently inferior, and thus compromise with it was immoral.

His successes as secretary of state are numerous. As a function of CONTAINMENT, he initiated the Manila Conference in 1954, resulting in the Southeast Asia Treaty Organization (SEATO). SEATO united eight nations in a defense pact. He then turned his sights to the Middle East, resulting in the Baghdad Pact, later renamed the Central Treaty Organization (CENTO), in 1955. This created a defense organization that included Turkey, Iraq, Iran, and Pakistan. In Europe he played a critical role in the Austrian State Treaty (1955) that created a neutral Austria returned to its pre-1938 borders. Perhaps his greatest success was the administration's ability to control the growing threat posed by the Soviet Union.

Dulles's critics viewed him as difficult, inflexible, and harsh. He stirred controversy and criticism by coining the term *massive retaliation* to signify that the United States would use nuclear weapons in response to Soviet aggression. He inadvertently precipitated the Suez Crisis of 1956 with his blunt refusal to assist Egypt in building the Aswan Dam. In an effort to fund the construction, Egyptian President Gamal Abdel Nasser seized the Suez Canal, leading to a secret plan between Israel, Great Britain, and France to invade Egypt. Eisenhower and Dulles were infuriated by the attack and pressured the U.S. allies to withdraw.

Suffering from cancer, Dulles resigned on April 15, 1959, and died the following month. Early critiques of the foreign policy of the Eisenhower administration focused on the role played by the secretary of state and contended that he wielded considerable influence over a passive president, so much so that many claimed the foreign policy of the United States was solely the foreign policy of Dulles. Revisionists, however, with the benefit of Eisenhower's PRESIDENTIAL PAPERS, paint a picture of an active president who possessed strong convictions about the direction of U.S. foreign policy. Still, Dulles was key in Eisenhower's diplomacy, making 60 trips abroad to advance policy.

Further reading: Guhin, Michael A. *John Foster Dulles: A Statesman and His Times.* New York: Columbia University Press, 1972; Townsend, Hoopes. *The Devil and John Foster Dulles.* Boston: Little, Brown, and Company, 1973.

—Elizabeth Matthews

E

Eagleton, Thomas (1929–) *U.S. senator*

A U.S. Senator from Missouri (1968–87), Thomas Eagleton entered presidential politics on July 13, 1972, when he was nominated for the vice presidency to run with George S. McGovern, the DEMOCRATIC PARTY's presidential nominee. However, 12 days into the campaign it was revealed that Eagleton had been hospitalized three times between 1960 and 1966 while suffering from emotional exhaustion and depression and had twice received electric shock therapy. The news ignited an intense nationwide debate about his ability to withstand the stress of the presidency should he have to succeed to the OVAL OFFICE. Eagleton came under increasing pressure, first from major newspapers, and later from party faithful, to leave the ticket. On July 31, 1972, at the request of McGovern, Eagleton withdrew his candidacy and subsequently was replaced by Sargent Shriver, a former director of the Peace Corps. Eagleton's RESIGNATION marked the only time in American political history that a vice presidential candidate withdrew from a ticket after being nominated by a major political party convention. McGovern, a senator from South Dakota, initially strongly supported retaining Eagleton as his running mate. However, as the debate over Eagleton's qualifications intensified and pressures for his resignation mounted, both men agreed that it would be best for him to drop out of the race so that the major issues of the time, such as the war in VIETNAM, could be discussed.

Further reading: Kneeland, Douglas E. "Eagleton Tells McGovern It Was 'the Only Decision.'" *New York Times,* 1 August 1972, p. A1; Naughton, James M. "Eagleton Withdraws From Election Race at Request of McGovern." *New York Times,* 1 August 1972, p. A1; White, Theodore H. *The Making of the President, 1972.* New York: Atheneum Publishers, 1973.

—Robert E. Dewhirst

economic policy

Although the business cycle was manifested from the beginning of the American republic, the political culture of the United States was steeped in *laissez-faire* assumptions that government ought not become intimately involved in the workings of the economy. Certainly the federal government had no mandate from the citizenry to try to moderate the ups and downs of the business cycle. As President Warren G. HARDING stated in 1921: "There has been vast unemployment before and there will be again. There will be depression and inflation just as surely as the tides ebb and flow." This thinking ended with the GREAT DEPRESSION, and in its wake Congress enacted the (Full) EMPLOYMENT ACT OF 1946 to hereafter guarantee that the federal government would be the guardian of national prosperity.

The conventional wisdom is that four goals are the cornerstone of economic policy: economic growth, full employment, stable prices, and a positive international balance of payments. It was 1946 when the first three goals were articulated as official government policy, whereas the fourth objective gained salience as the United States moved from being economically hegemonic within the world economy, in the years following WORLD WAR II, to later being faced with competition from nations with highly developed economies in Europe (the European Union) and Asia.

The importance of economic growth, full employment, and price stability were underscored in the declaration of policy in Section 2 of Public Law 79–304:

The Congress hereby declares that it is the continuing policy and responsibility of the federal government to use all practical means consistent with its needs and obligations and other essential considerations of national policy with the assistance and cooperation of industry, agriculture, labor, and state and local governments, to coordinate and utilize all its plans, functions, and resources for the purposes of creating and maintain, in a manner calculated to foster and promote free competitive enterprise and the general welfare, conditions under which there will be afforded useful employment, for those able, willing, and seeking to work, and to promote maximum employment, production, and purchasing power.

Because the economic dislocations during the Great Depression caused one in four American workers to become unemployed, the primary goal was "maximum employment"—but note that the statutory language does not require the federal government to guarantee *full* employment. Moreover the law does not stipulate the policy tools for carrying out this mandate. Indeed, "maximum production and purchasing power" are supposed to be achieved along with maximum employment.

Maximum production signifies economic growth, or increasing the total amount of goods and services produced by the American economy. For years it was measured as Gross National Product (GNP) but today the more commonly used index is Gross Domestic Product (GDP). The GNP and GDP are fairly close, differing mainly in whether non-U.S. residents in the United States or U.S. residents outside the United States are included in this calculation. GNP includes the value of goods and services produced by nonresidents located within the United States but excludes the value of those services and goods produced by U.S. residents working abroad. GDP excludes the former but includes the latter.

Maximum purchasing power means price stability—the avoidance of steadily rising prices for goods and services (inflation) or falling prices (deflation)—and is measured by a variety of indices, most prominently the Consumer Price Index (CPI) and the Producer Price Index (PPI). The CPI reflects the prices paid by consumers for goods and services; the PPI represents the prices paid by producers for raw materials, labor, and other resources needed to produce goods or services for sale.

American tourists travel abroad; the U.S. armed forces have bases around the world; Congress annually appropriates FOREIGN AID to assist less developed nations; companies located in the United States have established multinational corporations doing business in countries close and afar. Americans purchase goods and services produced abroad (imports) and sell to foreigners goods and services produced domestically (exports). This web of capital flowing to and from the United States is calculated as the balance of payments. It is generally more desirable to have a positive balance of payments, with moneys flowing into the United States, than the reverse (or a negative bal-

ance of payments), but no one answer is correct for all times and circumstances.

Also note that the 1946 act stimulated that maximum employment, production, and purchasing power are to be secured "in a manner calculated to foster and promote free competitive enterprise," which seemingly precludes the path taken by most European nations. What arguably qualifies as socialistic enterprises—the U.S. Postal Service holding the monopoly over delivery of first-class mail or Amtrak operating all passenger rail service—are rare in the United States as compared to Great Britain, France, or virtually any other Westernized nation. Thus, the 1946 act represents a commitment to private enterprise and seemingly a repudiation of socialism, or direct government ownership of the means of production. On the other hand, though not explicitly mentioned in the 1946 law, private enterprise and free markets are also jeopardized by private monopolies, which explains why ANTITRUST POLICY aimed at keeping markets competitive and curbing business concentration dates back to the late 19th century.

However, what is equally important about the declaration in the 1946 act is that the United States took a decisive step away from a pure free market economy based on private enterprise toward a "mixed" economy where a substantial share of the GNP or GDP is produced by local, state, and federal governments although the lion's share is still contributed by the private sector. Because the public sector has grown so large, and especially the federal government (whose budget surpassed the $2 trillion mark for fiscal year 2003), federal policy making can have an impact on the total economy through spending, taxing, and borrowing as well as through their manipulation of the money supply.

One final economic goal is more contested in the United States than in most other developed nations: redistribution of wealth. Apart from the moral dictates of social justice that society provide for the poor and underprivileged, the economic argument favoring a widespread distribution of income is that one powerful engine for maintaining economic growth and low unemployment is consumer spending—which represents a larger contribution to the GNP or GDP than government spending, business spending, or foreign investment. Obviously, poor people are limited in their ability to spend money, especially during periods of recession, which is why government payments to the poor in the form of welfare checks help improve the lives of the poor and also help increase the amount of spending by consumers on goods and services. There are many welfare programs provided by local, state, and federal governments, but Americans are much less supportive of economic equality, as a policy goal, as compared to Europeans. This, in turn, explains why the United States commits fewer public resources to social-welfare programs compared to any European nation.

The astute observer will immediately understand that the goals specified in the 1946 act are all important for a healthy economy, but they are not all entirely compatible. The best known example is what economists call the Dilemma Model, which argues that economic policy designed to achieve a lowering of the unemployment rate will predictably yield inflationary pressures, that is, higher prices. It is unlikely, therefore, that "maximum" employment, production, and purchasing power will coexist for long periods of time, to suggest that the better strategy for policy makers would be to use a mix of policies that optimize—rather than maximize—these divergent economic goals. But that is easier said than done.

See also ECONOMIC POWERS.

Further reading: Baily, Stephen K. *Congress Makes a Law.* New York: Columbia University Press, 1950; Frendreis, John P., and Raymond Tatalovich. *The Modern Presidency and Economic Policy.* Itasca, Ill.: F. E. Peacock Publishers, 1994.

—Raymond Tatalovich

economic powers

Although the EMPLOYMENT ACT OF 1946 charged the federal government with various economic responsibilities in the area of ECONOMIC POLICY, it included no mention of explicit powers—what economists call policy tools—for achieving those goals. Because its primary concern was to avoid any repeat of the GREAT DEPRESSION, even economic recession, policy makers have come to view the 1946 act as representing a call for "countercyclical" policy, which means that economic policy should aim at countering any extremes in the business cycle. During periods of economic downturn, policy seeks to stimulate the economy; when threatened with rising prices, policy should aim to dampen inflationary pressures. A countercyclical strategy for economic policy would require the government to exert powers over FISCAL POLICY and MONETARY POLICY.

Fiscal policy is manipulating taxes and spending, or the federal budget, to either increase or decrease aggregate spending in the economy. Since the 1930s fiscal policy is likely the most important power available to policy makers, because followers of Keynesian Economics (named for British economist John Maynard Keynes) believe that the impact of fiscal policy is more direct and immediate than with the monetary policy. If the problem is rising unemployment, then policy makers may seek to lower individual income taxes so consumers have more disposable income to spend, or reduce corporate taxes to encourage businesses to invest in new plant and equipment and increase production, as well as to increase federal expenditures even if the result is a widening of federal deficits. On the other hand,

if the problem is rising prices, then policy makers may seek to increase individual or corporate income taxes and reduce the level of government spending, because one conventional understanding of inflation is "too many dollars chasing too few goods and services."

Monetary policy involves manipulating the money supply and the flow of credit in our economy. It began with the FEDERAL RESERVE SYSTEM in 1913, enacted in response to bank failures, whereby 12 regional Federal Reserve Banks act as lenders of last resort providing loans to banks faced with "runs" on their deposits. From that humble beginning, again prompted by the economic trauma of the Great Depression, the "Fed" began to use its powers over monetary policy to stabilize the macroeconomy. Unlike fiscal policy, which is controlled by political leaders in the executive and legislative branches, the powers to shape monetary policy are held by the Federal Reserve Board of Governors, an independent body which is relatively insulated from both the presidency and Congress.

Monetary policy involves three policy instruments: the discount rate, reserve requirements, and open market operations. When banks borrow money from the Federal Reserve Banks, the price they pay is the discount rate, and obviously the price that local banks pay for an infusion of federal funds will, in turn, affect the rates of interest they must charge their customers who ask for bank loans. If the discount rate is increased, then interest rates charged by banks will increase and thus discourage the demand for bank loans; if the discount rate is decreased, then interest rates charged by banks will fall and thereby encourage the demand for bank loans.

Reserve requirements mandate that banks have sufficient cash on hand to accommodate withdrawals, but again, raising or lowering the reserve requirements will affect the quantity of money available to banks for making loans to businesses or consumers. Increasing the reserve requirement—from, say, 10 percent to 15 percent—means that banks must keep more cash in vaults and, therefore, contracts the supply of credit and ultimately the nation's money supply. In contrast, if the Federal Reserve Board authorized a cut in the reserve requirement from 15 percent to 10 percent, then local banks could use the extra money to grant more credit to businesses and consumers and ultimately increase the money supply. An increase in overall money supply, in turn, works to hold down interest rates, so there is an additional incentive for businesses and consumers to borrow money for investment or for purchases.

The Federal Open Market Committee (FOMC) operates through the Federal Reserve Bank of New York to buy and sell U.S. government securities on the open (free) market. This power is arguably the most important policy tool in the Fed's arsenal, given the fact that the federal government has sustained decades of budgetary deficits. If the federal government spends more money than it receives as revenue, then the federal government must borrow funds to close that gap between spending and revenue, often by borrowing from itself (for example, SOCIAL SECURITY funds that are held in a trust fund are often used to cover budget deficits) and from private sector banks and financial institutions.

A problem with fiscal policy is that budgeting is a shared power between the executive and legislative branches. Each year the president submits his budget, after which the Congress may make so many substantial changes that the congressional budget that results is very different from what the president originally requested. Because the fiscal year begins on October 1, the preceding February the president submits to Congress his "executive budget," which means that almost eight months is required to enact a budget that addresses whatever economic problem faces the nation, and then even more time is needed for those taxing and spending policies to "impact" businesses and consumers. In contrast, the Fed is able to act more quickly, although monetary policy will take longer than fiscal policy to have an impact on businesses and consumers.

A final consideration is whether there is a partisan bias to fiscal policy and, to a lesser extent, monetary policy whenever these economic powers are wielded by Democratic versus Republican political and administrative elites. Given that the DEMOCRATIC PARTY gets more electoral support from lower income voters and organized labor whereas the REPUBLICAN PARTY relies more heavily on the middle- and upper-class and business interests, some political scientists (Douglas A. Hibbs, Jr., for example) find evidence that Republican administrations favor a countercyclical policy that restrains inflationary pressures while Democratic administrations prefer an expansionary countercyclical policy geared to reducing the unemployment rate.

Further reading: Hibbs, Douglas A., Jr. *The American Political Economy: Macroeconomics and Electoral Politics in the United States.* Cambridge, Mass.: Harvard University Press, 1987; Keech, William R. *Economic Politics: The Costs of Democracy.* New York: Cambridge University Press, 1995; Markovich, Denise E., and Ronald E. Pynn. *American Political Economy: Using Economics with Politics.* Pacific Grove, Calif.: Brooks/Cole [Wadsworth] Publishing Company, 1988.

—Raymond Tatalovich

Economic Stabilization Act

In the late 1960s the dramatic economic expansion of the KENNEDY and JOHNSON years was in decline. Richard NIXON came to office in 1969 with declining economic conditions exacerbated by the United States's continued activity in the VIETNAM WAR. The years 1969 and 1970 saw severe upswings in the rate of inflation. Nixon initially tried to reduce inflation via monetary policy by limiting the amount of money in the economy. This was in response to the prevailing view of the day that the inflation was "demand pull," that is, increased demand decreased supply and thereby pulled prices up. This diagnosis was soon challenged when not only did inflation not decline but inflation began to rise, resulting in an extended period of stagflation. During this time, unemployment increased to 6 percent, while unemployment jumped 5 percent above average. Stagflation led to a reconsideration of the origins of the problem. Instead of "demand pull," some advisers noted that the trends were consistent with "cost push" inflation, which results when increasing costs of production push prices up regardless of patterns of demand. This trend was largely thought to be exempt from preventative policies, implying the needs for direct controls over prices.

Nixon was an advocate of free-market policies, but not so ideologically wed to them that he was immune from persuasion. The Democratic Congress, sensing Nixon's vulnerability on the issue, passed the Economic Stabilization Act of 1970. The act gave the president standby authority to set controls on wages, prices, and rents. Nixon, while noting his reservations about the powers given the president, signed it.

Though Nixon was given these powers, he did not initially use them. He continued to rely on the market to free the nation from the economic turmoil it found itself in. However, through the rest of 1970 and into 1971, economic conditions continued to deteriorate. In 1971 Secretary of the Treasury John Connally advised Nixon to invoke powers given under the act and impose wage and price controls. On August 15, 1971, Nixon imposed a 90-day freeze on wages and incomes. Most governmental actors heavily supported this freeze, as did the public.

The policy was imposed in four phases, and its success in meeting its objectives was uneven. For example, the Price Commission, which oversaw prices, allowed price increases to cover production costs as well as demand costs. Exemptions were permitted, and concessions were often made in reference to strong unions. As such, prices and wages were unevenly regulated and often dependent upon whether workers were unionized or nonunion. As such, prices were regulated more heavily than wages. Also exempted were food and energy, and when Phase III began, prices began to gradually increase as a result of sharp increases in these commodities. Spillover effects caused nonfood commodities and services to increase, and by the end of April 1974 (the sunset date for the act), it was commonly felt that the experiment had been a policy, though not a political, failure.

Further reading: Frendreis, John P., and Raymond Tatalovich. *The Modern Presidency and Economic Policy.* Itasca, Ill.: Peacock Press, 1994.

—Daniel E. Ponder

Education, Department of

The U.S. Department of Education is the cabinet-level agency responsible for national educational policy. The mission of the Department of Education is to ensure equal access to education and promote excellence in our nation's schools. The department's budget is $42 billion with a workforce of 5,000 employees.

Between 1867 and 1979, the federal government, through presidential action, reorganized and reinvented its role in education policy several times. On March 2, 1867, President Andrew JOHNSON signed Public Law 39–73 creating a Department of Education, an independent agency. The legislation was a response to a national call for a centralized governmental entity to collect and distribute information on the "condition and progress of education in the Several States and Territories. . . ." This legislation culminated several decades of unsuccessful attempts in creating a national educational office.

Beginning in 1869 and continuing for the next century, a series of organizational and name changes occurred. On July 1, 1869, the Office of Education was created within the DEPARTMENT OF THE INTERIOR. Nearly one year later, another name change ushered in the Bureau of Education. In 1911, within the Bureau of Education, a Division of Higher Education was created to meet the country's growing needs for postsecondary education.

The bureau lasted until 1929, when the name changed back to the Office of Education, a move seen as increasing the organization's stature. Ten years later, under Franklin Delano ROOSEVELT's NEW DEAL, the services of the federal government were bolstered in response to America's GREAT DEPRESSION. FDR requested a complete overhaul of the EXECUTIVE BRANCH. A plan was outlined by the President's Committee on Administrative Management (the BROWNLOW COMMITTEE). Part of the plan included the creation of a social welfare arm of the federal government, the Federal Security Agency (FSA). On July 1, 1939, the Office of Education was transferred under the FSA, the newly created agency responsible for health, education, and welfare. During the Depression, the Office of Education helped direct and coordinate the educational activities of the Federal Emergency Relief Administration, the CIVILIAN CONSERVATION CORPS, and the WORKS PROGRESS ADMINISTRATION.

In April 1953 President EISENHOWER officially changed the name of the Federal Security Agency (FSA) to the Department of HEALTH, EDUCATION, AND WELFARE (HEW). In 1979, following through on a campaign pledge, President Jimmy CARTER sought and won congressional support for the creation of an independent, cabinet-level Department of Education. On October 17, 1979, President Carter signed Public Law 96-88 creating the stand-alone department amid a storm of criticism from conservatives, liberals, labor, and the press.

Further reading: Lykes, Richard Wayne. *Higher Education and the United States Office of Education, 1867–1953.* Washington, D.C.: Bureau of Postsecondary Education, 1975; Miles, Rufus E. *The Department of Health, Education, and Welfare.* New York: Praeger Publishers, 1974; U.S. Department of Education, Office of the Secretary. *An Overview of the U.S. Department of Education.*
—Owen Holmes

education policy, American presidents and

Presidential involvement in education policy in the United States has been guided by two fundamental principles: first, that elementary and secondary education should be free and universal, and second, that public education should be largely the responsibility of state and local government rather than the national government. In order to examine how these two principles in various ways have undergirded the ideas and actions of American presidents regarding public education, it is useful to focus on three periods of American history. The first is during the early years of our nation, the second is WORLD WAR II and the subsequent two decades, and the third is the era from 1965 to 2002.

The Early Years of the Nation

The six presidents who served during the early years of the republic were largely opposed to direct involvement of the federal government in formal education. George WASHINGTON, John ADAMS, Thomas JEFFERSON, James MADISON, James MONROE, and John Quincy ADAMS all believed that an educated citizenry was vital for maintaining the stability of democratic political institutions and that the provision of public education should be centered at the state and local levels. They also supported the shift from the traditional private, primarily church-based educational system that existed during the colonial years to a free, universal public system.

In the writings of several of the six early presidents, emphasis is given to the idea that one of the major goals of public education should be to expose the young in a systematic, step-by-step method to superiority of democratic political philosophy and institutions associated with the American Constitution. According to historians Lorraine Smith Pangle and Thomas Pangle, there was no aim of public education that was more important than making sure that students grasped ideas concerning "the enormous advantages of modern constitutional democracy, that is, the kind of civil society created by the founding, over previous or traditional societies and forms of government."

A common set of principles and aims concerning public education as expressed in the writings of the early presidents is most clearly embodied in the thoughts of Thomas Jefferson. Like the other early presidents, Jefferson was convinced that while the new republic needed a national education vision and set of goals that would promote democratic values and institutions, it did not need a national school system. The establishment throughout the nation of local and neighborhood governments, centered on the involvement of local residents in the founding and oversight of public elementary schools, Jefferson contended, was absolutely essential for the flourishing of democracy. "Jefferson saw in the involvement of local adults in the establishment of schools for their children an educational experience valuable above all to the adults themselves— and through their example as active citizens, valuable to their children."

Although all six of the early presidents maintained that public education of children was the responsibility of state and local governments, several of them proposed that the federal government establish a national university in order to effectively prepare older students for national leadership positions. In 1790 President Washington requested that Congress authorize the establishment of a national university. Several other early presidents made proposals to amend the Constitution in order to found a national university. None of these proposals had sufficient support to be enacted.

Because there is no provision in the U.S. Constitution for federal government involvement in formal education, the power over education is reserved by the states which have delegated most of the responsibility for the operation of public education systems to local school districts. Limited by these constitutional constraints, American presidents have tended to be reluctant to exercise leadership in education policy. Abraham LINCOLN in 1862 signed the Morrill Land Grant Act, which provided grants of federal land to each state for the establishment of public colleges specializing in agriculture and mechanical arts. President Woodrow WILSON signed the Smith-Hughes Act of 1917, which initiated the first program of federal grants-in-aid to fund vocational education, and President Herbert HOOVER appointed a commission to explore the issue of establishing a U.S. department of education. These presidential actions, however, were the exceptions. It was not until World War II and thereafter that public education was part of the policy of most presidents.

World War II and the Following Two Decades
During World War II and the following two decades, presidents began to exercise more leadership in education policy. Presidential action was motivated by concerns such as the need to help the returning World War II veterans pay for their college expenses, the financial difficulty encountered by local school districts as they attempted to accommodate the dramatically increased "baby boom" enrollments, and the perception that the relatively low quality of the science and mathematics curricula of Ameri-

can public schools was limiting the economic and military power of the nation.

President Franklin D. ROOSEVELT's leadership contributed significantly to the passage of the 1944 Servicemen's Readjustment Act (GI Bill) which provided financial assistance to veterans enrolled in higher education programs; these benefits were later extended to Korean conflict-era veterans in 1952 and to Vietnam-era veterans in 1966. The GI Bill made it possible for more than two million veterans to attend college and played a key role in creating mass higher education in the United States.

President Harry S TRUMAN's administration supported three important education-related programs: The 1946 National School Lunch and Milk Act, which began the provision of federal grants and commodity donations for nonprofit lunches and milk served in public and private schools, the 1950 Federal Impacted Areas Aid Program authorizing federal aid to school districts in which large numbers of federal employees and tax-exempt federal property create either a substantial increase in public school enrollments or a significant reduction in local property tax revenues, and the establishment in 1950 of the National Science Foundation (NSF) with the goal of promoting scientific research and improving the quality of teaching in the areas of science, mathematics, and engineering.

In response to the Soviet Union's success in launching the first satellite into space in 1957, President Dwight D. EISENHOWER and the Democratic-dominated Congress saw the need for federal action to enhance the scientific and defense capabilities of the nation. The resulting 1958 National Defense Education Act provided federal financial support to strengthen the areas of science, mathematics, and foreign language instruction, and to establish a system of direct loans to college students. President Eisenhower's other notable education-related action was his 1957 deployment of federal troops to restore order around Central High School in Little Rock, Arkansas, and thereby enforce the public school desegregation decision of the Supreme Court.

Faced with domestic discord, a potential constitutional crisis, and international embarrassment, President John F. KENNEDY in 1962 responded as Einsenhower had done earlier in Little Rock during similar circumstances and called in federal troops to promote the desegregation of public schools. In this case, President Kennedy used federal troops to restore order and make it possible for James Meredith (a black student) to enroll at the all-white University of Mississippi. President Kennedy's administration also was active in the design and promotion of a federal-aid program for public elementary and secondary schools that would have enrolled large numbers of students from poor and low-income families. However, it was not until the presidency of Lyndon JOHNSON that Congress took favorable action on a similar presidential initiative.

The Era from 1965 to 2002

The civil rights movement of the mid 1960s and the war on poverty largely defined the domestic policy AGENDA of Lyndon B. Johnson and led his administration to initiate several highly significant and innovative education programs that were aimed at improving educational opportunities for children of poor families, enforcing court orders to end racial segregation of public schools, and expanding opportunities for Americans to attend college. Johnson hoped that the would be remembered as the "education president." He signed more than 60 education bills into law during his presidency. The three most important education-related initiatives of the Johnson administration were the launching of the Head Start Program in 1965, the enactment of the 1965 Elementary and Secondary Education Act (ESEA), and the passage of the 1965 Higher Education Act.

Head Start was designed to help break the cycle of poverty by providing preschool children of low-income families with a comprehensive program to help meet their emotional, social, health, and education needs. Grants are awarded by the DEPARTMENT OF HEALTH AND HUMAN SERVICES to community-based nonprofit organizations and to school systems.

The historic Elementary and Secondary Education Act of 1965 initiated the single largest program of federal aid to education. Schools with high concentrations of poor students are the principal beneficiaries of the ESEA, receiving funds for instructional materials and education research and training. The ESEA not only dramatically increased the amount of federal financial aid for poverty-impacted schools but it also had the effect of forcing school districts to end racial segregation in order to qualify for ESEA funding.

The 1965 Higher Education Act is the authorizing legislation for most of the federal government's higher education programs, in particular those that provide financial aid to students. The primary aim of this act has been to expand postsecondary education opportunities for low-income students and increase the affordability of higher education for many moderate-income families. The 1965 Higher Education Act also provides financial assistance to community colleges; historically black, hispanic, and tribal colleges; college libraries; and for faculty professional development.

President Richard M. NIXON demonstrated little educational policy leadership. Seldom demonstrating active resistance, his administration might best be characterized as having been largely indifferent to the efforts of Congress to expand the federal education programs begun during the Johnson presidency that emphasized expanding educational opportunities for the poor. In 1970, however, President Nixon did propose the establishment of a new federal agency (the National Institute of Education) aimed at promoting research on education.

Between 1908 and 1975, approximately 130 bills to form a federal department of education were introduced in Congress. In 1979 President Jimmy CARTER signed into law the creation of the U.S. DEPARTMENT OF EDUCATION (D.O.E.) largely due to the urging of the National Education Association, which had endorsed Carter for president in the 1976 election. Approximately 152 education-related programs, most of which had been located in the DEPARTMENT OF HEALTH, EDUCATION, AND WELFARE, were transferred to the new D.O.E.; however, a large number of present programs remain outside of the control of the D.O.E. and within the Departments of Health and Human Services, ENERGY, and DEFENSE.

High on President Ronald REAGAN's domestic policy agenda in 1981 was his intent to abolish the new Department of Education, which he believed was an intrusion upon local and state control of public education. However, the usefulness of maintaining a federal role in education became more apparent to REAGAN, and he grew to accept the idea of preserving the D.O.E. after the 1983 publication of the D.O.E.-sponsored report, entitled *A Nation at Risk: The Imperative for Education Reform.* In their highly negative critique of American public education, the authors of this report wrote that "if an unfriendly foreign power had attempted to impose on America the mediocre performance that exists today, we might have viewed it as an act of war." Fearing that the relatively low quality of education provided in American public schools was making for a decline in American brainpower and consequently reducing the economic competitiveness of the U.S. economy in comparison to other highly developed nations (notably Japan), the alarmist tome of *A Nation at Risk* resonated with top leaders in the Reagan administration and with many other Americans.

Although no federal legislation was enacted as a direct result of *A Nation at Risk,* the document did spur many state governments to begin a wave of education reform efforts. The publication of *A Nation at Risk* is often credited with ending President Reagan's opposition to the existence of the Department of Education, and it appeared to have motivated Reagan to engage in the cost-neutral activity of using the BULLY PULPIT of the presidency for preaching the virtues of excellence reform in education. However, President Reagan remained committed to reducing federal financial aid for public education, and many federal education programs (including Title I of the ESEA) experienced heavy budget cuts by the end of the Reagan presidency.

Like President Lyndon Johnson, each of the three most recent presidents (George H. W. BUSH, Bill CLINTON and George W. BUSH) has claimed that he wanted to be thought of as "the education president." All three of these presidents have made the issue of education reform a top priority on their domestic policy agendas.

President George H. W. Bush took an approach to education policy leadership that was similar to that of his predecessor, President Reagan. Believing that public education was the responsibility of the states, both Presidents Reagan and Bush mainly exercised a hortatory style of leadership, attempting to sell the general public and state education officials on the importance of pursuing education excellence reform. In 1991 President George H. W. Bush released *America 2000: An Education Strategy*. Although this proposal largely presented very broad goals for the future of American education, several specific policy preferences were included: rewarding high-achieving students and successful schools, merit pay and alternative paths of certification for teachers, a longer school year, national standards in core subjects and voluntary achievement tests to measure progress in those subjects, improved adult literacy programs, and expansion of school choice options through use of vouchers and the founding of more charter schools. The plan also called for maintaining a limited federal financial role in funding education reforms. Implementation of *America 2000* was not achieved during George H. W. Bush's administration; however, several of its features are found in the education reform plans of successor presidents Bill Clinton and George W. Bush.

The centerpiece of President Clinton's education agenda was his Goals 2000 proposal. Like George H. Bush's plan for education reform, Clinton's proposal also sought to shift federal education policy to focus on education standards, outcomes, and accountability. Although most of Clinton's plan was light on substantive content, several of its more specific components were enacted into law by Congress, including: (1) the 1994 Goals 2000: Educate America Act, which created the National Education Standards and Improvement Council to develop voluntary national skills standards for local school districts; (2) the 1994 reauthorization of the Head Start Program, which expanded the program's funding and requires that higher education performance standards must be met for recipient organizations to retain federal funding; (3) the 1994 reauthorization of the ESEA (Improving America's Schools Act), which significantly increased Title 1 funding for poverty-impacted schools, increased flexibility in the use of funds, and stressed standards-based accountability of performance; and (4) the 1998 Charter School Expansion Act, providing increased federal funding for charter school startups.

The Clinton administration also introduced several important higher education acts in an attempt to increase accessibility to college and technology training programs for low- and moderate-income students: a $1,500 income tax credit applicable to the cost of the first two years of college, provided for by the 1997 Taxpayer Relief Act; the Student Loan Act, which allows the federal government to make low-interest direct loans to college students; and the School-to-Work Opportunity Act, which increases funding for advanced technology training for students who plan to enter the workforce immediately after high school.

Like the activist style of education policy leadership demonstrated by President Lyndon B. Johnson in the mid 1960s, both Presidents Clinton and George W. Bush have been highly involved in the design and promotion of federal education programs. For instance, both Clinton and George W. Bush were active in the development and passage of reauthorizations of the Elementary and Secondary Education Act (ESEA). The central component of George W. Bush's education policy efforts was the design and eventual enactment in January 2002 of the No Child Left Behind Act (the most recent reauthorization of the ESEA).

Although the broad goals underlying the new laws were also found in George H. Bush's earlier America 2000 proposal and in Clinton's Goals 2000 initiative, George W. Bush's administration gave these goals greater specificity and increased the likelihood that they would be implemented. At the core of the 2002 No Child Left Behind Act are a number of policy implementation measures that will reach into virtually every public school district in the United States, and receipt of ESEA funding will be contingent upon a public school system's meeting the new federal mandates. They include (1) annual testing of students grades 3 through 8 in reading and mathematics; (2) the use of annual report cards showing school-by-school test scores in all school districts; (3) the requirement that every public school teacher must be highly qualified; and (4) the provision of supplemental education services and the offer of public school choice to students in schools that fail to meet adequate yearly progress targets.

Looking Backward

Thus, it is apparent that there has been a steady rise in the priority given education policy, and particularly to education reform issues, by presidents since the Reagan administration. Paralleling and supporting this increased presidential focus on educational policy has been the growth and maturing of the U.S. Department of Education. From its fledgling infancy in 1980, when it was attacked as an unnecessary intrusion into the education responsibilities of states and local school districts, the Department of Education has grown into a major institutional force in public education in the United States.

It should be noted that the recent federal education programs that have been promoted by presidents do not represent a radical departure from the tradition of state and local school district control of public education in the United States. State and local taxpayers have always paid for more than 90 percent of the costs of public elementary and secondary education (the federal government's contribution has never been more than 10 percent). And states have always borne more than 85 percent of the costs for higher education (the federal share has never been more than 15 percent).

Further reading: Dye, Thomas R. *Understanding Public Policy.* Upper Saddle River, New Jersey: Prentice Hall, 2002; National Commission on Excellence in Education. *A Nation at Risk.* Washington, D.C.: U.S. Government Printing Office, 1983; Pangle, Lorraine Smith, and Thomas L. Pangle. "What the American Founders Have to Teach Us About Schooling for Democratic Citizenship." In *Rediscovering the Democratic Purposes of Education,* edited by Lorraine McDonnell, Michael Timpane, and Roger Benjamin. Lawrence: University Press of Kansas, 2000; Stallings, D. T. "A Brief History of the U.S. Department of Education, 1979–2002." *Phi Delta Kappan* 83, no. 9 (May 2002).

—Lance Blakesley

Eisenhower, Dwight David (1890–1969) *thirty-fourth U.S. president*

Dwight David Eisenhower, the 34th president of the United States, was born on October 14, 1890, in a small rented house in Denison, Texas. In 1891, after facing some economic reversals, the family moved to Abilene, Kansas, where the father worked as a mechanic at the local creamery. Dwight David attended local grammar schools and attended Abilene High School, where he made passing grades, played football and baseball, and served as president of his senior class. Tutored by a friend, he passed a competitive exam that enabled him to attend West Point. A middling student, his quest for stardom on the football field was cut short by a serious knee injury.

After his graduation from West Point in June 1915, he went to Fort Sam Houston near San Antonio, Texas, where he met Marie Geneva Doud (Mamie). They married in Denver on July 1, 1916.

He served at several military bases, from Fort Oglethorpe through Camp Meade, including a stint in the Panama Canal Zone (1922–24). In preparation for higher command posts, he studied at the Command and General Staff School (1925–26, where he placed first in his class) and the Army War College (1928–29) at Fort McNair, Washington. After a year in Paris, he came to Washington, D.C., where he served as the special assistant to the assistant secretary of war. He was a speechwriter and special assistant for General Douglas MacArthur (1932–39), first in Washington, then in the Philippines.

With the outbreak of WORLD WAR II, Eisenhower returned to Washington, where his work caught the eye of Army Chief of Staff George C. MARSHALL. With that he was catapulted from what might have been an ordinarily successful career to the top of his profession. He was placed in command of the U.S. forces in Europe, overseeing the invasions of North Africa, Sicily, and Italy. As the supreme Allied commander of Operation Overlord, he oversaw one of the greatest and largest military undertakings in history, the invasion of France. He made the highly risky but ultimately successful decision on June 6, 1944, to commence the Allied landings at Normandy despite inclement weather. On May 7, 1945, he accepted Germany's surrender at a ceremony at Rheims. In November 1945 he succeeded General George C. Marshall as army chief of staff.

Though he first retired from the army in February 1948, and served for a short time as president of Columbia University, Eisenhower returned to service in April 1952 as the supreme commander of the new NATO staff. An affable, gregarious, and able individual who governed through indirection and mediation, Eisenhower's popularity was such that as early as 1948 representatives from both political parties in the United States encouraged him to run for president. In 1952 he agreed to seek the Republican nomination for president, winning the nomination by a large margin after a close fight in the Republican Party credentials committee. In the subsequent campaign against his Democratic opponent, Adlai STEVENSON, he promised to end the KOREAN WAR and went along with the rollback (the communists in Eastern Europe) themes of the REPUBLICAN PARTY. He was elected president on November 4, 1952, receiving 55 percent of the popular vote and 442

President Dwight David Eisenhower *(Library of Congress)*

electoral votes. In a repeat competition with Adlai Stevenson in 1956, he won by a somewhat larger margin: 57 percent of the popular vote and 457 electoral votes. Richard NIXON served with him as vice president throughout his two terms in office.

As president, Eisenhower's main goal was to contain Soviet expansionism, but to do so in a way that would not lead to war. Thus, he undertook a nuclear missile buildup, embraced treaties that drew a line around the Soviet Bloc (SEATO in 1954, the defense treaty with Nationalist China, 1954), announced what became known as the EISENHOWER DOCTRINE (that the United States had the right to aid any country in the Middle East threatened by communist aggression or subversion), and sent marines to Lebanon in 1958 to shore up a government feeling threatened by Nasser in Egypt. Viewing any new communist takeover in the Third World as having a possible domino effect in the world, he sent arms to bolster the Diem regime in Vietnam and supported covert actions to overthrow left-leaning governments in Iran, Guatemala, and Indonesia. During his last year in office, he planned for a U.S.-backed invasion at the BAY OF PIGS to overthrow Fidel Castro in Cuba.

Eisenhower also rejected, on several different occasions, pressures from within his inner circle to resort to the use of force in ways that could cause a broader war. Fulfilling his campaign promise, Eisenhower revived peace talks with North Korea and China, signing an armistice at Panmunjom in 1953 that separated Korea at the 38th parallel. (Dulles and others had pushed for an effort to win the war via an entry into Manchuria to the North.) After the French defeat at Dien Bien Phu in 1954, he decided against a direct U.S. military involvement in Vietnam even though most of his advisers were for it and some, including Admiral Arthur Radford, the chairman of the JOINT CHIEFS OF STAFF, favored the use of the nuclear bomb to aid the French. (The Geneva Conference on Indochina partitioned [April 26–July 21, 1954] Vietnam at the 17th parallel and provided for elections through Vietnam.) Later, in the fall of 1956, he decided not to intervene in Eastern Europe to aid the Hungarian uprising. Employing his best "hidden hand skills," he avoided the domestic political fallout that could have resulted from the reversal of Republican rollback policies. His broader concerns with peace found expression in his suggestion at the Geneva Summit in 1955 for an "Open Skies" proposal. His desire was to reduce the concerns of both the United States and the Soviet Union of a possible surprise attack from the other by opening up the air space of each country for surveillance activities by the other.

Eisenhower's major contribution to the domestic realm was in part motivated by domestic security concerns. Impressed with the ease with which German troops could move through Germany due to the autobahn, he pushed for and won the Federal-Aid Highway Act of 1956. The act provided for 40,000 miles of national highways that would literally unite the United States. When the Soviets fired their first Sputnik into space, he saw the United States's need to sharpen its scientific and technical skills. With the National Defense Education Act of 1958, Eisenhower hoped to encourage more students to become teachers. He realized that a competitive America needed more students trained in math and science. He also cooperated with Canada by building the Saint Lawrence Seaway that opened up the Great Lakes to oceangoing ships.

As a fiscal conservative, Eisenhower was successful in keeping the federal budget under control. He avoided a costly arms race during the first phase of the COLD WAR even though some critics argued that his defense budget put the United States at a military disadvantage relative to the USSR. He knew, from the reports of high-flying U-2 planes developed during his presidency, that the United States was not lagging behind the Soviet Union in its missile development. Politically, however, the need to keep the U-2 flight secret meant that he could not make this information public.

During his two terms in office he made five appointments to the U.S. Supreme Court, contributing to the perpetuation of an ideologically diverse body. Earl Warren, whom he named Chief Justice, led a liberal bloc that included William J. Brennan, another of Eisenhower's appointees. Three others named as associate justices—John Marshall Harlan, Charles E. Whittaker, and Potter Stewart—leaned in the conservative direction.

Critics would later charge that Eisenhower's HIDDEN HAND PRESIDENCY kept him from exercising moral leadership in two major issues that confronted him as president. Though he provided behind-the-scenes support for the army in the Army-McCarthy hearings of 1954, he never openly criticized the reckless tactics of the crusading anticommunist Senator Joseph R. McCARTHY of Wisconsin. In 1957 he sent federal troops to quell the potential for violence that was sparked by the integration of Central High School in Little Rock, Arkansas. He would countenance no violation of federal law, but he never publicly supported the ruling in *Brown v. Board of Education of Topeka* that separation of the races was inherently harmful to a whole group of people.

Somewhat ironically, Eisenhower's desire for better relations with the USSR was smashed when Francis Gary Powers was shot down in a U-2 spy plane over Russia on May 1, 1960, shortly before the Paris summit meeting, which was scheduled to deal with ARMS CONTROL issues. In an effort to show that he was in control of his own administration, Eisenhower publicly stated that he had known of the flight. In response, Soviet Premier Nikita Khrushchev decided to pull out of the conference. The breakup of the conference was one of Eisenhower's major disappointments as president.

Eisenhower, it seems, was willing to threaten the use of nuclear arms to prevent communist expansion but loath to ever use them. "War," as he noted in his memoirs, "is a clumsy political instrument." That process, as he noted, "has produced notable victories and notable men, but in temporarily settling international quarrels it has not guaranteed peace with rights and justice. War is stupid, cruel, and costly." One of his major goals as president was to prevent such wars from happening.

In his farewell address he warned that "we must guard against the acquisition of unwarranted influence, whether sought or unsought, by the military industrial complex." On another occasion he noted, "We kept the peace. People ask how it happened—by God, it didn't just happen, I'll tell you that."

On March 28, 1969, Eisenhower died at the Walter Reed Army Medical Center in Washington, D.C. A ceremony was held at Bethlehem Chapel in the Washington National Cathedral. His funeral took place at the Eisenhower Center in Abilene, Kansas. Dwight D. Eisenhower was buried in his army uniform.

Further reading: Ambrose, Steven E. *Eisenhower: Soldier, General of the Army, President-Elect 1890–1952.* New York: Simon and Schuster, 1983; ———. *Eisenhower: The President.* New York: Simon and Schuster, 1984; Burke, John P., and Fred I. Greenstein, with Larry Berman and Richard Immerman. *How Presidents Test Reality: Decisions on Vietnam, 1954 and 1965.* New York: Russell Sage Foundation, 1989; Eisenhower, Dwight D. *Waging Peace. 1956–1961.* Garden City, N.Y.: Doubleday and Co., Inc., 1965; Galambos, Louis. *The Diaries of Dwight David Eisenhower, 1953–1961.* Washington, D.C.: University Publications of America, 1980; Greenstein, Fred I. *The Hidden-Hand Presidency: Eisenhower as Leader.* New York: Basic Books, 1982; Kitts, Kenneth, and Betty Glad. "Improvisational Decision-Making: Eisenhower and the 1956 Hungarian Crisis." In *Reexamining the Eisenhower Presidency,* edited by Shirley Anne Warshaw. Westport, Conn.: Greenwood Press, 1993.

—Betty Glad and Donna Hedgepath

Eisenhower Doctrine

In 1957 the U.S. Congress passed a law authorizing the president to provide financial and military aid to any Middle Eastern nation that requested assistance against communist aggression. This policy became known as the Eisenhower Doctrine.

Following the Suez Crisis of 1956 and the resulting withdrawal of British and French forces from the area, EISENHOWER became concerned that the Soviets would attempt to fill the vacuum in the region. He believed the Soviets had designs on the oil of the Persian Gulf and that they intended to cut off its flow to weaken the Western allies. On January 5, 1957, Eisenhower delivered a special address to Congress, in which he declared that "Russia's rulers have long sought to dominate the Middle East." He requested economic and military assistance for Middle East nations and authorization to use the armed forces to protect the "territorial integrity and political independence of such nations" that requested the aid "against overt armed aggression from any nation controlled by International Communism."

Critics argued that the Eisenhower Doctrine was misdirected. Nations such as Egypt and Syria, who were unlikely to ask for U.S. assistance, were the ones most in danger of Soviet intervention. Arab nationalism, not communism, was the true threat to pro-Western countries such as Jordan and Lebanon. Although the House voted 355 to 61 in favor of the legislation, the Senate required considerable debate before passage was attained. Supporters of Israel had doubts about extending aid to Arab nations, while others feared it abridged the constitutional authority of the legislature. Despite the hesitation, in March, the Senate voted 72 to 19 to pass the legislation.

In April 1957 the Eisenhower Doctrine underwent its first test. The administration believed the life of King Hussein of Jordan was in danger from nationalist opposition. Eisenhower believed the problems were the fault of communists, and in order to save Jordan from disintegration, he sent the U.S. Sixth Fleet into the eastern Mediterranean and announced a $10 million economic grant to Jordan. The situation stabilized quickly and the Sixth Fleet was recalled in May.

In July 1958 Eisenhower put the doctrine into practice again when he sent U.S. Marines to Lebanon to protect its pro-Western government from a coup by pro-Nasser pan-Arab nationalists. The Lebanese government had requested the INTERVENTION, and the United States obliged out of concern that the Soviets were supporting Nasser's pan-Arabism movement. There was fear that a single Arab nation, as envisioned by pan-Arabists, would be anti-American and restrict access to Middle Eastern oil. Eisenhower told the American people that the purpose of the intervention was to protect Lebanon's integrity from "indirect aggression." The intervention was limited to securing the airfield and Beirut only, but no coup was attempted against the Lebanese government. U.S. troops were withdrawn in October.

Further reading: Divine, Robert A. *Eisenhower and the Cold War.* New York: Oxford University Press, 1981; Eisenhower, Dwight D. *Waging Peace: The White House Years, 1956–1961.* New York: Doubleday, 1965.

—Elizabeth Matthews

Eisenhower Executive Office Building   See EXECUTIVE OFFICE BUILDING, EISENHOWER.

Electoral College

Unlike the electoral process for members of Congress or governors, citizens do not directly elect the president of the United States. Instead, the president is chosen by a group of 538 electors that comprise the Electoral College. The Electoral College is an intermediary body that elects the president. It was established in Article II, Section 1, of the Constitution. The Founding Fathers put forth a few proposals for electing the president. One side argued that Congress should elect the president in a similar manner as in England where the Parliament elects the prime minister. The problem with this plan was that it posed a threat to the notion of SEPARATION OF POWERS; the legislature would have too much power over the EXECUTIVE BRANCH. Others wanted a direct election by the people. This proposal also received much criticism. First, opponents were concerned with the ability of the general public to choose the executive. With the lack of technology at the time, it would be extremely difficult for a resident of South Carolina, for example, to learn much about the governor of Massachusetts. Furthermore, the Founders did not want the most popular candidate to win but the most qualified. Also, slave states were concerned that they would have little influence over the election of the president if a popular vote were employed. The Founders compromised by creating the Electoral College. They did not debate this issue as much as some others, however, because everyone knew that George Washington would be elected the first president.

Here is how the Electoral College works. Each state receives a number of electors equal to the number of senators and representatives it has in Congress. For example, as of the 2000 presidential election, California had 54 electoral votes and Wyoming had three. (With the ratification of the TWENTY-THIRD AMENDMENT in 1961, the District of Columbia was also awarded three electoral votes.) A candidate must receive a majority of the electoral votes (270) to win the election. The electors meet in December in each state's capital to cast their ballots. In January a joint session of Congress opens and agrees to the electoral votes submitted by the states. If no candidate wins a majority, each state's House delegation is awarded one vote and they choose among the top three candidates. Thus, Wyoming and California have the same influence. The candidate who wins a majority of the states becomes president. The Senate uses the same process to choose the vice president. The House has picked the president only twice in the country's history (1800 and 1824).

The Electoral College no longer works in the way that was originally intended. Initially, several states' legislatures chose the electors, while others had a statewide vote. While not having a direct role, the people have more involvement today in the selection process than in the past. On Election Day, voters go to the polls and cast their ballots for a slate of electors. Electors are usually activist members of the party whose presidential candidate carried the state. A candidate who receives a plurality of the votes in the state receives all of the electoral votes; this is known as winner-take-all. Thus, if a candidate wins California by one vote, he receives all 54 electoral votes. Maine and Nebraska are the only states that do not choose their electors on a winner-take-all basis. Instead, they allocate their votes by congressional district with the plurality winner of the state receiving the remaining two votes.

However, in most states, electors are not bound by law to vote for the plurality winner. While the vast majority do, occasionally there is a "faithless elector" who votes his or her conscience instead of with the wishes of the state. There have been roughly half a dozen "faithless electors." None of them has ever been decisive. Because of the potential for faithless electors, some states have passed laws requiring the electors to vote as the state did. While these laws have never been challenged in court, it is unclear if they are constitutional.

People criticize the Electoral College for a variety of reasons. Most obvious, and perhaps most important from an opponent's standpoint, is that the popular vote winner might not be elected president. This happened in the 2000 presidential election when Al GORE won the popular vote by roughly 500,000 votes but lost the electoral vote. Before 2000, only three other times has the winner of the popular vote not won the presidency. In other elections, such as 1960 and 1976, a shift of a few thousand votes in a couple of states would have changed the outcome.

Critics also oppose the Electoral College because it can exaggerate the winner's victory, making it appear as if the public has given the newly elected president a mandate. For example, in 1984 Ronald REAGAN won 58.8 percent of the popular vote, but 98 percent of the electoral vote. In both 1992 and 1996, Bill CLINTON failed to win a majority of the popular vote, but still won roughly 70 percent of the electoral vote in both elections. Others assert that the College works to the advantage of the two major parties. Because of the winner-take-all system, it is nearly impossible for third party candidates to be successful. For instance, in 1992 Ross Perot carried 19 percent of the vote but did not come close to winning any electoral votes. Furthermore, some argue that it lowers voter turnout. If you are a Democrat in the state of Indiana, for example, where a Democratic candidate has not won the state since 1964, you might be less inclined to vote.

Citizens have put forth several proposals to amend or eliminate the Electoral College because of its perceived problems. The most obvious change would be to have a direct vote. Supporters argue that a popular vote election is the only way to insure "one person-one vote." Others have lobbied to modify the Electoral College by going to a winner-take-all district system like that used in Maine and Nebraska or a proportional plan where candidates would receive the same percentage of electoral votes as the popular vote they received in the state. Under this system, if a candidate received 45 percent of the popular vote in a state, he would win 45 percent of the state's electoral vote instead of nothing, as is the case under the current system.

On the other side, however, many claim the Electoral College has worked the way it was intended and should not be changed. Perhaps the most common argument supporters of the College make is that it protects the smaller states. Because of the two electors each state receives regardless of population, electors in Wyoming represent fewer people than electors in California. Without the Electoral College, supporters claim, a candidate could run solely in the most heavily populated states and win, while ignoring rural states. This is the main reason why, even though there have been calls to abolish the Electoral College, it is unlikely to happen. The less populated states have too much power in amending the Constitution. Critics of the College respond that candidates already pay less attention to less populated states under the current system by concentrating predominantly on "battleground states," such as Pennsylvania, Michigan, and Florida. In fact, a candidate could win California by one vote and another candidate could win 100 percent of the vote in the 15 smallest states, and the candidates would only break even.

Supporters of the Electoral College also claim that a direct election would raise the potential for voter fraud or recounts. Some also believe it provides minority voters with a greater voice in the election. For example, instead of comprising roughly 10 percent of the national electorate, in some states AFRICAN AMERICANS might make up 20–25 percent of a state's electorate. Whatever the case, while the Electoral College remains quite controversial, it is unlikely to be changed any time soon.

Further reading: Best, Judith A. *The Choice of the People?: Debating the Electoral College.* Lanham, Md.: Rowman & Littlefield, 1996; Longley, Lawrence D., and Neal R. Pierce. *The Electoral College Primer.* New Haven, Conn.: Yale University Press, 1996; Witcover, Jules. *No Way to Pick a President.* New York: Farrar, Straus, and Giroux, 1999.

—Matt Streb

electoral reform

Nearly every presidential election brings calls for reforming the selection process. It is fair to say that few are pleased with the way the United States selects its presidents. Generally speaking, presidential campaigns are criticized for being (1) too long (2–3 years); (2) too costly; (3) too "race horse" oriented; (4) not policy-related enough; and (5) that the "loser" could win the election. Calls for reform became especially urgent in the aftermath of the 2000 election debacle.

There is little that can be done to shorten the timing of a presidential election. Candidates feel they benefit by starting early, and no law can prevent a potential candidate from making themselves "available." Likewise, efforts to limit the negative effects of money have been unsuccessful, as big money continues to play a significant role in the election process. Efforts to get the media to focus less on the horserace (who is ahead) aspects of elections have been informal and slightly effective, as have calls for the media to focus more on policy and less on personality.

Fundamental reforms have often been proposed but rarely go far. Calls to abolish the ELECTORAL COLLEGE and have direct election of presidents satisfies a democratic urge, and would have averted the debacle of 2000 when the winner of the popular vote (Al GORE) lost the election, but vested party interests have been able to protect status quo. Other reform proposals have also faced difficulties as the forces defending the status quo have been able to delay or fend off reforms.

electronic surveillance

The authority of the executive to intercept information that is communicated through telephone or other electronic devices became a significant issue in the early 20th century with the wide distribution of the telephone.

The Supreme Court first addressed this issue in OLMSTEAD V. UNITED STATES (1928). It held that telephone communication was not tangible or property, and in the absence of any legislation, a warrant was not required for its interception.

The Federal Communications Act of 1934 made divulging or publishing the contents of any intercepted interstate or foreign wire or radio communications illegal. The Court ruled in successive cases of *Nordone v. United States* in 1937 and 1939 that any evidence resulting from warrant-less interceptions of electronic communications was impermissible in a criminal trial. The government interpreted this not as barring warrantless wiretaps but as barring their use as evidence in a criminal prosecution.

The Court ruled in *Silverman v. United States* (1961) that a conversation could be "seized" but that a warrant was required despite the fact that police did not enter the premise. In *Berger v. United States* (1967) in state cases, and in *Katz v. United States* (1967) in federal cases, the Court ruled that the Fourth Amendment's requirement of a judicial approval of a warrant applies to all communication where there exists a "reasonable expectation of privacy."

In the Omnibus Crime Control and Safe Streets Act of 1968, procedures were outlined that required that all intercepted communicators be approved by a judge based on probable cause that crimes were committed or about to be committed. In 1986 it was updated to include electronic mail, cellular phones, paging devices, and beepers, requiring Court approval based on probable cause when there exists a reasonable expectation of privacy.

NATIONAL SECURITY has been treated differently. Franklin ROOSEVELT ordered electronic surveillance without warrants for the defense of a nation. In addition, Justice White in the Katz case stated that no warrant should be required in cases of national security.

In *United States v. United States District Court* (1972), the Court ruled that warrant-less searches on domestic targets for purposes of internal security are unconstitutional. It recognized presidential claims but did not authorize warrantless searches for foreign intelligence.

From 1940 to 1978, the attorney general, without judicially sanctioned warrants, was authorized to approve presidential requests for electronic surveillance in national security matters.

The FOREIGN INTELLIGENCE SURVEILLANCE ACT (FISA; 1978) changed the rules by requiring that all electronic surveillance of targets in the United States for foreign intelligence be approved by the attorney general and by specially designated federal district judges. The attorney general, however, without judicial approval, may authorize electronic surveillance on targets not likely to involve Americans. FISA does not apply to electronic surveillance against intelligence targets outside the United States.

In the wake of the terrorist attack on September 11, 2001, Congress authorized the use of one warrant to cover multiple communication devices to reflect the contemporary communication patterns of people residing in the United States.

Electronic surveillance has evolved as property to be seized; however, very different rules have applied in the national security arena.

Further reading: Brown, William F., and Ameirco Cinquegrana. "Warrantless Physical Searches for Foreign Intelligence Purposes: Executive Order 12333 and the Fourth Amendment." *The Catholic Law Review* 35 (1985): 97; Lafave, Wayne R. *Search and Seizure: A Treatise on the Fourth Amendment,* 3d ed. St. Paul, Minn.: West Pub. Co., 1996.

—Frank M. Sorrentino

Emancipation Proclamation

Announced by Abraham LINCOLN on September 22, 1862, the Emancipation Proclamation declared that slaves in any state or part of a state that was in rebellion against the United States as of January 1, 1863, were "forever free." It also allowed for the enlistment of former slaves into the Union army and navy and committed the military to maintaining the freedom of the emancipated slaves.

The actual scope of emancipation was quite limited. Exempted were slave states that had remained loyal to the Union ("border states") and areas of the Confederacy already

under Union control. However, Lincoln's action had a significant effect on the course of the war. First, while emancipation did not effect areas already under Union control on January 1, 1863, it did apply to lands conquered after that date. Second, it also provided the Union with badly needed manpower. Third, it transformed the war from one merely to save the union to one to abolish slavery as well. This new moral cast in turn prevented the intervention of European powers on behalf of the Confederacy. Finally, it also accelerated the movement toward complete, national abolition.

Lincoln had approached emancipation cautiously, aware that Northern opposition was strong and that emancipation would strengthen Southern resolve to fight on while jeopardizing the loyalty of the border states. However, he eventually came to believe that emancipation was necessary in order to avert foreign intervention in the war, increase the recruitment of blacks into the army, and settle the slavery issue once and for all.

He spent the months after this decision waiting for a suitable Union victory after which he could announce the proclamation. During this time he began to lobby public opinion in support of emancipation through letters to major newspapers. Following the Union victory at Antietam, Lincoln officially signed and announced the policy. While well received by abolitionists, Republicans, and international opinion, the Proclamation was widely unpopular in the North. Democrats rallied in opposition to it, and in the November elections that year captured 35 Republican congressional seats, the state legislatures of three states, the governorship of two others, and generally improved their share of the vote by 5 percent.

Lincoln had based his proclamation on his power as COMMANDER IN CHIEF to suppress rebellion. Aware that the Proclamation rested on unsure constitutional footing, Lincoln strongly lobbied Congress for a constitutional amendment abolishing slavery, which he eventually signed (purely symbolically, as the president's signature is not necessary for CONSTITUTIONAL AMENDMENTS) in 1865.

Further reading: Donald, David Herbert. *Lincoln.* New York: Simon & Schuster, 1995; Paludan, Phillip Shaw. *The Presidency of Abraham Lincoln.* Lawrence: University of Kansas Press, 1994.

—Sean C. Matheson

Embargo Acts

A series of acts passed by the U.S. Congress between 1807 and 1809 halting trade with England and France, the embargo acts were passed with the full support of President Thomas JEFFERSON and were a response to British and French harassment of the U.S. merchant marine, caught in the cross fire of the war between France and England. The embargo originated primarily as a policy of protecting American citizens and ships from French and British plundering. Of especial concern was protecting American sailors from the detested British practice of impressment. However, over time, the embargo took on a coercive emphasis. Jefferson came to believe that the loss of American markets would be too great for the English and French to bear and that they would subsequently halt their offending actions. The first act was passed on Dec. 22, 1807, and four subsequent acts were passed expanding the scope of the embargo and tightening the rules for enforcement.

The embargo was a signal failure of Jefferson's presidency, as it achieved little of its desired ends. Neither the British nor the French were intimidated by the embargo, and the American people suffered considerable economic hardships. Enforcement of the embargo was particularly nettlesome. The potential profits of trade with England and France were too tempting to deter some Americans from evading the law and authorities. What is more, certain segments of the country, particularly New England, depended substantially on the ocean-carrying trade and were very reluctant to comply with a law that injured them disproportionately. The government's attempts to enforce the embargo by consolidating power in the presidency and violating the constitutional protections of the Fourth Amendment did little to stem evasions and did much to fuel resentment against the embargo and the government. In the face of widespread acknowledgment of the failure of the embargo and popular protests throughout the country, it was repealed in March 1809. Despite the widespread opposition to the embargo, and notwithstanding the excesses of the federal government in enforcing the embargo, Jefferson left office in 1809 revered and respected.

Further reading: Johnstone, Robert M., Jr. *Jefferson and the Presidency: Leadership in the Young Republic.* Ithaca, N.Y.: Cornell University Press, 1978; Spivak, Burton. *Jefferson's English Crisis: Commerce, Embargo, and the Republican Revolution.* Charlottesville: University Press of Virginia, 1979.

—Michael J. Korzi

Emergency Banking Act

The bank collapse that followed the depression of 1929 led Franklin D. ROOSEVELT to put forth two PROCLAMATIONS to summon Congress back into session, and to declare a "BANK HOLIDAY." When Congress reconvened it confronted emergency-banking legislation proposed by FDR. The Emergency Banking Act passed in 1933. It gave the president sweeping powers to deal with the bank crisis.

emergency powers

The Constitution makes no explicit reference to emergency powers of the presidency; however, presidents have made claims based on the preservation of the nation, prompting

the general welfare, or providing for the common good of the people.

The theory of emergency powers is also based on the concept of executive prerogative espoused by philosopher John Locke. Although a firm believer in a government of laws, Locke argued that in emergencies "the laws themselves . . . give way to the executive power, or rather to this fundamental law of nature and government . . . that as much as may be, all the members of society are to be preserved." This concept also supported by Jean-Jacques Rousseau, who stated: "It's advisable not to establish political institutions so strongly as to present a possibility of suspending their operations."

In the FEDERALIST PAPERS, both HAMILTON and MADISON argued that national preservation might be the cause for superseding constitutional restrictions. LINCOLN claimed that the presidential oath that required the president to "preserve, protect, and defend" the Constitution and uphold its provisions, along with the commander-in-chief clause, implies a grant of emergency powers.

Theodore ROOSEVELT argued that the presidency must advance the "public good." In his *Autobiography* (1913), Roosevelt developed the STEWARDSHIP THEORY, in which he advocated that it was not only the president's right "but his duty to do anything that the needs of the Nation demanded unless such action was forbidden by the constitution or by the laws."

In addition to these interpretations of the Constitution, there are statutory grants of power to the president from acts of Congress, which may be temporary or permanent. Furthermore, Congress may grant standby authority to the president and make them available with a formal declaration of the existence of a national emergency.

In wartime presidents have established several precedents of emergency powers. Lincoln, during the CIVIL WAR, unilaterally blockaded Southern ports, mobilized state militias, increased the size of the army and navy, supported those who established the state of West Virginia, authorized and appropriated funds for the purchases of ships and other war material. Lincoln did not call Congress into session but claimed his authority was based on the commander-in-chief clause. Congress ultimately approved Lincoln's actions retroactively.

Lincoln also suspended the writ of habeas corpus. In *Ex Parte Merryman,* Roger Taney ruled that Lincoln had unconstitutionally usurped Congress's authority to suspend the writ. Lincoln ignored the Courts. In addition, Lincoln used preemptive arrests and military courts to try civilians. In *EX PARTE MILLIGAN* (1866), the Supreme Court ruled that Lincoln's actions were unconstitutional; however, the Court acted after the war was over and Lincoln was dead.

During WORLD WAR I and WORLD WAR II, Woodrow WILSON and Franklin D. ROOSEVELT were granted broad statutory power to prosecute the war on both the military and economic fronts. It empowered the president to seize defense-related facilities, regulate food production, manufacturing, and mining, set prices, establish the Selective Service Act to raise an army, and pass the Espionage Act, which authorized the president to regulate and monitor communications.

Congress repeated these grants of authority to Roosevelt during WWII. Despite these generous grants of authority, both Wilson and Roosevelt extended their claims for voluntary press censorship. Roosevelt also claimed authority to ignore two Neutrality Acts passed by Congress. In addition, Roosevelt issued EXECUTIVE ORDERS for the internment of Japanese, Italian, and German Americans. The Courts did not challenge these claims of authority.

During the KOREAN WAR, however, TRUMAN was rebuffed when he ordered the seizure of the steel mills during a threatened strike. In YOUNGSTOWN SHEET AND TUBE CO. V. SAWYER (1952), the Court declared his actions unconstitutional because Congress considered and rejected that action in the passing of the TAFT-HARTLEY ACT of 1947.

The COLD WAR led many to worry that the emergency powers created the opportunity for abuse. In the aftermath of the VIETNAM WAR and WATERGATE, Congress attempted to reclaim its authority and to restrain the "imperial presidency." This resulted in the NATIONAL EMERGENCIES ACT of 1976, which officially terminated all states of emergencies and all presidential power emanating from these emergencies. It stated that when a president declares a national emergency, he must specify which standing authorities are being activated. Congress can override this action by a resolution that denies the emergency or the activation of statutory power. All non-overriding emergencies expire in one year unless the president gives 90 days notice to Congress. The act also mandates reporting and accounting requirements for each emergency declaration.

In 1977 Congress also revised the WWI Trading with the Enemy Act by limiting the president's use of economic controls during a presidential declared emergency. Emergency powers are an evolutionary concept dependent on the military, political, and economic climate of the nation.

Further reading: Fisher, Louis. *Presidential War Power.* Lawrence: University Press of Kansas, 1995; Franklin, Daniel. *Extraordinary Measures: The Exercise of Prerogative Powers in the United States.* Pittsburgh, Pa.: University of Pittsburgh Press, 1991.

—Frank M. Sorrentino

Employment Act of 1946

In the immediate postwar period, the U.S. government feared a return to the economic turmoil of the 1930s brought on by the potential for massive dislocation of workers following WORLD WAR II. Among the most important responses to these possibilities was a bill proposed by Senator James Murray (Dem.-Mont.), originally called the Full Employment Bill. Language in the original legislation would have given the federal government the authority to provide all Americans with significant employment opportunities commensurate with the notion that "all Americans . . . have the right to useful, remunerative, regular, and full time employment." Key to these provisions was the empowerment of the president to create a national production and employment budget, to be constructed by the BUREAU OF THE BUDGET. As such, the president was given, in the original legislation, the authority to provide the economic well-being of the nation, specifically through large employment projects.

The Murray Bill faced significant business opposition, though not on the idea that the national government should be given greater responsibility for regulating the economy. Instead, it was argued that "full" employment was neither desirable nor reachable. Ultimately, the term "full" was dropped from the bill, and the Employment Act of 1946 passed through Congress and was signed by President TRUMAN. The bill abandoned "full" employment and substituted language that called for maximum production, employment, and purchasing power.

Several institutional innovations accompanied the act. First, the president was charged with creating an Economic Report of the President, which would be written by a COUNCIL OF ECONOMIC ADVISERS (CEA), consisting largely of academic economists nominated by the president and confirmed by the Senate. Thus, as Eisner reports, the fact that the CEA would be at least partially responsible to Congress (as opposed to the BUREAU OF THE BUDGET [BOB], which was not) indicates that though there would be a new era of governmental direction of the economy, it would be shared with Congress and not governed by executive fiat. Additionally, the act created a Joint Economic Committee, further limiting the governing power of the president independent of Congress.

Nonetheless, the fact that Congress gave to the president a team of in-house economic advisers that would surely act in some coordinative capacity with the BOB meant that the executive would have enhanced symbolic and substantive power to regulate the direction of the macroeconomic policy. Presidents would be organizationally free to use the CEA as much or as little as they want, or to adopt Keynesian measures as they chose, contingent upon congressional cooperation.

Further reading: Eisner, Mark Allan. *The State in the American Political Economy: Public Policy and the Evolution of State-Economy Relations.* Englewood Cliffs, N.J.: Prentice Hall, 1995; Stein, Herbert. *Presidential Economics: The Making of Economic Policy from Roosevelt to Clinton,* 3d ed. Washington, D.C.: American Enterprise Institute for Public Policy Research, 1994.

—Daniel E. Ponder

Energy, Department of

The Department of Energy (DOE) was established in 1977 by the Department of Energy Organization Act. Creation of the DOE represented the third reorganization in the field of energy since the creation of the MANHATTAN PROJECT during WORLD WAR II. The Atomic Energy Act of 1946 replaced the Manhattan Project with the ATOMIC ENERGY COMMISSION (AEC), which absorbed the Manhattan Project's weapons development program and added nuclear energy production and nuclear medicine. Unable to respond effectively to the challenges of the environmental movement and apparent energy shortages (Grafton, 1983), the AEC was abolished in 1975 and replaced by the Energy Research and Development Administration (ERDA), which was given research and development responsibilities beyond nuclear power, and the Nuclear Regulatory Commission, which was responsible for safety regulation. The DOE absorbed ERDA along with the Federal Energy Administration, the Federal Power Commission, and energy-related programs scattered among other agencies.

Major DOE functions include conducting, coordinating, and funding basic and developmental research in energy production, including nuclear fission and fusion, coal liquefaction and gasification, solar, geothermal, and wind, as well as energy conservation. The DOE also continues nuclear weapons work begun in the Manhattan Project, although its current efforts are probably focused less on the development of new devices and more on maintaining an arsenal of aging weapons as well as supervising weapons destruction. In addition, it is developing techniques and locations for nuclear waste disposal.

Further reading: Duffy, Robert J. *Nuclear Politics in America.* Lawrence: University Press of Kansas, 1997; Grafton, Carl. "Response to Change: The Creation and Reorganization of Federal Agencies." In *Political Reform,* edited by R. Miewald and M. Steinman, 25–42. Chicago: Nelson-Hall, 1983.

—Carl Grafton

environmental policy

Presidential involvement in environmental policy-making is as old as the republic. It is useful to think about the evolution of environmental policy in the context of three broad eras. The first era runs from the Founding to the beginning of the last century (1789–1900). During this period national environmental policy primarily focused on the expansion of the country and the extraction of raw materials from newly conquered territory during the westward expansion. In the second era (roughly 1900 to the late 1960s) most environmental policy was focused on the conservation of public lands and, to a lesser degree, public resources. Since the late 1960s much of the environmental

policy agenda has centered on protecting and improving environmental quality. In each of these eras presidents have used their powers to advance or slow the development of policy within the constraint of the policy thrust of the era.

Presidents have two major roles in environmental policy: *policy formulation* and *policy implementation.* Policy formulation involves, first, the president in focusing public attention on a policy problem, defining the problem, and seeking to define the set of acceptable policy alternatives. Second, presidents make decisions about committing limited staff resources—both inside the White House and in the federal bureaucracies—to actual policy formulation. Finally, presidents must make decisions about how to allocate their personal political resources in mobilizing interest groups and marshaling public opinion in support of a chosen policy alternative. All of this is done within the context of competing policy initiatives on the president's broader policy agenda.

Presidential involvement in the generation of important environmental legislation is dependent on the public mood and the political style and policy interests of individual presidents. The 1970s is often referred to as the "environmental decade" due to the rise in public interest in environmental issues and the volume of important environmental legislation. Some find it ironic that this surge in environmental legislation in the 1970s took place under one of America's more conservative presidents, Richard NIXON. However, the rise in public attention to environmental issues made it difficult for President Nixon to oppose much of this legislation. Instead, he chose to support Democratic legislation and then claim credit for much of this legislation. As the public mood turned conservative in the 1980s another Republican, Ronald REAGAN, did not feel significant public pressure to advance environmental policies. Despite President CLINTON's stated commitment to environmental issues, few pieces of important legislation were passed during his administration. Continuing public conservatism combined with an opposition Republican Congress that was unfriendly to environmental concerns during most of his administration depressed important environmental legislation further.

Despite the conventional wisdom there is no evidence that Democratic presidents will be more focused and successful in pursuing environmental policy than will Republican presidents. On average, Democratic presidents between 1969 and 1998 signed about one piece (.90) of "important" environmental legislation for each year in office, while Republican presidents signed a little over one piece (1.23) of important environmental legislation per year in office.

As the CHIEF EXECUTIVE the president also controls, to some extent, how the federal bureaucracies will implement existing environmental policies. Congressional statutes generally provide presidents some discretion in the implementation of policy through the appointment of department heads and through EXECUTIVE ORDERS. In this way individual presidents can substantially influence environmental policy without formal legislation in the Congress.

President Reagan, who sought to weaken environmental regulation of business, appointed Anne Gorsuch to head the ENVIRONMENTAL PROTECTION AGENCY (EPA) and James Watt to head the DEPARTMENT OF INTERIOR. Both Gorsuch and Watt had long-standing differences with environmental advocates, and both sought to promote the president's agenda by changing how environmental statutes were implemented. President George W. BUSH appointed Christie Whitman to head the EPA during his first term, indicating that he would not substantially challenge the bureaucratic mission of the EPA.

Presidents can also use executive orders, which define for the BUREAUCRACY how statutes will be interpreted and enforced, to influence environmental policy. During the administration of Theodore ROOSEVELT Congress passed the Antiquities Act (1906), which allows the president "in his discretion, to declare by public proclamation historic landmarks" on public lands. Under the Clinton administration this law was interpreted as giving the president the authority to declare National Heritage Areas that would protect parts of public lands from mining and other sources of development. Though this outraged his conservative opponents, the federal courts upheld his authority to use the Antiquities Act in this manner. By "reinterpreting" existing statutes in this way presidents can often achieve goals that they could not achieve through statutory means, as in President Clinton's case, because they face an opposition Congress.

Further reading: Shanley, Robert A. *Presidential Influence and Environmental Policy.* Westport, Conn.: Greenwood Press, 1993; Soden, Dennis L. *The Environmental Presidency.* Albany, N.Y.: SUNY Press, 1999; Vig, Norman J. "Presidential Leadership and the Environment: From Reagan to Clinton." In *Environmental Policy,* 4th ed., edited by Norman J. Vig and Michael E. Kraft. Washington, D.C.: CQ Press, 2000.

—Sean Q. Kelly

Environmental Protection Agency (EPA)

The Environmental Protection Agency is the federal regulatory agency responsible for monitoring and implementing federal laws designed to protect the environment. Such issues as air, water, pesticide, waste, and toxic materials control come under its purview.

Created in 1970 under Reorganization Plan No. 3 during the NIXON administration, the EPA consolidated elements of five departments into a single agency responsible for environmental affairs. In 1992 during the CLINTON presidency, the EPA was granted cabinet-level status. The president appoints the EPA director, and appointees must be confirmed by the Senate.

During the Reagan administration, the EPA came under attack from Congress and environmental groups for underenforcing environmental protection laws. EPA administrator Anne Gorsuch, arguing that environmental rules and regulations had become too burdensome to business, failed to enforce existing laws, leading to her forced resignation.

Since its inception, the EPA has been mired in controversy. Seen as the bellwether of presidential intent, insiders closely monitor activities at the EPA to gain insight into the true nature of each administration. Some presidents, Clinton, for example, aggressively use the EPA as a tool to gain increased control over pollution. Other presidents, REAGAN and George W. BUSH, for example, are less interested in pollution control, allowing business interests to dominate policy at the EPA.

Era of Good Feeling

In the early 1800s, party conflict in the United States began to wane. The two existing parties, the Federalists and the Democratic Republicans, were engaged in party combat, but this declined when John ADAMS, the last Federalist president, left office in 1801. The Democratic Republicans began to dominate presidential elections, culminating in James Monroe's crushing defeat of Daniel Tompkins in 1816, coupled with the emerging Democratic-Republican control of Congress.

Though cracks in the existing partisan universe had been growing for some time, it was the WAR OF 1812 that marked the beginning of the end for the Federalists. Most Federalists opposed war with England, while Democratic Republicans did not. Most dramatic was the Federalists' participation in the Hartford Convention, called by New England Federalists in 1814 to vet their growing problems with the national government, which most directly grew out of their opposition to the war. It was at this convention that the possibility of seceding from the union was discussed, though rejected. Still, the Hartford Convention was seen by most Americans as being not only antiwar but anti-American. Any remaining support for the Federalists as a national party vanished virtually overnight, leaving Congress effectively a one-party legislature by 1815. Monroe's victory in the presidential election of 1816 marked the death-knell of the Federalists, leaving the whole of national politics a one-party affair, with MONROE winning reelection in 1820 virtually without opposition.

The term "era of good feeling" is somewhat of a misnomer, however. The mere fact that the period between 1815 and 1824 is seen as largely bereft of partisan conflict does not mean that it was free of political conflict. The recession of the Federalists portended a rise of a politics that was factional rather than partisan. Issues such as foreign policy declined in significance while issues such as slavery, which divided the country deeply along geographic as well as ideological lines, became the major focus of political unrest. The task of party leaders such as Henry CLAY and Martin VAN BUREN was to try to assemble governing coalitions that were strong enough to resist centrifugal forces of regionalism that threatened to explode the tenuous coalition on which the politics of the time were built. Ultimately, they were successful, but the underlying tensions remained just below the surface and constantly threatened to blow apart the fragile coalition that held the Democratic Republicans together.

The Era of Good Feeling found its demise in the presidential election of 1824, when Andrew JACKSON won the popular vote but failed to win an absolute majority of electoral votes, while John Quincy ADAMS came in second. The election was thrown into the House of Representatives, where Henry Clay threw his support to Adams. Clay, who had been a staunch political enemy of Adams, was given the post of secretary of state, a post which in that time was seen as being next in line for his party's nomination for the presidency. Supporters of Jackson were outraged at the "corrupt bargain" and formed a new party. Led by Martin Van Buren, a new party system was built around the supporters of Jackson (the origins of the DEMOCRATIC PARTY) and wrested the presidency from Adams in 1828. Thus began a new era of party competition in American politics.

Further reading: Hofstadter, Richard. *The Idea of a Part System: The Rise of Legitimate Opposition in the United States, 1780–1840.* Berkeley: University of California Press, 1969, 183–188; Kolodny, Robin. "The Several Elections of 1824." *Congress and the Presidency* 23 (Fall 1996): 139–164; Stewart, Charles, III. *Analyzing Congress.* New York: W. W. Norton, 2001, 96–98.

—Daniel E. Ponder

Ethics in Government Act of 1978

Congress passed the Ethics in Government Act of 1978, containing a provision for an independent prosecutor, after considerable debate over how best to provide a mechanism that would make such an official available, when necessary, to investigate high-level EXECUTIVE BRANCH wrongdoing when there might be a real or apparent conflict of interest by Justice Department officials who would normally be charged with investigating misdeeds. The need for such an official arose out of the legacy of WATERGATE, where a special prosecutor had been appointed by the attorney general to investigate possible crimes by presidential aides and the president but was summarily fired by an order from President NIXON, thus undermining any "independence" of the

position. That background framed the subsequent debate in Congress over how to fashion an independent prosecutor in a way that would avoid the pitfalls of Watergate.

The provisions in the 1978 law outlined the selection process, responsibilities, jurisdiction, tenure, and termination procedures for the special prosecutor (later renamed INDEPENDENT COUNSEL). Selection would be by a panel of three judges (Special Division) appointed by the Chief Justice of the United States, upon completion of a preliminary investigation by the attorney general where such inquiry yielded the conclusion that further investigation was warranted. The attorney general could remove the special prosecutor "only for extraordinary impropriety, physical disability, mental incapacity, or any other condition that substantially impairs the performance of such special prosecutor's duties," and such removal would be subject to judicial review. Termination of the official would occur when the special prosecutor notified the attorney general that the investigation was complete and a report was filed, or when the panel of judges determined that the inquiry had ended.

The act called for reauthorization for no more than five years at a time, which occurred in 1983, 1987, and 1994. Twenty investigations had been conducted under the act by the time it was due for its fourth reauthorization in 1999, but public dissatisfaction was so widespread by that point that it seemed likely that Congress would let the statute lapse. Many of the investigations created their own sensationalism, monopolized public attention for long periods of time, cost millions of dollars, escalated partisan tensions, and hounded their targets, often without yielding convictions and, thus, ruining reputations. The most expensive and most high-profile inquiries were the 1987 Iran-contra investigation of REAGAN administration officials, headed by Lawrence Walsh, and the inquiry begun in 1994 by Kenneth Starr to look into the prepresidential Whitewater real estate dealings of President CLINTON but which expanded in January 1998 to include the probe into Clinton's relationship with Monica Lewinsky and the possible charges of perjury and obstruction of justice associated with it.

The life of the Ethics in Government statute was a tumultuous one, in large part, because it made possible the targeting of executive branch officials on a low level of evidence. Challenges arose to its constitutionality by those who were subjected to it. In 1988 the Supreme Court considered a challenge to the law by Theodore Olsen, a Justice Department official at the time. In an unmistakable 8-1 decision (Scalia dissenting), Chief Justice Rehnquist's opinion for the Court in *Morrison v. Olsen* was a ringing endorsement of the law, upholding it against charges of violation of SEPARATION OF POWERS. Scalia's lone dissent, decrying the statute's interference with EXECUTIVE POWER and warning of the "vast power and the immense discretion that are placed in the hands of a prosecutor," turned out to be, in hindsight, a very prescient and, ultimately, accurate characterization. The law was not renewed after its 1999 lapse, and it ended with the submission of the final report of Kenneth Starr's inquiry of Clinton.

Further reading: Dole, Robert, and George J. Mitchell. *Report and Recommendations: Project on the Independent Counsel Statute.* Washington, D.C.: American Enterprise Institute and Brookings Institution, 1999; Fisher, Louis. *The Politics of Shared Power: Congress and the Executive,* 4th ed. College Station, Tex.: Texas A & M University Press, 1998, 136–142; Fisher, Louise. "The Independent Counsel Statute." In *The Clinton Scandal and the Future of American Government,* edited by Mark J. Rozell and Clyde Wilcox, 60–80. Washington, D.C.: Georgetown University Press, 2000; Harriger, Katy J. *The Special Prosecutor in American Politics,* 2d rev. ed. Lawrence: University Press of Kansas, 2000; "The President and the Independent Counsel: Reflections on Prosecutors, Presidential Prerogatives, and Political Power." *Presidential Studies Quarterly* 31, no. 2 (June 2001): 338–348.

—Nancy Kassop

executive agreements

An executive agreement is a concord or pact made by the president or his representatives with a foreign government or leader. Executive agreements are a powerful tool for the president because, unlike treaties, they do not require the ADVICE AND CONSENT of the Senate. However, many executive agreements require some expenditure of money and thus would require congressional authorization. Executive agreements give the president maximum flexibility, and as the United States has grown in power and as the international environment has become more globalized and interdependent the executive agreement has become the major vehicle for international agreements.

The authority for executive agreements is unclear—it may stem from the EXECUTIVE POWER clause, COMMANDER IN CHIEF clause, and/or from a statute or treaty. Executive agreements are not mentioned specifically in the Constitution as a presidential power, nor are they prohibited.

The framers of the Constitution created a system of CHECKS AND BALANCES in which all major decisions and commitments of the United States would have direct congressional involvement in the decision-making process. In *UNITED STATES V. CURTISS-WRIGHT* (1936), the Supreme Court seemed to put forward an almost limitless power of the national government in the field of FOREIGN AFFAIRS with the president as its chief agent. Justice Sutherland argued that the Constitution divided powers, that at the time of the American Revolution the individual colonies exercised domestic authority individually and could delegate it piecemeal. However, foreign and military authority

was in the purview of the British crown, then of the Continental Congress and finally the new constitutional government. The states never had these powers. In this theory, neither the national government nor the president is much hampered by the Constitution. The President has essentially the foreign policy authority of an 18th-century British monarch. This case suggests a theory of INHERENT POWERS or is similar to John Locke's PREROGATIVE POWERS.

The Court's decision in *United States v. Belmont* (1936) was extremely relevant. The case decided the president's authority to conclude unilaterally executive agreements connected to the 1933 recognition of the Soviet Union. Justice Sutherland stated, "Government power over external affairs is not distributed, but is vested exclusively in the national government and in respect to what was done here, the Executive had the authority to speak as the sole organ of that government." The Court concluded that executive agreements were the legal equivalent of treaties.

Executive agreements have a long history. Thomas JEFFERSON purchased the Louisiana territory in this manner. President MONROE negotiated the Rush-Bagot agreement (1817) with Great Britain, which limited naval forces in the Great Lakes. President TYLER annexed Texas by executive agreement because it probably would have been defeated by the treaty process. In 1898 MCKINLEY annexed Hawaii as a territory by the same process. Franklin ROOSEVELT utilized executive agreements to avoid the treaty process when he provided destroyers to Britain in exchange for British bases despite the fact that there were two neutrality statutes and that he thus altered the neutral status of the United States.

Congress unsuccessfully attempted to limit executive agreements with the Buche Amendment in 1953, which aimed at establishing congressional review of executive agreements and making them unenforceable as domestic law without accompanying legislation.

In 1972 Congress passed the CASE ACT, which requires transmittal of all executive agreements to the Congress and provides for submission of secret agreements to the relevant Senate and House Committees for purposes of confidentiality.

—Frank Sorrentino

executive branch

The departments and agencies of the federal government are part of the executive branch under the powers of the president as the nation's chief executive. While the "executive branch" is not mentioned in the Constitution, over time the size of the federal BUREAUCRACY has grown to the point where today, it is quite difficult to manage.

The job of CHIEF EXECUTIVE of the executive branch is performed by the president. Article II, Section 1, of the

Constitution: "The executive power shall be vested in a president. . . ." Article II, Section 3, says the president "shall take care that the Laws be faithfully executed. . . ." Thus the president is the chief executive officer with powers, duties, and responsibilities, some of which are shared with Congress.

executive departments See EXECUTIVE BRANCH.

Executive Office Building, Eisenhower (EEOB)

The OLD EXECUTIVE OFFICE BUILDING (OEOB), formerly known as the Old State, War, and Navy Building and now known as the Eisenhower Executive Office Building (EEOB), houses the nerve center of the EXECUTIVE BRANCH. The EEOB is next door to the White House. During the first BUSH administration's War on Terrorism, the EEOB housed the Coalition Information Center (CIC). The Bush White House used the CIC to coordinate the multiple flows of information from its allies and agencies and departments within the executive branch. The building was designed by Supervising Architect of the Treasury Alfred B. Mullett and was completed in 1888. It was created to house the growing staffs of the State, War, and Navy Departments. Built with flamboyant style during the post–CIVIL WAR resurgence, the EEOB is considered one of the finest examples of Second Empire French architecture. In 1930 the Navy vacated the State, War, and Navy Building, and it was renamed the Department of State Building. It was here (in Room 208) that Secretary of State Cordell Hull confronted Japanese envoys with evidence from the bombing of Pearl Harbor. In 1947 the STATE DEPARTMENT moved out, and in 1949 the building was renamed the Executive Office Building. The building became a historic landmark in 1971.

—Diane Heith

Executive Office of the President (EOP)

The Executive Office of the President is the institutional home for a variety of agencies that serve the president. Some of them are central to the exercise of presidential power, such as the WHITE HOUSE OFFICE, NATIONAL SECURITY COUNCIL, and OFFICE OF MANAGEMENT AND BUDGET. Some of them are primarily advisory to the president, such as the COUNCIL OF ECONOMIC ADVISERS and the OFFICE OF SCIENCE AND TECHNOLOGY POLICY. Some symbolize presidential priorities, such as the Office of National Drug Control Policy and the Council on Environmental Quality. The EOP functions more as a holding company than it does as a coherent organization. All of the units report to the president, and there is no central organizational control of the EOP short of the president.

For the first 150 years of the United States government the president did not have a large institutional capacity separate from the EXECUTIVE BRANCH of government, which contains the major departments and agencies of the government. The president himself did not have much personal professional assistance provided by the government; it was only in 1857 that the president was provided funds from Congress to hire a private secretary, and in 1929 governmental funding was provided for two more secretaries and an administrative assistant. That was to change with the coming of the NEW DEAL and the growth of government in the 1930s to deal with the GREAT DEPRESSION.

In response to governmental growth the 1937 BROWNLOW COMMITTEE's Report made proposals for strengthening the administrative capacity of the president to manage the executive branch, but it was not until 1939 that Congress granted the president limited reorganization authority, and Franklin D. ROOSEVELT used it to establish the Executive Office of the President. This was to lay the groundwork for the INSTITUTIONAL PRESIDENCY that grew to such broad scope and size in the second half of the 20th century. The president's organizational establishment grew to such size and importance that it was dubbed by some "the presidential branch" in contrast to "the executive branch."

The original units within the new EOP included the WHITE HOUSE OFFICE (the president's personal staff), the National Resources Planning Board, the Office of Government Reports, and the Liaison Office for Personnel Management. In addition, the BUREAU OF THE BUDGET, which had been created by the BUDGET AND ACCOUNTING ACT OF 1921, was transferred from the Department of the TREASURY to the newly created EOP. Since that time, more than 50 other units have been added to the EOP, most of them for short periods of time before they were abolished or transferred to other executive branch organizations.

The EOP now contains several major units that perform central functions of control and coordination for the president in the direction of the executive branch; others primarily provide advice and do not have independent power or staff to prevail over departments and agencies in the executive branch. Some units have come in and out of the EOP for temporary or symbolic purposes; they may play key roles for a few years but atrophy when a new president does not seek their advice. Since 1939 there have been about 50 units that have come and gone. At the beginning of the 21st century, there were about a dozen units.

First and foremost among the EOP offices is the White House Office, which contains the aides closest to the president and whose staff has numbered between 400 and 500 during the 1990s. The White House Office contains the president's top NATIONAL SECURITY, DOMESTIC POLICY, economic, and legal advisers. It also contains the major offices for outreach and communications, including the press secretary, speechwriters, public liaison specialists, intergovernmental affairs and political staffers, and the legislative liaison people. The White House Office also houses those staffers who conduct internal coordination for the presidency: the CHIEF OF STAFF, staff secretary, CABINET affairs, and scheduling. Finally, the Office of Management and Administration is split between the White House Office and the EOP.

Second to the White House Office in power, but first in size and institutional memory is the OFFICE OF MANAGEMENT AND BUDGET (OMB), which was created in 1970 when the name of the Bureau of the Budget was changed. The OMB has a full staff of about 500, most of them career civil servants. The agency is headed by a director and deputy who must be Senate confirmed (since 1974) and a politically appointed leadership of between 30 and 40. The main functions of the OMB include preparing the president's budget by refining agency requests and integrating them into the president's agenda before the budget proposal goes to Congress for consideration. The OMB budget examiners are experts in the budgetary issues in each department and agency in the executive branch and play an oversight and control function. The OMB also conducts "central legislative clearance" by examining all legislative requests from executive branch agencies before they go to Congress. OMB staffers often provide the institutional memory and administrative expertise to authoritatively advise the White House staff about the implementation implications of new policy proposals.

The NATIONAL SECURITY COUNCIL (NSC) staff is also central to each presidency. The NSC was created by the NATIONAL SECURITY ACT of 1947, and its official members include the president, vice president, the secretary of State, and secretary of Defense (with advice from the chairman of the JOINT CHIEFS OF STAFF and the director of the CENTRAL INTELLIGENCE AGENCY). The function of the NSC is to "advise the president with respect to the integration of domestic, foreign, and military policies relating to the national security." Most of the work of the NSC is carried out by its staff under the direction of the assistant to the president for national security affairs (often referred to as the NATIONAL SECURITY ADVISER). The National Security adviser and several of the top aides are in the White House Office, but the bulk of the staff are officially in the EOP, separate from the White House Office. (The reason for this split is that presidents do not want it to appear that they have large staffs, so only the top advisers are in the White House Office; the rest are in the EOP.)

The role of the NSC in coordinating national security policy has remained consistent across administrations, but how it exercises its power varies depending on the president. The NSC staff was quite small in the 1950s and 1960s but grew substantially in the 1970s when President NIXON used it for his major foreign policy initiatives, often at the expense of the STATE DEPARTMENT. Others, such as President George H. W. BUSH, used the NSC staff to coordinate but not to dominate national security policy making.

Because of the growing centralization of policy initiation and advice from the departments to the White House, the Domestic Policy Council was created by President Nixon in 1970. Nixon distrusted the departments and agencies and wanted to have his own capacity to develop policy and not have to depend on the career staffs in the executive branch. The staff of the council was about 70 people in the 1970s. The name of the Domestic Policy Council was changed to the Domestic Policy Staff in 1977 and the OFFICE OF POLICY DEVELOPMENT in 1981. Regardless of the name, the major DOMESTIC POLICY ADVISERS to the president have been located in the EOP since 1970.

Many cabinet departments and agencies play roles in U.S. trade with foreign nations, and the EOP's Office of U.S. Trade Representative, with about 200 staffers, coordinates broad governmental policies concerning international commerce. The COUNCIL OF ECONOMIC ADVISERS (CEA), with a staff of several dozen, prepares the president's economic report and advises the president on ECONOMIC POLICY. The Office of National Drug Control Policy (ONDCP) helps coordinate executive branch efforts to curb the sale and consumption of illegal drugs in the United States.

Other EOP units primarily provide advice to the president in their specialized areas of expertise, such as the Office of Science and Technology Policy (OSTP), the Council on Environmental Quality (CEQ), and the National Critical Materials Council. The OFFICE OF ADMINISTRATION provides administrative support for the EOP, including personnel services, physical space, and technology support.

Over the years, presidents have placed offices in the EOP that later were abolished or transferred to departments in the executive branch, for instance, the Office of Economic Opportunity (1964–75), the National Council on the Arts (1964–65), the Council on Wage and Price Stability (1974–81), the Office of Telecommunications Policy (1970–77), and the Office of Consumer Affairs (1971–73).

The EOP fills the function of a holding company for organizational units that are central to the presidency, but those units vary widely in their power and centrality to the president. Clearly the White House Office, OMB, and NSC are central to the core functions of the presidency. Other units provide useful advice, e.g., CEA and OSTP; and yet other units are placed in the EOP for symbolic and political reasons, e.g., CEQ and ONDCP. In the future it is likely that the EOP will house new units that will become central to all presidents, and that the EOP will also provide a useful organizational location for other units of temporary importance.

The Units in the EOP and Year Established

White House Office (1939)
Office of Management and Budget (1939, 1970)
Council of Economic Advisers (1946)
National Security Council (1949)
Council on Environmental Quality (1970)
Office of Science and Technology Policy (1976)
Office of Administration (1977)
U.S. Trade Representative (1979)
National Critical Materials Council (1984)
Office of National Drug Control Policy (1988)
National Space Council (1988)
Office of Faith-Based and Community Initiatives (2001)
Office of Homeland Security (2001)

—James P. Pfiffner

executive orders

An executive order is a directive, or order, issued by the president of the United States. Its purpose is to assist the president in his capacity as CHIEF EXECUTIVE of the nation. Originally, the executive order was intended for rather minor administrative and rule-making functions, to help the nation's chief administrative officer administer the laws of the nation more efficiently and effectively. However, over time, the executive order has become an important and sometimes controversial tool for the president to make policy without the consent of Congress as required by the Constitution.

As the nation's chief executive, the president bears significant administrative and managerial responsibilities. It is his job to "take Care that the Laws be faithfully executed" (Article II, Section 3, of the United States Constitution). Article II of the Constitution (Section 1) states that "The executive Power shall be vested in the President. . . ." In order to do his job, a president needs the power and authority to issue administrative orders and instruction. The executive order is an implied power, not specifically mentioned in the Constitution, but deemed essential for the functioning of government. Thus, presidents rely on executive orders to better fulfill their constitutional duties as chief executive. In fact, every constitutional democracy has some form of executive order, even if it is not named as such.

When Congress writes a law, it cannot cover every contingency or account for every aspect of implementation. Laws, in short, are not self-executing. Executive orders allow a president to fill in the missing pieces, or design administrative rules and regulations that govern the implementation of laws. Executive orders generally have the force of law. The courts have, for the most part, recognized and legitimized executive orders as legally binding.

George WASHINGTON issued the first executive order on June 8, 1798. It instructed heads of departments (CABINET officers) to make a "clear account" of matters in their departments. Under the national ADMINISTRATIVE PROCEDURE ACT of 1946, all executive orders must be published in the *Federal Register*. Congress, if it wishes, can overturn an executive order. Executive orders can also be challenged in court on grounds that they may violate the Constitution.

Over time, presidents have gone beyond the use of executive orders for merely administrative matters, and have begun to use orders to "make law" on more substantive and controversial matters. Increasingly, presidents have turned to administrative techniques such as executive orders in an effort to bypass the slow and frustrating process of going through Congress to pass legislation. Thus, presidents use orders along with PROCLAMATIONS, memoranda, findings, directives, and signing statements, to boost their administrative reach over policy. Such efforts to bypass Congress sometimes overstep the bounds of what is an appropriate use of administrative tools of the office. Presidents have been accused, with some justification, of "going around" Congress and "legislating" independent of Congress.

Presidents have used executive orders to implement some very controversial policies. In 1942, during WORLD WAR II, FDR interned Japanese-American citizens in detention centers. In 1948 Harry S TRUMAN integrated the military. In 1952 Truman attempted to seize control of steel mills. And in 1992 Bill CLINTON directed the Coast Guard to return Haitian refugees found at sea to Haiti. In 2001 President George W. BUSH issued a series of orders aimed at undermining terrorist organizations in the United States and abroad. All these acts were done through executive orders.

Many of these presidential efforts have been challenged in the courts. And while in general the courts have recognized the legitimacy and legality of executive orders, not all orders pass the test of constitutionality. In 1952, for example, during the KOREAN WAR, President Truman seized the nation's steel mills to prevent a work stoppage that might have negatively affected the war effort. The Supreme Court, in *YOUNGSTOWN SHEET AND TUBE CO. V. SAWYER*, decided that the president's actions were unconstitutional. Truman was forced to back down, but such limitations are the exception. Overall, presidents have been able to take control of a variety of significant policy areas through the use of administrative tools such as the executive order. They have become an important weapon in the president's arsenal and are likely to remain so into the future.

executive power

The president's executive power stems from two constitutional provisions: Article II, Section 1, states that "the executive power shall be vested in a President," and Article II, Section 3, empowers the president to "take care that the Laws be faithfully executed."

With the growth in size and power of the federal government, and with the corresponding growth of presidential power along with the size and scope of the EXECUTIVE BRANCH of government, came an increase in the executive power of the presidency. While controversial, this trend toward a more powerful executive has been hard to resist. Even with abuses of power such as the WATERGATE and IRAN-CONTRA scandals, it has been hard to scale back the powers of the presidency.

executive privilege

Executive privilege is not explicitly stated in the Constitution. It derives from the concept of SEPARATION OF POWERS, which provides each branch of government a degree of independence from the others. Executive privilege is the right of the president to withhold information from the Congress and from the courts.

The principal arguments in favor of this privilege are confidentiality and NATIONAL SECURITY. A president and his advisers need to discuss freely the various viewpoints and options in the development of public policy. These discussions need to be freewheeling and robust. Unpopular and controversial views are necessary for discussion but would be threatened if aides knew that their positions would be revealed without context. Confidentiality thus assures the president that he can operate independently and effectively in the political system.

National security by its nature requires secrecy and confidentiality, particularly when negotiating with foreign nations. Thus, executive privilege permits the president and the nation to have an effective foreign policy, which protects the interests of the nation.

There are, however, the needs of the other two branches of government. Congress has its own responsibilities with regard to legislation, budget, and the OVERSIGHT of executive departments. Can a committee investigating fraud, malfeasance, or incompetence in a federal agency request testimony and papers from the executive to implement their constitutional responsibilities? In addition, Congress also has important constitutional responsibilities with regard to national security, including declaring war, raising armies and navies, and ratifying treaties.

The courts also have important responsibilities with regard to fair trial and due process. Criminal procedure requires that the courts determine which information is needed for the prosecution and the defense in criminal trials.

The term executive privilege is of recent vintage but its practice dates back to George WASHINGTON, who refused to provide the House of Representatives with the working papers developed during the negotiations of the Jay Treaty and with regard to General Arthur St. Clair's failed expedition against the Indians. President EISENHOWER enlarged the concept of executive privilege particularly by refusing the demands of Sen. Joseph MCCARTHY's investigation of communism in the EXECUTIVE BRANCH.

The history of executive privilege generally followed a negotiated approach among the three branches until the Nixon administration. At one point, Attorney General Richard Kleindienst asserted that every employee and communication of the executive branch was covered by this privilege.

During the WATERGATE scandal, Richard NIXON was accused of covering up any connections to the White House of those individuals who were arrested during the burglary of the Democratic National Committee Headquarters. When it was revealed that a taping system recorded all conversations in the White House, both the courts and Congress moved to subpoena the tapes. Nixon argued that "[n]o President could function if the private papers of his office, prepared by his personal staff were open to public scrutiny." In addition, he further argued that if a president were personally subject to the orders of a court it would effectively destroy the status of the executive branch of government as an equal and coordinate element of government.

In UNITED STATES V. NIXON (1974), the Supreme Court unanimously rejected Nixon's claims of absolute executive privilege and ordered Nixon to turn over 64 tapes to a federal trial judge. The Court ruled that the prosecution and defense attorneys' need for compulsory means to obtain information, including the use of the subpoena to force persons to present vital information, overrides the executive's use of privilege. Lawyers, however, must persuade the trial judge that the information requested is relevant and cannot be found elsewhere. The judge makes an in camera (in chambers) inspection to determine if the information is relevant and thus released. Executive privilege is, therefore, not absolute but needs to be balanced against competing interests of the other branches of government.

Executive privilege issues and Congress are less resolved. The courts have never determined the constitutional limits of executive privilege to deny Congress information, preferring to allow the political process to resolve each dispute.

During the IRAN-CONTRA AFFAIR in 1986, President REAGAN waived all executive privilege and even allowed two former NATIONAL SECURITY ADVISERS to testify before Congress.

Executive privilege and national security remains more problematical. In the Nixon case, the Supreme Court supported claims of executive privilege where there was "a claim of need to protect military, diplomats or sensitive

National Security secrets." The Court believed that even an in camera review by a federal judge was unwise and an inclusion into political matters in which the courts are ill suited. The courts, however, have continued to urge the Congress and the president to negotiate in the field of national security, acknowledging each branch has primary responsibility in this area.

President CLINTON caused some important subsidiary issues with regard to executive privilege. The first was whether the Secret Service personnel guarding the president could be required to testify in a criminal proceeding. The District Court judge ruled that no such privilege exists in law or practice and furthermore, the SECRET SERVICE can not make a request of privilege; it must come from the president. The second issue is whether White House attorneys have a lawyer-client privilege relationship with the president. The courts ruled that White House attorneys are employed by the government and are counsels to the Office of the President and not the president personally, and thus no lawyer-client privilege exists.

Executive privilege remains an important and relevant dimension of the presidency. It is, however, not an absolute concept and works best when the needs and constitutional responsibilities of all three branches are recognized and respected.

Further reading: Berger, Raoul. *Executive Privilege: A Constitutional Myth.* Cambridge, Mass.: Harvard University Press, 1974; Rozell, Mark J. *Executive Privilege: The Dilemma of Secrecy and Democratic Accountability.* Baltimore, Md.: Johns Hopkins University Press, 1994.

—Frank M. Sorrentino

Ex parte Milligan, 71 U.S. (4 Wall.) 2 (1866)

This Supreme Court decision ruled that the military arrest, detention, and trial of a civilian outside of the theater of war was unconstitutional. During the CIVIL WAR, President Abraham LINCOLN unilaterally assumed extraordinary powers to prosecute the conflict. These powers included, among other things, the subjection of Rebel sympathizers to MARTIAL LAW. While the majority of the broad powers exercised by Lincoln were later retroactively ratified by Congress, his placement of civilians under the jurisdiction of military courts was never authorized by the legislature and at the time of his actions may have been contrary to federal law.

Lambdin P. Milligan was an Indiana resident and Confederate sympathizer who conspired to raid Midwestern prisons and free Southern prisoners of war. In 1864 Milligan was arrested and imprisoned by federal troops and in 1865 was sentenced to death. He petitioned a federal court to be discharged from prison, arguing that as a civilian living outside the theater of war he could not be lawfully arrested and confined by military authorities.

The Supreme Court ruled in favor of Milligan and concluded that the military tribunals established by Lincoln existed outside of the lawfully established judicial power. The Court reasoned that the power of the military authorities, insofar as they had jurisdiction over civilians, was limited to the theater of war. As long as the civilian courts were in operation, the Court reasoned, no civilian should have to appear as a defendant before a military tribunal. Since Indiana fell outside of the theater of war, the Court concluded that Milligan's trial and sentence were unlawful and that consequently he should be discharged.

Although all members of the Court agreed that the president could not unilaterally take the steps that Lincoln did, five justices concluded that subjection of civilians to military courts outside of the war zone could not be authorized, even by Congress. Chief Justice Salmon CHASE, along with three other justices, strongly disagreed with the majority's reasoning. The minority expressed concern that by gratuitously adding that Congress could not authorize expanded jurisdiction for such tribunals, the Court might be overly limiting the powers of government to meet future exigencies.

Milligan is in many respects the counterpoint to THE PRIZE CASES in Civil War jurisprudence. Unlike the latter decision, which was decided amid the clash of arms, *Milligan* was decided after hostilities had been concluded. With peace reestablished, the Court once again turned its attention to CIVIL LIBERTIES. Unfortunately, the *Milligan* precedent has not been uniformly applied in upholding the rights of citizens during wartime, as the Japanese internment cases during World War II illustrate. Nor has it been held to apply to enemy belligerents committing acts of war against the United States, as demonstrated in *Ex parte Quirin.* Nonetheless, *Milligan* was cited favorably in a Supreme Court decision following WORLD WAR II that struck down martial law in Hawaii and the decision remains good law today. The likelihood, however, of future courts applying it *during wartime* in defense of civil liberties against exercises of presidential power remains in question.

Further reading: Randall, J. G. *Constitutional Problems under Lincoln.* Urbana: University of Illinois Press, 1951; Rehnquist, William H. *All the Laws But One.* New York: Knopf, 1998; Rossiter, Clinton, and Richard P. Longaker. *The Supreme Court and the Commander in Chief.* Ithaca, N.Y.: Cornell University Press, 1976.

—Roy E. Brownell II

F

Fairbanks, Charles W. (1852–1918) *U.S. vice president*

The 26th vice president of the United States (1905–09) under Theodore ROOSEVELT, Fairbanks was an accomplished and influential public figure in the vice presidency. While Roosevelt and Fairbanks did not always see eye to eye on matters, Fairbanks remained a prominent public figure throughout his career. Part of the difficulty between Roosevelt and Fairbanks stemmed from the thwarted plan by Fairbanks to run for president after President MCKINLEY served out his term. McKinley's assassination elevated Vice President Roosevelt to the presidency, and the hopes and dreams of Fairbanks were put on hold and eventually ended in frustration. Roosevelt did not like or trust Fairbanks and only selected him as vice president to satisfy the conservative wing of the REPUBLICAN PARTY. As vice president, Fairbanks remained a darling of the conservatives but an outsider in the administration. In 1908 Fairbanks sought the Republican nomination for the presidency but was defeated by William Howard TAFT, who eventually won the office. Fairbanks again sought the party's presidential nomination in 1916 but again was unsuccessful.

Fair Deal

In his January 5, 1949, STATE OF THE UNION message, President Harry S Truman referred to his major domestic policy proposals collectively as the "Fair Deal." The Fair Deal included a civil rights bill that sought the elimination of racial discrimination in jobs, housing, voting rights, and access to education and public facilities, a new formula for farm subsidies known as the Brannan Plan, repeal of the TAFT-HARTLEY ACT concerning the federal regulation of labor unions, federal aid to elementary and secondary education, federal aid and guidance for housing construction and slum clearance, expansion of SOCIAL SECURITY coverage, and a comprehensive national health insurance program. Truman had proposed similar policies in the "21 Point

Charles Warren Fairbanks *(Library of Congress)*

Program" that he submitted to Congress on September 6, 1945. Truman's first civil rights bill, more modest and limited than his Fair Deal proposal, died in Congress in 1947. The Taft-Hartley Act of 1947 became law after Congress overrode his veto of it. Truman's vigorously repeated promise to labor leaders and union members to seek repeal of this law mobilized enthusiastic electoral and financial support from labor unions for Truman and the Democrats in the 1948 presidential and congressional elections. Likewise, Truman's issuance of an EXECUTIVE ORDER in 1948 to desegregate the military and his promise to AFRICAN AMERICANS to submit a stronger civil rights bill to Congress also helped Truman to win his upset victory in the 1948 presidential election and the Democrats to win control of Congress.

Truman emphasized that the Fair Deal was not merely a continuation of the NEW DEAL. Whereas the New Deal represented immediate federal intervention to an economic crisis, the Fair Deal used the New Deal as its ideological and programmatic foundation in order to make steady progress in improving the quality of domestic policies during a relatively prosperous, stable economic period. Some scholars have identified this difference as that between the New Deal's quantitative liberalism and the Fair Deal's qualitative liberalism.

Unfortunately for Truman and other Fair Dealers, the bipartisan conservative coalition of Republicans and southern Democrats in Congress defeated most Fair Deal proposals. The Housing Act of 1949, a heavily compromised, limited product of Truman's original proposal, was the only major Fair Deal bill to be enacted. Congress quickly and easily rejected the Fair Deal's most controversial legislation, namely, Truman's civil rights bill, repeal of the Taft-Hartley Act, and a comprehensive national health insurance program. Despite its legislative failure, the Fair Deal is especially significant for providing a partisan, ideological, and programmatic link between the New Deal of the 1930s and the NEW FRONTIER and GREAT SOCIETY of the 1960s.

Further reading: Hamby, Alonzo L., ed. *Harry S Truman and the Fair Deal.* Lexington, Mass.: D.C. Heath, 1974; Savage, Sean J. *Truman and the Democratic Party.* Lexington: University Press of Kentucky, 1997.

—Sean J. Savage

Fair Employment Practices Committee

Created in 1941, with Executive Order 8802 issued by Franklin D. ROOSEVELT, the Fair Employment Practices Committee's job was to eliminate discrimination based on race, color, national origin, or religion. Although of very limited utility, the committee did represent an effort, albeit a small one, to introduce fairness and equality into federal employment practices. Such efforts were quite controversial at the time, and FDR realized he had to move cautiously, but move he did, and the results, while of limited significance in impacting hiring practices, did send a powerful message, one that in the 1950s and 1960s became part of the civil rights movement. The committee was eliminated in 1946 in an amendment to an appropriation bill.

Fair Labor Standards Act (FLSA)

Passed in 1938, the Fair Labor Standards Act, sometimes referred to as the Wages and Hours Act, established federal standards for the minimum wage, overtime pay, equal pay, and child labor. One of FDR's NEW DEAL reforms, the administration suffered a series of political and judicial setbacks before FLSA finally became law. In 1985 the Supreme Court, in *Garcia v. San Antonio Metropolitan Transit Authority,* extended FLSA to state and local employees. FLSA is an example of the federal government extending its reach during the post-Depression, New Deal era. From this point on, the federal government took on a greater role in regulating commerce and labor practices and standards.

Faithful Execution Clause

Article II, Section 3, of the Constitution says that the president shall "take Care that the Laws be faithfully executed." The president is thus responsible, as the nation's CHIEF EXECUTIVE, to uphold the rule of law and the laws as passed by Congress.

Disputes over this clause have occurred frequently in history. Most recently, President NIXON in the WATERGATE crisis, and President REAGAN in the IRAN-CONTRA scandal, failed to execute the law and instead, superseded the law with their own chosen courses of action.

farewell addresses

These represent a genre of presidential rhetoric that arises from an opportunity given to all presidents who have completed their term in office. The farewell address is a way for the outgoing president to influence judgments on his administration through the use of language (by speaking in the role of president) and history (by bequeathing a legacy). Likened to the Greek concept of *kairos,* or an opportunity to make a fitting gesture, farewell addresses attempt to veil or unveil deeds done while in office, to influence coming legislative programs, and to mediate national values and identity.

According to Karlyn Kohrs Campbell and Kathleen Hall Jamieson, farewell addresses are "produced in response to a systemic need for a ritual of departure." As transitional moments that signal the end of one presidency and thus the beginning of another, a farewell address offers a president the opportunity to reflect upon his own administration and to attempt to establish the criteria by which that administration will be judged. In establishing this criteria, presidents can also hope to influence the nation's future by indicating the principles and policies that they understand as pivotal to that future. They are also important indicators of political continuity; farewell addresses help to smooth the transition between administrations and affirm the presidency as an institution that is greater than its individual occupants.

Farewell addresses are an indication of the rhetorical power of the presidency as an institution, for by the time a farewell address is given, the president has little practical political power remaining; these speeches allow presidents to make the most of their moral and persuasive power. In part, presidents can exercise this power because they are anticipating a removal from office and a return to the role of private citizen; they can therefore claim to be politically disinterested and focused only upon the future well-being of the nation as a whole. In this capacity, they can speak for the nation, invoking timeless principles to reflect upon the past and guide future action. Presidents will invoke God to both reaffirm the nation's covenant and special status and to ask Him to continue to protect the nation and to provide for it in the future.

Farewell addresses can be offered as special speeches (WASHINGTON, JACKSON, Andrew JOHNSON, TRUMAN, EISENHOWER, CARTER, NIXON, REAGAN, and CLINTON); they can be the final STATE OF THE UNION address (GRANT, Truman, FORD); or they can take the form of a final PRESS CONFERENCE (Lyndon JOHNSON). Presidents can offer more than one leave-taking, as Truman and Clinton did, offering farewells to the Congress, the press, the people, or, as in Nixon's case, to the White House staff.

Farewell addresses are often considered by pundits and the media to be poor examples of the rhetorical arts; in this they are misunderstood, although Nixon's, Carter's and Clinton's deserve their reputations as inferior speeches. Certainly Washington's, Jackson's, and Eisenhower's are well-remembered and often quoted, although this is probably due more to the nature of those presidents' legacies than to the eloquence of their farewell addresses. Eloquent farewells, according to Campbell and Jamieson, combine character, style, and recounting of presidential achievements in ways that recall the values shared by the entire nation.

Farewell addresses offer presidents the opportunity to enact the role of private citizen while remaining president, and thus also the opportunity to reflect upon the practices of the government with reference to timeless principles. Farewell addresses can be used to teach citizens about the government, foster an appreciation of the presidency as an institution, and smooth the transition between administrations. They reflect and exemplify the rhetorical power of the presidency.

Further reading: Campbell, Karlyn Kohrs, and Kathleen Hall Jamieson. *Deeds Done in Words: Presidential Rhetoric and the Genres of Governance.* Chicago: University of Chicago Press, 1990; Kaufman, Burton Ira, ed.

Washington's Farewell Address: The View from the Twentieth Century. Chicago: Quadrangle, 1969.
—Mary E. Stuckey & Colleen Blanchard

Farley, James A. (1888–1976) *postmaster general, national party chairman*

One of FDR's key political operators, Farley ran Roosevelt's successful 1928 bid for governor of New York and later helped secure the Democratic presidential nomination for FDR. He then was appointed national committee chairman of the DEMOCRATIC PARTY and later the postmaster general (where he ran FDR's patronage system). Farley was an old-style politician in the new world of Washington, D.C., politics. More accustomed to the party boss system of PATRONAGE and party decision making, Farley had difficulty transitioning to the new and different political dynamics brought on by the NEW DEAL with its executive leadership and interest-group politics. Farley and the president drifted apart, with Farley finally breaking with Roosevelt when Farley's hopes of becoming president foundered because FDR decided to seek a third term as president in 1940. Farley did not oppose Roosevelt in 1940 but, instead, withdrew from politics and public life.

Federal Bureau of Investigation (FBI)

The FBI was founded in 1908 by Attorney General Charles Bonaparte, during the presidency of Theodore ROOSEVELT. It was originally called the Bureau of Investigations but was renamed the Federal Bureau of Investigations in 1935. The bureau has had a controversial history. Initially there was great hesitancy over the creation of the bureau out of fear that it would create a national police force.

In 1910, during the uproar over "white slavery," Congress passed the Mann Act, which resulted in the arrest of controversial black heavyweight champion Jack Johnson. After World War I, Attorney General Palmer utilized the bureau to round up communists, socialists, and anarchists. The affair became known as the PALMER RAIDS and was widely viewed as a gross violation of CIVIL LIBERTIES.

J. Edgar HOOVER was appointed director in 1924. He quickly moved to reform the image and operations of the bureau. He emphasized that the bureau should be limited to enforcing federal statutes and that the qualifications and training of agents would be substantially upgraded. In addition, he established important systems of accountability. As a result of these efforts the bureau and Hoover became respected but also feared.

The role and the power of the bureau became transformed by its relationship with successive presidents and Hoover's exceptional skills as politician and promoter. In 1936 President Franklin ROOSEVELT expanded the FBI's role when he requested a report on fascist and communist activities. This was followed up in 1939 when Roosevelt requested the FBI to investigate espionage, sabotage, and violations of the "neutrality law." Roosevelt subsequently authorized the bureau to receive information regarding these activities from local police and from patriotic citizens. Hoover interpreted these directives as authority to develop files on citizens not under investigation for violating federal laws. During WORLD WAR II, the FBI began to publicize its new role. The FBI also began to provide information to Roosevelt on his political rivals and enemies.

With the beginning of the COLD WAR, the FBI began to investigate Soviet espionage activities and the Communist Party under the Smith Act. TRUMAN and EISENHOWER issued executive orders authorizing the FBI to investigate potential subversives. The FBI also cooperated with Sen. Joseph MCCARTHY and began to investigate all those individuals who they believed either knowingly or unknowingly promoted the Soviet cause. This included both the academic community and the entertainment industry.

Truman and Eisenhower also authorized the bureau to investigate all current and future government employees for potential threats to domestic and NATIONAL SECURITY. This further expanded the system of files and authorized the bureau to gather noncriminal material, including information regarding the personal life of many public officials and citizens.

During the 1950s and 1960s the FBI continued to raise the issue of communism both domestically and internationally. The FBI developed its Cointelpro operation (Counter Intelligence Program) to reduce communist-supported activity in the civil rights or anti–VIETNAM WAR movements. While the FBI made significant efforts against the Ku Klux Klan, it was heavily criticized by civil rights groups for not having significant numbers of AFRICAN AMERICANS as agents and for their relationship with local Southern police officers who were often indifferent in enforcing civil rights violations. Hoover bristled at the criticism leveled against the bureau. He responded with counterintelligence efforts to discredit Dr. Martin Luther King, Jr., the leading critic of the FBI.

The FBI continued to provide political intelligence to Truman, Eisenhower, and KENNEDY. It reached its height, however, when, during the 1964 Democratic National Convention in Atlantic City, Hoover provided 30 agents to help the Johnson campaign keep abreast of every move from all of Johnson's adversaries and attempts to disrupt the convention. The FBI also provided information to JOHNSON and NIXON on critics of the Vietnam War.

The Nixon administration requested information on all critics of the war in particular and of the administration in general, including reporters and political officials. The administration proposed the Houston Plan, which called for rounding up large numbers of citizens on mere suspicion, but retreated when the plan was objected to by Hoover. Hoover observed that the bureau was losing public support and no longer believed that supporting the presidential request was in the bureau's interest. Some have suggested that Hoover's reluctance to support presidential initiatives lead the Nixon administration to create "the plumbers," its own covert unit who were created to fix the leaks of government documents and to gather intelligence on other critics of Nixon.

The WATERGATE scandal involved the obstruction of justice concerning the investigation of those who burglarized the Democratic National Headquarters, several of whom were members of the illegal "plumbers" unit. Hoover and the bureau were praised for their resistance to these unconstitutional presidential requests.

During the Hoover years, the bureau was very successful in launching activities that led to both public and legislative support for the bureau. The bureau launched its 10 Most Wanted List, which brought tremendous positive publicity to the bureau when it inevitably got its man. Critics argued that the bureau focused on romantic or rogue criminals such as Machine Gun Kelly or Pretty Boy Floyd while avoiding the more potent threats of drug rings and organized crime. They argued that Hoover was concerned that the bureau's investigation into these areas could lead to its agents being corrupted because of the moneys involved with these activities.

The bureau also promoted Hoover as a sage. Hoover's book *Masters of Deceit* and other articles on communism were written by agents and published under Hoover's name. Hoover also worked with movie and television producers and newspaper reporters. The bureau provided them with stories and information in exchange for promoting the bureau, Hoover, and its ideology. Hoover also forged relationships with interest groups such as local police organizations and the American Legion, providing them with information and services in exchange for support and publicity. Hoover assiduously developed relationships with the leadership of Congress. He was assisted in this by the massive files that intimidated some of the bureau's critics.

When Hoover died in 1972, the bureau was being criticized for its political role, its publicity machine, and for not being more aggressive in enforcing civil rights. L. Patrick Gray, who replaced Hoover, became embroiled in the Watergate scandal. Clarence Kelly became director in 1973; he was a former agent who was Kansas City police chief. In 1975 Congress began to investigate the bureau. The revelations about its political activities and the Cointelpro operation led to further decline in public support and more restrictive rules of operation: The director would serve one term of 10 years and the bureau had to abide by strict rules regarding wiretaps and foreign intelligence.

Judge William Webster was appointed director in 1978 and was followed by Judge William Sessions in 1987 to enforce these new rules. They both focused on counterterrorism, political corruption, and white-collar crime. Judge Louis J. Freeh, a former agent, was made director in 1993. Freeh emphasized international crime and terrorism as the top priorities of the FBI.

Two events had a major impact on the FBI: one at Ruby Ridge, Idaho, where an FBI sniper killed federal fugitive Randal Weaver's wife, and the events at Waco, Texas, where 80 individuals died in a fire when the FBI sought to end a standoff with a heavily armed religious group. This led many to question the FBI's ability to handle a crisis.

In 2001 former U.S. Attorney Robert Mueller replaced Freeh. He was immediately thrown into the domestic war on terrorism following the attacks on the World Trade Center in New York and the PENTAGON. The bureau's inability to gather intelligence and prevent the terrorist attacks raised questions of the bureau's effectiveness.

The FBI has been a controversial institution since its inception. It has developed into the premier investigation agency in the world, yet its history also includes significant involvement in politics and lapses in performance. The FBI's challenges remain as demanding as ever. The threat of terrorism, with its menace of nuclear, biological, and chemical weapons, has become its highest priority. It must also adapt to a complex political environment that is ethnically, racially, and religiously diverse and remains concerned about CIVIL LIBERTIES.

Further reading: Garrow, David J. *The FBI and Martin Luther King, Jr.* New York: Penguin Books, 1983; Powers, Richard Gid. *Secrecy and Power: The Life of J. Edgar Hoover.* New York: Free Press, 1987; Sorrentino, Frank M. *Ideological Warfare: The FBI's Path Toward Power.* Port Washington, N.Y.: Associated Faculty Press, 1985; Ungar, Sanford J. *FBI.* Boston: Little, Brown, 1976.

—Frank M. Sorrentino

Federal Election Commission (FEC)

The Federal Election Commission was created in 1975 to help enforce the Federal Election Campaign Act (FECA). FECA provided for a new system of CAMPAIGN FINANCE for federal elections, and it was the job of the FEC to help monitor the act's implementation. As an independent regulatory agency, the FEC is designed to provide nonpartisan oversight of the financing of federal elections. Its functions are to make campaign finance information available to both candidates and the public, to enforce the provisions of the FECA, and to administer the public funding of presidential elections.

The president appoints the six members of the commission with the ADVICE AND CONSENT of the Senate. Each commissioner serves a six-year term with two seats becoming eligible for reappointment every two years. The law creating the commission stipulates that there must be four votes for any official action and that no more than three of the commission's members may be from the same political party. The position of FEC chair rotates each year among the commission members, and each member can serve in the capacity of chair once during his/her term.

The FEC is structured into different divisions according to their respective purposes. For example, the FEC's general counsel directs the agency's enforcement activities, and the Office of the General Counsel represents the commission in civil litigation and also prepares advisory opinions and regulations for the commission to consider. The INSPECTORS GENERAL monitors the agency's internal operations. The Office of Election Administration aids election officials, responds to inquiries, publishes reports, and conducts workshops related to election administration. The Public Disclosure Division receives and makes publicly available campaign finance reports filed by POLITICAL ACTION COMMITTEES and candidates for federal office.

The FEC's enforcement process starts when staff members review the campaign finance reports it receives. Oftentimes, discrepancies are resolved by asking the candidate or committee to file a revised report. Other discrepancies are referred to the commission for enforcement action. Enforcement actions also may be initiated by other government agencies or by private individuals or groups filing a complaint. If four or more commissioners find a reason to believe that a violation occurred, then the FEC pursues enforcement action against the alleged violator. If a violation is found to have occurred, the FEC often will try to settle the matter with the party involved, such as requiring a fine to be paid. If the two sides cannot reach a settlement, the FEC will pursue the matter in federal court. Although this may describe the general process of FEC enforcement actions, the reality is that the FEC has somewhat limited enforcement powers. As a result, FEC decisions have often fallen on deaf ears. For example, the FEC decided to fine both the CLINTON and Dole campaigns for irregular fundraising issues during the 1996 campaign; neither fine was paid.

The FEC often issues regulations implementing federal campaign finance laws as well as advisory opinions further interpreting the laws and regulations. Sometimes, though, such regulations and opinions have resulted in further controversy. For example, the FEC issued a series of advisory opinions interpreting the 1979 amendments to FECA, which were designed in part to address concerns raised by party organizations that the spending limits imposed on them forced the parties to choose between election-related media advertising on candidates and traditional grassroots party-building activities such as voter registration and get-out-the-vote drives. The FEC's opinions led to the advent of soft money, that is, unregulated and unrestricted party money often donated by corporations and unions that are otherwise banned from making contributions to political candidates. The use of soft money has grown since the 1980s, and soft money fundraising became a primary focus for presidential candidates. Congress finally banned soft money at the federal level through campaign finance reform legislation passed in 2002.

The FEC has also been the center of other reform proposals. Campaign finance reform efforts, like early versions of the McCain-Feingold bill in the Senate and its companion in the House (the Shays-Meehan bill), called for more enforcement power for the FEC as well as more funding for it to better monitor current campaign practices. The 2002 legislation included provisions increasing the level of penalties that the FEC could assess and requiring candidate disclosure reports to be filed more frequently.

Opponents of the McCain-Feingold/Shays-Meehan legislation argued that any problems with the federal campaign finance system could be resolved through greater disclosure to and rigorous enforcement by the FEC. The commission's critics contend that the FEC, even before the implementation of the 2002 law, has not sufficiently enforced the existing laws. For example, some criticize the FEC for failing to address substantively many of the complaints it receives. Instead, most complaints fall into a backlog within the agency and are subsequently dismissed as being too stale. Critics also contend that the FEC is too intrusively involved in the electoral process already, and its regulations provide too great of a regulatory burden.

Further reading: Corrado, Anthony, and Thomas E. Mann, Daniel R. Ortiz, Trevor Potter, and Frank J. Sorouf, eds. *Campaign Finance Reform: A Sourcebook.* Washington, D.C.: Brookings Institution, 1997; Federal Election Commission's web site http://www.fec.gov
—Victoria Farrar-Myers

federalism

The United States has a federal system, meaning power and responsibilities are divided between the national and state governments. Over time this division of power has created certain problems, even leading, in part, to CIVIL WAR.

In *The Federalist No. 45,* James MADISON wrote of how federalism would work:

> The powers delegated by the Constitution to the federal government are few and defined. Those which are to remain in state governments are numerous and indefi-

nite. The former will be exercised principally on external objects, as war, peace, negotiation, and foreign commerce. . . . The powers reserved to the several states will extend to all objects which, in the ordinary course of affairs, concern the lives, liberties, and properties of the people, and the internal order, improvement, and prosperity of the states.

Over time, the national government has grown in power and responsibility, but the states retain and continue to execute many powers. Often, conservatives call for devolving some powers to the states, but the larger trend over the past 70 years has been toward increased power for the national government.

Federalist Papers

The *Federalist Papers* are a series of 85 persuasive editorial essays published in New York newspapers following the CONSTITUTIONAL CONVENTION. Authored under the name of "Publius," the *Federalist Papers* were written by James MADISON, Alexander HAMILTON, and John JAY. In total, Hamilton composed 56 of the essays, Madison authored 21, Jay penned five, and Hamilton and Madison collaborated on three. These essays were designed to raise and debunk all the potential difficulties that opponents to the new Constitution might use to prevent its ratification. In addition to this decidedly political purpose, the *Federalist Papers* offer insight into the political philosophy held by the framers of the Constitution and the purpose of each component of the intricate governmental system they developed.

In the first essay, Hamilton noted that Publius would "discuss the following interesting particulars" throughout the essays:

> The utility of the union to your political prosperity—the insufficiency of the present confederation to preserve that union—the necessity of a government at least equally energetic with the one proposed, to the attainment of this object—the conformity of the proposed constitution to the true principles of republican government—its analogy to your own state constitution—and lastly, the additional security which its adoption will afford to the preservation of that species of government, to liberty, and to property.

To accomplish these tasks, Publius first had to address why the CONSTITUTIONAL CONVENTION, originally called only to modify the Articles of Confederation, became the drafting place for a new document of government. Further, the authors had to explain the creation of the new concept of federalism: the division of power between the states and the national government. After all, despite the failures of the

Articles of Confederation, many political leaders had a lasting distrust of a strong centralized government held over from the nation's days under English colonial rule. A theme that ran throughout the *Federalist Papers* was that the states would retain their own sphere of authority. In addition, Hamilton, Madison, and Jay had to justify the three national institutions of the legislative, executive, and judicial branches. In doing so, they strove to explain the functions of each institution's powers as well as their necessity.

Similarly, James Madison used *Federalist No. 10* and *No. 51* to address immediate issues at hand. In *#10* he justified the need for a large republic, representative government, and a system of majority rule to check against the tyranny posed by factions. In *#51* Madison addressed the need for SEPARATION OF POWERS and CHECKS AND BALANCES. These two essays, however, also serve as the best exposition of the political philosophy of the framers, their view of human nature, and the rationale behind the system of government created. In *#51* Madison expressed his oft-quoted view of the relationship between human nature and government as follows:

> If men were angels, no government would be necessary. If angels were to govern men, neither external nor internal controls on government would be necessary. In framing a government, which is to be administered by men over men, the great difficulty lies in this: you must first enable the government to control the governed; and in the next place oblige it to control itself.

Federalist No. 10 set out the sort of external and internal controls the Federalist viewed as necessary. A large republic diluted factions within the nation. The majority-rule system would obstruct tyranny by a minority faction. The intricate system of separation of power, checks and balances and the different constituencies and manners for selecting national government officials provided sufficient controls against the tyranny of the majority.

As for the Federalist view of the presidency, that can be found in essays *No. 67* through *No. 77*, each the work of Alexander Hamilton. In these essays, Hamilton justified the need for a single executive and how the creation of such was not returning the country back to a monarchy. He wrote in *Federalist No. 70*:

> Energy in the Executive is a leading character in the definition of good government. It is essential to the protection of the community against foreign attacks; it is not less essential to the steady administration of the laws; to the protection of property against those irregular and high-handed combinations which sometimes interrupt the ordinary course of justice; to the security of liberty against the enterprises and assaults of ambition, of faction, and of anarchy.

For Hamilton, a feeble executive was the equivalent of a bad government; the tools necessary to have a sufficiently energized executive were, in Hamilton's words, unity, duration, an adequate provision for its support, and competent powers. The executive's energy, however, would remain constrained by the need to be elected, by the powers and checks held by Congress, and ultimately by the authority of the people. The president would not become another king with absolute power; instead the president would be one of the "elective and periodical servants of the people" (*Federalist No. 69*) in whose hands the power of the government rested.

Further reading: Hamilton, Alexander, James Madison, and John Jay. *The Federalist Papers.* Edited by Clinton Rossiter. New York: Mentor, 1999.

—Victoria Farrar-Myers

Federalist Party

One of the first two parties established in the United States, the Federalists were a conservative, nationalist party, led by Alexander HAMILTON. The Federalist Party began during the final days of the WASHINGTON administration, and while it would not have been considered a true party by today's standards, one can see the roots of formal parties developing in this period.

Opposed by the Jeffersonians, the Federalists won control of the government in the post-Washington era, with John ADAMS as president, but with Alexander Hamilton exercising power behind the scenes. While in power, the Federalists passed the ill-advised ALIEN AND SEDITION ACTS. With the election of JEFFERSON to the presidency in 1800, the Federalists began to decline. After the WAR OF 1812 they became a weak party and began to wane.

Further reading: Chambers, William N. *Political Parties in a New Nation: The American Experience, 1776–1809.* New York: Oxford University Press, 1963; Hofstadter, Richard. *The Idea of a Party System; the Rise of Legitimate Opposition in the United States, 1780–1840.* Berkeley: University of California Press, 1969.

Federal Register Act of 1935

During the NEW DEAL, government agencies issued rules and regulations at a pace that far outstripped any previous era. To systematize and keep records of these voluminous regulations, Congress passed the Federal Register Act of 1935. This act created the *Federal Register,* where all proposed rules and regulations must be published. Prior to the act there was no systematic collection and publication of federal rules and regulations. Some were kept in the agencies, some in the White House, others were lost or misplaced. Today the *Federal Register*, issued every day, contains all rules, regulations, presidential PROCLAMATIONS, EXECUTIVE ORDERS, and other EXECUTIVE BRANCH documents. The Code of Federal Regulation (CFR) is the permanent repository for these documents and is responsible for their maintenance and upkeep.

Federal Reserve System

Control of MONETARY POLICY rests with the Federal Reserve System. The system is the product of seven major depressions in the 19th century (1837, 1847, 1857, 1864, 1873, 1883, and 1893). The National Monetary Commission was established so as to make a recommendation as to what to do. The result was the creation of the Federal Reserve System within the Federal Reserve Act of 1913. Most countries have one central bank. In the United States, this "central bank" is more compact. The Fed, as it has come to be known, was originally created to prevent adverse economic conditions, but its role has evolved so it has an active role in the whole of macroeconomic policy-making, maintaining where possible an optimal growth in the money supply with relative price stability.

Unlike FISCAL POLICY, which deals with taxing and spending and is broadly governed by CONGRESS AND THE PRESIDENT, monetary policy is the amount of money in play at any particular time in the economy. The Fed has three mechanisms for controlling monetary policy. First, it sets reserve requirements governing how much of each deposit a bank must keep on hand. Second, the Fed can buy or sell securities on the open market. Finally, it sets interest rates, which are the rates that banks charge one another for short-term overnight loans.

The system consists of a board of governors of the Federal Reserve Board, 12 Federal Reserve Banks, and the Federal Open Market Committee (FOMC). The regional banks are technically privately owned within their regions, their expenses paid largely through interest earned on their securities holdings and fees assessed to member institutions, which comprise about one-third of all commercial banks and all national banks.

However, the most potent control over monetary policy lies with the Board of Governors and the Federal Open Market Committee. The Board of Governors consists of seven members, who are appointed by the president, confirmed by the Senate, and serve 14-year staggered terms. A new governor is up in even-numbered years. The chair and the vice-chair serve four-year terms and can be reappointed as long as their full terms have not expired. The seven board members also sit on the FOMC along with five presidents of the regional banks (one of whom is always the president of the Bank of New York). Other members serve on a one-year, rotating basis. These committees are pivotal in decisions effecting the macroeconomy.

For example, inflation derives from a situation in which there is too much money in the economy. Consequently, demand for goods and services is high and manufacturers and providers have a difficult time keeping up. As a result, prices increase. To fend this off, the Fed, if it chooses to use all of the weapons in its arsenal, will take steps to take money out of the economy. It could increase the reserve requirement, increase the rate of interest (which would provide a disincentive to investors and slow down indicators such as new housing starts), and perhaps most important, the FOMC would buy government securities on the open market, which would take billions of dollars out of the economy. If unemployment (basically a lack of money in the economy) is the problem, the Fed could use each of its tools in an opposite fashion to stimulate activity by infusing money into the economy.

Further reading: Frendreis, John P., and Raymond Tatalovich. *The Modern Presidency and Economic Policy.* Itasca, Ill.: Peacock Publishers, 1994; Kettl, Donald F. *Leadership at the Fed.* New Haven: Yale University Press, 1986.
—Daniel E. Ponder

Federal Trade Commission Act

Passed in 1914 in tandem with the Clayton Act, the Federal Trade Commission Act marked the first major overhaul of the antitrust law since the Sherman Antitrust Act of 1890. This law established the Federal Trade Commission (FTC) as the agency charged with insuring the prohibition of "unfair methods of competition." President ROOSEVELT spearheaded the drive to redefine antitrust policy and place its enforcement within the hands of the EXECUTIVE BRANCH.

Further reading: Sklar, Martin J. *The Corporate Reconstruction of American Capitalism, 1890–1916.* New York: Cambridge University Press, 1988.

Ferraro, Geraldine Anne (1935–) *lawyer, politician*

Born in Newburgh, New York, on August 26, 1935, Geraldine Ferraro was the first woman to be nominated as a candidate for a major party's bid for the vice presidency. Running with Walter MONDALE on the Democratic ticket, she unsuccessfully vied for that office in 1984, losing to President Ronald REAGAN and Vice President George H. W. BUSH.

Graduating from Marymount College (1956) and Fordham University Law School (1960), she married John Zaccaro, a wealthy attorney and businessman. Practicing law privately until 1974, she then worked for a local district attorney in Queens County from 1974 to 1978. Her specialization was investigation of sex crimes and spousal abuse. This reinforced her desire to work on behalf of women.

In 1979 she won election to the U.S. House of Representatives from a relatively conservative Queens district. While in Congress, she continued to be a spokesperson for women's issues.

Active in feminist organizations such as the National Women's Political Caucus, Ferraro was also a protégé of Speaker Thomas O'Neill. In Congress she served on the powerful Budget Committee and became an important figure in the national DEMOCRATIC PARTY. After the 1980 presidential election, she served on the Hunt Commission and was an important supporter of the proposal to create "superdelegates" to the Democratic National Convention.

Backed by the National Organization for Women to be the vice-presidential nominee, Ferraro supported abortion rights, affirmative action, and economic equity legislation, and opposed mandatory school busing. She was opposed by many groups and experienced public criticism and scrutiny throughout her vice-presidential bid. At issue were not only her liberal positions but also her private life. Her husband's business affairs were questioned repeatedly during the campaign. She was asked about her ability to fulfill her domestic responsibilities, including her skill at baking blueberry muffins. Even the VICE PRESIDENT's wife, Barbara BUSH, called her "a four million dollar—I can't say it, but it rhymes with rich."

Democratic losses at the polls in 1984 were devastating and the Mondale/Ferraro ticket only carried one state, Minnesota, in the ELECTORAL COLLEGE. The extent to which the "Ferraro factor" played a significant role in this defeat, however, is debated. While she mobilized some women, among them liberal women and some Italian-American women, her liberal positions served to mobilize and catalyze organized opposition, such as displayed by the Catholic Church.

Still active in politics, Ferraro lost her bid for the U.S. Senate representing New York in 1992 and 1998. She has served as president of the International Institute for Women's Political Leadership and is a permanent member of the United Nations Commission on Human Rights, from 1993 to the present.

Further reading: Ferraro, Geraldine. *My Story.* Toronto: Bantam Books, 1985; Schramm, Peter, and Dennis Mahoney. *The 1984 Election and the Future of American Politics.* Durham, N.C.: Carolina Academic Press, 1987.
— Rebecca E. Deen

Field v. Clark

This is a Supreme Court decision that upheld the power of Congress to delegate broad power to the president in the field of international trade. In this case, several importers, led by Marshall Field & Company, challenged the constitutionality of Section 3 of the Tariff Act of October 1, 1890

(the McKinley Tariff Act). Passed in order to assist the president in negotiating reciprocal trade agreements, this statutory provision permitted free entry of foreign sugar, molasses, coffee, tea, and hides into the United States unless the president made a determination that the other nation's duties on American exports were "reciprocally unequal and unreasonable." If the president made such a finding, he could suspend free entry of the goods into the United States, resulting in the imposition of duties on them "for such time as he shall deem just."

In the suit, the plaintiffs argued that such a provision delegated to the president both the lawmaking and the treaty-making functions. The Court disagreed with the plaintiffs, concluding that the statute only authorized fact-finding (that is to say, execution of the law) by the president. Once the president made a factual determination, the Court reasoned, the statute then compelled him to suspend part of the statute. The Court's reasons were that a large number of statutes throughout the nation's history had delegated comparable powers of suspension to the president, and beginning with the Supreme Court case of *Brig Aurora v. United States* in 1813, courts had shown themselves unwilling to overturn broad delegations in the field of foreign commerce.

At the time, *Field*'s generous interpretation of Congress's power to delegate lent further support to maturing legal doctrine that would in time come to justify the future expansion of federal administrative activity. Although the Supreme Court would on two occasions in the 1930s strike down statutes as unconstitutional delegations of lawmaking authority, courts since that time have let stand even the most broad and seemingly standardless delegations. *Field* also presaged later decisions involving foreign affairs delegations such as *UNITED STATES V. CURTISS-WRIGHT*. The importance of *Field*, however, has waned somewhat since courts have come to uphold domestic delegations to the president with nearly the same frequency as delegations in the context of FOREIGN AFFAIRS. Nonetheless, the Supreme Court has insisted that the doctrine has less applicability in the latter realm.

Further reading: Barber, Sotirios A. *The Constitution and the Delegation of Congressional Power.* Chicago: University of Chicago Press, 1975; Larkin, John Day. *The President's Control of the Tariff.* Cambridge, Mass.: Harvard University Press, 1936; Schoenbrod, David. *Power without Responsibility.* New Haven, Conn.: Yale University Press, 1993.
— Roy E. Brownell II

Fillmore, Millard (1800–1874) *thirteenth U.S.*

president, U.S. vice president, U.S. representative
After Zachary TAYLOR's death, Millard Fillmore assumed the presidency (1850–53). At 5'9", with blue eyes and thin

gray hair, Fillmore was nonetheless an imposing figure. He took office as a crisis was looming over slavery, but as Harry TRUMAN said of him, "At a time we needed a strong man, what we got was a man that swayed with the slightest breeze."

Fillmore accepted the resignations of all department heads and appointed his own CABINET. This bold assertion of control, however, did not extend to the domain of public policy. Fillmore's Whiggish tendencies were self-limiting in an age when the hot issue of slavery needed political leadership.

Millard Fillmore was president during the "Great Guano Wars." Guano, bird droppings, was a much sought-after fertilizer. American business clashed with the Peruvian government over this odiferous issue. He who controlled foul excrement controlled a great deal of currency. Fillmore's government successfully negotiated a treaty with Peru granting American business the profitable rights to extract the guano from islands off Peru.

Shortly after taking office, Fillmore signed the Compromise of 1850. Under the compromise, California was admitted into the union as a free state, the borders of Texas were defined, the territories of New Mexico and Utah were established, and slavery was abolished in the District of Columbia.

The Compromise also contained the controversial Fugitive Slave Law, which required that Northerners help return escaped slaves to their Southern owners. The Compromise of 1850 may have postponed the CIVIL WAR, but it did little to end the strife caused by slavery. Fillmore was one of the pre–Civil War presidents who confronted the growing sectional split between North and South and was unable to prevent the problem from becoming a crisis. He tried to bargain and compromise, giving each side a bit of what they wanted, but satisfying no one. Fillmore was an accidental president lacking the authority or the will to take on the growing sectional rift, and in the end he failed to stem the tide of separation. He governed at a time when Congress's power overshadowed that of the presidency and he willingly allowed Congress to dominate. "With you," Fillmore told the Congress, "is the power, the honor, and the responsibility for the legislation of the country," adding, "My only desire is to discharge my duty." This minimalist view of presidential power, while honoring the Whig view of the Constitution, may not have been well suited to a time when factional and sectional cleavages threatened to destroy the nation.

In 1852 the Whigs refused to nominate Fillmore for another term as president. He ended up joining the nativist Know-Nothing party. As the 1856 presidential nominee of the Know-Nothings, Fillmore won only the state of Maryland. He was offered an honorary degree from Oxford University but declined, stating later, "I had not the advantage of a classical education, and no man should, in my judgment, accept a degree he cannot read."

President Millard Fillmore *(Library of Congress)*

Further reading: Rayback, Robert J. *Millard Fillmore: Biography of a President.* Buffalo, N.Y.: Henry Stewart, 1959; Smith, Elbert B. *The Presidencies of Zachary Taylor and Millard Fillmore.* Lawrence: University Press of Kansas, 1988.

films and the presidency

Initially, presidents were portrayed in commercial films with awe, reverence, and respect. Until the fallout from a variety of scandals, Hollywood tended toward fawning hero worship in its cinematic treatment of presidents—real or fictional—but in the past quarter century, the presidential image on film has gone through a roller-coaster ride of high worship and abject scorn.

Among the changes in film coverage in the past two decades is the increased use of the American president as a symbol, character, and key component in a wide variety of films. The presidency is a potent symbol of American politics and nationhood and has become an attractive focal point in countless movies. The presidency, once treated in popular art with respect, even reverence, has been transformed from national icon to pop idol, with all the negatives of familiarity that comes with pop-star status.

In the nation with no official RELIGION or sacred text and few unifying national symbols, the presidency has been converted into a high priest and symbolic representative. Our monuments to presidents tower over the Washington, D.C., landscape. We have a MOUNT RUSHMORE to honor our presidents. We erect grand palaces to their names in the form of PRESIDENTIAL LIBRARIES, the modern cathedrals of presidential worship. If you go to Disney World in Orlando, Florida, you can visit the Hall of Presidents. We have constructed the paraphernalia of quasi-religious worship to the men who serve as presidents. The presidency has become more than a political or constitutional institution. It is the focus of emotions, hopes, and aspirations. Since the VIETNAM WAR, the presidency has been the focal point for complex and contradictory attachments and emotions. As such, the good, the bad, and the ugly of the American presidency have become the focus of numerous films.

In the early days of moving pictures, the presidency drew very little attention. Rarely was the president portrayed as a fictional character in films, and while some historical portrayals made it to the screen (especially of Abraham LINCOLN), the presidency was infrequently a part of films.

Prior to the disillusionment of Vietnam, WATERGATE, the IRAN-CONTRA scandal, and the CLINTON sex scandals, presidents—when portrayed in films—were presented primarily as political giants, saints who oozed goodness. No president received a greater cinematic boost than Abraham Lincoln. With such films as *Abraham Lincoln's Clemency* (1910), *Lincoln's Gettysburg Address* (1912), *Lincoln the Lover* (1913), *Lincoln's Thanksgiving Story* (1914), *The Life of Abraham Lincoln* (1915), *The Lincoln Cycle* (1917), *The Highest Law* (1921), *The Heart of Lincoln* (1922), *The Dramatic Life of Abraham Lincoln* (1924), *Abraham Lincoln* (1930), *Of Human Hearts* (1938), *Lincoln in the White House* (1939), *Young Mr. Lincoln* (1939), and *Abe Lincoln in Illinois* (1940), a type of blind hero worship rose around Lincoln.

This began to change during the GREAT DEPRESSION, when the search for hope led some filmmakers to turn their attention to politics and the creation of presidential hero amid all the squalor and misery. In periods of crisis (the Depression) and war (WORLD WAR II), it is not unusual to see the president portrayed as heroic or as a savior. In time of stress, the public looks to the president for reassurance, comfort, and rescue. Films such as *Gabriel Over the White House* (1933) presented an activist, quasi-authoritarian president who (after the spirit of the angel Gabriel entered his body) accomplished miraculous deeds of reform and political regeneration, albeit in violation of constitutional restraints. This wishful thinking and hero worship presented the president as popular hero and savior.

In *The President Vanishes* (1934), an honest president, beset by a corrupt Congress, fakes his own kidnapping. In *The Phantom President* (1932), George M. Cohan plays the dual role of T. K. Blair, a cold, colorless presidential candidate, and a Blair look-alike, song-and-dance man Doc Varney. The political bosses have Varney run for president as Blair. Varney wins and stays on as president, "to run the country for the people's benefit."

Presidential cinematic hero worship continued into World War II as a patriotic fervor swept the nation and the film industry. Movies featuring pro-American and pro-presidential themes proliferated as Hollywood was enlisted to boost morale and support the war effort. It did so enthusiastically.

After the hot war, a COLD WAR developed between the United States and the Soviet Union. This ideological and geographical war led to a Red Scare in the United States (1947–55) and the result was the McCarthy Era. This period had a chilling effect on Hollywood, and most filmmakers shied away from overt political messages. The occasional cinematic representation of a fictional president can be found, such as in Frank Capra's *State of the Union* (1948), but the McCarthy Era is best known in Hollywood as the time of the blacklist and the retreat from social problems.

State of the Union, starring the popular duo of Spencer Tracy and Katherine Hepburn, has Tracy playing successful industrialist Grant Matthews, who goes after the Republican presidential nomination. The well-meaning Matthews is manipulated and, finally, seduced by the political bosses, and goes from man of integrity to political pawn. He becomes "one of them," but at his wife's urging, Matthews has a change of heart and, in true Capra fashion, once again becomes a man of integrity, speaking truth to power.

For roughly the next dozen years, political or social problem films declined, falling victim to the oppressive forces of MCCARTHYISM and the Hollywood blacklist. By the 1960s presidential films such as *Sunrise at Campobello* (1960), dealing with FDR's response to paralysis in his prepresidential years, and *PT 109* (1963), about John KENNEDY's bravery during WWII, presented a reverential, hero-worshiping portrayal of individual courage. It was politics at a distance; the personal was the political. And the president was the hero.

Some more complex presidential images were also evident in films such as *Advice and Consent* (1962), *The Manchurian Candidate* (1962), *The Best Man* (1964), and *Fail-Safe* (1964), but in general, the reverential depiction was the order of the day. For the most part, presidents were portrayed as "forceful, wise and selfless, they were stolid embodiments of republican virtue."

This changed rather dramatically in the post-Vietnam, post-Watergate era. The age of the heroic presidency gave way to demonization of the presidency and the decline of public trust in government. An age of cynicism enveloped the political landscape, and the cinematic portrayal of presidents reflected this shift.

Before Vietnam and Watergate, it was all but unthinkable to cinematically portray a real-life president in anything but a most flattering light. All presidential rogues were fictional characters. The fallout from Vietnam and Watergate changed everything.

All the President's Men (1978), starring Robert Redford and Dustin Hoffman as *Washington Post* reporters Bob Woodward and Carl Bernstein, dealt with the lies and corruption of Richard Nixon and started a flood of Nixon-bashing films from *Secret Honor* (1984), to *Dick* (1999), to Oliver Stone's biopic *Nixon* (1995).

Even when the president was not a central character, it was not unusual to present a president in less-than-flattering light. In *The Right Stuff* (1983), for example, Lyndon JOHNSON comes off as a buffoon, and George and Barbara BUSH as comic characters in *Naked Gun 2 ½: The Smell of Fear* (1991). It is the era of the post-heroic presidency, brought painfully to scale.

In the 1960s, as a result of the cultural rebellion of the period, we saw the rise of the antihero. This trend filtered its way into the presidential image as well. Commercial films are designed, first and foremost, to make a profit. Therefore, filmmakers are less likely to shape views than they are to reflect the ideas, biases, tastes, needs, and desires of their audience. Filmmakers give the audience "what it wants," and with the counterculture movement of the 1960s, Vietnam, then Watergate, the public grew cynical and films played to, fed, and exploited the dissatisfaction and disaffection of the American moviegoing audience, and thus the American voter. Slowly portraits of presidents as venal, corrupt, and self-serving began to appear. *Being There* (1979), about an amiable dunce becoming presidential timber, began to deflate the presidential image. Instead of simplistic adulation, a paradigm shift took place: it was now simplistic condemnation. Instead of hailing the chief, we were railing the chief. In *Wild in the Streets* (1968), when 14-year-olds get the right to vote, and age minimums for officeholding are eliminated, one of the new president's first acts is to forcibly place everyone over 35 in "retirement" camp. In *Putney Swope* (1969) we see President Mimeo, a marijuana-smoking midget, more interested in fooling around with the first lady than governing. In *The Virgin President* (1968), fictionalized President Fillard Millmore, a 35-year-old idiot, cannot even figure out that his CABINET is going to bomb China. And in *Hail to the Chief* (1972) a megalomaniac president orders his private police force to massacre hippies.

During the 1980s, life began to imitate art when an actor, Ronald REAGAN, actually became president. And as the memories of the turbulent '60s, Vietnam, and Watergate began to fade, we saw a revival of a more hopeful, even heroic (some would say imperial) presidency. Reagan, the star of such movies as *The Knute Rockne Story* (where he played George Gipp, "the Gipper") and *Bedtime for Bonzo* (where Reagan costarred with a chimp) began to mix up life and art.

Reagan told the Israeli prime minister that he would never let Israel down because he was there when the Americans liberated the Jews from Nazi concentration camps, and he would never, could never, forget. Of course, this never occurred. Reagan was not there when the allies liberated the Jews, but he has seen it in a movie! Reagan even drew ideas and inspiration from popular films, as when he announced that he would build a protective bubble (the strategic defense initiative) over the United States and named it after the movie *Star Wars*. And Reagan even challenged the Congress in cinematic language, telling them to "go ahead, make my day!," after another popular movie line.

By the 1990s, and the end of the cold war, the public's confusion regarding what it wanted and expected of the presidency worked its way into the movies. Conspiratorial or critical depictions of presidents such as *JFK* (1991) and *Nixon* (1995), mixed with lighthearted hopeful portrayals such as *Dave* (1993) and *The American President* (1995). If the images were mixed and mixed up, one thing was perfectly clear: The presidency had become a star of Hollywood movies.

Even a partial list of presidency-oriented films reveals just how popular and marketable the presidential image and office has become. From Oliver Stone's conspiracy homage in *JFK* (1991) to the president as liberal icon in *The American President*, to the president as *Star Wars* hero in *Independence Day* (1996), to president as comic relief in *Mars Attacks* (1998), to the president as supermacho man in *Air Force One* (1997), to the president as—well, as CLINTON—in *Wag the Dog* (1997), to Clinton as Clinton in *Primary Colors* (1998), presidential images cluttered the silver screen. And many of these films drew large audiences. Even *Beavis and Butthead Do America* (1997) had a not-so-lifelike president.

Further reading: Crowdus, Gary, ed. *The Political Companion to American Film.* Chicago: Lakeview Press, 1994; Genovese, Michael A. *The Political Film: An Introduction.* Needham Heights, Mass.: Simon & Schuster, 1998.

findings, presidential

The world of COVERT OPERATIONS must, by definition, be secret. And yet, a democracy must, by definition, be open. How, in a complex world, can the two competing needs be satisfied?

As covert operations came to greater use in the COLD WAR, then post–cold war, eras, the federal government groped for ways to keep these operations secret but also to ensure some ACCOUNTABILITY and control. Primary responsibility for covert operations falls under the purview of the president with the CENTRAL INTELLIGENCE AGENCY (CIA) as the primary agency to engage in these activities. When the president authorizes a covert operation he must give formal notice by filing a "presidential finding."

From TRUMAN to FORD, covert operations were not covered by "findings" but were initiated on the order of the president. As reports of misuse of the CIA surfaced, ways needed to be developed whereby a president could authorize covert operations and yet not be unaccountable.

In 1974 Congress passed the Hughes-Ryan Act, requiring the president to approve all covert operations and to inform the appropriate committees in Congress. This reporting was limited by the INTELLIGENCE OVERSIGHT ACT (1980) to include only two intelligence oversight committees.

In 1991 Congress passed another Intelligence Oversight Act, allowing the president greater flexibility to delay reporting "for a few days" in case of emergency. This 1991 act also made explicit the requirement that presidential findings be written, signed by the president, and submitted to Congress (to the "gang of eight" as it was called). This was an effort to correct the practice of the REAGAN administration that led to the Iran-contra scandal. The use of retroactive findings, another Reagan practice, was also outlawed by this act.

Further reading: Jeffreys-Jones, Rhodri. *The CIA and American Democracy.* New Haven, Conn.: Yale University Press, 1989; Johnson, Loch K. *America's Secret Power: The CIA in a Democratic Society.* New York: Oxford University Press, 1989.

fireside chats

Radio became a powerful tool for presidential persuasion during the presidency of Franklin D. ROOSEVELT. FDR used radio addresses (31 of them), known as "fireside chats," to educate and reassure the public in the midst of the GREAT DEPRESSION. They provided a powerful link between the president and the people. These fireside chats also revolutionized the way a president could connect directly with the people and also use a new technology to further presidential power. Roosevelt's charm, his reassuring voice, and the confidence that seemed to spring from his personality inspired many average citizens and helped stabilize the public mood in the volatile depression era. Increasingly, as technology advanced and the means of communicating with the people expanded, presidential "rhetoric" became more important. When the president could develop a direct link to the public, the possibility of his power and influence expanded. As the sole voice of the nation—or so presidents claim—the president is in a unique position to directly speak to and impose his presence on the public and the public agenda. FDR masterfully utilized radio addresses to develop such a link and increase his power in the political arena.

First Hundred Days

From March 9 to June 15, 1933, the famed First Hundred Days of the Franklin D. ROOSEVELT administration, Congress met in special session to respond to the GREAT DEPRESSION. During this time, Roosevelt led the heavily Democratic Congress in passage of an array of domestic legislation and took firm control of the nation's consciousness and its government.

By inauguration day, over half the nation's banks had declared bankruptcy or suspended operations. The new president immediately declared a 10-day "BANK HOLIDAY" for the banking industry while Congress took up an Emergency Banking Bill drafted by the White House. After its hasty passage, the statute sent federal auditors to review the nation's banks. Those deemed solvent were reopened amid a new atmosphere of confidence. During the Hundred Days, Congress also established the Federal Deposit Insurance Commission, which continues to this day to guarantee depositors' funds.

President Roosevelt's initial plan for the special session was to deal with the banking crisis and then send Congress home, but Congress's eagerness to be led encouraged the president to present to the legislators numerous other bills to address the continuing economic crisis.

Among the most significant acts passed by Congress in its extended session were those that created the famed "Alphabet Soup" agencies, such as the AAA, the CCC, the TVA, the FERA, CWA, PWA, and the NRA.

The AAA was the Agricultural Adjustment Administration, which provided cash subsidies to farmers to limit agricultural production, thus maintaining the incomes of farmers. The CCC was the CIVILIAN CONSERVATION CORPS, which sent millions of unemployed young men into military-style camps from which they ventured forth to plant trees, rebuild parks, and otherwise earn a monthly wage. The TVA, the TENNESSEE VALLEY AUTHORITY, grew into the nation's largest single provider of electricity. The Federal Emergency Relief Administration and its Civil Works Administration channeled millions of dollars to state relief agencies. The Public Works Administration concentrated on brick and mortar projects. As a consequence, the nation's parks are today outfitted with lodges, rest stations, and tourist facilities constructed in the architectural style of the 1930s. The National Recovery Administration, finally, oversaw a novel attempt to fight economic depression through government-business cooperation, aimed at reducing excess competition, which many economists believed to be at the root of the depression. The NRA's "codes of fair conduct" raised wages and encouraged the growth of labor unions. The NRA and the AAA were ruled unconstitutional by the Supreme Court in 1935 and 1936, respectively. Nevertheless, the First Hundred Days created numerous agencies that survived Court scrutiny and left a legacy of government activism that liberal presidents throughout the century looked to as a model.

Further reading: Leuchtenburg, William E. *Franklin Roosevelt and the New Deal, 1932–1940.* New York: Harper & Row, 1963; Schlesinger, Arthur M., Jr. *The Coming of the New Deal.* Norwalk, Conn.: Easton Press, 1987.
—Thomas S. Langston

first ladies

The American presidency, the most original political office created by the framers of the Constitution, unexpectedly spawned an influential albeit unofficial position simply called the first lady. To the 18th-century world accustomed to autocratic rulers, the proposed American presidency was an anomaly, unlike any other. It grew out of the faith that the Founders had in the demonstrated character of George WASHINGTON. The Founders' creative approach to the CHIEF EXECUTIVE has been matched over time by the evolution of the role of the first lady. The Constitution is silent on the position of the presidential spouse. An unofficial, unpaid position, the nation's first lady has evolved in its own right and was institutionalized by the beginning of the 20th century. The office now has a paid staff similar to that of the president. At its best, it is more than a symbolic, social role for the presidential spouse.

An examination of the rankings of first ladies by scholars helps to identify those who have made the most important contributions to defining the position, even though these ratings are of a much more recent vintage than the highly developed ones on presidents. In 1982, two scholars at Sienna College, Thomas O. Kelly II and Douglas A. Lonnstrom, surveyed historians at 102 randomly selected four-year colleges and universities—57 in the North and 45 in the South. Respondents rated the first ladies on a scale of one to five in 10 categories: background, value to country, integrity, leadership, intelligence, own person, accomplishments, courage, public image, and value to president. Overall rankings for the top five were (1) Eleanor ROOSEVELT, (2) Abigail ADAMS, (3) Lady Bird JOHNSON, (4) Dolley MADISON, and (5) Rosalynn CARTER. No attempt was made to subdivide the results into tiers or groups.

In 1993, with only slight revisions, the Sienna Research Institute replicated the 1982 study. The results were (1) Eleanor Roosevelt, (2) Hillary Rodham CLINTON, (3) Abigail Adams, (4) Dolley Madison, and (5) Rosalynn Carter. Although she had been first lady for only a short time, Clin-

ton already was rated among the top, pushing Johnson from third to sixth place.

That same year, the *Journal of American History* conducted a reader survey. The 1,047 respondents ranked Eleanor Roosevelt above all other females in the "most admired person in American history" category. Overall, she ranked as the sixth most admired person in our country's history. For a special April 1997 issue of *Life*, its editors surveyed historians, politicians, and writers. Eleanor Roosevelt was the only first lady—and the highest-ranking female— among America's 25 greatest heroes/heroines in that survey.

Her standing with the public is likely only to increase. With the unveiling of a memorial located in New York City's Riverside Park in 1996, she became the first presidential spouse commemorated in a public statue. Of greater significance is that the Franklin D. Roosevelt Memorial in Washington, D.C., which opened in 1997, is the first presidential memorial to depict a first lady also. That memorial is likely to engrave in the public psyche recognition of her as the greatest first lady.

While all first ladies did not perform equally in their White House positions, one indicator of performance is consistent. Marriages between active and flexible personalities are more like to produce spouses who treat each other and their staffs as professional equals. In short, they dignify others. Therefore, it is not surprising that Franklin Roosevelt supported Eleanor's growing public role, even after their intimate physical relationship ended.

Nor should it be surprising that Mary Todd LINCOLN was the first spouse to campaign with her husband. She was the most politically active first lady between Dolley Madison (her distant relative by marriage) and Eleanor Roosevelt. Her behavior subsequent to her traumatic losses of three sons and husband forever blemished her popular and historical reputation, but Mary Todd Lincoln, like her 20th-century counterpart Eleanor Roosevelt, blurred the lines between social and political affairs. In that same tradition, Betty FORD belatedly grew into an active political wife whose openness enhanced her stature. Rosalynn Carter became her spouse's equal before his political career began, while she was working with him to make the family peanut farm a success. As first lady, Mrs. Carter sat in on CABINET meetings and occasionally represented the president abroad. Hillary Rodham Clinton, who was given the opportunity to plan the president's health care reform proposal and to testify before Congress on its behalf, epitomized the political partner.

Political partnerships such as those mentioned are characteristic of some of the most enduring marriages among presidential couples. When both partners are mentally healthy, power may enhance rather than undermine their relationships. These pioneering first ladies, who were sometimes controversial, shared a common trait: each self-actualized through the political arena. In doing so, they became the first ladies who have done the most to create a dual presidency of first couples, regardless of gender.

Further reading: Caroli, Betty B. *First Ladies.* New York: Oxford University Press, 1987; Marton, Kati. *Hidden Power: Presidential Marriages That Shaped Our Recent History.* New York: Pantheon Books, 2001; Pederson, William D., and Frank J. Williams. "America's Presidential Triumvirate: Quantitative Measures of Character." In *George Washington, Foundations of Presidential Leadership and Character,* edited by Ethan Fishman, William Pederson, and Mark Rozell. Westport, Conn.: Praeger, 2001; Watson, Robert P. *The Presidents' Wives: Reassessing the Office of First Lady.* Boulder, Colo.: L. Rienner, 2000.

—William D. Pederson

First Lady's Office

The First Lady's Office facilitates presidential outreach, policy processing, and internal management. Of the three, however, outreach is indisputably the office's defining task. The office organizes every event in the White House, from state dinners to policy briefings, assuming responsibility for the delivery of the president's message to a variety of publics. Like other White House outreach offices, the development of this office in the modern presidency has been primarily driven by environmental factors, though their effect has been mediated by the political choices of the first lady (as the office executive) and by the president (as the CHIEF EXECUTIVE). These circumstances are well illustrated by the offices of Lou Henry HOOVER, Claudia Alta (Lady Bird) JOHNSON, Rosalynn CARTER, and Hillary Rodham CLINTON.

Throughout her years as first lady, Lou Henry Hoover had at least three full-time secretaries. A fourth secretary managed WHITE HOUSE social events, under Mrs. Hoover's direct and close supervision. This was the only member of the first lady's staff salaried by the government, with the others paid by the first lady. When her workload grew heavier—as when the deepening Depression led to increased public correspondence—Mrs. Hoover hired and paid additional staff. If President Hoover inaugurated the practice of a plural White House staff for the president's office, it may well be that Lou Henry Hoover did the same for the first lady's office.

Though earlier FIRST LADIES had drawn on the resources of the West Wing to manage their press relations and public outreach, Lady Bird Johnson had her own press secretary/staff director. Responsible for coordinating the first lady's public outreach, this individual did (or delegated) campaign- and policy-related speech writing, scheduling, and advance work. As in the past, a social secretary arranged events hosted by the president and/or the first lady. Two Interior Department detailees worked on beautification programs. Thus, the press secretary/staff director and social secretary (and their assistants) complemented one another functionally, while the detailees focused more narrowly on policy substance.

Rosalynn Carter's staffing arrangements set a new standard. During the presidential transition, study of Betty FORD's office identified the need for stronger management within the office and for better relationships with the West Wing. Mrs. Carter therefore named a project director specifically to supervise her policy-related work. At the same time, East Wing and West Wing correspondence was integrated as part of an effort to ensure efficiency and consistency. In 1978 passage of the WHITE HOUSE PERSONNEL AUTHORIZATION ACT formally authorized staff to assist the first lady. In 1979 Carter reorganized her office twice. Scheduling and advance positions were first established to handle the first lady's "political" travel. Then a second reorganization shifted the managerial task of staff supervision from the press secretary to a distinct staff director. This formal office structure continued, with slight modifications, in the REAGAN, BUSH, and CLINTON administrations.

During the Clinton administration, there were notable changes in the formal definition of the first lady's position, which had significant staffing implications. In *American Physicians and Surgeons, Inc. et al v. Hillary Rodham Clinton* (1993), the District of Columbia Circuit Court ruled on appeal that the contributions of first ladies were so historically consistent and extensive that the first lady was a *de facto* federal official. The Clinton administration interpreted this as an endorsement of the first lady's role as a senior presidential adviser. Throughout the Clinton administration, therefore, the first lady was staffed by domestic policy staff in the West Wing, in addition to her East Wing and Millennium Project staffs.

The evolution of the First Lady's Office has not been progressive or linear. First ladies TRUMAN, EISENHOWER, KENNEDY, and NIXON had fewer staff and less extensive political networks than did first ladies Hoover, Roosevelt, Johnson, Carter, Bush, and Clinton. Still, it is clear that the first lady's office has grown in size and specialization. The tasks assigned to staff members, the titles they have held, the discretion they have been granted—these organizational qualities constitute a powerful message about what is valued within and by a presidency. Having facilitated the first lady's political activism, developments in the first lady's office have also contributed to change in the wider polity.

Further reading: Anthony, Carl Sferrazza. *First Ladies: The Saga of the Presidents' Wives and Their Power.* New York: William Morrow, 1990; Caroli, Betty Boyd. *First Ladies,* expanded ed. New York: Oxford University Press, 1995.

—Mary Anne Borrelli

fiscal policy

The president's use of taxing and spending policies in order to achieve certain macroeconomic goals is called fiscal policy. Particularly since the NEW DEAL, the president has had the responsibility of trying to manage the economy by keeping full employment, holding inflation low, and simultaneously maintaining economic growth.

Origins of the president's use of fiscal policy go back as far as the beginnings of the Republic. Federalists wanted the central government to take a leading role in fostering economic growth and industrialization through funding internal improvements and the like. The LAISSEZ-FAIRE policies favored by the government up until the Depression limited the effectiveness of the types of policies. However, by the late 1930s, economic conditions in this country and the publication of J.M. Keynes's *The General Theory of Employment, Interest and Money* (1936), fiscal policy had become a major tool at the president's disposal. Not only did economic conditions demand that the federal government take a lead role in designing policy to deal with the depression, but Keynes's work gave theoretical justification for his doing so.

Keynes's argument was that slowdowns in the economy were caused by a decline in aggregate demand for goods and services. Through deficit spending (by a combination of lowering taxes and increasing spending) the government would increase aggregate demand and pull the economy out of recession. In times of rapid economic growth and inflation the opposite is done. By raising taxes and decreasing spending aggregate demand would decline and the economy would slow. This became the accepted theory of the economy from the late 1930s until the late 1970s, when it became clear that Keynesian theory had no suitable answer for the conditions of stagflation. However, presidents continued to use fiscal policy as a means for trying to control the economy.

Several factors weaken the president's ability to use fiscal policy. First, much of what influences the economy is out of the hands of the president. An independent Federal Reserve Board makes decisions about interest rates and the money supply which also have a strong effect on the economy. Second, from 1974, Congress limited the president's ability to set fiscal policy on his own, because Congress started setting its own budget and fiscal policies, many times independent of the president's agenda. Third, large deficits and the dramatic rise in spending on entitlement programs, which made spending control much more difficult, added to this problem.

Further reading: Savage, James D. *Balanced Budgets and American Politics*. Ithaca, N.Y.: Cornell University Press, 1988; Stein, Herbert. *Presidential Economics: The Making of Economic Policy from Roosevelt to Reagan and Beyond.* Washington, D.C.: American Enterprise Institute for Public Policy Research, 1988; Wildavsky, Aaron, and Naomi Caiden. *The New Politics of the Budgetary Process.* New York: Addison Wesley/Longman, 2001.

—Joseph Wert

Ford, Betty (Elizabeth Ann Bloomer Ford) (1918–)
first lady, social activist

As a young woman, Betty Ford pursued a career in dance, attending the Bennington School of Dance (summers, 1936 and 1937) and joining Martha Graham's auxiliary dance troupe in New York (1938–41). When she returned home to Michigan, she became a department store buyer. She married (1942) and divorced (1947) William C. Warren, before meeting Gerald R. FORD. The two married in 1948, dividing the wedding day between his congressional campaign and their ceremony.

The Fords had four children, Michael (born 1950), John (1952), Steven (1956), and Susan (1957). Gerald Ford's political career limited his home life; when he was elected House Minority Leader in 1965, it became nonexistent. Always the primary caregiver, Betty Ford effectively

First Lady Betty Ford *(Library of Congress)*

became a single parent even as she assumed a more visible political role. Suffering from the combined effects of strain and overmedication for chronic illness (arthritis and a pinched nerve), Ford consulted a psychiatrist. When she publicly discussed the value of this therapy, she made her first of several contributions to changing public perceptions of illness and treatment.

As the wife of Vice President and then President Ford, Betty Ford was distinguished by her traditionalism and her liberal feminism. Her "projects" were traditional, including art, dance, and children. Yet she conducted a PRESS CONFERENCE—the first held by a first lady since the Roosevelt administration—less than a month after she entered the White House. She lobbied for presidential appointments for women. When she was diagnosed with breast cancer and underwent a radical mastectomy, she commented on her medical condition. Approximately 56,000 letters arrived at the White House, many from cancer survivors who valued the first lady's leadership in educating the public about this disease. In her speeches, she insisted that women's family and career choices be honored, their contributions valued. Never popular with conservative Republicans, Ford nonetheless made numerous appearances and was well-received in the 1976 campaign.

Ford entered the Long Beach Naval Hospital rehabilitation clinic for drug and alcohol addiction treatment in 1978. Once again, stress and overmedication for chronic illness had compromised her health. Again, Ford discussed her treatment on behalf of public education. In 1982 she cofounded the Betty Ford Center for alcohol and substance abuse recovery.

Further reading: Ford, Betty. *A Glad Awakening.* New York: Doubleday, 1987; ———. *The Times of My Life.* New York: Harper and Row, 1978.

—Mary Anne Borrelli

Ford, Gerald R. (1913–) *thirty-eighth U.S. president*
Born Leslie King, Jr., July 14, 1913, his name was changed to that of his stepfather's when Gerald Ford was a toddler. Raised in Grand Rapids, Michigan, Ford received his B.A. in 1935 from the University of Michigan and his LL.B. from Yale University in 1941. During WORLD WAR II he served four years in the navy, first teaching aviators and then working as an aviation operations officer aboard the aircraft carrier the *USS Monterey.*

In 1948 he defeated Representative Bartel Jonkman in the Republican primary for the 5th District of Michigan and went on to win the general election. In his 25-year congressional career, he developed a conservative record on most issues including ECONOMIC POLICY, civil rights, and FEDERALISM. In foreign policy he was an internationalist,

generally in favor of the UNITED NATIONS and DÉTENTE with the Soviet Union.

As a member of the subcommittees of the Appropriations Committee that controlled the budgets of Defense and the CENTRAL INTELLIGENCE AGENCY, Ford began to develop both substantive expertise and a circle of influence. In 1963 he was elected chairman of the House Republican Conference, and only two years later he defeated then minority leader Charles Halleck (Indiana) for the position he would hold until assuming the vice presidency in 1973. As a party leader he was generally respected for his competence and known for his loyalty to Presidents EISENHOWER and NIXON.

Both his loyalty to the REPUBLICAN PARTY and his popularity among fellow members of Congress were instrumental in the choice to appoint him to the WARREN COMMISSION in 1963, which investigated the assassination of President KENNEDY. In 1968 presidential candidate Richard Nixon asked him to be his running mate. With an eye to possible Republican gains in the House that would enable him to run for Speaker, Ford declined.

His successful congressional trajectory was altered, however, in 1973 when President Nixon appointed Ford to the vice presidency after a plea of *nolo contendere* to income tax evasion forced Vice President Spiro AGNEW from that office. Ford was chosen both because of his loyalty and because of his likely confirmation by Congress, as required by the TWENTY-FIFTH AMENDMENT to the Constitution. Indeed, Ford underwent an extensive congressional confirmation process, and on December 6, 1973, he was confirmed and assumed office. Only eight months later, the so-called WATERGATE scandal's "smoking gun" tape recording became public, on which President Nixon was heard ordering the CIA to block the FBI's investigation of the scandal. Facing the near certainty of an IMPEACHMENT in the House and possible conviction in the Senate, President Nixon resigned the office of the presidency and on August 9, 1974, Vice President Gerald Ford assumed the presidency.

With a reputation for honesty, Ford was generally well liked by his former colleagues in Congress and immediately following his swearing-in he enjoyed a HONEYMOON PERIOD with Washington and the general public alike. Indeed, as he said in his first speech as president, ". . . this long national nightmare is over. Our good republic is a government of laws, not men. Here the people rule."

Whatever goodwill had accrued was swiftly demolished on September 8, 1974, when Ford issued a presidential pardon to Nixon for "all offenses against the United States." As Senator Marlow Cook of Kentucky said, "Doesn't he have any sense of timing?" referring to upcoming congressional elections. Indeed, in the MIDTERM ELECTIONS of 1974, Republican candidates were punished mightily at the polls. Democrats gained 43 seats in the House, three in the Senate, and won four gubernatorial races across the country.

In addition to the political fallout, the decision was criticized for the effect it had on the Watergate investigation's ability to seek other incidents. Though President Ford vigorously denied any deals were struck prior to his taking office or during his administration, politicians and the public were skeptical. This had profound implications on his ability to move his agenda through Congress, to react to domestic and foreign policy crises, and, ultimately, to win election in 1976.

With a solid Democratic majority in both the House and the Senate, and plummeting public approval after the pardon, President Ford had little political capital to accomplish his policy goals. The economic situation was dire and complex, as the country was experiencing both rising inflation and a stagnant economy leading to unemployment. Labeled "stagflation," this unusual economic condition forced the Ford administration to choose between fighting inflation and tackling unemployment.

In August of 1974, the Consumer Price Index (CPI) had risen 1.3 percent, which was the second largest monthly increase since the KOREAN WAR. By October it had risen another 0.9 percent. These conditions, combined with President Ford's own predisposition toward fiscal conservatism and deficit reduction, led him to combat inflation first, calling for a temporary tax surcharge on individuals and corporations in the upper income brackets. Additionally, he appealed to the public to participate in finding ways to lower prices. He created a volunteer organization, Whip Inflation Now, which citizens could join; they would receive WIN buttons to wear showing their support.

While centering his economic plan on fighting inflation jibed with President Ford's personal beliefs about fiscal responsibility, a number of economic indicators suggested mounting problems. At the beginning of his administration, unemployment levels were at 5.4 percent, gross national product was down, and the Dow Jones Index was down 99 points in August of 1974. In addition new housing starts had fallen 15 percent from July to August and the trade deficit was $1.1 billion. To combat these ills, President Ford advocated a cut in individual and corporate taxes; measures that would decrease dependence on foreign oil and consumption of fossil fuels; and attempts to reduce the size and scope of the federal government, in an effort to reduce spending to address the size of the federal deficit.

His promise to veto any congressional spending measures that were not offset by spending cuts was part of a larger veto strategy in dealing with the strong Democratic congressional control. With little political capital after the pardon, President Ford vetoed 61 bills in the 16 months he was president. Of those, Congress attempted to override 28 and was only successful on 12.

President Gerald R. Ford *(Library of Congress)*

In addition to the domestic policy concerns facing President Ford, there were a series of international incidents to which he had to respond as he tried to move his foreign policy forward. A decades-old fight between Greece and Turkey over Cyprus would be the first international crisis President Ford faced.

In July 1974 Turkey invaded Cyprus. This was a response to the overthrow of the Cyprus government and the installation of a pro-Greece government; Turkey feared abuse of the Turkish minority in Cyprus at the hands of the Greek military junta. Four days after Ford took office, talks sponsored by Secretary of State Henry KISSINGER broke down. When the United States sided with Turkey in the conflict, pro-Greece forces stormed the U.S. Embassy, killing Ambassador Rodger Davies.

Democrats in the Senate, led by Senator Henry "Scoop" Jackson (Dem.-Wash.), opposed the Ford administration's policy and sponsored a bill that ended aid to Turkey. On October 14, Ford vetoed that bill and the override attempt was unsuccessful. This was repeated again two days later, but the closer override vote motivated the administration to compromise, accepting an embargo of Turkey. Furious, Turkey retaliated by closing all military bases to the United States. These bases had been important military installations, housing Juniper missiles, CIA listening posts, and the U-2 spy planes.

Throughout the Nixon administration, COLD WAR tension had been easing between the United States and the Soviet Union, thus paving the way for smooth negotiations on trade and most favored nation (MFN) status. However, the Democratic majority, again led by Senator Jackson, forced the president to compromise. Passage of MFN status for the Soviet Union was tied to the USSR's unlimited acceptance of Jewish emigration. Though not what the administration had originally negotiated with the USSR, President Ford was forced to sign the bill on December 13, 1974, under threat of his veto being overridden.

President Ford took office at the very end of the U.S. involvement in the war in southeast Asia. In April 1975 the last of the U.S. troops and personnel were evacuated out of both Vietnam and Cambodia. On May 12, 1975, a U.S. cargo ship, the *Mayaguez,* was fired upon, seized, and boarded. Given that many at the time attributed this act of aggression to the new Cambodian government, this was widely seen as a test of the Ford administration's determination. President Ford ordered the military to take action. Though 41 American lives were lost, there was widespread public approval for the action.

Illustrating President Ford's political weakness was the challenge to his candidacy within his own party, by former governor Ronald REAGAN of California. Though Ford successfully won the Republican nomination, Reagan was a formidable opponent, supported ideologically by the conservative wing and regionally by the West and part of the South. Facing a strong Democratic challenger, former governor Jimmy CARTER of Georgia, Ford was also hampered by a slowing economic recovery, lingering public resentment over his pardon of Nixon, lackluster and uneven debate performances, and a series of political missteps. President Ford lost the election by 27 ELECTORAL COLLEGE votes and by 1.7 million popular votes.

Further reading: Firestone, Bernard J., and Alexej Ugrinsky, eds. *Gerald R. Ford and the Politics of Post-Watergate America.* Westport, Conn.: Greenwood Press, 1993; Greene, John Robert. *The Presidency of Gerald R. Ford.* Lawrence: University Press of Kansas, 1995; Porter, Roger B. *Presidential Decision Making: The Economic Policy Board.* New York: Cambridge University Press, 1980.

—Rebecca E. Deen

foreign affairs

While it is often assumed that the president makes foreign policy, and indeed that is often the case, nowhere in the U.S. Constitution does it clearly spell out what branch shall be in control of foreign affairs.

In fact, the foreign affairs powers are—like so many powers within the Constitution—shared by the president and Congress. While the president has certain advantages in the development of foreign policy, the Congress too has significant powers in this area.

Thomas JEFFERSON, articulating a widely shared view, once wrote that "the transaction of business with foreign nations is Executive altogether." And a casual observer of today's foreign policy process might well draw a similar conclusion—but the Constitution gives to the Congress legislative power, the power of the purse, the power to raise armies, to declare war, and a host of other powers in the area of foreign relations.

The president is constitutionally the COMMANDER IN CHIEF in times of war, and the president receives foreign emissaries. The president also heads the EXECUTIVE BRANCH of which the State and Defense Departments are a part.

Crises and war have tilted policy powers toward the presidency. This had been especially true from the 1940s (WORLD WAR II) on through the COLD WAR and continues today with the war against terrorism. Today, presidents claim inherent power to commit the United States to war and use EXECUTIVE AGREEMENTS in place of treaties in making policy. In part Congress has been guilty of delegating foreign policy power to the presidents; in part, the presidents have aggressively grabbed foreign policy powers; and in general, the courts and the public have sided with these presidential power grabs.

Further reading: Adler, David Gray, and Larry George, eds. *The Constitution and the Conduct of Foreign Policy.* Lawrence: University Press of Kansas, 1996; Corwin, Edward S. *The President, Office and Powers, 1787–1984: History and Analysis of Practice and Opinion.* Edited by Randall W. Bland, Theodore T. Hindson, and Jack W. Peltason. New York: New York University Press, 1984; Fisher, Louis. *Constitution Conflicts between Congress and the President,* 3d ed. Lawrence: University Press of Kansas, 1991; Glennon, Michael J. *Constitutional Diplomacy.* Princeton, N.J.: Princeton University Press, 1990; Koh, Harold Hongju. *The National Security Constitution: Sharing Power after the Iran-Contra Affair.* New Haven, Conn.: Yale University Press, 1990.

foreign aid

The United States, for humanitarian and political reasons, gives aid—financial, food, etc.—to other nations. While the percentage of the U.S. foreign aid ranks as one of the lowest of any developed nation, the massive size of the U.S. economy nevertheless means that the United States can use this aid to influence the behavior of other nations.

After WORLD WAR II, the MARSHALL PLAN and TRUMAN DOCTRINE infused money and aid into Europe, Greece, and Turkey, with massive amounts of aid, all designed to strengthen those governments and stem the tide of Soviet expansion.

Also after World War II, the United States set up an international monetary and relief regime, creating the International Monetary Fund, the World Bank, and other agencies to help nations in need, but also to impose market systems around the world.

In recent years, U.S. aid has been relatively miserly regarding foreign aid programs, and critics argue that the United States is missing an opportunity both to help nations in need and to exert greater influence across the globe.

Foreign Intelligence Surveillance Act (1978)

In the post–World War II era, presidents claimed broad inherent authority to authorize warrantless ELECTRONIC SURVEILLANCE of domestic communication. In 1978 Congress passed the Foreign Intelligence Surveillance Act, requiring that such instances of surveillance be based on a court order by a designated federal district court judge. Application for said surveillance must go through the attorney general. In the post-9/11 period, and with the passage of the USA PATRIOT ACT, the attorney general has greater authority to use surveillance.

Foreign Service

The Foreign Service is comprised of the professional diplomats responsible for the execution of U.S. foreign policy. Under the auspices of the U.S. DEPARTMENT OF STATE, foreign service employees are the career civil servants who deal with FOREIGN AFFAIRS and consular offices and staff U.S. embassies across the globe. Critics sometimes see the foreign service as too interested in smoothing over conflicts with DIPLOMACY rather than using force to solve international problems, but such criticisms, while common, have little merit. Diplomacy is vital to the protection of U.S. interests, and the creative use of diplomacy can be a great benefit to the nation.

former presidents

There has always been a bit of confusion regarding what role former presidents should play. Some, especially in the early decades of the republic, reentered politics. John Quincy ADAMS served in the House of Representatives for 16 years, and William Howard TAFT became Chief Justice of the Supreme Court. Some, like Herbert HOOVER, headed special commissions.

In recent years, former presidents' roles and lives have varied dramatically. Most ex-presidents wrote, and received a great deal of compensation from, memoirs. After his RESIGNATION, Richard NIXON spent two decades writing books and trying to reverse his WATERGATE-stained image. Gerald FORD, after a brief attempt at a political comeback, accepted a number of lucrative posts on corporate boards. Jimmy CARTER used his post-presidency to serve in a variety of ways, from hosting peace conferences, to monitoring elections around the world, to building low-income housing for Habitat for Humanity, and he won a Nobel Peace Prize. Ronald REAGAN was diagnosed with Alzheimer's Disease shortly after leaving office and withdrew from public life.

It was not until the Former Presidents Act of 1958 that federal funds went to assist ex-presidents. That act established a modest pension and staff and office allowance. Over the years the benefits have been increased, and SECRET SERVICE protection has been added. Also, the federal government supports the libraries of former presidents.

Forrestal, James V. (1892–1949) *government official*

James V. Forrestal was born in Beacon, New York, on February 15, 1892. He attended Dartmouth College and Princeton University but did not earn a bachelor's degree at either institution. He served in the U.S. navy during WORLD WAR I and became a successful Wall Street financier. When President Franklin D. ROOSEVELT appointed Forrestal undersecretary of the navy in 1940, Forrestal specialized in managing procurement for the navy. He subsequently served as secretary of the navy from 1944 to 1947 and as secretary of defense from 1947 to 1949.

After WORLD WAR II, President Harry S TRUMAN, Congress, and the military considered various proposals for replacing the Department of War and Department of the Navy as separate CABINET departments with a DEPARTMENT OF DEFENSE that would have authority over all branches of the military, including the air force as a new branch independent of the army. As secretary of the navy, Forrestal was a vigorous advocate of the navy's policy and budgetary interests and conflicted with Truman's priorities in first protecting the army's interests and then in trying to achieve an entirely unified military establishment. Nonetheless, Truman appointed Forrestal as the nation's first secretary of defense in 1947.

During his tenure as secretary of defense, Forrestal focused on resolving interservice rivalries among the armed forces over defense spending, military strategy, and weapons technology. In particular, Forrestal had to address such issues as the further development of missile technology and an increase in the number of long-range bomber planes. After the 1948 election, Truman decided to replace Forrestal with Louis Johnson. Shortly after Forrestal resigned, he entered the Bethesda Naval Hospital because of mental and physical exhaustion. He committed suicide by jumping from a hospital window on May 22, 1949.

Further reading: Millis, Walter, ed. *The Forrestal Diaries.* New York: Viking Press, 1951; Rogow, Arnold A. *James Forrestal: A Study of Personality, Politics, and Policy.* New York: Macmillan, 1963.

Four Freedoms

In 1941, with war in Europe threatening to involve the United States, President Franklin D. ROOSEVELT articulated his "Four Freedoms," an effort to develop a rationale or set of goals for the war. In his annual message, delivered on January 6, 1941, nearly a year before U.S. entry into the war, FDR set forth a series of universal truths centered around four freedoms all humans are to enjoy. As Roosevelt's message read,

> The first is freedom of speech and expression—everywhere in the world.
>
> The second is freedom of every person to worship God in his own way—everywhere in the world.
>
> The third is freedom from want—which, translated into world terms, means economic understandings which will secure to every nation a healthy peacetime life for its inhabitants—everywhere in the world.
>
> The fourth is freedom from fear—which, translated into world terms, means a worldwide reduction of armaments to such a point and in such a thorough fashion that no nation will be in a position to commit an act of physical aggression against any neighbor—anywhere in the world.

Roosevelt, acknowledging that this was asking for a great deal, denied that this was a utopian dream and insisted that it should be the benchmark for the postwar world. This vision was, in Roosevelt's words, attainable in "our own time and generation."

Fourteen Points

On January 8, 1918, in an address to a joint session of Congress, President Woodrow WILSON enunciated his goals for the peace that would follow the inevitable defeat of the Central Powers in WORLD WAR I. Wilson was an idealist, and these aims were based on his desire to make the world "safe for democracy."

The Fourteen Points, in brief, are as follows:

1. Open covenants of peace, openly arrived at; diplomacy shall proceed frankly and in the public view.
2. Freedom of navigation upon the seas, except when closed by international action.
3. The removal of all economic barriers among all nations.
4. The reduction of national armaments to the lowest possible levels.
5. An absolutely impartial adjustment of all colonial claims, observing the interests of the populations and the claims of the government whose title is to be determined.
6. The evacuation of all Russian territory and a settlement allowing for the independent determination of her own political development and national policy.
7. The evacuation and restoration of Belgium.
8. The freedom and restoration of French territory, including Alsace-Lorraine.
9. The readjustment of the frontiers of Italy along lines of nationality.
10. Autonomous development for the people of Austria-Hungary.
11. The evacuation and restoration of Rumania, Serbia, and Montenegro, with international guarantees of their integrity.
12. Assured autonomous development for the nationalities under Turkish control and the permanent guarantee of free passage for all nations through the Dardanelles.
13. The independence of Poland, with free access to the sea and international guarantees of economic independence and territorial integrity.
14. A general association of nations for the purpose of affording mutual guarantees of political independence and territorial integrity to all states.

While Wilson hoped to make these principles the basis for the peace settlement, he encountered initial opposition from the Central Powers. Facing defeat, however, in October 1918, the Germans requested an immediate cessation of fighting and the start of peace negotiations based on the Fourteen Points. At the same time, Austria-Hungary assumed a similar posture. Once Wilson had received assurances from the German chancellor, Prince Maximilian of Boden, that Germany would not renew the fighting, unrestricted submarine warfare would cease, and German armies would halt the practice of merciless destruction as they retreated, he informed the Allies of the German position and began discussions for the acceptance of the Fourteen Points as the basis for the peace negotiations. He succeeded, and the armistice agreement of November 11, 1918, included recognition of the Fourteen Points and additional elaborations made in subsequent addresses as the foundation for securing a peace settlement. The armistice came with reservations, however, concerning reparations and the freedom of the seas.

Even with the acceptance of the Fourteen Points in the armistice agreement, Wilson knew he needed to fight for his ideals to survive the negotiations for a final peace treaty. In light of this belief, Wilson became the first president to cross the Atlantic Ocean while in office, as he traveled to Paris to represent the United States at the peace conference in December 1918. Although Wilson faced some opposition from the Allies, especially France and its leader Georges Clemenceau, the TREATY OF VERSAILLES, signed on June 28, 1919, substantially honored his vision as enunciated in the Fourteen Points, with special satisfaction garnered with the acceptance of the LEAGUE OF NATIONS. Once the principle of the League was accepted, Wilson knew the practical goals of France, England, and Italy must be met as well. France desired a highly punitive settlement against Germany, particularly due to the harsh treatment it received following its defeat by Prussia in 1871. As a result of the compromise between the idealism of the Fourteen Points and the punitive demands of France, Germany felt betrayed by the Treaty. The terms were harsh; Germany lost significant territory, its military was substantially restricted, and the "War Guilt Clause" held Germany responsible for the war, thus requiring the country to pay crippling reparations. The terms of the Treaty of Versailles are seen as a leading cause of WORLD WAR II.

The Fourteen Points Address is widely regarded as Wilson's greatest speech. Although the Senate refused to ratify the Treaty, thus preventing the United States from joining the League of Nations, Wilson was awarded the 1919 Nobel Peace Prize for his role in founding the League and seeking a just peace to end World War I.

Further reading: Ferrell, Robert H. *Woodrow Wilson and World War I, 1917–1921.* New York: Harper and Row, 1985; Seymour, Charles. *Woodrow Wilson and the World War.* New York: United States Publishers Association, Inc., 1921.

—Elizabeth Matthews

Freedom of Information Act (FOIA)

The Freedom of Information Act became law in 1966 in an attempt to make federal records available to any person. Since its implementation, the FOIA has been used extensively by journalists in news gathering efforts, especially in investigative stories to uncover government wrongdoing. The federal government receives approximately 600,000 FOIA requests each year. However, President Lyndon JOHNSON was reluctant to sign the bill into law, and journalists' requests have been routinely met with hostility from government officials over the years, particularly during the presidency of Ronald REAGAN. The goal of the Reagan Administration was to enforce the letter of the law, but not the spirit of the law. The FOIA applies to federal agencies to make all records available for inspection and copying, and each agency is supposed to provide an index of available documents (to be updated every three months). An agency must respond to a written request for a record within 10 working days. If a delay occurs, an appeal must be sent to the head of the agency, which must respond within 20 working days. Extensions can be granted due to the large volume and backlog of requests. If time limits are not met, or

the person requesting the documents is denied, he or she can appeal in a federal district court. If the plaintiff wins, the government must pay all costs. Agencies covered by the act include departments within the EXECUTIVE BRANCH, or independent agencies such as the CIA or NASA. It cannot be used for the president and his immediate advisers, Congress, its committees, and agencies under its direct control (GENERAL ACCOUNTING OFFICE, Library of Congress), or the judicial branch. Nine exemptions exist to maintain confidentiality of documents. They include: NATIONAL SECURITY; agency management records; materials already kept secret by other laws; trade secrets or commercially viable items; inter- and intra-agency memos; personnel, medical, and similar files; material about ongoing civil and criminal investigations; reports by banks and financial institutions; and maps of oil and gas wells. Court decisions interpreting the FOIA usually fall into three categories: defining an agency record (a document must be in the legal possession of the agency); defining the ability of a third party to prevent the release of documents; or defining the nine exemptions. The PRESIDENTIAL RECORDS ACT (PRA), passed in 1978, also placed presidential documents under the governance of FOIA by making all records pertaining to the official functions and duties of the president the property of the U.S. government. Presidential LIBRARIES are the repositories for these records, which are eligible for access under the FOIA five years after a president leaves office. A president may restrict access to certain kinds of information for up to 12 years after he leaves office; after that time, the only exemptions allowed fall under the FOIA. The Reagan Administration was the first to be governed by the PRA, which took effect on January 20, 1981.

Further reading: Holsinger, Ralph, and Jon Paul Dilts. *Media Law,* 4th ed. New York: McGraw-Hill, 1997; Pember, Don R. *Mass Media Law.* Dubuque, Iowa: Wm. C. Brown Co., 1977.

—Lori Cox-Han

frontloading

Delegates to the national nominating conventions of the Democratic and Republican Parties choose presidential nominees during the summer prior to presidential election. State legislatures, in cooperation with political parties in that state, determine the timing and method of delegate selection. Beginning in the 1970s, binding preference primaries became the principal method by which delegates are chosen, with the majority of states holding primaries after April 1 of the election year. In 1988 states began to frontload the nomination calendar of events by moving primaries into the months of February and March. By the 2000 presidential election, 60 percent of states holding primaries did so before March 15 with a clear majority of the delegates to the national nominating convention selected.

Many states frontloaded their primaries after realizing that smaller states such as Iowa and New Hampshire, who selected their delegates earlier in the presidential nomination cycle, exhibit an extraordinary influence on the outcome of the nomination process. Essentially, the choices voters faced in later primaries became structured by the outcome of earlier primaries as losing candidates withdrew from competition. Thus, moving the primary date forward permitted states to increase their influence on the outcome of the nomination process. For example, the first group of states to bundle their primaries together early in the nomination cycle were Southern states who wished to see the DEMOCRATIC PARTY nominate a more moderate to conservative candidate; this became known as SUPER TUESDAY.

The impact of frontloading on the presidential nomination process is significant. First, bundling so many primaries together increases the importance of fund-raising to pay for the campaign in a large number of states early in the cycle. Second, running in many primaries concurrently changes the strategy necessary to win, emphasizing an air war campaign of television and radio advertising to reach caucus and primary voters. Third, frontloading restricts the field of viable candidates to established political figures. Momentum from performing well in the Iowa caucuses and in New Hampshire is no longer sufficient to carry lesser-known candidates to the presidential nomination as it did Jimmy CARTER in 1976. Generally, the media and voters in frontloaded states can only take seriously the better-known candidates who perform well in public-opinion preference polls, receive key endorsements from leading political figures, and then raise significant sums of money before the primaries even begin.

Further reading: Polsby, Nelson W., and Aaron Wildavsky. *Presidential Elections.* New York: Chatham House Publishers, 2000; Wayne, Stephen. *Road to the White House, 2000.* Boston: Bedford/St. Martin's, 2000.

—Randall E. Adkins

G

Gadsden Purchase

In 1852 Franklin PIERCE was elected president on a pledge to expand U.S. territory. One area ripe for expansion was near the U.S. border with Mexico. The president sent James Gadsden to negotiate for transit and other rights on behalf of the United States. After a complex set of negotiations, both with General Antonio Lopez de Santa Ana of Mexico, then with the U.S. Senate over treaty provisions, the treaty was finally approved in 1854. In the Gadsden Purchase, the United States acquired 39 million acres of land, far less than President Pierce had wanted. Pierce reluctantly agreed, however, as he felt this was the best deal to be had in a difficult situation. On June 30, 1854, the United States and Mexico exchanged ratified treaties, making the Gadsden Purchase the final acquisition of contiguous land attained by the United States.

Gallatin, Albert (1761–1849) *member of Congress, treasury secretary*

Born in Geneva, Switzerland, in 1761, Gallatin immigrated to America at the age of 19 and became active in the Jeffersonian Republican movement. He served in the House of Representatives from 1795 to 1801 and became the leading voice for tax cutting and the reduction of public debt.

Gallatin was a House member less than two weeks when he proposed the creation of a congressional watchdog committee to monitor government expenditures. This committee became known as the Ways and Means Committee and soon became an influential force in financial management in the new republic. Gallatin served on this committee until 1801 when President JEFFERSON appointed him secretary of the Treasury. In that post, Gallatin also served as a liaison between Jefferson and the Congress, helping the president exert a behind-the-scenes leadership over Congress.

In 1814 Gallatin served as a member of the Peace Commission in Ghent, from 1816 to 1823 as U.S. minister to France, and from 1826 to 1827 as minister to London. He died in 1849.

Further reading: Balinky, Alexander. *Albert Gallatin: Fiscal Theories and Policies.* New Brunswick, N.J.: Rutgters University Press, 1958; Walters, Raymond. *Albert Gallatin: Jeffersonian Financier and Diplomat.* New York: Macmillan, 1957.

Garfield, James A. (1831–1881) *twentieth U.S. president*

James A. Garfield had served as the nation's 20th president for only a few months before being struck down by an assassin's bullet in July 1881, although he did not succumb to blood poisoning, attributed to his doctors' use of unsterilized instruments and their bare hands, until September of that year. Garfield's six-month tenure in the White House ranks as the second shortest in history. Despite his brief time as president, Garfield had an effect, directly and indirectly, on the nation's and his party's politics.

Born November 19, 1831, Garfield graduated from Williams College in 1856. Shortly thereafter, he turned to public life and served as Ohio State senator from 1859 to 1861. In August 1861 he joined the Union Army, commissioned as a lieutenant colonel. He rose to the rank of major general before resigning in December 1863 to take a seat in the U.S. House of Representatives, to which he was elected in 1862. During the remainder of the CIVIL WAR, Garfield was considered among the ranks of the Radical Republicans. Although he later softened his stance during the Andrew JOHNSON presidency, he joined in voting to impeach Johnson. During his 18-year tenure in the House, Garfield served at various times as the chair of the Banking and Currency Committee, the chair of the Appropriations Committee, and as a member of the Ways and Means Committee. In addition, he also acted as counsel for Lambdin P. Milligan in the case *EX PARTE MILLIGAN* and, in doing so,

President James A. Garfield *(Library of Congress)*

became the first lawyer to argue his first court case in front of the Supreme Court. Garfield also was tainted by scandal during these years, as he was implicated in the Crédit Mobilier affair in which he allegedly accepted 10 shares of the company's stock and a $300 loan. Ultimately, Garfield testified to a congressional committee that he declined an offer to purchase stock but acknowledged that he accepted (but repaid) the loan. The scandal eroded some support back home and would again be raised during his presidential campaign.

Garfield originally did not seek the presidency in 1880, instead serving as the leader of those supporting Senator John Sherman from Ohio for the Republican nomination. The moderate wing of the GOP was split between Sherman and James G. Blaine of Maine. The conservatives in the party, the Stalwarts as they were known, favored Ulysses S. GRANT for an unprecedented third term. Despite having a plurality of initial support among Republican delegates, Grant supporters, led by Senator Roscoe Conking of New York, failed to secure key positions at the party's convention, such as permanent chairman or head of the Credentials Committee. James Garfield served as the Rules Committee chair and in that position secured the rejection of a procedural voting rule, the unit rule, crucial to Grant's

success. The convention went through an extended deadlock, and this provided Garfield the opportunity to emerge as a DARK HORSE candidate. On the 34th ballot, Wisconsin voted for Garfield; on the next, Indiana came on board. Finally, on the 36th ballot, Garfield secured the Republican nomination for the presidency. In an effort to placate the Stalwarts, Chester Alan ARTHUR, whose removal by President Rutherford B. HAYES as New York Customhouse Collector sparked an intraparty battle, was added to the party's slate as its vice-presidential candidate.

Garfield's Democratic opponent was Winfield S. Hancock, a general and military hero from the CIVIL WAR. The campaign was an undistinguished one, as the candidates differed little and did not campaign much. The most significant issue dividing the two was the tariff, on which Republicans favored a high protectionist tariff while the Democrats favored a policy of using the tariff for revenue only. An important moment in the campaign came when Garfield met with his GOP rival, Roscoe Conkling, resulting in what has been called the "Treaty of Fifth Avenue." Although the importance of this "treaty" has been debated, Garfield allegedly agreed to consult with Conkling and other Stalwarts on patronage issues; Conkling, in return, actively supported his party's nominee. Garfield won the presidency by a 214-155 margin in the ELECTORAL COLLEGE. In the popular vote, however, Garfield squeaked by with less than a 10,000-vote margin.

Any truce between Garfield and the Stalwarts that may have developed during the 1880 campaign evaporated early in the new president's term. Much like his immediate predecessor, Rutherford Hayes, Garfield became embroiled in a battle with Republicans in the Senate over the president's right to appoint EXECUTIVE BRANCH officials. Whereas Hayes and Garfield had their own ideas as to whom to nominate for CABINET and other positions, the Senate leadership, commanded by Roscoe Conkling, sought to dictate who would be appointed as a matter of senatorial courtesy. The issue first raised itself when the Stalwarts demanded that Garfield appoint Levi P. MORTON as secretary of the Treasury. The president viewed Morton, a New York banker, as too close to the financial establishment on Wall Street and as having too-conservative economic views. When Garfield did not adhere to the Stalwarts' wishes, the battle lines started to be drawn.

The issue came to a head when Garfield nominated for the position of the New York customhouse collector William H. Robertson, Senator Conkling's chief rival in New York and an ally of James BLAINE. Vice President Arthur urged Garfield to withdraw the nomination to preserve party unity. Garfield, however, saw the matter as one that impacted "the independence of the executive" (as he wrote in his diary) and as a war that was brought to his doorstep. The battle reached a point of brinksmanship in which Garfield withdrew all other nominations from consideration until the Senate dealt with the Robertson appointment. Conkling and fellow New York Senator Thomas C. Platt responded by resigning their positions with the idea that the New York legislature would validate their position by reelecting them. The legislature, however, did not do so, and as a result Conkling's days as a national political force were over. Garfield's legacy that emerged from this battle was one of greater control and independence for the CHIEF EXECUTIVE. Although the notion of senatorial courtesy continues in some fashion today and presidential appointments are far from sure things, Garfield's efforts mark an important milestone for the exercise of presidential authority.

On July 2, 1881, Charles J. GUITEAU shot Garfield twice, one bullet grazing the president's arm and the other entering his back, deflecting off a rib, and stopping near his pancreas. Guiteau came to Washington seeking an appointment to a diplomatic post as a reward for supporting Garfield in the 1880 election. When he did not receive such employment, he started stalking the president. After being arrested, Guiteau proclaimed, "I am a Stalwart; now Arthur is president." He was eventually convicted for Garfield's death and sentenced to die. Garfield did not pass away immediately from the gunshot wound, but survived over two more months, dying on September 19, 1881. His death, however, served as a catalyst for reform of the federal government CIVIL SERVICE system. Guiteau's actions were seen by the public as a consequence of the spoils system, where the winning president was allowed to appoint his loyal supporters to federal government positions. The new President Arthur surprised skeptics by calling for limited reform in his first annual message to Congress and supporting the PENDLETON ACT in his second message. Gains by the Democrats in Congress following the 1882 midterm election sped the prospects for reform along. In 1883 Congress passed and Arthur signed the Pendleton Act, the first major civil service reform for the federal government, requiring among other provisions merit selection of certain governmental employees.

See also ADVICE AND CONSENT.

Further reading: Doenecke, Justus D. *The Presidencies of James A. Garfield and Chester A. Arthur.* Lawrence: Regents Press of Kansas, 1981; Milkis, Sidney M., and Michael Nelson. *The American Presidency: Origins & Development, 1776–1993,* 2d ed. Washington, D.C.: CQ Press, 1994.

—Victoria Farrar-Myers

Garner, John Nance (1868–1967) *U.S. vice president* Vice president from 1933 to 1941, under President Franklin D. ROOSEVELT, Garner was dropped from the '42 ticket and replaced with Harry S TRUMAN. A devoted member of Congress, Garner, known as Cactus Jack, helped secure the Democratic nomination for FDR in 1932 and was instrumental in helping Roosevelt pass his NEW DEAL legislation. Garner's qualms about Roosevelt seeking a third term led to a rift between the vice president and the president. In December of 1939, Garner announced his intention to seek the presidential nomination in 1940, but FDR captured the nomination and the presidency.

GATT (General Agreement on Tariffs and Trade)
GATT helped provide a framework for the industrial nations to impose an open or free trade regime on the international economic system. An executive agreement legitimized the U.S. role in GATT, not a treaty. Over the years the international community has held roughly a dozen GATT meetings. GATT has provided the United States and its allies with a framework and a forum for the discussion of international trade and economic policy issues. In this way GATT has been valuable as a tool in the promotion of free trade and the development of international codes on trade and tariff matters. Such multilateral agreements became increasingly important in a more interdependent international economy.

gay men, lesbians, and the presidency
With the notable exception of the issue of gays in the military, there has been relatively little public or media attention paid to how the president affects the rights of gays and lesbians. In fact, the president has a powerful and varied impact on issues of concern to these groups, although most of what American presidents have done in this area has been done quietly. But the role of the president is quite important. The president can affect the rights of gay men and lesbians in any of the following ways:

1. Introduction and/or support of legislation;
2. Vetoing or threatening to veto legislation;
3. Issuing executive orders;
4. Informally pressuring executive officials to alter their behavior;
5. Hiring practices with respect to his staff;
6. Encouraging investigation and/or litigation by the Justice Department;
7. Appointments of judges, Supreme Court justices, and cabinet officials; and
8. Setting a public tone through the bully pulpit of the presidency.

Throughout most of American history, presidents paid little attention to gay and lesbian issues, as did the other branches of the federal government, as well as state governments. If any action was taken by the president it was usually in the form of his signing legislation restricting the liberties of gays and lesbians, such as the 1917 federal law that effectively excluded gay and lesbian aliens from the United States.

In the 1950s, gays and lesbians bore much of the brunt of the hysteria of MCCARTHYISM. In 1950 the Senate authorized an inquiry into the "employment of homosexuals and other moral perverts in Government." As a result, one of President EISENHOWER's first EXECUTIVE ORDERS was the 1953 order banning gays and lesbians from all federal jobs. The immigration ban on gays and lesbians was also made even tighter during the period.

The first president to take some active interest in issues of gay and lesbian rights was Jimmy CARTER. Although Carter actively campaigned for gay and lesbian votes, he was unwilling to speak out in favor of legal equality for gays and lesbians, and his aides described him as personally uncomfortable with homosexuality. Nonetheless, Carter's commitment to human rights and open government led to new responsiveness to gay and lesbian concerns. Under his administration, the OFFICE OF PUBLIC LIAISON was more open to hearing gay and lesbian concerns than under any previous administration. Further, President Carter supported New York Representative Bella Abzug's efforts to amend the 1964 CIVIL RIGHTS ACT to protect against discrimination on the basis of "sexual or affectional preference."

The relationship between the administration of President Ronald REAGAN and the gay and lesbian community was far chillier. The main fault line was the proper response to the rising AIDS epidemic during the 1980s. Gay and lesbian advocates, as well as much of the mainstream medical and public health professions, sought urgent and effective federal action to contain the epidemic. This was strongly resisted by an administration that was committed to shrinking the federal government outside of the military and also regarded gays and lesbians as outside of its electoral coalition.

Reagan's successor, President George H. W. BUSH, was significantly more welcoming to gays and lesbians and their concerns. In 1990 he signed the Hate Crime Statistics Act, which directed the Justice Department to collect statistics on hate crimes committed against various groups, including gays and lesbians. This was the first time that any federal law specifically mentioned sexual orientation and was the first legal expression of concern by the federal government for the rights of gays and lesbians. Bush also invited gay activists to the WHITE HOUSE for the signing ceremony—another first.

President Bush also signed the Ryan White Comprehensive AIDS Resources Emergency Act and the Americans with Disabilities Act in 1990, which protects persons with AIDS from discrimination. However, on issues such as the ban on gay and lesbian service members in the military and the exclusion of gays and lesbians from ROTC and the FBI, Bush's policies did not differ significantly from Reagan's.

Defeating Bush in 1992, Bill CLINTON became the first openly pro-gay rights president in U.S. history. Although he had no record of supporting gay rights as the governor of Arkansas, he campaigned hard for votes and money from the gay and lesbian community. Once in office, his record on gay and lesbian issues was variable. He attempted to fulfill his promise of ending the ban on gays and lesbians in the military but quickly backed down and agreed to the "don't ask, don't tell" policy, under which the number of gays and lesbians expelled from the military has actually increased. He also signed into law the Defense of Marriage Act, which preemptively denied federal recognition to same-sex marriage, should any state eventually decide to recognize such marriage. Nonetheless, Clinton was clearly more supportive of gay rights than any other president has ever been. He significantly increased funding on AIDS research services, prohibited federal agencies from denying security clearance on the basis of sexual orientation, and appointed numerous openly gay and lesbian officials to federal offices.

As of this writing, it is too early to evaluate the record of George W. BUSH. The relationship between the White House and gays and lesbians has been a varying one. It reached a low point in the age of McCarthyism. President Carter tried to address the issue quietly. President Clinton was willing to publicly support gay and lesbian rights to a limited extent. Most presidents have attempted to avoid dealing with the issue publicly, but many important issues of concern to gays and lesbians, and their opponents, are breaking into the public debate and will probably have to be addressed by future administrations. These include issues such as bringing sexual orientation within the protection of antidiscrimination and hate-crime laws, and the debate over gay and lesbian inclusion in the institutions of marriage and the military. These promise to be difficult, important, and controversial issues for future presidents.

Further reading: D'Emilio, John, William Turner, and Urvashi Vaid. *Creating Change: Sexuality, Public Policy and Civil Rights.* New York: St. Martin's Press, 2000; Gerstmann, Evan. *The Constitutional Underclass: Gays, Lesbians and the Failure of Class-based Equal Protection.* Chicago: University of Chicago Press, 1999.

—Evan Gerstmann

General Accounting Office (GAO)

Established by the BUDGET AND ACCOUNTING ACT OF 1921 to audit federal government expenditures and to assist Congress in its fiscal oversight role, the GAO gives

Congress a semi-independent source of information in its budget and fiscal dealings with the executive. It is directed by a comptroller general who is appointed by the president with the ADVICE AND CONSENT of the Senate for a 15-year term. Since the 1960s, the GAO has increased its visibility and responsibilities. This has led several presidents and their attorneys general to question the constitutionality of the GAO on the grounds that it is engaged in "executive duties" but is not under the control of the president. These objectives have gotten nowhere, and the GAO continues to clash with the president, especially over fiscal and budget projections.

Gerry, Elbridge (1744–1814) *U.S. vice president*

Gerry was one of the most influential men of the Founding era. A member of the Continental Congress, signer of the Declaration of Independence, member of Congress representing Massachusetts during the Articles of the Confederation period, Gerry attended the Continental Congress and advocated a stronger federal government but refused to support the new Constitution because he feared it gave too much power to the federal government and reserved too few powers to the states.

He was later elected to the House of Representatives, and in 1797 President John ADAMS sent Gerry, John MARSHALL, and Charles C. Pinckney to France in hopes of negotiating a peace treaty with the French. The Americans, without Gerry, returned to the United States when the French demanded payment of a bribe, an incident referred to as the XYZ AFFAIR, which led to an undeclared conflict with the French for several years.

Gerry was elected governor of Massachusetts in 1810 and 1811. Just before leaving office in 1812, Gerry's name became infamous when he redrew legislative districts to help his party win more seats. One of the redrawn districts resembled a salamander, and from then on such efforts at redrawing legislative districts for political gain were referred to as "gerrymandering."

In 1812 he was selected as James MADISON'S VICE PRESIDENT. In that office he was an outspoken advocate of the WAR OF 1812. He died in office on November 23, 1814.

Further reading: Austin, James T. *Life of Elbridge Gerry*, 2 vols. Boston: Wells and Lilly, 1828–1829; Billias, George Athan. *Elbridge Gerry: Founding Father and Republican Statesman*. New York: McGraw-Hill, 1976.

Gettysburg Address

In late June 1863, Lee's Army of Northern Virginia invaded the North and got as far as Gettysburg, Pennsylvania, where it encountered Meade's Army of the Potomac. Three days and some 40,000 combined casualties later, in one of the decisive events of the CIVIL WAR, the battle of Gettysburg was over, bringing the North a crucial victory. On November 19, 1863, the governors of the 18 Northern states organized a new cemetery in which they would rebury those who died during the battle. President Abraham LINCOLN was not the principal speaker at the dedication of the cemetery (that honor went to famed orator and eulogist Edward Everett). Yet Lincoln gave an address that at 272 words is one of the shortest—and one of the best—in U.S. history. There is no evidence that the original text was written, as myth would have it, on the back of an envelope during the journey from Washington, D.C., to Pennsylvania. It is much more likely that Lincoln, always a careful and precise wordsmith, would have been equally careful in his crafting of this address. At the time, the address was widely considered a rhetorical failure, for in its brevity, style, and form, it fell outside of the generally accepted rhetorical conventions of a eulogy.

Garry Wills argues that in this speech, Lincoln offers his interpretation of the meaning of the Civil War and thus transforms the national understanding of the Constitution and the American polity. By dating the inception of the Union to the Declaration of Independence ("Four score and seven years ago . . .") rather than to the signing of the Constitution, Lincoln forged a new understanding of that Union, grounding it in the eternal and universal principles of the Declaration ("All men are created equal") rather than in the legalisms of the Constitution, which endorsed, among other things, the institution of slavery. In so doing, Lincoln defined the American mission as one of ensuring and extending freedom. He thus redefined the cause of the Civil War—as one of opposing slavery rather than of defending union—and therefore also the challenge facing the nation once union had been restored. Lincoln was able to give transcendent meaning to the slaughter of the battlefield at Gettysburg, and thus to all of the bloody battlefields of that immensely bloody war. He did so by relying on timeless values and ideals—neither slavery nor the specific battles of the Gettysburg campaign are ever mentioned in the address. Lincoln could thus transcend the historical specificity of the moment while imbuing it with greater meaning.

That meaning was national in scope, and the address, as James M. McPherson notes, signals a transition in presidential rhetoric from the use of the word *Union* to *Nation*. Lincoln defined the nation as one that was dedicated to ideals of freedom and equality; the Constitution became not a definitive statement of American ideals, but a contingent embodiment of those ideals. It was subject to change, redefinition, elaboration, and refinement as the nation progressed. The Gettysburg Address is thus a stellar example of constitutive rhetoric, which creates or recreates community through language. In this case, Lincoln defined the national audience—and thus the nation—through a combination of deliberative and epideictic rhetoric that fused past, present, and future in a way that emphasized the significance of contemporaneous action in the processes of national development. In Lincoln's interpretation, the prosecution of the Civil War by the Northern armies thus enacted and forwarded the Founders' values and ensured that those values would continue to inform the nation that would follow the reunion after the war.

Further reading: McPherson, James M. *Battle Cry of Freedom: The Civil War Era.* New York: Ballantine Books, 1988; Wills, Garry. *Lincoln at Gettysburg: The Words That Remade America.* New York: Simon and Schuster, 1992; Zyskind, Harold. "A Rhetorical Analysis of the Gettysburg Address." *Journal of General Education* 4 (April 1950): 202–212.

—Mary E. Stuckey

gifts to the president

One role that is played by the president of the United States is that of pastor to the nation. Like those of other pastors, his flock is generous: A president typically receives some 15,000 gifts each year. A special suboffice of the Correspondence Office, the Gift Unit, with some five staffers, is the place to which all gifts are sent. The unit judges the acceptability of each one (acceptability is governed by law and by Article I, Section 9, of the Constitution) catalogs it, sends the notes of thanks, and handles its disposition.

Gifts come in several categories. If they come from foreign governments, they are adjudged to be gifts to the nation, not to the president personally. If these exceed a "minimum value" (currently defined as $250), they can be displayed temporarily in the WHITE HOUSE but then are sent to the NATIONAL ARCHIVES (to be part of the future presidential library) or to the Smithsonian Institution, to the Library of Congress, or to the of STATE DEPARTMENT for use in its official functions. If the gift is under the minimum value, it may be kept by the recipient. The State Department annually publishes a list of gifts to the nation from foreign governments. (In 1839, in spite of the protests of the U.S. Consul, the emperor of Morocco made a gift of a pair of lions to the United States. They were temporarily housed in one of the rooms of the consulate, then shipped to Philadelphia and auctioned off.)

A second category of gifts is those from private citizens—from anywhere in the world, but most come, of course, from domestic admirers. Some private gifts are returned; if they are kept and are valued at more than $100, they are reported to the Office of Government Ethics, which makes the list public. If the president is known to have a hobby or special personal interest, the White House is deluged with gifts to match. In shaking hands down a rope-line, a president is likely to be loaded up with gifts. The presidential aide follows him, gathers in the presents, and if necessary goes back up the rope-line and gets names and addresses of donors—so that thank-you notes can be sent. Many gifts come with truly touching sentiments. An elderly man sends the president his cherished grandfather clock; a fisherman puts his prize catch on ice and mails it to the White House (all food is destroyed unless it comes from close friends). Students of the presidency often overlook this pastoral role which the president—every president—assumes, and which has great meaning for thousands of American citizens.

In 1996 the National Archives and the White House Historical Association published a handsome catalog, "Tokens and Treasures: Gifts to Twelve Presidents,"—portraying some of the gifts presidents have received—both beautiful and not-so-beautiful, but fascinating.

At times, gifts are sent with a selfish purpose, i.e., for the self-promotion of the donor. The Gift Office consults with the White House counsel to help spot donations that may cause embarrassment.

Further reading: Patterson, Bradley H. *Ring of Power: The White House Staff and its Expanding Role in Government.* New York: Basic Books, 1988; *The White House Staff: Inside the West Wing and Beyond.* Washington, D.C.: Brookings Institution, 2000.

—Bradley H. Patterson

Goldwater, Barry M. (1909–1998) *U.S. senator, presidential candidate*

Barry M. Goldwater was born on January 1, 1909, and died on May 29, 1998. He was an Army Air Corps pilot in WORLD WAR II, an Air Force Reserve major general, and a successful businessman. He was also an accomplished photographer of the Arizona desert and its native American peoples. Elected to the U.S. Senate from Arizona in 1952, he served five terms in that body. He wrote the popular book The *Conscience of a Conservative* (1960), which helped establish him as the nation's most prominent conservative leader of the 1960s and early 1970s until his eclipse by Ronald REAGAN.

Goldwater opened his book by censuring fellow conservative Republicans who felt the need to soften their self-descriptions with such terms as "progressive conservative" or "conservative with a heart." Phrases of this sort, Goldwater asserted, amounted to admissions that conservatism was little more than a mechanistic economic theory and that conservatives were only concerned with defending the interests of the wealthy. Goldwater rejected both characterizations.

He saw conservatism as "the art of achieving the maximum amount of freedom for individuals that is consistent with the maintenance of social order" (Goldwater, 7). Since order was adequately maintained at home and accorded far too much emphasis in the many dictatorships abroad, Goldwater reasoned, conservatives should devote most of their attention to preserving and extending freedom. (Goldwater, 8) He saw the federal government as the primary threat to freedom in the United States.

In *Conscience* he defended what was then popularly known as states' rights, a phrase that had been appropriated by Southern defenders of racial discrimination. Goldwater used the term *states' rights* to mean minimal involvement by the federal government in state functions. For example, he advocated the elimination of federal grants-in-aid to the states. He argued that his advocacy of states' rights was not a defense of racial discrimination because the Fourteenth and Fifteenth Amendments of the U.S. Constitution, as well as the Civil Rights Act of 1866, already made virtually all forms of racial discrimination illegal. He defended his widely criticized vote in the Senate against the CIVIL RIGHTS ACT of 1964 on that basis.

In foreign policy Goldwater was aggressively anticommunist. He rejected the principle of nuclear disarmament negotiations between the United States and the Soviet Union when he wrote *Conscience* and wanted continued nuclear testing to perfect "small, clean nuclear weapons." (Goldwater, 104) He advocated supporting future uprisings in Eastern Europe by confronting the Soviet Union with tactical nuclear weapons (Goldwater, 115), and he suggested that such devices might also be used in the VIETNAM WAR.

Goldwater won the Republican nomination for president in 1964, thus wresting control of the GOP from East Coast moderates and liberals who had controlled it for many years. His nomination was considered a coup for conservatives, but it was probably facilitated by the fact that the nominee would face the popular and virtually unbeatable incumbent President Lyndon B. JOHNSON.

Goldwater's opponents frequently characterized him as an extremist. He threw this appellation in their faces in his nomination acceptance speech when he said: ". . . extremism in the defense of liberty is no vice. And . . . moderation in the pursuit of justice is no virtue."

He lost the presidential election with 36 percent of the popular vote, having carried only six states. At the time, his defeat was widely interpreted as signaling the demise of conservatism as a significant force in U.S. politics. However, it laid the groundwork for Ronald Reagan's successful campaign a decade and a half later.

Further reading: Goldwater, Barry. *The Conscience of a Conservative.* 1960. Reprint, Washington, D.C.: Regnery Gateway, 1990.

—Carl Grafton

Goldwater v. Carter, 444 U.S. 996 (1979)

This is a Supreme Court decision in which the Court declined to decide on the merits the question of President Jimmy CARTER's unilateral termination of the nation's Mutual Defense Treaty with Taiwan. In *Goldwater,* several members of Congress led by Senator Barry GOLDWATER challenged the treaty termination on constitutional grounds, claiming that they were denied their proper constitutional role in considering revocation of the treaty. They argued that a treaty could be terminated by the president only if accompanied by the ADVICE AND CONSENT of the Senate or approval of both houses of Congress.

As a preliminary step toward diplomatic recognition of the People's Republic of China (the Beijing government), President Carter in December 1978 announced he would terminate the nation's Mutual Defense Treaty with Taiwan. The President justified his actions by citing his power as COMMANDER IN CHIEF and his role as the nation's "sole organ" of DIPLOMACY, in particular, his RECOGNITION POWER. In response to the president's announcement, the Senate considered a resolution declaring that Senate approval was necessary for the termination of any treaty; however, no final vote was ever taken. Frustrated over what they perceived to be the failure of Congress to take a formal stance, the lawmakers brought suit.

The Constitution provides that two-thirds of the Senate must give advice and consent before the president can ratify a treaty. The Constitution, however, is silent as to treaty termination. The historical record preceding the suit provided little more guidance. Treaties had been repealed by the president acting in conjunction with both houses of Congress, acting with approval of the Senate, and acting unilaterally.

In *Goldwater,* no opinion of the Court commanded a majority of the justices but a majority concluded that the case should not be decided on the merits, effectively letting the president's revocation stand. Four justices, led by Justice William Rehnquist, concluded that the issue was a "political question" and thus beyond the competence of the Court. Justice Thurgood Marshall concurred in the result but did not provide his reasoning. Justice Lewis Powell reasoned that the case was not ripe since the Senate had not yet exercised all of its prerogatives. Justice William Brennan, in dissent, wrote that the case should have been decided on the merits in favor of the president. Justices Harry Blackmun and Byron White concluded that the case should have been heard on the merits but did not indicate whether they thought the president's actions were lawful or not. Thus, seven of the nine justices concluded that President Carter's actions should have been either left undisturbed or decided on the merits in the president's favor.

Not surprisingly, the EXECUTIVE BRANCH has interpreted *Goldwater* broadly to justify unilateral presidential treaty termination. The question remains, however, what, if any, limitations exist on the president's ability to terminate such agreements? To what extent can the Senate place conditions on its approval of treaties to ensure that congressional or Senate assent must be received before the president terminates them? Could either the Senate or both houses "veto" unilateral presidential treaty termination? As important as these questions are with respect to the president's FOREIGN AFFAIRS power, they are unlikely to be resolved judicially.

Further reading: Adler, David Gray. *The Constitution and the Termination of Treaties.* New York: Garland Publishing, 1986; Kraft, Victoria Marie. *The U.S. Constitution and Foreign Policy.* New York: Greenwood, 1991.

—Roy E. Brownell II

good neighbor policy

While the phrase was first used by President Herbert HOOVER, it is now associated with President Franklin D. ROOSEVELT to describe his policy toward Central and South America. In his 1933 inaugural address FDR said,

> I would dedicate this nation to the policy of the good neighbor—the good neighbor who resolutely respects himself and, because he does so, respects the rights of others—the neighbor who respects his obligations and respects the sanctity of his agreements in and with a world of neighbors.

Roosevelt hoped for improved economic and political relations, a nonintervening military stance, and to an extent, he was successful, especially during WORLD WAR II, when most Latin American nations supported the Allied war effort.

Further reading: Dozer, Donald M. *Are We Good Neighbors?: Three Decades of Inter-American Relations, 1930–1960.* New York: Johnson Reprint Corp., 1972; Gellman, Irwin F. *Good Neighbor Diplomacy: United States Policies in Latin America, 1933–1945.* Baltimore, Md.: Johns Hopkins University Press, 1979; LaFeber, Walter. *Inevitable Revolutions: The United States and Central America.* New York: W. W. Norton, 1984.

Gore, Albert A., Jr. (1948–) *U.S. vice president, U.S. senator, U.S. representative*

Al Gore was born in Washington, D.C., on March 31, 1948. His father was a liberal Democrat who represented the state of Tennessee in the U.S. House and the U.S. Senate for more than 30 years. Al Gore, Jr., received a B.A. in government from Harvard University in 1969, and he then served as an army reporter in Vietnam. Following his service in

Albert A. Gore, Jr. *(Office of the Vice President)*

Vietnam, Gore studied religion at Vanderbilt University and then worked as a reporter for the *Nashville Tennesseean.* When a U.S. House seat unexpectedly became available in 1976, Gore decided to run. He was successful, serving for four terms, until he was elected to the U.S. Senate in 1984. With an avid interest in public policy, Gore became an authority on national defense and environmental issues.

Gore began his quest for the presidency in 1988 when he was not yet 40 years of age. Running as a "New Democrat," Gore attracted support from the moderate wing of the party. However, despite winning seven Democratic PRIMARIES AND CAUCUSES, he withdrew because of his inability to draw sufficient support outside of the South. His moderate message did not appeal to liberal Democrats, many of whom continued to control the party, because of his image as somewhat of a stiff personality. In 1990 Gore was easily reelected to the U.S. Senate, and speculation arose yet again that he might seek the 1992 Democratic presidential nomination. When the republican incumbent, George H. W. BUSH, looked all but unbeatable as a result of the Gulf War, Gore decided not to run. However, Gore was chosen by the eventual Democratic nominee and fellow southerner Arkansas governor Bill CLINTON, to be his vice-presidential running mate. Clinton and Gore won the 1992 presidential campaign after a brutal election in which they urged voters to opt for change. Gore proved himself to be a tough campaigner in his second run for national office. As VICE PRESIDENT, Gore became a trusted adviser to President Clinton, and he continued his espousal of environmental causes and the use of modern technology. He was one of the most actively involved vice presidents in American history, and Clinton continually stressed that his relationship with Gore was both a friendship and a partnership.

His most recognized achievement as vice president was his leadership of the "Reinventing Government" initiative. In 1996 Gore moved into a second term as vice president when Clinton was reelected. However, during the campaign Gore had been heavily involved in party and fund-raising activities. Some independent political observers and Republicans charged Gore with having violated CAMPAIGN FINANCE laws, and they urged U.S. Attorney General Janet Reno to appoint an INDEPENDENT COUNSEL. Ultimately, she determined that there was not enough evidence to warrant such action. Gore claimed exoneration, while the Republicans charged a political cover-up.

Perhaps the most politically difficult period for Gore was the yearlong investigation and ultimate IMPEACHMENT of President Clinton in 1998–99. Although Gore himself was not personally responsible for the events surrounding Clinton, he could neither publicly defend the president's actions nor could he criticize them: He risked looking either too loyal to Clinton or not independent enough. Despite the Clinton scandal, and the fund-raising imbroglio, Gore ran for the Democratic nomination in 2000 with little serious opposition. The economy remained strong and the Clinton-Gore administration enjoyed a high level of public approval. Gore's only challenger in the Democratic primaries was former New Jersey senator Bill Bradley, who posed a threat to the vice president from within the liberal wing of the party. After defeating Bradley and securing the nomination, Gore ran behind the Republican nominee, Governor George W. BUSH, for several months leading up to the Democratic National Convention.

To many seasoned political observers, it seemed as if Gore just did not have what it takes to energize the Democratic base, let alone the general electorate. However, Gore delivered a well-received acceptance speech at the convention, and his support began to grow. Stressing the strong economy, the need to protect SOCIAL SECURITY and Medicare, and health care reform, Gore barely lost the 2000 election. Because of the necessity of the 25 electoral votes in Florida for either candidate to win, an automatic recount was instituted. After more than two weeks of manual recounts Bush officials sued to bring it to a close. Bush was certified the winner by the Florida secretary of state, upon which Gore challenged the decision on the basis of a flawed certification process. The matter came before the U.S. Supreme Court, where in a 5 to 4 decision, they ruled in favor of Bush.

Further reading: Caesar, James W., and Andrew E. Bush. *The Perfect Tie: The True Story of the 2000 Presidential Election.* Lanham, Md.: Rowman and Littlefield, 2001; Maraniss, David, and Ellen Nakashima. *The Prince of Tennessee: The Rise of Al Gore.* New York, N.Y.: Simon and Schuster, 2000; Nelson, Michael, ed. *The Elections of 2000.* Washington, D.C.: CQ Press, 2001; Pomper, Gerald M., ed. *The Election of 2000.* New York, N.Y.: Chatham House, 2001.

—Jean-Philippe Faletta

government corporations

On occasion, the federal government engages in activities that closely resemble a commercial venture that generates income and requires greater flexibility than the normal governmental agency might allow. When this happens the government often forms a government corporation. Examples would be the Federal Deposit Insurance Corporation, the Resolution Trust Corporation, the TENNESSEE VALLEY AUTHORITY, the U.S. Postal Service, and the Corporation for Public Broadcasting. These corporations are headed by a bipartisan board of directors or board of commissioners. In 1945 Congress passed the Government Corporation Control Act (31 U.S.C. 9101-9111) to better control these corporations. In recent years presidents have been less inclined to use government corporations, and the supervisory responsibility, once under the purview of the OFFICE OF MANAGEMENT AND BUDGET, has been taken up by the Congress. This has called into question precisely who is to oversee these government corporations, the president or Congress.

Gramm-Rudman-Hollings Act of 1985

This name was given to two budget-balancing legislative measures enacted in the 1980s that were designed to stem the growing budget deficit and require a balanced budget within a specified period of time. Gramm-Rudman-Hollings (GRH) was named after its three Senate sponsors, Phil Gramm (Rep.-Tex.), Warren Rudman (Rep.-N.H.), and Ernest Hollings (Dem.-S.C.).

Large tax cuts enacted in the early 1980s, coupled with significant increases in defense spending, produced ballooning deficits in the federal budget throughout the 1980s and early 1990s. The first GRH measure, the Balanced Budget and Emergency Deficit Control Act of 1985, was enacted hurriedly by Congress as a means to unblock the continuing executive-legislative budget stalemate that centered on Republican Presidents REAGAN and Bush's refusal to consider a tax increase, and Democratic Congresses that refused to consider deeper cuts in domestic federal programs. GRH required that deficit reduction occur by law in a yearly progression starting in 1986, so that the federal budget would be balanced by fiscal year 1991. If the projected deficit targets were not met, based on information provided by the Congressional Budget Office (CBO) and the OFFICE OF MANAGEMENT AND BUDGET (OMB), automatic cuts were to take place through a "sequestration process" according to a formula established by Congress. Cuts were to be made equally from defense and domestic programs, although some programs, such as SOCIAL SECURITY, were exempted from their automatic cuts. Further, various budget timetables and schedules were altered, including a requirement that the president submit his initial budget a month earlier.

The law's constitutionality was challenged in court (as the bill's sponsors had anticipated), and in the case of *Bowsher v. Synar* (1986), the Supreme Court struck down the provision of GRH that gave the head of the GENERAL ACCOUNTING OFFICE (GAO), called the INSPECTOR GENERAL, the power to order EXECUTIVE BRANCH budget cuts on the grounds that the GAO head was removable by Congress, thus making this grant of power a violation of the SEPARATION OF POWERS. This ruling in turn led Congress to enact the Balanced Budget and Emergency Deficit Control Reaffirmation Act of 1987, also known as GRH II. It also extended the deficit reduction timetable and placed additional limits on what could count toward deficit deductions.

The laws were widely criticized by budget experts, and the effects of these laws on the deficit were few. In fact, deficits continued to rise. The new procedures encouraged budget makers to rely on a series of accounting gimmicks to produce deficit-cutting numbers required by the law; yet deficits still rose, delays in the annual budget process increased, and Congress found itself relying ever more on temporary CONTINUING RESOLUTIONS to keep the government running. By 1992, in the final year of the George H. W. BUSH presidency, the year's deficit was nearly $300 billion. This occurred even though President Bush agreed to a tax increase in 1990. Balanced budgets were not achieved until the CLINTON presidency in 1998.

Further reading: Fisher, Louis. *The Politics of Shared Power.* College Station: Texas A&M University Press, 1998; Leloup, Lance T. *Budgetary Politics.* Brunswick, Ohio: King's Court Communications, 1977; Spitzer, Robert J. *President and Congress.* Philadelphia: Temple University Press, 1993.

—Robert J. Spitzer

Grant, Ulysses S. (1822–1885) *eighteenth U.S. president, military leader*

A hero of the CIVIL WAR, but at best a mediocre president, Grant was born on April 27, 1822, in Point Pleasant, Ohio.

President Ulysses S. Grant *(Library of Congress)*

He graduated from the U.S. Military Academy, West Point, in 1843.

After the turmoil of Civil War, IMPEACHMENT, and years of strife, the voters turned to a popular military hero for leadership. But Ulysses S. Grant, a stocky, hard-drinking, politically inexperienced executive, proved unfit for the task of being president.

In the post–Civil War years, the United States experienced an unparalleled period of growth. The railroads opened the West, and agriculture and industry flourished. Immigration also expanded greatly. The age of robber barons ensued, and the Congress as well as the Supreme Court lent support to corporate expansion and development. During this period, government grew as well.

The shrinking of the presidency continued during the Grant years (1869–77). Unlike his predecessor, who fought unsuccessfully to protect the authority of the presidency, Grant seemed more than willing to play the role of observer in the political pageant unfolding before him. After the executive-congressional hostility of the Andrew JOHNSON years, Grant made peace with Congress—but on Congress's terms.

Politically inept and managerially lax, Grant saw the presidency as a purely administrative office, not as a vehicle for national leadership. That suited the Congress just fine. During the Grant years, congressional power reached its zenith.

It was also during the Grant years that the first female candidate for president emerged. Victoria Woodhull (1838–1927), spiritualist, first woman to open a Wall Street brokerage firm, and newspaper publisher, ran for president in 1872 as the nominee of the newly formed Equal Rights Party. Lamentably, on election day Woodhull was in jail facing charges ranging from slander to adultery. Running as Woodhull's VICE PRESIDENT was Frederick Douglass, the first black vice presidential candidate.

Grant's limited view of his role as president not only fostered weak political leadership but allowed abuses of power and corruption to overwhelm his administration. A series of scandals plagued Grant's administration, including the Whiskey Ring scandal, bribery of CABINET officials, the CRÉDIT MOBILIER SCANDAL, and others. All attest to Grant's weak management of his own administration.

Grant was personally honest but irretrievably inept. He was never himself implicated in the scandals of the administration, but his lax management and naïve views allowed those whom he trusted to take advantage of their positions and to poison the administration.

During Grant's term RECONSTRUCTION continued, CIVIL SERVICE reform was promoted (unsuccessfully), and troubling military clashes with Native American tribes escalated. In 1873 an economic panic brought about a financial crash.

Grant left the presidency in 1877 after two terms. His last STATE OF THE UNION message was an astonishing admission of failure. It began, "It was my fortune, or misfortune, to be called to the office of CHIEF EXECUTIVE without any previous political training. From the age of 17, I had never even witnessed the excitement attending a Presidential campaign but twice."

Further reading: Carpenter, John A. *Ulysses S. Grant.* New York: Twayne, 1970; Mantell, Martin E. *Johnson, Grant, and the Politics of Reconstruction.* New York: Columbia University Press, 1973; McFeely, William S. *Grant, a Biography.* New York: W. W. Norton, 1981; Simpson, Brooks D. *Let Us Have Peace: Ulysses S. Grant and the Politics of War and Reconstruction, 1861–1868.* Chapel Hill: University of North Carolina Press, 1991.

Great Depression

The stock market crash of 1929 led to the Great Depression. It was the worst economic crash in U.S. History and lasted until WORLD WAR II. The Depression led to the election of Franklin D. ROOSEVELT in 1932, and allowed FDR to impose his NEW DEAL policies. The Depression marked the end of a period of REPUBLICAN PARTY domination in national politics and ushered in what were called the "New Deal era" and the "New Deal coalition." The 1932 presidential and the 1934 midterm congressional elections were "transforming elections" when the old dominating party (Republicans) gave way to a new one (Democrats). The Democrats were able to bring together a variety of electoral groups into a coalition sufficient to dominate national politics for nearly 50 years. But by the 1970s, the New Deal coalition began to disintegrate, and an era with no clear majority party followed.

greatness, presidential

The concept of presidential greatness emerged from scholarly efforts to rate the individual performances by U.S. chief executives in office and then rank them in relation to each other. This "rating game" of presidents dates back at least to the late 19th century. In the 20th century, after WORLD WAR II, a sophisticated social science approach developed through use of polls and application of social science methodology. Scholars attempted to better define what they were evaluating and what the ratings actually revealed. Critics tend to dismiss the approach as a mere game even today, but rating presidential performance at some level is an inevitable part of making political judgments. The recent phenomenon of a generic "Presidents Day," which honors all presidents without differentiation of performance, highlights the need for an accepted means to impartially identify presidents who have been great leaders worthy of public tribute.

British statesman and historian James Bryce (1838–1922) may have been the first to attempt to document presidential greatness. Bryce, who visited the United States in the 1880s and served as British ambassador to the United States from 1907 to 1913, wrote about presidential greatness in his *American Commonwealth* (1888).

It was a half-century before steps were taken to advance the rating of presidents from an individual, subjective effort toward an empirical one. Arthur M. Schlesinger, Sr., the Harvard historian, undertook a scientifically constructed survey in 1948 and again in 1962. In each he asked a group of scholars (historians, journalists, political scientists, and others) to rate the presidents in terms of their greatness. Schlesinger divided the findings into five groups corresponding to letter grading: greats, near-greats, average, below average, and failures. Because results of his comparative findings were published in general circulation periodicals, Schlesinger is credited with popularizing the rating-game approach to presidential greatness. His initial survey results tapped the American public's compulsion to compare most things, from sports teams to physicians to songs to colleges to political candidates, then to place them in rank-ordered lists. More substantively, the concept of greatness raised to public awareness the issue of standards in democratic elections. Schlesinger's poll identified half a dozen presidents as greats, including Abraham LINCOLN, George WASHINGTON, and Franklin ROOSEVELT, a finding replicated by virtually every subsequent poll of scholars. Most presidents, however, are clustered in the average category.

Toward Methodological Rigor
The Schlesinger studies spawned a host of other polls that seem to be continually conducted on topics from American presidents to FIRST LADIES to legislators to justices and others. However, the first to bring methodological rigor to Schlesinger's basic approach was Gary M. Maranell, a social scientist from the University of Kansas who created a poll based on social-psychological scaling methods and a much larger, less biased sample. He sent a survey questionnaire to nearly 600 American historians asking them to evaluate presidents on six different scales: prestige, strength, activeness, idealism, flexibility, and accomplishments. An additional scale was included to measure the amount of information that each respondent possessed on each president. Greater methodological rigor did not change the three greatest presidents: Lincoln, Washington, and Franklin Roosevelt. However, Thomas JEFFERSON and Theodore ROOSEVELT moved to the fourth and fifth slots in that tabulation.

Robert K. Murray and Tim H. Blessing of Pennsylvania State University developed the most comprehensive, systematic and scientific poll of presidential greatness. Their 19-page poll contained 400 questions that asked American historians for demographic data, presidential questions, evaluations of individual presidential actions, and a rating of the presidents. The sample, which included nearly 1,000 historians, was so broad that the ratings of most presidents are unlikely to undergo major changes from the categories in which this poll placed them. The top five greats, however, remained the same as in the Maranell study, with the exception that Franklin Roosevelt and George Washington switched second and third positions. The demographic findings from the poll suggested that the entry of larger numbers of women into the history profession contributed to the elevation of FDR at the expense of George Washington.

A sophisticated social science analysis of the rating games of presidents by Dean K. Simonton in 1987 found that six variables explain why presidents end up in the rating categories assigned to them by evaluators. These predictive variables are (1) length of presidential service; (2) whether the president was in office in wartime; (3) whether there was a scandal in the administration—Simonton's study found that a single scandal was powerful enough to undermine a two-term president; (4) assassination—an automatic boost to historical legacy; (5) whether the president was a war hero; and (6) intellectual brilliance. This social science study serves as a good contrast between historical rating games and the more scientific approaches used to explain human behavior. For example, Stanford University historian Thomas A. Bailey, a critic of the liberal bias he saw in the Schlesinger polls, wrote the first book on rating presidents (*Presidential Greatness,* 1966), in which he discussed 43 potential determinants of president performance ("measuring rods"). Only one, scandals, was found by Simonton's study to be meaningful.

Greatness as Mental Health
A bold theory to move beyond the historical rating game of presidents was advocated in 1972 by political scientist James David Barber. Building upon his earlier quantitative work on legislators, in his *Presidential Character,* Barber created a controversial classification (active-positive, active-negative, passive-positive, and passive-negative) scheme of presidents based upon mental health. He attempted to show how voters could identify the best presidential candidates based on candidate personality or "character." Retroactively applied to the presidents, his criteria show that the greats are essentially active politicians who enjoy their work and possess high self-esteem. These positive traits contrast sharply with the three other categories of presidents, all characterized as having low self-esteem.

In 1977 William D. Pederson began a series of quantitative checks on Barber's theory by juxtaposing the activity and flexibility scales from the Maranell study. His slightly revised fourfold classification scheme corresponds closely to Barber, with the added benefit that the extended analysis includes every American president from the Maranell study, not just 20th-century presidents. The "active-flexibles" (Barber uses the term "active-positives") are the presidents who are mentally healthiest. They include the MOUNT RUSHMORE quartet—named in the rating game polls—plus Franklin D. Roosevelt. These five "greats" are what psychologists might define as individuals who self-actualize through the political arena. They enjoy working on public policy issues and are the most political in terms of promoting democratic values.

Overall, this quantitative research has found that the active-flexible "greats," or self-actualizers, are different from the other three groups of presidents. The active-flexibles demonstrate great energy and enjoyment in public office. They exercise more than most presidents. As a group, active-positives are least likely to be lawyers; if they had law degrees they were quickest to give up law practice for politics. Ironically, Abraham Lincoln, the greatest president, is the major exception to that pattern. Lincoln, however, ran for political office earlier in his law career than any other lawyer-president.

The active-flexibles also seem to be the most decent or magnanimous presidents. The granting of AMNESTY and pardon tend to be unpopular with the public, who perceive it as a short-circuit of the normal judicial process, but the active-flexibles are willing to act against public opinion to promote justice. Active-flexible presidents grant more clemency that the other three groups of presidents combined.

The active-flexibles, overall, tend to be more open and to value equality more than other presidential types. Lincoln, for example, is renown for his "public opinion baths." Modern active-positives are more likely to rely on a decentralized staffing structure than the chain-of-command model. Other research supports the notion that these presidents harbor greater dislike of the need for SECRET SERVICE protection compared with the other types.

The greatness-as-mental-health approach helps to clarify many of the "near-great" rankings of presidents who are quite active in office but who seem often not to enjoy their work. Termed "active inflexibles," this group of presidents consists of individuals who appear to have been torn between their career choices. As presidents they either grant the most amnesty (e.g., Andrew JOHNSON) or refuse to grant any—suggesting an extremist dimension to their personalities. Collectively, they tend to be boss-centered chief executives, and working for them can be torturous, staff report. In addition, their insecurities trigger paranoia often manifested in desire for Secret Service protection.

In sum, there appears to be consensus among scholars between the rating-game approach and psychological classification schemes of political scientists, at least regarding which American presidents are among the top five. Five among the 40-plus presidents should be enough from which to discern clarification of what democratic politics admires in its best leaders as well as form a basis for seeking those characteristics in future presidential candidates.

Further reading: Bailey, Thomas A. *Presidential Greatness: The Image and the Man from George Washington to the Present.* New York: Appleton-Century, 1966; Maranell, Gary M. "The Evaluation of Presidents: An Extension of the Schlesinger Polls." *Journal of American History* 57, no. 1 (June 1970): 104–113; ——— and Richard A. Dodder. "Political Orientation and the Evaluation of Presidential Prestige: A Study of American Historians." *Social Sciences Quarterly* 51, no. 2 (September 1970): 415–420; Murray, Robert K., and Tim H. Blessing. *Greatness in the White House: Historians Rate the Presidents, Washington through Carter.* University Park: Pennsylvania State University Press, 1988; Pederson, William D., and Ann McLaurin, eds. *The Rating Game in American Politics.* New York: Irvington Publishers, 1987; Simonton, Dean K. *Why Presidents Succeed: A Political Psychology of Leadership.* New Haven, Conn.: Yale University Press, 1987.

—William D. Pederson

Great Society

In his first year in office, President Lyndon JOHNSON cast about for some sort of label for his administration. He had won his first election by being 100 percent for the NEW DEAL of Franklin Roosevelt, and Roosevelt's energetic liberalism had forever been his model of governance. As vice president, Johnson had lent his support to the NEW FRONTIER of President John KENNEDY, and in his first months as president he led Congress to pass the stalled legislative agenda of his successor. But what would be Johnson's own rallying cry, and his legacy?

White House intellectuals were put to work on a catch phrase. Their product, the "Great Society," was unveiled by the president in his commencement address at the University of Michigan, May 22, 1964. The country was at a turning point, the president said in that speech, part of his campaign for election to the presidency in his own right. For over a century after its birth, the nation had settled and subdued a continent. That had been a time of labor. For the past half century, Americans had "called upon unbounded invention and untiring industry" to create a society of plenty. The recent past had been a time for creating wealth. Now, Johnson intoned, "we have the opportunity to move not only toward the rich society and the powerful society, but upward to the Great Society . . . a place where men are more concerned with the quality of their goals than the quantity of their goods." The present, Johnson announced, was the opening of a new age, a time of labor and invention surely, but more importantly a time when beauty and the arts would be taken as seriously by government as the gross national product, where civil rights for all Americans would at last be achieved, where the cities would be rebuilt, the hungry would be fed, the young educated, and the poor lifted forever out of poverty.

If the rhetoric with which the Great Society was announced appears extreme, it must be remembered that the 1960s opened amid great optimism among America's policy-making and intellectual elites. Ending poverty was, indeed, supposed to be the easy part of achieving a Great Society. The harder task was to reach beyond old concerns such as economics, to answer a felt need in the country for less materialism and more spirituality.

The Great Society's legacy remains contested to this day. The Great Society raised expectations, its critics assert, to levels where frustration and even violent protests were virtually assured when Utopia was not realized. It was right to raise expectations, its defenders reply; the government still has much to do. What critics and supporters agree on is that the Great Society expanded the federal government's role in the lives of the American people. Federal aid to education was an important part of the Great Society, and the federal government has not, even in conservative times, looked back to the pre-Great Society days when local and state governments were on their own in meeting the educational needs of children. Civil rights, federally guaranteed health care for the elderly and the poor, along with such smaller but widely praised programs as Head Start, are also among the legacies of the Great Society.

Further reading: Divine, Robert A. *The Johnson Years, Volume Three: LBJ at Home and Abroad.* Lawrence: University Press of Kansas, 1994; Jordan, Barbara C., and Elspeth Rostow. *The Great Society: A Twenty-Year Critique.* Austin, Tex.: Lyndon Baines Johnson Library, 1986; Murray, Charles A. *Losing Ground: American Social Policy, 1950–1980,* 10th anniversary ed. New York: Basic Books, 1994; Schwarz, John E. *America's Hidden Success: A Reassessment of Twenty Years of Public Policy,* rev. ed. New York: Norton, 1988.

—Thomas Langston

Green Party of the United States, the

The "Greens" originated in Europe in the 1970s and have been on the rise in the United States for at least 15 years, first as an environmental movement and then as a political party active at the state level. The Green Party of the United States ("Green Party") is a confederation of these state Green parties that obtained official recognition from the FEDERAL ELECTION COMMISSION on November 8, 2001. The Green Party's national office was opened on February 20, 2002, and is located in Washington, D.C.

Although each state organization is unique and particularly adapted to its location, much like the various international Green organizations, they all share a basic set of core principles, including: environmentalism, social justice, grassroots democracy, and nonviolence. The Green Party adapted and expanded upon these "Key Green Values" in its detailed 2000 presidential election platform, which was built primarily around four elements: grassroots democracy and political reform, social justice and equal opportunity, environmental sustainability, and economic sustainability.

For the 2000 presidential election, the Green Party nominated Ralph Nader, the high-profile consumer watchdog, and Winona LaDuke to be the Green Party presidential and vice-presidential candidates. After extensive media coverage, the Green Party received 2.74 percent (2,882,955) of the national vote. For supporters and some political observers, this was generally regarded as a success due to the numerous obstacles faced by third parties in the United States (e.g., ballot access laws, media coverage, financial constraints). However, there were some political commentators who criticized the Green Party, believing that Ralph Nader had functioned as a "spoiler" by attracting Democratic votes and causing Democratic presidential candidate Al GORE to lose the electoral count in some key states.

While the Greens have not yet had any electoral victories at the national level (congressional, Senate, or presidential), they do hold several local elected posts in the United States, including city council, school board, and commission seats.

Further reading: Green Party of the United States. Available online. URL: http://www.greenparty.org/index.htm; Nader, Ralph. *Crashing the Party.* New York: Thomas Dunne Books/St. Martin's Press, 2002.

—Stephanie Mullen

Grenada invasion

Grenada is a small island nation, approximately 90 miles north of Venezuela. It has a population of less than 100,000 and its economy is based on agriculture and tourism. Grenada gained independence in 1974, establishing a constitutional monarchy with Eric M. Gairy as prime minister. The People's Revolutionary Army, led by Marxist Maurice Bishop, overthrew the Gairy government in 1979. Bishop was named prime minister and adopted a series of leftist policies. He gained economic and technical assistance from Cuba and the Soviet Union, leading to the construction of a modern airport runway at Point Salines (at the southwestern end of the island) and a stockpile of military equipment. Bishop failed to adopt a complete Marxist system and in October 1983 was overthrown and subsequently executed in a coup led by General Hudson Austin.

Fearing Cuba and the Soviet Union would use Grenada as a base for terrorist attacks or the support of leftist revolutions in Latin America, the Organization of Eastern Caribbean States (OECS) requested the assistance of the United States in restoring order and democracy to the island nation. On October 25, 1983, on orders from President Ronald REAGAN, approximately 1,900 Marines and several hundred troops from six Caribbean nations invaded Grenada in Operation Urgent Fury. Cuban and Grenadian forces resisted the invasion, but the island was occupied in several days. The United States suffered 18 dead and more than 100 wounded. Although the action appeared to be an unhampered military success, it was not without its problems. The soldiers suffered from a scarcity of accurate intelligence information, communication problems, and a lack of coordination.

The Reagan administration argued that American lives were endangered by the unstable situation created by the coup and subsequent imposition of MARTIAL LAW. Reagan said the action was particularly directed at protecting the lives of about 600 U.S. students at St. George's University School of Medicine. Many critics believed the primary goal of the invasion was to divert attention from the terrorist attack on a barrack in Beirut that killed 241 Marines on

October 23. Critics' claims are bolstered by the fact that the dean of the medical school had announced that his students were not in danger. Many claimed the invasion was an attempt to return a sense of patriotism and pride to the country brought on by a quick and decisive military victory. Regardless of the motives, the invasion was extremely popular in the Caribbean and the United States. Although some opposed it, most Grenadians welcomed the U.S. force. The international reaction was not so favorable. The UNITED NATIONS Security Council passed a resolution deploring the INTERVENTION by a vote of 11 to 1, with the one serving as a veto by the United States. The resolution passed the General Assembly by a vote of 108 to 9 (with 27 abstentions).

By mid-December all U.S. troops had been removed from Grenada, but noncombat personnel remained until 1985 to maintain law and order. A general election was held in December 1984 and Grenada returned to democratic rule. Democracy was restored, but prosperity was not. Little changed for Grenadians after the invasion, with little relief from unemployment and debt.

Further reading: Adkin, Mark. *Urgent Fury: The Battle for Grenada.* Lexington, Mass.: Lexington Books, 1989; Payne, Anthony, Paul Sutton, and Tony Thorndike. *Grenada: Revolution and Invasion.* New York: St. Martin's Press, 1984.

—Elizabeth Matthews

Group of Seven
Starting in 1975, presidents have participated in periodic summit meetings with the heads of other leading nations: Japan, West Germany, Great Britain, France, Canada, and Italy. Known as the "Great Seven," their meetings are designed to develop more coordinated and complementary economic policies in an increasingly interdependent world.

Guiteau, Charles J. (1841–1882) *assassin*
Charles Guiteau shot President James A. GARFIELD with a pistol on Saturday, July 2, 1881, at the Baltimore and Potomac Depot in Washington, D.C. Guiteau's motivation for the shooting stemmed from his failure to acquire a presidential appointment to a consul generalship. Garfield died on September 19, 1881, from complications associated with his wounds. As a result, Guiteau was indicted for the assassination on October 14, 1881. A lawyer by trade, Guiteau presented three arguments before a Washington, D.C., court to support his plea of "not guilty" to the murder charges that were filed against him. First Guiteau declared that he was insane. He also tried to convince the court that Garfield's death resulted from medical malpractice on the

part of his doctors since President Garfield died approximately two months after the shooting. Finally, Guiteau claimed that the court had no legal authority to try and sentence him for a crime because Garfield died in the state of New Jersey. Guiteau received a death sentence on January 26, 1882, and was hanged five months later on June 30. The assassination of President Garfield further fueled the political discourse on civil service reform in American politics that eventually led to reform in the federal personnel system. The Civil Service Reform Act of 1883 (known as the PENDLETON ACT) was enacted during the Chester Alan ARTHUR presidency. This act created a merit system to limit the role of political PATRONAGE in federal employment practices.

Further reading: Clark, James C. *The Murder of James A. Garfield: The President's Last Days and the Trial and Execution of His Assassin.* Jefferson, N.C.: MacFarland, 1993; Shafritz, Jay M., Albert C. Hyde, and David H. Rosenbloom. *Personnel Management in Government: Politics and Process.* New York: M. Dekker, 1986.

—Adam L. Warber

Gulf of Tonkin Resolution
In response to alleged attacks on two U.S. destroyers in the Gulf of Tonkin in August 1964, President Lyndon JOHNSON requested a congressional resolution authorizing him to take "all necessary measures to repel any armed attacks against the forces of the United States and to prevent further aggression." The Senate passed the Gulf of Tonkin Resolution (officially entitled "Joint Resolution to Promote the Maintenance of International Peace and Security in Southeast Asia") by a vote of 88 to 2, and the House voted 416 to 0 in favor. The only dissenters in the Senate were Wayne L. Morse of Oregon and Ernest Gruening of Alaska. Johnson used the Resolution as the constitutional authorization for escalation of the VIETNAM WAR.

In early 1964, President Johnson approved COVERT OPERATIONS against North Vietnam after concluding that South Vietnam would not survive without U.S. assistance. The covert plan, OPLAN 34A, included an enhanced propaganda campaign and increased South Vietnamese activity in the north, the interception of communist ships supplying the Vietcong, and information gathering for an eventual amphibious assault on the north. The key component of the intelligence gathering activities was the DeSoto missions, in which specially equipped destroyers would locate enemy radar facilities and chart and photograph the coast.

While conducting a DeSoto mission on August 2, 1964, the U.S. destroyer *Maddox* was fired on by North Vietnamese torpedo boats in the Gulf of Tonkin. No American casualties occurred, and Johnson determined no reprisals were necessary. The response, however, was to order the destroyer *C. Turner Joy* to join the *Maddox* in the Gulf of Tonkin. On August 4, both allegedly came under hostile attack. There is considerable debate over whether this second attack actually occurred, as no crewman immediately reported actually seeing enemy PT boats. Bad weather and nervous crewmen may have resulted in the false belief that they were under attack. Regardless, Johnson declared that the incidents were "deliberate attacks" and ordered air strikes on August 5 against targets in North Vietnam. On the same day, he submitted the Gulf of Tonkin Resolution to Congress. In addition to authorizing the president to take "all necessary measures" against aggressors, it declared that "[t]he United States regards as vital to its national interest and to world peace the maintenance of international peace and security in Southeast Asia" and the United States is prepared, "as the President determines, to take all necessary steps, including the use of armed force, to assist any member or protocol state of the Southeast Asia Collective Defense Treaty requesting assistance in defense of its freedom." The Resolution functioned as a virtual blank check for Johnson to escalate U.S. involvement in Vietnam as he saw fit.

As opposition to the war grew in the public and in Congress, the Senate repealed the Resolution in May 1970 on the initiative of Senator Robert Dole. Richard NIXON did not oppose the repeal of the Resolution, despite the fact that he had invoked it as justification for the bombing of Cambodia. Many members of Congress eventually felt misled by the Johnson administration because they were not informed of the circumstances leading to the incidents in the Gulf of Tonkin.

Further reading: Karnow, Stanley. *Vietnam: A History.* New York: Viking, 1983; Moïse, Edwin E. *Tonkin Gulf and the Escalation of the Vietnam War.* Chapel Hill: University of North Carolina Press, 1996.

—Elizabeth Matthews

Gulf War, Persian (1990–1991)

The Gulf War was fought by America and its allies to expel the army of Iraq from occupied Kuwait. President George H. W. BUSH's leadership during the crisis won him unprecedented public support and was considered the most important achievement of his administration.

On August 2, 1990, Iraqi troops invaded and occupied the oil-rich, but militarily vulnerable, neighboring nation of Kuwait. Iraq's leader, Saddam Hussein, may have been encouraged by mixed signals from the United States over its possible response to such a move. Five days later, Bush began a massive military buildup dubbed Operation Desert

Shield. Within two weeks, nearly 100,000 troops had been deployed in the Middle East. Only one congressional leader, Senate Armed Services Committee Chair Sam Nunn (Ga.), was informed before the buildup decision was implemented. Throughout the fall, Bush worked with considerable success to rally bipartisan and international support on behalf of military INTERVENTION, including several UN resolutions. Yet members of Congress argued with increasing force that congressional approval was necessary for any large-scale military action. Bush rejected the arguments at first, claiming that his commander-in-chief powers provided sufficient authority.

Two days after the November MIDTERM ELECTIONS, Bush announced that he was doubling the Middle East military presence, a move that emboldened congressional leaders and increased support for formal congressional deliberations. Senate Majority Leader George Mitchell (Dem.-Maine) stated flatly that the president had to come to Congress for a formal declaration. House Majority Leader Dick Gephardt (Dem.-Mo.) said that unilateral presidential actions might well provide grounds for IMPEACHMENT. Bush agreed to come to Congress, which considered two resolutions at the start of 1991. One, sponsored by Democratic leaders, called for continued use of sanctions; the other, sponsored by the Republicans and some Democrats, authorized Bush to use military force. On January 10, 1991, the sanctions resolution failed, and the Bush-backed force resolution was approved by both houses. The resolution stopped short of a formal declaration of war, but it gave Bush the necessary legal authority and specifically invoked the terms of the WAR POWERS RESOLUTION of 1973. Many within and outside of Congress applauded Congress's assumption of responsibility and its thorough and thoughtful debate.

Shortly after the January 15 deadline for Iraqi withdrawal, America and its 30 allies launched a massive air assault, consisting of about 100,000 air missions against targets in Kuwait and Iraq, dubbed Operation Desert Storm. On February 23, the allies launched a massive ground assault. In a campaign lasting only about 100 hours, demoralized and battered Iraqi troops were routed. Those not captured or killed were pushed back into Iraq. In all, 184 Americans were killed in action, compared with roughly 100,000 Iraqis killed.

Despite the stunning nature of the victory, the Bush administration decided against pushing all the way to Iraq's capital of Baghdad, leaving Saddam Hussein in power. This decision was later the subject of much criticism. By the time of the war's end, Bush's popularity stood at nearly 90 percent, the highest ever recorded for any sitting president. After the war, the allies imposed a strict inspection schedule to prevent Iraq from renewing its

President George H. W. Bush meets with U.S. troops in the Persian Gulf, 1991. *(George Bush Presidential Library)*

efforts to produce chemical, biological, and nuclear weapons. It also imposed a strict no-fly zone to limit Iraq's ability to project airborne force.

The war's successful conclusion seemed to dim Democratic prospects for winning back the White House, and several prominent potential Democratic contenders decided against entering the race. Yet memories of the Gulf victory faded, Americans became more concerned than ever with domestic problems, and the economy turned down, all of which paved the way for Bush's defeat in 1992 by Democrat Bill CLINTON.

Further reading: Fisher, Louis. *Presidential War Power.* Lawrence: University Press of Kansas, 1995; Spitzer, Robert J. *President and Congress.* New York: McGraw-Hill, 1993; Whicker, Marcia Lynn, James P. Pfiffner, and Raymond A. Moore, eds. *The Presidency and the Persian Gulf War.* Westport, Conn.: Praeger, 1999.

—Robert J. Spitzer

gunboat diplomacy

Gunboat diplomacy refers to efforts by one nation to intermediate, through the threat or use of force, the behavior or choices of another nation. In regards to the United States, gunboat diplomacy usually refers to military actions in the Caribbean or Central and South America. President Theodore ROOSEVELT is considered one of the key practitioners of gunboat diplomacy, as his actions leading to the development of the Panama Canal indicate.

H

habeas corpus, suspension of

Article I, Section 9, of the Constitution states that "the Privilege of the Writ of Habeas Corpus shall not be suspended, unless when in cases of Rebellion or Invasion the public safety may require it." Habeas corpus is a safety against false imprisonment and requires that a writ be issued and the accused be brought before a judge. Given that the habeas corpus suspension provision is in Article I, which specifies the powers of Congress, most authorities presumed that it was a power reserved for Congress.

Shortly after taking office, Abraham LINCOLN faced a CIVIL WAR. When the South fired on Fort Sumter, Congress was not in session. Lincoln did not call them back into session, and on his own claimed authority, he suspended the writ of habeas corpus. It is estimated that tens of thousands of civilians were arrested by the military during the Civil War. More than 4,000 were tried in military courts.

On March 3, 1836, Congress passed a Habeas Corpus Act, legalizing the suspension of the writ, but did not explicitly authorize Lincoln's action. After the war, the Supreme Court, in EX PARTE MILLIGAN, found the use of military courts and suspension of habeas corpus unconstitutional.

In the aftermath of the 9/11 tragedy, President George W. BUSH claimed authority to again suspend constitutional provisions relating to the imprisonment without charges against U.S. citizens.

Hagerty, James C. (1909–1981) *press secretary*

Hagerty served as press secretary to President Dwight D. EISENHOWER from 1953 to 1961. A former reporter for the *New York Times,* Hagerty had also served as press secretary to New York Governor Thomas E. Dewey before joining the Eisenhower presidential campaign in 1952. Hagerty, often referred to by Washington reporters as "the best Republican president who was never elected," was one of Eisenhower's closest and most trusted advisers. He was exceptionally skilled at the job due to his prior experience as a newspaper reporter, which allowed him to understand and meet the needs of members of the WHITE HOUSE PRESS CORPS. Eisenhower also had great confidence in his abilities to handle the White House press operations, which included issuing press releases, holding daily press briefings, preparing for presidential PRESS CONFERENCEs, and maintaining the president's overall public image. Hagerty understood how to use the news media, essential during the 1950s and the start of the television age, to the president's advantage. Eisenhower's press conferences were the first to be taped for later broadcast on television, and it was Hagerty's job to approve any portion that aired.

Eisenhower was known for many verbal miscues during interviews and press conferences, and Hagerty worked closely with reporters to check any material directly attributed to Eisenhower in news coverage. He also worked closely with EXECUTIVE BRANCH officials to brief Eisenhower prior to press conferences and was responsible for coordinating all news coverage of the administration among White House staff members. A key White House adviser in the handling of Eisenhower's heart attack in 1954, Hagerty skillfully managed the crisis from a public relations standpoint to avoid possible public panic. Through a carefully planned press strategy, Hagerty relied on frequent press briefings to maintain the public image that Eisenhower was in full control of government operations and focused the attention of news coverage on accurate medical details of the president's condition and recovery. The image-building campaign contributed to the public perception of Eisenhower as an active and capable leader, which helped to ensure his reelection in 1956. After leaving the White House in 1961, Hagerty worked for the American Broadcasting Company (ABC) until 1975.

Further reading: Allen, Craig. *Eisenhower and the Mass Media: Peace, Prosperity, and Prime-Time TV.* Chapel Hill:

University of North Carolina Press, 1993; Emery, Michael, and Edwin Emery. *The Press and America: An Interpretive History of the Mass Media.* Boston: Allyn and Bacon, 1996.

—Lori Cox-Han

Hamilton, Alexander (1755–1804) *secretary of the treasury, Revolutionary War leader*

It would be difficult to overstate the importance of Alexander Hamilton on the formation of the United States and the operation of the presidency. As George WASHINGTON's aide and secretary during the Revolutionary War, Hamilton, of humble birth, rose to prominence as a lawyer, member of the CONSTITUTIONAL CONVENTION (where he urged the development of a strong central government), and coauthor of the FEDERALIST PAPERS.

Although he never held elective office, he had a huge impact on the development of the United States. He served as Washington's secretary of the treasury and most influential adviser, and urged the development of a strong national government and capitalist economy. His rifts with Thomas JEFFERSON became legendary, and this split led to the development of political parties in the nascent United States. Hamilton became titular head of the FEDERALIST PARTY, Jefferson of the Republican (Democratic) party.

While he harbored presidential ambitions, Hamilton could be abrasive and arrogant. He settled for the exercise of power behind the throne. During the presidency of John ADAMS, another Federalist, Hamilton worked aggressively behind the scenes to undermine Adams's authority, contributing to Adams's loss of the presidency to Thomas Jefferson, in 1800.

In 1804 Aaron BURR, accusing Hamilton of slander, challenged him to a duel. Burr killed Hamilton in their duel in New Jersey on July 11.

Hamlin, Hannibal (1809–1891) *U.S. vice president*

The nation's 15th vice president, serving from 1861 to 1865, during the CIVIL WAR, Hamlin served previously in the House and Senate and was a vocal opponent of slavery. He broke with the DEMOCRATIC PARTY in 1856, became a Republican, and was elected governor of Maine in 1856. He resigned within a year to become senator from Maine.

Hamlin became Lincoln's loyal vice president during the president's first term, but in 1864 he was ousted from the nomination for another term by behind-the-scenes efforts by LINCOLN, who wanted Andrew JOHNSON as his vice president. Hamlin was stunned when he was not renominated as vice president but felt vindicated by the belief that he was Abraham Lincoln's choice. It was 25 years later that Hamlin learned that in fact, it was Lincoln who had maneuvered for Hamlin's removal.

Hampton & Co. v. United States, 276 U.S. 394 (1928)

Important for its impact on the DELEGATION OF LEGISLATIVE POWER, Hampton supported a congressional delegation of authority to the president.

The Tariff Act of 1922 gave the president authority to change the level of duties to ensure that domestic goods were not threatened by imports. Hampton, an importer, sued, challenging the delegation of a congressional power to the president. The Supreme Court upheld constitutionality of the Tariff Act and supported the delegation of tariff authority to the president, arguing:

> The true distinction is, between the delegation of power to make the law, which necessarily involves a discretion as to what it shall be, and conferring an authority or discretion as to its execution, to be exercised under and in pursuance of the law. The first cannot be done; to the latter no valid objection can be made.

Harding, Warren Gamaliel (1865–1923) *twenty-ninth U.S. president*

The 29th president of the United States, and one of the least effective, Warren G. Harding was born on November 2, 1865, in Corsica, Ohio. He attended Ohio Central College and worked as a newspaper editor before entering politics.

Warren G. Harding promised a "Return to Normalcy." An unlikely choice for president, Harding once confessed: "I like to go out into the country and bloveate" (loaf). At 6 feet tall, handsome, and charming (he looked like a president), Harding was passive and uninterested in the details of government. His nomination was so much of a surprise that the *New York Times* called Harding's Senate record "faint and colorless." The *Times* added, "We must go back to Franklin PIERCE if we would seek a president who measures down to his political stature." Harding was once employed as a schoolteacher but soon quit, saying it was the hardest job he ever had.

Harding was the first president to broadcast a speech over radio (dedicating the Francis Scott Key Memorial at Fort McHenry, in Baltimore, Maryland, on June 14, 1922) and the first to win an election in which women voted. His inauguration was the first ever described over radio. A British reporter described Harding's inaugural address as "the most illiterate statement ever made by the head of a civilized government." He is considered by many historians as the worst president in history.

Harding, a one-time small-town Ohio newspaper editor, had a strange way with words. He often left transitive verbs hanging mysteriously without the aid of direct objects: "I would like the government to do all it can to mitigate"; he invented words like "re-revealinent"; and he often spoke in trite banalities: "Despite all the depreciation, I cannot bring myself to accept the notion that the interrelation among our men and women has departed." H. L. Mencken dubbed these gems "Gamalielese" and said of Harding, "No other such a complete and dreadful nitwit is to be found in the pages of American History." Poet E. E. Cummings called Harding "[t]he only man, woman, or child who wrote a simple declarative sentence with seven grammatical errors. . . ."

A poor manager and disinterested president, Harding saw his role as primarily ceremonial. He did not attempt actively to lead Congress. This allowed Congress, determined to reassert its authority after Theodore ROOSEVELT and WILSON, to take command during the Harding years. Harding once admitted, "I am a man of limited talents from a small town. I don't seem to grasp that I am President." He once confessed to his secretary, "Jud, you have a college education, haven't you? I don't know what to do or where to

President Warren G. Harding (Library of Congress)

turn . . . Somewhere there must be a book that tells all about it . . . But I don't know where that book is, and maybe I couldn't read it if I found it! . . . My God, but this is a hell of a place for a man like me to be in!" His wife, Florence, kept a "little red book" in which she listed her husband's enemies.

Harding preferred women and gambling to politics and policy. He had a weakness for women, and had several long- and short-term relationships. His father once said of him, "If you were a girl, Warren, you'd be in the family way all the time. You can't say 'No.'"

During the Harding years (1921–23), American participation in the LEAGUE OF NATIONS died when the president announced he would not support U.S. membership in the League. Under Harding, the 1921 Washington Conference for the Limitation of Armament limited the spread of the arms race. The BUREAU OF THE BUDGET was created in 1921, and the president was required to submit a federal budget proposal to Congress.

The most noteworthy and notorious event of the Harding years centered around corruption, and the scandals ran deep. Harding himself was never implicated in these scandals, but he was guilty of lax management. He appointed friends and cronies, but he did not properly supervise them. Seeing that Harding was asleep at the wheel, they felt that they could take advantage of the president—and did.

Among the numerous scandals that plagued the Harding administration, the biggest was TEAPOT DOME. Harding's secretary of the interior, Albert B. Fall, was convicted of accepting a $100,000 bribe for granting oil leases under value to some "friends." He was the first CABINET member ever convicted of a crime while in office.

Fraud in the Veterans Bureau, graft in the Office of Alien Property Custodian, criminal conspiracy in the Justice Department (which was known as the "Department of Easy Virtue"), suicides, and a slew of other crimes and scandals haunted the administration. Harding's "friends" from the Ohio Gang used a weak and indifferent president to feather their financial nests, and the president remained blissfully unaware and pleasantly disinterested.

After being victimized by so many of his underlings, an exasperated Harding opined: "My god, this is a hell of a job! I can take care of my enemies all right. But my damn friends, my god-damn friends. They're the ones that keep me walking the floor nights!" He finally admitted, "I am not fit for this office and should never have been here."

On a trip to the West, Harding contracted several "unspecified" illnesses. He died in August 1923. After his death, his wife, Florence Harding, refused to permit an autopsy (fueling endless speculation of foul play).

After Harding's death, investigations into administrative corruption revealed a dark underbelly to the Harding team. Three high officials went to jail. One of the president's friends committed suicide, and a series of crimes were revealed. Until the NIXON years, the Harding Administration was considered the most corrupt in U.S. history.

Further reading: Murray, Robert K. *The Harding Era: Warren G. Harding and His Administration.* Minneapolis: University of Minnesota Press, 1969; Russell, Francis. *The Shadow of Blooming Grove; Warren G. Harding in His Times.* New York: McGraw-Hill, 1968; Trani, Eugene P., and David L. Wilson. *The Presidency of Warren G. Harding.* Lawrence: Regents Press of Kansas, 1977.

Harrison, Benjamin (1833–1901) *twenty-third U.S. president*

Benjamin Harrison, the grandson of the ninth president, William Henry HARRISON, served as the nation's 23rd president from 1889 to 1893. Harrison perhaps represents the epitome of the Whiggish conception of the presidency that dominated political thinking during the late 19th century. He passively allowed his party's leaders in Congress to set the political agenda while serving more as a figurehead of the American political system.

Harrison was born in North Bend, Ohio, on August 20, 1833. He graduated from Miami University in Oxford, Ohio, in 1852 and, after studying at a Cincinnati law firm, was admitted to the bar in 1854. Harrison was elected as Indianapolis city attorney in 1857, served as secretary for the Indiana Republican state central committee from 1858 to 1860, and worked as the state Supreme Court reporter during 1861–62. During the CIVIL WAR, he served in the Indiana Infantry Regiment from 1862 to 1865, rising to the rank of brigadier general. Following the war, Harrison returned to the practice of law in Indiana. He unsuccessfully sought the Republican nomination for governor in 1872. Four years later, he garnered the nomination but lost in the general election. Also that year, Harrison was first mentioned as a presidential candidate, although that push was limited to Indiana and Ohio, and quickly faded. In 1880 Harrison campaigned heavily for James GARFIELD and was rewarded with the offer of a CABINET position. Harrison declined, however, in favor of serving in the U.S. Senate, to which the Indiana legislature elected him in January 1881. Senator Harrison became known as the "soldier's legislator" for his strong backing of pensions for Civil War veterans. After six years in the Senate, Harrison lost his seat when the Democrats gained control of the state legislature.

In February 1888, Harrison declared himself a candidate for the Republican nomination for president. His campaign slogan became "Rejuvenated Republicanism." By that summer, Republican front-runner James G. Blaine, the party's standard-bearer four years earlier, withdrew

President Benjamin Harrison *(Library of Congress)*

from the race. At the party's convention, Harrison's supporters pursued a strategy in which they sought to make him the second choice of delegates favoring other candidates. The strategy worked as other candidates dropped out and Harrison gained support. He received the Republican nomination on the convention's eighth ballot. Harrison's Democratic opponent was incumbent President Grover CLEVELAND. The primary issue of the campaign was the tariff; Cleveland favored reducing the tariff while Harrison favored protectionism. Harrison conducted his campaign largely from his estate in Indianapolis. Making use of his gift at oratory, Harrison gave speeches from his front porch to voters who gathered to hear him. The close election resulted in a split between the popular and electoral vote. Cleveland outpolled Harrison by more than 100,000 votes, but Harrison garnered a majority of the electoral votes, a situation that was not replicated until the year 2000. An intraparty dispute with Tammany Hall led to Cleveland's defeat in New York, his home state, thus securing the ELECTORAL COLLEGE victory for Harrison.

Harrison entered the presidency at a time of recognized congressional dominance in the American political system. Moreover, the Republicans at the time followed the model of Whiggish party government. As party leader Senator John Sherman wrote to Harrison shortly after the latter's election to the White House, "The President should 'touch elbows with Congress.' He should have no policy distinct from his party and that is better represented in Congress than in the Executive." Harrison diligently followed the lead of the Republican majority in Congress following the 1888 election. Some of the most significant pieces of legislation of the last part of the 19th century became law during the Harrison presidency with little or no involvement of the CHIEF EXECUTIVE than the constitutionally required act of signing a bill into law. The SHERMAN ANTITRUST ACT of 1890 was the first act to attack monopolies. The McKinley Tariff Act created the most protectionist tariff during peacetime seen to date at that point in time. The Sherman Silver Purchase Act of 1890 was an apparent trade-off to obtain the support of members of Congress from Western silver-mining states for the McKinley Tariff Act. The result was a highly inflationary act that resulted in a significant depletion of the nation's gold reserves.

The Republican activity in Congress, however, may have gone too far for the voters. Following the 1890 MIDTERM ELECTIONS, the Democrats gained control of the House of Representatives by nearly a 3-1 margin over the Republicans. Emerging economic troubles attributed in part to the Republican policies further eroded support for the party and the president. In addition, Harrison became embroiled in intraparty disputes over patronage issues with several prominent Republican leaders, such as former Speaker of the House Thomas Reed, New York party boss Thomas C. Platt, and Pennsylvania boss Matthew Quay, as well as the wife of Secretary of State James G. Blaine. Harrison originally did not intend to seek reelection in 1892. He chose to do so because he believed that if he did not meet the challenges from within his party, he would be branded a political coward. The dissension within his party as well as the eroding public support for the Republicans contributed to Grover Cleveland's sound victory in the 1892 presidential election. Cleveland returned to the White House with a 277-145 victory over Harrison in the ELECTORAL COLLEGE.

The Harrison presidency was largely defined by domestic issues, in terms of the major legislation during his tenure, its effects, and in Harrison's Whiggish adherence to a passive role in the policy-making process. Nevertheless, he developed his own style of foreign policy, one that, when employed, appeared almost the antithesis of his approach to domestic politics. In the first part of the Harrison presidency, Secretary of State Blaine played a predominant role. A longtime Republican Party leader, Blaine returned to the position he held under Presidents Garfield and Arthur and was seen to cast a large shadow over the president's foreign policy. For example, one of the first foreign policy events to occur in the Harrison presidency was the Pan-American Trade Conference, the impetus of which Blaine spearheaded during his first tenure as secretary of State. But Blaine's deteriorating health provided the president the opportunity to assert himself, as did the increasingly strained relationship between the two throughout Harrison's presidency.

Harrison biographers Homer E. Socolofsky and Allan B. Spetter summarized the president's foreign policy "without exception, as vigorous, firm, belligerent, militant, and chauvinistic." Perhaps the best example of how these characteristics were put into practice was in 1891 when the president sent three warships to protect American interests during the Chilean civil war. A mob beat a group of American sailors on shore leave, and two were killed. Harrison threatened further action against Chile if his demands for restitution were not met; the Chilean leader's response was seen as an insult to the president and the nation. As diplomatic tensions rose, Secretary Blaine, without support from Harrison or his administration, sought to find a resolution, which might involve American concessions. Harrison, however, would not yield, issuing an ultimatum to Chile on January 21, 1892, and delivering what amounted to a war message to Congress four days later. Harrison's tactics worked, as the next day Chile yielded in the dispute and later sent a $75,000 payment to the injured sailors and the relatives of those killed. Harrison's approach to foreign policy was not limited to smaller nations, however. He brought a similar attitude, for example, to diplomatic negotiations with England in trying to resolve a long-standing dispute involving sealing in the Bering Sea and with Germany regarding restrictions on American pork in that country. As with Chile, Harrison's tactics in these negotiations were at times at odds with Secretary Blaine's more conciliatory approach to foreign policy. Finally, the Harrison administration in early 1893 tacitly supported the efforts of Americans, backed by the American minister in Honolulu, to coerce Queen Liliuokalani into relinquishing control over Hawaii. Harrison submitted a treaty annexing Hawaii to the Senate, but President Cleveland, who condemned the American minister's actions, subsequently withdrew it.

Further reading: Milkis, Sidney M., and Michael Nelson. *The American Presidency: Origin and Development, 1776–1993*, 2d ed. Washington, D.C.: CQ Press, 1994; Sievers, Harry J. *Benjamin Harrison*. Newtown, Conn.: American Political Biography Press, 1952; Socolofsky, Homer E., and Allan B. Spetter. *The Presidency of Benjamin Harrison*. Lawrence: University Press of Kansas, 1987.

—Victoria Farrar-Myers

Harrison, William Henry (1773–1841) *ninth U.S. president*

The ninth president, and the first elected Whig, William Henry Harrison was born in Virginia in 1773. After a career

President William Henry Harrison *(Library of Congress)*

in the military, Harrison became territorial governor and served in the House and Senate.

In 1841, at age 68 he was the oldest president ever elected (an honor he would hold until Ronald REAGAN). He delivered his 8,578-word inaugural address in a driving rainstorm, caught cold, and died a month later. He was the first president to die in office and served the shortest term in history. Andrew JACKSON derisively called Harrison "our present imbecile chief," and John Quincy ADAMS spoke of Harrison's "active but shallow mind."

Harrison was a Whig (smaller government) president who believed Congress should set the national agenda. He declared in his inaugural address:

> . . . it is preposterous to suppose that a thought could for a moment have been entertained that the President, placed at the capital, in the center of the country, could better understand the wants and wishes of the people than their own immediate representatives, who spend a part of every year among them, living with them, often laboring with them, and bound to them by the triple tie of interest, duty and affection.

Harrison did leave his footprints on one aspect of the presidency. His activist campaign of 1840, using placards, hats, effigies, campaign songs, banners, stump speeches, parades, and other electoral paraphernalia, was the beginning of modern public campaigning. In this sense, the Jacksonian revolution had truly transformed the presidency: Even Whig candidates had to appeal to the people for authority and power.

Further reading: Cleaves, Freeman. *Old Tippecanoe: William Henry Harrison and His Time.* New York: Scribner's, 1939; Peterson, Norma L. *The Presidencies of William Henry Harrison and John Tyler.* Lawrence: University of Press of Kansas, 1989.

Hatch Act

Congress passed the Hatch Act (originally called an "Act to Prevent Pernicious Political Activities") in August 1939 to regulate federal employees' involvement in political campaigns. Although the original act also prevented using public funds appropriated for public works on electoral efforts, the Hatch Act's more lasting importance stems from the limitations it places on political activity of federal employees. Among its most important provisions, the Hatch Act (Section 2) prohibited "any person employed in any administrative position by the United States . . . to use his official authority for the purpose of interfering with, or affecting, the election or the nomination of any candidate" for federal office. Section 9 provided in part, "No officer or employee in the EXECUTIVE BRANCH of the Federal Government, or any agency or department thereof, shall take any active part in political management or in political campaigns." Congress added a second Hatch Act in 1940. Section 12 of the second act added prohibitions on political activity for state and local government workers whose main employment was in a federally financed activity (e.g., through federal grants or loans). Section 9 and Section 12 were challenged as unconstitutional violations of the First, Fifth, Ninth, and Tenth Amendments. In 1947, however, the Supreme Court upheld these provisions in *United Public Workers v. Mitchell,* 67 S. CT. 556 (1947), and *Oklahoma v. United States Civil Service Commission,* 67 S. CT. 544 (1947). The Hatch Act's constitutionality also was challenged in 1974, and once again the Supreme Court upheld the act.

The Hatch Act has been amended over the years, most recently in 1993 to ease certain of its restrictions. The Internet is now filled with lists of "Do's and Don'ts" for federal employees. Among the permitted political activities, employees may be candidates for public office in nonpartisan elections, contribute money to political organizations, and campaign for or against candidates in federal elections. From the "Don't" list, federal employees, among other acts, may not use their official authority to interfere with an election; generally solicit or receive political contributions; be candidates for public office in partisan elections; or pursue political activity while on duty, in a government building, in a government uniform, or while using a government vehicle. The restrictions remain more stringent for certain government employees, generally those in positions nominated by the president and approved by the Senate.

The Hatch Act was brought to light in the wake of the 1996 presidential campaign, but ultimately provided little basis for any action. For example, Vice President Al GORE made campaign-related phone calls from a government building, an act that for most government employees would be a clear violation of the Hatch Act. The VICE PRESIDENT, however, is expressly exempt from the Hatch Act's provisions (as is the president). Also of note is John Huang, a former employee in the COMMERCE DEPARTMENT, and the question of whether he fund-raised for Democratic candidates before his resignation from that department was official. The issue of whether he violated the Hatch Act became moot, however, when Congress granted him immunity in exchange for his testimony to Congress.

Further reading: Heady, Ferrel. "The Hatch Act Decisions." *American Political Science Review*, 1947; Howard, L. V. "Federal Restrictions on the Political Activity of Government Employees." *American Political Science Review*, 1941; 5 U.S.C. §7321 *et seq.*; 5 CFR §734.304 (1999); Office of Special Counsel website http://www.osc.gov/index.htm.

—Victoria Farrar-Myers

President Rutherford B. Hayes *(Library of Congress)*

Hayes, Rutherford Birchard (1822–1893)
nineteenth U.S. president

The 19th president of the United States, Hayes was born on October 4, 1822, in Delaware, Ohio. He graduated from Kenyon College in 1842.

After the failed presidencies of JOHNSON and GRANT, in the midst of congressional ascendancy, Rutherford B. Hayes came along and arrested, but did not reverse, the trend toward congressional dominance. Grant left the presidency at perhaps the lowest ebb ever. Hayes, at 5'8", with a long beard, governed during what was called the Gilded Age. It was a time of economic growth, a rise in immigration, harsh labor-business disputes, and a growing women's movement.

Henry Adams said of Hayes, "He is a third-rate nonentity whose only recommendation is that he is obnoxious to no one." But Hayes was much more than this. His motto, "He serves his party best who serves his country best" is an admirable sentiment in any age.

The weakness of the presidency in this period was noticed by the observant Englishman Walter Bagehot, who found fault with the American constitutional system and the weakness of the presidency, writing: "The executive is

crippled by not getting the law it needs, and the legislature is spoiled by having to act without responsibility; the executive becomes unfit for its name, since it cannot execute what it decides on; the legislature is demoralized by liberty, by taking decisions of which others [and not itself] will suffer the effects."

Hayes came to the presidency after the hotly contested and harshly disputed election of 1876. One of the dirtiest campaigns in history featured two of the cleanest candidates ever. Samuel J. Tilden, governor of New York, won 51 percent of the popular vote and Hayes conceded defeat to a reporter. Republicans charged voter fraud in three southern states, and the disputed election went to the House of Representatives for resolution. Congress named a special commission to recommend a solution to the dispute. After a bizarre back-and-forth process, the commission awarded Hayes all the disputed votes, and he won the election. In "exchange," Republicans in Congress agreed to withdraw all federal troops from the South and end RECONSTRUCTION. Hayes was president. The charges of a stolen election hounded him, and opponents referred to Hayes as Rutherford FRAUD B. Hayes, and His Fraudulency.

Hayes kept to the Republican deal and ended Reconstruction. He also promoted CIVIL SERVICE reform and good government. He stood firm in asserting the rights of the executive in the face of congressional pressure. Historians generally rank Hayes in the average or below average category of presidents. His greatest contribution was to put a halt to the hemorrhaging of presidential power occurring in the aftermath of the Johnson impeachment and Grant presidency.

Further reading: Davison, Kenneth E. *The Presidency of Rutherford B. Hayes.* Westport, Conn.: Greenwood Press, 1972; Hoogenboom, Ari A. *The Presidency of Rutherford B. Hayes.* Lawrence: University Press of Kansas, 1988.

Health, Education, and Welfare, Department of (HEW)

Created in 1953, during the EISENHOWER administration, the department was reorganized in 1979 and split into the DEPARTMENT OF EDUCATION and the DEPARTMENT OF HEALTH AND HUMAN SERVICES (HHS). Most of HEW's responsibilities were transferred to HHS. During the 1960s, HEW was the place to be if you were an activist and a liberal. It was the center of action for most of President Lyndon JOHNSON's Great Society programs and was a hotbed of liberal policies. In later years, this made HEW a target for conservatives who saw the department as the centerpiece for the big-government programs they opposed.

Health and Human Services, Department of (HHS)

The Department of Health and Human Services was created when President Jimmy CARTER signed the Department of Education Organization Act. This act surgically removed the Office of Education from the Department of Health, Education, and Welfare (HEW) and it became its own department. Thus, HEW became HHS on May 4, 1980.

HHS is responsible in large part for administering and overseeing the various public assistance and health programs with which the national government engages. As such, its role in American national government and politics is enormous. HHS and the Departments of Defense and Treasury account for about three-quarters of all U.S. budgetary spending.

The role of HHS goes back almost to the Founding period. In 1798, for example, the first Marine Hospital, an ancestor of today's Public Health Service, was established for the care of sailors. Similarly, in 1862, Abraham LINCOLN established the Bureau of Chemistry, a precursor to the Food and Drug Administration. Vestiges of what would become the Food and Drug Act, the National Institutes of Health, the Social Security Act, and the Centers for Dis-

ease Control and Prevention all eventually came under the jurisdiction first of HEW and, eventually, HHS.

HHS is basically a purpose-based (as opposed to client-based) organization. In modern times, HHS has assumed or been delegated responsibility for such diverse programs as federal support for child care, the Human Genome Project, health care for homeless (under the auspices of the McKinney Act), various efforts at welfare reform, AIDS projects, and those dealing with diabetes, cancer screening, infant mortality, regulation of tobacco use by minors, and children's health insurance programs. One potential weakness of this range of programs is that, as a purpose-based organization, HHS cannot hope to speak for a unified set of health or welfare policies, nor can it coordinate activities so as to assure uniformity in policy execution.

Further reading: Fesler, James W., and Donald F. Kettl. *The Politics of the Administrative Process,* 2d ed. Chatham, N.J.: Chatham House, 1996, pp. 114–115.

—Daniel E. Ponder

health of presidents

Increased media attention to the presidency since the end of WORLD WAR II has intensified scrutiny of the president's health and extended attention from the physical health of presidents to that of vice presidents. More recently, the mental health of presidential and vice presidential candidates has been an issue of concern for both media and academia. Once taboo medical topics today are discussed openly. The death from illnesses that befell four sitting presidents—William Henry HARRISON, 1841; Zachary TAYLOR, 1850; Warren HARDING, 1823; and Franklin ROOSEVELT, 1945—as well as ASSASSINATIONS, various health conditions, and similar considerations prompted enactment of the disability (Twenty-fifth) amendment to the United States Constitution in 1967. This amendment specifies the procedure, although not a fail-safe mechanism, to be invoked should an ill president need to be removed from office.

Physical Health

John TYLER, the tenth president (1841–45), became the first vice president elevated to the presidency following the death of William Henry Harrison. The 68-year-old Harrison fell ill after delivering the longest inaugural address in American history without adequate clothing for the weather, and he died a month later. "His Accidency," as some dubbed Tyler, set the precedent for later successions.

By the 20th century, presidential vitality was a growing public concern, fueled by media coverage. Franklin Roosevelt kept his polio condition from the public by manipulating photographic coverage until his abbreviated fourth presidential term.

Dwight EISENHOWER between 1949 and 1956 suffered a series of heart attacks and strokes, both prior to and during his presidency. The first president to suffer a heart attack, at 70 years old he was the oldest president, up to that time, to leave office. Ronald REAGAN was believed by some to be too old to undertake the presidency, but he defied that barrier and at almost 70 years old became the oldest president at the time of inauguration. Media concern extended to vice-presidential health in the age of instantaneous news broadcasts. This was particularly true in the 2000 presidential race when Dick CHENEY was selected as George W. BUSH's vice-presidential nominee. He had survived three heart attacks prior to his election and a fourth during the infamous November recount. Initial refusal to discuss Cheney's health in detail followed the typical pattern among presidential candidates, but later coverage of the implant of his heart defibrillator in 2001 signaled more openness about serious matters that competent medical practitioners can manage through appropriate treatment.

Mental Health

Even more taboo than the physical health of presidents is the topic of mental health, which carries broad social implications in American culture. With the CHIEF EXECUTIVE's hands controlling use of nuclear weapons, mental health is a sensitive but relevant issue. As recently as the 1972 presidential race, Democratic candidate George MCGOVERN was forced to drop his running mate, Thomas EAGLETON, after the media broke stories about Eagleton's prior treatment for depression. There are memoirs of Bill CLINTON's staff seeking professional psychological help as well as reports that Richard NIXON faced such unrelenting stress during preliminary impeachment maneuvers that his staff agreed informally to block presidential use of nuclear weapons.

The overlap between physical and mental-health problems is evident in the case of Woodrow WILSON. Scholars suggest that Wilson had a history of deep-seated psychological conflicts with older male authority figures that they trace back to his demanding preacher father. Low self-esteem led to power-seeking compensation. About one-fourth of presidents follow this pattern of active politicians who sometimes exhibit blinding inflexibility in a crisis situation, impairing their judgment (e.g. Richard Nixon, Lyndon JOHNSON, Andrew JOHNSON). Woodrow Wilson also had a history of cardiovascular disease, leading to a series of strokes between 1896 and October 2, 1919, when he suffered a massive one that left him seriously impaired. Health issues during his presidency were critical factors in the defeat of his LEAGUE OF NATIONS initiative and in OVAL OFFICE intervention by Edith WILSON, his doting second wife who became *de facto* president.

Contrasting the active but inflexible presidents who seem to seek power as compensation for low self-esteem but derive little pleasure from the presidency, are an equal number of presidents—including the Mount Rushmore quartet plus FDR—who exhibit active and flexible personalities. This group of presidents self-actualized through the political arena. They enjoy working on public policy issues. Ironically, even though the presidency is pictured as a killer job because of inherent stress, these are the individuals who live the longest among presidents and outlive even their counterparts in the general public. A possible clue to this apparent contradiction is that these active and flexible chief executives are defined, in part, by their energy and engage in physical exercise that may effectively reduce stress for that personality type.

Further reading: Barber, James D. *Presidential Character: Predicting Performance in the White House.* Englewood Cliffs, N.J.: Prentice-Hall, 1972; Levin, Phyllis L. *Edith and Woodrow. The Wilson White House.* New York: Scribner, 2001; Lewis, Edward S., and William D. Pederson. "Theodore Roosevelt as a Model of Mental and Physical Fitness." In *Theodore Roosevelt: Many-Sided American,* edited by Natalie A. Naylor, Douglas Brinkley, and John Allen Gable. Interlaken, N.Y.: Heart of the Lakes Publishing, 1992; Pederson, William D. *The "Barberian" Presidency.* New York: P. Lang, 1989; ———, and Frank J. Williams. "America's Presidential Triumvirate: Quantitative Measures of Character." In *George Washington, Foundation of Presidential Leadership and Character,* edited by Ethan Fishman, William Pederson, and Mark Rozell. Westport, Conn.: Praeger, 2001.

—William D. Pederson

Helvidius-Pacificus Debates

The Helvidius-Pacificus debates took place during the European war of the 1790s involving Great Britain, Austria, Prussia, Sardinia, and the United Netherlands against France. Not wishing to involve the United States in another war, President George WASHINGTON was not sure how to respond to the conflict. He therefore requested members of his CABINET to advise him as to what he should do. Specifically, he wanted to know how they felt about him issuing a proclamation declaring that the United States would remain neutral in the war; and further, that citizens involving themselves in the war on either side would be punished. The request engendered a great deal of disagreement among his cabinet members, particularly between Alexander HAMILTON, Washington's secretary of the Treasury, who supported the issuing of the proclamation, and Thomas JEFFERSON, Washington's secretary of State, who opposed it. After listening to the argument on both sides, Washington decided to issue a NEUTRALITY PROCLAMATION, announcing that the United States would pursue a position "friendly and impartial" toward the belligerent powers.

Because of issuance of the Proclamation, Washington attracted much criticism, especially from citizens supporting France. Hamilton came to Washington's defense by writing a series of seven essays in the Philadelphia newspaper, *The Gazette of the United States,* under the pseudonym *Pacificus*—or lover of peace—defending the Neutrality Proclamation. An additional two essays, that were intended to be *Pacificus* essays but were eventually signed *Americanus No. I and No. II,* that appeared in Philadelphia published in *Dunlap and Claypoole's American Daily Advertiser,* were also supportive of the proclamation. James MADISON answered these arguments by writing five essays using the pseudonym *Helvidius*—or lover of liberty—that appeared in *The Gazette.* Madison agreed to respond to Hamilton only after Thomas Jefferson, in an impassioned appeal, asked Madison to ". . . take up your pen, select the most striking heresies and cut him [Hamilton] to pieces in face of the public."

Two major concerns related to the Neutrality Proclamation faced these writers. One involved the desire, on everyone's part, not to offend France, given how much this country had done for the United States during the American Revolution. Second, memories of the revolutionary war against Great Britain were still fresh in the minds of many citizens who were not eager to support Britain by declaring neutrality in the war. An even more important concern, particularly to those strict constructionists of the Constitution like Madison and Jefferson, was to make sure that such a proclamation did not unnecessarily extend the president's constitutional authority beyond reasonable limits.

Although the two opposing sides in this debate had their own distinct positions, neither side wanted the United States involved in another war. Where the two sides most differed was over the argument concerning presidential power. Neither Jefferson or Madison, as Democratic-Republicans, favored the possibility of the president extending his powers, and neither wanted George Washington to set this precedent. Hamilton, a Federalist, on the other hand, saw that the Neutrality Proclamation should most naturally come from the EXECUTIVE BRANCH since even though Congress had the right to declare war, it was the duty and the right of the executive to preserve the peace until the declaration of war was made. Of all the *Pacificus* and *Helvidius* essays written, *Pacificus No. 1,* written June 29, 1793 and *Helvidius No. 1,* written August 24, 1793, were probably the most important, since they focused primarily on the question of presidential power. Hamilton made a strong case justifying the president's authority to issue such a proclamation and further suggested that such a proclamation in no way would act contrary to the treaties we had with France, nor would

it undercut the gratitude we had expressed to France for its previous assistance in the war. Madison's first *Helvidius* letter, on the other hand, argued against the executive having such complete control over FOREIGN AFFAIRS that would allow the president the right to issue this proclamation, since the Constitution gives the legislature foreign policy authority in allowing it to make war and make treaties in cooperation with the executive. To think otherwise, Madison argued, comes very near to Britain's practice of insisting that treaty and war powers are really "royal prerogatives."

As a result of the Neutrality Proclamation and the attending debates that followed, George Washington both won and lost some political leverage. The Neutrality Proclamation did keep the United States out of war, but the courts refused to punish violators of the proclamation unless there was also an additional law that had been passed by Congress. Washington and Hamilton won the debate concerning the extension of presidential power in the area of foreign affairs—presidents since Washington have for years looked to the *Pacificus* argument to support their own extensions of authority in international affairs.

Further reading: Madison, James. *Writings.* New York: Library of America, 1999; Syrett, Harold C., ed. *The Papers of Alexander Hamilton.* New York: Columbia University Press, 1961–87; Thomas, Charles Marion. *American Neutrality in 1793: A Study in Cabinet Government.* New York: Columbia University Press, 1931.

—Byron W. Daynes

Hendricks, Thomas (1819–1885) *U.S. vice president*
Hendricks was the nation's 21st vice president. He served in the House and Senate and was a serious contender for the presidential nomination as a Democrat. He served as vice president under Grover CLEVELAND but died in office after barely a year. His death highlighted the problem of succession, as the Presidential Succession Act of 1792 allowed that the president pro tempore of the Senate and Speaker of the House assumed the presidency after the VICE PRESIDENT. At the time of Hendricks's death there was neither a president pro tempore nor a Speaker. In 1886 Congress again revised the succession line, placing CABINET members on the list to rise to the presidency should vacancies occur.

heroic leadership

That presidents must lead and govern in the times and circumstances during which they hold office is obvious. Yet discussions of leaders to their "followers" repeatedly invoke the assumption of a unified public psychology regardless of circumstances. Winston Churchill, it is assumed, spoke to the need of *all* the English for heroic leadership to define the country. Likewise, discussions of Franklin D. ROOSEVELT assume that *all* Americans (rich and poor) welcomed the heroic leadership necessary to save the American economic and political system. Yet in times of deep public division—with no extraordinary crises—the public is less apt to demand heroic measures and leaders who aspire to enact them.

There are two very different templates of leadership competing for public support in America at the turn of the 21st century. In the modern presidency, one has become traditional and well-known—the heroic model; the other is emerging and not yet well articulated—the *reflective.*

Heroic leadership in American society is the traditional. Its archetype is Franklin Roosevelt, its metaphor the hierarchy, and its motto: decide and command. The task of the heroic leader is to convince the public of what it is that he already thinks they *must* do. It envisions the leader as struggling against, and overcoming through determination, courage, or even artifice, the circumstances he must surmount. He is known for his authoritative views and acts, not his accessibility. He makes no concessions to the illusion of public intimacy, because the heroic leader stands above and beyond his supportive publics.

Reflective leadership, on the other hand, is personal and diffuse. It draws its authority not by being beyond people, but by being of and like them. It draws its legitimacy not by gathering up all available power, but by dispensing it. Its prototype, but not its archetype, is Bill CLINTON. President George W. BUSH seemed to be a possible exemplar—at least before 9/11. Its metaphor is the prism, and its motto is: select and reflect. It is not reflective in the introspective sense but rather in the sense of radiating outward.

The task of reflective leadership is to gather the disparate elements of a frayed or fractured political and cultural consensus and mirror them so that publics can see the basis for their common purposes. The reflective leader diffuses conflict, he does not sharpen it. It is leadership whose purpose is not to choose and impose, but to engage and connect. It is in a basic sense, restorative—although this need not make it conventional.

It is also profoundly interpersonal in nature. Freud (1920) believed that when crowds (publics) were beset by anxiety they turned to heroic leaders. Yet in doing so, they became disconnected from each other—allied only through their joint connection to the leader. This is one drawback of heroic leadership.

Reflective leadership, unlike heroic leadership, seeks to develop horizontal ties, not direct and hierarchical ones. The reflective leader does not bend the public to his will but rather leads by serving as an expression of a more common one. He does not so much command as explain. He

does not so much tell as ask. And he is not so much the author of the public's common interests as their reflection.

Reflective leadership is not passive. The leader must often fight against adversaries—including those who by temperament and psychology prefer strong answers to common purpose. What kind of circumstances give rise to such leadership?

Countries in which there are no great mobilizing crises, but which are nonetheless deeply divided, seem ripe for reflective leadership. It happens also when citizens feel separated from their major institutions and each other and because of technology and lifestyle have ceased to be connected with each other. The result is a political culture and system in which the issues that divide the country are less responsive to traditional heroic leadership—which relies on a strong psychological basis and urgent consensus that "something must be done."

Technology is part of the reason that reflective leadership has been gathering momentum. Bennett sees economic dislocation and anxiety as the cause of the public's disconnection from traditional ties. Robert Lane referred to this as "sociological release"—the freeing of people from formerly restricting but also connecting categories. He worried that the "colder" market of exchange had increasingly supplanted the domain of community. In such circumstances, absent a crisis, the public yearns for some sense of solidarity and a leader who promises to build it.

As political parties ceased to stand for broad inclusive views and policies, and as each new candidate refined party principles in their own idiosyncratic and politically self-interested way, there were less stable and consistent principles for supporters to attach themselves to and a corresponding rise in the number of independent voters. One consequence of this was not only the consolidation of candidate-centered politics and a corresponding rise in voters' connection to individual leaders and their specific personas and policies, but a dramatic rise in the transience of voters' attachments. You might be a Democrat and like Jimmy CARTER but not Walter MONDALE. You could like Bill Clinton but not Al GORE. If you were a Republican you could like George H. W. BUSH much better than you liked Bob Dole.

Segmented political markets, along with candidate-centered politics, led voters to expect that their specific, individual views would be catered to by candidates. And candidates rushed to reassure voters, through the symbols of intimacy like town meetings and policies derived from intensive use of focus groups that were doing so. As Bennett has insightfully noted, the combination of unrealistic public expectations of familiarity coupled with shallow political attachments gives rise to candidacies that focus on "responsiveness, intimacy (no matter how contrived) and continual reassurance. . . ."

The result is a paradox. After 9/11, the heroic presidency has gained force because it will take the single-minded determination of the president to mobilize all possible leadership resources to deal with the consequences of catastrophic terrorism. Yet at the same time America is still beset by deep political and cultural divisions. We need both heroic and reflective leadership, but can one president give us both? That remains to be seen. George W. Bush seems to be essentially a reflective leader ("I'm a loving man" he said after the 9/11 attacks), but also a determined and inspired one ("but I've got a job to do," and "this president has found his mission").

How well he is able to handle both kinds of presidential LEADERSHIP will be critical—both for his presidency and our country.

Further reading: Bennett, W. Lance. "The Culls Public: Bill Clinton Meets the New American Voter in Campaign '92." In *The Clinton Presidency: Campaigning, Governing, and the Psychology of Leadership*, edited by Stanley A. Renshon, 91–112. Boulder, Col.: Westview Press, 1995; Freud, Sigmund. *Group Psychology and the Analysis of the Ego in Standard Edition*, Vol. 18. 1920. Reprint, London: Hogarth Press, 1974; Renshon, Stanley A. "Political Leadership in a Divided Electorate: Assessing Character Issues in the 2000 Presidential Campaign." Cambridge, Mass: The John F. Kennedy School of Government, Harvard University, 2001.

—Stanley Renshon

hidden hand presidency

The concept of the "hidden hand" presidency was developed by Fred Greenstein to explain the behind-the-scenes maneuvering that enabled EISENHOWER to play an active role in shaping basic policies while safeguarding his public image as a warm, uncontroversial head of state.

Aware of the strengths and weaknesses of the people around him, he knew how to place them in the positions where they would serve him well. His organizational skills, moreover, made it possible for him to delegate policy details while reserving for himself the ability to deal with issues of major importance. In this way, he was able to avoid personal blame for choices that were controversial. In a subsequent study, Greenstein and several of his colleagues expanded the "hidden hand" analysis through a comparison of Eisenhower and JOHNSON's foreign policy making on two key decisions vis-à-vis Vietnam.

Building on these earlier works, Glad and Kitts have argued that Eisenhower also played an activist, and to some extent hidden hand, role in the formulation of U.S. policies relative to the Soviet Union. The Solarium studies, instituted shortly after the death of Stalin, enabled Eisenhower to embrace a CONTAINMENT doctrine opposed by many individuals in his own political party. Behind the scenes he shaped the assignments that would be given to each of the three task forces and influenced how they would be staffed.

At the time of the Hungarian uprising in 1956, the hidden hand was even more important. At the beginning of the crisis, Eisenhower took the question of the U.S. response off the agenda of the NATIONAL SECURITY COUNCIL, decided on his own not to intervene, and called off plans to promote military rebellion behind the Iron Curtain in Europe. The ambassador to the UNITED NATIONS, Henry Cabot Lodge, would not even move the matter from the UN Security Council to the General Assembly until it had become clear that the Soviets would intervene militarily, and the only realistic option for the West was to condemn the Soviet Union and provide relief for those who had engaged in the uprising. In short, Eisenhower knew how to play the game of "preventive politics and recognized the advantages of minimizing discourse on sensitive issues."

Though the president, through this strategy, was able to avoid criticisms that would undermine his authority as head of state, it had a downside. In failing to openly criticize the tactics employed by Senator Joseph McCARTHY and neglecting to take a public stand on the value of integration for the American people, he bought popularity at the expense of moral clarity.

Further reading: Greenstein, Fred I. *The Hidden-Hand Presidency: Eisenhower as Leader.* New York: Basic Books, 1982; Kitts, Kenneth, and Betty Glad. "Improvisational Decision-Making; Eisenhower and the 1956 Hungarian Crisis." In *Reexamining the Eisenhower Presidency,* edited by Shirley Anne Warshaw. Westport, Conn.: Greenwood Press, 1993.

—Betty Glad

high crimes and misdemeanors

Article II, Section 4, of the Constitution establishes that "The President, Vice President, and all civil Officers of the United States, shall be removed from Office on Impeachment for, and Conviction of, Treason, Bribery, or other high Crimes and Misdemeanors." As treason or bribery are defined offenses, debate on what constitutes an impeachable offense has centered on the meaning and scope of the phrase "other high Crimes and Misdemeanors." Specifically, two issues have dominated the debate. First, does the wording "other *high Crimes* and Misdemeanors" limit IMPEACHMENT to official (i.e., political) misconduct, and second, does the wording "Crimes and Misdemeanors" limit it to statutory offenses (i.e., actual violations of the law)?

The phrase "High Crimes and Misdemeanors" was borrowed from the British, who created impeachment in the 14th century. The common-law understanding of impeachment was that it was a political procedure reserved for those officials who would otherwise be beyond the reach of ordinary criminal redress. After examining some 300 years of British impeachment cases, Raol Berger (1973) found that they could be lumped into six categories, all of which are political in nature, but some of which are noncriminal: misapplication of funds, abuse of official power, neglect of duty, encroachment on or contempt for Parliament's prerogatives, corruption, and betrayal of trust.

The colonial and post-revolutionary American experience with impeachment was markedly different from the British practice, though, and this experience was evidenced in the CONSTITUTIONAL CONVENTION. The current language was adopted after an initial proposal that impeachment be for "maladministration" was rejected because it would have made the president subordinate to the good will of Congress. Alexander HAMILTON argued in *Federalist No. 65* that the language referred to political crimes, but James MADISON, who objected to the broader language initially proposed at the Convention, argued in the 1st Congress that "High Crimes and Misdemeanors" could include the unwarranted removal of a meritorious official for personal indiscretion. There is no indication that impeachment was intended to be limited to statutory offenses.

Despite this, during the aborted impeachment attempt of John TYLER and the IMPEACHMENT OF ANDREW JOHNSON the narrower definition of high crimes as actual legal violations was commonly accepted. An initial impeachment attempt against JOHNSON that listed his abuses of the office of the president was defeated because he had violated no laws. The second, successful attempt was therefore focused on a statutory offense—Johnson's violation of the TENURE OF OFFICE ACT.

By the time of the 1974 impeachment effort against Richard NIXON this narrow construction had been disregarded by all but the president's staunchest defenders. In addition to charges based on statutory violations (such as witness tampering, obstruction of justice, and income tax evasion), Nixon was also charged with abusing his powers by ordering the auditing of political enemies, bombing Cambodia, and ordering the surveillance of political enemies and White House employees. The proposed articles also included charges of personal, as well official, misconduct.

The debate over the IMPEACHMENT OF BILL CLINTON brought the definition of high crimes and misdemeanors to the fore. With generally solid evidence against the president, the critical issue was whether what Clinton "did" constituted an impeachable offense. Both sides tended to agree that impeachment was not limited to statutory violations, but they differed beyond that. Republicans tended to argue that statutory violations were a sufficient cause for impeachment, while Clinton's supporters contended impeachment was limited only to official misconduct.

A related issue in the Clinton impeachment was whether the same definition of high crimes and misdemeanors applied equally to all civil officers. The language of the Constitution does not distinguish between civil officers, and Clinton's opponents argued that the president could not be held to a higher threshold of impeachable offenses than other civil officers. If federal judges had been impeached and removed from office for obstruction of justice and perjury, then so, too should the president. Democrats contended that there was a fundamental difference between the single, electorally accountable president and the hundreds of life-tenured federal judges. Since the cost to the country of removing the president was much greater than the cost of removing one of those judges, the threshold had to be higher.

In the end, a modern consensus seems to exist that horrendous personal offenses such as murder can be impeachable, and that impeachable offenses need not be actual legal violations. Beyond that, the vagueness of the Constitution's wording, coupled with competing precedents and historical antecedents, promotes a context-dependent interpretation of the meaning of "other High Crimes and Misdemeanors."

Further reading: Berger, Raol. *Impeachment: The Constitutional Problems.* Cambridge, Mass.: Harvard University Press, 1973; Gerhardt, Michael. *The Federal Impeachment Process: A Constitutional and Historical Analysis.* Princeton, N.J.: Princeton University Press, 1996.
—Sean C. Matheson

Hobart, Garret (1844–1899) *U.S. vice president*
Active in state Republican politics in New Jersey, Hobart became the party's vice presidential candidate in 1896. With William MCKINLEY heading the ticket, the Republicans won and Hobart became the nation's 24th VICE PRESIDENT. Though lacking in experience at the federal government level, he served capably as vice president. In 1899 Hobart collapsed and never recovered. He died on November 21, 1899.

Homeland Security, Department of
Established in 2002, the new department consolidated a number of departments designed to fight terrorism and secure homeland security. Former Pennsylvania governor and later head of the Office of Homeland Security Tom RIDGE served as first head of the new department.

With more than 170,000 employees, a first-year budget of more than $37 billion, and 22 agencies placed under its control, the new Department of Homeland Security immediately became one of the largest and most powerful agencies in the federal government. Included in the department are such varied agencies as the SECRET SERVICE, the Federal Emergency Management Agency, the Customs Service, the Border Patrol, the Immigration and Naturalization Service, and a slew of other agencies.

honeymoon period

The *honeymoon* refers to the period of time immediately following the presidential election in which the public, mass media, and Congress withhold their criticism and give the benefit of the doubt to the newly elected president. It is during this time that presidents try to build a reservoir of goodwill from which they will be able to draw later in their term. During the honeymoon, the public still holds positive evaluations of presidents, media coverage of presidents is still favorable, and the Congress is still willing to give presidents an opportunity to present their legislative agendas.

Public Opinion

Immediately following presidential elections, the public is curious about the White House's new occupant and not yet ready to render a judgment of the president's performance. During this time, public opinion toward the president is generally positive. After about six months, however, almost all presidents since Franklin ROOSEVELT have experienced a substantial decline in public support.

Mass Media

Media coverage early in the term is usually favorable and often focuses on the president's agenda. Once the president has had the opportunity to present proposals from that agenda to the public and Congress, the media usually adopt a more critical perspective as their coverage reflects the more spirited and contentious discourse of the legislative process that takes place between the president and Congress.

Congress

Congress is almost always willing to give new presidents the opportunity to at least present their legislative agendas. Presidents are frequently able to get more of their legislation passed by Congress during their honeymoon. Paul Light has demonstrated that, between 1961 and 1978, 72 percent of a president's proposals sent to Congress in the first three months become law, while the rate of success drops to 39 percent in the second three months, and 25 percent in the third three months.

Further reading: Brace, Paul, and Barbara Hinckley. *Follow the Leader: Opinion Polls and the Modern Presidents.* New York: Basic Books, 1992; Light, Paul C. *The President's Agenda: Domestic Policy Choice from Kennedy to Clinton.* Baltimore, Md.: Johns Hopkins University Press, 1999; Ragsdale, Lynn. *Vital Statistics on the Presidency: Washington to Clinton.* Washington, D.C.: CQ Press, 1998.

—Adam B. Lawrence

Hoover, Herbert Clark (1874–1964) *thirty-first U.S. president*

Before becoming president, Herbert Hoover had already attained stature as a truly great and accomplished man, but his failed presidency forever tainted his once stellar reputation. Herbert Hoover was born on August 10, 1874, in West Branch, Ohio. He graduated from Stanford University in 1895.

If one could create a person with all the qualities essential for a great president, you might invent Herbert Hoover. His prepresidential career reveals one success after another. The "Great Engineer," as Hoover was called, brought to the presidency a reputation for skill, accomplishment, and public service that was truly impressive. He was food administrator during WILSON's presidency, secretary of commerce under HARDING and COOLIDGE, an able administrator, and a man of integrity. Few presidents stood so high in public esteem as they entered office. Yet this same man who had accomplished so much, and from whom so much was expected would, four years later, leave office amid scorn and abuse. This dramatic reversal is due to one thing: the GREAT DEPRESSION of 1929.

In presidential politics, as in life, much hinges on luck—good and bad. Napoleon, when choosing generals, would say "find me a man who is lucky." Herbert Hoover had the great misfortune to become president a few months before the depression struck. As the old blues song goes: "If it wasn't for bad luck, I wouldn't have no luck at all."

In October 1929 the stock market plunged. From a high of 469, it sunk to 85 by 1932. Unemployment soared. Some estimates put the unemployment rate at 35 percent. Businesses failed, banks closed, the poor took to the streets and to the roads.

Hoover at first responded with pep talks designed to instill confidence in the midst of chaos. "Prosperity is just around the corner," he would say. When that failed he turned to intervention in the economy, launching public works programs, tax reductions, and the establishment of a Reconstruction Finance Corporation. These small steps also failed. Former President Coolidge visited the White House and discussed the administration's efforts at reversing the depression. Coolidge told Hoover he could not understand why Hoover's relief efforts were so ineffective and why the president's critics were so vehement. "You can't expect to see calves running in the field the day after you put a bull to the cows," Coolidge said. "No," replied Hoover, "but I would expect to see contented cows."

President Herbert C. Hoover (Library of Congress)

As the Depression deepened, a BONUS ARMY, comprised of thousands of WORLD WAR I veterans marched on Washington demanding help. They set up shacks, and their makeshift town became known as "Hooverville," in which they kept warm with "Hoover blankets" (discarded newspapers).

In July of 1932, Hoover ordered the army to tear down the makeshift huts. U.S. troops went in carrying rifles with fixed bayonets, and they used tear gas and flamethrowers on the demonstrators, demolishing Hooverville. The nation, seeing this in movie-house newsreels, was stunned. Hoover appeared heartless as well as helpless.

Herbert Hoover was a talented, sincere man, overcome by events. He was the victim, not the master of these events. "This office is a compound hell," he said toward the end of his presidency. Upon leaving office in 1933, the Hoovers retired to Palo Alto, California, and Hoover worked on the development of the Hoover Library at Stanford University. Eventually he took a more active public opposition to Franklin D. ROOSEVELT's economic programs, writing the

highly critical book *The Challenge of Liberty.* After WORLD WAR II, President TRUMAN called Hoover back into public service, appointing the former president as chairman of the Famine Emergency Commission, and later appointing Hoover as chairman of the Commission on Organization of the Executive Branch (the "HOOVER COMMISSION"). Hoover died on October 20, 1964.

Further reading: Faushold, Martin L. *The Presidency of Herbert Hoover.* Lawrence: University Press of Kansas, 1985;————, and George Mazuzan, eds. *The Hoover Presidency: A Reappraisal.* Albany: State University of New York Press, 1974; Warren, Harris G. *Herbert Hoover and the Great Depression.* New York: Oxford University Press, 1959.

Hoover, J. Edgar (1895–1972) *FBI director*
John Edgar Hoover was appointed Director of the Bureau of Investigation (renamed the FEDERAL BUREAU OF INVESTIGATION in 1935) in 1924 and served in that capacity until his death in 1972.

Hoover took over the Bureau after the scandalous PALMER RAIDS, which were an abuse of the Bureau's investigative authority in their attempt to uncover communists, socialists, and anarchists. Hoover reformed the Bureau by instituting managerial systems for accountability, upgrading qualifications for agents, and establishing rigorous training for new recruits. In addition, he established a crime laboratory that became a model for forensic science and police organizations. Hoover established an outstanding reputation for himself and the FBI.

Hoover was also an outstanding bureaucratic politician. He cultivated relationships with presidents, members of Congress, interest groups, and the media.

In 1936 Hoover and Franklin ROOSEVELT agreed that the Bureau would report on "fascist and communist activities." In 1939 FDR directed Hoover to take charge of investigations involving espionage, sabotage, and violations of the neutrality laws and to receive information for the first time from local police and later from citizens pertaining to "subversive activities." Hoover interpreted these orders as the authority to collect and maintain files on noncriminal behavior. The FBI was thus transformed into an intelligence agency. Hoover also provided political intelligence for Roosevelt by investigating and reporting on critics of the administration.

After the war, Presidents TRUMAN and EISENHOWER issued EXECUTIVE ORDERS requiring security clearances for present and future federal employees. This further established the need and authority for internal security files. The Truman and Eisenhower administrations also authorized warrantless ELECTRONIC SURVEILLANCE for national security.

Hoover continued to provide political intelligence for presidents. During the 1964 Democratic Convention in Atlantic City, the FBI provided President JOHNSON with information regarding the activities of his critics.

President NIXON escalated the demands on the FBI and Hoover by seeking information on members of the press and any negative material on his "enemies." Hoover, however, objected to the Houston Plan, which called for massive arrests in case of disorder.

As a result of his relationship with various presidents, Hoover had established a massive file system on Americans and was therefore able to intimidate many of his critics. His relationship with key members of Congress and with interest groups further enhanced his political power.

Hoover was able to use his files to co-opt journalists and media executives who wanted inside information or access to his stories for television and film. In return, they would promote Hoover, the Bureau, and their ideology.

Hoover was the listed author of *Masters of Deceit,* a book that described the communist threat to America, as well as numerous scholarly articles on this and related security issues. These publications, which were actually written by agents, presented Hoover as a sage in America's war against "Godless Communism." Hoover also created "The 10 Most Wanted List," in which the FBI inevitably got their man. Critics contend that Hoover created a propaganda machine and that the favorable publicity served his and the Bureau's interests. In addition, they argued that he focused on rogue criminals and avoided the drug problem and organized crime because of their sophistication and their potential for inducing agents into corruption, which would endanger the vaunted reputation and power of the Bureau.

The VIETNAM WAR and the Civil Rights movement created difficulties for the Bureau. The civil unrest led to a program of counterintelligence (Cointelpro). Its revelation in the 1970s along with its other "political" and "illegal" activities severely damaged Hoover and the Bureau's reputation. Most devastating to its reputation was the campaign to discredit Dr. Martin Luther King, Jr., for being a critic of the Bureau.

At the time of his death, Hoover was under attack and his beloved Bureau was under siege. The great accomplishment of successfully building a great investigative agency was placed in the context of abuse of power.

Further reading: Gentry, Curt. *J. Edgar Hoover: The Man and the Secrets.* New York: Norton, 1991; Sorrentino, Frank M. *Ideological Warfare: FBI's Path Toward Power.* Port Washington, N.Y.: Associated Faculty Press, 1983; Theoharis, Athan, and John Stuart Cox. *The Boss: J. Edgar Hoover and the Great American Inquisition.* Philadelphia: Temple University, Press, 1988.

—Frank M. Sorrentino

Hoover, Lou Henry (1874–1944) *first lady*
Lou Henry Hoover had earned degrees from San Jose Normal School and Stanford when she married Herbert Hoover (1899). In the early years of their marriage, their shared interest in geology led them to collaborate in translating Chinese mining texts and *Agricola de re Metallica.* Herbert and Lou Henry Hoover had two sons, Herbert Clark Hoover, Jr. (born 1903) and Allan Henry Hoover (1907).

Their partnership continued in WORLD WAR I relief work, when Lou Henry Hoover was the fund-raiser and Herbert Hoover the administrator. She also had an independent agenda for social change. A strong supporter of Girl Scouting, she served as a national commissioner (1917–18), national board of directors chair (1925–28), vice president (1921 and 1925–29), and president (1922–25, 1933–37). She was also president of the Women's Division of the National Amateur Athletic Foundation, later renamed the National Women's Athletic Association. Her political interests led her to conduct the 1924 Women's Conference on Law Enforcement, called in response to the TEAPOT DOME SCANDAL and sponsored by the General Federation of Women's Clubs.

First Lady Lou Henry Hoover *(Library of Congress)*

In the presidential campaign and in the White House, Lou Henry Hoover was the first presidential wife to speak on national radio and to give formal speeches. Her other initiatives during the White House years included establishing Camp Rapidan, inventorying the contents of the White House, and refurbishing several rooms. She responded personally and supportively to innumerable citizens who requested her aid during the Depression. Though generally reluctant to challenge traditional social practices as first lady, she rejected segregationist standards and welcomed the wife of African-American Representative Oscar De Priest (Ill.-Dem.) to a tea for congressional wives.

After leaving the White House, Lou Henry Hoover continued her work in Girl Scouting and related organizations. By 1940 she and Herbert Hoover were once again active in war relief efforts and in fund-raising. She died suddenly and unexpectedly in 1944 of a heart attack.

Further reading: Mayer, Dale C., ed. *Essays on a Busy Life*. Worland, Wyo.: High Plains Press, 1994.

—Mary Anne Borrelli

Hoover Commissions

WORLD WAR II among other things, increased the number of administrative agencies in the federal government. The 80th Congress created the first Hoover Commission in 1947 for the stated purpose of integrating and reducing the number of agencies created during the pursuit of the war effort. The commission, formally called the Commission on the Executive Branch of Government and headed by former President Herbert HOOVER, did not call for a reduction in the number of agencies of the federal government but made the case for increasing the managerial capacities of the presidency by shoring up offices in the EXECUTIVE OFFICE OF THE PRESIDENT (EOP). These capacities could be increased by, among other things, giving the presidency full discretion over presidential organization and staff, strengthening the BUREAU OF THE BUDGET, locating a personnel office in the EOP, and creating a staff secretary in the White House to provide liaison between the president and his subordinates. It also called for agencies and departments to be reorganized so as to provide a clear, coherent rationale for each department and a greater degree of presidential control. All in all, 277 specific recommendations, not all governed by the same administrative theory, were put forward, most being organized around the values of hierarchical control, coherence in governmental organization, centralized authority, and organization by purpose. Many were adopted and put into effect.

In 1953 the second Hoover Commission was convened, this time under the formal designation of the Commission on the Organization of the Executive Branch of Government. In contrast to the first commission, the second Hoover Commission was charged with streamlining the public business, defining and setting limits on executive functions, and reducing or eliminating nonessential government services that competed with private business on the grounds that government had grown too large to be effectively managed. Unlike the first Hoover Commission, which boasted an impressive percentage of recommendations being implemented, the second commission saw relatively few of its recommendations adopted and those that were adopted were largely ineffective.

Further reading: Arnold, Peri E. *Making the Managerial Residency: Comprehensive Reorganization Planning, 1905–1996,* 2d rev. ed. Lawrence: University Press of Kansas, 1998; Fesler, James W. "Administrative Literature and the Second Hoover Commission Reports." *American Political Science Review 61* (March 1967); Shafritz, Jay. *The Dorset Dictionary of American Government and Politics.* Chicago: The Dorset Press, 1988, pp. 266–267.

—Daniel E. Ponder

Hopkins, Harry Lloyd (1890–1946)

During the 1930s and 1940s, Harry Hopkins was regarded as Franklin Roosevelt's most loyal policy adviser. President ROOSEVELT appointed Hopkins to serve as director of the Federal Emergency Relief Administration (FERA) in 1933. This NEW DEAL program disseminated federal grants to the states in an effort to provide financial relief to the poor. In the fall of 1933 Hopkins headed the Civil Works Administration (CWA) and was responsible for developing public works projects for the unemployed. In 1935 Hopkins was appointed to head another public works program known as the WORKS PROGRESS ADMINISTRATION (WPA). The programs of the WPA occasionally conflicted with those projects that were under the jurisdiction of the Public Works Administration (PWA) headed by Harold Ickes. The source of conflict partially stemmed from Ickes's philosophy that successful public works programs were those that produced financial results benefiting the nation's economy. Hopkins believed public works projects should be designed to eliminate unemployment, reduce the number of poor seeking federal relief assistance, and build the self-esteem of their recipients. Roosevelt eventually nominated Hopkins as secretary of Commerce in 1938 to replace Daniel C. Roper. Hopkins resigned his CABINET position in 1940 because of poor health. Apart from his role in federal relief programs, Hopkins also served as a valuable foreign policy adviser and performed many diplomatic roles during the Roosevelt presidency regarding American involvement in WORLD WAR II. In 1942 Hopkins assisted in the implementation of the Lend-Lease program and was appointed to serve on the Munitions Assignment Board (MAB). Hopkins accompanied Franklin Roosevelt to the Tehran Conference in the fall of 1943 to meet with Prime Minister Winston Churchill of Great Britain and Premier of the Soviet Union Joseph Stalin. The purpose of this meeting was to discuss Allied progress in the war and to address postwar policy issues. Hopkins served a key role at the Tehran Conference by participating in negotiations with British Foreign Secretary Anthony Eden and Soviet Foreign Commissar Vyacheslav M. Molotov concerning Turkey's role in the war and European security. During the first week of February in 1945, Hopkins attended the YALTA CONFERENCE to assist Roosevelt during his meetings with Churchill and Stalin. Following the death of President Roosevelt in April of 1945, Hopkins resigned from his duties in the EXECUTIVE BRANCH and began to prepare for retirement. Despite his frail health, Hopkins continued to offer his foreign policy advice and diplomatic skills at the beginning of the TRUMAN administration. Although he did not personally attend the POTSDAM CONFERENCE in the summer of 1945, Hopkins undertook a significant role in preparing the Truman presidency for its first encounter with Churchill and Stalin at this meeting. Hopkins retreated back into retirement during the fall of 1945 to cope with his failing health. He died on January 29, 1946.

Further reading: Adams, Henry H. *Harry Hopkins.* New York: Putnam, 1977; Hopkins, June. *Harry Hopkins: Sudden Hero, Brash Reformer.* New York: St. Martin's Press, 1999; McJimsey, George. *Harry Hopkins: Ally of the Poor and Defender of Democracy.* Cambridge, Mass.: Harvard University Press, 1987.

—Adam L. Warber

hotline

The Direct Communications Link (DCL) or hotline, as it is commonly called, is an evolving communications system that has linked the heads of state of the United States and Russia in times of crisis since 1963. During the CUBAN MISSILE CRISIS in the fall of 1962, President John F. KENNEDY and Premier Nikita S. Khrushchev averted a superpower showdown over Cuba through back-channel communications and restraint. Mutual consultation was achieved through diplomatic channels (ambassadors and envoys). With the possibility of a nuclear war starting in hours, not days, Kennedy and Khrushchev realized the two countries needed quicker forms of communication for consultation in times of crisis. Hence, negotiations were begun on a direct communications link between the two countries.

The DCL was originally established on June 20, 1963, through a memorandum of understanding between the United States and the Union of Soviet Socialist Republics (USSR). Originally, the hotline system consisted of two telegraph-teleprinter terminal points located in the United States and the USSR. The hotline in the United States is located in the PENTAGON with a link to the White House. In 1963 the DCL was able to transmit messages at 65 words per minute. The first reported use of the direct communications system occurred during the 1967 Middle East war, with subsequent uses in 1978 by President Jimmy CARTER to confer with Soviet leader Leonid Brezhnev about Afghanistan and in 1982 to inform President Ronald REAGAN that Brezhnev had died.

To date, the communications system has been upgraded three times. In 1971 the system was modernized from wire to satellite circuits. A satellite earth station (Detrick Earth Station) was constructed at Fort Detrick in Maryland. On September 4, 1985, President Reagan authorized NSDD-186 (National Security Decision Document) to upgrade the system's capabilities. The modernization included the addition of facsimile transmission of full pages of text and graphics to the teletype link and additional redundant transmission links. The Reagan Administration also created a Standing Subcommittee on Upgrades to set technical parameters and recommend overall enhancements to the DCL agreeable to both countries. In 1999 the United States and Russia included video-conferencing capabilities to enable each side to see and hear their counterparts during an emergency or crisis situation.

Further reading: Blechman, Barry M. "Efforts to Reduce the Risk of Accidental or Inadvertent War." In *U.S.–Soviet Security Cooperation: Achievements, Failures, Lessons,* edited by Alexander L. George, Philip J. Farley, and Alexander Dallin. New York: Oxford University Press, 1988; Direct Communication Link (DCL) / "Hotline" Between Washington and Moscow Policy (NSC-NSDD-186) http://209.207.236.112/irp/offdocs/nsdd/nsdd-186.htm (1 Sept. 2001); Agreement between the United States of America and the Union of Soviet Socialist Republics to Expand the U.S.-USSR Direct Communications Link http://www.state.gov/www/global/arms/treaties/hotexpa.html (1 Sept. 2001).

—Owen Holmes

housing policy

Concern for public housing is a relatively recent presidential phenomenon. While there were early expressions of concern and interest, the real attention of presidents to housing issues dates back to the 1940s. Prior to that time, the marketplace of the free enterprise system was seen as the most appropriate place for housing policy to evolve.

After WORLD WAR II, the goal of making home ownership available to returning veterans brought the federal government into the equation. The Housing Act of 1949 was the first federal effort to establish a uniform housing policy of encouraging home ownership.

It was not until the 1960s, when housing and urban renewal became linked, that the federal government got more directly involved. President KENNEDY's task force, followed by President JOHNSON's programs as part of his GREAT SOCIETY, placed housing on the presidential and national agenda. Johnson's Model Cities Program (1966) and Housing and Urban Development Act (1968) got the federal government active in the housing market, especially in development of low-cost housing for the poor.

Many of the federal government's housing programs and subsidies were cut during the Reagan presidency. In the first six years of the Reagan administration federal housing subsidies fell from $30 billion to $7.9 billion, and tax breaks were adjusted to favor commercial over residential construction.

Housing and Urban Development, Department of (HUD)

Responsible for programs related to housing and urban community development, this CABINET office was created in 1965 as a consolidation of several government agencies. During the Reagan years, mismanagement on a massive scale was revealed at HUD, as charges of corruption and favoritism in government contracting led to a series of personnel dismissals and scandals.

Federal housing projects began during WORLD WAR I. They were modest projects under the authority of the U.S. Housing Corporation. The program was a temporary one, designed to build houses for those working on the war effort. During the NEW DEAL, the Federal Housing Administration (FHA) was created, dealing with federal mortgage insurance. In 1937 the U.S. Housing Authority was created, issuing grants and loans to local community housing programs.

In an effort to unify several housing-related agencies, in 1942, FDR created, the National Housing Agency. Several years later, President TRUMAN created the Housing and Home Finance Agency.

After WORLD WAR II, a housing boom led to demands for greater federal involvement in housing. The Housing Act (1954) established a federal urban renewal program. When he took office, President KENNEDY proposed a CABINET-level department of Housing, but fears that Kennedy would appoint Robert Weaver, an African American, to head the new agency led to its demise.

As part of his GREAT SOCIETY program, President Lyndon JOHNSON proposed the creation of the Department of Housing and Urban Development (HUD). In 1965 this new cabinet agency was established. By the 1980s support for federal housing programs waned, as President REAGAN was ideologically opposed to such ventures. In the Reagan years, HUD was a scandal-plagued agency. By the 1990s HUD remained a mildly successful but often disappointing housing development agency of the federal government.

Hull, Cordell (1871–1955) *secretary of state*

The longest-serving secretary of State in U.S. history, Hull served Franklin D. ROOSEVELT for 11½ years. Of course, Roosevelt liked serving as his own secretary of State and was sometimes off put by Hull's deliberate and inflexible style. Thus, Hull's length of service should not be confused with influence, as FDR often worked around his secretary of State. Hull served FDR during the NEW DEAL and most of WORLD WAR II and was referred to by Roosevelt as the "father of the UNITED NATIONS." In 1945 Hull received the Nobel Peace Prize.

human rights

While the United States's stress on human rights in foreign policy is usually associated with the presidency of Jimmy CARTER, American concern goes back to the creation of the republic. The Declaration of Independence is a clear, eloquent statement of universal or unalienable human rights, and the Bill of Rights (first 10 amendments to the Constitution) serve as an attempt to codify such rights.

Throughout U.S. history presidents such as JEFFERSON (Declaration), LINCOLN (GETTYSBURG ADDRESS), Wilson (FOURTEEN POINTS), and FDR (FOUR FREEDOMS) emphasized universal human rights and the "unique" role or responsibility of the United States in advocating such rights.

With the COLD WAR, power politics replaced human rights concerns in the making of U.S. foreign policy, but in the 1970s President Carter reemphasized the role human rights would play in U.S. policy. With the collapse of the Soviet Union in 1989, the United States became the world's only superpower, and its responsibilities as well as its powers became more pronounced and more controversial. Presidents George H. W. BUSH and Bill CLINTON often spoke of human rights but failed to make them the centerpiece of policy. Early in the presidency of George W. BUSH, the tragic events of 9/11 overshadowed all other policy considerations, and the United States became a focus of criticism from human rights groups for its handling of foreign internees, children under the age of 16, and U.S. citizens imprisoned in Guantánamo Bay, Cuba, without a trial, without being charged with a crime, and without access to attorneys.

Further reading: Brown, Peter G., and Douglas MacLean, eds. *Human Rights and U.S. Foreign Policy: Principles and*

Application. Lexington, Mass.: Lexington Books, 1979; Frankel, Charles. *Human Rights and Foreign Policy.* New York: Foreign Policy Association, 1978; Muravchik, Joshua. *The Uncertain Crusade: Jimmy Carter and the Dilemmas of Human Rights Policy.* Lanham, Md.: Hamilton Press, 1986; Vogelgesang, Sandy. *American Dream, Global Nightmare: The Dilemma of U.S. Human Rights Policy.* New York: Norton, 1980.

humor

Presidents use humor and are the victims of humor. Presidents who made use of humor often did so, not merely with the goal of getting a laugh or gaining popularity in mind, but with the purpose of using humor to educate an audience. Abraham LINCOLN was known as a great storyteller, yet his stories had morals.

John F. KENNEDY used humor to highlight his wit, intelligence, and personality. Ronald REAGAN used humor to draw people toward him, as a way to demonstrate his warmth and everyman qualities.

Of course, humor can also be used to skewer presidents. Political cartoons were a means of bringing politicians down a peg or two, and often with devastating effect, as the work of Thomas Nast, Herblock, Garry Trudeau, and others demonstrates. Television's late-night comedians such as David Letterman and Jay Leno and shows such as *Saturday Night Live* and *The Daily Show* also use humor to devastating effect.

Humphrey, Hubert H. (1911–1978) *U.S. vice president*

Hubert H. Humphrey was born on May 27, 1911, in Wallace, South Dakota. Humphrey earned a B.A. in political science at the University of Minnesota in 1939 and an M.A. from Louisiana State University in 1940. While teaching at Macalester College in Minneapolis, he participated in the merger of the Farmer-Labor and Democratic parties of Minnesota in 1944. Humphrey was elected mayor of Minneapolis in 1945.

Elected to the Senate in 1948, Humphrey gradually distinguished himself as a leading liberal Democrat on such issues as civil rights, nuclear arms control, Medicare, AGRICULTURAL programs, and a more humanitarian foreign policy toward the Third World. As Senate minority and then majority leader during most of the 1950s, Lyndon B. JOHNSON of Texas valued Humphrey as his major liaison with northern liberals.

Humphrey briefly ran against Senator John F. KENNEDY for the 1960 Democratic presidential nomination. During Kennedy's presidency, Humphrey served as Senate majority whip and developed Senate support for such leg-

islation as the partial nuclear test ban treaty, Medicare, and the CIVIL RIGHTS ACT of 1964. After being elected vice president as President Johnson's running mate in 1964, Humphrey was a loyal, zealous advocate and spokesman for Johnson's foreign and domestic policies.

After Johnson withdrew from the presidential campaign of 1968, Humphrey entered the race. The Democratic national convention in Chicago, marred by antiwar protests and violence, nominated Humphrey for president. After narrowly losing the presidential election to Richard M. NIXON, Humphrey returned to the Senate in 1971 and died of cancer on January 13, 1978.

Further reading: Griffith, Winthrop, *Humphrey: A Candid Biography.* New York: Morrow, 1965; Humphrey, Hubert H. *The Education of a Public Man: My Life and Politics.* Garden City, N.Y.: Doubleday, 1976.

—Sean J. Savage

Humphrey's Executor v. United States, 295 U.S. 602 (1935)

This case establishes limits of presidential REMOVAL POWER. President Franklin ROOSEVELT asked Federal Trade Commissioner William Humphrey to resign. When Humphrey refused, Roosevelt notified him that he had been removed. Humphrey died in 1934 never having agreed to his removal. The executor of Humphrey's estate decided to sue for his salary that he contended was due him.

Roosevelt believed he was on solid legal ground to dismiss Humphrey. The Supreme Court in *MYERS V. UNITED STATES* (1926), sustained President WILSON's decision to dismiss a postmaster without the Senate's consent. Chief Justice William Howard TAFT delineated broad removal powers of the president and the unconstitutionality of the TENURE OF OFFICE ACT, which led to the IMPEACHMENT of President Andrew JOHNSON.

The Supreme Court had to address two questions: (1) Did the FEDERAL TRADE COMMISSION ACT limit the president's removal powers, except for the reasons stated, and (2) If the act did limit the president's removal power, was it constitutional?

Justice George Sutherland, speaking for a unanimous court, ruled that Roosevelt had exceeded his authority in dismissing Humphrey because it violated the SEPARATION OF POWERS principle. He stated that Myers was a "purely executive functionary," while Humphrey, as a Federal Trade Commissioner, occupied "no place in the executive department"; the FTC was "an agency of the legislative or judicial departments" which exercised "quasi-legislative or quasi-judicial powers." Congress therefore had the authority to set conditions for tenure of the commissioners, and

Congress could therefore "forbid their removal except for cause in the meantime."

The Court's decision was both praised and condemned. Many believed that it did not follow the precedent of the *Myers* case and would weaken presidential control and ACCOUNTABILITY. Supporters saw the decision as freeing the new regulatory tribunals from fear of reprisal. This would allow these new agencies to function as effective umpires in the complex modern economy that was emerging. *Humphrey's Executor* was never reversed and the principles were sustained and expanded in *Weiner v. United States* (1958) and *Morrison v. Olson* (1988).

Further reading: Corwin, Edward. *The President: Office and Powers 1789–1957*, 5th rev. ed. New York: New York University Press, 1984; Koenig, Louis W. *The Chief Executive*. Fort Worth: Harcourt Brace College Publishers, 1996.

—Frank M. Sorrentino

Hyde Park

Hyde Park is the ancestral home of Franklin ROOSEVELT. The family's name for the site was Springwood, although FDR preferred the name Krum (Crum) Elbow, claiming that Springwood was a pedestrian title, but Krum Elbow never gained acceptance. The Roosevelt residence became popularly known as Hyde Park from the name of the Dutchess County, New York, town two miles north of the estate. The president's father purchased the home and 110 acres in 1867. With subsequent land acquisitions, the estate expanded to 900 acres and continued to be a working, if not profitable, farm until the president's death. After several ren-

ovations, the home has 35 rooms and nine baths. The decor is that of when FDR lived there. FDR and his wife, Eleanor ROOSEVELT, are buried in the rose garden near the house.

During FDR's administration, Springwood was the "summer White House," especially useful since air conditioning was not widely used in Washington until after WORLD WAR II. The Franklin D. Roosevelt Library was constructed in 1939–40 on the family estate. After FDR's death, the library and accompanying museum were designated the Franklin D. Roosevelt National Historic Site. Now encompassing 254 acres, it is maintained by the NATIONAL ARCHIVES. Two miles to the east is the Eleanor Roosevelt National Historic Site, a 180-acre estate known as Val-Kill, the retreat that her husband purchased for her in the 1920s.

The FDR library became the first in a series of congressionally authorized presidential LIBRARIES, although the Rutherford B. Hayes Library that opened in 1916 was the first presidential library. Herbert HOOVER is unusual for having two libraries named for him. From the 1920s on the Hoover Institution at Stanford University housed his materials on international communism and related topics. In 1962 he opened his presidential library at his birthplace, West Branch, Iowa.

Further reading: Davis, Kenneth S. *FDR: The Beckoning of Destiny, 1882–1928, A History*. New York: Putnam, 1971; Dows, Olin. *Franklin Roosevelt at Hyde Park*. New York: American Artists Group, 1949; Steeholm, Clara, and Hardy Steeholm. *The House at Hyde Park*. New York: Viking Press, 1950.

—Thomas P. Wolf

I

illness See HEALTH OF PRESIDENTS.

Immigration and Naturalization Service v. Chadha, 462 U.S. 919 (1983)

This was a Supreme Court decision that struck down the LEGISLATIVE VETO as a violation of the constitutionally prescribed lawmaking procedure. The decision involved an alien, Jagdish Rai Chadha, who had had his deportation suspended by an immigration judge. Congress, however, had earlier empowered itself by statute to review any deportation suspensions. The Senate and the House of Representatives were each granted authority by the act to reject any determination that a deportation should be suspended by simply passing a resolution. The resolution did not have to pass the other house of Congress or be presented to the president for his signature or VETO. This statutory measure was a species of legislative veto, a venerable mechanism that had existed since the 1930s, through which either house of Congress or even certain congressional committees could "veto" actions taken by administrative agencies. In this instance, the judge's report was transmitted to Congress and the House passed a resolution concluding that Chadha should have his suspension of deportation revoked.

Chadha argued that the one-house veto violated the proper lawmaking procedure as provided in Article I of the Constitution, known as the PRESENTATION CLAUSE. Chadha reasoned that since the House action altered legal rights (in that he was to be deported), such an action constituted lawmaking and must follow the correct constitutional procedure.

The Court agreed with Chadha and concluded that the one-house resolution involved lawmaking and thus violated the Presentation Clause. The Court ruled that for federal law to be properly enacted the Presentation Clause's twin requirements must be met: bicameral passage of a bill and its presentation to the president for either his signature or veto. In *Chadha*, the Court ruled that Congress through its legislative veto effectively rendered a policy decision that circumvented presentment to the president, effectively depriving him of his veto power.

Ostensibly, *Chadha* dealt a severe blow to the power of Congress since as a legal matter it eliminated a potent and longstanding check on EXECUTIVE POWER. *Chadha* effectively nullified more than 200 legislative vetoes, more provisions of federal law than the Supreme Court had struck down in its entire history up to that point. After *Chadha*, however, Congress found new, creative approaches to ensure that the power it delegated to the EXECUTIVE BRANCH would be employed more to its liking. Use of legislative vetoes, therefore, persists to this day, albeit in more subtle forms. The reality is that both political branches find it convenient to continue using them: Congress gains from improved OVERSIGHT capability, and the executive branch enjoys more freedom from statutory restriction.

The Court's strict interpretation of the Presentation Clause in *Chadha* and in later striking down the Line Item Veto Act, stands in stark contrast, however, to the Court's loose treatment of the non-delegation doctrine, a principle that theoretically limits Congress in its delegations to the executive branch. The Court's permissive treatment of this doctrine has permitted agencies to perform their own lawmaking functions through the issuance of regulations. In the wake of *Chadha* courts have done little to resolve this tension in the jurisprudence of lawmaking.

Further reading: Craig, Barbara Hinkson. *Chadha: The Story of an Epic Constitutional Struggle.* New York: Oxford University Press, 1988; Fisher, Louis. "The Legislative Veto: Invalidated, It Survives." *Law & Contemporary Problems* 56 (autumn 1993): 273; Korn, Jessica. *The Power of Separation: American Constitutionalism and the Myth of the Legislative Veto.* Princeton, N.J.: Princeton University Press, 1996.

—Roy E. Brownell II

immigration policy

Until 1882, the United States placed no restrictions on immigration. For the 40 years after 1882, a number of restrictions were imposed, but apart from restriction against immigration from Asia, these restrictions were of limited utility. In 1921 and 1924, Presidents HARDING and then COOLIDGE promoted the Emergency Quota Act of 1921, then the Immigration Act of 1924. These acts imposed severe restrictions on the number of immigrants admitted to the United States, and discriminated specifically against southern and Eastern Europeans.

In 1943 President Franklin Delano ROOSEVELT got Congress to repeal Chinese exclusionary restrictions, and this was the beginning of a more open attitude regarding immigration of people of color. By the 1970s, immigration from Mexico and South and Central America caused a political backlash, and by the 1980s and 1990s an anti-immigration sentiment developed among some Americans. In the aftermath of the 9/11 tragedy, the Immigration and Naturalization Service (INS) came under fire and further tightened immigration policy.

immunity, presidential

The powers of the president are laid out in Article II of the Constitution, which makes no mention of immunity from civil lawsuits or criminal prosecution. Nonetheless, federal courts have held that the president is entitled to some immunity for several reasons. There is considerable evidence that the Founding Fathers believed that the president should have a certain degree of immunity, even if they did not explicitly say so in the Constitution. Also, many have argued that respect for the important principle of SEPARATION OF POWERS means that the president cannot be at the beck and call of the courts. The Supreme Court has also expressed concern that without immunity, the president might shrink from taking actions that are in the national interest but could potentially subject him to personal liability or even criminal prosecution. Finally, the Court has expressed concern that without immunity too much of the president's time might be taken up by legal proceedings.

On the other hand, there are competing concerns that argue against executive immunity, or at least for strictly limiting it. It is a well-known axiom that "no man is above the law." If a president is accused of violating the law, many argue that he should be as accountable as any other person.

The Supreme Court has tried to accommodate these competing interests and concerns. In *Bivins v. Six Unknown Named Agents of the Federal Bureau of Narcotics* (1971) the Court held that the Constitution gives individuals the right to sue federal officials who violate their constitutional rights. But in *Nixon v. Fitzgerald* (1982), the Court held that the president enjoys absolute immunity from civil suit that might arise from any action he undertakes within the "outer perimeter" of his official duties. Anything less might deprive the president of "the maximum ability to deal fearlessly and impartially" with the duties of his office.

Nevertheless, there are serious limits on the scope of executive immunity. In *CLINTON V. JONES* (1997), the Court held that the president is not entitled to even temporary immunity from civil litigation stemming from actions he undertook prior to his assuming the office of the presidency. The majority of the Court held that there was no "unequivocal common understanding" among the Constitution's framers that the president was entitled to absolute immunity during his term in office.

Furthermore, the president is not immune from lawsuits challenging his use of EXECUTIVE POWER. In *YOUNGSTOWN SHEET & TUBE CO., V. SAWYER* (1952) the Supreme Court held that President Harry S TRUMAN overstepped his Article II power when he ordered the secretary of Commerce to seize and operate most of the nation's steel mills during the KOREAN WAR. President Truman had argued that if a strike shut down the mills this would cripple the war effort and that he was therefore empowered as COMMANDER IN CHIEF to seize and operate the mills. The *Youngstown* case established the important principle that the Courts can prevent the president from overstepping his constitutional powers, even if he is not held personally liable for whatever damages his overstepping might have caused.

Finally, it is well established that the president is not immune from being subpoenaed to testify as a witness in a criminal case, although the courts must defer to his schedule, usually allowing taped or written testimony. President's Ulysses GRANT and Gerald FORD both gave depositions in criminal cases, and Presidents CLINTON and Jimmy CARTER both provided videotaped testimony in criminal trials.

Executive immunity is an important and complex issue in which the courts have strived to balance the values of presidential ACCOUNTABILITY with the unique demands and requirements of the office of the presidency. It is an area where there remain many unanswered questions and unresolved tensions, ensuring the law will continue to evolve.

Further reading: Miller, Randall K. "Presidential Sanctuaries after the Clinton Sex Scandals." *Harvard Journal of Law and Public Policy* 22 (1999): 647–692; Pious, Richard M. "The Paradox of Clinton Winning and the Presidency Losing." *Political Science Quarterly* 114 (1999): 591–592; Ray, Laura Krugman. "From Prerogative to Accountability: The Amenability of President to Suit." *Kentucky Law Journal* 80 (1992): 739–813.

—Evan Gerstmann

impeachment

Article II, Section 4, of the Constitution states that "The President, Vice-President and all civil Officers of the United States, shall be removed from Office on Impeachment for, and Conviction of, Treason, Bribery, or other high Crimes and Misdemeanors." The framers wanted to provide a process, however rarely it might be used, for removal of a sitting president who had abused his powers. The process they established was a delicate blend of both constitutional and political elements: The standard of conduct by which a president would be judged was the constitutional one of "treason, bribery, or other high crimes and misdemeanors," but the impeachment and removal procedures would be conducted by two political bodies, the House and the Senate, respectively, and the ultimate "punishment" of removal from office was, also, a political one.

In identifying the grounds for impeachment, the framers wanted these to be broader than simply the commission of a criminal offense but narrower than "maladministration," the vague standard proposed by George Mason at the CONSTITUTIONAL CONVENTION. James MADISON feared that a "maladministration" standard was so vague as to make a president too vulnerable to political attack, increasing the likelihood of abuse of the impeachment process. Alexander HAMILTON's view in *The Federalist No. 65* seems to capture best the essence of what the framers wanted, that the misconduct by the president must be political in nature and damaging to the nation. Of more recent vintage, the House Judiciary Committee report in the impeachment inquiry of Richard NIXON in 1974 clarified that description further by adding that "in an impeachment proceeding, a President is called to account for abusing powers that only a President possesses."

Impeachment and removal do not preclude indictment and prosecution of a president in the criminal justice system where his acts are criminal offenses. Rather, criminal prosecution is a wholly separate track, bringing a president into the legal system, whereas impeachment represents the judgment of the political system. Scholars presume that impeachment precedes any possible criminal indictment and prosecution, although there is not universal agreement on this issue. No sitting president has ever been indicted for a crime, although President Nixon was designated an "unindicted co-conspirator" for his role in the WATERGATE coverup in 1974.

The framers provided a two-step process, with impeachment charges determined by the House by majority vote and trial in the Senate on those charges approved by the House. The Chief Justice of the United States would preside at the trial, adding a judicial presence, and conviction by the Senate of any charge would require a two-thirds vote. The bar for conviction and removal was set high intentionally, demonstrating the gravity of such a judgment.

The two chambers also differed in their nature, a difference that was reflected in their institutional division of responsibilities and sequence of actions in the process. The House was closer to the passions of the people, and mirrored those emotional judgments, while the Senate was more deliberative and sober and more able to judge the long-term interests of the nation at a critical moment.

Three presidents in history have been the subject of impeachment inquiries: Andrew JOHNSON, Richard Nixon and Bill CLINTON. Johnson and Clinton were impeached by the House but escaped conviction in the Senate and thus remained in office. Nixon faced three articles of impeachment voted by the House Judiciary Committee, but he resigned from office before a vote on the House floor occurred.

The IMPEACHMENT OF ANDREW JOHNSON was rooted in the politics of RECONSTRUCTION. He was a Democratic former slave owner whom LINCOLN appointed to the "Union" ticket as vice president in 1864, and Lincoln's assassination elevated Johnson to the presidency, where he was responsible for implementing Reconstruction. He incurred the wrath of Republicans in Congress when he vetoed the TENURE OF OFFICE ACT in 1867, which they subsequently overrode, and then fired Secretary of War Stanton in 1868 after the Senate refused to approve this removal, as the act required. The House voted 11 articles of impeachment against Johnson, most focusing on his violation of the Tenure of Office Act. He was acquitted in the Senate, which fell short by one vote of the required two-thirds needed for conviction.

In 1974 Richard Nixon was the subject of an impeachment inquiry in the House for his misuse of the office to cover up the burglary of the Democratic National Committee headquarter in the Watergate Hotel complex in Washington, D.C., on June 17, 1972, by people hired by his reelection committee. Congress began to investigate the break-in and a connection with illegal fund-raising with a committee hearing by the Senate Select Committee on President Campaign Activities, headed by Senator Sam Ervin of North Carolina. At the same time, Archibald COX was appointed SPECIAL PROSECUTOR to determine if any of the executive branch officials should be charged with crimes. When the Ervin Committee learned of the existence of an OVAL OFFICE taping system, attention quickly turned to efforts by both the Senate Committee and Cox to obtain the tapes to see if they showed a White House conspiracy to obstruct the investigations. When, after a series of court battles and the firing of Cox, Nixon refused to turn over the tapes as ordered by a federal court, a House committee began its own inquiry into the Watergate cover-up and eventually started impeachment hearings. A Supreme Court decision on July 24, 1974, ordering Nixon to provide the tapes to the House committee, was followed three days later by the committee vote of three articles of impeachment against Nixon: obstruction of justice, abuse of power, and CONTEMPT OF CONGRESS. With the release by the president on August 5 of a tape that revealed that he had known of the cover-up since June 23, 1972, it was only four days later that Nixon resigned from office rather than face certain impeachment on the House floor.

The effort to impeach Bill Clinton differed from the Johnson and Nixon impeachments in that it involved private, not public, behavior, and the inquiry itself started as an investigation into his financial dealings before he became president. Only through the unusual twists and turns of the law under which an INDEPENDENT COUNSEL operated did the focus ultimately turn to Clinton's personal relationship with an intern in the White House. It was his unsuccessful efforts, under oath in legal proceedings, to refrain from divulging the full details of that relationship that provided the basis for his impeachment and Senate trial. He was impeached by the House on December 19, 1998, on two counts, perjury and obstruction of justice, and acquitted in the Senate on both charges on February 12, 1999.

The lesson from all impeachment efforts is that the burden of proof is on the accusers, who must meet an exceptionally high standard to convict and remove from office. Moreover, impeachments that are politically motivated and that do not have bipartisan support are doomed to fail. When Nixon's own party members informed him that they would not support him in the House, he knew that he could not survive in office. Conversely, Clinton's party stood by him throughout the process, and five Republican senators even crossed party lines to vote "not guilty" at the trial, and he prevailed against a deeply partisan effort to force him from office. Impeachment efforts are long, hard, complex and uncertain—and that is exactly what the framers wanted it to be.

Further reading: Adler, David Gray, and Nancy Kassop. "The Impeachment of Bill Clinton." In *The Presidency and the Law: The Clinton Legacy,* edited by David Gray Adler and Michael A. Genovese. Lawrence: University Press of Kansas, 2002, pp. 155–174; Black, Charles L. *Impeachment: A Handbook.* New Haven, Conn.: Yale University Press, 1974; Gerhardt, Michael J. *The Federal Impeachment Process: A Constitutional and Historical Analysis.* Princeton, N.J.: Princeton University Press, 1996; U.S. House Committee of the Judiciary. *Constitutional Grounds for Presidential Impeachment.* 93rd Congress, 2nd session, 1974.

—Nancy Kassop

impeachment of Andrew Johnson

The IMPEACHMENT of Andrew JOHNSON in 1868 was the sixth federal impeachment and the first impeachment of a U.S. president. The impeachment of Johnson was the first of an elected official since the first impeachment effort, against former Senator William Blount in 1798. The only impeachment in recent memory at the time of Johnson's trial was the quick and uncontested removal in 1862 of Judge West Humphreys, who had abandoned his office to accept a judicial position in the Confederacy. The impeachment of the president was an extraordinary drama that held potentially important constitutional and political implications.

Andrew Johnson was a Jacksonian Democrat from Tennessee with a long career in state and federal political office and a fiery personality. As a U.S. senator, he opposed Southern secession and chose to stay in the Senate after Tennessee did secede in 1861, the only Southern senator to do so. During the war, Johnson was an ardent supporter of the Lincoln administration, and when Union troops occupied Tennessee in 1862 he was appointed the military governor to oversee its pacification and reconstruction. Although a reliable Democrat, Johnson was a strong nationalist and populist with little sympathy for the secessionist planters. He was a zealous military governor, often declaring that "treason is a crime and must be made odious." Needing to overcome the perception of a partisan war and to expand his own electoral base, LINCOLN pursued a conscious strategy of bringing "War Democrats" into his administration. In 1864 Lincoln chose Johnson to be his running mate on a National Union ticket. In April 1865 Lincoln was assassinated just days after General Robert E. Lee surrendered at Appomattox, and during the long 19th-century congressional recess Johnson assumed the presidency.

The problem of peace had always been more politically complicated than the problem of war, and Johnson proved psychologically and politically incapable of making it any easier. Lincoln and the Republicans in Congress had already been at odds over such things as the timing and nature of emancipation during the war. As Union troops recaptured Southern territory, Lincoln had initiated a presidential reconstruction under military command. His "Ten Percent Plan" gave full presidential pardons to Southerners who were willing to swear their future loyalty to the Union, and new civilian state governments could be formed as soon as a population equivalent to 10 percent of the votes cast in the 1860 election was so declared "loyal." This plan was strongly denounced by Republican congressional leaders, but the issue was not resolved before the 1864 elections and the president's assassination. Upon taking office, Johnson followed Lincoln's model of exchanging pardons for Southern acquiescence to presidential plans for quickly restoring civilian state governments. Johnson adhered to the view that the Southern states had never left the Union, that the war had been an executive problem of mass lawlessness, and that the goal was simply to restore the "Union as it was" (except for slavery) as quickly as possible.

Sketch showing the U.S. Senate as a court of impeachment for the trial of Andrew Johnson *(Library of Congress)*

By the time Congress reconvened in December 1865, the president was prepared to declare the South pacified and the Thirteenth Amendment abolishing slavery ratified and to recognize the South's newly elected governments and federal representatives. The Republicans in Congress responded by refusing to seat the Southern representatives and creating a Joint Committee on Reconstruction to determine legislative policy regarding the South. In February 1866 Congress set new conditions before it would recognize Tennessee as having rejoined the Union. Two days later, Johnson surprised Congress by vetoing the first piece of RECONSTRUCTION legislation, the Freedmen's Bureau Bill. Soon thereafter, the president denounced the Radical Republicans in Congress as extremists and vetoed the Civil Rights Bill. Congress narrowly overrode that presidential veto, the first time a president had lost an override vote on an important piece of legislation. Over presidential objections that in turn fed Southern resistance, Congress sent the Fourteenth Amendment to the states for ratification. In preparation for the midterm congressional elections of 1866, Johnson encouraged the meeting of a National Union Party convention to push more favorable candidates. The president himself made an unprecedented national cam-

paign tour, denouncing his congressional opponents and using his control over executive offices to punish his political adversaries and obstruct congressional Reconstruction in the South. Nonetheless, the Republicans won significant victories across the North. With stronger veto-proof majorities, Congress dismantled Johnson's restored state governments and divided the South into military districts, required that all presidential orders to the military be approved by General Ulysses GRANT, and prohibited the president from removing EXECUTIVE BRANCH officials without Senate consent.

Throughout 1867, Radical Republicans in the House pursued impeachment investigations against the president. Three such attempts failed before Johnson attempted, for the second time, to remove Secretary of War Edwin Stanton from office and appointed a retired general to be the acting secretary in February 1868 without Senate consent, even as Stanton refused to leave the premises. This apparent violation of the terms of the TENURE OF OFFICE ACT of 1867, and clear defiance of Congress, gave new life to the impeachment movement and led the House first to pass an impeachment resolution in late February and then to pass detailed articles of impeachment against the president in March 1868. The first nine articles addressed the events surrounding the Stanton removal. The next day Radicals in the House were able more narrowly to win passage for two additional articles of impeachment, one censuring Johnson's speeches on the 1866 tour and the other a catchall charging general political resistance to Congress. The House chose eight managers to try their case before the Senate. The conservative John Bingham, who with another manager and Judiciary Committee Chairman James Wilson had long resisted the impeachment movement, was chosen by the managers to chair their committee. The ranks of the managers were numerically dominated by some of the most powerful Radicals in the House, including Thaddeus Stevens, Benjamin Butler, and George Boutwell. The president chose his counsel with care, selecting conservative Republicans Benjamin Curtis, William Evarts, and Henry Stanbery, and War Democrats William Groesbeck and Thomas Nelson. All were highly regarded in law and politics, and their ranks included a former Supreme Court justice, a former attorney general, and a future secretary of state. The capital was awash with rumors and suspicions, with Radical legislators fearing that Johnson would use the military against them and the president believing that Congress might attempt to suspend him from office even before an impeachment, and the president had to be persuaded not to attend the trial in person and defend himself directly.

The Senate, where the Radicals had less influence, immediately began lengthy wrangling over the proper procedures for a trial. The Constitution specified that Chief Justice Salmon CHASE would serve as the presiding officer of a presidential impeachment trial, and Chase, who had his own presidential ambitions and favored acquittal, quickly moved to expand his own role and organize the Senate as a distinct "court." The Democrats briefly stalled the proceedings by objecting to the participation of Senate president pro tem Benjamin Wade in the trial, since Wade would become president if Johnson were convicted. Ultimately, the Senate regarded the right of the states to be represented as overriding the potential conflict of interest, though Democrats noted the continued exclusion of the Southern states from representation in the Senate. Proceedings were further delayed as Johnson's counsel prepared their case, and the Senate sat as a court only during the afternoons. Radical Senator Charles Sumner had hoped the trial would last no more than 10 days, but the Senate did not even begin hearing testimony for five weeks. The facts of the case were hardly in dispute, however, and the real disagreements were over the applicable statutory and constitutional law and over the politics.

Despite encouragement by the House to move quickly, the Senate trial dragged on until the end of May. The Senate first voted on the catchall 11th article of impeachment

but fell one vote short of the two-thirds majority constitutionally required to convict. Seven Republican senators voted to acquit the president, along with all of the Democratic senators. The Senate then recessed for the Republican Party convention. At the convention, the moderate Ulysses Grant became the Republican nominee for the presidency and urged in his acceptance speech, "Let us have peace." The convention delegates adopted a resolution endorsing the impeachment but refusing to condemn the seven dissenting senators. When the Senate reconvened, it defeated the second and third articles of impeachment by the same margin before calling an end to the trial without voting on the remaining charges. The vote margin in the Senate was orchestrated by a number of moderate Republican senators who were unwilling to remove the president on these grounds and cautious about the prospect of moving the Radical Wade into the White House. In order to secure his acquittal, Johnson had agreed with the moderates to cooperate with congressional Reconstruction, though with a new secretary of war. The National Union Party had long since collapsed, and the Democratic Party convention passed over Johnson to nominate New York governor Horatio Seymour for the presidency.

Johnson quietly completed his term and returned to his home state. A few months before his death in 1875, he reclaimed his seat as a senator from Tennessee. Grant acknowledged the postbellum return of congressional dominance in national affairs and assured Congress in his inaugural address that "all laws will be faithfully executed whether they meet my approval or not." Radical Republicanism and Radical Reconstruction never fully recovered, and the REPUBLICAN PARTY and the federal government gradually turned their attention away from the South.

Further reading: De Witt, David Miller. *The Impeachment and Trial of Andrew Johnson.* New York: Russell & Russell, 1967; Les Benedict, Michael. *The Impeachment and Trial of Andrew Johnson.* New York: W. W. Norton, 1973; McKitrick, Eric L. *Andrew Johnson and Reconstruction.* Chicago: University of Chicago Press, 1960.

—Keith E. Whittington

impeachment of Bill Clinton

From January 1998 until February 12, 1999, the nation lived in suspended animation, as it witnessed the unfolding of the impeachment process against President Bill CLINTON. Not since President Andrew JOHNSON escaped removal from office by one vote in his impeachment trial in 1868 had the Senate been the focus of an effort to remove a president. President Richard NIXON resigned in August 1974 after the House Judiciary Committee passed three articles of impeachment against him for his participation in the cover-up of the June 23, 1972, WATERGATE burglary, and his departure from office prevented the full House and Senate from ever having to undertake their constitutional roles at that time. The Clinton impeachment, however, played out in full but ended well short of the two-thirds vote in the Senate needed for removal.

Bill Clinton was elected president in 1992 with a Democratic Congress, but the 1994 midterm congressional elections resulted in an historic upheaval, as Republicans won both houses for the first time in 40 years. With DIVIDED GOVERNMENT in place once again and throughout the remainder of both Clinton terms (and, for the first time with a Democratic president and a Republican Congress), partisan tensions were already evident.

Other factors surfaced that may have contributed to the eventual road to impeachment. First, the previous configuration of divided government with a Republican president and Democratic Congress, especially during the REAGAN and George H. W. BUSH years, was notable for some spectacular congressional investigations into those administrations (e.g., IRAN-CONTRA and the SAVINGS AND LOAN SCANDAL) and some highly contentious Senate confirmation hearings (e.g., the unsuccessful Supreme Court nomination of Robert Bork in 1986, the John Tower defeat in 1989, and the Clarence Thomas nomination in 1990). In addition to the fact that the majority party in Congress controls the subpoena power to conduct investigations, the ETHICS IN GOVERNMENT ACT OF 1978 provided another basis for congressional initiation of the process to appoint an INDEPENDENT COUNSEL with the power to investigate and prosecute high EXECUTIVE BRANCH officials, including the president, of wrongdoing. Use of these two tools by congressional Democrats against Republicans during the Reagan and Bush administrations left a legacy of resentment. With Clinton's election, and with Republican control of Congress, as of 1994, a political alignment existed, for the first time, that could reverse the partisan fortunes, putting investigatory power into the hands of the Republicans.

Second, Bill Clinton provided Republicans with a number of vulnerabilities that were ripe for political exploitation. He was elected president in 1992 amid rumors of extramarital affairs while serving as governor of Arkansas, requiring him to go public during the presidential campaign with an emphatic television denial of an illicit relationship with Gennifer Flowers. He survived that embarrassment, but this was the first of many incidents that would ultimately emerge that would taint Clinton with a whole range of claims of improper relationships with women other than his wife.

Thus, Republicans undertook multiple investigations of Clinton: Some inquired into his own personal conduct prior to coming to office, such as his long-dormant, failed real estate dealings back in Arkansas known as Whitewater, while others probed scandals within his administration, such as his summary firing of personnel in the WHITE HOUSE Travel Office, and still others included investigations into the conduct of CABINET officials such as Secretary of AGRICULTURE Mike Espy and Secretary of HOUSING AND URBAN DEVELOPMENT Henry Cisneros. But all of these pale in comparison to the impact of and massive diversion of national attention from the business of government that came with the revelation in the *Washington Post* on January 21, 1998, that Clinton had engaged in affair with a 22-year-old White House intern, Monica Lewinsky, beginning in November 1995.

The public learned of this affair as a result of yet another Clinton sexual encounter, this one stemming from an allegation of sexual harassment by Paula Jones, a former state worker in Arkansas who brought suit against Clinton in 1994 for his conduct with her in a hotel room at a 1991 convention in Little Rock. As the Jones civil case moved forward in late 1997, Jones's lawyers presented a list to the judge of people to be deposed, including Lewinsky, whose name showed up on a list of women with whom Clinton may have had relationships. Lewinsky sought advice from Clinton as to what she should say at the deposition, and he advised her to file a false affidavit, denying their relationship. It was this advice that gave rise, ultimately, to the impeachment charge against him of obstruction of justice. Clinton was then deposed in the Jones case on January 17, 1998, by Kenneth Starr, appointed as independent counsel to investigate Clinton's conduct in the Whitewater real estate matter, but whose authority had been expanded just the day before to include probing the possibility that Clinton may have obstructed justice in his advice to Lewinsky. Clinton was surprised at the questions at his deposition and denied having had a sexual relationship with Lewinsky. Once revealed, his repeated public denials of the alleged relationship did not put the issue to rest.

Clinton was next questioned by Starr and his associates in grand jury proceedings from the White House via closed-circuit television on August 17, 1998. He was asked very specific questions about the nature of his physical contact with Lewinsky, and, after being confronted with DNA evidence from a semen-stained dress submitted by Lewinsky, Clinton admitted to an "inappropriate" relationship with her that included "intimate contact" of a sexual nature, but he denied having had any form of sex with her. He denied numerous other charges and, most important, denied that he had testified falsely at the Jones deposition where he answered that he had not had sexual relations with Lewinsky.

In sum, Clinton's position was that he had not testified falsely at the Jones deposition nor had he testified falsely at the grand jury proceeding. A number of events occurred in rapid succession in the fall of 1998. On September 9,

Independent Counsel Starr submitted to the House a report of his investigation of Clinton, containing lurid sexual detail and concluding that the president may have committed the impeachable offenses of perjury and obstruction of justice. On October 8, 1998, the House of Representatives voted to begin an impeachment inquiry into Clinton's behavior in the Lewinsky matter and his related testimony under oath. The 1998 midterm elections intervened on November 3, and, contrary to long historical trends, the president's party gained five seats in the House and held their own in the Senate, faring better than expected. Though still remaining in the minority, however, these election results were the first real evidence of public reaction to the impeachment inquiry under full swing at that time.

On three days in mid-November, the House Judiciary Committee held a stormy set of hearings, followed by its submission to Clinton later that month of a written list of 81 questions for him to answer under oath. He continued to repeat all of his earlier denials in his written answers. A second set of House Judiciary Committee hearings was held in early December, and by mid-month, the committee approved four impeachment articles to send to the full House: perjury before the grand jury, obstruction of justice in the Jones deposition, perjury in the Jones deposition, and abuse of power. The House leadership rejected sending a censure proposal to the House floor. On December 19, 1998, the full House approved two impeachment articles (perjury before the grand jury and obstruction of justice in the Jones deposition) and rejected the other two (perjury in the Jones deposition and abuse of power).

Trial in the Senate began on January 14 with three days of opening arguments by the House managers, followed by three days of defense arguments by the president's legal team, headed by White House Counsel Charles Ruff and Deputy Counsel Cheryl Mills, and lawyers Gregory Craig and David Kendall. Former Senator Dale Bumpers, a longtime Clinton friend and fellow politician from Arkansas, added a folksy lecture to close the White House's presentation of its case on the third day, imploring the Senate not to convict and remove the president. A Senate effort to CENSURE passed 56-43 on February 12, 1999, but it did not meet the required two-thirds vote necessary to suspend Senate impeachment trial rules. The Senate then moved on to vote on the two articles of impeachment before them, failing in both cases to get the two-thirds vote of 67 senators needed to convict, or even a simple majority. On February 12, 1999, the Senate vote on Article I, perjury before the grand jury, failed by a 45-55 vote, with 10 Republicans joining all 45 Democrats in voting "not guilty." Article II, obstruction of justice in the Jones deposition, failed by a vote of 50-50, with five Republicans joining all 45 Democrats in voting "not guilty." Clinton survived the impeachment effort against him, holding all of his party in the Senate and losing the votes of only five Democrats on three of the votes in the House and one Democrat on the fourth vote. If there is any lesson to be learned from this effort, it may be that only where enough members of a president's own party acknowledge the sufficiency of the evidence against the president to make such an effort bipartisan (as in the Nixon attempt) will it make sense to pursue impeachment. Where the effort to impeach garners only partisan support and nothing more, history has shown that it is not likely to succeed, and, worse, it will expose the raw political motives of those who sought it.

Further reading: Baker, Peter. *The Breach: Inside the Impeachment and Trial of William Jefferson Clinton.* New York: Scribner, 2000; Kassop, Nancy. "The Clinton Impeachment: Untangling the Web of Conflicting Consideration." In *Presidential Studies Quarterly* 30, no. 2 (June 2000): 359–373; Posner, Richard A. *An Affair of State: The Investigation, Impeachment and Trial of President Clinton.* Cambridge, Mass.: Harvard University Press, 1999; Rozell, Mark J., and Clyde Wilcox. *The Clinton Scandal and the Future of American Government.* Washington, D.C.: Georgetown University Press, 2000.

—Nancy Kassop

impeachment of Richard Nixon

The impeachment attempt against Richard NIXON has emerged as the "gold standard" against which other presidential impeachment attempts are compared. The Nixon IMPEACHMENT was notable for the nature of the alleged offenses, the extensiveness of the compiled evidence, and the bipartisan coalition that supported it. However, as with Andrew JOHNSON and Bill CLINTON, Nixon's personality and the contemporaneous political environment are also important in understanding his impeachment.

The Nixon impeachment was the product of Nixon's combative and paranoid personality, a tumultuous domestic and international political environment, and Nixon's experience in the "stolen" 1960 presidential election and his narrow 1968 victory. Nixon's aggressive and staunch opposition to communism in his early political campaigns and his subsequent role on the House Un-American Activities Committee made him a favorite of conservatives and a pariah among liberals. His status as a political polarizer combined with his own paranoia to lead him to adopt a personalized conception of his political opponents that directly produced behaviors that led to his impeachment. His efforts to extract the United States from the VIETNAM WAR "with honor" were hampered, he believed, by the increasingly vocal antiwar movement that was being fed by leaks from his administration. Finally, in response to his near-loss of the 1968 election, Nixon was determined to "win big" in

1972, and he engaged in a serious of covert activities that would later form the basis for the WATERGATE crisis and lead directly to his impeachment.

The impeachment effort began with the Saturday Night Massacre, in which Nixon ordered the firing of special counsel Archibald COX. Attorney General Elliot Richardson and Deputy Attorney General William Ruckelshaus resigned in protest. When Congress reconvened two days later, 14 members of the House introduced impeachment resolutions to the Judiciary Committee. Over the next few months Chairman Peter Rodino organized a special impeachment staff separate from the regular Judiciary Committee staff and crafted special rules to guide the investigation and hearings. The committee began its work in January and by summer was ready for testimony from witnesses. By the time Judiciary Committee debate began on July 24, 1974, the committee had listened to 19 hours of taped Nixon conversations, heard testimony from nine witnesses, and produced 39 volumes of work.

The reelection conspiracy and subsequent cover-up conspiracy, while the essence of the Watergate scandal, were the subject of only one article of impeachment. The first article charged Nixon with obstruction of justice in investigation of the Watergate scandal. Nixon was alleged to have pressured the FEDERAL BUREAU OF INVESTIGATION to halt its investigation of the Watergate break-in, of asking the CENTRAL INTELLIGENCE AGENCY to convince the FBI to stop its work, of suborning perjury, of paying off witnesses, and of generally orchestrating a widespread and far-reaching cover up.

The second article charged that Nixon had abused his powers as president and specified a range of offenses that transcended the break-in of the Democratic National Committee offices and were rooted more in Nixon's concerns for silencing opposition to the Vietnam War. The article alleged, among others, misusing the Internal Revenue Service (to audit his opponents and critics), FBI, SECRET SERVICE, other EXECUTIVE BRANCH employees, and a secret unit (the "plumbers," to surveil and harass his opponents).

The third article charged Nixon with CONTEMPT OF CONGRESS for refusing to adhere to Judiciary Committee subpoenas. Beginning early in 1974 the Judiciary Committee issued multiple subpoenas for materials, principally audiotapes, relevant to their impeachment investigation. Nixon steadfastly refused to comply with the subpoenas, and his attempts to circumvent them fell apart when his transcripts of the audiotapes were shown to be inaccurate, incomplete, and misleading.

The fourth article charged Nixon with abusing his powers by initiating and then concealing the bombing of Cambodia. While the war in Vietnam may have contributed to Nixon's impeachment generally, this was the only article to deal with it directly. In March 1969 Nixon ordered the secret bombing of enemy supply lines (the "Ho Chi Minh Trail") running through Cambodia, an officially neutral nation. In April 1970 Nixon ordered American troops to invade Cambodia to destroy enemy bases and sanctuaries. To Nixon's opponents, these actions violated Article I of the Constitution, which gave Congress the sole power to declare war. To Nixon's supporters, the article was a galling attempt to attach blame for the Vietnam War to Nixon, who had actually extracted the United States from the conflict. The article was defeated by a vote of 12-26, with nine Democrats joining every Republican to oppose it.

The final article charged Nixon with income tax evasion and for government-funded improvements to his Key Biscayne, Florida, and San Clemente, California, residences, and for taking excessive deductions for the donation to the NATIONAL ARCHIVES of his vice-presidential papers. These were the only charges to remain from a string of proposed charges that included bribery by dairy lobbyists and representatives of the ITT Corporation. However, the evidence in support of them was at best unclear (Nixon's attorneys had advised that the deductions were legal), and Republicans and centrist Democrats did not want to hurt the impeachment effort by appearing to be piling on charges. Not unimportantly, the article also came up at the end of six days of debate, and all participants were exhausted. As a result, the article received the least amount of attention—just two hours (versus two days for Article One) and was defeated by the same 12-26 margin as Article Four.

While a majority of the committee Democrats supported all five charges and a majority of the Republicans opposed all five, a group of swing votes known as the "Fragile Coalition" or "Swing Seven" emerged as the driving force in the impeachment effort. Comprised of three Southern Democrats and four Republicans, the coalition eliminated potential articles (such as one involving bribery by dairy interests and the ITT Corporation), drafted much of the others, and shepherded the debates along. As neither side could win without the support of this centrist group, the group exercised great power over the tone and substance of the proceedings.

An estimated 70 million Americans observed part of the live proceedings (about half the American population) and another third saw excerpts on the news. Just 10 percent failed to observe any of the proceedings on television or the radio. The six days of debate also had a profound impact on public support for impeachment. Going in to the debates, a slight majority (53 to 40 percent) of the public favored impeachment. After the debates the American public favored impeachment by a nearly 40-point margin (66 to 27 percent).

On August 5 Nixon released to the SPECIAL PROSECUTOR the tapes that he had been holding back (the Supreme Court having ruled unanimously on July 24, the day the

Judiciary Committee debate began, that Nixon had to release the tapes). One, a tape of the Oval Office conversations of June 23, 1972, proved to be the "smoking gun" that established Nixon's complicity in the criminal cover-up of the Watergate break-in. Every one of Nixon's supporters on the House Judiciary Committee announced he now favored impeachment, and the possibility of a unanimous impeachment vote by the full House combined with certain conviction in the Senate forced Nixon to resign on August 9.

Further reading: Genovese, Michael A. *The Watergate Crisis.* Westport, Conn.: Greenwood Press, 1999; Matheson, Sean C. "Partial Justice: Congressional Argumentation and Presidential Impeachment." Ph.D. diss., University of Illinois, 2001.

—Sean C. Matheson

imperialism

Often used pejoratively, imperialism has come to mean domination or control by one state over another, usually to exploit the weaker nation. Imperialism also has come to mean hegemony, or domination by one power within an international regime.

However one defines the term, the United States became an imperial power in 1898 under President MCKINLEY when we gained control of the Philippines and Cuba. But it was not until after WORLD WAR II that the United States became *the* hegemonic power of the world.

With hegemony comes responsibility. The United States often became the policeman of the world. Hegemony brings power and wealth, but also costs. Some argue the costs are too high; others see great benefit from being the dominant nation. The pejorative meaning of imperialism was leveled against the United States before and during the 2003 war against Iraq. The United States, after going to the UNITED NATIONS in hopes of gaining approval for a military invasion of Iraq, ultimately bypassed the UN and, with what was called the "coalition of the willing" (essentially the United States and Great Britain), invaded Iraq and overthrew the government. Such actions by stronger nations against weaker ones inevitably bring out complaints of imperialism and militarism. The United States, with its imperial responsibilities as the only superpower in the world, felt it was justified in attacking Iraq due to the irresponsibility and dangers posed by Iraq's leader, Saddam Hussein.

imperial presidency

The most important principle for the framers of the Constitution in writing a charter for a new nation was that of limited government power. They were determined not to live under the same type of tyranny and absolute power of the royal monarchy that had promoted the colonists to leave England and come to America. To this end, the framers were careful to craft a governmental system that provided for a balancing of powers among the three branches and a monitoring function, whereby each branch would keep a watchful eye over the other two to insure that no one branch abused its power or usurped another's authority.

For the first 150 years, this structure worked relatively well. By 1973 historian Arthur M. Schlesinger, Jr., was able to coin the powerful and evocative phrase "the imperial presidency" and he wrote an influential book with that as its title to alert the American public that a momentous change had occurred in the nature of the office of the CHIEF EXECUTIVE. He wrote in 1974 that, "in the last year, presidential primacy . . . has turned into presidential supremacy. The constitutional presidency . . . has become the imperial Presidency and threatens to be the revolutionary Presidency." His focus was on "the shift in the constitutional balance . . . that is, the appropriation by the Presidency . . . of powers reserved by the Constitution and by long historical practice to Congress."

Schlesinger's immediate reference was to the presidency of Richard NIXON and to the charges of presidential abuse of power, stemming from (1) the investigation at that time of White House involvement in the WATERGATE scandal, and (2) Nixon's continuation of American involvement in the VIETNAM WAR. In trying to locate the initial source of a presidential predilection for absolute power, Schlesinger traced its roots back to Franklin ROOSEVELT and to the central role that the emergence of the United States as a world power played in foreign policy, beginning with WORLD WAR II. It was here that Schlesinger located the seeds of "the capture by the Presidency of the most vital of national decisions, the decision to go to war." He saw this as a global assumption of power by the chief executive, although he directed equal amounts of criticism toward the president for usurping power and toward Congress for abdicating its own constitutionally allocated war power.

Schlesinger suggests that Roosevelt followed a traditional path in fashioning the domestic policies of the NEW DEAL in the 1930s, and that he worked collaboratively with Congress, which granted him statutory authority to act. FDR involved Congress, also, in his foreign policy-making until just prior to the December 7, 1941, attack on Pearl Harbor, refraining from claims of inherent EXECUTIVE POWER. However, FDR's approach began to shift with a series of actions he took in the months before Pearl Harbor, and Schlesinger notes that "such a course . . . (would) . . . have produced a serious constitutional crisis had not the Japanese obligingly come to the rescue." In short, FDR began to change course during the war, as he started to rely more on his "commander-in-chief in wartime" powers and on EMERGENCY POWERS from his EXECUTIVE ORDERS and less on statutory authority from Congress, even for domestic policies. Thus, the wider latitude for independent policy-making in the foreign policy sphere that attaches to an "imperial" president soon expands to apply to DOMESTIC POLICY as well, especially, but not exclusively, in wartime.

TRUMAN's entry into the KOREAN WAR accelerated the claims to exclusive presidential power to decide when to commit the nation's military force, and Lyndon JOHNSON, in Schlesinger's opinion, continued that same approach, despite the GULF OF TONKIN RESOLUTION in August 1964, which Johnson viewed as politically helpful but not constitutionally necessary for authorizing the use of force in Vietnam. By the time that Richard Nixon confronted the continuation of the war in Southeast Asia in 1969, he relied increasingly on his power as COMMANDER IN CHIEF for support in ways that were never intended by the framers of the Constitution, who saw it as only to designate the president as the top officer in the armed forces but never as a source of constitutional authority for policy-making. When resort to this title is coupled with presidential appeals for the need to act to protect national security, it sets in place a difficult dynamic for the public to challenge.

The Nixon presidency provided an operative example of "the imperial presidency," if "imperial" connotes an approach to power that is absolute and elusive. In addition to Nixon's singular prosecution of the Vietnam War in the face of growing public and congressional opposition, a few other examples of his swelling of the powers of the presidency (and diminution of and disregard for the powers of Congress and the courts) included (1) his assertions of EXECUTIVE PRIVILEGE over his OVAL OFFICE tapes during the Watergate scandal and his refusal to comply with subpoenas and court orders for tapes and documents, (2) his effort to impound (or refuse to release) funds appropriated by Congress for programs he opposed, and (3) his unauthorized firing of Watergate Special Prosecutor Archibald COX. The common thread that runs through all of these actions is the claim that the president alone has the authority to decide, and that neither Congress not the courts has any constitutional power to oppose the president on these matters. Unilateral power in one branch is directly contrary to the system's checking and balancing principle that was so crucial to the framers in their careful construction of three coequal branches.

Further reading: Schlesinger, Arthur M., Jr. *The Imperial Presidency.* New York: Popular Library, 1974.
—Nancy Kassop

implied powers

The Constitution uses language that is general and at times undefined; as a consequence all of the powers which are granted to the president are not enumerated or explicitly stated but need to be inferred from the general principles of the document, the dominant political philosophies of the time, the concept of sovereignty, and the language

itself. Implied powers are all those powers that are not explicitly granted to the president but through precedent and court decisions have been accepted as presidential powers.

It is argued that these presidential powers are less legitimate than those explicitly granted by the Constitution. However, *IN RE NEAGLE* (1890) states that "any obligation fairly and properly inferable from the Constitution and the statutes is within the meaning of the word 'law' as if it were absolutely expressed therein."

The philosophy of John Locke is instrumental to understanding the Constitution. Locke believed in "executive prerogative" power, which in times of emergency gives the executive the authority to rule to preserve the government and the society.

The Constitution, however, does not explicitly acknowledge this principle. However, in *UNITED STATES V. CURTISS-WRIGHT* (1936) the Court upheld a congressional act giving the president the authority at his discretion to embargo arms to the parties in a South American war. The Court declared that the national government's authority in FOREIGN AFFAIRS comprises all the powers of a sovereign nation. It has "INHERENT POWERS." In addition, the president is the "sole organ of the federal government in the field of international relations." The president's power is therefore implied by his position as COMMANDER IN CHIEF and his authority to negotiate treaties. While this case has been controversial, it has established an important precedent with regard to increasing presidential powers as commander in chief and chief diplomat. Some scholars have argued that the prerogative power theory espoused by John Locke may be viewed as an implied power.

The removal of CABINET members has been a controversial issue. When Congress established four executive departments, it raised the question of whether the president can remove cabinet officers who were confirmed by the Senate without Senate consent. James MADISON argued that the Constitution implied that power—otherwise the president could not "take care that the Laws are faithfully executed." The Supreme Court supported that position in *Meyers v. United States* (1926). The Court has made exceptions to this rule with commissioners on the Independent Regulatory Commissions in *HUMPHREY'S EXECUTOR V. UNITED STATES* (1935), with officials engaged in adjudicative (judicial) functions in *WIENER V. UNITED STATES* (1958), and with independent prosecutors in *Morison v. Olson* (1988).

EXECUTIVE AGREEMENTS are also not mentioned in the Constitution. They are accords between two heads of government to follow a course of action. In *UNITED STATES V. BELMONT* (1936), the Court ruled that executive agreements were an international compact and were the equivalent of a treaty.

While the Constitution does not specifically grant presidents the power to recognize foreign governments, in Article II of the Constitution, the president is given the authority to appoint and receive ambassadors. This authority has been interpreted to imply the authority to recognize governments without the involvement of Congress. In GOLDWATER v. CARTER (1980), the Court even refused to reject the president's power to abrogate a defense treaty with Taiwan as part of his decision to establish diplomatic relations with the People's Republic of China.

Implied powers of the presidency have evolved over years and represent an important and significant dimension of presidential powers. They will remain controversial because of the lack of specificity in the Constitution and the disagreement over which powers can be reasonably implied or deduced.

Further reading: Fisher, Louis. *Presidential War Power.* Lawrence: University Press of Kansas, 1995; Koenig, Louis W. *The Chief Executive.* Forth Worth, Tex.: Harcourt Brace College Publishers, 1996; Pious, Richard M. *The Presidency.* Boston: Allyn and Bacon, 1996.

—Frank M. Sorrentino

impoundment of funds

Impoundment of funds occurs whenever the EXECUTIVE BRANCH through either action or inaction prevents the obligation or expenditure of budget authority provided by Congress. The practice is currently governed by the CONGRESSIONAL BUDGET AND IMPOUNDMENT CONTROL ACT OF 1974 (ICA).

Historically, impoundment has taken two basic forms. In its least controversial manifestation, impoundment has been carried out to promote efficiencies and address contingencies. This practice has been performed since the WASHINGTON administration. The logic behind this routine practice is that if a project could be completed for less than originally appropriated, then the extra funds ought to be returned to the TREASURY. By the same token, conditions change over the course of an appropriation cycle and full expenditure of funds often proves unnecessary. Before passage of the ICA, this rather prosaic form of impoundment was justified on either explicit or implicit statutory authority.

More controversial but of comparable vintage is the practice of the president impounding funds based on policy disagreements with Congress. Although often difficult to distinguish from routine impoundment, this form of withholding of funds implicates the relative constitutional powers of the political branches. The lion's share of these impoundments have occurred in areas affecting national defense, when presidents claimed constitutional authority as COMMANDER IN CHIEF to withhold funds. Although precedent in this regard dates back at least to the JEFFERSON administration, President Franklin ROOSEVELT was the first

president to impound such funds on a large scale. His successors did not hesitate to follow suit. Presidents TRUMAN, EISENHOWER, and KENNEDY each withheld funds for weapons systems they thought were overfunded. President Lyndon B. JOHNSON expanded the practice by impounding funds outside of the realm of national defense and generally without justifying his actions on national security grounds. His actions were later used as precedent by President Richard NIXON to impound funds on an even grander scale. Nixon went so far as to claim a generalized constitutional power to impound funds regardless of the subject matter. Whereas Johnson supported many of the programs for which he impounded funds, Nixon attempted to terminate entire domestic programs with which he disagreed.

Nixon's actions triggered a backlash on two fronts—both judicial and legislative. At the same time as Congress began to reassert its "power of the purse," private litigants challenged Nixon's actions in the courts. This spate of impoundment litigation, almost all of which was decided against the executive branch, culminated in the Supreme Court's decision in *Train v. New York.* In that case, the high Court ordered the director of the ENVIRONMENTAL PROTECTION AGENCY to release the impounded funds. Although the Court did not consider the constitutional issue of impoundment, the decision still amounted to a major setback to the president's claims of a generalized impoundment power.

Nixon's impoundments also prompted a major conflict with Congress, one which raised profound constitutional concerns. Through impoundment, the president appeared to be wielding an absolute veto of sorts; a device that distorted the standard lawmaking process. Instead of "faithfully executing" congressional enactments, the president seemed to be working actively to frustrate the will of the legislature. In Congress lawmakers reasserted their spending prerogatives through enactment of the ICA. While the statute did not prohibit impoundment, the ICA did make the expenditure of appropriated funds presumptively mandatory. The burden was placed on the president to garner subsequent legislative authority for his impoundments instead of leaving the onus on Congress to reappropriate the funds.

The ICA divided impoundment into two categories: recisions and deferrals. With recision, the president, with the assent of Congress, was granted the power to cancel budget authority previously authorized by Congress. The ICA mandates that whenever the president wishes to rescind spending he must first issue a special message to Congress. In order for the funds to be withheld, both houses must complete action on a recision bill approving the impoundment within 45 days of a continuous session. If Congress fails to act within the allotted time, the funds are to be released by the president. Deferral, on the other hand, involves the routine withholding or delay of an obligation or expenditure of budget authority. The deferral mechanism provides that the funds will remain unexpended unless overridden by an act of Congress. (This provision reflects an amendment passed in the late 1980s which brought the ICA into conformity with a federal court ruling that the LEGISLATIVE VETO provision found in the original statute was unconstitutional.) Deferrals are permitted only to provide for contingencies, to achieve savings through greater efficiency, or as specifically provided by law. No employee may defer budget authority for any other reason.

Although the ICA was amended in 1996 to provide the president with what was popularly known as a "line-item veto," that provision was struck down by the Supreme Court in 1998. Today, impoundment remains governed by the ICA framework, which is not radically different from what it was 25 years ago. At the same time, assertions of inherent presidential power to impound NATIONAL SECURITY funds have lain largely dormant since the 1960s.

Further reading: Brownell II, Roy E. "The Constitutional Status of the President's Impoundment of National Security Funds." *12 Seton Hall Const. L.J.* 1 (2001); Fisher, Louis. "Funds Impounded by the President: The Constitutional Issue." *Geo. Wash. L. Rev.* 38 (1969): 124; *Presidential Spending Power.* Princeton, N.J.: Princeton University Press, 1975; Pfiffner, James P. *The President, the Budget, and Congress: Impoundment and the 1974 Budget Act.* Boulder, Colo.: Westview Press, 1979.

—Roy E. Brownell II

inaugural addresses

According to Karlyn Kohrs Campbell and Kathleen Hall Jamieson, inaugural addresses as a genre of presidential speech are the rhetorical centerpiece of the rite of investiture that is the inauguration of a president. Inaugurals are a species of epideictic or ceremonial address, characterized by the nature of the occasion, the rhetorical link between past and future in present contemplation, and the affirmation of shared principles that will guide the new administration. In ceremonial addresses such as inaugurals, the focus is on the character of the speaker, which comes to represent the character of the audience. Inaugurals vary depending upon the rhetorical skill of the president, and because of the selective emphasis on aspects of our national traditions consistent with the party or political philosophy the president represents.

As a specific kind of ceremonial address, inaugurals are constitutive—they recreate the national community in terms specific to and chosen by the new president. Thus, LINCOLN's discussion of the causes of war in his first inau-

Bill Clinton, standing between Hillary Rodham Clinton and Chelsea Clinton, taking the oath of office of the president of the United States *(Library of Congress)*

gural and the magnificent plea of generosity that concludes his second reflected his understanding of national identity in the 1860s and his hopes for the nation's future. Similarly, Franklin ROOSEVELT's calm assurance that "[t]he only thing we have to fear is fear itself," in his 1933 inaugural defined the American polity as one that was courageous in the face of even the direst economic threat, and John KENNEDY's characterization of the American people as willing to "pay any price, bear any burden, meet any hardship, support any friend, oppose any foe, in order to assure the survival and the success of liberty" was based in COLD WAR imperatives and reflected the dominance of international affairs in defining the American people and the American mission in the middle of the 20th century.

In serving this constitutive function, inaugurals unify the people as one collective whole, providing final closure to the recently concluded national campaign (think of JEFFERSON's claim that "We are all Republicans, we are all Federalists" and the importance of the inaugural ritual after the contentious 2000 campaign). In order to provide this national reconciliation, inaugural addresses are full of affirmative rhetoric that calls upon shared national values and ideals and enunciates broad national political principles. Inaugurals set forth the principles that will guide the new administration, enunciate a general political philosophy, and call for contemplation rather than action.

Both as constitutive rhetoric and as unifying addresses, inaugurals also require presidents to formally acknowledge the constitutional limits on their power. So important is this element in fact, that Edward Chester claims that inaugurals are characterized by "Constitution worship." In enacting the presidential role for the first time, presidents must be careful not to overstep their bounds; they must be focused on their public rather than their private selves as well as on their public duties. Presidents express humility through respect for the Constitution and through dependence upon the beneficence of God. Discussion of specific policies is usually left out of inaugurals, as they tend to be more divisive than unifying, and such discussion is inappropriate to the inaugural occasion. Any mention of policy is thus based in tradition and is used to show veneration for the past as well as exemplify guidelines for the future; but the present is the pivot, and the mood is contemplative, not active.

Great inaugurals, like great speeches generally, are relatively rare. To be considered "great," an inaugural address must conceive of "the people" in a fresh, new, and plausible way (Lincoln's second), make traditional values come alive in a way that induces audience participation (FDR's first), and/or convey universal truths in way that speaks to the specificity of the times while also denoting greater and more lasting meaning (WASHINGTON's first).

Ascendant vice presidents, who attain office on the death or RESIGNATION of their predecessor, also give speeches that function as inaugurals, although they do not have the accompanying ritual and occasion. There have been nine such occurrences to date, eight deaths in office and one resignation. These vice presidents face a complicated rhetorical task, for they must combine the requirements of an inaugural with that of a eulogy and affirm the continuity of government even within the context of abrupt and often painful change. This can be done with great eloquence, exemplified by Lyndon JOHNSON's 1963 address before a joint session of Congress in which he acknowledged the tragedy of Kennedy's death. He combined eulogy with promise for the future, beginning the speech with the statement, "All I have I would have given gladly not to be standing here today," and ending it with his pledge of fidelity to the principles of the Kennedy administration: "Let us continue."

Gerald FORD remains the only vice president who ascended to office upon the resignation of the president. He could not offer a eulogy per se, but he handled that difficult transition with great aplomb, stating that "our long national nightmare is over" and emphasizing continuity in policy as well as change in leadership as a means of reassuring the nation and assuming power in his own right.

As these examples indicate, inaugurals mark transitions between the old administration and the new as well as between the division of the campaign and the emerging national unity under a new administration. As transitional moments they have important consequences for the definition of the national policy and the national self-identification.

Further reading: Campbell, Karlyn Kohrs, and Kathleen Hall Jamieson. *Deeds Done in Words: Presidential Rhetoric and the Genres of Governance.* Chicago: University of Chicago Press, 1990; Chester, Edward W. "Beyond the Rhetoric: A New Look at Presidential Inaugural Addresses." *Presidential Studies Quarterly* 10: 571–582; Germino, Dante. *The Inaugural Addresses of the American Presidents: The Public Philosophy and Rhetoric.* Lanham, Mass.: University Press of America, 1984.

—Mary E. Stuckey

inaugurations

The inauguration ceremony officially marks the beginning of a president's term, when he assumes the responsibility of the office. The Constitution (Article II, Section 1, Clause 7) requires the president to take the OATH OF OFFICE, but other than the oath of office, the customs and rituals surrounding the inauguration have evolved by practice rather than by statute.

WASHINGTON established several of the rituals surrounding presidential inauguration. At noon on April 30, 1789, on the balcony of the federal statehouse in New York City in front of a throng of people, Washington took the first oath of office with one hand on a Bible. At the end of the oath, he added, "So help me God!" To which the crowd of onlookers responded, "Long live George Washington, president of the United States." Subsequent presidents have adopted both the practice of taking the oath of office with one hand on the Bible and finishing the oath with the phrase "So help me God." It is not surprising that inauguration onlookers no longer salute the president with the "Long live . . ." chant, given its monarchical overtones.

After taking the oath, Washington retired inside to the Senate Chamber to give the nation's first inaugural address. He addressed his remarks to the members of Congress. However, four years later in his second inaugural address, Washington addressed the people directly in the shortest inaugural address ever given. (William Henry HARRISON in 1841 gave the longest.) Since then, presidents have given their inaugural addresses in front of the public. With the advent of radio and television, presidents have been able to reach a larger audience. Calvin COOLIDGE's 1925 inaugural address was the first to be broadcast live on radio, and Harry TRUMAN's 1949 inaugural address was the first to be televised nationally.

The inaugural address, not mentioned in the Constitution, has become the most visible and important part of the inauguration ceremonies. Washington's first inaugural address was unique in its humility. He noted how unqualified he was for office, having "inferior endowments from nature and unpracticed in the duties of civil administration" and expressed his reservations about leaving retirement at MOUNT VERNON to take on the duties of presidency. Only a president with as great a national reputation as Washington could make such a statement. After Washington listed his shortcomings, he thanked the people for the great honor they had bestowed upon him, invoked divine guidance, and promised to do his best, all common refrains in inaugural addresses that followed.

Subsequent presidents have used the inaugural address for additional purposes. JEFFERSON's inaugural address stressed the peaceful transfer of power from one party to another. Many presidents have used the inaugural addresses as an opportunity to interpret the election. JACKSON in his second inaugural address interpreted his election as a mandate to destroy the Second Bank of the United States. Another common practice is for presidents to preview their legislative agenda. Presidents usually stick to consensual and optimistic remarks in their inaugural addresses. With the exception of Ulysses S. GRANT, most presidents have resisted attacking their enemies in their inaugural addresses.

The nine vice presidents who ascended to the presidency from the vice presidency as a rule have not given full-fledged inaugural addresses, but most presidents have felt the need to address the country in a formal statement of some kind. FORD had a particularly difficult task, taking over after NIXON's RESIGNATION and having not been elected as vice president but appointed. In Ford's case, his speech, which he denied was an inaugural address, took the place of a popular election as imbuing Ford's presidency with legitimacy. Calvin COOLIDGE was the exception. After taking the oath of office on August 3, 1923, he made no public statement in part because he felt that he should address the Congress first, which was not to reconvene for another four months.

Historical and recent practice is for the president-elect to come to the WHITE HOUSE and make the trip to Capitol with the incumbent president, signaling a peaceful transition. There have been only three instances in which the incumbent president has refused to ride with the president-elect to the inauguration ceremonies: John ADAMS after the 1800 election, John Quincy ADAMS after the 1828 election, and Andrew JOHNSON after the 1868 election.

The inauguration takes place at noon on January 20 as set by the TWENTIETH AMENDMENT, which was passed in 1933. Before the Twentieth Amendment, the president was not inaugurated until early March, almost six months after the election. One of the purposes of the Twentieth Amendment was to shorten the amount of time a LAME DUCK PRESIDENT served. With the date moved up to January 20, a lame duck president only serves three months.

Further reading: Campbell, Karlyn Kohrs, and Kathleen Hall Jamieson, *Deeds Done in Words*. Chicago: University of Chicago Press, 1990; Fields, Wayne. *Union of Words: A History of Presidential Eloquence*. New York: Free Press, 1996.

—Terri Bimes

independent counsel

One of many post-WATERGATE reforms, the INDEPENDENT COUNSEL LAW was created as part of the ETHICS IN GOVERNMENT ACT OF 1978. The purpose of the provision was to employ procedures for probing wrongdoing within the EXECUTIVE BRANCH, thereby preventing self-examination of a presidential administration and hence a potential conflict of interest. The law was renewed at five-year intervals until 1992, when it was allowed to lapse. It was renewed in 1994 but died again in 1999.

According to the law's specifications, if an allegation of a serious crime involving a high official surfaces, the attorney general conducts a 30-day inquiry to determine whether the charges are credible. If so, the investigation continues for another 60 days. If at the end of this period the attorney general believes that further inquiry is needed, a three-judge panel selects an independent counsel, who conducts the probe and makes a recommendation on any legal action at its conclusion.

During the first five-year period of the Independent Counsel Law, three major investigations occurred. Two of the independent counsels probed alleged cocaine use by CARTER administration personnel, neither of which led to any indictments. A third probe, aimed at Secretary of Labor Raymond Donovan, started in 1981 and ended seven years later without any incriminating evidence.

President Ronald REAGAN signed a bill to extend the Independent Counsel Law in January 1983, though several amendments altered the original statute. For instance, the discretion of the attorney general in initiating the act was augmented; the standard for eliciting the act was lessened; the test for removal of the independent counsel was lowered; and the investigator was asked to follow DEPARTMENT OF JUSTICE guidelines whenever possible. During its second five-year run, the law led to the appointment of independent counsels to probe President Reagan's attorney general, Edwin MEESE, his assistant attorney general, Theodore Olson, and his deputy chief of staff, Michael Deaver. Although Meese and Olson were exonerated, Deaver was indicted and convicted. Revelations of illegal sales of weapons to Iran and diversion of profits to Nicaraguan contras, referred to as IRAN-CONTRA, led to an eight-year inquiry by Independent Counsel Lawrence Walsh. Although Walsh succeeded in getting 11 convictions of various Reagan administration personnel involved in Iran-contra, six persons subsequently had their convictions overturned. Walsh spent $48.5 million on the Iran-contra case. The 1987 reauthorization of the Independent Counsel Law was influenced by growing antagonism between the executive and legislative branches following the 1986 elections, by inter-chamber disputes within Congress, and by the influence of such groups as the American Bar Association and Common Cause. Just a year later, the law withstood a constitutional challenge emanating from the inquiry of Theodore Olson. Between 1987 and 1992, four more investigations by independent counsels were undertaken. Of these, three probed Reagan Administration personnel, including former White House aide Lyn Nofziger, Assistant Attorney General W. Lawrence Wallace, and Housing and Urban Development Secretary Samuel Pierce. Although Wallace was cleared and Nofziger had his conviction on violation of lobbying laws overturned, 17 convictions transpired in the Pierce inquiry, which lasted more than a decade and cost $28 million. In the final case during the aforementioned period, various officials from the George H. W. BUSH administration were charged with misuse of passport files from their background check of Bill CLINTON; no indictments were filed.

Criticized by both political parties as intrusive and ineffective, the Independent Counsel Act expired on December 15, 1992. However, several events transpired between 1992 and 1994 to cause its resurrection. For one, President H. W. Bush pardoned several Reagan presidency personnel involved in the Iran-contra scandal just nine days after the law's demise. Second, several charges against new president Bill Clinton were lodged, including the spring 1993 purge of the White House Travel Office and Clinton's ties to Whitewater, a failed Arkansas development venture. After an 18-month hiatus, the Independent Counsel Law was reauthorized on June 30, 1994.

During its most recent period of existence, the independent counsel law led to the appointment of eight special prosecutors, all probing Clinton administration personnel. Of these, one led to no indictments, one involving Secretary of Commerce Ron Brown was terminated after Brown's death in a plane crash, and two were in process when the law expired in 1999. An inquiry against Secretary of Agriculture Mike Espy produced 17 convictions and cost $17.5 million. An investigation of Henry Cisneros, President Clinton's secretary of Housing and Urban Development, led to one conviction and cost $7.3 million. The most costly and controversial investigation was by independent counsel Kenneth Starr, who moved from probing the Whitewater matter to the Monica Lewinsky scandal. Starr's report in the latter inquiry precipitated the IMPEACHMENT of President Bill Clinton in December 1998. Starr racked up 14 convictions and spent $43.6 million in the combined cases. When the Independent Counsel Law was not renewed in 1999, it expired for a second time. A total of 22 investigators spent more than $160 million during its start-and-stop existence.

Further reading: Eastland, Terry. *Ethics, Politics, and the Independent Counsel: Executive Power, Executive Vice, 1789–1989.* Washington, D.C.: National Legal Center for the Public Interest, 1989; Harriger, Katy. *Independent Justice: The Federal Special Prosecutor in American Politics.*

Lawrence: University Press of Kansas, 1992; Hoff, Samuel B. "Back from the Grave: The Death and Renewal of the Independent Counsel Law." Paper delivered at the National Social Science Association Conference, New Orleans, La., November 4–6, 1996; Kearnes, John. "The Independent Counsel Law and Its Impact on the Presidency." Paper delivered at the Annual Meeting of the Southern Political Science Association, Savannah, Ga., November 3–7, 1999.

—Samuel B. Hoff

Independent Counsel Law

Adopted in 1978 in the wake of WATERGATE scandal, the Independent Counsel Law's purpose was to ensure that investigations of criminal misconduct by either the president or other powerful executive officials were handled in a fair and impartial way. INDEPENDENT COUNSELs have been assigned to investigate a wide range of activities, including the IRAN-CONTRA scandal (President Ronald REAGAN), rumored cocaine use (Hamilton Jordan, President Jimmy CARTER's chief of staff), and allegations of personal and financial misconduct (President Bill CLINTON). Although initially hailed as a mechanism to ensure presidential ACCOUNTABILITY, the law came under attack in the 1980s and 1990s due to the perception that independent counsels had become partisan tools, overly costly, and out of control. The provision for the appointment of independent counsels expired in June 1999, when Congress declined to extend its charter. This closed the book on this act's tumultuous 20-year history.

President Richard Nixon's firing of Archibald COX, the first special prosecutor assigned to investigate Watergate, triggered serious doubts about the Justice Department's ability to conduct an independent investigation of the president, given that the ATTORNEY GENERAL is a presidential appointee. When Cox demanded that NIXON hand over the tape recordings of Oval Office discussions about the cover-up, Nixon called upon Attorney General Elliot Richardson to fire Cox. Instead, Richardson resigned. When the deputy attorney general also refused to carry out Nixon's order, the president turned to Solicitor General Robert Bork, who promptly fired Cox. This Saturday Night Massacre, as Cox's firing came to be known, raised many questions about the role of politics in what was supposed to be an independent investigation into presidential misconduct and started the chain of events that led to the creation of an Independent Counsel Act. More than five years of debate took place before Congress agreed on what kind of mechanism to create. Finally, an office of independent counsel was created with the passage of the ETHICS AND GOVERNMENT ACT OF 1978.

This act placed the attorney general in a central and potentially awkward position by making him the only governmental officer who could request the appointment of an independent counsel and giving him much discretion in that decision. The exact wording of the act reads that if the attorney general "receives information sufficient to constitute grounds to investigate," then he shall request an independent counsel, but the statute did not delineate what "sufficient grounds" were, leaving it to the attorney general to determine the definition on a case-by-case basis. The tenure of Janet Reno, Bill Clinton's attorney general, exemplified the difficulties that this discretion created. Reno confronted repeated controversies concerning her rulings on requests for independent counsels. During Clinton's first term, Reno came under attack from the president's allies for being too quick to appoint independent counsels, but during the president's second term, Reno was accused of shielding Clinton and Vice President Al GORE from an independent investigation of CAMPAIGN FINANCE irregularities in the 1996 campaign.

Once the attorney general decides that an independent counsel is needed, a special court composed of three federal judges selected by the Chief Justice of the United States decides whom to appoint. Once appointed, the independent counsel has considerable freedom to conduct his inquiry, with no significant monetary or time restrictions. The scope of the investigation is limited to a certain crime and related matters but may be expanded with the approval of the same three-judge panel that appointed the independent counsel. For instance, the independent counsel's investigation that originated with Clinton's handling of the Whitewater real estate development in Arkansas was permitted to spread to several seemingly unconnected topics: the White House Travel Office firings, the FBI files controversy, and Clinton's relationship with White House intern Monica Lewinsky. The act also obligates independent counsels to hand over information to Congress that they deem an impeachable offense. Thus, when Kenneth Starr, the independent counsel investigating Whitewater and other matters, found evidence that Clinton had perjured himself and obstructed justice in relation to his affair with Lewinsky, he furnished a detailed report of his findings to Congress, which led to the House of Representative's impeachment hearings against Clinton.

Both Republicans and Democrats have attacked the investigations conducted by independent counsels, questioning the resources, time, and even the motivations of the investigator. During the 1980s, Republicans were skeptical of the work of Independent Counsel Lawrence Walsh, who spent six years and more than $45 million investigating how much President Reagan and his aides knew about the Iran-contra arms deal. In the 1990s, Democrats railed against the performance of Independent Counsel Kenneth Starr and his successor, Robert Ray, who spent approximately $50 million and six years investigating President Clinton. In addition, four other independent counsel investigations of other top executive officials in the Clinton administration cost another $50 million. During its existence, there have been a total of 20 independent counsel investigations—seven of those investigations led to indictments and five investigations yielded at least one criminal conviction, although some of those were overturned on appeal. Partisans from both sides of the aisle hailed the expiration of the independent counsel provision. With the provision gone, authority to appoint special prosecutors will revert to the attorney general.

Further reading: Harriger, Katy J. *The Special Prosecutor in American Politics.* Lawrence: University Press of Kansas, 2000; Johnson, Charles A., and Danette Brickman. *Independent Counsel: The Law and the Investigations.* Washington, D.C.: CQ Press, 2001.

—Terri Bimes

inherent powers

As a matter of constitutional principle and practice, all governmental acts must be grounded in the Constitution. The president possesses powers that are enumerated in the text of the Constitution, including the authority to issue pardons and veto bills presented to him by Congress. Presidents also have claimed "inherent" powers, variously asserted as emergency, residual, or PREROGATIVE POWERS. For analytical purposes, the theory of inherent power should be understood as encompassing powers that are neither enumerated nor implied but which, nonetheless, are rooted in the four corners of the Constitution. As such, they are distinguishable from the theory of extra-constitutional powers, which are said to derive from some source beyond the Constitution.

The doctrine of inherent executive authority does not fit comfortably within a constitutional system that assigns specific powers, responsibilities, and duties. At bottom, the doctrine must confront conceptual and analytical difficulties involved in the determination of the basis and scope of inherent authority. For example, an inherent power cannot be said to derive from an enumerated power; otherwise, the distinction between implied and inherent powers will be eclipsed. Moreover, for obvious conceptual reasons, inherent powers may neither supersede nor conflict with the scope of the enumerated or IMPLIED POWERS of the president or Congress, lest they eviscerate the premise and promise of a written Constitution. As Chief Justice John MARSHALL declared in *MARBURY V. MADISON* (1803): "to what purpose are powers limited, and to what purpose is that limitation committed to writing, if these limits may, at anytime, be passed by those intended to be restrained."

Advocates of the doctrine of inherent EXECUTIVE POWER typically have conceived of it as a residual power and have sought to ground it in the vesting Clause of Article II, Section 1, which provides that "the executive power shall be vested in a President of the United States," and in the Take Care Clause of Section 3, which commands the president to "take Care that the Laws be faithfully executed," frequently in connection with the formulation, management, and conduct of foreign policy and national security matters. In 1793, in his famous defense of President George WASHINGTON's Proclamation of Neutrality, Alexander HAMILTON, writing as "Pacificus," applied the initial gloss on "executive power" in his claim of an inherent presidential power. Hamilton emphasized the differences between the Constitution's assignment to Congress in Article I of "all legislative powers herein granted" and what he argued was a more general grant of executive authority to the president in the Vesting Clause of Article II. Hamilton contended that the Constitution embodies an independent, substantive grant of executive power. The subsequent enumeration of specific executive powers was meant, he argued, to "specify and regulate the principal articles implied in the definition of Executive power." The nation's executive power, he explained, is vested in the president, and it is "subject to the *exceptions* and *qualifications* which are expressed" in the Constitution.

Hamilton's effort to adduce a substantive conception of executive authority, a residual executive power to conduct FOREIGN AFFAIRS independent of constitutional exceptions and qualifications, on the basis of differences in terminology between Articles I and II, is fraught with difficulties. The records of the CONSTITUTIONAL CONVENTION reveal no basis for ascribing any significance to the phraseology between the legislative powers "herein granted" and "the Executive Power." The curb on congressional power represented an effort to reaffirm the limits of FEDERALISM and the regulatory authority of Congress and allay concerns of the states, which feared for their legislative authority, rather than an effort to recognize a substantive conception of executive power. Nor is there any evidence in the Convention debates to suggest that the framers intended to vest the president with a broad grant of discretionary authority. The framers held a deep-seated aversion to executive power and sought to confine presidential authority. Pacificus's argument, moreover, that only those executive articles that were "principal" articles is at odds with the concept of inherent power, for there is nothing more inherent in executive authority than the power to require a subordinate to place an opinion in writing, a power enumerated in the constitutional text. In addition, Hamilton's argument about a residual executive power to conduct foreign policy is contradicted by his own explanations in the *FEDERALIST PAPERS* of the Convention's determination to carefully limit presidential power in foreign affairs. In *Federalist No. 69,* for example, he wrote that the COMMANDER IN CHIEF clause does not carry with it the authority to initiate war, a power, he explained, that was constitutionally vested in Congress. In *Federalist No. 75,* he observed that the president was not granted the power to make treaties because "the history of human conduct does not warrant that exalted opinion of human virtue" that would justify the placement of unilateral discretionary power in the president, a description that leaves no room for a residual executive authority in foreign affairs.

For all of its failings and deficiencies, at least Hamilton's theory of inherent authority perceives presidential powers as constitutionally limited. A version of his argument was given expression in Justice George Sutherland's convoluted opinion for the Court in UNITED STATES V. CURTISS-WRIGHT EXPORT CORP. (1936), in which he asserted that the external sovereignty of the nation is vested in the executive and not derived from the Constitution. Sutherland's opinion should be understood as an assertion of an extra-constitutional foreign affairs power which somehow inheres in the executive. According to Sutherland, internal and external powers differ in both origin and nature. Inside the CONSTITUTIONAL CONVENTION, he explained, the powers then possessed by the states were carved up and distributed to governmental departments. While domestic powers are derived from the Constitution, foreign affairs powers are not, since the states did not possess such powers at the time of the Convention. In his version of history, Sutherland contended that the powers of external sovereignty were transferred from the English Crown at the time of the American Revolution to the colonies in their collective capacity, and they remained in Congress under the Articles of Confederation, where they stayed until, for reasons of the need for expertise and secrecy in foreign relations, they were somehow granted to the president, although not by the Convention.

The poverty of Sutherland's revolutionary historical thesis has been thoroughly discredited by scholarly critiques and subsequent judicial opinions that have dismissed his theory as dicta. It has been pointed out, for example, that contrary to Sutherland's assertions, the states were sovereign under the Articles of Confederation and that they did, indeed, possess foreign affairs powers which, for reasons of prudence and expediency, they delegated to Congress. As a constitutional matter, Sutherland's bizarre thesis never had any standing. James MADISON made it clear that foreign relations powers, like domestic powers, are derived from the Constitution when he wrote in *Federalist No. 45* that "the powers delegated by the proposed Constitution are few and defined," and that they would "be exercised principally on external objects, as war, peace, negotiation, and foreign commerce."

In 1952 President Harry TRUMAN adduced an inherent executive power to seize the nation's steel mills to prevent a labor strike, which, he feared, would cripple the economy and jeopardize important foreign policy and national security objectives, including the KOREAN WAR. No statute authorized the seizure; indeed, Congress had, in the course of debates on the TAFT-HARTLEY ACT in 1947, considered vesting the president with such authority but rejected the idea. Consequently, Truman's claim of inherent executive power to seize the steel industry amounted to the proposition, in Lockean terms, not only that the president might act to meet an emergency in the absence of legislation but also in defiance of a legislative prohibition. In effect, Truman's assertion was tantamount to a declaration of presidential power to improvise legislation. In *YOUNGSTOWN SHEET & TUBE CO. V. SAWYER* (1952), the Supreme Court, in an opinion by Justice Hugo Black, rejected Truman's assertion of an inherent executive power. In a weighty concurring opinion, Justice Robert H. Jackson rejected the concept of "nebulous" inherent EMERGENCY POWERS erected on nothing more than the "will of the President." Jackson rebuked the argument that the vesting clause is a "grant in bulk of all conceivable executive power. . . ." Rather, it is to be regarded "as an allocation to the presidential office of the generic powers" enumerated in the Constitution, a view that reflects the framers' aim, as Madison explained, to "confine and define" executive power.

Youngstown's repudiation of Truman's claim of an inherent power left little life in the theory. In *NEW YORK TIMES V. UNITED STATES* (1971), the Court rejected the assertion of an inherent presidential power to halt publication of the Pentagon Papers.

Given the Court's repudiation of a presidential claim to an inherent emergency power, often styled as the Lockean Prerogative, there remains the question of the solution to emergency, for it was understood by the framers that the law may not provide an immediate remedy for every conceivable situation that the nation might encounter. The answer lay in the doctrine of retroactive ratification, an English practice by which governmental officials might find it necessary to violate the law in order to meet a crisis but would trust the legislature for protection in the form of an act of indemnity. In its application in America, a president might act illegally and turn to Congress for ratification of actions. Congressional ratification would hinge on the question of whether Congress shared the president's perception of emergency. The chief virtue in this practice was that it left to Congress, as the nation's lawmaking authority, the ultimate determination of the existence of an emergency, and it prevented the president from sitting as judge of his own cause, a principle of overarching importance in Anglo-American legal history. Examples include congressional ratification of Thomas JEFFERSON's purchase of supplies without authorization in response to a British attack on Chesapeake and retroactive authorization by Congress

of several of Abraham LINCOLN's unauthorized acts during the CIVIL WAR, including expenditures from the Treasury. The doctrine of retroactive ratification avoids the specter of a president judging his own act of usurpation and it incorporates elements of doctrines of separation of powers and CHECKS AND BALANCES, and in this way it maintains a semblance of constitutional government.

—David Gray Adler

Inspectors General (IG)

The offices of Inspector General were created in the aftermath of the WATERGATE scandal amid accusation of fraud, waste, and abuse within EXECUTIVE BRANCH agencies. The first IG was established in 1976, and in 1978 the Inspector General Act was passed. In 1988 significant amendments strengthened the 1978 act.

The Inspectors General have broad authority to "promote economy, efficiency, and effectiveness," and oversee executive branch agencies. They are responsible for uncovering fraud and abuse of power. They are nominated by the president with Senate confirmation and are nonpartisan watchdogs who monitor activities within executive branch agencies.

institutional presidency

The institutional presidency refers to the vast and complex organizational apparatus that has been cultivated over the latter half of the 20th century as a mechanism for assisting modern presidents with the day-to-day business of government. From its modest origins in 1939, the institutional presidency has grown into an increasingly specialized and highly differentiated organization. Over time, the institutional presidency has become more important, as presidents have increasingly sought to develop an independent, centralized capacity to oversee decision-making in the agencies of the EXECUTIVE BRANCH.

Origins

In the first one hundred days of his administration, President Franklin ROOSEVELT proposed an extensive legislative agenda designed to combat the economic hardships of the GREAT DEPRESSION. Roosevelt's NEW DEAL included measures to stimulate and regulate the financial, agricultural, and business sectors of the economy, and it provided for labor reform, SOCIAL SECURITY, soil conservation, and a number of public works projects. Roosevelt's relief program also led to the establishment of a host of regulatory agencies designed to implement the New Deal policies.

Roosevelt's New Deal established for the first time a permanent role for the president in the national policymaking process, effectively ushering in the modern presidency, but, without any preexisting organizational capacity in the White House, it was impossible for Roosevelt to ensure that the newly created agencies would implement his policies in an effective and efficient manner. The administrative capacity of the presidency at that time was simply insufficient to manage the new responsibilities of a modern presidency.

To address the problem, Roosevelt created the Committee on Administrative Management, known as the BROWNLOW COMMITTEE, to recommend reforms that would establish a presidential staff structure in the White House. The report concluded, simply and dramatically, "the President needs help," and cited the inability of the president's current staff to adequately assist Roosevelt with the growing complexity and magnitude of his work. Although Congress initially rejected the report's recommendations, Roosevelt was eventually awarded six new staff positions and the power to reorganize portions of the executive branch, subject to congressional veto. Exercising this newly acquired power, in 1939 Roosevelt created by executive order the EXECUTIVE OFFICE OF THE PRESIDENT (EOP).

Growth

Prior to 1939 the president was assisted by just a few aides, most of whom were from other agencies of the executive branch. In 1925 the total budget allotted for all personnel working for the president was $126,000. In 1939, the year of the Brownlow report, it was $250,000. In the year 2000 it was approximately $200 million. The first EOP housed five units, including the BUREAU OF THE BUDGET, the National Resources Planning Board, the Liaison Office for Personnel Management, and the Office of Government Reports. As of 2000 the EOP contained 12 organizational units and employed a combined staff of about 1,600.

Importance

The conclusion reached by the Brownlow Committee was accurate; the president did need help, and the White House staff has provided it. The development of the institutional presidency over the last half-century has provided presidents with a wealth of organizations. A brief consideration of the nature and functions performed by the core departments of the EOP illustrates the importance of the institutional presidency as a mechanism for shouldering the burdens of presidential governance.

The White House Office (WHO) Unlike other departments within the EOP, the WHITE HOUSE OFFICE is composed solely of presidential appointees. Over the years, several organizational units have been added to the WHO which perform a number of invaluable functions on behalf of the president. During the NIXON administration, a White House Communications Office was created for handling the president's relations with the media. During the FORD and CARTER presidencies an OFFICE OF PUBLIC LIAISON was created to maintain relations between the White House and various interest groups. Finally, the REAGAN Administration established in the White House Personnel Office a system for screening potential presidential nominees to ensure a strong ideological commitment to the Reagan agenda.

The Office of Management and Budget (OMB) The primary function of the OFFICE OF MANAGEMENT AND BUDGET is to prepare the president's annual budget request to Congress. Since the BUREAU OF THE BUDGET (BOB) was reorganized into the OMB and moved from the TREASURY DEPARTMENT into the EOP in 1970, it has taken on a political—in addition to just a professional—advisory role. The OMB not only coordinates executive agency spending requests but it also advises the president concerning the efficiency and effectiveness of various federal programs.

The National Security Council (NSC) The NATIONAL SECURITY COUNSEL was created in 1947 to encourage presidents to seek the advice of military leaders in planning national security policy. Although the NSC has little independent power and is designed to advise the president, some presidents have accorded more weight to the Council's advice than others. While TRUMAN's use of the NSC was limited until the KOREAN WAR, EISENHOWER gave its director the title of Assistant to the President. And, while KENNEDY abandoned the NSC during the early stages of his administration, it was revived after the BAY OF PIGS invasion. It was during the Nixon administration that the importance of foreign policy advice independent of the State and Defense Departments was permanently established in the White House under the strong leadership of Henry KISSINGER.

Can Presidents Manage the Institutional Presidency?

The EOP was intentionally developed to help modern presidents adjust to their new role under the bright lights at the center of the national policy-making stage. Today, the institutional presidency assists presidents with much of the governmental business in which they are involved, but the question of whether presidents can effectively manage the institutional presidency is not easily answered.

Presidents face formidable obstacles in their attempts to utilize White House staff as an instrument to pursue their policy objectives. First, the sheer size of the presidential BUREAUCRACY may prohibit a president's ability to manage the institutional presidency effectively. Generally speaking, a large bureaucracy will be less amenable to presidential management than a smaller one. Second, despite the appointments presidents are able to make, a sizable portion of the institutional presidency is passed down from administration to administration. As Hugh Heclo points out, once presidents assume office they realize the presidency is really a "deep structure" that they can change only slowly, if at all. Finally, Congress may make presidential attempts to manage the institutional bureaucracy more difficult by adding organizational units not desired by the president, as it did by adding the NSC during the Truman presidency. Or, Congress may choose to withhold funding or establish requirements for funding to be given to certain departments within the EOP.

Despite these obstacles, presidents can employ strategies to more effectively manage the institutional presidency. Presidents can enhance their effectiveness by establishing clear lines of responsibility for their staff members and carefully monitoring their performance. It was precisely this lack of presidential guidance that threatened to undermine the Reagan presidency when Oliver North attempted to conduct his own foreign policy in what history remembers as the IRAN-CONTRA AFFAIR. Presidents can also more effectively manage the institutional presidency by designing their staffs to compensate for their own personal weaknesses. George H. W. BUSH remained open to alternative views in matters of DOMESTIC POLICY in which his knowledge was relatively limited and he was politically vulnerable. In foreign policy, where Bush's expertise was much greater and he had strong public support, he relied on advice much less.

Further reading: Burke, John P. *Institutional Presidency: Organizing and Managing the White House from FDR to Clinton,* 2d ed. Baltimore, Md.: Johns Hopkins University Press, 2000; Committee on Administrative Management. *Administrative Management in the Government of the United States.* Chicago: Public Administration Service, 1947; Hart, John. *The Presidential Branch: From Washington to Clinton,* 2d ed. Chatham, N.J.: Chatham House, 1995; Heclo, Hugh. "The Changing Presidential Office." In *Politics and the Oval Office,* edited by Arnold Meltsner. San Francisco: Institute for Contemporary Studies, 1981; Kernell, Samuel. "The Evolution of the White House Staff." In *Can the Government Govern?,* edited by John E. Chubb and Paul E. Peterson. Washington, D.C.: Brookings Institution, 1989; Pfiffner, James P. *The Modern Presidency.* New York: St. Martin's Press, 1994.

—Adam B. Lawrence

intelligence oversight

The president is in charge of the CENTRAL INTELLIGENCE AGENCY as well as military intelligence, but Congress retains the OVERSIGHT responsibility for policies of the government. In order for Congress to do its job, it needs access and information, but by their very nature, intelligence activities are secret. This creates a conflict between the need to keep operations secret and the need for a democratic government to be open and ensure responsibility. This tension is usually resolved by EXECUTIVE BRANCH officials keeping the Congress minimally informed of covert or intelligence-related activities. Congress (usually congressional committees and subcommittees) reviews the policies and activity of U.S. intelligence agencies. This oversight became more important in the 1970s in response to charges of abuse of power by the intelligence agencies of the government. While the president is still granted wide latitude in the use of these agencies, on occasion Congress will become involved in investigations of potential abuses or illegalities.

Intelligence Oversight Act

Passed in 1980, this act is the result of Congress's frustration with the executive in the wake of the VIETNAM WAR and accusations of presidential abuses of the intelligence agencies during the WATERGATE scandal.

The CENTRAL INTELLIGENCE AGENCY (CIA) had, for nearly three decades, been a COVERT OPERATIONS wing of the EXECUTIVE BRANCH. When revelations of CIA assassination attempts as well as its efforts to unseat governments came to light, Congress enacted the Hughes-Ryan Amendment (1974), requiring the president to inform select congressional committees of any covert CIA operations. A month later the Senate established the Senate Select Committee to study government operations with respect to intelligence activities. Known as the CHURCH COMMITTEE and headed by Senator Frank Church (Dem.-Idaho), the committee revealed a series of shocking covert operations and recommended the establishment of permanent committees to oversee intelligence activities. These committees were established in 1976 and 1977.

The Senate Committee on Intelligence recommended a restructure charter for the intelligence community. While this charter was based in President Jimmy CARTER's Executive Order 12036, the president opposed giving the charter legislative approval, and it was not passed into law.

However, one part of the committee's recommendations, the INTELLIGENCE OVERSIGHT ACT establishing congressional OVERSIGHT powers, was passed in 1980. One controversial provision of the act required the president to submit a "finding" to the committee when a covert operation was being undertaken. This proved especially troublesome during the REAGAN administration when the president signed findings authorizing the sale of arms to a terrorist nation, Iran, as well as the use of profits from the ARMS SALES to support the antigovernment "contras" in Nicaragua. However, these findings were not submitted to Congress, and testimony before Congress was contradictory regarding when and even if a finding was signed at all.

President REAGAN testified to various versions at various times, and the truth is still elusive.

In response to the IRAN-CONTRA scandal, Congress passed the Intelligence Oversight Act of 1991, which further codified the responsibility of the president to notify Congress of covert actions. In 1991 President George H. W. Bush killed the act with a POCKET VETO. After a compromise between Bush and the Congress, a slightly watered-down bill was passed and eventually signed into law as the Intelligence Authorization Act of 1991.

Further reading: Paterson, Thomas G. "Oversight or Afterview? Congress, the CIA, and Covert Action since 1947." In *Congress and United States Foreign Policy: Controlling the Use of Force in the Nuclear Age*, edited by Michael A. Barnhart. Albany: State University of New York Press, 1987.

interest groups and the presidency

Throughout history, individuals and organizations seeking assistance and favor in terms of their interests have sought access to the power structure. Politics, in basic terms, is the process by which a society chooses: rates of taxation, the condition of air and water, war or peace. The Founders recognized that without some way to limit the activities of factions (opposing sides of an issue), the fledging republic would be short-lived. The proposal and result: the creation of a multilevel DIVIDED GOVERNMENT with many opportunities available for competition of various interests.

For much of our history, that competition took place on Capitol Hill and focused on the U.S. Congress. With the advent of the GREAT DEPRESSION and the subsequent election of Franklin Delano ROOSEVELT as president, the focus of access for such groups quickly tilted from the legislative to the EXECUTIVE BRANCH.

Upon taking the OATH OF OFFICE on March 4, 1933, Roosevelt became president during one of our nation's most challenging times. His administration faced domestic economic chaos. In his inaugural address, Roosevelt asked Congress for unprecedented powers to radically solve the American economic crisis.

In response to the crisis, he made the presidency accessible to banking, business, labor, and agricultural groups. Through their work, a torrent of legislation was drafted and became law in a very short period of time. Each bill addressed a key sector of economic and/or social renewal. With the establishment of a multitude of NEW DEAL government agencies and programs to manage such renewal, the executive branch became more visible, central, and powerful, and a more attractive target for interest groups.

Following Roosevelt's gesture of an open-door policy to various interest groups, subsequent chief executives have continued the practice, though modified to suit each president's style. Although Gerald FORD's White House was the first to formally organize an office in the West Wing to interact with such groups, other presidents have housed a similar operation to accommodate and manage interest group requests. Typically groups with the most access to the presidency are often sympathetic to an administration's position and/or policies. President CARTER's interest-group focus was focused on women's, consumers', and environmental groups. President REAGAN's focused more on business and religious organizations. Recent estimates indicate that leaders of 23,000 national organizations make the WHITE HOUSE a key stop during their visits to Washington.

Further reading: Brogan, Hugh. "The Era of Franklin Roosevelt, 1933–1938," in *The Longman History of the United States of America.* New York: William Morrow and Company, 1985; Mahood, H. R. *Interest Group Politics in America: A New Intensity.* Englewood Cliffs, N.J.: Prentice Hall, 1990; Orman, John. "The President and Interest Group Access." *Presidential Studies Quarterly* 18 (4), 1988; Patterson, Bradley H., Jr. *The White House Staff—Inside the West Wing and Beyond.* Washington, D.C.: Brookings Institution Press, 2000.

—F. Owen Holmes

Interior, Department of the

Created in 1849 as the fifth CABINET agency, the Department of Interior, headed by a secretary appointed by the president with the ADVICE AND CONSENT of the Senate, is today the nation's chief conservation agency, responsible for more than 500 million acres of federal land (about 29 percent of the U.S. land mass).

When created, the department was a grab bag of various responsibilities. It was especially active in developing the West. Today, under its jurisdiction are the census, public lands, patents, pensions, Indian Affairs, natural resources, national parks, dam and aqueduct construction, conservation, the National Park Service, the U.S. Geological Survey, the Fish and Wildlife Service, and a host of other activities.

international law

Dutch jurist Grotius is credited as the father or inventor of international law. In 1625 he wrote *The Law of War and Peace*, an attempt to devise a system of laws applicable to all peoples, places, and times. Today, international law remains an only partially realized dream. There are a variety of regimes and actors—the United States, the UNITED NATIONS, the World Court, and others—that form a web of partially binding rules and norms that make up a system of international law. Given that there is no one world government, there is no one power with sufficient authority to enforce international law.

The United States—and the president—is subject to a variety of international laws and as the world's only superpower, often takes upon itself the responsibility of trying to enforce those rules and norms it deems especially important. At other times, the United States goes to the United Nations for legitimacy and authority. And at other times, NGOs (nongovernmental organizations, such as the International Red Cross, Amnesty International, or Human Rights Watch) become involved.

In the absence of a compelling, binding, enforceable code of international law, the nations of the world will use such rules when it suits their needs and ignore them where possible. Power remains the coin of the realm. Largely, international law, then, becomes a tool for the big powers to impose their will on international events.

As the world becomes more globalized and interdependent, the need for governing rules and regulations will increase. This will give greater authority to international law and, over time, increase the power and authority of international organizations designed to insure enforcement.

intervention

Intervention is the introduction of military forces by one state into the territory of another state. Limited intervention is sanctioned by INTERNATIONAL LAW when one's citizens are in danger, by certain treaty arrangements, or for reasons of self-defense.

The United States has a long history of intervention, especially in this hemisphere. Dating back to the MONROE DOCTRINE, the United States has sought to quell rebellions, take land, and protect its citizens. Much of U.S. intervention is in the form of COVERT OPERATIONS. As the United States became the "hegemonic" power of the West, its responsibilities grew. This sometimes necessitated U.S. intervention into other nations either to enforce international norms, insure stability, or sometimes, to pursue U.S. interests. In such events, more often than not, "might makes right," that is, those nations with sufficient authority to impose their wills on weaker nations, whether right or wrong, can dictate events. As the world's most powerful nation, the United States has, from time to time, imposed its will via military and economic means, by threat, or by imposition of sanctions.

investigation of the presidency, congressional

As part of the OVERSIGHT responsibility exercised by the legislative branch, Congress, from time to time, holds hearings and investigations into EXECUTIVE BRANCH activities.

Often these investigations are serious and intended to assist Congress in the development of rules, standards, or legislation. Sometimes these investigations are merely efforts to embarrass the president and grab headlines.

The first congressional investigation of the executive took place in 1792 when the House examined the failed military expectation of General Arthur St. Clair against two Native-American tribes in Ohio. Since then Congress has investigated a number of executive operations.

The Supreme Court has helped define the parameters of these investigations. In *McGrain v. Dougherty* (1927) the Court ruled that anyone could be called before Congress to testify in an investigation. In *Sinclair v. United States* (1929) the Court ruled that Congress had broad powers to investigate the EXECUTIVE BRANCH.

In recent years congressional investigations into WATERGATE, IRAN-CONTRA, and the CLINTON scandals have grabbed headlines and put presidents on the defensive.

Iran-contra Affair

The Iran-contra Affair during the REAGAN administration raised major constitutional questions of who controls foreign policy. The affair involved two interconnected policies: (1) the sale of weapons to Iran for the stated purpose of supporting the "moderates" in Iranian government and for the implicit purpose of freeing American hostages, and (2) to assist in the financing of the contras—the opposition force determined to overthrow the Sandinista government of Nicaragua. The two policies became interconnected when profits from the arms sale to Iran were diverted to contras. The revelations of these details lead to the appointment of Laurence Walsh as special counsel and the convening of a Congressional Committee to investigate these activities. These two policies were brought together through the activities of Colonel Oliver North, who was a staff member of the NATIONAL SECURITY COUNCIL.

The Contra Dimension

Somoza's regime in Nicaragua was overthrown in 1979 by a group known as the Sandinistas who espoused Marxism. President CARTER provided aid to the new regime in the hope that would bolster the moderates in the group and keep the Sandinistas unaligned with the Cubans and the Soviets.

REAGAN abandoned the Carter policies and became the principal sponsor of covert military support of the contras to overthrow the Sandinista regime. Reagan compared the contras to the American Founding Fathers.

Leaders in Congress objected to this policy, leading to the passage of the first BOLAND AMENDMENT (1982), which stated that the CENTRAL INTELLIGENCE AGENCY and the Department of Defense were prohibited from using any

President Ronald Reagan and Senator Edmund Muskie listen as Senator John Tower (left) reports on his commission's investigation into the Iran-contra affair. *(Ronald W. Reagan Library)*

funds for the purpose of overthrowing the government of Nicaragua. The Reagan administration attempted to circumvent this policy by soliciting funds for the contras from other nations and wealthy individuals. In addition, it ordered the CIA to mine several ports. The administration argued that the purpose of the mining was to prevent arm shipments to revolutionary forces in El Salvador and not the overthrow of the Sandinistas.

Congress reacted by passing a second Boland Amendment in 1984 that was even more restrictive. It prohibited any direct or indirect military or paramilitary support for the contras whether by the CIA, the DEFENSE DEPARTMENT, or "any other agency or entity of the United States involved in intelligence activities." The supporters of the Boland Amendment believed they had utilized their constitutional authority of "the power of the purse," and that all activities by the United States government in support of the contras must cease.

Despite the Boland Amendment, the Reagan administration contended that they were committed to supporting the contras. They believed that because the National Security Council was not specifically mentioned and was not engaged in the gathering of intelligence, it would be able to coordinate activities in support of the contras. It was furthered argued that the president possessed the PREROGATIVE POWERS in foreign policy as implied in *UNITED STATES V. CURTISS-WRIGHT* (1936) and was free to act independently of Congress. The National Security Council under Colonel North continued to solicit funds from foreign nations and private citizens to support the contras.

The Iranian Dimension

In 1979 the shah of Iran, a staunch ally of the United States, was overthrown by an Islamic group hostile to the United States. The new government supported the taking of American Embassy personnel hostage for 444 days. The situation was exacerbated by the continual taking and torturing of hostages, including CIA operatives in the Lebanon. The administration policy was to encourage all nations not to sell arms to Iran and not to bargain with terrorists. Privately, they worried about the fate of the hostages and the potential loss of intelligence that might result from the torture.

Intelligence reports suggested that there was a faction within the government of Iran who were "moderates." These individuals wanted a more constructive relationship with the United States, and the sale of arms would bolster this faction and possibly facilitate the release of the hostages.

The National Security Council in 1985 decided to pursue this option. They authorized the Israelis to sell American-made missiles to Iran, and subsequently one American hostage was released. Hence, whether intended or not, it became perceived as an arms-for-hostage deal. A second Israeli sale of arms to Iran resulted in a second American hostage being released. As American involvement grew deeper, the administration decided to abandon this approach. In addition, under the Hughes/Ryan Act, a presidential finding must be prepared for all covert activities and reported to the Congress. No such finding was prepared before the first sale. Afterward, a finding was prepared that suggested that the administration understood the arms-for-hostage arrangement.

The administration then pursued a second approach in which the Defense Department would sell arms to intermediaries who in turn would sell the arms to Iran. This policy was approved despite the objections from Secretary of State Schultz and Secretary of Defense Weinberger. Former General Richard Secord was selected to be one of the intermediaries, who would then divert the profits to the contras in Nicaragua.

When news of the operation began to leak, uproar emerged. The administration appointed John Tower to investigate the affair. Lawrence Walsh was appointed special counsel, and Congress held hearings on both the ARMS SALES and the diversion of funds. Oliver North and National Security Counsel Advisor John Poindexter were convicted; however, these convictions were overturned by the Court of Appeals because substantial evidence in the trial was derived from their own testimony before Congress for which they were granted immunity.

The Iran-contra affair goes beyond the evaluation of policy. It involved fundamental questions of who controls foreign policy. The Reagan administration pushed the prerogative theory to a new level. It suggested that it could operate independently of Congress and the system of CHECKS AND BALANCES. Several questions were raised. When foreign governments and wealthy individuals contributed to the contras, were they given any consideration by the United States government? In addition, when private intermediaries purchased weapons from the Defense Department and sold them to the Iranians for a substantial profit, were the profits their rightful property to dispose of or the property of the government of the United States? In addition, is it the proper role of an advisory group such as the National Security Council—where there are no confirmation hearings, no procedures for IMPEACHMENT and removal, and no congressional OVERSIGHT—to engage in COVERT OPERATIONS?

Furthermore, it raises the question of an "off-the-shelf" intelligence agency operating under the sole authority and direction of the president and in some instances in direct opposition to the will of Congress. The Iran-contra Affair, hence, raised important issues relating to democracy, ACCOUNTABILITY, and the system of SEPARATION OF POWERS.

Further reading: Draper, Theodore. *A Very Thin Line: The Iran-Contra Affairs.* New York: Hill & Wang, 1991; Koh, Harold Hongju. *The National Security Constitution: Sharing Power after the Iran-Contra Affair.* New Haven, Conn.: Yale University Press, 1990; Walsh, Lawrence E. *Firewall: The Iran-Contra Conspiracy and Cover-Up.* New York: Norton, 1997.

—Frank M. Sorrentino

Iranian hostage crisis (1979–1980)

Early in November of 1979, roughly nine months after the shah of Iran had fallen from power, an angry mob in Tehran took over the American embassy compound and captured the U.S. diplomats working there. A similar embassy takeover had occurred earlier in the chaos that followed the Shah's departure, but that incident ended in short order when the forces of the Iranian revolutionary council cleared the embassy grounds of the rioters who had temporarily occupied it. This time was different. The Iranian government, such as it was, took no steps against the embassy occupiers whose actions, we later learned, had the full support of the Ayatollah Khomeini, the religious leader who was emerging as the new ruler of Iran.

For the next 444 days, all the days that remained in the Carter presidency, American diplomats were held hostage in a foreign land. That land was still in the midst of a revolution that eventually replaced an autocratic regime with a modern version of an ancient Islamic theocracy. The inability of the Carter administration to understand what was happening in Iran or to resolve the hostage crisis played a major part in Carter's failure to win a second term.

President Carter's problems bringing the hostages home was not for want of trying. In the weeks and months following the embassy takeover, the president condemned the hostage-taking, froze Iranian assets in the United States, imposed sanctions against the revolutionary regime, sent offi-

cial and secret emissaries to meet with various Iranian officials, closed the Iranian embassy in Washington, and offered to approve the formation of a UNITED NATIONS commission to investigate earlier American relations with the Shah. Though there were occasional false hopes that some of these diplomatic steps would lead to the safe release of the hostages, no real progress was made in the early months of the crisis.

When the president became convinced that he had exhausted every available avenue for DIPLOMACY, he authorized a daring rescue mission for late in the spring of 1980. The mission involved sending a small band of specially trained counterterrorism Delta Force troops into downtown Tehran in the dead of a moonless night. Good intelligence information suggested that the hostages were lightly guarded in the embassy compound. The hard part would be getting there.

Helicopters flying low to avoid radar detection had to travel hundreds of miles into the Iranian interior where they were scheduled to meet with American transport aircraft at a remote desert location. There the helicopters would refuel and pick up the Delta Force soldiers for the final leg of their long journey to the outskirts of Tehran. As it turned out, not enough helicopters made it to the designated desert rendezvous and the mission had to be aborted. A subsequent refueling accident added a tragic dimension to the failed mission and produced the only combat-related casualties of the Carter presidency.

After the unsuccessful rescue attempt, and the resignation of Secretary of State Cyrus Vance, who had opposed it, the Carter administration had very few options that were likely to bring the crisis to a peaceful conclusion. The president never contemplated giving in to demands to turn over the Shah or his financial assets, and he rejected the advice of his national security advisor, Zbigniew Brzezinski, who urged him to issue an ultimatum and punish Iran with military strikes if, as was likely, our terms for an immediate hostage release were not met. Between giving in and going all out, the only other option was to wait and hope for sanctions and diplomatic pressures to have some effect.

The hostages were still in captivity when Americans went to the polls in November of 1980, just a few days after a flurry of media coverage accompanied the first anniversary of their capture. The winner, Ronald REAGAN, had actively criticized Carter for his weakness in responding to the Soviet threat and implicitly for the handling of the hostage crisis.

During the transition, a diplomatic breakthrough finally came. The Iranian assets which had been frozen in American banks and other financial institutions became much more important after Iraq invaded Iran. A complicated arrangement, largely negotiated by Deputy Secretary of State Warren Christopher, was made to free the hostages in exchange for a release of most of the funds that had been held for over a year. President Carter was still monitoring the final details of the hostage release while dressing for the inauguration of his successor. By accident, or perhaps as a final insult to Carter, the actual release of the hostages did not occur until after Reagan had taken the OATH OF OFFICE.

The hostage crisis consumed enormous presidential time and energies in Carter's final year in office. He canceled primary campaigning against his challenger, Senator Edward Kennedy, in order to stay close to the White House and any unexpected crisis developments. This "Rose Garden" strategy may have helped Carter secure the Democratic nomination, but it became a campaign liability when the general election arrived with no resolution of the crisis in sight. Political strategists in both parties wondered if some last-minute deal with Iran, an "October surprise," would tip the balance in what was expected to be a close election. Since then, some have speculated that some members of Reagan's campaign team may have made contact with Iranians to prevent such a surprise.

In the end, there were no Iranian surprises in the 1980 presidential election. From a broader perspective, there were many surprises related to the revolution in Iran. Hardly any Western experts thought that the shah would be replaced by an aging cleric or that Islamic fundamentalism would reverse much of the social and material progress that had occurred in a rapidly modernizing Iran. When the hostage crisis began, it was nearly inconceivable that the sanctity of diplomatic immunity, widely accepted in the world community for hundreds of years, would be flagrantly and systematically violated.

President Carter, who made it his mission to secure the safe return of the hostages, counts the final resolution of the crisis as a success, even if it came at the expense of a second term. In his post-presidency, Carter has rarely expressed regret for any of the decisions he made while he was in the White House. But he has said, on more than one occasion, that he wishes he had sent one more helicopter into the Iranian desert.

Further reading: Christopher, Warren, ed. *American Hostages in Iran: The Conduct of a Crisis.* New Haven, Conn.: Yale University Press, 1985; Sick, Gary. *All Fall Down: America's Tragic Encounter with Iran.* New York: Random House, 1985.

—Robert A. Strong

Iraq War

In late March of 2003, the George W. BUSH administration, along with Great Britain and other nations, launched an assault on Iraq to overthrow the government of Saddam Hussein. For more than a decade, Hussein had violated UN resolutions, and the Bush administration made removing Hussein one of the central elements of its foreign policy. In commencing war with Iraq, the administration, while first going to the UNITED NATIONS for an authorizing resolution, decided to go to war without UN approval, causing a serious international backlash and a fissure in the traditional alliances. France, Germany, Russia, China, and a variety of other nations condemned the war. The Bush administration, seeing this as part of its new "preventive war" strategy, insisted that Iraq was developing weapons of mass destruction, aiding international terrorists, and threatening the region and the United States, and it had to be stopped "before" it caused harm. The administration formed its own coalition to fight the war, referred to as a "coalition of the willing" (primarily the United States and Great Britain) outside the United Nations and launched an air assault (known as "shock and awe") and a land invasion. It took less than a month to gain control of Iraq as the regime offered only limited opposition to the U.S. and allied forces. While the war was won quickly and at a minimal cost, the strategic doctrine that animated the military action, "preemptive" or "preventive" warfare, remained controversial. This controversial new security doctrine formed the basis of U.S. INTERVENTION and marked a dramatically new approach to foreign policy.

iron triangles

This metaphor of an iron triangle is used to describe the perceived "cozy relationship" between congressional committees, organized interest groups, and the executive bureaucracies in Washington. *Iron triangle* refers to both the shared *interests* of these three political actors, each at the apex of the triangle, and to the perceived *endurance* and *impenetrability* of this relationship by interests adverse to actors within the triangle.

According to the logic of iron triangles, these three political actors are responsive to overlapping constituencies. Congressional committee membership is thought to be a function of self-selection. Members of Congress (MC) seek membership on committees that reflect some dominant interest within their congressional district; committee membership provides the MC with the opportunity to pursue their interest in reelection by delivering the benefits of federal programs to an interested constituency within his or her district. For instance, MC from agricultural areas are thought to seek seats on the Agriculture Committee. United in their support from rural constituents, members on the committee seek to deliver benefits to their constituents while spreading the cost of those benefits to all Americans.

MC are supported, first, by organized interest groups in their efforts to secure benefits for their constituents and get reelected. Interest groups that represent narrow constituencies within the country (such as farmers) represent many of the same Americans who elected the members who sit on the Agriculture Committee. To the degree that interest-group representatives and MC have overlapping interests in serving their respective constituencies, they will often agree on the protection and expansion of programs within the jurisdiction of the committee.

While ostensibly under the control of the president, the federal bureaucracies have at least two other important constituents: Congress and the people that the bureaucrats are empowered to regulate (who are, in turn, constituents of MC). Maintenance and expansion of the budget and statutory authority of a BUREAUCRACY lie with Congress, most especially the congressional committee that has OVERSIGHT jurisdiction over the bureaucracy. For instance, the U.S. DEPARTMENT OF AGRICULTURE (USDA) will be especially responsive to the Agriculture Committee. In its regulatory function, the USDA will have significant interactions with interest groups who enjoy a special relationship with members of the Agriculture Committee. Thus the convergence of interests between these three actors is complete. Groups and interests outside of the iron triangle find it difficult, if not impossible, to gain entrée into this "cozy little triangle."

Iron triangles are thought to provide significant challenges to presidential LEADERSHIP. Actors within the triangle seek to maintain the status quo with respect to the policies and programs that benefit their shared constituencies. Presidents who pursue policy *change* may meet with significant resistance from the political interests of MC, interest-group representatives and their members, and bureaucrats, since each find some benefit in the status quo distribution of political benefits enforced by the iron triangle arrangement.

Generally speaking the metaphor of the iron triangle has been replaced by the concept of ISSUE NETWORKS. Issue networks suggest a more permeable structure of interests in Washington wherein membership in overlapping issue networks by these same political actors prevents the strict control of interests over the policy domains previously thought dominated by iron triangles.

Further reading: Cater, Douglass. *Power in Washington.* New York: Random House, 1964; Heclo, Hugh. "Issue Networks and the Executive Establishment." In *The New American Political System,* edited by Anthony King. Washington, D.C.: American Enterprise Institute, 1978; Lowi, Theodore J. *The End of Liberalism: The Second Republic of the United States,* 2d ed. New York: Norton, 1979; Shepsle, Kenneth A. *The Giant Jigsaw Puzzle: Democratic Committee Assignments in the Modern House.* Chicago: University of Chicago Press, 1978.

—Sean Q. Kelly

isolationism

While the United States has never been, nor could it be, isolated from the rest of the world, from time to time an isolationist sentiment gains hold over the public and government officials. Isolationism refers to the desire to retreat from or isolate oneself from the rest of the world.

In his farewell address George WASHINGTON advised Americans that "The great rule of conduct for us in regard to foreign nations is to have with them as little political connection as possible." This fear of what Thomas JEFFERSON dubbed "entangling alliances" with foreign nations has informed isolationist sentiment ever since. However, this isolationist thinking did not stop the United States from getting involved in the affairs of other nations. Indeed, over the decades as the United States became more powerful, it found itself less able to heed the warnings of Washington. Today, as the dominant world power, the United States could hardly isolate itself from the world or its concerns and problems. With a web of entangling alliances, economic integration, and security needs, the United States must remain a—if not *the*—significant actor on the world stage. It is often called upon and at other times chooses to involve itself in the world. International leadership is imposed by the power and reach of the United States, and it is therefore unlikely that the United States will or can become isolated from the concerns and problems of the world.

issue networks

An issue network usually begins to evolve within the institution of Congress. It is normally formed by a policy entrepreneur—someone interested in a particular issue that requires his/her personal leadership to achieve legislative activity. Key legislators and their staffs will be tapped to assist in lobbying other lawmakers and their respective party and issue caucuses (e.g., the Congressional Black Caucus) to vote in particular ways on the issue. The most successful issue networks, however, are those that have both an internal and external component, support from both inside and outside the institution of Congress. Such an external network includes outside interest groups, the media, and governmental actors such as the president and others in the EXECUTIVE BRANCH. Even minimal presidential involvement, such as a public statement of support or a letter to members of Congress at a key moment, lend credence to and garner additional backing for the issue network's efforts.

An expansive issue network provides an informational advantage to those who participate within the network and a disadvantage to those who are excluded or who are in opposition to it. This advantage is an incentive for legislators to join. This sort of network also is able to move beyond just the pursuit of votes to play an educational role that assists in widening the support network and, therefore, increasing the likelihood of legislative success. Clearly, creating such a network is a tremendous task that only sometimes results in passage of a bill. Those who rise to the challenge of policy entrepreneurship, therefore, must be extraordinarily committed to their cause, since the time and personal investment to create such a network can prove costly.

Further reading: Heclo, Hugh. "Issue Networks and the Executive Establishment." In *The New American Political System,* edited by Anthony King. Washington, D.C.: AEI Press, 1978; Kirst, Michael W., Gail Meister, and Stephen R. Rowley. "Policy Issue Networks: Their Influence on State Policymaking." *Policy Studies Journal,* 1984.

—Victoria Farrar-Myers

item veto

An item veto is the power of an executive to veto, delete, or send back to the legislative branch some section, portion, or part of a bill. Depending on how the power is defined, an item veto could apply only to appropriations bills or to all legislation. It could also be defined to allow the executive to reduce appropriations levels (an item-reduction power). Forty-three of 50 state governors possess some kind of item veto power. Except for a brief experiment with a limited item veto in 1997, the president does not possess an item veto.

Suggestions that the president be granted item veto powers first surfaced in the 1840s. The first codification of the item veto appeared in the Confederate Constitution of 1861, in which the Confederate president was given the power to veto parts of appropriations bills. President Jefferson DAVIS never exercised the item veto. After the CIVIL WAR, the item veto was adopted by Georgia in 1865 and Texas in 1866. Thereafter, the idea spread rapidly to most of the other states.

Ulysses S. GRANT became the first president to call for an item veto in 1873. Since then, many presidents and others have called for the power. Nearly 200 proposals to grant such a power have been proposed in Congress, usually based on the belief that presidents would use the power to eliminate wasteful or unnecessary spending. Opponents argued that the power would have no special fiscal effects, and that it would simply increase presidential leverage over Congress.

In 1996 Congress passed a bill granting the president a limited item veto–type power, called "enhanced rescission." The proposal had been included in congressional Republicans' 1994 "Contract With America." Under the law, presidents could sign bills into law but could block dollar amounts of discretionary budget authority, new spending items, and limited tax benefits within the bill while signing the remainder of the bill into law. The blocked amounts would remain vetoed unless Congress voted to pass them by majority vote, whereupon the president could veto them, and Congress could attempt to override the veto. In 1997 President Clinton used the power against 82 items in 11 bills. Several were challenged in court. In the case of *CLINTON V. NEW YORK* (1998), the Supreme Court struck down the new power, arguing that the power violated the "finely wrought" procedures of Article I, Section 7, of the Constitution by allowing the president to, in effect, rewrite legislation. The only way such a power could be granted to the president was by constitutional amendment.

Further reading: Spitzer, Robert J. "The Constitutionality of the Presidential Line-Item Veto." *Political Science Quarterly* (Summer 1997); *The Presidential Veto: Touchstone of the American Presidency.* Albany: State University of New York Press, 1988; "Symposium on The Line-Item Veto." *Notre Dame Journal of Law, Ethics & Public Policy* (1985).

—Robert J. Spitzer

J

Jackson, Andrew (1767–1845) *seventh U.S. president*
Andrew Jackson was the first political outsider to occupy the presidency. His six predecessors had all come to office after extensive political apprenticeships close to national power. His predecessors had also all enjoyed the benefits of a formal education and had all spent their lives near the Eastern Shore of the United States as well as, in several cases, in Europe.

Jackson was different. He was a self-made man, born March 15, 1767, in South Carolina, to a farming family of modest means. Serving in the militia during the Revolutionary War, the 13-year-old Jackson was wounded by a British officer for refusing to shine the officer's boots while being held a prisoner of war. After the war, Jackson read the law under the tutelage of an attorney in North Carolina, before making his way across the Appalachian Mountains to the new settlement of Nashville, where he established himself as a leading citizen of what became the state of Tennessee.

After serving as the prosecuting attorney for the federal government in Nashville and its environs, Jackson was sent to Washington, D.C., as Tennessee's first member of the House of Representatives. Within months of the expiration of his term in the House, the Tennessee legislature sent Jackson back to Washington to serve out a vacant Senate seat. In November of 1798, the year his brief time in the Senate ended, he was appointed to the Tennessee Superior Court, where he served until 1804.

Jackson's Popularity

Jackson's path to power in Tennessee took him through these various appointive and elected positions, but his popularity with the electorate and the elite in government rested upon more than Jackson's fitness for political or judicial offices. He was renowned in Tennessee for his physical courage, his sense of honor, and as a man, in his own words, who "can command a body of men in a rough way."

Jackson's temper was famous. In one incident, widely publicized by the opposition during his presidential election campaigns, Jackson dueled with another attorney, John Dickinson. The cause of the duel may have been an insult to Jackson's wife. Whatever the cause, Jackson's friends warned him of the likely outcome; Dickinson was widely regarded as the superior duelist. Jackson won the confrontation through discipline. Permitting his opponent to fire first, Jackson took Dickinson's bullet in his chest (where it remained until he died, being too close to his heart to permit surgery) and then carefully laid aim and killed the man.

As this episode is often interpreted to suggest, Jackson's sense of honor to his wife was intense. He had met Rachel Robards the year he moved to Nashville. Mrs. Robards was separated from her husband at the time, and Mr. Jackson sought to protect her from her sometimes-angry husband. Mr. and Mrs. Robards agreed to divorce and Rachel and Andrew were married in 1791. What they did not know is that Rachel's husband had not yet completed the divorce. Legally, Rachel was a bigamist and the future president an adulterer. When these charges were publicized, anonymously, during Jackson's presidential campaigns, they reinforced Jackson's hatred of his opponents and his desire to sharpen, rather than smooth over, the divisions between his party and that of the opposition.

During the WAR OF 1812, Jackson won fame that transcended the boundaries of Tennessee. Nicknamed "Old Hickory" by his troops in recognition of his toughness, he led his soldiers in the defeat of a force of 1,000 Creek Indians at the Battle of Horseshoe Bend in March 1814. His success in bringing the Creek War to an end earned Jackson appointment as a major general in the Regular Army, with responsibility for the 7th Military District of the United States, which included Louisiana.

On January 8, 1815, Jackson led a force made up of regular soldiers, sailors and marines, militiamen, volunteers, Indians, pirates and freed blacks, in a stunning defeat of veteran British troops. The battle took place after the Treaty of Ghent, formally ending the war, had been signed, but was important nonetheless. First, the peace treaty had

President Andrew Jackson *(Library of Congress)*

left open the possibility that Britain would seek to separate the broad expanse of Louisiana from the United States. Only Jackson's victory ensured the physical integrity of the nation. Second, the slaughter of 2,000 British troops in a conflict in which U.S. casualties numbered 21, was a source of immense pride for most Americans and reinforced confidence in their nation and its destiny.

After the War of 1812, Jackson had one more military service to perform for his nation. He was ordered by President James MONROE to check the incursion of Seminole Indians against settlers in Georgia. Exceeding his instructions, Jackson invaded Spanish Florida. Acting as a virtual warlord, Jackson captured the capital of Florida, executed two British subjects, whom he accused of aiding hostile Indians, and destroyed numerous Seminole villages. Jackson's actions caused controversy in Washington but had the practical consequence of hastening Spain's decision to relinquish Florida to the United States.

Presidency

Jackson's exploits had earned him a new nickname, "the Hero," and it was as the nation's most exalted war hero since George WASHINGTON that Jackson's supporters pressed him to run for president. In his first attempt at the office, in 1824, Jackson won a popular plurality but lost the election. In a crowded race with five principal contenders, no candidate won a majority of ELECTORAL COLLEGE votes, and the contest was decided in the House of Representatives. With the support of House Speaker Henry CLAY, the second-place finisher, John Quincy ADAMS, won the presidency.

In 1828 Jackson's men entered the contest with a grudge against the incumbent. Adams, they alleged, had won the White House through a "Corrupt Bargain" with Clay, whom Adams then appointed secretary of State, a traditional stepping-stone in those days to the presidency. Jackson won easily in 1828 and won reelection four years later. The enthusiasm for Jackson united a majority of voters across the nation and helped to transform the DEMOCRATIC PARTY into the nation's first *mass-based* partisan institution.

Jackson's presidency was marked by his handling of several crises. The first year of the Jackson presidency was absorbed by a scandal revolving about John Eaton, Jackson's secretary of War and a friend from Tennessee. Eaton's young bride, Peggy, had been married to another man when she and then-Senator John Eaton first came to the attention of Washington gossips as a couple. Jackson's wife, Rachel, had died while he was president-elect, and the slanders against his "little friend Peg" clearly reminded the president of the charges that had been hurled at his wife. The CABINET split over the Eaton affair, which was relayed to the nation through the popular press. Jackson stood by the Eatons and so did Martin VAN BUREN, who thereby earned the enduring gratitude of the president and positioned himself to follow Jackson into the presidency. The other significant crises of Jackson's presidency were less personal, beginning with the issue of Indian Removal. Demographic and economic pressures pitted settlers in Georgia against Indian tribes. Georgia claimed authority to remove Indians from their lands, in concert with the Indian Removal Act passed by Congress in 1830, which empowered the president to trade land in the "Great American Desert" for more desirable land coveted by whites. Despite Supreme Court rulings that upheld Indian tribal sovereignty and denied Georgia's authority to force the Cherokee off their land, President Jackson sided with Georgia's government. Under President Jackson's orders, the U.S. Army forcibly escorted 15,000 Cherokee Indians along the "Trail of Tears" to present-day Oklahoma.

In the Indian Removal controversy, Jackson sided against the Supreme Court and in favor of a popular mythic conception of the United States as a white settler society. Another myth about the United States that was popular at that time, especially in the South, was that the government represented a perhaps temporary union of convenience. This myth was anathema to Jackson, who demonstrated his devotion to the union in the NULLIFICATION Crisis of 1832. The crisis had come to a head in that year with South Carolina's issuance of a Nullification Ordinance declaring a newly passed tariff law null and void in that state. The issue of the tariff was resolved through compromise and a new tariff passed the next year. In the meantime, however, Jackson took the opportunity that South Carolina's defiance presented to thunder his support for the inviolability of the federal union. To underline how seriously he took South Carolina's thinly veiled threat of secession, he obtained from Congress a "Force Bill," authorizing the president to use military force to collect import duties and uphold national sovereignty.

President Jackson was strong for union, then, as he was strong for his friends and for the alleged right of white settlers to spread across the continent, but he was not in favor of a strong central government. Jackson had not entered the presidency with an agenda or platform. During his first term, however, as his supporters and opponents coalesced into rival parties, the president was forced by events to declare where he stood on a number of important issues. Increasingly, Jackson stood for limited central government, and therefore against internal improvements (interstate roads, bridges, and canals built with federal money), federal taxes, and the nation's central bank. His stand against the Second BANK OF THE UNITED STATES became the centerpiece of his bid for reelection and was the issue over which Jackson proclaimed a new theory of presidential power and forever changed the presidency.

In the Bank War the president declared himself the "direct representative of the American people" in their government, which was a novel perspective on the presidency. From this time forward, the presidency was to be a popular, democratic office, whose occupant was to be supported by the will of a mass party.

The Jacksonian revolution in government was made complete in 1840. In that year, the anti-Jacksonian Whigs defeated Jackson's handpicked successor, Martin Van Buren, who was up for reelection. They did so by offering to the people their own version of Old Hickory, in the persona of William Henry HARRISON, another hero of Indian warfare on the frontier.

Further reading: Latner, Richard B. *The Presidency of Andrew Jackson: White House Politics, 1829–1837.* Athens: University of Georgia Press, 1979; Myers, Marvin. *The Jacksonian Persuasion.* Stanford, Calif.: Stanford University Press, 1957; Remini, Robert V. *Andrew Jackson and the Course of American Empire, 1767–1821; Andrew Jackson and the Course of American Freedom, 1822–1832; Andrew Jackson and the Course of American Democracy, 1833–1845.* New York: Harper & Row, 1977, 1981, 1984; Ward, John William. *Andrew Jackson: Symbol for an Age.* New York: Oxford University Press, 1955; White, Leonard D. *The Jacksonians: A Study in Administrative History.* New York: Macmillan, 1954.
—Thomas Langston

Japanese-American internment

Seventy-four days after Pearl Harbor, President Franklin ROOSEVELT signed Executive Order 9066 authorizing the secretary of War and military commanders to establish military areas on the West coast—which included portions of western Washington and Oregon, California, and southern Arizona—from which were excluded more than 110,000 persons of Japanese ancestry. Approximately two-thirds of those involved were second-generation Japanese Americans, or Nisei, who were citizens. Many were young, with half of them being under 21 years of age. There were also quite a number of elderly citizens. The purpose of the president's executive order was to protect West Coast defensive war installations from possible espionage and sabotage. The secretary of War and military commanders were given the freedom to take any steps they deemed necessary to enforce compliance with the restrictions applicable to each military area. Commanding General John L. DeWitt of the Western Defense Command, who oversaw the entire operation, was very suspicious of all Japanese Americans, reasoning that "[a] Jap's a Jap . . . They are a dangerous element, whether loyal or not . . . The Japanese race is an enemy race and while many second and third generation Japanese born on U.S. soil, possessed of U.S. citizenship have become 'Americanized,' the racial strains are undiluted."

These internees were first housed in 12 temporary Assembly Centers, primarily located in California, and then they were sent to 10 poorly built, more permanent relocation centers. All of the relocation centers were barbed-wired and guarded concentration camps located in rural areas of California, Arizona, Arkansas, Idaho, Utah, Wyoming, and Colorado. In addition to the relocation centers, there were four temporary Justice Department internment camps located in New Mexico, North Dakota, Texas, and Montana, and two "citizen isolation" camps located in Utah and Arizona for those the government considered to be difficult cases. None of these encampments gave adequate protection from the extreme hot and cold temperatures. Of greatest concern to the internees as far as their living arrangements, according to Michi Weglyn, was feeling like ". . . debased human beings . . . being guarded night and day by soldiers up in guard towers." As one of the Japanese Americans stated on arriving at one of the internment camps: "This evacuation did not seem too unfair until we got right to the camp and were met by soldiers with guns and bayonets. Then I almost started screaming."

One of the worst long-range consequences of these repressive conditions was that there was no oversight over these military decisions that were made—no CHECKS AND BALANCES—since most of the important decision-makers were in full support of the military's decisions, including President Roosevelt, Earl Warren (then California attorney general and later chief justice of one of the most progressive Supreme Courts) and Supreme Court Justices William O. Douglas and Felix Frankfurter.

No espionage or sabotage activity was ever found linked to these internees. Nor were German Americans or Italian Americans incarcerated in such staggering numbers. Because of this, a federal commission in 1982 recognized that much of the motivation for the internment had been based on racial prejudice and the hysteria of the war years. By 1988 Congress finally passed and President REAGAN signed legislation that both apologized to those who had been incarcerated and paid $20,000 to each internee still living.

Further reading: DeWitt, Gen. J. L. *Final Report: Japanese Evacuation from the West Coast, 1942.* Washington, D.C.: U.S. Govt. print. off., 1943; Irons, Peter. *Justice Delayed: The Record of the Japanese American Internment Cases.* Middleton, Conn.: Wesleyan University Press, 1989; Weglyn, Michi. *Years of Infamy: The Untold Story of America's Concentration Camps.* New York: Morrow, 1976.
—Byron W. Daynes

Jaworski, Leon (1905–1982) *lawyer*

Leon Jaworski was a Texas attorney and a former president of the American Bar Association when he was selected to replace Archibald COX as the WATERGATE SPECIAL PROSECUTOR in November 1973. In fact, Jaworski had been asked to serve as special prosecutor before Cox had been approached, but he declined the offer because of his concern for lack of independence—exactly the quality that was responsible for Cox's dismissal. However, on October 30, a mere 10 days after the "Saturday Night Massacre" that had resulted in the firing of Cox, as well as the departure of the attorney general and the deputy attorney general, Jaworski was approached by Alexander Haig, Nixon's CHIEF OF STAFF, and was asked to consider, once again, taking the special prosecutor's position. After making very clear to Haig his demand for a guarantee of independence and getting it, he agreed to serve. One major revision in the provisions under which Jaworski served was that the regulation now contained a LEGISLATIVE VETO in it, requiring the consensus of eight members of Congress before the president could remove the special prosecutor.

Jaworski picked up where Cox had left off, and he had the immense responsibility of carrying the investigation to the Supreme Court. Jaworski ultimately received the tapes subpoenaed by Cox, providing him with enough evidence

to indict seven conspirators, including former Attorney General John MITCHELL, and White House aides Bob Haldeman and John Ehrlichman, on charges of conspiring to obstruct justice. Jaworski was also responsible for the position that a sitting president could not be indicted, and, thus, President NIXON was named, instead, as an unindicted coconspirator. Evidence gathered by Jaworski for use in the grand jury was ordered by District Court Judge Sirica to be given to the House Judiciary Committee as information to aid it in its impeachment investigation.

Jaworski requested 64 more tapes from the president, and, once again, the president balked, claiming that EXECUTIVE PRIVILEGE protected the confidentiality of his conversations with his White House aides, and, once again, the lower court ordered the president to comply. Nixon asked the Court of Appeals to overturn the District Court order, but Jaworski took the bold move of petitioning the U.S. Supreme Court under the Court's rule of "imperative public importance," asking it to bypass the Court of Appeals and take the case on an expedited basis. The Court agreed, and it heard oral argument in the case of *UNITED STATES V. NIXON* on July 8, 1974. The Court ruled 8-0 on July 24 that the president's claim of an absolute, unqualified privilege of confidentiality could not prevail over a subpoena for evidence needed in a criminal proceeding. It ordered him to release the tapes to Jaworski, but it took almost two weeks before Nixon began to comply. By July 27 the House Judiciary Committee had voted three articles of IMPEACHMENT against the president, and the process was in full motion. On August 9, 1974, Richard Nixon resigned from the presidency. Leon Jaworski had been the pivotal figure in this drama that ended with the first RESIGNATION from office of a sitting president.

Further reading: Dole, Robert, and George J. Mitchell. "Report and Recommendations: Project on the Independent Counsel Statute." Washington, D.C.: American Enterprise Institute and Brookings Institution, 1999, pp. 5–8; Jaworski, Leon. *The Right and the Power: The Prosecution of Watergate.* New York: Pocket Books, 1976.
—Nancy Kassop

Jay, John (1745–1829) *first chief justice of the U.S. Supreme Court, governor, diplomat*

One of the foremost men of the Founding era, John Jay was a diplomat, governor of New York, and was appointed by Washington as the first Chief Justice of the United States.

Jay was the primary author of the state constitution of New York. This constitution, with a fairly strong and independent governor, influenced the inventors of the governor's office and was used as a model of the presidency. Although he did not attend the constitutional convention,

Jay was a fervent supporter of the Constitution and wrote five of the FEDERALIST PAPERS (Nos. 2, 3, 4, 5, and 64).

As Chief Justice, Jay was asked by Washington to serve as envoy to England to resolve a dispute over the seizure of American ships by the British. The result, JAY'S TREATY, proved controversial but was approved by the Senate.

President WASHINGTON asked for an advisory opinion from the Supreme Court on the constitutionality of a matter of INTERNATIONAL LAW. Jay refused to comply with Washington's request on the grounds that it violated the SEPARATION OF POWERS. This set a precedent later Courts would follow.

Jay resigned from the Court, believing the judiciary was too weak to be a major player in the government. He ran for, and won, the governorship of New York, retiring from public life in 1801.

Jay's Treaty

President George WASHINGTON sent Chief Justice John JAY to England to negotiate a treaty to settle several disputes with Great Britain. The treaty settled some issues such as trade and treaty-removal questions, but it did not stop Britain from searching American ships.

The 1795 treaty was controversial in the United States and exposed the growing differences between the Federalists (Washington) and the Jeffersonian Democratic-Republicans. Senate ratification was difficult but achieved. Since the treaty required U.S. payment of some previously disputed debts, the House also had to ratify the spending of government money. After a bitter debate the expenditure was approved, but mobs burned Jay's effigy in the streets and Jeffersonians accused Washington of selling out to the British.

Further reading: Bemis, Samuel Flagg. *Jay's Treaty: A Study in Commerce and Diplomacy.* Westport, Conn.: Greenwood Press, 1957; Combs, Jerald A. *The Jay Treaty: Political Battleground of the Founding Fathers.* Berkeley: University of California Press, 1970; DeConde, Alexander. *Entangling Alliance; Politics and Diplomacy under George Washington.* Durham, N.C.: Duke University Press, 1958.

Jefferson, Thomas (1743–1826) *third U.S. president*

In his personal inventory of the trio of accomplishments of which he was most proud, Thomas Jefferson omitted his service as president of the United States (1801–09). Instead, Jefferson stated in his will that he wanted to be remembered for three things: (1) as author of the Declaration of Independence, (2) as author of the Virginia Statute of Religious Freedom, the model for the First Amendment to the U.S. Constitution, and (3) as founder of the University of Virginia. These three seminal contributions to the nation he helped to found endure as viable legacies of his creative genius, foundations upon which collective human rights—as well as individual dignity—continue to develop. It is ironic that he did not mention his presidency, since scholars rank him as one of the four greatest presidents in American history. Nor did Jefferson consider his service as the nation's first secretary of State under George WASHINGTON (1789–94), though he is also ranked by scholars as one of the best secretaries of state, among his top three accomplishments. Neither did he seek to be remembered as a lawyer, his chosen profession from 1767 to 1775, although he is considered by scholars to be one of the 10 lawyers who have most influenced development of American law. He overlooked, too, that he was founder of the world's oldest political party, and that he was the architect of his beloved MONTICELLO, which experts rank among the earliest great examples of American architecture. Jefferson's "short list" disregards the much longer list of his lifetime accomplishments, all of which support the conclusion that he is the greatest "Renaissance man" to hold the presidency.

Lawyer for Democracy

Jefferson was born into the Virginia gentry on the western fringe of Virginia on April 13, 1743. His father, a planter and surveyor, was also a local justice of the peace and member of Virginia's House of Burgesses. His mother was descended from one of the colonies' most prominent families, the Randolphs. He attended the College of William and Mary, and for five years he studied law with the colonies' most distinguished jurist, George Wythe, who became a father figure for Jefferson. In 1767 he was admitted to the Virginia bar, embarking on a successful eight-year career as a lawyer. Within two years of obtaining his license to practice the law, young Jefferson expanded his sphere of interest into politics. In 1769 Jefferson, like his father before him, took a seat in the Virginia House of Burgesses, his transition into a 40-year political career in legislative and executive branches of government. Only two years later, Jefferson demonstrated his innate abilities in the case of *Bolling v. Bolling* (1771), considered by some scholars as one of the greatest trials in American history. The case pitted defense attorney Jefferson against former mentor Wythe, who represented the plaintiff. The case between brothers involved technical issues of property and succession law. Jefferson bested Wythe, employing the same extraordinary ability to reason that he would later use on behalf of the colonies to best England.

Despite a dislike for lawyers, Jefferson used his professional skills on behalf of the independence movement. The Virginia legislature sent him to the Second Continental Congress in 1775, and the next year he drafted the Declaration of Independence, adopted on July 4, 1776, after some modification. In it, he used natural law jurisprudence to assert *the equal rights* of people and deliberately directed his rhetoric at the king rather than blame the British Parliament for violating the colonies. Jefferson had no intention of creating a situation in which the monarchy would be replaced by demagoguery. Later that year Jefferson turned his attention to religious freedom and composed the Virginia statute that his nearby neighbor and friend, James MADISON, would eventually advocate as a First Amendment guarantee within the Bill of Rights adopted during his presidency.

Jefferson's first executive experience was as Virginia's governor, elected in 1779 by the Virginia legislature. His was a controversial state performance that included a hurried departure from the Virginia capital to avoid the enemy—a scenario nearly duplicated on the national level by his protégé and presidential successor, James Madison, who had to flee Washington during the WAR OF 1812. Jefferson had the opportunity to rebut his legislative critics during a subsequent inquiry into his conduct, although latter-day partisan historians have tried Jefferson's protégé *in absentia.*

Jefferson's 33-year-old wife died in 1782 after a 10-year marriage, leaving him a widower with six children. The next year, as a member of his state's congressional delegation, Jefferson focused on drafting a plan with admission procedures for new states on the basis of equality. His rationale was later adopted as the basis for the better-known Northwest Ordinance of 1787, which also banned slavery from the new territory north of the Ohio River.

In 1784 Jefferson accepted the congressional appointment as U.S. minister to France, replacing Benjamin Franklin. Jefferson immersed himself in his diplomatic duties in France but found time abroad to write one of only two books he would author. *Notes on the State of Virginia,* published in 1785, reveals Jefferson's comparatively scientific outlook on society. Among topics he addressed was slavery, arguing for eventual emancipation. Jefferson returned from his five-year diplomatic assignment convinced of the need for a stronger U.S. government so that American foreign policy would be taken more seriously abroad.

His diplomatic service yielded political rewards. George Washington appointed him as the first secretary of State (March 22, 1790–Dec. 31, 1793). During his tenure, Jefferson established numerous diplomatic and administrative precedents, and he supported efforts by the Washington administration to maintain U.S. neutrality as war broke out between France and Great Britain in 1793. It was Jefferson's opposition to Alexander HAMILTON's influence on domestic and foreign policy that led to his resignation from Washington's CABINET at the end of 1793. Similarly, opposition to Hamilton was Jefferson's impetus for becoming one of the chief architects of America's first political party—the Democratic-Republican party, established to counter Hamilton's influence on Washington.

Transition to the Presidency

During the 1796 presidential election, Jefferson, champion of the new Democratic-Republicans, opposed John ADAMS, who had been Washington's two-term moderate Federalist VICE PRESIDENT. Adams received 71 ballots to Jefferson's 68 in the close ELECTORAL COLLEGE vote, making Jefferson vice president under election rules at that time. The new Federalist regime blocked Vice President Jefferson from the administrative policy-making process. In this vice-presidential vacuum, Jefferson turned his creative energies to compiling his second book, *Manual of Parliamentary Procedure,* containing precedents that the U.S. Senate still uses as a guide in conducting its legislative business.

The beginning of the end for the Federalists was in their overreaction to the challenge mounted by the Democratic-Republicans. The overreaction was manifested in passage by the Federalist Congress of the infamous ALIEN AND SEDITION ACTS of 1789, the massive assault on CIVIL LIBERTIES that made it a crime to criticize the policies of the Federalist administration. By reluctantly signing his party's congressional initiative, Adams effectively signed his own political death warrant. In the 1800 election, President Adams and Vice President Jefferson opposed each other. In close Electoral College balloting, Jefferson and Aaron BURR, his Republican vice-presidential running mate, tied for first with 73 votes each. Adams was third with 65 ballots, and the Federalist vice presidential candidate, Charles Pinckney, received 64. According to prevailing Electoral College rules, the election was thrown into the U.S. House of Representatives. The ambitious Burr broke his promise to acquiesce to Jefferson if there were a tie presidential vote. It took 36 additional ballots and, ironically, the support of Jefferson's nemesis, Hamilton, to sway the lame-duck Federalist House majority to support Jefferson. With Hamilton's support, 10 state delegations voted for Jefferson, four for Burr, and two divided delegations abstained. Jefferson was declared president on February 17, 1801, and Burr became vice president as well as a pariah to the Democratic-Republicans. Jefferson acknowledged the aid of his former archrival by placing a bust of Hamilton above the vestibule to Monticello, symbolic of how America's third president would govern.

Jefferson's Legacy to the Presidency

The most significant legacy of the Jefferson presidency was the establishment of a precedent in the United States for the peaceful transition of power from one political party to another. The orderly transfer of power between political parties was echoed in Jefferson's presidential rhetoric. In his first inaugural address, he proclaimed "We are all republicans: we are all federalists." He emulated George Washington's example of using the presidential power to pardon, first to grant clemency to those who had been jailed under the Alien and Sedition Acts and offering AMNESTY to others later in his term.

Even though he founded the first political party and governed through the Democratic-Republicans, Jefferson desired to eliminate partisan politics. He abandoned the FEDERALIST PARTY leadership of his predecessors in favor of a variety of informal methods to retain the loyalty of his moderate Republican CABINET appointees and members of Congress. Jefferson exhibited a strong work ethic and never used the veto. Most legislation originated with Jefferson and he shepherded his bills through the Congress, personally lobbying senators and representatives. He turned the presidential mansion into a social club where he wined and dined congressmen. Democratic-Republican majorities in Congress responded positively to his personal approach. His collegial manner was also evident with his cabinet, contributing to his ability to retain the loyalty of its members. James Madison, for example, served as secretary of state during both of Jefferson's presidential terms. The political spoils system was distasteful to Jefferson and he followed a moderate policy in his appointments and removals from executive positions in his administration. His reputation and his moderation drew others to him.

During his presidency, Jefferson attempted to make the position more democratic and less regal through a series of changes. He walked to his first inaugural ceremony without the escort that had become usual for the president-elect en route to his inauguration. He dressed simply and continued his daily practice of riding through the nation's capital. Jefferson submitted written annual messages to the Congress rather than appear in person to deliver his message, a technique he used to contrast the British king's annual appearance before Parliament. He abandoned formal PROTOCOL at the presidential house, eschewed holding birthday balls and weekly levees there for the socially elite in favor of opening it twice a year to the public.

In terms of public policy, Jeffersonian rhetoric called for limited government, states' rights, and neutrality in European affairs. To accomplish his public policy goals, he tried to reduce government expenditures by means such as closing half of the American embassies in Europe. He reduced the size of the army and navy in response to Republican fear of the potential threat to liberty they perceived in a standing military. Jefferson tried to dilute the power of the Federalist-dominated judiciary by repealing the Judiciary Act of 1800, which had created 16 new judgeships and a new circuit court system. His distant relative John MARSHALL outmaneuvered him by claiming for the Supreme Court of the United States the power of judicial

President Thomas Jefferson *(Library of Congress)*

review in *MARBURY V. MADISON* (1803) and thwarting the impeachment trial of Supreme Court Justice Samuel Chase when the Senate failed to convict Chase.

Despite Jefferson's often romantic and idealistic rhetoric, he also had a pragmatic side. He typically adjusted to reality when confronted by problems and opportunities. By late 1803 Jefferson had suppressed his constitutional prudery to accept Napoleon's offer to sell Louisiana to the United States for $15 million. The Senate ratified the LOUISIANA PURCHASE in October, and the size of the United States doubled under Jefferson's presidency. Consistent with his scientific inclinations, he authorized the Lewis and Clark expedition (1803 to 1806) and a second expedition to explore the southern boundary of Louisiana. In addition, Jefferson was the COMMANDER IN CHIEF during the four-year naval war with Tripoli that ended the practice of the United States having to pay tribute to Tripoli in exchange for Tripoli's protection of American merchant ships from Barbary pirates.

The Presidential Encore

Jefferson's first term successes led to an easy reelection in which he and his vice presidential running mate, New York Governor George CLINTON, swept 15 states to two in Electoral College balloting. They defeated Federalists Charles Pinckney and Rufus King.

The major issue facing the United States was the threat of being dragged into the Napoleonic wars. Jefferson opted for an economic rather than a military response. In December 1807 the Congress approved Jefferson's first EMBARGO ACT, which prohibited the export of American goods. The mixed results of this policy set the stage for the WAR OF 1812 during Madison's administration. When Jefferson's presidency expired, so did the Embargo Act, and Congress replaced it with the Nonintercourse Act.

The Legacy

Critics like to point out inconsistencies and flaws in Jefferson's record. For instance, during the Alien and Sedition Acts controversy, he secretly drafted the Kentucky Resolutions that would allow states to nullify federal laws that they considered unconstitutional, a position that ultimately was resolved by the CIVIL WAR. Jefferson supported Congress in making the African slave trade illegal even though he needed slaves to maintain Monticello and remained a slaveholder, freeing only a few of his slaves. His excesses in CIVIL LIBERTIES led to Justice Chase's IMPEACHMENT as well as the treason trial of Aaron Burr, whom John Marshall was forced to acquit. Critics also note the role of Jefferson's Embargo Act in starting the War of 1812.

Despite these flaws, Jefferson's positive political legacy far exceeds any shortcomings. And it also extends well beyond the three accomplishments that he specifically noted in his will. In most polls of experts, Jefferson is rated as one of the greatest American presidents. Only Abraham LINCOLN, Franklin ROOSEVELT, and George Washington are ranked higher. Jefferson, the "Renaissance man," was a blend of democratic idealism tempered by scientific method and pragmatism. In theory he subcribed to the philosophy of HUMAN RIGHTS, but practically he understood the nature of self-government and its limitations. His major contribution to the presidency was the precedent of peaceful transition between political parties. He was able to rally his allies and potential allies by exerting strong leadership in Congress and among his cabinet members using his considerable powers of informal persuasion. Jefferson was flexible in his leadership, capable of modifying idealism when political reality required it. He left a worldwide standard for democratic leadership for subsequent generations.

His death at Monticello on July 4, 1826, the 50th anniversary of the Declaration of Independence, is the stuff of legend, but legend is overshadowed by the legacy of Jefferson as a leader who moved democracy forward despite political challenges.

Further reading: Cunningham, Noble E. *In Pursuit of Reason: The Life of Thomas Jefferson.* Baton Rouge: Louisiana State University Press, 1987; Ellis, Joseph T. *American Sphinx: The Character of Thomas Jefferson.* New York: Knopf, 1997; Malone, Dumas. *Thomas Jefferson as Political Leader.* Westport, Conn.: Greenwood Press, 1979; McDonald, Forrest. *The Presidency of Thomas Jefferson.* Lawrence: University Press of Kansas, 1976; Onuf, Peter S., ed. *Jeffersonian Legacies.* Charlottesville: University Press of Virginia, 1993; Pederson, William D., and Ann McLaurin, eds. *The Rating Game in American Politics.* New York: Irvington Publishers, 1987; Peterson, Merrill D., ed. *Thomas Jefferson: A Reference Biography.* New York: Scribner, 1986; Tucker, Robert W. *Empire of Liberty. The Statecraft of Thomas Jefferson.* New York: Oxford University Press, 1990.

—William D. Pederson

Johnson, Andrew (1808–1875) *seventeenth U.S. president*

The first president to be impeached, Andrew Johnson's post–CIVIL WAR presidency was plagued with problems and crises. Born on December 29, 1808, in Raleigh, North Carolina, Johnson went on to become one of the least effective presidents in history.

The reaction against EXECUTIVE POWER that followed the Civil War led to a dramatic shrinking of executive power, as congressional government characterized the American system for 30 years. Congress could have had no better foil in beginning this process than the stubborn, rigid, and abrasive Andrew Johnson.

Johnson's Senate opponent, Steward of Nevada, described Johnson as "the most untruthful, treacherous, and cruel person who had ever held a place of power in the United States." No sooner did Johnson take the OATH OF OFFICE in 1865 than clashes broke out between the new administration and a Congress determined to reassert its power and shape the coming RECONSTRUCTION.

President Johnson played a pivotal role in the shrinkage of the presidency. He inherited a powerful wartime presidency but, in the aftermath of war, failed to successfully defend the prerogatives of the institutions and left the office weaker and more vulnerable to the will of Congress.

Johnson became embroiled in a divisive battle with Congress over Reconstruction. Johnson followed LINCOLN's lead in promoting a mild reconstruction designed to restore the Union quickly, but the Republican leadership in Congress, the "radicals," led by Senator Charles Sumner of Massachusetts, were determined to extract a hard price from the Southern states. The SEPARATION OF POWERS often sets up a tug-of-war between the executive and Congress for control of policy. The Republican Congress of the Reconstruction era had little patience for Johnson and was determined to undermine his efforts and grab control of policy. It did so on Reconstruction and, after the Republicans won a convincing victory in the 1866 MIDTERM ELECTIONS, passed measure after measure designed to strip the presidency of its powers.

Johnson seemed helpless in the face of the Congress. Determined to protect the authority of his office, Johnson fought back. The Radicals in Congress were livid when Johnson, during a congressional recess in December 1865, proposed a lenient reconstruction policy. When Congress reconvened, President Johnson announced that Reconstruction was complete and that every rebel state met his qualifications for readmission to the Union. However, it was anything but finished.

The Democrat Johnson and the Republican Congress engaged in open warfare. Congress dumped the president's plan for Reconstruction, replacing it with one of its own, a harsher peace than the president preferred. Congress pushed for the Fourteenth Amendment to the Constitution, which would forbid any state to deny any citizen "due process" or "equal protection" of the law. Johnson pressed Southern states to reject the amendment, but it passed anyway.

Johnson took his case directly to the people. His appeals fell mostly on deaf ears. Johnson engaged in bombast and name-calling. *The Nation* magazine characterized Johnson's charges as "vulgar, egotistical and occasionally profane."

When the congressional Radicals passed the TENURE OF OFFICE ACT, a blatant effort to reclaim the power possessed by the president to fire certain EXECUTIVE BRANCH employees without the consent of the Senate, Johnson reacted. He fired Secretary of War Edwin M. Stanton (who barricaded himself in his office in an effort to stave off removal) and claimed the act was an unconstitutional invasion of his power. This was just what the Congress needed to begin impeachment proceedings against Johnson.

The clashes between Johnson and the Congress grew angrier and angrier, with each side putting its worst foot forward. Efforts began in the House to develop articles of impeachment against Johnson. Finally, 11 articles of impeachment were brought against the president.

The impeachment effort against Andrew Johnson was a largely partisan, rather woolly affair. *New York Tribune* editor, Horace Greeley, called Johnson "an aching tooth in the national jaw, a screeching infant in a crowded lecture room," adding "There is no peace or comfort till he is out." Johnson's Republican congressional critics denounced him as "an ungrateful, despicable, besotted traitorous man—an incubus." Another said he dragged the robes of office

President Andrew Johnson *(Library of Congress)*

through "the purloins and filth of treason." And Johnson's advisers were referred to as "the worst men that ever crawled like filthy reptiles of the footstool of power." No accusation was too wild for the Johnson-bashers. He was accused of aiding in the assassination of Abraham LINCOLN, of fathering an illegitimate son, of conspiring to help the Confederacy rise again. The House voted to recommend articles of impeachment to the Senate, but after a Senate trial, the conviction failed by one vote: that of Kansas Republican Senator Edmund Ross. In the next election Ross was thrown out of office, but history remembers him as a hero who stood up for justice. In his prizewinning book *Profiles in Courage*, John F. KENNEDY praised Ross as a case study of integrity in the face of unyielding pressure.

Impeachment proceedings were instituted against President Johnson by the House of Representatives on February 24, 1868, with the following resolution: "Resolved: that Andrew Johnson be impeached of high crimes and misdemeanors." The charges brought against him included usurpation of the law, corrupt use of the veto power, interference at elections, and misdemeanors. Probably the most revealing was Article 10, which said it was an impeachable offense for the president to speak ill of Congress "with a loud voice."

After hearings on the charges, the House voted 126-47 to impeach Johnson, the first time in history a president had been impeached. This moved events to the Senate, where Chief Justice Salmon P. Chase was to preside over the trial against the president. Associate Justice Samuel Nelson of the Supreme Court administered the following oath to the Chief Justice: "I do solemnly swear that in all things appertaining to the trial of the impeachment of Andrew Johnson, President of the United States, now pending, I will do impartial justice according to the Constitution and laws. So help me God." This oath was then administered by the Chief Justice to the 54 members of the Senate.

The impeachment trial of Andrew Johnson lasted six weeks. The case against the president was weak and politically motivated.

The vote on May 16, 1868, to convict Johnson was 35 guilty, 19 not guilty, one short of the two-thirds needed to convict a president. The trial ended on May 26, 1868, with Johnson acquitted, but the president and the presidency had been put in its place. If Johnson had been convicted, the independence of the executive might have been all but destroyed. As it was, the presidency was severely weakened. Senator Trumball, who voted not guilty, gave his reasoning:

> Once set the example of impeaching the President, for what, when the excitement of the hour shall have subsided will be regarded as insufficient causes, . . . and no future president will be safe who happens to differ with a majority of the House and two-thirds of the Senate on any measure deemed by them important, particularly if of a political character. Blinded by partisan zeal, with such an example before them, they will not scruple to remove out of the way any obstacle to the accomplishment of their purposes, and what then becomes of the checks and balances of the Constitution, so carefully devised and so vital to its perpetuity? They are all gone.

All was not tragedy for Andrew Johnson. His most valuable achievement was the purchase of Alaska from Russia for $7.2 million in 1867. Derisively referred to as "Seward's Folly," "Seward's Icebox," or "Johnson's Polar Bear Garden" (Seward was secretary of State and chief negotiator of the deal), it was not long before the benefits of this purchase became clear.

Navigating the choppy waters of the post-Civil War era required tact, subtleness, nuance, and flexibility—qualities Johnson lacked in abundance. He could not bend, so Congress decided to try to break him.

Some historians give Johnson credit for protecting the authority of the presidency by preventing a coup by the Radicals in Congress, but the reality is probably that he much weakened the presidency by intemperate behavior and bad decision making, and invited a harsh response by a Radical Congress that was looking for an opportunity to humble the president and limit the presidency. Johnson gave them the opportunity.

Further reading: Beale, Howard K. *The Critical Year: A Study of Andrew Johnson and the Reconstruction.* New York: Harcourt Brace, 1930; Castel, Albert. *The Presidency of Andrew Johnson.* Lawrence: Regents Press of Kansas, 1979; Dewitt, David M. *The Impeachment and Trial of Andrew Johnson, Seventeenth President of the United States: A History.* New York: Macmillan, 1903; McKitrick, Eric L. *Andrew Johnson and Reconstruction.* Chicago: University of Chicago Press, 1960; Sefton, James E. *Andrew Johnson and the Uses of Constitutional Power.* Boston: Little, Brown, 1980; Trefousse, Hans L. *Andrew Johnson: A Biography.* New York: W. W. Norton, 1989.

Johnson, Claudia Alta (Lady Bird) (1912–)
first lady

Born Claudia Alta Taylor in Texas in 1912, Lady Bird was first lady to President Lyndon Baines JOHNSON (1963–69). Her mother, Minnie Pattillo Taylor, died when she was only five years old, thus she was raised by her father, Thomas Jefferson Taylor, with the help of family and servants. Indeed, it was a nursemaid who dubbed her "Lady Bird," saying that she was as pretty as a ladybird. A good student, she is a graduate of the University of Texas at Austin, with degrees in liberal arts and journalism. In 1934 she met and married Lyndon Johnson. The two have two daughters, Lynda Bird (1944) and Luci Baines (1947).

Lady Bird Johnson was a quintessential political wife, beginning when her husband ran for and won election to the U.S. House of Representatives in 1937. She fulfilled traditional expectations in providing unwavering support and using her good nature and charm to win admirers. Yet at the same time she provided substantial substantive assistance, first when Representative Johnson was called to active duty in WORLD WAR II, keeping his congressional office moving, and again when, in 1955, he had a severe heart attack, she maintained his office as Senate Majority leader.

When her husband rose to even greater prominence in accepting the Democratic nomination for the vice presidency in 1960, Lady Bird stepped up to the challenge. She took speech lessons and traveled with him speaking to crowds. Indeed, when President Johnson ran for election in 1964, Lady Bird was instrumental in his success in the South. She traveled across the region on the "Lady Bird Special," a train trip from Washington to New Orleans, campaigning for her husband. In this way, she helped to open the door for women to make campaign appearances on behalf of their husbands.

First Lady Claudia Alta Johnson *(Library of Congress)*

As wife of the VICE PRESIDENT and later as first lady, Lady Bird Johnson maintained a careful balance between traditional roles of the first lady (e.g., ceremony and entertaining) and policy work. While she did not have her own political aspirations, and indeed felt that it was the duty of the first lady to avoid controversy (for example, she did not share her own views regarding Vietnam or the civil rights movement), there were components of her husband's policy agenda on which she worked diligently. She believed strongly in Head Start, the public preschool program, and was named its honorary chairperson. However, she is best known for her campaign to clean and beautify not only the nation's highways but also its landscape generally. In some ways challenging expectations about the role of the first lady, she participated in legislative and lobbying sessions, advocating for the Highway Beautification Act. Though she was somewhat uncomfortable with the title of this legislation, her efforts were successful, as the act became law in October of 1965.

Further reading: Boller, Paul F., Jr. *Presidential Wives.* New York: Oxford University Press, 1988; Eksterowicz, Anthony, and Kristen Paynter. "The Evolution of the Role and Office of the First Lady: The Movement Toward Integration with the White House Office." In *Social Science Journal* 37 (2000): 547–563; Klapthor, Margaret Brown. *The First Ladies.* Washington, D.C.: White House Historical Association, 1989.

—Rebecca E. Deen

Johnson, Lyndon B. (1908–1973) *thirty-sixth U.S. president*

Born on August 27, 1908, near Stonewall, Texas, Lyndon Baines Johnson, the first of five children, grew up in a family where his father was a member of the Texas legislature. Johnson was particularly close to his mother, who instilled in her son a burning ambition for success. Johnson became a schoolteacher, but politics boiled in his blood. A tireless campaigner, Johnson seemed to hunger for office more than most, and he devoted his abundant energies to electoral politics in Texas and Washington, D.C.

After a distinguished career in Congress, Lyndon Johnson sought the presidential nomination of the Democratic Party in 1960. Johnson lost the nomination to John KENNEDY, who then asked Johnson to run as his vice president. Kennedy and Johnson won a close election and LBJ went on to serve a frustrating three years as vice president.

The sudden, tragic death of President Kennedy in 1963 put Lyndon Johnson in the White House. Johnson was an experienced legislator, a big (6'3") burly Texan who seemed larger than life. He was an overbearing, domineering man of monumental ambition, an earthy sense of HUMOR, and a need to be the center of attention.

Johnson's manners tended to be imperious. He often spoke of the "State of My Union Address," and of "My Supreme Court." After reviewing some Vietnam-bound marines, President Johnson started toward a helicopter. An officer stopped him, pointed to another chopper, and said, "That's your helicopter over there, sir." "Son," said LBJ, "they are all my helicopters."

At a White House luncheon, Bill Moyers was saying grace, when Johnson interrupted: "Speak up, Bill! I can't hear a damn thing." Moyers looked up and said quietly, "I wasn't addressing you, Mr. President."

Lyndon Johnson was a legislative genius. In 1965 and 1966, he and the 89th Congress passed an astounding array of bills: Medicare, Medicaid, the CIVIL RIGHTS ACT, the War on Poverty, the Air Pollution Control Act, the Elementary and Secondary Education Act. They also created the Departments of Transportation and of Housing and Urban Development. The number of major bills passed was truly amazing. While the table may have been set by

President Lyndon B. Johnson *(LBJ Library)*

John Kennedy, it was Johnson who got the bills through Congress.

Johnson's GREAT SOCIETY rivaled the NEW DEAL in size and importance. "There is but one way for a president to deal with the Congress," Johnson said, "and that is continuously, incessantly, and without interruption. If it's going to work, the relationship between the president and Congress has got to be almost incestuous." No other president had Johnson's understanding of the Congress or its members. He knew their strengths, weaknesses, what they liked to drink, and what they did in their spare time. He knew when to push, where to push, how far to push. "I pleaded, I reasoned, I argued, I urged, I warned," said Johnson of his lobbying efforts.

It all seemed so grand. Lyndon Johnson's remarkable legislative achievements in the wake of John Kennedy's tragic assassination seemed to confirm for many the wisdom of the strong-presidency model: The presidency was seen as the seat of wisdom, virtue, and effectiveness, and Lyndon Johnson looked like strong leader.

Just when the public was lulled into a false sense of complacency and security concerning the benevolence of presidential power, things began to change. And they changed quickly and dramatically. It started with the VIETNAM WAR.

U.S. involvement in Vietnam began quietly, escalated slowly, and eventually led to tragedy. By 1966 the United States was engaged in a war that it could not win and from which it could not (honorably) withdraw. It was a "presidential war," and it brought the Johnson administration to its knees.

As U.S. involvement escalated, and as victory seemed farther and farther away, blame was placed squarely on the shoulders of President Johnson. Although the Constitution gives the power to declare war to the Congress, in practice since the TRUMAN administration and the "Korean Conflict," presidents have often acted unilaterally in this regard. By the time Johnson came to office, presidents had been setting policy in Vietnam for 20 years, virtually unencumbered by the Congress. As U.S. involvement escalated, it was the president who was calling the shots. The tragedy of Lyndon Johnson is that after such a sterling start, after such great success, the blunder of Vietnam would overwhelm him and the nation. From such great heights, the president fell to such tragic depths. The nation was torn apart. The glue that bound Americans together had lost its adhesiveness, and in its place, divisiveness and conflict overtook the nation. The strong presidency, so long the savior of the American system, now seemed too powerful, too dangerous, too unchecked—in short, a threat. After years of hearing calls for "more power to the president," by the late 1960s the plea was to rein in the overly powerful "monster" in the White House.

It was a rude awakening. All the hopes, all the trust, all the expectations that had been entrusted to the presidency were being shattered. Johnson was compelled not to seek reelection in 1968 when faced with the near-certainty of electoral defeat.

As president, Lyndon Johnson rose to the heights, then hit rock bottom. He had a far-reaching and positive impact on the lives of black Americans. His Great Society programs greatly improved the quality of life for many Americans, especially the poor. But Vietnam haunted the Johnson legacy. It was his glaring weakness.

At first Johnson expanded the power of the presidency and generated high expectations for what the office could and should accomplish, but with Vietnam, support for the presidency went into free fall. He achieved much: the Civil Rights Act of 1964, the Economic Opportunity Act of 1984, Medicare, Medicaid, the Elementary and Secondary Education Act of 1965, the Higher Education Act of 1965, and the Voting Rights Act of 1965. But he failed mightily as well, in Vietnam and the domestic disturbances of the '60s.

After Johnson announced he would not seek another term as president, he went into a deep depression: "I've never felt lower in my life. How do you think it feels to be completely rejected by the party you've spent your life with, knowing that your name cannot be mentioned without choruses of boos and obscenities? How would you feel? It makes me feel that nothing's been worth it. And I've tried. Things may not have turned out as you wanted or even as I wanted. But God knows I've tried. And I've given

it my best all these years. I woke up at six and worked until one or two in the morning every day, Saturdays and Sundays. And it comes to this. It just doesn't seem fair."

In a book about his former boss, President Johnson, published in 1982, Press Secretary George Reedy wrote the following.

> He may have been a son of a bitch but he was a colossal son of a bitch. He also possessed the finest quality of a politician. It was a sense of the direction of political power—the forces that were sweeping the masses. He did not merely content himself by getting ahead of those forces. He mastered the art of directing them . . . Of all his qualities, however, the most important was that he knew how to make our form of government work. That is an art that has been lost since his passing and we are suffering heavily as a result.

Further reading: Bornet, Vaughn D. *Presidency of Lyndon B. Johnson*. Lawrence: University Press of Kansas, 1983; Califano, Joseph A. *The Triumph & Tragedy of Lyndon Johnson: The White House Years*. New York: Simon & Schuster, 1991; Goldman, Eric F. *The Tragedy of Lyndon Johnson: A Historian's Interpretation*. New York: Knopf, 1969; Kearns, Doris. *Lyndon Johnson and the American Dream*. New York: Harper & Row, 1976.

Johnson, Richard M. (1781–1850) *U.S. vice president*
Richard M. Johnson was the ninth VICE PRESIDENT of the United States. A hero of the WAR OF 1812, where he allegedly killed famed Chief Tecumseh, Johnson became a powerful member of Congress and later served as vice president under Martin VAN BUREN. Johnson failed to receive a majority of electoral votes and, consequently, the decision on the new vice president went to the Senate which elected him to the post.

Joint Chiefs of Staff (JCS)
The Joint Chiefs of Staff was created in 1947 by the NATIONAL SECURITY ACT, a postwar effort to make more orderly the nation's newly expanded military establishment. The idea for something like a JCS had been popular among military reformers for a long time before its creation. Secretary of War John C. CALHOUN, in fact, decades before the CIVIL WAR, had drafted plans for a "general staff" that would bring together in one place the leading officers of the different services and compel them to work together in making plans and offering advice to their civilian superior, the COMMANDER IN CHIEF. Calls for centralizing the military's leadership had proven liable over many years to attack from entrenched interests within the military. Efforts to centralize military decision-making also routinely encountered

opposition from members of Congress who preferred that the military remain divided and therefore weak in political influence.

While some progress toward a more rational organization of military expertise had been made in the United States in the aftermath of the SPANISH-AMERICAN WAR, only after WORLD WAR II did the nation's government create a modern defense apparatus, including a unified DEFENSE DEPARTMENT (at first known formally as the National Military Establishment), the CENTRAL INTELLIGENCE AGENCY, the NATIONAL SECURITY COUNCIL, and the JCS.

The members of the JCS are the chiefs of staffs of the army and the navy, the chief of naval operations, and the commandant of the marine corps, plus the chairman (CJCS), who can be from any of the services. All are appointed by the president, with Senate approval. All are under the command of their civilian superiors, the secretary of Defense and the president. The service chiefs serve one nonrenewable four-year term while, since 1967, the chairman has served a two-year term, which may be renewed once.

A major overhaul of the JCS was undertaken in the Goldwater-Nicholls Act of 1986. As a consequence of that legislation, the chairman's role has been strengthened considerably. The CJCS is now routinely placed in the chain of command, under the secretary of Defense and directly above the field commanders who direct men and women from the different services in joint operations. Thus the service chiefs are effectively frozen out of military command and are restricted to a strictly advisory position. The chairman, not the joint chiefs collectively, is now recognized in law as the president's supreme military adviser.

The CJCS's power was taken to its modern heights by General Colin POWELL, who served as CJCS for President George Herbert Walker BUSH and President Bill CLINTON.

Further reading: Kittfield, James. *Prodigal Soldiers.* Washington, D.C.: Brassey's, 1997; Korb, Lawrence J. *The Joint Chiefs of Staff.* Bloomington: Indiana University Press, 1976.

—Thomas Langston

judges, appointment of

Perhaps the most lasting legacy that a president of the United States leaves is the changed legal system that comes through his appointment of judges to the federal bench. During the average four-year term a president may appoint as many as two new Supreme Court justices, 20–30 court of appeals judges, and more than 100 district court judges. Because all of these judges enjoy life tenure, most will be issuing opinions on significant issues of constitutional and statutory law long after their appointing president has passed from the political scene. In studying the modern presidency, more and more scholars in recent years have begun to recognize the influential role that judicial appointments play in supporting presidential policy-making initiatives far into the future.

Appointments to the U.S. Supreme Court tend to garner the most attention by far. Article II, Section 2, of the U.S. Constitution vests presidents with the power to "nominate, and by and with the Advice and Consent of the Senate . . . appoint . . . Judges of the Supreme Court." Because Congress has not altered the size of the Court in well over a century (since 1869 the Court's maximum capacity has stood at nine justices), a modern president's capacity to influence the Surpreme Court through new appointments rests entirely on the fortuitous timing of individual justices' retirements. Thus while President Dwight EISENHOWER got to name five new justices to the Court during his eight years in office, President CLINTON nominated just two justices during an administration that ran the same length. President William Howard TAFT appointed six new justices during a single four-year term, while President Jimmy CARTER named not a single justice during his sole term in office. Some presidents have grown impatient waiting for such opportunities to arise: In 1965 President Lyndon Johnson helped lure Justice Arthur Goldberg off the Court with the promise of a UN ambassadorship, just so that he could name close friend and adviser Abe Fortas to the high Court in Goldberg's place.

When vacancies on the Supreme Court do in fact arise, the factors that enter into the selection of Supreme Court nominees vary widely from president to president, and sometimes even from vacancy to vacancy within a particular presidency. Since the 1950s, a candidate's so-called ideology (including perceptions of how he or she might vote on hot-button political issues such as abortion and school prayer) has been a dominant concern of the president and his advisers. Earlier administrations invested a modest amount of work into researching candidates; in the 1980s and early 1990s, Presidents REAGAN and George H. W. Bush dedicated unprecedented levels of administrative manpower toward comprehensively reviewing potential candidates' judicial opinions and/or law review articles for evidence of how they might rule on key issues of the day. Still, no amount of background research can predict with absolute accuracy how a new justice will vote once he finds himself on the high Court. President Eisenhower was clearly frustrated with the liberal voting patterns of two of his own Supreme Court selections, Chief Justice Earl Warren and Justice William Brennan—Eisenhower was rumored to have called their appointments "the two biggest mistakes" of his presidency. Similarly, conservative supporters of President George H. W. Bush would eventually be frustrated by Bush's selection of David Souter for the

Supreme Court in 1990; Souter went on to cast a key vote saving *Roe v. Wade* (the 1973 opinion recognizing a constitutional right to abortion).

A candidate's perceived judicial competence and integrity may also play a role in helping him or her secure a presidential appointment to the Supreme Court. Certainly, less-qualified nominees may reflect badly on the administration itself; they also stand a lesser chance of surviving Senate confirmation. During the past 60 years the American Bar Association has ranked every Supreme Court nominee on the basis of his or her qualifications to serve on the high Court. Thus when choosing nominees, presidents are quite conscious of how that candidate might be viewed by the ABA, as well as by other interest groups.

A president must also take into account the immediate political environment that surrounds a particular vacancy when choosing a nominee. For example, the public's interest in having a diverse Supreme Court may dictate that a president look to female candidates, or those who represent a racial or ethnic minority. When the Supreme Court's first African-American Justice, Thurgood Marshall, resigned from the Court in 1991, President George H. W. Bush and his aides felt considerable political pressure to replace him with another African-American candidate (they ultimately settled on Clarence Thomas, an African American then sitting on the U.S. Court of Appeals in Washington). President Reagan made good on his campaign promise to name the first female to the Supreme Court (he tapped Sandra Day O'Connor for the high Court in 1981). The religious affiliation of candidates has also played a role in securing Supreme Court nominations for certain individuals; the media has sometimes written of a "Jewish seat" or a "Catholic seat" on the Court, and presidents are often conscious of the need to foster religious diversity on the Court as well.

The age of prospective nominees can also be an important factor in garnering them consideration for the Supreme Court. In order to secure their legacies well into the future, presidents may lean toward younger nominees who may be able to sit actively on the Court for many decades. President Franklin D. ROOSEVELT's appointment of 40-year-old William Douglas to the Supreme Court in 1939 helped launch the longest tenure of any Supreme Court justice in history (he sat on the Court until 1975). More recently, President George H. W. BUSH's nomination of 43-year-old Clarence Thomas to the Supreme Court helped ensure that at least one conservative voice would be heard on the Court well into the 21st century.

Finally, the personal consideration of individual presidents sometimes figures heavily into the Supreme Court selection process as well. Three of President TRUMAN's four appointments were poker-playing companions of the president; Presidents KENNEDY and JOHNSON appointed mostly members of their respective administrations to the high Court. And while he did not know her well before 1993, President Clinton claimed that he was "personally" drawn to Supreme Court nominee Ruth Bader Ginsburg because of her inspirational story (the female nominee had been rejected for jobs out of law school, before ultimately leading a crusade for equal rights for women all the way up to the U.S. Supreme Court).

Of course the president's selection of a Supreme Court nominee represents only the first stage of the Supreme Court appointment process; the president must then help his nominee successfully navigate through what has become an increasingly arduous Senate confirmation process. For much of the 20th century the Senate—often controlled by the same party as that in the White House—rarely stood in the way of the president's nominations ot the high Court. Indeed between 1900 and 1967 just one of 40 presidential selections for the high Court failed to be confirmed. Since then, however, the Senate confirmation process has often become a source of political struggles waged between a president intent on using his Supreme Court nominees to advance his political agenda and a Senate just as determined to resist all such efforts. In 1968 President Johnson's attempt to promote Justice Abe Fortas to be Chief Justice ran into a torrent of resentment from senators who perceived that the president was trying to shoehorn a close friend into the Court's top post near the end of his own lame-duck presidency. (Fortas's nomination was eventually withdrawn.) The frequent state of divided party government, often pitting Republican Presidents against a Democratic-controlled Senate, has also contributed significantly to this contentious environment. President NIXON watched as two straight conservative nominees went down to defeat in the early 1970s. Perhaps the most heated confirmation battle of modern times occurred 15 years later, when President Reagan nominated arch-conservative Robert Bork to the Supreme Court in 1987. Bork's outspoken views on abortion, free speech, and other issues rankled many Senate Democrats; Bork's nomination was ultimately defeated when a coalition of moderate and liberal Republican Senators joined with Democrats to reject his confirmation by a 58-42 vote. In 1991 Clarence Thomas's nomination was nearly undermined by allegations that he had sexually harassed one of his employees a decade earlier: Thomas's seat on the Court was secured by an even narrower (52-48) margin.

Although Supreme Court appointments tend to attract tremendous attention from the press and the public at large, a president can exercise considerable influence over the legal landscape through strategic appointments to the lower federal courts as well. With the rise of the federal regulatory state and the proliferation of federal laws affecting all matters of criminal and civil activity in the United

States, more and more significant legal controversies have been initiated in the lower federal courts which enjoy jurisdiction over, among other things, all cases "arising under federal law." Responding to this increase in litigation at the federal level, Congress was forced to authorize many new federal judgeships during the middle-to-late 20th century. In all, the total number of federal district and circuit judgeships combined has risen from just over 200 in 1930 to well over 700 today. As a consequence modern presidents' opportunities to influence lower-court policy-making have multiplied steadily during this same period. Given the Supreme Court's limited caseload (the Court today hears on average less than 100 cases per year), presidential appointments to the lower courts enjoy a nearly unlimited capacity to fashion national law and policy that affect millions of Americans.

Still, a tradition of deferences to senators' preferences regarding appointments to federal judicial posts in their home states goes back almost to the beginning of the republic. Up until the 1970s, presidents yielded to the wishes of senators from their own party almost without exception, which limited their own ability to transform the federal judiciary in accordance with their specific ideological goals. President Jimmy Carter attempted to reform this system of senatorial prerogative, at least with regard to circuit court appointments, when his administration established by executive order the U.S. Circuit Judge Nominating Commission in early 1977. The commission was charged with recommending "qualified" persons to fill circuit court judgeships; resentful of their diminished role in the process, senators forwarded the names of candidates of their own directly to the White House, often circumventing the body entirely. Although the Carter administration's reforms opened the judiciary to unprecedented numbers of women and minorities, relations between the Carter White House and the Senate were often contentious.

Although his administration disbanded Carter's nominating commission, President Reagan did not entirely hand over the reigns of the lower court selections back to individual senators. In fact, more than any president who came before him, Ronald Reagan sought to utilize the selection of lower court judges as a means of advancing his administration's own ideological agenda. Thus both the Reagan White House and the Justice Department played an ongoing and active role in scrutinizing nominees for the federal courts during the 1980s, assessing their potential for taking conservative positions on issues important to the administration. By many accounts such efforts at administration paid dividends in helping to transform the legal landscape

in a more conservative direction. Subsequent presidents would adopt Reagan's strategy for their own purposes in the years to follow.

Recognizing the importance of strategically placed lower-court appointments, the Senate has begun to assert itself in recent years in this arena as well. Two of President George W. BUSH's court of appeals appointments were rejected by the Senate Judiciary Committee during his first two years in office, and many others were denied hearings by a Democrat-controlled Senate Judiciary Committee. Thus as the 21st century begins to unfold, appointments at all levels of the federal court system promise to receive considerable attention. Once considered just another means of PATRONAGE, judicial appointments now promise to find their way atop the agenda of any modern president interested in exercising his will on the legal system.

Further reading: Goldman, Sheldon. *Picking Federal Judges: Lower Court Selection from Roosevelt through Reagan.* New Haven: Yale University Press, 1997; Watson, George L., and Stookey, John A. *Shaping America: The Politics of Supreme Court Appointments.* New York: Harper-Collins, 1995; Yalof, David Alistair. *Pursuit of Justices.* Chicago: University of Chicago Press, 1999.

—David Yalof

Justice, Department of

This cabinet-level department serves the United States in enforcing the law in the public interest, and conducts all suits on behalf of the United States before the Supreme Court. Headed by the attorney general, who is appointed by the president upon advice and consent of the Senate, the official is often referred to as the nation's "top cop." While the ATTORNEY GENERAL'S OFFICE has existed since 1789, the department was not created until the Judiciary Act of 1870.

Because the attorney general is appointed by the president, there is some concern that allegations of EXECUTIVE BRANCH wrongdoing might not be fully and fairly investigated. This has led to efforts to appoint special prosecutors (during WATERGATE) and independent councils (during the CLINTON years).

The Justice Department became a focus of attention and controversy in the aftermath of the 9/11 crisis. Attorney General John ASHCROFT, in an effort to root out suspected terrorists, cut constitutional corners, and critics charged that he was undermining the Constitution, but the president and much of the public supported Ashcroft's effort.

K

Kellogg-Briand Pact

The multilateral treaty for the Renunciation of War as an Instrument of National Policy that "outlawed" war was named the Kellogg-Briand Pact. Cosponsored by U.S. Secretary of State Frank B. Kellogg and French Foreign Minister Aristide Briand, the pact was signed on August 27, 1928, in Paris by all the world's major military powers, and they pledged to "solemnly declare . . . that they condemn recourse to war for the solution of international controversies, and renounce it as our instrument of national policy." Lamentably, it did not prevent WORLD WAR II. While the Kellogg-Briand Pact did not accomplish its lofty goal, it remains one in a series of efforts at disarmament that have been ongoing but only marginally successful. The follow-up to these efforts can be seen in the STRATEGIC ARMS LIMITATIONS TALKS (SALT) agreements and other negotiated limits of weaponry.

Further reading: Ferrell, Robert. *Peace in Their Time: The Origins of the Kellogg-Briand Pact.* Hamden, Conn.: Archon Books, 1952.

Kennedy, Jacqueline (1929–1994) *first lady*

Jacqueline Lee Bouvier met John F. KENNEDY in 1951 while he was a member of the U.S. House of Representatives and she was the "Inquiring Photographer" for the *Washington Times-Herald*. They married in 1953, Kennedy's first year in the U.S. Senate. The couple had four children: a girl who died at birth in 1956, Caroline Bouvier Kennedy (1956–   ), John Fitzgerald Kennedy, Jr. (1960–1999), and Patrick Bouvier Kennedy, who died two days after birth in August 1963. Upon her husband's election to the presidency in 1960, Mrs. Kennedy became one of the youngest and most admired FIRST LADIES in history, due in part to her fashionable and trendsetting appearance and her commitment to the arts. She was an invaluable political asset to her husband on the campaign trail and

First Lady Jacqueline Kennedy *(Library of Congress)*

during state dinners and trips abroad. She spoke French, Spanish, and Italian and was greeted by adoring crowds on numerous international visits, including a trip to France, where she reportedly charmed French President Charles DeGaulle. The excitement of her visit prompted her husband to quip that he was the man who had accompanied Jacqueline Kennedy to Paris. Early in the Kennedy administration, Mrs. Kennedy devoted herself to the restoration of the WHITE HOUSE. She helped to set up the White House Historical Association as well as the White House Committee of the Fine Arts. She also procured legislation designating the White House as a museum and established the first-ever publication of a White House guidebook. In 1962 she gave a televised tour of the newly restored White

House to the nation. Mrs. Kennedy will be remembered most for her courage in the days following her husband's assassination on November 22, 1963. Her public composure and dignity during the funeral, which she had planned based on Abraham LINCOLN's funeral following his assassination in 1865, aided the nation in its grief. In 1968, following the assassination of Robert Kennedy, Mrs. Kennedy married Greek shipping magnate Aristotle Onassis. After Onassis's death in 1975, she worked as a book editor for Doubleday in New York until her death in 1994.

Further reading: Anderson, Christopher. *Jack and Jackie: Portrait of an American Marriage.* New York: Morrow, 1996; Goodwin, Doris Kearns. *The Fitzgeralds and the Kennedys.* New York: Simon and Schuster, 1987; Schlesinger, Arthur M., Jr. *A Thousand Days: John F. Kennedy in the White House.* Boston: Houghton Mifflin, 1965.

—Lori Cox-Han

Kennedy, John F. (1917–1963) *thirty-fifth U.S. president*

John Kennedy was a military hero in World War II, and a member of the House and Senate. John F. Kennedy, the Camelot president, wanted an activist administration, and after eight years of EISENHOWER the public seemed ready for action, but try as he might, President Kennedy's legislative proposals often fell prey to unresponsive leaders in Congress. Stymied by an intransigent Congress that took the system of CHECKS AND BALANCES quite seriously, the Kennedy legislative record was, at best, mixed. The first Roman Catholic to be elected president, and the youngest ever elected, Kennedy won the presidency by a razor-thin margin in 1960. Kennedy presided over the BAY OF PIGS fiasco in Cuba, placed military advisers in Vietnam, and successfully led the nation through the CUBAN MISSILE CRISIS, but his ambitious and progressive domestic initiatives often were blocked by a Congress controlled by conservatives in his own party. Kennedy did achieve tax cuts, actually passed later under LBJ, which stimulated economic growth, and he started the Peace Corps and placed civil rights reform on the presidential agenda, but overall he was stymied by a reluctant Congress.

This led to grumblings among the public and scholars: "How can the Congress stand in the way of progress? . . . there are too many checks on the presidency . . . We need *more* power for the president" went the refrains. If the presidency was good and just, it also deserved to be strong, and it was the Congress that stood in the way.

Kennedy was young, attractive, and elegant. He was remarkably photogenic, and he, his children, and his glamorous wife, Jackie, became American's royal family. It was the age of Camelot, a romanticized era when anything seemed possible. Kennedy exuded charm and sophistication. Author John Steinbeck remarked, "What a joy that literacy is no longer prima-facie evidence of treason." Only in later years would we learn of a darker side of Camelot: plots against Castro and the president's private affairs.

Washington reporters knew about President Kennedy's "active" private life, but at that time it was not considered relevant or proper to write about such private matters. Only later would the stories of Kennedy's dalliances become public knowledge.

The transformation of the president from chief clerk to tribune of the people was all but complete by the end of the NEW DEAL, but with the advent of television, the president had a new tool to reach directly to the people. Thus Kennedy could state that "only the president represents the national interest. And upon him alone converge all the needs and aspirations of all parts of the country, all departments of government, all nations of the world." That's quite a job description! And while constitutionally that description should be much in doubt, in practical terms that is precisely how presidents viewed themselves and how much of the public viewed them as well. Presidents did not give up their claim to a constitutional base of power. They merely grafted another power—tribune of the people—onto their already inflated job descriptions.

John Kennedy was president when television first became a factor in presidential politics. He took full advantage of this new tool for reaching out to the public. His televised PRESS CONFERENCES were virtuoso performances, as he stood there cool, calm, witty, intelligent. The camera loved him. Politics was beginning to cross the line into entertainment, and the president was becoming a national celebrity.

Kennedy summoned the nation to action. If Eisenhower left much undone, Kennedy was determined to get much done. He realized that revolutions are not built on electoral victories, so he pragmatically pursued a reformist agenda.

The White House, he asserted, "must be the center of moral leadership." But on some of the pressing moral issues of the day, Kennedy was a reluctant reformer. He avoided civil rights until it became politically unacceptable to do so. Was this wisdom or cowardice? As FDR knew, it was dangerous to get too far out in front of public opinion. Kennedy waited until the civil rights issue gained prominence, then became its champion.

As Kennedy took office, the Civil Rights movement was picking up steam. Several violent confrontations between demonstrators and police officials made headline news. In Mississippi and Alabama, reactionary governors tried to prevent black students from enrolling in state universities. Riots followed. "Freedom riders" flocked into the

President John F. Kennedy *(Library of Congress)*

South, hoping to work for racial equality. At first Kennedy was a "reluctant revolutionary," but as events built to the boiling point, the president intervened. Blacks desperately needed the moral force of the presidency to help their cause. Kennedy obliged. Speaking over national television from the OVAL OFFICE, Kennedy said the nation faced a "moral crisis as a country and a people." This cannot be the land of the free "except for the Negroes . . . The heart of the question is whether all Americans are to be afforded equal rights and equal opportunities, whether we are going to treat our fellow Americans as we want to be treated." Then, in an especially moving passage, he said, "We cannot say to 10 percent of the population that you can't have that right; that your children can't have the chance to develop what-

ever talents they have; that the only way that they are going to get their rights is to go into the streets and demonstrate. I think we owe them and we owe ourselves a better country than that."

Another Kennedy priority was to land a man on the moon. The "space race" with the Soviets pushed Kennedy to promote space exploration, and the president promised to land a man on the moon by the end of the decade (an American landed on the moon by 1969). Kennedy set in motion an ambitious and successful space program that involved new technologies and gave the nation a great sense of accomplishment.

Elsewhere in his domestic program, Kennedy faced frustration after frustration. His efforts at developing a

"NEW FRONTIER" of domestic programs failed to pass a Democrat-controlled Congress, and Kennedy had to settle for a few meager victories, such as tax cuts and small spending increases in the president's projects.

In FOREIGN AFFAIRS Kennedy began his administration with a blunder. The president approved of plans, drawn up during the Eisenhower administration, for an invasion of communist-controlled Cuba by Cuban refugees trained and supported by the United States. When the invasion faltered, Kennedy refused to allow the U.S. military to intervene, thereby guaranteeing the failure of the mission. The "Bay of Pigs" taught the young president lessons. "How could I have been so stupid?" he asked. "It's a hell of a way to learn things." He took full public responsibility for the disaster (and his popularity shot up afterward).

President Kennedy was cautious about committing U.S. combat forces in Vietnam, and he extended but did not guarantee long-term U.S. support of South Vietnam. Kennedy had several successes in foreign policy: the ALLIANCE FOR PROGRESS in Latin America, protection of Berlin against Soviet threats, the Peace Corps, and, most dramatically, the Cuban missile crisis.

In October 1962 intelligence reports revealed that the Soviet Union was building nuclear missiles sites in Cuba. The president demanded their removal and ordered a naval quarantine of the island. After several tense days, when the world was poised on the brink of nuclear war, the Russians backed down and removed the missiles.

The threat of nuclear war changed Kennedy from a belligerent "cold warrior" to a man determined to reduce the risk of nuclear annihilation. In 1963 the United States and Soviet Union signed the Nuclear Test Ban Treaty, which barred atmospheric testing of nuclear weapons. It may have been Kennedy's greatest accomplishment. In a speech, he discussed the futility of the arms race: "For in the final analysis, our most basic common link is that we all inhabit this small planet. We all breathe the same air. We all cherish our children's future. And we are all mortal . . . Let us reexamine our attitude toward the COLD WAR, remembering that we are not engaged in a debate, seeking to pile up debating points."

On November 22, 1963, while on a political fence-mending visit to Dallas, Texas, President Kennedy was assassinated. He served as president for only one thousand days. Questions of what might have been linger. His charm, elegance, and vision brought a whole generation of young men and women into public service. His call for a caring, compassionate America, his call for sacrifice, and his inspiring image of a better America still animate political action. His achievements as president cannot be measured simply by his accomplishments or his failures (Bay of Pigs, Vietnam). It is not merely a question of what John Kennedy did,

it is also a question of what he brought out in the nation: a spirit of sacrifice, a notion that public service was honorable, a call to be our better selves. As Thomas Cronin has written, "His greatness lies less in what he achieved than in what he proposed and began." Cronin added: "In the end he had an impact on all of us who lived in his country at the time. If nothing else he made people think of politics, the presidency, and government in different ways. His impact has less to do with conventional legislative or administrative achievements than it does with attitudes, values, and symbols. His ultimate contributions were far more than the sum of his record in the White House." And James MacGregor Burns offers this verdict in his book *The Power to Lead:*

> In the longer and broader judgment of history . . . he will be seen as a politician of extraordinary personal qualities who rhetorically summoned the American people to a moment of activism and greatness, who fell back on a conventional politics of brokerage, manipulation, and consensus once he attained office, who found the institutional constraints on action—especially in Congress— far more formidable than he had expected, who was intellectually too much committed to existing institutions to attempt to unfreeze them but lacked the passionate moral commitment necessary to try to transcend the restraints—and then, in his third year in the presidency and his last year on earth, he began to find his true direction and make a moral and political commitment to it.

He may have been a man with personal flaws, but he appealed to the better angels within the American people. He was inspired and inspiring.

In his book *In Search of History: A Personal History,* Theodore H. White wrote:

> So the epitaph on the Kennedy Administration became Camelot—a magic moment in American history, when gallant men danced with beautiful women, when great deeds were done, when artists, writers and poets met at the White House, and the barbarians beyond the walls held back.

Which is, of course, a misreading of history. The magic Camelot of John F. Kennedy never existed . . . the knights of his round table were able, tough, ambitious men, capable of kindness, also capable of error . . . What made them a group and established their companionship was their leader. Of them all Kennedy was the toughest, the most intelligent, the most attractive—inside, the least romantic. He was a realistic dealer in men, a master of games who understood the importance of ideas. He assumed his responsibilities fully. He advanced the cause of America at home and abroad. But he posed for the first time the great questions of the sixties and seventies: What kind of people are we Americans? What do we want to become?

Further reading: Giglio, James N. *The Presidency of John F. Kennedy.* Lawrence: University Press of Kansas, 1991; Parment, Herbert S. *Jack: The Struggles of John F. Kennedy.* New York: Dial, 1980; ———. *JFK: The Presidency of John F. Kennedy.* New York: Dial, 1983; Reeves, Richard. *President Kennedy: Profile of Power.* New York: Simon & Schuster, 1993; Schlesinger, Arthur M., Jr. *A Thousand Days: John F. Kennedy in the White House.* Boston: Houghton Mifflin, 1965; Sorensen, Theodore C. *Kennedy.* New York: Harper and Row, 1965.

Kennedy, Robert F. (1925–1968) *U. S. senator, U. S. attorney general*

Robert F. Kennedy was born on November 20, 1925, in Brookline, Massachusetts. He earned his bachelor's degree at Harvard University in 1948 and his law degree at the University of Virginia in 1951. Kennedy managed his brother John F. KENNEDY's 1952 Senate campaign and 1960 presidential campaign. During most of the 1950s, Kennedy served in several investigative, committee staff positions in the Senate. In particular, Kennedy was the chief counsel for a Senate committee investigating labor racketeering from 1957 to 1959.

After he was appointed ATTORNEY GENERAL in 1961, Kennedy focused his efforts on investigating and prosecuting gangsters, labor racketeers, and the Ku Klux Klan. In addition to his aggressive agenda as attorney general, Kennedy was a close political and policy adviser to his brother John, especially during the CUBAN MISSILE CRISIS of 1962. After John F. Kennedy's assassination in 1963, Robert F. Kennedy continued to serve as attorney general until he resigned in order to be elected to a U.S. Senate seat from New York in 1964.

As a liberal Democrat, Kennedy generally supported President Lyndon B. JOHNSON's GREAT SOCIETY programs. Kennedy specialized in developing innovative policies for reducing urban poverty and economically revitalizing inner-city neighborhoods.

A critic of Johnson's policies in the VIETNAM WAR, Kennedy announced his presidential candidacy on March 15, 1968. Two weeks later, Johnson announced to the nation that he would not seek another term as president. Although he competed against another Democratic presidential candidate, Senate Eugene MCCARTHY of Minnesota, for the support of antiwar activists in the primaries, Kennedy formed a coalition that included blacks, Latinos, youths, and blue-collar whites. Kennedy won the Indiana and Nebraska primaries but lost in Oregon. After announc-

ing his victory in the California primary on the evening of June 5, 1968, Kennedy was assassinated.

Further reading: Hilty, James W. *Robert Kennedy: Brother Protector.* Philadelphia: Temple University Press, 1997; Schlesinger, Arthur M., Jr. *Robert Kennedy and His Times.* Boston: Houghton Mifflin, 1978.

—Sean J. Savage

King, William Rufus de Vane (1786–1853) *U.S. vice president*

The thirteenth vice president, serving under Franklin PIERCE, William Rufus King served as a member of Congress, diplomat, senator, and president pro tempore of the Senate. He was an exceptionally close friend to James BUCHANAN.

He was a defender of the slave system yet sought compromises with the abolitionists. In 1852 the Democrats selected King as their vice-presidential candidate as a way to appease the Buchanan wing of the party. During the campaign King was diagnosed with tuberculosis and went to Cuba in hopes of regaining his health. He was elected vice president while in Cuba and was unable to return to the United States to take the OATH OF OFFICE. A special law was passed allowing him to take his oath in Cuba. King never recovered and died on April 18, 1853. Thus, for most of Pierce's presidency, the nation did not have a vice president.

Kissinger, Henry (1923–) *secretary of state, national security adviser*

He was born Heinz Alfred Kissinger in Furth, Bavaria, in 1923 to a middle-class Orthodox Jewish family. He and his parents, Louis and Paula, and his brother, Walther, fled Nazi Germany in 1938 and settled in New York City, where Heinz changed his name to Henry and became a naturalized American citizen. After high school, he planned to be an accountant and took evening courses at the City College of New York. He was drafted into the army during WORLD WAR II and developed an interest in FOREIGN AFFAIRS. His superiors became aware of his intellect, and he served for three years as an intelligence officer in occupied Germany. He left the army in 1947 and entered Harvard to complete his undergraduate education.

At Harvard he studied under William Yandell Elliott, one of the powers in the government department and a strong anticommunist, who placed Kissinger as executive director of Harvard's International Seminar. Through this position, Kissinger made contacts with many future world leaders. He completed his M.A. degree in 1952 and his Ph.D. at Harvard in 1954 with a dissertation on the aftermath of the Napoleonic Wars, *A World Restored:*

Metternich, Castleraugh and the Problems of Peace: 1812–22, in which he praised Metternich for his use of balance of power in order to preserve world order.

Henry Kissinger continued to meet prominent leaders during his work at the Council of Foreign Relations from 1955 to 1957, and his duties there resulted in his book on *Nuclear Weapons and Foreign Policy* (1957), in which he criticized Secretary of State John Foster DULLES's policy of massive retaliation of nuclear weapons and instead advocated a more traditional form of DIPLOMACY.

He returned to Harvard as a professor of government and international affairs in 1957, and in 1960 he became involved in New York Republican Governor Nelson Rockefeller's presidential race as a foreign policy adviser. When ROCKEFELLER lost the nomination to Richard NIXON, Kissinger moved to John KENNEDY's campaign, and after the election, he remained at Harvard while serving as a part-time foreign policy consultant to the White House. He never gained entry into the inner circle of Kennedy advisers, but the Lyndon JOHNSON administration used his services more extensively when Kissinger engaged in secret negotiations through contacts made at the Harvard seminar to end the VIETNAM WAR. The talks, though, were not successful.

He worked again as a foreign policy adviser for Rockefeller during the presidential race in 1968, but when Rockefeller lost the nomination a second time to Nixon, Kissinger advised Vice President Hubert HUMPHREY in foreign affairs while at the same time providing information to the Nixon camp on negotiations between the United States and North Vietnam.

When Nixon entered the presidency, he appointed Kissinger as his NATIONAL SECURITY ADVISER. These two people worked closely together in foreign affairs and centralized decision-making power in the White House while excluding other areas of the foreign policy BUREAUCRACY. Kissinger's prominence overshadowed Secretary of State William Rogers, who was replaced by Kissinger as secretary of State in 1973. For two years Kissinger held the dual roles of secretary of State and national security adviser to the president.

Although the Vietnam War was the central foreign policy issue during the Nixon administration, Henry Kissinger was involved in other significant foreign affairs matters, including his secret negotiations with Chinese and Soviet leaders which led to the reopening of U.S.-Chinese relations with Nixon's trip to China in 1972 and the Nixon-Brezhnev summit of May 1972. He spent two years in negotiations with the North Vietnamese, which resulted in a cease-fire prior to the 1972 election and a signed agreement in 1973. His efforts over Vietnam earned him the Nobel Peace Prize in 1973.

Kissinger's reputation increased in stature as Nixon's declined on the heels of WATERGATE. He was able to arrange disengagement agreements between Israel and Egypt and Israel and Syria during the Yom Kippur War. After Nixon resigned from office, Kissinger remained as Gerald FORD's secretary of State, but he relinquished his role as national security adviser to Brent Scowcroft in 1975. During the 1976 presidential campaign, Kissinger's handling of foreign relations became as issue. Ronald REAGAN accused Kissinger's détente policy with the Soviet Union of working to the disadvantage of the United States, and Jimmy CARTER criticized Kissinger's morally deficient foreign policy, which lacked a focus on HUMAN RIGHTS.

Kissinger acted in an advisory capacity to Reagan and George H. W. Bush from 1981 to 1992. He established Kissinger Associates as an international consulting firm on foreign affairs for private clients. He is best known for his intellect and his imaginative integration of the realist approach to foreign relations, but he is also criticized for his egotism, secretive nature, and lack of human compassion in the arena of foreign affairs.

Further reading: Isaacson, Walter. *Kissinger: A Biography.* New York: Simon and Schuster, 1992; Prados, John. *Keepers of the Keys: A History of the National Security Council from Truman to Bush.* New York: Morrow, 1991; Starr, Harvey. *Henry Kissinger: Perceptions of International Politics.* Lexington: University Press of Kentucky, 1984.

—Michael G. Krukones

kitchen cabinet

CHIEF EXECUTIVES frequently rely on an informal group of loyal and trusted advisers, referred to as the "kitchen cabinet," rather than the formal CABINET to assist them with policy and managerial advice. The development of a kitchen cabinet dates back to the Andrew JACKSON presidency (1829–37). Anti-Jacksonian newspapers, such as the *Telegraph,* began to report in 1831 that a select group of advisers rather than the formal cabinet were exerting political influence over Jackson's policy agenda. Senator George Poindexter of Mississippi, a defender of states' rights, is often credited with coining the phrase "kitchen cabinet" in the *Telegraph* during the spring of 1832. Poindexter, a supporter of Vice President John C. CALHOUN, who was another proponent of states' rights, eventually believed that Secretary of State Martin VAN BUREN exerted greater influence over Jacksonian policy than Calhoun. Jackson frequently sought policy advice from a core set of individuals, such as Secretary of State (and later vice president) Martin Van Buren, Secretary of War John H. Eaton, and presidential advisers William B. Lewis and Amos Kendall (later appointed as postmaster general). Unlike the formal cabinet, membership in the kitchen cabinet greatly fluctuates throughout a president's term. A few advisers may serve as temporary members in a kitchen cabinet when a president seeks their assistance on a specific policy area that requires a degree of expertise and technical advice. There may be instances when the policy views of a kitchen-cabinet member deviate from the president's policy goals. This difference of opinions might lead the president to remove an adviser from the kitchen cabinet. Chief executives choose from a variety of individuals when they form their kitchen cabinets. Members might include key secretaries from the formal cabinet, senators and representatives serving in Congress who share the same policy views as the president, White House aides, political cronies inside and outside of Washington politics, presidential friends and family members, or other governmental officials. A few FIRST LADIES, such as Edith Wilson, Rosalynn CARTER, and Hillary Rodham CLINTON were active and valuable members in their husbands' kitchen cabinets. Members of the kitchen cabinet derive their status and influence directly from the president, whereas formal cabinet members possess statutory authority. The kitchen cabinet lacks a defined organizational structure and no formal meetings are held on a regular basis. Some scholars have suggested that kitchen cabinets fulfilled those administrative and political functions that the contemporary White House staff eventually assumed after its creation in 1939. Although modern presidents have increasingly relied on their White House staff rather than the cabinet as a collective body for advice, they occasionally rely on an inner core of loyal advisers that serve as a kitchen cabinet. Karen P. Hughes, counselor to the president, and Karl C. Rove, senior adviser to the president, were active kitchen cabinet participants during the first year of the George W. BUSH administration.

Further reading: Cole, Donald B. *The Presidency of Andrew Jackson.* Lawrence: University Press of Kentucky, 1993; Latner, Richard B. *The Presidency of Andrew Jackson: White House Politics, 1829–1837.* Athens: University of Georgia Press, 1979.

—Adam L. Warber

Knox, Philander Chase (1853–1921) *senator, secretary of State, attorney general*

Philander Knox was one of the most influential figures of his era. After serving as chief counsel for the Carnegie empire, Knox served as attorney general to William MCKINLEY and Theodore ROOSEVELT. Knox believed that trusts should be regulated but not busted, and he sought strict enforcement of the SHERMAN ANTITRUST ACT. He created the antitrust division of the DEPARTMENT OF JUSTICE but, ironically, never sought a criminal prosecution of violation of the Sherman Antitrust Act.

Knox also served as William Howard TAFT's secretary of State, a post wherein he sought to implement DOLLAR DIPLOMACY to protect U.S. interests. During the presidency of Woodrow WILSON, Knox served in the Senate where he vigorously fought against Wilson's TREATY OF VERSAILLES and LEAGUE OF NATIONS.

Korean War

The Korean War is considered the first "war" of the COLD WAR. On June 24–25, 1950, North Korean forces, supported by communist China, attacked South Korea. President TRUMAN, in an effort to combat communist aggression and expansion, called for an emergency session of the UNITED NATIONS Security Council. The Council passes a resolution condemning the invasion.

President Truman ordered U.S. forces—headed by General Douglas MacArthur—into action. Truman made his decision without formal congressional authorization (although only a handful in Congress opposed the use of troops). Truman acted on the claimed authority to act as COMMANDER IN CHIEF absent congressional authorization. This bold claim of a previously unrecognized and constitutionally questionable power worked. Truman, acting alone, had committed the United States to war.

The war ended, a draw, in 1953. More than 150,000 Americans were killed or wounded.

Korematsu v. United States, 323 U.S. 214 (1944)

During WORLD WAR II, the fear that the West Coast of the United States might be attacked by the Japanese, or that Japanese-Americans might not be loyal to the United States, sparked calls for the internment of Americans with Japanese ancestry. President ROOSEVELT was pressed to act, and he signed an executive order, the result of which was the establishment of a series of internment centers located along the West Coast.

Designed to protect the West Coast from anticipated espionage and sabotage, the order affected more than 110,000 persons of Japanese ancestry, incarcerating them in relocation centers located in rural areas of California, Arizona, Arkansas, Idaho, Utah, Wyoming, and Colorado. Fred T. Korematsu was one of the internees, a citizen of Japanese descent, who was arrested and convicted by a federal district court for violating an exclusion order from the San Leandro, California, military areas. Korematsu challenged the constitutionality of the exclusion order and the entire detention program. His conviction was sustained by the Ninth Circuit Court but then taken up by the Supreme Court because of the importance of the constitutional questions.

The majority opinion, delivered by Associate Justice Hugo Black, revealed support for the war crisis at hand.

Black cites the decision that had been made a year prior to *Korematsu* in the case of *Hirabayashi v. United States* (1943) (320 U.S. 81 [1943]) where the Court had justified a curfew order against those of Japanese ancestry in the military areas. Black further indicated that it was not beyond the war powers of CONGRESS AND THE PRESIDENT to exclude and confine particular persons during war, whether they be citizens or not. While he admits Japanese Americans are undergoing some hardship as a result of this incarceration, he explains it away by suggesting it is part of war.

There were three important dissents as well in this case. Justice Owen Roberts, Jr., asserted that Korematsu's constitutional rights had been violated by this incarceration and had been done so exclusively because of his ancestry. Justice Frank Murphy felt this entire operation fell into the "ugly abyss of racism." He argued for limits on military discretion during times of war. Justice Robert H. Jackson's dissent was perhaps the most important of all, as he pointed to the great danger of having the Supreme Court justify racial discrimination as being more serious than the U. S. Army's program of apprehending and deporting these people.

Forty years after the decision, Fred Korematsu won a pyrrhic victory of sorts, as a federal district court on April 19, 1984, for the first time in history, vacated the criminal conviction that had been sustained by the Supreme Court. Judge Marilyn Hall Patel found for the court that the federal government had omitted essential information and misled the Supreme Court, violating their ethical obligations to the court (see 584 F. Supp. 1406 [N.D. Cal. 1948]). In addition to this decision, in 1988 Congress passed a law granting Korematsu and the other living Japanese Americans $20,000 to help compensate every Japanese American incarcerated. Finally, President Bill CLINTON in 1998 recognized the sacrifices and struggles of Fred Korematsu by granting him a Presidential Medal of Freedom, the country's highest civilian award.

Further reading: Irons, Peter. *Justice Delayed: The Record of the Japanese American Internment Cases.* Middleton, Conn.: Wesleyan University Press, 1989; *Korematsu v. United States,* 323 U.S. 214 (1944).

—Byron W. Daynes

L

Labor, Department of

The Department of Labor was created in 1913. Its roots can be traced to 1884, when Congress established a Bureau of Labor under the Interior Department. In 1888 an independent Department of Labor was established, but it did not have CABINET status. In 1903 a Department of Labor and Commerce was created, and finally, in 1913, Labor became a separate department with cabinet status.

Headed by a secretary who is appointed by the president with consent of the Senate, the Department of Labor is responsible for a variety of federal laws that affect workers, including unemployment insurance, worker's compensation, minimum wage, occupational health and safety, antidiscrimination policies, protection of pension rights, job training, and the strengthening of collective bargaining

President Franklin ROOSEVELT appointed Frances PERKINS secretary of Labor. Perkins was the first woman to serve in the cabinet. She was instrumental in the development of several NEW DEAL programs, especially SOCIAL SECURITY and the FAIR LABOR STANDARDS ACT of 1938.

labor policy

Before 1900, the federal government was only sporadically involved in labor policy, leaving to private enterprise or the states primary responsibility for setting policy in this area. By the 1900s the development of a national and international economic role of the United States led presidents to become more involved in labor policy.

Teddy ROOSEVELT intervened in an anthracite coal strike in 1902, promoted child labor laws, pushed for the protection of women in the workplace, and called for better health protection in business.

During the WILSON presidency, the LABOR DEPARTMENT was created and the president selected former United Mine Workers official William B. Wilson as the first labor secretary. U.S. entry into WORLD WAR I brought about a new relationship between the Wilson administration and labor as the president resuscitated labor and industry during the war.

After a series of strikes, Wilson created the National War Labor Board in 1918 to regulate labor during the war, but after the war relations between the government and labor worsened, and in 1919 a series of strikes brought about increased action. In 1919 and 1920 Wilson convened industrial conferences in hopes of improving relations.

By the 1920s the Republicans controlled the White House and Congress, and policy continued to be designed to create cooperation between industry and labor, with Commerce Secretary Herbert HOOVER taking a lead role.

The NEW DEAL and the administration of Franklin D. ROOSEVELT marked a major turning point in government-labor relations. The federal government established the legal framework for labor-industry interaction and regulated child labor rules, working-hour limits, and wage rates. During this period, the federal government clearly superceded the states in establishing national standards for labor-industry relations.

With the NATIONAL INDUSTRIAL RECOVERY ACT (1933) and the establishment of government agencies such as the National Recovery Administration (NRA), the National Labor Board (NLB), and later the National Labor Relations Board (NLRB), the federal government became referee and rule-maker for labor rights and standards. This led to an increase in labor organizing, and the beginnings of organized labor as a key element of the FDR, and later the Democratic, NEW DEAL coalition. And while the judiciary found several New Deal labor laws unconstitutional, this did not stop FDR from pursuing his goals, as Congress enacted the National Labor Relations Act, or WAGNER ACT, guaranteeing workers the right to unionize and to pursue collective bargaining.

After the war, Congress, led by the Republicans, passed the TAFT-HARTLEY ACT (1947) limiting labor's power to unionize, but this did little to halt the power of labor in American politics throughout the 1950s and 1960s. By the

1980s, union membership declined and labor lost some of its political clout. Today, labor remains an important part of the Democratic political coalition.

Further reading: Forbath, William E. *Law and the Shaping of the American Labor Movement.* Cambridge, Mass.: Harvard University Press, 1991; Millis, Harry A., and Emily C. Brown. *From the Wagner Act to Taft-Hartley, A Study of National Labor Policy and Labor Relations.* Chicago: University of Chicago Press, 1950; Tomlins, Christopher L. *The State and the Unions: Labor Relations, the Law, and the Organized Labor Movement in America, 1880–1960.* New York: Cambridge University Press, 1985.

La Follette, Robert M. (1855–1925) *governor, U.S. senator*

Known as "Fighting Bob," La Follette was a U.S. senator from Wisconsin and was known for his "militant liberalism" and reformist orientation. A gifted public speaker, this activist Republican unsuccessfully sought the party's presidential nomination for president, then left the party in 1924 to run as the progressive candidate for president and received 16.6 percent of the popular vote. La Follette fought for greater citizen participation in politics, higher taxes on the wealthy, and corporate regulatory reforms. He was a progressive governor of Wisconsin, serving from 1901 to 1906.

lame duck presidents

The phrase "lame duck" implies that a person is incompetent. The term originates with an English play in 1771. In the play, individuals who did not pay their debts were described as "waddl[ing] out like lame ducks." The phrase quickly was adopted for political use. Prior to 1933, a president who lost an election in November continued to serve as president until March of the following year. A president serving in that awkward scenario for 120 days was termed a lame duck, since the president no longer had the support of the nation nor was he responsible for the future of the nation. On January 23, 1933, Congress ratified the TWEN-TIETH AMENDMENT to shorten the tenure of a lame duck by beginning the presidential and vice presidential terms on January 20, rather than March 4. The amendment was proposed and passed because the time between November 1932 and Franklin ROOSEVELT's inauguration in March of 1933 was some of the most harrowing of the GREAT DEPRESSION, and the nation was forced to wait 120 days for the individual who promised to solve the nation's problems. However, the term now refers to a different situation entirely. On March 21, 1947, Congress proposed an Amendment to the Constitution, which would limit to two

terms the tenure of the president of the United States. The Twenty-second Amendment was ratified in 1951. President Franklin Roosevelt's four electoral victories and 12 years in office spurred Congress to propose and pass the amendment. The rules change has had consequences for the office of the presidency. Since the ratification, only Dwight EISENHOWER, Ronald REAGAN, and Bill CLINTON have managed a reelection. A president who does not achieve a second term must endure a tarnished legacy, but a president who does achieve a second term is considered a lame duck. A second-term president who cannot run again loses his electoral connection, his electoral imperative, and the power to bargain with others. At the same time, the second-term president is also free from the constraints of popular demands. More importantly, a lame duck president can lock in the next president to decisions neither the incoming president nor the country want. Ultimately, a second-term president runs the risk of irrelevancy.

Further reading: Briggs, James. "Origins of English Sayings and Idioms." http://www.briggsl3.fsna.co.uk/book/d.htm.

—Diane Heith

law enforcement powers

Technically, the president is the nation's chief law enforcement officer. Article II, Section 3, of the Constitution says the president "shall take care that the Laws be faithfully executed." This task is performed primarily through the ATTORNEY GENERAL and the DEPARTMENT OF JUSTICE.

Prior to the 20th century, the law enforcement responsibilities of the federal government were fairly limited. Over time the federal government and the president, the Department of Justice, and later the FEDERAL BUREAU OF INVESTIGATION became a central focus of law enforcement.

In the 1960s, crime became an important issue in presidential campaign politics, and presidents were increasingly compelled to develop elaborate anticrime proposals. Presidential interest in crime fluctuates with the rise and fall of the crime rates and of the public concern for crime.

leadership, presidential

Political leadership has been a key concern of Plato, Aristotle, Machiavelli, and many contemporary students of management and primate studies, but only recently have leadership studies received the attention they deserve in American political science. The traditional concern has been that the study of individual leaders will result in an idiopathic analysis of how one man or woman influences particular events. General theories are now being developed—offering understandings about the bases of political authority, of how leaders define their goals, relate to others, employ various techniques of influence. Nor are leadership goals and skills seen as an alternative to an analysis of broader environment factors. Rather, leaders are seen as responding to a variety of contextual factors that provide opportunities for, and limits to, what they can do. As Max Weber pointed out some time ago, leaders may have authority because followers view them as having a (possibly a God-given) right to rule. Or their powers may be founded on superior wisdom and access to information that others lack. Or they may have special emotional or spiritual ties to their followers. In some cases, as Machiavelli has suggested, there may be another factor at work. Acquiescence to the claims of a leader may be based on fear of reprisals, though only tyrants will make this the major base of their rule.

American presidents who have been successful have relied on a blend of all these appeals. Coming to office via elections that are viewed as legitimate is only the beginning. They must appear wise and committed to the general welfare of the American people. Rewards and punishments are at their disposal to win over other actors in the political system. A strong emotional connection to the public may not always be evident, but for presidents such as Franklin D. ROOSEVELT, Dwight David EISENHOWER, and John KENNEDY, it was certainly an asset.

The difficulty of the tasks the leader undertakes, as James M. Burns has noted, will vary with his or her goals. The transformational task that Burns posits requires a leadership that can raise followers above their everyday concerns to the expression of "higher levels of motivation and morality." But to do so, his enterprise will run counter to many vested interests and norms associated with an earlier regime. Franklin D. Roosevelt, for example, was already having problems with conservatives in his own party by the late 1930s. Lyndon JOHNSON, when he signed the CIVIL RIGHTS ACT of 1964, knew that he was writing off the DEMOCRATIC PARTY in the South for years to come. The transactional leader, more common to the American political system, has a somewhat easier task. His job is to act as a kind of broker, negotiating between the competing demands of the various actors within the political system to maintain both his position and some sort of order. Dwight David Eisenhower, committed to peace and a conservative political order, was particularly skilled along these lines, as Fred Greenstein has pointed out. The tactics of a hidden hand presidency were especially suited to the maintenance of a regime. Structural contexts, of course, provide limits and opportunities for any American president. The transformational leader cannot function in a time when most influentials and the public, as a whole, as reasonably satisfied with the status quo, as Bill CLINTON found out in his first two years in office. But neither does standing pat

work when people feel they are in a crisis situation, as Herbert HOOVER discovered in 1932.

Cyclical events and historical trends will also impact what a president can do. Any person coming to the presidency of the United States today has more power at his disposal than presidents in time past. As Richard Pious has pointed out, every president whose assertion of some new power had been met with political acquiescence has added to what are considered to be the legitimate powers of the office. Moreover, the rise and dissipation of broader political and social constellations may enhance or limit what a president can realistically hope to achieve. As Stephen Skowronek has shown, Presidents JEFFERSON, JACKSON, LINCOLN, and Franklin Roosevelt were at the beginning of new constellations of thought and interests and had considerable leeway in directing the nation in a new direction. John Quincy ADAMS, PIERCE, Hoover, and CARTER (and Clinton, we would add) are more closely aligned with the tail ends of old regimes that were falling out of favor. Regardless of their efforts to work with or augment formerly popular policies, their options were limited.

Specific situational factors, too, can impact how presidents make decisions. Foreign policy crises and other high-stress situations are apt to narrow the range of alternatives the president and his advisers consider and promote the reliance "on stereotypic images of the enemy and misperceptions the situation . . . they are dealing with." From their study of 16 crises from WORLD WAR II to the post-World War II period, Snyder and Dieing conclude that "stereotypic thinking, restricted search for alternatives, and impaired ability to estimate the consequences of action." In exceptional cases, however, such as Eisenhower's response to the Hungarian uprising in 1956, and Kennedy's handing of the CUBAN MISSILE CRISIS, empathy with the enemy may lead to the search for non-provocative responses.

A president's past investment in a particular policy line, too, may trap him in a line of behavior that is counterproductive. Lyndon Johnson's response to negative feedback during the VIETNAM WAR is suggestive along these lines. Even after the new secretary of Defense, Clark CLIFFORD, told him that the Vietnam War was unwinnable, Johnson could not openly reverse himself.

At another level of analysis, one must recognize that the U.S. presidency is not comprised of only one person. The individual who wins the office of president is but the center of advisers who process information for him and act on his behalf. Though he has considerable flexibility in the choice of particular advisers and the decisional structures that will best suit his style, the variety of tasks the contemporary president must perform has led to the development of a complex and increasingly specialized support system. Most often his personal advisers perform instrumental services for the him—organizing his efforts generally or in a particular arena of action, following through on his decisions to make sure that the appropriate follow-up takes place. At CAMP DAVID, for example, Cyrus Vance, Zbigniew Brzezinski, and Rosalynn CARTER all assured President Carter that he should adhere to his mission, even when matters looked bleak. But occasionally, advisers may act as strategic actors, devising ways to place their own imprint on policies. Col. Edward M. House undercut Woodrow Wilson's policy objectives at the Paris Peace Conference in 1919, and Brzezinski shaped Jimmy CARTER's advisory process in a way that encouraged Carter to embrace a strategic tilt toward China that put his SALT II Agreement with the Soviet Union at risk.

As the foregoing suggests, the values, the personality traits, and the skills of specific presidents influence the directions they take and the ways in which they process information, organize their staffs, and exercise power. A president's worldview, as James David Barber has argued, sets the direction that he takes. His style is relevant to the way he works and manages issues, people, and organizations. His character—the underlying, more enduring aspect of his personality—is relevant to his ability to learn, to work, and to exercise power. In zeroing in on the president's characteristics, M. Brewster Smith's map is particularly useful. The president's character, as he suggests, can be assessed in terms of three kinds of processes—his reality testing, self/other relationships, and ego defensive maneuvers. The latter, as Greenstein has noted, are the techniques a person employs to avoid awareness of "deeper, anxiety-producing conflicts."

Indeed, the U.S. presidency provides temptations—a screen upon which men may act out some of their own psychological needs. An angry or insecure president may project aggressive impulses onto foreign adversaries in ways that aggravate conflict. The office, moreover, provides many opportunities for the fulfillment of the kinds of narcissistic needs delineated in Heinz Kohut's work on the development of the self. An approving audience (the public) provides a mirror for the president's idealized self. The great presidents of the past, with whom he may identify, may serve to immerse him into a powerful, collective personae. And the powerful leaders on the world stage with whom he consorts may come to represent to him an idealized "other" in what Kohut calls the twin-ship relationship. The result may be to feed a kind of grandiosity in which a president overestimates his ability to control events. These kinds of considerations may explain how two otherwise very competent presidents, Richard NIXON and Bill Clinton, made the mistakes they did—one in the WATERGATE fiasco, the other in the Monica Lewinsky affair.

Rather than focusing on presidential vulnerabilities, Fred Greenstein has suggested that American presidents be evaluated in terms of six relevant skills. Thus, we should look at their ability to communicate with their followers, to hold up a vision of where they want to go, and how they exercise control over their organization. The relevant political, cognitive, and emotional skills are also delineated. No one president, he suggests, will excel in all these areas. Indeed, he shows each president since Franklin D. Roosevelt as having in some ways a unique profile. Useful as this approach is, we might also attempt to piece together a model of what the political equivalent of a grand master in chess might look like (a quest suggested earlier by Irving Janis). A strategically sophisticated president will have an ability to articulate the concerns of a significant public, provide some answers to those concerns, and face tradeoffs he may be forced to make. His organizational skills will be apparent in his ability to delegate while reserving for himself the ability to make final decisions. Emotional skills may be manifested in his ability to promote honest feedback from his own inner circle, as well as his ability to form and maintain working alliances with other political influentials where it is mutually beneficial. No one president, of course, is apt to meet all these standards, but a political grand master will do well on most of these measures. To be considered "great" however, his skills must fit the times. A would-be transformational leader is only apt to be successful if his aspirations fit the times. Even then, fortune will play a role in his later reputation. His success or his failures are influenced by factors outside his control, but in the long run he will be judged by what he actually accomplished.

Further reading: Barber, James David. *The Presidential Character: Predicting Performance in the White House,* 4th ed. Englewood Cliffs, N.J.: Prentice Hall, 1992; Burns, James MacGregor. *Leadership.* New York: Harper & Row, 1978; George, Alexander L., and Juliette L. George. *Woodrow Wilson and Colonel House: A Personality Study.* New York: Dover Publications, 1964; Glad, Betty. *Jimmy Carter: People, Politics and the Making of the U.S. Foreign Policy* (forthcoming); "When Governments are Good." In *The Moral Authority of Government: Essays to Commemorate the Centennial of the National Institute of Social Sciences,* edited by M. Kennedy, R. G. Hoxie, and B. Repland. New Brunswick, N.J.: Transaction Publishers, 2000; Greenstein, Fred I. *The Hidden-Hand Presidency: Eisenhower as Leader.* New York: Basis Books, 1982; ———. *The Presidential Difference: Leadership Style from FDR to Clinton.* Princeton, N.J.: Princeton University Press, 2000; Holsti, Ole R. "Crisis Management." In *Psychological Dimensions of War,* edited by B. Glad. Newbury Park, Calif.: Sage Publications, 1990; Janis, Irving Lester. *Crucial Decisions: Leadership in Policymaking and Crisis Management.* New York: The Free Press, 1989; Skowronek, Stephen. *The Politics Presidents Make: Leadership from John Adams to Bill Clinton.* Cambridge,

Mass.: Belknap Press, 1997; Smith, M. Brewster. "A Map for the Analysis of Personality and Politics." *Journal of Social Issues* 24, no. 3 (1968): 15–28.

—Betty Glad

League of Nations

In January 1918 President Woodrow WILSON made a speech to Congress outlining his program for peace at the end of the war in Europe. His guiding principles were brought together under the rubric of his FOURTEEN POINTS. The last of these principles was Wilson's proposal for an international League of Nations that would work to maintain world peace. In Wilson's eyes, the League was the most important feature of the Paris Peace Conference, and it was the main object of his efforts. In the end, Wilson was willing to sacrifice other elements of his Fourteen Points to get the League, a fact the other allies quickly understood.

The purpose of the League of Nations was to maintain world peace through world public opinion, resorting to military force only if necessary. In Wilson's words, the League would organize "the moral force of the world." Instead of focusing on the more traditional balance of power, the League would preserve the territorial integrity and political independence of member nations and foster cooperation among all. However, the League at first excluded Germany and did not include the Soviet Union, and the defeat of the TREATY OF VERSAILLES by the U.S. Senate kept America out of the League as well, undermining its effectiveness.

The most controversial aspect of the Treaty was the issue of participation in the League, outlined in Article X of the Covenant of the League. Wilson considered that article to be the heart of the charter, for it bound signatories "to respect and preserve against external aggression the territorial integrity and . . . political independence of all . . . members of the League." Many Republican senators had reservations about Article X, arguing that the United States would be under no obligation to act in defense of other nations unless Congress voted on the matter. Wilson said Article X was permissive in nature and did not infringe upon the constitutional authority of Congress to initiate military action. The Senate was more suspicious, knowing that a president could work things in such a way that Congress would have no choice but to authorize military force. Wilson himself had demonstrated that power in Mexico in 1914 and Germany in 1917. Thus, to a large extent the resistance of many senators was a matter of protecting congressional prerogatives.

Opposition to the League was partisan, but the partisans were joined by isolationists and immigrant groups, such as German- and Irish-Americans offended by some of the provisions. Opponents, led by Henry Cabot Lodge, made Wilson aware of their problems with the League and urged him to separate it from the larger and more immediate issue of peace. Wilson refused, obstinately pledging to bring back from Paris a Treaty and Covenant so intertwined that they could not be separated. He succeeded, and when the Senate defeated the Treaty, it killed American participation in the League.

Further reading: Blum, John Morton. *Woodrow Wilson and the Politics of Morality.* Boston: Little, Brown, 1956; Clements, Kendrick A. *The Presidency of Woodrow Wilson.* Lawrence: University Press of Kansas, 1992; Cooper, John Milton, Jr. *The Warrior and the Priest: Woodrow Wilson and Theodore Roosevelt.* Cambridge, Mass.: Belknap Press of Harvard University Press, 1983.

—David A. Crockett

legislative leadership

Major Pierre L'Enfant, principal designer of the nation's capital, had more than space in mind when he located the president and Congress at opposite ends of Pennsylvania Avenue. The Congress would be housed atop Jenkins Hill, giving it the high ground. The president would find his home about one mile away, at the end of a long street that would serve as a threadlike link connecting these two institutions. Not only did the Constitution separate the executive and legislative branches, but geography as well would keep these two branches apart.

For the U.S. system to work, however, both branches must find ways to bridge the gap, to join what is separated. The Founders saw the SEPARATION OF POWERS not as a weakness (as we tend to see it today), but as a strength, as a way to ensure deliberation and thoughtfulness, as a way to prevent tyranny. But how does a president develop the syncopation of the branches necessary to make the system of separate institutions sharing power work? How can a president couple what the Founders decoupled?

Beyond question, the relationship between the president and Congress is the most important one in the American system of government, and while the president spends a great deal of time and energy courting the media and appealing to the public, he does so in order to gain leverage with Congress. For, in the long run, presidents must get Congress to formally or tacitly accept their proposals, lest they run the risk of deadlock, delay, or failure. After all, only Congress can allocate resources, and presidents who consistently attempt to go around the Congress cannot long succeed. The president may not like it, but he cannot live without Congress.

While there are a select few areas in which presidents may act semi-independently of the Congress, most of the president's goals require a partnership with Congress. This is no easy matter. As one longtime presidential adviser has noted, "I suspect that there may be nothing about the White House less generally understood than the ease with which a Congress can drive a President quite out of his mind and up the wall."

In matters requiring legislative authorization, the Congress ultimately has the upper hand. Though the president may be seen as leader of the nation, agenda setter, vision builder, or legislator in chief, it is often the Congress that has the final say. And since there are multiple veto points in Congress, any of which may block a president's proposal, the forces wishing to prevent change almost always have the upper hand. The American system has many negative veto points but few avenues for positive change.

In the expectations game, the president is supposed to dominate Congress. But public expectance notwithstanding, the president's legislative powers are constitutionally (Article II, Section 3) quite thin. He has the VETO POWER, reports on the state of the Union, and extraconstitutionally may suggest legislation, lobby Congress, set the agenda, and build coalitions, but overall his *powers over* Congress are very limited.

In this sense, the Constitution sets up what Edward S. Corwin refers to as an "invitation to struggle" over political control of the Constitution (the power of the government). Another way to look at it is to see the Constitution as creating a situation in which "guerrilla warfare" between the president and the Congress is almost inevitable. Since Congress has "all legislative powers" and the president has limited legislative powers, conflict is built into the system.

Originally (constitutionally) the Congress was established as the dominant branch of government, and the first few presidents were only minimally involved in the legislative process. The Founders' vision soon gave way to political reality, and slowly presidents began to pull power into the White House, and generally the Congress was a willing participant in giving more and more power to the presidency. Today, as Robert Spitzer describes it, "What was designed as a congressionally centered system has evolved into a presidentially centered, or 'executive-hegemonic,' system." Still, the Congress has a way of frustrating even the most skilled of presidents.

While the image or expectation of the president is as "chief legislator" who "guides Congress in much of its lawmaking activity," the reality is quite different. The decentralized nature of the Congress, the multiple access and veto points within the congressional process, the loosely organized party system, the independent-entrepreneurial mode of the legislators, and the weakness of the legislative leadership all conspire against presidential direction and leadership. As George Edwards points out, this means that presidents impact Congress only "at the margins" and are more "facilitators" than leaders.

Lest the system break down into hopeless gridlock, the president and Congress must find ways to work together. The theory upon which the U.S. government is based hinges on some cooperation between these two branches. As Justice Robert Jackson wrote in 1952, "While the Constitution diffuses power the better to secure liberty, it also contemplates that practice will integrate the dispersed powers into a workable government."

Under what conditions is a president most likely to establish his agenda and get congressional support? Put another way, when is Congress most likely to follow a president's lead?

Several factors lead to presidential success when dealing with Congress. First, in a crisis, the president is accorded a great deal of deference, and the Congress usually backs up the president, as was generally the case after the 9/11 attack against the United States. Second, when a president has a clear electoral mandate (when the campaign was issue-oriented, the president wins by a wide margin, and the president's party has a sizable majority in Congress), the Congress sometimes will follow. Third, the president can exert pressure on members of Congress when he, the president, wins the election by a landslide *and* runs ahead of the members in his or her own district (this is usually referred to as "presidential COATTAILS"). Fourth, high levels of presidential popularity are often said to be a source of power over Congress, but how easily can presidents translate popularity into power? Many social scientists are suspicious, believing that popularity has only a marginal impact on presidential success within Congress, while others argue that popularity does translate into power.

Fifth, skill does make a difference, but how much of a difference? As is the case with popularity, scholars disagree about the importance of skill in legislative success, with some arguing that skill is of little importance, while others see skill as very important.

High skill levels can give a president greater leverage to win in the congressional process. A variety of skills—knowledge of the congressional process and needs; good timing, bargaining, deal-making, persuasion, and coalition-building skill; moving the public, setting the agenda, self-dramatization, arm-twisting, trading, consultation and co-optation, and even threats—can be used to advance the president's goals.

Lyndon JOHNSON, arguably the most skilled of the modern presidents vis-à-vis Congress—who also came into office on the heels of the martyred President KENNEDY, won election by a huge landslide, and had a huge partisan majority and a shattered opposition in Congress—explained that there was only one way to deal with Congress and that is continuously, incessantly, and without interruption. If it's really going to work, he noted, the relationship between the president and Congress has got to be almost incestuous. He's got to know them even better than they know themselves. And then, on the basis of this knowledge, he's got to build a system that stretches from the cradle to the grave, from the moment it is officially enrolled as the law of the land.

Lyndon Johnson could be a presidential pit bull, but he was afforded that luxury only partly due to personal skills. LBJ had, as mentioned earlier, other significant advantages that made his power more robust and his threats more credible (compare the resources Johnson had to the more meager power resources of President Clinton). One of the most important of these power resources is party support.

Partisan support in Congress is the sixth major factor shaping presidential success in Congress. Lyndon Johnson had such a large majority in Congress that, even if several dozen Democrats abandoned the president, he could still get his majority in Congress. George H. W. BUSH, on the other hand, faced a Congress in the control of the opposition, and he was thus stymied in Congress. Bill CLINTON had a paper-thin majority, and any defections undermined his legislative hopes. This forced Clinton to do a great deal of vote-trading and deal-making with congressional Democrats in order to get his 1993 deficit-reduction bill passed by Congress, as not one Republican voted for the president's proposal. In fact, deal making is a very common form of presidential leverage in attempting to extract votes from a recalcitrant Congress. Reagan's budget director David Stockman noted that "the last 10 or 20 percentage of the votes needed for a majority of both houses on the 1981 tax cut had to be bought, period. . . . The hogs were really feeding."

Related to this is the seventh factor: the nature of the opposition in Congress. How many votes do they have? How ideologically driven are they? How willing are they to work with the president? In 1981 President REAGAN faced a Senate controlled by his own party but a House controlled by the Democrats. Reagan was able—via skill, luck, and circumstance—to win over enough Democrats (referred to as the "Boll Weevils") to win several significant legislative battles. By contrast, while President Clinton had majorities in both houses, the Republican opposition was so ornery (Senator Dole of Kansas, in the first six months of Clinton's term, seemed determined to bring the Clinton presidency down) and so unified (on Clinton's 1993 economic package, not one Republican senator supported the president) that Clinton had an amazingly difficult time getting a win.

Because of the nature of partisan politics, the eighth factor that shapes presidential success or failure in Congress is the nature of consultation between the two branches. One of the lessons President Clinton learned is that a president must consult not only with his own partisans but with the opposition as well. There are so many veto points in the legislative process that attempting to gain cooperation and agreement must be the first step. If a president sets up an effective legislative liaison office and he can co-opt the Congress, he can often gain support.

Finally, the type of agenda a president pursues has a significant impact. George H. W. Bush had a very thin legislative agenda, and he pursued it only halfheartedly. Bill Clinton had a very ambitious agenda, making it more difficult to get the Congress to go along.

In recent years, presidents have spent less time "going Washington" and more time "going public." The inside bargaining skills necessary to cut deals have been replaced by or supported by efforts at self-dramatization. In the loose bargaining regime of the Congress, presidents feel their time is better spent appealing directly to the public for support (which may translate into clout in Congress). But ultimately presidents must cut deals in Congress.

Can presidents lead Congress? Yes, but not often and not for long. A mix of skill, circumstances, luck, popularity, party support, timing, and resources need to converge if the syncopation of the branches is to occur.

Further reading: Bond, Jon R., and Richard Fleisher. *The President in the Legislative Arena.* Chicago: University of Chicago Press, 1990; Edwards, George C., III. *At the Margins: Presidential Leadership of Congress.* New Haven, Conn.: Yale University Press, 1989; Fisher, Louis. *Constitutional Conflicts between the Congress and the President,* 3d rev. ed. Lawrence: University of Kansas Press, 1991; Peterson, Mark A. *Legislating Together.* Cambridge, Mass.: Harvard University Press, 1990; Spitzer, Robert. *President and Congress.* New York: McGraw-Hill, 1993; ———. *The Presidential Veto.* Albany: State University of New York Press, 1988.

legislative veto

A power developed in the 1930s to provide a means for Congress to maintain control over the actions of administrative agencies, yet to also allow agencies, and the president, to retain discretion to act. This power is created when Congress passes legislation, duly signed by the president, that gives Congress the ability to block or "veto" subsequent administrative actions without giving the president any say over the blocking actions themselves. A legislative veto differs from regular legislative action in that the former does not cross the president's desk, although the law creating the power does. For example, Congress passed a law that was signed by the president in 1980 that required the Federal Trade Commission (FTC) to present to Congress any proposed FTC regulations, which would then automatically take effect 90 days after receipt by Congress, unless both houses of Congress voted by concurrent resolution to strike down any of the rules. Concurrent resolution votes do not cross the president's desk (they are traditionally reserved for internal congressional matters or expressions of congressional opinion). Congress has enacted legislative vetoes that could be invoked by two houses of Congress, one house of Congress, or even by a congressional committee.

Legislative vetoes came to be relied on increasingly by Congress in the 1970s and early 1980s. From 1970 to 1980, for example, 423 legislative veto provisions were imbedded in laws. Presidents since Herbert HOOVER have objected to the legislative veto, yet have invariably signed bills into laws with such provisions in them, arguing that the device was an abuse of congressional power, and that it circumvented constitutional presentment of bills to the president. Proponents of the power argued that it was a legitimate and useful way for Congress to maintain control of the federal BUREAUCRACY.

These arguments came to a head in the 1983 Supreme Court case of INS V. CHADHA, in which the Court struck down the legislative veto power, arguing that it violated presentment and (in the case of one-house legislative vetoes) bicameralism. In the aftermath of the ruling, Congress repealed legislative veto provisions; yet it also continued to employ the power, sometimes by agreements imbedded in congressional reports instead of in law. By one count, from 1983 to 1997, more than 400 legislative vetoes have been enacted into law. For example, an appropriations bill for fiscal year 1996 required the General Services Administration to obtain approval from the House and Senate Appropriations Committees if it decided to spend more for certain construction projects than had been authorized. The persistence of these arrangements in the face of the *Chadha* case underscores their mutually beneficial nature for Congress and federal agencies.

See also PRESENTATION CLAUSE.

Further reading: Fisher, Louis. *The Politics of Shared Powers.* College Station: Texas A&M University Press, 1998; Korn, Jessica. *The Power of Separation.* Princeton, N.J.: Princeton University Press, 1996; Spitzer, Robert J. *President and Congress.* Philadelphia: Temple University Press, 1993.

—Robert J. Spitzer

Lend-Lease Act

The Lend-Lease Act was President Franklin D. ROOSEVELT's main mechanism for aiding the United States' WORLD WAR II allies to defeat Hitler. It was a turning point of the war, for it put the full industrial and economic might of the United States behind Britain's war effort. British Prime Minister Winston Churchill famously characterized Lend-Lease as "the most unsordid act in the history of any nation."

FDR committed the United States in late 1939 to providing war materials to Britain on a cash-and-carry basis, but by the summer of 1940 the new prime minister, Churchill, pointed out that British cash reserves were dwindling. The British financial situation became critical by early December 1940, right after FDR's reelection to his third term, and the president proposed the concept of Lend-Lease. In a radio broadcast to the American people on December 17, FDR told Americans that, if a neighbor's house catches on fire, the proper response is not to charge him cash to borrow a garden hose to douse the flames, but to lend the hose willingly. The program thus would provide goods to Britain on the condition that it returns or provides for their replacement at the conclusion of the war. FDR spelled out the details of the initiative to the American people in his annual message of January 6, 1941.

Democratic leaders placed the bill before Congress four days later with the symbolic number H.R. 1776. The legislation enabled the U.S. government to "sell, transfer title to, exchange, lease, lend, or otherwise dispose of" a long list of defense supplies to "any country whose defense the President deems vital to the defense of the United States." Repayment was to be made "in kind or property, or any other direct or indirect benefit which the President deems satisfactory." The act prohibited U.S. naval vessels from transporting the defense supplies or from entering combat zones to facilitate such exchanges. The bill sailed through Congress on March 11, 1941, after FDR accepted minor limitations on the administration of the program. "The words and acts of the President and the people of the United States," said Churchill, "come to us like a draft of life, and they tell us by an ocean-borne trumpet call that we are no longer alone."

Lend-Lease aid was extended to China later in the spring of 1941 and to the Soviet Union in the fall. By the end of World War II, more than 40 countries had received Lend-Lease aid. The original legislation provided for up to $7 billion in appropriations through June 30, 1942, but this total would grow to more than $50 billion by the time President Harry S TRUMAN ended the program on August 21, 1945. Approximately $40 billion went to Britain and about $11 billion to the Soviet Union. Some of this aid was repaid by "reverse lend-lease," through which recipient countries provided roughly $8 billion in aid to U.S. military forces abroad. Final and full repayment arrangements with most Lend-Lease recipient countries were reached by 1960. The Soviet Union repaid only about one-third of the aid it received, however, and a final deal was not cemented until 1972, with $722 million to be paid through installments through 2001.

Further reading: Dallek, Robert. *Franklin D. Roosevelt and American Foreign Policy, 1932–1945.* New York: Oxford University Press, 1979; Kimball, Warren F. *The Most Unsordid Act: Lend-Lease, 1939–1941.* Baltimore, Md.: Johns Hopkins University Press, 1969; Gilbert, Martin. *The Second World War: A Complete History.* New York: H. Holt, 1989.

—Douglas M. Brattebo

libraries, presidential

Presidential libraries serve as repositories of PRESIDENTIAL PAPERS, documents, oral histories, audio/video recordings, and other historical records of a presidential administration. Other historical records may include donated materials from CABINET members, contemporaries, and advisers. Generally the libraries are built with private donations, transferred to the federal government and maintained with federal funds. Once transferred to the federal government, the NATIONAL ARCHIVES and Records Administration (NARA) is responsible for the maintenance and operation of the facilities. NARA currently operates and maintains 10 presidential libraries and two materials projects (NIXON and CLINTON). Often associated with the libraries are museums that house and display personal items of each president and first lady, provide an historical overview of their lives, and conduct seminars, conferences, and other programming related to the particular president and his administration.

The NARA-managed libraries include (in alphabetical order): George Bush Library (College Station, Tex.); Jimmy Carter Library (Atlanta Ga.); Dwight D. Eisenhower Library (Abilene, Kans.); Gerald R. Ford Library (Ann Arbor, Mich.); Herbert Hoover Library (West Branch, Iowa); Lyndon B. Johnson Library (Austin, Tex.); John F. Kennedy Library (Boston, Mass.); Ronald Reagan Library (Simi Valley, Calif.); Franklin D. Roosevelt Library (HYDE PARK, N.Y.); Harry Truman Library (Independence, Mo.). These facilities offer scholars and the general public access to more than 400 million pages of text, 10 million photographs, 15 million feet of film, and nearly 100,000 hours of recorded material (audio/video). Currently, five of the NARA libraries (Roosevelt, Truman, Kennedy, Johnson, and Ford) provide grants-in-aid to scholars conducting research.

The two materials projects under the auspices of NARA include the Nixon Presidential Materials Project and the Clinton Presidential Materials Project. Once a president leaves office, NARA establishes a presidential project where papers and documents of the former CHIEF EXECUTIVE are stored until the creation of a presidential library. President Clinton's papers are being held by the William J. Clinton Presidential Materials Project in Little Rock, Arkansas, while the Clinton Presidential Center is being built. Upon completion of the facility, the Clinton library will become the 11th facility maintained by NARA.

The case of President Nixon's papers is significantly different. President Nixon's papers are administered under the terms of the Presidential Recordings and Materials Preservation Act. The Richard Nixon Library and Birthplace in Yorba Linda, California, was privately built and is privately maintained. It is not part of the NARA's holdings. Archives of the Nixon Library include prepresidential papers (1913–68) and postpresidential papers (1974–94).

President Franklin Delano ROOSEVELT was the first chief executive to turn over both his personal and presidential papers to the government for preservation, and the Franklin D. Roosevelt Library was the first presidential library to be administered by NARA. Before 1939, papers of U.S. presidents were thought to be the personal property of each individual. In the absence of a formal system to acquire, catalog, and archive such papers, many important documents relating to the American presidency and its occupants were lost and/or destroyed. One former president, Chester Alan ARTHUR, is reported to have burned three trash cans of his papers the day before he died. Fortunately, papers of 23 of the first 29 presidents are housed under the auspices of the Library of Congress.

There are many "firsts" in presidential library history. The first facility to be called a presidential library is located in Ohio. The Rutherford B. Hayes Presidential Center is not part of the 10 presidential libraries administered by NARA. However, the Hayes Center is the only library named for a 19th-century president. It is supported by private funding and the Historical Society of Ohio. The library, built in 1916, houses HAYES's personal library, including 12,000 volumes, along with archival material from his military and political career. Material from Hayes's presidency (1877–81) is also part of the holdings.

The annual cost to the U.S. Treasury to maintain the 10 federally administered libraries is approximately $38 million.

Further reading: Rutherford B. Hayes Presidential Center: www.rbhayes.org; Overview of Presidential Libraries of the National Archives and Records Administration: http://www.nara.gov/nara/president/overview.html; NARA Presidential Libraries and Projects: http://www.nara.gov/nara/president/address.html.

—Owen Holmes

Lieberman, Joseph (1942–) *U.S. senator*

The Democratic senator from Connecticut who ran as VICE PRESIDENT in 2000, Lieberman is noteworthy because he was the first Jewish candidate for one of the top spots on a national ticket. As a senator Lieberman was a moderate

Democrat who was one of the early critics of President CLINTON on the "character" issue. This made him attractive to vice president Al GORE, as a potential vice presidential running mate, as Gore sought to distance himself from President Clinton on issues of character. Lieberman planned to seek the Democratic nomination for president in 2004.

Lincoln, Abraham (1809–1865) *sixteenth U.S. president*

America's 16th president was elected twice, first in 1860 and again in 1864 when Abraham Lincoln insisted that the regularly scheduled presidential election be conducted during the CIVIL WAR, even though he expected to lose. During a wartime administration he (1) preserved the Union in the face of a devastating Civil War, (2) ended the institution of slavery in the United States, (3) promoted the American experiment in self-government by upholding the electoral process despite the national schism, and (4) advocated a magnanimous reconstruction policy. Not only do experts consistently rank him as the greatest American president, but also they regard his leadership style as one of the greatest gifts of American democracy to the world.

Origins

Lincoln's rags-to-riches myth epitomizes the self-made man of the 19th century, but in reality his origins were more complex. He was a classic psychological outsider—the most marginal president in American history. Physically, he was too tall, too skinny, and, perhaps, too ugly to be a successful politician. Layered onto his appearance was the additional hindrance of his border-state birth on February 12, 1809, in Kentucky. The only male child to survive infancy among his siblings, young Abraham Lincoln grew up on the American frontier as his father moved the family first to Indiana and then to Illinois. Comparative research suggests that by the time he was a teenager, Lincoln's family had achieved middle-class status, contrary to popular Lincoln lore. Nonetheless, he remained a frontier hick by both New England and aristocratic Southern standards. His speech and dress did little to dispel his hick reputation. He married up when he wed Mary Todd, a member of one of the most prominent families in Lexington, Kentucky, known at that time as "the Athens of the West." Mary Todd married Abraham Lincoln against the wishes of her socially-conscious relatives in Springfield, Illinois. Lincoln possessed intelligence and energy, qualities more important to Mary Todd than appearance. They seemed an odd couple to observers who could not see beyond the contrast of the lovely Mary and homely Abe, separated by more than a foot in height, but united by a passion for politics and mutual desire to see Abraham Lincoln as president of the United States.

On a deeper level, they had the shared childhood trauma of losing their mother at a young age, perhaps the root cause of the moodiness that both endured as adults. If their frontier insecurity about "fitting in" with Easterners made them marginal, Abraham suffered the additional impediment of being an intellectual outsider due to his lack of formal education. Mary Todd, by contrast, was well educated and she used her greater sophistication to groom her gangly spouse for higher political office.

Like other future political leaders, Lincoln had taken a long time to decide what to do with his life. He held a series of jobs—a farmer's field hand, a deckhand on Mississippi flatboats, a postmaster, a surveyor, a militiaman, and a storekeeper. He even considered becoming a blacksmith. Ultimately he rejected his father's model of working with his back in favor of working with his brain. In the process, Abraham Lincoln became an autodidact.

Politics and Law

In 1832 he ran for the Illinois statehouse and lost. More important historically than his defeat in that first election was the fact that Lincoln ran for public office five years before he became a lawyer—earlier than any other lawyer who went on to become president. In politics he found an activity in which he was competent and which he enjoyed for its own sake so much that he sought the same office in 1834, and won the first of four terms as an Illinois state legislator. In an extremely short time, consistent with an individual who has resolved a postponed identity crisis, Lincoln emerged from nowhere to become the Whig floor leader in the Illinois legislature. He would spend the rest of his life seeking or serving in a political office, except for a five-year hiatus after his single term in the U.S. House of Representatives (1846–48).

To pursue his preferred professional activity, it was necessary for Lincoln to use the law as a means to support his wife and their growing family. He had received his law license in 1836 and became a junior partner of John Todd Stuart, who introduced Lincoln to his cousin Mary Todd. It was the first of three law practices for Lincoln. In 1841 he became a partner of Stephen T. Logan. Three years later, he established his own law practice with William H. Herndon, treating Herndon as an equal business partner instead of the way he had been treated in his first two practices. Except for the single congressional term, Lincoln spent the next 17 years in Springfield practicing law and developing his own jurisprudence. It was a busy practice involving mostly state circuit courts, arguing hundreds of cases before the Illinois Supreme Court and federal courts during the Golden Age of American jurisprudence, when outdated English precedents were replaced by American cases as part of its jurisprudential development. In the process, Lincoln became one of Illinois' best-known lawyers.

He was offered the position of chief counsel for a major railroad just prior to assuming the presidency. Lincoln, of course, chose politics instead of a law career and certain wealth. Ironically, choosing the political arena fulfilled both areas of Lincoln's competence, in a sense, because he served as president during a period of continual constitutional crisis in which he made constitutional law and established himself as one of America's greatest legal minds.

Transition to the Presidency

With the demise of the Whigs, Lincoln became a Republican candidate for the U.S. Senate, representing the antislavery party that he had helped to organize in Illinois. Through this election, Lincoln established a national reputation although he lost the battle for the Senate seat in a contest finally decided by the Illinois legislature. He engaged in the seven now-famous debates against "the Little Giant," incumbent senator and noted orator Stephen A. Douglas. Lincoln effectively challenged the amorality of "popular sovereignty" as advocated by Douglas, just as he had challenged the irrational notion of "concurrent majority" when it was offered by John C. CALHOUN, the eminent and successful Southern politician, "the Marx of the Master Class." In contrast, Lincoln, with classical prudence, advocated an end to the spread of slavery into the new territories but upheld protection of it in the South as guaranteed by the Constitution while suggesting a long-term natural rights jurisprudence, which emphasized the moral equality basis of the Declaration of Independence.

Douglas won the first battle by retaining his Senate seat, but they met again two years later as candidates for the American presidency. Douglas became the candidate of the Northern Democrats with anti-secessionist Herschell V. Johnson from Georgia as his running mate. Southern Democrats supported vice president John C. Breckenridge of Kentucky and Senator Joseph Lane of Oregon as their candidates. John BELL of Tennessee and Edward Everett of Massachusetts were the candidates of the Constitutional Unionists. Abraham Lincoln emerged as the dark-horse compromise candidate of the unified, antislavery REPUBLICAN PARTY. His vice-presidential running mate was Senator Hannibal HAMLIN of Maine. The Republican ticket won 39.8 percent of the popular vote for a plurality. Douglas-Johnson received 29.5 percent, Breckinridge-Lane got 18.1 percent, and Bell-Everett took 12.6 percent.

The Persistent Lawyer President

The South was in the midst of a revolutionary situation, inflamed by radicals. With the expansion of the United States, the historic control by the South of the U.S. Senate, the Supreme Court, and the presidency was doomed, especially after Lincoln's election. Unwilling to accept Lincoln's constitutional guarantee of slavery only in the South, seven

President Abraham Lincoln *(Library of Congress)*

Deep South states had seceded from the Union by early 1861. In their zeal to retain slavery, the secessionists fired first at Fort Sumter, which momentarily worked in Lincoln's favor and ultimately led to the South's defeat, given Lincoln's consummate political performance in the OVAL OFFICE. Congress was in recess so Lincoln turned to John Locke's philosophy of an executive assuming the "prerogative" power to guide his actions. Facing a Civil War that escalated into tragedy on a scale previously unknown in the American experience, Lincoln used the most extraconstitutional measures ever exercised by a CHIEF EXECUTIVE until that time. Roger B. Taney, a provincial and paternal Jacksonian justice from the border state of Maryland, was mired by both inclination and origin in the legal positivism of a white majority. He was unable to comprehend the values of the emerging Republican Party, much less those of the audacious frontier lawyer who was advocating an equality alien to Taney's Southern roots.

Lincoln insisted on preserving the Union, in part because it had provided him with the opportunity to fulfill himself and because its government, as he clearly articulated, represented "the last best hope of mankind." He was aware that all autocratic governments in the world at that

Engraving showing the assassination of Abraham Lincoln by John Wilkes Booth at Ford's Theatre *(Library of Congress)*

time expected—even hoped—that the American democratic experiment would fail. Lincoln was severely criticized for the extraconstitutional measures he employed to meet the national crisis, but his steps paled in comparison to those used by Jefferson DAVIS in his reactionary Confederacy, which aped the 1787 U.S. Constitution, except in practice. Taney's blinders were obvious to anyone acquainted with Andrew JACKSON, Taney's political hero, and the measures Jackson had imposed in New Orleans to deal with dissent during the WAR OF 1812. Lincoln's critics have labeled him a "constitutional dictator," but that term rings hollow because Lincoln fully appreciated that Congress would have the ultimate power to rule on his presidential actions. Moreover, Lincoln's entire personal and political philosophy opposed autocrats. Even when he fully expected to lose reelection, he sustained the electoral tradition in an atmosphere conducive to self-made dictators. Perhaps even more impressive is that he upheld the democratic process for the public good even while privately he was grieving the loss of his favorite son and facing a seemingly unending series of military commanders who could not win battles.

Presidential Precedents

Lincoln was a president with a constitutional purpose even without an impressive electoral mandate initially. The prudent lawyer-president improvised as he faced challenges and in the process turned in a consummate presidential performance. At first willing to allow the South to keep its "peculiar institution" since it was guaranteed in the U.S. Constitution, Lincoln tried only to prevent the spread of slavery, consistent with the Northwest Ordinance of 1787 and the Missouri Compromise of 1820. He later abandoned that initial goal in favor of measures necessary to preserve the Union when it became apparent that the very survival of the Union was at risk after Southern radicals pushed for and achieved secession.

The secession crisis forced Lincoln into a delicate balancing act, trying to keep the border states in the Union while at the same time countering the move of the secessionists. Relying on his OATH OF OFFICE and the powers of the COMMANDER IN CHIEF, Lincoln took extraconstitutional steps to meet the military crisis with the understanding that, ultimately, congressional ratification of his actions would be necessary. Meanwhile, he blocked Southern ports, doubled the armed forces, spent Treasury funds, and suspended the writ of *habeas corpus*. Congress eventually approved most of his war measures.

The short-term rebellion deepened into a protracted Civil War. Rather than caving in to the pressures of the wartime situation, he improvised with incompetent military leaders until General Ulysses S. GRANT demonstrated his understanding of tactics needed to win the unconventional war. Critics have portrayed Grant as a butcher because he, like his commander in chief, realized that the South must be militarily defeated to preserve the Union. Even so, Lincoln was unwilling to subject soldiers on either side to more bloodshed than was absolutely necessary to quell the revolution. He adopted the codified rules of war proposed by Francis Lieber, the foremost political scientist of the 19th century, in *Instructions for the Government of Armies of the United States in the Field*. The same rules that Lincoln adopted for the Civil War were the basis of the international rules of the law of war at The Hague and Geneva in the 20th century. In addition to extending the law to warfare, Lincoln refused to expand the war abroad, prudently insisting on "one war at a time."

As the Civil War ground on, Lincoln revised his initial conservative stance of endorsing the South's constitutional right to slavery. Confederate refusal to compromise prolonged the war and as it dragged on, Lincoln formulated a plan to end slavery by reconciling the Declaration of Independence with the U.S. Constitution. Equality and nationhood replaced slavery as well as any further serious talk of a compact of sovereign states. This was an *ad hoc* practical and philosophical policy that Lincoln formulated gradually between his single term in Congress and the presidency. The EMANCIPATION PROCLAMATION was a war measure, a policy which would liberate both blacks and whites in the South from their physical and intellectual bondage to an indefensible institution at odds with democratic ideals. The proclamation sent messages to abolitionists in the North, to Europeans who recognized the inconsistency between America's ideals and constitutional limitations, and, of course, to slaves. Lincoln had never been an abolitionist crusader; in fact, he perceived them to be nearly as impossible to reason with as the firebrand plantation owners were. On the other hand, his ever-active and flexible personality allowed him to convert challenges to opportunities, and he took advantage of the situation to advance democratic values.

Unlike most warrior executives, at the same time that Lincoln focused on defeating the South militarily, he reached beyond the bayonet for the olive branch. He became the Great Reconciler by advocating a RECONSTRUCTION policy of "with malice toward none," virtually unprecedented magnanimity from a president confronted with a bloody civil war. While Lincoln focused on winning the Civil War to preserve the Union, he deferred to a Republican-controlled Congress, which enacted other key parts of its platform to benefit an emerging middle class. Among the legislative acts were the Land Grant College Act (Morrill Act, 1862), which in some ways was the first significant piece of social legislation in American history; the Homestead Act, 1862; and the Pacific Railroad Act (transcontinental railroad). Lincoln expected and allowed Congress to perform its constitutional duty. Unlike some presidents, specifically his immediate predecessor, Lincoln understood that the role of government is to work for the welfare of people in areas where they are unable to help themselves individually. He defined the United States as a Union with a government of, by, and for the people. The one-time politician who was willing to protect the South's "peculiar institution," and who said at times that his policy was "to have no policy," crafted his GETTYSBURG ADDRESS into an eternal echo of democratic values which have come to define self-government at home and abroad.

He lacked executive experience, but Lincoln's style was evident from the start. He brought the best minds and voices into his CABINET, treating them as political equals even though some of them initially considered him to be their inferior. As long as they performed competently and consistently with his aims, Lincoln delegated and allowed them maximum latitude. Most of them came to appreciate Lincoln's political style. His "public-opinion baths," resulting from his open-door policy, kept him aware of the public pulse. His personal treatment of others earned their respect and trust. His public addresses reinforced public support.

The Legacy

Lincoln's presidential performance was so deft that it often was misunderstood while he was in office and even afterward. He broke boundaries. He was a man of many dimensions. Lincoln was autocratic in imposing extraconstitutional measures to deal with the war, but as a lifetime Whig lawyer, he was a conservative. At other times he seemed to be a passive victim, more controlled by events than controlling them, as he saw it. Nevertheless, Lincoln emerges as the foremost democratic leader in history. More books, journals, and newsletters, as well as organizations, are devoted to Lincoln than to any other democratic leader.

It was an assassin's bullet that turned the often-vilified President Lincoln into an icon. He was the first president to be assassinated and his violent death turned him into an American saint overnight. That sainthood threatens to mask the human who deserves to be remembered as a democratic leader who understood leadership. Evidence of his leadership is his record of advancing democratic values while fulfilling his own lifelong ambition to attain the presidency, the most original political office created by the framers in 1787.

Further reading: Fletcher, George P. *Our Secret Constitution. How Lincoln Redefined American Democracy.* New York: Oxford University Press, 2001; Neely, Mark E. Jr. *The Fate of Liberty: Abraham Lincoln and Civil Liberties.* New York: Oxford University Press, 1991; Pederson, William D., and Norman W. Provizer, eds. *Leaders of the Pack.* New York: P. Lang, 2003; ———— and Ann McLaurin, eds. *The Rating Game in American Politics.* New York: Irvington Publishers, 1987; Pessen, Edward. *The Log Cabin Myth. The Social Backgrounds of Presidents.* New Haven, Conn.: Yale University Press, 1984; Williams, Frank J., William D. Pederson, and Vincent J. Marsala, eds. *Abraham Lincoln. Source and Style of Leadership.* Westport, Conn.: Greenwood Press, 1994; ———— and William D. Pederson, eds. *Abraham Lincoln: Contemporary. An American Legacy.* El Dorado Hills, Calif.: Savas Publishing, 1996.

—William D. Pederson

Lincoln, Mary Todd (1818–1882) *first lady*

Mary Todd Lincoln, wife of America's greatest president, Abraham LINCOLN, was the most active political spouse between Dolley MADISON (her distant relative by marriage) and Eleanor ROOSEVELT. These FIRST LADIES blurred the traditional lines between social and political affairs for presidential spouses.

Mary Todd was a Southern belle from one of the most eminent families in Lexington, Kentucky, "the Athens of the West." Henry CLAY was a family friend and Mary Todd's maternal uncles were U.S. senators from Kentucky and Louisiana. She was unusually well educated for a female of her era. She learned to act in school, loved the opera, and was fluent in French. Her older sister married a lawyer who was an aspiring Illinois politician, the circumstance that brought the 21-year-old Mary Todd to the state where her first cousin was lawyer partner to Abraham Lincoln.

Superficially, the match between Lincoln and Mary Todd seemed incongruous. From a social standpoint, she married down to a man nearly a decade older, more than a foot taller, and lacking social status and graces. Yet their mutual Kentucky origins, Whig partisanship, appreciation of literature, and, most important, their love and ambition for a political life brought them together. After a broken engagement, they finally married on November 4, 1842, and four sons were born over the next decade (Robert Todd, 1843; Edward Baker, 1846; William Wallace, 1850; and Thomas "Tad," 1853). Mary reared her sons under conditions much harsher than any she had ever experienced in her upbringing and still refined her spouse's outward appearance and encouraged his political ventures with one exception. She blocked his acceptance of the governorship of Oregon, which might have ended his national political advancement.

Abraham had a Republican platform for the nation; Mary Todd had a corresponding agenda for herself and the presidential mansion. She represents the transition from Dolley Madison's Washington social emphasis to Eleanor Roosevelt's national political activism. At a time when most political wives were invisible, Mary Todd Lincoln was as assertive as her spouse when she arrived at the presidential mansion. She embarked on a major redecoration and refurbishment with the goal of transforming it into a national and international symbol of the American presidency; similarly, Abraham continued completion of the dome of the Capitol during the CIVIL WAR as a symbol of belief in the continuation of the Union. Mary overspent her project, repeating Abraham's action while pursuing his mission of developing Illinois during his service as a state legislator in Springfield. Running the presidential mansion was Mary's domain, politicians soon discovered. She hosted elegant parties there, as well as receptions, to bolster the national spirit. Again tracking her husband's behavior, Mary organized the first dinner of the new administration to honor the diplomatic corps, thereby putting the secretary of State in his place, just as the president had done to this one-time presidential competitor. Mary Todd, ever the social-conscious hostess, created a new salon boasting dominant political and literary figures that she invited to the executive mansion. The Marine band played "The Mary Lincoln Polka" and a foreign correspondent for the first time referred to the president's wife as first lady.

Her efforts to influence political PATRONAGE yielded mixed results but did not induce her to modify her approach. Even when the capital was under a military threat, Mary Todd insisted on remaining there with the president. She encouraged his afternoon carriage rides and attendance of the theater as means of relaxation from his presidential burdens. With characteristic energy, she visited military hospitals and even reviewed Union troops on occasion. Her personal relationship with African Americans exceeded her husband's. Elizabeth Keckley, her dressmaker, for example, was a close friend while she remained in Washington, D.C. Both raised funds for the Contraband Relief Association.

Unfortunately, her energetic agenda to prove her right to preside in the nation's capital even though she had lived on the frontier and had Confederate relatives was undermined by the emotional toll extracted by the deaths of her spouse and all but one son. High-strung and given to mood swings, Mary Todd reached her breaking point and turned to spiritualism and engaged in bizarre behavior. In 1875 her oldest son committed her to an asylum for a short confinement. That episode continues to influence scholars who do not balance that dramatic portion of her life against her multiple contributions to the 16th presidency.

Further reading: Baker, Jean H. *Mary Todd Lincoln: A Biography.* New York: Norton, 1987; Ostendorf, Lloyd, and Walter Oleksy, eds. *Lincoln's Unknown Private Life: An Oral History by His Black Housekeeper Mariah Vance, 1850–1860.* Mamaroneck, N.Y.: Hastings House, 1995; Turner, Justin, and Linda Levitt Turner, eds. *Mary Todd Lincoln—Her Life and Letters.* New York: Knopf, 1972.

—William D. Pederson

Little v. Barreme, 6 U.S. (2 Cranch) 170 (1804)

This Supreme Court decision affirmed the constitutional authority of Congress to restrain the president's COMMANDER IN CHIEF power by defining the scope of hostilities. During the quasi-war between the United States and France in the late 1790s, Congress passed a number of statutes suspending intercourse between the two nations. The acts authorized the president to instruct commanders of armed vessels "to stop and examine any ship or vessel of the United States on the high sea" suspected of violating the statute. Following examination, if the commanders were convinced the ship was bound or sailing *to* any port within the territory of France, the commander could send the vessel back to the United States for adjudication. Following enactment of this legislation, the secretary of the Navy issued orders that authorized commanders to seize not only any ship heading to a French port but also any ship having departed *from* a French port. Pursuant to such orders, Captain George Little intercepted a Danish vessel, *The Flying Fish,* which was sailing *from* a French port. Captain Little sent the vessel to the United States, whereupon he was sued for damages by the Danish owners of the vessel.

The decision, delivered through Chief Justice John MARSHALL, concluded that Congress, by only authorizing seizure of vessels heading toward French ports, effectively prohibited any interception of vessels heading from French ports. The Court concluded that Captain Little would have to pay damages to the shipowners despite the orders given by his superiors in the EXECUTIVE BRANCH. The Court, however, did not rule out whether the president could have ordered the seizure of such vessels absent congressional intent otherwise.

The *Little* decision is important with respect to the Constitution's allocation of war powers between the president and Congress. In *Little,* the Court held that statutory silence by Congress on the question of vessels coming from France constituted a prohibition of such activity. Consequently, *Little* is frequently cited by advocates of a more powerful Congress and a more restrained executive who contend that the president altogether lacks or enjoys at best only circumscribed inherent power in the realm of national security affairs. Subsequent cases, on the other hand, such

as *DAMES & MOORE v. REGAN,* have held the opposite of *Little*—that statutory silence in FOREIGN AFFAIRS constitutes implicit authorization or at least no prohibition to presidential action. The relationship between *Little v. Barreme* and *Dames & Moore v. Regan* is unclear and it mirrors the judiciary's inconsistent approach to exercises of presidential power. At a minimum, *Little* suggests that Congress in authorizing limited hostilities has the authority to set at least some parameters on the president's use of force.

Further reading: Glennon, Michael J. "Two Views of Presidential Foreign Affairs Power: *Little v. Barreme* or *Curtiss-Wright?*" *Yale J. Int'l Law* 13, no. 5, 1988; *Constitutional Diplomacy.* Princeton, N.J.: Princeton University Press, 1990; Sofaer, Abraham. *War, Foreign Affairs, and Constitutional Power.* Cambridge, Mass.: Ballinger Pub. Co, 1976.

—Roy E. Brownell II

Louisiana Purchase

From the time of the American Revolution, the potentially volatile nature of the Western lands was a matter of great concern for Americans, involving as it did claims (legitimate and spurious) by various states, the federal government, Native Americans, and the foreign powers of Britain, France, and Spain. The Treaty of Paris in 1783 had ceded control over Trans-Appalachian lands to the Mississippi River to the United States, secured navigation rights on the Mississippi for both the United States and Britain, and divided the Continent among competing powers. Access to the port at New Orleans subsequently became a matter of great significance, as upwards of one-third to one-half of American goods passed through the port by the turn of the century, with an increase anticipated.

Thomas JEFFERSON exhibited concern about the West, and especially about New Orleans, early on, and was thus chagrined to discover in 1802 that Spain had retroceded Louisiana to France. But American negotiators Robert Livingston and James MONROE were surprisingly offered the territory by France early in 1803 and concluded a treaty on April 30 of that year. The treaty required Senate approval under Article II, and, more important, presented a constitutional problem for Jefferson, given that his well-established principles of government of limited powers and strict constitutional construction were now challenged by the possibility of undertaking an action for which he had no constitutional authority. Jefferson at first contemplated proposing a constitutional amendment that would authorize the purchase, and even drafted a proposal, but, in the end, fearing, in part, that there was insufficient time to get an amendment ratified (Napoleon had given the United States six months to approve the purchase), and knowing that he would need both Senate and House approval for the purchase (to approve the treaty and to appropriate the funds for it), he simply called Congress back into session in October and won approval from both houses. Approval of the Purchase made for a fascinating reversal of political identities, involving support for expansion and overlooking of constitutional limitations by Jeffersonian Republicans, including John BRECKINRIDGE and John Taylor, and the questioning of federal expansion by Federalists, including Alexander HAMILTON and Fisher Ames. (The Marshall Court, not the greatest source of support for Jeffersonian principles, later provided legal sanction for the acquisition in *Sere v. Pitot* [1810] and *American Insurance Co. v. 356 Bales of Cotton* [1828].)

The aftermath of the Purchase is more important, and as interesting, as the contestations contained in the original acquisition. The purchase doubled the land mass of the United States, incorporating land that would constitute 10 new states, and gave impetus to the continental westward expansion fully envisioned by only a few in the Founding generation. It established national control over a considerable portion of the public lands, control that was typically not relinquished when the states were carved out of the territory, thus leaving a rather large federal presence within the borders of the states. In addition, the Purchase incorporated into the Union tens of thousands of people largely unknown in the eastern areas, French and Spanish speakers with different religious and political backgrounds, making newly minted citizens out of people who did not emigrate to the country by choice.

Most important, perhaps, the Purchase set the stage for the expansion of slavery into the western territories, a move that prompted long struggles about the institution across the decades. The geographic divisions that eventually united the North and the West on this issue culminated with LINCOLN's reentrance into public life in the 1850s as the head of the REPUBLICAN PARTY. His election in 1860 brought the persistent friction of the previous years to a head, producing secession and the outbreak of civil war.

In terms of its effect on the exercise of executive authority, the Louisiana Purchase is perhaps most notable for the relative lack of attention paid to Jefferson's actions, the general approach seeming to be that actions so useful to the success of the American enterprise are inherently justifiable, and that raining down legal objections reveals a lack of attention to the realities of political life. The relative niceties of constitutional interpretation, exacerbated in this instance by the presence in the executive office of an otherwise strict constructionist, take on a secondary importance given the grand scope of the Purchase and its utility for the country. But the exercise of power undertaken in the Purchase set an important precedent for subsequent presidents (and legislatures), and the expansion and extension of federal power assisted the later growth of presidential power.

—Richard Dougherty

loyalty-security programs

Loyalty programs designed to increase U.S. security date back to the early days of the republic. Even the Continental Congress took steps to remove those loyal to the Crown from public employment.

It was not until the COLD WAR era that these loyalty-security programs began to raise serious questions of civil liberty violations by the government. In the late 1940s and 1950s fear of communist subversion and of communist infiltration led to demands that the government institute programs designed to weed out subversives. Facing pressure from the Red Scare and demands by Senator Joseph MCCARTHY (Rep.-Minn.) the Truman administration instituted a number of programs in hopes of muting these fears.

Executive Order 9300 (8 Fed. Reg. 1701, 1943), for example, created a WORLD WAR II Interdepartmental Committee on Employee Loyalty Investigations to investigate federal employees. Later the FBI was used to investigate alleged subversives. Executive Order 9835 (12 Fed. Reg. 1935, 1947) required a loyalty investigation of all those employed by the federal government.

This "Loyalty Order" brought about the creation of a Loyalty Review Board, along with regional boards under the purview of the Civil Service Commission. Executive Order 10450 (18 Fed. Reg. 2489, 1953), known as the Security Order, superceded the Loyalty Order and expanded both statute and EXECUTIVE ORDERS controlling security programs.

As the Red Scare waned, so too did demands for loyalty programs, and some died of underuse while others were withdrawn. By the 1960s, demands for loyalty programs all but disappeared.

M

Madison, Dolley (1768–1849) *first lady*

Perhaps one of the best-known and -loved FIRST LADIES in American history, Dolley Madison served as the head of the most prominent political and social circles for almost 50 years. After her first husband succumbed to yellow fever, Dolley married James MADISON in 1794. As the wife of the secretary of State, from 1801 to 1809 Dolley Madison performed the functions of first hostess of Washington, D.C., during Jefferson's administration. She broke precedent by inviting women to White House soirees and encouraging them to engage in political discussions at these events.

After her husband's election to the presidency in 1808, Dolley assumed the formal duties of first lady. In that capacity, she had three major tasks: redecorating the White House, fulfilling the duties of the nation's hostess, and rescuing priceless artifacts during the WAR OF 1812 invasion. Mixing both Republican and High Federalist styles, Mrs. Madison created an eloquently fashioned WHITE HOUSE with the help of architect Benjamin Henry Latrobe. Her simple style won Dolley much fame as she established the role of first lady as the nation's hostess. Her quick tact soothed many political quarrels and divisions that festered during her husband's presidency.

By far, her most remarkable contributions occurred in the summer of 1814, during the British invasion of Washington. Even though the president had left town to supervise the army, Mrs. Madison remained at the White House. As the British approached the city, Dolley packed important state papers and expensive silver in wagons and sent them to the Bank of Maryland for safekeeping. At the last moment, Mrs. Madison supervised the rescue of Gilbert Stuart's full-length portrait of George Washington. After sending the painting to a nearby farm, Dolley escaped by wagon before the troops descended upon the capital, eventually burning the White House. President Madison was condemned for his leadership during the War of 1812, but Dolley Madison received much praise for her heroic actions. The Madisons retired to Montpelier, Virginia, but upon

First Lady Dolley Madison *(Library of Congress)*

her husband's death in 1836 Dolley returned to Washington, D.C., and lived a prominent and respected life until her death in 1849.

Further reading: The Dolley Madison Project: http://moderntimes.vcdh.virginia.edu/madison/index.html; Zall, Paul. *Dolley Madison.* Huntington, N.Y.: Nova History Publications, 2001.

—Colleen Shogan

305

Madison, James (1751–1836) *fourth U.S. president*
The fourth president of the United States, James Madison served two terms. His presidency remains largely overshadowed by that of Thomas JEFFERSON, his predecessor, mentor, and former boss while two-term secretary of State. As a result, Madison's presidential legacy is often overlooked, even though it is substantial. He was America's first great political scientist, and he was America's most constitutionally circumspect wartime CHIEF EXECUTIVE. Concurrently, Madison's spouse, Dolley, set a standard as America's great first lady.

Origins of a Philosophical Politician

Madison, born on March 16, 1751, in Port Conway, Virginia, was the eldest of 12 children in a planter family that moved in the early 18th century to Orange County, where their plantation, Montpelier, ultimately encompassed five thousand acres. Although Madison hated the institution of slavery, he—like Jefferson—depended upon the slave system to maintain his lifestyle.

Classically educated at the College of New Jersey in Princeton (later Princeton University), Madison received his bachelor's degree in 1771. He considered a career in the church or in law but was content reading widely from the Enlightenment and classical philosophers, especially their views on legal and political systems. Madison knew a great deal about the law, including INTERNATIONAL LAW, yet he never sought to practice law. At the age of 25, the young political philosopher entered politics with election to the Virginia convention that voted for independence. Madison, who fulfilled himself throughout his life as a practicing politician, remained politically active in executive or legislative capacities until the end of his presidency.

First Great American Political Scientist

The title "Father of the Constitution," conferred upon Madison, reflects the key role that he played in the 1787 Philadelphia Convention. He was principal author of the Virginia Plan, which served as the working model for the delegates. He designed a new kind of constitution that rejected the extremes of a unitary government like the one the colonists had experienced under King George as well as the confederal government that Americans had concocted in the Articles of Confederation and Perpetual Union. Exceeding their charge to revise the Articles of Confederation, the Philadelphia delegates adopted Madison's federal solution to the eternal problem of how to handle power. For his solution, Madison returned to his classical background, drawing upon Aristotle's moral principle of the golden mean to reject both extremes in government. The unitary model posed dangers to individuals' freedoms while the confederal model invited anarchy, as evidenced by Shays's Rebellion under the Articles of Confederation.

Madison's enduring legacy as a political theorist arose from his participation with Alexander HAMILTON and John JAY in writing a series of newspaper columns to help gain ratification of the new federal constitution. Later compiled as *The FEDERALIST PAPERS* (or *The Federalist*), these essays collectively are regarded as America's unique contribution to 2,500 years of Western political thought. Madison believed that he had constructed the solution for preventing entropy in good government. His solution was based upon a mixed polity, as Aristotle suggested first, combined with CHECKS AND BALANCES and implementation of a federal system over a large geographical area to dilute the power of factions, a novel approach. At the CONSTITUTIONAL CONVENTION, Madison joined Alexander Hamilton in calling for a strong presidency.

Madison realized not only that a structural mechanism of FEDERALISM to offset decay in government was needed, but also that leaders with character, or virtue, would be necessary for the new experiment in self-government to succeed. The Founders were willing to create the presidency, the constitution's most original office, since they knew George WASHINGTON, who had proven that he could be entrusted with power, would hold the new office. Both Jefferson and Madison were cautious in their exercise of presidential power. Madison, like Washington, viewed the president as a nonpartisan and virtuous umpire.

Transition to the Presidency

Madison had extensive legislative experience before assuming the presidency. He had served as a member of the 1776 Virginia Constitutional Convention and served terms in the Continental Congress (1780–83). He assumed the de facto role of floor leader for the new federal constitution as a member of the Virginia delegation to the 1787 Philadelphia Convention. Following ratification of the Constitution, he was elected to the U.S. House of Representatives and in 1789 became de facto floor leader of that new legislative body. Madison had considered a Bill of Rights unnecessary during the Constitutional Convention but changed his mind while campaigning for his new House seat, as he found that voters wanted one. As a result, he led the movement to adopt the Bill of Rights.

Madison's leadership in the House soon evolved into that of opposition leader against the commercial and manufacturing interests of Alexander Hamilton. After Thomas Jefferson resigned from George Washington's CABINET in opposition to Hamilton, Madison helped to organize the Democratic-Republicans in the Congress to counter the Hamiltonian Federalists. Madison retired from the U.S. House of Representatives in 1797 after four terms and joined Jefferson's opposition to the Federalist enactment of the ALIEN AND SEDITION ACTS of 1798—the nation's first massive legislative act that violated civil rights and CIVIL LIBERTIES.

The Federalists wanted to retain power indefinitely, but Jeffersonian forces prevailed. After his electoral victory, Jefferson appointed Madison as his secretary of State (1801–09). Madison democratized the PROTOCOL of the State Department, a parallel to Jefferson's democratization of the presidency itself.

First Presidential Term

Madison was not Jefferson's first choice as his successor, but Madison inherited the Republican presidential nomination in 1808. He ran with Jefferson's second-term vice president, George CLINTON, a former New York governor. Madison won 122-47 electoral votes, eclipsing Charles C. Pinckney of South Carolina, who also had run unsuccessfully in 1804.

Madison, the first president to have been a congressman, viewed the legislative and executive branches as partners. He assumed the presidency in an era of growing congressional power subsequent to development of its nominating caucus that elected presidents. Unfortunately, Madison misjudged his CABINET appointees and he acted as his own secretary of State until James MONROE accepted that position. For three years, Madison attempted to negotiate with the British, who raided American ships and impressed sailors and disregarded the rights of neutral nations. Critics argue that Madison allowed the Congress to shape foreign policy, but British arrogance allowed Madison little choice but to become the first president to seek a congressional declaration of war, which was declared on June 8, 1812, on votes of 79 to 49 in the House and 19 to 13 in the Senate.

In 1704 Madison had married Dolley Payne Todd, who became the president's hostess and dominated the social scene, providing entertainment for members of Congress and the cabinet based upon skills she had perfected while acting as Jefferson's presidential hostess. Dolley and James Madison were equals in their marriage who treated each other and everyone else with dignity. She enjoyed others whether playing cards, going to the racetrack, or dipping snuff with Henry CLAY. Unlike Jefferson's social events, which were restricted to males, First Lady Dolley Madison's included the wives and daughters of politicians. She became so popular through parties and entertaining on Lafayette Square that after her husband's death, the United States House of Representatives in 1844 unanimously voted her a seat in the House.

George Clinton, Madison's VICE PRESIDENT, died on April 20, 1812, leaving dissident Republicans without a candidate to run against Madison in that year's election. The congressional caucus selected him in May for renomination and gave their ticket regional balance through Elbridge GERRY of Massachusetts. Federalists selected DeWitt Clinton of New York and Jared Ingersoll of Pennsylvania. Madison took 128 electoral votes to Clinton's 89; Gerry won the

President James Madison *(Library of Congress)*

vice presidency over Ingersoll 131-86. Democratic Republicans retained control of both chambers of Congress.

Second Term

Presidents elected twice typically enjoy less successful second terms, but James Madison's second term may enhance his reputation as president among future analysts. However, presidential reputations tend to correspond to wartime success. The WAR OF 1812 was popular in the West, which was growing in political influence, but highly unpopular in New England. In addition to New England opposition bordering on disloyalty, the war went badly. On August 16, 1812, General William Hull surrendered Fort Detroit without a shot. Congress had not prepared the military for war as Madison had requested. The battle score in 1813 was mixed but included carrying the war into Canada with victories at York (Toronto), the capital of Upper Canada, where American troops burned public buildings. British retaliation on August 23, 1814, included burning the WHITE HOUSE, the Capitol, and other buildings. By then, American resolve had grown. The British failed to capture Fort McHenry in Baltimore and the American fleet on Lake Champlain defeated a British squadron. Meanwhile, Madison had begun negotiations with the British, who signed the

Treaty of Ghent. Belatedly, the nation learned that General Andrew JACKSON's troops had massacred the British force in New Orleans.

Critics argue that the peace treaty changed little, which is an assertion open to debate. For most Americans, belief that U.S. forces had defeated the world's dominant naval power a second time was a morale builder. By standing up to British arrogance, the United States confirmed its independence to the world. The United States gained equal commercial footing with Britain. Britain recognized American rights on the Mississippi and the Great Lakes. Perhaps the most important legacy from the War of 1812 was presidential—Madison followed the Constitution in asking Congress for a declaration of war, and he observed civil liberties protected by the Constitution and the Bill of Rights, thereby affirming and upholding the entire concept of democratic self-government.

By the end of his administration, Madison called for a broad national program that included rechartering the BANK OF THE UNITED STATES, a small defense force, a program of internal improvements, and a national university. He had assisted Jefferson in founding the University of Virginia and later served as its rector for eight years after Jefferson's death in 1826.

The Constitutional Legacy

The reputation of America's shortest president, only 5'5" tall and barely 100 pounds, has been cut shorter through comparisons to presidential giant Thomas Jefferson, his predecessor in the White House, and statesman giant Henry Clay, Madison's congressional contemporary. Henry Adams, grandson-historian of Federalist John ADAMS, emitted the first scholarly scoff at Madison's supposed "executive weakness" by claiming that Madison was forced to become a Federalist to govern properly. Madison, however, never trampled civil liberties like the political party of the historian-scholar's grandfather. Madison overlooked Henry Clay's disdain for him and added Clay to the peace delegation that negotiated the Treaty of Ghent, just as he later recruited James Monroe, who had been his competitor for the presidency, to his cabinet.

Political scientists, who have built on the early and traditional judgments of historians in contrasting HAMILTON's bold call for activist CHIEF EXECUTIVEs to the seemingly more modest Madisonian view of presidential power, forget that Madison sided with Hamilton on the CREATION OF THE PRESIDENCY. Madison's presidential character was more active and flexible, traits common to great presidents, than often is credited. Small of stature, Madison grew in leadership capacity while president when challenged with complex issues. Like other early great presidents, Washington and Jefferson, Madison was a naturally magnanimous leader, as demonstrated by his appointments of rivals Monroe and Clay as well as his pardon of General Hull following court-martial for the Fort Detroit fiasco. Madison, like Washington, issued multiple amnesties.

Overall, scholars rank Madison only in the top quarter of presidents, below the great and near-great echelons. Still, in time, his reputation and ranking may rise among scholars. The tendencies of subsequent presidents to engage in warlike behavior abroad absent congressional endorsement and for activist presidents to violate civil rights and liberties on a massive scale during wartime boosts Madison's legacy of faithfulness to republican ideals that potentially will enhance his reputation. In the closing decades of the last century, Madison was honored by his nation. The annex to the Library of Congress was named the James Madison Memorial Building in 1981, and Montpelier, Madison's Orange County home, now owned by the National Trust for Historic Preservation, was opened to the public in the 1990s. A growing number of publications about him have appeared in recent years suggesting renewed study of his presidency.

Madison left the United States much stronger than it was before his presidency. Unlike James BUCHANAN, the 15th president who is often mislabeled a Madisonian president, Madison confronted reality and demanded that the world's powers treat the United States as an independent nation. He preserved the world's first great experiment in self-government, perpetuating it for successors to build on his constitutional legacy.

Further reading: Brant, Irving. *James Madison.* Indianapolis: Bobbs-Merrill, 1941–61; Fishman, Ethan, William D. Pederson, and Mark J. Rozell, eds. *George Washington. Foundation of Presidential Leadership and Character.* Westport, Conn.: Praeger, 2001; Rakove, Jack N., ed. *James Madison and the Creation of the Republic.* Glenview, Ill.: Scott, Foresman/Little, Brown Higher Education, 1990; Rutland, Robert A., ed. *James Madison and the American Nation, 1751–1836: An Encyclopedia.* New York: Simon and Schuster, 1994; Sheldon, Garrett W. *The Political Philosophy of James Madison.* Baltimore, Md.: Johns Hopkins University Press, 2001.

—William D. Pederson

managerial presidency

The president is the CHIEF EXECUTIVE officer of the government. This job entails managerial responsibilities. The president manages a staff, the executive office of the president (EOP), the CABINET, and a sprawling BUREAUCRACY.

Some presidents employ a managerial style of presidential LEADERSHIP (NIXON and REAGAN), using EXECUTIVE ORDERS and PROCLAMATIONS, signing statements, the appointment process, and regulatory and budgetary discretion to set policy.

See also ADMINISTRATIVE PRESIDENCY.

Manhattan Project

Dramatic scientific breakthroughs in the 1930s led to the belief that nuclear energy could be used to develop a weapon of mass destruction. As WORLD WAR II began, fears that the Germans were developing such a weapon led Albert Einstein to encourage the U.S. development of such a weapon.

President Franklin D. ROOSEVELT agreed, and in 1942 the Manhattan Engineer District, or the Manhattan Project, was born. Under the Army Corps of Engineers and headed by General Leslie Groves, most of the work for the Manhattan Project took place in Los Alamos, New Mexico, under the guidance of the enigmatic scientist J. Robert Oppenheimer. It was the first major scientific effort undertaken by the federal government and ended up costing more than $2 billion. This later led President TRUMAN to note, "We have spent $2 billion on the greatest scientific gamble in history—and won."

When Truman became president in April of 1945, he was not aware that the United States was developing this weapon. In July of 1945 the first test of an ATOMIC BOMB proved successful. This led to the bombing of Hiroshima and Nagasaki in Japan and an end to World War II.

manifest destiny

This was an accepted tenet by most Americans in the 19th century proclaiming that the United States had a God-given right to expand its territory in North America. The phrase "manifest destiny" is attributed to John L. O'Sullivan, editor of the *Democratic Review*. He first used the phrase in the summer of 1845 to justify the U.S. annexation of Texas. President POLK had used similar arguments in his inaugural address. It became a powerful symbol of action that justified and animated the nation's move west and the annexation and conquering of the western regions from Mexico. Today, "manifest destiny" has a pejorative ring to it, but in its time, it was a crusader's cry for expansion and control of other peoples and regions.

See also FOREIGN AFFAIRS, MONROE DOCTRINE.

Marbury v. Madison, 1 Cranch 137 (1803)

This case is the first case in which the U.S. Supreme Court declared an act of Congress unconstitutional. The case underscores a political conflict between President Thomas JEFFERSON, a Democratic-Republican, and a Supreme Court that was dominated by the FEDERALIST PARTY under Chief Justice John MARSHALL.

William Marbury, et al., were nominated by John ADAMS as Justices of the Peace in the District of Columbia. These nominations, all Federalist, referred to as the "Midnight Appointments," occurred in the final days of the Adams presidency and were confirmed by the Senate.

Adams signed the commissions and Marshall affixed the Great Seal of the United States to them. However, Marshall, who was assuming the position of chief justice, did not have time to deliver all the commissions.

In 1801 the Supreme Court ordered James MADISON to show cause why it should not issue a writ of mandamus compelling him to deliver his commission to Marbury. Jefferson was outraged because he believed that the Federalists had abused their authority by stacking the Judiciary with potential cronies and because the Court was audacious in considering a claim to order the EXECUTIVE BRANCH. Marshall and the Federalists knew any decision commanding the executive would be ignored.

The issues before the court were (1) Did Marbury have a right to the commission and (2) If he has a right and that right has been violated, does the Court have a remedy?

The Court concluded that Marbury did have a right to the commission. Marshall made a distinction between political acts of the executive in which the courts could not interfere and ministerial acts which required no discretion, such as the delivery of a commission in which the courts could compel action.

Marshall concluded, however, that the writ could not be issued because the Congress, in Section 13 of the Judiciary Act of 1789, had unconstitutionally added to the original jurisdiction of the Supreme Court, which authorized writs of mandamus. Marshall, by claiming the Court did not have the power to issue a writ, claimed a much higher power to declare acts of Congress unconstitutional. While Madison technically won the case, Marshall and the Federalists were able to criticize the administration and to politically establish the principle of judicial review.

Legally, it is unclear that Congress could not add to the original jurisdiction of the Supreme Court, or whether the authority to issue a writ adds to original jurisdiction.

Marshall, who served until 1835, however, never held another act of Congress to be unconstitutional.

Further reading: Clinton, Robert L. *Marbury v. Madison and Judicial Review.* Lawrence: University Press of Kansas, 1989; Van Al Styne, William W. "A Critical Guide to Marbury v. Madison." *Duke Law Journal* (1969): 1–47.

—Frank M. Sorrentino

marque and reprisal

Article I, Section 8—the War Clause—of the Constitution vests in Congress the exclusive authority to initiate military hostilities on behalf of the American people. Consistent with this constitutional theory, the CONSTITUTIONAL CONVENTION granted to Congress the power to issue "letters of marque and reprisal." Dating back to the Middle Ages, when sovereigns employed private forces in retaliation for an injury inflicted by the sovereign of another state or his subjects, the practice of issuing reprisals gradually evolved into the use of public armies. By the time of the Convention, the framers considered the power to issue letters of marque and reprisal sufficient to authorize a broad spectrum of armed hostilities short of declared war. In other words, it was regarded as a species of imperfect war, in contrast with a declared or perfect war. James MADISON and Alexander HAMILTON, who not only helped to write the Constitution but also defended and explained it, agreed that the authorization of reprisals was an act of war and belonged to Congress. In 1793, as secretary of State, Thomas JEFFERSON said of the authority necessary to issue a reprisal: "Congress must be called upon to take it; the reprisal being lodged with them by the Constitution, and not with the executive."

Congress frequently has exercised its power to grant letters of marque and reprisal. For example, it passed some 20 statutes from 1798 to 1799 that authorized a limited naval war against France. In *Bas vs. Tingy* (1800), the Supreme Court held that Congress has the exclusive power to authorize both limited and general war-making, including the authority to determine its place, scope, and duration. As such, the Constitution precludes unilateral presidential acts of war-making, such as covert wars, which are the modern equivalent of the private, undeclared wars of the 18th century.

—David Gray Adler

Marshall, George C. (1880–1959) *military leader, diplomat, secretary of state, secretary of defense*

One of the greatest of the unsung heroes of American history, George C. Marshall served his country as army chief of staff, secretary of state, and secretary of defense. During WORLD WAR II, Franklin ROOSEVELT named Marshall U.S. Army chief of staff, and he became an influential adviser to the president. When Truman became PRESIDENT in 1945, he tapped Marshall to be his secretary of state. In 1947 Marshall developed a strategy for rebuilding Europe. Known as the MARSHALL PLAN, it is largely credited with restabilizing Europe after World War II.

After suffering from kidney disease, Marshall resigned his post in 1948. A year later, Truman asked Marshall to serve as president of the American Red Cross, a post he held for a short time when the KOREAN WAR began. Truman then asked Marshall to return to the administration as secretary of Defense, a post he held until his resignation in September 1951. In 1951 Marshall was awarded the Nobel Peace Prize.

Marshall, John (1755–1835) *chief justice of the United States, secretary of state, representative, Revolutionary War leader*

John Marshall was the fourth chief justice of the United States (February 4, 1801–July 6, 1835). By implementing

George WASHINGTON's national values on the Court, Marshall helped to define the nation and ranks as its greatest justice.

Born on the Virginia frontier on September 24, 1755, and the oldest of 15 children, Marshall developed a love of English literature instilled by his father, ultimately reflected in some of Marshall's classic case language on the Supreme Court. Through his mother, a member of the prominent Randolph family, Marshall was a distant relative of Thomas JEFFERSON. During the Revolutionary War, Marshall fought in several battles, served as the deputy judge advocate, and endured Valley Forge. His disdain for provincialism and weak government was reinforced by his military experience as well as his lifelong admiration of George Washington, his father's boyhood friend. Marshall eventually wrote the first multivolume biography of Washington.

After military service, Marshall studied law with George Wythe at the College of William and Mary. He entered law practice in 1780 and married in 1783, relying on his legal work to support his wife, Mary Willis "Polly" Ambler, and their 10 children. Marshall, like his father, found time to engage in local politics. His episodic service in the Virginia House of Delegates between 1782 and 1795, as well as the Governor's Council of State from 1782 to 1784, reinforced his disdain for parochial state government. He was a delegate to the Virginia convention to ratify the U.S. Constitution in 1788.

Marshall rejected early offers to serve in the Washington and John ADAMS administrations, finally accepting John Adams's request that he serve on a three-man diplomatic team to negotiate a treaty with France. Refusal to pay financial tribute to the French made Marshall a national hero in the so-called XYZ AFFAIR. At the urging of George Washington, Marshall ran for the congressional seat from Richmond and served as the only Federalist from Virginia in the U.S. House of Representatives from 1798 to 1800. In May 1800, Marshall was confirmed as secretary of State for less than one year, but he acted as a *de facto* president due to Adams's frequent absences from the nation's capital.

Marshall was Adams's second choice for chief justice after the resignation of Oliver Ellsworth. John JAY declined the post, and on January 20, 1800, President Adams turned to his loyal secretary of State to become the nation's fourth chief justice. The Senate confirmed the nomination on January 27. Adams signed the commission of this "midnight justice" on January 31, 1801. Marshall served as chief justice for 35 years, spanning five subsequent presidential administrations—Jefferson, MADISON, MONROE, J. Q. Adams, and JACKSON. He remained active on the court until his death on July 6, 1835.

As chief justice, Marshall made the Supreme Court a coequal branch of American government and implemented the nationalistic economic and political visions of Alexander HAMILTON and George Washington. He persuaded his colleagues to refrain from issuing seriatim opinions and instead to adopt a single opinion, giving the high court a collective and authoritative voice. Marshall delivered 519 of the 1,215 opinions of the Court during his long tenure. In addition to his unusual energy, he had learned astute political skills from his prior legislative and executive experience. His essential political moderation combined with a sense of HUMOR and warm social skills allowed him to educate others. In contrast to Thomas Jefferson, who espoused equality but practiced aloofness, Marshall enjoyed mingling with all kinds of people. With the single exception of his distant relative Jefferson, Marshall maintained friendships even with those who opposed his nationalist policies. Even in Jefferson's case, Marshall took a cue from his political hero, George Washington, by demonstrating classical magnanimity when Jefferson needed financial support during his final years.

In his classic decisions, Marshall's jurisprudence was neither consistently activist nor restraintist. Although he established judicial review (MARBURY v. MADISON, 1803), the Marshall Court did not strike down another act of Congress. His even handling of the 1805 impeachment trial of Justice Samuel Chase contributed to the acquittal and also promoted moderation. In his longest opinion, and the one he considered the most disagreeable, Marshall used a narrow definition of treason to acquit Aaron BURR, Jefferson's first-term VICE PRESIDENT (*U.S. v. Burr*, 1807).

Marshall's reflections of George Washington's values are reflected in the famous Yazoo land case (*Fletcher v. Peck*, 1810), in which he asserted judicial nationalization by restricting state authority and encouraged national economic development. His touchstone case (*McCulloch v. Maryland*, 1819) used a broad interpretation of IMPLIED POWERS that would provide the constitutional basis for the federal government's involvement in public policy. His final classic statement of nationalism came in the so-called steamboat case (*Gibbons v. Ogden*, 1824), which emancipated national commerce from the free trade obstructions of the states. On the other hand, one of his last decisions (*Barron v. Baltimore*, 1823) limited the Bill of Rights to the federal rather than state governments.

Overall, Marshall aimed for the middle path, consistent with his own moderate Federalist perspectives that promoted cosmopolitan views for a developing nation rather than provincial and proprietary states. In short, Marshall adapted George Washington's classical prudence and moderation along with Alexander Hamilton's economic nationalism and executive energy through a judicial forum. Marshall's outgoing personality, industriousness, democratic instincts, and balanced behavior shaped his leadership during his long tenure as the Chief Justice. While he was not the first Chief Justice of the United States, Marshall set precedents for the court that echoed those set for the presidency by his political hero and first CHIEF EXECU-TIVE. Standards that still resonate throughout American jurisprudence have earned for Marshall the enduring rank of greatest among U.S. Supreme Court justices.

Further reading: Hobson, Charles F. *The Great Chief Justice: John Marshall and the Rule of Law.* Lawrence: University Press of Kansas, 1996; Johnson, Herbert A. *The Chief Justiceship of John Marshall, 1801–1835.* Columbia: University of South Carolina Press, 1997; Newmyer, R. Kent. *John Marshall and the Heroic Age of the Supreme Court.* Baton Rouge: Louisiana State University Press, 2001; Pederson, William D., and Norman W. Provizer, eds. *Leaders of the Pack. Polls and Case Studies of the Great Supreme Court Justices.* New York: P. Lang, 2003; Smith, Jean E. *John Marshall: Definer of a Nation.* New York: H. Holt & Co., 1996; Robarge, David. *A Chief Justice's Progress. John Marshall from Revolutionary Virginia to the Supreme Court.* Westport, Conn.: Greenwood Press, 2000.

—William D. Pederson

Marshall, Thomas R. (1854–1925) *U.S. vice president*

Although Marshall is best known for saying "What this country needs is a good five cent cigar," he also served as the 28th VICE PRESIDENT during a turbulent time in U.S. history. He had been a small-town lawyer for more than 30 years and had never held political office when he ran for governor of Indiana in 1908 at the age of 54. Despite being a reluctant candidate, this Democrat won a usually Republican state in a Republican year nationally. Marshall gained considerable fame as a reform governor and after being reelected in 1910 came to be seen as a contender for the Democratic nomination for president in 1912. The presidential nominee, Woodrow WILSON, did not think highly of Marshall, once calling him "a small caliber man." But Wilson relented and *Time* magazine stated that Thomas Marshall "had the humility the vice presidency requires." Marshall had the wit to poke fun at himself and at the then, unimportant office which he held for eight years, from 1913 to 1921.

Marshall played very much a background role during the Wilson presidency. Although he did oppose some of the administration's policies, he felt the need to keep some of his views to himself in the interest of party harmony. On numerous occasions, Marshall was asked about being president in the event something happened to Wilson, but he always demurred to respond. Marshall never got that chance, even though Wilson suffered a stroke, because Wilson continued in office for an additional 18 long months.

Thomas Marshall was the first vice president to preside over CABINET meetings even though he had little impact. This limited role reflected his conception of himself as more a member of the legislative than EXECUTIVE BRANCH.

No doubt Marshall could have had more influence during Wilson's illness, but he was completely ignored by the ailing president and especially his wife, Edith Wilson, who apparently exercised complete control over who saw the president. Wilson's confidants may have been more concerned with losing their power than in preserving the stability of the country. This historic but unfortunate period in American history was one more impetus for Congress to pass the TWENTY-FIFTH AMENDMENT to the Constitution, which more clearly defined presidential DISABILITY. Given the times, Thomas Marshall served the country well.

Further reading: Bailey, Thomas A. *Woodrow Wilson and the Great Betrayal.* New York: Macmillan, 1945; Light, Paul C. *Vice-Presidential Power.* Baltimore, Md.: Johns Hopkins University Press, 1981.

—Steven A. Shull

Marshall Plan

After WORLD WAR II, Europe saw its economies devastated. Infrastructure had been destroyed, leading to joblessness and diminished capacities for production. The United States saw many of its trading partners (and, by extension, security interests) in danger of economic collapse. At least two consequences were feared. First, if the United States had fewer trading partners because of the potentiality of failed economies in Europe, U.S. trade would diminish, leading in turn to rising unemployment and overproduction. Second, if those economies collapsed, it was feared, communist ideology would spread via the Soviet Union, considered by many in the American foreign policy establishment to be an expansionist nation.

In articulating the doctrine of "enlightened self-interest," Secretary of State George C. MARSHALL, in a speech at Harvard University, June 5, 1947, promoted a plan for pumping money into European economies for the purpose of rehabilitating and reconstituting them so as to stave off economic collapse. The plan was conditioned on the provision that the economies (16 in all) would act together to estimate their needs and plan their recovery on a cooperative basis. The 16 affected countries and the Anglo-American occupied zone of Germany subsequently made requests of the United States in loans and gifts in the amount of $21 billion for the years 1948–52. By the end of 1951, when the plan was terminated, these countries had received more than $12 billion under the auspices of the European Recovery Program, which became the official title of the Marshall Plan. The plan was widely hailed as a success and, in some circles, credited with staving off a worldwide depression.

The Marshall Plan is also commonly seen as one of the origins of the COLD WAR. Scholars generally agree that the plan was one of the early events that led to the period of prolonged tensions with the Soviet Union and a cornerstone of the doctrine of CONTAINMENT. This, along with the TRUMAN DOCTRINE, the creation of NATO, and the Berlin airlift, heavily influenced the direction of the Cold War. Indeed, while the Soviet Union was technically invited to join the Marshall Plan, the plan was constructed in such a way that it virtually guaranteed Soviet nonparticipation. The plan worked so well that it has since entered the lexicon of American political parlance and is often used to refer to any large investment of money directed at a particular social problem, such as a "Marshall Plan for cities."

Further reading: Grantham, Dewey. *Recent America: The United States Since 1945.* Arlington Heights, Ill.: H. Davidson, 1987; Kindleberger, Charles P. *The Marshall Plan Days.* Boston: Allen and Unwin, 1987.

—Daniel E. Ponder

martial law

Martial law is an extreme measure usually reserved for wartime emergencies. While the Constitution makes no provisions for the executive to suspend constitutional law, martial law entails the temporary replacement of civilian rule by a form of military rule.

There has never been a case of absolute or complete martial law. Throughout U.S. history, several limited declarations of martial law have occurred. For example, agents of the president (usually military officers) have declared limited martial law in 1814, when General Andrew JACKSON, prior to the Battle of New Orleans during the WAR OF 1812, declared martial law in the region. In 1899, with President MCKINLEY's approval, a military commander declared martial law in Idaho to combat labor unrest. The only president to directly invoke martial law was Abraham LINCOLN, who, during the CIVIL WAR, put several areas of the nation under martial law.

The courts have been suspicious of the exercise of martial law, but they are reluctant to directly confront a president during a crisis. If the courts do stand up to this exercise of presidential prerogative, it is usually after the crisis has passed, as was the case when the Court declared Lincoln's exercise of martial law unconstitutional in 1866 after the Civil War ended.

See also EX PARTE MILLIGAN.

Mayaguez incident

On May 12, 1975, soon after the fall of Saigon, Cambodian forces seized the merchant ship *Mayaguez* off the disputed island of Poulo Wai in the Gulf of Siam, taking hostage its crew of 39. The ship was painted black and showed no flag at the time of its seizure, and it was outside international shipping lanes when seized by Cambodia. The ship carried DEPARTMENT OF DEFENSE cargo, though apparently no arms. Almost immediately American political and military leaders feared a repeat of the 1968 seizure of the *Pueblo* by North Korea.

President Gerald FORD made the determination that the seizure was an act of piracy, and the administration demanded the immediate release of the ship. Cambodian forces then moved the crew to the mainland. Ford unilaterally ordered U.S. military forces to free the ship and crew. American air strikes destroyed several naval vessels, and Marines invaded Koh Tang Island, coming under unexpectedly heavy fire. The crew, however, had already been moved. Naval forces then bombed the mainland, while simultaneously commandeering the *Mayaguez*. Again, however, the crew was not on board. Throughout the course of the operation the Marines lost 41 men to accident or enemy fire. The *Mayaguez* crew was soon released, though apparently not in response to the military action. Nevertheless, the effort, coupled with the release of the crew, prompted a surge in Ford's approval ratings of 11 points.

The *Mayaguez* rescue mission was the first real test of the WAR POWERS RESOLUTION. Ford complied with the provision that required him to report to Congress within 48 hours, but he consulted only selected members of Congress, arguing that in the midst of a crisis "it is impossible to draw the Congress in with the decision-making process in an effective way." When Democratic leaders questioned why they had not been consulted prior to the initiation of military action, Ford responded, "It is my constitutional responsibility to command the forces and to protect Americans." Accusations that Ford had broken the law disappeared with the rise in approval ratings.

Declassified documents have led some to argue that Ford's military action was less a genuine rescue mission than a punitive action, taking advantage of an opportunity to appear tough. The Marine assault was called a success even though no hostages were rescued, and despite the fact that the intelligence failure led to a larger loss of life than the number of actual captives. The purpose behind the bombing of the Cambodian mainland, in light of the administration's lack of knowledge of the whereabouts of the hostages, remains unclear. However, the operation was the biggest political victory of the Ford presidency. It allowed a weakened president to look presidential, and to take back some of the NATIONAL SECURITY agenda from Congress.

Further reading: Ford, Gerald R. *A Time to Heal.* New York: Harper & Row, 1979; Greene, John Robert. *The Presidency of Gerald R. Ford.* Lawrence: University Press of Kansas, 1995; Lamb, Christopher Jon. *Belief Systems and Decision Making in the Mayaguez Crisis.* Gainesville: University of Florida Press, 1989.

—David A. Crockett

McCarren Internal Security Act

An effort to undermine communist organizations within the United States, the McCarren Internal Security Act (1950), named after its chief sponsor Senator Pat McCarren (Dem.-Nev.), became law over the veto of President TRUMAN.

A response to the Red Scare and anticommunist fears of the COLD WAR, this act required communist organizations to register with the DEPARTMENT OF JUSTICE and to fully disclose all finances and membership, made promotion of totalitarianism in the United States a crime, prohibited communists from getting passports, prohibited employment of communists in the defense industry, allowed for the arrest and internment of communists during an emergency, limited entry visas into the United States, and required the development of a list of subversive organizations.

The bill passed both Houses of Congress with ease, but President Truman, citing the bill's violation of CIVIL LIBERTIES and arguing that the bill went too far, vetoed it. Congress easily overrode the veto. The Truman administration underenforced the act, but the EISENHOWER administration took it more seriously. Subsequent administrations also underenforced the act.

McCarthy, Eugene J. (1916–) *U.S. senator, U.S. representative*

Eugene Joseph McCarthy was a notable war veteran who turned politician. He was born in Watkins, Minnesota, in 1916. He attended St. John's University and the University of Minnesota, where he studied economics and sociology. McCarthy briefly taught at St. John's University before enlisting in the army in 1943, where he served as an intelligence officer during the remainder of WORLD WAR II. Following the end of the war, McCarthy was enlisted to run for the U.S. House of Representatives in 1948. As a liberal, pro-organized labor Democrat, he led other fellow Democrats in forming the Democratic Study Group, as an alternative to Republican public policies. He served in the U.S. House from 1949 to 1959. He ran for the U.S. Senate and became one of 13 liberal Democrats who defeated Republicans in the MIDTERM ELECTIONS of 1958. Despite this, McCarthy never assumed the vigorous leadership role that he had played in the House. However, he did manage to become very involved in FOREIGN AFFAIRS. He supported the GULF OF TONKIN RESOLUTION in 1964, which eventually led to the expansion of U.S. involvement in Vietnam. However, he became a vocal opponent of Lyndon JOHNSON's policies in Vietnam by early 1967. By the end of that year, McCarthy decided to seek the Democratic presidential nomination, after other more popular antiwar political figures had declined to run. Although he believed that he had no hope of winning the nomination, he was entering the race in order to force the issue of a negotiated settlement to the military conflict in Vietnam, an option that he felt was absent in the political debate. McCarthy galvanized the hopes of many college students, who turned out in droves at the site of the first primary, New Hampshire. He won 42 percent of the vote to Johnson's 49 percent, and 20 of the 24 delegates. This stunning event led to the entrance of Robert F. KENNEDY into the race, who was then beaten by McCarthy in the Oregon primary. Facing an almost certain loss to McCarthy in Wisconsin, Johnson decided to withdraw from the race on March 31, 1968. From that point on, until Kennedy was assassinated after his victory in the California primary on June 4, 1968, McCarthy and Kennedy faced each other in a series of primaries. Vice President Hubert H. HUMPHREY, who had been campaigning for delegates in non-primary states, won the Democratic presidential nomination at the contentious Democratic National Convention in Chicago in August of that year. On election day, Humphrey lost the presidential election in a close contest to Richard M. NIXON. In 1969 McCarthy surprised many by resigning from the Foreign Relations Committee, and he declined to seek reelection to the U.S. Senate in 1970. He made attempts to run for president again in 1972 and 1976, and ran for his old Senate seat again in 1982, where he lost. McCarthy has written poetry and several books and has done numerous speaking tours.

Further reading: Callahan, John. "The Good McCarthy: Saint Gene." *The New Republic*, 15 April 1991; Sann, Paul. *The Angry Decade: The Sixties.* New York: Crown Publishers, 1979.

—Jean-Philippe Faletta

McCarthy, Joseph R. (1908–1957) *U.S. senator*

Joseph R. McCarthy, senator from Wisconsin, had the distinction of having an "ism" named after him. His rabid anticommunist approach to politics in the 1950s, combined with the fact that by 1954 he was only the third member of the U.S. Senate to be censured, made him a well-known, if not well-liked, politician on the national level.

Joseph Raymond McCarthy was born on November 14, 1908, on his family's farm in Grand Chute, Wisconsin. He went to school until the eighth grade and did not continue his education until he was 19 when he completed high school in one year. He entered Marquette University, received a law degree, and began a law practice. Within four years he became a judge in the Tenth District of the Wis-

consin Circuit Court. In 1942 he entered the Marine Corps as a first lieutenant. While in the service he broke his leg at a shipboard party. (Later he claimed that he had received the injury in combat.) In 1944 he unsuccessfully ran against Alexander Wiley for a Senate seat from Wisconsin. Two years later he defeated incumbent Senator Robert La Follette, Jr., in the Republican primary and won an easy victory in the general election.

In the Senate McCarthy was involved in accepting kickbacks from Pepsi-Cola totaling $200,000 for his role in ending postwar sugar rationing six months early, which benefited the soft-drink manufacturer. He also received $10,000 from the prefabricated housing industry after speaking for this style of housing and against public housing for veterans. He continued to emphasize this position as a member of the newly created Senate Housing Committee.

By 1950 Joseph McCarthy realized that he needed a new idea to get his name in the headlines in preparation for his reelection race in 1952. At the prompting of some friends, McCarthy decided to take on the issue of communism, and on February 9, 1950, he gave his first speech against communism before the Republican Women's Club in Wheeling, West Virginia, in which he stated that, "I have here in my hand a list of 205 cases of individuals who appear to be either card-carrying members or certainly loyal to the Communist Party." The numbers of communists changed with different speeches he made, and on February 20 he gave a six-hour speech on the Senate floor indicating communist infiltration in the State Department, which he stated had 81 communist members.

In the early 1950s Joseph McCarthy was riding a crest of popularity, and he was reelected to the Senate in 1952. In May 1954 he convened the Army-McCarthy hearings to investigate communism in the army. The hearing proved to be McCarthy's undoing, and his tactics were shown to have gone beyond the level of human decency. With the assistance of President EISENHOWER and Edward R. Murrow's unedited film of the hearings, the army was cleared of charges leveled against it, and McCarthy and his philosophy began a steep decline.

On December 2, 1954, the Senate by a vote of 67 to 22 censured McCarthy for "conduct contrary to Senatorial traditions." His influence in the Senate was at an end, and he began to drink heavily, which led to his death from alcohol-induced cirrhosis of the liver on May 2, 1957. He was 48 years old.

Further reading: Herman, Arthur. *Joseph McCarthy: Reexamining the Life and Legacy of America's Most Hated Senator.* New York: Free Press, 2000; Rovere, Richard H. *Senator Joe McCarthy.* New York: Harcourt, Brace, 1959.

—Michael G. Krukones

McCarthyism

"McCarthyism" encompasses both the whole "Red Scare" period of the early COLD WAR and the specific activities of Wisconsin senator Joseph MCCARTHY.

The domestic communism issue was already heated before McCarthy adopted it. The House Un-American Activities Committee had investigated communist influence in the entertainment industry, using subpoena power to force citizens to testify about present and past political associations. Unfriendly witnesses were blacklisted and found employment difficult.

The most serious allegation of the period was that there were government officials working for Soviet intelligence. The perjury conviction of Alger Hiss (for denying he was a spy) intensified the fear of internal subversion. Republicans attacked Harry TRUMAN for being dismissive of the dangers of disloyalty. In response, Truman issued an EXECUTIVE ORDER mandating that federal employees be checked for subversive affiliations.

McCarthy injected himself into this controversy by announcing in Wheeling, on February 9, 1950, that "I have here in my hand" a list of subversives in the STATE DEPARTMENT. He had no list, but the charges were sensational and they unavoidably made headlines. He suggested, for instance, that Secretary of State Dean ACHESON and Gen. George Marshall deliberately shielded State Department communists. McCarthy flaunted his contempt for evidence, saying, "I don't answer accusations, I make them."

Truman was openly combative toward McCarthy, calling him "the greatest asset the Kremlin has." He urged the Senate Foreign Relations Committee to investigate McCarthy's allegations. The committee issued a report calling the charges "a fraud and a hoax." But when several Democrats on that committee were defeated in the 1950 elections, it was taken to mean that McCarthy, not Truman, had the public's ear.

Dwight EISENHOWER's election in 1952 changed the political calculus. Eisenhower disliked McCarthy's crudeness and his attack on MARSHALL, but he thought that Truman had created publicity for McCarthy by publicly confronting him, and Eisenhower was determined not to "get down into the gutter with that guy." Some have credited him with waging a successful "hidden hand" campaign against McCarthy, denying him publicity and permitting him to discredit himself, but Eisenhower said little about the CIVIL LIBERTIES of citizens McCarthy investigated.

McCarthy eventually began an investigation of the armed forces, which culminated in a widely viewed televised hearing. The public perceived his manner to be belligerent, a perception crystallized for history when army counsel Joseph Welsh asked in a legendary exchange, "Have you left no sense of decency?" McCarthy's popularity rapidly waned; by this time, many anticommunist activists had decided he was becoming an albatross. He was censured by the Senate in 1954 and died in 1957. The "domestic communist" political comet died out by the second Eisenhower election in 1956.

Recently revealed intelligence from Soviet and American sources has tended to confirm the charges against Hiss and indicated a larger sphere of espionage than some believed at the time. But even those most convinced that there were real national security risks in the period condemn McCarthy as a demagogue. "McCarthyism" resulted in the loss of civil liberties and livelihood by some citizens and forced more to speak, behave, and even think with caution. Neither president was able to prevent that most corrosive effect.

Further reading: Greenstein, Fred. *The Hidden-Hand Presidency: Eisenhower as Leader.* Baltimore, Md.: Johns Hopkins University Press, 1994; Haynes, John Earl. *Red Scare or Red Menace: American Communism and AntiCommunism in the Cold War Era.* Chicago: Ivan R. Dee, 1996; Oshinsky, David. *A Conspiracy So Immense: The World of Joe McCarthy.* New York: Free Press, 1985; Schrecker, Ellen. *Many Are the Crimes: McCarthyism in America.* Boston: Little, Brown and Co., 1998; Thompson, Francis. *The Frustration of Politics: Truman, Congress, and the Loyalty Issue.* Rutherford, N.J.: Fairleigh Dickinson University Press, 1979.

—Marc Lendler

McGovern, George (1922–) *U.S. senator, U.S. representative*

Although George McGovern was not able to achieve the presidency in 1972 against Richard NIXON, his ideas and behavior showed him to be a man of principle in an era when values were rapidly changing. His upright character was greatly influenced by his family. He was born in Avon, South Dakota, on July 19, 1922, in a farming community steeped in populist belief. His father was a Methodist minister who set down a strict code of conduct for the family which included no drinking or smoking. The family moved to Mitchell, South Dakota, when George was six, and he attended elementary and high school there, becoming a member of the high school debate team. His experience in debating won him a scholarship to Dakota Wesleyan University in 1940, piqued his interest in politics, and allowed him to meet his wife, Eleanor Stegeberg.

His college studies were interrupted by WORLD WAR II. He enlisted in the U.S. Army Air Force in 1942 and flew 35 combat missions as a B-24 pilot over Germany, Italy, and Austria. After the war McGovern returned home to finish his degree at Dakota Wesleyan University. He studied for a year as a seminary student but eventually went on to Northwestern University for graduate work in history. After receiving his M.A. degree in 1949, he returned to his alma mater as a professor of history and political science and continued his graduate work in his free time and summers, completing his doctorate in 1953.

During his years in graduate school, George McGovern drew closer to the Democratic left in his political beliefs. He grew increasingly concerned that the interests of the average person in South Dakota were not being heard because of the dominance of the REPUBLICAN PARTY in the state. In 1953 McGovern left his teaching post and became executive secretary of the South Dakota DEMOCRATIC PARTY, which was in an extremely weak position in the state. He helped to revive the party and ran for the House of Representative in 1956, winning the seat to become the first Democrat to be elected from South Dakota in 22 years. He lost a Senate race in 1960 to Karl Mount but was appointed director of the new Food for Peace program by President KENNEDY. In 1962 he resigned this position to run for the Senate seat from his home state and won this race.

In the Senate, McGovern was a strong supporter of Presidents Kennedy and JOHNSON's domestic programs, but he was increasingly disenchanted with the administration's policy toward Vietnam. He called upon President Kennedy to withdraw American advisers from Vietnam, but later reluctantly voted for the GULF OF TONKIN RESOLUTION, which gave President Johnson additional power over the conflict. He was asked by some members of his party to challenge Johnson in the 1968 primaries, but he refused to do so and backed Hubert HUMPHREY.

In 1969 McGovern headed the Democratic Reform Commission (the MCGOVERN-FRASER COMMISSION) on revising delegate selection to the Democratic convention after the debacle of 1968. This position made him a strong contender for the 1972 presidential nomination. He announced his candidacy in January 1971 and built up support over the next year and a half in his party, taking a populist stand on domestic issues and an antiwar stand on Vietnam. He won the presidential nomination at the Democratic convention in July 1972, but his campaign was marred by a divided party and poor campaign planning, which included having to drop his vice presidential running mate, Senator Thomas EAGLETON, for Sargent Shriver after Eagleton's prior depression was made public. McGovern could not gain any momentum in the campaign against a strong incumbent, President Nixon, especially after Nixon claimed that the Vietnam conflict would soon be ended. McGovern gained 38 percent of the popular vote and won only Massachusetts and the District of Columbia with 17 electoral votes. He returned to the Senate in 1974 but lost his reelection bid in 1980. After his defeat he founded Americans for Common Sense to challenge the growing political right wing in the nation.

Further reading: Anson, Robert Sam. *McGovern: A Biography.* New York: Holt, Rinehart, and Winston, 1972;

White, Theodore. *The Making of the President.* New York: Atheneum Publishers, 1973.

—Michael G. Krukones

McGovern-Fraser Commission

The 1968 Democratic Convention in Chicago proved to be one of the most controversial in history. Excluded from meaningful participation in many states during the selection of delegates to the convention, Eugene McCarthy's supporters called for a study of (1) the process by which delegates were selected and (2) the relationship between the national and state parties. In the end, the DEMOCRATIC PARTY set into motion an unprecedented wave of reform in the presidential nominating process that lasted through the mid-1980s. The chair of the Democratic National Committee, Fred Harris, appointed a Commission on Party Structure and Delegate Selection. Led by Senator George MCGOVERN and later by Representative Donald Fraser, the committee held 17 regional meetings from 1969 to 1972, producing a report for the DEMOCRATIC PARTY entitled *Mandate for Reform.*

The McGovern-Fraser Commission Report rewrote the Democratic Party's delegate selection rules to be consistent with two general principles. First, rules and procedures of the national party would take precedent over state and local parties. Second, the power of delegate selection would rest with party activists and candidates instead of state and local party officials. More specifically, the commission recommended a number of additional changes to the Democrats' presidential selection process. Among the more important were:

State and local parties would abide by written, clearly defined, easily accessible rules of procedure. Party meetings would be held on uniform dates, at uniform times, in public places of easy access, and publicized well in advance. Any interested Democrat had the right to participate on full and equal terms. There would be abolition of the "unit rule," with preference given to proportional allocation of delegates. Delegate selection procedures would be held during the year of the election. Gender, racial, and age (under 30) composition of state delegations would mirror the state's gender, racial, and age makeup.

The consequences of these reforms were not immediately evident in the technical language of the resolution adopted by the commission but evolved over the next two decades as the Democratic Party continued to reform the process in response to the requests of state and local party officials. Specifically, states found that binding preference primaries were the easiest method by which to fully comply with the recommendations of the commission. Finally, the REPUBLICAN PARTY organized the Delegates and Organization Committee, which made similar recommendations, and eventually many of the reforms were codified in state laws.

Further reading: Busch, Andrew E. *Outsiders and Openness in the Presidential Nominating System.* Pittsburgh, Pa.: University of Pittsburgh Press, 1997; Shafer, Byron. *Quiet Revolution: The Struggle for the Democratic Party and the Shaping of Post-Reform Politics.* New York: Russell Sage Foundation, 1983.

—Randall E. Adkins

McKinley, William (1843–1901) *twenty-fifth U.S. president*

President at the dawn of the nation's imperial rise, 1896–1901, President McKinley did not seek to build empire, but when circumstances presented the opportunity, he did not shrink from the task. Born on January 29, 1843, McKinley attended Allegheny College but left school prior to graduating. The presidency of William McKinley, 5'7" and about 200 pounds, marked the beginning of a shift away from congressional government toward a presidency-centered system.

McKinley was something of a paradox. Frequently portrayed as personally weak, he nonetheless (albeit reluctantly) exerted presidential and American power on the world stage. In some ways he displayed a regressive brand of conservatism, promoting high tariffs and embracing jingoistic IMPERIALISM. Yet he also led the nation into the global arena, declaring, "Isolation is no longer possible or desirable." He expanded American and presidential power and began the nation's venture into empire and imperial conquest. He helped transform the role of president from national clerk to national leader.

In truth, McKinley was more swept up by events than in control of them. It was a time of growth and change. Henry Jones Ford, whom scholar Edward S. Corwin called "the real herald of the twentieth-century presidency," wrote the influential book, *The Rise and Growth of American Politics,* in 1898. Ford predicted the rise of presidential power:

> It is the product of political conditions which dominate all the departments of government, so that Congress itself shows an unconscious disposition to aggrandize the presidential office. . . . The truth is that in the presidential office, as it has been constituted since Jackson's time, American democracy has revived the oldest political institution of the race, the elective kingship. It is all there: the precognition of the notables and the tumultuous choice of the freemen, only conformed to modern conditions.

A passive president was no longer possible. Events demanded a bolder, more assertive leadership. As America became a global power, it became a presidential nation. Thus, some historians refer to William McKinley as the first modern president.

President William McKinley *(Library of Congress)*

McKinley, aided by his experience as a congressman, developed a sound working relationship with Congress. But it was not executive-legislative relations alone that marked a change in power. Dramatic changes in foreign relations brought forth a new presidency. The SPANISH-AMERICAN WAR, in 1898, was a major transforming event in the life of the nation. The war itself, referred to as "the splendid little war," lasted only a few months, but its impact was revolutionary. After the U.S. victory, Spain lost nearly all its colonial interests in the Americas, and the United States became a recognized world power—an imperial power that controlled and occupied nations outside its borders. The United States now controlled the fate of Cuba, the Philippines, and Puerto Rico. As a result of the Paris Peace Treaty in December 1898, the United States had become an imperial or colonial power.

McKinley was unsure what to do about these new responsibilities. "I don't know what to do with them," he confessed. Rudyard Kipling advised McKinley to "[t]ake up the White man's burden" and civilize the Filipinos. Perplexed, the president turned to God. "I walked the floor of the White House night after night until midnight; and I am not ashamed to tell you . . . I went down on my knees and prayed almighty God for light and guidance more than one night. And one night it came to me this way—I don't know how it was, but it came." Giving the islands back to Spain "would be cowardly and dishonorable." Transferring them to France or Germany "would be bad business and discreditable." The Filipinos were, he said, "unfit for self-government—and they would soon have anarchy and misrule over there worse than Spain's was." He concluded "that there was nothing left for us to do but take them all, and to educate the Filipinos, and uplift and civilize and Christianize them, and by God's grace do the very best we could by them, as our fellow-men for whom Christ also died." And so, McKinley decided to keep the Philippines to bring Christianity to the natives. When told that the Filipinos were already Roman Catholics, McKinley said, "Exactly."

During the McKinley presidency a significant shift in power occurred. The Congress declined and the executive rose. The Constitution's meaning changed as well, as McKinley, along with Teddy ROOSEVELT and Woodrow WILSON, would extend presidential power to fill America's new global role. In the area of FOREIGN AFFAIRS, McKinley greatly enhanced presidential authority. He conducted a presidential war, largely on his own claimed authority; he acquired the Philippines (using an EXECUTIVE AGREEMENT and bypassing the Senate); he and Secretary of State John Hay established an OPEN DOOR POLICY for China; in 1900, without congressional approval, he dispatched 5,000 troops to China to suppress the Boxer Rebellion. By waging war, acting unilaterally, bypassing Congress, establishing an empire, and doing this "solely" on executive authority, McKinley shifted the balance of power (especially in foreign affairs) in favor of the presidency.

In September 1901 McKinley traveled to Buffalo, New York, to open the Pan-American Exposition. As he greeted visitors, he noticed a man whose hand seemed to be wrapped in a bandage. As McKinley reached out to shake the man's other hand, two shots rang out from a concealed pistol. On September 14 the president died. "Good Lord," exclaimed Senator Mark Harerce, "that Goddamn cowboy [Theodore Roosevelt] is president of the United States."

Further reading: Gould, Lewis L. *The Presidency of William McKinley.* Lawrence: University Press of Kansas, 1980; Morgan, H. Wayne. *William McKinley and His America.* Syracuse, N.Y.: Syracuse University Press, 1963.

McNamara, Robert (1916–   ) *secretary of defense, president of the World Bank*

As secretary of defense under Presidents KENNEDY and JOHNSON, Robert McNamara had a significant impact over organization and policy. He expanded the power of the secretary's post and reorganized the department and its budget powers.

McNamara was the president of Ford Motor Company when he was chosen to serve in the Kennedy administration. He restructured the Pentagon budgeting by institut-ing the Systems Analysis and Planning, Programming, Budgeting System (PPBS) to budget-making.

McNamara urged the development of a strategy of mutually assured destruction (MAD) where deterrence was maintained by a second strike capability. He also promoted a strategy shift in NATO from the doctrine of massive retaliation to a flexible response capability.

In the Johnson administration, McNamara emerged as one of the leading hawks on Vietnam. Doubts about America's role led him to shift to an antiwar perspective, and he soon found himself out of the administration and, in 1968, head of the World Bank.

media and the presidency

The presidency was not meant to be an institution constantly on public display. WASHINGTON tried to project the presidency as a sedate ministerial position. However, as soon as the presidency began, extensive media coverage also followed. In the beginning, the relationship between PRESIDENTS AND THE PRESS was one of collusion and conflict. Political parties and interest groups controlled the press until the CIVIL WAR. Different political groups ran presses that were unapologetic tools of propaganda. If the president wanted a speech printed word for word with no critical commentary, the president's own partisan press would oblige, while the opposing press would strongly attack the president.

This partisan relationship with the media lasted until the emergence of penny presses and other independent newspaper outlets. As printing technology improved, newspapers were able to print thousands of copies and sell these copies for a profit. With this emergence of a more independent media and an era of a weakened presidency after the Civil War, presidents did not spend as much time trying to influence media coverage. This changed in the beginning of the 20th century with the presidency of Theodore ROOSEVELT (Ponder, 1999). The powerful newspaper publisher Joseph Pulitzer attacked Roosevelt as unfit for the office of the presidency, but Roosevelt fought back. He held regular PRESS CONFERENCES, inviting only sympathetic members of the press. Roosevelt also understood the nature of the "personal presidency." He continued a tradition of close contact with the press that had started when he was governor of New York. He let the press follow him on almost any occasion, including vacations. With these efforts, Roosevelt received tremendous media attention. He knew his popularity depended upon good press coverage, and he helped to establish the tradition in modern presidencies of focusing on media relations. His BULLY PULPIT was meant to encourage citizens to put pressure on Congress to support his programs.

The importance of the media as the connection between the president and the people was highlighted when Richard NEUSTADT described real presidential power as the "power to persuade." According to Neustadt, if presidents cannot convince the American public, the press, and members of Congress to follow their leadership, their presidencies become impotent. The primary way to bring about this influence with the public is through the media. Since the 1920s, presidential press conferences have become a normal occurrence at the White House (Ponder, 1999), and presidents have institutional offices that focus exclusively on media relations.

Another Roosevelt completely reworked the relationship between the president and the media. Franklin Roosevelt used the radio to make his case for the NEW DEAL after his election in 1932. His famous FIRESIDE CHATS brought the presidency into the home of every American with a radio. With public support and large Congressional majorities, Roosevelt dominated the agenda in Washington. His relationship with the press was so strong that few media reports ever discussed his considerable physical disabilities.

With the advent of television, a revolution in media coverage of the presidency was born. Television news coverage of the presidency has made the president the nation's center of attention. A president who can manage to have positive media coverage on the news can ensure control of the nation's political agenda. The KENNEDY presidency, with its Camelot surroundings, was the perfect marriage of the presidency and the news media. The telegenic Kennedys caught the imagination of the nation with everything from televised press conferences to footage of the Kennedy children greeting their father as he arrived on AIR FORCE ONE or the White House lawn.

The end of this cordial relationship between the media and the president came with the VIETNAM WAR and WATERGATE. The television coverage of the Vietnam War showed that the JOHNSON and NIXON administrations were lying about the progress of the war. This difficult time for presidential press relations was then immediately followed by the Watergate scandal. In Watergate, media coverage of the presidency shifted from being a friendly conduit between the president and American citizens to being part an investigative prosecution of presidential misdeeds.

The post-Watergate era created a relationship of cynicism between the presidency and the media. The cynicism led to the press questioning almost all of the official statements coming from presidential administrations. This new relationship put presidential administrations into a difficult circumstance. Presidents need the press to communicate with American citizens, yet do not want the intense scrutiny that accompanies press coverage in the post-Watergate era. This cynicism bred press "feeding frenzies." These frenzies led to massive negative media coverage of such events as drug use among President CARTER's advisers, IRAN-CONTRA during the Reagan years, Whitewater and the Lewinsky scandals during Bill CLINTON's presidency.

In order to combat negative press coverage, presidential administrations relied heavily on their ability to frame media coverage of the president. President NIXON created an Office of Communications to complement his press secretary in getting his message across to the media and the public. Nixon's successors have all heavily invested in attempting to manage the press. Ronald REAGAN's advisers attempted to control the coverage of the president by having a theme of the day that network news shows could convert into easy sound bites and nice pictures.

Bill Clinton's communications operators reveled in their ability to "spin" the media to get their message out. The 1992 Clinton campaign followed the lead of Ross Perot, an independent candidate for president, and tried to bypass traditional press outlets such as the network news shows. Clinton appeared on friendly national talk shows like *Larry King Live* and also gave extensive time to local news outlets because they were less negative than national news programs.

Another major development in the relationship between the media and the presidency has been the diversification of communication outlets. These new outlets, including 24-hour cable news shows, Internet websites, and political talk shows on the radio, offer presidents both opportunities and challenges. With these many outlets, presidential administrations cannot frame issues on all of these different communication venues. Presidential administrations are, in effect, on a seven-day-a-week, 24-hour-a-day news cycle. Everything presidents and their families do is covered extensively. The coverage of the president is so pervasive that the media often ignores Congress and the Supreme Court. Because of this attention, presidents can control the policy-making agenda. Conversely, the intense media coverage of the institution can destroy presidencies if events and circumstances create massive amounts of negative media attention.

Further reading: Genovese, Michael. *The Presidential Dilemma: Leadership in the American System.* New York: HarperCollins, 1995; Ponder, Stephen. *Managing the Press: Origins of the Media Presidency.* New York: St. Martin's Press, 1998; Sabato, Larry J. *Feeding Frenzy: Attack Journalism and American Politics.* Baltimore, Md.: Lanahan Edition, 2000; Warshaw, Shirley Anne. *The Keys to Power: Managing the Presidency.* Longman: New York, 2000.
—Matthew Corrigan

Meese, Edwin, III (1931–   ) *U.S. attorney general*
Longtime Ronald Reagan adviser Ed Meese served first as counselor to the president and later as ATTORNEY GENERAL. Meese was a part of the "troika" that, along with James BAKER and Michael Deaver, ran the Reagan White House in the first term. Meese handled primarily policy matters, with

Baker serving as manager and CHIEF OF STAFF and Deaver dealing with politics and communication.

In 1985 Meese became attorney general, where his very conservative views caused controversy. His efforts to curb drugs and pornography drew attention but few results. He promoted the adherence to "original intent" by judges, yet he argued against such a view when it might limit the power of President REAGAN. He developed an ideological screening system for prospective judges that helped the administration select judges sympathetic to the president's views.

In 1984 Meese was investigated by an INDEPENDENT COUNSEL and was cleared of charges of ethics violation. In 1987 a second independent counsel was appointed to investigate allegations of wrongdoing, and again the counsel found insufficient evidence to warrant prosecution.

Merryman, Ex parte, 17. Cas 144 (CC. Md. 1961)

The opinion of the case was written by Chief Justice Roger B. TANEY in 1861. Taney had issued a writ of habeas corpus on May 26, 1861, for John Merryman, a citizen of Maryland who was arrested by U.S. military authorities and imprisoned at Fort McHenry in Baltimore. General Cadwalader, the commander, refused to produce Merryman in Taney's circuit court on the grounds that President LINCOLN had authorized the suspension of the privilege of the writ of habeas corpus.

Lincoln believed that Washington was in jeopardy, with secessionists in Virginia on one side and Maryland filled with rebel sympathizers on the other. The mayor of Baltimore was pro-Confederate and mobs were attacking Union troops, bridges were sabotaged, and there was a possibility that Maryland's legislature might vote to secede. Lincoln decided to declare MARTIAL LAW and to suspend the writ of habeas corpus permitting military authorities to arrest without warrants any Confederate sympathizers. Lincoln also suppressed opposition newspapers and ordered censorship of postal and telegraph communications.

Taney wrote, "I had supposed it to be one of those points in which there is no difference of opinion on all hands that the privilege of the writ could not be suspended except by an act of Congress." He noted that the clause permitting suspension was in Article I, Section 9, of the Constitution, which describes the powers of Congress and makes no reference to the executive. He also noted that Chief Justice John MARSHALL and constitutional scholar Joseph Story believed only Congress could suspend the writ.

Taney made no attempt to enforce his decision but sent a copy to Lincoln, who ignored it. Taney previously had also written the majority opinion in the Dred Scott decision, which was widely condemned in the North.

Congress voted in 1863 to affirm Lincoln's decision. Lincoln, while never formally responding, stated that the Constitution "is silent as to which branch or who is to exercise the powers of suspension . . . and the provision was plainly made for a dangerous emergency, it cannot be believed that the framers intended that in every case, the danger should run its course until Congress be called together."

While the Supreme Court never ruled on this question directly, the issue of the courts attempting to cut executive powers in times of emergency has remained problematical.

Further reading: Neely, Mark E., Jr. *The Fate of Liberty: Abraham Lincoln and Civil Liberties.* New York: Oxford University Press, 1991; Pious, Richard M. *The Presidency.* Boston: Allyn and Bacon, 1996.

—Frank M. Sorrentino

Mexican War   (1846)

Arguably the first "presidential war," this conflict between the United States and Mexico over territorial borders in the Southwest led to a U.S. victory and expansion of U.S. territory. President POLK created a conflict with Mexico because he coveted land that was under Mexican control (Texas). The exact circumstances remain murky, but it is believed that Polk ordered General Zachary TAYLOR to occupy land under the control of Mexico. When Mexican forces attacked, Polk asked Congress for a declaration of war. Congress gave Polk his declaration, and the war was short. Under the Treaty of Guadalupe Hidalgo, the United States got 522,568 square miles of territory (Texas to California) and the United States paid Mexico $15 million.

midterm elections

Midterm, or off-year, elections fall in between presidential elections. During midterm elections, the president is not on the ballot, but the entire House of Representatives as well as one-third of the Senate is up for reelection. Though the president is not running for reelection, he may still play a major role in the outcome of the midterm election. Off-year elections are often perceived as an indicator of the public's approval of the president. If the president is quite popular, such as Ronald REAGAN was in 1986, he will actively campaign for his party's congressional candidates. On the other hand, if the president is not well-favored by the public, such as Lyndon JOHNSON in 1966 or Bill CLINTON in 1994, he will play a less active role, since most candidates do not want to be associated with an unpopular president.

One general characteristic of midterm elections is the phenomenon of midterm loss. Midterm loss refers to the tendency of the president's party to lose seats in Congress in off-year elections. Before 1998 the president's party had lost seats in the House of Representatives in every midterm election since 1934. While seat losses always occurred, the size varied. In some elections, such as 1986, the president's party only lost five seats in the House of Representatives. In others, such as 1994, the president's party lost an astonishing 53 seats, giving Republicans control of the House for this first time since 1952. The size of this loss was attributed to the public's referendum on Bill Clinton. While Clinton would be easily reelected just two years later, in 1994 his popularity was quite low. The president had failed miserably trying to pass his universal health-care plan and middle-class tax cut. Barely 40 percent of the public approved of Clinton's job as president.

Even when presidents have been popular at the midterm, they have almost always lost seats. Some argue that midterm elections are really referendums on the president's performance, especially regarding the economy. If the president is popular and the economy is performing well, his party will lose fewer seats. If the president is not popular and/or the economy is stagnant, his party will lose more seats. There is evidence that the president's popularity and the state of the economy impact the number of seats the president's party will lose. The problem with this justification, however, is that it never explains why popular presidents should lose seats in the first place.

While the performance of the president and the state of the economy are generally accepted as indicators regarding the size of the midterm loss, political scientists have failed to provide a clear-cut explanation for why the loss occurs in the first place. One of the first explanations regarding midterm loss is the "surge and decline" theory, first proposed by Angus Campbell. Campbell argued that members of Congress ride the president's COATTAILS into office during presidential election years (the "surge" aspect of the theory). In other words, if a Republican presidential candidate is popular, chances are that people will vote for a Republican congressional candidate as well. Independent voters may be especially more likely to vote for the same party for Congress as they did for president. Also, the winning presidential candidate's party is likely to have higher turnout than normal, giving the party more seats. Two years later, the president is no longer on the ballot, so the coattails do not exist. Independent voters are less likely to have a party preference, if they vote at all. Turnout from the president's party is also likely to decline. As a result, the president's party loses seats (the "decline" aspect of the theory). The problem with this theory is that more recent research has found virtually no differences between presidential-year and midterm electorates (except that fewer people vote at midterm). Also, we have seen a weakening of presidential coattails. For example, in 1992 the Democrats actually *lost* seats in the House even though Bill Clinton easily beat George H. W. BUSH in the presidential election.

Others have put forth a "presidential penalty" explanation. They argue that the midterm electorate penalizes the president's party for being the party in power even if the president is popular. The reason the electorate punishes the president's party is that evidence shows that voters at the midterm are more likely to be negative. Also, some voters do not want the presidency and Congress to be controlled by the same party. However, whether people consciously act to create DIVIDED GOVERNMENT is a contentious debate among political scientists.

Because of the 1998 midterm elections, the puzzle became even muddier. Bill Clinton's DEMOCRATIC PARTY did not lose seats but actually *picked up* five seats in the House. The reason for the Democrats' gains can likely be attributed to a prosperous economy and satisfaction with Clinton's job as president but also to the negative reaction regarding Clinton's impeachment. While the public did not support Clinton's actions, they did not think he should be impeached. House Republicans continued to push for impeachment against the public's will, and this likely resulted in a backlash against the GOP.

The results of midterm elections in the future remain unclear. Normally the president's party could expect to lose seats in Congress and it was just a matter of how many. This trend is likely to continue, but the gains made by Democrats in the 1998 election have added more uncertainty to future outcomes.

Further reading: Campbell, Angus. "Surge and Decline: A Study of Electoral Change." *Public Opinion Quarterly* 24 (1960): 397–418; Campbell, James. "The Revised Theory of Surge and Decline." *American Journal of Political Science* 31 (1987): 965–979; Erikson, Robert S. "The Puzzle of Midterm Loss." *Journal of Politics* 50 (1988): 1011–1029.

—Matt Streb

Missouri v. Holland, 252 U.S. 416 (1920)

In 1913 Congress passed a law regulating the killing of migratory birds. Lower courts struck down the law, arguing that the states, under the Tenth Amendment, had the authority to regulate such activities, not the Congress. In 1916 President WILSON entered into an agreement, the Migrating Birds Treaty, with Great Britain (acting on behalf of Canada) and in 1918 Congress passed and President Wilson signed legislation implementing this treaty. In spite of the lower court's 1913 decision, this treaty was upheld as legally valid. Missouri appealed the case to the Supreme Court. By a 7 to 2 vote the Supreme Court sided with the president, granting the federal government significant authority to enter into treaties that would be legally binding on the states, and thereby granted to the federal government broad TREATY POWERS.

Mitchell, John (1913–1988) *U.S. attorney general*

A former Nixon law partner in New York, Mitchell managed NIXON's presidential campaign in 1968 and became attorney general in 1969. He was a close Nixon adviser and was selected to head the president's reelection bid, but Mitchell resigned in March of 1972, well ahead of the election. Soon, reports linking Mitchell to campaign illegalities began to surface. As the WATERGATE scandal picked up steam, revelations and accusations against Mitchell increased. Privately, the president asked Mitchell to take full responsibility for the crimes of Watergate, but Mitchell refused.

As the Watergate saga unfolded, it was revealed that as ATTORNEY GENERAL, Mitchell had indeed been engaged in a series of questionable and many illegal activities including approving the "Liddy Plan" (named after its author, G. Gordon Liddy) for a series of illegal acts aimed at Democrats, anti-Nixon protesters, and antiwar activists.

In March of 1974 Mitchell was indicted by a federal grand jury for conspiracy, obstruction of justice, and perjury. He stood trial and on January 1, 1975, was found guilty on all counts. He is the only attorney general in U.S. history to be convicted of federal crimes. He served in federal prison for 19 months.

Mondale, Walter F. (1928–   ) *U.S. vice president*

Walter "Fritz" Mondale, the highly regarded senator from Minnesota, was selected by Jimmy CARTER as his vice presidential running mate in 1976. In the aftermath of the WATERGATE scandal the Democrats won the White House and Mondale was given a great deal of clout in the Carter White House. Mondale helped the outsider Carter familiarize himself with how Washington, D.C., operated, assisted in the selection of CABINET and staff members, helped draft legislative proposals, and served as a key adviser to the president. When the Carter-Mondale ticket lost in 1980, Mondale geared up for a run at the presidential nomination in 1984.

He won the DEMOCRATIC PARTY nomination and selected Geraldine A. FERRARO as his running mate, the first woman ever selected for such a place on the ticket. But the Mondale-Ferraro ticket was defeated in 1984 by Ronald REAGAN and George H. W. BUSH.

monetary policy

The federal government attempts to influence or control the level of interest rates, the growth rate of the money supply, and regulatory conditions in the financial markets. This is what is meant by monetary policy. While presidents have a fairly limited impact on monetary policy, their primary sources of power are their ability to appoint members of the Federal Reserve Board and the board chairman (that is where "real" monetary policy is made), and in their ability to influence policy by rhetoric and persuasion.

Further reading: Kettl, Donald. *Leadership at the Fed.* New Haven: Yale University Press, 1986; Mayer, Thomas, ed. *The Political Economy of American Monetary Policy.* New York: Cambridge University Press, 1990; Woolley, John T. *Monetary Politics: The Federal Reserve and the Politics of Monetary Policy.* New York: Cambridge University Press, 1984.

Monroe, James (1758–1831) *fifth U.S. president*

Born on April 28, 1758, in Westmoreland, Virginia, James Monroe graduated from the College of William of Mary in 1776.

The last of the "Virginia Dynasty" (four of the first five presidents were from Virginia), James Monroe, a rugged six-footer with gray-blue eyes and stooped shoulders, was more caretaker than leader. Chosen for the nomination by the congressional "King Caucus," Monroe presided over relative peace and prosperity, in a time that a Boston newspaper proclaimed an ERA OF GOOD FEELINGS.

Although personally forceful, Monroe could also be stiff and formal. John ADAMS ungraciously called him "dull, heavy, and stupid." Others saw him as honest and straightforward.

Henry CLAY was still the very powerful Speaker of the House, and Congress continued to dominate the political arena. Monroe was unable to control his party and thus, it, and the Congress at times, controlled him. Monroe also had a limited view of the executive's role in the political system. Having said all this, it may come as something of a surprise that Monroe was a fairly successful president with several significant accomplishments. Monroe saw himself as head of the nation, not of a political party. Being "above politics" had its consequences. The FEDERALIST PARTY all but disappeared in the aftermath of the WAR OF 1812, and new conflicts—those taking place *within* the REPUBLICAN PARTY—animated politics. Internal strife and rivalries, jockeying for inside position in the selection of presidents, sectional disputes, all caused powerful cleavages.

If all were of one party, at least on the surface, partisan party leadership became all but impossible. Monroe, who had a somewhat ambitious program, found it difficult to promote that program while remaining true to his republican principles. Stripped of the opportunity for party leadership and hemmed in by self-imposed philosophical constraints, Monroe groped for a viable leadership style, but his meager efforts to influence Congress met with stiff opposition from Speaker Clay, who denounced Monroe:

> The constitutional order of legislation supposed that every bill originating in one house shall there be delib-

erately investigated, without influence from any other branch of the legislature, and then remitted to the other House for a free and unbiased consideration. Having passed both houses, it is to be laid before the president—signed if approved, if disapproved to be returned with his objections to the originating House. In this manner, entire freedom of thought and action is secured, and the president finally sees the proposition in the most matured form which Congress can give to it. The practical effect, to say no more, of forestalling the legislative opinion, and telling us what we may or may not do, will be to deprive the president himself of the opportunity of considering a proposition so matured and us the benefit of his reasoning, applied specifically to such a proposition; for the Constitution further enjoins upon him to state his objections upon returning the bill.

The tide of power had shifted to the Congress, and it jealously guarded its institutional position. While King Caucus was in decline, the power of congressional committees was on the rise. In this so-called era of good feeling, Monroe tried to become a nonpartisan chief of states, but Congress wanted no part in it. After Monroe won a second term as president, Speaker Clay concluded, "Mr. Monroe has just been reelected with apparent unanimity, but he has not the slightest influence on Congress. His career is closed. There was nothing further to be expected by him or from him." Some era of good feeling!

In spite of these restrictions, Monroe left his mark on America. During his presidency, five new states were added to the union, a series of wars with Native-American nations took place, the United States won control of Florida from Spain, and the Missouri Compromise was reached. The Missouri Compromise was an attempt to strike a peaceful balance between the slave and free states. The issue of slavery was reaching a boiling point. Monroe's solution was resettlement of blacks back to Africa. It was not much of a solution. The split over slavery led to secessionist calls by some Southern states. The "compromise" was that for every slave state added to the union, a free state had to be added. Thus, Missouri came in as a slave state, Maine as a free state. It also set up a boundary in the Louisiana Territory, north of which was free, while south was slave. This compromise merely postponed confrontation. Thomas JEFFERSON wrote of the compromise: "This momentous question, like a fire-bell in the night, awoke and filled me with terror. I considered it at once as the knell of the Union. It is hushed, indeed, for the moment. But this is a reprieve only, not a final sentence."

It was in FOREIGN AFFAIRS that Monroe is best remembered. After the collapse of the Spanish empire, several European powers attempted to make political headway in the Americas. In response to fears that France, Russia, or

President James Monroe *(Library of Congress)*

Britain might set up colonies in the hemisphere, President Monroe included the following policy pronouncement, known as the MONROE DOCTRINE, in his 1823 State of the Union message:

> The occasion has been judged proper for asserting, as a principle in which the rights and interests of the United States are involved, that the American continents, by the free and independent condition which they have assumed and maintain, are henceforth not to be considered as subjects for future colonization by any European powers.

He added:

> . . . We owe, it therefore, to candor and to the amicable relations existing between the United States and those powers to declare that we should consider any attempt on their part to extend their system to any portion of this hemisphere as dangerous to our peace and safety. With the existing colonies or dependencies of any European power we have not interfered and shall not interfere. But with the Governments who have declared

their independence and maintained it, and whose independence we have, on great consideration and on just principles, acknowledged, we could not view any interposition for the purpose of oppressing them, or controlling in any other manner their destiny, by any European power in any other light than as the manifestation of an unfriendly disposition toward the United States.

In so announcing, Monroe reinforced a president's power to take the initiative and make policy in foreign affairs. This MONROE DOCTRINE was not confirmed by Congress, nor did Monroe have to enforce it during his presidency, but it became one of the pillars of U.S. foreign policy. In an age of relative executive weakness, the president could still pull his weight in the making of foreign policy.

Early in Monroe's presidency, Supreme Court Justice Joseph Story noted that "the Executive has no longer a commanding influence. The House of Representatives has absorbed all the popular feeling and all the effective power of the country." Overstated perhaps, but close to the point. In spite of governing in an era of congressional ascendancy, Monroe did manage to strengthen the power of the presidency in foreign affairs and postpone sectional disputes that were soon to change the era of good feelings to the era of bad feelings and secessionist revolts.

Further reading: Ammon, Harry. *James Monroe: The Quest for National Identity.* New York: McGraw-Hill, 1971; Cresson, William P. *James Monroe.* Chapel Hill: University of North Carolina Press, 1946; Cunningham, Noble E. *The Presidency of James Monroe.* Lawrence: University Press of Kansas, 1996; Dangerfield, George. *The Era of Good Feeling.* New York: Harcourt Brace, 1952.

Monroe Doctrine

As the European imperial powers eyed lustfully the nations of Central and South American, President James MONROE, in his annual message to Congress on December 2, 1823, set forth the Monroe Doctrine, declaring that it was the policy of the United States to resist all European intervention in the Western Hemisphere.

While the United States did not have the military clout in 1823 to fully enforce such a doctrine, over time, the Monroe Doctrine became established as a core principle of American foreign policy.

In 1899 the Monroe Doctrine was endorsed by Congress, and in 1904 President Teddy ROOSEVELT expanded the doctrine, claiming the right to intervene in the hemisphere if "chronic wrongdoing or impotence" by a Western Hemisphere nation endangered stability. This became known as the "Roosevelt Corollary" to the Monroe Doctrine, and protest from many Latin American nations led to

rescinding the corollary in 1928 (although this did not prevent U.S. INTERVENTION in the region).

Monticello

Located in Charlottesville, Virginia, Monticello was the plantation home of the third president of the United States, Thomas JEFFERSON. Jefferson designed the home himself at the age of 26. Monticello is the only house in America on the UNITED NATIONS' prestigious World Heritage List of sites that must be protected at all costs. Monticello is an example of Roman neoclassicism architecture. Jefferson's first design contained only 14 rooms. He redesigned and redesigned the structure until it included 43 rooms, a pavilion, and a terrace. Construction of the first design began in 1769 and was completed by Jefferson's trip to Europe in 1784. The redesign and remodeling began in 1796 and was completed by 1809. Monticello was a Southern plantation and utilized slaves: In a typical year, Jefferson owned about 200. During his life, Jefferson freed two slaves and did not pursue those who ran away. In death, he freed five. All freed slaves were members of the Hemings family. Jefferson died on July 4, 1826, at Monticello.

—Diane Heith

monuments, presidential

Across the nation are to be found numerous monuments to presidents and the presidency. In Washington D.C., the WASHINGTON, JEFFERSON, LINCOLN, and Franklin ROOSEVELT monuments dot the landscape and serve both as tourist attractions and ways to honor our great presidents.

Presidential birthplaces and residences also memorialize our presidents, with Washington's MOUNT VERNON, Jefferson's MONTICELLO, MADISON's Montpelier, JACKSON's The Hermitage, and FDR's HYDE PARK being the most visited.

More than 30 national parks are named after presidents as are a number of cities and states. MOUNT RUSHMORE in South Dakota has chiseled replicas of Lincoln, Washington, Jefferson, and Teddy ROOSEVELT.

A number of presidents are honored with presidential LIBRARIES, maintained (with the exception of the Nixon Library in Yorba Linda, California) by the NATIONAL ARCHIVES and Records Administration.

Even Disney World, in Orlando, Florida, memorializes presidents with its Hall of Presidents.

Morgenthau, Henry, Jr. (1891–1967) *secretary of the treasury*

Longtime friend and close political adviser to Franklin D. ROOSEVELT, Morgenthau was appointed to several key positions when FDR was governor, and when Roosevelt became president he made Morgenthau his secretary of the Treasury. One of the, if not the most, conservative members of FDR's inner circle, toward the end of WORLD WAR II, Morgenthau advocated harsh treatment of Germany after the war. Morgenthau's plan was warmly received by both Churchill and Roosevelt initially but over time was rejected. Morgenthau served President TRUMAN briefly but resigned his post in July 1945.

Morris, Gouverneur (1752–1816) *politician*

One of the more influential of the Founders, Morris helped write the state constitution of New York (with its rather strong CHIEF EXECUTIVES), was a signer of the Articles of Confederation, and served as a Pennsylvania representative to the CONSTITUTIONAL CONVENTION, where he supported "an Executive with sufficient vigor to pervade every part" of the new system. As one of the chief advocates of a strong executive, Morris helped guide the framers in the invention of the presidency. He promoted the veto power, long tenure, reelection eligibility, and election by the people.

As a member of the Committee of Style, Morris helped write the final draft of the Constitution. He is credited with writing the famous words in the Constitution, "We the people . . .".

Morton, Levi P. (1824–1920) *U.S. vice president*

Morton, a wealthy businessman, was elected to the House of Representatives in 1878. President GARFIELD appointed him minister to France, where he was known for the lavish parties he threw. He returned to the United States in 1885 and unsuccessfully sought Senate seats in 1885 and 1887. In 1888 Benjamin HARRISON selected Morton to run as his vice president. Morton's independence angered some Republicans and in 1892 he was dropped from the ticket. In 1895 he was elected governor of New York.

Mount Rushmore

Located near Keystone, South Dakota, this monument consists of the heads of presidents WASHINGTON, Theodore ROOSEVELT, LINCOLN, and JEFFERSON (roughly 60 feet high each) carved into the Black Hills. A well-known tourist attraction, the idea for this monument was originated in 1923 by Doane Robinson, secretary and historian of the South Dakota Historical Society. Sculptor John Gutzon Borglum supervised the project. It was dedicated on August 10, 1927, with President Calvin COOLIDGE presiding at the ceremony. The project continued for over a dozen years and Borglum died just prior to its completion.

Mount Vernon

The first president of the United States, George Washington once said of his Virginia home, "I can truly say I had rather be at home at Mount Vernon with a friend or two about me, than to be attended at the seat of the government by the officers of State and representatives of every power in Europe." Washington and his wife Martha lived at Mount Vernon for 45 years. Washington inherited the estate after the death of his brother Lawrence's widow in 1761. Washington expanded the house and property from 2,000 acres to nearly 8,000 acres, including five working farms. As a working Southern farm, Mount Vernon employed slaves. By 1799 more than 300 slaves lived at Mount Vernon. On his death, George Washington freed 123 slaves at Mount Vernon who belonged to him. The remaining slaves belonged to the estate of Mrs. Washington's first husband and could not be freed by Washington. A foundation has restored the home to its appearance in 1799, the last year of George Washington's life. It is one of the most visited historic homes in America, after the White House.

—Diane Heith

Myers v. United States, 272 U.S. 52 (1926)

This case was the first of several 20th-century decisions which defined the extent of the president's authority to remove EXECUTIVE BRANCH personnel. The Court held by a vote of six to three that Congress could not obstruct the CHIEF EXECUTIVE's authority to fire executive officials. The majority opinion was written by Justice William Howard TAFT, the nation's 27th president and the only former president to serve the Supreme Court.

The etiology of the Myers case began in several 19th-century disputes over attempts by Congress to involve itself in presidential removal actions. The 1867 TENURE OF OFFICE ACT, which mandated Senate approval of executive branch removals, became the primary impetus for the IMPEACHMENT of President Andrew JOHNSON in 1867. Though the latter act was repealed in 1887, Congress passed similar legislation which remained in force. One such law was an 1876 statute which required senatorial ADVICE AND CONSENT in the removal of all first-, second-, and third-class postmasters.

In 1920 President Woodrow WILSON and Congress battled over removal power issues. Wilson at one point ordered the postmaster general to remove Frank S. Myers, a first-class postmaster from Portland, Oregon. Myers, a Democrat who had been involved in Wilson's reelection campaign, was appointed in July 1917 for a four-year term. He was removed partly because he lost support of DEMOCRATIC PARTY leaders in Oregon. Myers challenged his termination as a violation of the 1876 statue. He sued to recover his lost salary in the Court of Claims. After the latter court ruled against Frank Myers and he died shortly thereafter, the administrator of his estate appealed to the Supreme Court. The case was heard twice by the justices and was pending for almost two years before the decision was released.

Writing for the majority, Chief Justice Taft declared the 1876 statute unconstitutional and affirmed the decision of the Court of Claims. Taft's opinion reviewed the position of the Constitution's framers on the president's removal power authority, the 1789 debate in Congress addressing the issue, the Article II, Section 2, appointment clause, and earlier Supreme Court rulings on the matter. Taft asserted that by requiring the Senate participation in removal decisions, the CHIEF EXECUTIVE would lose the "unity and coordination" essential for effective administration.

Justices Louis Brandeis and James McReynolds—both appointed by Wilson—dissented, along with Oliver Holmes. Of the dissents, Brandeis's was by far the longest. He contended that Senate participation in removal of executive officials was justified by the SEPARATION OF POWERS doctrine. On the other hand, Justice Holmes released a three-paragraph dissent which emphasized the power of Congress to create and abolish departments. Justice McReynolds traced the history of laws that restricted independent presidential REMOVAL POWER.

Though the Myers case seemingly ended the removal power controversy once and for all, presidents would enjoy just nine years of a unrestricted authority to fire underlings. Starting with the 1935 *Humphrey's Executor v. United States* case, chief executives would lose the unlimited ability to terminate certain executive branch personnel, a trend which would continue for the remainder of the century.

Further reading: Corwin, Edward S. *The President's Removal Power Under the Constitution.* New York: National Municipal League, 1927; Fisher, Louis. *Constitutional Conflicts Between Congress and the President.* Princeton, N.J.: Princeton University Press, 1985; Hart, James. *Tenure of Office under the Constitution: A Study in Law and Public Policy.* Baltimore, Md.: Johns Hopkins University Press, 1930; Humphrey's Executor v. United States, 295 U.S. 602, 1935.

—Samuel B. Hoff

N

National Archives

The National Archives and Records Administration, or NARA, is the federal agency charged with identifying, managing, preserving, and making available the records of the federal government. All government records not restricted by law become part of the historical record and are to be made available to scholars, the public, and government officials.

Established in 1934 and incorporated into the General Services Administration in 1949, NARA became an independent executive agency in 1985. The NARA is headed by the archivist of the United States, who is a presidential appointee requiring Senate confirmation. There is no fixed term for the archivist, who can be removed only for "cause."

NARA supervises the presidential library system (all presidential LIBRARIES except the Nixon library in Yorba Linda, California, which is privately operated, are under its control). It also preserves and makes available material and papers from each of the nine (Hoover to REAGAN) presidential libraries under its supervision.

NARA's Office of the Federal Register publishes the *Federal Register, Code of Federal Regulations, U.S. Government Manual, Weekly Compilation of Presidential Documents, Public Papers of the Presidents, and Codification of the Presidential Proclamations and Executive Orders.*

On display at the National Archives building in Washington, D.C., is an original of the Declaration of Independence and the U.S. Constitution. The Archives has more than 1.6 million cubic feet of records, with more than 6.5 million photographs, more than 100,000 motion pictures, 2 million maps and charts.

National Economic Council (NEC)

Established by executive order in 1993, at the beginning of the first CLINTON administration, the National Economic Council was designated to coordinate economic policy-making and advice to the president and to monitor depart-mental actions to make certain that they remained consistent with presidential policy. To these ends, it was mandated to serve as a central coordinating body to resolve disagreements among economic policy units in the EXECUTIVE OFFICE OF THE PRESIDENT (EOP) (COUNCIL OF ECONOMIC ADVISERS [CEA] and the OFFICE OF MANAGEMENT and Budget [OMB]) and in key EXECUTIVE BRANCH agencies such as the TREASURY DEPARTMENT and to facilitate communication of those policy decisions to the media and to the public. The NEC handled both domestic and international economic issues.

The NEC consisted of a formal council structure as well as an operational staff of about 20 professionals under the direction of an assistant to the president for economic policy. Formal NEC membership included the president, the vice president, 11 cabinet-level secretaries and agency administrators, chair of the CEA, director of OMB, the NATIONAL SECURITY ADVISER, and assistants to the president for ECONOMIC POLICY, DOMESTIC POLICY, and science and technology policy.

The NEC's inception was related to the administration's desire to both emphasize economic issues and to address the deficiencies of economic policy-making units in previous administrations. Lack of means to facilitate conflict resolution among key presidential economic advisers, fragmentation between domestic and international economic policy-making, and inadequate utilization of executive branch economic analysis and information had often produced inferior economic advice to the president in the past. Moreover, the lack of an institutional mechanism in the EOP to communicate substantive economic policies effectively to the public and Washington officialdom through the media had also undermined past administrations' economic policy agendas. The NEC was thus established to improve upon past efforts in these regards by adapting an "honest broker" role to facilitate the inclusion of views from a variety of sources into economic decision-making and to effectively communicate those decisions.

The division of labor and maintenance of good relationships and teamwork among the NEC and other EOP economic advisory offices (the CEA and OMB) as well as the NATIONAL SECURITY COUNCIL was a major challenge facing this new economic policy-making process. Certain functions remained under the sole purview of the previous units, while other roles were shared with the NEC. The CEA continued to perform a number of established functions including preparation of the annual economic report of the president. OMB, with its staff of more than 500 professionals, was still responsible for preparing the president's budget and for providing detailed programmatic review, but the NEC was authorized to assess and coordinate broad-based budgetary, tax, and fiscal issues such as those that would be presented in the STATE OF THE UNION ADDRESS. Over the course of the eight years of the Clinton administration, the NEC coordinated economic policy analysis on a wide variety of issue areas including but not limited to the 1993 budget, SOCIAL SECURITY reform, climate change, the Hope scholarship tax credit, and automobile trade negotiations with Japan.

While the NEC role was primarily that of a facilitator and coordinator, from time to time it served other functions as well. For example, it developed policy related to the administration's Community Development Financial Institutions Initiative, it participated in congressional negotiations leading to legislation establishing the Empowerment Community Enterprise Zone Initiative, and it served as a contact point in the White House for the business community.

The NEC was considered by policy-making participants to have been generally successful at operating as an "honest broker" in part because NEC Directors Robert Rubin, Laura Tyson, and Gene Sperling and NEC deputy directors and staff were able to foster confidence among other Clinton administration officials that their policy positions would be factored into economic policy making and presidential advice. Improved public communication of economic policies was facilitated through NEC staff work as well. To this end, the NEC regularly prepared talking points for administration officials before they presented policies to the public and press.

In a study of economic policy making during the Clinton administration, Orszag, Orszag, and Tyson concluded that this application of the "honest broker" role in a White House economic policy unit did enhance White House economic policy making significantly. It encouraged a more thorough and thoughtful policy process, it aided in avoiding both substantive and political missteps, it helped to assemble informational resources from other governmental agencies, and it constrained turf competition and press leaks. Moreover, the NEC was considered successful because its role and functions were supported by the president throughout his two terms in office, and NEC directors and staff experienced frequent access to the president.

At the end of his presidency, President Clinton considered the NEC to have been one of the most important structural policy-making contributions introduced in his administration. After some discussion and debate among economic and budgetary policy advisers in the George W. BUSH administration, the NEC structure and process was retained for the new administration. Lawrence Lindsay was appointed by President Bush to be its new director.

Further reading: Destler, I. M. *The National Economic Council: A Work in Progress.* Washington, D.C.: Institute for International Economics, 1996; Orszag, Jonathan, Peter Orszag, and Laura Tyson. *The Process of Economic Policy-Making During the Clinton Administration.* Unpublished paper prepared for the Conference on American Economic Policy in the 1990s at the Center for Business and Government, JFK School of Government, Harvard University, June 27–30, 2001.

—Shelley Lynne Tomkin

National Emergencies Act

The U.S. Constitution makes no provision for emergency rule in times of crisis. However, from time to time, presidents have declared that national emergencies exist and have employed extra-constitutional powers to meet these emergencies. Some EMERGENCY POWERS were merely claimed by presidents, others were delegated to the president by Congress.

During the VIETNAM WAR, concerns grew about possible presidential abuse of emergency powers and a Special Committee on the Termination of the National Emergency was established in 1972. When it was discovered that four national emergencies still technically existed, the committee was renamed the Special Committee on National Emergencies and Delegated Emergency Powers. The committee drafted the National Emergencies Act that tightened up the rules for declaring and terminating national emergencies. In 1985 the act was amended to give Congress, via a joint resolution, the right to negate the declaration of a national emergency.

National Industrial Recovery Act (NIRA)

As one of the most important elements of President Franklin ROOSEVELT'S NEW DEAL program, the NIRA was signed into law on June 16, 1933. Its purpose was to stimulate the American economy of the GREAT DEPRESSION. The NIRA was an attempt at economic planning by implementing a corporatist state approach to policy-making.

The NIRA suspended the antitrust laws and utilized industrial codes to establish set prices and production schedules, divide market share, and negotiate labor practices. The underlying assumption was that the American economy was suffering from deflation and that the solution was in establishing a governmental price above the market price that would insulate corporations from cutthroat competition. This would sustain the various enterprises by insuring profits leading to economic recovery and gradual reduction of unemployment.

The NIRA under its mercurial leader, Hugh S. Johnson, pushed through 557 codes covering virtually all aspects of the American economy through its Blue Eagle Campaign. The sheer scope and complexity of the task overwhelmed the NIRA, leaving many of the codes to be written by the various industries. The result was cartelization and higher prices.

According to its supporters, the NIRA encouraged labor union collective bargaining and helped to abolish child labor.

In May 1935 the Supreme Court ruled in SCHECHTER POULTRY CORP. V. UNITED STATES that the NIRA unconstitutionally delegated legislative authority to the executive by setting goods at a price that no competitor could beat. American values of individualism, competition decentralization, and the rule of law were deemed more important than this economic plan.

The New Deal experiment in economic corporation planning was over; however, Roosevelt continued to harbor visions for economic planning—but plans were pushed aside by the oncoming war.

Further reading: Bellush, Bernard. *The Failure of the NRA.* New York: Norton, 1975; Brand, Donald. *Corporatism and the Rule of Law: A Study in the National Recovery Act Administration.* Ithaca, N.Y.: Cornell University Press, 1988.

—Frank M. Sorrentino

national security

While somewhat imprecise in definition and boundaries, generally, *national security* refers to efforts to protect the United States and its citizens from threats of a military, political, economic, or environmental danger. In the aftermath of the SEPTEMBER 11, 2001, ATTACKS on the United States, that definition has been expanded to encompass threats of terrorism as well as cyberthreats. While it cannot be found in the Constitution, it is generally assumed that primary responsibility for national security rests with the president.

The president, as the diplomat-in-chief and primary foreign policy maker of the United States, is held responsible for defining and insuring the national security of the nation. While the Congress has constitutional responsibilities as well as political interests in national security issues,

the public, and even the Congress, generally look to the president for leadership in this area. Thus in routine, and even more so in crisis areas, the president is the focus of attention as well as power in national security matters.

The president usually takes the lead in formulating a national security policy. By national security policy, we mean the assessment of threats and the resources and strategy available to meet those threats. Resources are divided into hard (military) and soft (diplomacy; for example, economic power). Strategy refers to the ideas that animate policy. A national security policy is designed to protect the United States and its vital interests and promote American values and interests in a potentially hostile world. During the COLD WAR, a containment policy guided U.S. national security policy. In the aftermath of the September 11, 2001, attacks on the United States, President George W. BUSH developed a new policy designed to promote U.S. military superiority and the use of preemptive strikes against potential enemies.

See also DEPARTMENT OF HOMELAND SECURITY, NATIONAL SECURITY ACT, NATIONAL SECURITY ADVISER.

Further reading: Boll, Michael. *National Security Planning: Roosevelt through Reagan.* Ithaca, N.Y.: Cornell University Press, 1988; Crabb, Cecil V., and Kevin V. Mulcahy. *American National Security: A Presidential Perspective.* Pacific Grove, Calif.: Brooks/Cole, 1991.

National Security Act

In the aftermath of WORLD WAR II, a new conflict emerged, this time between the United States and its allies in the West, and the Soviet Union and its allies, primarily in Soviet-controlled Eastern Europe. Known as the COLD WAR, this conflict between "democracy and communism" defined the period from 1947 to 1989 when the Berlin Wall (separating East and West Berlin) fell and the Soviet Union imploded, ending the Cold War.

As tensions between the United States and Soviet Union escalated after World War II, the United States, led by President Harry S TRUMAN, developed a policy of CONTAINMENT of Soviet expansion. This policy was followed by all subsequent U.S. presidents and it led to the end of the Cold War. One of Truman's early efforts was to develop what became known (sometimes derisively) as "the National Security State," or, the militarization of U.S policy. The National Security Act of 1947 was a key element in this development.

The act combined the army, navy, and air force into a "National Military Establishment" and created the NATIONAL SECURITY COUNCIL and the CENTRAL INTELLIGENCE AGENCY (CIA), all under the control of the president. In 1949 the act was amended to replace the National Military Establishment with the DEPARTMENT OF DEFENSE.

The National Security Act greatly expanded the powers of the president. Over time presidents asserted broad claims of unilateral power, used the CIA for a series of COVERT OPERATIONS around the globe, and eclipsed Congress in the making of foreign policy.

After the end of the Cold War, the structures and institutions created by the National Security Act remained in place and continued to give presidents power in making U.S. foreign policy.

national security adviser

The national security adviser is an outgrowth of the creation of the NATIONAL SECURITY COUNCIL (NSC) by the NATIONAL SECURITY ACT of 1947. The adviser serves the president by coordinating the resources of government departments and agencies and advising him on foreign, military, and intelligence affairs, as well as domestic and economic matters. As written, the National Security Act did not provide for a national security adviser and the National Security Council operated mainly as a facilitator of interagency cooperation.

Originally, the NSC had no substantial role in the formation and implementation of policy. President TRUMAN relied heavily upon his secretary of State and close advisers for national security policy. The first "true" adviser was Robert Cutler, who served under President EISENHOWER (1953–55). Over time the position of National Security Adviser grew in power and stature, but there have been times when the position declined in importance and access to the president relative to other presidential advisers (during the Reagan administration, for example). At times the adviser has clashed with the secretaries of Defense and State over the substance and direction of policy and with the director of the CENTRAL INTELLIGENCE AGENCY regarding intelligence matters. The position was elevated to CABINET status under President CARTER. This status was later revoked by President REAGAN. Presidents tend to schedule private meetings with their adviser (and other staff as needed) on a frequent basis rather than attending sessions of the National Security Council. Hence, the adviser is often in a unique position to influence the president's position on a variety of policy issues. Some advisers have had so much influence and access to the president that they also served as a quasi-secretary of State (KISSINGER under Nixon; Brzezinski under Carter). In fact, Kissinger was named secretary of State in 1973 while maintaining his position as National Security Adviser (the only person to hold both positions concurrently).

Throughout the brief history of the National Security Council, the council and the adviser have seen both expanded and diminished roles and influence within the EXECUTIVE BRANCH—depending on the needs and predilections of the administration in power. The size of the council, the number of standing committees, and budget allotment have fluctuated substantially as well. At times, presidents have relied more upon personal friends and their secretaries of State and Defense for advice and guidance in matters of NATIONAL SECURITY. At other times, the adviser has been one of the most powerful men in government. What seems to matter most regarding the influence and status of the adviser is the organizational style and preferences of the incumbent president and those he chooses to rely upon for counsel. The position of national security adviser has been dominated by white males. Colin POWELL (1987–89) became the first African American to hold the position and Condoleezza Rice (also an African American) became the first woman to hold the office (2001–present). Rice had also served at the National Security Council under President George Herbert Walker BUSH. The NSC employs approximately 44 people with an annual budget of $7 million.

Further reading: Berman, Larry. *New American Presidency.* Boston: Little, Brown, 1987; www.whitehouse.gov/nsc; www.polisci.com.

—Joseph Smaha

National Security Council (NSC)

The creation of the National Security Council grew out of the realization at the end of WORLD WAR II that there needed to be better coordination of military and diplomatic agencies and their objectives in dealing with U.S. national security matters. James FORRESTAL, secretary of the Navy in 1945, advocated the establishment of an agency to act in an integrative manner with foreign and defense policy areas of government. He did not see Presidents ROOSEVELT or TRUMAN possessing the ability to perform this function.

This new bureau would be modeled on the British War Cabinet and chaired by the president. It would review issues of NATIONAL SECURITY, provide advice to the president, and expect that advice to be implemented by the president. Thus, the NSC would not only integrate various policy areas but would also act as a check on the president in his role of initiator of foreign policy.

The NATIONAL SECURITY ACT of 1947 created the NSC headed by the president with the secretaries of State and Defense as its key members. Other secretaries from executive departments could be asked to come to the meetings. The head of the CENTRAL INTELLIGENCE AGENCY (CIA), established under the same act, was to report to the NSC and attend the meetings as an observer and resident adviser. Recommendations could be made to the president on matters of national security, but the NSC staff, headed

President Ford meets with his National Security Council to discuss the *Mayaguez* situation, May 13, 1975. *(Ford Library)*

by a civilian executive secretary and appointed by the president, played no role in the formulation and implementation of NATIONAL SECURITY policies.

Behind the function of assisting the president on national security matters, Congress intended the NSC to create a more collegial decision-making process in foreign policy. The fear was that national security matters had become too centralized in the White House.

In reality, though, the NSC has become an instrument used by presidents to carry out their own views of U.S. foreign policy. As part of the EXECUTIVE OFFICE OF THE PRESIDENT, the NSC is independent of outside control and responsible only to the president. While Congress establishes the budget for the NSC, the budget's limits can be ignored by having staff members transferred on loan to the NSC from other agencies.

Presidents have used the NSC in a variety of ways. President Truman believed that the NSC was created to check his authority, and he, therefore, viewed the council only as an advisory body and went to few meetings until the onset of the KOREAN WAR. As a former military leader, President EISENHOWER used the NSC in a more formalistic way by holding weekly meetings even when they were not necessary. He expanded the size of the NSC, and, most important, he created the position of assistant to the president for national security affairs to head the NSC staff.

President John KENNEDY substituted the formal structure of the NSC under Eisenhower with a looser, more informal decision-making model. Scheduled meetings were deemphasized, and during the CUBAN MISSILE CRISIS, he relied on an ad hoc group of associates, the ExCom, rather than the entire NSC. The president also reduced the staff and responsibilities of the NSC. Lyndon JOHNSON did not change the national security system formulated under Kennedy, although there was some reduction in advisory staff.

Richard NIXON made some significant changes to the NSC, including tripling the size of the NSC staff to about

50 and appointing Henry KISSINGER as his NATIONAL SECURITY ADVISER. Kissinger shifted the advisory role of his position to one of direct engagement in diplomatic negotiations, and he became the center of attention when Secretary of State William Rogers resigned in 1973. At this point Kissinger assumed the secretary of State role along with his national security position. National security matters became centralized in the hands of Nixon, Kissinger, and the NSC staff, and during the WATERGATE scandal, Kissinger played an even greater role in FOREIGN AFFAIRS.

Under President FORD, Brent Scowcroft became national security adviser while deferring to Kissinger in his role of secretary of State. President Jimmy CARTER attempted to reduce the policy influence role of the NSC. His secretary of State, Cyrus Vance, became the chief policy formulator, but Carter's national security adviser, Zbigniew Brzezinski, gained more status in the administration as Carter relied more on Brzezinski. Vance resigned in 1980 over the attempt to rescue American hostages in Iran, and Brzezinski played the prime role in foreign policy in Carter's last year in office.

Ronald REAGAN reduced the emphasis on the NSC that had been evident in the past dozen years. The president took a less involved approach to foreign affairs and allowed CABINET secretaries and other subordinates to make more daily decisions in this area. This tactic, though, backfired during the IRAN-CONTRA scandal in 1986, which showed the negative consequences of lack of presidential involvement with national security matters. President George H. W. BUSH was more actively involved in national security policy and had a good working relationship with his national security adviser, Brent Scowcroft. At the same time, Bush held few meetings of the NSC and was very informal in his approach to national security affairs.

President CLINTON's imprint on the NSC was to enlarge the membership of the agency and place greater emphasis on economic issues in formulating national security policy. Besides the president, VICE PRESIDENT, secretaries of State and Defense, who are prescribed by statute along with the CIA director and chairman of the JOINT CHIEFS OF STAFF, the new membership of the NSC included the secretary of the Treasury, the U.S. representative to the UN, the assistant to the president for national security affairs, the assistant to the president for ECONOMIC POLICY, and the CHIEF OF STAFF for the president.

Upon entering office in January 2001, President George W. BUSH appointed Condoleezza Rice as his national security adviser.

Further reading: Boll, Michael M. *National Security Planning: Roosevelt through Reagan.* Lexington: University Press of Kentucky, 1988; Destler, I. M., Leslie H. Gelb, and Anthony Lake. *Our Own Worst Enemy: The Unmasking of American Foreign Policy.* New York: Simon and Schuster, 1984; Prados, John. *Keepers of the Keys: A History of the National Security Council from Truman to Bush.* New York: Morrow, 1991.

—Michael G. Krukones

National Security Directives (NSDs)

Primary responsibility for setting national security policy rests with the president. It is through national security directives that presidents establish policy. NSDs are not new, but that term only began during the presidency of George H. W. BUSH. Prior to that time, NATIONAL SECURITY COUNCIL (established in 1947) policy guidelines were known merely as NSC and numbered sequentially. Often NSDs are classified "secret" and do not become widely known. This has caused concern among members of Congress who fear that policy is being made without any ACCOUNTABILITY.

National Treasury Employees Union v. Nixon, 492 F. 2d 587 (D.C. Cir. 1974)

This case, ultimately decided against President NIXON, is important because it reaffirmed the standard that when statutes conflict, the Court is empowered to determine which law a president is to enforce. In the case, President Nixon failed to implement a provision of the Federal Pay Comparability Act of 1970 (FPCA), on the grounds that another law, the ECONOMIC STABILIZATION ACT of 1970, gave him latitude in choosing different courses of action to pursue. The courts were put in a precarious position and ultimately decided the case on rather narrow grounds, remanding the case to a district court. The administration, recognizing it might face a more expansive defeat in district court, eventually agreed to comply with the FPCA provisions.

Native American policy

While Congress exercises plenary power over the nation's policy concerning American Indians, presidents have historically been involved in three main areas of policy action: They have conducted treaty negotiations with members of indigenous nations, directed military engagements with and against them, and have overseen the administration of policy through the EXECUTIVE BRANCH and its attendant departments and agencies.

In the early republic, American Indians were important as trading partners and as military allies. They were also often military opponents as well. Indian land, once appropriated through treaty or conquest, was an important source of revenue for the new American government. (By 1850, land sales comprised 80 percent of the revenues in the federal budget.) Early United States policy toward American Indians was thus aimed at attaining land, promoting trade, and avoiding as well as prosecuting military actions. These priorities are reflected in the number of treaties negotiated: Between 1789 and 1829, 119 treaties between the United States and indigenous nations were signed and ratified. Between 1829, when Andrew JACKSON took office, and 1871, when Congress officially ended treaty-making with native nations, a further 262 treaties were ratified. The first Removal Treaty (signed with the Choctaw at Dancing Rabbit Creek in 1830) was ratified during Jackson's administration, paving the way for the eventual removal of some 70,000 American Indians from what is now the Southeastern United States, and the deaths of thousands more along what came to be known as the "Trail of Tears."

Many presidents first attained national prominence as "Indian Fighters"; a number of them also presided over military engagements while in office. Some of the better known of these engagements include the Red Stick War, prosecuted by James MADISON; the 1832 Black Hawk War; and James K. POLK's MEXICAN WAR. During the CIVIL WAR, Abraham LINCOLN authorized the largest public execution in American history, hanging 38 Dakota (Sioux) for their participation in an "uprising" in Mankato, Minnesota, in 1862.

Following the CIVIL WAR, there were numerous "Indian Wars" on the Great Plains as the U.S. government sought to wrest control of the West from its original inhabitants. These wars involved dramatic—and often sensationalized—conflicts such as "Custer's Last Stand," the pursuit of the Nez Perce under Chief Joseph, and the three-year campaign to capture Geronimo. These conflicts were often accompanied by stark brutality, exemplified in the massacres at Sand Creek and Wounded Knee. Whatever the tactic, the results were the same: the deaths of large numbers of indigenous people, the cession of millions of acres of land, and the restriction of the remaining natives to land set aside (often by EXECUTIVE ORDER) as reservations.

Whenever possible, presidents have preferred to conduct their relations with American Indians through administrative rather than military channels. The Non-Intercourse Act of 1790 gave the federal government the exclusive right to negotiate with Native Americans. Such negotiation was originally conducted through the War Department. In 1824 the Office of Indian Affairs was officially organized there, and the Office of the Commissioner of Indian Affairs was authorized in 1832. An advisory council was added to that office during the GRANT administration. In 1849 administrative functions relevant to American Indians were moved to the DEPARTMENT OF THE INTERIOR. Reorganized and renamed the Bureau of Indian Affairs (BIA) as a result of the "Indian New Deal" in the 1940s, the BIA remains within Interior today.

Few contemporary presidents have taken much real interest in Native American policy, but their actions have both mirrored public attitudes toward American Indians and led to important changes. Dwight EISENHOWER, for instance, publicly called the infamous Public Law 280, which sought to terminate federal recognition of indigenous nations, "unchristian," then signed it into law. A decade later, Lyndon JOHNSON oversaw legislation (the Indian Civil Rights Act) that extended most of the protections of the Bill of Rights to Native Americans.

Richard NIXON was the strongest presidential supporter of American Indian rights. He ended termination, began the era of "self-determination" which stresses government-to-government relations with indigenous nations, returned some 48,000 acres of sacred land to Taos Pueblo, and became an advocate for strong tribal governments. This last position was controversial, for it exacerbated strife within native communities and led the Nixon administration to sanction the largest deployment of U.S. forces on American soil since the Civil War, against some 200 protestors at Wounded Knee, South Dakota, in 1973.

Nixon's successors have continued his policy of self-determination, have appointed American Indians to manage the BIA, and have signed legislation aimed at protecting indigenous religious freedom and burial rights and mandating repatriation of sacred and funerary objects. Thus, the federal government remains an important player in Native American policy, but American Indian issues generally command little in the way of presidential attention.

Further reading: Champagne, Duane, ed. *Native America: Portrait of the Peoples.* Detroit: Visible Ink Press, 1994; Dippie, Brian W. *The Vanishing American: White Attitudes and U.S. Indian Policy.* Lawrence: University Press of Kansas, 1982; Prucha, Francis Paul, ed. *Documents of United States Indian Policy,* 2d ed. Lincoln: University of Nebraska Press, 1990.

—Mary E. Stuckey

NATO treaty

In the aftermath of WORLD WAR II, conflicts between the United States and the Soviet Union led to a COLD WAR. The United States and Europe, in an effort to develop mutually supportive security arrangements, formed the North Atlantic Treaty Organization (NATO). The original NATO countries were the United States, Canada, Belgium, Denmark, France, Iceland, Italy, Luxembourg, the Netherlands, Norway, Portugal, and the United Kingdom.

The NATO treaty, legitimizing U.S. entry into the NATO agreement, was approved by the Senate on July 21, 1949, during the TRUMAN administration. NATO's coordinated efforts to limit Soviet expansion were largely responsible for limiting Soviet influence and ending the cold war. In the post-cold war era several new nations, many in Eastern Europe, have been added to NATO.

Neagle, In Re, 135 U.S. 1 (1890)

This case addresses the meaning of the EXECUTIVE POWER of the president and how to take care that the laws are faithfully executed. Does this clause authorize the president to act in what he believes to be the public interest, so long as it does not conflict with specific laws and other constitutional provisions, or does a president require a specific statute to authorize his actions?

The facts of this case are complex. Supreme Court Justice Stephen J. Field, whose judicial circuit included California, was being threatened by David Terry. The attorney general assigned David Neagle, a federal marshal, to protect Field while in California. When Neagle saw Terry make a threatening move toward Field, Neagle killed Terry.

Neagle was charged with murder by the state of California. The Justice Department sought Neagle's release on a writ of habeas corpus because his actions were done "in pursuance of the law of the United States." However, Congress had not expressly authorized the president or his deputies to assign federal marshals to protect federal judges.

The Supreme Court held that the government had an obligation to protect its judges and that the president, as the executive, was in the best position to perform this function. Therefore, his assigning of a marshal was proper and "under the authority of the United States." The president must also enforce the Constitution and the general peace of the land.

This case was cited as precedent for EXECUTIVE POWER in the *In Re Debs* 1895 case, where President CLEVELAND sought an injunction to stop the PULLMAN STRIKE, despite there being no specific authorizing law. The Court ruled that every government was free to utilize the Courts for the protection of the general welfare.

However, during the KOREAN WAR, President TRUMAN seized the strike-torn steel mills. The Court in *YOUNGS-TOWN SHEET AND TUBE CO. V. SAWYER* (1952) held that the president had exceeded his power because Congress, when debating the TAFT-HARTLEY ACT, considered that option but ultimately rejected it. The *In Re Neagle* case has defined executive powers broadly, unless it contradicts specific legislative or constitutional provisions.

Further reading: Corwin, Edward. *The President: Office and Powers 1789–1957,* 5th rev. ed. New York: New York University Press, 1984; Fisher, Louis. *Constitutional Conflicts between Congress and the President,* 3d ed. Lawrence: University Press of Kansas, 1991; Koenig, Louis W. *The*

Chief Executive, 6th ed. Fort Worth, Tex.: Harcourt Brace College Publishers, 1996.

—Frank M. Sorrentino

Neustadt, Richard M. (1919–2003) *scholar*

One of the founders of modern presidential studies, his 1960 book *Presidential Power* was a groundbreaking work that looked at the informal powers of the president as the key to leadership. Neustadt served as an adviser to many presidents. The best-book award of the Presidency Research Group is named in his honor. Richard Neustadt also received the first Presidency Research Group Career Service Awards in 2003. His impact on the study of the presidency has been enormous, and his emphasis on presidential prestige, bargaining, and reputation broadened the study of leadership in the executive office at a time when most scholars examined primarily the legal and constitutional sources of presidential power.

Neutrality Proclamation (1793)

The relative tranquillity of the first WASHINGTON administration was abruptly interrupted by the news from Europe in April of 1793 that the much-anticipated war among the powers of France, Great Britain, Prussia, Sardinia, and Holland had broken out. Washington, desirous of pursuing a policy of strict neutrality, sought advice from his CABINET concerning the circumstances facing America, a situation complicated by the existence of a Treaty of Alliance and Treaty of Amity and Commerce with France, dating from 1778. Secretary of Treasury HAMILTON advised that Washington could and should take broad measures to ensure American neutrality, including suspending or even nullifying the treaties with France, given the change in the French government that had recently taken place. JEFFERSON, generally well disposed to the new republican government in France, argued against the issuance of a proclamation on both legal and policy grounds, though even he acknowledged the necessity of the United States staying out of the conflict.

The Neutrality Proclamation was issued by Washington on April 22, 1793, though the name is somewhat misleading, in that it carefully avoids the term neutrality, heavily laden as that term is in INTERNATIONAL LAW. (The term "impartial" is used in the opening paragraph.) The publication of the Proclamation was met with some derision in the public presses, especially by the friends of republican France. The most notable of these pieces were written by Veritas, suspected to be Philip Freneau, publisher of the *National Gazette* and friend to Jefferson.

The real import of the debate over the Neutrality Proclamation, though, came in the following months. In the response to the criticism of the administration, Hamilton authored the essays of "Pacificus," which appeared in June and July of 1793, in the *Gazette of the United States*. James MADISON, having been spurred on to reply to Hamilton by Jefferson, did so with some ambivalence (an effort he described as "the most grating one I ever experienced"). Madison's replies, penned under the pseudonym "Helvidius," appeared in August and September, also in the *Gazette*. The HELVIDIUS-PACIFICUS debate joined in these two series of essays has stretched its influence across American political history, establishing, to some extent, the contours of the debate concerning presidential control over FOREIGN AFFAIRS, especially over war and treaty obligations.

Hamilton's seven Pacificus essays make two major assertions and numerous practical judgments about the political circumstances involved in the issuance of the Proclamation. The most developed arguments concern the authority of the executive to issue the document and the responsibilities of the United States in regard to the two treaties with France. To the first question, Hamilton adopts his recognizably broad view of EXECUTIVE POWER, justifying Washington's action as a legitimate exercise of the executive power vested in him by Article II of the Constitution; he argues that executive power is lodged wholesale in the president, the Constitution providing legislative influence on that distribution only by specific exceptions and qualifications explicitly set forth therein. The president, then, in issuing the Proclamation, is simply recognizing the official status of the United States, one that has not been altered by a congressional declaration of war. To the second question, concerning which he is on considerably shakier ground, he argues that the change in the French government (still not settled, as we later see) militates in favor of suspending our treaty obligations. Even if it did not, the treaties were triggered only by a defensive action, and the French, he argues, were responsible for the outbreak of war.

Madison's Helvidius responses focus almost exclusively on the question of the extent of executive power to make war and treaties and reject what is said to be the view of Pacificus that the president's authority in issuing the Proclamation was an extension of his exclusive power over war and treaties. Hamilton's Pacificus did not really make that extreme argument; he did not, for instance, claim that the Proclamation established a fixed policy of the United States, one that Congress could not later change if it desired to put the nation at war. While Pacificus argued for a broad understanding of executive power, Madison had also done so in the First Congress's considerations of the REMOVAL POWER and thus would be hard-pressed as Helvidius to refute such a claim. Instead, he more narrowly focused on the interpretation of the treaty obligations and on articulating a thoughtful and persuasive understanding of executive power, one Hamilton would in fact find little with which to disagree.

The arrival in America of the French ambassador, Edmond Genet, in April of 1793, greatly complicated the neutrality question. Genet was intent on rallying support for the French cause, including fomenting rebellion in the Western lands against England and Spain and promoting privateering against British ships. The too-strenuous negotiations with the United States, in part led by his desire to promote the seizing of prizes and adjudication of such in American ports, added to the tensions between Hamilton and Jefferson within the administration. The practical outcome of the immediate controversy, though, was decided more by the frenetic activity of Genet than anything else, for in the end all sides, including Jefferson, turned against him, demanding his ouster. The French government, by now in the hands of the Jacobins, was not opposed to the recall, and by the winter Genet was gone from Philadelphia, but he spent his remaining years in New York, never to return to France.

Response to the issuance of the Proclamation in fact broke along familiar lines, most decisive being that of the relative sympathy with or for the French Revolution. In the end, there was little practical disagreement not only between Pacificus and Helvidius but also among all others involved in consideration of the Proclamation, including Jefferson, who acknowledged that it behooved the United States to stay out of the war enveloping Europe. Neutrality was the only viable political option, given the status of the U.S. armed forces, the economic needs of the country, and the practical political consequences of intervening in the conflict.

Further reading: Casto, William R. "Pacificus and Helvidius Reconsidered." *Northern Kentucky Law Review* 28 (2001): 612–639; Elkins, Stanley, and Eric McKitrick. *The Age of Federalism: The Early American Republic, 1788–1800.* New York: Oxford University Press, 1993; McDonald, Forrest. *The Presidency of George Washington.* Lawrence: University Press of Kansas, 1974.

—Richard J. Dougherty

New Deal

In his acceptance speech at the Democratic National Convention in 1932, Franklin D. ROOSEVELT said, "I pledge to you, I pledge to myself, to a new deal for the American people." Thus the New Deal, FDR's domestic programs to combat the GREAT DEPRESSION, got its name. The New Deal was a series of experiments in getting the nation out of the depression by establishing new programs of social welfare and government-subsidized work. It marked the greatest expansion of federal power into the economic and domestic policy arena in the nation's history and created dozens of new federal programs, among them SOCIAL

SECURITY, the TENNESSEE VALLEY AUTHORITY (TVA), and a slew of programs known by their letters (e.g., "CCC" for CIVILIAN CONSERVATION CORPS). The New Deal marked a more activist role of the federal government. From that point, the federal government took on added responsibility for programs to alleviate poverty and promote growth. It also signified a more activist, powerful and personal presidential office.

New Freedom

New Freedom was the name given to Woodrow WILSON's domestic-policy agenda during the presidential campaign of 1912. The New Freedom contained several planks: strengthened antitrust laws, tariff reform, and an overhaul of the banking and currency system. Each of these programs would help to "emancipate" free enterprise from concentrations of both private and governmental power. Associating his domestic platform with the term New Freedom was originally a response to Theodore ROOSEVELT's New Nationalism, but the New Freedom program eventually evolved into a broadly based set of initiatives for the expansion of federal ECONOMIC POWERS during Wilson's first term as president.

The defining feature of Wilson's New Freedom was its antitrust program. In the 1912 presidential campaign, Wilson and Theodore Roosevelt offered contrasting visions of how the national government should deal with the nagging problem of business monopoly. Roosevelt's strategy, as outlined in his New Nationalism program, was to create a commission that would distinguish "good trusts" from "bad trusts." In contrast, Wilson pursued a regulatory approach that sought to limit the expansion of governmental power. Statutes would specify exactly those practices that are allowed and those that are forbidden. This would rein in big business while avoiding creation of a discretionary national BUREAUCRACY.

After winning the presidential election, Wilson faced the task of getting his program through Congress. His task was made easier by the presence of Democratic majorities in both the House and Senate. Wilson, making the most of his position as party leader, experienced great success in pushing his New Freedom agenda through Congress in the first two years of his presidency. In October 1913 the Underwood Tariff became law. Two months later Wilson signed the Federal Reserve Act, which restructured the banking and currency system. The next year Wilson signed both the Clayton Antitrust Act and the FEDERAL TRADE COMMISSION ACT. In a bid to appeal to progressive Republicans, Wilson backed away from his distrust of discretionary bureaucracy and instead created an expert regulatory commission remarkably similar to Roosevelt's designs.

New Freedom constituted both a constitutional and a political watershed, providing the foundation for the trans-formation of the federal government into a modern administrative state with distributive and regulatory roles. With respect to the presidency, Wilson's New Freedom laid the groundwork for the expansion of executive authority during the NEW DEAL and beyond, as well as pushing the presidency into a more active lawmaking arena by making the president the legislative leader of his party. Relying heavily on the advice and guidance of progressive lawyer and future Supreme Court justice Louis Brandeis, Wilson initially envisioned New Freedom as a way to restore and maintain vigorous competition among smaller actors in the marketplace. New Freedom originally represented a Jeffersonian desire to enhance the viability of small-scale capitalism by using the federal government as a referee and temporary change agent in its endeavor to ensure socioeconomic fairness. Nevertheless, as the realities and inevitability of industrial capitalism became obvious, and as the need to respond to Roosevelt's comparatively active conception of the government's role in economic affairs became evident, New Freedom grew into a blueprint for a more vigorous policy of government-centered social and economic reform.

The most significant aspect of New Freedom was its gradual redefinition of the presidency from an office that was designed by the framers of the Constitution to lead a largely agrarian society of entrepreneurs, artisans, and farmers into the head of an industrial-era administrative state. Prior to Wilson's tenure in office, neither the Congress nor the president had much authority or ability to confront the problems caused by mass industrialization. New Freedom involved a radical reconceptualization of governmental authority and EXECUTIVE POWER by requiring a vigorous executive, along with the required regulatory apparatus, to regulate the economy and redistribute its resources according to notions of social justice. The New Freedom program had a profound impact on the evolution of presidential LEADERSHIP during the 20th century. Without the precedents laid down by Wilson and his administration, the NEW DEAL and the GREAT SOCIETY would have been all but impossible. Wilson's expansion of executive administrative capacities and his willing use of the presidency for legislative purposes allowed FDR to elaborate on an existing pattern rather than experiment in the wholesale transformation of government during a time of great upheaval for the United States.

Further reading: Cooper, John Milton, Jr. *The Warrior and the Priest: Woodrow Wilson and Theodore Roosevelt.* Cambridge, Mass.: Belknap Press of Harvard University Press, 1983; Dawley, Alan. *Struggles for Justice: Social Responsibility and the Liberal State.* Cambridge, Mass.: Belknap Press of Harvard University Press, 1991; Sklar, Martin J. *Corporate Reconstruction of American Capitalism, 1890–1916: The Market, The Law, and Politics.* New

York: Cambridge University Press, 1988; Skowronek, Stephen. *Building a New American State: The Expansion of National Administrative Capacities 1877–1920*. New York: Cambridge University Press, 1982.

—Terri Bimes and Lori Cox-Han

New Frontier

The name given to the domestic programs of President John F. KENNEDY, the New Frontier came to symbolize energy, vigor, and progress for a generation. The phrase "new frontier" was first used in Kennedy's acceptance speech at the Democratic National Convention in Los Angeles, California, in 1960. Kennedy's New Frontier was a mixture of expansive rhetoric and bold policy initiatives. Consisting of a civil rights initiative, a full employment program, tax reduction, federal aid to education, medical insurance for the elderly, aid to depressed areas, the elimination of discrimination in employment based on sex, age, religion, and place of national origin, as well as the establishment of the Peace Corps, Kennedy's agenda marked the renewal of government activism in the aftermath of the more conservative EISENHOWER years. While President Kennedy wanted to reinvigorate government, in office, his agenda was thwarted by a Congress controlled by his own party. Given that President Kennedy served less than a term in office, it is difficult to say how he might have fared had he been given the opportunity to serve out his full term as president.

New York Times v. United States, 430 U.S. 713 (713) (The Pentagon Papers Case)

In 1971 the U.S. Supreme Court faced the following issue for the first time in its history: Can the president order a newspaper to cease publication of classified government documents, where no statute prohibited such publication, on the grounds that unauthorized public disclosure might damage NATIONAL SECURITY? In effect, does a president have inherent executive authority to censor of impose prior restraint on a publication?

This case began with the appearance on the front page of *The New York Times* on June 13, 1971, of the first installment of a series of articles that reprinted part of a top secret DEFENSE DEPARTMENT study of the history of American involvement in Vietnam over three decades. The study had been stolen from the Defense Department by one of its employees, Daniel Ellsberg, and given to the *Times* so that the public might be informed about the conduct of the U.S. government that led to a deepened involvement in Vietnam. That conduct had never before been revealed, and exposure of it here would lay bare the deception that underlay it. After the first two parts of the series had been

published by the *Times,* Attorney General John MITCHELL sent a telegram to the paper's publishers, asking them to refrain from further publication, warning them that publication of this material violated the Espionage Act of 1917. (In fact, later judicial proceedings ruled that this was *not* violated here, since the statue did not prohibit "publication" of classified information.) The *Times* refused to comply with the attorney general's request, and the Justice Department filed a motion in federal district court for an injunction that would order the paper to cease publication. The district court judge issued that injunction, the first ever against a newspaper in the United States, but abolished it four days later after a federal court in Washington refused to issue a similar order against *The Washington Post* for the same purpose. Cases from both Washington and New York reached the Supreme Court simultaneously.

Thus began this spectacular and historic case that probed the contours of the First Amendment and the question of whether a president possesses the power, solely on his own and without statutory authorization, to circumscribe that amendment's protection. A Supreme Court decision in the Pentagon Papers case affirming the newspaper's right to publish was soon followed by a separate government effort to criminally prosecute Ellsberg and his codefendant, Anthony Russo, for their role in the removal of the study from the Defense Department. This second case created even more embarrassment for the government when evidence of its misconduct during the trial came to light, including illegal entry into the office of Ellsberg's psychiatrist by men hired by the White House staff and offers of an FBI directorship to the presiding trial judge by the president's chief domestic aide, John Ehrlichman. Consequently, the trial judge declared a mistrial and dismissed all criminal charges against Ellsberg and Russo.

The speed with which the Pentagon Papers case raced through the federal court system was evidence, in itself, of its dramatic significance. Freedom of the press, unfettered by government restraint, is one of the cornerstones of democracy. If the government, and, for that matter, if a president alone, could decide what information a paper could and could not print, democracy would lose all meaning. From start to finish the case took 17 days, with Supreme Court review granted on June 25, oral argument on the 26th, and a 6-3 decision on the 30th.

The Court issued a three-paragraph, unsigned, per curiam opinion, holding only that "any system of prior restraints of expression comes to this Court bearing a heavy presumption against its constitutional validity." The Court agreed with the lower court rulings that "the Government had (has) not met that burden."

Each justice of the Court then followed with a separate opinion, six concurrences and three dissents. Justices Black and Douglas maintained a near-absolute position against any inherent executive restriction of publication. Justice Brennan followed closely behind, scolding the government for premising its power on the claim that publication here "could" or "might" or "may" damage the national interest without any proof that it, in fact, would do so. For Brennan, only where government could prove "that publication must inevitably, directly and immediately cause the occurrence of an event kindred to imperiling the safety of a transport already at sea . . ." would he find sufficient justification for overriding the First Amendment's ban on prior restraint and for issuing an interim restraining order.

Other concurring justices criticized the government for fueling public skepticism through excessive classification but based their judgments mostly on the absence of statutory authority for the president to restrain publication during national emergencies. Of particular note was an unsuccessful effort in 1917 to insert such a provision in the Espionage Act. The fact that Congress rejected that effort was conclusive evidence of congressional intent to deny such power to the president, according to Justice White's concurrence, despite the fact that White readily conceded that disclosure of the documents in this case "will do substantial damage to public interests."

The dissenters were most critical of the "unseemly haste" with which the Court proceeded and the inability of the justices to give "reasonable and deliberate judicial treatment" to the case. They complained about the lack of time to develop an adequate record, the inordinate time pressure under which the parties labored to prepare for argument, and the fact that judges at all levels in both cases were unable to know all of the facts before ruling.

Despite the focus on the First Amendment here, the legacy of this case is far greater for what it reaffirms about the relationship among the three branches. The Court here was, in effect, asked by the president to do what Congress had already declined to do: provide a president with unlimited power to decide what information newspapers can publish. Instead, the Court made clear to the CHIEF EXECUTIVE that there are limits on the president's power that the judiciary will enforce.

Equally, there are individual liberties, as in the First Amendment here, that courts are prepared to protect, absent compelling proof by a president of the need to override those freedoms.

Further reading: Department of Defense. *United States-Vietnam Relations, 1945–1967.* Washington, D.C.: U.S. Government Printing Office, 1971; Rudenstine, David. *The Day the Presses Stopped: A History of the Pentagon Papers Case.* Berkeley: University of California Press, 1996; Ungar, Sanford. *The Papers and The Papers.* New York: Columbia University Press, 1989.

—Nancy Kassop

Nixon, Richard M(ilhous) (1913–1994) *thirty-seventh U.S. president*

Born on January 9, 1913, in Yorba Linda, California, Nixon graduated from Whittier College in 1934, then went to Duke Law School. Brilliant but deeply flawed, in 1974 Richard M. Nixon became the first and only president to resign from office (to avoid IMPEACHMENT and conviction) for abuse of power and criminal behavior. He remains an enigma and a paradox.

Nixon was a complex, multidimensional figure. He was not, as some of his critics suggest, a shallow, one-dimensional person. He was a man of many contradictions. There were, as cartoonist Herblock oversimplified, two Nixons: the good Nixon and the bad Nixon, and they existed side by side within the man.

Simple, easy descriptions do not apply to Richard Nixon. Was he, as Garry Wills suggests, "the least authentic" man alive? The "Market's servant?" "Plastic?" Was he, as Irving Grant wrote, "a synthetic figure?" Or was he, as Theodore White has written, "a quintessentially insecure man . . . uncomfortable with people?" Does Henry KISSINGER's "the essence of this man is loneliness" apply? Or do Nixon's own "I'm an introvert in an extrovert's profession," and "I'm not a lovable man" apply? Arthur Miller wrote that he "marched instinctively down the crooked path," and George V. Higgins said that he was "a virtuoso of deception." Columnist Murray Kempton wrote that Nixon was "the President of every place in the country which does not have a bookstore." Nixon's own CHIEF OF STAFF, Bob Haldeman, likened Nixon to a piece of quartz crystal: "He was very complex, with all kinds of light and dark faces, depending on where you're looking from."

Longtime Nixon friend and speechwriter Raymond Price sees his former boss as something of a paradox. Theodore White also noticed the paradoxical quality of Nixon, when he wrote of "the essential duality of his nature, the evil and the good, the flights of panic and the resolution of spirit, the good mind and the mean trickery." And former White House aide William Safire sees Nixon as a complex man with multiple layers, best seen as a layer cake, with the icing (Nixon's public face) "conservative, stern, dignified, proper. But beneath the icing one finds a variety of separate layers which reveal a complex, sometimes contradictory, paradoxical human being." One part of Nixon, Price writes, is exceptionally considerate, exceptionally caring, sentimental, generous of spirit, kind. Another part is coldly calculating, devious, craftily manipulative. A third part is angry, vindictive, ill-tempered, mean-spirited. Price notes that those close to Nixon often referred to his "light side" and his "dark side" and suggests that over the years the light side and the dark side "have been at constant war with one another." Because of this, Price notes, "he has always needed people around him who would help the light side prevail." Interestingly, Price points out "the extent to which the dark side grew not out of his nature, but out of his experiences in public life." The light side–dark side assessment of Nixon is frequently referred to, especially by Nixon insiders. Some staffers (e.g., Bob Finch) appealed to Nixon's better side, while others (e.g., Chuck Colson) appealed to the dark side. For the most part, the latter dominated in the White House. This light side–dark side quality of Nixon made him a sort of Dr. Jekyll and Mr. Hyde character.

Bob Haldeman once described Nixon as "the weirdest man ever to live in the White House," and John Ehrlichman described his former boss as "the mad monk." Nixon has been a fascinating subject for analysis precisely because he is so puzzling. As columnist Hugh Sidey has said, "He is an absolutely sinister human being, but fascinating. I'd rather spend an evening with Richard Nixon than with almost anybody else because he is so bizarre. He has splashes of brilliance. He is obscene at times; his recall is almost total; his acquaintanceship with the world's figures is amazing. He is a fascinating human being."

In FOREIGN AFFAIRS, Nixon was an innovative thinker and grand strategist. Understanding that the United States was entering an "age of limits," Nixon attempted to refashion U.S. power and position in the world while maintaining international leadership. The Nixon years were a time of dramatic, bold, innovative approaches and overtures in the field of foreign affairs. They were years when the conventional wisdom was challenged and conventional solutions eschewed for a new strategic approach to foreign policy.

It was a new era that brought about an opening of relations with China, DÉTENTE with the Soviet Union, a strategic arms limitation agreement with the Soviets. It was a period when America's military involvement in Vietnam and Southeast Asia was expanded, then ended, and when a relatively new approach and strategic orientation was introduced into American foreign policy thinking.

Under Richard Nixon and Henry Kissinger, a reexamination and reorientation of the U.S. role in the world produced a different strategic vision. There was recognition of the changing role and capacity of the United States, recognition of the limits of power, and an attempt to match America's strategic vision with its capabilities. Had it not been for WATERGATE and the self-destruction of the Nixon presidency, there is no telling how the early stages of the Nixon foreign policy revolution might have eventually changed the United States and the world.

In collaboration with Henry Kissinger, Nixon promoted a far-reaching, forward-thinking approach to foreign policy that had a momentous impact on the world. As Crabb and Mulcahy note: "Nixon's impact was felt in several ways—the theoretical framework in which his foreign policy initiatives were cast (the so-called NIXON DOCTRINE), in the specific content of the policies themselves

President Richard M. Nixon (*Library of Congress*)

(for example, in détente and the normalization of Sino-American relations), and in the process by which these policies were formulated, especially regarding the role of Kissinger and his White House staff."

As was the case in so many other aspects of his presidency, the foreign policy Nixon promoted was full of irony and contradiction. How could one of America's premier anticommunists open the door to China and promote détente and ARMS CONTROL with the Soviet Union? How could the politician who kept promoting an "America First" attitude negotiate a deal with the Soviets that effectively granted them equality with the United States? How could a president who promoted American hegemony relinquish economic power and prestige? What accounts for these metamorphoses?

Even Nixon's most skeptical critics recognized that this truly was a different and more sophisticated approach to American foreign policy. Nixon had a vision—a new strategic orientation—and attempted to take the steps necessary to bring that vision to fruition. One could argue that Nixon's vision was inappropriate or incorrect, but that Nixon had an integrated, complex, and sophisticated worldview seems clear.

Nixon had a clearer idea of where he wanted to lead the nation in foreign affairs than in any other area of policy. Nixon felt that the domestic arena could be run by a CABINET, but only the president could lead in foreign policy. Foreign policy was Richard Nixon's domain, the area in which he felt most comfortable, most in command. And Nixon had some definite ideas about where he wanted to lead the nation, the Western alliance, and the world.

Nixon came to office (1969) at a time when U.S. foreign policy was ripe for reexamination and redesign. The post-World War II consensus that had guided the nation for 25 years was collapsing, and America's role in the world was going through some convulsive changes. By the late 1960s, an era of U.S. foreign policy was coming to an end.

For the two decades immediately following WORLD WAR II, the United States served as the dominant, hegemonic power of the West. It was the beginning, many thought, of the "American Century," a period in which the United States would provide a benevolent leadership and direction. After the decline of Great Britain in the postwar era, the United States inherited hegemonic control, which placed it in the lead of the Western alliance. This role was challenged by the Soviet Union in the years following World War II, but by virtue of vast military and economic superiority, the United States was able to spread its protective umbrella over Western Europe and eventually over much of the rest of the world.

Empire was costly, but in the 1940s and 1950s, the United States had the resources to spend. We could afford a costly web of military ventures and economic aid to contain the expansion of communism, but by the 1960s, America's role was proving to be a burden—a burden costly in lives and resources. By the time Richard Nixon took office, the American empire seemed to be in the early stages of decline.

The combination of the VIETNAM WAR and the multiple changes taking place in the world left the United States without an acceptable road map for the future. Strategically the United States was adrift and foundering. The war in Vietnam deeply divided the American people. Relations with the Soviet Union were in flux. As the Soviets approached strategic parity with the United States, questions of how best to deal with the Russians proved confounding. Should the United States continue CONTAINMENT? Search for coexistence? Move to confrontation? These questions confused us at a time when a further COLD WAR belief was being dispelled. The assumption regarding monolithic communism was being reexamined because of deep rifts between the Soviet Union and China, and trouble with the communist satellite states. Tight bipolarity seemed to be giving way to a kind of global pluralism, and the United States was without a plan for dealing with these changes.

Other changes in the world proved equally perplexing to the American policy makers. Members of the Western alliance, which the United States had dominated for 20 years, were showing signs of independence as the European economies rebounded from the war with vigor and American economic dominance was being threatened. The Third World and less-developed nations were becoming more independent and nationalistic, the oil-producing nations were forming a cartel, and the post–World War II world seemed to be going through changes that the United States could neither control nor comprehend.

The world was becoming more complex, more interdependent, and less amenable to U.S. dominance, at a time when America's resources—military and economic—were declining relative to the demands placed upon the United States. Nothing seemed to be working as it should. The center did not hold. Amid this policy incoherence and confusion, the time was right for a fundamental change in American foreign policy. But how could the United States respond to this changing world?

Vietnam was the most glaring symptom of America's relative decline. Henry Kissinger recognized this "new" relationship when he wrote in his memoirs:

> We were in a period of painful adjustment to a profound transformation of global politics; we were being forced to come to grips with the tension between our history and our new necessities. For two centuries America's participation in the world seemed to oscillate between over-involvement and withdrawal, between expecting too much of our power and being ashamed of it, between optimistic exuberance and frustration with the ambiguities of an imperfect world. I was convinced that the deepest cause of our national unease was the realization—as yet dimly perceived—that we were becoming like other nations in the need to recognize that our power, while vast, had limits. Our resources were no longer infinite in relation to our problems; instead we had to set priorities, both intellectual and material.

Gone were the days when American power was so preponderant that the United States seemed capable of solving problems by simply overwhelming them with America's superior economic or military power. The world had changed; the United States had changed. Not having overwhelming resource superiority, the United States had to be more careful, more selective. But how does one adjust responsibilities to match declining power while still exerting hegemonic control?

In effect, Nixon and Kissinger attempted to deal with relative decline by developing slightly more modest international commitments (the Nixon Doctrine), developing a new international system (Nixon's ambitious "Grand

Design" or "structure of peace"), exerting dramatic international leadership (shuttle diplomacy), and refashioning our relationships with the two most powerful communist nations (détente with the Soviet Union, opening the door to China). Charles E. Osgood called the new strategy "military retrenchment without political disengagement." And Nixon attempted to deal with the overextension of American power, not by retreating from American globalism, but in an orderly, controlled readjustment, a measured devolution. In light of the new limits on America's capabilities and resources, the United States could not bear the international burdens it had accumulated for the last 25 years. Now the United States would have to settle for less, set clearer priorities, and redefine the national interest. But could this be done while still playing the role of hegemon?

Nixon attempted to implement a new "Grand Strategy" for foreign affairs, but like so many aspects of his presidency, grand designs gave way to petty politics, and Nixon's ambitious plans were eventually crushed by the weight of the Watergate scandal.

In DOMESTIC POLICY, Nixon was often a reluctant reformer. Pushed by a Congress controlled by the Democrats, Nixon promoted a "new Federalism" to devolve some federal power back to the states, imposed wage and price controls during an economic slump, created the ENVIRONMENTAL PROTECTION AGENCY, and witnessed the first moon landing on July 20, 1969.

Because the opposition party controlled Congress, Nixon devised an "administrative strategy" to govern. He attempted, where possible, to bypass Congress and use administrative discretion to the limit and beyond. This administrative strategy was an innovation that would later be used by President REAGAN with great success. The swelling of the ADMINISTRATIVE PRESIDENCY added to the tools of presidential LEADERSHIP.

Presidential IMPOUNDMENT OF FUNDS had become a major issue in the Nixon years. Due to the claims of power by Richard Nixon, the courts faced a series of cases questioning the legality of impoundment.

The roots of impoundment can be traced to Thomas JEFFERSON's refusal, in 1803, to spend $50,000 appropriated by Congress, but the issue of impoundment did not reach the Supreme Court until 35 years later when, in *Kendal v. United States ex rel Stokes,* the Court ruled against the EXECUTIVE BRANCH in an instance in which the postmaster general refused to release funds.

Impoundment as a political issue did not, however, become important until the Nixon administration. President Nixon made the impoundment of funds a weapon in making policy, even when that policy ran counter to the expressed wishes of Congress. A number of cases reached the courts. Most of these cases were decided against the president.

These impoundment cases serve as an example of the courts standing up to the president. In case after case, courts throughout the country ruled against impoundments and ordered the president to release congressionally appropriated funds. Arthur Miller once noted that the power of the president to impound funds could be exercised "to the extent that the political milieu in which he operates permits him to do so." In the case of the Nixon administration, it was an example of presidential overload. The political system could take a lot, but it could not take this many intrusions into the realm of congressional policy making.

The courts were joined by the Congress, which wanted the funds released, and this coalition was able to halt a president who seemed determined to breach the boundaries of the political milieu in which he was operating.

The presidential scandal known as Watergate was the most serious presidential scandal in United States history. In it, the president was implicated in a variety of crimes, including obstruction of justice, bribery, criminal conspiracy, election fraud, destruction of evidence, and a host of other crimes and questionable activities.

Could a sitting president be indicted in a criminal case? Special Prosecutor Leon JAWORSKI was unsure, instead naming Nixon an "unindicted coconspirator" in the case dealing with the president's top staffers. The people with whom the president conspired were all convicted and sent to prison for Watergate offenses. Nixon received a pardon from Gerald FORD.

As the Watergate investigations drew the noose tighter and tighter around the president's neck, it became clear that Nixon would be impeached by the House and convicted by the Senate. The Supreme Court decision in *UNITED STATES V. NIXON* (1974) compelled the president to release tape recordings (while also adding to the power of the presidency by establishing judicial recognition of limited "EXECUTIVE PRIVILEGE") that clearly established that fact that Nixon was involved in criminal behavior. From that point on, what little support Nixon had quickly evaporated. In order to escape impeachment, Nixon resigned from office on August 9, 1974. He is the only president to resign his office. The House Judiciary Committee approved three articles of impeachment against President Nixon:

Article I
In his conduct of the office of president of the United States, Richard M. Nixon, in violation of his constitutional oath faithfully to execute the office of President of the United States and, to the best of his ability, preserve, protect, and defend the Constitution of the United States, and, in violation of his constitutional duty to take care that the laws be faithfully executed, has prevented, obstructed, and impeded the administration of justice, in that:

On June 17, 1972, and prior thereto, agents of the Committee for the Re-election of the President committed unlawful entry of the headquarters of the Democratic National Committee in Washington, District of Columbia, for the purpose of securing political intelligence. Subsequent thereto, Richard M. Nixon, using the powers of his high office, engaged personally and through his subordinates and agents, in a course of conduct or plan designed to delay, impede, and obstruct the investigation of such unlawful entry; to cover up, conceal and protect those responsible; and to conceal the existence and scope of other unlawful covert activities.

Article II

Using the powers of the office of President of the United States, Richard M. Nixon, in violation of his constitutional oath faithfully to execute the office of President of the United States and, to the best of his ability, preserve, protect, and defend the Constitution of the United States, and in disregard of his constitutional duty to take care that the laws be faithfully executed, has repeatedly engaged in conduct violating the constitutional rights of citizens, impairing the due and proper administration of justice and the conduct of lawful inquiries, or contravening the laws governing the agencies of the executive branch and the purposes of these agencies.

Article III

In his conduct of the office of President of the United States, Richard M. Nixon, contrary to his oath faithfully to execute the office of President of the United States, and, to the best of his ability, preserve, protect, and defend the Constitution of the United States, and in violation of his constitutional duty to take care that the laws be faithfully executed, has failed without lawful cause or excuse to produce papers and things as directed by duly authorized subpoenas issued by the Committee on the Judiciary of the House of Representatives . . . In refusing to produce these papers and things, Richard M. Nixon substituted his judgment as to what materials were necessary for the inquiry, interposed the powers of the Presidency against the lawful subpoenas of the House of Representatives, thereby assuming to himself functions and judgments necessary to the exercise of the sole power of impeachment vested by the Constitution in the House of Representatives.

In all of this, Richard M. Nixon has acted in a manner contrary to his trust as President and subversive of constitutional government, to the great prejudice of the cause of law and justice, and to the manifest injury of the people of the United States. Wherefore Richard M. Nixon, by such conduct, warrants impeachment and trial, and removal from office.

The aftermath of Watergate led to a decline of the presidency and a rebirth of congressional power. A transformation began to take place. As a result first of Vietnam, then of Watergate, our superman became an imperial president. The presidency had become a danger to the republic, using its power not for the public good but for self-aggrandizement. A new image of the presidency developed.

Watergate turned out to be the final nail in the coffin of the unambiguous acceptance of the strong-presidency model. The twin effects of Vietnam and Watergate led to an era of deep cynicism regarding politics and the presidency. Scholars and the public began to condemn the "excesses" of presidential power, characterized as the IMPERIAL PRESIDENCY, and called for a corralling of a presidency perceived as acting above the law. It was a presidency-curbing, if not presidency-bashing, period.

Reacting against the excesses of power in the Johnson and Nixon presidencies, the Congress attempted to reassert its power by taking a series of presidency-curbing steps, the most notable being the passage of the WAR POWERS RESOLUTION, which attempted (with little subsequent success) to curb the president's war powers. The presidency-curbing era also ushered in a period in which the public did an about-face regarding their trust in and support of presidents and the presidency. Any and all presidential acts were suspect; virtually no support was given for presidential initiatives; and a weak-presidency model (though not a strong-Congress model) prevailed. In the MIDTERM ELECTIONS of 1974, a new breed of activist Democrats was elected to the Congress. Weaned not on FDR's greatness but on JOHNSON's and NIXON's excesses, this new generation of legislator was less deferential to presidents, less willing to bow to claims of presidential prerogative, and more willing to challenge presidents directly. As a result, the legislative initiatives of Presidents Ford and CARTER would fall victim to the Congress's revised, more suspicious attitude toward presidential power.

Further reading: Ambrose, Stephen E. *Nixon.* New York: Simon Schuster, 1987–1991; Genovese, Michael A. *The Nixon Presidency: Power and Politics in Turbulent Times.* New York: Greenwood Press, 1990; Morris, Roger. *Richard Milhous Nixon: The Rise of an American Politician.* New York: Holt, 1990; Parmet, Herbert S. *Richard Nixon and His America.* Boston: Little, Brown, 1990; Safire, William. *Before the Fall: An Inside View of the Pre-Watergate White House.* Garden City, N.Y.: Doubleday, 1975.

Nixon Doctrine

Initially called the "Guam Doctrine," and more widely referred to as "Vietnamization," this policy began the gradual withdrawal of American forces from Vietnam. It was eventually broadened into a worldwide strategy in which the United States would manage its treaty obligations by limiting its involvement in local wars. In effect, it served to extricate the United States from the VIETNAM WAR while seeking to avoid future Vietnam Wars.

Announced by President Richard NIXON on Guam Island in July 1969, the policy called for the gradual removal of American combat forces from Southeast Asia and their replacement with South Vietnamese forces. U.S. troop reductions had already begun a month earlier in June 1969 and continued until 1975. The Nixon administration pushed for increased military aid to South Vietnam in order to modernize its forces, but Congress steadily reduced this aid until 1975, when it eliminated it altogether.

In explaining the doctrine to the American public in a televised address on November 3, 1969, Nixon outlined the three elements of the doctrine: First, the United States would keep all of its treaty commitments. Second, the United States would provide a nuclear shield "if a nuclear power threatens the freedom of a nation allied with us or of a nation whose survival we consider vital to our security." Third, in nonnuclear situations the U.S. would provide military and economic assistance but would "look to the nation directly threatened to assume the primary responsibility of providing the manpower for its defense."

While directed initially at Asia, the doctrine was also used to manage conflicts in the Middle East and to reassure Latin American countries who had grown increasingly nervous about previous U.S. INTERVENTIONS.

—Sean C. Matheson

Nixon v. Administrator of General Services (1977)

This case dealt with a 1974 agreement between Richard NIXON and the administrator of General Services to take control of and eventually destroy many of the estimated 42 million pages of documents and 880 tape recordings. Nixon and the General Services Administration (GSA) had agreed that Nixon could not take any of the original documents for three years, but then could withdraw all material except the tape recordings, which he could not gain access to for five years. By September 1, 1979, Nixon could indicate which tapes he wanted destroyed, and by September 1, 1984, or at his death, whichever came first, all the tapes were to be destroyed.

Once the public heard of this agreement, Congress introduced the Presidential Recordings and Materials Preservation Act (S 4016), that would have the administrator of the GSA take control of all presidential materials and have them screened by government archivists to determine which materials were personal and should be returned to the president and which materials had historic worth. The act was signed into law by President Gerald FORD on December 19, 1974 (Pub. L. 93–526, 88 Stat. 1695). The

next day, Nixon filed suit in district court challenging the act's constitutional validity. Nixon maintained that this law violated SEPARATION OF POWERS, presidential privilege, his own privacy rights, his First Amendment rights, and the Bill of Attainder clause of the Constitution. The district court held that Nixon's constitutional challenges to the act had no merit.

The case was then appealed to the Supreme Court, where Justice William Brennan delivered the majority decision with six other justices agreeing in part with his opinion. Chief Justice Burger and Justice Rehnquist dissented. Brennan did not feel this act violated separation of powers, nor did the act violate confidentiality or invade Nixon's privacy, since Nixon's private materials would be returned to him. The Court majority agreed that the act was not a punitive bill or unconstitutional.

Justice Stevens's concurrence indicated that it was not right to single Nixon out and humiliate him, but he agreed with the rest of the majority decision. Justice White's concurrence argued that Nixon's own private material should be returned despite the fact that it might have historic worth. Justice Blackmun's concurrence suggested he was not sure that the act necessarily served the CHIEF EXECUTIVE's functions, while Justice Powell agreed in his concurrence that many constitutional questions remained to be answered as far as presidential confidentiality.

Justice Burger in his dissent argued that the act violated the principle of separation of powers interfering with the power of the president to conduct his office and exchange advice with his staff. Justice Rehnquist's dissent suggested that the decision supported the power of Congress to seize official papers of outgoing presidents threaten future presidents and their personal communications. He was also concerned about the lack of agreement concerning what "historical significance" meant.

Had it not been for this decision and Congress's quick action, materials from the Nixon administration would have been lost to history. The decision also confirmed that presidential IMMUNITY is a qualified power, and that presidential records are "public" and not "private" information. However, questions raised by the dissenters regarding presidential communication and the effect of intrusion on future presidents have yet to be answered.

Further reading: McGowan, Carl. "Presidents and their Papers." *Minnesota Law Review* 68 (1983): 409–437; *Nixon v. Administration of General Services*, 443 US 425 (1977).

—Byron W. Daynes

nominating candidates for president

Almost immediately after a presidential election, political pundits start speculating about potential candidates for the next election. While the discussion might seem absurd given that the winner of the most recent election will not even be inaugurated for another two months, in reality, potential candidates are always testing the waters to determine whether they have a legitimate chance of being elected president.

One aspect of presidential elections that has changed over the years is that aspirants are now announcing their candidacies much earlier. According to Michael G. Hagen and William G. Mayer, during the 1950s and 1960s, the average number of days that candidates declared their intention to run before the party's convention was roughly 140. In 1996 that number rose to 475 days. Candidates were announcing their presidential ambitions a year and a half before the actual election. In fact, in 1952 Democratic candidate Adlai Stevenson did not announce his intention to run until his party's convention. In 1996 Republican Phil Gramm made his decision 535 days before the convention.

The time between the last presidential election and the next election's first caucus is called the Invisible Primary. Many candidates "run" during this period, but few actually make it to the first primary or caucus; the Invisible Primary is a political version of the "survival of the fittest." For example, in 2000 half of the Republican field had already suspended their campaigns before the Iowa caucus. This process is called the "winnowing of candidates."

How are those that survive the Invisible Primary able to do so? First, candidates must have strong campaign organizations and grassroots supporters. This is especially important in states like New Hampshire, where "retail politics" is still popular. More important, candidates must be able to raise substantial amounts of money. The rule of thumb is that you must raise at least $20 million to have a legitimate chance of winning the nomination. Candidates such as John Kasich in 2000 realized they could not raise this kind of money, so they dropped out. Also, candidates must do well in early polls. There is added emphasis placed on the Iowa straw-poll held the summer before the election year. A straw poll is an unscientific poll that attempts to determine who is leading the race. In reality, one must be extremely cautious of straw poll results because candidates are literally paying supporters to vote. Because of the unscientific nature of the poll, they tell us little, but candidates and the media place great importance on these polls. CNN, while constantly questioning the validity of the poll, still showed daylong coverage of the 1999 Republican Iowa straw poll. Even though one can question thier validity, candidates place great emphasis on doing well in the straw polls and spend substantial amounts of money on them. Failure to meet expectations can already mean the end of the road for some candidates. After his poor sixth-place finish in 1999, Republican Lamar Alexander suspended his campaign.

While raising money and strong campaign organizations might allow presidential hopefuls to survive the Invisible Primary, candidates need strong showings in the early PRIMARIES AND CAUCUSES to remain in the field. If candidates are able to last until the Iowa caucus or the New Hampshire primary, most do not make it much further than that. Using the 2000 Republican nomination as an example again, Orrin Hatch dropped out immediately after a poor showing in Iowa; Gary Bauer did so after getting trounced in New Hampshire; and Steve Forbes called it quits after two subpar performances in Iowa and New Hampshire and failure to repeat his 1996 performance in Delaware. Just two weeks into the primary season, the Republican field had already been cut in half. All of these candidates failed to establish momentum.

Obtaining momentum, or "Big Mo" as it is referred to by some, can have a large impact on the success of a candidate's chances of winning the nomination. Momentum is important because it gives the candidate press coverage (usually positive) and legitimacy, both of which make it easier to raise money. In 1976 Democratic long shot Jimmy CARTER emerged from nowhere to win the Iowa caucus and the New Hampshire primary. The momentum Carter obtained from these victories carried him all the way to the Democratic nomination. However, it is not always necessary that one win an early primary to build momentum. Sometimes a strong second-place (or occasionally even a third-place) showing is enough to energize a candidate's campaign. In 1984 Gary Hart received only 16.5 percent of the Democratic vote in the Iowa caucus compared to Walter Mondale's 48.3 percent, but Hart received the favorable press coverage because of his surprise showing and went on to win the New Hampshire primary. Success is not always based on winning, but on how the media reports that the candidate did.

Recently, the ability of candidates to build momentum has diminished because of a process known as frontloading. Frontloading is the trend of states moving their primaries closer to the start of the primary calendar. States have started to frontload because they want more of a voice in who the parties' nominations will be. States such as California and New York moved their primaries from June to late March in 1996 but still failed to have an impact on the nomination. As a result, California moved its primary even earlier in 2000 (March 7). Because a state as large as California now has more influence over the nomination, other states began moving their primaries earlier in the season to avoid being left out of the process.

The effects of frontloading have been substantial. Frontloading helps well-financed or front-runner candidates immensely because it creates less of an opportunity for an outside candidate to build momentum. Jimmy Carter benefited from his win in Iowa because he had roughly a month before the next primary. This gave him the opportunity to use his momentum to raise substantial amounts of money. Outsider candidates do not have the same luxury today. In 2000 Senator John McCain surprised Republican front-runner George W. BUSH with a commanding victory in New Hampshire. However, McCain had to turn around and compete in Delaware just four days later and South Carolina a little more than a week after New Hampshire. The immediate primaries gave McCain little time to cash in on his success in New Hampshire. Because Bush was so well funded, his loss in the first primary and the short time to the next primary did not hurt him.

While frontloading has consequences on the campaign, many political scientists argue that it also impacts the voter. Some argue that frontloading keeps voters from receiving much information about candidates because the primary season is almost over before it starts; voters do not have enough time to thoroughly access candidates' strengths and weaknesses. While parties have tried to combat the problems of frontloading by awarding bonus delegates to those states that hold their primaries later in the year, these efforts have been largely unsuccessful. It is unlikely that the problem of frontloading will disappear any time soon.

Further reading: Ceaser, James W., and Andrew E. Busch. *The Perfect Tie: The True Story of the 2000 Presidential Election.* Lanham, Md.: Rowman & Littlefield, 2001; Polsby, Nelson W., and Aaron Wildavsky. *Presidential Elections: Strategies and Structures of American Politics.* 10th ed. New York: Chatham House, 2000; Wayne, Stephen J. *The Road to the White House 2000.* Boston, Mass.: Bedford/St. Martin's, 2001.

—Matt Streb

nuclear command procedures

Since the dawn of the nuclear age, one of the most important tasks of a president is to command the nation's nuclear forces. But one man—alone—could not, or should not, be able to plunge a nation into nuclear war. Thus, certain controls needed to be developed on the use of nuclear weapons. Nuclear strategists developed the Single Integrated Operational Plan (SIOP), a planned response to possible nuclear weapons use. If NORAD, the North American Aerospace Defense Command, detects an attack on the United States, they are to inform the president, who has minutes to consult with advisers, evaluate his SIOP options, decide, then order a response.

If the president decides to retaliate he must transmit the launch codes (kept by a military officer who is always in the vicinity of the president), which are in "the football" (a briefcase), to the military. Once the order is authenticated, the order is carried out.

nuclear weapons policy

In 1945 the nuclear age began when the United States dropped two bombs on Hiroshima and Nagasaki, Japan. From that day on, the world's powers have wrestled with how to prevent their further use. When the Soviet Union acquired nuclear weapons and their means of delivery, a policy of "deterrence" was developed. As long as the adversary of a nuclear first strike feared retaliation, a deterrence effect would prevent launching a nuclear strike. Deterrence dominated strategic thinking for 50 years.

With the spread of nuclear weapons a "nonproliferation" strategy was developed to halt the spread of these weapons. But France, Great Britain, China, Israel, India, North Korea, and other nations acquired nuclear weapons, thus undermining efforts to limit the spread and danger of use. In recent years, with the collapse of the Soviet Union and rise of international terrorism, efforts were developed to eliminate and disarm nuclear weapons, as well as prevent them from getting into the hands of rogue states and terrorist organizations.

nullification

Nullification was the doctrine urged by a number of writers and politicians in the early 19th century that held that the states could declare a federal law to be unconstitutional and therefore null and void. Although the term itself is a general one, as in the "judicial nullification" of unconstitutional laws, it is generally used to refer to the doctrine of state nullification.

The doctrine of nullification is based on the theory that the federal union is a compact of independent sovereign states. As such, the federal government can only exercise the powers specifically delegated to it by the Constitution, strictly constructed. The doctrine of nullification held that the Supreme Court, as a branch of the federal government, could not have the final word on whether the acts of the federal government exceeded the bounds of the Constitution. As the creators of the federal compact, the individual states have the right to evaluate the constitutionality of federal actions for themselves. The doctrine had its origins in the Virginia and Kentucky resolutions of 1798, secretly authored by James MADISON and Thomas JEFFERSON respectively. The resolutions were a response to the congressional passage of the ALIEN AND SEDITION ACTS and argued that the statutes exceeded congressional authority. Although the resolutions did not indicate what specific actions the states should take, the Virginia resolution called for the state governments to "interpose" themselves between the citizenry and the federal government acting unconstitutionally, and Jefferson's draft of the Kentucky resolution argued for the states' right "to nullify [such unconstitutional laws] on their own authority." No actions were ever taken in that case, but the resolutions became founding texts of the Jeffersonian DEMOCRATIC PARTY. A number of states passed similar resolutions in subsequent years.

The doctrine of nullification was given its strongest form and most sophisticated defense in response to the passage of the highly protectionist Tariff of Abominations of 1828. Supported by Northern manufacturing interests, protective tariffs were bitterly opposed in the South, which depended on international trade. In 1828 the South Carolina state legislature published the "Exposition and Protest," which was secretly written by Vice President John CALHOUN. In the Exposition and elsewhere, Calhoun argued that the protectionist tariff was unconstitutional and that state nullification was the appropriate response. Calhoun repeated and further developed the central elements of the compact theory of the federal union. Calhoun was explicit, however, that the states had the right to take necessary steps to prevent the enforcement of unconstitutional federal laws within their boundaries but could be overruled by the passage of a constitutional amendment authorizing the disputed federal action. He also added the innovation that nullification ordinances could only be issued by state popular conventions, not state legislatures. Such a convention met in South Carolina in November 1832 and directed the state government to block the collection of the federal tariff duties in state ports. President Andrew JACKSON responded with a strongly worded nationalist proclamation, and the Force Bill was introduced in Congress authorizing the use of the military to collect the tariff. Calhoun resigned from the administration to become a senator from South Carolina. Henry CLAY helped broker a compromise in the U.S. Senate by which both the Compromise Tariff of 1833 that abandoned protectionism and the Force Bill were passed. The South Carolina convention rescinded its original nullification ordinance but passed a new ordinance nullifying the now-symbolic Force Bill. Although the compact theory of the federal union was still widely held after 1833, and was the theoretical foundation for the right of secession, the specific doctrine of state nullification found little serious support thereafter.

Further reading: Ellis, Richard E. *The Union at Risk: Jacksonian Democracy, States' Rights and the Nullification Crisis.* New York: Oxford University Press, 1987; Freehling, William W. *Prelude to Civil War: The Nullification Movement in South Carolina,* 1816–1836. New York: Oxford University Press, 1992.

—Keith E. Whittington

O

oath of office

Article II, Section 1, of the U.S. Constitution mandates that before the president "enter on the execution of his office, he shall take the following oath or affirmation: 'I do solemnly swear (or affirm) that I will faithfully execute the office of president of the United States, and will to the best of my ability, preserve, protect, and defend the constitution of the United States.'" The oath itself reflects the framers' concern that the executive be given energy without compromising safety, and that any monarchial tendencies should be minimized whenever possible.

As Karlyn Kohrs Campbell and Kathleen Hall Jamieson note, "Inauguration is a rite of passage, a ritual of transition in which a newly elected president is invested with the office of the presidency." The inaugural event is comprised of many elements: the inaugural address, the presence of the people as witnesses to the oath-taking, poetic readings and/or music. But it is the act of taking the oath of office that makes the president the president, legally investing him in office. Following John F. KENNEDY's assassination, for instance, Lyndon B. JOHNSON took the oath of office on AIR FORCE ONE; he gave no inaugural address, and there were no other elements of the inaugural ritual. Nonetheless, Johnson was fully authorized as president

The idea of an oath was first mentioned at the CONSTITUTIONAL CONVENTION as a suggestion that the officers of the states be required to support the federal government. That was agreed to without significant debate, although there was some concern that officers of the states had to pledge loyalty to the general government, and that federal officers had no such mandate regarding the states. During this discussion, Elbridge GERRY, delegate from Massachusetts, suggested that members of the national government be required to support the federal government, a suggestion that was agreed to without dissent, although the efficacy of oaths in general was debated. As James Wilson of Pennsylvania put it, "A good government did not need them, and a bad one could not or ought not to be supported." The

Gerald R. Ford is sworn in as president by Chief Justice Earl Warren. *(Ford Library)*

idea of an oath seemed attractive to the delegates, who could find no positive harm and some potential good in it. Concerned about the mutual support of the national government for the states and vice versa, the oath of office seemed to reassure them that the primacy of the Constitution, reassuring each level of its own importance in its own sphere, would be supported if not guaranteed. There was little debate concerning the wording of the oath of office.

The framers did not consider the oath by itself to be either a panacea or a solution to the various concerns about the potential monarchial nature of the executive office. In *Federalist No. 64,* John JAY lists "oath-taking" among the reasons (the others being honor, reputations, conscience, the love of country, and family affections and attachments) that promote an individual's "fidelity to the nation." The oath is but one element of the presidency that prevents it from being the potentially monarchial institution that the framers so feared. The presidential pledge to defend the Constitution is often cited as a reason for pursuing CENSURE and/or IMPEACHMENT. Violation of the oath of office is widely considered to be clear evidence of the commission of a "high crime or misdemeanor" and is considered evidence of an impeachable offense.

Despite its importance in investing the president and in underlining the limited nature of presidential power, there is little or no mention of the oath of office, its origins, or its implications in the presidential literature.

Further reading: Campbell, Karlyn Kohrs, and Kathleen Hall Jamieson. *Deeds Done in Words: Presidential Rhetoric and the Genres of Governance.* Chicago: University of Chicago Press, 1990; Madison, James. *Notes of Debates in the Federal Convention of 1787.* Edited by Adrienne Koch. Athens, Ohio: Ohio University Press, 1966; Rossiter, Clinton, ed. *The Federalist Papers.* New York: Mentor, 1961.

—Mary E. Stuckey

Office of Administration

The Office of Administration is a unit of the EXECUTIVE BRANCH responsible for the "housekeeping" functions of the WHITE HOUSE (e.g., payroll, accounting, data processing, computer use, purchasing). Established in 1977, and officially part of the EXECUTIVE OFFICE OF THE PRESIDENT (EOP), the Office of Administration is the primary unit giving the president and top staff administration technical support. The office is headed by a director appointed by and responsible to the president.

Office for Emergency Management (OEM)

Part of the EXECUTIVE OFFICE OF THE PRESIDENT (EOP), the Office of Emergency Management (OEM) was established during WORLD WAR II by President Franklin D. ROOSEVELT to assist in the war effort. OEM was headed by a presidential assistant with the title Liaison Officer for Emergency Management. By the 1950s OEM became inactive but it has never been formally eliminated.

Office of Federal Procurement Policy (OFPP)

Part of the OFFICE OF MANAGEMENT AND BUDGET, the OFPP is responsible for coordinating contracting for products and services of the federal government. In 1972 Congress's Commission on Government Procurement recommended the creation of a central procurement office. Spearheaded by Senator Lawton Chiles (Dem.-Fla.), the OFPP was eventually created to fulfill this goal.

Office of Homeland Security (OHS)

In the aftermath of the 9/11 terrorist attack, the Bush administration established by Executive Order 13228 the Office of Homeland Security. Headed by Tom RIDGE, former governor of Pennsylvania, the office was to promote homeland security from terrorist attacks. The OHS was in the WHITE HOUSE OFFICE, and the director reported to the president. Initially, the president instructed Ridge not to testify before Congress. This caused a significant backlash and the president was compelled, in June 2002, to recommend that Congress create a cabinet-level DEPARTMENT OF HOMELAND SECURITY.

Office of Information and Regulatory Affairs (OIRA)

The Office of Information and Regulatory Affairs within the OFFICE OF MANAGEMENT AND BUDGET (OMB) is a key unit within the executive office of the president that reviews regulatory actions proposed by the departments and agencies and government requests for information such as surveys to the private sector and other government agencies. OIRA was established in 1980 at the end of the CARTER administration under the auspices of the Paperwork Reduction Act of 1980 in order to spearhead an effort to reduce federal paperwork burdens on the private sector, to develop more efficient management of government information, and to conduct research to facilitate its mission. OIRA was formally established on April 1, 1981, at the beginning of the REAGAN administration, by virtue of Executive Order 12,291.

Most of OIRA's staff time was soon focused on its role in reviewing agency regulatory proposals through cost-benefit analysis, which weighs the economic costs of proposed regulations against their benefits in behalf of the public interest. By virtue of EO 12,291, OIRA was empowered to review proposed regulations and to require agencies to conduct regulatory impact analysis (RIA's). It became a centralized mechanism to assist the president in controlling regulatory activity in the EXECUTIVE BRANCH agencies. OIRA is professionally staffed by career civil servants consisting primarily of economists and attorneys, and it is directed by a politically appointed administrator.

From 1981 to 1985, in keeping with President Reagan's policy and ideological inclinations, OIRA led the charge to reduce federal regulations. In implementing this mandate, OIRA became a lightning rod for tensions between a free- market Republican president and Democratic members of Congress. Criticisms of OIRA centered around the idea that OIRA's authority had been expanded beyond what Congress intended in the Paperwork Reduction Act and that OIRA's decision-making processes were both hidden from public scrutiny and responsible for unwarranted delays in the regulatory review process. OIRA was also perceived as being overly politicized in the way it conducted its analysis, favoring business interests over the "public interest." At the time there were both congressional and judicial challenges to OIRA including congressional oversight hearings, critical General Accounting Office (GAO) reports, and threats from Congress to cut off OIRA's appropriations.

Congressional–White House tensions continued during the George H. W. BUSH presidency. In early 1990 the Supreme Court in *Dole v. United Steelworkers of America* ruled that OMB through OIRA had overstepped its authority to curb agency-promulgated rules that mandated industry to make health- and safety-related information concerning their products available to consumers and employees. The Senate refused to confirm the administration's choice for OIRA administrator and stopped OIRA's reauthorization. Thus OIRA operated with an acting career-level administrator, and by 1990 OIRA staff had dropped to 40 from a high of 80 professionals at the beginning of the Reagan administration. From 1990 to the end of the Bush administration the administration's regulatory activity was shifted to the Competitiveness Council, a White House office headed by Vice President Dan QUAYLE.

While Vice President Al GORE had been one of OIRA's most vociferous critics, it is significant that when President CLINTON took office in 1993, OIRA was not eliminated but was merely retooled in a way that ushered in a new era in OIRA's 13-year history. Gore headed an ad hoc working group charged with rewriting OIRA's marching orders that consulted with representatives from both industry and the public-interest community.

On September 30, 1993, President Clinton signed EO 12,866. The new EXECUTIVE ORDER addressed some of the criticisms of OIRA's regulatory review that had plagued the previous two administrations. The process was made more open to the public by mandating that documents exchanged between OIRA and the agencies were to be made public at the end of the review process. To curb delays in completing regulatory reviews within OIRA, a 90-day deadline was mandated. To promote better relations between OIRA and affected executive branch regulatory offices, OIRA interest group communications were to be shared with the relevant agency within 10 days. Moreover, OIRA staff were instructed to work more "cooperatively" with the agencies. The executive order restricted OIRA's review to matters involving economic impacts of more than $100 million. This mandate allowed the agencies to handle "routine" mattes without undue OIRA interference. To address the criticism that OIRA staff had tilted in favor of quantifiable cost factors at the expense of more qualitative considerations such as future health and public safety, the Clinton executive order mandated that agencies factor in qualitative measures of costs and benefits that are difficult to quantify.

Studies conducted during President Clinton's two terms in office found less acrimonious relationships between OIRA and the agencies, and between the OIRA and the Congress, than during the two previous administrations. Moreover, the public was afforded a greater opportunity to provide input into rule-making and OIRA

review. In sum, under President Clinton, OIRA adopted a middle-ground approach to regulatory analysis. While eliciting less acrimony than in the past, it also did not abandon its centralized authority over agency rule-making—thereby adhering to Clinton's "New Democratic" third way approach.

Early OIRA actions under President George W. BUSH assumed a generally more conservative and pro-business stance. OIRA's new director, John Graham, a Harvard expert in "risk analysis," was considered to be more antiregulatory than middle-of-the-road. Moreover, in the early months of the Bush administration, the White House decided to revisit, postpone, or eliminate a sizable number of regulations promulgated at the end of President Clinton's second term, many of which had been developed after a number of years of research and analysis. These included regulations dealing with workers' safety, ergonomics, drinking water safety, and national parkland.

Other decisions made within the first year of the Bush administration continued institutional trends set during the Clinton administration. Significantly, the Bush administration decided not to replace EO 12,866 and its directives remain in effect. So, too, continuing the trend toward making OIRA's regulatory review process more accessible to public scrutiny, Director Graham announced in October of 2001 that OIRA would begin designing a process that would make lists of regulations under review and correspondence between agencies and OIRA and between OIRA and outside interest groups available to the public on-line through OMB's website.

Further reading: Duffy, Robert J. "Regulatory Oversight in the Clinton Administration." *Presidential Studies Quarterly* 27 (Winter 1997); Tomkin, Shelley L. *Inside OMB, Politics and Process in the President's Budget Office.* Armonk, N.Y.: M. E. Sharpe, 1998; West, William F., and Andrew W. Barrett. "Administrative Clearance Under Clinton." *Presidential Studies Quarterly* (Spring 1996).
—Shelley Lynne Tomkin

Office of Intergovernmental Affairs

While the EXECUTIVE POWER of the federal government is vested in one element—the presidency—executive power in our federal system as a whole is divided far and wide: among 50 states, 3,043 counties, 19,372 cities, 16,629 townships, 13,726 school districts, 34,683 special districts, and 558 federally recognized Indian tribes. A president who vows to tackle the issues of drugs, crime, poverty, welfare tightening, educational reform, cleaning the environment, or homeland defense will find himself having to deal with many if not most of those 88,061 elements of our administratively highly diverse nation. He must reach out to governors, county executives, mayors, tribal councils, and hundreds of others—because, whatever their party, each of them wields governmental power.

Presidents have long recognized this fact. In March of 1953 President EISENHOWER recommended that the Congress enact a statute creating a Commission on Intergovernmental Relations "to eliminate friction, duplication and waste from Federal-State relations." Under the chairmanship of Meyer Kestenbaum of Chicago, the commission issued a report in June of 1955 which included the recommendation that each president have "a Special Assistant . . . to serve with a small staff as the President's chief aide and adviser on state and local relationships. He should give his exclusive attention to these matters throughout the government. He would be the coordinating center." Eisenhower approved that recommendation, created the position, and in October of 1955 named Kestenbaum as the special assistant. The Office of Intergovernmental Affairs has endured at the White House.

President JOHNSON asked Vice President HUMPHREY (a former mayor) to oversee that office; President NIXON assigned the function to Vice President AGNEW (a former governor). In neither case was this arrangement an effective one, primarily because neither of those two vice presidents was held in high regard by the president. The recent presidents have elevated the director of the office to the level of assistant to the president, or deputy assistant, with from six to eight staffers.

As is obvious, there is a blizzard of relationships intertwining each of the various domestic departments with the nation's state, city, and local governing officials. Most of the nation's domestic assistance programs may be federally financed, but they are in fact administered by state or local governments. For this reason, the governors and mayors and country officials are desperately insistent that they be consulted in the design and operating rules of major federal programs; they want "in" on program decision-making processes, especially those of the White House. It is the function of the Office of Intergovernmental Affairs to try to ensure that this consultation takes place—to do more than merely liaison business, but to bring governors and mayors together with senior policy makers. The office has counterparts in the CABINET departments; the group of them meet periodically with the White House intergovernmental affairs staff to exchange information about what problems are bubbling up in the system and what steps can be taken to resolve them.

For their part, the governors, the mayors, the country officials descend on Washington not only individually; they are very well organized. There is the National Governors Association, the U.S. Conference of Mayors, the National League of Cities, and the National Association of Counties—all with offices and staffs in Washington, all holding national meetings (at which they expect the president to speak), at which they pass resolutions which may support (or oppose) the president's policies. The White House intergovernmental staffers are regular attendees at these sessions and may have a behind-the-scenes hand in the language of these resolutions.

A governor will try to telephone the president or meet personally in the OVAL OFFICE; the Intergovernmental Affairs staff will provide the briefing. In 1989 the George H. W. BUSH staffers organized an Education Summit conclave of the nation's governors with the president. The CLINTON staffers would combine forces with the cabinet departments to set up a "Federal Agency Showcase" at each governors' conference: a series of information booths about the work and programs of each of the departments.

One of the matters preoccupying all the White House Intergovernmental Affairs offices ever since the REAGAN administration has been the drafting of a document—a presidential EXECUTIVE ORDER—which would lay out the basic principles of a proper division of labor between the federal government and the states. Needless to say, the Reagan White House favored maximum delegation of power and functions to the states; its Executive Order 12612 did just that. The Clinton administration had quite a different set of priorities and issued Executive Order 13083, revoking the Reagan order and setting out nine categories in which federal actions would override state authority. The Intergovernmental Affairs staff was caught in the middle of the explosion of opposition from the state and local representatives and spent a year working out a compromise. The new George W. Bush administration is expected to revisit the issue.

There is one characteristic which distinguishes the Intergovernmental Affairs Office from just about every other office in the White House: the requirement that it work across party lines. Governors, mayors, and country officials are Democrats, are Republicans. Irrespective of party alignment, they wield governmental power. Be it handling natural disasters or designing homeland security, attention to partisan attachments is overridden by the necessities of formulating joint action.

Further reading: Elving, Ronald D. "They're Really Listening in the White House Office of Intergovernmental Affairs." *Governing Magazine* (December, 1989); Patterson, Bradley H. *Ring of Power: The White House Staff and its Expanding Role in Government.* New York: Basic Books, 1988; *The White House Staff: Inside the West Wing and Beyond.* Washington, D.C.: Brookings Press, 2000.
—Bradley H. Patterson

Office of Management and Budget (OMB)

Congress passed the BUDGET AND ACCOUNTING ACT OF 1921, creating the BUREAU OF THE BUDGET (BOB). In 1970 the BOB was renamed the Office of Management and Bud-

Office of Policy Development 351

get. OMB advises the president on budget and management policies. OMB is one of the most powerful arms of the presidency due to the fact that virtually all policy and spending proposals must go through OMB. Since the 1970s, OMB has been at the center of presidential policy making.

Office of Personnel Management (OPM)

The Office of Personnel Management was created by the Civil Service Reform Act of 1978 to partially replace the workings of the Civil Service Commission. The Civil Service Commission (CSC) was abolished by the 1978 act, which divided up the responsibilities of the old CSC into two new offices. The Merit Systems Protection Board hears appeals from federal employees over adverse personnel decisions of individual agencies or the OPM itself. The Office of Personnel Management took on the purely personnel functions of the old commission, serving as the body which administers and enforces the civil service laws and regulations.

In order to be hired for a federal CIVIL SERVICE job, one must take a competitive examination. These are administered by the Office of Personnel Management. While the authority to hire, promote, discipline, and terminate employees ultimately lies with heads of individual agencies, overall policy is set by OPM, and individual agencies may be required to get OPM approval for certain personnel policies they may follow.

Reform that ultimately led to the creation of the OPM was a long time coming. The Civil Service Reform Act of 1978 was the first major reform of the CIVIL SERVICE system since the passage of the PENDLETON ACT of 1883, which set up the civil service system and created the Civil Service Commission. This commission was a three-member, bipartisan commission whose job it was to oversee virtually all aspects of federal government personnel policy—including hiring and firing, but also hearing appeals from employees who were harmed by decisions of the commission. These dual, conflicting functions of the CSC were part of the reason for the enactment of the Civil Service Reform Act of 1978.

In addition to this criticism, many experts believed the CSC had become too centralized and controlled the personnel function too tightly. In addition, some believed the personnel function had become too cumbersome and was not responsive enough to both the government and the changing needs of the federal workforce. All of these criticisms culminated in the reform that was passed during the Carter administration.

Further reading: Fesler, James W., and Donald F. Kettl. *The Politics of the Administrative Process.* Chatham, N.J.: Chatham House Publishers, 1996.

—Joseph Wert

Office of Policy Development

A White House structure dedicated to developing DOMESTIC POLICY is a relatively contemporary invention. Prior to the administration of Franklin D. ROOSEVELT, there was little White House control over domestic policy development; this was left to the individual executive agencies and departments. What policy development did go on in the Roosevelt White House was largely accomplished through ad hoc committees and working groups. It was not until the Truman administration that the White House began to exert concerted control over the domestic policy-making process. Even in this administration, however, few staffing structures were institutionalized. While the shift toward White House control of domestic policy development is gradual and marked by fits and starts, many believe the NIXON administration is when the shift was clearly cemented. It was during his administration that the first White House advisory structure for domestic affairs was created: the Urban Affairs Council. In the same act that authorized the OFFICE OF MANAGEMENT AND BUDGET, a Domestic Policy Council was also instituted.

Whatever a president's preferred staffing structure and policy goals, presidential domestic policy-making requires a commitment of White House personnel. The nature of domestic policy-making necessitates coordination across a set of diverse and often conflicting policy arenas. Agencies and departments in the federal government, because they are charged with implementation, have a vested interest in policy development. The challenge of the White House domestic policy staff is to coordinate among these groups in a way that protects the president's policy preferences.

Many factors influenced the development of a White House structure for domestic policy. The advent of such a structure was part of a general trend, quickened in the administration of Franklin D. Roosevelt and fully functioning in the Nixon administration, of increased White House control over the EXECUTIVE BRANCH of government. Some have pointed to a parallel pattern of a decreased use of the president's CABINET and a proliferation of White House personnel.

The extent to which individual presidents prioritize domestic policy making also affects the size and shape of the White House staffing structure. For example, President Dwight D. EISENHOWER's expertise and agenda focused on foreign policy; this was reflected in his White House organization. President Lyndon B. JOHNSON, by contrast, did use White House staff in domestic policy making, though he relied not on a formal policy council but rather on small working groups and task forces.

The relationship between a president and his predecessor also can have an effect on the organization of the White House staff. President Richard M. NIXON had a relatively large domestic policy structure that maintained tight control over policy development. President Gerald FORD, in the wake of the WATERGATE scandal and his subsequent pardoning of Nixon, wanted to eschew Nixon's large formal structure, creating only an Economic Policy Board in response to the growing economic crisis. Difficulties in transitions can occur without a national crisis. When George H. W. BUSH took office after REAGAN's second term, his personnel housecleaning included restructuring the domestic policy staff, significantly downsizing it. This, of course, was also a reflection of his greater focus on foreign policy.

Like Ford, when he took office Bill CLINTON faced significant economic challenges—and indeed had made several campaign promises regarding the economy. These priorities were reflected in his staffing structure as he chose a broad-reaching Office of Policy Development, to which reported the Domestic Council, NATIONAL ECONOMIC COUNCIL, and the Environmental Policy Council. Policy development in the first two areas was housed squarely in the White House. Indeed, both an economic plan and a policy to change health-care policy were high on the president's agenda. As a result, the Domestic Council and the Economic Council staff often competed for scarce resources.

The Clinton administration's vision of domestic policy was one in which the lines separating traditional policy areas (e.g., agriculture, education, labor, etc.) were blurred. As a result, a primary function of the Domestic Policy Council was to coordinate policy makers and to maintain an open channel of communication with the various cabinet secretaries who served on the Domestic Policy Council. Most of the policy development, however, took place in small working groups staffed by White House personnel.

In the White House of George W. BUSH, the Office of Policy Development is comprised of two advisory structures, the Domestic Policy Council and the National Economic Council. As in the previous administrations, the Domestic Policy Council is charged with coordinating policy development across a variety of policy areas (e.g., education, health, welfare, justice, FEDERALISM, transportation, environment, labor, and veterans' affairs). The National Economic Council coordinates economic policy making, advises the president on issues of domestic and international economics, and monitors the implementation of ECONOMIC POLICY.

Further reading: Domestic Policy Council. *The White House, President George W. Bush.* White House Connections: http://www.whitehouse.gov/dpc/ (1/15/2002); National Economic Council. *The White House, President George W. Bush.* White House Connections: http://www.whitehouse.gov/nec/ (1/15/2002); Patterson, Bradley H. *The White House Staff: Inside the West Wing and Beyond.* Washington, D.C.: Brookings, 2000; Walcott, Charles, and Karen M. Hult. *Governing the White House: From Hoover through LBJ.* Lawence: University Press of Kansas, 1995;

Warshaw, Shirley Anne. *The Domestic Presidency: Policy Making in the White House.* Boston: Allyn and Bacon, 1997.
—Rebecca E. Deen

Office of Price Administration (OPA)

Fear of inflation as the United States faced entry into WORLD WAR II sparked the creation of the Office of Price Administration (OPA). In April of 1941 (prior to the bombing of Pearl Harbor) FDR established the OPA. In March of 1942 the OPA imposed price controls, and these efforts increased in April of 1943 when FDR ordered a wage and price freeze. These controls lasted until June of 1946 and were generally seen as effective.

Office of Public Liaison

Since Franklin Delano ROOSEVELT's EXECUTIVE BRANCH became a focus for interest groups, part of the NEW DEAL coalition and programs, subsequent CHIEF EXECUTIVES have continued to accommodate important policy players in the West Wing. Presidents since FDR have devoted a segment of White House staff attention to the accommodation, tracking, and management of certain groups' interest in administration policies and/or programs. Regardless of the issue (civil rights, ARMS CONTROL, SOCIAL SECURITY, and/or tax reform), organized interests automatically include the White House in their tour of duty.

Initially, accommodation was informal. However, as the complexity and intensity of interaction grew with the West Wing, presidents have had to formalize an office to coordinate these vital interest group interactions. While an institutional role for interest group liaison took root, conceptually, under NIXON, it is widely agreed that President FORD instituted a formal structure. A new office, the White House Office of Public Liaison (OPL), was created.

On September 12, 1974, President Ford appointed William J. Baroody, Jr., as assistant to the president for public liaison. According to the announcement, Baroody's duties included work with "farm, labor, veterans, business, civic, academic, ethnic, consumer, youth, senior citizens and professional groups." Such an assemblage of special interests in the executive branch is very helpful to a sitting president—electorally and legislatively. Not only are groups utilized by the White House to provide a connection to a given community (civil rights, business, consumer, environmental), they are also utilized to "lobby" Congress in order to move forward an administration's agenda.

Goals and staffing have fluctuated with each administration. Several obvious factors influence the flavor of an administration's public liaison operation, including the party of the president, whether liberal, conservative, or moderate in politics. Other key factors include the personalities of the chief executives and the ties that they, their aides, and advisers have with such groups prior to reaching the White House.

Interest group interaction at any level of government is an important part of the democratic process and is safeguarded by the U.S. Constitution. However, criticisms of this activity, whether focused on Congress or the White House, have been voiced, particularly as reported abuses and excesses of campaign contributions cloud the goals of such access.

Further reading: Patterson, Bradley H., Jr. *The White House Staff: Inside the West Wing and Beyond.* Washington, D.C.: Brookings Institution Press, 2000; Pika, Joseph. "Opening Doors for Kindred Souls: The White House Office of Public Liaison." In *Interest Group Politics,* 3d ed, edited by Allan J. Cigler and Burdett A. Loomis. Washington, D.C.: CQ Press, 1991; Presidential Documents. *Gerald R. Ford, 1974* 10, no. 37, pp. 1142–1143. Superintendent of Documents, U.S. Government Printing Office.

—Owen Holmes

Office of Science and Technology Policy (OSTP)

A subunit of the EXECUTIVE BRANCH, the Office of Science and Technology Policy is headed by a director who serves as primary science adviser to the president. Established in 1976, the office faced elimination during the REAGAN years, but the scientific community as well as members of Congress intervened to save the office.

Office of the U.S. Trade Representative (USTR)

In 1980, President CARTER established the Office of U.S. Trade Representative. Part of a reorganization plan approved by Congress, the office promotes trade. Successor to the President's Special Representative for Trade Negotiations (STR) created by President KENNEDY in 1963, the new office is headed by the U.S. trade representative, a CABINET-level official with ambassadorial rank.

Office of War Mobilization (OWM)

Created to bring a "more efficient coordination of the mobilization of the nation for war," the OWM was part of the Office for Emergency Management (OEM). The OWM was established in May of 1943 with President Franklin D. ROOSEVELT's Executive Order 9347 and headed by James F. Byrnes (who became so influential he was sometimes called an "assistant president"). Byrnes's rise in power led to congressional efforts to claim some modicum of control over the OWM and in 1944, despite efforts by FDR to block passage, he signed the War Mobilization and Reconversion Act, giving the director of OWM

a two-year term and making the OWM director subject to Senate confirmation.

Old Executive Office Building (OEOB)

The Old Executive Office Building, located directly adjacent to the White House on Pennsylvania Avenue, has served many functions. It was originally built to consolidate the headquarters of the Departments of State, War, and the Navy. In 1999 President Bill CLINTON signed legislation renaming the national landmark in honor of President Dwight D. EISENHOWER. Now called the EISENHOWER EXECUTIVE OFFICE BUILDING (EEOB), it continues to house many White House offices and staff.

First known as the State, War, and Navy Building, it was constructed over a 17-year period and was occupied in January of 1888. President WASHINGTON decided on the location in 1796, satisfying his desire for the executive departments (Treasury, State, War, and the Navy) to be colocated near the White House. Construction of the executive department buildings did not commence right away, since work crews were completing the U.S. Capitol. Over the course of the next 70 years, facilities for the Treasury, State, War, and Navy Departments were constructed, reconstructed, and remodeled in response to war (British invasion of the capital in 1814) and the rapid growth of the federal BUREAUCRACY.

On March 3, 1871, due to what seemed to be a constant and costly effort to rebuild or renovate existing facilities, Congress authorized a half million dollars for the construction of a single building to house State, War, and Navy. Subsequent appropriations were necessary to complete construction. The final cost of the building totaled more than $10 million.

The building stands unique among the city's landmarks and monuments. The French Second Empire style is a sharp contrast to Washington's predominant Georgian and Greek revival styles as embodied by the White House, Treasury, and other government buildings.

The architect, Alfred Mullett, chose French Second Empire as it was his specialty in the style. Mullett was supervising architect of the Treasury with responsibility for oversight and design of post offices, customshouses, mints, and federal courthouses. Nearly all of Mullett's projects were of the French Second Empire style. Few have survived modernization trends of the 20th century.

The building has been the occupational home to many of our country's finest public servants. Future presidents worked there, mostly in military capacities. Theodore ROOSEVELT and Franklin Delano ROOSEVELT served as assistant secretaries of the Navy, 1897–98 and 1913–18, respectively. William Howard TAFT was secretary of War, 1904–08, and Dwight D. Eisenhower was military aide to

General Douglas MacArthur, 1933. The first presidential PRESS CONFERENCE was held in 1950 in the Indian Treaty Room. President Eisenhower held the first televised presidential press conference in 1955 in Room 474.

Further reading: Executive Office of the President, Office of Administration. *The Old Executive Office Building: A Victorian Masterpiece.* Superintendent of Documents, U.S. Government Printing Office, 1984.

—Owen Holmes

Olmstead v. United States, 277 U.S. 438 (1928)

Olmstead v. United States was a 1928 decision by the U.S. Supreme Court that concerned the Fourth Amendment right against unreasonable searches and seizures and the use of wiretapping by federal agents. Roy Olmstead and several other suspected bootleggers were being investigated for violating the National Prohibition Act and bribing Seattle police as part of this criminal conspiracy. Without a search warrant or any other court order, federal agents tapped Olmstead's telephone from public telephone wires outside of his property. The conversations heard by agents were used to prosecute and convict Olmstead. Olmstead appealed to the federal court of appeals for the ninth circuit, but this court upheld his conviction. Olmstead then appealed to the Supreme Court.

In a narrow, controversial 5-4 decision, the Supreme Court ruled against Olmstead. Chief Justice William H. Taft wrote the majority opinion stating that the protection of the Fourth Amendment does not extend "beyond the possible practical meaning of houses, persons, papers, and effects." Olmstead's conversation was an intangible communication, rather a tangible possession, which he chose to conduct and transmit through public property, i.e., telephone wires. Thus, the exclusionary rule established by the Supreme Court in 1914 in the *Weeks* decision does not apply and such evidence is admissible in court. Taft concluded that it is a responsibility of Congress, not the Supreme Court, to decide whether or not to protect the privacy of phone conversations.

Justice Louis Brandeis's dissenting opinion emphasized the need for the Supreme Court to actively and flexibly use its power of judicial review in order to protect personal privacy from unconstitutional government intrusions as science and technology progress and create more threats to privacy though such devices as wiretaps. Brandeis asserted that the original intent of not only the Fourth and Fifth Amendments but also of the Bill of Rights was to protect "the right to be alone." In 1967 the Supreme Court overturned the *Olmstead* decision in *Katz v. United States* and *Berger v. New York.*

Further reading: Fisher, Louis. *American Constitutional Law.* New York: McGraw-Hill, 1990.

—Sean J. Savage

open door policy

Most U.S. presidents have promoted free trade and open access to ports and an "open door" to trade, but the "open door" policy most specifically refers to efforts by President MCKINLEY in 1899 and 1900 to open ports and gain trade access to China.

Oswald, Lee Harvey (1939–1963) *alleged assassin*

Accused assassin of President John F. KENNEDY, Oswald worked at the Texas School Book Depository in Dallas at the time of Kennedy's assassination. He was a disaffected communist sympathizer who had renounced his citizenship and defected to the Soviet Union, where he married a Russian woman before returning to the United States. There is evidence, however, of a double life, for while Oswald belonged to the pro-Castro Fair Play for Cuba Committee, he was also involved with anti-Castro Cuban exiles.

Kennedy visited Texas in November 1963 in an attempt to shore up political support for his 1964 reelection bid. He was in Dallas on November 22, riding in a motorcade that included Texas governor John Connally. The accusation is that Oswald shot at Kennedy with a rifle from the sixth floor of the book depository, hitting Kennedy twice, once fatally in the head. One bullet also wounded Governor Connally. Kennedy died early that afternoon. Oswald later killed a Dallas police officer, and he was apprehended in a theater. Two days later, while being transferred to a different jail, Oswald was shot and killed on national television by Dallas nightclub owner Jack Ruby.

Before his death, Oswald denied his guilt. The circumstances surrounding Kennedy's assassination, especially persistent reports of gunfire from multiple locations and Ruby's ties to organized crime, caused conspiracy theories to persist. President JOHNSON convened the Warren Commission, headed by Chief Justice Earl Warren, which concluded that Oswald acted alone. In 1979 the House Select Committee on Assassinations declared that there was a high probability of a second gunman.

The most immediate consequence of Kennedy's assassination was the elevation to the presidency of Lyndon Johnson. Concern about presidential succession and presidential DISABILITY also led to the passage of the Twenty-fifth Amendment.

Further reading: Clarke, James W. *American Assassins: The Darker Side of Politics,* 2d rev. ed. Princeton, N.J.: Princeton University Press, 1990; Kurtz, Michael L. *Crime of the Century: The Kennedy Assassination from a Historian's Perspective,* 2d ed. Knoxville: University of Tennessee Press, 1993.

—David A. Crockett

The Oval Office during the Kennedy administration *(Kennedy Library)*

Oval Office

The informal name given to the president's office in the West Wing of the WHITE HOUSE (so named because it is oval in shape), the original Oval Office was built during the TAFT presidency in 1909; the current Oval Office was built in 1934 during the presidency of Franklin D. ROOSEVELT. It opens onto the Rose Garden. The ceiling of the office is decorated with a medallion representing the presidential seal. It is sometimes called "the most intimidating room in the world," and "the world's greatest home-court advantage." Visitors often find themselves awed to be in the Oval Office.

oversight, congressional

As CHIEF EXECUTIVE, the president is the head of the EXECUTIVE BRANCH of government, but he shares power with Congress. One of the functions of Congress is to serve as a watchdog over executive branch activities, supervising the business of government. Congress fulfills the task by annual hearings on agency budget requests, when calling CABINET officials and others to testify, and through the GENERAL ACCOUNTING OFFICE audits of agencies.

Most visible are special hearings, called to investigate the executives. WATERGATE and IRAN-CONTRA are two cases where the Congress exercised its oversight function and held special hearings to investigate supposed executive branch wrongdoing.

Presidents see these oversight activities as intrusive, and to a degree, they may be, but overall, they serve a useful and important function in keeping the executive branch accountable.

Further reading: Aberbach, Joel D. *Keeping a Watchful Eye: The Politics of Congressional Oversight.* Washington, D.C.: Brookings Institution, 1990; Dodd, Lawrence C., and Richard L. Schott. *Congress and the Administrative State.* New York: Wiley, 1979.

P

Palmer Raids

After WORLD WAR I, the United States experienced significant political turmoil, which included racial violence, labor strikes, and social unrest. Many of these events mirrored those in Europe. Many political leaders believed that these events were related to the Bolshevik Revolution in Russia in 1917 and the founding of the Communist Party in the United States, which received resources from Moscow. Many of the initial members were recent immigrants from eastern and southern Europe. The party, with its ties to the labor movement and to the immigrant communities, was perceived as being the spearhead of this political turmoil.

President Woodrow WILSON's attorney general, A. Mitchell Palmer, blamed a series of terrorist bombings on the "Bolsheviks." He believed that the "foreign element" was a threat to American values and to American security.

In the summer of 1919 Palmer ordered an investigation into radical groups and individuals. This resulted in the creation of dossiers on all who were perceived to be radical aliens and supporters. In autumn 1919 federal agents began a series of roundups which resulted in some evidence of explosives. On December 21, 1919, the government deported 249 aliens.

In early 1920 Palmer ordered another series of raids. They entered—without warrants—homes, businesses, social clubs, and political meetings in search of radical aliens. This resulted in more than 4,000 individuals being taken in custody, leading to 591 deportations.

The raids were criticized by such leading legal scholars as Felix Frankfurter, Roscoe Pound, and Zacharian Chafee, who denounced these raids as "unconstitutional." Later, as the perceived threat of the radical aliens diminished, more widespread criticisms ensued, damaging the political reputation and career opportunities of Palmer.

The raids, however, served to intimidate many radicals and diminished the effectiveness of the radical movement. Lastly, the Palmer Raids served as a prologue to the anticommunist movement following WORLD WAR II.

Further reading: Coben, Stanley. *A Mitchell Palmer, Politician.* New York: Columbia University Press, 1963; Morray, Robert. *Red Scare: A Study in National Hysteria.* Minneapolis: University of Minnesota Press, 1955; Sorrentino, Frank. *Ideological Warfare: The FBI's Path Toward Power.* Port Washington, N.Y.: Associated Faculty Press, 1985.

—Frank M. Sorrentino

Panama Canal Treaties

In the 1976 presidential campaign the Panama Canal was a major issue in the Republican primaries. Ronald REAGAN challenged Gerald FORD with the claim that his administration was planning to give away our canal. "We paid for it, it's ours, and we should tell Terrijos and company [the Panamanian leaders] that we are going to keep it," Reagan told cheering crowds in his nearly successful bid for the nomination.

Candidate Jimmy CARTER wisely said little about an issue that was dividing his Republican opponents, but shortly after his election he decided to make the renegotiation of canal arrangements a top priority. The justice for doing so was clear. The creation of the state of Panama during Theodore ROOSEVELT's presidency had been accompanied by a 1903 treaty giving the United States permanent control over a zone on either side of the proposed canal that would cut across the center of the new nation. In the 1970s the canal was a neocolonial legacy of America's brief flirtation with IMPERIALISM at the beginning of the 20th century and a vulnerable strategic asset that could easily be attacked by Panamanian nationalists.

The best way to protect the canal was to voluntarily turn it over to the Panamanians in exchange for special privileges regarding its administration. This had been recognized by foreign policy experts since the Johnson presidency, but every attempt to rewrite the canal agreements met with immediate congressional and public opposition.

The popular position on this issue was always the one that Ronald Reagan adopted in the 1976 campaign.

Jimmy Carter understood the political dangers of pursuing a new and fairer relationship with Panama but went ahead with this initiative because it was the right thing to do. The negotiations with Panama were difficult but eventually produced two agreements—one turning the canal over to the Panamanians at the end of the century and another giving the United States special consideration in how the canal would be administered after the transfer of ownership.

Carter's real problems were not in Panama but involved finding two-thirds of the Senate to vote for ratification of treaties that remained unpopular. His ability to win ratification was in some ways a model of executive-legislative relations. The president did everything he could to win Senate support. He personally briefed individual senators and leading citizens from their states. He addressed the nation, massaged Senate egos, traded administration favors, and endorsed some of the amendments to the resolution of ratification that would give senators an opportunity to say that they had revised and improved specific treaty provisions.

One of those amendments, sponsored by Arizona's Senator Dennis DeConcini, explicitly stated that the United States could intervene in Panama when the safety of the canal was threatened. DeConcini's amendment gave the administration the last few votes it needed to win ratification of the first Panama treaty but almost destroyed both treaties by offending Panamanians.

Carter's eventual success in winning 68 Senate votes for the Panama treaties came at a high price. The effort to win ratification distracted him from other pressing issues including domestic energy policies and controversial ARMS CONTROL negotiations with the Soviet Union. The treaties gave the right wing of the REPUBLICAN PARTY an effective issue with which to raise money and recruit candidates. In the 1978 congressional elections, only seven of the 20 senators up for reelection who had voted for ratification were able to secure another term. Still more senators who supported the treaties—and one president—failed to win reelection in 1980.

Further reading: Jorden, William J. *Panama Odyssey.* Austin: University of Texas Press, 1984; Moffett, George D. *The Limits of Victory: The Ratification of the Panama Canal Treaties.* Ithaca, N.Y.: Cornell University Press, 1985.
—Robert Strong

Panama Refining Co. v. Ryan, 293 U.S. 388 (1935)

This 1935 case is important as it was the first time the Supreme Court invalidated a delegation of congressional power to the president. In the early days of the GREAT DEPRESSION, a glut of oil drove prices down. In 1933 Congress authorized the president to stop what was called "hot oil" (smuggled across state lines) from being transported. Through a series of EXECUTIVE ORDERS, President ROOSEVELT attempted to enforce the prohibition. The Panama Roofing Company sought to prevent enforcement. In January 1935 the Supreme Court invalidated the delegation of congressional power to the president.

pardon power

The president has few independent powers that derive from the Constitution and can be exercised unilaterally (without congressional approval). But Article II, Section 2, of the Constitution gives the president almost absolute and unregulatable "Power to grant Reprieves and Pardons for Offenses against the United States, except in cases of Impeachment." The courts have given the president wide latitude in the area of pardons and reprieves (*ex parte Grossman* [1925] and *Klein v. United States* [1872]).

While the pardon power may be constitutionally beyond the control of Congress, on several occasions presidents have suffered political damage in issuing controversial or unpopular pardons. In 1974 Gerald FORD granted Richard NIXON a "full, free, and absolute pardon" for all acts as president. Many argue that the fallout from this pardon cost Ford the 1976 election.

Perhaps the most egregious misuse of the pardon power occurred when President George H. W. BUSH pardoned six participants in the IRAN-CONTRA scandal, including former Defense secretary Caspar Weinberger. These pardons prevented evidence—most notably, Weinberger's diary entries—from being used in court, evidence that might have established perjury, an impeachable offense, by then–VICE PRESIDENT Bush. In effect, Bush was pardoning himself when he pardoned Weinberger.

In the waning days of the Clinton presidency, CLINTON issued a number of controversial pardons to donors and friends. Included in the list was a pardon for the president's brother who, in his youth, was convicted on drug charges.

parliamentary reforms

The U.S. system of a SEPARATION OF POWERS is often compared (usually unfavorably) to the British Parliamentary form of democracy. Reformers who wish to introduce parliamentary reforms into the United States point to several possible changes: a "question time" wherein presidents would be compelled to face Congress to answer direct questions from members; allowing members of Congress to serve in the president's CABINET; or allowing a vote of "no confidence" to be made regarding the president and the calling of new national elections. The chances of such reforms passing (most would require a constitutional amendment) are slim at best.

parties, political See DEMOCRATIC PARTY; REPUBLICAN PARTY.

party conventions

Every summer during presidential election years, the two major parties (and often minor parties as well) gather for their national conventions. The national convention is where the delegates who were selected in the PRIMARIES AND CAUCUSES officially nominate the presidential and vice presidential candidates as well as pass the party's platform.

At one time, political observers considered the party convention to be extremely important and the public closely followed its events. The original party conventions were held in the "smoke-filled rooms" where party leaders quizzed potential candidates and debated which candidate was most acceptable. It was often unclear who the nominee would be before the convention began. Conventions were considered to be "brokered conventions" in which there was not much agreement on issues and candidates. In fact, in 1924 it took the Democrats 103 ballots to nominate John W. Davis.

Today, the party convention is much different. Generally, few disagreements exist between party members (and those that do are usually hidden from the media) and there is little surprise regarding who the party's presidential nominee will be. In fact, not since 1952 has one of the two major parties' presidential candidates required more than one ballot to secure the nomination. This has led many to complain that conventions are purely theatrical events that are designed as pep rallies for the parties and fail to give the public much more than propaganda. It was for this reason that, during the 1996 REPUBLICAN PARTY convention, *Nightline*'s Ted Koppel declared the convention unworthy of further coverage and left.

Koppel is not alone in his view about the newsworthiness of conventions. Both television coverage and the percentage of households watching the conventions have declined substantially over the years. Initially, when television began broadcasting the conventions, the media provided gavel-to-gavel coverage. Because of the unpredictability of the conventions, the three major networks wanted to be sure to capture any disagreements live. The public was consumed with the conventions as well. As the number of households owning televisions grew, the number of people watching the conventions rose substantially as well.

Because of the constant media coverage and large audience, parties quickly realized that the potential existed to persuade many voters. The nominating convention became a springboard for the party's candidate in the fall campaign. Party leaders also realized, however, that because so many people were watching, the event had to be flawless. Viewers could not see a party divided on the issues or potential nominees; the party needed to appear united, whether in fact it was or not. Also, parties could not afford mistakes, such as the one made at the 1972 Democratic convention in which George MCGOVERN gave his acceptance speech at 2:48 A.M. to a paltry television audience. The convention had to be completely scripted. As a result, party conventions lost their spontaneity, thereby losing the interest of the media as well as the public. Instead of gavel-to-gavel coverage, the major networks covered the two major parties' 2000 conventions for a total of 8½ hours (although cable stations such as C-Span continued longer coverage). Not only did the length of television coverage decline, but so did the number of viewers. Surveys conducted by the Annenberg Public Policy Center and the Shorenstein Center for the Press, Politics, and Public Policy indicated that roughly half of the television audience reported that they saw some of the conventions, but most of those viewers only watched a few minutes.

A typical party convention is four days long (Monday through Thursday). While there is not a rigid schedule that parties must follow, generally both the Democrats and the Republicans adhere to a similar format. The first two days of the convention are devoted to party business, such as passing the platform, and high-ranking party officials give speeches. Traditionally, the Keynote Address is given the first night. The goal of the Keynote Address is to unite the party and heal any divisions that might have occurred during a bitter primary battle. However, the Keynote Address is not necessarily the most important speech delivered at the beginning of the convention. In fact, in 2000 the Republicans opted not to have a Keynote Address, while the Democrats' Keynote Address, given by Congressman Harold Ford, Jr., of Tennessee, was not shown in its entirety by most newscasts. Instead, other speeches draw more attention from the public and the press. In 2000 viewers were interested in hearing presidential candidates John McCain's and Bill Bradley's endorsements of their former opponents. Other speeches can be quite controversial, such as Republican Pat Buchanan's speech in 1992 attacking Bill CLINTON and the DEMOCRATIC PARTY. In recent conventions, the candidates' wives have also addressed the delegates.

The third convention night is devoted to the official nomination process of the president and the vice president (although the Republicans used a rolling nomination in 2000 in which a few states' delegates voted each night). In the past, there was some uncertainty about who the vice-presidential candidate would be going into the convention. In 1956, for example, Democratic nominee Adlai STEVENSON let the delegates chose between Estes Kefauver and

John F. KENNEDY. George H. W. BUSH stunned many when he picked Dan QUAYLE as his vice-presidential candidate at the 1988 Republican convention. More recently, however, the president has selected his vice-presidential candidate before the convention.

The fourth night is when the presidential nominee makes his acceptance speech. The acceptance speech is crucial because it is the first time the candidate speaks before such a large audience. This is really the first chance the candidate has to "turn the public on" to his candidacy. For example, during the 2000 acceptance speeches, George H. W. Bush questioned Bill CLINTON's and Al GORE's leadership abilities, while Gore presented himself as his "own man," trying to separate himself somewhat from Clinton. Acceptance speeches can cause a jump in the candidate's popularity, but they can also hurt a candidate as well. Walter MONDALE's promise to raise taxes in 1984 certainly did not help his chances in November.

Because the conventions are so scripted today, many question their purpose. Others argue that conventions are not meaningless but in fact serve the important role of uniting the party. Traditionally, candidates have received a "convention bounce" in their public approval ratings after the convention. In fact, every candidate since George McGovern in 1972 received some sort of post-convention boost. The bounces are often short-lived, such as Bob Dole's in 1996, but in some cases they are longer lasting. In 2000 Al Gore erased a 19-point deficit and remained basically even with George W. BUSH until Election Day. Though the conventions certainly are not the old-fashioned gatherings of the past, supporters of conventions argue that they remain important because of the convention bounce.

Further reading: Polsby, Nelson W., and Aaron Wildavsky. *Presidential Elections: Strategies and Structures of American Politics*, 10th ed. New York: Chatham House, 2000; Wayne, Stephen J. *The Road to the White House 2000*. Boston, Mass.: Beford/St. Martin's, 2001; Witcover, Jules. *No Way to Pick a President*. New York: Farrar, Straus, and Giroux, 1999.

—Matt Streb

Patriot Act See USA PATRIOT ACT.

patronage

By *patronage*, we mean the appointment of supporters or party members to government posts as a reward for services or help in the previous election. Since the time of President Andrew JACKSON, who is credited with introducing a "spoils system" (to the victor go the spoils), patronage has been a common feature of politics. Critics argued that patronage had a corrupting influence in politics, that it brought unqualified people to government posts, and that it was inefficient. Even presidents complained that they often felt overburdened by job seekers. In 1881 a disgruntled job seeker, Charles GUITEAU, assassinated President James A. GARFIELD. This prompted the passage of the Civil Service Act of 1883 (the PENDLETON ACT). This act created a merit system for CIVIL SERVICE and also created the Civil Service Commission. Today presidents appoint approximately 5,000 people to EXECUTIVE BRANCH posts.

Further reading: MacKenzie, G. Calvin. *The Politics of Presidential Appointments*. New York: Free Press, 1981; Patterson, Bradley H., Jr. *The Ring of Power*. New York: Basic Books, 1988; Tolchin, Martin, and Susan Tolchin. *To the Victor: Political Patronage from the Clubhouse to the White House*. New York: Random House, 1971; Van Riper, Paul P. *History of the United States Civil Service*. Evanston, Ill.: Row, Peterson, 1958.

Pendleton Act

The Pendleton Act marked a clear change in direction toward the idea of merit hiring in the CIVIL SERVICE. Its central target was the spoils system, in which government jobs were parceled out on the basis of PATRONAGE. The spoils system developed in the early 19th century and was based on the principle of rotation in office, in which the victors in elections divided the "spoils." This system prevented the establishment of an entrenched BUREAUCRACY and was seen as more democratic, especially by Jacksonian forces. The spoils system explicitly linked jobs to party loyalty and constituted the primary mechanism of the machinery of government. However, frequent turnover in government service led to inefficiency, and party leaders forced appointees to contribute time and money to party affairs. Leaders were constantly harassed by job seekers, and a modernizing world required people to have special skills.

By the 1880s Congress and other political bosses had practical control over the president's APPOINTMENT POWER, hampering his ability to act as the administrative head of government. President Rutherford B. HAYES waged a running battle with Congress over civil service reform. James A. GARFIELD inherited this battle, and his presidency was symbolic of the dueling factions within the REPUBLICAN PARTY. His vice president, Chester ARTHUR, came from the patronage pro-spoils wing of the party. The Pendleton Act was prompted initially by Garfield's assassination. Charles Guiteau was supposedly a demented job seeker who had expected to receive a presidential appointment upon Garfield's election in 1880. When he did not receive one, Guiteau shot Garfield, reportedly saying, "I am a Stalwart; now Arthur is president."

With Garfield's assassination, public opinion turned against the spoils system, presenting government reformers with an ideal opportunity. Despite a background soaked in the spoils system, the new president recognized the need for movement on the issue and supported limited civil service reform. Democratic gains in the 1882 MIDTERM ELECTIONS magnified the danger for Republicans, and Arthur called on Congress to pass the act, named for its author, Democratic senator George Hunt Pendleton of Ohio. Arthur signed the bill into law in 1883.

The Pendleton Act "classified" certain government jobs, establishing competitive merit exams for entrance and promotion. The measure was designed to provide for a better allocation of positions and higher quality personnel. The law also established a permanent bipartisan Civil Service Commission, appointed by the president with the consent of the Senate, to control the exams and investigate enforcement. The president had the power to expand the classified service by executive order. The act sparked fears in some quarters of an aristocracy of officeholders, probably to the advantage of the more highly educated East, but the law had limited application at first. In its initial form the act only applied to employees in Washington, D.C., major customhouses with 50 or more employees, and certain post offices. Most federal employees were not covered by the act.

Despite its limited application, the law marked a clear change in direction toward the idea of merit hiring and a ban on solicitations of campaign funds from federal employees. Over the next few years the number of classified employees rose as defeated presidents sought to protect their supporters in office by expanding the classified list. In 1883 there were less than 15,000 classified jobs. By 1897 there were 86,000, nearly half of all federal employees. Theodore ROOSEVELT made great use of EXECUTIVE ORDERS to further expand the classified service.

Further reading: Garraty, John A. *The New Commonwealth, 1877–1890.* New York: Harper & Row, 1968; Milkis, Sidney M., and Michael Nelson. *The American Presidency: Origins and Development, 1776–1998,* 3d ed. Washington, D.C.: CQ Press, 1999; Morgan, H. Wayne. *From Hayes to McKinley: National Party Politics, 1877–1896.* Syracuse, N.Y.: Syracuse University Press, 1969.

—David A. Crockett

Pentagon, the

Constructed between 1941 and 1943, the five-sided Pentagon building consists of five concentric pentagons around a center courtyard. Under the wartime vision of Franklin D. ROOSEVELT, it was at the time the U.S. DEPARTMENT OF WAR. During construction, 13,000 workers were employed, 6,000,000 cubic feet of earth was removed, and nearly 42,000 concrete pilings were driven. The Pentagon covers an area of 35 acres.

The Pentagon is often used synonymously for the DEPARTMENT OF DEFENSE, as it houses the headquarters of the U.S. Department of Defense and the departments of Army, Navy, and Air Force. It currently employs approximately 23,000 individuals.

In the SEPTEMBER 11, 2001, ATTACKS one of the four hijacked planes was flown into the western portion of the building, killing 125 and causing approximately $700 million in damage to the structure.

Further reading: Locher, James R., and Sam Nunn. *Victory on the Potomac: The Goldwater-Nichols Act Unifies the Pentagon.* College Station: Texas A&M University Press, 2002; U.S. Government. *Pentagon—The Amazing Story of America's Defense Department Headquarters Building History, Renovation, and Repair after 9/11.* Progressive Management, 2002.

—Paul Rexton Kan

Perkins, Frances (1880–1965) *secretary of labor*

The first woman in American history to serve in a president's CABINET, Frances Perkins was secretary of Labor in the Franklin ROOSEVELT administration. Although her nomination was controversial initially, she ultimately served longer than any member of Roosevelt's cabinet, from 1933 until 1945, when she resigned two months after President Harry TRUMAN took office. Overall, she helped develop and win passage of several key components of what came to be known as President Roosevelt's NEW DEAL.

As secretary of Labor, one of her best-known policy preferences was for winning governmental legal protection of workers instead of relying on their collective efforts made through unionization. Hence, she never held strong ties to organized labor, whose unions often supported Roosevelt's election efforts and key policy initiatives. Nonetheless, she played a leading role in developing and pressing for passage of numerous major labor reforms enacted during the Roosevelt administration. In 1934 the president selected her to lead his committee to develop plans for a comprehensive retirement system—SOCIAL SECURITY—which became law the following year. She later played a key role in planning and winning passage of the FAIR LABOR STANDARDS ACT of 1938. In addition, as a cabinet member she was a leading supporter of establishing federal public works projects, adopting minimum wage legislation, limiting the employment of children under age 16, creating the CIVILIAN CONSERVATION CORPS, compensating unemployed workers, and passing maximum hour legislation. Her administrative legacy included reinvigorating and rebuilding the DEPARTMENT OF LABOR and strengthening its Bureau of Labor Statistics.

Prior to serving in the Roosevelt administration, she was a teacher and social worker and activist. She later held several administrative positions, including executive secretary of the New York City Consumers' League, executive secretary of the New York Committee on Safety, and executive director of the New York Council of Organization for War Service. Subsequent state positions she held included membership on the governing board of the New York Department of Labor and administrative head of the New York Department of Labor.

After leaving the cabinet she was a member of the U.S. Civil Service Commission from 1946 to 1953. She later lectured on problems of labor and industry and taught at Cornell University until her death in 1965.

Further reading: Martin, George. *Madam Secretary: Frances Perkins.* Boston: Houghton Mifflin, 1976; Perkins, Frances. *The Roosevelt I Knew.* New York: Viking Press, 1946.

—Robert E. Dewhirst

pets, presidential

Most presidents, like most citizens, have had a great affection for animals, and many cared deeply for their pets. President JEFFERSON taught his pet mockingbird Dick to sing along as he played the violin. President Andrew JACKSON's pet parrot had to be removed from Jackson's memorial service at his home, the Hermitage, because the bird was shouting obscenities, undoubtedly learned from the former president.

President James GARFIELD had a pet dog named Veto. President William MCKINLEY had a pet parrot named Washington Post. And Teddy Roosevelt had a one-legged chicken for a pet. CALVIN COOLIDGE kept a pet raccoon named Rebecca.

In modern times presidential pets have at times attracted a great deal of media attention. Much was made of Franklin D. ROOSEVELT's Scottish terrier, Fala, riding on an American battleship. Of course FDR used the criticism to turn the tables on his critics, mocking them for their obsession with such trivialities in wartime.

During the presidency of George H. W. BUSH, the presidential dog, Millie, "wrote" a best-selling book. This got Millie on the cover of *Life* magazine. And during the Clinton presidency Socks, the family cat, became a minor celebrity, with the likeness of the cat available on T-shirts from Washington, D.C., kiosks.

Linking the president to his pets humanizes the president and makes him more accessible to the general public. Love of a pet is something that presidents share with the average citizen, and this connects the president to the public they are to lead.

Philadelphia Plan

The first federal affirmative action program, the seeds of the Philadelphia Plan can be traced to the last years of the Lyndon JOHNSON presidency when Executive Order 11248 (1965) required government contractors to hire minorities and women in the Philadelphia area. The GENERAL ACCOUNTING OFFICE (GAO) argued that the plan was "unauthorized," and the plan was withdrawn.

Richard NIXON reintroduced the plan in 1969 against stiff opposition from labor and Comptroller General Elmer Staats. But Nixon persisted, and the Third U.S. Circuit Court of Appeals agreed with the president's position in *Contractors Ass'n of Eastern Pa. v. Secretary of Labor* (1971).

Pierce, Franklin (1804–1869) *fourteenth U.S. president*

As the conflict over slavery escalated, the new president, the handsome 5'10" Franklin Pierce, declared in his inaugural address, "I believe that involuntary servitude, as it exists in different States of this Confederacy, is recognized by the Constitution. I believe that it stands like any other admitted right, and that the States where it exists are entitled to efficient remedies to enforce the constitutional provisions." Such sentiments, while comforting to the Southern states, did little to calm the approaching storm.

Pierce was a native of New Hampshire and a lawyer by training. He became speaker of the New Hampshire Assembly in 1830 and then served in the U.S. Congress and then the Senate from 1833 to 1842. After serving as a brigadier general in the MEXICAN WAR, Pierce returned to his law practice in New Hampshire. Pierce, who had penetrating dark eyes and a drinking habit that led adversaries to call him "a hero of many a well-fought bottle," was a believer in limited government and was perceived as a "Doughface," a Northerner who supported the South. It was his support of the South that helped to make Pierce the compromise choice as the Democratic nominee when all the other candidates at the 1852 Democratic National Convention were unable to win a clear majority. In 1853 Pierce won over his Whig opponent (and former commander) Winfield Scott and became the 14th president of the United States.

Pierce assumed office during a time of great turmoil—both in his personal life and in the country. When Franklin Pierce's longtime friend Nathaniel Hawthorne, author of *The Scarlet Letter,* heard of Pierce's election, he wrote to his friend: "Frank, I pity you—indeed I do, from the bottom of my heart." Pierce was probably the last president who might have been able to prevent the CIVIL WAR. His inability to resolve what may have been an unsolvable situation contributed to the coming Civil War. During his presidency, a new political alignment was emerging. The Whigs

President Franklin Pierce *(Library of Congress)*

were collapsing and a new Republican faction was forming. This instability, mixed with deep sectional divisions, made Pierce's efforts at party control of the legislative difficult. In addition to the political strife, Pierce suffered a personal tragedy when, two months before his inauguration, Pierce and his wife Jane lost their only remaining child (two others had already died) in a terrible train accident.

Of course, slavery remained the most important and most divisive issue of the era. The controversial Kansas-Nebraska Act of 1854 repealed the Missouri Compromise of 1820 and allowed settlers in Kansas and Nebraska to decide the question of slavery for themselves. Senator Stephen DOUGLAS played the lead role in passage of the Kansas-Nebraska Act, as it was an era when senators were more "event-making" than presidents. In general, the North opposed the bill, but Pierce supported it, hoping to diffuse the tension over the slavery controversy. It was too little, too late, as slavery polarized the nation and took it to the brink of Civil War. The Pierce administration was not a total failure. In 1853 the United States acquired land, now south-ern Arizona and New Mexico, from Mexico for $10 million in the GADSDEN PURCHASE. This purchase made possible a direct rail link across Texas and the newly acquired territories all the way to California. Pierce also attempted, but failed, to acquire Cuba for the United States. Following his mishandling of the Bleeding Kansas turmoil, the DEMOCRATIC PARTY refused to consider him for renomination.

Pierce was a weak president in a time that cried out for leadership. Theodore ROOSEVELT called Pierce "a small politician, of low capacity and mean surroundings, proud to act as the servile tool of men worse than himself but also stronger and abler." Harry TRUMAN referred to Pierce as "another one that was a complete fizzle. Pierce didn't know what was going on, and even if he had, he wouldn't of known what to do about it." And Herbert Agar wrote that of "all presidents . . . none was more insignificant than Mr. Pierce." Historians generally rate Pierce in the below average or failure category of presidents. He was unable to stem the tide of secession and had neither the imagination nor the skill to impose a solution on the fractious politics of the pre–Civil War nation. Pierce died, all but forgotten, in Concord, New Hampshire, on October 8, 1869.

Further reading: Gara, Larry. *The Presidency of Franklin Pierce.* Lawrence: University Press of Kansas, 1991; Hoyt, Edwin P. *Franklin Pierce: The Fourteenth President of the United States.* New York: Harper & Row, 1972.

pocket veto

The pocket veto power allows the president to prevent enactment of a bill, thereby killing the bill, but without returning the bill to Congress. Unlike the regular or return veto, use of the pocket veto by presidents is carefully circumscribed by the Constitution. According to Article I, Section 7, of the Constitution: "If any Bill shall not be returned by the President within ten Days (Sundays excepted) after it shall have been presented to him, the Same shall be a Law, in like manner as if he had signed it, unless Congress by their Adjournment prevent its Return, in which case it shall not be a Law." A regular or return veto is exercised when the president vetoes a bill by returning it to the house of origin. The pocket veto power may only be used when two circumstances apply: congressional adjournment and prevention of bill return by the president to Congress. Since the pocket veto is not returned to Congress, it cannot be subject to an override vote, making the power an absolute veto.

While the Constitution's founders were adamantly opposed to an absolute veto for the president, the pocket veto was inserted to guard against the possibility that Congress could pass a bill but then quickly adjourn as a way of avoiding a veto before the president had a chance to return the bill. Congress's only alternatives to dealing with a pocket veto are to either stay in session for at least 10 days after the passage of a bill that may be subject to veto, so that the bill can be returned to Congress, or start from scratch and repass the bill when Congress reconvenes.

Ambiguities have persisted regarding pocket veto use. In recent decades, many have argued that the pocket veto should only be used at the end of a two-year Congress, since both CONGRESS AND THE PRESIDENT now designate agents to receive vetoed bills and other messages during adjournments and other times when governing leaders are not in the nation's capital. This position has received support in several court cases. In recent years, presidents including George H. W. BUSH and Bill CLINTON have exercised controversial "protective returns," whereby they have claimed to simultaneously exercise both a return veto and a pocket veto, on the same bill, in an apparent effort to expand the pocket veto power.

Further reading: Spitzer, Robert J. *The Presidential Veto: Touchstone of the American Presidency.* Albany: State University of New York Press, 1988; "The 'Protective Return' Pocket Veto." *Presidential Studies Quarterly* (December 2001); U.S. House Judiciary Committee. Subcommittee on the Legislative Process. *Hearings on HR 849, A Bill to Clarify the Law Surrounding the President's Use of the Pocket Veto.* July 26, 1990.

— Robert J. Spitzer

political action committees (PACs)

Political Action Committees (PACs) are the political fundraising arms for many interest groups, labor unions, corporations, and politicians themselves, raising millions of dollars and contributing them to individual candidates and political parties. PACs originally were created by organized labor in 1943 to avoid federal campaign law that prevented them from directly participating in federal elections. Business-related PACs followed suit, providing corporations with more flexibility in being involved in political endeavors. Both labor and business PACs raise funds from individual union members, employees, stockholders, and other groups and associations; by doing so, and because such PACs are distinct entities from their respective unions or corporations, PAC contributions to federal campaigns are not deemed illegal (as they would otherwise if they came directly from their respective organizations' treasuries). Although other organizations, such as ideological groups or trade associations, are not necessarily barred from contributing to federal candidates, they too have made extensive use of PACs as separate entities from their primary group. Similarly, PACs affiliated with politicians, known as leadership PACs, allow elected officials and candidates to raise and contribute funds to party-building efforts through their PACs without sacrificing their own electoral war chests.

The CAMPAIGN FINANCE reforms of the 1970s saw the PAC go from a murky legal status to a legitimate means for getting funds to federal candidates. According to the Center for Responsive Politics, in 1974 PAC contributions totaled around $15 million and by 1997–98 their contributions totaled around $220 million. In addition, the number of PACs has grown in the wake of these reforms. In 1974 there were 608 total PACs registered with the FEDERAL ELECTION COMMISSION; by the 1998 election cycle there were 3,798. The overall number is impressive, but even more interesting is that a large part of this growth has occurred because of a great increase in the use of PACs by corporations rather than by the traditional labor union sector. PAC money tends to follow whichever party is in the majority in Congress, although PACs provide a bulk of their contributions to incumbents regardless of their party. This trend became even more evident with the Republican takeover of both Houses of Congress in 1994.

Although PACs were once seen as the scourge of the campaign finance system, some reformers now view them as a somewhat tolerable part of the system because PACs are subject to federal reporting laws and contribution limits. PACs are limited to contributing to any individual candidate $5,000 per election cycle. Moreover, with the advent of the public financing system for presidential elections, a candidate's impetus for raising money from PACs is limited. For example, in the 2000 presidential primary season, less than 1 percent of the close to $343 million raised by all presidential candidates came from PACs.

Nevertheless, many critics of PACs feel that they undermine ACCOUNTABILITY in the system, drive the cost of campaigns up, open up avenues for special interests to influence politics, and help corporations and labor unions to participate in a system that legally they have been banned from helping directly. In addition, certain PAC activities are not regulated, thus providing avenues for these organizations to circumvent legally the limitations they face. For example, PACs have increasingly made use of noncoordinated issue ads. Such ads have become a source of controversy because of their close nature to expressly advocating the election or defeat of a candidate or party. Further, PACs have worked hard to court the political parties by assisting them in cultivating soft money (unregulated, undisclosed funds) contributions from their ranks, thus opening yet another loophole in the already shaky campaign finance system.

Further reading: The Center for Responsive Politics: http://www.opensecrets.com; Sabato, Larry. *PAC Power: Inside the World of Political Action Committees.* New York: Norton, 1984.

—Victoria Farrar-Myers

Polk, James K. (1795–1849) *eleventh U.S. president*

President from 1845 to 1849, during which occurred a war with Mexico (which he may have provoked), Polk expanded the nation's borders and extended the country across the continent to the West Coast. Born on November 2, 1795, in Near Pineville, Mecklenburg County, North Carolina, Polk graduated from the University of North Carolina at Chapel Hill in 1818.

After the Whig difficulties with Whig president John TYLER, the Democrats were able to elect the first DARK HORSE in history. James Polk was not considered a candidate when the Democratic convention began; in fact, his name did not even appear on the first seven ballots. After a stalemate between Martin VAN BUREN and Lewis CASS, the convention turned to a compromise candidate, the 5'8", white-haired James Polk.

Referred to as "Young Hickory" because he was a protégé of Andrew JACKSON, Polk was a strong, assertive president who expanded the office and used war to expand America. While he accomplished much, he had his critics. John Quincy ADAMS said of Polk:

> He has no wit, no literature, no point of argument, no gracefulness of delivery, no elegance of language, no philosophy, no pathos, no felicitous impromptus; nothing that can constitute an orator, but confidence, fluency, and labor.

In his inaugural address, Polk enunciated an expansive view of the presidency:

> Although . . . the Chief Magistrate must almost of necessity be chosen by a party and stand pledged to his principles and measures, yet in his official action he should not be the President of a part only, but of the whole people of the United States. While he . . . faithfully carries out into the executive department of the Government the principles and policy of those who have chosen him, he should not be unmindful that our fellow-citizens who have differed with him in opinion are entitled to the full and free exercise of their opinions and judgments, and that rights of all are entitled to respect and regard.

Historian Page Smith called Polk "a petty, conniving, irascible, small-spirited man," and historian Bernard De Voto said that "Polk's mind was rigid, narrow, obstinate, far from first-rate."

Like his mentor Andrew Jackson, Polk saw the presidency as an office of force and leadership. In his first two years in office, his fellow Democrats controlled both houses of Congress, and Polk used this opportunity to chart a bold course in DOMESTIC POLICY, referred to as the "New Democracy." With Polk in the lead, Congress passed tariff

President James K. Polk *(Library of Congress)*

reductions and established an independent treasury system, but it was in FOREIGN AFFAIRS that Polk really left his mark.

It was a time of MANIFEST DESTINY, a phrase coined by John L. O'Sullivan, editor of the *Democratic Review*. It reflected the spirit of expansionism, territorial and otherwise. The movement westward was in full swing, and the age recognized few limits. Was manifest destiny merely a rationale for aggressive acquisition, belligerent and militaristic, or was it the realization of a providentially blessed grand design? Whatever it was, Polk exploited the nationalistic mood and led the nation to significant territorial expansion.

Polk's expansionist agenda advocated annexation of Texas and expansion of the Oregon border. Getting the Texas territory required some sleight of hand. After being rejected in an effort to purchase the Texas territory from Mexico, Polk ordered General Zachary TAYLOR to lead an expedition into Texas. In April 1846, U.S. and Mexican troops clashed, setting off a war in which the United States acquired Texas, New Mexico, and California. By brute force, Polk acquired a tremendously valuable chunk of land. Next to JEFFERSON's purchase of the Louisiana Territory, this was the most important acquisition of land in U.S. history. Abraham LINCOLN, a congressman at the time, spoke of Polk and the MEXICAN WAR, calling the president "a bewildered, confounded, and miserably perplexed man."

Acquisition of new territory raised thorny issues of sectional balance and slavery. A storm was brewing. From this point until the time of CIVIL WAR, slavery and sectional rivalries would dominate American politics.

Polk was a powerful, assertive president who expanded the Jacksonian model of presidential power. Under his leadership, the president began openly to coordinate the development of the federal budget. He chose to serve only one term, but it was a time of great change and expansion.

Further reading: Bergeron, Paul H. *The Presidency of James K. Polk.* Lawrence: University Press of Kansas, 1987; McCormac, Eugene I. *James K. Polk, A Political Biography.* Berkeley: University of California Press, 1922; McCoy, Charles A. *Polk and the Presidency.* Austin: University of Texas Press, 1960; Sellars, Charles G., Jr. *James K. Polk, Continentalist: 1843–1846.* Princeton, N.J.: Princeton University Press, 1966.

polls See POPULARITY AND THE PRESIDENCY.

popularity and the presidency

Public approval of presidents is crucial to the legitimacy of the presidencies in the modern era. However, the Founders originally created a system to shield presidents from popular opinion. In theory, the use of the ELECTORAL COLLEGE as a method of electing presidents would keep the mass public from dictating the actions of the CHIEF EXECUTIVE. The changes that states made to choose electors by the popular vote by the mid 1800s reflected the reality that presidents need the consent of the governed to govern effectively. Lincoln's famous statement that "[p]ublic sentiment is everything. With public sentiment nothing can fail, without it nothing can succeed" highlights the necessity of presidents to gain public support for their leadership.

Theodore ROOSEVELT recognized the importance of public opinion when he courted extensive media coverage of his presidency at the beginning of the century. Roosevelt held PRESS CONFERENCEs, invited reporters to follow him on vacation, and sought to control the headlines for the major newspapers reporting out of Washington. Franklin ROOSEVELT depended upon his popularity with the people to fortify his leadership during the GREAT DEPRESSION and WORLD WAR II.

Franklin Roosevelt was the first president to make extensive use of radio as a form of mass communication. His FIRESIDE CHATS allowed Roosevelt to talk directly to American people without the intervention of the newspaper media.

Presidential popularity entered a new era in the 1950s with two major developments. First was the introduction of reliable public opinion polling by the use of the telephone. Seeking to avoid the polling disasters of 1936 (when *Literary Digest* predicted a victory for Alf Landon in the presidential race) and the "Dewey Defeats Truman" headline wrongly described the 1948 presidential race, the Gallup and the Roper organizations began producing accurate polling results in the 1950s. As the science of survey research improved, both the media and political advisers began to pay tremendous attention to polling results. Since the 1950s, the Gallup organization has been consistently asking the question of a national sample of adults, "Do you approve or disapprove of the job ———— is doing as President?". This approval question has become the measure of presidential popularity.

The second major development was the widespread accessibility and use of television as a way to market political candidates and parties. Political operatives realized the power of television advertising to reach voters. Television news conferences, interviews, debates, and commercials would be employed by all major political candidates and officeholders to get their messages out to voters. Since the 1950s, the view and image that voters have of presidents are shaped by their presence on television.

Commentators and scholars have examined the importance of presidential popularity. Some have argued that presidents and their advisers are "concerned primarily with maintaining public support" as the major goal of presidential administrations. Kernell has documented the various ways that presidents try to maintain public support. He highlights the importance of public relations efforts by presidential administrations to maintain their public standing. Other commentators believe that presidential popularity has its limits as being an effective tool for governing. Edwards provided data to show that popular presidents may have little effect on the legislative process in Congress.

Yet modern presidential administrations focus heavily on keeping presidents in good public standing. The presidency of Bill CLINTON was a constant effort to maintain public popularity. With the IMPEACHMENT OF BILL CLINTON in 1999 by the House of Representatives, public approval of his presidency not only remained high but actually increased. Many observers believe that this public approval ensured that the U.S. Senate would not remove Clinton from office.

At the beginning of the 21st century, presidential popularity has become an important measure of the success or failure of modern presidents.

Further reading: Brace, Paul, and Hinckley, Barbara. *Follow the Leader: Opinion Polls and the Modern Presidents.* New York: Basic Books, 1992; Edwards, George.

Presidential Influence in Congress. San Francisco, Calif.: W. H. Freeman, 1980; *Gallup Poll Monthly.* Princeton, N.J.: Gallup Organization, 2000; Genovese, Michael. *The Presidential Dilemma: Leadership in the American System.* New York: Harper Collins, 1995; Kernell, Samuel. *Going Public: New Strategies of Presidential Leadership.* Washington, D.C.: CQ Press, 1986.

—Matthew Corrigan

postmodern presidency

This is a term used by political scientist Richard Rose, as well as Bruce Miroff in his essay "Courting the Public: Bill Clinton's Postmodern Education," in *The Postmodern Presidency: Bill Clinton's Legacy in U.S. Politics.* Miroff argues that Bill CLINTON's popularity resulted from his being "a postmodern character attuned to a postmodern moment in American political history." Miroff defines postmodern character as "a political actor who lacks a stable identity associated with ideological and partisan values and who is, thereby, free to move nimbly from one position to another as political fashion dictates." The postmodern moment of the 1990s "is an era where the organizing themes of modern American politics—the heroic presidency, the COLD WAR, the conflict between Democratic liberalism and Republican conservatism—are superseded by fleeting images and issues that do not produce any consistent or coherent political understanding."

Miroff finds the roots of Clinton's postmodern style in his personal history. His shift from a left-liberal MCGOVERN organizer in 1972 to a founder of the moderate DEMOCRATIC LEADERSHIP COUNCIL in the 1980s revealed an ideological adaptability well suited to postmodern politics. During this transformation, Clinton demonstrated an increasing affinity for business values and discourses, applying the concepts of "profitability" and "bottom line" to governmental policy. Given the shifting electoral "market" involving a public no longer strongly grounded in ideological and partisan values, dogmatic adherence to core values is risky and prevent necessary adaptation, as Clinton's Republican opponents in Congress eventually discovered.

Clinton's postmodern methods involved constant polling and spinning current events to maximum political advantage. The increasingly postmodern tilt of the national media, "emphasizing discontinuity and irony over consistency and conviction" boosted the effectiveness of such tactics. "The new political culture, like the new popular culture, is skeptical of certainties and fixities and welcoming of novelties so long as they provide the audience with the satisfactions it seeks at the moment." Clinton mastered those public needs sufficiently to overcome the scandals and impeachment that resulted from questionable private and public activities.

Clinton's postmodern legacy, to Miroff, involves a limited policy record but great creativity in the style of governance he employed. His impressive survival skills, involving a strongly tactical approach to governing and a flexible and shifting agenda, may well prove a useful model for future presidents. In that sense, though his policy record is more modest than Ronald REAGAN's, Clinton's ultimate conduct of the presidency may have greater import for his successors in office. Public exhaustion with scandal, though, prompted a temporary departure from irony in the victory of George W. BUSH in the 2000 election.

In his concluding essay in *The Postmodern President,* Steven Schier notes that Clinton's governing style proved indispensable, given the dispersed power and harsh partisanship dominating Washington political institutions during the 1990s. Despite the seeming vacation from irony resulting from the election of George W. Bush, postmodern governing tactics may well become the lasting legacy of the Clinton presidency. Clinton's variable identity helped him greatly because of the characteristics of the Washington political establishment in the 1990s, traits likely to persist indefinitely. That establishment has "no clear partisan or ideological profile but instead a muddle of conflicting power centers with a cumulative bias toward stasis." Since "no partisan nor programmatic governing coalition consistently prevails" in this establishment, presidents will continue to need great "political and personal flexibility."

The postmodern aspects of Clinton's presidency are ultimately evidence of a major change in the institutional evolution of the presidency, defined as the "preemptive presidency." With the "institutional thickening" of relationships between Congress, interest groups, and the BUREAUCRACY in recent decades, presidents must act disruptively to create new political arrangements. The presidential task is to "construct some new political arrangements that can stand the test of legitimacy with other institutions of government as well as the nation at large." Clinton's postmodern style is a flexible set of tactics aimed at creating new political arrangements beneficial to the president. Instead of creating new institutional arrangements, though, the tactics became raw survival skills in Clinton's second term. The postmodern celebration of irony and appearances helped him to survive.

That era may already be over. Miroff concludes that "perhaps only a dramatic economic or social issue that galvanizes the public and redraws the map of partisan cleavages will move Americans beyond postmodern detachment and irony."

Further reading: Rose, Richard. *The Postmodern President.* Chatham, N.J.: Chatham House Publishers, 1991.

—Steve Schier

Potsdam Conference

The last allied summit conference of WORLD WAR II, the Potsdam Conference, held from July 17 to August 2, 1945, in Cecilienhof Palace in Potsdam, a suburb of Berlin, Germany, led to several significant decisions regarding the shape of the postwar world, including the occupations of Germany, the ATOMIC BOMB, the timing of Russia's entry in the war with Japan, and the borders of central and Eastern Europe. This was President TRUMAN's first meeting with British Prime Minister Churchill and his only meeting with Joseph Stalin of the Soviet Union.

POTUS (President of the United States)

"POTUS" is the internal WHITE HOUSE acronym for "President of the United States." It is typically used as a label on one key of the telephone receiving set of those very few White House staff officers whom the president is likely to call directly. When it lights up, the staffer answers with especial alacrity. "VPOTUS" is another such acronym—meaning, of course, the VICE PRESIDENT. The SECRET SERVICE, in its own communications systems, uses not so much these acronyms but coded nicknames for the president, the vice president, and every senior officer who usually accompanies the president on trips.

—Bradley H. Patterson

Powell, Colin (1937–) *secretary of state*

Colin Powell was born on April 5, 1937, to Jamaican immigrant parents in Harlem, New York. He found his calling as a cadet in the Pershing Rifles, the Reserve Officer Training Corps of City College of New York. As a young officer of the army, he served as a military adviser in Vietnam in 1962. In 1971 the army sent Powell to George Washington University, where he earned a master's in business administration. In the next year his career took a decisive turn when he was admitted to the prestigious White House Fellows program.

From 1972 until his retirement from the army, Powell distinguished himself in a succession of Washington, D.C., postings, while taking care to serve the tours of duty as a field commander essential to promotion to the highest ranks. In 1979 Powell became the youngest brigadier (one-star) general in the army and served as the senior military assistant to the secretary of Energy. Ten years later, Powell became the youngest, and the first African-American, chairman of the JOINT CHIEFS OF STAFF (CJCS), a four-star position. In the years in between, he served, among other places, in both the PENTAGON and the White House.

As chief military assistant to Caspar Weinberger, secretary of Defense during President Ronald REAGAN's first term in office, Powell helped draft a list of restrictive criteria of when a president might legitimately use military force. This statement, which became known as the Weinberger Doctrine, sought to codify the professional military's

understanding of the lessons of the VIETNAM WAR. As NATIONAL SECURITY ADVISER (NSA) to President REAGAN after the IRAN-CONTRA scandal, Powell reorganized the NATIONAL SECURITY COUNCIL according to the recommendations of the Tower Commission.

As the chairman of the Joint Chiefs from September 1989 to October 1993, Powell put to use this accumulated experience to become the most powerful CJCS in history. Contrary to stereotype, the senior military leadership in the United States is typically more reluctant to use force than are senior civilian politicians. In the GULF WAR and in the U.S. response to crisis in the Balkans, Chairman Powell restricted and slowed the introduction of U.S. troops. Conforming to stereotype, the professional military is more reluctant than are civilian leaders to change internal military policies. Powell spoke for the military when he successfully lobbied behind the scenes to prevent President Bill CLINTON from overturning outright the ban on open homosexuality in the armed forces.

While serving under both Presidents George Herbert Walker BUSH and Bill Clinton, Powell was so influential on behalf of the profession he served, in fact, that some critics accused him of creating a crisis in civil-military relations, which is founded in the United States on the principle of strict civilian control.

Upon retirement from military service, General Powell kept alive speculation about a possible run for the presidency while authoring a best-selling autobiography and making numerous public appearances. After the election of 2000, Powell accepted George W. BUSH's offer to be secretary of State in the new administration.

Further reading: Kohn, Richard H. "Out of Control: The Crisis in Civil-Military Relations." *The National Interest* (Spring 1994); Powell, Colin L., with Joseph E. Persico. *My American Journey.* New York: Random House, 1995.

—Thomas Langston

prerogative power

In addition to the specific powers allocated to the president in Article II of the Constitution and any other powers that Congress may, from time to time, delegate by law to the CHIEF EXECUTIVE, presidents have also claimed that, during emergencies, they must have the discretion to act in the best interests of the nation, regardless of whether they can point to explicit authority in the Constitution or delegations from Congress. The theory underlying such a claim is one of "prerogative," a concept that owes its origins to the writings of the 17th-century British political philosopher John Locke and to the practices of the Stuart kings of that period. The essence of prerogative power is that it provides an executive with absolute, unlimited, and exclusive authority—

power that is nowhere expressly stated but that derives from the nature of government, and from *any* government's inherent right of self-preservation. Such a right of self-preservation emerges during times of crisis, when presidents often need to act quickly and without clear guidance from Congress. It is at these times that presidents look to the notion of prerogative as a basis for taking actions that may be "extraconstitutional," or outside of the Constitution.

Locke wrote of prerogative in his *Second Treatise on Civil Government* (1690). He defined it as "this Power to act according to discretion, for the public good, without the prescription of the Law, and sometimes even against it. . . ." Thus, he acknowledged that rulers might need to act when the law was silent, and might even need to act contrary to law, if the danger to the nation was sufficiently grave.

Two corollaries, however, were necessary when prerogative was exercised, and these were consistent with the social contract between the people and the government that was so central to Locke's work: (1) the executive must report his actions immediately to the people, and (2) the people would hold the president accountable for these acts: If his actions met with public approval, he would be vindicated, but if they were disapproved, he was ultimately responsible for them and was at the mercy of the people's judgment. For a president in the American system, this translated into: A president may have discretion to act outside of or even contrary to existing law during times of emergency, but he is obligated to report his actions at once to Congress and the public and to accept their judgment as the embodiment of the public will. Congress may approve retroactively, may do nothing, or may disapprove. The people also hold power in their hands to bring the president to account politically, and they can use the ballot box at the next election to express disapproval, or may start the impeachment process, if they believe the president abused his power. Equally, the courts may rule on whether a president exceeded his constitutional authority: Such a ruling may well depend on the extent to which a court believed that a crisis was genuine and that there was no other alternative for a president than to resort to extraconstitutional power.

Although there is no provision in the Constitution for EMERGENCY POWERS, scholars believe that the framers, who were very familiar with Locke's work and who drew upon much of it and that of other social contract theorists in drafting the Constitution, did not reject the idea that presidents might one day need to rely on the doctrine of prerogative if it was necessary to save the nation. Moreover, Richard Pious notes that the OATH OF OFFICE that a president takes refers only to his duty to "preserve, protect, and defend" the Constitution, without also mentioning in it an obligation to faithfully uphold the law. This omission leads Pious to conclude that the framers were well aware that there might be times when a president, in order to "preserve" the Constitution, might need to act contrary to the law or where no law existed.

Some examples of presidents who have relied on this unilateral power during crises are: (1) Abraham LINCOLN's suspension of the writ of habeas corpus in July 1861, authorizing seizure of thousands of civilians suspected of sympathizing with the South, where the constitutional provision for suspension left unstated whether Congress or the president possessed such power. Lincoln's suspension was declared unconstitutional by the Supreme Court in *EX PARTE MILLIGAN*, 71 U.S. (4 Wall.) 2 (1866), when it was used to arrest citizens outside of the theater of war and where the civil courts were operating; (2) Franklin ROOSEVELT's claim in September 1942 that, if Congress refused to repeal a provision of the Emergency Price Control Act that he believed was hindering the war effort, he would take the action himself, stating, "I shall accept the responsibility, and I will act. . . . . When the war is won, the powers under which I act automatically revert to the people—to whom they belong;" and (3) Harry TRUMAN's order to Secretary of Commerce Sawyer to seize the steel mills in April 1952 in order to avert a labor strike, which might jeopardize the production of steel needed for the ongoing KOREAN WAR, an action which the Supreme Court held unconstitutional in *YOUNGSTOWN SHEET AND TUBE COMPANY V. SAWYER*, 343 U.S. 579 (1952).

The notion of an executive prerogative to determine whether conditions warrant taking the law into one person's hands is a mischievous one that is completely at odds with the principle of a government of constitutionally limited powers. The ultimate question, when such power is at issue, is whether a president's use of such enormous and unlimited authority on his own judgment is legitimate and necessary. Thus, the sole guarantee against unbridled use and abuse of such power is the responsibility of the people and the other branches to hold the president accountable for his actions.

Further reading: Locke, John. "Of prerogative." In *Two Treatises of Government.* Edited by Peter Laslett, 159–168. Cambridge: Cambridge University Press, 1960; Pious, Richard M. *The American Presidency.* New York: Basic Books, Inc., 1979, pp. 44–84; Pyle, Christopher H., and Richard M. Pious. *The President, Congress and the Constitution.* New York: The Free Press, 1984, pp. 49–73; Schlesinger, Arthur M., Jr. *The Imperial Presidency.* New York: Popular Library, 1974, pp. 19–21.

—Nancy Kassop

presentation clause

The presentation clause is one of several constitutional provisions that insures presidential involvement in the legislative process by requiring in Article I, Section 7, that "Every Bill which shall have passed the House of Representatives and the Senate, shall, before it becomes a Law, be presented to the President of the United States. . . ." Upon presentation, the president may either approve the bill by signing it within 10 days of presentment, or veto it (see VETO POWER).

The Constitution further stipulates in section 7 that "Every Order, Resolution, or Vote to which the Concurrence of the Senate and House of Representatives may be necessary . . . shall be presented to the President . . . before the Same shall take Effect. . . ." This latter paragraph was added to avoid a situation in which Congress might seek to enact legislation by giving it some other name as a way of avoiding presidential review. Presentment is not required for congressional enactments that are expressions of opinion, or that involve internal administrative matters, including concurrent resolutions (passed by both houses) and simple resolutions (passed by one house). In Article V Congress may avoid presentment when it approves CONSTITUTIONAL AMENDMENTS by a two-thirds vote in both chambers and then sends proposed amendments directly to the states for ratification. Aside from these exceptions, there was general agreement at the CONSTITUTIONAL CONVENTION that the president should retain this final say over legislation.

Even though the president must deal with legislation within 10 days of presentment, considerable flexibility exists regarding the actual presentment process. After a bill is passed by both houses of Congress, presentment may be delayed if the president is out of the country or otherwise indisposed. In a case heard before the U.S. Court of Claims (*Eber Bros. Wine and Liquor Corp. v. U.S.* [1964]), the court ruled that during a presidential absence, Congress could present bills to the president abroad, hold them for presentment until the president's return, or present bills at the WHITE HOUSE as though the president were there.

The question of presentment played a key role in a constitutional challenge to the LEGISLATIVE VETO. In 1983, the Supreme Court ruled in *INS v. CHADHA* that the congressional practice of using simple and concurrent resolutions to control EXECUTIVE BRANCH actions was unconstitutional. In 1998 the Court also struck down a limited ITEM VETO in *CLINTON v. NEW YORK*, arguing that it violated the constitutional procedures for presenting legislation to the president.

See also VETO POWER.

Further reading: Craig, Barbara Hinkson. *Chadha: The Story of an Epic Constitutional Struggle.* New York: Oxford University Press, 1988; Fisher, Louis. *Constitutional Conflicts between Congress and the President.* Lawrence: University Press of Kansas, 1997; Spitzer, Robert J. *President and Congress.* New York: McGraw-Hill, 1993.

—Robert J. Spitzer

presidency, theories of the

A great deal of work among presidency scholars concerns itself with only one of the many "hats" that a president wears and thus contributes to partial theories about particular aspects of the presidency. Different scholars have in this way developed theories about presidential influence on congressional vote outcomes, the "rally" phenomenon whereby the public often but not always rallies in support of a president during a crisis, and the influence of public opinion on presidents, and presidents on public opinion. As a consequence of such studies, the presidency subfield has many theories. But can there be *a theory* of the presidency?

A limited but influential number of presidency scholars take as their subject the sum total of a president's responsibilities. The president, these authors remind us, are first and foremost *leaders,* but why are some leaders more successful in the presidency than others? How, in other words, can presidents combine their many responsibilities, the many hats they wear, to get what they want from their time in office?

Presidential Leadership, Presidential Power

In the most influential single work on the presidency, *Presidential Power,* by Richard NEUSTADT, first published in 1960, Neustadt examines the conditions under which modern presidents successfully exercise influence over the government. Neustadt finds that presidents can only rarely succeed by issuing orders. Rather, "presidential power is the power to persuade," and because the Constitution disperses power throughout the government, Neustadt concludes that "the power to persuade is the power to bargain." The president, Neustadt advises, has no choice but to be a politician and to guard his power carefully. Neustadt's perspective is not self-consciously scientific. He does not explicitly write in terms of dependent and independent variables and does not seek to quantify the measurement of key concepts such as power, reputation, or prestige. Nevertheless, his work has been a model for many scholars in the field.

Other influential theoretical perspectives on the president as a leader have been offered by Theodore Lowi, *The Personal President* (1985), Richard Pious, *The American Presidency* (1979), James McGregor BURNS, *The Power to Lead* (1984), James David Barber, *Presidential Character* (1992), and Stephen Skowronek, *The Politics Presidents Make* (1993). All of these scholars, like Neustadt, seek to explain why some presidents, such as Franklin ROOSEVELT, seem to have had so much greater success than others, such as Dwight EISENHOWER.

Moralists

One body of work, exemplified by Burns and Barber, stands out for its explicit moral dimension. For Burns, presidents succeed when they become "transformative" leaders, who through their leadership raise the "the level of human conduct and the ethical aspirations of both leader and led." Theoretically, Burns may be said to offer a refinement of the dependent variable of presidential power. It is not power itself that concerns Burns, but its use in service of moral enlightenment. The independent variables associated with "good," or transforming, presidential LEADERSHIP are found, ultimately, in the individual president and his character.

Burns is thus joined by James David Barber and others in a common pursuit of the psychological underpinnings of effective presidential leadership. Barber's work famously offers a typology of presidential dispositions toward power. Those presidents who both enjoy wielding power and have an activist temperament are usually the "best" presidents. Those for whom the office is more burden than joy, and yet who are driven to activism, tend to become trapped in office pursuing losing strategies.

Another group of scholars look more to the structure of government than the psychology of presidents in the effort to understand why some presidents succeed while others fail. Among this group, which might be termed the "constitutional school," significant work has been done by, among others, Richard Pious and Theodore Lowi.

Constitutionalists

Pious argues that the personal qualities of a president pale in significance to a president's constitutional resources and constraints. "[T]he fundamental and irreducible core of presidential power rests," Pious writes, "not on influence, persuasion, public opinion, elections, or party, but rather on the successful assertion of constitutional authority to resolve crises and significant domestic issues." Only if he husbands his constitutional authority can a president influence events.

Similarly, Theodore Lowi and Jeffrey Tulis ground their theories of presidential leadership on their understanding of the office's constitutional foundation. Lowi's argument starts by asserting that modern presidents are all but doomed to fail. The dependent variable, in other words, is destined to have the same value for every president. What explains persistent presidential failure? Lowi contends that modern presidents, beset by the legacies of Franklin Roosevelt, seek routinely to "run the country." But no one, not even the president, "runs" the United States, and presidents who try to do so end up either as obvious or hidden failures. Hidden failures, according to Lowi, use overblown rhetoric to persuade the public of a success that is beyond any president's reach, no matter what his personality or the rightness of his intentions.

Historical-Pattern Seekers

Several political scientists, working from the perspective of what is sometimes called the "new institutionalism," view the president as an institutional actor whose incentives are structured by his historical environment. Along these lines, a significant step forward in theorizing about presidential leadership across the broad sweep of U.S. history was taken recently by Stephen Skowronek.

Skowronek seeks to explain different outcomes, differences as it were in the dependent variable of presidential success, with systematic differences in a president's resources for leadership, changes among independent variables. Skowronek identifies two key independent variables: the resilience of the "regime" that defines a president's policy direction and commitments, and the president's affiliation with that regime. The most successful presidencies, Skowronek argues, are those in which a leader such as Franklin Roosevelt comes to office opposed to a crumbling regime. The individual in office makes a difference, but not as much difference as in many other comprehensive theories of the presidency.

From Presidential Theories to a Theory of the Presidency?

To some scholars, the presidency subfield lags behind other niches within political science. Its practitioners, from this perspective, rely too often on qualitative descriptions rather than quantitative measurements and futilely seek to build theories upon a foundation of historical complexity. "If we want to build a theory of the presidency," Terry Moe has written, "this is perhaps the most important place to begin: by simplifying away the burdensome complexities of the personal presidency."

Formal theory, Moe and others contend, provides the way out of the thicket of history. Formal theory, or rational choice theory, uses mathematical tools to explore the power of the presidency in a consistent way. The president's use of the veto has been scrutinized from a rational choice perspective, as has the president's role as a bargainer in "principal-agent" relations with members of the BUREAUCRACY.

Formal theorists claim for their perspective a unique ability to overcome the problem for theory allegedly posed by the small number of presidents. In congressional studies, where formal theory is widely utilized, there are thousands of votes to be analyzed, and the postulates of formal theory can be tested by statistical analysis of those votes. In the presidency subfield, the analogue to the congressional vote cannot be the individual presidency, because their number is too small, but rather a particular presidential behavior that is numerous and clearly identifiable, such as the use of the veto or the decision to issue an EXECUTIVE ORDER.

Different Theories for Different Questions

The most likely scenario for the future of presidency theory is that there will be a multitude of theories and continued debate over the appropriate way to theorize the presidency. Scholars most interested in developing causal inferences that can be tested by statistical means will be drawn toward game theory, spatial theory, expected utility theory, and other variants of formal theory. Their work promises particular progress in building bridges between the presidency subfield of political science and the subfields of congressional studies and public administration. Those most interested in the presidency as the fulcrum of national power will likely continue to utilize and develop theories about presidential leadership and will likely continue to combine empirical questions (how do presidents act?) with normative questions (how *should* they act?). Other scholars will work the vineyards of partial theories for partial aspects of the presidency, or reject causal theory altogether in favor of an "interpretive" approach that seeks to understand the "meaning" rather than the causes of presidential action.

Further reading: Edwards, George C., III. "Studying the Presidency." In *The Presidency and the Political System,* 2d ed., edited by Michael Nelson. Washington, D.C.: CQ Press, 1988; Miroff, Bruce. "Let a Hundred Theories Bloom." In *PRG Report: Newsletter of the Presidency Research Group of the American Political Science Association* (Fall 1997); Moe, Terry. "Theory and the Future of Presidential Studies." In *Ibid.;* Tulis, Jeffrey K. "The Interpretable Presidency." In *The Presidency and the Political System,* 2d ed., edited by Michael Nelson. Washington, D.C.: CQ Press, 1988.

—Thomas Langston

Presidency Research Group (PRG)

The Presidency Research Group, a subdivision of the American Political Science Association (APSA), was founded in 1979 and received formal recognition from APSA in 1981. It is the nation's premier academic organization promoting the study of the American presidency.

presidential papers

The materials that form the internal record of an administration are called the "presidential papers." In the early days of the republic these records were haphazardly kept, if kept at all, but over time, as the historical importance of these records became more obvious, methods were devised to protect them into the future.

At first, presidents themselves, or their families, kept their records and made them available as they saw fit. In the modern era, presidential LIBRARIES were created to house their—often heavily edited—materials. The federal government, recognizing the importance of preserving these materials, sought ways to guarantee their safety and make them available to scholars and the public. The Presidential Libraries Act of 1955 (69 Stat. 695) gave FORMER PRESIDENTS complete control of the papers. The presi-

dent could deed what papers he wished to the federal government, which would maintain the building and records deeded over. The government agreed to abide by whatever rules and restrictions the president imposed on use of the materials. After the 1955 act, a system of presidential libraries began to emerge, with each outgoing president paying careful attention to promoting their legacy via libraries.

During the Watergate scandal, Congress feared that President NIXON might destroy valuable records upon leaving office. They passed the Presidential Recordings and Materials Preservation Act of 1974 (88 Stat. 1965), giving the federal government, under control of the Archivist of the United States, custody of presidential materials.

The PRESIDENTIAL RECORDS ACT of 1978 (92 Stat. 2523) revised the 1974 Act and made presidential materials federal property. Presidents still constructed elaborate libraries, but the Archivist of the United States controlled presidential papers. The Presidential Libraries Act of 1986 (100 Stat. 495) set limits on the presidential libraries.

Presidential papers are a vital part of the scholarly evaluation of a president and his administration. Without these papers, our nation and our government would be the poorer.

See also PUBLIC PAPERS OF THE PRESIDENT.

Presidential Personnel Office (PPO)

Up until the 1940s, in the presidency of Franklin ROOSEVELT and some of his administrative reforms, political PATRONAGE was handled almost exclusively by the national parties. Even after civil service reform with the PENDLETON ACT of 1883, which would significantly reduce the number of federal jobs that the president needed to fill, the parties took the major responsibility of filling these jobs. With the Roosevelt administration, patronage decisions began shifting to the White House. From then on, the history of the White House personnel office has been one of increasing size and centralization.

Although Roosevelt was the first president to bring this function into the White House, it was with TRUMAN that the first White House personnel office was established, when he appointed one man to take charge of the personnel function. EISENHOWER, being from a military background, adopted a more formal style, creating an office of special assistant to the president for personnel management.

The process of centralization and growth continued at a more rapid pace during the Johnson and Nixon administrations. Both presidents showed great interest in playing an active role in the appointment process—JOHNSON in order to get the best-qualified people; NIXON in order to gain control over the BUREAUCRACY. It wasn't until the FORD administration that the White House Personnel Office was renamed the Presidential Personnel Office.

Hoping to distinguish its personnel practices from Nixon's, Ford renamed the office and reduced its size to about 35 employees.

The centralization process was temporarily reversed during the CARTER administration. This stemmed from two things—a power struggle between two of Carter's aides that left the PPO floundering for direction, and Carter's lack of interest in personnel matters. In spite of this lack of interest, Carter operatives set precedent by beginning their search for appointees even before he was elected, a practice that continued after him. This was particularly true of the younger BUSH, whose transition team was busy filling positions before the outcome of the election was known.

The decentralization that occurred during the Carter administration was abruptly reversed in the REAGAN and George H. W. BUSH Administrations. Both of these presidents centralized all appointments in the White House as a matter of policy, a practice continued by both CLINTON and the younger Bush, thus following the adage, "personnel is policy." When this practice is combined with the fact that the number of political appointments has been increasing, the job of the PPO is becoming more time-consuming and complicated.

Further reading: Mackenzie, G. Calvin, ed. *The In-And-Outers.* Baltimore, Md.: Johns Hopkins University Press, 1987; Weko, Thomas. *The Politicizing Presidency.* Lawrence: University Press of Kansas, 1995.

—Joseph Wert

Presidential Records Act (PRA)

In 1978 Congress passed and President CARTER signed into law a transfer of ownership of presidential records, from private to public. The Presidential Records Act (PRA) (44 U.S.C. B2201–2207) governs the official documents from presidents, vice presidents, and their staffs serving after January 20, 1981. The PRA gives the White House guidelines that govern the maintenance, storage, and release of presidential documents. The PRA also allows "the incumbent President to dispose of records that no longer have administrative, historical, informational, or evidentiary value, once he has obtained the views of the Archivist of the United States on the proposed disposal." In addition, the PRA routinized a process for public access to presidential documents via the FREEDOM OF INFORMATION ACT (FOIA) beginning five years after the end of the president's term in office. However, the PRA does allow the president to invoke as many as six specific restrictions to public access for up to 12 years. In 2000 the 12-year restriction and subsequent release of the REAGAN information produced a firestorm of debate when the George W. BUSH administration attempted to limit the release of any information relating to current administration members. Scholars, members of the media, Congress, and

the national archivists all expressed dismay and frustration at the return to document restrictions. After leaving the White House, the documents of an administration are housed within the President's Library and Museum (the Nixon Archives remain the exception to this rule). Due to the legal disputes stemming from the WATERGATE scandal, the Nixon Archives are currently housed in Maryland at the National Archives Depository.

Further reading: www.nara.gov

—Diane Heith

presidential succession laws

Article II of the Constitution provides for Congress to determine "what officer shall then act as President" should both the president and vice president be killed or incapacitated at the same time. This situation is known as "double vacancy." The nation has been without a vice president 18 different times in its history, making this scenario a valid concern for continuity and stability in the EXECUTIVE BRANCH.

Congress passed the first succession law in 1792. It provided that the president pro tempore of the Senate would act as president in the event of a double vacancy, followed by the Speaker of the House. The nation would conduct a special election to a full four-year term the following November, unless the vacancy occurred in the last six months of a term. James MADISON objected to the law, arguing that the inclusion of legislators in the line of succession violated the principle of SEPARATION OF POWERS. The sequence specified in the law was partly motivated by Federalist antipathy for Thomas JEFFERSON, Washington's secretary of State.

The problem with the 1792 law was that the lack of a president pro tempore and Speaker would leave the nation without a president in the event of a double vacancy. In fact, when Chester ARTHUR took over as president following the assassination of James GARFIELD in 1881, the next three positions in the line of succession were vacant. There was no VICE PRESIDENT, the Senate was evenly divided, and the Speaker would not be in place until the House convened in December. A similar circumstance took place when Thomas HENDRICKS, Grover CLEVELAND's vice president, died in 1885. In 1886 Congress passed a new succession law. This time the line began with the CABINET secretaries in the order in which the departments were created. The new law left the question of special elections uncertain. It also made it highly unlikely that the new acting president would come from a political party different from that of the replaced president. This would presumably reinforce the continuity and stability of government policy.

When Harry TRUMAN assumed the presidency following the death of Franklin ROOSEVELT, he became concerned about the prospect of having no vice president for nearly four years. He objected to the 1886 law on the grounds that it violated democratic principles by allowing the president to appoint his successor. Truman urged revision of the 1886 law. He argued that the Speaker was closest to the president and vice president in terms of popular selection, since he is elected every two years and has the more recent mandate. Although Truman's suggestion enjoyed only lukewarm support, he persisted in pushing his bill, even after the REPUBLICAN PARTY gained control of Congress in 1947. Congress passed a new succession law in July 1947.

The current law channels succession first through the Speaker, then the president pro tempore, and finally through the cabinet secretaries in the order in which the departments were created. The law explicitly rejects the idea of a special election, saying the acting president will serve "until the expiration of the then current presidential term." The law applies not only to death, RESIGNATION, removal, and DISABILITY, but also failure to qualify. Thus, in the case of a deadlocked election, the Speaker must first resign his position as Speaker and representative, then act as president for the remainder of the current presidential term, or until the failure to qualify is rectified.

The 1947 law was criticized on the grounds that congressional positions are not chosen on the basis of their qualifications for the presidency. The law also makes it more likely that an acting president will be from a party different from the replaced president. Concern heightened after the assassination of John KENNEDY. Lyndon JOHNSON had a history of heart trouble and both of his designated successors—the Speaker and the president pro tempore—were quite elderly. The TWENTY-FIFTH AMENDMENT, passed partly because of concern over the 1947 act, now makes double vacancy highly unlikely.

Further reading: Feerick, John D. *From Failing Hands: The Story of Presidential Succession.* New York: Fordham University Press, 1965; Silva, Ruth C. *Presidential Succession.* Ann Arbor: University of Michigan Press, 1951.

—David A. Crockett

presidential transitions

The transition of the presidency symbolizes the essence of democracy: the peaceful change of political power from one set of rulers to the political opposition. But in an operational sense, each transition presents the challenge to the incoming administration to take control of the government and implement its policy agenda. This entry will take up each of these fundamental aspects of transition in turn.

A democratic polity fundamentally depends on the transition of power from one leader to another and more profoundly from the control of a political party representing one set of priorities to a regime representing another

approach. Throughout the history of the world these transitions have most often been accompanied by violence and the force of arms. Modern democracies have made significant progress in the passage of power through the peaceful means of more or less democratic elections.

The politics and the organization of the transfer of power are most often complicated endeavors. In the United States the transition of power from one president to the next has always been peaceful, though it often entails political conflict. Transitions involving the succession of a VICE PRESIDENT at the DEATH OF A PRESIDENT contain their own perils but involve little planning. Transitions from a president to an elected successor of the same political party are peaceful and orderly, though there are often undercurrents of conflict as the newly elected president attempts to put his own stamp on the office. The most challenging transitions involve changing administrations from one political party to another, and these have been the focus of recent scholarly attention.

Over the first century and a half of the American republic, presidential transitions may have signified important changes in the direction of government, but the administrative dimensions were comparatively simple because the institution of the presidency itself was relatively small. As the scope of the national government began to expand in the mid 20th century and as the EXECUTIVE BRANCH grew to millions of employees, the challenge of taking over this huge enterprise grew correspondingly. And as the size of the presidency itself (EXECUTIVE OFFICE OF THE PRESIDENCY) grew to assert control over the executive branch, transitions became much more formalized and complicated.

The change of parties that came with the election of President EISENHOWER foreshadowed large changes in policy direction and control of the executive branch, but aside from some advisory groups, the transition organization was not a large one. When John KENNEDY was campaigning for the presidency in 1960, he asked Clark CLIFFORD and Richard NEUSTADT each to write a memo for him about actions he should take if he were elected. Each of the memos provided judgments about initial actions to take along with recommended personnel and organizational decisions that needed immediate consideration. Kennedy used their advice during his transition into office, and because of his administrative difficulties before inauguration, he asked Congress to pass the Presidential Transition Act of 1963, which provided administrative expenses for both incoming and outgoing administrations.

When Richard NIXON was elected in 1968, he engaged in policy and personnel planning but did not feel that an elaborate transition effort was required, in part because of his eight years experience as vice president during the EISENHOWER administration. It was left to presidential candidate Jimmy CARTER to initiate the modern era of elaborate transition planning. Carter had been governor of Georgia and had relatively little Washington experience; he also felt that systematic preparation was necessary and in the summer of 1976 he established a transition project in Atlanta to prepare a plan of action should he be elected. His staff conducted a series of budget and policy studies and set up a "talent inventory program" of potential nominees for political appointments.

Four years later another state governor without Washington experience, Ronald REAGAN, initiated a transition planning operation in the spring of 1980. The operation was much more elaborate than the Carter effort, with hundreds of people organized into working groups. After the election more than one hundred transition teams were formed for the various federal agencies. The agency teams submitted reports to transition headquarters, a large office building in Washington, D.C. The transition BUREAUCRACY was so large that its leaders had a difficult time controlling the activities of all of the teams throughout the government.

George H. W. BUSH was the vice president when he was elected to the presidency in 1988 and felt that the Reagan transition was larger than necessary, though succeeding to the presidency was less complicated since he was a sitting vice president. On the surface the Bush transition was smooth, but there were undercurrents of conflict between the Reagan appointees, many of whom expected to stay in office, and the need of the Bush team to place its own people in office, and the turnovers in political personnel turned out to be significant.

When Bill CLINTON was elected he chose to run his transition from Little Rock, Arkansas. There were several teams of advisers in Washington preparing policy plans, organization, and political appointments, and the bilocation of the work made the transition difficult. The transition also lost some momentum as rival factions struggled over control of the new administration. Clinton made good progress in putting together his CABINET, despite some misfires; but delays in appointing the White House staff caused significant delays in getting the administration up and running.

In contrast to Clinton, President-Elect George W. BUSH set up a relatively organized transition in 2000–2001 despite the five-week delay in determining who was the winner of the election. His team decided to begin the transition even before the outcome of the election was determined. Bush was able to designate his White House staff and cabinet and begin his administration smoothly, particularly given the uncertainty of the election outcome. The relatively smooth transition into office, however, did not translate into the expeditious appointment of the top levels of the executive branch, which had been slowing over the past several decades.

Each new administration must deal with the basic requirements of taking control of the executive branch and establishing a new presidency. These tasks include appointing the cabinet, designating a White House staff, making executive branch political appointments, and articulating a policy agenda.

While the cabinet does not play the most important role in advising the president as it once did, appointing cabinet secretaries is one of the most visible public actions that presidents-elect perform. Cabinet appointments send important symbolic signals as to the direction and ideological makeup of the new administration. Cabinets are often used to demonstrate ideological breadth in reaching out to the faction of the party that the presidential nominee defeated, and they are used to demonstrate inclusiveness of the administration in terms of geography, ideology, race, and gender.

Bill Clinton said that he chose a cabinet that "looked like America," in appointing more women and minorities than previous cabinets had contained, but the Clinton transition also illustrated the point that the White House staff has in recent decades overshadowed cabinet members in dominating advice to the president. Clinton spent most of his time early in the transition in carefully assembling his cabinet and put off designating his White House staff until January 1993. As a result, there was much infighting, and the administration took more time than usual in establishing who was in charge of different parts of the administration. The widely accepted conclusion of the Clinton experience was that designating the top levels of the White House staff cannot be put off until late in the transition.

The most frustrating part of most recent transitions into office has been the job of making presidential appointments. These appointments are crucial to running the executive branch, yet it has been taking longer to bring the people in a new administration on board. In the Kennedy administration it took an average of 2.4 months to appoint the top members of the new administration, but it took President Clinton an average of 8.5 months to make his top appointments. The reason for this slowing of the appointments process is the increasing of the number of political appointments available to presidents and the centralization of control in the PRESIDENTIAL PERSONNEL OFFICE.

In addition to the administrative aspects of transitions, new presidents need to establish a policy agenda that will be presented to Congress. Doing so necessarily involves planning in order to narrow the general promises of the campaign to narrowly focused options that the president-elect can choose and present to Congress early in the administration. Doing this in an organized way means that the top White House staff has to agree on who is in charge.

The challenge of presidential transitions is to achieve the appropriate balance of change and continuity. The new administration must take control of the executive branch of government and pursue its policy agenda, but at the same time, it must shift gears from campaigning to government and assure the American public and the international community that ongoing business of the U.S. government will continue with competence and good leadership.

—James P. Pfiffner

presidents and the press

The relationship between the president and the American press has a long and colorful history. The press has always been among the most influential political actors with which presidents must contend. American newspapers during the late 18th and early 19th centuries were highly partisan in both their political loyalties and coverage of events in Washington. By the mid 19th century, with advanced printing capabilities and a desire to provide more objective news coverage for increasing circulations, newspapers began to cover the White House as a formal beat. News coverage of the presidency dramatically increased during the administration of Theodore ROOSEVELT, who cultivated positive press coverage in an attempt to maintain strong ties to the American public.

During the 20th century, with the rise of the RHETORICAL PRESIDENCY and the continual expansion of media technology, presidents have increasingly relied on the press to communicate their vision to both the American public and other important political actors. However, the White House and the Washington press corps have often struggled to define the political agenda. Each wants to control the content of the news, but like it or not, one cannot do its job without the other. Reporters have maintained a presence at the White House for more than 100 years, but an ideal relationship where each side was satisfied with the other has never existed between the president and the press. This love-hate relationship has also been fueled over the years by a credibility gap between an investigative press and a government bent on managing news.

The news media can help in getting out the president's message but has also been known to distort the message. The press, however, can be useful to a president by providing information about current events, keeping the EXECUTIVE BRANCH apprised of major concerns of the public, enabling executives to convey their messages to the public and political elites, and allowing the president to remain in full public view on the political stage. A cyclical view of the relationship between the press and the president has been shown to exist, and it is based on both cooperation and continuity between the two institutions. While the extent of cooperation varies throughout different time periods of each administration, the relationship is not always adversarial, since each side must cooperate with the other to get its job done. The growth of the president's communication staff in recent years can be attributed to the systematic

approach of handling the news media, not to a desire to control the content of the news. The larger news outlets have also kept up with this level of growth, putting some members of the White House press corps on equal footing with the president's communication advisers. And since both the president and major news organizations gain from coverage that is favorable and prominent, both sides try to work together to avoid conflict. However, reporters on the White House beat are rarely experts on the policy issues that presidents promote, and stories can often lack substance.

White House reporters are most often comfortable reporting on what they know best, which is the politics of Washington: suspected scandal, dissension within an administration, verbal and visual gaffes, and tactical political blunders. Few are policy experts, but most have expertise in covering the horse-race aspect of politics. This contributes to the focus on politically oriented, rather than policy oriented, stories. Presidents have attempted control over the news with the knowledge of the news media's preference to report on politics, but only the subject matter can be controlled, not the tone of the news. The president makes news by virtue of being the ideological symbol of American democracy and leadership to both journalists and the public. The president's relationship with the press is a combination of strengths and weaknesses. Presidential power can be undermined both by a failure of the administration to effectively manage the news, and by news-gathering norms within the journalism industry and the skepticism of the press. While presidents can usually enjoy deference from the press in terms of coverage during times of crisis or on certain ceremonial occasions, usually reporters place presidential actions within a political context that reduces the symbolic nature of the presidency to that of just another politician seeking to retain political power.

The president is under constant scrutiny by the press but must be careful in his criticisms of reporters, who can not only give voice to his opponents but can present the news as unflattering to the president's public image. Several factors can increase the tensions between the president and the press. Presidents have historically viewed the press as a hindrance in achieving the public's support for policies, due mostly to the content of most news originating from the White House. First, an administration, as well as other top government officials, often attempts to use the press to its advantage through leaks. Often, top aides or even the president himself will leak information as a trial balloon to test public reaction to a proposed policy. In this instance, the press agrees to serve as a communication tool of the government in order to remain competitive with other news outlets. Second, many stories on the president tend to have a superficial or trivial quality. Stories focusing on the personal aspects of the president's life often gain more prominent coverage than stories analyzing policies. Again,

President Ford answers some questions from the press. *(Library of Congress)*

competition among reporters, as well as a lack of expertise on many national political issues, fuels this type of coverage. Finally, while most studies on media coverage of news show no systematic bias along partisan or ideological lines, distortion still occurs in coverage of the president.

The presentation of news contains a structural bias in how stories are selected, since not all issues receive coverage. Due to deadlines and limited time and/or space for stories, important issues are often oversimplified. The president relies on two groups of advisers within the White House in an attempt to control his own public image and that of his administration—the press office and the Office of Communications. The press secretary heads the press office and is responsible for preparing press releases, coordinating news, and holding daily press briefings for the White House press corps as well as facilitating the needs of reporters who cover the president. The press secretary also serves as an important public spokesperson for the president and as a liaison between reporters and the White House. The role of the WHITE HOUSE OFFICE OF COMMU-NICATIONS, created during the administration of Richard

NIXON, is to coordinate news throughout the EXECUTIVE BRANCH. Under the leadership of Communications Director David Gergen during the REAGAN years, the use of this office to effectively manage the president's public image and promote news about the president's legislative agenda became an increasingly important aspect of the overall White House communication strategy. The Office of Communications develops a long-term public relations strategy and also coordinates presidential coverage in regional and local media outlets. Advisers usually spread the "line of the day" throughout the administration, which then takes it to the press; the office also takes the White House message directly to the people when necessary. The ultimate goal is to set the public agenda through the use of focus groups, polls, sound bites, and public appearances by the president.

Press coverage of the president and the way stories out of Washington are generated have continued to evolve into the 21st century as a result of the increasing technological capabilities of the news media as well as the changing political environment. Intense competition between the various media for both audience and advertising revenue has altered both the content and tone of many political stories. Newspapers now compete with television as a result of CNN's emergence during the 1980s, which created the 24-hour news cycle. Now, other all-news networks, such as MSNBC, compete to have the most up-to-the-minute news headlines available. The Internet has also influenced both the availability and quality of political news. Competition and the dramatically short news cycle have often resulted in the use of questionable news sources and many factual errors in reporting, all done with the zeal to become the "first" to provide an "exclusive" to the American audience. As the first baby-boomer president raised during the television age, Bill CLINTON routinely used alternative media formats such as talk shows and town hall meetings to speak directly to the American people, often bypassing the traditional Washington press corps. These factors, among others, have led news coverage of both politics in general and the presidency in particular to become more personal, intrusive, and obsessed with scandal.

Further reading: Edwards, George C., III. *The Public Presidency: The Pursuit of Popular Support.* New York: St. Martin's Press, 1983; Emery, Michael, and Edwin Emery. *The Press and America: An Interpretive History of the Mass Media.* Boston: Allyn and Bacon, 1996; Graber, Doris. *Mass Media and American Politics.* Washington, D.C.: CQ Press, 2002; Grossman, Michael Baruch, and Martha Joynt Kumar. *Portraying the President: The White House and the News Media.* Baltimore, Md.: Johns Hopkins University Press, 1981; Paletz, David L. *The Media in American Politics: Contents and Consequences.* New York: Addison-Wesley, 2002.

—Lori Cox-Han

President's Foreign Intelligence Advising Board

Established by President EISENHOWER in 1956, the President's Foreign Intelligence Advisory Board (PFIAB) advises the president on foreign policy matters. Established by executive order 12331, the board's responsibilities vary with each president, and members of the board are appointed by the president.

President's Intelligence Oversight Board (PIOB)

Created in 1976 by President Gerald FORD's Executive Order 11905, the PIOB was deemed necessary after revelations of scandal and criminality on the part of U.S. intelligence agencies. The PIOB is a three-member board, appointed by the president, is served by a small staff, and has no subpoena powers. Its job is to serve as a watchdog over actions by the intelligence community. It is for the most part, a paper tiger, as PIOB serves the president, and if the president does not want PIOB to have teeth, it

becomes weak and ineffective. For example, PIOB did not know of the crimes of the Iran-contra scandal during the Reagan years, because the president and his top aides were deeply involved in these crimes and did not want PIOB to investigate. Thus, the PIOB is only as effective or ineffective as the sitting president wants it to be.

press conference

Press conferences provide the president with an opportunity to make news by formally interacting with the White House press corps. Press conferences have become an institutionalized tradition in which all presidents are expected to participate. A written transcript is kept of all questions and answers, and most presidents begin the session with a prepared opening statement. Since they were first televised live in the 1960s, press conferences have become less about informing reporters and the public about important issues and more about controlling the president's public image.

The number of press conferences held by each president during the last century has varied greatly. Theodore ROOSEVELT held some of the earliest press conferences, which were informal sessions with the press on Sundays to combat the lack of interesting news from Washington in Monday's newspapers. William Howard TAFT was the first president to hold regular press conferences, which occurred twice a week, until he stopped the practice after "an unfortunate session" with reporters. Woodrow Wilson, Warren G. HARDING, Calvin COOLIDGE, and Herbert HOOVER (until the onset of the GREAT DEPRESSION) returned to the practice of regular press conferences, usually twice-weekly formal events. Each also required reporters to submit their questions in advance. Franklin D. ROOSEVELT changed that requirement, as well as the formal setting for press conferences. FDR enjoyed an effective relationship with the press, due in part to his frequent and informal meetings with the WHITE HOUSE PRESS CORPS in the OVAL OFFICE. FDR held a total of 881 press conferences while in office, a yearly average of approximately 70. He was famous for his congenial personality toward the press and his "off-the-record" remarks. Through press conferences, FDR was a master at news management and was able to capture many headlines throughout the nation's newspapers.

Following FDR's 12 years in office, no other president would come close to matching the number of press conferences held. Harry S Truman, who averaged 38 per year, returned press conferences to more formal events and moved the location in 1950 out of the Oval Office and into the EXECUTIVE OFFICE BUILDING. Truman and his advisers began to exercise more control over the content and structure of press conferences, relying on preconference briefings and an increased use of prepared opening statements. Truman also earned a reputation for his "shoot-from-the-hip" speaking style that would regularly produce unpredictable yet quotable comments. Dwight D. EISENHOWER would be the first president to encounter television cameras during a press conference, and he allowed taping for later television release. John F. KENNEDY was innovative with his groundbreaking use of live televised press conferences, which both the press and public found highly entertaining. Lyndon JOHNSON could never match the Kennedy style during press conferences and would contribute to the growing credibility gap with inaccurate reports on the VIETNAM WAR. The frequency of press conferences would drop during the presidency of Richard NIXON, who believed that the mystique of the presidency must be maintained through limited public appearances. Nixon was also famous for his great disdain of the press and averaged only 6.5 press conferences per year. Gerald FORD, during his brief tenure in office, as well as his successor, Jimmy CARTER, both attempted to restore credibility to the White House and its relationship with the press by increasing the number of press conferences after the Nixon years. Both used these opportunities to speak bluntly to the press about the problems facing the nation in the mid-to-late 1970s. While neither received high marks for style during press conferences, both Ford and Carter were known for their substantive knowledge of government policies.

While his public skills earned him the nickname of the "Great Communicator," Ronald REAGAN held even fewer press conferences than Nixon did, averaging only 5.5 per year. This was due to his unfavorable performances, since Reagan often made misstatements and verbal gaffes during the give-and-take of questions from reporters. In an attempt to better control these events, Reagan's advisers implemented new rules for press conferences, including assigned seats for those in attendance (which provided a seating chart for Reagan to reference when calling on reporters) and insisting that reporters raise their hands before asking a question. George H. W. BUSH would hold more press conferences than Reagan and would also begin the practice of holding joint press conferences with foreign leaders. Bill CLINTON would continue this practice, although he would not hold many formal press conferences, particularly during his second term. However, he always performed well in these impromptu sessions, deftly fielding questions from seasoned White House correspondents. Since the Reagan years, presidents have held fewer formal press conferences where they appear alone before the White House press corps, relying more on regional and foreign press conferences as well as joint appearances with foreign dignitaries.

Further reading: Edwards, George C., III. *The Public Presidency.* New York: St. Martin's Press, 1983; Emery, Michael, and Edwin Emery. *The Press and America: An Interpretive History of the Mass Media.* Boston: Allyn and Bacon, 1996; Ragsdale, Lyn. *Vital Statistics on the Presidency.* Washington, D.C.: CQ Press, 1996.

—Lori Cox-Han

press secretary See WHITE HOUSE PRESS SECRETARY.

primaries and caucuses

Primaries and caucuses are methods used to choose delegates to represent the states at the parties' national conventions. Initially, primaries and caucuses were a Progressive Movement creation to make the presidential nomination process more democratic. While primaries existed during the first half of the 20th century, their influence was minimal. Party leaders ignored the primaries because primaries gave them less power to choose the nominee. In fact, few participated in primaries because it was a sign of weakness (though John KENNEDY was an exception in 1960).

The role of primaries changed immensely following the events of the 1968 Democratic National Convention. Because of tensions surrounding the VIETNAM WAR, the DEMOCRATIC PARTY was divided over their nominee. Party leaders chose the VICE PRESIDENT at the time, Hubert H. HUMPHREY, to be the Democratic candidate. This move infuriated rank-and-file members because Humphrey supported U.S. involvement in Vietnam and was nominated without having entered a single primary. As a result of the outrage, the Democrats established the MCGOVERN-FRASER COMMISSION to address the party's nomination process.

While there were several effects of the McGovern-Fraser reforms, the most important is that they led to an increase in the number of primaries. In 1968 states held a total of 30 Democratic and Republican primaries. By 2000 that number increased to 88. In a primary, voters go to the polls to cast their ballots for a delegate who is pledged to one of the candidates. There are two common types of primaries: open and closed. An open primary is one in which eligible voters do not need to be registered party members. In other words, a Democrat could vote in the Republican primary (she would forfeit her ability to vote in the Democratic primary, however). In a closed primary, only registered party members may vote. A subset of the closed primary is the independent primary that is open only to members of the party and those not registered with another party. Some states have a blanket primary that is open to any registered voter and all candidates for each office are listed on the same ballot regardless of party. The constitutionality of blanket primaries has come under close scrutiny; in 2000 the Supreme Court declared California's blanket primary to be unconstitutional.

A caucus is much more confusing (and less common). While the rules of a caucus vary by party and state, members in a precinct gather in a selected location (such as a church or a person's home) to discuss the candidates and choose delegates. The Iowa Caucus is the most famous caucus because it is normally the first state in the nomination process. In the case of Iowa, the caucus actually has four different stages (i.e., precinct, county, congressional district, and state convention): In each one delegates are selected to attend the next level. However, if a candidate wins the precinct level, then they usually control the other levels as well. The caucus may seem somewhat odd in comparison to the more traditional primary, but many people claim it has distinct advantages over the primary. The most common argument may be that it is "old-fashioned democracy." People get together, discuss the merits of the candidates, and then vote. Also, in caucuses candidates are likely to focus more on grassroots campaigning than mass advertising, which could make voters more knowledgeable about their choices. The major downside to caucuses, however, is that turnout is extremely low. According to Stephen J. Wayne, only 915 people participated in Wyoming's 1996 Republican caucus!

Whether the state conducts primaries or caucuses, delegates are apportioned one of two ways. Under winner-take-all rules, the candidate who receives a plurality (the most) of the votes obtains all of the state's delegates. Winner-take-all rules can apply either at the state level or by congressional district. Under winner-take-all statewide rules, the candidate that wins the most votes obtains all of the state's delegates. In a winner-take-all by congressional district system, the candidate who wins the most votes in a congressional district is awarded all of that district's delegates. The person that wins the most votes statewide receives the state's bonus delegates. Republicans generally elect their delegates on a winner-take-all basis, but not in all cases. The 2000 New Hampshire Republican primary used proportional rules for delegate selection.

The second way to allocate delegates is proportionally. Under proportional rules, a candidate receives the same percentage of delegates as the percentage of votes that they won. For example, if a candidate wins 50 percent of the vote, s/he would receive 50 percent of the delegates. All Democratic primaries and caucuses allocate delegates proportionally. The Democrats have instituted a 15 percent threshold that candidates must meet in order to receive delegates. If a candidate wins less than 15 percent, their votes are discounted and the remaining candidates' percentages are recalculated. Many scholars argue that dividing delegates proportionally is a disadvantage to the party because it can create divisive primaries that make it difficult for a front-runner to emerge.

Democrats have also added something called a superdelegate. Superdelegates are Democratic elected officials and party leaders who are allowed to vote for the party's nominee at the national convention. Superdelegates were designed to give the party elite some control over the nomination once again. In 2000, 18 percent of the delegates at the Democratic National Convention were superdelegates. Superdelegates have had the effect of reinforcing the front-runner's status since most support the establishment candidate. For example, even if Bill Bradley had been able to mount a serious campaign against Al GORE in 2000 by winning a few primaries, he still would have had to overcome the immense advantage Gore had from the superdelegates.

There have been several calls to reform the current primary and caucus system. One possible reform is to hold a national primary in which each state's primary or caucus would be held on the same day. While the public supports this idea, it is unlikely to receive support from many state legislatures. Smaller states would be concerned that candidates would never visit because the contenders would focus all of their attention on states with more delegates. Others maintain that the national primary gives the front-runner a large advantage because it prevents other candidates from building momentum.

Another possible reform is to hold regional primaries. This idea was sparked by SUPER TUESDAY, when most Southern states decided to hold their primaries on the same day to give the South a greater voice in the nomination process. Under a regional system, Iowa and New Hampshire would remain first, and then the regions would rotate the order in which their primaries are held every four years. Several states have already begun to clump together their primaries and caucuses, but we are still a long way from a nationally coordinated regional primary. Like the national primary, a regional system may not happen any time soon because it would require unprecedented cooperation from the states, and it still does not get around the fact that some region will have to go last.

A third reform, the one that has come closest to being implemented, is "the Delaware Proposal." Under this plan, the smallest populated states would come first, followed by the largest populated states. At the 1996 Republican National Convention, the delegates passed this plan to be implemented in 2000. However, the Democrats did not go along, so the Republicans did not follow through. Democrats were concerned that predominantly white, small-populated states would determine the nominee and that urban areas would have little voice in the nomination. The future of "the Delaware Proposal" is dependent on both parties supporting it.

Further reading: Ceaser, James W., and Andrew E. Busch. *The Perfect Tie: The True Story of the 2000 Presidential Election.* Lanham, Md.: Rowman & Littlefield, 2001; Mayer, William G., ed. *In Pursuit of the White House*

2000: How We Choose Our Presidential Nominees. New York: Chatham House Publishers, 2000; Polsby, Nelson W., and Aaron Wildavsky. *Presidential Elections: Strategies and Structures of American Politics,* 10th ed. New York: Chatham House Publishers, 2000; Wayne, Stephen J. *The Road to the White House 2000.* Boston, Mass.: Beford/St. Martin's, 2001.

—Matt Streb

The Prize Cases, 67 U.S. (2 Black) 635 (1863)

This is a Supreme Court case decided during the CIVIL WAR that concluded that President Abraham LINCOLN possessed the constitutional authority to impose a blockage on Southern ports in response to the Confederacy's assault on Fort Sumter in April 1861. With Congress out of session, President Lincoln took a series of extraordinary measures designed to counter the rebellion. Among these responses to the attack was Lincoln's unilateral imposition of a blockade on Southern ports. Once Lincoln called Congress back into session during the summer of 1861, Congress passed legislation retroactively ratifying the president's actions including his imposition of the blockade.

A legal dispute arose when several vessels and their cargoes were individually captured and brought in as prizes by Union ships prior to congressional ratification of Lincoln's actions. In *The Prize Cases,* the owners of the captured ships argued that President Lincoln exceeded the scope of his constitutional authority by unilaterally imposing the blockade. The key question was whether the rebellion constituted a war under the Constitution. The shipowners argued that absent a declaration of war by Congress no legal state of war existed between North and South at the time of the prizes' capture and hence Lincoln's action was unlawful.

In a 5-4 decision, the Court ruled that the South through its attack on Fort Sumter created a state of civil war. Thus, the majority concluded that Lincoln's actions did not amount to a presidential declaration of war but merely constituted a response to a *de facto* state of war. Or in the words of the Court: "The President was bound to meet . . . [the war as] it presented itself, without waiting for Congress to baptize it with a name. . . ."

Without conceding that the president possessed independent constitutional powers to act as he did, the Court also supported its decision by reasoning that statutes passed by Congress provided retroactive legislative sanction to Lincoln's actions. In so doing, the Court seemed to hint that unlawful acts performed by the president could be cured by subsequent congressional action. Finally, the Court further reasoned that Congress under the acts of February 28, 1792, and March 3, 1807, among others, authorized the president to suppress insurrection.

Four justices dissented, however, contending that no state of war can exist without a congressional declaration and that the congressional acts of 1795 or 1807 did not and could not (as they sought) delegate to the president the authority to declare war. The dissenters argued that a legal state of war did not exist until Congress assembled and recognized the war in the summer of 1861. Consequently, the dissenters contended that any capture of prizes before that time was unlawful.

The Prize Cases is a decision often cited by advocates of presidential power in support of the position that the president possesses broad inherent authority to make war in response to armed attacks. Those favoring a more restrained role for the president focus more on the retrospective ratification of President Lincoln's actions by Congress and on the dissenting opinion.

Further reading: Randall, J. A. G. *Constitutional Problems under Lincoln.* Urbana: University of Illinois Press, 1951; Rossiter, Clinton, and Richard P. Longaker. *The Supreme Court and the Commander in Chief.* Ithaca, N.Y.: Cornell University Press, 1976.

—Roy E. Brownell II

proclamations

Presidents have issued nearly seven thousand proclamations since George WASHINGTON issued his Proclamation of Neutrality of 1793. In general, proclamations have the binding force of law (assuming Congress does not block a proclamation).

For the most part, proclamations have dealt with declaring special "days" (e.g., National Cheese Day) or special recognitions (i.e., honoring an especially noteworthy achievement). But increasingly, presidents of the modern era, employing an ADMINISTRATIVE PRESIDENCY strategy for governing, have used proclamations to establish substantive policies absent congressional consent.

Further reading: Office of the Federal Register. *Codification of Presidential Proclamations and Executive Orders, April 13, 1945–January 20, 1989.* 1990; U.S. House Committee on Government Operations. *Executive Orders and Proclamations: A Study of a Use of Presidential Power.* 85th Cong., 1st sess., 1957. Committee Print.

protection of the president See SECRET SERVICE.

protocol, presidential

Protocol refers to established rules or customs of ceremony, manners, and etiquette. It comprises the rules of conduct that apply to a particular person, title, or occasion. Because of America's commitment to democratic equality, we have always been wary of high protocol as practiced by American officials at home and abroad. The president is guided in such matters by the chief of protocol, who is head of the protocol office. The office is responsible for arranging visits of state and other events and advising the president on proper procedures.

When a foreign head of state, or member of another nation's royal family visits the United States, there are certain practices and procedures that are to be followed, lest a public embarrassment, or worse, international incident result from an unintended insult or snub. Though the rules of protocol are often formal to the point of stuffiness, following them allows for top-level visits and meetings without the fear that an unintentional slight will interfere with the business of government or DIPLOMACY.

public papers of the president

Started in 1957, the *Public Papers of the Presidents of the United States* series is the official annual compilation of PRESIDENTIAL PAPERS. The *Public Papers* series is considered a comprehensive public source of data on the American presidency and has aided those presidency scholars interested in a more institutional approach to studying the office, since the data available now spans numerous administrations. This allows researchers to employ a comparative methodological approach to understanding the institution of the American presidency. The National Historical Publications Commission originally suggested this endeavor because no uniform compilations of presidential messages and papers existed. The *Public Papers* is now the annual version of the *Weekly Compilation of Presidential Documents*, which began publication in 1965. Both are published by the Office of the Federal Register, NATIONAL ARCHIVES and Records Service, and are printed by the Government Printing Office. Administrations included in the series of *Public Papers* include Presidents HOOVER, TRUMAN, EISENHOWER, KENNEDY, JOHNSON, NIXON, FORD, CARTER, REAGAN, George H. W. BUSH, and CLINTON. The papers of President Franklin ROOSEVELT were published privately prior to the creation of the official *Public Papers* series. Other privately published series of presidential papers by scholarly presses include: *The Papers of James Madison,* published by the University of Chicago Press; *The Papers of Woodrow Wilson* by Princeton University Press; and *The Papers of Dwight David Eisenhower* by Johns Hopkins University Press. Other series of presidential papers include *The Adams-Jefferson Letters: The Complete Correspondence Between Thomas Jefferson and Abigail and John Adams,* published by the University of North Carolina Press, and *The Writings of George Washington from the Original Manuscript Sources, 1745–1799,* published by the George Washington Bicentennial Commission. The working papers for each administration since President Herbert HOOVER are also available in presidential LIBRARIES, and for administrations prior to Hoover, the papers are housed at the Library of Congress. At present, volumes of the *Public Papers* are published approximately twice a year, and each volume covers approximately a six-month period. The papers and speeches of the President of the United States that were issued by the Office of the Press Secretary during the specified time period are included in each volume of the *Public Papers.* These include: press releases, presidential PROCLAMATIONS, EXECUTIVE ORDERS, addresses, remarks, letters, messages, telegrams, memorandums to federal agencies, communications to Congress, bill-signing statements, transcripts from presidential press conferences, and communiqués to foreign heads of state. The material is presented in chronological order, and the dates shown in the headings are the dates of the documents or events. Remarks are checked against a tape recording, and any signed documents are checked against the original, to ensure accuracy. The appendices in each volume of the *Public Papers* are extensive and include listings of: a digest of the president's daily schedule and meetings and other items issued by the WHITE HOUSE PRESS SECRETARY; the president's nominations submitted to the Senate; a checklist of materials released by the Office of the Press Secretary that are not printed full-text in the book; and a table of proclamations, EXECUTIVE ORDERS, and other presidential documents released by the Office of the Press Secretary and published in the *Federal Register.* Each volume also includes a foreword signed by the president, several photographs chosen from White House Photo Office files, a subject and name index, and a document categories list. Between 1965 and 1976, only selected press releases from the *Weekly Compilation* were contained in the *Public Papers.* Beginning in 1977 with the administration of Jimmy CARTER, no editing has been done, and all press releases have been included in the *Public Papers* since that time.

Further reading: Edwards, George C., III, and Stephen J. Wayne. *Studying the Presidency.* Knoxville: University of Tennessee Press, 1983; Ragsdale, Lyn. *Vital Statistics on the Presidency: Washington to Clinton.* Washington, D.C.: CQ Press, 1996.

—Lori Cox-Han

Pullman Strike

The depression of 1893 hit the nation at the beginning of Grover CLEVELAND's second presidency. Many of the employees of the Pullman Sleeping Car Company lived in the model town of Pullman, outside of Chicago. George Pullman, in an attempt to secure his profits during the depression, slashed the wages of his employees. When a delegation of workers begged for an interview in May 1894, Pullman fired three of its members, prompting workers to strike. The striking workers were joined by the American Railway Union, led by Eugene DEBS. When Pullman refused to negotiate, union members boycotted Pullman, refusing to work on any train that carried a Pullman car. The boycott affected 27 states, halting most rail traffic west of Chicago. The strikers squared off against an alliance of management called the General Managers Association, which had formed a working alliance with Attorney General Richard Olney. A federal district court in Chicago issued an injunction against the union, prohibiting any striker from obstructing the mail or interstate commerce.

Cleveland determined that federal troops were necessary to protect government property and to ensure mail delivery. Relations with his own party were already strained due to the repeal of the Sherman Silver Purchase Act. Nevertheless, without consulting state and local officials, and against the vigorous objections of Illinois Governor John P. Altgeld, Cleveland dispatched federal troops to enforce the injunction. Violence erupted as mobs destroyed hundreds of rail cars. State militia and police also got involved, resulting in several deaths and many more wounded. Debs and 70 other union members were arrested, and the boycott was smashed.

Although Cleveland and the federal troops got the credit for ending the violence, Cleveland's actions angered many Democrats, who looked with suspicion on any domestic exercise of centralized power. Cleveland had not relied on statutory authority for his actions, since Congress had not authorized use of military force. Instead, he relied on constitutional authority. The Supreme Court ratified the constitutionality of his actions in 1895 when it argued in *In re Debs* that the president enjoys general powers under Article II of the Constitution to take any measures necessary to protect the peace of the United States. The decision represented an expansion of the president's police powers and an expanded view of presidential authority.

Cleveland's actions were very damaging politically. He incurred the hatred of both labor and many members of his own party. Altgeld determined to drive Cleveland and his allies from power. At a Jefferson's birthday celebration of party leaders, Altgeld said, "To laud Clevelandism on Jefferson's Birthday is to sing a *Te Deum* in honor of Judas Iscariot on a Christmas morning." During the 1894 midterm election, South Carolina Governor Ben Tillman campaigned against his own president, saying, "When Judas betrayed Christ, his heart was not blacker than this scoundrel, Cleveland, in deceiving the Democracy. He is an old bag of beef, and I am going to Washington with a pitchfork and prod him in his old fat ribs." The DEMOCRATIC PARTY resoundingly repudiated Cleveland in 1896.

Further reading: Morgan, H. Wayne. *From Hayes to McKinley: National Party Politics, 1877–1896.* Syracuse, N.Y.: Syracuse University Press, 1969; Welch, Richard E., Jr. *The Presidencies of Grover Cleveland.* Lawrence: University Press of Kansas, 1988.

—David A. Crockett

qualifications of the president and vice president

The question of qualifications for the president and VICE PRESIDENT appeared late at the constitutional convention. The issue of qualifications is tied to the selection process, and the framers saw no need to establish qualifications for an office if qualifications already existed for those whose task was to choose that position. For most of the convention the delegates assumed that other "qualified" officials, most likely Congress, would choose the president. Thus, the issue of qualifications did not arise until delegates rejected congressional selection and invented the ELECTORAL COLLEGE. There was little debate at the convention about the specific qualifications, but it is possible to ascertain some explanation for them from later defenses of the Constitution.

The guiding principle behind the qualifications is that the greater the powers of the office, the higher the qualifications. Thus, for the presidency the framers wanted someone who was "preeminent for ability and virtue," and who had a "continental reputation." Two assumptions lay behind the age requirement of 35 years. First, the framers believed that age brings maturity and wisdom. Although the passage applies to senators, James MADISON's argument concerning age in *Federalist No. 62* makes the point. There he argues that high political positions require "greater extent of information and stability of character," and that such positions require that the individual "should have reached a period of life most likely to supply these advantages." Second, the framers believed that greater age would allow electors to evaluate an individual's record, abilities, and reputation. They believed that an individual's true characteristics would manifest themselves by this age. John JAY, in *Federalist No. 64,* argues that "by excluding men under thirty-five . . . it confines the electors to men of whom the people have had time to form a judgment, and with respect to whom they will not be liable to be deceived by those brilliant appearances of genius and patriotism which, like transient meteors, sometimes mislead as well as dazzle." Thus, the age requirement works in conjunction with the chan-

neling function of the selection system, for people of great ability and ambition who want the job will spend their energy establishing a distinguished record of service to the state, taking risks for long-term glory and honor.

The citizenship and residency requirements had more immediate purposes. The requirement that the president be a natural-born citizen prevented any invitation of a foreign monarch to rule the United States, a persistent rumor and not an uncommon practice at the time. The requirement that the president be 14 years a resident of the United States barred British sympathizers who fled to England during the American Revolution. It also barred popular military leaders, such as Baron Frederick Von Steuben of Prussia, from eligibility. An alternative requirement that the president be 21 years a resident would have excluded three of the delegates at the convention.

Prior to the Twelfth Amendment the qualifications for vice president were identical to those for the president, since the vice president was the runner-up in the election. When the TWELFTH AMENDMENT eliminated the dual-vote mechanism and created a ticket, it also explicitly stated that "no person constitutionally ineligible to the office of President shall be eligible to that of vice-president of the United States." The TWENTY-SECOND AMENDMENT adds a further qualification to both jobs by disqualifying anyone who has already been elected twice, or who has been elected once after serving more than half of another president's term.

There remain some ambiguities and peculiarities with respect to the citizenship and residency requirements. For example, the citizenship rule may bar some officers from their place in the line of succession. In recent years this has included secretaries of State Henry KISSINGER and Madeleine Albright. Some have questioned whether the citizenship requirement disqualifies someone born of American parents on foreign soil. Finally, some have asked whether the residency rule requires 14 consecutive years in the United States prior to an election—an interpretation that would have barred Herbert HOOVER and Dwight

EISENHOWER from serving. Senator Thomas Eagleton of Missouri sought to pass a constitutional amendment in 1983 repealing the citizenship and residency qualifications in favor of an 11-year citizenship requirement.

Further reading: Ceaser, James W. *Presidential Selection: Theory and Development.* Princeton: Princeton University Press, 1979; Hamilton, Alexander, James Madison, and John Jay. *The Federalist Papers, Nos. 62 and 64.* New York: Signet Classic, 1961; Milkis, Sidney M., and Michael Nelson. *The American Presidency: Origins and Development, 1776–1998,* 3d ed. Washington, D.C.: CQ Press, 1999.

—David A. Crockett

Quayle, J. Danforth (1947–) *vice president*

After serving as Republican Senator from Indiana, Quayle became VICE PRESIDENT under President George H. W. BUSH from 1989 to 1993. Quayle's selection was a surprise, as this little-known politician had been an undistinguished senator for less than a decade. Since he was youthful and telegenic, it was hoped that Quayle would inject a youthful vigor into the campaign, as well as shore up Bush's support among the conservative wing of the party.

As vice president, Quayle faced a good deal of criticism as an intellectual lightweight who could not spell "potato" (he put an 'e' on the end of the word). He became—somewhat unfairly—a national joke as late-night television hosts used Quayle as the butt of endless jokes and jabs.

President Bush kept Quayle away from the administration's power core, but he did give Quayle responsibility as head of the President's Council on Competitiveness, where Quayle promoted deregulation of business.

R

rating the president

A popular U.S. pastime is to rank and rate. More than a mere parlor game, the rating of presidents demonstrates what our values are, and in a way, who we are. In 1948 Harvard historian Arthur Schlesinger polled 48 historians, asking them to place presidents into categories. The presidents rated as "great" were LINCOLN, WASHINGTON, Franklin ROOSEVELT, WILSON, JEFFERSON, and JACKSON. In 1962 Schlesinger asked more historians to weigh in, with similar results except for Jackson, who dropped to the "near great" category.

In 1993 historians Robert K. Murray and Tim H. Blessing distributed a 19-page, 383-question list to 846 historians. The results were similar to Schlesinger's results. Updated versions of their poll continued to be consistent with previous findings.

Reagan, Ronald (1911–) fortieth U.S. president

Ronald Reagan, the 40th president of the United States, was born on February 6, 1911, in Tampico, Illinois, to parents John Edward "Jack" Reagan and Nelle Wilson Reagan. His father, an itinerant shoe salesman, moved the family to Chicago, Galesburg, Monmouth, and finally Dixon, Illinois, where the Reagan family resided until Ronald won success as an actor in Hollywood. Though Jack was an alcoholic, Nelle provided a relatively stable environment for her sons (John Neil, the oldest, and Ronald), volunteering for work in the PTA, the Disciplines of Christ Church, and at local prisons. Reagan describes this period as the happiest time of his life. By the time of his senior year at Northside High School in Dixon, he was tall, handsome, athletic, and popular, and was serving as president of the student body. At Eureka College (also in Illinois), where he majored in economics and sociology, he was an average student. Reagan played the lead in several plays and was on the debate team and the student newspaper, where he developed skills that would serve him well in his future careers.

Graduating in the midst of the GREAT DEPRESSION, Reagan was fortunate to find a job as a radio sportscaster in Davenport, Iowa. Taking descriptions of baseball games in Chicago off the telegraph wires, he did play-by-play descriptions as if he were on the spot, foreshadowing his later acting career. In 1937, with the help of an actress friend, he secured a screen test at Warner Brothers, was awarded a studio contract, and moved to Hollywood, where he made movies for more than 10 years. Although he

RATING THE U.S. PRESIDENTS: MURRAY AND BLESSING POLL

Great	Near-Great	Above-Average	Average	Below-Average	Failure
Abraham Lincoln	Theodore Roosevelt	John Adams	William McKinley	Zachary Taylor	Andrew Johnson
Franklin D. Roosevelt	Woodrow Wilson	Lyndon B. Johnson	William Taft	Ronald Reagan	James Buchanan
George Washington	Andrew Jackson	Dwight D. Eisenhower	Martin Van Buren	John Tyler	Richard Nixon
Thomas Jefferson	Harry S Truman	James K. Polk	Herbert Hoover	Millard Fillmore	Ulysses S. Grant
		John Kennedy	Rutherford B. Hayes	Calvin Coolidge	Warren G. Harding
		James Madison	Chester A. Arthur	Franklin Pierce	
		James Monroe	Gerald Ford		
		John Quincy Adams	Jimmy Carter		
		Grover Cleveland	Benjamin Harrison		

President Ronald Reagan *(Library of Congress)*

mostly starred in B films, his performance as a lead in *Kings Row* suggested that he might become a major motion picture star. During WORLD WAR II, Reagan served with the Army Air Force First Motion Picture Unit in Culver City, making training films for pilots. Due to bad eyesight he was barred from combat.

After the war, Reagan's efforts to build on the promise of his earlier career in films was thwarted by his decision to leave Warner Brothers, a decline in the studio system, and the rise of television. As president of the Screen Actors Guild from 1947 to 1952 (and again from 1959 to 1960) and later as spokesman for General Electric, he built an alternative career for himself, honing some increasingly conservative political views and developing the political and speaking skills that were to later propel him into the U.S. presidency. During this period he worked with studio heads dedicated to keeping communists out of the industry, served as a friendly witness to the House Un-American Activities Committee, and gave information to the FBI on the political views of some of his left-wing colleagues. His motivation, Reagan argued, was that he came face to face with communists as they worked to infiltrate the movie industry and overthrow democracy.

His preoccupation with politics at this time contributed to his divorce in 1949 from Jane Wyman (who had

become a major star, winning an Oscar for *Johnny Belinda* in 1948). Later, in March 1952, he married Nancy Davis, who would become a full partner in his subsequent political career. Reagan's children with Jane Wyman were Maureen and Michael. His children with Nancy Davis were Patti and Ronald Prescott.

By the early 1960s, Reagan's political transformation was complete. From a supporter of Franklin D. ROOSEVELT'S NEW DEAL, he came to oppose most social welfare programs as an abridgment of individual liberty and a violation of the principle of the free market. In 1963 he formally changed his political affiliation from Democrat to Republican. In 1964 he gave a nationally televised speech supporting Barry Goldwater's candidacy for president that marked him as a rising conservative voice in the party. Five years later Reagan was elected as the Republican governor of California for his first of two terms. His bids for president in 1968 and 1976 failed, but Reagan's close finish to Gerald FORD (just 60 votes short of receiving the 1976 Republican nomination) set him up as a major Republican candidate for 1980.

Running as a Washington outsider, Reagan struck a responsive chord with a public seeking reassurance and strong leadership following the turbulent WATERGATE and Vietnam years. He was aided by the runaway stagflation and the IRANIAN HOSTAGE CRISIS that had marked President Carter's last year in office. Reagan took approximately 51 percent of the popular vote, to Democrat Jimmy CARTER's 41 percent and independent John ANDERSON's 7 percent of the vote. Because Reagan won 489 electoral votes to Jimmy Carter's 49 and the Republicans gained control of the U.S. Senate, his election was perceived as a landslide.

As president, Reagan undertook a revolution designed to increase defense spending, cut back on big government, reduce taxes, and deregulate industry. This philosophy, called supply-side economics (named "trickle-down theory" in an earlier incarnation) was based on the premise that the marketplace created prosperity and that the less involved the government was in the lives of individuals and businesses, the more prosperous the nation would be. Support for his first budget was enhanced by the charm and bravery he showed after a would-be assassin, a mentally ill drifter, nearly felled him with a bullet to his chest on March 30, 1981. By 1983 the economy did respond with lower unemployment and increased productivity. Other factors—the tight money policies of the Federal Reserve Board and the drop in world oil prices and a short-lived recession—contributed to the drop in the inflation rate (from 13 percent when Reagan took office to a 4 to 5 percent range in his second term).

The Reagan policies, however, hid certain costs. Decreased federal spending on the rate of growth in social programs mainly shifted the burden for the programs to individual states. Reagan's refusal to raise taxes or to scale back his ambitious defense spending produced a budget deficit that tripled the overall national debt by the time he left office. The U.S. trade deficits quadrupled, turning the United States from the greatest creditor nation into a debtor nation. The gap between the rich and the poor also increased, as did the number of children living in poverty.

In his foreign policies Reagan sought to roll back Soviet gains through an ambitious military modernization program that included funding of programs such as the MX missile and B-1 bomber. For him, the world was divided into two camps, good versus evil, with only two possible outcomes— winning or losing. A critic of ARMS CONTROL efforts such as SALT I and II, Reagan argued that arms control had weakened the American military position in relation to the Soviet Union. Furthermore, he countered the prevailing strategic nuclear doctrine MAD (Mutually Assured Destruction) with the STRATEGIC DEFENSE INITIATIVE (SDI). Ignoring questions about the feasibility of the SDI program, Reagan could move ahead on a military buildup to counter an expansionistic Soviet Union, assured that a defense against Soviet retaliation could be built for the American people.

As a part of this anticommunist effort, the administration undertook steps to roll back Soviet and Cuban influence in Central America. The administration funded and trained contra fighters from a base in Honduras to counter the Sandinista takeover in Nicaragua. A U.S. invasion of Grenada in late October 1983 led to the overthrow of a pro-Cuban Marxist regime, and also muted criticism over Reagan's Lebanese policies that might otherwise have been politically devastating. (A few days earlier, a truck packed with explosives killed 230 Americans at the Marine headquarters at the Beirut airport. This peacekeeping mission had been transformed by mission creep into a force supporting an unpopular Christian minority government. In February 1984 Ronald Reagan redeployed the Marines to offshore vessels.)

During Reagan's second term, domestic political constraints placed limits on the president's foreign policy choices. The Democrat-led Congress worked to halt his military modernization programs (including the MX and B-1). Congressional leaders who opposed the administration's repudiation of the un-ratified SALT II Treaty threatened to cut off all funding for SDI. They succeeded in passing the BOLAND AMENDMENT that outlawed the use of public funds to support Nicaraguan contra military operations.

Attempts to get around some of these constraints led to Reagan's biggest political crisis. In late 1986 news leaked out that the NATIONAL SECURITY COUNCIL staff had shipped arms to Iran in exchange for hostages. The administration then admitted that profits from those sales had been used to fund the contras fighting the Sandinistas. Not only did the exercise counter the Boland Amendment, it ran contrary to the administration's own policy not to deal with terrorists. The subsequent scandal led to the establishment of a presidential commission to inquire into the matter, congressional hearings, and the appointment of an independent prosecutor. Though Reagan denied any knowledge of the arms-for-hostages deals, the presidential commission indirectly critiqued him for his laid-back, delegating management style that made this whole operation possible.

The excesses of the IRAN-CONTRA affair illustrated the political costs that came with Reagan's hands-off leadership style. Reagan, who saw himself as chairman of the board to a CABINET that served as his board of directors, remained disengaged from the daily operations of the White House. This situation led to high levels of infighting and turmoil among central advisers and created conditions that allowed the excesses of Iran-contra to flourish unchecked.

The result of the Iran-contra affair was a plunge in Reagan's approval ratings from 65 percent in 1986 to 52 percent in January 1987. Thirty-three percent of those polled said that they did not believe he was telling the truth about Iran and the hostage deal. However, what might have been a political slide was reversed by Reagan's decision to move forward in the Intermediate Nuclear Forces (INF) negotiations with Soviet leader Mikhail Gorbachev. The INF Treaty, signed in their third meeting in 1987 and eliminating a whole class of intermediate-range nuclear weapons, was the major foreign policy highlight of the Reagan presidency. In his postpresidential autobiography, *An American Life,* Ronald Reagan notes the irony that the man who had spent much of his life warning about the threat of communism and calling the Soviet Union an "evil empire," was also the president who extended his "hand with warmth and a smile to its highest leader." Reagan argued that he had not changed, but that the Soviets had. Yet President Reagan, unlike some of his advisers, saw that Mikhail Gorbachev's offer of an arms deal was very close to his own original demands on the Soviets. There was now an opportunity to transform the U.S.-Soviet competition into a more trusting relationship.

When Reagan left office in January 1989, spending on defense had increased, relations with the USSR were better (his proponents would argue that his defense buildup had forced Gorbachev to make the concessions he did), and this cheerful, sunny-but-tough leader had made Americans feel good about themselves. The size of the U.S. government, however, had not been drastically cut, though there had been a shift in service from welfare to defense sectors, and the size of the national debt was at an all-time high. Overall, Reagan's critics argued that the prosperity of the 1980s came at the expense of future generations. Still, Ronald Reagan left office with the highest rating of any president since Franklin Roosevelt, and two-thirds of those polled approved of his overall performance in office. Ronald Reagan, in short, was a man whose tough talk and antigovernment stances were tempered by a charm and leadership style that resonated with the American public in the 1980s.

Further reading: Cannon, Lou. *President Reagan: The Role of a Lifetime.* New York: Putnam, 1982; ———. *The Role of a Lifetime.* New York: Simon and Schuster, 1991; Meese, Edwin, III. *With Reagan: The Inside Story.* Washington, D.C.: Regnery Gateway, 1992; Schultz, George. *Turmoil and Triumph: My Years as Secretary of State.* New York: Charles Scribner's Sons, 1993; Wills, Garry. *Reagan's America: Innocents at Home.* Garden City, N.Y.: Doubleday, 1987.

—Jean Garrison and Betty Glad

Reagan v. Wald, 468 U.S. 222 (1984)

In 1963, via the Trading with the Enemy Act (TWEA), the United States declared an embargo on Cuba. This act authorized the president to impose trade and travel restrictions. In 1977 President CARTER eased the travel ban to Cuba, but in 1982 President REAGAN reimposed these restrictions.

In 1977 Congress amended TWEA to restrict the president to imposing restrictions only in times of war or emergency. The following year Congress amended the Passport Act of 1926 to further limit a president's ability to impose travel restrictions. U.S. citizens, wishing to travel to Cuba, brought suit against President Reagan, challenging his power to reimpose travel restrictions absent war or emergency. While an appeals court struck down the travel ban, the Supreme Court, in a 5-4 vote, upheld the ban, giving the president wide latitude in this area and embracing as expansive view of the president's FOREIGN AFFAIRS powers.

recess appointment

Anticipating that there would be long periods in which the Congress would not be in session, Article II, Section 2, of the Constitution grants the president "Power to fill up all vacancies that may happen during the Recess of the Senate, by granting Commissions which shall expire at the end of their next session."

Thus, in certain circumstances, presidents can appoint people to government posts that require Senate confirmation without such confirmation. Sometimes used to circumvent the normal confirmation process (especially for controversial nominees), this power has on occasion been quite problematic.

Ronald REAGAN used this process to appoint a revolving-door list of nominees to the Legal Services Corporation (LSC). Reagan opposed the LSC's mission (providing legal assistance to the poor in civil cases), and rather than have his nominees to the LSC board of directors face this congressional appointment process, he would fill posts temporarily with recess appointments.

While recess appointments to the bench have been controversial, the courts, in *United States v. Alloco* (1962) and *United States v. Woodley* (1983), have determined that a president can make recess appointments to fill openings.

recognition power

This is the power to grant or deny other governments' legitimacy as sovereign nations. Once recognition is granted, official legal and diplomatic relations between the countries can commence. Recognition may apply to a new nation as well as a new government in an existing nation. This power is evidently granted solely to the president of the United States in the following passage of the Constitution, Article II, Section 3: "he shall receive Ambassadors and other public ministers." The power of recognition today is accepted by most as a uniquely executive function; however, at the time of the Founding and thereafter, there was disagreement on the scope of the power.

At the time of the Founding, the settled understanding of recognition was that it was more a ceremonial duty than a discretionary action. Governments had a right to send ambassadors; the only issues to decide, simple ones, were whether the official's credentials were in order and whether the government was the actual controlling authority in the country. Consistent with this perspective, the Constitution lists the power to receive ambassadors in Section 3 of Article II, while the powers to make treaties and appoint ambassadors, presumably the major foreign policy powers short of war-making, are listed in Section 2 of Article II. Alexander HAMILTON in *Federalist No. 69* argued that the receiving of ambassadors is "more a matter of dignity than authority. It is a circumstance which will be without consequence in the administration of government." It would merely be easier, Hamilton continued, for the president to receive ambassadors than to convene the Congress for the purpose. The reception of ambassadors would be "ceremonial," foreign policy decisions being made by the president with collaboration of the Senate only in treaties and nominations of foreign ministers. The issue would turn out to be much more complicated.

Almost immediately the power to receive ambassadors became controversial in the wake of the French Revolution. WASHINGTON agreed to receive French ambassador Edmund Genet, a representative of the new republican regime of France, although some advisers suggested refusing to receive Genet, thus illustrating that recognition was a more complex affair than Hamilton had indicated in the *Federalist*. Washington in 1793 also issued a proclamation, now referred to as the NEUTRALITY PROCLAMATION, which implied that the United States was not obligated, as a 1778 treaty with France held, to aid France in its current war with England. Hamilton, writing under the pseudonym "Pacificus," publicly defended the president's right to issue the proclamation and also established a more full-bodied notion of the recognition power, now claiming that the power entailed a unilateral presidential right to decide the United States's obligations to foreign countries. James MADISON responded under the pseudonym "Helvidius" that the Constitution gives no such exclusive power to the president. Although it might be necessary, Madison argued, to refuse to recognize a government because of its despotism, this question could not be left solely to the executive and was "certainly not to be brought by any torture of the words, within the right to receive ambassadors."

Despite Madison's and others' protestations, and notwithstanding the Senate's role in approving ambassadorial nominations and treaties, over time the recognition power has come to be accepted as firmly within the ambit of presidential powers. However, even as late as 1833, the renowned Justice Story would offer that Congress might, at least theoretically, challenge a president's recognition of a government or even themselves recognize a government or nation the president had refused. These clashes, though, have largely remained theoretical.

The power of recognition carries with its considerable responsibility, as presidential decisions on recognition can have important foreign policy implications. For instance, a decision may significantly affect the internal politics of a nation-state (and thus the larger world) or a decision may bring forth praise or opprobrium for the president and the United States in the eyes of the international community. Presidents may choose to exercise the power of recognition positively or negatively and also in a qualified sense. In the most common application, presidents use the power to acknowledge the sovereignty and legitimacy of a particular government and thereby accord the nation legal and diplomatic status. Recently, in 1995, for example, President William CLINTON recognized the government of Vietnam and thereby established the legitimacy of diplomatic and trade relations between the two countries. In the negative sense, the president can refuse to recognize a government, thereby denying it of full diplomatic and legal relations with the United States. Woodrow WILSON famously exercised this right in 1913 when he refused recognition of the Huerta government in Mexico. Importantly, Wilson justified his actions by arguing that the United States may refuse to grant recognition to governments because of their despotic ways. Since the administration of Dwight EISENHOWER, similarly, presidents have refused recognition to Fidel Castro's Cuba. Presidents may also grant a limited type of recognition, like that adopted by Richard NIXON toward China in the 1970s. China would be granted full recognition by the CARTER administration later in 1979.

Congress has at times attempted to assert a role in the process of recognition. For instance, in its authorization of military action against Spain in 1898, the U.S. Congress declared the Cuban insurgents the legitimate sovereigns of Cuba. Nevertheless, the decision did not establish precedent and there was disagreement at the time over whether recognition per se was really Congress's aim in its statement. Congress can attempt to deny funds to embassies and ambassadors as well, but this avenue is generally not pursued. Finally, Congress may certainly express its opinions on recognition, as Speaker Newt Gingrich did supporting recognition of Taiwan in the 1990s, but these views have no binding effect on the nation's policy or the president's possible course of action.

Further reading: Adler, David Gray. "The President's Recognition Power." In *The Constitution and the Conduct of American Foreign Policy,* edited by David Gray Adler and Larry N. George. Lawrence: University Press of Kansas, 1996; Corwin, Edward. *The President's Control of Foreign Relations.* 1917. Reprint. New York: Johnson Reprint Corp., 1970; Story, Joseph. *Commentaries on the Constitution of the United States.* Boston: Hilliard, Gray, and Company, 1833; Wirls, Stephen H., and Daniel C. Diller. "Chief Diplomat." In *Powers of the Presidency,* 2d ed. Washington, D.C.: CQ Press, 1997.

—Michael Korzi

reconciliation bills

Putting the federal budget together is a complex and contradictory task. High demands and limited resources make for competing interests struggling for their share of the economic pie. As a way to move this ungainly process ahead, the 1974 CONGRESSIONAL BUDGET AND IMPOUNDMENT CONTROL ACT established, among other things, a "reconciliation" process to further budget decision-making.

Reconciliation is a stage in the budget process where broad outlines of spending are "reconciled" with policy goals of the president and Congress, and, hopefully, brought into line with expected revenues. This reconciliation process was designed to give Congress a better way to facilitate budget decision making, but it has become a way for the president and Congress to resolve their budget disputes. In the 1980s Ronald REAGAN's OFFICE OF MANAGEMENT AND BUDGET used reconciliation as a key point in the budget battle to promote the president's spending goals. In 1985 Congress tightened the spending side of this process with the GRAMM-RUDMAN-HOLLINGS ACT. In 1990 the Omnibus Budget Enforcement Act further institutionalized the reconciliation process.

The president is required to sign all reconciliation bills. This encourages bargaining and agreement between the president and Congress over budget priorities.

Reconstruction

In the period following the CIVIL WAR, efforts to reconnect and reconstruct the South became so politicized that this led to the IMPEACHMENT of one president and the possibility of a corrupt bargain that decided a presidential election. Covering the years roughly from 1865 to 1877, Reconstruction was planned by President Abraham LINCOLN, but it was left to his successor, Andrew JOHNSON, to implement the program. Conflicts between Johnson and the Republican majority over Reconstruction policy led to the passage of the Civil Rights Act of 1866 and the Reconstruction Act of 1867. While President Johnson vetoed the Reconstruction Act, Congress was able to override the veto.

Johnson and the Congress got into battle after battle until the passage of the TENURE OF OFFICE ACT in 1867 led to a direct confrontation that ended in the impeachment, though not the conviction, of President Andrew Johnson.

Reconstruction ended in 1876 when a "deal" was brokered to give Rutherford B. HAYES the presidency in a disputed election, in exchange for removing federal troops from the South.

Reform Party of the USA

The Reform Party of the United States began as a political movement called United We Stand America (UWSA), led by Henry Ross Perot. In 1995, disappointed with the lackluster performance of the Republican-controlled House of Representatives and Senate, Ross Perot and many UWSA members announced that they would create the Reform Party. This new party was legally formed in each state, which meant that voters could change their voter registration to the Reform Party.

In the 1996 presidential election, the leader of the Reform Party, Ross Perot, selected economist Dr. Pat Choate as his vice-presidential running mate. Even though the Perot/Choate ticket received $29.5 million in federal matching funds and had agreed to spending limits, they were not invited to participate in the televised presidential DEBATES. Their campaign sued the Presidential Debate Commission but in the end their attempt to be included in the debate was unsuccessful. In the election Ross Perot's Reform Party received 9 percent of the popular vote, which qualified it for official party status. In the fall of 1997 the National Reform Party was officially formed at a convention in Kansas City.

One of the star Reform Party candidates was former professional wrestler Jesse Ventura. Although he was expected to come in third place in the 1998 gubernatorial election in Minnesota, he ended up winning with the support of more than 61 percent of the registered voters. Ventura was the first Reform Party candidate elected to high office at the state or federal level, but he later renounced his association with the party when Patrick J. Buchanan, the conservative commentator and columnist who was twice a candidate for the Republican presidential nomination, became the Reform Party's presidential candidate in 2000.

From 1999 onward, internal disagreement, disorganization, and legal action over who should lead the party in the 2000 presidential election resulted in a splinter group leaving the official Reform Party and fielding their own presidential candidate. However, a federal judge ruled that the $13 million in federal election matching funds be given to the original Reform Party, which eventually fielded Pat Buchanan as its presidential candidate, with Ezola B. Foster as his vice-presidential running mate. Neither were included in the respective presidential and vice-presidential debates.

The Reform Party received less than 1 percent of the vote in the 2000 presidential election. While the Reform Party was unsuccessful at the ballot box, it did raise the profile and promote discussion of particular campaign issues, such as the North American Free Trade Agreement (NAFTA), CAMPAIGN FINANCE reform, and term limits for politicians. For students of American politics, the Reform Party also raised institutional questions, such as the role of third parties in the modern electoral process and the role of a charismatic leader in third party development.

Further reading: Buchanan, Patrick J. *A Republic, Not an Empire.* Washington, D.C.: Regnery Pub., 1999; Perot, Ross. *United We Stand.* New York: Hyperion, 1992.
—Stephanie Mullen

regulatory policy

The president is one of the key political actors in the development of the regulatory policies of the federal government. The government issues rules and regulations governing administration and policy matters, large and small. All proposed regulations must be published in the *Federal Register* and face potential challenges from the public, interest groups, or other officials.

A president can shape the direction of policies by the use of regulations, and this can have a dramatic impact. Since the time of the NEW DEAL, the number of federal regulations has risen, and a president may use his influence over these regulations to change the course of policy.

Reid v. Covert, 351 U.S. 487 (1956); 354 U.S. 1 (1957)

Could an EXECUTIVE ORDER or treaty limit the constitutional right of a U.S. citizen? In *Reid v. Covert* the Supreme Court ruled that a citizen's constitutional rights take precedence over EXECUTIVE AGREEMENTS.

Clarice Covert was a U.S. citizen living in England with her serviceman husband. She was accused of killing her husband and was tried and convicted by a court-martial. She challenged the legality of the court-martial, claiming she was denied her constitutional rights to a trial by jury. The government argued that a 1942 executive agreement with Great Britain granted American military officials jurisdiction in this case.

In 1956 the Supreme Court upheld the conviction, but in a rehearing a year later, the Court ruled that the executive agreement deprived Covert of her constitutional rights. The Constitution, thus, takes precedence over executive agreements.

religion

Perhaps surprisingly, religion has only rarely been a key issue in presidential elections or presidential politics. The Constitution bars the imposition of religious tests on federal officeholders, and while Protestants dominated the political scene, religion was not a controversial element of presidential politics. Candidates and presidents were expected to be Protestants, but beyond that, religious questions rarely intruded into the public debate surrounding the presidency.

It was not until 1928 that a major party nominated a non-Protestant, Catholic Alfred E. Smith, governor of New York, for president. While his Catholicism was an issue in the campaign, in all likelihood, Smith would have lost the election to Herbert HOOVER regardless of the issue of religion.

In 1960 the Democrats again nominated a Catholic, John KENNEDY, and in a very close election, Kennedy won the White House. Since that time, the religion of candidates has not been a wedge issue. All nominees have been from Christian denominations and there seems to be very little religious bigotry remaining among Christian denominations.

Religion only occasionally plays a role in presidential politics as such issues as abortion or capital punishment raise important issues. But generally, issues of importance are not translated primarily into religious issues in the United States. Even divorce (Ronald REAGAN is the only divorced president in history) is no longer an issue in presidential politics.

With the rise of the fundamentalist right in American presidential politics, there is increased pressure on candidates to publicly discuss their religious convictions and how their policies are influenced by such beliefs. Beginning with Jimmy CARTER, who openly discussed his Christian beliefs, and later with Ronald Reagan, who often made a public demonstration of his Christianity, presidential candidates and presidents have been more and more likely to "talk religion." George W. BUSH actively courted Christian fun-

damentalist groups, and part of his "compassionate conservatism" admittedly comes from his religious faith. His effort to replace social welfare as we know it with "faith-based initiatives," which allowed for religious groups to receive federal funds for working in social welfare activities, is just one indication of how religion guides the Bush presidency.

Further reading: Hutcheson, Richard G., Jr. *God in the White House: How Religion Has Changed the Modern Presidency.* New York: Macmillan, 1988; Stokes, Anson Phelps. *Church and State in the United States,* 3 vols. New York: Harper, 1950.

removal power

The Constitution is silent on who shall have the power to remove EXECUTIVE BRANCH officials from their posts. In *Federalist No. 77,* Alexander HAMILTON wrote that as the Senate had the ADVICE AND CONSENT power, they should also have removal power. James MADISON argued for sole presidential authority in removing executive branch officers.

Over the years, the removal power has been a source of conflict and controversy. In 1867 the removal power was the source of a conflict that led to the IMPEACHMENT of Andrew Johnson, when the Congress argued that the president had violated the TENURE OF OFFICE ACT of 1867 by firing his secretary of War.

Subsequently the Supreme Court has, for the most part, sided with the presidency in removal cases. In cases such as *Shurtleff v. United States* (1903), *Wallace v. United States* (1922), and most authoritatively in *MYERS v. UNITED STATES* (1926), the Court has granted wide latitude to the president in removing executive branch officials.

Further reading: Corwin, Edward S. *The President's Removal Power under the Constitution.* New York: National Municipal League, 1927.

reorganization power

As the nation's CHIEF EXECUTIVE, the president is responsible for managing the EXECUTIVE BRANCH of government. From time to time, presidents propose measures to reorganize the executive branch. Congress will sometimes delegate to the president the authority to implement reorganization plans. Historically, Congress has been wary of presidential efforts to reorganize the federal branch of government, fearing that the president might encroach on the Congress's power, but from time to time, events propel action, as was the case with the creation of the OFFICE OF HOMELAND SECURITY, later DEPARTMENT OF HOMELAND SECURITY. In the wake of the SEPTEMBER 11, 2001, ATTACKS, the need for some agency to coordinate homeland security policy became obvious. After some haggling back and forth, President George W. BUSH finally called for the creation of a CABINET department to deal with the issue. Congress approved of the creation of a new superagency that consolidated a variety of existing agencies under one institutional umbrella.

Republican Party

The Republican Party, sometimes called the GOP for "Grand Old Party," is one of the two major parties in American politics and government. It was established in 1854. The location of its founding, either Ripon, Wisconsin, or Jackson, Michigan, is still a matter of historical dispute. Many of the first Republicans were previously members of the Free Soil Party, the Whig Party, and the Know-Nothing Party. The disintegration of the Whig and Know-Nothing parties had been accelerated by intra-party conflicts over slavery, but the Free Soil Party had been established in 1848 for the purpose of opposing the extension of slavery into new territories. Although the Free Soil Party's anti-slavery position was moderate and based on economics rather than morality, this shared policy position gave the Free Soilers a degree of unity and common purpose that the other founders of the Republican Party generally lacked. Although the Free Soil Party formally ended in 1852, its opposition to the extension of slavery was adopted by the Republican Party in its platform for the 1860 presidential election. The Republicans won the election with Abraham LINCOLN as their nominee for president.

Lincoln, a former Whig congressman from Illinois, was actually a compromise candidate for the Republican presidential nomination and did not receive a majority of the popular votes in the 1860 presidential election. Shortly before his assassination in 1865, Lincoln emphasized the need for the federal government to reconcile with the defeated South after the CIVIL WAR. Most Republicans in Congress, though, opposed Lincoln's conciliatory policies, which Andrew JOHNSON, Lincoln's successor, tried but failed to continue, especially after his IMPEACHMENT and trial by Congress. Despite some differences among Republicans on how to treat the occupied South during Reconstruction and AFRICAN AMERICANS as former slaves, the Republican Party soon became the majority party in voter registration outside of the South, and especially in the Northeast and Midwest. This enabled the Republicans to win most presidential elections and to usually control Congress from 1860 until 1932.

During this time period, the Republican Party found a broad, diverse coalition outside of the South. African Americans overwhelmingly identified with the Republican Party because of its association with Abraham Lincoln and the Democratic Party's domination by pro-segregation Southern whites. Most native-born white Protestants in the Northeast and Midwest, regardless of socioeconomic or urban-rural differences, were Republicans. Several big city Republican machines, such as those of Philadelphia and Chicago, had loyal followings among Italians, Jews, and other non-Irish ethnic groups. In terms of intra-party ideological and policy differences, the Republican Party during this period consisted of two major wings or factions: progressive and conservative, the latter sometimes referred to as "Old Guard." Progressive Republicans emphasized such issues as the advancement of civil rights for African Americans, the conservation of forests and other national resources, women's suffrage and the prohibition of alcohol, reforming big business, and ending corrupt machine politics in both major parties. The conservative wing emphasized the protection and advancement of big business interests through high protective tariffs, the gold standard, a tight money supply, opposition to most business and labor reform legislation, and an American foreign policy that actively intervened on behalf of American economic interests abroad.

These differences between the two wings of the GOP were most evident and detrimental to party unity in the 1912 presidential election. As a former Republican president running as the Progressive Party's nominee, Theodore ROOSEVELT opposed the conservative Republican incumbent, William H. TAFT, who sought reelection. Although Roosevelt and Taft attracted a total of nearly 60 percent of the popular votes, the Democrats won both the presidential election and majorities in Congress.

Republican voter registration, however, still exceeded that of the DEMOCRATIC PARTY. Consequently, the Republicans won the 1920, 1924, and 1928 presidential elections by wide margins and controlled both houses of Congress from 1921 until 1931. Throughout the 1920s and early 1930s, the conservative, pro-big business Republicans dominated both these three presidencies and the Congress. After the beginning of the GREAT DEPRESSION, however, a significant minority of Republican voters, especially economically distressed farmers, voted for Franklin D. ROOSEVELT and, to a lesser extent, for Democratic congressional nominees in 1932. During his first term, Roosevelt's personal leadership skills and NEW DEAL policies helped to attract some previously Republican progressives, farmers, African Americans, and non-Irish Catholics and Jews into the Democratic Party as he gained their votes in his 1936 landslide reelection. The Democrats controlled the presidency for 20 consecutive years under Franklin D. Roosevelt and Harry S TRUMAN and both houses of Congress for 18 of those 20 years. With the Democrats also having a wide lead over Republicans in voter registration, the Democrats dominated both foreign and domestic policy making.

From the time of Roosevelt's reelection in 1936 until the 1980 election of Ronald REAGAN as a conservative Republican president, the Republicans were divided about how to challenge the Democratic Party in presidential elections. Progressive Republicans wanted to generally advocate and pursue the same policy goals as the Democrats while asserting greater efficiency and competence in achieving or managing such policies as civil rights, federal aid to education, and antipoverty programs. This approach, derided as "Me Tooism" or a "Dime Store New Deal" by conservative Republicans, was personified by such Republican presidential aspirants as Thomas Dewey and Nelson ROCKEFELLER. Conservative Republicans, such as Barry GOLDWATER and Ronald REAGAN, wanted to emphasize clear ideological and policy differences with the more liberal, non-Southern Democrats. This was especially true after the 1968 election bitterly divided the Democrats on COLD WAR foreign policy.

With party loyalty declining and ticket splitting increasing among American voters by the late 1960s, Republicans won all but one of the presidential elections from 1968 until 1992. Most voters seemed to prefer Republican presidential nominees on economic, foreign policy, and social issues, especially on crime and race, during this period. However, they failed to become the new majority party in voter identification and did not win control of Congress until 1994. Republicans also controlled the Senate from 1981 until 1987. During the 2000 presidential election, Republican presidential nominee George W. BUSH was faced with the challenge of retaining the loyalty of conservative Republican activists on divisive social issues such as abortion and gun control while appealing to more moderate Republican and independent voters.

Further reading: Larson, Arthur. *A Republican Looks at His Party.* New York: Harper, 1956; Rae, Nicol C. *The Decline and Fall of the Liberal Republicans.* New York: Oxford University Press, 1989.

—Sean J. Savage

resignation

Only one U.S. president has resigned from office: Richard M. NIXON. Two vice presidents, John C. CALHOUN (in 1832 over states rights disputes) and Spiro T. AGNEW (in 1974 when faced with criminal charges) have resigned their positions.

Article II, Section 1, of the Constitution says that when a president resigns, the office devolves on the vice president, and the TWENTY-FIFTH AMENDMENT says that if a president resigns the VICE PRESIDENT "shall become president." The procedure for a presidential resignation is that the president must sign a letter of resignation addressed to the secretary of State. The secretary of State informs the vice president that he or she is to assume the presidency.

President Richard M. Nixon, when faced with the certainty of IMPEACHMENT by the House and conviction in the Senate over the crime of WATERGATE, announced his res-

ignation on August 8, 1974, effective at noon the following day. At that time, Nixon's vice president, Gerald FORD, was sworn in as president, announcing "our long national nightmare is over."

retreats, presidential

Busy executives need "downtime," a place to relax, or a getaway location in which to work, away from the glare of cameras and the daily pressures of the normal workplace. In the early days of the republic, when the United States was a small coastal nation, most of the presidents had country estates, often their own homes, where they could go for rest and relaxation.

George WASHINGTON's MOUNT VERNON, JEFFERSON's MONTICELLO, and MADISON's Montpelier serve as examples of the use of a presidential estate as a retreat. In the modern period, Franklin ROOSEVELT had HYDE PARK in New York, KENNEDY had Hyannisport on Cape Cod, LBJ had his Texas ranch, NIXON had his San Clemente "western White House" in California, the Carters had their Plains, Georgia, home, REAGAN had a sprawling ranch north of Santa Barbara in California, George H. BUSH had a Kennebunkport, Maine, home, and his son, George W. BUSH has a ranch in Crawford, Texas. The Clintons did not have a home outside of Washington D.C. (they had lived for years in the Arkansas Governor's Mansion) until the end of his presidency, when they bought a home in New York.

The "official" presidential retreat, CAMP DAVID in rural Maryland in the Catocin Mountains, was acquired in 1939 by FDR. This 143-acre location was built by the CIVILIAN CONSERVATION CORPS and the WORKS PROGRESS ADMINISTRATION. It takes a half-hour helicopter ride to make the 70-mile trip from the White House to Camp David. The National Park Service maintains the grounds. FDR called it Shangri-la, after the mythical city of the James Hilton novel, *Lost Horizon.* Roosevelt used the retreat for relaxation and work, especially during WORLD WAR II, when Winston Churchill was a frequent guest.

During the EISENHOWER years, the president renamed the retreat "Camp David" after his father and his grandson. It was at Camp David that President Carter had one of his greatest successes, when he used the retreat for peace discussions between Egyptian president Anwar Sadat and Israeli prime minister Menachem Begin. The result was the CAMP DAVID ACCORDS.

rhetorical presidency, the

"The rhetorical presidency" is a term first coined in 1981 by James W. Ceaser, Glenn E. Thurow, Jeffrey Tulis, and Joseph M. Bessette and amplified in Tulis's 1987 book. According to these scholars, the rhetorical presidency marks a shift in the presidency from the "head of government" to "the leaders of the people." It is "based on words, not power," and engenders inflated expectations of the office and its occupant.

There are three elements that facilitated the development of the rhetorical presidency: a modern doctrine of presidential LEADERSHIP; the decline of the political parties, which brought with it changes in the processes of nominating presidential candidates and electing presidents; and the growth of the mass media. All of these factors have shifted influence away from political institutions and toward the individual person of the president. This shift is understood as antithetical to the Founders' conception of the office as well as being potentially antidemocratic and dangerous to the principles of republican government.

A number of scholars have contributed to the literature on the rhetorical presidency. In general they agree that the constitutional system as a whole has been weakened by presidential attempts to build a direct relationship between themselves and the electorate and that the institution has been eroded by presidential dependence upon the mass public rather than the political parties to both govern and maintain their status as national political leaders. This direct and dependent relationship with the American public is thought to have changed both the presidency and the entire political system. It is demarcated by an increase in the amount of presidential speech as well as the purpose and meaning of that speech. This increase is in turn considered indicative of an erosion of traditional means of governance, and a replacement of deliberative, policy-oriented speech with epideictic ceremonial address. Presidents once sought a deeply personalized relationship with the mass public as a tool of governance, a resource with which they could increase their leverage over the political system. They have subsequently been trapped by this relationship and must now spend increasing amounts of time tending to the electorate rather than managing the government.

The rhetorical presidency is thus a construct that enables an understanding of the presidency as an institution. Those who research in this area are interested in an alleged shift from the framers' conception of the office as a deliberative, largely administrative entity, toward a more publicly oriented institution. The rhetorical presidency, which in political science is generally understood as focusing on instrumental rather than constitutive consequences of rhetoric, is often associated with similar conceptions of the office, broadly known as the "public presidency." Specifically, this work is often grounded in Theodore J. Lowi's notion of the "plebiscitary president," and with Samuel Kernell's research on "going public," the presidential use of public persuasion in order to influence Congress on specific legislation. Scholars thus often conflate connected but not identical terms and use "the rhetorical presidency" to refer to the study of presidential communication generally, rather than to a specific set of arguments about the institutional consequences of changes in broad patterns of presidential communication.

The rhetorical presidency has been criticized in both its pure and its more popularized forms. These criticisms come from three important directions. First, quantitative scholars have examined the extent, purpose, and effectiveness of presidential strategies of public persuasion and have found that they apply only, in George C. Edwards III's felicitous phrase, "at the margins." That is, presidents do not avail themselves of this sort of persuasion all that often, and when they do, the strategies are not necessarily effective.

Second, institutionalists have increasingly begun to understand some of the institutional changes associated with the rhetorical presidency as part of the general growth in the executive's administrative apparatus. Thus, the rhetorical presidency is understood by some to be functionally the same as the institutionalized presidency.

Finally, scholars with a historical focus have challenged the idea that the elements focused upon by Ceaser, Thurow, Tulis, and Bessette are unique to the late 20th century. Much of this work investigates the persuasive strategies of 19th-century presidents and finds that presidents as persuaders have a good deal more in common than scholars of the rhetorical presidency assert.

These controversies point to the theoretical and empirical richness of this area of scholarly endeavor. Presidential communication continues to garner a great deal of well-deserved attention from historians, political scientists, and those in the field of speech communication. Current research focuses on the persuasive techniques of individual and/or sets of presidents, on both instrumental and constitutive consequences of presidential rhetoric, on historical conceptions of presidential persuasion, on the persuasive capacities of particular speeches and/or sets of speeches, on institutional requirements for and responses to the need for presidential rhetoric, on the influence of the mass media, and on the impact of presidential persuasion on Congress and on public opinion. The rhetorical presidency as a theoretical construct has generated a vibrant area of research, characterized more by its growing diversity than by its degree of substantive agreement on the exact nature, extent, and functioning of the role of communication and communicative strategies in the presidency and the EXECUTIVE BRANCH.

Further reading: Ceaser, James W., Glenn E. Thurow, Jeffrey Tulis, and Joseph M. Bessette. "The Rise of the Rhetorical Presidency." *Presidential Studies Quarterly* 11 (1981): 158–171; Kernell, Samuel. *Going Public: New Strategies of Presidential Leadership,* 2d ed. Washington, D.C.: CQ Press, 1993; Lowi, Theodore J. *The Personal President: Power Invested, Promise Unfulfilled.* Ithaca, N.Y.: Cornell

University Press, 1985; Stuckey, Mary E., and Frederick J. Antczak. "The Rhetorical Presidency: Deepening Vision, Widening Exchange." In *Communication Yearbook 21,* edited by Michael E. Roloff, 405–442. Thousand Oaks, Calif.: Sage, 1998; Tulis, Jeffrey. *The Rhetorical Presidency.* Princeton, N.J.: Princeton University Press, 1987.

—Mary E. Stuckey

Richardson, James D. (1843–1914) *U.S. representative*

James D. Richardson represented his district in Tennessee in the U.S. House of Representatives for 10 Congresses (1885–1905) and served as minority leader during the 57th Congress. He left his mark on presidential studies, however, by compiling and publishing the *Messages and Papers of the Presidents.* Congress authorized Richardson to undertake this endeavor in 1894. The task of compiling the papers alone took four years, three years longer than Richardson originally anticipated; he admitted that he had no idea of the difficulty he would incur while tracking down every presidential communication—PROCLAMATIONS, addresses, messages and communications to Congress, and EXECUTIVE ORDERS—since the ratification of the Constitution. The result of Richardson's diligence is a 10-volume comprehensive collection of presidential statements from George WASHINGTON through Benjamin HARRISON, later supplemented to include the messages of William MCKINLEY, Theodore ROOSEVELT, and William Howard TAFT. As Richardson states in his *Prefatory Note* to the collection, the "messages of the several Presidents of the United States—annual, veto, and special—are among the most interesting, instructive and valuable contributions to the public literature of our Republic." The papers are supplemented by an encyclopedic index, which Richardson hoped would allow readers to familiarize themselves with facts and events of American political history. The index also helped correct what Richardson realized was a shortcoming in his project after publishing the first two volumes. Richardson originally omitted communications with Congress that simply nominated people to office, transmitted treaties, or submitted a report from Executive Department heads without any presidential recommendation for action. Richardson decided that having an "accurate and exhaustive" collection of papers meant that these presidential communications should be included. Thus, in subsequent volumes, he included previously omitted entries, even though they were out of chronological order, and relied on the index to enable the reader to find them. Richardson, who fought in the Confederate army during the CIVIL WAR, complemented his collection on U.S. presidents by compiling and editing the messages, proclamations, and INAUGURAL ADDRESSES of Jefferson DAVIS, as well as important diplomatic correspondence of the Con-

federacy. Richardson, in his *Prefatory Notes* to the *Messages and Papers of the Presidents,* offered his view that the collection of papers from the Civil War era "should enkindle with the heart of every citizen of the American Republic, whether he fought on the one side or the other in that unparalleled struggle, or whether he has come upon the scene since its closing, a greater love of country, a greater devotion to the cause of true liberty, and an undying resolve that all the blessings of a free government and the fullest liberty of the individual should be perpetuated."

Further reading: Richardson, James D. *A Compilation of the Messages and Papers of the Presidents.* New York: Bureau of National Literature, 1911; *The Messages and Papers of Jefferson Davis and the Confederacy Including Diplomatic Correspondence, 1861–1865.* Edited by Allan Nevins. New York: Chelsea House-R. Hector, 1966.

—Victoria Farrar-Myers

Ridge, Tom (1945–) *secretary of homeland security, governor*

In an effort to combat terrorism after the SEPTEMBER 11, 2001, ATTACKS, President Bush appointed Tom RIDGE, former governor of Pennsylvania, head of the newly created OFFICE OF HOMELAND SECURITY (OHS). Ridge was sworn in on October 8, 2001. He was to develop and implement a comprehensive national strategy to protect the U.S. homeland against terrorist threats. While Ridge was given significant responsibilities, he was not granted a great deal of political authority to accomplish his task. To try and correct this problem President Bush, in June of 2002, recommended, and the Congress approved, the creation of a CABINET-level DEPARTMENT OF HOMELAND SECURITY, with Ridge as its first secretary.

Rockefeller, Nelson A. (1908–1979) *U.S. vice president*

Nelson A. Rockefeller was born on July 8, 1908, in Bar Harbor, Maine. After Rockefeller was graduated from Dartmouth College in 1930, he worked in his family's various business interests, including an oil company in Venezuela from 1935 to 1940. His experience in Venezuela made him more interested in public service, especially American foreign policy toward Latin America. President Franklin D. ROOSEVELT appointed Rockefeller, a Republican, Coordinator of Inter-American Affairs in 1940 and assistant secretary of state in 1944. Rockefeller later advised President Harry S TRUMAN on foreign economic aid.

By the time Dwight EISENHOWER was elected president in 1952, Rockefeller had become known as a liberal Republican who favored a bipartisan, internationalistic foreign policy. Eisenhower appointed Rockefeller under-secretary of health, education, and welfare in 1953 and special assistant to the president in 1954. Frustrated by Eisenhower's cautious policies, Rockefeller left the Eisenhower administration in 1955. Rockefeller's upset victory in New York's gubernatorial election of 1958 soon led to speculation that he would run for president in 1960.

Serving as governor of New York from 1959 until 1973, Rockefeller used his state policy efforts and record as the foundation for many of his domestic policy proposals in his brief, unsuccessful efforts to secure the Republican presidential nomination in 1960, 1964, and 1968. During his governorship, the New York state government significantly expanded the state's university system, social welfare programs, civil defense, and water pollution control policies. Rockefeller resigned as governor in 1973 in order to establish a policy study commission and served as VICE PRESIDENT under Gerald R. FORD from 1974 until 1977. He died of a heart attack on January 27, 1979.

Further reading: Desmond, James. *Nelson Rockefeller: A Political Biography.* New York: Macmillan, 1964; Persico, Joseph E. *The Imperial Rockefeller.* New York: Simon and Schuster, 1982.

—Sean J. Savage

Roosevelt, Anna Eleanor (1884–1962) *first lady, social reformer*

The daughter of Anna Hall and Elliott Roosevelt, Eleanor Roosevelt was born into a socially and politically distinguished family. Orphaned as a young girl, she had a childhood that was notable for its lack of close family ties. Distance characterized her marriage, as well. Her five children—Anna (born 1906), James (1907), Franklin (1909, who lived only a few months), Elliott (1910), Franklin (1914), and John (1916)—seemed closer to their paternal grandmother, Sara Delano Roosevelt, than to herself. Her 1918 discovery of the affair between her husband, Franklin, and Lucy Mercer predictably strained her marriage.

If her personal relationships were difficult, her social and political connections were resilient and formidable. From the earliest years of her marriage, she participated in the progressive network of women reformers that had its national center in New York City. During WORLD WAR I she was an active member of the Red Cross. Subsequently, she established stronger affiliations with the League of Women Voters, the Women's Trade Union League, and the Foreign Policy Association. During the 1920 presidential campaign, she consulted with Louis Howe and Stephen Early to refine her political and media skills.

When Franklin ROOSEVELT was paralyzed by polio in 1921, Eleanor Roosevelt became his surrogate in New York

First Lady Eleanor Roosevelt *(Library of Congress)*

and DEMOCRATIC PARTY politics. She gained recognition for her fund-raising, writing, and speaking abilities. By 1925 she was editing the *Women's Democratic News,* teaching at the Todhunter School in New York City, and was a partner in the Val-Kill furniture factory. When Franklin was elected governor of New York in 1928, however, she drastically curtailed her activism.

As first lady, though, she resumed her role as a liberal advocate. She encouraged women to become involved in politics, through speeches and publications. She lobbied on behalf of women's appointments and invited appointees to the White House and to her press conferences. Her HUMAN RIGHTS agenda included proposals to hire blacks in government jobs (including the White House), to pass a federal antilynching law, and to end racial discrimination in the armed forces, industry, and public housing. She was active in the NAACP and the National Urban League, and a strong supporter of Howard University. During WORLD WAR II, she argued that unions should retain their rights to collective bargaining and to strike, stressed the loyalty of Japanese-Americans, and opposed anti-Semitism. Her column, *My Day,* was syndicated and appeared in newspapers six days a week for almost 30 years—and yet she also published several books and innumerable articles. As first lady, she also delivered approximately 1,400 speeches, lectures, radio broadcasts, and short statements.

In 1945 she was appointed a U.S. delegate to the UNITED NATIONS. By 1947 she was offering to resign, because she so strongly disagreed with the TRUMAN administration's Palestinian policy. Continuing in office, she chaired the UN Commission that negotiated the Universal Declaration of Human Rights, adopted by the General Assembly in 1948. She was politically active throughout the 1950s, speaking against Senator Joseph MCCARTHY and working for presidential candidate Adlai STEVENSON. When she died in 1962, she was chairing the President's Commission on the Status of Women.

Further reading: Beasley, Maurine, ed. *The White House Press Conferences of Eleanor Roosevelt.* New York: Garland Publishing, 1983; Roosevelt, Eleanor. *The Autobiography of Eleanor Roosevelt.* New York: Harper, 1961.

—Mary Anne Borrelli

Roosevelt, Franklin D. (1882–1945) *thirty-second U.S. president*

Franklin Roosevelt presided over our nation as no other CHIEF EXECUTIVE of the 20th century. His confidence and optimism pervaded the government during its slow recovery from the GREAT DEPRESSION and through victory in Europe during WORLD WAR II. His faith in government and in the ability of the EXECUTIVE BRANCH to steer the nation through trying times set a standard that all other presidents of the century were judged against.

Franklin Roosevelt was born on January 30, 1882, in HYDE PARK, New York, at the home of his father, James Roosevelt, and his mother, Sara. Franklin's early education was overseen by private tutors. At 14, Franklin matriculated at Groton Academy, a private boarding school in Connecticut favored by wealthy Protestant families in the Northeast. Its founder, the Reverend Endicott Peabody, impressed upon his pupils their duty as "Christian gentlemen" to serve the less fortunate and to strive always to excel. At graduation, Franklin and his classmates gave their attention to their commencement speaker, Franklin's cousin, Theodore ROOSEVELT, then VICE PRESIDENT of the United States.

In 1900 Franklin Roosevelt and his recently widowed mother packed their bags and headed to Harvard College. At college, Franklin was an average student, though he distinguished himself on the school newspaper, the *Crimson.* Roosevelt was so interested in this outlet for his burgeoning gifts of persuasion, in fact, that he stayed at Harvard an extra year, taking graduate courses so that he could serve as editor in chief of the newspaper. Socially, Mrs. Roosevelt oversaw her son's introduction to Boston society from her new home in Boston, while back in Cambridge, the young Roosevelt joined the Fly Club after being rejected by the ultimate private society on Harvard's campus, Porcellian.

For a young man emerging from this privileged educational and social background, the law was a natural calling, and Franklin Roosevelt enrolled after Harvard in Columbia University's School of Law. When he passed the New York Bar examination, he dropped out of law school and took up practice as an attorney. In March of 1905, Franklin Roosevelt wed his fifth cousin (his parents had themselves been sixth cousins), (Anna) Eleanor ROOSEVELT. The Reverend Peabody officiated at the ceremony. The young couple settled into domestic life on the fashionable Upper East Side of Manhattan. When not working on cases, Franklin and his bride might be found at the family estate along the Hudson River, at Hyde Park.

Early Political Career

Franklin Roosevelt was saved from a life of easy wealth and the casual practice of law by a call to politics. In 1910 the leaders of the DEMOCRATIC PARTY in the Hudson River area sent an emissary to Hyde Park to recruit Franklin to run for a seat in the state house. When Franklin at first replied that he would have to consult with his mother, he received a brusque reply that led him immediately to cast off his hesitation and accept the offer of the party's support. When the incumbent House member learned who was to replace him on the ballot, however, he felt insulted and refused to give up his seat. Roosevelt, undeterred, managed to secure the party's backing instead for the open state senate seat in his district. With his famous name and natural charm, he won his first election and was reelected in 1912. In 1913, with the presidency temporarily in the hands of the Democratic Party, thanks in large part to Theodore Roosevelt's bid for the presidency in 1912 as an independent, Roosevelt was offered the position of assistant secretary of the Navy in the Woodrow WILSON administration.

In Washington, Roosevelt served with energy and distinction. President Wilson refused to consider Roosevelt's request for active duty during WORLD WAR I and the assistant secretary held his post until he gained the vice presidential nomination in the Democrats' futile effort to hold the EXECUTIVE BRANCH in the aftermath of an unpopular war. No one blamed the vice-presidential nominee for the defeat of the ticket in 1920, however, and the experience gained Roosevelt useful media exposure and nationwide contacts within the party.

A year later, Roosevelt, once again practicing law, was at the family's vacation home at Campobello Island, New Brunswick. After a strenuous day's activities, he came down with an illness that was diagnosed as poliomyelitis. From polio, Roosevelt lost almost total use of his lower body and would spend the rest of his life confined to a wheelchair.

President Franklin D. Roosevelt *(Library of Congress)*

Roosevelt's experience with a grave illness tested his strength in more ways than the merely physical. His mother wished for Franklin to go into semiretirement and live out his life as a well-cared-for semi-invalid. Before, what Mother had wanted, she had typically gotten. This time, however, Franklin rebelled. He had always sought to lead an active life and still had considerable unrealized political ambitions. Eleanor supported his efforts at recovery and urged him not to go into seclusion. As first lady, Eleanor replied once to an unkind question regarding whether her husband's illness "had affected his mind" with the insightful reply that she believed it had made him more compassionate toward those who suffered. Many historians and presidential analysts agree with Mrs. Roosevelt that in battling a serious, debilitating illness, Franklin matured considerably and gained the poise and equanimity that served him so well as president during two extended crises.

In 1928 Roosevelt entered the race for New York governor. In New York that year, while the Republican Herbert HOOVER won the state, so did the Democrat Franklin Roo-

sevelt. He won reelection in 1930. As governor of the Empire State, Roosevelt worked through the state legislature to secure tax relief for farmers, expand state highways, extend assistance to the unemployed, and defend workers' rights to unionize. Governor Roosevelt also brought down utility prices and punished corrupt local officials.

Roosevelt's largely successful term as governor of New York made him a front-runner for the presidency in 1932. Roosevelt entered the convention in that year with a majority of delegates, but under the rule the Democrats then used at their conventions, it took two-thirds to win the nomination. Roosevelt therefore made a deal with conservative Southerners in the party and accepted the vice-presidential candidacy of John Nance GARNER of Texas, in exchange for the nomination for president. Roosevelt broke with tradition and appeared personally before the convention to accept their nomination for the presidency.

After defeating the Republican incumbent, Herbert Hoover, in the general election, President-Elect Roosevelt earned the unfortunate distinction of being the only president-elect to be the target of an assassination attempt. Uninjured by the would-be assassin, Roosevelt responded coolly to an assault that left four others wounded and one dead.

Presidency

In March of 1933, when Roosevelt took office, the nation's industrial output was only half of what it had been just four years before. Fifteen million American workers were unemployed. Uncounted others had been removed from the official tally of the unemployed only because they had stopped looking for work. Roosevelt's response to the Great Depression was signaled by his INAUGURAL ADDRESS.

"So first of all let me assert," Roosevelt famously proclaimed, "my firm belief that the only thing we have to fear is fear itself." Roosevelt's programs were numerous and sometimes contradictory, but his optimism in the face of difficulty was something Americans learned they could count on during his lengthy presidency. To meet the demands of the present crisis, Roosevelt in his Inaugural went on to preach the superiority of spiritual over material values and to extol the virtues of discipline and presidential LEADERSHIP. "If we are to go forward," Roosevelt intoned, "we must move as a trained and loyal army willing to sacrifice for the good of a common discipline." The people of America, Roosevelt said, were "willing to submit [their] lives and property to such discipline because it makes possible a leadership which aims at a larger good." As for Congress's role in the days ahead, it must, Roosevelt plainly asserted, lead, follow, or get out of his way.

The numerous programs of the FIRST HUNDRED DAYS and the many hundreds of days of legislative action that followed through the 1930s never did lift the nation from depression. Innovations adopted in the name of economic relief left lasting legacies nonetheless. These legacies were deepened by the extraordinary length of the Roosevelt presidency, and by the fact that President Roosevelt, unlike any other president, led the nation through not just one, but two, epochal crises.

Franklin Roosevelt won four consecutive presidential elections, overturning the precedent established by George WASHINGTON, which informally limited presidents to two consecutive terms. In his first election, Roosevelt won 57.40 percent of the popular vote. His coalition was united primarily against the ineffectual presidency of incumbent Herbert Hoover. In 1936 Roosevelt fought aggressively in the campaign to sharpen the differences between his program and the Republicans' plans for "enslavement for the public." With regard to his enemies, Roosevelt said, "I welcome their hatred." In the beginning of his second term, Roosevelt stumbled politically. He overreached when he tried to pass through Congress a COURT PACKING plan that would have enabled the president to attain a pro-NEW DEAL majority on the Supreme Court by immediately increasing the Court's membership. The plan was eventually dropped. Roosevelt also overreached in his second term when he took the unusual step of intervening personally in Democratic congressional races in 1938. Roosevelt wanted to force conservatives out of the party and make the two-party system more ideologically coherent. What he discovered was that congressional elections are almost impossible to control from Washington, D.C., even for a highly popular president.

In 1940 Roosevelt's popular majority declined, but he still won close to 55 percent of the vote, with more than 60 percent of the nation's eligible voters turning out on Election Day. Through one full term and the start of another, after his 1944 election victory, "Dr. New Deal" was replaced by "Dr. Win the War," in Roosevelt's own terminology. In World War I, the United States had entered the conflict late, had failed to establish the terms of an enduring peace in Europe after the war, and had thereafter returned to an isolationist foreign policy. Under Roosevelt's deft statesmanship and political maneuvering, the United States entered World War II before its final battles were to be won; it established the conditions for a lasting peace between the major West European and Asian combatants; and the nation accepted continued responsibility as a world leader after the war was won.

In his three-plus terms, President Roosevelt presided over a number of complementary "revolutions" in American life and governance.

First was a revolution in the implicit social contract that binds the American people to their government. From the 1930s forward, the American people would look, under conservative as well as liberal presidents, to the national government for help in times of need. The system of SOCIAL SECURITY, established in the so-called Second New Deal of 1935, is the bedrock upon which has been built the modern American welfare state. In the modern welfare state, the great majority of Americans, not just the relatively small number of the nation's poor, are popularly considered to be "entitled" in retirement to monetary assistance from the federal government. When the nation's economy dips into recession, moreover, the president is now expected to lead the federal government in providing help to those hurt by the slump. As a consequence of Roosevelt's efforts on behalf of the public, and his masterful use of rhetoric to explain his actions, the term *liberalism* was redefined in America in the 1930s to mean the active use of government power to secure basic needs of the people.

Second, President Roosevelt oversaw a fantastic expansion of the presidency, from an office to an institution. Under Roosevelt, the White House staff became considerably more numerous and professional than before, and their jobs became offices that future presidents would also fill as a matter of routine. Numerous executive agencies and regulatory bodies were established under the Roosevelt presidency, and these too expanded the reach of the executive across the nation and throughout the government. The post-Roosevelt presidency, in addition, was a media-enhanced, nuclear institution. Roosevelt's Inaugural Address was one of the first to be broadcast nationally on radio. His success at speaking to the people in plain and familiar terms was famously maintained through 27 FIRESIDE CHATS delivered over radio. As for the nuclear aspect of modern presidential power, the ATOMIC BOMB was not ready for use until Harry TRUMAN assumed the presidency following Roosevelt's death, but it was the creation of the top-secret MANHATTAN PROJECT, started at the direction of President Roosevelt.

Third, President Roosevelt's leadership forged an enduring coalition within the Democratic Party. The "New Deal" Democratic Party brought together urban workers, including large numbers of immigrants and Catholics, with farmers and their dependents. Additionally, the New Deal Democratic Party was deeply tied to the expansion of organized labor. Southern whites were the remaining pillar of the New Deal Democracy. This coalition, like all others in a two-party system covering a vast territory such as the United States, possessed huge contradictions. Eventually, it would fall as the people of the nation forced its parties to address issues that cut across old party lines, namely, civil rights and the War in Vietnam. While it lasted, however, the New Deal Party was one of the more successful party "regimes" in U.S. electoral history.

Further reading: Burns, James McGregor. *Roosevelt: The Lion and the Fox.* New York: Harcourt, Brace, 1956;

Freidel, Frank. *Franklin D. Roosevelt: A Rendezvous with Destiny.* Boston: Little, Brown, 1990; Lowi, Theodore. *The Personal President: Power Invested, Promise Unfulfilled.* Ithaca, N.Y.: Cornell University Press, 1985; Schlesinger, Arthur M., Jr. *The Age of Roosevelt.* Boston: Houghton Mifflin, 1957.

—Thomas Langston

Roosevelt, Theodore (1858–1919) *twenty-sixth U.S. president*

A larger-than-life character, Theodore Roosevelt was one of the most significant presidents in U.S. history. Serving from 1901 to 1909, he was a man of robust appetites who loved politics, embraced power, and expanded the scope and size of the presidency.

Puffy face, droopy mustache, pince-nez eyeglasses with thick lenses, prominent teeth, and a high voice—Theodore Roosevelt (TR) helped transform the presidency and convert the office into a truly national leadership institution. It was in the Roosevelt era that the presidency began to resemble the institution with which we are familiar today.

TR was an activist who stamped his personality onto his age. The sheer force of his will compelled action. Roosevelt exerted policy leadership as a "conservative-progressive" à la Disraeli. He transformed the presidency into a more public office, using (some would say abusing) the BULLY PULPIT to elevate the RHETORICAL PRESIDENCY to new heights, and developing a more sophisticated relationship between the president and the press.

At the turn of the century, the presidency was a mere suggestion of what it was to become, and MCKINLEY did not fully exploit the opportunity to gain power afforded by the rise of the United States as a world power. TR would not let the opportunity slip through his hands. He loved power, relished in its exercise, and sought to dominate. He seized power. The result, he later boasted, was that "I did and caused to be done many things not previously done by the President and the heads of the departments. I did not usurp power, but I did greatly broaden the use of executive power. In other words, I acted for the public welfare, I acted for the common well-being of all our people, whenever and in whatever manner was necessary, unless prevented by direct constitutional or legislative prohibition." Under TR, the presidency became the center of the political universe. His gravitational pull, his flair for self-dramatization, allowed the president to direct the government and set the political agenda.

Louis Hartz called TR "America's only Nietzschean president." A contemporary of Roosevelt's said, "At every wedding, Theodore wants to be the bride. At every funeral he wants to be the corpse." "He is," said Henry James, "the very embodiment of noise." And muckraker Ida Tarbell wrote of TR, "I felt his clothes might not contain him, he was so steamed up, so ready to go, to attack anything, anywhere." Roosevelt's need to lead every parade compelled him to exert himself, even force himself, to center stage. He courted and cultivated public opinion; he was the president as national celebrity. Did any other president delight in the exercise of power as much as Teddy Roosevelt? Few presidents *needed* power as much as TR. Few *needed* to achieve greatness as much as TR, but conditions, as he recognized, were not ripe for greatness. "If there is not the great occasion," he noted, "you don't get *the* great statesman; if Lincoln had lived in times of peace no one would have known his name now." "If this country could be ruled by a benevolent czar," he wrote in 1897, "we would doubtless make a good many changes for the better."

TR had an obsession with masculinity bordering on the pathological. As Bruce Miroff writes, "He portrayed a world divided between the timid men of words, sitting in the stands and carping at their betters, and the heroic men of action, gladiators in the political arena." In a 1910 speech at the Sorbonne in Paris, Roosevelt said:

> It is not the critic who counts; not the man who points out how the strong man stumbles, or where the doer of deeds could have done them better. The credit belongs to the man who is actually in the arena, whose face is marred by dust and sweat and blood; who strives valiantly; who errs, and comes short again and again, because there is no effort without error and shortcoming; but who does actually strive to do the deeds.

He "reserved his greatest contempt for 'emasculated sentimentalists.'" TR believed in the strenuous life, enjoying gymnastics, riding, and swimming. He once said of his sons, "I would rather one of them should die, than have them grow up weaklings." In Roosevelt, masculinity merged with moral righteousness to form "an ego of heroic proportions."

TR was among a mere handful of presidents who greatly increased the authority and responsibility of the office. He may have built on the foundation of predecessors, but few presidents did as much as TR to fundamentally alter the presidency. He changed the office whereas others held it. He led where others presided.

The America of Roosevelt's era was a more urban, industrial nation; a nation ready to take its place on the world stage. In 1890 there were 63,000,000 Americans. By 1900 the U.S. population was more than 75,000,000. When TR left office, the number had risen to more than 90,000,000.

It was also an age of political change. The Progressive Movement was sweeping America, promoting activist government, presidential LEADERSHIP, more open political participation, and the control of corporate capitalism. Roosevelt fit perfectly in this new era.

Roosevelt had an expansionist view of presidential power, to say the least. He *personalized* the office, linking policy to personality. In his *Autobiography* (1913), TR described the theory that guided his behavior as president:

> My view was that every officer, and above all every executive officer in high position, was a steward of the people bound actively and affirmatively to do all he could for the people, and not to content himself with the negative merit of keeping his talents undamaged in a napkin. I declined to adopt the view that what was imperatively necessary for the Nation could not be done by the president unless he could find some specific authorization to do it. My belief was that it was not only his right but his duty to do anything that the needs of the Nation demanded unless such action was forbidden by the Constitution or by the laws.

In his first annual message to Congress, TR summed up his view of how American society had changed and how the role of government needed to change as well.

> When the Constitution was adopted, at the end of the eighteenth century, no human Wisdom could foretell the sweeping changes, alike in industrial and political conditions, which were to take place at the beginning of the twentieth century. At that time it was accepted as a matter of course that the several States were the proper authorities to regulate, so far as was then necessary, the comparatively insignificant and strictly localized corporate bodies of the day. The conditions are now wholly different and wholly different action is called for.

If the president was to be the "steward of the people," he was also to be the centerpiece of political action. Roosevelt not only changed the way the presidency was viewed but also changed the way it operated, establishing a very close and personal relationship between the president and the public. This connection may have had its roots with Andrew JACKSON, but it came into full bloom with TR. He helped turn the executive into a personal presidency and a people's presidency, using the bully pulpit to reach out to the people. Here, the RHETORICAL PRESIDENCY was born. And TR scoffed at his critics:

> While President I have *been* President, emphatically; I have used every ounce of power there was in the office and I have not cared a rap for the criticisms of those who spoke of my "usurpation of power"; for I knew that the talk was all nonsense and that there was no usurpation.

President Theodore Roosevelt *(Library of Congress)*

> I believe that the efficiency of this Government depends upon its possessing a strong central executive, and wherever I could establish a precedent for strength in the executive . . . I have felt not merely that my action was right in itself, but that I was establishing a precedent of value.

TR extended authority farther than any other peacetime president. His linking of the president to the public established a new theory of government. The president, to Roosevelt, was the chief spokesman for the people.

Roosevelt was a whirlwind who sought to dominate events utterly, and he often did. He asserted a claim that the president should be the nation's chief legislator, and he pushed himself deeper into the legislative arena than any of his predecessors. TR outlined his proposals in public speeches and messages to Congress. He even went so far as to draft bills and send them to Congress. In the past, this was done behind the scenes for fear that the presidents might be accused of overstepping their SEPARATION OF

POWER bounds, but Roosevelt was very open about this. He also worked very hard lobbying Congress on behalf of his legislative proposals. "A good executive," he asserted, "under the present conditions of American political life, must take a very active interest in getting the right kind of legislation." (He once lamented, "Oh, if I could only be President and Congress together for just ten minutes!"). To Roosevelt, the president was not only the voice of the people but of the legislature as well.

In 1904–1905 Roosevelt added a critical tool to the president's power when he intervened militarily in Santo Domingo. Done ostensibly to protect the interests of U.S. companies, Roosevelt defended his decision on grounds that the United States had a right to establish and guarantee hemispheric order. The United States was to be sheriff of the hemisphere. "It is our duty," he said, "when it becomes absolutely inevitable to police these countries in the interest of order and civilization." This act—the Roosevelt corollary to the MONROE DOCTRINE—added a significant weapon to the president's already enlarging arsenal. In a speech directed to the United States's Latin American neighbors, Roosevelt said:

> It is not true that the United States feels any land hunger or entertains any projects as regards the other nations of the western hemisphere save such as for their welfare. All that this country desires is to see the neighboring countries stable, orderly and prosperous . . . if a nation shows that it knows how to act with reasonable efficiency and decency in social and political matters, if it keeps order and pays its obligations, it need fear no interference by the United States. Chronic wrongdoing, or an impotence which results in a general loosening of the ties of civilized society may in America, as elsewhere, ultimately require intervention by some civilized nation, and in the western hemisphere the adherence of the United States to the Monroe Doctrine may force the United States, however reluctantly, in flagrant cases of such wrongdoing or impotence, to the exercise of an international police power.

Roosevelt's ambitious legislative agenda, known as the SQUARE DEAL, included antitrust legislation, the Hepburn Act, conservation, the creation of a Department of Commerce and Labor, and a host of other ideas.

If TR was innovative in the domestic arena, he was even more activist and controversial in FOREIGN AFFAIRS. McKinley introduced America to the world stage; Roosevelt was determined to dominate it. He talked of speaking softly but carrying a big stick; he increased the size of the navy, imposed a deal that led to the building of the Panama Canal, and brokered a peace agreement ending the Russo-Japanese War (for which he was the first Ameri-

can president to receive a Nobel Peace Prize). When the Senate refused to ratify a treaty with the Dominican Republic, TR merely ignored the will of the Senate and signed an EXECUTIVE AGREEMENT. Roosevelt defended this decision: "The Constitution did not explicitly give me power to bring about the necessary agreement with Santo Domingo," Roosevelt wrote in 1913. "But, the Constitution did not forbid my doing what I did. I put the agreement into effect, and I continued its execution for two years before the Senate acted; and I would have continued it until the end of my term, if necessary, without any action by Congress." Teddy Roosevelt was no wallflower.

Teddy Roosevelt changed the Constitution: not the wording, but the interpretation and understanding of the scope and nature of EXECUTIVE POWER. He stretched the constitutional elastic further than any president since LINCOLN, and in doing so, helped invent a "new" institution. He redefined the presidency.

Upon leaving office TR said: "No President has ever enjoyed himself as much as I have enjoyed myself, and for the matter of that I do not know any man of my age who has had as good a time. . . ."

Further reading: Gould, Lewis L. *The Presidency of Theodore Roosevelt*, rev. ed. New York: Oxford University Press, 1975; Miller, Nathan. *Theodore Roosevelt: A Life*. New York: William Morrow and Company, 1992; Morris, Edmund. *The Rise of Theodore Roosevelt*. New York: Coward, McCann and Geoghegan, 1979.

rulemaking power

The president is the CHIEF EXECUTIVE officer of the federal government. Executives need some administrative rulemaking discretion in order to do their job. Thus, some flexibility in allowing presidential rulemaking is necessary.

In the post–WORLD WAR II era, however, presidents have attempted to broaden the scope of rulemaking, possibly encroaching on legislative terrain. Presidents have done so as a way to circumvent the legislature and expand the scope of presidential power.

The ADMINISTRATIVE PROCEDURE ACT of 1946 (APA) set up some parameters but was unclear about the president's RULEMAKING POWER, and the Supreme Court ruled in 1992 that the APA does not apply to the president (*Franklin v. Massachusetts*) but to agencies.

The APA requires agencies to give public notice when proposing new rules, allow for public input, then publish all rules in the *Federal Register*.

Presidents can exert some measure of control over rulemaking by agency heads to establish rules and procedures. The proposed rules must then go through the APA process. A determined president can attempt to influence policy via an administrative strategy, a part of which includes changes in rulemaking. This would be considered an element of the ADMINISTRATIVE PRESIDENCY.

Further reading: National Academy of Public Administration. *Presidential Management of Rulemaking in Regulatory Agencies.* Washington, D.C.: The Academy, 1987; Strauss, Peter L., and Cass R. Sunstein. "The Role of the President and OMB in Informal Rulemaking." *Administrative Law Review* 38 (1986): 181–207.

Rumsfeld, Donald (1932–   ) *secretary of defense*
Born in Chicago, Illinois, in 1932, Donald Rumsfeld has held prestigious positions in the military, business, and government for more than half a century. Graduating from Princeton in 1954, Rumsfeld joined the U.S. Navy as a naval aviator. He became active in government by first working for Representative Dave Dennison of Ohio in 1958 and then for Representative Robert Griffin of Michigan in 1959. In 1962, after a brief stint in investment banking, he was elected to the U.S. House of Representatives from Illinois at the age of 30.

Reelected to Congress three times, he resigned in 1969 to serve in the administration of President Richard NIXON. He served in several positions, first as assistant to the president, then as member of the CABINET (1969–72), as counselor to the president and as director of the Economic Stabilization Program. President Nixon then appointed him ambassador to NATO, where he served from 1973 to 1974. When President FORD assumed office after Nixon's RESIGNATION, Rumsfeld chaired the transition team. He also served as CHIEF OF STAFF (1974–75) and as the 13th secretary of Defense (1975–77), the youngest in U.S. history. In 1977 he was awarded the highest honor granted to a civilian, the Presidential Medal of Freedom.

Throughout the 1980s and 1990s he was active in the business community, serving as CEO and chair of numerous companies. In 1978–85 he was the CEO, president, and chair of G. D. Searle and Co., a pharmaceutical company, and won several awards for his leadership. He has served on many boards and commissions in the REAGAN, BUSH, and CLINTON administrations, among them: the President's General Advisory Committee on Arms Control (1982–86); the National Commission on the Public Service (1987–90); chairman, Commission on the Ballistic Missile Threat to the United States (1998–99). He is also on the board of trustees of the Gerald R. Ford Foundation, the Eisenhower Exchange Fellowships, the Hoover Institution at Stanford University, and the National Park Foundation.

In 2001 President George W. BUSH chose Rumsfeld to once again hold the position of secretary of defense. In agreeing to serve, Rumsfeld joined a list of people who had worked as high-level officials in the administration of his father, President George H. W. Bush: VICE PRESIDENT Dick Cheney (former secretary of Defense); Secretary of Defense Colin POWELL (chair of the JOINT CHIEFS OF STAFF); and NATIONAL SECURITY ADVISER Condoleezza Rice (special assistant to the president for national security affairs and senior director for Soviet affairs at the NATIONAL SECURITY COUNCIL).

Prior to the SEPTEMBER 11, 2001, ATTACKS, the focus of Secretary Rumsfeld's tenure was on advocating, shaping, and implementing a national missile defense system, revamping the military's pay scale, and improving the living conditions for U.S. military troops. In the events that followed September 11, 2001, Secretary Rumsfeld has captured the media's attention and received favorable attention from pundits and news analysts for his plainspoken and direct style with the media. As the administration's lead spokesperson for the "War on Terrorism," Secretary Rumsfeld has been charged not only with helping to shape the administration's policies on counterterrorism, the military action against the Taliban militia in Afghanistan and the Al Qaeda terrorist network, but also as a primary conduit of information to the news media.

Further reading: Biography of Donald Rumsfeld. http://www.defenselink.mil/bios/secdef_bio.html. (downloaded 12/15/2001); "The Bush All-Stars," *The New York Times,* 22 January 2001, sec. A, p. 18; White House press release, November 3, 1975; http://www.ford.utexas.edu/library/exhibits/cabinet/rumsfeld.htm. (downloaded 2/15/2001).

—Rebecca E. Deen

S

salaries and perquisites

President George W. BUSH receives an annual salary of $400,000, double the salary that President Bill CLINTON received. The presidential pay raise was passed by Congress in the closing days of the 106th Congress and signed into law by President Clinton on December 21, 2000. The last presidential pay raise dates back to 1969, when the salary was increased from $100,000 to $200,000. The president will also receive a $50,000 expense account, a budget to refurbish the White House, and an entertainment allowance.

Although approved in 2000, the pay increase could not take effect until the next president took office. Article II, Section 1, of the Constitution stipulates that the president's compensation shall not be increased or diminished during the term that he holds office. The framers passed this provision to guard the independence of the executive. Under the Articles of Confederation, some state legislatures had in effect bribed governors with pay increases in exchange for support for specific policies. By preventing alterations of an incumbent president's salary, the framers hoped to prevent this kind of corruption.

The first president, George WASHINGTON, was offered a $25,000 salary, which he turned down. Translated into current dollars, Washington's salary would have totaled approximately $4.5 million dollars as calculated by the Congressional Research Service. The president's salary remained at $25,000 until 1873, when it was increased to $50,000. Though presidential salaries have been increased on a handful of occasions since then, they nonetheless have failed to keep up with inflation. Increased presidential power in the 20th century did not translate into increased real incomes.

In addition to his monetary compensation, the president is entitled to live in the White House for free, receives free use of AIR FORCE ONE and a fleet of helicopters, and free medical care through the U.S. Navy. The White House has many amenities: a movie theater, a bowling alley (installed under President NIXON), a gym, a heated swimming pool, plus a small barbershop, dentist office, and medical clinic. Presidents also have access to CAMP DAVID, a cabin retreat about 50 miles northwest of Washington in the Catoctin Mountain National Park. Although many presidents have used Camp David to host foreign leaders and to conduct important negotiations, presidents may use this retreat for rest and relaxation as well.

After departing from office, presidents continue to receive significant rewards. In addition to an annual pension, retiring presidents now receive up to $150,000 a year to maintain an office and staff. The first lady also receives a $20,000 annual pension. Retired presidents and FIRST LADIES also receive SECRET SERVICE protection for 10 years after leaving office.

Further reading: Light, Paul C. "A President's Just Due." *Government Executive Magazine*, 1 July 1999.

—Terri Bimes

savings and loan scandal

The S & L crisis of the 1980s was the result of three factors. First, Congress, though the Garr-St. Germain Depository Institution Decontrol Act of 1982, deregulated banks and savings and loan institutions. Second, President REAGAN dramatically reduced the number of federal bank auditors. Third, a number of unscrupulous bankers saw an opportunity to loot their banks and did so.

Roughly 1,500 S & L's went under, with losses estimated at $500 million. Taxpayers had to foot the bill because of the guaranteed investment protection of the federal government as established after the GREAT DEPRESSION.

Schechter Poultry Corp. v. U.S., 295 U.S. 495 (1935)

Acting under its authority to regulate interstate commerce (U.S. Constitution, Art. I, Section. 8, Clause 3), and as part of Franklin D. Roosevelt's NEW DEAL anti-Depression policy, Congress passed the NATIONAL INDUSTRIAL RECOVERY ACT (NIRA) of 1933. The NIRA authorized the EXECUTIVE BRANCH to create "codes of fair competition" for businesses, including standards for wages, hours, and working conditions.

The Schechter Poultry Corporation received chickens from outside New York State, slaughtered them in New York City, and sold them to local retailers. The corporation was convicted in federal district court of violating several standards established under the NIRA by the National Recovery Administration. After a federal court of appeals upheld these convictions, the corporation appealed to the U.S. Supreme Court. Voting 9-0, the Court overturned the convictions on two grounds. First, the corporation was engaged in intrastate commerce that had merely an indirect effect on interstate commerce and therefore could not be regulated under Congress's power to regulate interstate commerce. Second, because the NIRA contained no intelligible standards to guide the executive branch in the formation of the codes, Congress had unconstitutionally delegated its legislative power to an agency of the executive branch.

The Supreme Court later abandoned the direct/indirect effects distinction (*National Labor Relations Board v. Jones & Laughlin Steel Corp.*, 301 U.S. 1 [1937]; *Wickard v. Filburn*, 317 U.S. 111 [1941]). It has since routinely upheld congressional regulations of business activities that have only a very indirect effect on interstate commerce. It has also not enforced the "nondelegation" doctrine since the *Schechter* decision.

Further reading: Mason, Alpheus Thomas, and Donald Grier Stephenson, Jr. *American Constitutional Law: Introductory Essays and Selected Cases.* Upper Saddle River, N.J.: Prentice Hall, 2002; O'Brien, David M. *Constitutional Law and Politics: Struggles for Power and Governmental Accountability.* New York: W. W. Norton, 2000.

—Michael Comiskey

science adviser

Having a science adviser became indispensable in the post-WORLD WAR II era as science and technology became more important and more complex elements of the presidential agenda.

The role of science adviser was informal and episodic until the early 1960s, when President KENNEDY institutionalized the position, creating the OFFICE OF SCIENCE AND TECHNOLOGY (OSTP). In the JOHNSON administration, the science adviser was an important staffer, especially as ARMS CONTROL became a more visible presidential issue. Subsequent presidents used, or failed to use, the science adviser as they deemed necessary.

science policy

Article I, Section 8, of the U.S. Constitution established the patent system "to advance the Progress of Science and the useful Acts." But it has not been until recently that the federal government took seriously a mission to promote science and technology. A good deal of the impetus for this concern stemmed from WORLD WAR II and the COLD WAR, when scientific knowledge and military superiority were linked. In recent years the government has also promoted scientific and technological innovations to spur the economy.

Beginning with World War II, science policy (along with technology) became an important component of the White House. President EISENHOWER, encouraged by concern over the Soviet launch of Sputnik in 1957, created the President's Science Advisory Committee, and his successor President KENNEDY further institutionalized science advising by creating the OFFICE OF SCIENCE AND TECHNOLOGY POLICY (OSTP).

After Kennedy, science advising was closely linked to military policy and arms control issues. Today, presidents rely on a wide range of experts as policy-making has become more complex and as technological advances and scientific discoveries produce rapid change.

seal, presidential

The presidential seal (Great Seal of the Office of the President) is a variation of the Great Seal of the United States of America. The Great Seal is a symbol of the nation and embodies the beliefs and philosophy of the Founders. The first presidential seal was authorized for design by a committee formed in 1777. However, due to the American Revolutionary War, the actual design was not completed until 1782. The actual first die cut is on display in the NATIONAL ARCHIVES. The Great Seal is on display in the Exhibit Hall of the U.S. Department of State in Washington, D.C.

The use of the presidential seal (and other official seals of the government) is strictly controlled by United States Code, Title 18, Section 713. The front of the presidential seal is used only on documents. It may also appear on medals, publications, stationery, flags, monuments, and architecture. The Code stipulates penalties of fines and/or imprisonment for unauthorized use of the presidential and other official governmental seals.

The current presidential seal was first publicly displayed during the 1949 Inauguration of President Harry S TRUMAN. In the fall of 1945, President Truman, through an EXECUTIVE ORDER, authorized a change in the presidential seal. The changes included a modification to the 1880 seal first used by President Rutherford B. HAYES. The 1880 seal depicted, for the first time in our history, an American eagle facing a talon of arrows, a symbol of war. Truman's new seal depicted the American eagle facing a talon of olive branches, symbolizing peace.

Further reading: *The Great Seal of the United States.* U.S. Department of State, Bureau of Public Affairs. Washington, D.C.: Superintendent of Documents, U.S. Government Printing Office, September 1996.

—Owen Holmes

SEATO Treaty

Envisioned as the Asian counterpart to NATO, the SEATO Treaty (Southeast Asia Collective Defense Treaty) was agreed upon on February 19, 1955, during the EISENHOWER presidency. The original members were the United States, France, and the United Kingdom, along with Australia, New Zealand, Pakistan, the Philippines, and Thailand.

Secret Service

The U.S. Secret Service considers itself the nation's premier law-enforcement agency, protecting the EXECUTIVE BRANCH's top political leadership. Created in 1865, the Secret Service has from its beginnings been a part of the TREASURY DEPARTMENT.

Today the law specifies that the service's protectees include the president, the VICE PRESIDENT, the president-elect, and the vice president-elect—who cannot decline the protection—and may include (a) their immediate families, (b) FORMER PRESIDENTS, their spouses, and their children under 16, (c) foreign heads of state visiting the United States, (d) some U.S. envoys on special missions abroad, (e) if the president directs, White House staff members who have received threats on their lives, and (f) major candidates for president (if the coverage is approved by a committee of five House and Senate leaders). The Secret Service also has a Foreign Missions Section which provides protection to the Washington embassies of foreign nations.

All this adds up to a substantial task. In 1996, during the fiftieth-anniversary celebration of the UNITED NATIONS, more than 150 foreign chiefs of state were gathered in New York City. The events of September 11, 2001, have opened up a grim new dimension to the challenges facing the U.S. Secret Service. Fortunately, after some years of inadequate interagency coordination (as documented by the WARREN COMMISSION following the assassination of President KENNEDY), the Secret Service is now tied closely to the entire U.S. intelligence community, both overseas and at home.

The service has some 5,100 employees, 2,200 of them agents. It works out of 126 field offices in the United States and in 14 foreign cities, including Moscow, Hong Kong, and Bangkok.

At the White House, the Secret Service's Uniformed Division staffs the outer perimeter of guardhouses and protective equipment (some patrol on bicycles); the inner perimeter consists of agents in civilian clothes who guard the president's and vice president's persons, and the two first families. There is a Technical Security Division, which designs and installs detection equipment at White House entrances, and a Protective Research Division, which has consulted with psychiatric experts to try (not successfully so far) to develop a predictable "profile" of an assassin. Protective Research also maintains a list of several thousand persons who are considered threats to the president, and a "watch list" of several hundred who are known to be dangerous. The service has a computerized collection of handwriting samples—the largest database of its kind.

At Beltsville, a Washington suburb, the service runs the James J. Rowley Training Center, where each new agent spends 10 weeks, plus regular repeat visits during his or her career. A presidential limousine rolls down a mock "Main Street," a "president" greets crowds on a rope-line; then there is an "AOP"—an "attack on the principal"—during which new recruits receive a realistic and highly effective introduction to presidential protection. State and local law enforcement officers are invited to use the facilities at the Rowley Training Center; this helps not only to upgrade local capabilities but cements the close professional cooperation between the Secret Service and state and local officers, who must constantly work together in their protective duties.

Presidential trips, especially those abroad, present a special challenge. In his first seven years in office, President CLINTON made some 2,500 appearances in more than 800 cities here and abroad; the first lady visited 83 countries. Advance teams always include Secret Service representatives; the total Secret Service contingent on a foreign trip is very large. Will the presidential limousine fit through the palace gates? One of the limos is flown over and tested. When President EISENHOWER visited Greece, the schedule called for a helicopter trip from Athens to the cruiser *Des Moines* offshore. Would its flotation gear work? The Secret Service dunked the helicopter to find out. Some foreign nations do not approve of the carrying of weapons even by law enforcement personnel; the Secret Service must negotiate individual arrangements with host countries. The establishment of Secret Service field offices in foreign capitals facilitates the coordination that is indispensable. Said one spokesman: "Our agent in Moscow not only knows the territory there, but he has also created close liaison arrangements with the host country security services. He makes that bridge from the Service here to the right people over there. We work very closely with foreign nations' security and police forces."

Sadly and ironically, the increases in the responsibilities of the Secret Service have come as a response to tragedies. Its presidential protective function was added to its original anticounterfeiting role only after President

MCKINLEY was assassinated in 1901. Its protection was extended to presidential candidates only after Robert Kennedy was killed. Its function to protect foreign leaders in the United States resulted from an incident in Chicago during the visit of French President Georges Pompidou. CARTER White House aides vetoed the installation of magnetometers at White House entrances until a man walked in with a gun and said, "Take me to the president!" The stone bollards were set up outside the White House only after the bombing of our troop quarters in Beirut; the gates themselves were heavily reinforced after a man crashed his car through a gateway on Christmas morning. The closing of Pennsylvania Avenue came only after the Oklahoma City car-bomb disaster. Commented one Secret Service veteran: "Protection is reaction to what happened yesterday!"

The total budget of the Secret Service for FY 2001 was $826.6 million; the Service does not make public the precise amount for its presidential protective functions.

Further reading: Melanson, Philip H. *The Politics of Protecton: The U.S. Secret Service in the Terrorist Age.* New York: Praeger, 1984; Patterson, Bradley H. *The White House Staff: Inside the West Wing and Beyond.* Washington, D.C.: Brookings Institute, 2002.

—Bradley H. Patterson

Seery v. United States, 127 F. Supp 601 (1955)

Maria Jeritza Seery, an opera singer and naturalized American citizen, sued the government for compensation for damages that resulted when the U.S. Army seized an estate she owned in Austria and, during WORLD WAR II, used it as an officer's club. While the United States had entered into an agreement with Austria, paying $15.4 million for all claims against the United States, Ms. Seery (who was offered $600 by the Austrian government) sued the United States claiming that even though the government entered into an agreement with Austria, it could not deny her Fifth Amendment rights to just compensation for taking her property.

The government, relying on the Court's logic in *U.S. v. Belmont* (1937) and *U.S. v. Pink* (1942), which supported EXECUTIVE AGREEMENTS, asserted the legality of this agreement. Lawyers for Seery, while recognizing the Court's previous approval of the legitimacy of executive agreements, argued that these previous cases did not deprive a U.S. citizen of constitutional rights.

The Court ruled that an executive agreement could not deprive U.S. citizens of these constitutional rights. Seery was eventually awarded $11,000.

This case is one of two key cases decided in the 1950s (the other being *REID v. COVERT,* 1957) that limited the president's power to issue executive agreements.

Senior Executive Service (SES)

The Senior Executive Service (SES) was established by the Civil Service Reform Act of 1978. The SES consists of the three highest grade levels of administrative personnel in the federal CIVIL SERVICE: ES-1, ES-2, and ES-3. The SES formulates and applies policies for recruiting, promoting, compensating, and placing bureaucrats of the SES. These bureaucrats have less job protection than other civil servants, but they are also eligible for competitive cash bonuses if they provide especially meritorious service.

In order to share and further enhance their administrative skills and experiences with other agencies in the federal BUREAUCRACY, SES bureaucrats rotate among different agencies in order to improve the performance of those other agencies. Agency review boards then determine if these SES bureaucrats will receive bonuses for their administrative achievements. These boards also have the authority to remove SES bureaucrats from the SES and demote them if they fail to accomplish their administrative goals.

The use of rotation among agencies for new administrative challenges and improved organizational performance, competitive bonuses, and the possibility of demotion for failure was adopted from the personnel practices in private corporations. The SES personnel system also introduced greater presidential control of the highest-grade civil servants by authorizing the president to ultimately decide which SES bureaucrats would receive the largest bonuses. Unofficially, yet more significantly, however, this presidential influence on the SES and the status of the director of the OFFICE OF PERSONNEL MANAGEMENT (OPM) increased the potential for a president to recognize and reward SES bureaucrats who were politically loyal to his policy agenda within the federal bureaucracy.

Further reading: Dresang, Dennis L. *Public Personnel Management and Public Policy.* New York: Longman, 1991; Wilson, James Q. *Bureaucracy.* New York: Basic Books, 1989.

—Sean J. Savage

separation of powers

Power in the American governmental system is divided in two directions: horizontally, across the three branches, and vertically, between the national government and the states. The horizontal division is described as SEPARATION OF POWERS, or the allocation of constitutional authority among the three coequal branches: legislative, executive, and judicial.

The concept of dividing power among different institutions with different responsibilities owes its existence to French philosopher Baron de Montesquieu's 1748 work, *The Spirit of the Laws,* in which he noted that to protect liberty and to avoid tyranny, legislative and EXECUTIVE

POWER must be in separate hands. But it was James MADI-SON, in *The Federalist No. 47*, who refined Montesquieu's theory and posited that Montesquieu could not have meant that the branches were to be completely sealed off from one other, with no opportunity to participate in the acts of the others.

Madison reasoned, instead, that Montesquieu must have meant only that the hands that exercise "the *whole* power of one department" should not be permitted to possess "the *whole* power of another department." (emphasis in original) Moreover, Madison in *The Federalist No. 51* warns of the need for "auxiliary precautions" in order to control human nature and to keep government power limited. To this end, he proposes some measure of flexibility in the separation of powers, rather than a strict separation. As evidence, he states in *No. 47* that no state constitution at that time provided for a system "in which the several departments of power have been kept absolutely separate and distinct."

Thus was born the twin corollaries of separation of powers and checks and balances, much like two sides of the same coin, mutually dependent and reinforcing: Separation of powers allocates powers, while CHECKS AND BALANCES ensures that each branch "watches over" the other two to guarantee that no branch encroaches upon another. The opening clause in each of the first articles of the Constitution, known as the "distributing clauses," announces the locus of power for each institution: Article I states that "All legislative Powers herein granted shall be vested in a Congress of the United States. . . .;" Article II states that "The executive Power shall be vested in a President of the United States of America. . . .;" and Article III states that "The judicial Power of the United States shall be vested in one Supreme Court, and in such inferior courts as the Congress may from time to time ordain and establish." The structure that Madison sought so carefully to establish was calibrated to allow each branch to play a partial role in the actions of the others as well as to react to official acts of the others. Thus, the president is *part* of the legislative process, proposing bills at the beginning of the process, negotiating the language and provisions with Congress, and signing or vetoing at the end. The Senate is *part* of the appointment process, with the power to grant or deny confirmation to the president's executive and judicial branch nominees. The judiciary has the power to declare unconstitutional acts of the legislature or of the executive. The chief justice presides over the Senate in an IMPEACHMENT trial of the president or a federal judge.

Scholars have been dissatisfied with the misleading nature of the label "separation of powers." Richard NEUSTADT, in his 1960 *Presidential Power*, suggested that it is far more accurate to say that ours is "a government of separated institutions sharing powers." More recently, Charles O. Jones has modified Neustadt's description to suggest that our system can best be described as one "where . . . separated institutions *compete* for shared powers." It is this overlapping quality that lends a distinctive character to the sharing of powers among the branches. Louis Fisher has noted that the branches engage in a "constitutional dialogue" with each other, almost as a continuous series of actions and reactions. For example, Congress may pass a law, which the Court may declare unconstitutional. Congress may then go back and rework the law to address the Court's objections. Upon a new legal challenge, perhaps, the Court will find the revised law constitutionally acceptable. Thus, a "conversation" has occurred between the branches, and both reached agreement after an initial conflict.

Of primary importance to the framers when they imported the principle of separation of powers into the structure of the government they were creating under the Constitution were the following features: (1) that it would divide power so as to protect liberty, and (2) that it would allow for policies to gather consensus through a democratic process of bargaining, negotiation, and compromise from among disparate political elements, ensuring that government would be insulated from acting on the fleeting passions of the day, and that decisions would have the benefit of careful deliberation and popular support before becoming official policy. One consequence of this gradual process is the frequent criticism that government under separation of powers is slow, incremental, and inefficient. To this, Justice Brandeis responded, in his eloquent dissenting opinion in *MYERS V. UNITED STATES* (1926), that "[t]he doctrine of the separation of powers was adopted by the Convention of 1787, not to promote efficiency but to preclude the exercise of arbitrary power. The purpose was, not to avoid friction, but, by means of the inevitable friction incident to the distribution of the governmental powers among three departments, to save the people from autocracy."

Further reading: Fisher, Louis. *Constitutional Dialogues: Interpretation as Political Process*. Princeton, N.J.: Princeton University Press, 1988; Hamilton, Alexander, James Madison, and John Jay. *The Federalist Papers*. Edited by Clinton Rossiter. New York: New American Library, 1961; Jones, Charles O. *The Presidency in a Separated System*. Washington, D.C.: The Brookings Institution, 1994, p. 16; *Myers v. United States*, 272 U.S. 52 (1926); Neustadt, Richard E. *Presidential Power: The Politics of Leadership*. New York: John Wiley and Sons, Inc., 1964, p. 42.

—Nancy Kassop

September 11, 2001, attacks

On September 11, 2001, members of a terrorist organization, later identified as al-Qaeda, hijacked four planes and flew two into the World Trade Center in New York City and one into the Pentagon Building in the Washington, D.C., area; the fourth was downed in Pennsylvania. The attack shocked the nation and mobilized the Bush administration into action. By October President George W. BUSH launched a U.S. attack on the Taliban government of Afghanistan, the country hosting Osama bin Laden and his al-Qaeda organization. The United States, with the help of other nations, brought down the Taliban government and disrupted al-Qaeda's operations. Well-financed and internationally based, al-Qaeda continued its activities but on a smaller scale.

Three different military responses emanated from the events of September 11, 2001. The first was the war against international terrorism, with special focus on the al-Qaeda terrorist organization headed by Osama bin Laden. The second military action was designed to overthrow the Taliban government in control of Afghanistan. The third action was the overthrow of Saddam Hussein and the government of Iraq.

September 11, or 9/11 as it was called, galvanized the public behind the leadership of President Bush and greatly expanded the power of the president. President Bush made use of his REORGANIZATION POWER to form the DEPARTMENT OF HOMELAND SECURITY and signing into law the USA PATRIOT ACT. As part of the effort to subdue terrorists, the Bush administration imprisoned an unknown number of people in an internment center in Guantanamo Bay, Cuba, where prisoners were held without being charged with a crime, without access to the courts, without access to an attorney, and where children under the age of 16 were held without charges. Under normal circumstances, such actions would be considered serious and impeachable violations of the Constitution, but in the crisis atmosphere following 9/11, the president was granted wide latitude in his attempts to stop terrorism.

sequestration

Sequestration was the process whereby money that had been authorized by Congress to be spent in the current fiscal year's budget was "sequestered" or withdrawn from the budget. This process was based on provisions of the Balanced Budget and Deficit Reduction Act of 1985 (GRAMM-RUDMAN-HOLLINGS ACT). The bill was an attempt to control the massive deficits of the 1980s.

In the original version of the bill, specific deficit targets were set. If those targets were met in the budget process, the procedures in the bill would not take effect. If, however, the deficit targets were not reached, the bill required the comptroller general to initiate a series of across-the-board budget cuts that would bring the deficit figures down to the stipulated target. The procedure required that half of these cuts come from defense and half from non-defense spending.

A year after the bill was passed, suit was filed in federal court. In 1986 the Supreme Court, in *Bowsher v. Synar,* held that portion of the act unconstitutional that gave the comptroller general, an officer of the legislative branch, the power to make the cuts, which is an executive function. The Court argued that since the comptroller general could conceivably be dismissed by a joint resolution of Congress, granting this power in that office was unconstitutional.

The sequestering procedures were changed by the Budget Enforcement Act of 1990. Instead of requiring action of the comptroller general, the sequesters were made automatically. Whenever a category of discretionary spending exceeded their target spending for the fiscal year, the offending category's budget was cut across the board the following fiscal year to make up that difference. This change was an important step in making the deficit reduction plans workable through the mid to late 1990s.

Further reading: Schier, Steven. *A Decade of Deficits.* Albany: State University of New York Press, 1992; Wildavsky, Aaron, and Naomi Caiden. *The New Politics of the Budgetary Process.* New York: Addison Wesley/Longman, 2001.

—Joseph Wert

Seward, William Henry (1801–1872) *secretary of state, U.S. senator, governor*

Born 60 miles northwest of New York City in 1801, Seward graduated Phi Beta Kappa from Union College in 1820 and was admitted to the bar in 1822. Entering politics as an anti-Masonic state senator, he served two terms as governor of New York as a Whig (1839–43). He pursued an activist course consistent with an emphasis on the sort of internal improvements advocated by the Whig Party and won approval for enlarging the Erie Canal. His many proposals for social reform anticipated the Progressive agenda of the early 20th century. Among reforms he achieved were better treatment of prisoners, the insane, debtors, and immigrants. Among actions that gained him a reputation in some quarters as a radical was his championing of a law encouraging rescue of free AFRICAN AMERICANS kidnapped into slavery. Seward earned the everlasting enmity of nativists by his support of immigration and equal educational opportunity for Irish Catholic children. Elected to the U.S. Senate in 1849 and again in 1855, Seward continued to support internal improvements and restrictions on slavery. Although he had built a reputation as a passionate opponent of slavery and maintained a close association with legendary slave rescuer Harriet Tubman, his commitment to preserving the Union put him in opposition to radical abolitionists. However, as did LINCOLN, he opposed the Fugitive Slave Law, the Kansas-Nebraska Act, and the Dred Scott decision. In the course of arguing the case for free labor as against slave labor, he delivered two speeches that gained him both acclaim and notoriety: the so-called Higher Law Speech (1850) and the so-called Irrepressible Conflict Speech (1858).

Partly because of the opposition of nativists, he lost the Republican nomination for president to Abraham Lincoln (1860). To the displeasure of some cabinet members, as secretary of state he gradually became Lincoln's closest confidant as well as social companion. After Lincoln rejected Seward's proposal of an outsized role for himself as a virtual "president in fact," Seward came to see that he had much in common with Lincoln—adherence to principle tempered by pragmatism, a deep commitment to saving the Union, principled opposition to slavery, and a taste for storytelling and down-to-earth HUMOR. He faced much opposition from Radical Republican members of Congress and others who viewed him as too moderate on slavery, including especially Salmon P. CHASE, secretary of the treasury. Late in 1862, Republican senators came close to demanding Seward's resignation. Bringing together Republican senators and cabinet members to save Seward, Lincoln denied excessive influence by Seward and noted the CABINET's support for major decisions. Unwilling to dissent in an open meeting, Chase embarrassed himself by staying silent and felt compelled to offer his resignation the next day. Having succeeded in blunting the senators' attacks on Seward, Lincoln was then free to refuse both Chase's resignation and one Seward had offered earlier.

After convincing Lincoln to suspend the writ of habeas corpus, Seward for a time administered a policy of detention of those deemed a threat to the Union. For this role he was roundly criticized. Seward's greatest accomplishment as secretary of state consisted of the complex DIPLOMACY that kept Great Britain and France from recognizing and assisting the Confederacy. After he miraculously survived an assassination attempt by one of Booth's co-conspirators, Seward continued as secretary of State under Andrew JOHNSON and succeeded in getting the French to withdraw troops from Mexico and in negotiating the purchase of Alaska. He died at his home in Auburn, New York, in 1872.

Further reading: Taylor, John M. *William Henry Seward: Lincoln's Right Hand.* New York: HarperCollins, 1991; Van Deusen, Glyndon G. *William Henry Seward.* New York, N.Y.: Oxford University Press, 1967.

—James E. Underwood

Sherman, James S. (1855–1912) *U.S. vice president*
James "Sunny Jim" Sherman served as vice president under William Howard TAFT from 1909 to 1912. Sherman suffered from Bright's Disease, a kidney ailment. In 1912 he was nominated for a second term as the Republican vice-presidential candidate but fell ill and on October 30 died of complications of Bright's Disease. With less than a week to go before the election and the Republicans without a vice presidential candidate, the party quickly selected Columbia University president Nicholas Butler to replace Sherman. Woodrow WILSON won the 1912 election, as the Republican vote was split between Taft and third-party hopeful Teddy ROOSEVELT.

Sherman Antitrust Act
Named after its chief legislative sponsor, Republican Senator John Sherman of Ohio, the Sherman Antitrust Act, passed in 1890, attempted to break up trade conspiracies, collusion, and monopolies in business. Signed into law by President Benjamin HARRISON on July 2, 1890, it was the nation's first antitrust law and became the basis of antitrust actions by President Theodore ROOSEVELT and others.

signing statements
Customarily, when a president signs a significant piece of legislation, he will issue a signing statement giving his reasons for supporting the bill. In the 1980s President REAGAN used signing statements in a new way, directing agencies to enact the new law in a manner described in the signing statement. On occasion, this interpretation was at variance with the intent of Congress. Reagan thus enlarged the ADMINISTRATIVE PRESIDENCY and used it to influence policy, going around the Congress.

Further reading: Garber, Marc N., and Kurt A. Wimmer. "Presidential Signing Statements as Interpretations of Legislative Intent." *Harvard Journal on Legislation* 24 (1987): 363–395; Rogers, Lindsay. "The Power of the President to Sign Bills after Congress Has Adjourned." *Yale Law Journal* 30 (1920): 1–22.

situation room
Colloquially termed the "Sit Room," this facility is the cardiac center of the staff of the NATIONAL SECURITY COUNCIL at the White House. Prior to 1961, the operating national security agencies—State, Defense, and the intelligence community—would have messengers hand-carry to the White House envelopes of paper copies of the messages which the agencies selected from their internal exchanges. The situation room was set up by President KENNEDY and was a resultant of four concurrent developments in the area of national security organization and operations. First, the BAY OF PIGS disaster had revealed the inadequacies of the tactical direction and control of national security crisis oper-

ations. Second, Kennedy, distrusting what he considered was the archaic structure and methods of the DEPARTMENT OF STATE, insisted on strengthening the role of the president and of the White House itself in national security policy making. Third, new developments in communications technology were enabling policy makers in Washington to communicate, in a secure mode, with military, diplomatic, and intelligence units stationed around the world. Fourth, Secretary of State Rusk, himself aware of State's outmoded procedures, had already established an Operations Center as part of his own office. The Sit Room got its baptism of fire during the CUBAN MISSILE CRISIS, because, as author Graham Allison emphasized, it "made it possible for political leaders in the basement of the White House to talk directly with commanders of destroyers stationed along the quarantine line"—a development "unique in naval history and, indeed, unparalleled in modern relations between American political leaders and military organizations."

In the years since, the Situation Room has been constantly expanded and improved. Today any and all important communications from the 500,000-plus that are exchanged daily between State and its posts abroad, between the DEPARTMENT OF DEFENSE and its commanders and tactical units on duty or engaged in operations overseas, and in the entire intelligence community can be—and are—instantly and electronically relayed to the Sit Room's computers. The experienced Sit Room staff of 25 professionals (on 24-hour duty) produces a weekly checklist reminding the agencies of the topics of prime interest to the White House; based on the president's priorities, they can raise or, in a crisis, lower the threshold for detailed material to be vacuumed in. If incoming information is judged incomplete, the Sit Room staff will instruct agencies or posts abroad to fill in the gaps. The Sit Room computers are programmed to admit or select out preselected data, or to create personalized "profiles" for senior recipients. Satellite photos, pictures, and radar images from manned or drone aircraft can be posted on the Sit Room screens. The staff daily prepares four or more summaries of the most important of all this material and sends the printed copies of all important messages to the responsible officers on the National Security Council staff.

Besides the computer bay, there are two conference rooms in the facility, one of them handling secure television feed, conference-style, from several top advisers simultaneously who themselves may be in distant locations.

The situation room has thus become the central instrument for assisting and enabling the president, the VICE PRESIDENT, and their senior White House advisers to be instantly aware of events throughout the world and of lower-level policy exchanges throughout the community of national security agencies. This is a new and extremely significant development in American public administration.

More than being aware, the president is now in a position to assert not just strategic but tactical supervision over what individual posts and units far away are planning or doing. This development has generated controversy, raising the question in the minds of both soldiers and diplomats and of senior policy leaders too—about the desirability of the CHIEF EXECUTIVE's becoming involved in operational matters. Could the president become overwhelmed with details to the detriment of his ability to concentrate on major policy issues? Those who argue for this new presidential ability point out that some decisions about "operational" moves are so sensitive and have such consequences that they are really matters of policy. The Constitution itself, one recalls, establishes the president as "Commander-in-Chief" and states quite simply that "The executive Power shall be vested in a President. . . ."

Further reading: Allison, Graham T. *The Essence of Decision: Explaining the Cuban Missile Crisis.* Boston: Little, Brown, 1971; Patterson, Bradley H. *The White House Staff: Inside the West Wing and Beyond.* Washington, D.C.: Brookings Institution, 2000.

—Bradley H. Patterson

Social Security
One of the key elements in the Social Security Act (1935), Social Security, or old-age insurance, was one of the chief legacies of Franklin ROOSEVELT and the NEW DEAL. It was the first modern effort at what became known as the welfare state, which included unemployment compensation, welfare, public health benefits, and old-age benefits. Since its inception, Social Security has become an important political issue, with Democrats using the fear that Republicans might cut Social Security benefits as a key campaign theme. In the 1970s, the cost of Social Security made it a target for cuts, but political support—especially among senior citizens—was so powerful that it has become something of a political untouchable. President REAGAN, in fact, tried to cut Social Security benefits on several occasions but was forced to retreat in the face of political pressure.

Further reading: Berkowitz, Edward D. *America's Welfare State: From Roosevelt to Reagan.* Baltimore, Md.: Johns Hopkins University Press, 1991; Light, Paul. *Artful Work: The Politics of Social Security Reform.* New York: Random House, 1985.

solicitor general
The Office of the Solicitor General (OSG) was created in 1870, by the same legislation that created the DEPARTMENT OF JUSTICE. Envisioned to aid the OFFICE OF THE

ATTORNEY GENERAL, the solicitor general was also to assume the duties of the attorney general should that position be vacated. A part of the Department of Justice and reporting directly to the deputy attorney general, the OSG represents the United States in the federal court system.

From the very first solicitor general, Benjamin Helm Bristow of Kentucky, the office has taken the lead in the government's business before the Supreme Court. A significant component of the OSG's activity is in the appellate process. All petitions, by any entity in the federal government, to the Supreme Court for writs of certiorari (requests to the Court that they hear a case) are funneled through the OSG. Any cases involving federal agencies eligible for the federal appeals process are screened by the OSG. That office then decides whether to seek a hearing before the Court. Thus, the OSG serves an important function for the court system by limiting the number of requests for certiorari that the Court receives each year. If the Court agrees to hear the case, the OSG oversees the litigation, from writing the briefs and petitions to conducting the oral arguments. Most of the cases are argued by the solicitor general or an attorney from the OSG. The assignment of attorneys is under the purview of the solicitor general.

In addition to arguing cases before the Court, the OSG is responsible for coordinating the government's position on all cases that affect the federal government. That is, if the government has been named as a party to the suit, or is otherwise affected by the action, the OSG determines the government's position and acts in its interests. Indeed, Seth Waxman, solicitor general from 1997 to 2001, argued that the most important responsibility of the OSG is to be the singular legal voice of the federal government, always seeking to establish justice.

The OSG files amicus curiae briefs (friend of the Court briefs) on cases affecting the federal government. The OSG amicus activity is far greater than any other group that regularly appears or files briefs before the Court. As a frequent filer of amicus briefs, the solicitor general has the unique privilege of occasionally articulating his position orally before the Court. The Court will also, at times, request the participation of the OSG, by asking that office to file amicus briefs.

As might be expected since the OSG represents the federal government before the Supreme Court, the OSG is frequently successful, both when the United States is a litigant and when the OSG files an amicus curiae brief. In terms of actually winning cases on the merits, the U.S. government has won an average of 63 percent of all cases between 1953 and 1991 (Epstein et al. 1996, 569). The solicitor general does even better when participating as an amicus than when the government is a direct party to a case. In fact, from 1952 to 1990, no presidential administration won less than 65 percent of its cases as an amicus,

and the KENNEDY administration won a high of 87.5 percent of its cases (Epstein et al. 1996, 551).

Further reading: Caplan, Lincoln. *The Tenth Justice: The Solicitor General and the Rule of Law.* New York: Knopf, 1987; Epstein, Lee, Jeffrey Segal, Harold Spaeth, and Thomas Walker. *The Supreme Court Compendium.* Washington, D.C.: CQ Press, 1996; Waxman, Seth P. "Presenting the Case of the United States As It Should Be: The Solicitor General in Historical Context." Address to the Supreme Court Historical Society, June 1, 1998.

—Rebecca E. Deen

space policy

On October 4, 1957, in the midst of the COLD WAR, the Soviet Union shocked the West with the launching of Sputnik, the world's first satellite. The fear that the United States was losing the "space race" galvanized America behind the space program. Congress passed the National Aeronautics and Space Act of 1958, thus also creating the National Aeronautics and Space Administration (NASA).

In 1961 the Soviets launched the first manned spacecraft to orbit. President KENNEDY responded with a mobilization of U.S. efforts to land the first man on the moon—and the race was on. And on July 20, 1969, Neil Armstrong and "Buzz" Aldrin were the first humans to set foot on the moon.

Since that time the U.S. space program has progressed in an uneven manner, with advances and setbacks affecting commitment and budget policy. In 1988 Congress established the National Space Council to advise presidents on space policy. The Council was formally created a year later by EXECUTIVE ORDER.

In the early 1980s President REAGAN proposed an elaborate ballistic missile defense program, the STRATEGIC DEFENSE INITIATIVE (SDI) which Reagan dubbed "Star Wars" after the popular movie. After Reagan, commitment to Star Wars wavered until President George W. BUSH revived the program.

Spanish-American War

In 1898 the United States emerged as a world and an imperial power. The Spanish-American War involved a dispute with Spain over refusal by Spain to grant independence to Cuba. The war was short, and after the U.S. victory, Cuba was granted independence, the United States annexed Puerto Rico and Guam, and eventually annexed the Philippines. President MCKINLEY, thus, helped usher the United States into great-power status, the presidency was elevated and empowered as the chief operational arm of America's international power, and the United States acquired control of nations in our backyard and across the globe, making the United States an "imperial" power for the first time.

special prosecutor

Prosecution of crimes in the federal justice system is the routine responsibility of federal prosecutors in the DEPARTMENT OF JUSTICE, under the supervision of the OFFICE OF THE ATTORNEY GENERAL. But when the person suspected of official misconduct is either the president to whom the attorney general owes his appointment or other high administration officials who are, also, politically allied with the top Justice Department administrators, the prospects for a real or perceived conflict of interest increase, and the public needs better assurance that impartial justice will be done. To that end, when such circumstances exist, there has been a tradition of appointing "independent" prosecutors, separate from the traditional U.S. attorneys in the Department of Justice and, thus, removed from the political pressures that operate on those attorneys.

The concept of independent prosecutors outside of the regular justice system, appointed for the precise purpose of removing politics from prosecution, has a rich tradition in the United States, at both the state and federal levels. It did not begin with the appointment of WATERGATE Special Prosecutor Archibald COX in 1973, but rather, with the appointment by President COOLIDGE of two special counsels to investigate the TEAPOT DOME SCANDAL in 1924, when Attorney General Daugherty and his Justice Department were implicated in the charges, and by President TRUMAN in 1952 when he appointed a special counsel to investigate tax scandals that involved a former commissioner of Internal Revenue and the assistant attorney general who headed the Justice Department's tax division. At the state level, New York has long used special prosecutors in its investigations of public corruption: Thomas Dewey was appointed to prosecute racketeering in New York City in the 1930s and 1940s, and Governor ROCKEFELLER appointed Maurice Nadjari as a special prosecutor in 1972 to look into allegations of corruption in the city's criminal justice system.

But it *was* the selection of Archibald Cox by Attorney General Elliott Richardson in May 1973 that forms the modern frame of reference for special prosecutors. Cox was a Harvard law professor who was selected by the attorney general to investigate and prosecute any misconduct among administration officials stemming from the June 17, 1972, break-in at the Democratic National Committee headquarters in the Watergate Hotel in Washington. Richardson granted Cox full independence to pursue the investigation wherever it would lead, and the Justice Department regulation authorizing his office and functions permitted his removal by the attorney general only for "extraordinary improprieties." Yet, by October 1973, when Cox subpoe-

naed tapes of Oval Office conversations between President NIXON and his aides about the Watergate break-in, the president balked. Although a federal district court ordered Nixon to surrender the tapes to Cox, he refused and ordered Cox to cease any further requests for tapes. Cox announced publicly that he would not comply with a future ban, and within hours, Nixon ordered Richardson to fire Cox. What followed has been dubbed "the Saturday Night massacre" for the series of rapid-succession actions that left many heads rolling. Richardson refused to fire Cox, since the attorney general did not believe that Cox had committed "extraordinary improprieties," the only reason for which he could be fired. Richardson submitted his own resignation to the president, who then ordered the deputy attorney general, William Ruckelshaus, to fire Cox. Ruckelshaus's refusal to carry out the deed resulted in his own termination from office, followed shortly thereafter by an order to the SOLICITOR GENERAL, Robert Bork, to fire Cox. Bork complied with the order, and Cox was removed as special prosecutor. He was eventually replaced, under a different charter, by Leon JAWORSKI. Two other special prosecutors ultimately completed the Watergate inquiry.

The specter of a president who was able to instigate the firing of a prosecutor whose investigation had moved uncomfortably close to the OVAL OFFICE pointed out the deficiencies of the regulation that had authorized Cox's office. Congress considered numerous proposals for a more secure and less vulnerable special prosecutor. The ETHICS IN GOVERNMENT ACT of 1978 included a permanent provision for the appointment of special prosecutors under an elaborate process, when certain threshold requirements were met. It was the product of an intense effort to improve upon the Watergate model, so that future special prosecutors could be free from presidential intimidation.

Under the 1978 law, upon receipt of allegations of violation of federal criminal law by certain high EXECUTIVE BRANCH officials, the attorney general was to conduct a preliminary investigation. If the attorney general concluded that further investigation was warranted, that information would be turned over to a three-judge special division court of the Court of Appeals for the District of Columbia, chosen by the Chief Justice of the United States. The special division would select a special prosecutor. Removal would be by the attorney general, for "extraordinary impropriety," and could be reviewed by the special division upon the special prosecutor's request. The act was to be renewed for no more than five years at a time.

Its renewal in 1982 brought a name change from "special prosecutor" to "INDEPENDENT COUNSEL" and a revision of the reasons for removal from "extraordinary impropriety" to "for good cause." By the time the act had lapsed in 1999 and Congress had decided not to renew it in 2000, 21 independent counsels had been appointed under the act's provisions since 1978. The constitutionality of the act was challenged in the Supreme Court case of *Morrison v. Olson,* 487 U.S. 654 (1988), and the Court upheld the law by an 8-1 decision (Scalia, dissenting).

Reasons for its nonrenewal centered primarily on the inability to separate independent prosecution from partisan politics. This failure reached a peak in the three investigations of President CLINTON (Whitewater, White House Travel Office/Vince Foster suicide, and the Lewinsky scandal) most especially in the highly charged Lewinsky inquiry by Kenneth Starr that led to the House IMPEACHMENT of Clinton in December 1998 and the Senate trial in January 1999. Public dissatisfaction with Starr's conduct and with the excessive length and cost of his inquiry (five years and $50 million) seemed to seal the fate of the law when it ran out in 1999. Without permanent statutory provisions governing the selection and operation of independent counsels when the need arises, there has been, by default, a reverting back to the original system of appointment by an attorney general on an ad hoc basis.

Further reading: Dole, Robert, and George J. Mitchell. *Project on the Independent Counsel Statute.* Washington, D.C.: American Enterprise Institute and The Brookings Institution, 1999; Harriger, Katy J. *The Special Prosecutor in American Politics.* Lawrence: University Press of Kansas, 2000; Spitzer, Robert J. "The Independent Counsel and the Post-Clinton Presidency." In *The Presidency and the Law,* edited by David Gray Adler and Michael A. Genovese, 89–107. Lawrence: University Press of Kansas, 2002.

—Nancy Kassop

speechwriters

Speeches are an integral part of modern presidential LEADERSHIP. As the RHETORICAL PRESIDENCY evolved and expanded during the 20th century, so too did the importance of presidential speechwriters. Those men and women involved in the research and writing of presidential speeches can play a key role in policy making as they help to shape the president's policy goals and initiatives. Major public addresses, particularly the STATE OF THE UNION ADDRESS and major policy addresses, set the president's legislative agenda for both the public and Congress. Major speeches and other public appearances are examples of how a president attempts to sell his agenda or other presidential actions, not only to the public but to the news media and other political actors as well.

The technological developments of the mass media in recent years have allowed presidents to go public more often and with much greater ease. As such, presidential speechwriters are now an integral part of the White House staff, and some have been extensively involved in the development of White House communication strategies for pres-

idents during the television age. When considering the history of presidential speeches, some early presidents relied on the help of others to write their speeches, most notably George WASHINGTON, Andrew JACKSON, and Andrew JOHNSON, but most wrote their own.

Thomas JEFFERSON, John ADAMS, James MADISON, and Abraham LINCOLN are all known for their eloquent and effective speeches that they authored themselves. By the 20th century, the public leadership strategies and the increased attention placed on public addresses by Theodore ROOSEVELT and Woodrow WILSON gave rise to the need for permanent speechwriters within the White House. Wilson was the first to revive the practice of delivering the State of the Union message in person to members of Congress, abandoned in 1796, which has since become the key presidential address each year. Beginning with Warren HARDING, ghostwriters were used, since it was unthinkable that a president would deliver someone else's words during a public address. Harding hired the first official White House speechwriter, journalist Judson Welliver, who maintained a low public profile. By the time Franklin D. Roosevelt entered the White House, presidential speeches became more of a collaborative effort between the president, his advisers, and his speechwriters. Other modern presidents, most notably John F. KENNEDY, Richard NIXON, Ronald REAGAN, and Bill CLINTON, were also extensively involved in the writing and phraseology of their major public addresses. While the organization of key advisers and other staff throughout the White House can differ for each administration, the general practice for most modern presidents when writing an important speech to outline major policy initiatives is to circulate a draft for input from various policy experts as well as the speechwriters. However, some presidents have struggled with effective coordination between those setting the policy and those in the speechwriting office drafting the remarks about policy. Access to the president by speechwriters does not always occur, but it is essential for those drafting remarks to clearly understand a president's view of a particular policy.

Further reading: Gelderman, Carol. *All The Presidents' Words: The Bully Pulpit and the Creation of the Virtual Presidency.* New York: Walker and Co., 1997; Kernell, Samuel. *Going Public: New Strategies of Presidential Leadership.* Washington, D.C.: CQ Press, 1997; Kessel, John H. *Presidents, the Presidency, and the Political Environment.* Washington, D.C.: CQ Press, 2001.

—Lori Cox-Han

spending power

In a literal sense, only Congress is authorized to spend "the people's" money. Article I, Section 9, of the Constitution states, "No Money shall be drawn from the treasury, but in

Consequence of Appropriations made by Law." And James MADISON, in *Federalist No. 48* wrote that "the legislative department alone has access to the pockets of the people."

However, over time presidents have inserted themselves into the budget and spending policies to the point where today, although Congress passes budgets and authorizes spending, the president exerts a great deal of influence over spending—by influencing and recommending legislation through the OFFICE OF MANAGEMENT AND BUDGET and by pressing Congress to accept his budget.

Further reading: Fisher, Louis. *Presidential Spending Power.* Princeton, N.J.: Princeton University Press, 1975; Sidak, J. Gregory. "The President's Power of the Purse." *Duke Law Journal* (1989): 1162–1253; Stith, Kate. "Congress's Power of the Purse." *Yale Law Journal* 97 (1988): 1343–1396.

Square Deal

Thrust into the presidency in 1901 upon William MCKINLEY's assassination, Theodore ROOSEVELT had to cope with the societal dislocations produced by rapid industrialization, unfettered capitalism, and urbanization. The American people demanded far-reaching reforms, and Roosevelt harnessed the aspirations of the Progressive Era to retool government institutions. TR called his DOMESTIC POLICY, which staked out a new central ground in American politics, the Square Deal. Roosevelt's Square Deal policies would chart a segment of his evolution from self-described "enlightened conservative" in 1903 to "radical liberal" in his presidential years.

Roosevelt spelled out the broad guiding principles of the Square Deal in his September 1903 "Class Government" speech at the New York State Fair. The thrust of the speech was that presidential LEADERSHIP should work toward the commonwealth by regulating the economy so that no sector—business, labor, or consumers—would have an unfair advantage. Government's role was to referee the marketplace by standards of "honesty, decency, fair-dealing and common sense," not to guarantee outcomes. The speech, however, gave no details about how Roosevelt would deal with difficult issues.

From the outset of his presidency, Roosevelt was keenly aware of the antireformist bent of the conservative wing of his REPUBLICAN PARTY in Congress. TR thus exercised EXECUTIVE POWER to address public concerns and waited to push his strongest legislation. In early 1902 Roosevelt breathed new life into the SHERMAN ANTITRUST ACT (1880) by bringing suit against the Northern Securities Corporation, a holding company of major railroads and banks. Roosevelt's purpose was to show that the EXECUTIVE BRANCH possessed more power than the moneymen of the era. His administration would utilize the Bureau of Corpo-

rations (created in 1903) to bring more than 40 additional antitrust suits throughout his presidency. Later in 1902 TR intervened in the anthracite coal strike, winning concessions for labor and setting the precedent of facilitating such settlements. The Elkins Act of 1903, making it illegal for railroads and shippers to offer rebates, was a hint of legislative successes to come.

Roosevelt was elected to a full term in 1904 and sought to use his popular mandate to surmount congressional resistance to his Square Deal legislative reforms. TR appealed directly to the public from the BULLY PULPIT of the presidency. The Hepburn Act (1906) empowered the Interstate Commerce Commission to set maximum railroad shipping rates, paving the way for the creation of many of today's regulatory agencies. Roosevelt also succeeded in getting both the Pure Food and Drug and Meat Inspection acts through Congress in 1906, putting in place the bedrock of government protection of consumers. TR ultimately would advocate greater economic redistribution in the form of an enlarged pension system for veterans, workman's compensation, and health and retirement insurance—programs that would come into being during subsequent decades.

The Square Deal helped move the United States away from laissez-faire economics and was a crucial precursor of the modern regulatory and distributive state. Presidents William TAFT and Woodrow WILSON would build on the Square Deal to further enlarge government's role in the economy. The Square Deal, coupled with TR's expansive view of presidential power, helped prepare the way for the arrival of the modern presidency under Franklin D. ROOSEVELT. After TR, the power of the president would depend foremost on the success of his political relationship with the American people, who would look to him to initiate policy and guarantee fairness. Subsequent CHIEF EXECUTIVES have attached labels to their domestic agendas (NEW DEAL, FAIR DEAL, GREAT SOCIETY, New Convenant) to capture the spirit of their initiatives.

Further reading: Blum, John Morton. *The Republican Roosevelt,* 2d ed. Cambridge, Mass.: Harvard University Press, 1977; Himmelberg, Robert F. *Business and Government in America since 1870,* Vol. 2: *The Monopoly Issue and Antitrust, 1900–1917.* New York: Garland, 1994; Mowry, George E. *The Era of Theodore Roosevelt, 1900–1912.* New York: Harper, 1958.

—Douglas M. Brattebo

staff, presidential

There are two varieties of presidential staff: institutional and personal. Presidential institutional staff are those men and women in the EXECUTIVE OFFICE OF THE PRESIDENT who, except for their top political leadership, have career status and serve from presidency to presidency. Personal presidential staff are those who serve at the president's pleasure, either in the WHITE HOUSE OFFICE or its closely associated units (if any are detailed or assigned to the personal staff, their status, if they are careerists, is only in the home agencies from which they have come). The Executive Office of the President, established by Franklin ROOSEVELT in September 1939, now has 12 units of presidential staff.

The President's Institutional Staff

Six of the 12 units of the Executive Office constitute the institutional staff of the president; they are: the OFFICE OF MANAGEMENT AND BUDGET (OMB) (about 527 people; created in 1921 and moved into the Executive Office as its first unit in 1939); the COUNCIL OF ECONOMIC ADVISERS or CEA (about 35 people; created in 1946); the OFFICE OF SCIENCE AND TECHNOLOGY POLICY (about 40 people; created in 1962); the Office of the United States Trade Representative (about 203 people, created in 1963); the COUNCIL ON ENVIRONMENTAL QUALITY/Office of Environmental Quality (about 24 people; created in 1969); and the Office of National Drug Control Policy (about 115 people; created by EXECUTIVE ORDER in 1971, by statute in 1988).

These six offices are continuing offices of the presidency. Each is headed by one or more leaders who are nominated by the president and confirmed by the Senate; those heads are expected to—and frequently do—testify before congressional committees. While several of these six units have additional noncareer appointees as part of their leadership, almost all of their staffs are professionals with career CIVIL SERVICE status. Their files are kept from administration to administration and form the institutional memory of the presidency; their papers (except those of CEA, and some of OSTP) are "agency records" which come under the purview of the Federal Records Act and are subject to FREEDOM OF INFORMATION ACT lawsuits. For more detailed information on these six offices, readers are referred to the pertinent sections of this encyclopedia.

The President's Personal Staff

Five of the 12 units of the Executive Office of the President constitute the personal staff of the president. They are: the White House Office (about 462 people, plus some 4,200 others when one includes the SECRET SERVICE units which protect the first family, the White House Military Office, interns, and volunteers); the vice president and his staff and residence (about 75 people); the Executive Residence (about 95 people); the NATIONAL SECURITY COUNCIL staff (about 225 people); and the OFFICE OF POLICY DEVELOPMENT (the economic and domestic policy advisers, about 60 people); White House maintenance and support personnel from the National Park Service (100), the General Services Administration (133), and the U.S. Postal Service (21). The 12th unit of the Executive Office, the OFFICE OF ADMINISTRATION, has 202 people, nearly half of whom are in direct support of the White House; the others serve the Executive Office generally.

The president's personal staff—the total White House staff community—thus numbers about 5,500 men and women. As members of the personal staff, none of them have career tenure in their White House positions; they all serve at the president's pleasure. They have no statutory duties other than to assist and advise the president. They are not confirmed by the Senate. They do not formally testify before congressional committees (except in unusual circumstances of scandalous or allegedly criminal behavior). Their official papers are PRESIDENTIAL PAPERS and come under the purview of the PRESIDENTIAL RECORDS ACT—immune from FREEDOM OF INFORMATION ACT lawsuits.

While it is theoretically possible, the advent of a new president never means that 5,500 people are replaced. Perhaps 1,200 of them will change. Nearly 4,300 of them, however, are technical and support professionals, and as such are invited to continue on into the next administration. Some of them serve succeeding presidents for 20, 30, and 40 years (the record is 50). They have a dual pride: for the president who is their boss, and for the office—the presidency—which is sustained by their dedicated expertise.

There are 130 separately identifiable units in the modern White House staff. There are 48 policy offices (two newly created examples are the Deputy National Security Adviser for Combating Terrorism, and the Director of the OFFICE OF HOMELAND SECURITY and his growing group of assistants). There are 31 supporting policy offices (for example the spouse of the vice president, the CHIEF OF STAFF to the first lady). There are 51 professional and technical offices (such as the SITUATION ROOM of the National Security Council, the Executive Clerk, the staff at CAMP DAVID, the 900-member White House Communications Agency, which handles the president's secure communications, and the crews who fly AIR FORCE ONE and the Marine One helicopter).

The costs of the White House—its total budget—are extremely difficult to ascertain. Besides the amounts publicly attributed to the Executive Office institutions, White House costs are contributed by many different agencies: STATE, DEFENSE, TREASURY, INTERIOR, the General Services Administration, the NATIONAL ARCHIVES and Records Administration, and a dozen or more agencies which send detailees (staff borrowed from other agencies) to the White House. A competent estimate of the annual total White House budget is more than $730,000,000.

Running the modern White House is a management challenge of the first magnitude. The senior policy officers are driven men and women, handling matters of crucial sensitivity under stressful pressures. The jurisdictional divisions among those 130 White House offices have to be kept clear; for example, the Office of Presidential Personnel controls the patronage process—others keep out; the counsel advises the president on legal matters—others don't play at being counsel; the legislative affairs director governs contacts on the Hill—other staffers are not welcome up there unless they speak with one voice.

Deadlines are merciless, egos are big, working hours are awesome. Thanks to beepers and cell phones, staffers are never off duty; their family life is constantly at the mercy of overriding presidential requirements. The White House is a glass house, with both the klieg lights and the heat of acrimonious criticism streaming in—from the press, from Congress, from interest groups. The White House staff environment has been described as a magnetohydrodynamic plasma of pressures, conflicts, diverse personalities, and fast-moving events.

Yet however specialized and separate the jurisdictions, however pressured the demands, however inflated the egos, all those 130 offices must work in exquisitely organized synchronization to support presidential initiatives. A forthcoming major address, an important new initiative in a message to the Congress, or the run-up to a summit conference requires tightly managed coordination among all staff units—from the speechwriters to the Secret Service, from the communications spinners to the Social Office. There is one supercoordinator who is the system manager for the whole White House community: the CHIEF OF STAFF. The chief is guardian of the president's schedule, doorway, and in-box. Discussions of tough issues are first rehearsed in his office. He is both diplomat and disciplinarian, son of a bitch and smoother of ruffled feelings. One chief of staff veteran described that position in two words: "javelin catcher." To further efficiency, the White House offers the personal presidential staff some privileges: personal contact with the president, social occasions at the residence, meals in the White House mess, travel in limousines or on Air Force One. A few staffers succumb to the temptation to let these privileges go to their heads, make stupid mistakes—and pay the price. They are a tiny minority, however. In spite of all pressures and sacrifices, service on the presidential staff is an honor and is almost without exception rendered—usually anonymously—by men and women of true brilliance and high personal integrity. In presidency after presidency, the governance of the nation is made more effective thanks to the competence and dedication of the presidential staff.

Further reading: Kernell, Samuel, and Samuel Popkin, eds. *Chief of Staff: Twenty-Five Years of Managing the Presidency.* Berkeley: University of California Press, 1986; Patterson, Bradley H. *Ring of Power: The White House Staff and its Expanding Role in Government.* New York: Basic Books, 1988; ———. *The White House Staff: Inside the West Wing and Beyond.* Washington, D.C.: Brookings Institution, 2000.

—Bradley H. Patterson

Starr Report (1998)

Kenneth Starr was appointed as INDEPENDENT COUNSEL on August 5, 1994, in order to continue the ongoing investigation into Whitewater and the death of Vincent Foster that had been begun by Robert Fiske. Attorney General Janet Reno expanded Starr's jurisdiction in March 1996 to include an examination of the dismissal of staff in the White House Travel Office, and again in June of that year to investigate the charges that the Clinton administration had misused confidential FBI files. Clinton's reputation had seen better days by the end of 1997. The investigation of Whitewater had been successful, resulting in several convictions and guilty pleas. However, the White House Travel Office and FBI files probe seemed to be languishing. In fact, Starr stunned the country on February 17, 1997, with his announcement that he was resigning as independent counsel to accept a position at Pepperdine University. Four days later, he reversed his decision.

On January 16, 1998, Reno and the Justice Department again expanded Starr's jurisdiction to now include the investigation of possible subornation of perjury, obstruction of justice, and the intimidation of witnesses surrounding the affair between President Clinton and White House intern Monica Lewinsky. This added assignment helped to create the impression that Starr was on a vendetta to get Clinton after the earlier investigations had failed to bear fruit in terms of incriminating evidence against the president.

In terms of the nearly yearlong investigation into the Lewinsky matter, Starr prevailed in legal disputes after the White House tried to place one hurdle after another in his path. Their arguments ranged from EXECUTIVE PRIVILEGE to attorney-client privilege to the position that the SECRET SERVICE agents responsible for Clinton's protection should not be compelled to testify with respect to his actions. Starr also took flak for forcing Monica Lewinsky's mother to the stand, as well as for his efforts to obtain a list of the purchases Lewinsky had made at a bookstore. Starr paid a price for these techniques. However, at this point in the investigation, Lewinsky was not cooperating with the Office of the Independent Counsel. After Lewinsky replaced her original attorney, William Ginsburg, with two seasoned veterans, the investigation quickly progressed. In his role as the independent counsel, Starr was never able to effectively counter the charges streaming from the White House that this was a one-man partisan witch-hunt of the president. He was also regularly accused of leaking grand jury testimony. With respect to Lewinsky's blue dress and the accompanying DNA evidence, Starr was labeled with being obsessed with sex. However, many argue that Clinton would have never told the truth without such irrefutable evidence.

Out of this aforementioned investigation, he forwarded a report on the Lewinsky matter to the U.S. House of Representatives on September 11, 1998, with the conclusion that President Clinton may have engaged in impeachable offenses. The report was criticized for the salacious details of Clinton's relationship with Lewinsky. Starr and his legal team decided to record the details of the affair according to Lewinsky. The content of the report was deeply divisive. Some argued that it was impossible to discuss the legal and constitutional issues at stake without including those details. Others believed that they were included only to politically weaken Clinton.

Once the Starr Report was submitted, Henry Hyde (Rep.), chairman of the House Judiciary Committee, decided to submit a list of 81 questions to Clinton regarding the details of the scandal. When the president responded to the questions with legalistic technical answers, the Republican members of the committee decided to move forward. The hearings that followed were acrimonious and partisan. Also, many felt that Starr was mistaken in his decision to testify before the House Judiciary Committee. This report and subsequent testimony eventually resulted in the U.S. House of Representatives approving two articles of IMPEACHMENT on December 19, 1998. The first article dealing with perjury passed by a vote of 228 to 206. The second article on obstruction of justice passed on a 221 to 212 vote. Both articles were, for the most part, voted on along party lines. However, on February 12, 1999, the U.S. Senate voted not to remove Clinton from office. Neither article was able to raise even a simple majority in favor of the president's removal from office.

Further reading: Rozell, Mark J., and Clyde Wilcox, eds. *The Clinton Scandal and the Future of American Government.* Washington, D.C.: Georgetown University Press, 2000; Wayne, Stephen J. "With Enemies Like This, Who Needs Friends." *Presidential Studies Quarterly* (Summer 1999): 773–79; Zaller, John R. "Monica Lewinsky's Contribution to Political Science." *PS: Political Science and Politics* 31 (1988): 183–189.

—Jean-Philippe Faletta

State Department

One of the four original cabinet posts (JEFFERSON was the first secretary of State), the State Department is today one of the keys to presidential control of foreign policy making and implementation. While some presidents prefer to make foreign policy directly out of the White House (e.g., President NIXON), most presidents rely heavily on the State Department and the secretary of State. The secretary is appointed by the president with the advice and consent of the Senate. The secretary is almost always a key adviser and part of the president's "inner cabinet."

statement and account clause

In an effort to establish some openness and accountability in public financing, the framers of the Constitution, in Article I,

Section 9, Clause 7, call for the federal government to issue "a regular Statement and Account of the Receipts and Expenditures of all Public Money." This report "shall be published from time to time." Financial openness, an essential component of democratic ACCOUNTABILITY, is thus embedded in the U.S. Constitution.

State of the Union addresses

State of the Union addresses are one of the few actions (nominations being another) and the only speech required by the U.S. Constitution which states that the president ". . . shall, from time to time, give Congress information on the state of the union . . ." (Article II, Section 3). George WASHINGTON began the practice of supplying this information in the form of a yearly message.

The Constitution does not mandate the scheduling of the address, but it is given by tradition in January or early February. At the president's request, Congress sends an invitation to the White House, which the president then accepts, and the speech is then scheduled. It is always given in the House chamber, reflecting its symbolic importance as a message to both Congress and the American people. Members of the House, the Senate, and the Supreme Court all attend, as do all but one member of the president's CABINET (who remains in a secure location to provide leadership in the case of catastrophe).

From Washington's administration into Franklin D. ROOSEVELT's, the State of the Union address was called "the annual message," reflecting both the language in the Constitution and the tradition that the message was generally sent to Congress rather than orally delivered to it. Prior to Woodrow WILSON's administration, the message was important, but it did not garner the attention it now does. Now, of course, the address receives considerable attention from both the public and the national media. It is always televised live and is carried on all major networks. It is accompanied by great fanfare and expectation, for it is the only annual event in which the branches of government appear together and are collectively exhorted to specific policy action by the president.

Few presidents, no matter how poor their communicative skill, fail to take advantage of this opportunity. As Karlyn Kohrs Campbell and Kathleen Hall Jamieson note, the State of the Union address gives the president the opportunity to enact his unique position as the sole voice of the nation. In thus speaking, the president becomes in effect the national historian, as he reflects upon the past in ways that allow him to reconstitute the present and rhetorically project the nation into the future. He does this through an enumeration of values which are given meaning through concrete historical circumstances.

These addresses are deliberative in form, moving from values to assessments to recommendations. The focus is on connecting national values to national policies. Generally speaking, they change slightly in emphasis over a president's administration, with the first prefiguring the goals and ideals of the administration, those in the middle looking both forward and backward offering impetus to the president's program, and the final address recapitulating the accomplishments of the administration. The final State of the Union address may thus either complement or sometimes serve as a farewell address.

Despite this temporal variation, State of the Union addresses are generally characterized by three elements: a public mediation on values, an assessment of current information and issues, and policy recommendations. All State of the Union addresses also involve the creation and celebration of national identity, which, because it is used to tie together the past, present, and future, functions rhetorically to sustain both the nation and the presidency as an institution.

State of the Union addresses are rooted in values, which are in turn grounded in a particular president's interpretation of national history. This history is nearly always an optimistic one, even in times of great national travail. It is used to celebrate the national ethos, to offer evidence for the assertion that our national problems will be solved, and to set the stage for the implicit argument that the president's policy proposals are "nonpolitical" and bipartisan, that they serve the national interest and not the narrow political interest of the president or his political party.

This reflection on national values as a guide to action is followed, in most cases, by an examination of enduring national issues. Usually, these issues are discussed in relatively generalized if not abstract terms and function as a rhetorical bridge between the national values of the speech's introduction and the recommendations that will form its conclusion.

The policy recommendations are often the longest section of the addresses and comprise what is generally referred to as a "laundry list" of specific legislative proposals. This section of the address prefigures the president's budget proposals, which are usually sent to Capitol Hill shortly after the speech is delivered. While purely symbolic proposals are there as well, the proposals that are included in the address generally have broad support within the administration and the president's party and represent the president's legislative agenda for the coming year and, to some degree, for the remainder of his term.

As television has become increasingly important, presidents have sought to capitalize on the "good visuals" of the State of the Union address. The setting and occasion serve presidents well in this regard, but there have been some innovations as well. Most notably, in 1982 Ronald REAGAN invited Lenny Skutnik, whose actions following a plane crash at Washington National Airport were used in the address as an example of American heroism, to be present in the House chamber during the address. Since that time, it has become common for presidents to introduce one or more exemplary citizens as visual props for the address.

While largely deliberative, State of the Union addresses also contain elements of epideictic address, in which the character of the president serves to exemplify the character of the nation. These addresses thus serve as powerful affirmations of the strength and power of the presidency and of the nation. They are important opportunities for the display of presidential LEADERSHIP—the best example being Bill CLINTON's performance in the midst of the Lewinsky crisis, which is often credited with resuscitating his presidency. As in that case, all State of the Union addresses are important rhetorical and political occasions, serving to unify the nation and to underline the enduring nature of the presidency as an institution.

Further reading: Campbell, Karlyn Kohrs, and Kathleen Hall Jamieson. *Deeds Done in Words: Presidential Rhetoric and the Genres of Governance.* Chicago: University of Chicago Press, 1990; Fields, Wayne. *Union of Words: A History of Presidential Eloquence.* New York: Free Press, 1996; Gellerman, Carol. *All the President's Words: The Bully Pulpit and the Creation of the Virtual Presidency.* New York: Walker and Co., 1997; Roderick, P. Hart. *The Sound of Leadership: Presidential Communication in the Modern Age.* Chicago: University of Chicago Press, 1987.

—Mary E. Stuckey and Colleen Blanchard

Stevenson, Adlai E. (1835–1914) *U.S. vice president*

Vice president during Grover CLEVELAND's second presidential term, Stevenson was a powerful leader of the DEMOCRATIC PARTY in Illinois, and grandfather of Adlai Stevenson III, the Democratic Party nominee for president in 1952 and 1956. In 1900 Stevenson was again nominated for VICE PRESIDENT on a ticket with William Jennings BRYAN. They were defeated by MCKINLEY.

Stevenson, Adlai E., II (1900–1965) *governor, diplomat*

Adlai Ewing Stevenson was born in Los Angeles on February 5, 1900, and grew up in Bloomington, Illinois. He came from a political family that included Jesse Fell, his maternal great-grandfather, a prominent Republican and LINCOLN supporter, as well as his paternal grandfather, Adlai E. STEVENSON, who was Grover CLEVELAND's VICE PRESIDENT in Cleveland's second term from 1893 to 1897. Stevenson attended preparatory school at Choate and went on to Princeton, where he graduated in 1922. He continued his education at Harvard Law School but returned to Bloomington to work as assistant managing editor of the family paper, *The Daily Pantagraph,* while the Illinois courts probated his grandfather's will. Stevenson reentered law school at Northwestern University and graduated in 1926. His marriage to Ellen Borden, a Chicago socialite, in 1928 lasted until their divorce in 1949, and they had three sons: Adlai E. Stevenson III, Borden Stevenson, and John Fell Stevenson.

Adlai Stevenson joined a conservative Chicago law firm, Cutting, Moore, and Sidley, but moved into government in Washington with various federal agency appointments in the early 1930s during the NEW DEAL. Returning to Chicago in 1935, his interests in FOREIGN AFFAIRS grew as leader in the Council on Foreign Relations and in the Committee to Defend America by Aiding the Allies. He returned to Washington in 1940 as special assistant to Secretary of the Navy Frank Knox and after WORLD WAR II moved to the STATE DEPARTMENT and was involved as the U.S. delegate to the Preparatory Commission of the UN Organization in 1946. He was encouraged to run for governor of Illinois in 1948 and soundly defeated the incumbent, Dwight Green, in a landslide. During his administration he reorganized the state police force and improved the educational system, highways, and welfare programs in the state.

With Stevenson's rising reputation as governor, President TRUMAN proposed that Stevenson seek the Democratic nomination for president in 1952. Stevenson preferred to run for a second term as governor, but the convention delegates drafted him, and he accepted the nomination at the convention in Chicago. He selected Senator John Sparkman from Alabama as his running mate but was not able to overcome a very popular Dwight EISENHOWER, whose war experience placed him at an advantage over Stevenson, who was forced into defending Truman's foreign policy of CONTAINMENT against communism. After the election Stevenson traveled extensively, continued his law practice, and became a fund-raiser for the DEMOCRATIC PARTY. In 1956 he actively sought the presidential nomination with Senator Estes Kefauver of Tennessee as his running mate. His emphasis on foreign affairs and support for ending H-bomb tests weakened his position against a strong President Eisenhower, and he lost the race a second time by an even wider margin than in 1952.

Stevenson again returned to his law practice, and in 1960 he stated that he would not seek the presidential nomination but would accept another draft. After John KENNEDY's election as president, Adlai Stevenson hoped for the position of secretary of State, but he instead was offered the role of U.S. ambassador to the UNITED NATIONS. In this appointment he defended U.S. policy in areas such as opposing the admission of the People's Republic of China to the UN and challenging Soviet strategy during the CUBAN MISSILE CRISIS. At the same time Stevenson became disillusioned with certain U.S. policies, such as the BAY OF PIGS invasion of Cuba in 1961, and began to discuss ways to end U.S. involvement in Vietnam with Secretary General U Thant. During a stop in London upon returning from addressing the Economic and Social Council in Geneva, he died suddenly on July 14, 1965.

Further reading: Baker, Jean H. *The Stevensons: A Biography of an American Family.* New York: Norton, 1996; Broadwater, Jeff. *Adlai Stevenson and American Politics: The Odyssey of a Cold War Liberal.* New York: Twayne, 1994; McKeever, Porter. *Adlai Stevenson: His Life and Legacy.* New York: Morrow, 1989.

—Michael G. Krukones

stewardship theory   See PRESIDENCY, THEORIES OF THE.

Stimson, Henry L.   (1867–1950)   *secretary of state, secretary of War, diplomat*

Stimson served nearly every U.S. president from Teddy ROOSEVELT to Harry TRUMAN. His most prominent appointments were as President TAFT's secretary of war, COOLIDGE's governor general of the Philippines, Herbert HOOVER's secretary of state, where clashes with Hoover made him somewhat ineffective, and as Franklin Roosevelt's secretary of war during WORLD WAR II. ROOSEVELT chose Stimson, a Republican, to demonstrate his BIPARTISANSHIP in foreign policy.

Strategic Arms Limitation Talks   (SALT)

For over a decade from 1968 to 1980, the negotiation of treaties involving limitations on long-range missiles, warheads, and bombers (what came to be known as the Strategic Arms Limitations Talks or SALT) were high politics for the two COLD WAR superpowers and major issues for all the presidents from Lyndon JOHNSON to Ronald REAGAN. Discussions at the highest levels or ceremonies celebrating the signing of new ARMS CONTROL agreements were on the agenda when Johnson met Kosygin in Glassboro, New Jersey, when NIXON traveled to Moscow in 1972, when FORD went to Vladivostok in 1974, and when CARTER had his 1979 summit with Brezhnev in Vienna.

From the beginning, negotiations between the two cold war rivals about how many and what kinds of weapons each could aim at the other were understandably difficult. Johnson's advisers, led by Secretary of Defense Robert MCNAMARA, tried to convince the Soviets that defensive missile systems, which both nations were developing in the 1960s, should be abandoned. These antiballistic missiles, or ABMs, were expensive, unreliable, and likely to fuel an arms race since any effectiveness they possessed could easily be overcome by the deployment of still more offensive weapons.

Ironically, from the outset of these negotiations American officials argued that both superpowers would be better off without defensive missiles. Instead, they should accept their mutual vulnerability. If each recognized their vulnerability to total destruction, they might exercise greater caution in cold war confrontations. Agreements to willingly maintain and manage that vulnerability might even contribute to better relations and ensure a stable balance of power.

Johnson had hoped to begin formal talks about strategic arms during his last year in office but had to put those plans on the shelf when Soviet tanks rolled into Czechoslovakia. After a presidential election and some delay, the Nixon administration adopted a negotiating position that was largely based on the Johnson plans and eventually negotiated an ABM treaty severely restricting the development and deployment of missile defenses. That treaty, together with a looser set of temporary restrictions on offensive strategic weapons, became known as SALT I.

Moving beyond the 1972 agreements was not easy. It took seven years and three presidents to settle on a second set of arms limitations, known as SALT II. The provisions of SALT II were complicated, involving different caps on different types of delivery systems and very few restrictions on the new technologies that were making all strategic weapons more accurate and more lethal.

More important, the SALT process, which was always closely connected to the DÉTENTE, suffered from the general deterioration of U.S.-Soviet relations in the second half of the 1970s. While the ratification of SALT II was officially withdrawn from Senate consideration after the Soviet invasion of Afghanistan, it was in serious political trouble well before Soviet troops arrived in Kabul.

Critics on the right, led by Ronald Reagan, were afraid that strategic arms agreements were lulling the Congress and the American people into a dangerous complacency about a growing Soviet military threat. Moreover, Reagan and his neoconservative supporters (including some former SALT negotiators) claimed that the Soviet Union cheated on existing arms control commitments and would only respond to an aggressive American strategic military buildup. SALT II, Reagan said in the 1980 campaign, was fatally flawed and should be rejected. By the time these political attacks from the right were gaining strength, there were very few effective advocates for the kind of complicated arms control that was emerging from years of tedious negotiations between the superpowers. The left would have to wait for the mid 1980s when the simple idea of a "nuclear freeze" and the apparent dangers of a revitalized cold war and arms race could generate a national grassroots protest movement.

Students of the presidency have studied the SALT process for what it tells us about the broader issues of the cold war and the ways that presidents manage, or mismanage, complicated political-military issues. According to Henry KISSINGER, the internal negotiations within the federal BUREAUCRACY about the development of strategic arms control proposals were always more difficult than the subsequent negotiations with the Soviet Union. And all of these negotiations had to be done under the shadow of the constitutional requirement for Senate ratification of any treaties they might produce. There were very few issues in the cold war era that were as complex or as politically vexing as the various stages and steps that led to the success of SALT I and the failure to ratify SALT II.

Further reading: Newhouse, John. *Cold Dawn: The Story of SALT.* New York: Holt, Rinehart and Winston, 1973; Talbott, Strobe. *End Game: The Inside Story of SALT II.* New York: Harper & Row, 1979.

—Robert Strong

Strategic Defense Initiative (SDI)

On the evening of March 23, 1983, President Ronald REAGAN addressed Americans on national television and announced: "I am directing a comprehensive and intensive effort to define a long-term research and development program to begin to achieve our ultimate goal of eliminating the threat posed by strategic nuclear missiles."

President Reagan's announcement had two immediate effects. First, it stunned many Americans, especially those accustomed to a U.S.-Soviet balance of terror predicated on nearly four decades of strategic nuclear offensive forces. Second, it polarized debate in the United States across a wide spectrum: politicians, scientists, engineers, the military, the clergy, and eventually millions of American citizens. Indeed, it was only a matter of hours before Senator Ted Kennedy attached the label "Star Wars" to the program that became officially the Strategic Defense Initiative (SDI), assigned to a new DEPARTMENT OF DEFENSE agency, the Strategic Defense Initiative Organization (SDIO).

SDI was a major sticking point in relations between the United States and Soviet Union. The Soviets felt that a missile shield would render their country vulnerable to a first strike and leave them incapable of responding. It was also clear to the Soviet leadership that developing and deploying a missile defense system of their own would be prohibitively expensive. So convinced that SDI would change the strategic relationship between the superpowers and could lead to a more pacific international environment, Reagan also considered sharing the technology with the Soviets in exchange for deep cuts in their strategic rocket forces.

In May 1993, in an attempt to jettison the acrimony surrounding SDI and to refocus research and development activities, the CLINTON administration changed the program's name to simply Ballistic Missile Defense and the agency to the Ballistic Missile Defense Organization (BMDO). In late 2001 the administration of George W. BUSH formally notified Russia of its intention to withdraw from the Antiballistic Missile Treaty in order to concentrate on moving forward with a missile defense program. In early 2002 the Bush administration refocused the program on countering missile threats from "rogue states" and renamed BMDO the Missile Defense Agency.

Further reading: Missile Defense Agency. "Fact Sheet: Ballistic Missile Defense Challenge." Washington, D.C.: Missile Defense Agency, January 2002; "Fact Sheet: Ballistic Missile Defense Approach." Washington, D.C.: Missile Defense Agency, January 2002; Newhouse, John. "The Missile Defense Debate." *Foreign Affairs* (July/August 2001): 97–109.

—Paul Kan

succession

Immediate presidential succession is established in Article II, Section 1, Clause 6, of the U.S. Constitution, which provides that "In case of the Removal of the President from Office, or of his death, Resignation, or Inability to discharge the Powers and Duties of the said Office, the Same shall devolve on the Vice President," with Congress given the authority to establish the line and circumstances of succession beyond the vice president. Two of these circumstances, death and incapacity, have been the principal issues surrounding presidential succession.

The first presidential succession law was passed in 1792 and made the president pro tempore of the Senate, followed by the speaker of the House, next in the succession line. Succession beyond the speaker was not established, nor were provisions for the selection of a new VICE PRESIDENT set forth.

The death of William Henry HARRISON in 1841 served as the first test of the presidential succession. Upon Harrison's death, Vice President John Tyler took the presidential OATH OF OFFICE, a move that caused immediate controversy. While Tyler contended that Harrison's death made him the president, opponents argued that he merely inherited the "powers and duties" of the presidency, not the presidency itself. Despite the controversy, the Tyler Precedent held, and in eight subsequent cases of presidential death or RESIGNATION, the vice president has assumed the office of the presidency without serious questions of the legitimacy of the ascension being raised.

While the "death" issue was settled early in the nation's political history, the problem of presidential DISABILITY remained unresolved. After being shot in 1881, James GARFIELD lingered for 80 days. Because Garfield was still alive, and fearing a backlash if he attempted to step in, Vice President Chester ARTHUR remained impotently in the shadows. The problem of presidential inability reached its most serious point following Woodrow Wilson's stroke in 1919. WILSON suffered from the effects of his stroke for the final 18 months of his presidency, and for six of those months very few people were allowed to see him. His condition was kept secret from the CABINET and Congress, and after Secretary of State Robert Lansing convened the cabinet more than 20 times in order to take care of pressing government business, Wilson fired him. Following his 1955 heart attack, Dwight EISENHOWER implemented an ad hoc system to conduct his responsibilities, but it was not until the assassination of John KENNEDY that efforts to provide for a more clearly defined law of succession made headway.

The result was the TWENTY-FIFTH AMENDMENT, which created the modern law of succession. It provided for filling vacancies in the vice presidency (Section 2), and for the incapacity of the president to fulfill his duties and responsibilities, whether his inability be self-declared (Section 3) or determined by the vice president and a majority of the cabinet officers (Section 4). Codifying the Tyler Precedent, it also clearly set forth in Section 1 that the vice president becomes president. To date, the Twenty-fifth Amendment has been implemented four times: with the resignations of Spiro AGNEW and Richard NIXON; the selection of Nelson ROCKEFELLER as Gerald FORD's vice president; and when Ronald REAGAN underwent anesthesia during surgical procedures in the 1980s.

The current line of succession now begins with the vice president, then moves to the speaker of the House, the president pro tempore of the Senate, the secretary of State, the secretary of Treasury, the secretary of Defense, the attorney general, and the remaining cabinet secretaries in order of the creation of their department: Interior, Agriculture, Commerce, Labor, Health and Human Services, Housing and Urban Development, Transportation, Energy, Education, and Veterans Affairs.

Further reading: Feerick, John D. *The Twenty-Fifth Amendment: Its Complete History and Earliest Applications.* New York: Fordham University Press, 1976.

—Sean C. Matheson

summit meetings

Summitry began in WORLD WAR II, largely through the efforts of Winston Churchill, who, although the oldest of the trio that included Franklin ROOSEVELT and Joseph Stalin, nonetheless flew frequently to meet with the other two, either individually or together. The 1941 meeting of Churchill and FDR off the coast of Canada at Placentia Bay was the first summit meeting.

Although there were meetings among heads of state before World War II (See Erik Goldstein in Dunn), it was the improved communication and transportation that facilitated the gatherings that became a diplomatic hallmark of the last half of the 20th century. The telegraph, radio, and the telephone permitted diplomats to prepare, and if desirable modify up to the last minute, agenda and ground rules. The days- or weeks-long ocean voyages, such as the one taken by Woodrow WILSON to reach Versailles, were replaced by air flights of mere hours.

It was not until 1950 that the term "summit" came into use. Churchill, concerned about the growing hostility between the opposing sides in the COLD WAR, called for a "parley at the summit" to ease tension. With the death of Stalin, the animosity was moderated between the two "superpowers," the Soviet Union and the United States. Churchill's desire for a summit meeting was realized when the superpowers met in Geneva, along with France and Britain.

Journalistic use of the term "summit meeting" has been imprecise: The narrowest and probably most useful refers to those person-to-person meetings of the heads of state of major nations that are intended to result in the conclusion of major foreign policy decisions. That is the use here, with a focus on summitry by American presidents.

There are two evident facets to summit meetings: substance and symbolism. Media coverage, which by the last years of the 20th century was worldwide and often instantaneous, made summit sessions media events whether or not much of substance was achieved. Meetings that are largely ceremonial may have significance for a nation in attendance, especially when its leader needs his or her stature to be validated at home and in the international community. Impressions can be more significant than substance. When Khrushchev and KENNEDY met at Vienna in 1961, no decisions resulted, but the Soviet leader evidently miscalculated the resolve and the competence of the youthful president, newly in office.

What can be considered a subcategory of summitry are meetings of heads of state at the funeral of a leader of a major nation. These tend to be more ceremonial than substantive since little planning precedes these events. Sufficient prior negotiation is crucial for successful substantive results.

Some heads of state have more freedom of action in conducting foreign policy. A British prime minister, leading a nation of declining international significance, has wide flexibility in these matters, while despite leading the world's most powerful nation, the American president must have treaties ratified by the U.S. Senate. Carter's difficulty in getting the SALT II Treaty approved is an example, albeit one that was undermined by the Soviet invasion of Afghanistan.

In general, summitry is resented by the career foreign services of the nations participating in these high-level gatherings. Career diplomats prefer the meticulous, back-and-forth, confidential negotiations of their trade rather than the dramatic, sometimes unexpected, outcomes that may arise at summit meetings. Margaret Thatcher and Nikita Khrushchev had little sympathy for their foreign service professionals and were not reluctant to ignore their counsel. Without the continual advice of diplomatic professionals, provocative proposals may be offered.

As did Thatcher, American presidents have frequently circumvented career diplomatic professionals and utilized other advisers in preparation for summit meetings. NIXON preferred to work primarily with White House staff. For major foreign policy issues, he frequently bypassed his first secretary of State, William Rogers, and the STATE DEPARTMENT to rely on his NATIONAL SECURITY ADVISER, Henry KISSINGER, who arranged the first U.S.-China summit meeting. Understandably, Rogers resented this practice; Kissinger replaced him in Nixon's second administration.

The use of summits by a new president is difficult to predict, as Reagan's conduct demonstrates. He assiduously declined to pursue this form of DIPLOMACY during his first four years in office, even to the extent of not attending the funerals of Leonid Brezhnev, Yuri Andropov, and Konstantin Chernenko, the Soviet leaders who died during 1982–85. Yet in the span of less than three years, November 1985–May 1988, REAGAN attended four summits: Geneva, Reykjavik, Washington, and Moscow.

For his first, in Geneva, Reagan was most fully prepared, having absorbed briefings on issues and Soviet behavior. Despite that preparation, little of substance emerged from the meeting, but the two leaders established a comfort level with each other. This rapport was crucial for their remaining summits. The Reykjavik summit was intended to advance the agenda for the subsequent Washington summit. Unexpectedly, Reagan announced he was willing to destroy the American stockpile of strategic arms, an offer that posed potential disaster for the Western alliance. Soviet opposition to the Reagan's Strategic Defense Initiative squashed the weapons concord, but it was unlikely that the American Senate would have ratified the proposal.

Although the Washington summit merely witnessed the signing of the previously negotiated Intermediate Nuclear Force Treaty, its larger significance was the warm welcome for the Soviet leader when he left his limousine to greet sidewalk crowds. At the Moscow summit, Reagan received a similar reception from Soviet citizens, who were harshly restrained by Soviet police. His television speech to the Soviet nation, in which he appealed for that populace to have more freedom, was also a triumph.

Presidents may use summit meetings to increase their domestic standing. Nixon's trip to China was probably the most effective in achieving that.

The "G" meetings began as the GROUP OF SEVEN gatherings among the major economic powers to discuss and formulate international economic policy. The precursor to the G-7 was the "Library Group" (White House Library) meetings of finance ministers that began in 1973. Two of those officials, West Germany's Helmut Schmidt and France's Valery Giscard d'Estaing, soon were their nations' heads of state and were instrumental in moving the discussion of ECONOMIC POLICY to a higher level, the leaders of the principal economic nations. The G-7 also included the United States, Britain, Japan, Italy, and Canada. Later Russia was invited to attend, creating the "Group of Eight," or G-8. These meetings are distinctive among summits in that they are regularly scheduled, rather than being convened expressly to acquaint heads of state with each other or to address a major issue, such as ARMS CONTROL. Summits have become a feature of major power diplomacy, achieving significant results on occasion, but they are invariably media events, and with consequences that may not be apparent at the time.

Further reading: Dunn, David H., ed. *Diplomacy at the Highest Level.* New York: St. Martin's Press, 1996; Fairbanks, Charles H., Jr. *The Allure of Summits.* Washington, D.C.: Foreign Policy Institute, 1988; Wilson, Theodore A. *The First Summit: Roosevelt and Churchill at Placentia Bay, 1941.* Lawrence: University Press of Kansas, 1991.

—Thomas P. Wolf

Super Tuesday

To increase the influence of southern states on the Democratic nomination process, the Southern Legislative Conference designed a regional primary called Super Tuesday, first held in early March of the 1988 presidential election. Bundling southern primaries began informally during the 1984 election in order to increase the influence of voters who preferred that a more moderate to conservative candidate win the Democratic nomination. In essence, southerners recognized that smaller states selecting delegates earlier in the presidential selection calendar, such as Iowa and New Hampshire, were realizing a disproportionate influence on the nomination outcome. In recent election cycles, Super Tuesday grew beyond the South to include primaries throughout the country, in total selecting more than one-half of the delegates to the national nomination conventions.

Super Tuesday produces a number of consequences for presidential nominations. First, media attention immediately shifted to candidates who naturally appealed to southern voters. As states outside the South began participating in Super Tuesday, attention again shifted to candidates who could perform well in multiple regions of the country. Second, campaigns switched to "air-war" strategies of television and radio advertising to reach caucus and primary voters. Finally, Super Tuesday winnowed the field of candidates, generally leaving only the front-runner. Any

other candidates remaining in the field are typically financially insolvent and/or mathematically eliminated from winning the competition.

In the first Super Tuesday held in 1988, Governor Michael DUKAKIS, Senator Al GORE, and Jesse L. Jackson divided the Democratic popular vote and delegate count evenly. The lone southern candidate, Gore, could not capitalize on the changes in the primary schedule and withdrew from the race soon thereafter. On March 10, 1992, the architects of Super Tuesday achieved their objective when Governor Bill CLINTON ascended to the position of frontrunner with convincing victories over his closest rival, former Senator Paul E. Tsongas of Massachusetts, in six southern states. That same day incumbent President George H. W. BUSH decisively won the six southern primaries plus contests in Massachusetts and Rhode Island. Four years later Senator Bob Dole closed the door on his nearest rival, commentator Patrick J. Buchanan, by sweeping the southern states plus Oregon. On March 7, 2000, 16 states held nomination contests. Both Al Gore and George W. BUSH swept the majority of those states, leaving their chief rivals to soon withdraw from competition.

Further reading: Norrander, Barbara. *Super Tuesday: Regional Politics and Presidential Primaries.* Lexington: University Press of Kentucky, 1992.

—Randall E. Adkins

symbolic presidency

As the only (with his VICE PRESIDENT) nationally elected officer of the government, with sworn responsibilities to the entire nation and its "sacred" document, the Constitution, the president, whatever his actual qualities as a person, stands as the preeminent symbol of national identity. As the symbol of the nation, the president embodies the beliefs and values of the American people and fulfills emotional and psychological needs among the population.

Given the absence in the American constitutional system of any rival to the president as the center of public attention, the presidency's symbolic importance was foreordained when the Constitution was adopted. But the symbolic potential of the presidency has been realized, and given substance, by particular presidents.

George WASHINGTON's most valuable qualification for the presidency was perhaps his symbolism. He was not simply a hero of American independence but *the* hero of the new nation. In truth, it could be said today that the nation won its independence only through General Washington's perseverance against the enemy and his stoic loyalty to an often ungrateful government. Though Washington had his enemies as president, none could deny that he was the one known as "Father of His Country." To all presidents since, and to all Americans, the presidency is the office of national "fatherhood."

An extraordinary change occurred in the presidency's symbolic meaning with the rise of Andrew JACKSON to the office. The framers had intended to keep the people in their collective capacity at a safe distance from the government, the presidency included. But as the American citizenry became imbued with democratic beliefs, they took possession of the presidency and made it their prize. Andrew Jackson proclaimed the new social contract between the president and the people when he declared himself the people's "direct representative" in their government.

Abraham LINCOLN also added enormously to the symbolism of the presidency. In upholding the principle of constitutional union, Lincoln solidified the nation as an organic whole, and the president's place at its heart. Through his words, Lincoln gave meaning to the war effort. This was not a mere matter of poetry. When Lincoln spoke the famous lines of the GETTYSBURG ADDRESS, for instance, he spoke symbolically of the nation and suggested that the Constitution was meaningful only in the context of the Declaration of Independence and the latter's promise of equality. These words had consequences. Because Lincoln meant what he said on this and similar occasions, and because enough people who heard his words had faith in them, the CIVIL WAR became a war for freedom as well as union, demonstrating that symbols are not merely vessels to be filled with the beliefs of their admirers but are active participants in shaping beliefs and turning beliefs into actions.

Presidential symbolism has helped presidents achieve lasting fame and inspired the nation during crises. Like any powerful tool, however, it can do harm as well as good. Presidents who otherwise might have enjoyed more suc-cess, such as Herbert HOOVER, Lyndon JOHNSON, Richard NIXON, and Jimmy CARTER, have failed in office in part because they could not rise to the symbolic demands of the job.

Moreover, the thirst for symbolic demonstrations of presidential LEADERSHIP may be undermining the rationality of American democracy. By equating the presidency with democracy, we risk trading the appearance of democratic rule for the real thing. Some political scientists argue, for instance, that recent presidents, including Ronald REAGAN and George Herbert Walker BUSH, have attempted to lull a passive public into acceptance of their rule by providing spectacles of presidential omnipotence, such as small-scale but media-worthy uses of military force abroad. Other analysts caution that President Bill CLINTON's insinuation of symbolic kinship with the people while he was under IMPEACHMENT turned what should have been a constitutional struggle into a contest over personal likability. Whatever the merits of these specific claims, the people who come into possession of the American presidency will continue to be clothed in the heavy raiment of presidential symbolism.

Further reading: Hinckley, Barbara. *The Symbolic Presidency: How Presidents Portray Themselves.* New York: Routledge, 1990; Langston, Thomas. *With Reverence and Contempt: How Americans Think About Their President.* Baltimore, Md.: Johns Hopkins University Press, 1995; Miroff, Bruce. "The Presidency and the Public: Leadership as Spectacle." In *The Presidency and the Political System,* 4th ed., edited by Michael Nelson. Washington, D.C.: CQ Press, 1994.

—Thomas Langston

T

Taft, William H. (1857–1930) *twenty-seventh U.S. president*

William Howard Taft is the only president to have also served as chief justice of the United States (1921–30). Born into a prominent Republican family in Ohio, Taft set his sights on a judicial career aimed ultimately at a seat on the Supreme Court. His rise to national prominence came almost exclusively by appointment rather than election to higher office. Appointed as assistant county prosecutor of Hamilton County (1880), assistant county solicitor of Hamilton County (1885), judge of the Superior Court of Ohio (1887), SOLICITOR GENERAL of the United States (1890), judge of the Sixth Judicial Circuit Court (1892), first governor general of the Philippines (1900), and secretary of war (1903) in the Theodore ROOSEVELT administration, Taft made his way to the heights of national Republican politics, positioning himself along the way for an appointment as chief justice of the United States. When the aging Democratic appointee Chief Justice Melville Fuller refused to retire, Taft sought the presidency instead, using Roosevelt's help in engineering the Republican presidential nomination in 1908. Democrats complained that Roosevelt had handpicked his successor and dubbed the nomination "a forced succession to the presidency." Elected in the midst of rising progressive protest, Taft soon found himself "a fish out of water" in the White House and unable to handle the rising tide of the progressive movement.

Much to the chagrin of Roosevelt, who had been led to believe that his successor would retain most of the CABINET, Taft proceeded to supplant Roosevelt appointees with his own loyalists, many of them corporate lawyers. Although committed to the domestic and international policies of his predecessor, Taft's legalistic style, Ohio conservatism, and political inexperience as a popular leader led to two major missteps in his first two years in office—the Payne-Aldrich Tariff Act of 1909 and the Ballinger-Pinchot controversy. Those missteps widened the split within the REPUBLICAN PARTY between the "stand-pat" and the pro-

gressive wings of the party, led Taft to unwisely attempt a purge of progressive Republican legislators, encouraged the return of Theodore Roosevelt to the national stage in 1910, and produced the split between Taft and Roosevelt at the 1912 Republican convention and the loss of the White House to the Democrats.

Payne-Aldrich Tariff

During the Roosevelt administration, public complaints against the "trusts" and the traditional high tariff policies of the Republican Party continued to grow. As a celebrated "trust-buster," Roosevelt was sympathetic to the movement to lower tariffs that sustained the trusts but he recognized that tariff revision was a no-win issue that would unleash political forces that inevitably would jeopardize the reelection of a president. He left the issue for his successor to tackle. Taft biographer Henry Pringle dubbed the issue Roosevelt's "legacy of doom." Taft summoned a special session of Congress in March 1909 to address the issue head-on. Aligning himself with the "stand-pat" Republican leaders of Congress with whom Roosevelt had been feuding, he was informed that he would be given a chance to shape the final bill when it reached the conference committee stage. By then it was too late to produce the significant downward revisions that the public had been led to expect. Taft then compounded his problems with the disappointed progressive wing of his party by subsequently describing the bill as "the best tariff bill that the Republican Party ever passed." The president's allegedly unholy alliance with the congressional leadership infuriated progressives, who concluded that Taft had been less than candid in portraying himself as a Roosevelt progressive.

The Ballinger-Pinchot Controversy

The second major political controversy that defined the Taft presidency as antiprogressive was the Ballinger-Pinchot controversy, in which Taft collided with Gifford Pinchot, head of the Forestry Service. Pinchot was a close friend and political ally of Roosevelt and a leader of the true believers of the progressive conservation movement. When Pinchot observed the appointment of Secretary of the Interior Richard A. Ballinger and the legalistic policies of the new president that questioned Roosevelt's withdrawal of federal lands by EXECUTIVE ORDER for conservation purposes, Pinchot was incensed and launched a guerrilla war against the administration and its land use policies. Seizing upon the charges of a minor official of the General Land Office, Pinchot asserted that Ballinger had nefariously facilitated an attempt by a syndicate of bankers to gain control of federal coal lands in Alaska through fraudulent means. Seeking a change in administration policies or political martyrdom, Pinchot persisted in his attacks on Ballinger and forced Taft to fire him for insubordination. Believing Ballinger to be innocent of the Pinchot charges, Taft stubbornly refused to accept Ballinger's resignation until well after significant damage had been done to the president's reputation as a progressive defender of Roosevelt's conservation policies.

Taft's alliance with the standpat leaders of Congress did produce a number of legislative dividends—the Mann Elkins Act of 1910 which strengthened the regulatory powers of the Interstate Commerce Commission, a postal savings bank bill, congressional approval of Roosevelt's withdrawal of public lands, a Tariff Board committed to setting tariff rates in a more scientific manner than the logrolling legislative process, a constitutional amendment permitting the income tax, and continued appropriations for a larger navy. Whatever legislative benefits Taft reaped from his alliance with the standpat congressional leadership were quickly overshadowed by Roosevelt's triumphant return from his yearlong sojourn to Africa and Europe. When Roosevelt embarked on a speaking tour of the West in the fall of 1910, he pointedly refused to endorse his successor's record and immediately became a lightning rod for disenchanted progressives who yearned for his return to the White House in 1912.

Taft's political ineptness and the fallout from the Payne-Aldrich Tariff and the Ballinger-Pinchot affair contributed to a stunning defeat of Republican regulars in the congressional midterm elections of 1910. Democrats erased an 80-vote Republican majority in the House and captured control by a 68-vote margin. Republicans lost eight Senate seats but retained control of the Senate. As voting returns came in on election eve, a stunned Taft lamented that the election result was "not only a landslide but a tidal wave and holocaust all rolled into one general cataclysm." Reelection in 1912 appeared highly doubtful.

With the House under Democratic control, Taft's ability to lead Congress in his last two years in office was diminished significantly. Nevertheless, he gamely summoned a special session of the newly elected Congress in March 1911 to push a Canadian Reciprocity Agreement which, if passed,

President William H. Taft *(Library of Congress)*

would have moved the United States closer to a commercial union with Canada. However, when a new nationalist Canadian government was elected that was committed to preventing the agreement from being approved, the Reciprocity Agreement collapsed completely. Taft, nevertheless, continued to address issues that were within his control as CHIEF EXECUTIVE. He continued to oversee the completion of the Panama Canal. He extended the merit system to 70,000 additional federal employees. He initiated twice as many antitrust suits as had his "trust-busting" predecessor. And, most significantly for the modern presidency, he sought to rationalize the budget-making process by centralizing budgetary control in the White House. His proposal for reform, however, was eventually adopted by Congress in the BUDGET AND ACCOUNTING ACT OF 1921. Finally, Taft made six appointments to the Supreme Court, including the appointment of aging southern Democrat Edward White as Chief Justice, an unprecedented act of BIPARTISANSHIP that left open the possibility that Taft might some day yet be elevated to the Chief Justiceship. Taft's six appointments coupled with his later influence over appointments as Chief Justice gave him significant influence over the direction of the Court in the first three decades of the 20th century. Roosevelt and Woodrow Wilson may have dominated American presidential and electoral politics during their tenure, but Taft quietly controlled the realm of national judicial politics until his death in 1930. At least two-thirds of the appointments to the Court between 1900 and 1930 were directly or indirectly influenced by Taft.

In the realm of FOREIGN AFFAIRS, Taft continued the internationalist defense and foreign policies of his predecessor. He initiated a more aggressive policy of "DOLLAR DIPLOMACY" in the hope of using American investments and commercial expansion to generate political stability in foreign lands. A fervent believer in the rule of law, he also sought vigorously to negotiate arbitration treaties with European powers that would have included even questions of "national honor." When the Senate, however, attached objectionable reservations, he refused to submit the treaties to Britain and France for ratification. Finally, Taft is remembered for his pacifist approach to the Mexican Revolution of 1911. When disturbances occurred on the American-Mexican border and spilled over onto U.S. territory, he refused to bend to popular pressures and send the army into Mexico, arguing that "I seriously doubt whether I have such authority [to intervene] under any circumstances, and if I had, I would not exercise it without express congressional approval." Believing INTERVENTION to be the wrong policy because it would jeopardize the lives of 40,000 Americans living in Mexico, the president conveniently hid behind a literalist view of his powers as COMMANDER IN CHIEF. A close evaluation of his view, however, indicated that he would have had no reservations about ordering military intervention if he had been faced with a genuine emergency and the loss of American lives.

Taft is also remembered for his titanic struggle with Roosevelt for the Republican nomination in 1912. Although he defeated Roosevelt at the Republican convention and was renominated, Roosevelt bolted from the Republican Party, accepted the nomination of the Progressive "Bull Moose" Party, and proceeded to divide the Republican vote in the general election, paving the way for the election of Woodrow WILSON. Taft, nevertheless, was relieved that he had preserved the Republican Party as the party of constitutional conservatism committed to "the absolute independence of the judiciary."

The Taft-Roosevelt struggle of 1912 led Roosevelt to publish his *Autobiography* (1913) in which he asserted his famous "STEWARDSHIP THEORY," which that maintained that a president could do anything necessary to protect the national interest that was not forbidden by the Constitution or statutory law. Taft responded in a series of lectures published as *Our Chief Magistrate and His Powers* (1916) with the constitutionalist-literalist theory of presidential power.

This theory maintained that the president did not possess unlimited inherent presidential powers and that a president could not roam at will doing good unless his power was rooted in specific grants of EXECUTIVE POWER in the Constitution or statutory law. These theories of executive power have remained fixed in our political culture and reflect the nation's need to call upon different kinds of presidential LEADERSHIP at different times. Taft's statement of the limited nature of presidential power remains one of his most important contributions to our understanding of the legal limits within which the presidency must operate in a constitutional democracy.

Further reading: Anderson, Donald F. *William Howard Taft: A Conservative's Conception of the Presidency.* Ithaca, N.Y.: Cornell University Press, 1973; Anderson, Judith I. *William Howard Taft: An Intimate History.* New York: Norton, 1981; Coletta, Paolo E. *The Presidency of William Howard Taft.* Lawrence: University Press of Kansas, 1973; Pringle, Henry F. *The Life and Times of William Howard Taft.* Toronto: Farrar & Rinehart, 1939.

—Donald F. Anderson

Taft Commission

In early 1911, President TAFT called together the President's Commission on Economy and Efficiency. The commission, known as the Taft Commission, was the second presidential effort at administrative reorganization. It had initially received Congressional blessing due to a run of federal budget deficits at that time. Taft seized the opportunity as a way of bringing the EXECUTIVE BRANCH under more central control.

The commission consisted of several well-known scholars, including its chair, political scientist Frederick Cleveland, and member Frank Goodnow, one of the founders of American public administration. The commission made several recommendations, which could broadly be put into three categories: the improvement of the administration of government, the reorganization of the executive branch, and changes in budgeting practices. Some of the recommendations relating to improving the administration of government were improvements in personnel records and in the distribution of governmental materials. Under the category of the overall reorganization of government, recommendations involved rearranging cabinet-level departments so that agencies with similar purposes would be grouped together. A final set of recommendations dealt with the budgeting process. The commission recommended the establishment of an executive budget, something that Taft had been pushing for.

President Taft implemented many of the recommendations regarding administrative practices, but Congress refused to back the commission's proposals regarding the reorganization of the executive branch. Congress was also initially reluctant to initiate an executive budget. However, less than 10 years after the recommendations were made, Congress passed the BUDGET AND ACCOUNTING ACT OF 1921, which enacted an executive budget.

Further reading: Arnold, Peri. *Making the Managerial Presidency.* Lawrence: University Press of Kansas, 1998; Skowronek, Stephen. *Building a New American State.* New York: Cambridge University Press, 1982.

—Joseph Wert

Taft-Hartley Act

Officially named the Labor-Management Relations Act of 1947, the Taft-Hartley Act was cosponsored by Republican Senator Robert A. Taft of Ohio and Republican Representative Fred Hartley of New Jersey. This legislation by the Republican-controlled 80th Congress was enacted despite the veto of Democratic President Harry S TRUMAN. The Taft-Hartley Act amended the WAGNER ACT of 1935, reduced the economic and political powers of labor unions, and increased their legal accountability to the federal government.

The provisions of the Taft-Hartley Act included Section 14(b), which authorized states to enact "right to work" laws. These state laws prohibit "closed shops," i.e., mandatory union membership. This act of Congress also banned "check off" practices in which employers collected union dues from their employees. It also prohibited financial contributions from labor unions in federal primary and election campaigns, required union officials to swear anticommunist affidavits and file copies of their unions's constitutions with the secretary of Labor. It also authorized "cooling off" periods of 60 to 80 days to prohibit strikes during national emergencies.

The Taft-Hartley Act was one of the most divisive, partisan legislative issues of the late 1940s. Supporters of this law claimed that it reduced and deterred irresponsibility and abuses of power by labor leaders toward the economy, NATIONAL SECURITY, the political system, and their own union members. Labor leaders, who overwhelmingly opposed this law, and their staunchest allies in Congress, mostly non-Southern liberal Democrats, denounced the Taft-Hartley Act as the "slave labor law" and were determined to eventually repeal it, especially Section 14(b). Although most Southern Democrats in Congress voted for this bill in Congress and to override Truman's veto of it, Truman dramatized the Taft-Hartley Act during his 1948 presidential campaign as a stark policy difference between the two major parties. He also warned voters that it was a precedent for harsher antilabor laws in the future if Republicans retained control of Congress and won the presidential election of 1948.

Truman's frequent denunciations of the Taft-Hartley Act mobilized the active political support of labor unions, which was crucial to Truman's upset victory and the election of a Democratic-controlled Congress, but the Democrats failed to repeal the Taft-Hartley Act. The Landrum-Griffin Act of 1959 was the next major federal law regulating labor unions.

Further reading: Lee, R. Alton. *Truman and Taft-Hartley.* Westport, Conn.: Greenwood Press, 1966; McClure, Arthur F. *The Truman Administration and the Problems of Postwar Labor, 1945–1948.* Rutherford, N.J.: Farleigh Dickinson University Press, 1969.

—Sean J. Savage

Taney, Roger R. (1777–1864) *chief justice of the United States*

Roger Brooke Taney was the fifth chief justice of the United States (March 28, 1836–October 12, 1864). In addition to being the first Catholic to serve on the high court, Taney brought Jacksonian jurisprudence to it.

Taney lived out his privileged and provincial life in the same tidewater area of Maryland where his ancestors had settled in the 1660s. Born on St. Patrick's Day 1777 in Calvert County, he was the third of seven children—three daughters and four sons. The son of an aristocratic tobacco grower, Taney maintained his family's religious, social, and economic status quo in Maryland, a border state that would exhibit strong Confederate support. Taney's father, an oldest son, had inherited the family estate and continued to favor the practice of primogeniture, even after it was abolished in Maryland. The destiny of Roger, as second-born son, was determined by his father, who chose his profession, his college, his training, then established the pattern of Roger's early professional life. Roger entered Dickinson College in Carlisle, Pennsylvania, at age 15 and was graduated in 1795. Afterward, he studied law with a prominent judge on the Maryland General Court in Annapolis. Admitted to the bar in 1799, he practiced briefly in Annapolis before he moved to Frederick in 1800 and finally settled in Baltimore in 1823. The very visible hand of the elder Taney extended to arranging for Roger to succeed him in the Maryland legislature. The same year that young Taney was admitted to the bar he was elected to the Federalist seat formerly filled by his father, even though he was only 22 years old and had lived away from home for the previous six years while in college and reading law. Taney misjudged the electorate, however, and was defeated for reelection during the Jeffersonian landslide the next year. He managed a local political comeback, but his poor eyesight and his paralyzing stage fright limited the appeal of electoral politics.

In 1806 Taney solidified his social status through marriage to the daughter of a wealthy plantation family. Her brother, one of Roger's childhood friends who also became a lawyer, was Francis Scott Key, later famous for writing "The Star-Spangled Banner." Roger and his wife had six daughters and one son. The son died in infancy.

A leader of Maryland's FEDERALIST PARTY, Taney supported the WAR OF 1812, unlike many New England Federalists. The demise of the Federalist Party, a distrust in large commercial monopolies, and the War of 1812 combined to shift Taney toward Jacksonianism. In 1816 he was elected to the Maryland Senate but served only one term. By 1826 he had become a staunch Democrat, and in 1827 he was elected as Maryland's attorney general. From that post, Taney led state support for Andrew JACKSON during the 1828 presidential campaign and was eventually rewarded by Jackson with appointment as the ATTORNEY GENERAL of the United States. This competent lawyer and the charismatic president complemented each other as a team. Jackson gave orders; Taney delivered legal justifications for them.

Taney also served briefly as secretary of War and was a loyal general in the president's war against the BANK OF THE UNITED STATES. Taney reversed his earlier support for the national bank to such a degree that he drafted Jackson's 1832 veto message that declared the bank unconstitutional, thus reversing John Marshall's landmark *McCulloch v. Maryland*, 1819. After two of Jackson's secretaries of the Treasury refused to withdraw federal deposits from the Bank, Taney accepted Jackson's appointment as Treasury secretary and executed the president's directive. Congress retaliated by refusing to confirm Taney, making him the first CABINET nominee rejected by the Senate.

Jackson did not forget his loyal supporters and friends. He already had appointed three Jacksonian jurists to the high court when two more vacancies occurred. Jackson previously had nominated Taney as an associate justice, but the Senate rejected that nomination. After the death of Chief Justice John MARSHALL in 1835, Jackson subtly resubmitted Taney as Marshall's replacement concurrent with his proposal of another nominee to fill the still-vacant associate justice seat. The appointment of the first Catholic to the Supreme Court by a president who himself was the son of immigrant Irish parents boosted the increasing importance of the Irish Catholic vote for the DEMOCRATIC PARTY during a period of heavy Catholic immigration to the United States.

Taney's appointment to the Supreme Court proved a double-edged sword because of his Jacksonian jurisprudence. As chief justice, Taney had power to overturn the legacy of John Marshall, but instead he merely modified it to allow greater leeway for entrepreneurs at the state and local levels during the national expansion westward that was concomitant with economic development. In 1837 Taney wrote what is often regarded as his finest opinion, the *Charles River Bridge Company v. Warren Bridge Company*. As was typical in the vast majority of his decisions, Taney in this 4-3 case deferred to state legislatures.

On the other hand, Taney's implementation of Jacksonian democracy led to disastrous results on HUMAN RIGHTS. Taney's legal positivism, allowing white majority rule, conflicted with the natural law tradition found in the Declaration of Independence, which Abraham LINCOLN would draw on for the new REPUBLICAN PARTY. Taney, unlike Jackson, manumitted his slaves, but his ultimate solution to the problem of slavery was to allow colonization abroad. His fundamental hierarchical view of life is probably accurately reflected in his 1857 *DRED SCOTT* decision, even though its activist basis conflicted with Taney's traditional judicial restraint. Like his father, who supported primogeniture beyond its legal life, Taney supported the slavocracy despite rapidly changing conditions. The 7-2 decision against Scott declared a major part of the Missouri Compromise unconstitutional, as well as insisted that Africans could be citizens of states, but never citizens of the United States with a right to sue in federal court. This "self-inflicted wound," generally regarded as the Court's worst decision, polarized the entire nation, gave the issue to the emerging Republican Party, and set the stage for Southern secession. If that single decision had been an aberration in Taney's subsequent behavior on the court, it might lessen his legacy without undermining it. Regrettably, he continued his obdurate behavior toward the Lincoln administration. Taney criticized Lincoln in the John Merryman case for suspending the writ of *habeas corpus* but conveniently overlooked Andrew Jackson's much more egregious behavior after the Battle of New Orleans in 1812, as well as Jefferson DAVIS's liberal suspension of the writ of *habeas corpus*. Both Andrew Jackson and his legal apologist Roger Taney have slipped from the great to near-great categories in the respective polls of scholars rating presidents and justices.

Further reading: Pederson, William D., and Norman W. Provizer, eds. *Leaders of the Pack: Polls and Case Studies of Great Supreme Court Justices.* New York: P. Lang, 2003; Swisher, Carl B. *Roger B. Taney.* New York: Macmillan, 1935; Walker, Lewis. *Without Fear or Favor.* Boston: Houghton Mifflin, 1965.

—William D. Pederson

tariff policy

Tariff policy is the policy of the American government with regard to duties on imports to the United States. Because of its constitutional responsibility for regulating foreign commerce, Congress has always maintained a substantial role in the establishment of tariff policy; however, during the past century the role of the president in tariff and trade policy has grown substantially. The tariff played a large role in American politics in the 19th and early 20th centuries, dividing the major political parties and causing considerable controversy. The first tariff act passed by the U.S.

Congress was the Tariff Act of July 4, 1789. The act had a dual purpose, as most tariff legislation would: It was passed to supply the federal government with revenue but it also had the impact of protecting certain industries and interests in the United States. Protection would always be the more controversial of these two purposes, and the revenue purpose of tariff legislation would be decidedly less important with the institution of the federal income tax in 1913.

Many of the major political, and especially partisan, battles of the 19th century revolved around the tariff. A critical point of the administration of Andrew JACKSON was the threatened secession of South Carolina prompted by the Tariff Act of 1828, the so-called Tariff of Abominations. The election of 1888, moreover, was primarily organized around the tariff issue. Although all partisans in the 19th century generally agreed with using tariffs to raise revenue, there was distinct disagreement on whether to protect American businesses or allow free trade. Whigs, and then Republicans after them, were normally of the protectionist bent, while Democrats sided with the "tariff for revenue only" as they often phrased it. When Whigs/Republicans controlled the federal government they either maintained or established high tariffs (e.g., the Tariff of 1842 and the McKinley Tariff of 1890), while Democrats sought to dismantle protectionism (e.g., the Walker Tariff of 1846).

While there was considerable contestation surrounding the tariff in the 19th and early 20th centuries, few disputed the hegemony of Congress on the issue. Later in the 20th century, however, Congress came to take on a less dominant role on the issue, according presidents more discretion and authority to negotiate trade and tariff agreements with other nations. This changing of roles was consistent with the need felt by many experts, including some in Congress, that free trade was more conducive to economic progress. Congress, with its emphasis on local districts and interests, was always hard-pressed to refrain from "protecting" businesses; presidents, with their national constituency and thus wider perspective, were often more willing to lower tariffs and promote free trade. The watershed piece of legislation increasing presidential authority was the Reciprocal Trade Agreement Act of 1934. The act was a response to the signal failure of the protectionist Smooth-Hawley Tariff Act of 1930, which had provoked angry reactions from other nations due to its high duties and imposts. The new legislation gave the president authority, subject to certain restrictions, to negotiate joint tariff reduction agreements with foreign nations. The trend toward cooperative negotiation of tariff schedules between countries was formalized internationally with the GATT (General Agreement on Tariffs and Trade), signed in 1947 by 23 nations, including the United States, and since signed by most other nations. The Trade Expansion Act of 1962 affirmed and extended the president's role in the negotiating and setting of tariff policies and the United States's subsequent participation in the "Kennedy Round" of GATT trade negotiations resulted in substantial lowering of tariffs.

Although presidents still dominate tariff policy, Congress has reasserted itself in recent years. With growing protectionist forces worrying that tariffs were being set too low, Congress passed the Trade Act of 1974, which placed restrictions on presidential discretion to negotiate tariff reductions (for example, it revived the role of the Tariff Commission, now renamed the International Tariff Commission, in investigating and redressing claims of businesses against tariff reductions). The act also, however, gave the president "fast-track" authority, which served to strengthen presidential power, or at least initiative, in this area. Congress further restricted presidential discretion in the 1988 Omnibus Trade Act, which required the United States to retaliate against other nations' unfair trade policies.

The 1990s provided mixed signals with regard to the tariff issue. Presidents and free trade activists won significant victories with the passage of the North American Free Trade Agreement (NAFTA) in 1993 and the GATT overhaul of 1994, which led to the creation of the World Trade Organization (WTO). However, Congress has failed to reauthorize "fast-track" procedures since 1993, and the WTO has provoked significant public backlash, culminating in the protests and riots in Seattle, Washington, at the meeting of the WTO in 1999.

Further reading: Destler, I. M. *American Trade Politics,* 3d ed. Washington, D.C.: Institute for International Economics, 1995; Diller, Daniel C., and Dean J. Patterson. "Chapter 6: Chief Economist." In *Powers of the Presidency,* 2d ed. Washington, D.C.: CQ Press, 1997; Dobson, John M. *Two Centuries of Tariffs.* Washington, D.C.: Government Printing Office, 1976.

—Michael Korzi

tax policy

"No taxation without representation!" was a battle cry of the Revolutionary War. But truth be told, most of us do not like taxes even with representation. There is a general agreement that U.S. tax policy be based on three themes: equity, efficiency, and simplicity. Beyond that, there is little agreement and lots of parties in disagreement.

It should not be surprising that due to their saliency, tax issues are important political hot potatoes. Questions such as what the level of taxation ought to be, who should pay, to what extent tax policy stimulates or dampens economic growth, raise the hackles of voters.

The income tax was instituted in 1913 with the passage of the Sixteenth Amendment, and since that time Democrats have generally sought to raise taxes on the wealthy and corporations and use those tax revenues for social and welfare programs, while Republicans have generally favored cutting taxes, especially for the wealthy and corporations, and limiting spending on social welfare programs. And of course, promising an across-the-board tax cut is a good way for all politicians to attract votes.

Prior to WORLD WAR II, federal revenues and federal taxes remained low. But with war, and in the postwar age of COLD WAR and U.S. hegemony, the tax burden increased as U.S. world power and responsibility increased.

The first major foray into postwar tax reform came as a result of candidate John Kennedy's promise to "get the country moving again." Thus, KENNEDY proposed a business tax cut in 1961 and a cut on income taxes for individuals in 1963. His proposals for cutting tax loopholes, however, were not passed by Congress.

While Kennedy's policies helped stimulate economic growth, President Lyndon JOHNSON tried to fund two wars simultaneously without raising taxes: LBJ would not fund a war on poverty and a war in Vietnam, and an economic slowdown ensued. He did, however, promote the Tax Reform Act of 1969, which became law in the early days of the NIXON presidency.

Jimmy CARTER attempted to simplify the tax code (he called the code "a disgrace to the human race"). While the Revenue Act of 1978 did become law, it did little to structurally change the tax code.

Ronald REAGAN, it is said, never met a tax he liked, and during his presidency he made tax-cutting a prime goal. He was successful in the first year of his presidency, passing the Economic Recovery Tax Act of 1981, cutting taxes on the wealthy and corporations, as well as reducing overall taxes by about 30 percent.

After early victories, Reagan faced a more determined opposition by the Democrats. A series of laws scaled back some of the Reagan tax cuts, but overall, Reagan held much of his ground. But during the Reagan years, the federal deficit skyrocketed. When Reagan took office, the United States was the world's largest creditor nation; when he left office it was the world's largest debtor nation. In 1986 some tax loopholes were closed and a modest increase in corporate taxes became policy.

Reagan's successor, George H. W. BUSH, after pledging "Read my lips, no new taxes!" ended up raising taxes in 1990. President CLINTON attempted to make taxes more progressive but had only limited success. And during his campaign for the presidency, candidate George W. BUSH, learning the lesson from his father's mistakes, promised and delivered on a significant tax cut in 2001.

Taylor, Zachary (1784–1850) *twelfth U.S. president, Army general*

Zachary Taylor, a general and the first president elected with no previous political experience, served 16 months as president before dying in office. "Old Rough and Ready,"

President Zachary Taylor *(Library of Congress)*

Taylor was a hero of the MEXICAN WAR and very popular with the public when he became president. However, politically he was an outsider with no clear agenda, and he resisted any sort of compromise with Congress, thus severely limiting the influence of his presidency.

Zachary Taylor was born in Virginia on November 24, 1784, and then was taken as an infant to Kentucky. His family's plantation prospered, and by 1800 they owned 10,000 acres and many slaves. Wishing to pursue a military career, Taylor received his first commission as an officer in 1808 and won distinction as a captain serving in the WAR OF 1812. Taylor also won fame as an Indian fighter, having earned the nickname "Old Rough and Ready" fighting the Seminole Indians in Florida from 1837 to 1840. In 1845 Texas was granted statehood, causing tension with Mexico. President James POLK ordered Taylor and his troops into the area to drive back any attempt by Mexico to reclaim the land. After winning two stunning victories and defeating the Mexican army at Buena Vista despite being outnumbered by almost 4 to 1, General Zachary Taylor was a national hero.

Taylor was at first reluctant to enter politics. He did not align himself with any particular political party, thinking of himself as an independent. Because he was a wealthy slave-owner and a war hero, the Whig Party nominated him in 1848, hoping he would oppose the Wilmot Proviso's prohibition on the extension of slavery into the territory acquired during the Mexican war. In fact Taylor opposed the idea of extending slavery into the new territories. In the end, however, Taylor declared himself a Whig. On November 7, 1848, Taylor and Millard FILLMORE barely edged out the Democrat Lewis CASS of the Free Soil Party.

Taylor's election was the last gasp of a dying Whig Party. Given Taylor's Whig view of a limited presidency, he neglected the possible role of legislative leader and even eschewed PATRONAGE as beneath him. Taylor's self-imposed limitations prevented him from attempting the exercise of strong presidential LEADERSHIP.

> "The Executive . . . has authority to recommend (not to dictate) measures to Congress. Having performed that duty, the Executive department of the Government cannot rightfully control the decision of Congress on any subject of legislation . . . the . . . veto will never be exercised by me except . . . as an extreme measure, to be resorted to only in extraordinary cases. . . ."

The issue of slavery dominated Taylor's short time as president. The threat of disunion haunted the politics of the day. Taylor, a Southerner and a slaveowner, was appalled by talk of secession but felt helpless in the face of fast-moving events. On July 4, 1850, Taylor developed gastroenteritis and died five days later. Upon Taylor's death, Vice President Fillmore assumed the presidency and quickly endorsed the Compromise of 1850, which effectively negated the influence of Taylor's presidency.

Taylor is generally rated in the below-average category by presidential historians. He was a better military leader than president, and he was unable—like so many of the pre-Civil War presidents—to effectively stem the tide of secession that ultimately led to the CIVIL WAR. In Taylor's case, the limits placed upon his powers were as much self-imposed as they were imposed from Congress or circumstances. His Whig view of the presidency prevented him from exerting strong leadership at a time when strong leadership might have averted war. Taylor's was a failure of will as well as imagination. Of Taylor, Polk said, "General Taylor is, I have no doubt, a well-meaning old man. He is, however, uneducated, exceedingly ignorant of public affairs, and I should judge, of very ordinary capacity."

Further reading: Hamilton, Holman. *Zachary Taylor.* Indianapolis: Bobbs-Merrill, 1941–51; Pechman, Joseph A. *Federal Tax Policy,* 5th ed. Washington, D.C.: Brookings Institution, 1987; Smith, Elbert B. *The Presidencies of Zachary Taylor and Millard Fillmore.* Lawrence: University Press of Kansas, 1988.

Teapot Dome scandal

The most notorious event of the Warren HARDING presidency centered around corruption. The Harding scandals ran deep. The president was never implicated in these scandals, but he was guilty of lax management. Harding appointed friends and cronies, but he did not properly supervise them. Seeing that Harding was asleep at the wheel, they felt that they could take advantage of the president, and they did.

"Teapot Dome" refers to an oil reserve in Wyoming under control of the federal government. Harding's secretary of the Interior, Albert B. Fall, gave control of the lands to business interests. Fall received an estimated $300,000 in return, and he received an additional $100,000 in another deal for oil rights in Elk Hill, California.

The scandal was not made public until after Harding's death. Fall was sentenced to jail. He was the first CABINET member ever convicted of a crime while in office.

television and the president

The invention of television at the start of the 20th century would have a profound impact on the American political process during the latter half of the century, particularly for presidential politics. Most presidential scholars attribute the start of the television age of politics to the 1950s, when Dwight EISENHOWER became the first president to utilize the rapidly expanding medium as a means to more effectively communicate with the American public. Thanks to television coverage, the Eisenhower administration became much more visible than any other before it through the use of filmed PRESS CONFERENCES for later use by the networks, televised cabinet meetings, and televised fireside chats. Following the election of John F. KENNEDY in 1960, the use of television as a means for presidential communication increased dramatically. Where Eisenhower had been somewhat reluctant in his use of television, Kennedy and his advisers saw the expanding medium as an excellent governing tool for the president to expand his influence and power over national politics. By the mid-1960s, the president had become a central focus of news from Washington and began to have more power over shaping the national agenda by rapidly reaching, through both television and print media sources, his national audience. The ability to help shape public opinion, through televised and highly covered speeches and press conferences, began to provide the president an important advantage during the legislative process. As the influence of television increased, presidents worked even harder to keep the initiative and control over the policy agenda coming out of the White House.

Presidential LEADERSHIP in the television age requires effective communication skills and the ability to positively shape public opinion in ways that match the needs of the medium—the presidential image is crucial. The president now utilizes television on a regular basis to go public by creating a myriad of photo opportunities and instant news in an attempt to speak directly to the American public about his policy agenda. As the national symbol of American leadership, this is a great advantage for the president in his relationship with Congress and other key political actors. Television is now the most prominent feature in the development of a White House communication strategy, especially since the introduction of CNN during the 1980s and other all-news cable networks, like MSNBC, during the 1990s. This has created a 24-hour news cycle, which leaves the president little time when his activities are not in full view on center stage. The president has emerged, especially during the television age, as a dominant rhetorical figure in American politics, representing a national constituency with many opportunities to influence the national agenda. However, most presidents are limited in their capacity to control both the image and the message of their administrations.

Presidents are capable of developing successful communication strategies, especially in their use of television, to get their message out to the American public, although some presidents have been more successful than others. During the television age, only three presidents have been considered skillful in their use of television—Kennedy, Ronald REAGAN, and Bill CLINTON. The impact of Kennedy's skillful use of television has had a lasting impact on the office of the presidency. His use of live televised press conferences, his eloquent speaking style, and the youthful images of both his family and administration on American television screens set a standard that his successors had difficulty matching. Kennedy also had the advantage of the uniqueness of the new medium, yet many presidents that followed him have longed for that golden, innocent era of the early 1960s, when personal and political scandal did not dominate political reporting from Washington. The current political environment with the news media, and in particular television, that presidents must face, which has steadily evolved since Vietnam and WATERGATE, is one that breeds mistrust, cynicism, and fierce competition among members of the White House press corps and their respective publications and news shows. While the administrations of Lyndon JOHNSON, Richard NIXON, Gerald FORD, and Jimmy CARTER could never quite capture the style and mystique presented by Kennedy on television, the Reagan administration was especially skilled at controlling the images that came out of the White House to provide a complete media package to sell both the president's image and his agenda.

Reagan, nicknamed the "Great Communicator," exhibited a style and ease in front of the television cameras due to his prior experience as an actor that was tailor-made for television in the 1980s. George H. W. BUSH was not able to master the use of television in the same manner as Reagan, and he worked hard to distance himself from the stagecraft

of the Reagan years in his communication strategy. Bill Clinton, the first president raised during the television age, often relied on alternative television opportunities like talk shows and live town meetings to bypass the traditional Washington press corps and speak directly to the American people. And while television events such as those worked well for Clinton by giving him more options in delivering his message unfiltered to the audience, television in a more general sense has also adversely affected the leadership potential for presidents. Television coverage of politics, and in particular the presidency, has not only personalized and politicized the functioning of the national government; but the immediacy of television coverage has also accelerated the decision-making process for presidents. The up-close-and-personal look at our presidents that television now provides through the plethora of public venues has also altered the political environment in which the president must lead. Americans have come to expect that the personal lives of presidents will make news, which has also desensitized the public to the tabloid-style reporting about personal indiscretions. Presidents must now pay close attention to their image as it is portrayed on television, but determining what is good for the president in terms of control over the message may not be the same as providing substantive information about the political process for the American electorate.

Further reading: Ansolabehere, Stephen, Roy Behr, and Shanto Iyengar. *The Media Game: American Politics in the Television Age.* New York: Macmillan, 1993; Han, Lori Cox. *Governing from Center Stage: White House Communication Strategies During the Television Age of Politics.* Creskill, N.J.: Hampton Press, 2001; Kerbel, Matthew Robert. *Remote and Controlled: Media Politics in a Cynical Age.* Boulder, Colo.: Westview Press, 1998; Kernell, Samuel. *Going Public: New Strategies of Presidential Leadership.* Washington, D.C.: CQ Press, 1997.

—Lori Cox-Han

Tennessee Valley Authority Act

Signed into law by Franklin ROOSEVELT in 1933, the Tennessee Valley Authority Act was a regional development program, grand in scope and progressive in design, that crossed state boundaries and was intended to promote the public use of natural resources. Aimed at one of the most depressed regions of the country, the act harnessed the hydroelectric power available in the region and put it to the goal of regional economic development.

Sponsored in the Senate by George Norris (Rep.-Neb.), the act transformed the Tennessee Valley into an energy-producing region, as well as flood control and agricultural development. The act created thousands of jobs, brought electricity to the region, improved navigation, built dams, and controlled floods. Roosevelt hoped the TVA would be a model program that could be replicated, but opposition in Congress and by elements of the private sector prevented the expansion of such programs. Today, the TVA is an independent corporate agency of the federal government.

Further reading: Chandler, William U. *The Myth of TVA.* Cambridge, Mass.: Ballinger Pub. Co., 1984; Morgan, Arthur E. *The Making of the TVA.* Buffalo, N.Y.: Prometheus Books, 1974.

Tenure of Office Act (1867)

Because the American Constitution is silent on whether the president possesses the exclusive authority to remove EXECUTIVE BRANCH personnel, and due to the reticence of the judiciary to intervene in such controversies in the 19th century, CONGRESS AND THE PRESIDENT were left to define the extent of this power.

During the initial federal Congress in 1789, both chambers debated REMOVAL POWER legislation, agreeing that the CHIEF EXECUTIVE had the sole right to fire subordinates. A major removal power controversy ensued in 1833, when President Andrew JACKSON fired Treasury Secretary William Duane when he failed to heed Jackson's orders to remove all deposits from the BANK OF THE UNITED STATES. The Senate passed a resolution condemning the action, which was quickly attacked by the Jackson administration. In 1863 Congress passed a bill establishing a comptroller of the Currency within the Treasury Department, who was removable only by joint president-Senate consent.

The 1867 Tenure of Office Act went much further than the 1863 law, mandating that all cabinet secretaries could be removed only with Senate permission. In his March 2 veto of the bill, President Andrew JOHNSON claimed that an exclusive removal power by the president was consistent with the intention of the Constitution's framers. His veto was overridden by both chambers the same day. President Johnson, who informed Congress in December 1867 that all of the administration's cabinet secretaries agreed that the Tenure of Office Act was unconstitutional, pushed the issue. Having suspended Secretary of Defense Edwin Stanton in August 1867 and transferred authority to Ulysses GRANT, the president fired Stanton on February 21, 1868, after Grant returned the post to Stanton. Three days later, the House of Representatives impeached Johnson on 11 articles—the alleged violation of the Tenure of Office Act paramount among them—by a straight party vote. The Senate acquitted Johnson following a trial which lasted from March 5 to May 26, 1868.

The 1867 Tenure of Office Act would be subsequently criticized by five chief executives over the next two decades, including Ulysses Grant, who evidently viewed the latter law in a different light upon becoming president. On March 3, 1887, the law was repealed. However, separate laws passed in 1872 and 1876 required Senate consent for removal of certain categories of postmasters. It was the 1876 law that would be tested in the 1926 *MYERS V. UNITED STATES* case.

Further reading: Benedict, Michael. *The Impeachment and Trial of Andrew Johnson.* New York: Norton, 1973; Hart, James. *Tenure of Office under the Constitution: A Study in Law and Public Policy.* Baltimore, Md.: Johns Hopkins Press, 1930; Hoff, Samuel B. "The Separation of Powers Doctrine and Its Relation to Presidential Removal Power, 1789–1900." *Political Chronicle* 11 (Spring 1999): 13–24; Morganston, Charles. *The Appointment and Removal Power of the President of the United States.* Washington, D.C.: Government Printing Office, 1929; *Myers v. United States,* 272 U.S. 52 (1926).

—Samuel B. Hoff

term and tenure of office

An early proposal at the constitutional convention called for a seven-year presidential term with no reeligibility, with the president chosen by Congress. Alexander HAMILTON suggested lifetime tenure for the president, but his argument gained few supporters. It soon became apparent that the issue of term length was intricately connected to those of reeligibility and selection. If selection were to be done by the legislature, the term would have to be longer and there could be no reeligibility, which would make the president too dependent on Congress. On the other hand, if reeligibility were desirable, terms would have to be shorter and selection done by some mechanism other than the legislature. Thus, the final arrangement called for four-year terms with unlimited reeligibility, and selection by an ELECTORAL COLLEGE.

Alexander Hamilton outlines the argument for four-year terms in *Federalist No. 71.* His two concerns are the "firmness," or independence, of the president in the execution of his constitutional duties, and stability in the administration of government. While acknowledging the need for public opinion to govern the conduct of public officials, Hamilton argues that when the people seek things contrary to their interests, "it is the duty of the persons whom they have appointed to be the guardians of those interests to withstand the temporary delusion in order to give them time and opportunity for more cool and sedate reflection." Thus, in order to have the freedom to act against public opinion, the president needs to have a relatively long term. Hamilton is aware that the president's independence will decline somewhat in an election year, but his hope is that a four-year term will give the president enough time to pursue worthy goals and to persuade the public of their virtue.

Hamilton outlines the argument for unlimited reeligibility in *Federalist No. 72*. Again, the primary goal is "stability of the system of administration." Hamilton argues that reeligibility gives presidents incentives to pursue good works and to perform well, knowing that the people will evaluate their conduct in four years. In turn, the people will have the freedom, if they approve of the president's performance, "to continue him in the station in order to prolong the utility of his talents and virtues, and to secure to the government the advantage of permanency in a wise system of administration." Hamilton criticizes term limits—in this case a one-term limit—for forcing "a disgraceful and ruinous mutability in the administration of the government." He believes that forcing change for no reason will encourage new presidents to change or reverse the policies of their successors. Term limits rob the nation of experience, especially in cases of emergencies. Perhaps most ominously, term limits might cause someone to attempt to seize power.

Despite Hamilton's arguments, the issue of unlimited reeligibility has always been an uneasy one for Americans. JEFFERSON provided the philosophical justification for the two-term tradition when he argued that a president elected for multiple terms might "degenerate into an inheritance." Jefferson's concern about the potential for tyranny superseded Hamilton's concern for stability. Thus, Jefferson strongly supported the principle of rotation in office, as did his immediate successors. Later, the Whig Party, which supported legislative supremacy, argued for a one-term presidency, something both elected Whigs succeeded in accomplishing. Presidents such as GRANT, Theodore ROOSEVELT, and WILSON sought third terms, but no one was successful before Franklin ROOSEVELT. Roosevelt based his decision to run for a third term in part on the international crisis in Europe and Asia, essentially supporting Hamilton's argument with respect to experience during emergencies. In reaction to his success, however, an alliance of Republicans and conservative Democrats pushed a term-limit amendment, ratified as the TWENTY-SECOND AMENDMENT in 1951. The largely partisan effort was couched as an argument between two camps: those who wanted to protect the people from an overly personalized presidency against those who argued that the people could vote an incumbent out of office.

Presidents EISENHOWER, REAGAN, and CLINTON—the three presidents the Twenty-second Amendment has affected—have argued for repeal of the amendment. Others throughout history, including JACKSON, Wilson, Lyndon JOHNSON, and CARTER, have advocated a one-term six-year presidency, to free the CHIEF EXECUTIVE from reelection pressures.

Further reading: Hamilton, Alexander, James Madison, and John Jay. *The Federalist Papers.* Edited by Clinton Rossiter. New York: New American Library, 1961; Milkis,

Sidney M., and Michael Nelson. *The American Presidency: Origins and Development, 1776–1998*, 3d ed. Washington, D.C.: CQ Press, 1999.

—David A. Crockett

textbook presidency

This conceptualization of the presidency is most closely associated with the second edition of Thomas CRONIN's *The State of the Presidency*. There he defines it as "the cult of the presidency" or "a chief executive who is generally benevolent, omnipotent, omniscient, and highly moral." This refers to the way that academic textbooks conceived the office of the CHIEF EXECUTIVE in the quarter century following Franklin ROOSEVELT.

For journalists and academicians writing in the aftermath of WORLD WAR II, the second Roosevelt was the epitome of national leadership for our government. Beginning with that administration, textbook authors persistently proclaimed that a powerful national government was essential with a strong president asserting leadership. The news media echoed that contention. In Cronin's words, the president was assumed to be "the embodiment of all that is good in America: courage, honesty, integrity, and compassion."

As the only office filled by the electorate as a whole, the presidency was the sole voice that could speak for the entire nation. Individual actions by a president might be questioned, but pundits and professors did not doubt the uniquely central function of the presidency.

FDR was praised for his masterful responses to the GREAT DEPRESSION and World War II, TRUMAN for his reaction to the Soviet threat, EISENHOWER for ending the Korean conflict, KENNEDY for his promise to put an American on the moon, and Lyndon JOHNSON for enacting meaningful civil rights legislation. In contrast to these textbook presidents were the records of their predecessors, HARDING, COOLIDGE, and HOOVER, who were deemed ineffective—to have let down the nation. Proponents of the textbook presidency could not condone the putative absence of initiative that resided in the White House of the 1920s.

James MacGregor Burns and Clinton Rossiter were representative of political scientists that touted the crucial leadership role of the president, with Burns notably critical of Congress, which he found nearly paralyzed by the conservative coalition of right-wing Republicans and Southern Democrats. Congress could obstruct but not lead. Rossiter posited a set of presidential roles, among which was "world leader," certainly a status never envisioned by the Founding Fathers.

According to Cronin, the textbook presidency exhibited two central dimensions. One was the omnipotent-competent dimension, in which the president is the key factor in achieving progress for America and exercising leadership in the international community. In the second or moralistic-benevolent dimension, the president served to symbolize what is and has been good for the American people. He is a figure that is almost ordained to be the best choice to lead the nation, if only for a brief period.

The origins of the textbook presidency are the consequence of seven sources: One, the president's emergence as the free world's leader; two, the nation's need for a symbol of reassurance; three, the liberal orientations of commentators and textbook authors; four, the expansion of the purview of the national government while Congress slowly surrendered power to the president; five, the nation's desire for loyalty to the governance system and yearning for national stability; six, the difficulty in conducting research on the presidency; and seven, the onset of television coverage of the presidency including campaigns, which increased massively in the 1960s.

The epitome of the textbook presidency arose with the administration of KENNEDY and the Camelot myth (named after the popular Broadway musical of the day). The young, handsome, witty, and presumably athletic president and his high-fashion wife were the culmination of the view that wisdom resided principally in the country's national office, which now manifested an attractive vitality as well. The trend toward what Arthur Schlesinger would later call the IMPERIAL PRESIDENCY, in reference to the Johnson-Nixon years, reached its zenith with the youthful Kennedy, who was a sharp contrast with the three older presidents that immediately preceded him.

Kennedy and his advisers were skillful with and at ease with the media. The new president benefited from the popularity of Theodore H. White's *The Making of the President 1960,* an account that reported and analyzed the event in unprecedented detail. Where Eisenhower had carefully restricted his PRESS CONFERENCES and appeared uneasy in that milieu, Kennedy was relaxed but alert and congenial, almost reveling in the experience. In sum, he seemed the ideal president for the television age. His television skills were magnified by the emergence of the half-hour evening newscasts of the three national networks. Those newscasts had an insatiable demand for material. Since members of Congress represented only their respective states or districts, and therefore held little attraction for most members of the national viewing audience, the president became the focus of nearly every evening's political news segment. In other words, the CHIEF EXECUTIVE was transformed into the "prime time president." This scenario mandated daily reports in which either the president appeared at some function or a White House reporter commented on one or more topics for which there was no videotape of the president available.

In the late 1960s and early 1970s, disillusionment with the textbook view set in. First with the opposition to Lyndon JOHNSON's insistence on pursuing the war in Vietnam, then with NIXON's conduct of that war and the WATERGATE affair, and finally with the recognition that neither FORD nor CARTER exemplified the lofty national leadership of the 1930–65 era. Neither sought to exercise their presidential duties at that level. On the contrary, Carter explicitly sought to demonstrate that the inhabitant of the OVAL OFFICE was merely a regular citizen, albeit one that exercised extraordinary powers and responsibilities, but only for a brief time.

With the demise of the textbook presidency, attention was directed to why it had developed. One source was the constraints on studying the office. Scholars and journalists lacked access to information that was essential in achieving a sufficiently accurate view of a president's tenure. While in office, a president's staff offered information favorable to the incumbent. After leaving office, a president's memoirs and those of his staff reinforced the positive portrait of that administration, often with an overly dramatic pen. Eventually, scholars might attain a more balanced evaluation of a presidency when records were declassified. An example was Fred Greenstein's groundbreaking *The Hidden-Hand Presidency,* which demonstrated Eisenhower was a skillful, insightful, and partisan politician, and able to conceal that from the press while he was in office. Greenstein demolished the contention that Ike was inarticulate and uninformed on issues. Instead, Ike intentionally misled the press, responding in a discursive manner to their questions, and thereby avoided further inquiries on a topic or revealing his intentions.

It took the veteran actor, Ronald REAGAN, to reverse the trend toward a passive presidency, and perhaps restoring the textbook one. In the eyes of many, he achieved that, despite his emphasis on shrinking government, especially the national one. For others, still skeptical of a president that dominated the national and international scenes, the IRAN-CONTRA affair confirmed their view that presidential power was too easily misused. Some considered that secret venture, an impeachable action, one worse than any prior or subsequent president had perpetrated—at least, to the end of the 20th century.

Despite the immense popular approval of his conduct of the GULF WAR, George H. W. BUSH was unable to maintain that high level of public approval or to gain reelection. His successor, Clinton, who presided over the longest stretch of economic vitality in the nation's history, never achieved the "cult of the presidency" status associated with the textbook version. His ability to do that was undermined by questions about his personal life, which the Monica Lewinsky episode confirmed, and the deep animosity toward him that bolstered persistent efforts to defame and remove him from office.

In an ironic twist, the younger BUSH, elected by the narrowest and most controversial of margins, may in the aftermath of the September 11, 2001, attacks emerge as the closest example of the textbook presidency since the 1960s.

That was the concern of those, especially civil libertarians, who were apprehensive about the powers given to the EXECUTIVE BRANCH following the 9/11 carnage. Yet the unquestioning aura that surrounded the textbook presidency is unlikely to be revived in the face of the cynical public and commentators, especially the comedic ones, who appeared to be firmly imbedded in the national culture as the 21st century began.

Further reading: Cronin, Thomas E. *The State of the Presidency.* Boston: Little, Brown, 1980.

—Thomas P. Wolf

third party candidates

The story of third parties and their candidates in America is one littered with false starts and dead ends. Third party candidates have campaigned under different banners (i.e., Anti-Masonic, Free Soil, Whig-American, Populist, Progressive, American Independents, Independents, and Reform). They have captured as low as 2 percent of the votes in presidential elections (1948) to 27 percent (1912) and have "spoiled" two-party elections. In 1992 Ross Perot, an Independent, established a movement that has become known as the Reform Party. Through his grassroots efforts, he and his organization split the presidential vote between incumbent President George Herbert Walker BUSH and challenger Bill CLINTON. Perot garnered 19 percent of the electorate's votes. Clinton won the presidency.

Nationally, third parties and their candidates have often represented a "voice in the wilderness" attempting to focus attention away from the major American two parties (Republicans and Democrats). Often third party candidates have been unsuccessful in their ultimate goal—reaching the presidency. This failure may stem from a lack of resources, which diminishes the ability of a third party candidate to cast his message broadly. However, third party candidates have often struck a chord with enough of a segment of the voting public to gain the attention of the two major parties. Issues as varied as the right to vote for women (Prohibition and Socialist Parties), child labor laws (Socialist Party), immigration restrictions (Populist Party), income tax (Populist and Socialist Parties), SOCIAL SECURITY (Socialist Party), and balancing the national budget (Reform Party) have been influenced on the national level by third parties.

At the state level, nearly half have had third party candidate successes for governor, mostly in the late 1800s and early 1900s. In 1910 Hiram Johnson, a Progressive third party candidate, won the governorship of California with nearly 50 percent of the vote. Much of California's political development and current structure is owed to the efforts of Governor Johnson and the Progressive Party. Minnesota's governorship went to Reform candidate Jesse Ventura in 1998. And in 1990, former Connecticut U.S. Senator Lowell Weicker won that state's gubernatorial contest with 40 percent of the vote.

Voter identification as "Independent" or as having no alignment with either of the major parties is on the rise. Growth of third parties in U.S. elections was greatest in the 1990s. In each of the election years before 1992 (1968, 1972, 1976, 1980, 1984, 1988), the number of third or minor parties hovered around the mid-thirties. In 1992 and 1994, the number of parties jumped significantly with 69 in 1992 and 51 in 1994.

Third parties and their candidates will continue to have a difficult road to travel in American politics. However, if the trend continues of voters labeling themselves Independent rather than Republican or Democrat, coupled with the use of technology, chiefly the Internet, third party candidates may have a better opportunity to reach their niche populations and build broader coalitions in electoral politics at all levels.

Further reading: Beck, Warren A., and David A. Williams. *California: A History of the Golden State.* Garden City, N.Y.: Doubleday and Company, 1972; Gillespie, J. David. *Politics at the Periphery: Third Parties in Two Party America.* Columbia, S.C.: University of South Carolina Press, 1993; King, Gary, and Lyn Ragsdale. *The Elusive Executive: Discovering Statistical Patterns in the Presidency.* Washington, D.C.: CQ Press, 1988; White, John Kenneth, and Daniel M. Shea. *New Party Politics: From Jefferson and Hamilton to the Information Age.* Boston: Bedford/St. Martin's, 2000.

—F. Owen Holmes

Thomas, Norman (1884–1968) *activist*

Pastor, civil libertarian, public intellectual, and repeated presidential candidate, Norman Thomas was a visible and influential figure in 20th-century America. Promoting a brand of non-Marxist Christian socialism, Thomas became a voice of conscience for his generation.

During WORLD WAR I, Thomas formed the National Civil Liberties Bureau, an organization that later became the American Civil Liberties Union. At the end of the war, Thomas joined the Socialist Party of America but rejected the Soviet model of socialism.

In 1924 he ran unsuccessfully for governor of New York, then in 1925 and 1927 for mayor of New York City. He first ran for president in 1928 as the Socialist Party candidate. He ran as the Socialist candidate for president in every election from 1928 to 1948. In 1932 he received nearly 900,000 votes, his best showing.

Although he spoke out against U.S. participation in WORLD WAR II, once war came he supported the president and the war effort. After the war, Thomas supported the development of the UNITED NATIONS. Later, he helped form the antinuclear group SANE. He died in 1968 at the age of 84.

title, president's

The framers of the presidency engaged in the difficult task of inventing an office with powers and limitations. But what to call this new executive? King? Out of the question. What title suited the CHIEF EXECUTIVE officer in a constitutional republic?

The framers decided on *president* as a term implying "to preside." It was not an "action" word, implying central leadership, but a term more managerial in scope. The term "president," or "president of the United States of America," as the Committee of Detail of the CONSTITUTIONAL CONVENTION submitted on August 6, 1787, was coined by James WILSON, who prepared the Committee of Detail's draft that was presented to the full convention.

How then should this president be addressed? Several alternatives were discussed at the convention, including "Serene Highness," "Elective Highness," and "Elective Majesty." Wilson himself suggested "His Excellency." The convention could not decide and so, for a time, the president was (quite democratically) referred to as "Mr. President."

During the presidency of George WASHINGTON, a controversy brewed over what the president should be called. Should he have a regal title? Some in the Senate proposed "His Elective Majesty" or "His Elective Highness," or "His Mightiness." John ADAMS, Washington's VICE PRESIDENT, proposed the wordy "His Most Benign Highness" and "His Highness, President of the United States and Protector of Their Liberties." This suggestion brought sneers from senators who shouted "His Rotundity" and "His Superfluous Excellency" at Adams.

In the end, the House of Representatives decided the issue, simply calling Washington "President of the United States" (although privately, Washington preferred being called "the general").

Tompkins, Daniel D. (1774–1825) *U.S. vice president*

Tompkins served as sixth VICE PRESIDENT from 1817 to 1825 under President James MONROE. Tompkin's health deteriorated almost immediately after taking office; he developed serious financial problems and began to drink heavily. Historians have often held Tompkins up to ridicule. Surprisingly, he was nominated for a second term as vice president and was reelected. In 1822 he returned to his home on Staten Island and never again returned to Washington, D.C.

Tower Commission

Formally known as the President's Special Review Board, but more popularly known as the Tower Commission after its chair, the Tower Commission was formed in December 1986 to investigate the role of President Ronald Reagan's National Security Council's (NSC) staff in what has become known as the IRAN-CONTRA AFFAIR.

The commission, established by President REAGAN, was composed of John Tower, a former senator from Texas; Edmund Muskie, a former senator from Maine and secretary of State under President Jimmy CARTER, and Brent Scowcroft, former NATIONAL SECURITY ADVISER to President Gerald FORD. President REAGAN directed the Tower Commission to avoid assessing any possible criminal actions and instead focus on the role and procedures of how the NSC had acted and should act in the future.

The Iran-contra affair involved officials in Reagan's NSC staff in 1985–86 secretly selling arms to Iran in exchange for that nation's help in winning the release of American hostages held by terrorists in Lebanon. Moreover, part of the income from the Iranian ARMS SALES financed a secret fund used to buy weapons and equipment to support contra forces trying to overthrow the government of Nicaragua. Such aid to the contras violated the second BOLAND AMENDMENT, a law passed in 1984 prohibiting any form of military aid to the Nicaraguan rebels. The Tower Commission's investigation focused in particular on the actions of John Poindexter, national security adviser to President Reagan, 1985–86; Robert McFarlane, national security adviser to President Reagan, 1982–85; Oliver North, a lieutenant colonel in the Marines and a member of the NATIONAL SECURITY COUNCIL staff; and Richard Secord and Albert Hakim, partners in "Enterprise," an organization involved in shipping arms internationally.

The Tower Commission confronted several significant obstacles during its brief three-month investigation. First, complicating the commission's work were the efforts of two rival investigations of the Iran-contra affair. Judge Lawrence Walsh was appointed as an INDEPENDENT COUNSEL focusing on possible criminal acts committed during the affair. In addition, select Senate and House committees were holding hearings looking into Iran-contra allegations. Even more importantly, the Tower Commission was not given such key investigative tools as the power to subpoena witnesses, grant witnesses immunity, or even take sworn testimony. Hence, government agencies such as the FEDERAL BUREAU OF INVESTIGATION and major subjects of the investigation, such as North, Poindexter, and Secord, declined to provide the commission either essential information or testimony.

The Tower Commission made its report in late February 1987. The commission criticized President Reagan's leadership style for being "disengaged" from his administration's foreign policy making. The commission accused the president of delegating too much responsibility to his advisers and NSC staff and for personally being unaware of key aspects of their operations. The commission's recommendations included proposing that NSC actions be subject to legal review by attorneys in either the Justice or State departments. However, the commission declined to recommend stronger reform measures, such as laws banning NSC implementation of policies or prohibiting the use of private individuals to help implement American diplomatic or covert activities. Although the president ignored most of the commission's recommendations, he did accept the resignation of his CHIEF OF STAFF, Donald Regan, soon after the release of the report.

Further reading: Cohen, William, and George Mitchell. *Men of Zeal*. New York: Viking, 1988; Koh, Harold. *The National Security Constitution: Sharing Power After the Iran-Contra Affair*. New Haven, Conn.: Yale University Press, 1990; President's Special Review Board. *The Tower Commission Report*. New York: Bantam Books, 1987.
—Robert E. Dewhirst

town meetings and the presidency

Vehicles for presidential communication with the public from FIRESIDE CHATS to whistle-stop tours have long been part and parcel of the White House communications function. The CLINTON White House was the first to experiment with large-scale use of the White House "town meeting" to facilitate direct interaction between the president and the citizenry. While the "town meeting" formats varied widely in their presentation, they shared the common characteristic of providing some opportunity for "nonelites" to interact directly with the president and/or at times with Vice President GORE or CABINET officials.

Most of the "town meetings" were conducted outside of Washington and involved an issue-based focus. Formats also varied from "Ask Bill" events in the first term, in which the president moved through the audience with a microphone, "talk show–style," to events in which a media personality such as Larry King or Tom Brokaw would pose questions to the president that had been called in by viewers. Some town meetings were launched exclusively by the White House and others were cosponsored with interest communities. Often large cosponsored town meetings featured the president along with other public officials who were available to field questions. Topics for town meetings during the first term included the first Clinton budget and economic plan and health care. In June of 1994 Vice President Gore participated in a live on-line town meeting—the first of its kind conducted by a nationally elected public official.

During President Clinton's first term, some observers faulted the "town meetings" for "overexposing" the president and/or allowing too many questions in disparate areas that left the audiences with no coherent message. President Clinton also expressed frustration that press accounts of town meetings were distorted in their focus on one or two peripheral questions raised during the session, or, according to Clinton, emphasizing "whatever [story] was breaking in the news at any given time."

Some of the town meetings became more carefully constructed as educational vehicles and included more structured citizen interaction during President Clinton's second term. Those led by the president focused on subjects such as gun violence, education, race in America (as part of the president's Initiative on Race), SOCIAL SECURITY, and medicare reform. Surrogates conducted town meetings on sustainable growth (EPA Director Carol Browner) and the U.S. operation in Kosovo (Madeline Albright). On November 1, 1999, the president took part in the first on-line town meeting between a sitting president and the general public. The event was cosponsored by the Democratic Leadership Forum and included satellite hookups with various Democratic governors and mayors around the United States.

The wide-scale use of "town meetings" in the Clinton administration can be traced to a number of sources. "Public interest"–based incentives included the motivation to spur citizenship engagement among the electorate. The town meetings were also designed to advance the president's interests and agendas by selling preset policy agendas after the fact (health care) and/or pretesting public reaction to various policy options before publicly launching proposals (the national discussion on Social Security). To this end, the meetings were also intended to constitute one way of allowing the president to communicate with his national constituency directly while circumventing what the White House perceived to be a "hostile press." President Clinton's natural gift for connecting with audiences and individuals in this format also undoubtedly encouraged their use. According to observers, President Clinton's capacities in this regard were twofold—encompassing the ability to project empathy to individuals in the audience and a pedagogical facility to explain and simplify complex policy options to audience participants as well as to interact with policy experts who were sometimes part of the discussions.

Among the most constructive town meeting formats utilized during the Clinton administration were three town meetings which examined various options for reforming the Social Security system. The town meetings were presented as part of a "national discussion on Social Security," that the administration hoped would culminate in a bipartisan agreement at the end of 1998, which did not come to fruition. Nonetheless, the town meetings themselves were extremely well implemented and can serve as a model for presidents in the future who wish to both educate and receive feedback from citizens with respect to complex, politically sensitive issues.

Cosponsored at the White House's request by AARP and the Concord Coalition—two groups that held opposing views on the future disposition of Social Security—the three forums were held in different geographical regions on the United States over a six-month period. In addition, a third group, Americans Discuss Social Security (ADSS), was brought in as a partner in the planning of the forums. ADSS had been a trailblazer in spearheading the use of new technologies to enhance a more direct and interactive linkage between the public and decision makers.

Led by President Clinton in two of the forums and by Vice President Gore in one meeting, the town meetings included a bipartisan representation of congressional members, experts, and other interested parties representing different shades of opinion on the topic, and an interactive audience that had been randomly selected from the public at large. Satellite hookups connected the main meetings with smaller forums in different locations. Open citizen participation was greatly facilitated by the "uncontrolled audience" selection method used to choose both the audiences for the forums and the individuals who would ask questions of the expert panelists.

Use of the town meeting format by future White Houses will most likely hinge on the president's command of public policy issues, rhetorical abilities, and willingness to accept feedback from nonelites. While the forums can continue to serve a valuable public relations function for the White House and the president, they also hold the potential to transform the proverbial BULLY PULPIT into a more interactive, responsive, and educational mode of presidential communications with the public.

Further reading: Drew, Elizabeth. *On the Edge: The Clinton Presidency.* New York: Simon and Schuster, 1994; Tomkin, Shelley L. *The National Discussion on Social Security; Civic Engagement From the White House* (unpublished research).

—Shelley L. Tomkin

trade policy

Constitutionally, Congress has the power "to regulate Commerce with foreign Nations." And so it was in the early decades of the republic. Tariff policy dominated discussion for the first 150 years of the nation's history, but since the 1930s, the presidency has come to dominate in the making of trade policy.

Today, presidents are expected to set policy through leadership, international negotiations, and the imposition of protectionist regulations. The Congress has delegated con-

siderable authority to the president over trade policy and presidents are today the primary makers of U.S. trade policy.

Trade policy deals with issues of import and export of goods. Tariffs, taxes, export controls, subsidies, quotas, are all used to influence policy.

In general, presidents have promoted free trade, but for either economic or political reasons, may promote protectionist policies. The administration of George H. W. BUSH promoted open trade and entered negotiations with Mexico and Canada to develop a free trade zone. The CLINTON administration inherited a North American Free Trade Agreement (NAFTA) and was able to push the legislation though a reluctant Congress. Clinton became an important spokesman for free trade internationally.

Bush's son, President George W. BUSH, spoke as a free trader but, for electoral reasons, promoted trade protections on steel imports. As the world's leading economic power, the United States has a significant impact on how other nations practice trade policy. In general, it is believed that free trade benefits U.S. interests.

Further reading: Bhagwati, Jagdish. *Protectionism.* Cambridge, Mass.: MIT Press, 1988; Destler, I. M. *American Trade Politics,* 2d ed. Washington, D.C.: Institute for International Economics, 1992.

transition

President George W. BUSH's transition into office was one of the shortest, but most efficiently run, in recent times. Because of the growth of the size and scope of the national government, transitions since the 1970s have been elaborately planned and bureaucratized. There never seems to be enough time to fully prepare to take over the government. Yet because of the delay in the authoritative outcome of the 2000 election, the incoming Bush administration had five fewer weeks for officially preparing to take office, about half as much time as other administrations. Surprisingly, under the circumstances, they accomplished the major tasks of the transitions—designating a White House staff, naming a CABINET, and laying the groundwork for their initial policy agenda—with dispatch.

While the outcome of the election was still in doubt the Bush team could not occupy the building set aside and prepared for the transition team or use funds provided in the Presidential Transition Act. So on November 27 the Republicans opened up a temporary transition headquarters in McLean, Virginia, that was supported by privately raised funds. Once the Supreme Court had made its ruling in BUSH v. GORE on December 12, the Bush people were allowed to move into the government-provided transition building and use public funds for their transition into office.

One of the main reasons that the transition went so smoothly was that Bush put his vice-presidential running mate, Dick CHENEY, in charge of the transition. They avoided the major problems that the CARTER team suffered in 1976 when the transition planners clashed with those running the Carter campaign immediately after the election victory. Thus much time was lost in 1976. In addition to effective control of the transition, the major asset that Cheney brought to the transition and administration was a depth of experience in government. After serving in the NIXON administration, Cheney had been deputy and then CHIEF OF STAFF for President FORD, member of Congress from Wyoming, and secretary of Defense during the earlier Bush administration, including during the GULF WAR.

The choice of Cheney as vice-presidential running mate was crucial in several other ways. In contrast to many vice presidential candidates in U.S. history, Cheney was not chosen primarily for electoral purposes; Wyoming brought few electoral votes, and Cheney was not a dynamic campaigner. Cheney's presence on the ticket was reassuring to voters because of his impressive experience, but his most important contribution would come in governance. As with Clinton's choice of GORE in 1992, Cheney was chosen for his experience, competence, and his relationship with the head of the ticket. While Gore had played an important policy and political role as vice president, Cheney was to break the mold of vice presidential importance to an administration. Cheney ran the transition and dominated most of the organizational and policy deliberations early in the administration. Administration officials took pains to emphasize that all final decisions were in fact made by President Bush and that Cheney's role was primarily advisory.

—James P. Pfiffner

Transportation Department

Responsible for coordinating the nation's transportation policy, the Transportation Department (DOT) became a cabinet-level agency in 1966. It is responsible for a variety of federal programs relating to transportation, highway planning and construction, railroads, urban mass transit, and highway and waterway safety.

Treasury, Department of the

The Treasury Department is the second-oldest CABINET agency (the STATE DEPARTMENT is the oldest). It is responsible for the nation's money and for the management of the nation's finances. It ranks as one of the most important and powerful departments of the government.

Alexander HAMILTON served as the first secretary of the Treasury, stabilizing the U.S. currency and establishing a BANK OF THE UNITED STATES. The secretary of the Treasury has often been an important adviser to the president. This has especially been the case in the post–WORLD WAR II era when the United States emerged as the dominant power of the West, and in the post–COLD WAR era when the U.S. became even more powerful on the international scene.

Treaty of Versailles

In January 1918, President Woodrow WILSON drafted the FOURTEEN POINTS, summarizing a set of principles he hoped would become the foundation of a treaty setting conditions for peace following WORLD WAR I. These principles included lenient terms for the defeated powers and an international LEAGUE OF NATIONS to maintain world peace. Wilson's central objective at the Paris Peace Conference in 1919 was the Covenant establishing the League. However, in order for Wilson to get the support of Allies for the League, he had to compromise many other aspects of his Fourteen Points, including reparations, territorial demands, disarmament of Germany, and placing the entire guilt for the war on Germany. Germany objected to the treaty but signed it under duress in June 1919.

Wilson's principal task was obtaining Senate ratification of the treaty. Wilson had enjoyed six years of Democratic control of Congress during his two terms as president, but that support had steadily weakened with each election cycle. Just before the 1918 midterm election, Wilson appealed to the public to return Democratic majorities to the House and Senate. The appeal to party loyalty in the middle of a war backfired, however, and Republicans took control of both houses of Congress. Thus, in a scenario in which Wilson needed two-thirds support of the Senate for treaty ratification, he now faced a body controlled by the opposition, led by Senate Foreign Relations Committee Chairman Henry Cabot Lodge, a man who detested Wilson and sought to undermine his efforts.

Despite the need for a supermajority, Wilson's treatment of the Senate throughout the treaty process harmed the larger drive for ratification. Wilson needed to address Senate concerns about the treaty, but his general demeanor toward the Senate exacerbated relations and contributed to the treaty's eventual defeat. Wilson rejected any significant Republican participation in the treaty process, despite the fact that several leading party officials supported an international league. He refused to provide a copy of the proposed draft when requested by the Senate. He refused to heed the signals of discontent, blasting his critics for their "careful selfishness" and "comprehensive ignorance of the state of the world." Wilson's unwillingness to compromise played right into Lodge's hands.

Lodge enjoyed party solidarity on the question of reservations to the treaty, but Wilson believed that reservations would necessitate renegotiation of the entire treaty. Instead of dealing with the Senate, Wilson chose to tour the country in a defiant attempt to drum up public support for the treaty. His tour was cut short by illness, and on October 2 he suffered a massive stroke that virtually incapacitated him. Wilson became even more resistant to compromise and moderation, and the Senate rejected the treaty in November 1919. Domestic and international support for the treaty persisted, and many influential Democrats counseled compromise, but Wilson remained steadfast, and the final effort at ratification fell short in March 1920. Lack of American membership in the League greatly hampered its effectiveness.

Further reading: Blum, John Morton. *Woodrow Wilson and the Politics of Morality.* Boston: Little, Brown, 1956; Clements, Kendrick A. *The Presidency of Woodrow Wilson.* Lawrence: University of Kansas Press, 1992; Cooper, John Milton, Jr. *The Warrior and the Priest: Woodrow Wilson and Theodore Roosevelt.* Cambridge, Mass.: Belknap Press of Harvard University Press, 1983.

—David A. Crockett

treaty power, the

Article II, Section 2, of the Constitution grants to the president the "Power, by and with the Advice and Consent of the Senate, to make Treaties, provided two thirds of the Senators present concur." The architecture of the treaty power reflects the preference of the CONSTITUTIONAL CONVENTION for collective decision making, joint participation, and consensus in the conduct of foreign policy. Until the last days of the convention, the framers' draft plan vested the treaty power solely in the Senate.

However, delegates from the large states, including Virginia's James MADISON, were uncomfortable with the proposition that the Senate alone would make treaties. Since large-state delegates had lost their campaign for proportional representation in both houses, they sought means to control the Senate, in which states enjoyed equal representation. In early September, the Committee on Postponed Parts recommended the addition of the president as a treaty-making partner. The convention's adoption of the proposal signaled not only the framers' preference for group decision-making in foreign as in domestic matters, but also their aim to infuse the conduct of foreign policy with the doctrines of SEPARATION OF POWERS and CHECKS AND BALANCES.

The inclusion of the president in the treaty power did not, in any way, signal an intention to give the president unilateral power in foreign relations. On the contrary, the role assigned to the Senate ensured discussion and debate, and an airing and consideration of the various economic, political, and security interests among the states. The two-thirds majority vote for the approval of treaties acted to check presidential interests.

The ADVICE AND CONSENT requirement drew upon English law and history. The framers borrowed the phrase from parliamentary practice, which was descriptive of continuous participation in lawmaking. In English usage, the phrase denoted legislative authorization: The King could not enact or make law without the advice and consent of both houses of Parliament. Thus the framers' employment of the familiar formula reflected their determination to exalt the Senate as a principal in the realm of international relations.

The convention debates reveal no support for unilateral EXECUTIVE POWER to make treaties. Indeed, those who spoke in the convention lauded a Senate role in treaties and legislative control of FOREIGN AFFAIRS generally. The framers' disposition was succinctly stated by Alexander Hamilton in *Federalist No. 74:* "The history of human conduct does not warrant that exalted opinion of human virtue which would make it wise in a nation to commit interests of so delicate and momentous a kind, as those which concern its intercourse with the rest of the world, to the disposal of a magistrate created and circumstanced as would be a president of the United States."

The framers' use of the formula of "advice and consent," moreover, meant to convey Senate participation in all stages of treaty making—negotiation, discussion, and decision. It is not suggestive in any way of a treaty-making process that is divided into two distinct stages: negotiation by the president and approval by the Senate. But the phrase is otherwise employed in the appointment clause to indicate a process that does depend on exclusive and sequential steps: The president "shall nominate, and by and with the Advice and Consent of the Senate, shall appoint Ambassadors."

When George WASHINGTON first communicated with the Senate on the question of the appropriate procedure for treaties, he assumed the process of negotiating treaties was a matter of joint participation. He advised a Senate committee that oral communications would best serve the active, continuous, and consultative role of the Senate. Washington, moreover, repeatedly expressed his intention to send "propositions" to the Senate, a solicitation of Senate "advice" on treaties.

In a well-known message to the senate on August 21, 1789, Washington stated his intention to meet with senators in the Senate chamber "to advise with them on the terms of the treaty to be negotiated with the Southern Indians." Washington, consistent with the framers' expectations, intended to seek the Senate's advice before, not after, the negotiation of a treaty. Washington's meeting with the Senate the following day did not go well; both sides were disappointed. When the senators announced that they would not commit themselves to any positions that day, Washington felt inconvenienced by the trip. He returned two days later and obtained the Senate's answers to his questions and its consent to the treaty, but he never again went to seek the Senate's advice on a treaty proposal.

There is nothing in that episode that would yield a conclusion that Washington had determined to exclude the Senate from any role in the negotiation process. Oral communication proved to be impracticable, but Washington continued to seek the Senate's advice through written communications rather than personal appearances. Senators were asked to approve the appointment of treaty negotiators and to advise on their negotiating instructions. Since the earliest days of the republic, there have been many examples of executive and Senate discussions regarding treaty negotiations.

The 20th century, however, witnessed the erosion of this joint effort and the assumption by presidents that negotiation was an exclusively executive concern. In short, the role of the Senate has been diminished by presidential resort to unilateral EXECUTIVE AGREEMENTS which circumvent altogether the role of the Senate in the formulation of international pacts.

While the Constitution requires joint action by the president and Senate in making treaties, it is silent on the repository of the authority to terminate treaties. The framers certainly were aware of the fact that treaties, for a variety of reasons, might require termination, and INTERNATIONAL LAW provided rules and regulations to govern their repeal. Madison and John JAY, among others, seemed to believe that treaties ought to be terminated by the president and the Senate, and, historically, some have. But the record also includes repeal by congressional action as a whole and by unilateral executive action, including President Jimmy CARTER's termination with Taiwan, and President George W. BUSH's termination in 2002 of the 1972 Anti-Ballistic Missile (ABM) Treaty with Russia. Carter's action resulted in a lawsuit in which the Supreme Court declined to reach the merits of the case and dismissed is as "nonjusticiable." The practical effect of the decision left President Carter's act of termination intact. While the question of the authority to terminate treaties was left unresolved, it seemed likely to become prominent again.

The president and the Senate may clash over the continued meaning of a treaty. Once a treaty takes effect, the president is principally responsible for its interpretation and implementation. A treaty is a law, and under the Constitution the president is charged with its faithful execution, but a president may not "reinterpret," that is, ascribe to a treaty a meaning contrary to what the Senate understood it to mean at the time it granted its consent. Disagreements arose, for example, between the president and the Senate on the interpretations of the ABM Treaty, on the question of the amenability of that treaty to the development of new weapons systems. Perhaps, as a result, the Senate will carefully examine future treaties and make publicly known in clear terms its understanding of particular treaty provisions.

—David Gray Adler

Truman, Harry S (1884–1972) *thirty-third U.S. president*

Harry S Truman was born in Lamar, Missouri, on May 8, 1884. He was the oldest of three children born to John and Martha Truman. The Truman family moved to Independence, Missouri, in 1890. John Truman was a farmer who also invested in real estate and sold livestock. After Harry Truman graduated from high school, he joined the Missouri national guard and also moved to Kansas City, Missouri. Truman worked at a variety of clerical jobs, most notably at a bank. Truman enjoyed the city life and, like his father, tried but failed to become wealthy through several investments. Harry Truman also became active in the Masons and in the "Goats," a faction of the Jackson County Democratic party. The Goats were led by Tom Pendergast, a machine boss and contractor in Kansas City, and often competed against the "Rabbits," a rival Democratic faction.

John Truman had long been active in the Goats and had influenced the development of his elder son's party identification and ideology as an anti-Wall Street, agrarian, populist Democrat who revered Andrew JACKSON and William Jennings BRYAN. Ironically and tragically, John Truman died as a result of working as a road overseer, a patronage job given to him by Tom Pendergast, in 1914.

Harry Truman returned to the family farm in order to live and work there after his father died. Upon the American entry into WORLD WAR I in 1917, Truman became the captain of an army artillery unit after he and other members of the Missouri national guard were federalized into the regular army. His artillery unit experienced extensive combat service in France. Truman was popular with the men in his unit for his fairness, decisive leadership, and bravery under fire. After the war, Truman and Eddie Jacobson, a corporal in his army unit, opened a haberdashery in Kansas City. Although this store was popular with veterans who had served with Truman, the business failed and closed because of the 1920–21 recession.

Jim Pendergast was Tom Pendergast's nephew and had served with Truman in World War I. The Pendergasts were Irish Catholics and were suspected of associating with the urban corruption of Kansas City by many rural Protestants in Jackson County. Jim Pendergast, therefore, perceived Truman as an attractive vote-getter and ticket balancer for his family's political machine. Pendergast approached Truman and offered him the opportunity to run as the machine's candidate for a seat on the county court in 1922. Truman accepted the offer.

This county "court" was actually a public works agency, which administered Jackson County's roads, bridges, construction projects, and public institutions. Truman was elected as a county "judge" in 1922, defeated for reelection in 1924, and then elected as presiding judge in 1926. During his eight-year tenure as presiding judge, Truman gener-

President Harry S Truman (center) with Soviet premier Joseph Stalin (left) and British prime minister Winston Churchill (right) *(Library of Congress)*

ally deferred to Tom Pendergast on patronage jobs while the machine boss usually gave Truman the discretion to emphasize efficiency, honesty, and professionalism in improving the county's public infrastructure, services, and finances.

Harry Truman was reluctant to run for the Democratic senatorial nomination of 1934, but Tom Pendergast insisted. Truman doubted that he could win an aggressively contested statewide primary, but he energetically campaigned throughout Missouri as the most enthusiastic, unequivocal advocate of Franklin D. Roosevelt's NEW DEAL. After winning the Democratic primary, he was easily elected to the U.S. Senate in November.

Initially derided as the "Senator from Pendergast" by some of his colleagues, Truman soon won the respect of many senators for his integrity, diligence, and deference to nine more experienced, senior senators. Despite Truman's loyal support for New Deal legislation, Roosevelt's controversial and doomed COURT PACKING PLAN, and pre–Pearl Harbor defense and foreign policies, ROOSEVELT usually favored Missouri's more conservative, senior Democratic senator, Bennett Clark, on PATRONAGE and other federal matters affecting Missouri. With the Pendergast machine in shambles because of Tom Pendergast's conviction and imprisonment for income-tax evasion, it seemed unlikely that Truman would be renominated in 1940. His Democratic opponents, though, split the anti-Pendergast votes, and Truman benefited from sudden, unexpected support from Bob Hannegan and other machine politicians in St. Louis. Consequently, Truman was narrowly renominated and reelected in 1940.

During his first term in the Senate, Truman had specialized in legislation affecting railroad and airline regulation. In 1941 he was appointed chairman of a special committee to investigate waste, fraud, and inefficiency in defense spending. As Truman provided nonpartisan, honest, dedicated leadership to this task, his reputation and status within the Senate grew further. He also attracted more favorable attention from Roosevelt and the media.

By 1943 Truman was a popular speaker at Democratic fund-raising dinners and other party functions. Truman had promoted Bob Hannegan's election as Democratic National Committee (DNC) chairman in 1944. With the help of urban machine bosses and party contributors, Hannegan lobbied Roosevelt to choose Truman as the best compromise candidate for VICE PRESIDENT as the 1944 Democratic National Convention.

Hannegan and other advocates of Truman's candidacy emphasized that the Missouri senator's legislative record was liberal enough to satisfy AFRICAN AMERICANS, organized labor, and big city mayors. On the other hand, Truman's independence and integrity, most prominently demonstrated in his chairmanship of the special committee on defense spending, made him acceptable to the Southern conservatives who dominated the Senate's committee system. The Southerners also respected Truman's insistence in 1937 on voting for Byron "Pat" Harrison of Mississippi, an increasingly anti-New Deal Democrat, for Senate majority leader instead of the eventual winner, Alben BARKLEY of Kentucky, a Roosevelt loyalist. Depite pressure from the White House and Tom Pendergast to vote for Barkley, Truman had already promised Harrison his support.

Roosevelt and Hannegan finally pressured Truman into becoming Roosevelt's running mate. Between the time of the Democratic National Convention of 1944 and Roosevelt's death on April 12, 1945, Roosevelt rarely saw or spoke with Truman. Consequently, Truman felt unprepared and inadequately informed in making the transition to the presidency. His first major presidential decision was to order the dropping of ATOMIC BOMBS on the Japanese cities of Nagasaki and Hiroshima in August 1945. Japan soon agreed to an unconditional surrender.

With the end of WORLD WAR II, Truman was confronted with the challenges of ending the wartime controls over the American economy, rebuilding a devastated Western Europe, and working on the growing diplomatic tensions with the Soviet Union. The American public was increasingly frustrated with the continuation of shortages in consumer goods and housing, rising inflation, and the slow demobilization of the armed forces. This frustration contributed to Truman's low public-approval ratings and the election of Republican majorities to both houses of Congress in 1946. A bipartisan coalition of Republicans and conservative southern Democrats passed the TAFT-HARTLEY ACT, which limited the power of labor unions, in 1947 and overrode Truman's veto of it. This bipartisan coalition also defeated a civil rights bill that Truman submitted in 1947.

While Truman and the Republican-controlled 80th Congress were at a stalemate on major domestic policy issues, Truman succeeded in securing bipartisan support for his foreign and defense policies. In particular, Congress appropriated substantial funds for the MARSHALL PLAN, which rebuilt Western Europe, and for the TRUMAN DOCTRINE. With the development of the COLD WAR with the Soviet Union and its allies in eastern Europe, the Truman Doctrine was the president's formal promulgation that the United States would stop or limit the further expansion of communist aggression or infiltration by providing economic and military aid to noncommunist governments. In particular, Truman persuaded Congress to appropriate funds to aid noncommunist governments in Greece and Turkey in 1947. After Soviet-backed East German forces isolated American-protected West Berlin, Truman ordered an airlift of consumer goods into West Berlin in 1948. These COLD WAR events and Truman's responses to them contributed to bipartisan congressional support for the creation of and American membership in the North Atlantic Treaty Organization (NATO), established in 1949. Consisting of the United States and mostly West European nations, NATO was one of several regional, multinational collective security alliances that developed during the Truman administration in order to deter communist expansion in the world.

Despite Truman's success in strengthening and expanding Roosevelt's practice of a bipartisan, interventionistic foreign policy, it seemed unlikely that he would win the 1948 presidential election. Truman's 1947 civil rights bill had antagonized the most stridently anti–civil rights southern Democrats. His cold war foreign policy alienated some liberals and leftists who perceived Truman as too belligerent and uncompromising toward the Soviet Union. Consequently, the most committed southern segregationists created the States Rights Democratic Party, and liberals most opposed to Truman's cold war foreign policy formed the Progressive Party. Throughout the presidential campaign of 1948, J. Strom Thurmond, the States' Rights Democratic nominee for president, and Henry Wallace, the Progressive presidential nominee, threatened to deprive Truman of enough normally Democratic votes so that Truman would lose the election. Major public opinion polls also showed the Republican presidential nominee, Thomas E. Dewey, the governor of New York, with a comfortable lead. A liberal, pro–civil rights Republican who generally supported Truman's foreign policy, Dewey avoided divisive domestic issues and emphasized the broad themes of national unity and the need for greater competence in the presidency in his rhetoric.

By contrast, Truman emphasized specific domestic policy issues such as inflation, housing, farm programs, and union rights in his speeches. He frequently blamed the "do nothing Republican Congress" for the nation's economic problems and warned voters that the election of a Republican president and continuation of a Republican-controlled Congress threatened the domestic policy accomplishments of the New Deal.

Truman won an upset victory and the Democrats won control of Congress in the 1948 elections. Truman collectively referred to his domestic policy proposals as the FAIR DEAL. His top priorities in the Fair Deal were civil rights, housing construction, national health insurance, a new method for subsidizing agriculture, and federal aid to education. Except for the Housing Act of 1949, most major Fair Deal bills died in Congress.

The communist conquest of all of mainland China in 1949 and the outbreak of the KOREAN WAR in 1950 forced Truman to focus on foreign policy for the remainder of his administration. Careful to avoid a direct military conflict with the Soviet Union, which now possessed atomic bombs, Truman wanted to protect South Korea as an anticommunist American ally by fighting a defensive, limited war. China's massive counterattack against American and other United Nations forces reaffirmed Truman's caution and led him to remove General Douglas MacArthur of command of American forces in the Far East on April 11, 1951. MacArthur had repeatedly disagreed with Truman's strategy in Korea.

Truman's removal of MacArthur made his KOREAN WAR policy in particular and his presidency in general even more unpopular and controversial with Congress, the public, and the media. Congress and the media also conducted highly publicized investigations of collusion between gangsters and big-city Democratic politicians and allegations of bribery and favoritism in income tax and federal loan cases among several Truman appointees. These investigations led the Truman administration to be characterized as the "mess in Washington." Frustration about the emergence of communist China and the stalemate in the Korean War contributed to charges that Truman was "soft" on communism both at home and abroad. Republican Senator Joseph MCCARTHY of Wisconsin was the most prominent leader of the "Red Scare" of the early 1950s.

After announcing in March 1952 that he would not seek another term as president, Harry Truman then concentrated on trying to end the Korean War to the satisfaction of American and South Korean policy interests and to elect a Democratic successor, Governor ADLAI STEVENSON of Illinois. The Republicans nominated Dwight EISENHOWER, a retired army general and popular hero of World War II, for president. Eisenhower easily defeated Stevenson, and the Republicans won control of Congress in 1952.

Harry Truman left the White House in January 1953 with low public-approval ratings. By the early 1960s, however, Truman was ranked as a "near-great" president, along with such presidents as Andrew JACKSON and Theodore Roosevelt, primarily because of his foreign policy accomplishments. Truman died on December 26, 1972.

Further reading: McCoy, Donald R. *The Presidency of Harry S. Truman.* Lawrence: University Press of Kansas, 1984; McCullough, David. *Truman.* New York: Simon and Schuster, 1992; Savage, Sean J. *Truman and the Democratic Party.* Lexington: University Press of Kentucky, 1997.

—Sean J. Savage

Truman Doctrine

WORLD WAR II profoundly changed the nature of the United States in the international community. Its entry into the war constituted a marked shift from its isolationist past, most notably the Neutrality Acts of the 1930s. After the war ended, the United States began to accept a more activist role in the world as events outpaced older modes of isolationist thinking. In particular, the United States began to more forcefully define its interests in terms of security and economic imperatives. The dominant perspective that emerged from this paradigm shift was that the United States could no longer remain inactive in world politics as it had in the period after WORLD WAR I. This new paradigm, which took the form of CONTAINMENT, found its earliest and most forceful voice in the Truman Doctrine, put forward by President Harry S Truman in 1947.

In 1947 a civil war raged in Greece, which pitted communism against ideals of free government. Britain informed the United States that it was withdrawing troops from the region. The Truman administration, fearing a "domino effect" of communist aggression, supported a bill to provide aid to Greece and Turkey. On May 12, 1947, in an address to Congress, Truman laid the groundwork for what would become known as the Truman Doctrine, with implications reaching far beyond the boundaries of Greece and Turkey. In that speech, Truman made the case that the United States would support interventionist policies in combating communist aggression. Specifically, he advocated providing military and economic aid to those countries that would resist "totalitarian aggression." The speech was focused on Greece and Turkey, though clearly the doctrine itself applied to a new interventionist foreign policy. The Soviet Union was not directly involved in the Greek civil war but would come to be most heavily affected by the Truman Doctrine in that the new policy was, along with the MARSHALL PLAN, a fundamental part of the U.S. policy of containment. Indeed, the Truman Doctrine is usually noted as the first affirmative step in laying the boundaries of the COLD WAR.

Further reading: Kegley, Charles W., Jr., and Eugene R. Wittkopf. *American Foreign Policy: Pattern and Process,* 2d ed. New York: St. Martin's Press, 1982.

—Daniel E. Ponder

Twelfth Amendment

The Twelfth Amendment changed the presidential selection system, providing for separate ballots for both president and VICE PRESIDENT. As originally written, Article II of the Constitution created a dual-vote system in which each presidential elector cast two votes for president, with at least one of those votes cast for someone from a different state than the elector himself. The intent of this dual-vote mechanism was to force electors to consider people with a national reputation. Whoever received a majority of the votes became president, and whoever came in second became vice president.

The creators of this system did not anticipate the rise of political parties, and very quickly the Federalists and Democratic-Republicans plotted to nominate the equivalent of a national ticket by throwing away enough second votes to ensure the proper selection of a president and vice president from the same party. The dual-vote mechanism created a strategic problem of electing a partisan ticket in a nonpartisan system. The result in 1796 was an EXECUTIVE BRANCH occupied by two political enemies, John ADAMS and Thomas JEFFERSON. The result in 1800 was electoral deadlock. Even though Democratic-Republicans agreed that Jefferson was their presidential candidate and Aaron BURR their vice-presidential candidate, the two men ended up tied in electoral votes, throwing the election into the House of Representatives for a contingency election. It took 36 ballots for Jefferson to win the necessary majority of states.

This near disaster indicated how problematical the original system was. Fears arose that an organized minority party could easily elect the majority party's vice-presidential candidate as president. The dual-vote mechanism also undermined the unitary nature of the presidency and called into question the legitimacy of the selection process. So, the Democratic-Republican Congress proposed the Twelfth Amendment in 1803. It was ratified the following year.

The first change enacted by the amendment was the elimination of the dual-vote mechanism. The new system called for each elector to vote separately for president and vice president, with a majority of votes necessary to win. This creation of a national ticket makes it highly likely that both the president and vice president will come from the same party, thus reinforcing the unitary nature of the executive branch. The second change enacted by the amendment was the reduction in the number of candidates, from five to three, from which the House would elect a president

in a contingency election. This was an acknowledgment of the emerging two-party system. The third change enacted by the amendment concerned the vice president. Since the vice president is no longer the second place finisher in the electoral tally, the amendment extends the qualifications for the presidency to the vice presidency. In the event of a contingency election, the amendment also calls for the selection of a vice president in the Senate, which would choose from the two highest electoral vote winners. Finally, the amendment states that the vice president shall act as president if no president has been chosen by March 4.

The amendment solved some problems but created others. First, the amendment greatly diminished the stature of the vice president for more than 100 years, moving him from an individual of national reputation to a mere ticket balancer. Second, the amendment effectively killed the FEDERALIST PARTY, and in the nonpartisan ERA OF GOOD FEELING actually made contingency elections more likely.

Further reading: Ceaser, James W. *Presidential Selection: Theory and Development.* Princeton, N.J.: Princeton University Press, 1979; McCormick, Richard P. *The Presidential Game: The Origins of American Presidential Politics.* New York: Oxford University Press, 1982; Milkis, Sidney M., and Michael Nelson. *The American Presidency: Origins and Development, 1776–1998,* 3d ed. Washington, D.C.: CQ Press, 1999.

—David A. Crockett

Twentieth Amendment

The Twentieth Amendment eliminated the lengthy "lame duck" session of Congress following a presidential election and addressed some technical defects in the presidential selection system. As originally written, the Constitution called for Congress to convene on the first Monday in December. This led to a variety of problems. First, following election years there was a 13-month gap between the election of members of Congress and their entry into office. By that time, there were only 11 months left before those members faced another election. Second, the second congressional session always convened after an election—after its successors had been elected but before they had taken office. This biennial lame duck session of Congress included many defeated members and could cause mischief for an incoming president who had to wait until March 4 to take office. Such a dynamic could cause tremendous uncertainty on policy grounds, especially when the presidential transition involved a change of parties. This problem was highlighted by the fractious transition between Herbert HOOVER and Franklin ROOSEVELT.

The lame duck session of Congress also created potential constitutional problems, for that session would be responsible to choose a president and vice president in a contingency election, not the newly elected Congress. The experiences of previous contingency elections in 1801 and 1825 demonstrated the problems with such a system. Congress might improperly influence a new president, or a president might improperly influence defeated members of Congress hoping for a federal appointment. In an era of faster transportation and communications, such a gap between election and inauguration seemed unnecessary.

The Twentieth Amendment cleared Congress in March 1932 and became part of the Constitution less than a month before Roosevelt's inauguration. The amendment changed the start of the congressional term to January 3 and the start of the presidential term to January 20. This change eliminated the lame duck session of Congress, reduced the time between a president's election and his inauguration (thus reducing the length of the transition), and began congressional terms prior to the start of presidential terms. If a contingency election is necessary, it will be the newly elected Congress that handles the task, rather than the outgoing members.

The amendment also irons out some technical ambiguities of the presidential selection system by declaring that the vice president-elect will be inaugurated if the president-elect dies before his term begins. If a president has not been chosen by the beginning of the term, due to ELECTORAL COLLEGE or contingency election deadlock, or is found to be unqualified, the vice president-elect will act as president until a president is chosen. The amendment also calls for Congress to pass laws providing for cases in which there is a problem with both the president-elect and the vice president-elect.

There remains ambiguity about what would happen if the winner of an election dies before electoral votes are counted (thus before the individual is technically the president-elect), but after the votes are cast by the electors. Party rules allow political parties to deal with the question of a candidate dying prior to the meeting of electors but after the popular vote. Congress can legislate for the former scenario but has not done so.

Further reading: Kyvig, David E. *Explicit and Authentic Acts: Amending the U.S. Constitution, 1776–1995.* Lawrence: University Press of Kansas, 1996; Milkis, Sidney M., and Michael Nelson. *The American Presidency: Origins and Development, 1776–1998,* 3d ed. Washington, D.C.: CQ Press, 1999.

—David A. Crockett

Twenty-fifth Amendment

In 1967 the Twenty-fifth Amendment became part of the U.S. Constitution. It deals with vacancies in the vice presi-

dency. It allows a president to fill a vacancy in the vice presidency by nominating and, with the ADVICE AND CONSENT of the Senate, filling the vacancy.

The Twenty-fifth Amendment also deals with presidential DISABILITY. If for any reason the president cannot fulfill his duties or becomes incapacitated, the VICE PRESIDENT discharges the duties of the presidency as acting president. It also accounts for situations (for example, when the president has a medical operation) when the president voluntarily and temporarily relinquishes his power to the vice president.

More difficult is the situation in which a president for some reason is unable to discharge his duties. Here, the vice president and a majority of the CABINET can declare a president disabled, and the vice president assumes the duties of the presidency, becoming acting president.

Twenty-second Amendment

The Twenty-second Amendment states that no person may be elected to the office of president more than twice outright, nor more than once if succeeding a previous CHIEF EXECUTIVE with more than two years remaining in a term. Proposed in 1947, this amendment was ratified in 1951.

The question of how long the president would serve was extensively debated at the CONSTITUTIONAL CONVENTION of 1787. The decision to allow the chief executive perpetual reelection capability was intricately related to the agreed-upon four-year length for a single term. When George WASHINGTON stepped down after two terms as the nation's first president under the Constitution, no subsequent president for another 135 years seemed willing to challenge what was viewed as an unbreakable tradition.

The conditions confronting the United States in 1940 led President Franklin ROOSEVELT, a Democrat, to seek a third term. Not only did he win that year but he was reelected to a fourth term in 1944 as well. Vice President Harry TRUMAN succeeded to the presidency after Franklin Roosevelt's death in April 1945. After Republicans took control of both chambers of Congress in the 1946 MIDTERM ELECTIONS, they quickly proposed the amendment limiting the chief executive's tenure. Forty-one states ratified the amendment within four years.

Before the Twenty-second Amendment was enacted, 15 presidents served for one term and 11 served two terms. After Truman's presidency, four presidents served one term or less; four were reelected to a second term, though Richard NIXON resigned with more than two years remaining in his second term; and one, Lyndon JOHNSON, served out the year remaining in John KENNEDY's term and was elected on his own for a term in 1964.

Supporters of the Twenty-second Amendment argue that the majority of the American public favors the two-term limit for the president. They likewise point to the more than 270 resolutions introduced in Congress by 1947 proposing the two-term restriction. According to its proponents, the amendment has prevented the corruption, arrogance, and laziness which unlimited reeligibility fosters, and is consistent with the limits placed on many American governors.

Opponents of the Twenty-second Amendment state that the people are being deprived of the right to express their will to reelect a popular incumbent. They contend that the amendment could force out a leader in the middle of a national crisis. According to its antagonists, the amendment has produced scandals and failed administrations in part because it diminishes the stature of the presidency, rendering a second-term incumbent a feckless lame duck. Among those who have campaigned for repeal of the Twenty-second Amendment are Presidents Dwight EISENHOWER and Ronald REAGAN, who ironically became victims of their party's frustration and haste over four successive defeats to Democrat Franklin Roosevelt.

In recent years there has been a movement by states to restrict the number of congressional terms, though the method of doing so has been rejected by the Supreme Court. Meanwhile, studies of second-term presidencies since the ratification of the Twenty-second Amendment have revealed that chief executives veto more, possess less public support, face a more unified opposition party, and have less success in getting their priorities through Congress than in their initial term.

Further reading: *Limiting Presidential and Congressional Terms.* Washington, D.C.: American Enterprise Institute for Public Policy Research, 1979; Polen, George. *Should Our President Be Elected for Eight Years?* New York: Schmidt, 1898; Spangler, Earl. *Presidential Tenure and Constitutional Limitation.* New York: University Press of America, 1977; Stathis, Stephen. *Presidential Tenure: A History and Analysis of the President's Term of Office.* Washington, D.C.: Congressional Research Service, 1981; Zucker, Frederick. "The Adoption of the Twenty-second Amendment." Ph.D. diss., Pennsylvania State University, 1959.

—Samuel B. Hoff

Twenty-third Amendment

The Twenty-third Amendment granted voting rights in presidential elections to residents of Washington, D.C. As originally written, the Constitution called for "each state" to appoint electors to choose the president. Since the Federal District is not a state, its residents had no role in choosing the president and vice president. Article I, Section 8, of the Constitution gave Congress the power to fix the loca-

tion of the national government, created from a cession of land in order to keep the district free from the direct influence of any specific state. Congress has jurisdiction over the Federal District. Some scholars argue that the framers did not anticipate a large permanent population in the district distinct from the surrounding states, and that they expected residents to remain citizens of the state from which they came. Nevertheless, citizens of the Federal District were just as much citizens as those from other states, with the same responsibilities with respect to taxation and military service, but with no voice in choosing members of the federal government.

The issue of political participation by the Federal District had a long history, going back as far as 1818, when James MONROE supported representation in Congress. The effort gained momentum in the civil rights era as political leaders sought to address the issues of race and denial of the franchise. Initial proposals began by supporting full and proportional representation, including provisions for congressional representation, but the House of Representatives limited the proposals to the question of electoral votes, fearing that the wider proposal would be opposed by Southern legislators. The final amendment gives Washington, D.C., the number of electors equal to the number it would have if it were a state. The only qualification to this rule is that the Federal District may have no more electors than the least populous state. This makes sure that Washington, D.C., with its greater population, does not have any more influence than smaller states. The practical effect of this rule is that the Federal District has three electoral votes. The amendment itself was proposed in June 1960 and ratified in April 1961. No state outside the former Confederacy failed to ratify the amendment, but no former Confederate state supported it. Since its ratification, the district has always voted for the Democratic presidential candidate.

The amendment has the technical effect of creating an even-numbered pool of electoral votes. Prior to its ratification, the nation usually conducted presidential elections based on an odd number of electoral votes, making a tie (and thus a House contingency election) highly unlikely in a two-party race. Although still a remote possibility, a tie has been possible ever since 1961. The nation came closest to this scenario in the disputed election of 2000.

Later attempts to grant Washington, D.C., statehood or full representation in Congress have failed. Congress passed an amendment concerning congressional representation in 1978, but an amendment that would give congressional representation to a liberal Democratic stronghold gained no traction at the state level.

Further reading: Anastaplo, George. *The Amendments to the Constitution. A Commentary.* Baltimore, Md.: Johns

Hopkins University Press, 1995; Kyvig, David E. *Explicit and Authentic Acts: Amending the U.S. Constitution, 1776–1995.* Lawrence: University Press of Kansas, 1996.

—David A. Crockett

two presidencies

In 1966 Aaron Wildavsky argued that presidential influence with Congress differs so much in foreign and domestic policy that there are, in effect, "two presidencies." (Wildavsky's work and all others mentioned appear in edited work cited in the bibliography.) Wildavsky advanced the idea of using the content of policy to distinguish among presidents' powers in dealing with Congress. During the past 35 years, scholars have made numerous theoretical and empirical arguments and interpretations about the two presidencies thesis. Cumulative research on the two presidencies has guided much of our understanding of presidential-congressional relations in the post–WORLD WAR II era. It has greatly helped us understand these two American political institutions. The literature has developed to such an extent that I edited a collection of research on the two presidencies in 1991.

Wildavsky's classic article argued that examining such policy differences would provide important opportunities for comparison, which he felt was lacking in the literature on the presidency. This first quantitative look found that Congress supported the president's foreign policy initiatives 70 percent of the time compared with about 40 percent for DOMESTIC POLICY. Research 14 years later updated Wildavsky's data through 1975, finding that the gap in presidential success had narrowed from 55 percent congressional support in foreign policy to 46 percent approval of domestic initiatives. When Lance LeLoup and Steven Shull looked at issues within both domestic and foreign policy, they observed considerable variation.

Congressional Quarterly's box score of presidential initiatives to Congress was the database for these first studies. Because *CQ* stopped collecting these data after 1975, scholars have sought to measure the two presidencies differently. All the subsequent studies have used presidential positions on congressional votes rather than presidential initiatives and so the measures are not directly comparable. Thus, the emphasis shifted from presidential actions to presidential reactions.

Lee Sigelman and Harvey Zeidenstein use only key votes (among all roll-call votes on which presidents take positions) in criticizing the box score for including inconsequential and noncontroversial matters. Perhaps not surprisingly, both authors find a more limited two presidencies difference than did earlier authors. However, because *CQ's* key votes measure is so different from its BOX SCORE, both conceptually and empirically, scholars necessarily

make different assumptions when using different measures. Most authors today think *CQ's* more recent measure of success better reflects concurrence of preference rather than presidential influence in Congress.

Later articles have added other considerations, such as variation by party, member status, chamber, and ideology. Zeidenstein finds chamber important, while for George Edwards, party rather than chamber or even policy is the explanation for the observed differences. Richard Fleisher and Jon Bond find that the two presidencies occurrence depends on party and works for Republican presidents only. Duane Oldfield and Wildavsky contend that societal changes have diminished the president's influence in foreign policy. However, other authors have found two presidencies differences with other *CQ* indicators, such as its support measure.

Terry Sullivan argues that the two presidencies theory is more about winning than support. His analysis uses a data set composed of presidential head counts compiled by their own administrations. Russell Renka and Bradford Jones suggest that the two presidencies in the REAGAN administration and in George H. W. BUSH's first year resulted from presidential minority party status. Other scholars are finding a reemergence of the two presidencies. The more recent focus is to expand the typology into subareas of domestic (such as civil rights and the environment) and foreign policy (such as defense and trade). Some authors have discussed coding and data problems with such groupings and others argue that economic and budget matters may need separate consideration. When subareas are considered, greater variation often appears than when issue areas are aggregated into only two groups. Both content-based and analytical typologies have been utilized in subsequent research along with the original two presidencies notion.

Has the two presidencies thesis enhanced our ability to compare presidents and our understanding of presidential-congressional relations? After 35 years the two presidencies still is not a theory, but it has made and will continue to make a contribution toward our understanding. It shows the utility of a policy approach for studying presidential-congressional relations. Typologies even as simple as the distinction between domestic and foreign policy do encourage such comparison, a first step in theory building. Perhaps a continuum is preferable to the two-part typology of domestic versus foreign. Apart from expanding the categorizations, we should derive them empirically rather than intuitively.

Much of the earlier two presidencies research relied on descriptive statistics, while multivariate analysis has been more common in recent research. Since 1991 we have seen two presidencies analyses at the most disaggregated level (the roll-call vote) as well as at more aggregated levels of analysis (such as annually). Also, subsequent research has examined other aspects of the relationship between

CONGRESS AND THE PRESIDENT, including major legislation, presidential position taking, comparing presidents' legislative success and support, and even nonlegislative actions, such as EXECUTIVE ORDER issuance. These expansions frequently find significant differences by domestic and foreign policy.

Scholars must be more innovative in sorting through the challenges posed to the two presidencies thesis than we have been during its first 35 years. Otherwise, it will not endure as the major paradigm of presidential-congressional relations for the next century. We need better concepts and measures and clearer explication of the underlying concept. The many interpretations of the two presidencies thesis have not always praised it but they have not buried it either. The two presidencies provides an important pedagogical tool for comparing and understanding, if not yet in fully explaining or predicting, presidential relations with Congress. Continuing the research beyond presidential success and/or support in Congress, and even to other actors, would allow a better assessment of the generalizability of the two presidencies thesis.

Further reading: Shull, Steven A. *Presidential-Congressional Relations: Policy and Time Approaches.* Ann Arbor: University of Michigan Press, 1997; ———, ed. *Two Presidencies: A Quarter Century Assessment.* Chicago: Nelson-Hall Publishers, 1991.

—Steven A. Shull

two-term tradition

The Constitution leaves open the number of terms a president may serve. While there is no constitutional limit, President George WASHINGTON decided to step aside after his second term, thereby setting a precedent that evolved into the two-term tradition. That tradition was followed until Franklin D. ROOSEVELT decided to seek a third, and eventually fourth, term.

As a reaction against FDR, Republicans led the effort to codify into law the two-term limit. This led to the passing of the TWENTY-SECOND AMENDMENT (1951). Now, presidents are limited by law to no more than two full terms.

Tyler, John (1790–1862) *tenth U.S. president*

Born on March 28, 1790, in Charles City County, Virginia, Tyler graduated from the College of William and Mary in 1807. John Tyler was the nation's first "President by act of God." When William Henry HARRISON died in 1841, one month after his inauguration, the six-foot-tall, blue-eyed John Tyler, his vice president, became president. Or did he? At that time, it was unclear whether a vice president who replaced a president became acting president or president.

President John Tyler *(Library of Congress)*

In the House of Representatives, John McKeon of Pennsylvania introduced a resolution giving Tyler the title "Acting President." The resolution did not carry. Tyler acted swiftly, claiming both the office and title of president. While critics dubbed Tyler "His Accidency," the new president was determined to exercise fully his new powers, much to the dismay and disappointment of his fellow Whigs.

Asserting and actually grabbing power are two different things. Tyler faced an early test of strength with "his" CABINET (Harrison holdovers, all). Daniel Webster, the secretary of State, tried to put Tyler in his place, announcing at the first cabinet meeting,

"Mr. President," he said at the first cabinet meeting, "I suppose you intend to carry on the ideas and customs of your predecessor, and that this administration inaugurated by President Harrison will continue in the same line of policy under which it has begun. It was our custom that the cabinet of the deceased President, that the President should preside over us. Our custom and proceeding was that all measures whatever, however, relating to the administration were brought before the cabinet, and their settlement was decided by a majority—each member, *and the President, having one vote.*"

After a short pause, Tyler responded:

I beg your pardon, gentlemen. I am sure I am very glad to have in my cabinet such able statesmen as you have proved yourselves to be, and I shall be pleased to avail myself of your counsel and advice, but I can never consent to being dictated to as to what I shall or shall not do. I, as President, will be responsible for my administration. I hope to have your cooperation in carrying out its measures; so long as you see fit to do this, I shall be glad to have you with me; when you think otherwise, your resignations will be accepted.

Cabinet resignations followed shortly. Tyler was a believer in states' rights, and as he vetoed bill after bill of the Whig legislative agenda, he alienated his Whig cohorts and his cabinet. On September 11, 1841, every member of his cabinet, except Webster, sent Tyler their resignations. Four years later Tyler's veto of a minor revenue bill was overturned by Congress—the first override in history. (Tyler was also the first president to face an impeachment resolution, which failed to get the necessary votes.) Tyler became, in Henry CLAY's words, "a President without a party."

In domestic affairs, Tyler's vetoes led to gridlock, as the Whig Tyler repudiated nearly every plank of the Whig program. Tyler wanted to run for reelection but was, not surprisingly, repudiated by the Whigs.

As an example of Tyler's stubbornness and difficulties with Congress, the case of Caleb Cushing is illustrative. Tyler nominated Cushing for secretary of the Treasury. When the Senate refused to confirm Cushing, the president immediately renominated him. Hours later, after the Senate once again rejected Cushing, Tyler sent Cushing's nomination to the Senate for a third time. For the third time in one day, the Senate refused to confirm a president's cabinet appointment.

In between vetoing legislation, Tyler had time to father 15 children (the last, Pearl, was born when Tyler was 70), by far the most productive president in history in this area. Historians generally rate Tyler in the below average category of presidents.

Further reading: Chitwood, Oliver P. *John Tyler: Champion of the Old South.* New York: Appleton, 1939; Young, Stanley P. *Tippecanoe and Tyler, Too!* New York: Random House, 1957.

U

United Nations

The United Nations (UN) was created in 1945. Designed to promote peace, security, and welfare, the UN is located in New York City. The president appoints the U.S. ambassador to the UN with the advice and consent of the Senate.

The UN Security Council, a committee of 15 nations, has primary responsibility for promoting peace and security. On rare occasions, the Security Council will recommend UN-sanctioned use of force. This occurred, for example, in 1950 when the UN authorized military force to prevent North Korea from overtaking South Korea, and in 1990 when force was authorized to remove Iraq from Kuwait.

The United Nations Participation Act of 1945 set out guidelines under which U.S. forces could come under the control of the UN. It reads, in part,

> The President is authorized to negotiate a special agreement or agreements with the Security Council which shall be subject to the approval of the Congress by appropriate Act or joint resolution, providing for the numbers and types of armed forces, their degree of readiness and general location, and the nature of facilities and assistance, including rights of passage, to be made available to the Security Council on its call for the purpose of maintaining international peace and security.

United States v. Belmont, 301 U.S. 324 (1937)

This was a Supreme Court decision that acknowledged the power of the president to conclude international agreements under his own constitutional authority and without either the ADVICE AND CONSENT of the Senate or approval of both houses of Congress.

In 1933 President Franklin D. ROOSEVELT exchanged diplomatic notes with Maksim Litvinov, the Soviet commissar for foreign affairs, formalizing relations between the United States and the USSR. Included among these diplomatic notes was an agreement known as the Litvinov

Assignment which resolved how claims held by the nationals of each country were to be settled. As part of the assignment, the Soviet Union assigned to the U.S. government all its outstanding claims against American nationals to help meet the U.S. claims against the USSR. President Roosevelt did not submit the agreement to the Senate or to Congress as a whole.

The executors of the estate of August Belmont, the assets of which had been appropriated by the Soviet nationalization decrees of 1918, sought to block the U.S. government's recovery of these funds. The executors argued, among other things, that the president could not conclude a valid international agreement absent the advice and consent of the Senate or congressional approval. They also contended that the presidential action could not prevail against conflicting state law.

The Court rejected the executors' arguments. In *Belmont* and in the later related decision, UNITED STATES V. PINK, the Court formally acknowledged the president's ability to conclude binding agreements with other nations based solely on his own authority, compacts known as sole EXECUTIVE AGREEMENTS, and to settle claims. Although the Court did not directly conclude that the president's actions prevailed over conflicting state law, it hinted that external affairs would take precedence over countervailing state action. This latter question would be addressed once and for all in *Pink*.

Clearly, *Belmont* accentuated presidential power in FOREIGN AFFAIRS and contributed to the rapid growth of sole executive agreements as a means of implementing U.S. foreign policy. Presidential gains in *Belmont* regarding executive agreements would later be reaffirmed by *PINK* AND *DAMES & MOORE V. REGAN*, both of which upheld presidential power to settle claims unilaterally.

In the wake of *Belmont* at least two major questions remain unresolved. The first is the relationship between sole executive agreements and treaties. That the two are interchangeable is highly unlikely. Were it otherwise, the advice and consent power of the Senate would be completely eviscerated. To a great extent, whether an agreement is concluded through sole executive agreement, congressional-executive agreement or the treaty process often depends more on political accommodation between the branches than on any legal formula.

The second question is the relationship between executive agreements and federal law. While *Belmont* hinted and *Pink* established the principle that executive agreements will control vis-à-vis countervailing state law, whether such compacts enjoy supremacy over countervailing federal law is entirely another matter. A federal statute passed following an executive agreement would seem likely to prevail over unilateral presidential action so long as the statute did not interfere with an area of exclusive presidential authority, such as diplomatic recognition.

Further reading: Henkin, Louis. *Foreign Affairs and the U.S. Constitution.* Ardsley-on-Hudson, N.Y.: Transnational Publishers, 1996; Millet, Stephen M. *The Constitutionality of Executive Agreements: An Analysis of United States v. Belmont.* New York: Garland, 1990; Tribe, Laurence H. *American Constitutional Law.* New York: Foundation Press, 2000.

—Roy E. Brownell II

United States v. Curtiss-Wright Export Corporation, 229 U.S. 304 (1936)

In 1934 Congress passed a statute that authorized President Franklin D. ROOSEVELT to impose an embargo on arms shipments to Bolivia and Paraguay, then involved in armed conflict in the Chaco, if he determined that it would contribute to the restoration of peace. FDR made the finding and exercised the delegation of contingent authority. The Curtiss-Wright Export Corporation was indicted in January 1936 for conspiring to violate the resolution, but it demurred on grounds that the resolution represented an unconstitutional delegation of power. The Supreme Court, in an opinion by Justice George Sutherland, upheld the delegation against the charge that it was unduly broad. In a convoluted opinion, Sutherland strayed from the issue and, in some ill-considered dicta, asserted that the president is the "sole organ" of American foreign policy, and that the powers of the office are derived not from the Constitution but from the nation's international sovereignty.

Sutherland's theory of an inherent presidential power over FOREIGN AFFAIRS, which is derived from an extra-constitutional source, stems from his bizarre reading of Anglo-American legal history. According to his version, domestic and foreign affairs are different, "both in respect of their origin and nature." The "domestic or internal affairs" are confined by the reach of the Constitution. But authority over foreign affairs is not dependent upon a grant from the constitution since the powers of external sovereignty "passed from the Crown not to the colonies severally, but to the colonies in their collective and corporate capacity of the United States of America." Sutherland's historical thesis has no foundation, and it is exploded by the fact that in 1776 states were sovereign entities. Proof is found in Article II of the Articles of Confederation, which stated: "Each state retains its sovereignty, freedom and independence, and every power . . . which is not . . . expressly delegated to the United States, in Congress assembled." The sovereign states delegated various foreign affairs powers to Congress, among them authority over war and peace, and treaties and alliances. That grant, alone, destroys Sutherland's premise that foreign relations powers stemmed from "some other source" than the states.

Even if it were assumed that the power of external sovereignty had been by some method transferred directly from the Crown to the Union, it remains to be explained why that power would be vested in the president. As Justice Felix Frankfurter stated, "the fact that power exists in the government does not vest it in the President." The Court, moreover, has ruled on several occasions that the sovereign power over foreign affairs is held by Congress. There is nothing in Sutherland's theory to explain the location of this power in the presidency. Finally, Sutherland was plainly in error in his contention that the conduct of foreign policy is not restricted by the Constitution. James MADISON put the question beyond doubt when he wrote in *Federalist No. 45* that "the powers delegated by the proposed Constitution are *few and defined.* . . . [they] will be exercised principally on external objects, as war, peace, negotiation, and foreign commerce," to demonstrate that foreign relations powers were derived from the Constitution. Since *Curtiss-Wright,* the Court consistently has taken the position that powers are tethered to the Constitution, and Sutherland's discussion of inherent presidential power was sharply dismissed as "dictum" by Justice Robert H. Jackson in *YOUNGSTOWN SHEET AND TUBE CO. V. SAWYER* (1952).

In his assertion that the president is the sole organ of foreign affairs, Sutherland misappropriated the phrase from a speech delivered in the House of Representatives by then-congressman John Marshall, who noted that "the President is the sole organ of the nation in its external relations . . . of consequence, the demand of a foreign nation can only be made on him." At no point in his speech did Marshall argue that the president's exclusive authority to communicate with a foreign nation included a power to formulate or develop policy. All Marshall had in mind was the president's role as the sole organ of communication with other governments, a rather unremarkable point, at that, since officials had acknowledged since the Founding that the president was the "sole" channel of communication with foreign nations. Thus it was Sutherland who infused a purely communicative role with a substantive policy-making function and thereby manufactured a great power out of the Marshallian "sole organ" doctrine. Of course, Sutherland's doctrine completely undermines the framers' penchant for collective decision-making in foreign affairs and their strong aversion to executive unilateralism. And given the allocation of foreign relations power to both CONGRESS AND THE PRESIDENT, the claim is by definition indefensible.

In spite of its flaws, the sole organ doctrine has been frequently invoked by presidents in support of their unilateral acts in the realm of international relations, a practice which is likely to continue.

—David Gray Adler

United States v. District Court, 407 U.S. 297 (1972)

This Supreme Court decision ruled that the president lacks the inherent constitutional power to authorize warrantless ELECTRONIC SURVEILLANCE of individuals or organizations suspected of being domestic security threats. In this case (popularly known as *Keith* after the federal judge, Damon Keith, whose ruling was appealed), the Court ruled that the Fourth Amendment prohibition against unreasonable searches and seizures governs the actions of the EXECUTIVE BRANCH in initiating electronic surveillance against such individuals. For over a quarter century prior to *Keith*, presidents had authorized warrantless surveillance of individuals they viewed as a threat to domestic security. Up until that time, Supreme Court precedent and relevant federal law had left open to question whether the president possessed such authority.

Keith stemmed from a criminal proceeding in which three defendants were charged with conspiracy to destroy government property. One of the defendants, who was also charged with the bombing of a CENTRAL INTELLIGENCE AGENCY building, had had his conversations overheard by federal agents pursuant to a warrantless wiretap authorized by the attorney general. The defendants attempted to compel the government to reveal certain surveillance information so that a hearing could be conducted to determine whether the information constituted unlawfully acquired evidence. Judge Keith concluded that the surveillance was indeed unlawful and ruled that the evidence be disclosed to the defendants for examination. The government, which had contended that its authority derived from both the president's inherent power to protect the NATIONAL SECURITY and the 1968 Omnibus Crime Control and Safe Streets Act, appealed Judge Keith's decision.

The Supreme Court decided against the government, concluding that neither the 1968 statute nor the president's inherent power conferred sufficient authority to the ATTORNEY GENERAL to initiate such surveillance. The Court reasoned that the potential for executive abuse of power was too great; that government officials could easily interpret legitimate dissent to be sedition and wiretaps could end up having a chilling effect on freedom of speech and association.

The Court expressly noted that the decision did not define the scope of the president's surveillance power with respect to the intelligence activities of foreign powers or their agents, either inside or outside of the United States. Instead, the Court indicated that the decision only circumscribed the president's power to place surveillance on domestic organizations composed of U.S. citizens not involved with foreign interests. Of course, the Court's analysis presupposes that the origin of the threat—whether foreign or domestic—can be determined prior to commencement of the surveillance.

In its decision, the Court encouraged Congress to fill the void in existing federal law with respect to the electronic surveillance of domestic security threats. Congress accepted this invitation six years later with the passage of the FOREIGN INTELLIGENCE SURVEILLANCE ACT (FISA). This statute created special procedures for authorizing surveillance of this kind. In its consideration of FISA, however, Congress left for another day the question of whether the EXECUTIVE BRANCH could place warrantless wiretaps on the phones of a U.S. citizen involved with a foreign power or could conduct a warrantless search of his or her residence or office. The latter issue arose briefly but remained ultimately unresolved following the investigation of Aldrich Ames.

Further reading: Banks, William C., and M. E. Bowman. "Executive Authority for National Security Surveillance." *Amer. Univ. L. Rev.* 50 (2000); Cinquegrana, Americo R. "The Walls (and Wires) Have Ears: The Background and First Ten Years of the Foreign Intelligence Surveillance Act of 1978." *U. Penn. L. Rev.* 137 (1989).

—Roy E. Brownell II

United States v. Nixon, 418 U.S. 683 (1974)

After some of President Nixon's supporters and staff persons had been indicted by a grand jury on March 1, 1974, for obstructing justice and conspiracy to defraud the United States, the grand jury also named President NIXON as an unindicted coconspirator. During this same time, the special prosecutor filed a motion to subpoena certain tapes of conversations and meetings between the president, staff persons, and aides. To protect these tapes, President Nixon claimed EXECUTIVE PRIVILEGE and filed a motion to quash the subpoena. Rather than handing over the 43 subpoenaed tapes to the House Judiciary Committee, on April 30, 1974, Nixon released 1,254 pages of edited transcripts of portions of 20 of the subpoenaed conversations. The D.C. district court denied the president's motion to quash the subpoena and ruled that the SPECIAL PROSECUTOR had made a legitimate request that was privileged, issuing an order for an in camera examination of the subpoenaed materials. The court also discounted Nixon's claim that the dispute between the president and special prosecutor was an intra-executive conflict and was thus inappropriate for the court to intervene and that the court had no authority to question his executive privilege.

The Supreme Court accepted a writ of certiorari filed by the United States from the Court of Appeals to review the case. Given that Nixon had appointed four members of the Court—Chief Justice Burger, and Justices Blackmun, Rehnquist and Powell—advantages for victory seemed to rest with the president.

While Justice Rehnquist did not participate in this decision—since he had just recently been employed in Nixon's Justice Department—the Court unanimously joined Chief Justice Burger in a strong 8-0 majority decision against the president.

The first issue that Burger addressed was whether the Court had the authority or jurisdiction to look into the president's concerns. Burger concluded that the Court did have authority to oversee executive operations. Burger next asked the question whether it was proper for the Court to look at this dispute between the president and the special prosecutor. The Court ruled that this dispute was justiciable since it was not an EXECUTIVE BRANCH dispute between a subordinate and superior officer, as the special prosecutor was not an officer that could be removed by the president without agreement by eight designated leaders of Congress. The Court had given the special prosecutor plenary authority to examine any offenses coming out of the 1972 presidential election.

Burger next took up the president's request to have confidential conversations between the president and his advisers protected. Burger denied that the president had an absolute privilege of confidentiality and made it clear that the Court has the final say as to the claim of executive privilege. The Court decided that it was not enough to claim or demand that SEPARATION OF POWERS and confidentiality of a president's high-level communications should be enough to protect a president from the judicial process under all circumstances, since needs of the judicial process may outweigh executive privilege. While presidential communication cannot be absolutely protected, it should be protected, but cannot be so protected when there is a need of relevant information for possible criminal prosecutions.

Under normal circumstances, then, the Court indicated that presidential conversations should be accorded a high degree of respect. This, then, in no way places the president above the law.

The effect of this decision certainly limited President Nixon in using executive privilege to protect communications and avoid judicial oversight of presidential actions. Yet normal protection of communication was taken from the realms of tradition and officially recognized as a power of the president in this case. Thus, this decision limited EXECUTIVE POWER in this particular case but in the future may contribute to the expansion of presidential power in formally recognizing this power.

The decision also played an important role in making it much easier for the members of Congress on the House Judiciary Committee to vote for IMPEACHMENT once House members understood the sort of tapes that were in Nixon's possession.

In less than three weeks after this particular case was decided, the president became the first and only president to resign his office.

Further reading: Friedman, Leon, ed. *U.S. v. Nixon: The President Before the Supreme Court.* New York: Chelsea House Publishers, 1974; Kurland, Philip B. *Watergate and the Constitution.* Chicago: University of Chicago Press, 1978; *United States v. Nixon,* 418 U.S. 683 (1974).

—Byron W. Daynes

United States v. Pink, 315 U.S. 203 (1942)

This Supreme Court decision reaffirmed the president's power to conclude international agreements with foreign nations without the ADVICE AND CONSENT of the Senate or other form of congressional approval. The decision also established that the president's actions in this respect will control even in the face of countervailing state law.

Much like its sister opinion, *UNITED STATES V. BELMONT,* *United States v. Pink* stemmed from a dispute arising from President Franklin D. ROOSEVELT's diplomatic recognition of the USSR in 1933. The president's recognition was carried out through an exchange of diplomatic notes with the Soviet commissar of foreign affairs, Maksim Litvinov.

Incident to the formalization of relations between the two nations was an agreement over the legal claims and counterclaims of each nation, known as the Litvinov Assignment. This agreement was premised on the understanding that all Soviet claims were to be released and turned over to the U.S. government and that the USSR would be duly notified of the amounts realized by the U.S. government. This compact was concluded as a sole EXECUTIVE AGREEMENT in that it was not submitted to either the Senate or to Congress as a whole.

Pursuant to state law, the New York superintendent of insurance, Louis H. Pink, took possession of the assets of a Russian insurance company that had continued to do business in the United States despite the nationalization of the company's assets in the Soviet Union. After paying all the domestic claims on the company's assets, the superintendent had $1 million left over with which to pay the claims of foreign creditors. The majority of these payments, however, were suspended pursuant to the executive agreement, pending the claim of the U.S. government. This provision placed the agreement in contravention of state law, and Pink challenged the federal government's authority to seize the assets.

In *Pink,* the Supreme Court formally concluded what it had hinted in *Belmont,* that the Litvinov Assignment would take precedence over state law. The Court also reaffirmed that the Senate was not required to play a role in the conclusion of sole EXECUTIVE AGREEMENTS. At the same time, *Pink* cemented the relationship between the president's hitherto disputed authority to settle claims and his undisputed power to recognize foreign governments. Both *Pink* and *Belmont* had the effect of emboldening the president in NATIONAL SECURITY affairs, leading to an increase in the use of sole executive agreements.

What the Court did not clarify in *Pink* (or in subsequent cases) was which international agreements required Senate advice and consent (or congressional assent) and which did not. Certainly the two are not interchangeable, since that would run afoul of constitutional text. The answer to this question has essentially come to be governed more by the give-and-take of the political process than by any legal doctrine. Neither did the Court clarify whether an executive agreement counter to federal law would be upheld. Presumably, unless the president were acting pursuant to his exclusive powers such as diplomatic recognition, he could not act counter to federal law.

Further reading: Henkin, Louis. *Foreign Affairs and the U.S. Constitution.* Ardsley-on-Hudson, N.Y.: Transnational Publishers, 1996; Tribe, Laurence H. *American Constitutional Law.* New York: Foundation Press, 2000.

—Roy E. Brownell II

United We Stand America (UWSA)

A surprisingly successful third party movement that appeared on the American political landscape in the 1990s, the United We Stand America (UWSA) organization had a rather unorthodox beginning when, on February 20, 1992, successful American businessman and philanthropist Henry Ross Perot appeared as a guest on *Larry King Live,* a television talk show on the Cable News Network (CNN), and stated that he would run for president if Americans would get his name placed on the ballot in all 50 states.

What followed was a citizen's initiative with unprecedented "grassroots" support and successful ballot signature campaigns in the states of California and Texas. However, in July 1992, less than six months after he had first publicly

expressed the desire to run for president, Perot stated that he would not seek that office in the 1992 presidential election, because he felt that he could not win against an invigorated DEMOCRATIC PARTY with Bill CLINTON as their newly nominated candidate, but he would leave his name on the state ballots he was already on so it could be used as a protest vote.

By the fall of 1992, Perot was officially on the ballot in all 50 states as a candidate for president of the United States. Overwhelmed by public support for his candidacy, Perot changed his mind and officially announced his candidacy. He fought on the issues of CAMPAIGN FINANCE reform, opposition to the North American Free Trade Agreement (NAFTA), and deficit and debt reduction. Perot's vice presidential running mate was James Stockdale, a distinguished former POW.

Even though he was not a major party candidate, Perot was included in all of the presidential DEBATES in October 1992. His aggressive television advertising campaign included conventional 30-second spots and introduced half-hour paid "infomercials" shown during prime time on major U.S. television networks. The strategy portrayed Perot as the ultimate outsider (he had never held elected office, worked in a BUREAUCRACY, or studied public policy) who was prepared to discuss the real issues and present practical solutions. The presentations often included Perot's colorful graphs and down-to-earth HUMOR. Perot also successfully introduced the use of the "800" number as a tool to recruit volunteers and donations for his campaign. It is also noteworthy that Perot did not hold traditional PRESS CONFERENCEs, preferring instead to appear regularly on *Larry King Live* in order to communicate his message to potential voters. While the Reform Party began the campaign with between 5 percent and 7 percent support in the electoral polls, on election day Perot received almost 20 percent of the vote.

In January of 1993, Ross Perot transformed the UWSA into a watchdog group with chapters in every state. By 1994 the Republicans desperately wanted to tap into the Perot support base, and in September the House Republican Conference promulgated its 10-section "Contract with America" as a joint campaign platform for Republican candidates across the country. The "contract" was drafted specifically to appeal to UWSA members on fiscal and government reform issues. The Republicans did manage to take control of the Congress and Senate in the 1994 elections for the first time in 40 years. However, dissatisfaction with what the Republicans managed to accomplish with their majorities in both houses of the legislature eventually motivated those involved with the UWSA movement to found the Reform Party of the United States.

See REFORM PARTY OF THE USA.

Further reading: Jelen, Ted G. *Ross for Boss.* Albany: State University of New York Press, 2001; Perot, Ross. *United We Stand.* Concord, N.H.: Hyperion Press, 1992.

—Stephanie Mullen

urban policy See HOUSING POLICY, DEPARTMENT OF HOUSING AND URBAN DEVELOPMENT.

USA PATRIOT Act (Uniting and Strengthening America by Providing Appropriate Tools Required to Intercept and Obstruct Terrorism Act; USAPA)

In response to the changed conditions and newly perceived threat assessment after the SEPTEMBER 11, 2001, ATTACKS Congress, at the request of President George W. BUSH, passed the USA PATRIOT Act (115, Stat. 272). President Bush signed the act into law on October 26, 2001. The new law gave the president sweeping new powers in the domestic arena and with respect to U.S. intelligence agencies. The law diminishes many of the CHECKS AND BALANCES characteristic of U.S. law and weakens the role of the courts in checking abuses of power by the government. Civil libertarians claim the law violates the rights of U.S. citizens, but the president claims these powers are necessary to combat terrorism.

Further reading: McCarthey, Michael T. "USA Patriot Act." *Harvard Journal on Legislation* 435 (2002); "USA Patriot Act, the Good, the Bad, and the Sunset." *Human Rights* 29, no. 1 (Winter 2002); Tepker, Harry F. "The USA Patriot Acts." *Extensions* (Fall 2002).

U-2 incident

At their 1955 meeting, Nikita S. Khrushchev declined President EISENHOWER's "Open Skies" proposal that would have allowed the two major powers to fly over and photograph each other's territory. In 1956 the United States began secret overflights of the USSR using the newly developed high-altitude U-2 plane equipped with high-definition cameras. Each flight required the approval of Eisenhower who, despite the pending Paris conference that held promise for a limited nuclear test ban treaty, authorized what proved to be the final U-2 mission.

On May 1, 1960, Francis Gary Powers, departed in a U-2 from Peshawar, Pakistan, on a 3,800-mile trip over the Soviet Union to Bodo, Norway. During the mission, a Soviet rocket intercepted the U-2. Although Powers had the means to destroy the plane and kill himself, he did neither, giving the Soviets irrefutable evidence that the United States was conducting aerial espionage over Soviet territory.

When Powers did not land in Norway, the American cover story was that he had suffered a oxygen deficit and probably crashed while skirting the USSR on a mission to record meteorological data, the non-espionage task of U-2 planes. Soon the Soviets released photographs of the plane wreckage and a few days later announced that Powers was captured alive and would be tried as a spy.

American, British, French, and Soviet heads of state arrived in Paris for the May 16, 1960, summit only to have it canceled when the Soviet leader refused to participate unless Eisenhower formally apologized for the U-2 flights. Eisenhower's trip to the USSR, scheduled to follow the Paris meeting, also was canceled. His foreign policy endured further embarrassment with the cancelation of his ill-advised June trip to Japan to sign the renewal of the U.S.-Japanese Mutual Defense Treaty.

In August 1960 the United States launched a satellite whose photography capability, passing over the USSR, far surpassed that of the U-2. Powers was given a 10-year sentence, three years of which were to be served in prison. On February 10, 1962, he was swapped in Berlin for the master Soviet spy Rudolf Abel.

Further reading: Beschloss, Michael R. *Mayday: Eisenhower, Khrushchev, and the U-2 Affair.* New York: Harper & Row, 1986; Powers, Francis Gary. *Operation Overflight: The U-2 Pilot Tells His Story for the First Time.* New York: Holt, Rinehart, and Winston, 1970; Wise, David, and Thomas B. Ross. *The U-2 Affair.* New York: Random House, 1962.

—Thomas P. Wolf

V

Vacancies Act

While the Constitution, in Article II, Section 2, says that the president appoints all officers of the United States with the ADVICE AND CONSENT of the Senate, there are times when, due to death or illness, heads of executive departments will be unable to fulfill their posts. When this happens, Congress has, through a series of statutes, granted the president the power to make temporary appointments to fill vacancies. Congress has attempted to control the length of service of these temporary officeholders, but on occasion, presidents press the temporary occupant to stay on the job beyond the statutory limits.

Van Buren, Martin (1782–1862) *eighth U.S. president*

Andrew JACKSON's handpicked successor, the 5'6" Martin Van Buren, dubbed "the little magician" because of his political adroitness, was no Jackson. Alexis de Tocqueville was right: Jackson's successors would be enfeebled. And surprisingly, Van Buren was weak in an area for which his skills were legend: as a politician.

President Van Buren's critics could be devastating. John Quincy ADAMS wrote: "There are many features in the character of Mr. Van Buren strongly resembling that of Mr. Madison—his calmness, his gentleness of manner, his discretion, his easy and conciliatory temper. But MADISON had none of his obsequiousness, his sycophancy, his profound dissimulation and duplicity." Folk hero and Tennessee Congressman Davy Crockett said:

> Van Buren is as opposite to General Jackson as dung is to diamond . . . [He] travels about the country and through the cities in an English coach; has English servants, dressed in uniform—I think they call it livery . . . no longer mixes with the sons of little tavern-keepers; forgets all his old companions and friends in the humbler walks of life . . .; eats in a room by himself; and is so stiff in his gait, and prim in his dress, that he is what the

President Martin Van Buren *(Library of Congress)*

English call a dandy. When he enters the Senate-chamber in the morning he struts and swaggers like a crow in a gutter. He is laced up in corsets, such as women in town wear, and, if possible, tighter than the best of them. It would be difficult to say, from his personal appearance, whether he was a man or woman, but for his large red and gray whiskers.

Two weeks after his inauguration, an economic panic hit the U.S. economy: the Panic of '37. Cautious and unsure of himself, Van Buren's response to the panic was modest.

As the depression worsened, Van Buren exercised caution, not leadership. His lukewarm response to the crisis led his critics to dub him "Martin Van Ruin."

In the aftermath of Jackson's expanded presidency, Congress reasserted its prerogatives and the presidency once again began to shrink. This dynamic and elastic institution, stretched by Jackson, now contracted in the face of an assertive Congress. While Van Buren helped shape the politics of the two-party system in the United States, he was unable to put it to full presidential use, and Congress, not the president, rose to the forefront. While historians recognize Van Buren as one of the master politicians of his age, they generally rate him in the average or below-average category of presidents. He was unable to translate his political skill into presidential LEADERSHIP, and while he did govern in especially difficult times, a truly masterful politician might have found other ways to manage the business of the presidency in those trying times.

Further reading: Cole, Donald B. *Martin Van Buren and the American Political System.* Princeton, N.J.: Princeton University Press, 1984; Niven, John. *Martin Van Buren: The Romantic Age of American Politics.* New York: Oxford University Press, 1983; Remini, Robert V. *Martin Van Buren and the Making of the Democratic Party.* New York: Columbia University Press, 1959; Wilson, Major L. *The Presidency of Martin Van Buren.* Lawrence: University Press of Kansas, 1984.

Vandenberg Resolution

Sponsored by the chairman of the Foreign Relations Committee, Senator Arthur F. Vandenberg (Rep.-Mich.), this 1948 act represented a U.S. commitment to regional collective security as a part of the United Nations Charter and helped bring about U.S. development of the North Atlantic Treaty Organization (NATO).

Passed in the early days of the COLD WAR, the Vandenberg Resolution was part of President TRUMAN's containment policy. Its passage was an example of comity and cooperation between the president and Congress over COLD WAR policy.

veto power

The veto power is the power of the president to prevent bills passed by Congress from being enacted into law. According to Article I, Section 7, of the Constitution, the president faces four possible actions to dispose of legislation: approval, whereby the president signs the bill into law; withholding of the presidential signature, whereupon the bill automatically becomes law after 10 days (Sundays excepted) without signature; the regular or return veto, where the president returns the bill to the house of origin, including a statement of objections; or the POCKET VETO, which may occur when the president objects to the bill in question, but Congress, by its adjournment, prevents return of the bill, whereupon withholding of the presidential signature causes the bill to die. The regular veto may be overridden, and the vetoed bill enacted into law by Congress, with a two-thirds vote in each house; a pocket-vetoed bill dies, forcing Congress to reenact the bill when it next convenes if it chooses to do so. The veto power is one of the few express powers granted to the president that formally involves the CHIEF EXECUTIVE in the legislative process, illustrating the sharing of governing powers among the branches of government, a fact also seen in its location in Article I, which is otherwise devoted to the legislative branch.

The country's Founders believed that an independent executive under the new constitution would need a qualified veto power to protect the EXECUTIVE BRANCH from legislative encroachments on EXECUTIVE POWER, even though many in America still remembered the oppressive veto practices of the British king and his appointed colonial governors before the Revolutionary War. The Founders were adamant, however, that the president's veto not be absolute (that is, Congress should have the ability to override the veto), as was that of the British monarchs. The Founders expected that the veto would be used to block legislation that was hastily conceived, unjust, or of dubious constitutionality. In addition, the power was not considered to be a purely negative action. Often called the "revisionary power," the veto was conceived as a creative, positive device whereby the president could bring a bill back to Congress for a final round of debate and consideration. This more constructive purpose for the veto has been mostly lost in the intervening years.

Early presidents used the veto power cautiously and sparingly, giving rise to claims that the Constitution somehow countenanced restrictions as to numbers or kinds of bills vetoed. Neither claim is substantiated by the Constitution itself or the debates of the time. From the first veto by President George WASHINGTON in 1792 until 1868, presidents vetoed 88 bills, reflecting presidents' more limited involvement in legislative matters. After the CIVIL WAR, veto use exploded. From then to the present, presidents have vetoed more than 2,500 bills. Most of these vetoes are attributable to the proliferation of private pension and related private relief bills, many of which involved dubious claims.

Recent scholarship has demonstrated that the veto power continues to be a major presidential tool for influencing the legislative process. One appealing trait of the veto for presidents is its effectiveness. Of the approximately 1,500 regular vetoes applied by presidents from 1792 to 2000, only about 7 percent have been overridden by

Congress. When that figure is broken down between public and private bills, the record is somewhat less impressive for important legislation, as about 20 percent of public bills have been overridden. Nevertheless, a presidential success rate of 80 percent for public bills poses a daunting challenge for a Congress contemplating override.

Presidents are more likely to use vetoes when Congress is controlled by the opposing political party, a circumstance that has been typical since 1968. Thus, Presidents FORD, REAGAN, George H. W. BUSH, and CLINTON after 1994 (when the Republicans won control of Congress) used the veto power, and the threat of the veto, to leverage concessions, alter legislation, and push Congress closer to presidential preferences. The veto threat has come to be understood in recent years as an especially potent force in shaping legislation, with recent presidents typically using veto threats against dozens of bills per year. In addition, vetoes are more likely to occur when the president lacks congressional experience, when the president's public standing is low, and during the second and fourth years of a presidential term. Presidents who rely too much on vetoes and veto threats are likely to be perceived as too obstructionist, a view that may harm the president's public standing. In recent decades, Presidents Ford and George H. W. BUSH sustained such criticisms for their frequent veto use. Congress is more likely to override a veto when party control is split between the two branches, when the president's popular support is low, after a midterm election, and in times of economic crisis.

In 1996 Congress approved by statutory enactment a limited ITEM VETO for the president, called enhanced rescission. President Clinton exercised the power in 1997, but in the case of CLINTON V. NEW YORK (1998), the Supreme Court ruled the power unconstitutional, saying that the president could only be given an item veto through constitutional amendment.

Further reading: Cameron, Charles M. *Veto Bargaining.* New York: Cambridge University Press, 2000; Jackson, Carleton. *Presidential Vetoes.* Athens: University of Georgia Press, 1967; Spitzer, Robert J. *The Presidential Veto: Touchstone of the American Presidency.* Albany: State University of New York Press, 1988; U.S. Senate Library. *Presidential Vetoes, 1989–2000.* Washington, D.C.: U.S. G.P.O., 2001; Watson, Richard A. *Presidential Vetoes and Public Policy.* Lawrence: University Press of Kansas, 1993.

—Robert J. Spitzer

vice president

For almost all of the 16 weeks of the CONSTITUTIONAL CONVENTION of 1787, there was no idea that a "vice president" would be needed in the new government. Early on, the delegates had voted to have the nation's president be chosen by the legislature—which could also fill any vacancy in that top office. It was only toward the end of the assembly, when the convention decided to reverse its earlier decision and approved the proposal by its Committee on Remaining Matters to select the president by an electoral college system, that it became necessary to provide for a second or standby person to be selected as well.

The vice presidency, as designed then and as it exists today, is an unusual office in that it has its place in both the legislative and the executive branches—in the former as president of the Senate (with the ability to vote only if the Senate is equally divided) and in the latter as becoming president of the United States in case of PRESIDENTIAL DEATH, DISABILITY, or removal from office. During the convention debates, delegate George Mason voiced apprehension about this duality, alleging that the vice president "was a dangerous Officer . . . who . . . is made president of the Senate, thereby dangerously blending the executive and legislative powers."

Mason's concern did not convince his fellow delegates; the electoral system of the Constitution initially (that is, from 1789 to 1804) provided that in choosing the president, electors would vote for two persons; the one who received a majority of the total electoral vote would become president, and the runner-up would become the vice president. In effect this meant that both candidates were to be considered as being of presidential caliber. As Delegate James Iredell put it:

> "two men . . . in office at the same time; the President, who will possess in the highest degree, the confidence of the country, and the Vice-President, who is thought to be the next person in the Union most fit to perform this trust."

Our first two vice presidents (John ADAMS and Thomas JEFFERSON) indeed met that standard.

In 1804 the TWELFTH AMENDMENT was ratified requiring the electors to vote separately for the two offices. The result was that the stature and capabilities of those proposed for the vice-presidential office suffered. Choices for that office tended to be made on the basis of partisanship instead of merit; in fact the parties, rather than the presidential candidate, usually did the selecting—which meant that for the pair that was elected, the vice president felt little if any sense of obligation to the president.

Nine times in American history, vice presidents have succeeded to the presidency because of the death or RESIGNATION of the CHIEF EXECUTIVE.

During the terms of office of most of our first 31 presidents, even if there was compatibility between the two men, the vice president was nonetheless considered to be more a part of the legislative branch than the executive. John Adams as vice president did give President WASHINGTON advice and at times met with the CABINET (but did not preside in Washington's absence). He did spend much time presiding over the Senate (and was called upon to break Senate deadlocks 29 times). As president, Adams suggested to Vice President Jefferson that the latter take on certain assignments, but Jefferson, feeling that he was primarily part of the legislature, declined. President POLK consulted with Vice President George DALLAS; President MCKINLEY regularly sought advice from Vice President Garret HOBART. Thomas MARSHALL was the first vice president to preside over cabinet meetings (when WILSON was at Versailles)—but it was Wilson who said, "The chief embarrassment in discussing his [the vice president's] office is, that in explaining how little there is to be said about it one has evidently said all there is to say."

Calvin COOLIDGE (under HARDING) and John GARNER and Henry Wallace (under Franklin ROOSEVELT) attended cabinet meetings. Garner advised Roosevelt on legislative strategy; WALLACE was chairman of the Economic Defense Board, of which seven cabinet officers were members. Vice presidents in most other instances—up through Harry TRUMAN's administration—were rarely in touch with their presidents; on some occasions there was outright hostility. When he had one, the vice president's office was in the Capitol, not anywhere in the EXECUTIVE BRANCH.

At the time of the party convention in July of 1944, when Harry Truman was nominated to join with Franklin Roosevelt on the ticket, Truman had not even seen Roosevelt for more than a year; Roosevelt himself had commented "I hardly know Truman." Truman did attend the few cabinet meetings held during the mere 38 days when Roosevelt was in Washington between January 20 and April 12, 1945, noting in his memoir "It has always been my feeling that this office, which is the second highest honor that can be bestowed by the American people, has great inherent and potential dignity that has been sadly neglected." Alben BARKLEY attended Truman's cabinet meetings and, by statute, was made a member of the NATIONAL SECURITY COUNCIL (NSC).

After experiencing the dramatically sudden succession of Harry Truman to the presidency in the midst of war, President Dwight EISENHOWER resolved to bring his vice president regularly and systematically into his circle of executive branch policy advisers. Vice President NIXON was a standing member of the cabinet and came to 171 meetings, chairing at least 20 of them in Ike's absence. He attended 217 National Security Council meetings, presiding over 26 of them; in all those sessions he sat opposite the president at the table. The vice president received all cabinet and NSC papers prior to the meetings (his staff once observed that, at the beginning, their office did not even possess an approved high-security filing cabinet to store such papers). Nixon's policy assistant attended the post-cabinet debriefing meetings of the other cabinet assis-

tants at the White House and attended the sessions of the NSC Planning Board. Nixon was a member of 173 meetings of the legislative leaders with the president, chairing two of them. The president also made Vice President Nixon the chair of the President's Committee on Government Contracts.

As vice president, Nixon initiated another vice-presidential "first": extensive travel representing the United States, and its president, abroad. At the president's request he and Mrs. Nixon, in the fall of 1953, undertook a 69-day trip to 14 countries in Asia, Southeast Asia, and the Middle East. He went to Austria in 1956 to dramatize the plight of the Hungarian refugees, paid an official visit to Brazil in 1956, and in a second trip to Latin America in 1958, visited every country in South America except Brazil. (He had a narrow escape from a communist mob in Caracas.) In 1959 Nixon opened the American National Exposition in Moscow—engaging in the famous "kitchen debate" with Premier Nikita Khrushchev, later going to Poland.

Nixon still had no office in the executive branch, however, and no place even to sit at the White House while waiting for meetings to commence. At the 1960 election neared, Nixon's presidential ambitions led him to seek more responsibilities—and more personal publicity—but, as author Stephen Ambrose recounts, Eisenhower was reluctant to accede.

A particularly significant change in the role of the vice president occurred in 1961, when President KENNEDY asked Vice President Lyndon JOHNSON to move his principal office downtown, into the EXECUTIVE OFFICE BUILDING, next to the White House. Johnson brought staff with him, some 23 in all, while retaining vice-presidential office space on Capitol Hill. Johnson had been made chair of the Space Council, and among the duties given him by the president was to conduct a special study on the advisibility of the United States building a commercial supersonic transport plane. Johnson's considerable ambitions, however, were far greater than any of his assignments from Kennedy; he was frustrated at not being given missions of substantive responsibility. One Johnson intimate commented, "The years as vice president were the most miserable years of his life."

Under Johnson, Hubert HUMPHREY's role was also minimized. Historian David Halberstam recounts: "Humphrey was not invited to meetings, not informed of important memos or the drift of the policy. He was, in effect, frozen out." When Humphrey gave a speech about education policy, Johnson, at the Ranch, called in reporters to tell them: "Boys, I've just reminded Hubert that I've got his balls in my pocket."

Richard Nixon started out by giving his vice president, Spiro AGNEW, the responsibility for liaison with governors and mayors and other local officials, but Agnew used his access to the OVAL OFFICE to spend time pleading for more staff, increased prerogatives, and additional perquisites. In the end, the Agnew choice was a disaster, but a significant development occurred in the history of the vice-presidential office: The Budget of the United States, beginning in February of 1970, contained a new authorizing line: "For expenses necessary to enable the Vice President to provide assistance to the President in connection with specially assigned functions . . . $700,000."

Jerry FORD gave Vice President Nelson ROCKEFELLER what looked like, on paper, a limitless charter, but Rockefeller's advocacy for domestic program initiatives collided with Ford's budget priorities—a divergence which diminished the effectiveness of their relationship.

President CARTER added another feature to the vice presidency: working office space in the West Wing itself. The vice president's large, ceremonial office was still across the street, in the Executive Office Building, and Mondale's staff now numbered 60. The two men were close; MONDALE did not have firm, set assignments but gave advice unobtrusively and frequently on a wide range of issues. From joint experiences, in the campaign period, the two staffs were close as well.

The cordial relationship between the president and his vice president continued in the REAGAN administration; George H. W. BUSH had weekly private luncheons with the president; as chair of the Task Force on Regulatory Relief he was put in charge of handling issues of regulatory reform needing top-level attention; for a time he was even designated foreign affairs "crisis manager." The vice presidential staff had by this time increased to 90.

George H. W. Bush, of course, became the first vice president since Martin VAN BUREN to be elected directly to the presidency himself.

As president, Mr. Bush had Vice President QUAYLE continue the regulatory reform responsibility; by statute Quayle was also chair of the Space Council. As a former senator, Mr. Quayle kept up his contacts at the Capitol and attended the weekly Republican Caucus luncheons, bringing back important intelligence to the White House. Quayle visited 42 countries, meeting with their heads of state and cabling personal reports back to the president. The vice president was included as one of the "Big Eight" who managed the GULF WAR, but when he argued that our forces should have gone further into Iraq, President Bush commented in his diary, "It doesn't help Quayle with me, and it doesn't help him at all."

It has been in the presidencies of William J. CLINTON and George W. BUSH that the vice presidential role has had its most expansive development. Vice Presidents GORE and CHENEY have been involved in literally every aspect of presidential decision-making—NATIONAL SECURITY matters, DOMESTIC POLICY, and political planning. The Gore assignments were more formalized, in dozens of EXECU-TIVE ORDERS and presidential announcements; the Cheney responsibilities have been equally comprehensive but almost nowhere are they set forth in public documents. Gore, of course, with the president's support, was aiming to succeed Clinton in 2000; Cheney has publicly denied any presidential ambitions.

Is it now fixed that vice presidents will follow the Mondale/Gore/Cheney model of total participation in presidential decision-making? By no means. Each future president and each future vice president will determine their unique personal relationship; the Constitution is silent on what that relationship is to be. But the presidential–vice presidential environment is not a tabula rasa. Step by step, a pattern of relationships has been established, and a very evident and impressive set of expectations has been created. "Whenever possible," recommended the Twentieth Century Task Force on the Vice Presidency, "the vice president should serve as general adviser to the president on the full range of presidential issues and concerns." That is the more likely future.

Further reading: Williams, Irving G. *The American Vice Presidency: New Look*. Garden City, N.Y.: Doubleday, 1954; Patterson, Bradley H. *Ring of Power: The White House Staff and Its Expanding Role in Government*. New York: Basic Books, 1988; ———. *The White House Staff: Inside the West Wing and Beyond*. Washington, D.C.: Brookings Institution, 2000.

—Bradley H. Patterson

Vietnam War

The Vietnam War was one of the most difficult and divisive wars in history. It began in the post-WORLD WAR II era when the French could no longer maintain its empire and the United States felt compelled to assume control lest the communists take power.

A series of presidents made commitments and escalated U.S. presence in Vietnam, but it was Lyndon JOHNSON who sent in fighting forces and escalated year after year. U.S. troops and bombing did not bring an end to the war between North Vietnam and the U.S.-supported South Vietnam. As the war dragged on, protests grew on the home front. LBJ was so politically damaged he decided not to run for reelection in 1968. Richard NIXON was elected with a "plan" to end the war, but Nixon had no real plan, and the fighting and bombing increased.

Nixon tried to bomb the enemy into submission, but even with dramatically escalated bombing, the North would not give in. Nixon, determined to attain "peace with honor," finally gave in and signed a deeply flawed peace accord that signaled the end of U.S. involvement but was almost certain to mean victory for the North. Shortly after

U.S. withdrawal, and after Nixon's RESIGNATION, the North took control of Vietnam.

The Vietnam War was a "presidential war," and opposition to that war began a backlash against presidential power that lasted for more than a generation. Trust in presidents and trust in government declined, and the presidency was placed in a defensive posture. A period of suspicion of presidential activities began, and when Vietnam was followed by the Nixon scandals of WATERGATE, a presidency-bashing mood enveloped the nation. From that point on, the public became more wary of presidential initiatives, the press grew more adversarial, and the Congress was more assertive. The legacy of Vietnam extended even further, as U.S. servicemen and -women returned from that unpopular war not as heroes but to a nation that wanted to ignore, condemn, or forget their contribution.

voting rights

Only in the last 50 years have presidents become involved in voting rights issues. Prior to that time the states and Congress had prime responsibility in this area.

With the rise of the modern civil rights movement in the 1950s and 60s, presidential politics became entwined with civil and, as an extension, voting rights. Passage of the CIVIL RIGHTS ACTS of 1957 and 1964, and then the Voting Rights Act of 1965 linked presidents to policy shifts in this area. And with the 1965 Voting Rights Act, enforcement power was given to the JUSTICE DEPARTMENT, further enhancing the presidential role in the area of voting rights.

Subsequent legislation, especially amendments to the Voting Rights Act in 1970, 1975, and 1982, extended presidential involvement. And by the 1990s, the issue had bipartisan support and had ceased to be a political issue.

Further reading: Grofman, Bernard, and Chandler Davidson, eds. *Controversies in Minority Voting: The Voting Rights Act in Perspective.* Washington, D.C.: Brookings Institution, 1992; Lawson, Steven F. *In Pursuit of Power: Southern Blacks and Electoral Politics, 1965–1982.* New York: Columbia University Press, 1985; Thernstrom, Abigail M. *Whose Votes Count? Affirmative Action and Minority Voting Rights.* Cambridge, Mass.: Harvard University Press, 1987.

W

Wagner Act

Sponsored by New York Democratic Senator Robert F. Wagner, this act was designed to promote better relations between business and labor and to protect workers' rights to organize. President Roosevelt was a late and reluctant supporter of the bill. The Supreme Court struck down the act as unconstitutional in May 1935. Roosevelt used the Court's decision as a whipping boy in the 1936 presidential race, and in 1937 the Court, responding perhaps to the '36 election returns, found the newly passed Wagner Act constitutional. In 1947 the TAFT-HARTLEY ACT superseded the Wagner Act.

Wallace, George (1919–1998) *governor*

The fiery populist and governor of Alabama, Wallace came to national attention when, in 1963, he attempted (unsuccessfully) to block enrollment of African-American students at the University of Alabama. In 1968 he ran for president as a third party candidate and received nearly 10 million votes. In 1972 he sought the Democratic nomination for president but was shot by a would-be assassin and exited the race, confined to a wheelchair.

Wallace, Henry A. (1888–1965) *U.S. vice president*

In 1933 President Franklin ROOSEVELT appointed Wallace as secretary of Agriculture. Wallace was very popular in the farm states, and FDR chose Wallace to replace John Nance Garner as his vice-presidential running mate in 1940. As VICE PRESIDENT, Wallace headed the Board of Economic Warfare, the only vice president ever to hold an administrative post.

Wallace's strongly liberal positions and his internationalist sentiments alienated many key southern Democrats, and in 1944 FDR dropped him from the ticket, choosing Harry S Truman as his vice president. To the surprise of some, Wallace campaigned vigorously for FDR in 1944, and later FDR named Wallace secretary of Commerce.

After Roosevelt's death, Wallace and Truman had a falling out over Truman's foreign policy positions, and Wallace became a vocal critic of the president. In September of 1946 Truman fired Wallace.

In 1948 Wallace ran against Truman as the Progressive Party's candidate for president. His candidacy, along with that of South Carolina senator Strom Thurmond, who also bolted the Democratic Party and ran for president, made a Democratic Party meltdown and a Truman defeat in 1948 a very real possibility. In the end, Truman was able to achieve an upset victory in 1948, with Wallace receiving only 2 percent of the popular vote.

war, declaration of

The War Clause of the Constitution grants to Congress the "Power . . . to declare War." At the time of the CONSTITUTIONAL CONVENTION, writers on the Law of Nations—now INTERNATIONAL LAW—observed that warfare should be preceded by a declaration of war. The Swiss jurist Emmerich de Vattel, regarded by the framers of the Constitution as the most authoritative writer on the Law of Nations, explained the purpose of such a proclamation: It informed the adversary, neutral nations, and subjects or citizens of the sovereign nation commencing the war. It also was held that a declaration of war should be preceded by a "conditional declaration of war"—the presentation of an ultimatum that afforded a final opportunity to redress grievances and avoid the calamities of war. It was recognized, of course, that war might be commenced without a declaration of war by the outbreak of mutual hostilities. A nation eschewing a formal proclamation might obtain the advantage of surprise.

Under the Constitution, a declaration of war is proclaimed by a joint resolution or an act of Congress that authorizes war or an act of war. A formal declaration is not required, but the United States may lawfully commence war or military hostilities only by explicit congressional authorization. The president is empowered by his designation as COMMANDER IN CHIEF to repel sudden invasions of the United States, but he has no constitutional authority to initiate hostilities. The framers' decision to withhold from the president the power to initiate war marked a radical departure from the prevailing model for conduct of FOREIGN AFFAIRS and war-making, which vested plenary authorization in an executive. The records of the convention reflect the delegates' fear of unilateral EXECUTIVE POWER and their commitment to collective decision-making, the cardinal principle of republicanism. Various members of the convention who spoke on the issue of the war power agreed that the prerogatives of the English monarchy, which included the war power, were not suitable to a republic.

Early judicial decisions affirmed that it is for Congress, alone, to choose between peace or war, and that the president is limited to repelling sudden invasions of the United States. In *Bas v. Tingy* (1800), *Talbot v. Seeman* (1801), and *LITTLE V. BARREME* (1804), the Supreme Court held that for the United States to lawfully initiate war, it must be declared or explicitly authorized by Congress, as it did in the quasi-war with France from 1798 to 1799, when it passed 20 statutes that authorized President John ADAMS to use force against France. In 1806, in *United States v. Smith,* the question of whether the president may initiate hostilities was decided on circuit by Justice William Paterson, who had been a leading delegate to the Constitutional Convention: "Does he [the president] possess the power of making war? That power is exclusively vested in Congress. . . ." He stated: "There is a manifest distinction between our going to war with a nation at peace, and a war made against us by actual invasion, or a formal declaration. In the former case, it is the exclusive province of Congress to change a state of peace into a state of war." The Supreme Court has never held that the president has constitutional authority to initiate war. In December 1990, as the United States prepared for war against Iraq in Kuwait, U.S. district Judge Harold H. Green agreed in *Dellums v. Bush* (D.D.C. 1990), that the Constitution grants to Congress the sole authority to commence hostilities on behalf of the American people.

Early presidents exhibited their respect for the War Clause by refusing the opportunity to initiate hostilities and by deferring to Congress requests for the use of military force. In 1792 President George WASHINGTON received a request from the governor of the Southwest Territory to initiate military hostilities against the Chickamaugas, whom it was feared were preparing to launch an attack. Washington refused and explained that such measures "must result from the decision of Congress who solely are vested with the powers of war." As president, Thomas JEFFERSON acknowledged the limitations of his authority. In his first annual message to Congress in 1801 he reported the arrogant demands made by the pasha of Tripoli. Unless the United States paid tribute, the pasha threatened to seize American ships and citizens. Jefferson responded by sending a small squadron to the Mediterranean to protect against the threatened attack. He then asked Congress for further guidance, stating he was "unauthorized by the Constitution, without the sanction of Congress, to go beyond the line of defense." It was left to Congress to authorize "measures of offense." Jefferson's understanding of the War Clause underwent no revision. In 1805 he informed Congress of the dispute with Spain over the boundaries of Louisiana and Florida. Jefferson warned that Spain evidenced an "intention to advance on our possessions until they shall be repressed by an opposing force. Considering that Congress alone is constitutionally invested with the power of changing our condition from peace to war, I have thought it my duty to await their authority for using force."

Other early presidents, including James MADISON, James MONROE, and Andrew JACKSON and, later, Abraham LINCOLN, also refused to lay claim to any constitutional authority to initiate hostilities, a power which they understood to be the sole repository of Congress. But since 1950, presidents frequently have initiated military hostilities in defiance of the War Clause. Presidents Harry TRUMAN, Lyndon JOHNSON, Richard NIXON, Gerald FORD, Jimmy CARTER, Ronald REAGAN, George W. BUSH, and Bill CLINTON fall into this category.

In the course of American history, Congress has passed resolutions declaring general war on 11 occasions, although it is commonly, but erroneously, said that Congress has declared war on only five occasions. In WORLD WAR II alone, Congress issued six declarations of war—against Japan, Germany, Italy, Bulgaria, Hungary, and Romania. Over the years, moreover, Congress has passed conditional declarations of war, contingent declarations of war, and dozens of statutes authorizing limited war or acts of war, all in the exercise of its constitutional power to determine war and peace. But the steady pattern of presidential usurpation of the war power raises serious questions about the continued application of the War Clause to the use of U.S. force abroad. Congress, undoubtedly, has plenary authority over the issue of going to war, but the relevant question is whether it has the political will to protect its constitutional power. In *YOUNGSTOWN SHEET & TUBE CO. V. SAWYER* (1952), Justice Robert H. Jackson wrote of ineffectual judicial efforts to maintain congressional power over emergencies that apply equally to the preservation of the War Clause: "We may say that power to legislate for emergencies belongs in the hands of Congress, but only Congress itself can prevent power from slipping through its fingers."

—David Gray Adler

War, Department of

Established in 1789, the War Department was one of four original cabinet posts. First headed by Henry Knox, the secretary was appointed by the president, with the advice and consent of the Senate.

In the post–WORLD WAR II era the Department of War became the DEPARTMENT OF DEFENSE, as part of a major reorganization under the NATIONAL SECURITY ACT of 1947.

war, undeclared

The War Clause of the Constitution (Article I, Section 8) provides: "The Congress shall have power . . . to declare war [and] grant letters of Marque and Reprisal." By virtue of this grant, the Constitution places in Congress the authority to initiate military hostilities against foreign adversaries. The commencement of war may be preceded by a congressional declaration of war, which names an enemy of the American people, but it is not necessary. All that is required under American law before hostilities are initiated is a congressional act that authorizes the use of force against a named adversary. Thus Congress may engage the nation in war, whether it is declared or undeclared.

The war power includes the authority to determine the scope of hostilities, the power, as James Madison explained, to "commence, continue or conclude" war. Congress may declare or authorize a "perfect" or general war, or an "imperfect" or limited war. In 1782 the Federal Court of Appeals distinguished the two kinds of war: "A perfect war is that which destroys the national peace and tranquillity, and lays the foundation of every possible act of hostility. The imperfect war is that which does not entirely destroy the public tranquillity, but interrupts it only in some particulars, as in the case of reprisals."

Since the early days of the republic, the courts have held that it is for Congress, alone, to engage in general or limited wars. As a means of authorizing limited or imperfect war, Congress may choose to exercise its power to issue "letters of marque and reprisal." Dating back to the Middle Ages when sovereigns employed private forces in retaliation for an injury caused by the sovereign of another state or his subjects, the practice of issuing reprisals gradually evolved into the use of public armies. By the time of the convention, the framers considered the power to grant letters of MARQUE AND REPRISAL sufficient to authorize a broad spectrum of armed hostilities short of declared war.

In the undeclared or "quasi-war" with France in 1798–99, Congress enacted more than 20 statutes authorizing limited naval war against France. In *Bas v. Tingy* (1800), the Supreme Court held that the body of statutes enacted by Congress had authorized imperfect, or limited war, which Congress is entitled to limit, "in place, in objects, and in time." In 1991 Congress exercised its authority to initiate an undeclared war when, by status, it authorized President George H. W. BUSH to engage in war to drive Iraq's army out of Kuwait.

Congressional control of limited war, the authority to prosecute an undeclared war through the passage of statutes, has given way to executive aggrandizement of the war power. Presidential usurpation of the war power has become a commonplace, a condition based on the erroneous assumption that the president possesses as COMMANDER IN CHIEF the constitutional authority to engage in lesser acts of military activities in the absence of a congressional declaration or authorization of war. Of course, there is in our constitutional architecture no support for such a proposition. As Alexander HAMILTON explained in *Federalist No. 69*, the president, in his capacity as commander in chief, is limited to repelling sudden attacks against the United States and conducting war, once "authorized or begun." Moreover, this claim of what amounts to a dual authority over the war power would eviscerate the constitutional grant of the war power to Congress. As a direct riposte to the claim of presidential power to order acts of war, we may consider what Thomas JEFFERSON said in 1793 of the authority necessary to issue a reprisal: "Congress must be called upon to take it; the right reprisal being expressly lodged with them by the Constitution, and not with the executive."

Nonetheless, presidents since 1950 frequently have engaged the nation in unilateral, undeclared, and unauthorized large-scale wars in Korea and Vietnam, and relatively smaller military operations in Grenada and Panama, as well as unauthorized missile strikes against Libya and Iraq. In 1999 President Bill CLINTON ordered, in conjunction with NATO but without congressional authorization, massive air strikes for 78 days against Yugoslavia to prevent Slobodan Milosevic from destroying Kosovo's ethnic Albanians. While perhaps morally justified, Clinton's unilateral acts took presidential war-making to a new pitch when, for the first time, a U.S. president violated a congressional vote that refused to authorize the military operation.

In most cases of presidential war-making, Congress has failed to vigorously protest the usurpation of its constitutional authority to determine war and peace. Thus, executive usurpation has been accompanied by an equally disturbing practice of congressional acquiescence and even abdication of its power. In response to the diminution of legislative control over war making, Congress passed the WAR POWERS RESOLUTION OF 1973 over President Richard NIXON's veto. The purported aim of the law was to restore congressional control over undeclared wars and military operations, but it was suffused with flaws and defects. The chief vice involved a provision that required the president to "consult" with Congress in all possible circumstances before committing military forces to hostilities or where hostilities were imminent. First, consultation does not meet the constitutional requirement of congressional authorization. Second, the provision unconstitutionally delegates the war power to the president by allowing him to determine when to engage the nation in military hostilities. Congress may not constitutionally delegate discretion to the president to choose the time, the place, and the enemy of the American people, even for a short period of time. The act has not been taken seriously either by presidents, who routinely ignore consultation requirements and criticize it as an encroachment on their authority as commander in chief, or by Congress, which refuses to hold the executive accountable to the requirements of the statute. In October 2002 Congress passed legislation authorizing President George W. BUSH to use military force against Iraq to defend America's security interests. That resolution represented another unconstitutional delegation of the war power, since it afforded the president a blank check of authority to determine whether the United States should make war against Iraq, a decision granted by the Constitution solely and exclusively to Congress.

—David Gray Adler

war messages

Prosecuting wars is one of the president's most clearly delineated constitutional powers. As COMMANDER IN CHIEF of the nation's armed forces, the president has tremendous—although not unlimited—power in wartime. War has often been a powerful legitimating factor in the expansion of presidential power, but the mere fact of armed conflict does not automatically guarantee that the president will be allowed—by the people, the Congress, or the courts—to aggrandize his office. While declaring war remains the sole province of the Congress, there has been no such declaration since WORLD WAR II. Military conflicts are now carried out under the provisions of the 1973 WAR POWERS RESOLUTION.

Regardless of the legal requirements, acts of war must be legitimated and justified through presidential rhetoric. According to Karlyn Kohrs Campbell and Kathleen Hall Jamieson, war rhetoric has five pivotal characteristics: The president argues that the decision to go to war is a momentous one and was arrived at thoughtfully as a result of due deliberation, not caprice; the use of force is justified through a chronicle or narrative of events; the audience is exhorted to display unanimity of purpose and total commitment to the war effort; the president justifies the use of force and his assumption of the powers of commander in chief; and finally, throughout the justificatory speech, strategic misrepresentations will play a key role.

War rhetoric generally begins with claims that the decision to go to war is the president's weightiest responsibility, and that it was made calmly, rationally, and with deliberation. The language will be formal if not legalistic and will place a clear emphasis on the necessity for the president's actions. As Robert L. Ivie says, "War is recommended by the president only after demonstrating that peaceful methods—such as remonstrance, expostulations, negotiation, and embargo—have failed to restore the ideal or to prevent the disharmony."

This claim will then be supported by a recitation of evidence, usually presented in the form of a narrative. This story of events demonstrates that the nation's values are somehow imperiled, and that the defense of those values requires the commitment of arms. It will also be used to insist that the decision to place the nation on a war footing is disinterested and is in defense of principles. An adversary will be clearly identified, and a history of forbearance and of attempts to solve the problem through less drastic means will be included. This narrative will contain what Campbell and Jamieson call "strategic misrepresentations," as the president is engaging in justificatory rather than deliberative rhetoric; he is engaged in advocacy and will present the strongest case legitimating the decision to go to war rather than an objective, forensic discussion of the pros and cons of this decision.

Following the explanatory narrative, the audience will be exhorted to unify behind the nation's armed forces and its commander in chief and to be completely committed to the war effort. Patriotic appeals thus play a large role, as presidents encourage what public opinion scholars refer to as the "rally effect," or the (often sharp) rise in presidential approval ratings following a decision to go to war. The national unity indicated by such a rise in approval is specifically requested by the president as a requirement for the successful prosecution of the war. Finally, war messages include notice that the president is actively assuming the role of commander in chief. Like INAUGURAL ADDRESSES, war rhetoric is rhetoric of investiture, and it legitimates and marks the assumption of specific duties and powers. The use of similar power by previous presidents will be invoked as precedents. Other forms of justification include the need to "protect American lives," previously existing agreements and/or treaties, and the nature of a particular crisis, which may require immediate or special sorts of action.

Because of the legitimating power of war rhetoric, "war" is an important metaphor in presidential speech: Lyndon JOHNSON declared war on poverty, for instance, and Gerald FORD declared war on inflation. Generally speaking, the war metaphor is less effective in DOMESTIC POLICY than it is in foreign affairs, for war rhetoric seems to be most powerful when there is a specific, clearly delineated enemy who can be understood as posing a legitimate threat to the nation or its interests.

Further reading: Bostdorff, Denise. *The Presidency and the Rhetoric of Foreign Crisis.* Columbia, S.C.: University of South Carolina Press, 1993; Campbell, Karlyn Kohrs, and Kathleen Hall Jamieson. *Deeds Done in Words: Presidential*

Rhetoric and the Genres of Governance. Chicago: University of Chicago Press, 1990; Ivie, Robert L. "Presidential Motives for War." *Quarterly Journal of Speech* 60 (1974): 337–345.

—Mary E. Stuckey & Colleen Blanchard

War of 1812

The seminal event of James Madison's presidency was the ill-advised War of 1812. Upon taking office, Madison's most pressing issue was how to keep the United States out of war. France and Britain were still engaged in the Napoleonic wars, and both nations, but most especially Britain, seized American ships at sea and impressed American sailors into service on British warships. Pressure for war was strong, and MADISON finally gave in to congressional pressure and somewhat reluctantly asked for a declaration of war (the first president to do so). In this, Madison followed rather than led. Had he more forcefully exerted presidential LEADER-SHIP, war might have been averted.

The war was badly managed by Madison. The most humiliating moment came when, in August 1814, British troops attacked Washington, D.C., and burned the Capitol building and the White House. Madison was forced to flee the Capitol and witnessed the burning of the White House from the Virginia Hills. His wife, Dolley MADISON, remained just long enough to save some priceless objects, among them Gilbert Stuart's portrait of George WASHINGTON.

The War ended inconclusively. Madison's performance as commander in chief, while personally courageous, was strategically flawed. Even Gaillard Hunt, one of Madison's more sympathetic biographers, found the president's leadership lacking: The hour had come but the man was wanting. Not a scholar in governments ancient and modern, not an unimpassioned writer of careful messages, but a robust leader to rally the people and unite them to fight was what the time needed, and what it did not find in Madison.

war powers

Although not mentioned in the Constitution, the term *war powers* refers to the complex of powers granted chiefly to Congress, but also to the president, to preserve and protect the nation. War powers apply to every facet of NATIONAL SECURITY, from the maintenance of peace to the declaration of neutrality to the prosecution of war.

The nation's war powers are drawn exclusively from the Constitution, which, according to the courts, grants to the government all those powers necessary to its preservation. Accordingly, Article I, Section 8, the War Clause, provides, "The Congress shall have power . . . to declare war [and] grant Letters of Marque and Reprisal." This constitutional grant vests all war-making powers in Congress, which, the

Court has held, has the sole and exclusive authority to change a state of peace into a state of war. As James MADI-SON observed, Congress possesses the authority to "commence, continue, or conclude" a war. For the purpose of making that judgment, the Constitution vests Congress with several specific powers to control war and military matters: to raise and support armies and provide and maintain a navy, to make regulations of the land and naval forces, to call forth the militia, and to provide for organizing, arming, and disciplining the militia. The president's war powers are derived from the COMMANDER IN CHIEF Clauses of Article II, and they are decidedly narrow. Alexander HAMILTON, an advocate of EXECUTIVE POWER, explained in *Federalist No. 69* that the president is empowered to repel sudden attacks against the United States. As commander in chief, he is "first General and admiral" of the military forces, and he is to conduct war when "authorized" by Congress. The president has no constitutional power to commence military hostilities.

In the CONSTITUTIONAL CONVENTION, the initial discussion and debates on the war power, on May 29, focused on the seventh paragraph of the Randolph Plan, which stated that the executive "ought to enjoy the executive rights vested in Congress of the Confederation." Delegates expressed concern that such a grant of authority might vest the president with the power of war and peace, to which they were opposed. James WILSON sought to assure his colleagues on two points: (1) the power of war and peace was considered by the Law of Nations to be a legislative, not an executive, power; and in any case (2) the prerogatives of the British monarchy are not a suitable guide, since some of the prerogatives were legislative in nature, including the power of war and peace. James Madison agreed that the war power was legislative in character, and no delegate asserted otherwise. There was no vote on Randolph's proposal, but the discussion reflects an understanding that the power of war and peace—that is, the power to initiate war—did not belong to the executive but to the legislature.

On August 6 the Committee of Detail circulated a draft constitution that declared, "The Legislature of the United States shall have the power . . . to make war." The proposal echoed the Articles of Confederation, which granted to the Continental Congress the "sole and exclusive right and power of determining on peace and war." When the War Clause was debated on August 17, Charles Pinckey opposed vesting the power in Congress since it was "too slow," and he preferred the Senate as a repository of the war power. Pierce Butler "was for vesting the power in the President, who will have all the requisite qualities, and will not make war but when the nation will support it." Butler's view shocked Elbridge GERRY, who said that he "never expected to hear in a republic a motion to empower the Executive alone to declare war." Butler stood alone in the convention: There was no support for his opinion and no second to his motion.

Madison and Gerry were less than satisfied with the proposal to vest the legislature with the power to make war, and they persuaded the delegates to substitute "declare" for "make," thus "leaving to the Executive the power to repel sudden attacks." The meaning of the motion is pellucidly clear. Congress was granted the power to make—that is, initiate—war; the president, for obvious reasons, could act immediately to repel sudden attacks without authorization from Congress.

The debates and the vote on the War Clause leave no doubt that Congress alone possesses the authority to initiate war. The war-making authority was deliberately withheld from the president, who was given only the authority to repel sudden attacks. Confirmation of this understanding was provided by ratifiers in various state conventions. For example, Wilson, a principal architect of the Constitution, told the Pennsylvania ratifying convention, "This system will not hurry us into war; it is calculated to guard against it. It will not be in the power of a single man, or a single body of men, to involve us in such distress; for the important power of declaring war is vested in the legislature at large." The record reveals that no member for any state ratifying convention held a different understanding of the meaning of the war clause.

The Constitutional Convention's decision to withhold the power to initiate war from the president signaled a marked departure from existing models of government, which placed the war power, indeed, virtually all FOREIGN AFFAIRS powers, in the hands of the executive. The framers' rejection of the prevailing models is attributable to both their deep fear of unilateral executive power in foreign and domestic affairs and their attachment to collective decision making, the core principle of the republican ideology that they embraced. The FEDERALIST PAPERS gave full vent to these concerns, principles, and values. In Federalist No. 69, Alexander Hamilton carefully distinguished the king's possession and control of foreign affairs powers, including the war power which, he sharply noted, was vested in Congress. In Federalist No. 75, he explained the framers' rationale for the radical break from executive control of foreign policy. "The history of human conduct does not warrant that exalted opinion of human virtue which would make it wise in a nation to commit interests of so delicate and momentous a kind, as those which concern its intercourse with the rest of the world, to the sole disposal of . . . a president." In 1798, Madison wrote to Thomas JEFFERSON, "The Constitution supposes, what the History of all Governments demonstrates, that the Ex. Is the branch of power most interested in war, and most prone to it. It has accordingly with studied care, vested the question of war in the legsl."

Several early judicial decisions upheld the framers' understanding of the War Clause. No court since has departed from this early view. In 1800, in *Bas v. Tingy,* the Supreme Court held that it is for Congress alone to declare an imperfect or limited war on a perfect or general war. In *Talbot v. Seeman* (1801), Chief Justice MARSHALL wrote for the Court that the "whole powers of war" are "vest[ed] in Congress." In *United States v. Smith* (1806), Justice William Paterson, riding circuit, denied that the president possessed constitutional authority to initiate military hostilities. Paterson, a delegate to the Constitutional Convention, stated that "it is the exclusive province of Congress to change a state of peace into a state of war." The Supreme Court has never held that the commander in chief clause confers any power to initiate war.

The constitutional design for war commanded and largely received adherence for the first 150 years of the nation's history. Early presidents—Washington, Adams, and Jefferson, and Madison, MONROE, and JACKSON—refused to initiate military hostilities without authorization from Congress, which they understood to be the sole repository of the power to commence war. There was no departure from this understanding of the war clause through the 19th century. In 1846 President James K. POLK sent an army into a disputed border area between Texas and Mexico; it defeated the Mexico forces. In a message to Congress, Polk advanced the rationale that Mexico had invaded the United States, which compelled Congress to declare war. If Polk's rationale was correct, then his action could not be challenged on constitutional grounds, since it had been established at the dawn of the republic that the president had the authority to repel sudden attacks. If, however, he was disingenuous—if he had in fact initiated military hostilities—then he had clearly usurped the war-making power of Congress. Polk laid no claim to a constitutional power to make war. Although Congress declared war, the House of Representatives censured Polk for his actions because the war had been "unnecessarily and unconstitutionally begun by the President of the United States." Representative Abraham LINCOLN voted with the majority against Polk. As president, Lincoln maintained that only Congress could authorize the initiation of hostilities. None of his actions in the CIVIL WAR constituted a precedent for presidential initiation of war. Moreover, in the *PRIZE CASES* (1863), the Supreme Court upheld Lincoln's blockade against the rebellious Confederacy as a constitutional response to sudden invasion, which began with the attack on Fort Sumter.

Since the KOREAN WAR, presidents and members of Congress have claimed for the executive a unilateral power to commence war without authorization from Congress. Since then, a steady pattern of presidential war-making has developed: Lyndon JOHNSON and Richard NIXON in

Vietnam; Gerald FORD in Cambodia; Jimmy CARTER in Iran; Ronald REAGAN in Lebanon and Grenada; George H. W. BUSH in Panama; Bill CLINTON in Iraq and Yugoslavia. Defenders have frequently invoked the Commander in Chief Clause as justification for presidential use of force. This argument is unpersuasive. As Hamilton explained in *Federalist No. 69*, the title confers no war-making power whatever; it only vests the president with the authority to repel sudden attacks on the United States, and to direct war, "when authorized or begun." Defenders have also advanced the Vesting Clause (Article II, Section 1) as a source of unilateral presidential war-making power, but this claim is of no moment. In fact, in the framers' discussion of the Randolph Plan, the claim that the grant of executive power includes the authority to initiate hostilities was considered and rejected in the convention, indeed, it triggered great alarm. But Madison and Wilson allayed concerns when they observed that under the Law of Nations, the war power is legislative, not executive, in nature.

Revisionists have contrived additional legal arguments to defend executive war-making. This argument rests on the premise that presidents have frequently exercised the war power without congressional authorization. Defenders have compiled lists that assert between 100 and 200 unilateral acts, each of which is said to constitute a legitimizing precedent for future wars. The argument fails, however, in detail and conceptions. The lists are inaccurately compiled. They typically begin with an assertion that president John ADAMS engaged in unilateral war-making with France in 1798. The claim is false: Adams took no independent action. Congress passed some 20 statues authorizing his wartime acts, which the Court said in *Bas v. Tingy* (1800), amounted to authorization of limited war. Many of the episodes cited on the defenders' lists involved acts of war by a military commander, not authorization from a president. If practice establishes law, as the revisionists contend, then the conclusion of this argument is that every commander of every military unit possesses the war power. Moreover, it is to be noted that of the relatively few instances in which presidents have personally usurped the war power, they have not pretended to rely on their authority as commander in chief or as CHIEF EXECUTIVE. Rather, they have made false claims of authorization—by altering facts, by treaty, by statute, or by INTERNATIONAL LAW. Yet, it cannot be maintained that constitutional power, including the war power, can be acquired through practice. Justice Felix Frankfurter affirmed a fundamental principal of Anglo-American jurisprudence when he stated: "Illegality cannot attain legitimacy through practice." The revisionists' arguments for a unilateral executive war-making power find no support in the Constitution, but this fact has not deterred presidential usurpation of the war power for much of the last half-century.

—David Gray Adler

War Powers Resolution

The Constitution grants Congress the power to declare war. However, over time, presidents have encroached on this congressional power, often with the tacit approval of the Congress itself. Toward the end of the war in VIETNAM, Congress made an effort to reclaim some of its lost war power and passed the War Powers Resolution (1973). President NIXON vetoed the bill, but Congress was able to override the president's veto. The resolution called for prior consultation with Congress when the president intends to send U.S. troops into potential combat situations, for the president to report to Congress on all military ventures and set up a "time clock" for presidential military engagements, and allowed Congress to terminate any military campaigns. After more than 30 years, most scholars believe the War Powers Resolution has not been effective in limiting presidential war power.

Further reading: Fisher, Louis. *Presidential War Power.* Lawrence: University Press of Kansas, 1995; Glennon, Michael J. *Constitutional Diplomacy.* Princeton, N.J.: Princeton University Press, 1990; Keynes, Edward. *Undeclared War: Twilight Zone of Constitutional Power.* University Park, Pa.: Penn State University Press, 1991; Koh, Harold. *The National Security Constitution: Sharing Power after the Iran-Contra Affair.* New Haven, Conn.: Yale University Press, 1990; Wormuth, Francis D., and Edwin B. Firmage. *To Chain the Dog of War: The War Power of Congress in History and Law.* Dallas, Tex.: Southern Methodist University Press, 1986.

Warren Commission

Formally termed the President's Commission on the Assassination of President John F. KENNEDY, the Warren Commission was created to investigate all aspects of the murder of both the president and his alleged assassin, Lee Harvey OSWALD. The murder of Oswald soon after his arrest eliminated the possibility of a trial and a legal path toward learning Oswald's explanation of what happened and why. With the goal of answering these and other questions, on November 29, 1963, President Lyndon B. JOHNSON announced the formation of a commission. He named Earl Warren, the Chief Justice of the United States, to head the commission, which soon was known by the name of its chair. The commission included two U.S. senators, Richard B. Russell, a Democrat from Georgia, and John S. Cooper, a Republican from Kentucky; two members of the House of Representatives, Gerald R. FORD, a Republican from Michigan, and Hale Boggs, a Democrat from Louisiana; plus two attorneys with extensive government experience, Allen Dulles, a former director of the CENTRAL INTELLIGENCE AGENCY, and John J. McCloy, a former president of the International Bank for Reconstruction and Development.

The Warren Commission's 10-month investigation included hearing the sworn testimony of 552 witnesses and reviewing files, documents, and other evidence gathered by several federal, state, and local law enforcement agencies investigating the murders. In particular, the commission's investigation avoided exploring Oswald's motives and instead focused on his personal background and the possibilities of any ties between his actions and the governments of two countries he had visited previously—the Soviet Union and Cuba.

The commission submitted its report, featuring 26 volumes of hearings and exhibits, to President Johnson on September 27, 1964. The president immediately made the document public. Overall, the commission found that the murder of President Kennedy was not part of any conspiracy, either domestic or foreign-based. The report said that the president was murdered by three shots fired by Oswald from a rifle positioned at a window on the sixth floor of the Texas School Book Depository in Dallas, Texas. The commission also asserted that Oswald acted alone and that he did not know Jack Ruby, a Dallas nightclub owner who murdered Oswald. Finally, the commission criticized some practices of the SECRET SERVICE and the FEDERAL BUREAU OF INVESTIGATION and made recommendations for improving the protection of the president.

The commission's report, which initially was welcomed with fanfare, subsequently attracted often-intense criticism. The validity of the report was questioned as theories of conspiracy to murder the president continued circulating at an accelerated pace for more than two decades after his death. Ultimately, the Warren Commission's report became one of the most controversial documents in American history. Numerous books, newspaper articles, television and radio documentaries, congressional committees, and even motion pictures subsequently challenged many aspects of the commission's findings while formulating conspiracy theories to explain what really happened. Two of the best known critiques were published in the mid-1960s—*Inquest*, by Edward Epstein, and *Rush to Judgment*, by Mark Lane. Another prominent examination, by William Manchester, was commissioned by the Kennedy family. His effort, published in 1967 as *The Death of a President*, supported the conclusions of the Warren Commission. Many of these reports attacked theories postulated by one another, as well as challenging the validity of the Warren Commission's effort. Ultimately, the death of Oswald, coupled with gaps in the existing evidence, suggests that the complete story of what happened, sought by the Warren Commission, likely will never be known.

Further reading: Epstein, Edward Jay. *Inquest*. New York: Viking Press, 1966; Lane, Mark. *Rush to Judgment*. Greenwich, Conn.: Fawcett Publications, 1967; Manchester, William. *The Death of a President*. New York: Harper & Row, 1967; United States Warren Commission. *Report of the President's Commission on the Assassination of President John F. Kennedy*. New York: McGraw-Hill, 1964.

—Robert E. Dewhirst

Washington, George (1732–1799) *first U.S. president*
George Washington, the first president of the United States of America, was born on February 22, 1732, in rural Virginia. As a teenager, Washington began working as a land surveyor. At the ripe age of 20, he became a public figure in the colonies by serving as a district adjutant, a post he acquired after his brother Lawrence's death. Part of his duties as adjutant included training the soldiers of the local militia. In this capacity, Washington gained his first experience as a military commander.

During the French and Indian War, Governor Dinwiddie of Virginia made Washington a lieutenant colonel in the colonial militia. Washington enjoyed mixed success as a young commander. Although he learned about several French advances preemptively, he eventually lost his protectorate, Fort Necessity, to the enemy in July 1754. Despite this failure, Washington continued to fight in the war, serving as an assistant to General Braddock. During the unsuccessful campaign at Fort Duquesne, Washington fought bravely beside Braddock. Throughout the fighting, two horses were shot from underneath him, yet Washington survived the battle. After this courageous expedition, Washington was named commander in chief of the Virginia militia.

In 1759 Washington married the wealthy widow Martha Dandridge Custis and took up residence at MOUNT VERNON. During this time, Washington worked as a gentleman farmer. He became a member of the Virginia House of Burgesses and quickly joined the vocal opposition movement that criticized British colonial policies. On June 15, 1775, the Continental Congress named George Washington the commander in chief of the Revolutionary army. Although Washington was not a military genius, his strategy during the war proved effective. Acutely aware that an outright defeat of the British was unlikely, Washington persistently harassed the enemy and relied upon surprise attacks and skillful retreats to win the war.

Upon arriving in Boston in 1775, Washington found the rebel forces poorly organized and trained. Despite this adversity, Washington managed to repel British forces from occupying Boston. Facing likely defeat, Washington and the army crossed the Delaware River on Christmas night in 1776, surprising the British at Trenton and nearby Princeton. A number of subsequent defeats instigated a movement within the Continental Congress to remove Washington as commander in chief, but after emerging from a brutal winter at Valley Forge in the spring of 1778, the Revolutionary army regained lost ground. By 1780 the arrival of French troops assured an American victory. The British general Cornwallis surrendered to Washington at Yorktown on October 19, 1781.

During his time as the Revolutionary War general, Washington exercised deference to Continental Congress, thus contributing to his reputation as a disinterested republican who exercised controlled ambition and exhibited laudable character. Washington's contribution as a military general was not simply winning the war but his subordination of military strength to democratic principles. Because of his republican restraint, Washington immediately became a national hero of almost astronomical renown.

After the war, Washington hoped to retire to Mount Vernon and resume his work as a farmer. Although there was a movement to crown him as king, Washington made it widely known that he disapproved of this idea, and he chastised those individuals who suggested a monarchical plot. In a letter to Colonel Lewis Nicola, who advocated crowning Washington "King George I of the United States," Washington wrote, "You could not have found a person to whom your schemes are more disagreeable." Washington's rejection of a kingship is perhaps his greatest republican contribution to American democracy.

President George Washington *(Library of Congress)*

In 1783 Washington officially retired from the army, but it soon became clear that the Articles of Confederation were too weak to sustain a national government. In 1787 Washington reluctantly abdicated his retirement and served as a delegate to the CONSTITUTIONAL CONVENTION. After arriving in Philadelphia, the assembled delegates quickly elected Washington as chairman of the convention. Even though Washington did not speak often during discussions, it is believed that his presence profoundly influenced the design of the Constitution. First, Washington's mere participation in convention proceedings gave the document an air of legitimacy. Second, the delegates widely believed that Washington would serve as the first president, which encouraged them to endow the office with substantial powers. Attendee Pierce Butler wrote that the powers of the presidency would not have been so extensive "had not many of the members cast their eyes toward General Washington as President; and shaped their Ideas of the powers to be given to a President, by their opinions of his Virtue." After the states ratified the Constitution, the ELECTORAL COLLEGE elected Washington unanimously to serve as the nation's first president. Washington was inaugurated on April 30, 1789, in New York City. After the administration of the oath, Washington gave a short speech, thus establishing the customary Inaugural Address given by all new presidents who assume the office.

Because he was the first citizen to serve as president of the United States, Washington faced the difficult task of instituting precedents, particularly during his first term of office. The presidency was a blank slate, and Washington believed it was his duty to give the office a semblance of form and function. In one of his first actions, Washington decided he would be called "Mr. President" instead of a more regal title, such as "Your Excellency." In doing so, Washington imbibed the presidency with reverence and respect but minimized the monarchical trappings of the office. Washington also established other precedents. He created the CABINET, instituted a two-term limit that was observed until the presidency of Franklin ROOSEVELT, and fortified the constitutional authority of the national government vis-à-vis state governments. Furthermore, Washington determined that the president could speak to the American people without using the states as an intermediary. In his presidential PROCLAMATIONS and declarations, Washington directly addressed the American people, not the state governments.

Some of Washington's endeavors to establish meaningful precedents did not always proceed smoothly. In an attempt to fulfill the ADVICE AND CONSENT clause in Article II of the Constitution, President Washington appeared before the Senate to ask its advice for a treaty with the Creek Indians in August of 1789. Unwilling to debate the matter of the treaty while Washington sat in the chamber, the Senate decided to postpone any decisions on the matter until a later date. Angry and frustrated with his colleagues' indecision, Washington left the Senate, vowing never "to go there" again. Washington's less than satisfactory experience led to future presidents eschewing the practice of publicly visiting the Senate for advice and consultation before negotiating treaties with foreign nations.

In an attempt to establish an executive office that was above partisanship, Washington chose men with eminent reputations from a variety of backgrounds and beliefs to serve in his first cabinet. Washington's disdain for localism and sectionalism led him to select individuals from every state to serve in the EXECUTIVE BRANCH. Throughout his presidency, Washington struggled to contain the conflict that arose between Secretary of Treasury Alexander HAMILTON and Secretary of State Thomas JEFFERSON. In his first term, Washington was largely successful in his efforts to mediate the differences between these two factions, which eventually evolved into the Federalist and Republican parties. The most significant compromise of Washington's first term involved the nation's financial system. In 1790 it was decided that the national government would assume the debts of the states, which mostly originated from the North. In return, the permanent capital of the United States would be located not in New York or Philadelphia, but on the southern Potomac River. Washington, Hamilton, and Jefferson approved of the deal, and the compromise appeared to minimize the principal differences that existed between the men. However, in his second term, as war broke out between England and France, Washington found it increasingly difficult to straddle the ideological divide that festered between the nascent Federalists and Republicans.

Washington did not want to serve a second term. In 1792 he asked James MADISON to prepare a farewell address. Urged by Hamilton, Jefferson, Madison, and other political elites to serve another term, Washington acceded. On February 13, 1793, Washington was reelected unanimously to the presidency. His second term proved more tumultuous and controversial than his first four years in office.

The first major crisis Washington faced was the WHISKEY REBELLION in western Pennsylvania. Enraged by a federal tax on whiskey imposed by Hamilton, farmers who distilled their grain crop into whiskey instigated a short uprising. In July of 1794 insurgents surrounded exciseman John Neville's mansion and fired shots. Two men were killed in the skirmish. A few weeks later, six thousand men met on Braddock's Field and threatened to take Pittsburgh by force if the whiskey tax was not repealed. Although Hamilton urged the president to call out the militia immediately and put down the rebellion, Washington moved slowly and cautiously. He issued a proclamation, warning that he would not hesitate to assemble the militia if order was not restored to the region. He also sent several commissioners to western Pennsylvania to survey the situation.

First Lady Martha Washington *(Library of Congress)*

When the commissioners' reports did not satisfy Washington, he ordered the militia to march at the end of September. Washington joined the troops at Carlisle and rode with them during part of their expedition. His decisive actions were widely praised throughout the country, although Thomas Jefferson ardently disapproved of Washington's military response.

By 1793 the international situation had become delicate. England and France were embroiled in a world war, and members of Washington's cabinet began to choose sides. Jefferson and his allies supported France, whereas Hamiltonians advertised their strong preference for England. During the spring, a new French foreign minister called Citizen Genet arrived in the United States. Genet's attempt to persuade Americans to support the French angered Washington, who had declared that the United States would remain neutral in the conflict. Eventually, the French government dismissed Genet from his duties and Washington granted him asylum in the United States. Since Genet would have certainly faced the guillotine if he had returned to France, Washington's actions were considered a great overture of kindness and compassion.

In the meantime, Washington sent John JAY, the Chief Justice of the United States, to negotiate a treaty with England to improve relations between the two nations. When Jay finally sent his proposed treaty to Washington in 1795, the president was disappointed. Although the treaty allowed the United States to trade with England, it placed several restrictions on American shipping, particularly in the Caribbean. When the treaty became public, its weaknesses proved quite unpopular. As copies of the treaty were burned in public, both Jay and Hamilton faced heavy criticism. Despite the controversy that surrounded it, Washington signed the Jay Treaty, reasoning that some concessions from the British were better than nothing at all. The House of Representatives, in a desperate attempt to stop the treaty, asked Washington to provide them with all correspondence related to Jay's negotiations in England. Realizing the dangerous implications of setting such a precedent, Washington refused, claiming that the Constitution did not require him to do so. Washington's decision to withhold his correspondence with Jay strengthened the independent leadership authority of the presidency.

The Jay Treaty was not the pinnacle of Washington's presidential LEADERSHIP, but it did prevent the United States from forming an alliance with France, which might have thrown the young nation into a war it was unprepared to fight. Even though Washington opposed factional politics, the disputes over the United States's international position during the war solidified the appearance of political parties. In spite of this development, Washington continued to serve as a disinterested republican, refusing to side publicly with either Hamilton's Federalists or Jefferson's Republicans.

If Washington had desired a third term of office, he could have easily won reelection, but by 1796 Washington had decided that he would retire from the presidency. In September he issued his Farewell Address, which was printed in newspapers across the country. In his message, Washington warned citizens that foreign alliances were unwise, condemned the formation of political parties, and stressed the importance of religion and morality in republican government. Although Alexander Hamilton helped the president write the document, all of the ideas and beliefs contained within it belonged to Washington. The Farewell Address is considered one of the most important state papers in American presidential history.

Washington's last public act demonstrated that the source of his honor was his willingness to refuse power. Much like the Roman hero Cincinnatus, who returned to his farm after fighting battles for his country, Washington spent the remainder of his life at Mount Vernon. On December 14, 1799, George Washington died at the age of 67. In his will, Washington freed the slaves of Mount Vernon and left ample provisions for their livelihood. His estate supported families of freed slaves until 1833. Throughout the nation, citizens mourned the loss of America's most eminent Founding Father. A tribute in the House of Representatives described Washington as "First in war, first in peace, first in the hearts of his countrymen."

Further reading: Brookhiser, Richard. *Founding Father: Rediscovering George Washington.* New York: The Free Press, 1996; Elkins, Stanley, and Eric McKitrick. *The Age of Federalism: The Early American Republic, 1788–1800.*

New York: Oxford University Press, 1993; McDonald, Forrest. *The Presidency of George Washington.* Lawrence: University Press of Kansas, 1974; Phelps, Glenn A. *George Washington and American Constitutionalism.* Lawrence: University Press of Kansas, 1993; Washington, George. *George Washington: A Collection.* Edited by W. B. Allen. Indianapolis: The Liberty Fund, 1988.

—Colleen J. Shogan

Watergate

Watergate was the most serious scandal in the history of U.S. presidential politics. It was unusual in presidential history because for the first time the president himself was deeply involved in the crimes of his administration.

The roots of Watergate extend as far back as the war in Vietnam and the divisiveness it caused at home. Richard NIXON was elected president in 1968 in the midst of that long divisive war. He was elected, in part, on his promise to end the war, but when he became president, he realized that getting out of Vietnam would be no easy task. Public protests against the war exerted much pressure on Nixon to bring the war to an end, but the president could find no way to get out of Vietnam "with honor." The war dragged on, and antiwar protests spread. Out of his determination not to be destroyed by the war, as his predecessor Lyndon B. JOHNSON was, Nixon proceeded on a path of leak plugging, wiretapping, a secret war in Cambodia, and a series of criminal acts that in the end led to his downfall and fed the already significant erosion of public trust in government.

"Watergate" is a generic term that originally only referred to the break-in of the Democratic National Committee (DNC) headquarters located in Washington, D.C., at the Watergate office complex, but it has come to be an umbrella term, under which a wide variety of crimes and improper acts are included. Watergate caused the downfall of a president. It led to jail sentences for more than a dozen of the highest-ranking officials of the administration. It was a traumatic experience for the nation. Why Watergate? How could it have happened? How could someone as intelligent and experienced as Richard Nixon behave so criminally and so stupidly? How could someone so adroit and practiced in the art and science of politics behave so foolishly? How could a "third-rate burglary" turn into a national disaster? How could Richard Nixon have done it to himself?

In essence, Watergate involved three separate, but interconnected, conspiracies. The first conspiracy was the Plumbers conspiracy, which took place during Nixon's first term (1969–73). This involved plugging leaks and "getting" Nixon's political enemies, illegal wiretapping, the break-in of the office of psychiatrist of Pentagon Papers distributor Daniel Ellsberg, and other acts, done in some instances for ostensible NATIONAL SECURITY reasons and at other times for purely political reasons. The purpose of this conspiracy was to destroy political enemies and strengthen the president's political position.

The second conspiracy was the reelection conspiracy. This grew out of lawful efforts to reelect the president but degenerated into illegal efforts to extort money; launder money; sabotage the electoral process; spy; commit fraud, forgery, and burglary; play "dirty tricks"; and attack Democratic front-runners. The purposes of this conspiracy were to (a) knock the stronger potential Democratic candidates (Senators Hubert HUMPHREY, Edward Kennedy, Edmund Muskie, and Henry "Scoop" Jackson) out of the race; (b) accumulate enough money to bury the Democratic opponent by massively outspending him; and (c) thus guarantee the reelection of Richard Nixon. This conspiracy was conscious, deliberate, and organized.

The third conspiracy was the cover-up conspiracy. Almost immediately after the burglars were caught at the Democratic National Committee headquarters in the Watergate office complex, a criminal conspiracy began that was designed to mislead law enforcement officers and protect the reelection bid of the president, and then after the election, to keep the criminal investigations away from the White House. To this end, evidence was destroyed, perjury was committed, lies were told, investigations were obstructed, and subpoenas were defied. The purpose of the cover-up was to contain the criminal charges and protect the president. This conspiracy was less conscious, almost instinctive. It was deliberate but poorly organized.

One can divide Watergate activities into four categories: the partisan arena, the policy arena, the financial arena, and the legal arena. The partisan activities include acts taken against those of the opposition party and those deemed to be "enemies" of the administration. They include wiretapping and break-ins, the establishment of the Houston Plan, the plumbers and the "enemies list," forged STATE DEPARTMENT cables, and political dirty tricks.

Policy activities include the stretching of presidential power beyond legal or constitutional limits. Examples include the secret bombing of Cambodia, the impoundment of congressionally appropriated funds, attempts to dismantle programs authorized by Congress, the extensive use of EXECUTIVE PRIVILEGE and underenforcement of laws such as the CIVIL RIGHTS ACT of 1964. When Nixon's defenders answer charges against the president by saying that "everybody does it," they are most often referring to this area of behavior.

In the financial arena, both Nixon's political and personal finances deserve mention. On the political front, the "selling" of ambassadorships, the extortion of money in the form of illegal campaign contributions, and the laundering of money must be included. In Nixon's personal finances, such things as "irregularities" in income tax deductions and questionable "security" improvements in his private Florida and California homes, paid for with tax dollars, are included.

Finally, in the legal arena, illegal activities of the Nixon administration include obstruction of justice, perjury, criminal cover-up, interference with criminal investigations, and destruction of evidence. It was the criminal cover-up that eventually led to Nixon's forced RESIGNATION.

Categorizing and classifying Watergate behavior does a disservice to the drama and suspense of the unfurling of this political mystery. The story of Nixon's rise and fall, of his choices at several important points in the story, and of his ultimate collapse is what makes this drama so poignant and tragic.

Watergate has had a profound and largely negative impact on American politics in the 25 years since that scandal was uncovered. It has spawned a distrust in government among the American people, led to a series of laws that were enacted to prevent future Watergates but have made it more difficult to govern, unleashed a hostile and highly investigatory press, increased partisan sniping in the political arena, and led to a more divisive relationship between the president and Congress. Further, the unintended consequences of the post-Watergate reforms have left presidents more vulnerable, or at least thinking they are so, and less able to function effectively as presidents.

Watergate spawned a variety of legislative responses. In the aftermath of Nixon's abuses, the Congress went through a period of legislative activism that resulted in the passage of the Budget Control and Impoundment Act (1974), the WAR POWERS RESOLUTION (1973), the CASE ACT (1972), the Federal Election Campaign Act (1974), the ETHICS IN GOVERNMENT ACT (1978), the PRESIDENTIAL RECORDS ACT (1978), the NATIONAL EMERGENCIES ACT (1976), the Government in Sunshine Act (1976), the Federal Corrupt Practices Act (1977), and the FOREIGN INTELLIGENCE SURVEILLANCE ACT (1978), plus laws relating to privacy in banking and to setting up a vehicle for creating special prosecutors and the FREEDOM OF INFORMATION ACT (1974). These efforts were designed to limit and shrink imperial executive claims to republican proportions. Many think the reaction against presidential power went too far. Today, presidents often seem encumbered by too many checks, with too few balances.

The abuses known as Watergate were the most pervasive and systematic subversion of the political rights of American citizens and sabotage of the democratic electoral process in the history of the United States. Never before had so many done so much to so many at so high a level in violation of laws and norms of this nation. Watergate went beyond the presidential corruptions of the past, for while most previous corruption involved isolated crimes or greed for money, Watergate was systematic and comprehensive and aimed at the rights of citizens and the democratic electoral process. And the president was right in the middle of the corruption. Among the casualties of Watergate are a president who was named as an unindicted coconspirator by a grand jury and who was eventually forced to resign (he was also disbarred), a VICE PRESIDENT who pleaded no contest to income tax evasion and who was forced to resign (he too was disbarred), an attorney general who went to jail, a former secretary of Commerce who went to jail, a CHIEF OF STAFF who went to jail, a president's counsel who went to jail, a president's chief domestic adviser who went to jail, a president's appointments secretary who went to jail, a president's personal attorney who went to jail, and the list goes on. More than two dozen administration figures went to jail because of Watergate.

Thomas Paine once said that in America, the Constitution is king. The downfall of Richard Nixon struck a blow for the concept that no man is above the law, not even the president. Though Nixon could attempt to justify his actions in a 1977 interview with David Frost by saying, "When the President does it, that means that it is not illegal"; this view was rejected by nearly all segments of the American system. The words of Supreme Court Justice Louis Brandeis remained operative: "If Government becomes the lawbreaker, it breeds contempt for law." Reverence for the laws, Abraham LINCOLN once said, should "become the political religion of the nation."

Further reading: Genovese, Michael A. *The Watergate Crisis.* Westport, Conn.: Greenwood Press, 1999; Kutler Stanley. *The Wars of Watergate.* New York: Norton, 1992.

welfare policy

Prior to the GREAT DEPRESSION/New Deal era, welfare was handled by private and church organizations or local governments. But the extent of hardship caused by the 1929 depression proved too much, and demands that the federal government get involved proved irresistible.

Under President Franklin D. ROOSEVELT, the beginnings of the modern welfare system began to take shape. Roosevelt signed the Social Security Act in 1935, and the welfare state was born. During the NEW DEAL, a variety of social welfare programs designed to help those in need extended the reach of the federal government and gave jobs, hope, and help to those affected by the Depression.

After WORLD WAR II, many of the Roosevelt NEW DEAL programs were ingrained into the American system, and SOCIAL SECURITY, aid to families with dependent children (AFDC), and other programs maintained widespread public support. Under President TRUMAN, welfare was expanded to include aid for the disabled and was pushed for government-paid medical programs.

President KENNEDY sent Congress the first presidential message devoted exclusively to the subject of welfare. In 1962 Congress passed the Public Welfare Amendment. It was under Kennedy's successor, Lyndon JOHNSON, that a significant expansion of federal welfare took place. As part of his GREAT SOCIETY program, LBJ helped create the Medicare and Medicaid programs that Harry Truman had envisioned.

Over time, however, a backlash against the cost and consequences of welfare led to demands for change. President NIXON proposed a dramatic revamping of welfare, calling for a guaranteed income as part of his Family Assistance Plan (FAP). Nixon failed to persuade Congress and the FAP was eventually dropped. The same fate befell Jimmy CARTER's efforts at welfare reform.

The first open assault on welfare took place in the Reagan years. In 1981, as part of the Omnibus Budget Reconciliation Act, REAGAN got Congress to make dramatic cuts in aid to families with dependent children programs. Then, in 1988, Reagan supported the Family Support Act, adding some benefits to welfare recipients.

Welfare continued to produce political backlash, and during his campaign for president, candidate Bill CLINTON promised to end welfare "as we know it." With a push from the Republican-controlled Congress, Clinton signed a welfare reform bill that cut welfare and compelled a work program. Along with these cuts, Clinton continued to gain small increases in health care for the poor.

Further reading: Berkowitz, Edward D. *America's Welfare State: From Roosevelt to Reagan.* Baltimore, Md.: Johns Hopkins University Press, 1991; Burke, Vincent J., and Vee Burke. *Nixon's Good Deed: Welfare Reform.* New York: Columbia University Press, 1974; Patterson, James. *America's Struggle Against Poverty, 1900–1980.* Cambridge: Harvard University Press, 1981; Trattner, Walter. *From poor Law to Welfare State,* 4th ed. New York: Free Press, 1989.

The West Wing television program

First aired on NBC in 1999, the television show *The West Wing* became a huge popular and critical success, winning nine Emmy awards in its first season.

The story of a president (Josiah "Jed" Bartlet, played by Martin Sheen) and his top staff focuses on the inner workings of the White House. Displaying a liberal stance, the program has, in some ways, become the "loyal opposition" to the George W. Bush presidency, a shadow government of "what might be." The deliberate contrast between the Nobel Prize–winning Bartlet and the less highly regarded Bush contrasts the real president with the fictional character in a way that challenges and critiques the real president.

Often witty, sometimes edgy, and at times, semi-serious in its attempt to discuss and debate public policy issues, *The West Wing* looks at the people, politics, processes, and policies of the federal government from an insider perspective in a way that is both engaging and challenging.

Further reading: Rollins, Peter C., and John E. O'Connor. *The West Wing: The American Presidency as Television Drama.* Syracuse: Syracuse University Press, 2003; and Keith Topping, *Inside Bartlet's White House: An Unofficial and Unauthorized Guide to* The West Wing. London: Virgin Books, 2002.

Wheeler, William A. (1819–1887) *U.S. vice president*

Nineteenth VICE PRESIDENT of the United States, Wheeler served from 1877 to 1881 under President Rutherford B. HAYES. The election of 1876 was a disputed election, but eventually, after much political wrangling, Hayes and Wheeler won. Hayes and Wheeler became close friends and Hayes often consulted Wheeler on government business.

Whig Party

The opposition to President Andrew JACKSON brought together persons and interests from across the nation. In the North, industrial and financial leaders were alarmed at Jackson's Bank War. In the West, supporters of House Speaker Henry CLAY and his "American System" were angered at Jackson's veto of internal improvements that would promote the settlement of the West. In the South, states' rights advocates were antagonized by Jackson's forceful response to talk of secession during the NULLIFICATION crisis of 1832 and 1833.

There were policy differences among these factions, but they could agree on their disdain for President Jackson, whom they thought fancied himself no mere CHIEF EXECUTIVE but "King Andrew." Thus they took as their label the term "Whig," the name of the antimonarchical faction in English politics.

In theory, Whigs opposed Jackson's popularization of the presidency as demagoguery. In practice, the Whigs' only success in presidential contests came when they copied Jacksonian practices by nominating comparative political novices for president, and by downplaying issues in favor of hero worship. The first Whig president, William Henry HARRISON, was championed by the Whigs in 1840 as the candidate not of any set of policies but as a man who had lived in a log cabin and enjoyed drinking hard cider. (The Whigs charged that the Democratic incumbent, President Martin VAN BUREN, preferred champagne.)

The only other presidential election that the Whigs won was the one of 1848, when they ran Zachary Taylor, a leading hero of the recently completed MEXICAN WAR. Like Harrison before him, Taylor died in office.

The Whig Party collapsed under the pressure of slavery and its extension to the territories. Northern antislavery Whigs abandoned the party for the Republicans in the 1850s, and Southerners turned to the DEMOCRATIC PARTY. The Whig Party's demise came in 1860, when a Whig remnant stumped for John BELL for president on the Constitutional Union ticket, while former Whig Abraham LINCOLN won the presidency as a Republican.

Further reading: Holt, Michael F. *Rise and Fall of the American Whig Party: Jacksonian Politics and the Onset of the Civil War.* New York: Oxford University Press, 1999; Howe, Daniel Walker. *The Political Culture of the American Whigs.* Chicago: University of Chicago Press, 1979.

—Thomas Langston

Whig presidency

In speeches and pamphlets, the Whigs, the congressional opponents of Andrew Jackson, elaborated on the theme of a congressionally dominated government, in which the president would be the mere *executor* of the laws. Senator Henry CLAY, a leading Whig, proclaimed that "On principle, certainly, the executive ought to have no agency in the formation of the laws." The Whigs were particularly offended at Jackson's interpretation of his reelection. To Jackson, the election of 1832 had settled a great contest over policy. To the Whigs, a presidential election merely placed a man in the post of the presidency.

Of course the Whigs were the out party when they developed these views. How well did their theories hold up when they at last captured the presidency? Only two Whigs were elected president. William Henry HARRISON died shortly after entering office and was succeeded by John TYLER, who had broken with his former party, the Democrats, over Jackson's leadership. As president, however, Tyler refused to be but another member of his CABINET, which is what his Whig secretaries wished for him to be, and he refused as well to follow his new party's legislative agenda. The next Whig president, Zachary TAYLOR, had been innocent of any political affiliation until he ran for president. Before his death in office, he fought with Whig leaders in Congress over the Compromise of 1850, which he opposed. To threats of secession from the South, he replied with a pledge personally to lead the army against any state that rebelled, and to hang the rebels. His successor, Millard FILLMORE, differed in his policies, but not in his vigorous efforts to influence the legislative process.

The Whig presidency was, then, more a matter for theory than practice, even during the Whig Party's existence. Some scholars argue that the most Whiggish presidents were not in fact Whigs. Abraham LINCOLN, though forceful in the exercise of WAR POWERS, left much power in the hands of cabinet members and Congress, reflecting his background in the Whig Party. To a limited extent, Thomas JEFFERSON, and to a great extent, James MADISON and James MONROE, also extolled comparative weakness in their offices and permitted Congress to establish the policies that they then executed.

In the 20th century, William Howard TAFT, a Republican, argued against Theodore ROOSEVELT's STEWARDSHIP THEORY of the presidency and cautioned that "There is no undefined residuum of power" available to the executive. Nonetheless, Taft at the same time lectured that "The Constitution does give the President wide discretion and great power, and it ought to do so." Taft's understanding of the presidency was "Whiggish," but it was hardly purely so. More modern writers in the Whiggish tradition argue for constitutional or statutory changes that would restrict the president's powers. Normatively, but not empirically, these writings are the heirs of the Whig presidency.

Further reading: Langston, Thomas. *With Reverence and Contempt: How Americans Think about Their President.* Baltimore, Md.: Johns Hopkins University Press, 1995; Lind, Michael. "A Radical Plan to Change American Politics." *Atlantic Monthly* (August 1992); Lowi, Theodore J. *The Personal President: Power Invested, Promise Unfulfilled.* Ithaca, N.Y.: Cornell University Press, 1985; Pious, Richard M. *American Presidency.* New York: Basic Books, 1979; Taft, William Howard. *Our Chief Magistrate and His Powers.* New York: Columbia University Press, 1916.

—Thomas Langston

Whiskey Rebellion

The Whiskey Rebellion of 1794 is widely regarded as one of the first tests of federal and presidential authority in the United States. Persuaded by Alexander HAMILTON, the federal government began levying a tax on whiskey in 1791 in an effort to decrease the nation's war debt. Farmers in western Pennsylvania, who distilled their grain crop into whiskey for easier transportation across rough terrain, found themselves unable to evade this excise. Despite Congress's ameliorating attempt to remove the strictest provisions of the tax, tension mounted steadily in the region. In the summer of 1794, four counties grew openly hostile toward the federal government and its whiskey excise.

The region's two Democratic Societies, particularly the society of Mingo Creek, were rumored to be the source of the escalated discontent. Inspired by the example of France, Democratic Societies discussed politics, spread political information, and celebrated patriotism. The members of these political clubs were self-professed Republican followers of Thomas JEFFERSON and James MADISON. The

Whiskey Rebellion culminated in a July 1794 raid on exciseman John Neville's mansion in which two men were killed. The following weeks were filled with passionate rhetoric and threats to seize Pittsburgh by force; in early August, 6,000 men gathered at Braddock's Field to protest the tax on whiskey.

On August 7, President WASHINGTON announced in a proclamation that he intended to call out the militia to quell the rebellion in western Pennsylvania. After federal commissioners reported that law and order had not been restored to the region, Washington ordered 13,000 militia, assembled from Pennsylvania, Maryland, Virginia, and New Jersey, to march on September 25. With this action, Washington established the precedent that the national government could quell an insurrection in one state by assembling militia from other states. President Washington and Hamilton joined the militia in Carlisle and rode at the head of the troops, encountering no resistance. The leaders of the rebellion were captured, and all were acquitted except two, whom Washington eventually pardoned.

Across the country, Washington's decision to call out the militia was extremely popular. As the embodiment of a patriot king standing above the fray, President Washington emerged from the Whiskey Rebellion stronger than ever. By quelling the rebellion, Washington exercised his broad EXECUTIVE POWER to "preserve and protect" the laws of the United States. Washington's decisiveness during the controversy substantiated the legitimacy of the young republic and fortified the president's constitutional role to "take care that the laws be faithfully executed."

Further reading: Boyd, Steven R., ed. *The Whiskey Rebellion: Past and Present Perspectives.* Westport, Conn.: Greenwood Press, 1985; Slaughter, Thomas P. *The Whiskey Rebellion: Frontier Epilogue to the American Revolution.* New York: Oxford University Press, 1986.

—Colleen Shogan

Whiskey Ring

The presidency of Ulysses S. GRANT was one of the more corrupt in history. Although Grant largely escaped responsibility for the scandals, the one crisis that drew closest to the president was the Whiskey Ring scandal.

Whiskey distillers regularly sought to evade taxes by bribing tax officials. In 1874 Secretary of the Treasury Benjamin H. Bristow launched an investigation that pointed to, among others, Orville E. Babcock, one of Grant's closest friends and aides. Although Grant must have known Babcock's involvement, the president gave a deposition defending Babcock, and Babcock was acquitted.

Grant then named Babcock a federal inspector of lighthouses (really) and forced Bristow out of the CABINET.

White House, the

These three words have two meanings—a building, and an institution.

As a building: "the White House" is what is formally termed "the Executive Residence"—the famous 132-room structure and its 18 acres at 1600 Pennsylvania Avenue.

Its site in the then raw, new "federal city" of 3,210 souls was picked by George WASHINGTON, and in the competition among architects, Washington approved the winning design by Dublin-trained builder James Hoban. The cornerstone was laid on October 13, 1792. The building was budgeted to cost $400,000, but Washington, who played an active role in directing the construction, asked Hoban to cut down its size and cost. Even then, Thomas JEFFERSON (one of the losing architectural competitors) commented that the new mansion was "big enough for two emperors, one Pope and the Grand Lama."

Funds were raised from the government's sale of lands in the District and were also contributed by Virginia and Maryland—but were still insufficient to complete the building eight years later. Washington's second term as president had ended in 1797, and it was our second president, John ADAMS, who, with his wife, Abigail Adams, was the first president to occupy the semicompleted mansion, in November 1800. Outside were waste-pits, rubbish, and mud, and the entrance was via temporary wooden stairs and a platform. Water was carried in from a spring five blocks away. Inside, there were no bathrooms. Abigail's laundry, hung to dry in the unfinished East Room, flapped in the winter winds.

Jefferson was the first president to serve a full term in the White House; he hired architect Henry Latrobe to finish the structure, and to add low pavilions (including a henhouse) on the east and west ends as service facilities. Latrobe continued his work with President and Dolley MADISON, but the fire which the British set on August 24, 1814, ruined some of the new building and much of its furnishings. One of those who fled from the burning mansion wrote in her diary, "It is not likely that Washington will ever again be the capital of our country."

Hoban returned to rebuild the walls; President MONROE installed new furniture, and on January 1, 1818, a New Year's Day reception was held in the refurbished mansion. The South Portico was finished in 1824, the North Portico not until 1829. Water was piped in beginning in 1833 and finally pumped in from the Potomac River in 1859.

Nineteenth and early 20th-century presidents changed decor and furnishings again and again—to comport with the latest (changing) styles.

Until 1902 the executive mansion was not only the residence of the first family but the office area for the president, whose study was on the second floor. The CABINET and other meetings were held on the second floor as well, and soon offices, frequented by secretaries and even by office-seekers, invaded the first family's living space and practically destroyed their privacy.

It was Theodore ROOSEVELT who, in 1902, demolished what then were greenhouses at the west end, and built a West Wing with a basement and two stories. With the OVAL OFFICE, the Cabinet Room, and staff offices in the West Wing, the Executive Residence at last became the first family's home, separate from the president's working offices and those of his staff.

In January 1948 President TRUMAN noticed vibrations in the flooring of the residence (the story is told that he saw the piano slide along the floor) and a series of investigations were initiated, culminating in a thoroughgoing examination of the entire structure. The building was found to be so dangerously deteriorated that it had to be evacuated immediately. The first family moved into BLAIR HOUSE across the street. In April of 1949 the Congress passed Public Law 40 establishing a Commission on the Reorganization of the Executive Mansion and in June appropriated $5.4 million for reconstruction (the final total spent was $5.761 million). The commission found that the deterioration was so widespread that the entire interior had to be gutted, leaving only the walls and the roof. The furnishings were carefully preserved. It was only on March 17, 1952, that the first family could move back into a sturdily and beautifully rebuilt White House.

Today the White House is the only chief-of-state residence in the world open, free, to the public; typically, 1.5 million visitors walk through each year. A Visitor's Office in the nearby DEPARTMENT OF COMMERCE buildings hands out the day's ticket supply to the public (it is often exhausted early each morning, except in wintertime). A separate Visitors Office in the White House itself makes arrangements for private and VIP tours.

There are three categories of staff who care for the residence: (a) the 90-plus White House employees who, under the direction of the chief usher, directly serve the first family (some of them have been there for 50 years); (b) the 100 National Park Service men and women who do the grounds maintenance and run the public Visitors Office as well as a White House Museum Storage Facility for spare furnishings and a nursery and greenhouse; and (c) a curator and a staff of four who are in charge of the publicly exhibited White House furnishings—which belong to the people of the United States. The curator is also on the prowl to reacquire some of the original White House furnishings, which, prior to 1902, were often taken away or sold off by outgoing first families.

In 1999 the National Park Service, in cooperation with 11 other agencies that have stewardship responsibilities for the White House, published a "Comprehensive Design Plan and Draft Environmental Impact Statement for the

The White House, ca. 1960 *(John F. Kennedy Library)*

White House and the President's Park." The 408-page document underscored the severe deficiencies that decades of growth in White House activities, staff, and tourists are causing in the service and support facilities at the Executive Residence, i.e., for parking, for visitors, for the news media, for deliveries, for official vehicles, and for special events. The plan proposed the creation of large, new underground facilities—under the Ellipse, under Pennsylvania Avenue, and under West Executive Avenue, and proposed a new museum/visitor center with orientation exhibits, with a pedestrian tunnel leading to the White House. As of this publication date, these proposals are still pending.

As an institution, "the White House" means the president and his staff (see several other sections in this encyclopedia, e.g., WHITE HOUSE OFFICE and STAFF, PRESIDENTIAL). "The executive power," says Article II of the Constitution, "shall be vested in a President of the United States of America." It is the president, aided by his staff, colloquially and collectively referred to as "the White House," who directs and commands the 14 cabinet departments and 17 executive agencies of the EXECUTIVE BRANCH whose heads serve at his pleasure. (Some 41 independent regulatory boards and commissions also are a part of the Executive Branch, but since their heads or members are by law appointed by but not removable by the president, his direction over them is highly attenuated.)

Perhaps the most significant development in the last half-century of American public administration has been the slow but steady shift of policy development, policy coordination, policy explication, and, to some extent, policy implementation from the line departments and agencies to the institution of the White House and to its large, strong, and energetic staff. While the departments and agencies still spend money and run programs (often devolving them upon state and local governments), on important matters, policy control is centralized at the White House. New initiatives are developed under White House leadership. Senior White House staffers pull the many affected departments together, dovetailing their mutually supporting resources and forcing the settlement of their frequent and sometimes pernicious differences. White House speechwriters draft the presidential policy announcements, the White House press secretary or other top White House officers explain and defend policies from the Briefing Room podium. The White House tightly manages the communications operations of its own staff and of all of the leaders of the line agencies. The White House Office of Presidential Personnel controls the 5,842 patronage appointments made in the EXECUTIVE BRANCH; in campaign season, the White House CHIEF OF STAFF typically demands sign-off rights on all the expenditures of the party's National Committee.

Especially dramatic has been the shift of control in national security affairs. The 24-hour duty officers in the White House SITUATION ROOM read—and pass upward within the White House—all important incoming and outgoing messages to or from U.S. diplomats, commanders, and intelligence chieftains. The president very frequently hosts, or travels to attend, face-to-face meetings with other world leaders—in summit conclaves or one on one. In between such top-level conferences, presidents pick up the telephone—literally hundreds of times—and negotiate personally with other chiefs of state. NATIONAL SECURITY ADVISERs themselves meet top government executives of other nations, in their own White House offices.

Modern technology now gives unbelievably potent meaning to the constitutional COMMANDER IN CHIEF role by enabling the president, if he wishes, to follow the events of any battlefield minutely, look at live pictures from drone aircraft, view the movements of both friendly and enemy forces, and give not just strategic but tactical direction to American soldiers anywhere, anytime. In the air war over Bosnia in 1998, the bombing targets were often personally approved by the American president and his British, German, French, and Italian opposite numbers. Such is the potency today of the institution called "the White House."

Further reading: Patterson, Bradley H. *Ring of Power: The White House Staff and Its Expanding Role in Government.* New York: Basic Books, 1988; ———. *The White House Staff: Inside the West Wing and Beyond.* Washington, D.C.: Brookings Institution, 2000; White House Historical Association and the National Geographic Society. *The White House: An Historic Guide.* Washington, D.C.: The Association, 1991.

—Bradley H. Patterson

White House Advance Office

If only for security reasons, there is no such thing as an impromptu presidential trip. Every presidential move beyond the White House grounds is an expedition, planned minute by minute ahead of time. In addition to assuring his personal protection, trip planners are aware that a CHIEF EXECUTIVE is never not president, never on vacation. For 24 hours a day it must be possible for him to reach anyone in the entire U.S. NATIONAL SECURITY community—any commander, any ambassador. And as chief diplomat himself, the contemporary president wants to be able to telephone any other CHIEF OF STATE in the world. Finally, as every politician knows, a presidential trip is also wonderful theater: each city an act, every stop a scene. It is unbeatable newsmaking—and political gold. (President CLINTON put in some 2,000 appearances in more than 800

foreign cities or destinations, plus some 450 appearances at public events in the Washington area.)

A presidential trip, therefore—particularly a presidential journey abroad—is a massive undertaking, involving many elements of the modern WHITE HOUSE: the communications and press offices, the speechwriters, the domestic or economic or national security policy staffs, the SECRET SERVICE, the FIRST LADY'S OFFICE, the medical staff, the 900-person unit (WHCA—the White House Communications Agency) that handles his encrypted communications, the scheduling group, the social office, AIR FORCE ONE and *Marine One,* and (if it is a domestic trip) the political, legislative and intergovernmental affairs staffs too.

Precisely akin to the coordination that occurs to support an ordinary day in the OVAL OFFICE, the integration of trip-planning efforts is equally indispensable but involves much more pressure and faster movement. The coordinator is the Advance Office. NIXON was the first president to organize a formal White House Advance Office, after his 1968 campaign. At first volunteers were used, and still are, but the contemporary White House has a full-time presidential Advance Office staff of some 16. In addition the VICE PRESIDENT now has his own four-person Advance Office and the first lady has an advance person as well.

The concept and purpose of each trip will have been worked out ahead of time, by White House policy and communications staffs, and approved by the president. Once that has been done, the Advance Office designates a "staff lead" and assembles the first advance group to get on a plane and begin the process; an Advance Office "ringmaster" takes charge at home base. While disasters, funerals, and crises may require immediate presidential movement, most president trips have lead time, of days or weeks, perhaps even months for a summit conference abroad. If there is time, the Advance Office will start with a "site survey" and a list of a thousand questions, e.g., what "events" are scheduled? Which stops will most effectively reinforce a presidential policy or theme? What will be the "storyboard" (background) for each photograph? Will the presidential limousine fit through the palace gates?

Next comes the "pre-advance"; for an international trip this is a group of 40 or more staffers from the several White House offices and also includes representatives of the national news networks. They will have a thousand more specific questions, e.g., will the president be free to have a live call-in media event with a huge foreign audience? Will the press room be adequately equipped and wired to handle the large press contingent? Does the local hospital have a supply of the president's blood? Their checklist is pages long.

Finally the main advance team itself deploys and stays on the scene—checking off every detail—until the president arrives. Advancemen are diplomats with steel shoulders. They absolutely ensure that every one of the thousands of arrangement details is handled without a hitch but give all the credit to the local hosts. They are anonymous, entirely behind the scenes; their job is to produce, apparently effortlessly, a total visit, which adds both to the president's reputation and to the luster of the presidential office itself.

Further reading: Patterson, Bradley H. *Ring of Power.* New York: Basic Books, 1988; ———. *The White House Staff: Inside the West Wing and Beyond.* Washington, D.C.: Brookings Institution, 2000.

—Bradley H. Patterson

White House "czars"

At times, in the day-to-day process of governing, presidents will be shaken up by a very special category of problems which surge into the White House policy machinery. These will be issues of bewildering complexity—cutting across many boundary lines of departmental jurisdiction; they will be urgent, requiring response so immediate that any delay opens the president to the charge of falling down on the job; and they will be seen as incapable of being managed by existing institutional arrangements. Some of these will be old problems which a president insists on tackling in new ways; some will arise from sudden, new circumstances; a few may be national crises of frightening severity.

The president's response will be quickly to augment his White House or Executive Office resources and call in a special person with expertise and stature, i.e., create a White House "czar." All the recent presidents have used this technique.

The question arises: How much power does a White House "czar" have and how is the "czar's" office organized as a basis for that power? There are four options. First, a White House special coordinator can be set up in business with only a presidential statement as mission and charter. This was the model that President CLINTON employed in June 1993; he simply made the announcement that he was ". . . appointing an AIDS Policy Coordinator who will . . . oversee and unify governmentwide AIDS efforts." When this officer resigned 13 months later, her parting shot of advice for her successor was: "Get more clarity, right from the beginning."

The second option is to issue a presidential EXECUTIVE ORDER, establishing the "czar's" position and stating the mission and functions. Such an executive order is likely to have more specificity than a mere presidential statement, and it has staying power; it can be revoked or amended only by another presidential executive order. However, unless it is issued to carry out a specific provision of a statute, even a presidential executive order is only a general admonition, applying only to the officers within a president's own administration, telling them how they should behave. Every such general executive order contains a caveat such as "This order does not create any right or benefit, substantive or procedural, enforceable at law or equity by a party against the United States, its departments, agencies or instrumentalities, its officers or employees, or any other person,"—i.e., no legal commitments for any new programs or any new money.

President BUSH chose this second option when he set up the OFFICE OF HOMELAND SECURITY in October of 2001. The order was full of wide-ranging language but the actual verbs used were significant. The new White House "czar" was to "develop and coordinate the implementation of a comprehensive national strategy . . .," "coordinate the executive branch's efforts . . .," "work with the executive departments and agencies . . .," "identify priorities . . .," "work with Federal, State and local agencies . . .," "facilitate . . .," "coordinate and prioritize . . .," "ensure that, to the extent permitted by law . . .," "review and assess the adequacy of . . .," "strengthen measures . . .," "develop criteria . . .," "review plans . . .," "encourage and invite the participation of . . .," "develop . . . proposals for presidential action . . . for submission to the Office of Management and Budget . . ."

As for budget authority, the new Homeland Security "czar" was to scrutinize the "level and use of funding in departments and agencies for homeland security-related activities and, prior to the [OMB] Director's forwarding of the proposed annual budget submission to the President for transmittal to the Congress, shall certify to the Director the funding levels that [he] . . . believes are necessary and appropriate. . . ." This language gave the new "czar" an exceptional measure of influence—but still, only the president has the power of decision and action.

The third option for establishing a central coordinator is to have the coordinator's mission and functions put into a statute. A law has even longer staying power than an executive order; it remains in effect until changed by CONGRESS AND THE PRESIDENT. This is the form used for the Director of the Office of National Drug Control Policy. The law authorizes the drug "czar" to "review the annual budgets" which the operating agencies send to the OFFICE OF MANAGEMENT AND BUDGET and "make recommendations to the President respecting such budgets before they are submitted to the Congress . . ."; to "review the allocation of personnel to and by such departments"; and to "evaluate the performance and results achieved by Federal drug enforcement" as well as to point out how such performance could be enhanced if additional programs and activities were employed.

Did the fact that these authorities were statutory endow the drug "czar" with extra clout? The "czar" of the Clinton period recently reflected on what happened when he began to make recommendations about the drug budget of the DEPARTMENT OF DEFENSE. The Pentagon's protests were so furious, he recalled, that "it was like setting fire to a cathedral on Easter Sunday." The fourth option is to transform the "czar" from being a coordinator to being an operating agency, i.e., enacting a law taking pieces out of several of the departments and combining them into a single line agency, the director of which would have full operating authority over all of its functions.

Readers will appreciate the cathedral conflagrations that such proposals would ignite within the CABINET and among protective legislators and interest groups. Besides a "czar's" organizational arrangements, there are other elements that can greatly contribute to the officer's effectiveness, e.g., the language which the president uses to describe the job and to endorse the appointee, the president's giving the "czar" a berth in the West Wing, and granting quick access to the OVAL OFFICE. The president can also direct that the White House "czar" be the principal spokesperson on the issues—in the press briefing room and on national media, and can make it equally clear that when he or she does so, the "czar" indeed speaks for the president. The mood of the nation counts mightily; no cabinet officer wants to appear reluctant or unsupportive of a "czar's" initiative when the country is in a crisis period.

In the end, the organization and work of the White House continues to be subject to long-lived verities. In his historic 1939 Executive Order 8248 establishing the EXECUTIVE OFFICE OF THE PRESIDENT, Franklin Roosevelt specified that "In no event shall the Administrative Assistants be interposed between the President and the head of any department or agency." A decade later the first Hoover Commission warned that "Statutory authority over the operating departments should not be vested in any staff members or staff agency of the President's Office." However *influential* a White House "czar" may be, the "czar's" *power* is nothing but the president's power.

Further reading: Foreman, Christopher H., Jr. "AIDS and the Limits of Czardom." In *Comments Presented to the National Commission on AIDS*. Washington, D.C.: Brookings Institution, 1992; Patterson, Bradley H. *The White House Staff: Inside the West Wing and Beyond*. Washington, D.C.: Brookings Institution, 2000.

—Bradley H. Patterson

White House–department relations

The central role of the White House in the totality of the executive branch stems, on the one hand, from a long-standing prescription of nine cogent words, and on the other hand from the realities of modern public administration.

"The executive Power shall be vested in a President," says Article II of the Constitution. However expanded has become the EXECUTIVE BRANCH, however numerous have become its departments and agencies and their chieftains, the EXECUTIVE POWER still rests in the hands of a single, not a plural, head.

If there ever was a period in American history when a circumscribed set of public policy issues could be confined to the jurisdictional boundaries of a single department—e.g., FOREIGN AFFAIRS to the DEPARTMENT OF STATE, legal affairs to the DEPARTMENT OF JUSTICE—those times are long gone. Today's public administrators live and work in a multidimensional policy world; every single major issue of public policy cuts across the authorities of multiple departments. The problem of homeland defense is the most recent and potent example; it sweeps through the interests of 124 bureaus in 16 departments and agencies—and totally wipes out what perhaps once was a distinction between "domestic" and "foreign" affairs.

To tackle a major issue in such a multijurisdictional environment, can any one department or agency be assigned to act as the supervisor, or even the coordinator, of all the others? Impossible. Only in the White House do all the lines come together; only the president and his Executive Office (institutional) and White House (personal) staffs can help him effectively deal with these crosscutting issues. In contemporary executive governance, policy development, policy coordination, policy explication, and, to some extent, policy implementation have been sucked away from the departments and agencies and drawn into the White House, with its large and active groups of assistants. The drafters of Article II had more foresight than they even imagined.

But statutory authorities, expertly specialized personnel, substantial appropriated funds, and years-long experience reside not in the White House but in the departments and agencies; no White House "czar" of however exalted a stature or title, can operate, build, buy, grant, or contract for anything or hire or fire any tenured employee. All such functions are still carried out only in the line agencies. Accomplishing the business of governance, therefore, requires effective White House/departmental relationships. The president "takes care that" the laws are faithfully executed, but the actual execution is in the departments and agencies.

The president and staff at the White House look at those cabinet departments and agencies, however, with some misgivings. While they may be appointed by the president, the leaders of the departments are confirmed by the Senate, must testify and defend their actions to both Senate and House, depend for their finances on the Congress, and are subject to highly politicized congressional investigations. Departments are peopled by civil or military careerists, whose policy priorities may not be anywhere near those of the president. Departments are hectored by the press, departmental papers are subject to FREEDOM OF INFORMATION ACT lawsuits, and their leaderships, both political and career, are subject to the ceaseless pressures from powerful outside advocacy groups. The result of being so besieged by such strong centrifugal forces is that departments tend to yield to many of these forces and become advocates for policy directions quite different from those pursued by the president. "The CABINET is the enemy of the president," said one government veteran.

How do these rather iffy relationships impact the functioning of government? The first step in the White House/departmental policy process, especially as it relates to sensitive and controversial issues, is gathering information. Washington is awash in information: from the electronic and print media, from millions of pieces of mail, communications from tens of thousands of interest groups and special pleaders, data from the far-flung federal BUREAUCRACY. The more sensitive and controversial the issue, the greater the volume—*except there is a question:* how much of this flood of information is pertinent and how much of it is accurate? Will the operating federal officials themselves forward timely and candid information to the president, especially when something is going wrong? Often not. In recent years, therefore, the White House has turned to employing unremittingly meticulous methods to corral information from every corner of the executive branch—a practice that has frequently soured White House departmental relationships.

Franklin ROOSEVELT told his assistant James H. Rowe, Jr., "Your job is to be bird-dog. . . . Just run around town and find out what's happening." In Arthur Schlesinger's words:

> Roosevelt's persistent effort . . . was to check and balance information acquired through official channels by information acquired through a myriad of private, informal and unorthodox channels and espionage networks. At times he seemed almost to pit his personal sources against his public sources.

Contemporary presidents employ sophisticated systems—and the latest technology—to permit them, if they desire, to uncover even the smallest details of federal operations. The White House SITUATION ROOM of the NATIONAL SECURITY COUNCIL demands a copy of every important incoming and outgoing communication in the national security community, reaching into State, Defense, and the entire intelligence community. It, or the president himself if he desires, can look at satellite or drone-acquired pictures of any battlefield. Some military officers blanche at such a degree of intrusiveness.

EISENHOWER instituted, and every subsequent president has continued, a requirement that each operating department and agency send the White House a weekly report on its significant activities (hopefully including problems as well as accomplishments). The stack of submissions goes to the secretary of the cabinet, who selects, edits, and

amalgamates them into a single weekly Cabinet Report—which goes to the president and the senior White House staff. The president scribbles commentaries and instructions on the margins, often with great candor, enhancing—sometimes putting a sharp edge into—the White House/departmental relationship. In the subsequent stages of policy development, those interdepartmental processes, too, are under firm White House control. Senior White House staff, not cabinet members, chair standing or ad hoc working groups and closely supervise the drafting of option papers. The final memorandum for the president's decision is almost always a White House staff product. For meetings with the president, the White House CHIEF OF STAFF will determine which department heads get into the OVAL OFFICE; he is a vital guarantor of healthy White House/departmental relationships, however, because he will make sure not only that attendance is limited but also that no essential participant is left out. With few exceptions, White House staffers, all the way up to and including the chief of staff, are keenly aware that they must not use their central position to skew the presentation of competing points of view. They are honest brokers and as such enhance rather than undermine White House/departmental relations.

One type of presidential activity has vastly expanded in the last half century: the president's conduct of personal DIPLOMACY. Besides attending frequent summit conferences, the modern president is constantly on the telephone with other chiefs of state abroad—engaging in serious negotiations. Will State and our ambassadors overseas be kept informed? When American military forces are operating abroad, the U.S. president will often require that, for instance, the Air Force get his advance approval for their target lists. Some DEPARTMENT OF DEFENSE leaders are very unhappy with such White House oversight.

In the Eisenhower years, the cabinet met practically every Friday morning, the department heads engaging with the president in candid discussion of domestic issues. This practice has come to a halt; in the CLINTON years the cabinet was sometimes convened under the chairmanship of only the White House chief of staff—leaving some cabinet heads to wonder whether they were still "in the loop."

Each president must balance his need for strong central control and for dispatch with the equally important requirement for maintaining healthy White House/departmental relationships. In view of the inherent misgivings at both ends of this relationship, it is a rocky road.

Further reading: Patterson, Bradley H. *Ring of Power: The White House Staff and Its Expanding Role in Government.* New York: Basic Books, 1989; ———. *The White House Staff: Inside the West Wing and Beyond.* Washington, D.C.: Brookings, 2000; Reich, Robert B. *Locked in the Cabinet.* New York: Knopf, 1997.

—Bradley H. Patterson

White House Office

This institutional title, in its narrow and proper use, is the name of one of the 12 units listed in the Budget of the United States as being the component parts of the EXECUTIVE OFFICE OF THE PRESIDENT. The 12 are: the president and the White House Office; the OFFICE OF POLICY DEVELOPMENT (the economic and domestic policy assistants and their staffs); the NATIONAL SECURITY COUNCIL, i.e., the staff of the council; the executive residence, i.e., the White House mansion; the VICE PRESIDENT and his staff and residence; the OFFICE OF ADMINISTRATION; the OFFICE OF MANAGEMENT AND BUDGET; the COUNCIL OF ECONOMIC ADVISERS; the Office of National Drug Control Policy; the OFFICE OF SCIENCE AND TECHNOLOGY POLICY; the United States Trade Representative; and the Council on Environmental Quality.

The White House is the largest of the 12; it is composed of the president and most of his personal staff. The White House Office group numbers approximately 3,100 people; it includes the FIRST LADY'S OFFICE, the assistants and their helpers for legislative liaison, political affairs, intergovernmental relations, presidential personnel, communications, press, public liaison, speechwriting, scheduling, advance, faith-based and community initiatives, AIDS policy coordination, strategic initiatives, the new OFFICE OF HOMELAND SECURITY, and the COUNSEL TO THE PRESIDENT; it includes the staff and CABINET secretaries and the White House CHIEF OF STAFF, and it also includes essential but less well-known support units such as the executive clerk, the Correspondence and Records Management offices, the Travel Office, the telephone operators, and the 2,200-person White House Military Office.

"The White House Office," a de jure term, should not be confused with "The White House Staff." The whole community of the White House Staff, de facto, is considerably larger: All of the first five of the above list of 12, and half of the sixth, plus the SECRET SERVICE units directly protecting the two first families—a total of some 5,500 men and women.

The budget of the White House Office is defended before the House and Senate Appropriations Committees by the director of the Office of Administration; personal assistants to the president do not (except in cases of criminal or scandalous conduct) testify before congressional committees.

While every person working in the broadly-defined "White House Staff community" serves in the White House at the pleasure of the president, those in the White House Office group who handle policy matters are the most likely to change with each change of administration. Those serving in the White House Office support units are traditionally invited to stay from president to president, and form an invaluable cadre of skilled, experienced men and women who, totally unknown to the American public, serve the presidential office with anonymous professionalism.

See also PRESIDENTIAL STAFF.

Further reading: Patterson, Bradley H. *Ring of Power: The White House Staff and Its Expanding Role in Government.* New York: Basic Books, 1988; ———. *The White House Staff: Inside the West Wing and Beyond.* Washington, D.C.: Brookings, 2000.

—Bradley H. Patterson

White House Office of Communications

Created by Richard NIXON in 1969, the White House Office of Communications serves as the public relations apparatus for the president. The impetus for the creation of this addition to the White House staff came mostly from Nixon's desire to maintain better control over his media image during the 1968 presidential campaign. Following Nixon's election, the office was created as an agency to supervise all of the information services from the EXECUTIVE BRANCH.

The responsibilities of Herb Klein, the first director of Communications, were different from those of Ron Ziegler, Nixon's press secretary. While Ziegler, head of the Press Office, was responsible for preparing press releases, holding daily press briefings for the White House press corps, and facilitating the needs of reporters who covered the president, Klein was charged with promoting the president and his legislative agenda with those members of the news media outside of Washington—regional and local television, radio, and print media outlets. Since its creation, the role of the Office of Communications has continued to expand in an attempt to control both the public agenda and the image of the president in the news media. And while the exact functions of the office can vary depending on the individual director and the needs of the president, general responsibilities have included coordinating local and regional media coverage when a president travels outside of Washington, coordinating White House luncheons for non-Washington journalists, and providing technical expertise in the use of television and radio for presidential appearances. The importance of this type of media coordination has increased since the Nixon administration and WATERGATE due to the increased adversarial relationship between the president and the WHITE HOUSE PRESS CORPS.

The news media has become increasingly obsessed with covering conflict, which often results in serious discussions of policy issues within the White House being depicted as dissent among top presidential ADVISERS. As a result, the goal of the White House is to stop any news reports of internal conflict and push for positive coverage of the president's policy agenda. The Office of Communications handles this through a long-term public relations strategy. Advisers usually spread the "line of the day" throughout the administration, which then takes it to the press; the office also takes the White House message directly to the people when necessary. The ultimate goal is to set the public agenda through the use of focus groups, polls, sound bites, and public appearances by the president. This allows ample opportunities for the president to dodge the hostile White House press corps and to rely on alternative modes of communication.

Members of the news media have also come to rely on the information provided through the Office of Communications. Staff members work hard to facilitate the needs of journalists and to make their jobs in covering the president easier in the hopes of gaining more favorable coverage for the White House. For example, the Office of Communications provides press releases, fact sheets, and other background information on policies, radio actualities, satellite feeds, and a variety of daily photo opportunities that provide a positive spin on the president's activities. This can be especially helpful to smaller news organizations, which in recent years have had diminished operating budgets and increased competition within the industry. Cultivating a positive image in the eyes of Americans through a well-planned communication strategy is now a top priority for presidents, and as a result, communication strategies have become an important and permanent part of the everyday operation of the White House.

Since the presidency is now more institutionalized and politicized, presidents and their staffs have found it necessary to learn over time how best to control the image that Americans have of their president through the news media. By the time Ronald REAGAN took office in 1981, the Office of Communications had become an important and permanent institutional aspect of governing. The administration decided early in 1981 to continue the practice of holding White House luncheons for out-of-town editors and publishers. Various departments within the Office of Communications headed up the efforts to cater to the needs of the local news media, which included telephone interviews with the president and other key administration officials for local television and radio stations, news briefings for out-of-town press representatives, and mailing fact sheets about Reagan's policy initiatives to local news editors and publishers.

The use of a radio actuality service, similar to the ones used by the Nixon and CARTER administrations, was also continued. Local radio stations around the country could call in to the White House on a toll-free number and receive a ready-to-use news clip from the "White House Broadcasting Service," as it was called during the Reagan years. During Reagan's eight years in office, the strategy to gain coverage for administration policies in the local press became much more aggressive than with previous administrations. Realizing the impact and influence that the White House would have on small news operations across the country, efforts were made to contact radio stations directly to promote the actuality service, and to contact local newspapers with White House statements for inclusion in their stories.

Certain states would also be targeted if news out of Washington was of particular interest to citizens in the area to increase the coverage on the president's policies. This continued during the George H. W. BUSH and CLINTON administrations as the Office of Communications maintained its role as a public relations outlet for the White House. Under Clinton, the Office of Communications devised several new techniques to keep in touch with both the press and the public in the new computer age while attempting to control the message about presidential policies. These included an increased access to information through a White House WEBSITE, which provided information available to computer users such as Clinton's public remarks, his daily schedule, transcripts of press briefings, and photos. A White House e-mail address was also set up to respond to questions from citizens about Clinton's policies.

Further reading: Kessel, John H. *Presidents, the Presidency, and the Political Environment.* Washington, D.C.: CQ Press, 2001; Maltese, John Anthony. *Spin Control: The White House Office of Communications and the Management of Presidential News.* Chapel Hill: University of North Carolina Press, 1994.

—Lori Cox-Han

White House Office of Legislative Affairs

Every law the president's EXECUTIVE BRANCH administers, every new activity it wishes to undertake, every dollar it plans to spend—must be approved by the Congress. One thousand, one hundred twenty-five nominees to senior federal positions, and all new federal judges, require Senate confirmation; each treaty the president signs must be ratified there. Thus does our Constitution require presidential-legislative collaboration. Moreover, the president is required by statute to furnish Congress with even the most sensitive intelligence information, and for their part neither the Senate nor the House hesitate to mount invasive investigations into any—repeat any—aspect of executive branch operations or of presidential activity.

Over the last 50 years, presidents have built an "ambulatory bridge" across this constitutional gulf; it is the White House Office of Legislative Affairs. TRUMAN had a couple of staffers who focused on this work, but it was EISENHOWER who created the office, strengthened it with senior people, and designated his deputy chief of staff (General Wilton Persons) as its director. Every president since has continued to make the Office of Legislative Affairs a principal part of his White House staff.

The office, with some 24 staffers (many of them usually with long experience on the Hill), is typically organized into a Senate section and a House section; a special unit focuses on the handling of congressional correspondence; there also may be an officer who concentrates on expediting Senate confirmation of presidential nominees. A strict rule is laid down: Since the White House must speak with one voice to members of Congress, no one else on the president's staff is to conduct congressional lobbying without the imprimatur of the Legislative Affairs Office. Even the CHIEF OF STAFF—who cannot avoid congressional contacts and often carries great weight on the Hill—complies with this rule.

In no way is Legislative Affairs limited to a White House office. Every CABINET department (and major operating agency) has a congressional affairs group. The heads of these departmental units are, themselves, usually selected by the White House Legislative Affairs director—giving the director a cabinet-wide circle of helpers, who add their information to the White House store, who often meet as a group on the call of the White House, and who can therefore be expected to conduct their own lobbying on the Hill in precise coordination with—i.e., at the direction of—the White House office.

The senior Legislative Affairs staffers view their mission in the White House as much more than being message-carriers or lobbyists for the president's policies; they need to be in on the policies' development as well as their implementation. They join domestic or economic policy formulation meetings at the White House; they arrange for and accompany the very frequent visits which senior White House policy assistants make to individual senators or representatives or committee staffs—negotiating the delicate and controversial compromises which are often required in the language of bills or committee reports. One important White House policy office, the NATIONAL SECURITY COUNCIL, has its own legislative liaison unit—which does its work in close collaboration with the central liaison group.

In addition to leaning on that departmental circle of associates—and on cabinet members personally whenever heavyweight influence is called for—the White House Legislative Affairs Office leaves no resource untouched to accomplish its never-ending mission for the president. The most potent weapon in their arsenal is the president himself. Often a group of legislators will be called into the OVAL OFFICE (the Legislative staff handles the invitations and helps prepare the briefing papers). Eisenhower, for instance, regularly met with legislative leaders on Tuesday mornings. If a senator or representative is undecided but "leaning" about an important piece of legislation, a presidential telephone call is arranged (more briefing papers). A single legislator may be invited to meet with the president—with press stationed outside the door to put the visitor's newly minted decision on the record.

The Legislative Affairs Office will call on the White House Public Liaison director to sponsor White House meetings of leaders of influential outside interest groups. Cabinet members will be invited to speak to such groups;

"talking points" and supporting literature will be distributed, questions asked and answered. But beyond that a caution: No one in the executive branch, even the president, can expend public funds specifically to organize a lobbying campaign on Congress. If asked "What can we do to help?" the White House sponsors can only say, "Here are the senators or congresspeople handling this issue; *you* know what next steps to take!" A rare but potent device is sometimes employed: If a legislator is on the point of deciding not to support the administration, and his vote is essential, calls may be made to the defector's major local contributors: "Do you realize what Senator X or Congressman Y is doing to our president?!" This technique is called "the hotfoot"; some presidents have been known to blanch at using it, but. . .

A presidential trip is scheduled; the Legislative Affairs Office will fight to reserve seats for key congressional supporters on AIR FORCE ONE. If it is a domestic trip, the senators from the destination states and the representatives from the affected districts need to be considered as presidential guests. A foreign trip often may include specially chosen legislators; for the funeral of Itzhak Rabin, an entire separate plane was chartered to carry selected Hill people to Israel. A state dinner is being held; the LA office will squeeze the social secretary to include influential lawmakers on the invitation list. Senators and congresspeople flood the White House with requests for patronage appointments; staffers may intervene with their White House colleagues in the PRESIDENTIAL PERSONNEL OFFICE. A popular musical opens at the Kennedy Center; office staffers will press for seats in the well-furnished president's box. Every senator and congressperson is allocated spaces on the much-sought-after White House "special tour"—separate from the public tours and afforded to selected visitors to the White House. Does the Legislative Affairs Office up the allocations to some and cut back those to other who are less supportive? Yes—as with all the above perks and privileges. Are "score-cards" kept? Usually not in writing.

While Congress is in session, on the Hill, the legislative staffers, all equipped with cell phones, move at a breathless pace. Consider this description by Nick Calio, Legislative Affairs Director for both Presidents BUSH:

> The most important thing was, we were on Capitol Hill all the time—I mean, all the time. We became familiar sights; people on both sides of the aisle were very comfortable with seeing us; they expected to see us. They consequently would talk to us, all the time. You didn't have to bargain to get a conversation, to find out what somebody was thinking. You would assimilate the information and thus keep your finger on the pulse and sense the mood and have a feel for what was going on. . . . We hung out all over; we would place ourselves all over the Capitol. When the bells went off, the call was "Who's

taking elevators? Who's taking subway? Who's taking stairs?" We would cover all of them. We also could get into places where most lobbyists couldn't get. On the House side we had people at the top of the steps, right where members come in; we had other people at the bottom, where the elevators were, then down by the subways where they were coming across. We covered all the doors. We would catch 'em everywhere.

A principal purpose of insisting on such direct, personal encounters was to procure as accurate a nose-count as possible of supporters and opponents; estimates from staffers do not equal the reliability of face-to-face exchanges with members. An illustration of determined and effective White House legislative liaison work occurred in October of 1981 when President REAGAN moved to sell sophisticated AWACS aircraft to Saudi Arabia. The Senate could vote to prohibit the sale; many favoring Israel were planning to block the president's initiative. Experienced Legislative Affairs Director Max Friendersdorf escorted senator after senator into the Oval Office: "We were moving people in and out of this building like we were showing it for sale," he recalled. To cap the forthcoming debate, Senate Majority Leader Howard BAKER needed a letter from the president describing the detailed U.S.-Saudi agreements that had been made to ensure the safety of the planes' equipment, where they would fly, how they would be operated, under what conditions the resulting intelligence could be shared, and why the planes would represent no threat to Israel.

For 10 days, drafts of that letter had been done and redone, Friedersdorf taking it up to individual doubting senators for comment, then taking it back—to State, to Defense, to the JOINT CHIEFS OF STAFF, to the NATIONAL SECURITY COUNCIL "four, five, and six times," Friedersdorf remembered. The final letter, which Baker was given to use just before the roll call, helped gain the president his 52-48 victory. Legislative liaison staffers always keep a final admonition in mind. In the words of Pat Griffin, President CLINTON's Legislative Affairs chief: "People would say, 'You've got to screw this guy!' You know, if you're leaving town and that was the last day, that's fine, but *we'd* be back tomorrow and the next day and the next day. You never make enemies; you tried never to make enemies."

Further reading: Collier, Kenneth E. *Between the Branches: The White House Office of Legislative Affairs.* Pittsburgh, Pa.: University of Pittsburgh Press, 1997; Patterson, Bradley H. *Ring of Power: The White House Staff and Its Expanding Role in Government.* New York: Basic Books, 1988; ———. *The White House Staff: Inside the West Wing and Beyond.* Washington, D.C.: Brookings Institution, 2000.

—Bradley H. Patterson

White House Office of Political Affairs

Reagan political affairs director Lyn Nofziger was once asked what, in the White House, did he consider was political. His answer: "Everything." In recognition of that fact, the contemporary White House staff includes an Office of Political Affairs—which can concern itself with any and every segment of White House activity. Every presidential decision is political in the broad sense that it tests the limits of consensus in the country. Partisanship in its narrow meaning colors each presidential decision as well; a president's approval rating may soar or slump as a result of success or failure even in NATIONAL SECURITY matters.

Political advice-giving goes back decades, but the Office of Political Affairs as a distinct White House unit with that name was established in 1980. It typically has a dozen staffers headed by a deputy assistant to the president.

The office is usually divided by regions so that each staff member concentrates on a group of neighboring states. If the president, the VICE PRESIDENT, or either of the two spouses plans domestic travel, the staff specialists from the regions to be visited prepare briefing materials about the political situation in the states on the itinerary, identifies which congressmen and senators should be on the plane, counsels on which local party leaders should be invited to be in the arrival ceremonies, and advises which local groups most deserve VIP attention.

The principal objective of the Political Affairs Office is not to control every presidential decision but to ensure that political pluses and minuses are included in the mix of considerations when policies are being debated—especially in the domestic sphere. This is known as "policy management." By his attendance at senior staff meetings, the political affairs director is able to track controversial issues bubbling up in the White House policy machinery, becomes aware of the economic and social (and therefore the political) impact of any forthcoming decision, and often invites affected community and organizational leaders—and contributors—to meet with the White House policy aides, giving these leaders the opportunity to have their voices heard. PATRONAGE is handled by the PRESIDENTIAL PERSONNEL OFFICE, and the Political Affairs Office may intervene in the appointment process. This is rare, however, since getting involved in many such cases would sap the office's limited time and staff.

The Political Affairs Office is of course the link from the White House to the party's National Committee and from the White House to the party state committees across the nation. The office calls upon any and all White House staff resources to help accomplish its mission, fighting on behalf of its party constituencies for time on the president's schedule, for invitations to state dinners, for seats on AIR FORCE ONE, and for places in the president's box at Kennedy Center performances.

The office looks upon the political appointees in the other-than-national-security CABINET departments as a circle of allies. Special electronic or written materials will be circulated to this circle so that the top political leadership throughout the EXECUTIVE BRANCH will be apprised of the president's priorities and activities and can be tasked to amplify the president's messages and themes.

At campaign time, all of the above activities are multiplied in number and intensity. Furthermore, a sitting president's campaign for a second term is completely controlled by the White House Political Affairs Office. Consider this excerpt from the account of a meeting of political aides in the CLINTON White House with the leadership of the Democratic National Committee as the 1996 campaign took shape:

> It was agreed that all matters dealing with the allocation and expenditure of monies involving the DNC, including, without limitation, the DNC's operating budget, media budget, coordinated campaign budget and any other budget or expenditure . . . are subject to the *prior* approval of the White House.

The Political Affairs Office is at the center of two other sets of linkage: with outside private political consultants and with pollsters.

Using campaign consultants is now a universal practice of those running for office—of congressmen, senators, and presidents. These men and women are outside of the government, but a president will give his contingent of outside advisers practically free access to the White House. Being paid for by the party national committee, they can do and say things which the White House Political Affairs staffers, as federal employees, cannot. The inside staffers must sometimes race to keep abreast of the consultants' activities.

A second omnipresent element in the political side of the presidency is poll-taking. This activity is also paid for by the party national committee, but the results are pumped immediately and directly into the White House. And not just during campaigns; throughout a presidency, politically financed polls (their questions often drafted in the White House itself) are sampling public sentiment. "Not to determine policy, but to help devise effective ways of explaining policy," the pollsters profess, but a critic commented: Too much emphasis on polling "turns leadership on its head."

A final quotation from Political Affairs Director Nofziger's quotation is memorable: "I will let Mr. Meese and Mr. Baker and Mr. Deaver and all those good guys worry about Reagan being president. They like government, they want to run government, they can run the government. I'm much more interested in making sure we go on running it."

Further reading: Patterson, Bradley H. *Ring of Power: The White House Staff and Its Expanding Role in Government.* New York: Basic Books, 1988; ———. *The White House Staff: Inside the West Wing and Beyond.* Washington, D.C.: Brookings Institution, 2000; Tenpas, Kathryn Dunn. "Institutional Politics: The White House Office of Political Affairs." *Presidential Studies Quarterly* (Spring 1996).

—Bradley H. Patterson

White House Personnel Authorization Act

The "swelling of the presidency," to use Thomas E. Cronin's apt phrase, caused a congressional reaction attempting to grapple with the expansion and growing power of the president's staff. In the aftermath of the VIETNAM WAR and WATERGATE, Congress made several attempts to control presidential power. Many congressional critics pointed to the growth of the president's staff as a sign of encroaching power. In 1978 the White House Personnel Authorization Act (PL 95-570) was Congress's attempt to gain some measure of control over the president's staff. While allowing for continued growth in the size of the staff, the act attempted—unsuccessfully—to make the president's staff slightly more accountable to Congress. Vice President Walter MONDALE is credited with lobbying Congress to weaken many provisions in the bill, which was passed during the CARTER years.

White House photographer

Presidents are very much aware of the fact that what they do during each day of their time in office adds to their niche in history. Each day's events, therefore, are meticulously recorded. Of course the nation's media—video, audio, film, and print outlets—cover newsworthy presidential activities, but those are only a selected fraction of a CHIEF EXECUTIVE's life. A president wants history to be aware of just about everything he does—newsmaking or not. A White House diarist keeps tab on how every waking minute is spent—who it is that attends any meeting with the president, whoever speaks with him on any phone call. The White House Records Office (or the NATIONAL SECURITY COUNCIL) files away every piece of paper that has been shown to the president. A White House Military Office video team tapes each important presidential event. Not surprisingly, every president, beginning at least with ROOSEVELT, has also added a White House photographer as part of his staff, whose still camera will capture the chief executive's hour-by-hour existence.

FDR's photographer (Abbie Rowe) was a National Park Service employee (and he stayed on the staff until 1967). Robert Knudsen, employed by the navy, served from

1946 to 1974. Johnson was the first president to create the position of personal photographer to the president (it was Yoichi Okamoto, employed by the U.S. Information Agency). By this time, the White House photography operation had expanded greatly: Besides the personal photographer there was a director of the Photography Office and three assistant photographers plus a photo lab in a separate building in Georgetown, where reportedly as many as 30 people worked. By the end of the Johnson administration there were an estimated 500,000 photographs of his presidency on file.

NIXON (using Ollie Atkins), FORD (using David Kennerly), CARTER (using a group that included Billie Shaddix), REAGAN (using Michael Evans), George H. W. BUSH (using David Valdez), CLINTON (using Bob McNeeley and Sharon Farmer), and George W. BUSH (using Eric Draper) have continued the tradition. The personal photographer usually changes with each president; the director of the photo office is often a long-serving person on the military payroll, as are the three or four assistant photographers and as are the 30 or so technicians in the photo lab which is at present located with the White House Communications Agency at the Anacostia Naval Air Station. The personal photographer (who usually has an office in the West Wing basement) and the assistant photographers study each day's schedule in advance and plan how they will cover each public or private event, each taking a "zone" to shoot from. All have security clearances entitling them to walk in on any meeting. What they seek is the "memorable moment" (for instance, President Clinton, arriving in New Zealand, walking down the stairway of AIR FORCE ONE and being greeted by a swarm of half-naked Maori chieftains). What they avoid is the posed picture. Every ambassador, after presenting his credentials, receives an autographed picture; every White House corridor glows with dramatic shots of recent presidential or first lady events. The photographers use digital equipment; the discs are inserted into a computer and the best shots marked for inserting onto the WHITE HOUSE WEBSITE and for preservation in the NATIONAL ARCHIVES. In the first six and one half years of the Clinton administration, the photographers used 76,000 rolls of film. "Our purpose is to serve the American democracy by creating a visual record of its presidency," explained photographer Sharon Farmer. "We are creating a legacy, not for public relations purposes, but as an archive for the future." And the VICE PRESIDENT now has his own official photographer as well.

Further reading: Patterson, Bradley H. *Ring of Power: The White House Staff and Its Expanding Role in Government.* New York: Basic Books, 1988; ———. *The White House Staff: Inside the West Wing and Beyond.* Washington, D.C.: Brookings Institution, 2000.

—Bradley H. Patterson

White House press corps

The White House press corps first received working space within the White House during the administration of Theodore ROOSEVELT, who included press quarters within the new West Wing built in 1904. Roosevelt actively cultivated a positive relationship with Washington reporters in an attempt to gain favorable coverage for his administration and legislative agenda. The White House Correspondents' Association was formed in 1914, which contributed to the trend of professionalization of reporters within the newspaper industry during the early part of the 20th century.

The White House press corps experienced tremendous growth during the 1930s and 1940s, particularly during the years of the Franklin D. ROOSEVELT's presidency, as presidential influence over national politics increased under the New Deal programs. Also, FDR's frequent and informal meetings with the White House press corps in the OVAL OFFICE were newsworthy events for reporters. His use of PRESS CONFERENCES and his effective news management efforts contributed to the need for the White House to be covered in various media outlets, since much of the news in Washington was beginning to be generated from the EXECUTIVE BRANCH.

During the 1930s, more than 350 reporters covered the Washington beat. By the 1990s, more than 1,700 people held White House press credentials, and while all are not considered "regulars" on the White House beat, the sheer size of the press corps has necessitated a more formalized daily press briefing than in years past. The emergence of the television age during the 1950s, and television's expansive growth during the 1960s and 1970s, greatly contributed to the growth in the size of the White House press corps.

Other factors contributing to the increase in number of reporters on the White House beat include the increased importance and size of the federal government and the role it plays in the lives of individuals, which requires reporters from non-Washington media outlets to cover policy-making at the national level. Also, the number of foreign correspondents covering the White House has increased in recent decades, as other countries have a greater need to understand the impact of American policies in their own countries. The prominence of the White House beat has also increased within the journalism industry and is now viewed as one of the premier assignments in most news organizations. Throughout the 20th century, prominent reporters who covered the White House beat often played an important role in shaping the image of presidents in their respective media outlets as well as in the eyes of the American public. Therefore, presidents and their advisers during the modern era have actively developed strategies in an attempt to manage and control the news of their administrations in the national media.

The reporters who regularly cover the White House now include representatives from a variety of media outlets, including the top daily newspapers (*New York Times, Washington Post, Los Angeles Times, Wall Street Journal, USA Today*); the big three weekly news magazines (*Time, Newsweek, U.S. News and World Report*); the major networks (ABC, CBS, NBC, Fox, CNN, MSNBC); and the major wire services (Associated Press, United Press International, Reuters). During the early part of the 20th century, the most notable reporters in Washington included such luminaries as Walter Lippmann and Arthur Krock; during the last 50 years many high-profile journalists have covered the White House beat, including James Reston of the *New York Times,* David Broder of the *Washington Post,* Helen Thomas of UPI, Sam Donaldson of ABC, and Wolf Blitzer of CNN, to name just a few. The growth in the size of the White House press corps has also contributed to the expansion of both the White House Press Office and the WHITE HOUSE OFFICE OF COMMUNICATIONS, which must handle the increased demands of Washington reporters.

Further reading: Edwards, George C., III. *The Public Presidency: The Pursuit of Popular Support.* New York: St. Martin's Press, 1983; Emery, Michael, and Edwin Emery. *The Press and America: An Interpretive History of the Mass Media.* Boston: Allyn and Bacon, 1996; Kessel, John H. *Presidents, the Presidency, and the Political Environment.* Washington, D.C.: CQ Press, 2001.

—Lori Cox-Han

White House press secretary

As the importance of the president's relationship with the press increased throughout the 20th century, so too did the role of the White House press secretary in managing that relationship. The press secretary heads the White House press office and is responsible for preparing press releases, coordinating news, and holding daily press briefings for the White House press corps. This person must also facilitate the needs of reporters who cover the president and must sometimes meet with the reporters privately to provide information about the president's legislative agenda and policy goals.

The press secretary also serves as an important public spokesperson for the president and is a liaison between reporters and the White House. As the job has continued to evolve, it is especially important for press secretaries to accurately reflect the views and policy goals of the administration. However, press secretaries are handicapped in this regard if the president or other top administration advisers do not provide him or her with up-to-date or accurate information to be provided to the White House press corps. To effectively perform the duties of the job, a press secretary must maintain credibility with members of the press in both the quality of information provided and facilitating access to top administration officials.

Some press secretaries have had closer working relationships with the presidents they have served than others, and some, but not all, have been considered top advisers to the presidents in setting their strategies for handling the press. George Akerson, appointed by Herbert HOOVER in 1929, was the first official White House press secretary. Stephen Early, serving during the administration of Franklin D. ROOSEVELT, and James HAGERTY, press secretary to Dwight EISENHOWER, were considered two of the most capable of all press secretaries ever to hold the position. Both were former journalists themselves, and both had close working relationships with their respective bosses, which earned each of them the necessary respect and credibility among members of the White House press corps. Hagerty was particularly a close adviser to Eisenhower and played a crucial role in the public relations strategy surrounding the president's heart attack in 1954; his effective CRISIS MANAGEMENT helped to avoid public panic over Eisenhower's condition. Pierre Salinger, press secretary to John F. KENNEDY, was influential in developing the television strategy, including live coverage of press conferences, utilized by Kennedy during the early 1960s as television began to gain more prominence in presidential politics.

The difficulties associated with the job can become obvious when presidents are not always forthcoming with essential information, as with the growing creditability gap that Lyndon JOHNSON perpetuated during the VIETNAM WAR or his refusal to provide the press with advance information about his travel plans. Each of Johnson's four press secretaries (Salinger, George Reedy, Bill Moyers, and George Christian) were at various times put to task by the White House press corps for the lack or inaccuracy of information given to them by Johnson or other advisers. Presidential scandals can also provide a difficult situation for the press secretary as they are point person for providing information to the press. Notable examples include Ron Ziegler's lack of factual information as NIXON's press secretary during WATERGATE, and Mike McCurry's attempts to positively spin the public scandal surrounding Bill CLINTON's IMPEACHMENT. Ron Nessen, a former journalist, had a difficult relationship with the press as Gerald FORD's press secretary. Nessen, who was known for his quick temper with members of the press, often exacerbated the already hostile situation between the White House and reporters that existed following the Watergate scandal and Nixon's overall inaccessibility to the press.

Despite Ford's attempts to provide a more open relationship between himself and reporters, Nessen lost credibility in the eyes of the press in his attempts to inflate the actions and accomplishments of Ford. Both Jody Powell, Jimmy CARTER's press secretary, and Marlin Fitzwater, who served both Ronald REAGAN and George H. W. Bush, were considered effective in the job due to the respect they earned among members of the White House press corps and their attempts to attend to the day-to-day needs of reporters in meeting their deadlines. Dee Dee Myers, the first of four press secretaries during the Clinton administration, became the first woman to hold the job in 1993.

Further reading: Edwards, George C., III. *The Public Presidency: The Pursuit of Popular Support.* New York: St. Martin's Press, 1983; Emery, Michael, and Edwin Emery. *The Press and America: An Interpretive History of the Mass Media.* Boston: Allyn and Bacon, 1996; Kessel, John H. *Presidents, the Presidency, and the Political Environment.* Washington, D.C.: CQ Press, 2001.

—Lori Cox-Han

White House scheduling office

The most precious commodity in the White House is the president's time. Crowds of petitioners compete for this scarce resource (usually a thousand a week); correspondingly there has to be a very strict White House staff procedure for allocating it. The scheduling office, typically headed by a deputy assistant to the president with a staff of 11, manages this process under the close supervision of the CHIEF OF STAFF. An inviolable rule is that no other person in the White House makes scheduling commitments except these two officers. "Even President [George H. W.] Bush would not put anything on his schedule without calling me!" explained his scheduler.

Of course a fraction of the president's day is preordained as routine: the daily NATIONAL SECURITY briefing, for example. For nonroutine appointments, there are several steps in the process.

First, every proposal for a piece of the schedule must be in writing. Oral arrangements carry too great a risk of miscommunication and dropped balls.

Second, every such proposal must be sponsored/ endorsed by a senior White House staff officer. The Legislative Affairs director signs off on every congressional schedule-appointment; the NATIONAL SECURITY ADVISER approves the recommended meeting with every foreign VIP, the Intergovernmental Affairs director evaluates the request of any governor.

One of the scheduling office's functions is to look ahead—months, perhaps years ahead—and try to estimate not only the known and easily identifiable events in which the president will normally participate, but to put its finger on the goals, the prime objectives the president wants to accomplish in his presidency—and try to plan for them and

make room to achieve them, while warding off the cascade of pressures from the lesser priorities.

A scheduling committee, chaired by the CHIEF OF STAFF (and including the schedulers of the VICE PRESIDENT and of the first lady) meets weekly to go over the pile of proposals. The governing standard is: Will this schedule item clearly support (or at least not detract from) the "policy theme" of the week to which the president and the White House are anxious to draw national attention? White House "sponsors" are quizzed, the political pros and cons deliberated. Campaign times raise other priorities, and periods of national crisis will of course wash out all nonurgent requests. Of the total thousand of requests coming in each week, 98 out of every 100 are denied. (Those meetings or appearances rejected but still deemed worthy may be assigned to appropriate CABINET officers to handle as surrogates.)

If a meeting is agreed to for the OVAL OFFICE, the chief of staff will have the deciding voice as to who must be sure to attend—and who will not. (If a policy debate is foreseen, the chief of staff may also schedule a rehearsal meeting in his own office—to flush out the agreed-upon or compromisable lesser matters and to hone sharply the arguments on the core substance.)

The approval of a schedule proposal is only the starting point of a carefully orchestrated procedure, which the scheduling office manages. A scheduling "desk" officer tracks—and puts in writing—the arrangements and assignments for each event. If the occasion means that the president is to leave the White House grounds, the SECRET SERVICE is notified. If remarks are appropriate, the speechwriters are alerted. The responsible White House office is assigned to prepare briefing materials for the boss. If the residence or the south lawn are to be used, the social office takes responsibility for the arrangements. If the scheduled event is a newsmaker, the press secretary will be alerted and the communications office will include notice of this occasion in its weekly "amplification" calls to the various cabinet departments.

In drawing up the schedule, there is always caution: Is the president being given enough quiet time of his own to think, to read, to deliberate? In the end, will the schedule reflect not the allegedly worthy "activities" sought for by others, but the *achievements* of the president himself? That is the overriding criterion.

A little-known officer on the scheduling office staff is the presidential diarist. To her come reports from the telephone operators, the ushers, the Secret Service, and the Office of Oval Office Operations, so that she can put on her computer a minute-by-minute record of the president's working life: everybody who met with him or talked with him on the telephone, when and on what subject, when his day started and when it ended. The result is an exceedingly useful compendium for current scheduling purposes and for the archivists of the future.

Further reading: Patterson, Bradley H. *Ring of Power.* New York: Basic Books, 1988; ————. *The White House Staff: Inside the West Wing and Beyond.* Washington, D.C.: Brookings, 2000.

—Bradley H. Patterson

White House website

The first White House website was inaugurated during the CLINTON presidency. While the White House web page has yet to realize its full potential as a means to engage the public more actively in interactive governance, it has developed new applications and complexity during its seven years of existence. Unveiled in October of 1994, the Clinton site evolved and kept pace with the rapid development of the Internet revolution. Anticipating the potential for interaction between the citizenry and their government brought forth by the Internet, the Clinton administration established a White House director for e-mail and electronic publishing in 1993 to create a White House website and to encourage e-mail contacts from the public to the White House.

The web page offered opportunities for the public to receive White House press briefings, policy speeches and statements, proposed legislation, major documents such as annual budgets, links with other EXECUTIVE BRANCH agencies, and radio addresses. Links to a "virtual library," which offered opportunities to search for documents by type, date, and keyword, were also provided. On a lighter note, the site offered virtual tours of the White House, audio messages from the president, a children's section including information about Socks, the first family's pet, and the opportunity for children to send e-mail messages to the first family.

Within a short time, the website was attracting attention from the rapidly growing Internet community, with a million hits being recorded in a six-month period in 1995 and 900,000 connections in one month in 1996. A study in 1997 concluded that the White House website dramatically increased public access to information regarding Clinton administration policies and assisted the public in seeking information from the EXECUTIVE BRANCH. By the end of President Clinton's second term, interactivity had increased. A specially constructed web section designed around the January 2000 STATE OF THE UNION ADDRESS provided background information related to the policy proposals in the address through links to other web pages. So too, the public was given an opportunity to provide feedback and views through e-mail messages to the White House.

When George W. BUSH took office in January 2001, the first White House website "cybertransition" took place.

Instantaneously, all Clinton site documents, pictures, and information links were transferred to an archival site under the auspices of the NATIONAL ARCHIVES. In its place appeared a much more basic initial site for President Bush. A couple of months into the Bush administration, the website was criticized as not measuring up to its predecessor with respect to both availability and interactivity. In response, an improved site was relaunched at the beginning of September 2001. The new site featured Spanish translations, sections for children, audio and video of recent presidential speeches, a voice synthesizer for the visually impaired, photo essays of President Bush's first 100 days in office, and press briefings categorized by subject matter.

Further reading: Davis, Richard. *The Web of Politics: The Internet's Impact on the American Political System.* New York: Oxford University Press, 1999; Diamond, Edwin, and Robert H. Silverman. *White House of Your House: Media and Politics in Virtual America.* Cambridge, Mass.: MIT Press, 1995.

—Shelley Lynne Tomkin

Wiener v. United States, 357 U.S. 349 (1958)

The Supreme Court case was the third in a series of 20th-century decisions that defined the parameters of presidential REMOVAL POWER. It followed the *MYERS V. U.S.* (1926) and *HUMPHREY'S EXECUTIVE V. UNITED STATES* (1935) decisions. In the latter case, the Court unanimously ruled that it was unconstitutional for the president to remove a member of the Federal Trade Commission—an EXECUTIVE BRANCH regulatory agency—without cause. The Humphrey ruling represented the first significant limitation on presidential removal authority; the Wiener decision continued the trend.

The circumstances of the Wiener case began in 1948, when President Harry TRUMAN created the War Claims Commission as a quasi-judicial body charged with adjudicating individual and organizational claims for compensation emanating from America's participation in WORLD WAR II. The commission was to be composed of three persons nominated by the president and confirmed by the Senate. The term of office of members was to expire after the deadline for filing claims, which would have allowed originally appointed personnel to serve until March 30, 1955.

Commission member Myron Wiener was nominated by President Truman in February 1950 and confirmed in June of that year. Dwight EISENHOWER, elected president in 1952, sought to replace War Claims Commission members in late 1953, ostensibly with Republican partisans. When Wiener and another commission member refused to resign, they were fired by Eisenhower. Wiener led a challenge to the action, asserting that commissioner terms were fixed and not based on party affiliation. After a controversy ensued over the fired commissioners and Congress delayed in naming replacements, the Eisenhower White House created another body, the Foreign Claims Settlement Commission, as part of the 1954 Reorganization Plan. When the plan became effective in July 1954, the Eisenhower administration terminated the War Claims Commission and shortly thereafter withdrew the list of nominees.

In 1954 a District Court dismissed Wiener's suit; an appeal was likewise dismissed that year. In 1956 the Court of Claims dismissed Wiener's action. But on June 30, 1958, a unanimous Supreme Court reversed the Court of Claims ruling. In his opinion on behalf of the Court, Justice Felix Frankfurter noted the similarity between the case and *Humphrey's Executor* as it pertained to the type of executive branch agency involved. He contended that presidents do not have a unilateral right to fire subordinates in the absence of statutory removal language. Just as the Wiener decision was influenced by the precedent set in *Humphrey's Executor v. U.S.*, so Wiener impacted on two REMOVAL POWER cases decided a generation later, *Bowsher v. Synar* (1986) and *Morrison v. Olson* (1988).

Further reading: *Bowsher v. Synar*, 478 U.S. 714 (1986); Corwin, Edward S. *The President's Removal Power Under the Constitution.* New York: National Municipal League, 1927; Hoff, Samuel B. "The President's Removal Power: Eisenhower and the War Claims Commission Controversy." *Congress and the Presidency* 18, no. 1 (Spring 1991): 37–53; *Humphrey's Executor v. United States*, 295 U.S. 602 (1935); Jones, Norville. "Constitutional Law—President's Power to Remove Member of Adjudicatory Agency When Statute Creating Body is Silent on Removal Question." *George Washington Law Review* 27 (1958): 129–132; *Morrison v. Olson*, 487 U.S. 654 (1988); *Myers v. United States*, 272 U.S. 52 (1926).

—Samuel B. Hoff

Wildavsky, Aaron (1930–1993)

Aaron Bernard Wildavsky (May 31, 1930–Sept. 4, 1993), born in Brooklyn, the son of Ukrainian immigrants, was a graduate of Brooklyn College who earned his M.A. and Ph.D. at Yale. As a scholar of the presidency he is best known for his coauthorship with Nelson W. Polsby of *Presidential Elections: Strategies of American Electoral Politics* (1964), which immediately became a textbook best-seller and appeared in eight revisions prior to his death; his 1996 article in *Transactions,* "The Two Presidencies," which suggested that a president has substantial autonomy in foreign policy but Congress imposes greater constraints on the domestic side; and his *Politics of the Budgetary Process* (1964), which emphasized the human, incremental factors of national budgeting. After multiple revisions, the book

was replaced by his *The New Politics of the Budgetary Process* (2d ed., 1992).

Unlike conventional textbooks, *Presidential Elections* demonstrated how voters' choices were influenced by nominating rules, why particular candidates were successful, and why the ELECTORAL COLLEGE was not likely to be abolished or even reformed. Whether one agreed with his Two Presidencies theory or not, it stimulated numerous commentaries.

In his latter years, Wildavsky's political science research was primarily in public policy, where he became a frequent critic of environmentalism and what he considered its underlying antidemocratic premises.

Further reading: Polsby, Nelson W. "The Contributions of President Aaron Wildavsky." *PS* 18, no. 4 (1985); ———, and Aaron B. Wildavsky. *Presidential Elections: Strategies of American Electoral Politics.* New York: Scribner, 1964; Shull, Steven A., ed. *The Two Presidencies: A Quarter Century Assessment.* Chicago: Nelson-Hall Publishers, 1991; Wildavsky, Aaron B. *The New Politics of the Budgetary Process*, 2d ed. New York: HarperCollins, 1992; ———. *The Politics of the Budgetary Process.* Boston: Little, Brown, 1964; ———. "The Two Presidencies." *TransAction* 4 (December 1966): 7–14.

—Thomas P. Wolf

Wilson, Edith (1872–1961) *first lady*

Edith Wilson was the second wife of President Woodrow Wilson, and first lady following the death of Wilson's first wife. Born in Virginia, Edith Bolling married a Washington, D.C. jeweler named Norman Galt, who died suddenly in 1908, leaving his profitable business to his widow. Wilson's first wife, Ellen, died in August 1914. Mutual friends introduced Edith to the president in March 1915, and romance quickly followed. The two were married that December. Edith proved to be an able first lady. She took a great interest in her husband's success and served as his close confidante, ultimately usurping the role created by Colonel Edward House. In turn, Wilson shared state secrets with her.

Edith's most controversial role came during the Senate debate over the TREATY OF VERSAILLES. Edith accompanied Wilson to Paris for the peace negotiations in early 1919, and she went with him on his national tour later that year urging Senate ratification of the treaty. Illness caused Wilson to abandon his tour, and in October 1919 he suffered a large, debilitating stroke. Firmly rejecting RESIGNATION as an option, Edith, along with Wilson's personal physician, Admiral Cary Grayson, hid the true extent of Wilson's illness.

In effect, Edith became the gatekeeper for the president, screening all papers, business, and visitors. She decided who would have access to the president, and few saw Wilson during this time. Edith played a significant role in approving new CABINET selections, as well as supporting Wilson in his rejection of compromise on the LEAGUE OF NATIONS. Some believed that she ran the country for the balance of Wilson's second term, and she was the subject of a variety of verbal attacks, including charges that she was the "presidentress" or the "first woman president," and that she was running a "petticoat government." It remains uncertain how much power Edith actually wielded, and she maintained that she never made any important independent decisions. If nothing else, however, her zealous role as gatekeeper prevented Wilson from having access to the normal range of advice.

Edith survived her husband by 38 years and remained active in Democratic politics. She died in 1961.

Further reading: Smith, Gene. *When the Cheering Stopped: The Last Years of Woodrow Wilson.* New York: Morrow, 1964; Weaver, Judith L. "Edith Bolling Wilson as First Lady: A Study in the Power of Personality, 1919–1920." *Presidential Studies Quarterly* (1985); Wilson, Edith Bolling. *My Memoir.* Indianapolis: Bobbs-Merrill, 1939.

—David A. Crockett

Wilson, Henry (1812–1875) *U.S. vice president*

An influential CIVIL WAR–era senator from Massachusetts, Wilson was one of the nation's leading voices against slavery. First elected to the Massachusetts legislature as a Whig, Wilson left the party in 1848 over the issue of slavery and helped form the Free Soil Party. In 1854 he joined the American, or Know-Nothing, Party but left in 1955 to join the Republicans. He served in the Senate from 1855 to 1873 and during the CIVIL WAR was chairman of the Senate Committee on Military Affairs. An advocate of harsh treatment for the Southern states after the Civil War, he voted for the IMPEACHMENT of President Andrew JOHNSON in 1868.

In 1873 Wilson was nominated to run on the ticket as President GRANT's vice president. Though tainted by accusations of corruption in the CRÉDIT MOBILIER SCANDAL, Wilson survived the charges and became VICE PRESIDENT. Just after the election he suffered a severe stroke. He attempted to return to his duties but was unable to effectively assume his responsibilities. A second stroke on November 22, 1875, ended his life, and left the vice presidency vacant for a year and a half.

Wilson, James (1742–1798) *Supreme Court justice*

James Wilson was one of only six signers of both the Declaration of Independence and the Constitution, but he was also a land speculator, an able legal theorist, Pennsylvania representative to the Continental Congress, architect of the Pennsylvania Constitution of 1790, and an associate justice of the Supreme Court. One of the most theoretically systematic and enigmatic of the Founding figures, Wilson was loved by few, respected by many, and was often embroiled in controversy. He was burned in effigy, arrested twice, and hounded by his creditors in his final days.

Nicknamed "James de Caledonia," Wilson was born in Scotland and moved to the United States in 1757 after receiving his education at St. Andrews. After arriving in Pennsylvania, Wilson studied law with John Dickinson. In 1774 Wilson published *Considerations on the Nature and Extent of the Legislative Authority of the British Parliament,* in which he held that "All men are, by nature, equal and free." Wilson's reputation grew on account of this writing, and he was subsequently selected by Pennsylvania as a delegate to the Second Continental Congress. As the cry for independence from Great Britain grew, Wilson recommended a political arrangement similar to the present-day British Commonwealth but was willing to sign the Declaration of Independence.

Pennsylvania returned Wilson to Congress in 1785. It was owing to his position there that Wilson influenced the shaping of the Constitution in 1787. Wilson spoke more at the convention than any other person besides Gouverneur MORRIS, but his influence was more limited than that of several other delegates. His argument, for instance, that the chief goal of government was the improvement of the mind was altogether ignored. He chiefly influenced the structuring of FEDERALISM and the presidency. Wilson's "pyramid" theory of government called for a powerful general government that draws its power from the consent of the governed rather than from the states. Wilson held that states had lost their sovereignty when they had entered into compact with the Continental Congress. This argument convinced few people at the convention but likely shaped Abraham LINCOLN's understanding of the nature of the Union.

Wilson was a strong "presidentialist" at the CONSTITUTIONAL CONVENTION. Wilson called for a unitary presidency and an absolute presidential veto, and he argued against any Senate involvement in presidential appointments. He also argued arduously against House selection of the presidency. After the convention, Wilson was instrumental in securing Pennsylvania's ratification of the Constitution by his deft handling of questions about the document. His speech in its favor was widely influential throughout the states.

Wilson was picked by WASHINGTON to serve as an associate justice of the Supreme Court. A strong advocate of judicial review, Wilson penned an important opinion in *Chisholm v. Georgia,* a decision that led to the adoption of the Eleventh Amendment. In the 1790s Wilson's service on the Court became increasingly interrupted as he fled his creditors when his land deals fell through.

Further reading: Beer, Samuel. *To Make a Nation: The Rediscovery of American Federalism.* Cambridge, Mass.: Belknap Press of Harvard University Press, 1993; Bradford, M. E. *Founding Fathers.* Lawrence: University Press of Kansas, 1994; Smith, Page. *James Wilson: Founding Fathers.* Chapel Hill: University of North Carolina Press for the Institute of Early American History and Culture, 1956.

—Michael E. Bailey

Wilson, Woodrow (1856–1924) *twenty-eighth U.S. president*

The only president (1913–21) to have earned a Ph.D. (from Johns Hopkins University), Woodrow Wilson, who was president of Princeton University and reform governor of New Jersey, resumed the activist tone of presidential LEADERSHIP established by Teddy Roosevelt. At 5'11", 170 pounds, at times aloof, withdrawn, and temperamental, Wilson, like TR, added to the presidency and cemented the role of world leader into the office.

Wilson was a progressive, activist reformer, who used party and popular leadership to move Congress. He was also a wartime president who not only exerted extraconstitutional leadership in war but in the aftermath of the war promoted an expansive and idealistic peace.

TR called Wilson "a Byzantine logothete." One of the most complex and fascinating presidents in U.S. history, Wilson seemed motivated by a mix of Puritan idealism, burning ambition, and intellectual superiority. He saw the world in starkly simplistic terms as a struggle between good and evil. This made it difficult for Wilson to compromise.

In a way there were three different Wilson presidencies: the very successful domestic reformer of the first term; the very successful war president during WORLD WAR I; and the idealistic, but in the end tragic, crusader for world peace toward the end of his presidency.

Woodrow Wilson was a political scientist who got the opportunity to put his academic theories of the presidency into practice (and wouldn't all countries be better off if political scientists ran things . . .). In his twenties he wrote: "the President is at liberty, both in law and conscience, to be as big a man as he can." A quarter century later, Wilson had a chance to do just that.

Congressional Government (1885), Wilson's first book, was critical of the Founding Fathers and of the Constitution. They had so distributed power and responsibility as to make leadership virtually impossible:

> The forms of government in this country have always been unfavorable to the easy elevation of talent to a sta-

> tion of paramount authority; and those forms in their present crystallization are more unfavorable than ever to the toleration of the leadership of the few.

The president Wilson saw in the 1890s was a clerk; Wilson wanted him to be a leader. At the turn of the century, Wilson's thinking underwent a change. In a new edition of *Congressional Government*, written in 1900, Wilson argues that the war with Spain had set in motion changes in the distribution of power that altered his earlier ideas. The war had brought the United States into global politics, and:

> [w]hen foreign affairs play a prominent part in the politics and policies of a nation, its executive must of necessity be its guide, must utter every initial judgment, take every first step of action, supply the information upon which it is to act, suggest and in large measure control its conduct. The President of the United States is now, as of course, at the front of affairs.

When Wilson delivered the lectures that were to be published in 1908 as *Constitutional Government in the United States* he was more optimistic about the possibilities of leadership. He saw the role of the president as:

> [t]he leader of his party and the guide of the nation in political purpose, and therefore in legal action.
>
> [The president was now seen] as the unifying force in our complex system.
>
> [The president's] is the only national voice in our affairs. Let him once win the admiration and confidence of the country and no other single force can withstand him. . . . If he rightly interprets the national thought and boldly insists upon it, he is irresistible; the country never feels the zest for action so much as when its President is of such insight and calibre. Its instinct is for unified action and it craves a single leader.
>
> [The President's] office is anything he has the sagacity and force to make it.
>
> The Constitution bids him speak, and times of stress and change must more and more thrust upon him the attitude of originator of policies. His is the vital place of action in the system.

Wilson broke precedent by personally addressing a special session of Congress—the first time this occurred since the presidency of John ADAMS. This was the beginning of an annual tradition, when the president delivers his STATE OF THE UNION to Congress himself.

In 1913, shortly after his inauguration, Woodrow Wilson held the first presidential PRESS CONFERENCE. Soon the press conference became institutionalized, and Wilson used this format to promote both himself and his policies.

Wilson aggressively pursued his legislative agenda in Congress. In his first term, he used party and popular leadership as a source of domestic reforms, known as the NEW FREEDOM. Legislation to break monopolies, assist unions, and lower tariffs were passed. Child labor laws, a newly created Federal Reserve, and a series of other laws all were passed as well. Wilson noted that "[i]t is only once in a generation that a people can be lifted above material things. That is why conservative government is on the saddle two-thirds of the time." Thus, when he became president he pushed and pushed hard to achieve as much as possible, but there was also a dark side to his leadership. Wilson's attitude about race relations led him further to impose segregation in several government departments, and his administration engaged a massive internal repression during World War I.

A Supreme Court test of the president's REMOVAL POWER was decided in *MYERS v. UNITED STATES*. In that case, Frank S. Myers was named a first-class postmaster by President Woodrow Wilson in 1917. In 1920 Wilson asked for Myer's resignation, but Myers refused. In February of that year, Myers was removed from office by order of the postmaster general, acting under direction of President Wilson. Myers protested, citing the act of Congress of July 12, 1876, which said that removal of a first-class postmaster could be effective only if the president acted with the consent of the Congress. Wilson neither requested nor received such consent.

The Supreme Court, with Chief Justice William H. TAFT writing the majority opinion, denied Myers's claim (brought by his heirs) and ruled in favor of the president's act of removal. Taft based his decision on the premise that this point was thoroughly argued by the First Congress (many members of which participated in the Constitutional Convention), and they had decided that the president did have the removal power. Taft argued that:

> The ordinary duties of officers prescribed by statute come under the general administrative control of the president by virtue of the general grant to him of the executive power, and he may properly supervise and guide their construction of the statues under which they act in order to secure that unitary and uniform execution of the laws which Article II of the Constitution evidently contemplated in vesting general executive power in the President alone. . . . Finding such officers to be negligent and inefficient, the President should have the power to remove them.

Wilson's great success as a reformer during his first term led to easy reelection, as Wilson promised to keep the United States out of war in Europe. But war was in the cards, and Wilson soon became a war president. During

President Woodrow Wilson and his wife, Edith Bolling Galt Wilson, riding to his second inauguration in the backseat of a convertible, March 4, 1917 *(Library of Congress)*

the war, Wilson demonstrated skill and determination. On January 8, 1918, he delivered his "FOURTEEN POINTS" speech to Congress, a comprehensive postwar plan for peace, calling for greater justice for small nations, self-determination for "enslaved" nations, and arbitration of international dispute.

After the war, Wilson went to work building a lasting peace. He went to Europe to negotiate not only a settlement to the war but a plan for peace as well. The result was the TREATY OF VERSAILLES, which Wilson brought back to the United States for Senate approval. (He won a Nobel Peace Prize for his efforts). The Senate, now controlled by Republicans, balked at the plan, rejecting Wilson's scheme, along with the LEAGUE OF NATIONS the president was proposing.

Wilson took his case directly to the people. World War I was to "make the world safe for democracy," and Wilson was not about to let the Senate interfere with his ambitious and idealistic plans for a League of Nations and postwar peace. Wilson was too rigid to compromise. He wanted it all and would settle for nothing less. His inability or unwillingness to compromise with Senate Republicans doomed the treaty.

As matters went from bad to worse, Wilson became more and more rigid. He took an exhausting national tour on behalf of "his" treaty. Soon fatigue and illness overtook him. Finally, he suffered a stroke that left him bedridden.

During his incapacitation, Edith WILSON, his wife, all but ran the country, leading critics to protest, "We have a petticoat government." The physically weakened Wilson remained uncompromising about the League of Nations. His all-or-nothing attitude led to nothing. Wilson's presidency ended with a debilitated and disappointed president, unable to achieve his final and biggest victory.

If failure marked the end of the Wilson presidency, we should not forget how much success there was: major domestic reforms, victory in war, an idealistic (if unsuccessful) hope for the future. "Whatever his failings," wrote historian John Morton Blum, "he phrased and symbolized some of the best hopes of liberalism and its possibilities for the country and the world." Wilson played the part of president as prime minister, leading party, public, and legislature. He expanded and strengthened the presidency. He demonstrated that the presidency could truly be a place of moral leadership.

Further reading: Baker, Ray S. *Woodrow Wilson: Life and Letters.* Garden City, N.Y.: Doubleday, 1927–39; Clements, Kendrick A. *The Presidency of Woodrow Wilson.* Lawrence: University Press of Kansas, 1992; Knock, Thomas J. *To End All Wars: Woodrow Wilson and the Quest for a New World Order.* New York: Oxford University Press, 1992; Link, Arthur S. *Woodrow Wilson.* Princeton, N.J.: Princeton University Press, 1947–1965.

Works Progress Administration (WPA)

Established via an EXECUTIVE ORDER in May of 1935 by Franklin D. ROOSEVELT executive order, as an offshoot of the Emergency Relief Appropriations Act, the WPA was designed to respond to the massive unemployment of the GREAT DEPRESSION by creating government-funded jobs. Headed by Harry HOPKINS, the WPA reflected FDR's desire to promote work over welfare. The WPA faced severe political opposition from business (which warned of unfair competition for wages and workers), labor (which feared loss of its membership and low wages), and from conservatives (who opposed government-created jobs programs). In spite of this vocal opposition, the WPA did make a difference in the lives of millions of poor Americans and in the development of the American infrastructure. WPA

projects led to the construction of 350 airports, a half million miles of new roads, nearly 80,000 new bridges, more than 8,000 parks, and thousands of new buildings. In 1939 it was renamed the Works Projects Administration.

World War I

World War I, 1914–18, marked in many ways the dramatic expansion of presidential power. Ironically, it exposed the limits of presidential power as well.

Prior to the start of World War I, the United States was an emerging imperial power. While President Woodrow WILSON campaigned for his second term on the theme "he kept us out of war," when the United States was finally drawn into the war, Wilson greatly expanded presidential authority. He broke precedent and delivered his call for a declaration of war in person to the Congress. No president had so addressed the Congress since John ADAMS.

Wilson took control of the war effort and heightened the use of presidential rhetoric, calling for "New Freedom" reforms and emerging as a leading international spokesman for reform. Many scholars credit Wilson with using the president's BULLY PULPIT to create what is called the RHETORICAL PRESIDENCY.

As a wartime president, Wilson sought and used power to the hilt. His "FOURTEEN POINTS" address in 1918 sought to reshape the course of international DIPLOMACY for a postwar world. At the Paris Peace Conference he pushed for the creation of a LEAGUE OF NATIONS and was hailed as the chief spokesman for reform, but his vision of a new world met resistance in the U.S. Congress. Wilson, a Democrat, arrogantly refused to bargain and deal with Congress over provisions in the postwar regime, and the Congress refused to ratify the TREATY OF VERSAILLES, thus preventing U.S. entry into the new League of Nations. For a time, the United States retreated into ISOLATIONISM, and Wilson, ill and defeated, sank into a state of depression.

During the war, Wilson greatly added to the power of the presidency. He also became an international leader and much admired figure in the world, but at home, after the war, the Congress frustrated his dreams and put a halt to his efforts at forging world peace.

Further reading: Ambrosius, Lloyd E. *Wilsonian Statecraft: Theory and Practice of Liberal Internationalism during World War I.* Wilmington, Del.: SR Books, 1991; Ferrell, Robert H. *Woodrow Wilson and World War I, 1917–1921.* New York: Harper&Row, 1985; Kennedy, David M. *Over Here: The First World War and American Society.* New York: Oxford University Press, 1980; Schaffer, Ronald. *America in the Great War.* New York: Oxford University Press, 1991.

World War II

Like Abraham Lincoln in the CIVIL WAR, and Woodrow WILSON in WORLD WAR I, Franklin D. Roosevelt greatly expanded the scope of presidential power during World War II.

WORLD WAR II also transformed the United States into the dominant, or hegemonic, power of the world. This added to the powers and responsibilities of the presidency and contributed to the president-centric system of the COLD WAR era.

Prior to the war, the United States was an isolationist power, still focused on efforts to get out of the GREAT DEPRESSION and not inclined to get involved in "Europe's war." But Roosevelt coaxed, prodded, and pushed the nation toward support of England, and with the passage of the LEND-LEASE ACT in 1941, the United States began down the road to all-out involvement.

With the surprise attack in Pearl Harbor by the Japanese on December 7, 1941, the war began for the United States. In war, presidents grab and are given extraordinary power. Roosevelt exercised this power with great skill. Working closely with British Prime Minister Winston Churchill, Roosevelt led the way to the defeat of Germany and the Axis powers. He also shattered precedent by seeking a third, then fourth, term as president. He expanded the powers and prerogatives of the presidency during the war and emerged as *the* leader of the alliance. Roosevelt authorized the research and development of the first atomic weapon but died shortly before it became operational. The final victory would be overseen by FDR's successor, Harry TRUMAN. After the war, the United States became *the* world power, challenged for dominance by the Soviet Union. Thus, the end of World War II reconfigured international power and led to the start of the cold war between the United States and the Soviet Union.

Further reading: Blum, John M. *V Was for Victory: Politics and American Culture during World War II.* New York: Harcourt Brace Jovanovich, 1976; Burns, James MacGregor. *Roosevelt: The Soldier of Freedom.* New York: Harcourt Brace Jovanovich, 1970; Larrabee, Eric. *Commander-in-Chief: Franklin Delano Roosevelt, His Lieutenants, and Their War.* New York: Harper & Row, 1987.

X

XYZ Affair

The XYZ Affair refers to the attempt of three secret agents (X, Y, and Z) acting on behalf of the French foreign minister, Prince Talleyrand, to extort bribes from three American envoys sent to France on a 1797 peace mission. Hostilities between the United States and France had begun to escalate in the 1790s during George WASHINGTON's administration. The French were particularly angered by JAY'S TREATY of 1796, which moved the United States closer to France's enemy, Great Britain. The French, feeling betrayed by the United States, started to attack American ships and seize their cargoes. In response, Washington appointed Charles Cotesworth Pinckney as minister to France to negotiate a peace settlement. Pinckney's trip to Paris was in vain. The French government refused to meet with him.

In 1797 the new president, John ADAMS, sent another peace mission to France. In addition to Pinckney, he asked two other distinguished politicians, Elbridge GERRY and John Marshall, to join the mission. The three envoys arrived in Paris in October 1797 and requested a meeting with the French government. After waiting three days to be seen, the envoys met very briefly with French Foreign Minister Talleyrand. Then, a few days after this initial meeting, the three secret agents visited the American envoys to relay Talleyrand's terms of negotiations. The agents' names were Jean Conrad Hottinguer, Pierre Bellamy, and Lucien Hauteval, but the American envoys called them X, Y, and Z in their official dispatches. The secret agents made the following demands of the Americans: In order for negotiations to proceed, a bribe of $250,000 to Talleyrand would be needed. In addition, the Americans would have to provide a loan of $10,000,000 for the Republic of France as compensation for Adams's hostile remarks about France in a speech to Congress in May 1797. When Agent X asked if America would accept this offer, Pinckney indignantly replied, "No! No! Not a sixpence."

In March 1798 Adams received official dispatches from the American envoys in France, some of which were written in code, relaying the events that had transpired. After decoding the dispatches, Adams addressed Congress, informing them that the peace mission to France had failed and asking for war preparations against France. Upon request of the Republicans, who had always been more sympathetic to the French cause than the Federalists and who were suspicious of Adams's motives, the president released the full text of the dispatches to Congress. These dispatches were soon leaked to the press. When the public found out about the XYZ Affair, there was a large groundswell of support for Adams's war efforts. Two years of naval conflict with France followed before a peace settlement was reached in 1800.

Further reading: DeConde, Alexander. *The Quasi-War: The Politics and Diplomacy of the Undeclared War with France, 1797–1801.* New York: Scribner, 1966; Elkins, Stanley, and Eric McKitrick. *The Age of Federalism: The Early American Republic, 1788–1800.* New York: Oxford University Press, 1993; Stinchcombe, William C. *The XYZ Affair.* Westport, Conn.: Greenwood Press, 1980.

—Terri Bimes

Y

Yakus v. United States, 321 U.S. 414 (1944)

During WORLD WAR II, the head of the OFFICE OF PRICE ADMINISTRATION set limits on prices. His authority to do so was delegated to the executive by Congress through the Emergency Price Control Act of 1942 and the Inflation Control Act of 1942.

This delegation of power was challenged by Yakus, who was accused of selling beef at prices in excess of government regulations, but the Supreme Court found in *Yakus v. United States* that Congress could delegate some powers to the executive under prescribed circumstances.

Yalta Conference

From February 3 to 4, 1945, the "Big Three," Franklin D. ROOSEVELT, Churchill, and Stalin, met at the Crimean resort city of Yalta to discuss issues relating to the post-WORLD WAR II peace. Issues such as postwar reparations, the division of Germany, the UNITED NATIONS, and the fate of the eastern European nations were discussed. Also at Yalta, it was decided that the Soviet Union would enter the war against Japan.

Youngstown Sheet and Tube Company v. Sawyer, 343 U.S. 579 (1952) (The Steel Seizure Case)

In April 1952, the Supreme Court faced the question of whether a president possesses inherent EXECUTIVE POWER in times of emergency. This issue arose when President Harry TRUMAN seized the nation's privately owned steel mills after the companies announced that they would halt production because of a labor dispute. The United States was engaged in the KOREAN WAR at the time, and there was a continuing need for steel production in order to insure that American military forces would be supplied with munitions.

By EXECUTIVE ORDER on the eve of the announced strike, President Truman authorized Secretary of Commerce Charles Sawyer to seize and administer the steel mills. Truman claimed sweeping authority from the Constitution, laws, and as president and COMMANDER IN CHIEF of the armed forces. He did *not* act under the TAFT-HARTLEY ACT of 1947, which was the federal law that regulated labor disputes and which provided the president with an option to call for an 80-day cooling-off period in such circumstances. Moreover, when Congress enacted Taft-Harley, it had considered and rejected a proposal to provide the president with the authority to seize private property during emergencies. For the six Supreme Court justices in the majority that declared Truman's action unconstitutional, it was this expressed refusal by Congress in 1947 to extend seizure authority to presidents that was the reason upon which all six agreed that Truman's action was constitutionally invalid.

The steel companies sued the president, and the federal district court enjoined the enforcement of the executive order and declared the seizure unconstitutional. The Court of Appeals for the District of Columbia stayed the lower court opinion, and three days later, the Supreme Court agreed to hear the appeal. Within the next five weeks, the Court heard oral argument and delivered its 6-3 decision in *Youngstown Sheet and Tube Company v. Sawyer.*

The central issue in the case was whether there was valid authority for Truman's action. In Justice Black's opinion for the Court, he posited that authority "must stem either from an act of Congress or from the Constitution itself." Black noted that there was no statute that expressly extended such authority to the president and none from which it could be implied. He then proceeded to reject Truman's claims for authority from the Constitution—claims that were not based in any expressed provision, but, rather, "implied from the aggregate of his powers under the Constitution." Truman maintained that this "aggregate of powers" was drawn from primary reliance on three clauses in Article II: the executive power clause in Section 1; the commander in chief clause in Section 2; and the "take care" clause in Section 3.

The Court refuted all of these claims. It found that presidential seizure of private property by executive order amounted to "law-making," and that "the Constitution is neither silent nor equivocal about who shall make laws which the President is to execute." Moreover, determining the measures taken to resolve labor disputes, where national interests were involved, was "a job for the Nation's lawmakers, not for its military authorities." Finally, the Court rejected reliance on the "take care" clause by noting that the president's power under this clause "refutes the idea that he is to be a lawmaker."

Each of the other five justices in the majority wrote separate concurring opinions, although Jackson's concurrence is the most frequently cited for its analysis of the intersecting nature of presidential and congressional powers and for his framework of the circumstances that should guide these branches in their use of power, relative to each other. Although the president was the chief loser in the outcome of this case, Congress did not escape unscathed, either, as Jackson cautioned that "[we] may say that power to legislate for emergencies belongs in the hands of Congress, but only Congress itself can prevent power from slipping through its fingers."

Chief Justice Vinson, joined by Justices Reed and Minton in his dissent, maintained that other presidents had acted during emergencies in the past without congressional authority to protect legislative programs until Congress was able to act, and that such precedents (such as *U.S. v. Midwest Oil Company*) had been approved by the Court. This line of reasoning by the dissent ran completely counter to the majority by maintaining that as long as there was no statue expressly *prohibiting* the president from acting, it was permissible for him to take actions during a national emergency *until* Congress could act. The majority, however, interpreted Congress's refusal to extend seizure power to the president from the Taft-Hartley debates as sufficient evidence of congressional intent to disallow this action, whereas the dissent was unpersuaded without an express prohibition of executive seizure.

The issue for the majority would have been much less clear—and more pristine, constitutionally—if Congress had not addressed it during the Taft-Hartley debates. Then, the justices would have had to confront the pure issue of whether a president may act during a time of crisis on his own inherent authority and upon his singular determination that the gravity of the circumstance demanded immediate, unilateral action. In fact, careful examination of the opinions of the concurring justices in *Youngstown* reveal that perhaps as many as four of them would agree that, in the absence of congressional intent, they recognized some inherent executive power to act during national crises. When these votes are added to the three dissenters, the result is that there is considerable support for such presidential action, as long as it does not conflict with Congress. The legacy of this case, then, is a far more mixed one that it seems at first glance. It does make clear to presidents that their actions are subject to judicial review, and that even in emergencies, they may not act contrary to Congress's expressed or implied intent. But where Congress has not acted and where its intent is unknown, the president has some latitude to act during emergencies.

Further reading: Fisher, Louis, and Neal Devins. *Political Dynamics of Constitutional Law,* 2d ed. St. Paul, Minn.: West Publishing Co., 1996, pp. 172–182; Marcus, Maeva. *Truman and the Steel Seizure Case.* New York: Columbia University Press, 1977.

—Nancy Kassop

Appendix I

SECTIONS OF THE U.S. CONSTITUTION DEALING WITH THE PRESIDENCY

Article II—The Executive Article
Nature and Scope of Presidential Power

Section 1: The executive Power shall be vested in a President of the United States of America. He shall hold his Office during the Term of four Years and, together with the Vice President, chosen for the same Term, be elected as follows:

Each State shall appoint, in such Manner as the Legislature thereof may direct, a Number of Electors, equal to the whole Number of Senators and Representatives to which the State may be entitled in the Congress: but no Senator or Representative, or Person holding an Office of Trust or Profit under the United States, shall be appointed an Elector.

The Electors shall meet in their respective States, and vote by Ballot for two Persons, of whom one at least shall not be an Inhabitant of the same State with themselves. And they shall make a List of all the Persons voted for, and of the Number of Votes for each; which List they shall sign and certify, and transmit sealed to the Seat of the Government of the United States, directed to the President of the Senate. The President of the Senate shall, in the Presence of the Senate and House of Representatives, open all the Certificates, and the Votes shall then be counted. The Person having the greatest Number of Votes shall be the President, if such Number be a Majority of the whole Number of Electors appointed; and if there be more than one who have such Majority and have an equal Number of Votes, then the House of Representatives shall immediately choose by Ballot one of them for President;

and if no person have a Majority, then from the five highest on the List the said House shall in like Manner choose the President. But in choosing the President, the Votes shall be taken by States, the Representation from each State having one Vote; A quorum for this Purpose shall consist of a Member or Members from two thirds of the States, and a Majority of all the States shall be necessary to a Choice. In every case, after the Choice of the president, the person having the greatest Number of Votes of the Electors shall be the Vice President. But if there should remain two or more who have equal Vote, the Senate shall choose from them by ballot the Vice President.

The Congress may determine the Time of choosing the Electors, and the Day on which they shall give their Votes; which Day shall be the same throughout the United States.

No Person except a natural born Citizen, or a Citizen of the United States, at the time of the Adoption of this Constitution, shall be eligible to the Office of President; neither shall any Person be eligible to that Office who shall not have attained to the Age of thirty five Years, and been fourteen Years a Resident within the United States.

In Case of the Removal of the President from Office, or his Death, Resignation, or Inability to discharge the Powers and Duties of the said Office, same shall devolve on the Vice President, and the Congress may by Law provide for the Case of Removal, Death, Resignation, or Inability, both of the President and Vice President, declaring what Officer shall then act as President, and such Office shall act accordingly, until the Disability be removed, or a President shall be elected.

The President shall, at stated Times, receive for his Services, a Compensation, which shall neither be increased nor diminished during the Period of which he shall have been elected, and he shall not receive within that Period any other Emolument from the United States, or any of them.

Before he enter on the Execution of his Office, he shall take the following Oath or Affirmation:—"I do solemnly swear (or affirm) that I will faithfully execute the Office of President of the United States, and will to the best of my Ability, preserve, protect and defend the Constitution of the United States."

Powers and Duties of the President

Section 2: The President shall be the Commander in Chief of the Army and Navy of the United States, and of the Militia of the several States, when called into actual Service of the United States, he may require the Opinion, in writing, of the principal Officer in each of the executive Departments, upon any Subject relating to the Duties of their respective Offices, and he shall have the Power to grant Reprieves and Pardons for Offences against the United States, except in Cases of Impeachment.

He shall have Power, by and with the Advice and Consent of the Senate to make Treaties, provided two thirds of the Senators present concur; and he shall nominate, and by and with the Advice and Consent of the Senate, shall appoint Ambassadors, other public Ministers and Consuls, Judges of the Supreme Court, and all other Officers of the United States, whose Appointments are not herein otherwise provided for, and which shall be established by Law: but the Congress may by Law vest the Appointment of such inferior Officers, as they think proper, in the President alone, in the Courts of Law, or in the Heads of Departments.

The President shall have Power to fill up all Vacancies that may happen during the Recess of the Senate, by granting Commissions which shall expire at the End of their Session.

Section 3: He shall from time to time give to the Congress Information of the State of the Union, and recommend to their Consideration such Measures as he shall judge necessary and expedient; he may, on extraordinary Occasions, convene both Houses, or either of them, and in Case of Disagreement between them, with Respect of the Time of Adjournment, he may adjourn them to such Time as he shall think proper; he shall receive Ambassadors and other public Ministers; he shall take Care that the Laws be faithfully executed, and shall Commission all of the Officers of the United States.

Section 4: The President, Vice President and all civil Officers of the United States, shall be removed from Office on Impeachment for, and Conviction of, Treason, Bribery, or other High Crimes and Misdemeanors.

Amendment XII (1804)

The Electors shall meet in their respective states and vote by ballot for President and Vice President, one of whom, at least, shall not be an inhabitant of the same state with themselves; they shall name in their ballots the person voted for as President, and in distinct ballots the person voted for as Vice President, and they shall make distinct lists of persons voted for as President, and of all persons voted for as Vice President, and of the number of votes for each, which lists they shall sign and certify, and transmit sealed to the seat of the government of the United States, directed to the President of the Senate;—The President of the Senate shall, in presence of the Senate and House of Representatives, open all the certificates and the votes shall then be counted;—The person having the greatest number of votes for President, shall be the President, if such number be a majority of the whole number of Electors appointed; and if no person have such majority, then from the persons having the highest numbers not exceeding three on the list of those voted for as President, the House of Representatives shall choose immediately, by ballot, the President. But in choosing the President, the votes shall be taken by states, the representative from each state having one vote; a quorum for this purpose shall consist of a member or members from two thirds of the states, and a majority of all the states shall be necessary to a choice. [And if the House of Representatives shall not choose a President whenever the right of choice shall devolve upon them, before the fourth day of March next following, then the Vice President shall act as President, as in the case of the death or other constitutional disability of the President.]—The person having the greatest number of votes as Vice President, shall be the Vice President, if such number be a majority of the whole number of Electors appointed, and if no person have a majority, then from the two highest numbers on the list, the Senate shall choose the Vice President; a quorum for the purpose shall consist of two thirds of the whole number of Senators, and a majority of the whole number shall be necessary to a choice. But no person constitutionally ineligible to the office of President shall be eligible to that of Vice President of the United States.

Amendment XX (1933)
Section 1.

The terms of the President and Vice President shall end at noon on the 20th day of January, and the terms of Senators and Representatives at noon on the 3rd day of January, of the years in which such terms would have ended if this article had not been ratified; and the terms of their successors shall then begin.

Section 2.

The Congress shall assemble at least once in every year, and such meeting shall begin at noon on the 3rd day of January, unless they shall by law appoint a different day.

Section 3.

If, at the time fixed for the beginning of the term of the President, the President elect shall have died, the Vice President elect shall become President. If a President shall not have been chosen before the time fixed for the beginning of his term, or if the President elect shall have failed to qualify, then the Vice President elect shall act as a President until a President shall have qualified; and the Congress may by law provide for the case wherein neither a President elect nor a Vice President elect shall have qualified, declaring who shall then act as President, or the manner in which one who is to act shall be selected, and such person shall act accordingly until a President or Vice President shall have qualified.

Section 4.

The Congress may by law provide for the case of the death of any of the persons from whom the House of Representatives may choose a President whenever the right of choice shall have devolved upon them, and for the case of the death of any of the persons from which the Senate may choose a Vice President whenever the right of choice shall have devolved upon them.

Section 5.

Sections 1 and 2 shall take effect on the 15th day of October following the ratification of this article.

Section 6.

This article shall be inoperative unless it shall have been ratified as an amendment to the Constitution by the legislatures of three fourths of the several States within seven years from the date of its submission.

Amendment XXII (1951)
Section 1.

No person shall be elected to the office of the President more than twice, and no person who has held the office of President, or acted as President, for more than two years of a term to which some other person was elected President shall be elected to the office of the President more than once. But this Article shall not apply to any person holding the office of President when this Article was proposed by the Congress, and shall not prevent any person who may be

holding the office of President, or acting as President, during the term within which this Article becomes operative from holding the office of President or acting as President during the remainder of such term.

Section 2.

This article shall be inoperative unless it shall have been ratified as an amendment to the Constitution by the legislatures of three fourths of the several States within seven years from the date of its submission to the States by the Congress.

Amendment XXIII (1961)
Section 1.

The District constituting the seat of Government of the United States shall appoint in such manner as the Congress may direct:

A number of electors of President and Vice President equal to the whole number of Senators and Representatives in Congress to which the District would be entitled if it were a State, but in no event more than the least populous State; they shall be in addition to those appointed by the States, but they shall be considered, for the purposes of the election of President and Vice President, to be electors appointed by a State; and they shall meet in the District and perform such duties as provided by the twelfth article of amendment.

Section 2.

The Congress shall have power to enforce this article by appropriate legislation.

Amendment XXIV (1964)
Section 1.

The right of citizens of the United States to vote in any primary or other election for President or Vice President, for electors for President or Vice President, or for Senator or Representative in Congress, shall not be denied or abridged by the United States or any state by reasons of failure to pay any poll tax or other tax.

Section 2.

The Congress shall have power to enforce this article by appropriate legislation.

Amendment XXV (1967)
Section 1.

In case of the removal of the President from office or of his death or resignation the Vice President shall become President.

Section 2.

Whenever there is a vacancy in the office of the Vice President, the President shall nominate a Vice President who shall take office upon confirmation by a majority vote of both Houses of Congress.

Section 3.

Whenever the President transmits to the President pro tempore of the Senate and the Speaker of the House of Representatives his written declaration that he is unable to discharge the powers and duties of his office, and until he transmits to them a written declaration to the contrary, such powers and duties shall be discharged by the Vice President as Acting President.

Section 4.

Whenever the Vice President and a majority of either the principal officers of the Executive departments or of such other body as Congress may by law provide, transmit to the President pro tempore of the Senate and the Speaker of the House of Representatives their written declaration that the President is unable to discharge the powers and duties of his office, the Vice President shall immediately assume the powers and duties of the office as Acting President.

Thereafter, when the President transmits to the President pro tempore of the Senate and the Speaker of the House of Representatives his written declaration that no inability exists, he shall resume the powers and duties of his office unless the Vice President and a majority of either the principal officers of the executive departments or of such other body as Congress may by law provide, transmit within four days to the President pro tempore of the Senate and the Speaker of the House of Representatives their written declaration that the President is unable to discharge the powers and duties of his office. Thereupon Congress shall decide the issue, assembling within forty-eight hours for that purpose if not in session. If the Congress, within twenty-one days after receipt of the later written declaration, or if Congress is not in session, within twenty-one days after Congress is required to assembly, determines by two thirds vote of both houses that the President is unable to discharge the powers and duties of his office, the Vice President shall continue to discharge the same as Acting President; otherwise, the President shall resume the powers and duties of his office.

Amendment XXVI (1971)

Section 1.

The right of citizens of the United States, who are 18 years of age or older, to vote shall not be denied or abridged by the United States or any state on account of age.

Section 2.

The Congress shall have power to enforce this article by appropriate legislation.

Appendix II

CHRONOLOGY OF PRESIDENTIAL ELECTIONS

★ ————————————————————————————————

1789 and 1792

Less an election than a coronation, George Washington was unanimously selected president by the Electoral College. In 1789 he received all 69 electoral votes. In 1792 he received all 132 electoral votes. John Adams was selected vice president. There was no campaigning and no popular vote.

1796

The first presidential election in which political parties played a role, the race was between John Adams, a Federalist, and Thomas Jefferson, a Democratic-Republican. When George Washington decided not to seek a third term the partisan split between the nascent parties became open political warfare. While there was no public campaigning to speak of, the election was hotly contested. Adams received 71 electoral votes, Jefferson won 68. Adams was elected president and Jefferson—as runner-up—was made vice president.

1800

In 1800 Adams and Jefferson had their rematch, with Jefferson winning 73 electoral votes to Adams's 65. This election marked the beginning of the congressional nominating caucus, "King Caucus," wherein the party members in Congress gathered to agree upon their party's nominee. This election, a hard-fought partisan contest, marked the first time control of the presidency shifted from one party to another.

1804

As the Federalist Party declined and the Jeffersonians rose, the 1804 election was a landslide victory for the incumbent.

Jefferson won 160 (82 percent) electoral votes to Charles C. Pinckney's 14.

1808

The Jeffersonians, now referred to as Republicans, maintained control of the presidency in 1808. The congressional caucus nominated James Madison, Jefferson's hand-picked successor, and he was easily elected president defeating Charles C. Pinckney and winning 122 (70 percent) of the electoral votes. George Clinton was elected vice president.

1812

Once again, the Democratic-Republican congressional caucus selected James Madison as their standard-bearer. Elbridge Gerry, the governor of Massachusetts (and still famous as the man after whom "gerrymandering" was named) was the vice-presidential candidate. Madison ran against and beat DeWitt Clinton 128-89 in the Electoral College.

1816

In another Democratic-Republican landslide, James Monroe won 183 (84 percent) electoral votes to 34 for Rufus King. This election marked the end of the Federalists.

1820

With virtually no opposition party to speak of, James Monroe was reelected with 231 of 232 electoral votes! John Quincy Adams won the one remaining electoral vote.

1824

In the election of 1824, the "King Caucus" system of nominating presidential candidates came under strain. As the nation became more democratic, and as voting rights were expanded, the closed nature of the caucus system came under fire. The 1824 race was between four serious candidates, but the race really boiled down to a contest between John Quincy Adams and the populist Andrew Jackson. No candidate was able to win a majority of the Electoral College vote. Jackson won 38 percent to Adams's 32 percent and Jackson led in the popular vote 43 percent to 30. The race was thus thrown into the House of Representatives (as per the Twelfth Amendment). After a series of back-room efforts to garner enough votes to win, John Quincy Adams was selected president. Adams won 13 state votes in the House, Jackson only seven.

1828

In the election of 1828, Andrew Jackson won his revenge and the presidency. He ran against John Quincy Adams and in this election, Jackson won the popular vote 56 percent to 44; and the electoral vote 178 (68 percent) to 83.

1832

Andrew Jackson easily won reelection in 1832, winning 56 percent to 38 percent of the popular vote and 77 percent of the electoral vote against opponent Henry Clay.

1836

Martin Van Buren, Andrew Jackson's protégé, won the presidency in 1836 against a field of rivals. Van Buren won 51 percent of the popular vote and 58 percent of the electoral votes.

1840

Van Buren sought reelection in 1840 but the Whig Party's candidate, William Henry Harrison, exploited rifts over slavery and tariffs and won the presidency. Harrison received 53 percent of the popular vote and 80 percent of the electoral vote.

1844

In 1844 John Tyler, who as vice president had become president after the death of President Harrison, sought the nomination for himself, but the Whigs chose Henry Clay instead. In the election, James K. Polk, a Democrat, won the presidency, gaining nearly 50 percent of the popular vote and 62 percent of the electoral vote.

1848

President Polk announced that he would serve only one term as president, and the 1848 race boiled down to a contest between Whig Zachary Taylor against Democrat Lewis Cass. Taylor won with 47 percent of the popular vote to 43 for Cass. He won in the Electoral College 163 to 127.

1852

As the nation wrestled with the political and moral dimensions of slavery, the election of 1852 proved unusual in that both parties, eager to bypass any discussion of the most central issue of the day, all but ignored the slavery question and conducted a campaign oblivious to the conflict in their midst. In 1852 Democrat Franklin Pierce beat Whig Winfield Scott in the popular vote 51 to 49 percent and the electoral vote by a 254 (80 percent) to 42 vote.

1856

The Whig Party was in decline and the issue of slavery threatened to destroy the Union. James Buchanan, the nominee of the Democrats, rather handily beat the candidate of the newly formed Republican Party, John C. Fremont, and American Know-Nothing/Whig Candidate Millard Fillmore. Buchanan won the popular vote 45 percent to Fremont's 32 and Fillmore's 22 percent. He also won nearly 60 percent of the electoral vote.

1860

With the Union collapsing as Southern states threatened to secede, the election of 1860 proved one of the most important in U.S. history. The Republicans nominated Abraham Lincoln, and three other parties challenged for the White House: The Democratic Southern Party nominated John C. Breckinridge, the Constitutional Union Party chose John Bell, and the Northern Democrats selected Stephen Douglas. Lincoln won less than 40 percent of the popular vote but 59 percent of the electoral vote. As the Union broke apart, Abraham Lincoln took office.

1864

In the middle of the Civil War, a presidential election took place. Abraham Lincoln ran against Democrat George B. McClellan. Lincoln won 55 percent of the popular vote and 91 percent of the electoral vote.

1868

In the aftermath of the Civil War, following the impeachment of President Andrew Johnson, and in the midst of Reconstruction, the election of 1868 was won by Civil War hero Republican Ulysses S. Grant. He beat Democratic rival Horatio Seymour 53 to 47 percent in the popular vote, and 73 to 27 percent in the electoral vote.

1872

The popular Grant easily won reelection in 1872. Grant won nearly 56 percent of the popular vote against Democrat Horace Greeley. He won 81 percent of the electoral vote.

1876

The election of 1876 was one of the most controversial in U.S. history. Republican candidate Rutherford B. Hayes received 48 percent of the popular vote; Democrat Samuel J. Tilden won 51 percent. In the Electoral College Tilden led Hayes 184 to 165. Tilden was one electoral vote short of victory. The votes in the southern states were in dispute (Florida, Louisiana, and South Carolina, plus one vote from Oregon). After weeks of partisan bickering, a deal was believed to be struck between Hayes's supporters and the southern states whereby the states would swing their votes to Hayes in exchange for Hayes putting an end to Reconstruction and removing Northern troops from the South. This "deal" called Hayes's legitimacy into question and he was often referred to as "Rutherfraud B. Hayes."

1880

This Gilded Age election pitted Republican James A. Garfield against Democrat Winfield S. Hancock. The close election results found Garfield barely winning the presidency, with both candidates winning slightly more than 48 percent of the popular vote, but emerging victorious in the electoral vote 214 to 155.

1884

The presidential election of 1884 was marked by the "character" issue, when Democrat Grover Cleveland was accused, during the campaign, of fathering a child out of wedlock. Cleveland took full responsibility and went on to win the presidency, defeating Republican James G. Blaine by a 48.5 percent to 48.3 percent popular margin, and a 219 to 182 electoral margin.

1888

President Cleveland was ousted from the White House in the election of 1888. Benjamin Harrison, grandson of William Henry Harrison, ninth president of the United States, beat Cleveland in a close election, with Harrison winning 48.7 percent of the popular vote to Cleveland's 47.8 percent, and 233 electoral votes to Cleveland's 168.

1892

In the election of 1892, Grover Cleveland came back to recapture the presidency. He beat former rival Benjamin Harrison 46 to 43 percent in the popular vote, and 62 to 33 percent in the electoral vote. This was the first time a defeated president ever came back to reclaim office.

1896

As the United States was poised to assume a larger role in the international community, the election of 1896 found Republican William McKinley against populist Democrat William Jennings Bryan. McKinley won 51 percent of the popular vote to Bryan's 48 percent, and 271 electoral votes to Bryan's 178.

1900

The 1900 presidential election was a rematch between Democrat William Jennings Bryan and Republican president William McKinley. As he had in 1896, Bryan stumped across the country, giving more than 600 speeches in 24 states (at the time, this type of campaigning was unheard of). He focused on similar issues as he had during his 1896 campaign, including stopping monopolies and trusts and the coining of silver. McKinley, campaigning on a prosperous economy, won by almost an identical margin as he had in 1896. He garnered 51.6 percent of the popular vote and 292 electoral votes.

1904

After William McKinley's death, Theodore Roosevelt became one of the most popular presidents in history. Roosevelt was a champion of the Progressive Movement and pushed labor and electoral reforms. His campaign slogan was "a Square Deal," which promised assertive presidential leadership. The Democrats nominated Alton Parker, a man with no national reputation. Because the outcome was a foregone conclusion, neither candidate campaigned much. Roosevelt easily won, winning 56.4 percent of the popular vote and 336 electoral votes.

1908

With Theodore Roosevelt's decision not to seek reelection because of increasing tension with many conservatives in the Republican Party, William Howard Taft won the party's nomination. Taft was not a typical candidate; he once admitted that he "hated" politics. The Democrats once again turned to two-time presidential candidate William Jennings Bryan. With a robust economy, the support of Roosevelt, and a Democratic candidate that did not excite many in his own party, Taft defeated Bryan, carrying 51.6 percent of the popular vote and 321 electoral votes.

1912

Upset with William Taft's inability to advance the Progressive agenda, former President Theodore Roosevelt entered the 1912 presidential election as a third party candidate. Roosevelt's entrance into the race deeply divided the Republican Party and allowed New Jersey governor Woodrow Wilson to easily win the election. Wilson won 41.9 percent of the popular vote to Roosevelt's 27.4 percent and Taft's 23.2 percent. He also carried 435 electoral votes compared to Roosevelt's 88 and Taft's 8. Roosevelt's showing was the best for a third party candidate in history.

1916

With the threat of World War I on the horizon, voters reelected Woodrow Wilson. The incumbent, however, again failed to win a majority of the vote and won only 277 electoral votes. Supreme Court justice and progressive Charles Hughes carried 46.1 percent of the popular vote and 254 electoral votes. Wilson ran on the platform of remaining neutral in the World War, which was popular with an isolationist public. Also, his reform legislation helped neutralize Hughes's progressive background.

1920

In 1920 both parties settled on compromise candidates, neither of whom were highly regarded. Ohio governor James M. Cox ran against an unknown senator from the same state, Warren Harding. Harding, whose private life included adultery, a penchant for poker games, and a love of alcohol when drinking it was prohibited by the Eighteenth Amendment, promised to bring the country "Back to Normalcy." That message, along with an appealing public image, carried the Republican to an easy victory. He won more than 60 percent of the popular vote and 404 electoral votes.

1924

After the scandal-ridden years of the Harding administration, the Republican Party turned to a candidate whose nickname was "Silent Cal" and who was notorious for taking long naps. Even with Harding's scandals, a booming economy helped Coolidge easily beat West Virginia Congressman John Davis and Progressive candidate Robert La Follette. Coolidge won more than 50 percent of the popular vote and 382 electoral votes in the three-person race .

1928

With incumbent Calvin Coolidge choosing not to run for reelection, the door to the presidency opened for a man who had never sought elective office. Herbert Hoover, the secretary of Commerce under Harding and Coolidge, continued the Republican domination of presidential elections in the 1920s. He easily beat Democrat Al Smith, garnering more than 58 percent of the popular vote and 444 electoral votes. Hoover's famous campaign slogan was "A chicken in every pot and two cars in every garage." Smith became the first Catholic to run for the presidency and was hurt by the public's fear that he would be beholden to the wishes of the pope. Smith's opposition to Prohibition also was not popular with voters.

1932

In the midst of the greatest depression in U.S. history, Franklin Roosevelt easily defeated incumbent Herbert Hoover. Roosevelt won more than 57 percent of the popular vote and 472 electoral votes. Hoover, whose laissez-faire approach to emerging from the depression was not popular among voters, won the fewest votes of any Republican candidate since William Howard Taft in 1912. Roosevelt's victory was the first of four and the beginning of a massive change in the role of the federal government regarding social welfare policy.

1936

The 1936 election may most be remembered for the inaccurate prediction by *Literary Digest* that Kansas governor Alf Landon would defeat incumbent Franklin Roosevelt. In reality, Roosevelt won in a landslide, winning more than 60 percent of the popular vote and 523 electoral votes; he lost only the states of Maine and Vermont. It was the largest victory since James Monroe. The Digest's inaccurate prediction occurred because its sample was comprised of those on automobile registration lists, most of whom were Republican. While criticized by some and mostly ineffective at ending the depression, Roosevelt's New Deal programs remained immensely popular with the American public.

1940

In 1940 Franklin Roosevelt ran for an unprecedented third term. Roosevelt's popularity remained high and his "New Deal Coalition" remained strong. Roosevelt would run against Republican Wendell Willkie with a new running mate. Vice President John Nance Garner, a conservative Southerner, had become disenchanted with FDR's liberal New Deal programs. Roosevelt shocked many by choosing liberal Henry Wallace as his running mate. Even with the change, Roosevelt easily defeated Willkie, winning 55 percent of the popular vote and 449 electoral votes. A major issue of the election was the potential involvement in World War II.

1944

In the midst of World War II and the first election since the bombing of Pearl Harbor, Franklin Roosevelt was elected to an unprecedented fourth term. Roosevelt's "New Deal Coalition" remained strong as he carried 53 percent of the popular vote and 432 electoral votes. Republican Thomas Dewey won 46 percent of the popular vote and 99 electoral votes. Perhaps the most important aspect of the 1944 election was the decision by the Democrats to nominate Missouri senator Harry Truman for vice president. With Roosevelt's health failing, it was clear to most that he would not survive the term and his vice president would ascend to the presidency.

1948

With declining public approval ratings for President Harry Truman, Republicans believed they had the best chance to recapture the presidency since Herbert Hoover lost in 1932. Pollsters were so convinced of the election outcome between Truman and New York governor Thomas Dewey that they stopped polling in September, more than two months before the election. In an incredible upset, Truman defeated Dewey, winning 49.5 percent of the popular vote and 303 electoral votes. In one of the most famous pictures in American politics, Truman held a copy of the *Chicago Tribune* that declared "Dewey Defeats Truman." Third party candidate Strom Thurmond ran in opposition to the moderate civil rights plank in the 1948 Democratic Party and won 39 electoral votes (all from the Deep South).

1952

In 1952 Republicans won the presidency for the first time in almost 25 years. War hero and general Dwight Eisenhower carried 55 percent of the popular vote and 442 electoral votes in his defeat of Illinois governor Adlai Stevenson. In addition to Eisenhower's immense popularity, the declining popularity of President Harry Truman and Stevenson's recent divorce hurt the Democrats. Perhaps the most interesting aspect of the election did not involve either presidential candidate: Addressing charges of a "slush fund" given to him while senator of California, Republican vice-presidential candidate Richard Nixon delivered his "Checkers" speech. The public's positive response to the speech kept him on the Republican ticket.

1956

In a rematch of the 1952 election, Dwight Eisenhower again easily beat Adlai Stevenson. Eisenhower won more than 57 percent of the popular vote and 457 electoral votes. Eisenhower had strong public approval ratings largely because of his leadership during the cold war and a strong economy.

1960

In one of the closest elections in history, Massachusetts senator John Kennedy narrowly defeated Vice President Richard Nixon. Kennedy won the popular vote by less than one-tenth of 1 percent and carried 313 electoral votes. Charges of voter fraud were rampant in two close (and large) states—Illinois and Texas. Had Nixon carried these states, he would have won the election. The 1960 election was notable for two firsts. Kennedy became the first Catholic president and questions about his Catholicism were raised throughout the campaign. The first televised debates were also held in 1960. Many consider Nixon's performance in the first debate to have lost the election (although there is little empirical evidence to support that claim).

1964

Even though many Democrats wanted to nominate Robert Kennedy, incumbent Lyndon Johnson won the nomination. Johnson, helped by the reaction to John Kennedy's assassination a year earlier, easily defeated Arizona senator Barry Goldwater in the general election. Johnson won 61 percent of the popular vote and 486 electoral votes. Many considered Goldwater, with his support of states' rights, too conservative. He carried only the five states of the Deep South and his home state.

1968

In 1968 incumbent Lyndon Johnson decided not to run for reelection because of low public approval ratings over his handling of the Vietnam War. Robert Kennedy quickly emerged as the front-runner on the Democratic side but was assassinated after the California primary. The Democrats nominated Vice President Hubert Humphrey, who did not run in a single primary. This upset many of the "doves" in the party who supported Kennedy or Senator Eugene McCarthy. On the Republican side, Richard Nixon made a comeback after defeats in the 1960 presidential and 1962 California gubernatorial elections. George Wallace ran as a third party candidate on a states' rights platform. In the three-way race, Nixon carried 301 electoral votes to Humphrey's 191 and Wallace's 46.

1972

In 1972 Richard Nixon easily defeated Senator George McGovern to win reelection. McGovern, generally considered too liberal for mainstream America, stressed his opposition to the war in Vietnam, but to little avail. Nixon won an astounding 61 percent of the popular vote and lost only traditionally liberal Massachusetts and the District of Columbia. McGovern even lost his home state of South Dakota. While the election was not close, its place in history is assured: It was during the 1972 election that burglars broke into the DNC headquarters at the Watergate hotel. The Watergate scandal would eventually lead to Nixon's resignation.

1976

With the resignation of Richard Nixon because of the Watergate scandal, Gerald Ford became the first appointed president (he was appointed by Nixon to be vice president after Spiro Agnew resigned). Ford's pardon of Nixon upset many voters, and a relatively obscure governor from Georgia, Jimmy Carter, narrowly defeated the president. Carter beat Ford in the popular vote 50 percent to 48 percent and in the electoral vote 297 to 240. Had Ford carried Ohio and Hawaii, two states that were quite close, he would have won the election.

1980

Stuck with a struggling economy, an inability to pass his legislation, and the failure to rescue American hostages from Iran, Jimmy Carter became the first elected president since Herbert Hoover not to win reelection. Former California governor and actor Ronald Reagan asked the voters if they were better off than they were four years ago. The voters resoundingly answered "no," giving Reagan a majority of the popular vote and more than 90 percent of the electoral vote. In the South, at the time a traditional Democratic stronghold, Carter won only his home state of Georgia.

1984

In one of the biggest blowouts in history, incumbent Ronald Reagan easily defeated former Vice President Walter Mondale. Reagan won close to 59 percent of the popular vote and lost only Mondale's home state of Minnesota and the traditionally Democratic District of Columbia. While some questioned Reagan's ability to be president for another term because of his age, he was still quite popular. Mondale lost a great deal of support from moderates when he promised to raise taxes.

1988

Massachusetts governor Michael Dukakis had a commanding lead over sitting Vice President George H. W. Bush in the summer of 1988. That lead quickly diminished, however, after Bush successfully portrayed Dukakis as being soft on crime and defense, unpatriotic, and unemotional. The campaign will be remembered for the notorious Willie Horton commercial that many believed had racial overtones and a Dukakis commercial in which the governor rode around in a tank. Bush won by smaller margins that his Republican predecessor, Ronald Reagan, but still carried 53 percent of the popular vote and 426 electoral votes.

1992

George H. W. Bush, considered to be unbeatable by many Democrats just a year earlier, lost to Arkansas governor Bill Clinton. Bush, the incumbent, had public approval ratings close to 90 percent just a year earlier because of his handling of the Gulf War. However, Clinton, who survived numerous scandals during the primaries, including charges of adultery, draft-dodging, and pot-smoking, focused on a struggling economy. Clinton only received 42 percent of the vote because of the strong showing of independent Ross Perot, but carried 370 electoral votes.

1996

Bill Clinton, whose presidency was considered "dead in the water" just two years earlier as a result of the Democrats' poor showing in the 1994 midterm elections, rebounded to easily defeat Senate Majority Leader Bob Dole. As in 1992, Clinton failed to win a majority of the vote but won 379 electoral votes. The 1996 election is widely considered to be one of the least dramatic elections of the 20th century, and voter turnout was the lowest since 1924.

2000

In perhaps the most controversial presidential election in history, Texas governor George W. Bush lost the popular vote to Vice President Al Gore by more than 500,000 votes but won a slim majority of electoral votes. Controversy over the results in the state of Florida led to more than five weeks of recounts, discussion of voting irregularities, claims by African Americans of being kept from voting, and court cases, ended only by a decision of the Supreme Court to stop the recounting. In the end, Gore, helped by a booming economy but hurt by his lack of a clear message, the scandals of the Clinton administration, and his perceived "wooden" personality, lost an election many believe he should have won.

Selected Bibliography

Major Reference Works on the Presidency

Goldsmith, William M. *The Growth of Presidential Power: A Documented History,* 3 vols. New York: Chelsea House, 1974.

Graff, Henry F., ed. *The Presidents: A Reference History.* New York: Scribner's, 1984.

Greenstein, Fred I., Larry Berman, and Alvin S. Felzenberg with Doris Lidtke. *Evolution of the Modern Presidency: A Bibliographical Survey.* Washington, D.C.: American Enterprise Institute, 1977.

Levy, Leonard W., and Louis Fisher, eds. *Encyclopedia of the American Presidency,* 4 vols. New York: Simon & Schuster, 1994.

Nelson, Michael, ed. *Guide to the Presidency.* Washington, D.C.: Congressional Quarterly Press, 1989.

———. *The Presidency, A to Z.* Washington, D.C.: Congressional Quarterly Press, 1992.

Shane, Peter M., and Harold H. Bruff, eds. *The Law of Presidential Power.* Durham, N.C.: Carolina Academic Press, 1988.

Whitney, David C., and Robin Vaughn Whitney, eds. *The American Presidents,* 8th ed. Pleasantville, N.Y.: Reader's Digest, 1996.

Other Important Works

Abbott, Philip. *Strong Presidents: A Theory of Leadership.* Knoxville: University of Tennessee Press, 1996.

Abraham, Henry J. *Justices and Presidents,* 2d ed. New York: Oxford University Press, 1985.

Abrams, Herbert L. *"The President Has Been Shot": Confusion, Disability and the 25th Amendment.* Stanford: Stanford University Press, 1994.

Adler, David Gray, and Larry N. George, eds. *The Constitution and the Conduct of Foreign Policy.* Lawrence: University Press of Kansas, 1996.

Arnold, Peri E. *Making the Managerial Presidency.* Princeton, N.J.: Princeton University Press, 1986.

Asher, Herbert. *Presidential Elections and American Politics,* 5th ed. New York: Harcourt Brace, 1992.

Baker, Nancy V. *Conflicting Loyalties: Law and Politics in the Attorney General's Office 1789–1990.* Lawrence: University Press of Kansas, 1992.

Barber, James David. *The Presidential Character: Predicting Performance in the White House,* 4th ed. Englewood Cliffs, N.J.: Prentice-Hall, 1992.

Barilleaux, Ryan J., and Barbara Kellerman. *The President as World Leader.* New York: St. Martin's Press, 1991.

Bennett, Anthony *The American President's Cabinet: From Kennedy to Bush.* New York: St. Martin's, 1996.

Bennis, Warren. *On Becoming a Leader.* Reading, Pa.: Addison-Wesley, 1989.

———, and Bert Nanus. *Leaders: Strategies for Taking Charge.* New York: HarperCollins, 1986.

Berman, Larry. *The New American Presidency.* Boston: Little, Brown, 1987.

Bessette, Joseph M., and Jeffrey Tulis, eds. *The Presidency in the Constitutional Order.* Baton Rouge: Louisiana State University Press, 1984.

Best, Judith A., et al. *The Choice of the People? Debating the Electoral College.* Lanham, Md.: Rowland & Littlefield, 1996.

Blakesley, Lance. *Presidential Leadership: From Eisenhower to Clinton.* Chicago: Nelson-Hall, 1995.

Bond, Jon R., and Richard Fleisher. *The President in the Legislative Arena.* Chicago: University of Chicago Press, 1990.

Brace, Paul, and Barbara Hinckley. *Follow the Leader: Opinion Polls and the Modern Presidents.* New York: Basic Books, 1992.

Brody, Richard A. *Assessing the President: The Media, Elite Opinion, and Public Support.* Stanford, Calif.: Stanford University Press, 1991.

Bryce, James. *The American Commonwealth.* New York: MacMillan, 1888.

Buchanan, Bruce. *The Presidential Experience: What the Office Does to the Man.* Englewood Cliffs, N.J.: Prentice-Hall, 1978.

Bunce, Valerie. *Do New Leaders Make a Difference?: Executive Successions and Public Policy under Capitalism and Socialism.* Princeton, N.J.: Princeton University Press, 1981.

Burke, John P. *The Institutional Presidency.* Baltimore: Johns Hopkins University Press, 1992.

Burns, James McGregor. *Deadlock of Democracy.* Englewood Cliffs, N.J.: Prentice-Hall, 1963.

———. *Presidential Government: The Crucible of Leadership.* Boston: Houghton Mifflin, 1965.

———. *Roosevelt: The Lion and the Fox.* San Diego: Harvest/HBJ, 1984.

———. *The Power to Lead: The Crisis of the American Presidency.* New York: Simon & Schuster, 1984.

———. *Leadership.* New York: HarperCollins, 1978.

———. *Roosevelt: Soldier of Freedom.* New York: Harcourt Brace, Jovanovich, 1970.

Campbell, Colin. *Managing the Presidency: Carter, Reagan and the Search for Executive Harmony.* Pittsburgh: University of Pittsburgh Press, 1986.

Cannon, Lou. *President Reagan: The Role of a Lifetime.* New York: Touchstone, 1991.

Caroli, Betty Boyd. *First Ladies.* New York: Oxford University Press, 1987.

Carrodo, Anthony. *Creative Campaigning.* Boulder, Colo.: Westview, 1992.

Carter, Jimmy. *Keeping Faith: Memoirs of a President.* New York: Bantam Books, 1982.

Ceasar, James W. *Presidential Selection.* Princeton, N.J.: Princeton University Press, 1979.

Corvitz, L. Gordon, and Jeremy A. Rabkin, eds. *The Tethered Presidency.* Washington, D.C.: American Enterprise Institute, 1989.

———. *The President: Office and Powers, 1978–1984,* 5th ed. New York: New York University Press, 1984.

Corwin, Edward S. *Total War and the Constitution.* Westminister, Md.: Knopf, 1947.

Covington, Cary R., and Lester G. Seligman. *The Coalition Presidency.* Chicago: Dorsey Press, 1989.

Cox, Gary W., and Samuel Kernell, eds. *The Politics of Divided Government.* Boulder, Colo.: Westview, 1991.

Crabb, Cecil V., and Pat Holt. *Invitation to Struggle: Congress, the President, and Foreign Policy,* 3d ed. Washington, D.C.: Congressional Quarterly Press, 1989.

———. *Presidents and Foreign Policymaking.* Baton Rouge: Louisiana State University Press, 1986.

———, and Kevin V. Mulcahy. *American National Security: A Presidential Perspective.* New York: Harcourt Brace, 1990.

Cronin, Thomas E., ed. *Inventing the American Presidency.* Lawrence: University Press of Kansas, 1989.

———. *The State of the Presidency,* 2d ed. Boston: Little, Brown, 1980.

Cronin, Thomas E., with Michael A. Genovese. *The Paradoxes of the American Presidency.* New York: Oxford University Press, 1998.

———, and Sanford Greenberg, eds. *The Presidential Advisory System.* New York: Harper & Row, 1969.

———, ed. *Rethinking the Presidency.* Boston: Little, Brown, 1982.

———, and Rexford Tugwell, eds. *The Presidency Reappraised.* New York: Praeger, 1977.

Dallek, Robert, *Hail to the Chief: The Making and Unmaking of American Presidents.* New York: Hyperion Books, 1996.

Darman, Richard. *Who's In Control? Polar Politics and the Sensible Center.* New York: Simon & Schuster, 1996.

Davis, James W. *The American Presidency,* 2d ed. Westport, Conn.: Praeger, 1995.

———. *The President as Party Leader.* New York: Praeger, 1992.

DeGrazia, Alfred. *Congress and the Presidency.* Washington, D.C.: American Enterprise Institute, 1967.

Donald, David H. *Lincoln.* New York: Simon & Schuster, 1995.

Draper, Theodore. *A Very Thin Line; The Iran-Contra Affair.* New York: Touchstone Books, 1991.

Edwards, George C. *Presidential Influence in Congress.* San Francisco: W. H. Freeman, 1980.

———. *The Public Presidency.* New York: St. Martin's Press, 1983.

———. *At the Margins: Presidential Leadership in Congress.* New Haven, Conn.: Yale University Press, 1989.

———, John H. Kessel, and Bert A. Rockman, eds. *Researching the Presidency: Vital Questions, New Approaches.* Pittsburgh: University of Pittsburgh Press, 1993.

———, and Stephen Wayne. *Presidential Leadership: Politics and Policy Making,* 3d ed. New York: St. Martin's Press, 1994.

Ellis, Richard, and Aaron Wildavsky. *Dilemma of Presidential Leadership.* New Brunswick, N.J.: Transaction Publishers, 1989.

Fishel, Jeff. *Presidents and Promises.* Washington, D.C.: Congressional Quarterly Press, 1985.

Fisher, Louis. *The Constitution Between Friends.* New York: St. Martin's Press, 1978.

———. *Presidential War Power.* Lawrence: University Press of Kansas, 1995.

Franklin, Daniel P. *Extraordinary Measures*. Pittsburgh: University of Pittsburgh Press, 1991.

Gardner, John W. *On Leadership*. New York: Free Press, 1990.

Genovese, Michael A. *The Supreme Court, the Constitution, and Presidential Power*. Landham, Md.: University Press of America, 1980.

———. *The Nixon Presidency: Power and Politics in Turbulent Times*. Westport, Conn.: Greenwood Press, 1990.

———. *The Presidency in an Age of Limits*. Westport, Conn.: Greenwood Press, 1993.

———, with Thomas E. Cronin. *The Paradoxes of the American Presidency*. New York: Oxford University Press, 1998.

———. *The Watergate Crisis*. Westport, Conn.: Greenwood Press, 1999.

———. *The Presidency and Domestic Policy*, with William W. Lammers. Washington, D.C.: CQ Press, 2000.

———. *The Power of American Presidency, 1789–2000*. New York: Oxford University Press, 2001.

———. *The Presidency and the Law: The Clinton Legacy*, with David Gray Adler. Lawrence: University Press of Kansas, 2002.

———. *The Presidential Dilemma: Leadership in the American System*. New York: Longman, 2003.

Greenstein, Fred. *The Hidden-Hand Presidency: Eisenhower as Leader*. New York: Basic Books, 1982.

Gregg, Gary L. *The Presidential Republic: Executive Representation and Deliberative Democracy*. Lanham, Md.: Rowland & Littlefield, 1997.

Grover, William F. *The President as Prisoner*. New York: State University of New York Press, 1989.

Hamilton, Alexander, James Madison, and John Jay. *Federalist Papers*. New York: New American Library, 1961.

Hargrove, Erwin C. *The Power of the Modern Presidency*. New York: Knopf, 1974.

———, and Michael Nelson. *Presidents, Politics and Policy*. Baltimore: Johns Hopkins University Press, 1984.

Harriger, Katy J. *Independent Justice: The Federal Special Prosecutor in American Politics*. Lawrence: University Press of Kansas, 1992.

Hart, Roderick. *The Sound of Leadership*. Chicago: University of Chicago Press, 1987.

———. *The Presidential Branch*. Chatham, N.J.: Chatham House, 1995.

Hess, Stephen. *Organizing the Presidency*. Washington, D.C.: Brookings, 1976.

Hughes, Emmet John. *The Living Presidency*. New York: Coward, McCann and Geoghegan, 1973.

Jamieson, Kathleen Hall. *Packaging the Presidency*. New York: Oxford University Press, 1996.

Johnson, Haynes, and David Broder. *The System*. Boston: Little, Brown, 1996.

Johnson, Loch K. *Secret Agencies: U.S. Intelligence Agencies in a Hostile World*. New Haven, Conn.: Yale University Press, 1996.

Johnson, Richard T. *Managing the White House*. New York: HarperCollins, 1974.

Jones, Charles O. *The Presidency in a Separated System*. Washington, D.C.: Brookings, 1994.

Kallenbach, Joseph E. *The American Chief Executive*. New York: Harper & Row, 1966.

Kernell, Samuel M. *Going Public: New Strategies of Presidential Leadership*. Washington, D.C.: Congressional Quarterly Press, 1993.

———, and Samuel Popkin, eds. *Chief of Staff*. Berkeley: University of California Press, 1986.

Kessel, John H. *Presidential Campaign Politics*. Chicago: Dorsey Press, 1988.

King, Gary, and Lyn Ragsdale. *The Elusive Executive: Discovering Statistical Patterns in the Presidency*. Washington, D.C.: Congressional Quarterly Press, 1988.

Koenig, Louis W. *The Chief Executive*, 5th ed. San Diego: Harcourt Brace Jovanovich, 1986.

Koh, Harold Kongju. *The National Security Constitution: Sharing Power After the Iran-Contra Affair*. New Haven, Conn.: Yale University Press, 1990.

Kutler, Stanley K. *The Wars of Watergate*. New York: Knopf, 1990.

Lammers, William W. *Presidential Politics: Patterns and Prospects*. New York: HarperCollins, 1976.

Laski, Harold. *The American Presidency*. New York: Harper & Brothers, 1940.

LeLoup, Lance T., and Steven A. Shull. *Congress and the President: The Policy Connection*. Belmont, Calif.: Wadsworth, 1993.

Leuchtenburg, William E. *In the Shadow of FDR: From Harry Truman to Ronald Reagan*. Ithaca, N.Y.: Cornell University Press, 1983.

Levine, Myron A. *Presidential Campaigns and Elections*. Itasca, Ill.: F. E. Peacock, 1995.

Light, Paul C. *The President's Agenda*. Baltimore: Johns Hopkins University Press, 1982.

———. *Vice Presidential Power: Advice and Influence in the White House*. Baltimore: Johns Hopkins University Press, 1984.

Loevy, Robert D. *The Flawed Path to the Presidency*. Albany: State University of New York Press, 1995.

Lowi, Theodore J. *The Personal President: Power Invested Promise Unfulfilled*. Ithaca, N.Y.: Cornell University Press, 1985.

Maltese, John. *Spin Control: The White House Office of Communications and the Management of Presidential News*. Chapel Hill: University of North Carolina Press, 1992.

Mansfield, Harvey C., Jr. *Taming the Prince: The Ambivalence of Presidential Power.* New York: Free Press, 1989.

Maraniss, David. *First in His Class: The Biography of Bill Clinton.* New York: Touchstone, 1995.

Mayer, Jane, and Doyle McManus. *Landslide: The Unmaking of the President, 1984–1988.* Boston: Houghton Mifflin, 1988.

Mayer, William G., ed. *In Pursuit of the Presidency: How We Choose Our Presidential Nominees.* Chatham, N.J.: Chatham House, 1995.

Mayhew, David. *Divided We Govern.* New Haven, Conn.: Yale University Press, 1991.

Milkis, Sidney M. *The President and the Parties.* New York: Oxford University Press, 1993.

———, and Michael Nelson. *The American Presidency: Origins and Development,* 2d ed. Washington, D.C.: Congressional Quarterly Press, 1994.

Miroff, Bruce. *Icons of Democracy.* New York: Basic Books, 1993.

———. *Pragmatic Illusions: The Presidential Politics of John F. Kennedy.* New York: David McKay, 1976.

Morris, Richard S. *Behind the Oval Office: Winning the Presidency in the 1990s.* New York: Random House, 1997.

Mosley, Zelma, Joseph Pika, and Richard A. Watson. *The Presidential Contest.* Washington, D.C.: Congressional Quarterly Press, 1992.

Mullen, William F. *Presidential Power and Politics.* New York: St. Martin's Press, 1976.

Murray, Robert K., and Tim H. Blessing. *Greatness in the White House: Rating the Presidents, Washington through Carter.* University Park: Pennsylvania State University Press, 1988.

Nathan, Richard. *The Administrative Presidency.* New York: John Wiley and Sons, 1983.

Neustadt, Richard E. *Presidential Power.* New York: Wiley, 1960.

———. *Presidential Power and the Modern Presidents.* New York: Free Press, 1990.

O'Toole, James. *Leading Change: The Argument for Values-based Leadership.* New York: Ballantine Books, 1996.

Patterson, Thomas E. *Out of Order.* New York: Vintage Books, 1994.

Peterson, Mark A. *Legislating Together.* Cambridge, Mass.: Harvard University Press, 1990.

Pfiffner, James P., ed. *The Managerial Presidency.* Pacific Grove, Calif.: Brooks/Cole, 1991.

———. *The Strategic Presidency: Hitting the Ground Running,* 2d ed. Lawrence: University Press of Kansas, 1996.

Phelps, Glenn A. *George Washington and American Constitutionalism.* Lawrence: University Press of Kansas, 1994.

Pika, Joseph A., Norman C. Thomas, and Richard A. Watson. *The Politics of the Presidency.* Washington, D.C.: Congressional Quarterly Press, 1993.

Pious, Richard. *The American Presidency.* New York: Basic Books, 1979.

———. *The Presidency.* Boston: Allyn and Bacon, 1996.

Podhoretz, John. *Hell-of-a-Ride: Backstage at the White House Follies, 1989–1993.* New York: Simon & Schuster, 1993.

Polsby, Nelson W. *Political Innovation in America.* New Haven, Conn.: Yale University Press, 1985.

———, and Aaron Wildavsky. *Presidential Elections.* Chatham, N.J.: Chatham House, 1995.

Quayle, Dan. *Standing Firm.* New York: Harper Paperbacks, 1995.

Ragsdale, Lyn. *Presidential Politics.* Boston: Houghton Mifflin, 1993.

———. *Vital Statistics on the Presidency.* Washington, D.C.: Congressional Quarterly Press, 1995.

Reagan, Ronald. *An American Life: The Autobiography.* New York: Simon & Schuster, 1990.

Reich, Robert. *Locked in the Cabinet.* New York: Knopf, 1997.

Rimmerman, Craig A. *Presidency by Plebiscite.* Boulder, Colo.: Westview, 1993.

Robinson, Donald L. *"To the Best of My Ability": The Presidency and the Constitution.* New York: Norton, 1987.

Rockman, Bert. *The Leadership Question: The Presidency and the American System.* New York: Praeger, 1984.

Rose, Richard. *The Postmodern President: The White House Meets the World.* Chatham, N.J.: Chatham House, 1991.

Rosenstiel, Tom. *Strange Bedfellows: How Television and the Presidential Candidates Changed American Politics, 1992.* New York: Hyperion Books, 1993.

Rossiter, Clinton. *The American Presidency.* New York: Harcourt, Brace and World, 1956.

———. *Constitutional Dictatorship: Crisis Government in the Modern Democracy.* Princeton, N.J.: Princeton University Press, 1948.

Sabato, Larry. *Feeding Frenzy.* New York: Free Press, 1991.

Schlesinger, Arthur M., Jr. *The Cycles of American History.* Boston: Houghton Mifflin, 1986.

———. *The Imperial Presidency.* Boston: Houghton Mifflin, 1973.

Shogan, Robert. *The Riddle of Power.* New York: Dutton, 1991.

Shull, Steve A., ed. *The Two Presidencies: A Quarter Century Assessment.* Chicago: Nelson-Hall, 1991.

Shultz, George P. *Turmoil and Triumph: My Years as Secretary of State*. New York: Scribners, 1993.

Simonton, Dean Keith. *Why Presidents Succeed*. New Haven, Conn.: Yale University Press, 1987.

Sindler, Allan P. *Unchosen Presidents*. Berkeley: University of California Press, 1976.

Skowronek, Stephen. *The Politics Presidents Make*. Cambridge, Mass: Belknap, 1993.

Smith, Hedrick. *The Power Game: How Washington Works*. New York: Ballantine, 1988.

Sorensen, Theodore C. *Watchman in the Night*. Cambridge, Mass.: MIT Press, 1975.

———. *Why I Am A Democrat*. New York: Henry Holt, 1996.

Spitzer, Robert J. *President and Congress: Executive Hegemony at the Crossroads of American Government*. New York: McGraw-Hill, 1993.

———. *The Presidential Veto: Touchstone of the American Presidency*. Albany: State University of New York Press, 1988.

Stewart, James B. *Blood Sport: The President and His Adversaries*. New York: Simon & Schuster, 1996.

Stockman, David A. *The Triumph of Politics: The Inside Story of the Reagan Revolution*. New York: Avon, 1987.

Stuckey, Mary E. *The President as Interpreter-in-Chief*. Chatham, N.J.: Chatham House, 1991.

Sundquist, James L. *Constitutional Reform and Effective Government*. Washington, D.C.: Brookings, 1986.

Tatalovich, Raymond, and Bryon W. Daynes. *Presidential Power in the United States*. Belmont, Calif.: Brooks/Cole, 1984.

Thurber, James A., ed. *Divided Democracy*. Washington, D.C.: Congressional Quarterly Press, 1991.

———, ed. *Rivals for Power: Presidential-Congressional Relations*. Washington, D.C.: Congressional Quarterly Press, 1996.

Troy, Gil. *Affairs of State: The Rise and Rejection of the Presidential Couple since World War II*. New York: McGraw Hill, 1997.

Tulis, Jeffrey K. *The Rhetorical Presidency*. Princeton, N.J.: Princeton University Press, 1987.

Walsh, Kenneth T. *Feeding the Beast: The White House vs. Press*. New York: Random House, 1996.

Walsh, Lawrence E. *Firewall*. New York: Norton, 1997.

Warshaw, Shirley Anne. *Powersharing: White House-Cabinet Relations in the Modern Presidency*. Albany: State University of New York Press, 1996.

———. *The Domestic Presidency*. Boston: Allyn and Bacon, 1997.

Watson, Richard A. *Presidential Vetoes and Public Policy*. Lawrence: University Press of Kansas, 1993.

———. *The Presidential Contest*. New York: Wiley, 1984.

Wayne, Stephen J. *The Road to the White House, 1996*. New York: St. Martin's Press, 1996.

Weko, Thomas J. *The Politicizing Presidency: The White House Personnel Office, 1948–1994*. Lawrence: University Press of Kansas, 1995.

Whitcover, Jules. *Crapshoot: Rolling the Dice on the Vice Presidency*. New York: Crown, 1992.

Wildavsky, Aaron. *The Beleaguered Presidency*. New Brunswick, N.J.: Transaction Publishers, 1994.

Wills, Garry. *Certain Trumpets: The Call of Leaders*. New York: Simon & Schuster, 1994.

Wilson, Robert A., ed. *Character Above All: Ten Presidents from FDR to George Bush*. New York: Simon & Schuster, 1995.

Woodward, Bob. *The Agenda: Inside the Clinton White House*. New York: Simon & Schuster, 1994.

Bibliography by President

George Washington

Brookhiser, Richard. *Founding Father: Rediscovering George Washington.* New York: The Free Press, 1996.

Ferling, John E. *George Washington: Anguish and Farewell.* Boston: Little, Brown, 1969.

———. *Washington, The Indispensable Man.* Boston: Little, Brown, 1974.

———. *The First of Men: A Life of George Washington.* Knoxville: University of Tennessee Press, 1988.

Freeman, Douglas S. *George Washington: A Biography,* 7 vols. New York: Schribner's, 1948–57.

Phelps, Glenn A. *George Washington and American Constitutionalism.* Lawrence: University Press of Kansas, 1993.

Schwartz, Barry. *George Washington: The Making of an American Symbol.* Ithaca: Cornell University Press, 1987.

Smith, Richard N. *Patriarch: George Washington and the New American Nation.* Boston: Houghton Mifflin, 1993.

John Adams

Adams, Charles F. *The Life of John Adams,* rev. ed., 2 vols. Philadelphia: Lippincott, 1871.

Brown, Ralph A. *The Presidency of John Adams.* Lawrence: Regents Press of Kansas, 1975.

Ellis, Joseph J. *Passionate Sage: The Character and Legacy of John Adams.* New York: W. W. Norton, 1993.

Ferling, John E. *John Adams: A Life.* Knoxville: University of Tennessee Press, 1992.

Kurtz, Stephen G. *The Presidency of John Adams: The Collapse of Federalism, 1785–1800.* Philadelphia: University of Pennsylvania Press, 1957.

Smith, Page. *John Adams,* 2 vols. Garden City, N.Y.: Doubleday, 1962.

Thomas Jefferson

Brodie, Fawn M. *Thomas Jefferson: An Intimate History.* New York: W. W. Norton, 1974.

———. *The Process of Government Under Jefferson.* Princeton, N.J.: Princeton University Press, 1978.

Cunningham, Nobel E. *In Pursuit of Reason: The Life of Thomas Jefferson.* Baton Rouge: Louisiana State University Press, 1987.

Ellis, Joseph T. *American Sphinx: The Character of Thomas Jefferson.* New York: Random House, 1997.

Fleming, Thomas J. *Man from Monticello: An Intimate Life of Thomas Jefferson.* New York: William Morrow and Company, 1968.

Johnstone, Robert M., Jr. *Jefferson and the Presidency, Leadership in the Young Republic.* Ithaca, N.Y.: Cornell University Press, 1978.

Malone, Dumas. *Jefferson and the Ordeal of Liberty.* Boston: Little, Brown, 1962.

———. *Thomas Jefferson as a Political Leader.* Berkeley: University of California Press, 1963.

———. *Jefferson the President: First Term, 1801–1805.* Boston: Little, Brown, 1970.

———. *Jefferson the President: Second Term, 1805–1809.* Boston: Little, Brown, 1974.

McDonald, Forrest. *The Presidency of Thomas Jefferson.* Lawrence: Regents Press of Kansas, 1976.

Padover, Saul K. *Jefferson.* New York: Merton, 1952.

Peterson, Merrill D. *The Jefferson Image in the American Mind.* New York: Oxford University Press, 1960.

Randall, Willard S. *Thomas Jefferson: A Life.* New York: Holt, 1993.

Tucker, Robert W. *Empire of Liberty: The Statecraft of Thomas Jefferson.* New York: Oxford University Press, 1990.

James Madison

Brant, Irving. *James Madison,* 6 vols. Indianapolis: Bobbs-Merrill, 1941–61.

Ketcham, Ralph L. *James Madison: A Biography.* New York: Macmillan, 1971.

Matthews, Richard K. *If Men Were Angels: James Madison and the Heartless Empire of Reason.* Lawrence: University Press of Kansas, 1995.

McCoy, Drew R. *The Last of the Fathers: James Madison and the Republican Legacy.* New York: Cambridge University Press, 1989.

Rakove, Jack N. *James Madison and the Creation of the American Republic.* New York: HarperCollins, 1990.

Rutland, Robert A. *The Presidency of James Madison.* Lawrence: University Press of Kansas, 1995.

James Monroe

Ammon, Harry. *James Monroe: The Quest for National Identity.* New York: McGraw-Hill, 1971.

Cresson, William P. *James Monroe.* Chapel Hill: University of North Carolina Press, 1946.

Cunningham, Noble E. *The Presidency of James Monroe.* Lawrence: University Press of Kansas, 1990.

Dangerfield, George. *The Era of Good Feelings.* New York: Harcourt Brace, 1952.

John Quincy Adams

Bemis, Samuel F. *John Quincy Adams and the Foundations of American Foreign Policy.* New York: Knopf, 1949.

———. *John Quincy Adams and the Union.* New York: Knopf, 1956.

Hecht, Marie B. *John Quincy Adams: A Personal History of an Independent Man.* New York: Macmillan, 1972.

Nagel, Paul C. *John Quincy Adams.* New York: Knopf, 1998.

Weeks, William Earl. *John Quincy Adams and American Global Empire.* Lexington: University Press of Kentucky, 1992.

Andrew Jackson

Cole, Donald B. *The Presidency of Andrew Jackson.* Lawrence: University Press of Kansas, 1993.

Latner, Richard B. *The Presidency of Andrew Jackson: White House Politics, 1829–1837.* Athens: University of Georgia Press, 1979.

Remini, Robert V. *The Age of Jackson.* Columbia: University of South Carolina Press, 1972.

———. *Andrew Jackson and the Course of American Empire, 1767–1821.* New York: Harper and Row, 1977.

———. *Andrew Jackson and the Course of American Freedom: 1822–1832.* New York: Harper and Row, 1981.

——— *Andrew Jackson and the Course of American Democracy, 1833–1845.* New York: Harper & Row, 1983.

Schlesinger, Arthur M., Jr. *The Age of Jackson.* Boston: Little, Brown, 1945.

White, Leonard D. *The Jacksonians: A Study in Administrative History, 1829–1861.* New York: Macmillan, 1954.

Martin Van Buren

Cole, Donald B. *Martin Van Buren and the American Political System.* Princeton, N.J.: Princeton University Press, 1984.

Curtis, James C. *The Fox at Bay: Martin Van Buren and the Presidency, 1937–1841.* Lexington: University of Kentucky Press, 1970.

Niven, John. *Martin Van Buren: The Romantic Age of American Politics.* New York: Oxford University Press, 1983.

Remini, Robert V. *Martin Van Buren and the Making of the Democratic Party.* New York: Columbia University Press, 1959.

Wilson, Major L. *The Presidency of Martin Van Buren.* Lawrence: University Press of Kansas, 1984.

William Henry Harrison

Cleaves, Freeman. *Old Tippecanoe: William Henry Harrison and His Time.* New York: Scribner's, 1939.

Peckham, Howard H. *William Henry Harrison: Young Tippecanoe.* Indianapolis: Bobbs-Merrill, 1951.

Peterson, Norma L. *The Presidencies of William Henry Harrison & John Tyler.* Lawrence: University Press of Kansas, 1989.

John Tyler

Chitwood, Oliver P. *John Tyler: Champion of the Old South.* New York: Appleton, 1939.

Young, Stanley P. *Tippecanoe and Tyler, Too!* New York: Random House, 1957.

James K. Polk

Bergeron, Paul H. *The Presidency of James K. Polk.* Lawrence: University Press of Kansas, 1987.

McCormac, Eugene I. *James K. Polk, A Political Biography.* Berkeley: University of California Press, 1922.

McCoy, Charles A. *Polk and the Presidency.* Austin: University of Texas Press, 1960.

Sellers, Charles G., Jr. *James K. Polk, Jacksonian: 1795–1843.* Princeton, N.J.: Princeton University Press, 1957.

———. *James K. Polk, Continentalist: 1843–1846.* Princeton, N.J.: Princeton University Press, 1966.

Zachary Taylor

Hamilton, Holman. *Zachary Taylor,* 2 vols. Indianapolis: Bobbs-Merrill, 1941–51.

Smith, Elbert B. *The Presidencies of Zachary Taylor and Millard Fillmore.* Lawrence: University Press of Kansas, 1988.

Millard Fillmore

Rayback, Robert J. *Millard Fillmore: Biography of a President.* Buffalo, N.Y.: Henry Stewart, 1959.

Smith, Elbert B. *The Presidencies of Zachary Taylor and Millard Fillmore.* Lawrence: University Press of Kansas, 1988.

Franklin Pierce

Gara, Larry. *The Presidency of Franklin Pierce.* Lawrence: University Press of Kansas, 1991.

Hoyt, Edwin P. *Franklin Pierce: The Fourteenth President of the United States.* New York: Harper & Row, 1972.

James Buchanan

Curtis, George T. *Life of James Buchanan, Fifteenth President of the United States,* 2 vols. New York: Harper, 1883.

Klein, Philip S. *President James Buchanan: A Biography.* University Park: Pennsylvania State University Press, 1962.

Smith, Elbert B. *The Presidency of James Buchanan.* Lawrence: University Press of Kansas, 1975.

Abraham Lincoln

Cox, LaWanda C. *Lincoln and Black Freedom: A Study in Presidential Leadership.* Urbana: University of Illinois Press, 1985.

Fehrenbacher, Don E. *The Leadership of Abraham Lincoln.* New York: Wiley, 1970.

Findley, Paul A. *Lincoln, the Crucible of Congress.* New York: Crown, 1979.

Handlin, Oscar, and Lilian Handlin. *Abraham Lincoln and the Union.* Boston: Little, Brown, 1980.

Herndon, William H., and J. William Weik. *Herndon's Lincoln: The True Story of a Great Life, the History and Personal Recollections of Abraham Lincoln,* 3 vols. Chicago: Belford, Clarke, 1889.

Oates, Stephen B. *Abraham Lincoln: The Man Behind the Myths.* New York: Harper & Row, 1984.

Paludan, Philip S. *The Presidency of Abraham Lincoln.* Lawrence: University Press of Kansas, 1994.

Sandburg, Carl. *Abraham Lincoln: The Prairie Years,* 2 vols. New York: Harcourt Brace, 1926.

———. *Abraham Lincoln: The War Years,* 4 vols. New York: Harcourt Brace, 1939.

Wills, Garry. *Lincoln at Gettysburg: The Words That Remade America.* New York: Simon & Schuster, 1992.

Andrew Johnson

Beale, Howard K. *The Critical Year: A Study of Andrew Johnson and the Reconstruction.* New York: Harcourt Brace, 1930.

Castel, Albert. *The Presidency of Andrew Johnson.* Lawrence: Regents Press of Kansas, 1979.

DeWitt, David M. *The Impeachment and Trial of Andrew Johnson, Seventeenth President of the United States: A History.* New York: Macmillan, 1903.

McKitrick, Eric L. *Andrew Johnson and Reconstruction.* Chicago: University of Chicago Press, 1960.

Sefton, James E. *Andrew Johnson and the Uses of Constitutional Power.* Boston: Little, Brown, 1980.

Trefousse, Hans L. *Andrew Johnson: A Biography.* New York: W. W. Norton, 1989.

Ulysses S. Grant

Carpenter, John A. *Ulysses S. Grant.* New York: Twayne, 1970.

Mantell, Martin E. *Johnson, Grant, and the Politics of Reconstruction.* New York: Columbia University Press, 1973.

McFeely, William S. *Grant, A Biography.* New York: W. W. Norton, 1981.

Simpson, Brooks D. *Let Us Have Peace: Ulysses S. Grant and the Politics of War and Reconstruction, 1861–1868.* Chapel Hill: University of North Carolina Press, 1991.

Rutherford B. Hayes

Davison, Kenneth E. *The Presidency of Rutherford B. Hayes.* Westport, Conn.: Greenwood Press, 1972.

Hoogenboom, Ari A. *The Presidency of Rutherford B. Hayes.* Lawrence: University Press of Kansas, 1988.

Morgan, H. Wayne. *From Hayes to McKinley: National Party Politics, 1877–1896.* Syracuse, N.Y.: Syracuse University Press, 1969.

James A. Garfield

Booraem, Hendrik. *The Road to Respectability: James A. Garfield and His World, 1844–1852.* Lewisburg, Pa.: Bucknell University Press; Cleveland: Western Reserve Historical Society Press, 1988.

Doenecke, Justus D. *The Presidencies of James A. Garfield and Chester A. Arthur.* Lawrence: Regents Press of Kansas, 1981.

Peskin, Allan. *Garfield: A Biography.* Kent, Ohio: Kent State University Press, 1978.

Chester A. Arthur

Doenecke, Justus D. *The Presidencies of James A. Garfield and Chester A. Arthur.* Lawrence: Regents Press of Kansas, 1981.

Reeves, Thomas C. *Gentlemen Boss: The Life of Chester Alan Arthur.* New York: Knopf, 1975.

Grover Cleveland

McElroy, Robert M. *Grover Cleveland, The Man and the Statesman: An Authorized Biography,* 2 vols. New York: Harper and Row, 1923.

Merrill, Horace S. *Bourbon Leader: Grover Cleveland and the Democratic Party.* Boston: Little, Brown, 1957.

Nevins, Allan. *Grover Cleveland: A Study in Courage.* New York: Dodd, Mead, 1932.

Welch, Richard E. *The Presidency of Grover Cleveland.* Lawrence: University Press of Kansas, 1988.

Benjamin Harrison

Sievers, Harry J. *Benjamin Harrison: Hoosier Statesman from the Civil War to the White House: 1865–1888.* New York: University Publishers, 1959.

———. *Benjamin Harrison: Hoosier Warrior: 1833–1865, Through the Civil War Years,* 2d ed. New York: University Publishers, 1960.

———. *Benjamin Harrison: Hoosier President: The White House and After.* New York: University Publishers, 1968.

William McKinley

Gould, Lewis L. *The Presidency of William McKinley.* Lawrence: University Press of Kansas, 1980.

Morgan, H. Wayne. *William McKinley and His America.* Syracuse, N.Y.: Syracuse University Press, 1963.

Theodore Roosevelt

Blum, John M. *The Republican Roosevelt,* 2d ed. Cambridge, Mass.: Harvard University Press, 1977.

———. *The Progressive Presidents: Roosevelt, Wilson, Roosevelt, Johnson.* New York: W. W. Norton, 1980.

Cooper, John M., Jr. *The Warrior and the Priest: Theodore Roosevelt and Woodrow Wilson.* Cambridge, Mass.: Harvard University Press, 1983.

Gould, Lewis L. *The Presidency of Theodore Roosevelt,* rev. ed. New York: Oxford University Press, 1975.

Miller, Nathan. *Theodore Roosevelt: A Life.* New York: William Morrow and Company, 1992.

Morris, Edmund. *The Rise of Theodore Roosevelt.* New York: Coward, McCann and Geoghegan, 1979.

Mowry, George E. *Theodore Roosevelt and the Progressive Movement.* Madison: University of Wisconsin Press, 1946.

———. *The Era of Theodore Roosevelt, 1900–1912.* New York: Harper and Row, 1958.

William Howard Taft

Anderson, Judith I. *William Howard Taft: An Intimate History.* New York: W. W. Norton, 1981.

Burton, David. *The Learned Presidency: Theodore Roosevelt, William Howard Taft, Woodrow Wilson.* Rutherford, N.J.: Fairleigh Dickinson University Press, 1988.

Coletta, Paolo E. *The Presidency of William Howard Taft.* Lawrence: University Press of Kansas, 1973.

Mason, Alpheus T. *William Howard Taft: Chief Justice.* New York: Simon & Schuster, 1965.

Pringle, Henry F. *The Life and Times of William Howard Taft: A Biography,* 2 vols. New York: Farrar, Straus, 1939.

Woodrow Wilson

Baker, Ray S. *Woodrow Wilson: Life and Letters,* 8 vols. Garden City, N.Y.: Doubleday, 1927–39.

Blum, John M. *The Progressive Presidents: Roosevelt, Wilson, Roosevelt, Johnson.* New York: W. W. Norton, 1980.

Canfield, Leon H. *The Presidency of Woodrow Wilson: Prelude to a World in Crisis.* Rutherford, N.J.: Fairleigh Dickinson University Press, 1966.

Clements, Kendrick A. *The Presidency of Woodrow Wilson.* Lawrence: University Press of Kansas, 1992.

Cooper, John, Jr. *The Warrior and the Priest: Theodore Roosevelt and Woodrow Wilson.* Cambridge, Mass.: Belknap Press, 1983.

Knock, Thomas J. *To End All Wars: Woodrow Wilson and the Quest for a New World Order.* New York: Oxford University Press, 1992.

Link, Arthur S. *Woodrow Wilson and the Progressive Era, 1910–1917.* New York: Harper & Row, 1954.

———. *Woodrow Wilson,* 5 vols. Princeton, N.J.: Princeton University Press, 1947–65.

———. *Wilson: The Struggle for Neutrality, 1914–1915.* Princeton, N.J.: Princeton University Press, 1960.

———. *Wilson: Confusions and Crises: 1915–1916.* Princeton, N.J.: Princeton University Press, 1964.

———. *Woodrow Wilson and a Revolutionary World, 1913–1921.* Chapel Hill: University of North Carolina Press, 1982.

Walworth, Arthur C. *Woodrow Wilson,* 3d ed. New York: W. W. Norton, 1978.

Warren G. Harding

Downes, Randolph C. *The Rise of Warren Gamaliel Harding: 1865–1920.* Columbus: Ohio State University Press, 1970.

Murray, Robert K. *The Harding Era: Warren G. Harding and His Administration.* Minneapolis: University of Minnesota Press, 1969.

Russell, Francis. *The Shadow of Blooming Grove: Warren G. Harding in His Times.* New York: McGraw-Hill, 1968.

Sinclair, Andrew. *The Available Man: The Life Behind the Masks of Warren Gamaliel Harding.* New York: Macmillan, 1965.

Trani, Eugene P., and David L. Wilson. *The Presidency of Warren G. Harding.* Lawrence: Regents Press of Kansas, 1977.

Calvin Coolidge

Fuess, Claude M. *Calvin Coolidge, The Man from Vermont.* Boston: Little, Brown, 1940.

McCoy, Donald R. *Calvin Coolidge, The Quiet President.* Lawrence: University Press of Kansas, 1988.

Murray, Robert K. *The Politics of Normalcy: Governmental Theory and Practice in the Harding-Coolidge Era.* New York: W. W. Norton, 1973.

Herbert Hoover

Best, Gary D. *Herbert Hoover: The Postpresidential Years, 1933–1964,* 2 vols. Stanford, Calif.: Hoover Institution Press, 1983.

Burner, David. *Herbert Hoover: A Public Life.* New York: Knopf, 1979.

Fausold, Martin L., *The Presidency of Herbert Hoover.* Lawrence: University Press of Kansas, 1985.

Fausold, Martin L., and George Mazuzan, eds. *The Hoover Presidency: A Reappraisal.* Albany: State University of New York Press, 1974.

Hoff-Wilson, John. *Herbert Hoover, Forgotten Progressive.* Boston: Little, Brown, 1975.

Nash, George H. *The Life of Herbert Hoover: The Engineer, 1874–1914.* New York: W. W. Norton, 1983.

Schwarz, Jordan A. *The Interregnum of Despair: Hoover, Congress, and the Depression.* Urbana: University of Illinois Press, 1970.

Smith, Richard N. *An Uncommon Man: The Triumph of Herbert Hoover.* New York: Simon & Schuster, 1984.

Warren, Harris G. *Herbert Hoover and the Great Depression.* New York: Oxford University Press, 1990.

Franklin D. Roosevelt

Abbott, Philip. *The Exemplary Presidency: Franklin D. Roosevelt and the American Political Tradition.* Amherst: University of Massachusetts Press, 1990.

Burns, James M. *Roosevelt: The Lion and the Fox.* New York: Harcourt Brace, 1956.

———. *Roosevelt: The Soldier of Freedom.* New York: Harcourt Brace, 1970.

Dallek, Robert. *Franklin D. Roosevelt and American Foreign Policy, 1932–1945.* New York: Oxford University Press, 1979.

Davis, Kenneth S. *FDR, Into the Storm 1937–1940: A History.* New York: Random House, 1993.

Freidel, Frank B. *Franklin D. Roosevelt,* 4 vols. Boston: Little, Brown, 1952–73.

———. *Franklin D. Roosevelt: A Rendezvous with Destiny.* Boston: Little, Brown, 1990.

Leuchtenberg, William E. *Franklin D. Roosevelt and the New Deal, 1932–1940.* New York: Harper and Row, 1963.

Miller, Nathan. *FDR: An Intimate History.* Garden City, N.Y.: Doubleday, 1983.

Morgan, Ted. *FDR.* New York: Simon & Schuster, 1985.

Schlesinger, Arthur M., Jr. *The Age of Roosevelt,* 3 vols. Boston: Houghton Mifflin, 1957–60.

Tugwell, Rexford G. *FDR: The Architect of an Era.* New York: Macmillan, 1967.

Harry S Truman

Daniels, Jonathan. *The Man of Independence.* Philadelphia: Lippincott, 1950.

Donovan, Robert J. *Conflict and Crisis: Presidency of Harry S. Truman: 1945–1948.* New York: W. W. Norton, 1977.

———. *Tumultuous Years: The Presidency of Harry S. Truman, 1949–1953.* New York: W. W. Norton, 1982.

Ferrell, Robert H. *Harry S. Truman: A Life.* Columbia: University of Missouri Press, 1994.

———. *Harry S. Truman and the Modern American Presidency.* Boston: Little, Brown, 1983.

Lacey, Michael J., ed. *The Truman Presidency.* New York: Cambridge University Press, 1989.

McCoy, Donald R. *The Presidency of Harry S. Truman.* Lawrence: University Press of Kansas, 1984.

McCullough, David G. *Truman.* New York: Simon & Schuster, 1992.

Dwight D. Eisenhower

Alexander, Charles C. *Holding the Line: The Eisenhower Era, 1952–1961.* Bloomington: Indiana University Press, 1975.

Ambrose, Stephen E. *Eisenhower: President and Elder Statesman, 1952–1969.* New York: Simon & Schuster, 1984.

———. *Eisenhower: Soldier and President.* New York: Simon & Schuster, 1990.

Greenstein, Fred I. *The Hidden-Hand Presidency: Eisenhower as Leader.* New York: Basic Books, 1982.

Pach, Chester J. *The Presidency of Dwight D. Eisenhower.* Lawrence: University Press of Kansas, 1991.

Parmet, Herbert S. *Eisenhower and the American Crusades.* New York: Macmillan, 1972.

John F. Kennedy

Beschloss, Michael R. *The Crisis Years: Kennedy and Khrushchev, 1960–1963.* New York: Edward Burlingame Books, 1991.

Giglio, James N. *The Presidency of John F. Kennedy.* Lawrence: University Press of Kansas, 1991.

Miroff, Bruce. *Pragmatic Illusions: The Presidential Politics of John F. Kennedy.* New York: McKay, 1976.

Parmet, Herbert S. *Jack: The Struggles of John F. Kennedy.* New York: Dial, 1980.

———. *JFK: The Presidency of John F. Kennedy.* New York: Dial, 1983.

Reeves, Richard. *President Kennedy: Profile of Power.* New York: Simon & Schuster, 1993.

Schlesinger, Arthur M., Jr. *A Thousand Days: John F. Kennedy in the White House.* Boston: Houghton Mifflin, 1965.

Sorensen, Theodore C. *Kennedy.* New York: Harper and Row, 1965.

Wills, Garry. *The Kennedy Imprisonment: A Mediation on Power.* Boston: Little, Brown, 1982.

Lyndon B. Johnson

Bornet, Vaughn D. *Presidency of Lyndon B. Johnson.* Lawrence: University Press of Kansas, 1983.

Califano, Joseph A. *The Triumph & Tragedy of Lyndon Johnson: The White House Years.* New York: Simon & Schuster, 1991.

Caro, Robert A. *The Years of Lyndon Johnson: The Path to Power.* New York: Knopf, 1982.

———. *Means of Ascent.* New York: Knopf, 1990.

Dallek, Robert. *Lone Star Rising: Lyndon Johnson and His Times, 1908–1960.* New York: Oxford University Press, 1991.

Dugger, Ronnie. *The Politician: The Life and Times of Lyndon Johnson: The Drive for Power, from the Frontier to Master of the Senate.* New York: W. W. Norton, 1982.

Goldman, Eric F. *The Tragedy of Lyndon Johnson: A Historian's Interpretation.* New York: Knopf, 1969.

Kearns, Doris. *Lyndon Johnson and the American Dream.* New York: Harper and Row, 1976.

Richard M. Nixon

Ambrose, Stephen E. *Nixon.* New York: Simon & Schuster, 1987–91.

Brodie, Fawn M. *Richard Nixon: The Shaping of His Character.* Cambridge, Mass.: Harvard University Press, 1983.

Evans, Rowland, Jr., and Robert D. Novak. *Nixon in the White House: The Frustration of Power.* New York: Vintage, 1971.

Genovese, Michael A. *The Nixon Presidency: Power and Politics in Turbulent Times.* New York: Greenwood Press, 1990.

Hersh, Seymour M. *The Price of Power: Kissinger in the Nixon White House.* New York: Summit Books, 1983.

Hoff-Wilson, Joan. *Nixon Reconsidered.* New York: Basic Books, 1994.

Litwak, Robert S. *Détente and the Nixon Doctrine: American Foreign Policy and the Pursuit of Stability, 1969–1976.* New York: Cambridge University Press, 1984.

Morris, Roger. *Richard Milhous Nixon: The Rise of an American Politician.* New York: Holt, 1990.

Parmet, Herbert S. *Richard Nixon and His America.* Boston: Little, Brown, 1990.

Safire, William. *Before the Fall: An Inside View of the Pre-Watergate White House.* Garden City, N.Y.: Doubleday, 1975.

Gerald R. Ford

Cannon, James M. *Time and Chance: Gerald Ford's Appointment with History.* New York: HarperCollins, 1994.

Greene, John R. *Gerald R. Ford: A Bibliography.* New York: Greenwood Press, 1994.

———. *The Presidency of Gerald R. Ford.* Lawrence: University Press of Kansas, 1995.

Reeves, Richard. *A Ford, Not a Lincoln.* New York: Harcourt Brace Jovanovich, 1975.

TerHorst, Jerald F. *Gerald Ford and the Future of the Presidency.* New York: Third Press, 1974.

Jimmy Carter

Campbell, Colin. *Managing the Presidency: Carter, Reagan, and the Search for Executive Harmony.* Pittsburgh: University of Pittsburgh Press, 1986.

Fink, Gary M. *Prelude to the Presidency: The Political Character and Legislative Leadership-Style of Governor Jimmy Carter.* Westport, Conn.: Greenwood Press, 1980.

Hargrove, Erwin C. *Jimmy Carter as President: Leadership and the Politics of the Public Good.* Baton Rouge: Louisiana State University Press, 1988.

Jones, Charles O. *The Trusteeship Presidency: Jimmy Carter and the United States Congress.* Baton Rouge: Louisiana State University Press, 1988.

Kaufman, Burton Ira. *The Presidency of James Earl Carter, Jr.* Lawrence: University Press of Kansas, 1993.

Lynn, Laurence E., Jr. *The President as Policy Maker: Jimmy Carter and Welfare Reform.* Philadelphia: Temple University Press, 1981.

Ronald Reagan

Campbell, Colin. *Managing the Presidency: Carter, Reagan, and the Search for Executive Harmony.* Pittsburgh: University of Pittsburgh Press, 1986.

Cannon, Lou. *President Reagan: The Role of a Lifetime.* New York: Simon and Schuster, 1991.

Dallek, Robert *Ronald Reagan: The Politics of Symbolism.* Cambridge, Mass.: Harvard University Press, 1984.

Greenstein, Fred I. *The Reagan Presidency: An Early Assessment.* Baltimore: Johns Hopkins University Press, 1983.

George H. W. Bush

Campbell, Colin, and Bert A. Rockman, eds. *The Bush Presidency: First Appraisals.* Chatham, N.J.: Chatham House, 1991.

Duffy, Michael. *Marching in Place: The Status Quo Presidency of George Bush.* New York: Simon & Schuster, 1992.

Hill, Dilys M., and Phil Williams, eds. *The Bush Presidency: Triumphs and Adversities.* New York: St. Martin's Press, 1994.

Kolb, Charles. *White House Daze: The Unmaking of Domestic Policy in the Bush Years.* New York: Free Press, 1994.

Bill Clinton

Drew, Elizabeth. *On the Edge: The Clinton Presidency.* New York: Simon & Schuster, 1994.

Hohenberg, John. *The Bill Clinton Story: Winning the Presidency.* Syracuse, N.Y.: Syracuse University Press, 1994.

Maraniss, David. *First in His Class: A Biography of Bill Clinton.* New York: Simon & Schuster, 1995.

Oakley, Meredith L. *On the Make: The Rise of Bill Clinton.* Washington, D.C.: Regnery, 1994.

Renshon, Stanley A., ed. *The Clinton Presidency: Campaigning, Governing, and the Psychology of Leadership.* Boulder, Colo.: Westview Press, 1994.

Woodward, Bob. *The Agenda: Inside the Clinton White House.* New York: Simon & Schuster, 1994.

George W. Bush

Bruni, Frank. *Ambling Into History: The Unlikely Odyssey of George W. Bush.* New York: HarperCollins, 2002.

Greenstein, Fred I., ed. *The George W. Bush Presidency.* Baltimore, Md.: Johns Hopkins University Press, 2003.

Lind, Michael. *Made in Texas: George W. Bush and the Takeover of American Politics.* New York: Basic Books, 2002.

Minutaglio, Bill. *First Son: George W. Bush and the Bush Family Dynasty.* New York: Times Books, 1999.

Index

Boldface page numbers denote extensive treatment of a topic. *Italic* page numbers refer to illustrations; *c* refers to the Chronology; and *m* indicates a map.

Supreme Court **122–124** *See also*
courts and the president
appointment of justices 10,
122–123, **278–280**
Buckley v. Valeo (1976) **48**, 69
Bush v. Gore (2000) **64–65**, 124
Clinton v. City of New York
(1998) **101**, 140
Clinton v. Jones (1997)
100–101, 238, 243, 244
congressional investigations of
the presidency and 259